8/5

D0793382

Index Herbariorum

Part I, edition 7

REGNUM VEGETABILE
A series of publications for plant taxonomists
VOLUME 106

Index Herbariorum

A guide to the location and contents of the world's public herbaria

General editor: F. A. Stafleu

Index Herbariorum

Part I *The Herbaria of the world*

SEVENTH EDITION

Compiled by
Patricia K. Holmgren, Wil Keuken *and* Eileen K. Schofield

BOHN, SCHELTEMA & HOLKEMA, UTRECHT/ANTWERPEN
DR. W. JUNK B.V., PUBLISHERS, THE HAGUE/BOSTON
1981

© 1981, Frans A. Stafleu, Utrecht, The Netherlands
No part of this book may be reproduced by film, microfilm or any other means without written permission from the publisher.

ISBN 90 313 0478 6

First edition, Utrecht 1952, Regnum Vegetabile vol. 2[a]
Second edition, Utrecht 1954, Regnum Vegetabile vol. 2[b]
Third edition, Utrecht 1956, Regnum Vegetabile vol. 6
Fourth edition, Utrecht 1959, Regnum Vegetabile vol. 15
Fifth edition, Utrecht 1964, Regnum Vegetabile vol. 31
Sixth edition, Utrecht 1974, Regnum Vegetabile vol. 92
Seventh edition, Utrecht 1981, Regnum Vegetabile vol. 106

Library of Congress Cataloguing in Publication Data

QK96.R4 vol. 106, etc. [QK75] 581'.012s **81-12261**
ISBN 90-313-0478-6 (v. 1) [580'.74'2] AACR2

Distributors:
for the United States and Canada
Kluwer Boston, Inc.
190 Old Derby Street
Hingham, MA 02043
USA

for all other countries
Libresso Distribution Center
P.O. Box 23
7400 GA Deventer
The Netherlands

WITHDRAWN

NATURAL HISTORY MUSEUM
OF LOS
library
LOS ANGELES COUNTY
WITHDRAWN

Printed in the Netherlands

Contents

Preface

The Introduction to the Index Herbariorum, printed in the first four editions of this *Herbaria of the World*, is not reproduced here again. Readers interested in the history of this book are referred to the earlier editions.

This seventh edition was compiled by Patricia K. Holmgren (New World herbaria), W. Keuken (Old World herbaria), and Eileen K. Schofield (Old World herbaria).

We are grateful to all curators who provided information on their herbaria for edition 7. It is not possible to acknowledge them all by name, but we offer a special thanks to the following for help with herbaria in the geographical areas listed in parentheses: Janice Coffey (U.S.S.R.), Mireya D. Correa A. (Central America), Thomas S. Elias (People's Republic of China, U.S.S.R.), Ramón Ferreyra (Peru), Enrique Forero (Colombia), Lauritz B. Holm-Nielsen (Ecuador), Vivian Wu Koyama (translation of Chinese), María Lebrón-Luteyn (Latin America), James L. Luteyn (People's Republic of China), Scott A. Mori (Brazil), Ghillean T. Prance (Brazil), Dennis W. Woodland (Canada), and Elsa M. Zardini (Argentina). Several reference works were useful to us: *Botany in China, report of the Botanical Society of America Delegation to the People's Republic, May 20-June 18, 1978*, edited by Anitra Thorhaug [United States-China Relations Program, Stanford University, 1978]; *Catálogo de los herbarios institucionales Mexicanos*, by J. Rzedowski [Sociedad Botánica de México, México, D.F., Mexico, 1976]; *Herbaria of the Soviet Union*, by I. T. Vassilczenko and L. I. Vassiljeva [Soviet Sciences Press 1–59. 1975]; *Phytotaxonomy in the People's Republic of China*, by B. Bartholomew, R. A. Howard and T. S. Elias [Brittonia 31:1–25. 1979]; *Mycology in Brazil: Available infrastructure for its development*, by Oswaldo Fidalgo and Vera Lucia Bononi de Camargo Penteado [Taxon 28: 435–464. 1979].

Secretaries play an insufficiently appreciated role in the production of books. We are indebted to several secretaries, especially to Carma L. Park and Linda D. Marschner.

This index contains all information received up to 1 November 1980. Even though questionnaires for updating were sent to all herbaria listed in the previous edition, we did not receive replies to all. In a few cases the information presented here is therefore marked "information 1974." Information on personnel is given only for those herbaria who provided recent information.

Wil Keuken and Eileen Schofield left IAPT-Utrecht and the New York Botanical Garden respectively since the completion of the manuscript. We are grateful to both for their important share in compiling this new edition. A very special word of thanks and appreciation goes to Wil Keuken who was involved in the compilation of all seven editions.

PATRICIA K. HOLMGREN
FRANS A. STAFLEU

A

AARHUS: *Herbarium Jutlandicum, Botanical Institute, University of Aarhus,* (**AAU**), 68 Nordlandsvej, DK-8240 Risskov, **Denmark.**
Telephone: 06/210677.
Status: University.
Foundation: 1963. *Number of specimens:* 400.000.
Herbarium: General, especially Europe, tropical Asia and S. America.
Important collections: K. Larsen (Thailand, 25.000), Kerr, Maxwell (Thailand), L. Holm-Nielsen, Løjtnant & Øllgaard (50.000, Ecuador), Rechinger (Fl. Iranica duplicate set). All these collections with many types.
    Director: K. LARSEN, 1926 (Leguminosae of Tropical Asia, particularly Caesalpiniaceae, Zingiberaceae, S.E. Asia).
    Curator: I. NIELSEN, 1946 (Mimosaceae of Tropical Asia).
    Staff members: P. FROST-OLSEN, 1946 (*Aphanes, Alchemilla*).
    L. B. HOLM-NIELSEN, 1946 (Flora Ecuador, Passifloraceae, Helobiales, *Phyllanthus*).
    S. LAEGAARD, 1933 (Biosystematics).
    SUPEE S. LARSEN, 1939 (*Bauhinia*, palynology, Caesalpiniaceae).
    B. LØJTNANT, 1946 (Orchidaceae, especially *Cranichis*).
    L. MATHIESEN, 1928 (Algae).
    B. ØLLGAARD, 1943 (Flora Ecuador, Pteridophytes, especially *Lycopodium*).
    S. SVANE, 1925 (Lichens).
    E. WARNCKE, 1939 (Bryophytes).
Specialization in research: Taxonomy (experimental and classic), phytogeography, Flora of Thailand, Flora of Ecuador, Danish and Mediterranean flora.
Associated botanic garden: Botanic Garden, Aarhus and Experimental Fields of the Botanical Institute.
Loans: To recognized botanical institutions.
Periodical and serial works: Herbarium Annual Report, Lindbergia.
Exchange: Available: Flora exsiccata Jutlandica, Flora exsiccata Germanica-Schleswig-Holstein, bryophytes and phanerogams from Scandinavia, Europe, S.E. Asia (limited), and tropical S. America (limited). Desired: Worldwide.

ABERCORN: *International Red Locust Control Service,* (**LCS**) – *see* LCO.

ABERDEEN: *Herbarium, Department of Botany, The University,* (**ABD**), Aberdeen, AB9 24D Scotland, **Great Britain.** (Information 1974)
Status: University.
Foundation: 1860. *Number of specimens:* 70.000.

Herbarium: Flora of Great Britain and Thailand.
Specialization in research: Taxonomy and ecology of British flora, taxonomy of flora of Malaysia.
Associated botanic garden: Cruickshank Botanic Garden.
Loans: To recognized institutions.

ABERYSTWYTH: *The Painter Herbarium, Department of Botany,* (**ABS**), University College of Wales, Aberystwyth, Wales, **Great Britain.** (Information 1974)
Status: University.
Foundation: 1872. *Number of specimens:* 29.000.
Herbarium: Great Britain (Shropshire, West Wales).
Important collections: Rev. H. Painter.
Specialization in research: Welsh flora, population studies.
Associated botanic garden: The College Botany Garden.

ABIDJAN: *Herbarium, Centre ORSTOM d'Adiopodoumé,* (**ABI**), B.P. 20, Abidjan, **Ivory Coast.** (Information 1974)
Status: State institute.
Foundation: 1946. *Number of specimens:* 10.000.
Herbarium: Flora of Côte d'Ivoire and adjacent countries.
Specialization in research: Flora of West Africa.
Associated botanic garden: Yes, including a collection of medicinal plants.
Loans: On request.

ABIDJAN: *Herbier National de Côte d'Ivoire (Université d'Abidjan),* (**UCJ**), B.P. 4322, Abidjan, **Ivory Coast.**
Telephone: 44.47.25.
Foundation: 1946. *Number of specimens:* 22.000.
    Director and Curator: LAURENT AKÉ ASSI (Taxonomy).

ABILENE: *Herbarium, Department of Biology, Hardin-Simmons University,* (**HSU**), 2200 Hickory Street, Box N, HSU Station, Abilene, Texas 79698, **U.S.A.**
Telephone: 915/677-7281, ext. 396.
Foundation: 1960. *Number of specimens:* 2.000.
Herbarium: Vascular plants of Taylor County, Texas.
    Director and Curator: H. TAYLOR RANKIN, 1934.
Exchange: Upon mutual agreement.

ABU DHABI: *Herbarium, Department of Biology, United Arab Emirates University,* (**ABDH**), P.O. Box 15551, Al Ayn, Abu Dhabi, **United Arab Emirates.**

Telephone: 77700-77280.
Status: University.
Foundation: 1979. *Number of specimens:* 2.000.
Herbarium: Local flora, especially desert species.
Director and Curator: ALY ALY EL-GHONEMY, 1932 (Ecology).
Staff member: MARIAM EL-FAROUKY, 1955.
Specialization in research: Floristic analysis, range ecology, vegetation mapping, ecosystem analysis, native plants of economic importance.
Exchange: Possible.

ADA: *Herbarium, Biology Department, East Central Oklahoma State University,* (**ECSC**), Ada, Oklahoma 74820, **U.S.A.**
Telephone: 405/332-8000, ext. 495 or 500.
Foundation: 1915. *Number of specimens:* 6.000.
Herbarium: Mainly local collections used for teaching taxonomy.
Director and Curator: CLYDE E. BUTLER, 1929 (Plant physiology).
Specialization in research: State and local flora; plant distribution in Oklahoma.
Loans: Usual regulations.

ADDIS ABABA: *Herbarium, Biology Department, Haile Selassie I University,* (**ETH**), P.O. Box 1176, Addis Ababa, **Ethiopia.** (Information 1974)
Status: National herbarium, administered by Biology Dept. of University.
Foundation: 1959 (as part of Forest Research Institute). *Number of specimens:* 8.000.
Herbarium: Flora of Ethiopia and adjacent countries.
Specialization in research: Ethiopian flora.
Loans: To recognized botanical institutions.

ADDIS ABABA: *Herbarium, International Livestock Centre for Africa,* (**ILCA**), P.O. Box 5689, Addis Ababa, **Ethiopia.**
Foundation: 1976. *Number of specimens:* 7.500.
Herbarium: Fodder plants, mainly Leguminosae and Gramineae; flora of semi-arid areas of Africa.
Director: DAVID PRATT.
Curator: LOUTFY BOULOS.
Specialization in research: Livestock research, introduction of fodder plants.
Loans: To recognized botanical institutions.
Exchange: Desired: Plants of dry regions of Africa, especially Central and East Africa.

ADELAIDE: *State Herbarium of South Australia,* (**AD**), Botanic Garden, North Terrace, Adelaide, South Australia 5000, **Australia.**
Telephone: 08-2233038.
Status: State Government of South Australia: Botanic Gardens, Department for the Environment.
Foundation: 1954. *Number of specimens:* 400.000.
Herbarium: Worldwide, but mainly Australian; collection of cultivated specimens separately.

Important collections: J. M. Black, J. B. Cleland (including fungi), R. S. Rogers (Orchidaceae), R. Schomburgk, R. Tate. The greater part of the higher plant collections of the Botany Department of the University of Adelaide is housed in AD on permanent loan.
Director: T. R. N. LOTHIAN, 1915.
Curator: J. P. JESSOP, 1939 (General flora).
Staff members: W. R. BARKER, 1948 (Scrophulariaceae, Stackhousiaceae).
  R. J. CHINNOCK, 1943 (Myoporaceae).
  N. N. DONNER, 1921 (Lichens).
  E. J. MCALISTER, 1942 (Cultivated plants).
  MUNIR AHMAD ABID, 1936 (Chloranthaceae, Verbenaceae).
  H. R. TÖLKEN, 1940 (*Kunzea*).
  J. Z. WEBER, 1930 (*Cassytha*).
  D. J. E. WHIBLEY, 1936 (*Acacia*).
Specialization in research: Australasian flora.
Associated botanic garden: Adelaide Botanic Gardens.
Loans: To recognized botanical institutions.
Periodical and serial works: Journal of the Adelaide Botanic Gardens.
Exchange: Available: Vascular plants from Australia. Desired: All groups, especially from areas with a Mediterranean climate.

ADELAIDE: *Herbarium, Botany Department, University of Adelaide,* (**ADU**), Adelaide, South Australia 5001, **Australia.** (Information 1974)
Status: University.
Foundation: 1874 (University), herbarium a few years later. *Number of specimens:* 45.000.
Herbarium: Mainly algae of southern Australia, also Solomon Islands, Antarctic and sub-Antarctic; teaching collections of other groups.
Specialization in research: Marine algae, ecology of Australian arid plants.
Associated botanic garden: Informal close relations with Adelaide Botanic Garden.

ADELAIDE: *Herbarium, Waite Agricultural Research Institute, The University of Adelaide,* (**ADW**), Private Bag No. 1, Glen Osmond, South Australia 5064, **Australia.**
Telephone: 08-797901.
Status: A foundation of the University of Adelaide.
Foundation: Waite Institute 1924, Herbarium 1933. *Number of specimens:* 55.000.
Herbarium: Australian phanerogams, particularly of agricultural and weedy interest.
Important collections: Albert Morris (plants from arid regions of Australia), D. E. Symon (Australian phanerogams, particularly Solanaceae).
Director: J. QUIRKE, 1924 (Soil chemistry and physics).
Curator: D. E. SYMON, 1920 (Phanerogams, especially Solanaceae).
Specialization in research: Australian genera,

mainly Solanaceae.

Associated botanic garden: The Waite Arboretum.

Loans: In general to recognized botanical institutions.

Periodical and serial works: Report of the Waite Agricultural Research Institute.

Exchange: Available: Duplicates of varied local collections, chiefly phanerogams. Desired: Agricultural and weedy plants, Solanaceae from anywhere.

Remarks: Dr. P. H. B. Talbot, Mycologist, listed in Ed. 6, has since died and the greater part of the J. B. Cleland fungal collection has now been transferred to AD.

ADMONT: *Benediktiner Abtei Admont "Obersteirisches Herbar,"* (**ADMONT**), Benediktiner Abtei Admont/Naturhistorisches Museum, A-8911 Admont, **Austria.**

Telephone: 03613/23120.

Status: Monastery.

Foundation: 1866 (herbarium). *Number of specimens:* 2.760.

Herbarium: Obersteirische Flora.

Curator: GÜNTER MORGE, 1925 (Entomology, forestry) [only working in Admont in October and November].

Specialization in research: Entomology, forestry.

Loans: Possible, but only on request to the following address: Prof. Dr. Günter Morge, Academy of Agricultural Sciences of GDR, Walther Rathenau Strasse 3, DDR-13 Eberswalde-Finow.

Remarks: There are two more herbaria of this monastery: the "Herbarium Universale" with 21.416 specimens and the "Italian Herbar" with 3.432 species, both on permanent loan to Graz (GJO).

ADRIAN: *Herbarium, Biology Department, Adrian College,* (**ADR**), Adrian, Michigan 49221, **U.S.A.**

Telephone: 517/265-5161.

Status: Private institution.

Foundation: 1930. *Number of specimens:* 7.500.

Herbarium: Plants of Michigan, lower peninsula and vicinities.

Director and Curator: K. S. XAVIER, 1930; 517/265-5161, ext. 237 (Orchid taxonomy; palynology).

Staff member: IDA MAY JOHNSON, 1917.

Specialization in research: Cloning of plants by plant tissue culture.

Associated botanic garden: Michigan Ecological Garden; Dawson Arboretum.

Loans: To all recognized institutions or individuals.

Exchange: Local collections.

AGANA: *Herbarium, University of Guam,* (**GUAM**) — *see* MANGILAO.

AKUREYRI: *Herbarium, Náttúrugripasafnic á Aku-*

reyri (*Akureyri Museum of Natural History*), (**AMNH**), Hafnarstraeti 81, P.O. Box 580, 600 Akureyri, **Iceland.**

Telephone: (96)2 23 97.

Status: Municipal.

Foundation: Museum 1951, herbarium 1960. *Number of specimens:* 50.000.

Herbarium: Icelandic and European vascular plants (30.000), Icelandic cryptogams: lichens, fungi, mosses (20.000).

Important collections: Herbarium of Steindór Steindórsson (about 5.000).

Director: HELGI HALLGRÍMSSON, 1935 (Icelandic macromycetes).

Staff member: JÓHANN PÁLSSON, 1931, Director of Botanic Garden (Icelandic phanerogams, Gramineae).

Specialization in research: Icelandic flora of vascular plants and fungi.

Associated botanic garden: Botanic Garden of Akureyri (Lystigardur Akureyrar), P.O. Box 95.

Loans: Usual regulations.

Periodical and serial works: Acta Botanica Islandica (Timarit um íslenzka grasafraedi).

Exchange: Available: Icelandic vascular plants. Desired: Arctic and boreal plants.

ALAMOSA: *Herbarium, Adams State College,* (**ALAM**), Alamosa, Colorado 81102, **U.S.A.**

Telephone: 303/589-7767.

Foundation: 1925. *Number of specimens:* 9.000.

Herbarium: Vascular plants and lichens of the San Luis Valley, Colorado.

Director: HOBART N. DIXON, 1933 (Distributional ecology of vascular plants).

Exchange: Yes.

ALBANY: *Herbarium, New York State Museum, Biological Survey,* (**NYS**), 3132 CEC, Albany, New York 12230, **U.S.A.**

Telephone: 518/474-5809.

Status: New York State Department of Education.

Foundation: 1836. *Number of specimens:* 225.000.

Herbarium: Emphasis on flora of New York; fungi, lichens, bryophytes, vascular plants, pollen, spores, anatomical sections.

Important collections: C. H. Peck, H. D. House, S. J. Smith, R. A. Latham, M. A. Curtis, C. Dewey, H. P. Sartwell, J. Torrey, E. Tuckerman, P. D. Kneiskern, J. V. Haberer, L. S. Rose, I. W. Clokey, C. F. Austin, B. D. Gilbert, C. S. Sheldon, E. Brainerd, S. P. Sargent, E. P. Bicknell.

Director: HUGO JAMNBACK.

Curator of Bryophytes, Lichens, and Vascular Plants: CHARLES J. SHEVIAK, 1947 (Systematics and evolution of North American orchids; flora of northeastern and midwestern U.S.; biogeography of eastern North America).

Curator of Fungi: JOHN H. HAINES, 1938 (Systematics of Hyalosyphaceae).

3

Staff members: RICHARD S. MITCHELL, 1938 (Polygonaceae systematics and morphology; New York flora; adaptability of aquatic plants).

DONALD M. LEWIS, 1927 (Palynology).

Specialization in research: Flora of New York State; systematics of aquatic plants; biosystematics of orchids; systematics of fungi; palynology.

Loans: To recognized botanical institutions.

Periodical and serial works: New York State Museum Bulletin.

Exchange: Available: New York plants. Desired: Bryophytes and higher plants of eastern North America.

ALBION: *Herbarium, Department of Biology, Albion College,* (**ALBC**), Albion, Michigan 49224, **U.S.A.**

Telephone: 517/629-5511.

Status: Private college.

Foundation: 1940. *Number of specimens:* 9.000.

Herbarium: Mainly Michigan flora.

Important collections: C. W. Fallass, William J. Gilbert.

Director and Curator: EWELL A. STOWELL, 1922 (Morphology and taxonomy of fungi and vascular plants).

Loans: Usual regulations.

Exchange: Limited.

ALBUQUERQUE: *Herbarium, Rocky Mountain Forest and Range Experiment Station, Albuquerque Unit,* (**ALBU**), 2205 Columbia SE, Albuquerque, New Mexico 87106, **U.S.A.**

Telephone: 505/766-2384.

Number of specimens: 750.

Herbarium: New Mexico and Arizona plants used for forage.

Important collections: H. W. Springfield, C. P. Pase.

Director: EARL F. ALDON, 1930 (Forest hydrology).

Curator: CHARLES P. PASE, 1926 (Range ecology).

Staff member: DAVID SCHOLL, 1941 (Soil scientist).

Specialization in research: Mine reclamation; range management.

ALBUQUERQUE: *Herbarium and Museum of Botany, Department of Biology, University of New Mexico,* (**UNM**), Albuquerque, New Mexico 87131, **U.S.A.**

Telephone: 505/277-5330; 277-2604.

Status: A section of the Museum of Southwestern Biology, Department of Biology, University of New Mexico.

Foundation: 1928. *Number of specimens:* 85.000.

Herbarium: Flora of New Mexico and surrounding areas.

Important collections: Cacti of New Mexico and other southwestern areas.

Director and Curator: WILLIAM C. MARTIN, 1923; 505/277-2604 (Floristics).

Staff members: KAREN CLARY (Ethnobotany).

ANNE CULLY (Ethnobotany).

PAUL KNIGHT (Ethnobotany).

MOLLIE STRUEVER (Ethnobotany).

Specialization in research: Floristics; vegetation surveys; threatened and endangered species; ethnobotany; seed germination.

Loans: 6 months, or more if in initial request; extensions granted upon request.

Exchange: Limited.

ALDERNEY: *Herbarium, Alderney Society and Museum,* (**ALD**), Alderney, Channel Islands, **Great Britain.**

ALEXANDRIA: *Department of Botany, Faculty of Science, The University,* (**ALEX**), Moharram Bey, Alexandria, **Egypt.** (Information 1974)

Herbarium: Mediterranean flora.

ALGER: *Herbarium, Laboratoire de Botanique de la Faculté des Sciences, Université d'Alger,* (**AL**), Alger, **Algeria.** (Information 1964)

Status: University.

Foundation: 1911. *Number of specimens:* 350.000.

Herbarium: Mainly northern Africa and Mediterranean Region.

Important collections: Types of A. N. Pomel, J. A. Battandier, L. C. Trabut (spermatophytes, bryophytes), R. Maire (spermatophytes, fungi).

Associated botanic garden: Botanic Garden of the University of Alger.

Loans: To recognized botanical institutions.

Periodical and serial works: Flore d'Afrique du Nord.

ALICE SPRINGS: *Herbarium of the Northern Territory of Australia,* (**NT**), Box 2134, Arid Zone Research Institute, Alice Springs, N.T. 5750, **Australia.**

Telephone: 089-522344.

Status: Department of Primary Production, N.T. Government.

Foundation: 1954. *Number of specimens:* 65.000.

Important collections: G. M. Chippendale, D. J. Nelson, R. E. Winkworth, R. A. Perry; Arid Zone Land Surveys.

Director of Department: A. D. L. HOOPER (Land conservation, agriculture).

Curator: J. R. MACONOCHIE, 1941 (Cycadaceae, Leguminosae, arid zone ecology).

Staff members: T. S. HENSHALL (Chenopodiaceae).

P. K. LATZ (Cyperaceae, Gramineae, ethnobotany).

A. S. MITCHELL (Malvaceae, economic botany).

Specialization in research: Flora of the Northern Territory, arid and subtropical Australia; medicinal and fodder plants.

Loans: To recognized botanical institutions.

Periodical and serial works: Northern Territory Botanical Bulletin.

Exchange: Desired: Arid zone plants.

ALLAHABAD: *Botanical Survey of India, Central Circle,* **(BSA),** 10 Chatham Lines, Allahabad-211002, **India.**
Telephone: 52087.
Status: Government of India.
Foundation: 1962. *Number of specimens:* 42.000.
Herbarium: Plants of eastern Uttar Pradesh and Madhya Pradesh, including plants of tribal use.
    Director: R. K. CHAKRAVERTY, 1939 (Plant physiology, economic botany, taxonomy of angiosperms).
    Curator: A. K. MUKHERJEE, 1932 (Taxonomy of angiosperms, ecology).
    Staff members: R. D. DIXIT, 1942 (Taxonomy of pteridophytes).
    J. LAL, 1945 (Morphology and taxonomy of bryophytes).
    RAM LAL, 1938 (Taxonomy of angiosperms).
    O. P. MISHRA, 1939 (Taxonomy of angiosperms).
    G. P. ROY, 1939 (Biosystematics of angiosperms).
    A. N. SINGH, 1943 (Taxonomy of angiosperms).
    R. C. SRIVASTAVA, 1954 (Taxonomy of angiosperms).
    D. M. VERMA, 1937 (Taxonomy of angiosperms).
    Specialization in research: Floristics; introduction and maintenance of medicinal, endangered and endemic species in Experimental Garden.
    Associated botanic garden: Experimental Garden.
    Loans: To recognized botanical institutions.

ALLENDALE: *Herbarium, Department of Biology, Grand Valley State College,* **(GVSC),** Allendale, Michigan 49401, **U.S.A.**
Telephone: 616/895-6611.
Foundation: 1964. *Number of specimens:* 3.000.
Herbarium: Primarily native vascular plants of western, lower peninsula of Michigan.
    Director and Curator: JOHN P. SHONTZ, 1940 (Plant ecology; local vascular plants).
    Staff members: FREDERICK BEVIS, 1934 (Flora of Michigan's upper peninsula).
    WILLIAM REDDING, 1928 (Aquatic vascular plants and non-vascular plants).
    Loans: Usual regulations.
    Exchange: Upon request.

ALLENTOWN: *Herbarium, Department of Biology, Muhlenberg College,* **(MCA),** Allentown, Pennsylvania 18104, **U.S.A.**
Telephone: 215/433-3191.
Foundation: 1890. *Number of specimens:* 52.000.
Herbarium: New Jersey and eastern Pennsylvania.
Important collections: Harold W. Pretz, Bayard Long, Robert L. Schaeffer, Jr.

Director: JAMES R. VAUGHAN, 1928 (Biochemistry).
Curator: ROBERT L. SCHAEFFER, JR., 1917 (Local flora).
    Specialization in research: Local flora.
    Loans: According to standard procedures.
    Exchange: No.

ALMA: *Herbarium, Biology Department, Alma College,* **(ALMA),** Alma, Michigan 48801, **U.S.A.**
Telephone: 517/463-2141.
Status: Private college.
Foundation: 1886. *Number of specimens:* 20.000.
Herbarium: Primarily vascular plants of central Michigan.
Important collections: A. Stilwell, E. Transeau, R. Kapp.
    Director and Curator: RONALD O. KAPP, 1935 (Palynology; plant ecology).
    Staff member: RICHARD ROEPER, 1938 (Mycology).
    Loans: No special restrictions.
    Exchange: Limited.

ALMA ATA: *Herbarium of the Botanical Institute of the Academy of Sciences of the Kazakh S.S.R.,* **(AA),** Kirova St. 103, Alma Ata 2, 480100 **U.S.S.R.**
Status: State institute.
Foundation: 1933. *Number of specimens:* 225.000 (150.000 phanerogams, 75.000 cryptogams).
Herbarium: Mainly plants of Kazakhstan.
    Director: P. M. MYRZAKULOV.
    Curator of Vascular Plants: V. P. GOLOSKOKOV.
    Curator of Cryptogams: M. P. VASYAGINA.
    Specialization in research: Flora of Kazakhstan and ancient Mediterranean.
    Periodical and serial works: Flora of Kazakhstan, Botanical Material of the Herbarium of the Botanical Institute of the Acad. Sci. Kaz. SSR, Opr. Kazakhstan.

ALPINE: *Herbarium, Department of Biology, Sul Ross State University,* **(SRSC),** Alpine, Texas 79830, **U.S.A.**
Telephone: 915/837-8112.
Foundation: 1946. *Number of specimens:* 27.000.
Herbarium: Plants of Trans-Pecos, Texas and the Chihuahuan Desert.
Important collections: Barton H. Warnock (vascular plants of Trans-Pecos, Texas).
    Director and Curator: A. MICHAEL POWELL, 1937 (Asteraceae; trees and shrubs of Trans-Pecos, Texas).
    Staff member: JOHN M. MILLER, 1952 (Systematics; phytochemistry).
    Specialization in research: Systematics and coevolutionary biology of the Chihuahuan Desert; phytochemistry.
    Loans: To recognized institutions; specimens must be annotated.

5

Massachusetts (MASS), Amherst.

ALTA LOMA: *Herbarium, Life Science Division, Chaffey College,* (**CHAF**), 5885 Haven Avenue, Alta Loma, California 91701, **U.S.A.**
Telephone: 714/987-1737.
Foundation: 1960. *Number of specimens:* 6.000.
Director and Curator: RICHARD M. BEEKS.

ALVA: *Herbarium, Northwestern Oklahoma State University,* (**NWOSU**), Alva, Oklahoma 73717, **U.S.A.**
Telephone: 405/327-1700.
Foundation: 1913. *Number of specimens:* 1.500.
Herbarium: Mainly northwestern Oklahoma.
Important collections: G. W. Stevens (1913–1915).
Director and Curator: PAUL F. NIGHSWONGER, 1923 (Vascular plants).
Loans: Usual regulations.

AMARILLO: *Herbarium, U.S. Soil Conservation Service,* (**USSC**), Herring Plaza, Box H-4358, Amarillo, Texas 79101, **U.S.A.**
Remarks: Herbarium dispersed several years ago. Staff members have small personal herbaria for use in training personnel in plant identification and management.

AMES: *Herbarium, Department of Botany, Iowa State University,* (**ISC**), Stange Road and Osborne Drive, Ames, Iowa 50011, **U.S.A.**
Telephone: 515/294-3413; 294-3522.
Foundation: 1870. *Number of specimens:* 350.000.
Herbarium: Comprehensive for state of Iowa; general for U.S.; exceptional collections of Gramineae and Leguminosae.
Important collections: J. P. Anderson (Alaskan and boreal plants), C. C. Parry (western U.S.), D. Isely (legumes), R. W. Pohl (tropical American grasses).
Director and Curator: RICHARD W. POHL, 1916 (Taxonomy and cytology of Central American Gramineae).
Staff members: DUANE ISELY, 1918 (Taxonomy of U.S. Leguminosae).
NELS LERSTEN, 1932 (Systematic anatomy, especially seeds of Leguminosae).
Specialization in research: Systematics of American Gramineae and Leguminosae.
Loans: To recognized botanical institutions for revisionary studies.
Periodical and serial works: Iowa State Journal of Research.
Exchange: Desired: Gramineae and Leguminosae from any area.

AMHERST: *Herbarium, Amherst College,* (**AC**), Amherst, Massachusetts 01002, **U.S.A.**
Foundation: 1829. *Number of specimens:* 84.000.
Remarks: The Amherst College herbarium has been placed on permanent loan to the University of

AMHERST: *Herbarium, Department of Botany, University of Massachusetts,* (**MASS**), Amherst, Massachusetts 01003, **U.S.A.**
Telephone: 413/545-0831.
Foundation: 1900. *Number of specimens:* 230.000 (including Amherst College herbarium).
Herbarium: Worldwide, especially New England vascular plants.
Important collections: Original herbaria of Addison Brown, W. W. Denslow, and A. S. Goodale; Amherst College; Otto Degener, A. C. Smith.
Curator: HARRY E. AHLES (Flora of eastern U.S.; weeds).
Staff members: HOWARD D. BIGELOW (Fleshy fungi).
MARGARET B. BIGELOW (Pyrenomycetes).
EDWARD L. DAVIS (Angiosperm taxonomy).
RUDOLF M. SCHUSTER (Bryophytes).
OTTO L. STEIN (Morphogenesis).
OSWALD TIPPO (Ethnobotany).
JAMES W. WALKER (Palynology).
ROBERT T. WILCE (Algology).
Loans: To recognized botanical institutions.
Exchange: Available: Mostly U.S. vascular plants, Desired: All vascular plants.

AMOY: *Herbarium, Amoy University,* (**AU**) — *see* XIAMEN.

AMSTERDAM: *Herbarium, Hugo de Vries-laboratorium,* (**AMD**), Plantage Middenlaan 2A, 1018 DD Amsterdam, **Netherlands.**
Status: University of Amsterdam.
Foundation: About 1700. *Number of specimens:* 175.000.
Herbarium: Worldwide, mainly Europe.
Director: A. D. J. MEEUSE, 1914 (General systematics, S. African flora, morphology, phylogeny).
Curator: A. A. STERK, 1931 (Biosystematics).
Staff members: F. BOUMAN, 1941.
F. D. BOESEWINKEL, 1937 (Morphology).
P. F. M. COESEL, 1941 (Systematics of algae).
L. DIJKHUIZEN, 1922 (Biosystematics).
A. C. ELLIS-ADAM, 1937 (Systematics of algae).
B. V. GEEL, 1947 (Palynology).
M. C. GROENHART, 1935 (Ecology).
T. VAN DER HAMMEN, 1924 (Palynology).
L. DE LANGE, 1925 (Ecology).
A. A. MIDDELDORP, 1949 (Palynology).
J. C. M. DEN NIJS, 1946 (Biosystematics).
J. WIEGERS, 1947 (Ecology).
T. A. WIJMSTRA, 1932 (Palynology).
Specialization in research: European flora (Ecology, biosystematics, palynology); palynology of South America.
Associated botanic garden: Hortus Botanicus of the University of Amsterdam.
Loans: To recognized institutions.

Periodical and serial works: Contributions.

Exchange: European plants.

AMSTERDAM: *Department of Systematic Botany, Vrije Universiteit,* **(AVU)**, De Boelelaan 1087, 1081 AV Amsterdam, **Netherlands.**

Telephone: 020-5483534.

Status: Department of the Biological Laboratory of Vrije Universiteit.

Foundation: 1951. *Number of specimens:* 30.000.

Herbarium: Spermatophytes, marine and freshwater algae of W. Europe, marine algae of Netherlands West Indies.

Director: M. VROMAN, 1927 (Systematics and ecology of marine and freshwater algae).

Curators: J. H. IETSWAART, 1940 (Biosystematics of spermatophytes).

H. STEGENGA, 1947 (Flora of the marine algae of Netherlands).

Staff members: J. VAN DER HEIDE, 1932 (Ecology of freshwater algae).

H. HILLEBRAND, 1943 (Ecology of freshwater algae).

J. KUIPER, 1953 (Biosystematics of *Acrochaetium*).

J. SIMONS, 1940 (Biosystematics and ecology of Zygnemales).

H. J. SLUIMAN, 1953 (Biosystematics of *Coleochaete*).

Specialization in research: Taxonomy, biosystematics and ecology of macroscopic algae; biosystematics of spermatophytes.

Associated botanic garden: Botanical Garden of Vrije Universiteit, van der Boechorststraat 8, 1081 BT Amsterdam.

Loans: To recognized botanical institutions.

Exchange: Available: Marine algae of Netherlands and Netherlands West Indies. Desired: Marine and freshwater algae.

ANAHEIM: *Herbarium, Orange County Department of Agriculture,* **(ANA)**, 1010 South Harbor Boulevard, Anaheim, California 92805, **U.S.A.**

Telephone: 714/774-0284.

Status: County government.

Foundation: 1950. *Number of specimens:* 1.000.

Herbarium: Local species; noxious weeds; some ornamental trees, shrubs.

Director: WILLIAM AMLING, 1925.

Curator: DELIA B. SMITH (Botanist).

ANGERS: *Herbier Lloyd,* **(ANG)**, Place des Halles, Angers, **France.**

ANGERS: *Herbier de la Faculté Libre des Sciences,* **(ANGUC)**, 3 Place André Leroy, B.P. 808, 49005 Angers Cedex, **France.**

Telephone: (41) 88 33 12.

Status: Facultés catholiques de l'Ouest.

Foundation: 1876. *Number of specimens:* 250.000–

300.000.

Herbarium: Bryophytes, lichens, Charophytes, vascular plants.

Important collections: Original herbarium of J. Harmand (Lichens, about 30.000); herb. F. Hy (Charophyceae).

Director: ROBERT CORILLION, 1908 (Charophyceae, phanerogamae).

Curator: MICHELINE GUERLÉSQUIN, 1928 (Charophyceae).

Staff members: PAULETTE LAMANT, 1930 (Technical assistant).

SIMONE LEMOYNE, 1912.

MARTHE NORMANT, 1917 (Secretary).

Specialization in research: Charophyceae: systematics, morphology, biology, caryology, phytosociology, phytogeography; flora and vegetation of West France and the valley of the Loire.

Loans: Short loan (six months maximum) for dried exsiccata.

Periodical and serial works: Travaux et mémoires du Laboratoire de Biologie végétale et de Phytogéographie.

Exchange: Reprints only.

ANGUIL: *Herbario, Estación Experimental Regional Agropecuaria, Instituto Nacional de Tecnología Agropecuaria,* **(ANGU)**, Casilla de Correo 11, 6326 Anguil, La Pampa, **Argentina.**

Telephone: Anguil 7.

Foundation: 1954. *Number of specimens:* 6.000.

Herbarium: Flora of La Pampa.

Important collections: Guillermo Covas, Eduardo Cano, Mario Frecentese.

Director: ABEL BERNARDÓN, 1926 (Pastures).

Curator: GUILLERMO COVAS, 1915 (Breeding of forage plants; taxonomy of grasses; flora of La Pampa).

Specialization in research: Flora of La Pampa; taxonomy of grasses.

Loans: Usual regulations.

Periodical and serial works: Apuntes para la Flora de La Pampa.

Exchange: Yes.

ANGWIN: *Herbarium, Biology Department, Pacific Union College,* **(PUA)**, Angwin, California 94508, **U.S.A.**

Telephone: 707/965-6227.

Status: Private college.

Foundation: 1967. *Number of specimens:* 20.000.

Herbarium: Nampa County, California, and Klamath Mountains of northern California and southern Oregon.

Director and Curator: GILBERT JEROME MUTH, 1938 (Floristic computerized data retrieval).

Specialization in research: Computerized data retrieval system for herbarium label data.

Loans: Yes.

7

Exchange: Limited.

ANKARA: *Ankara Üniversitesi Eczacilik Fakültesi Herbaryumu,* (**AEF**), Farmakognozi ve Farmasötik Botanik Kürsüsü, Tandogan, Ankara, **Turkey.**
Telephone: 232120/47.
Status: Faculty of Pharmacy.
Foundation: 1967. Number of specimens: 10.000.
Herbarium: Native and mostly medicinal plants of Turkey.
Important collections: Valeriana, Allium, Helichrysum, Dryopteris, Asplenium.
Director: NEVIN TANKER, 1931 (Asphodeline, Cyclamen, Juniperus).
Curator: MEHMET KOYUNCU, 1944; 232120/45 (Valeriana, Allium, Muscari, Ornithogalum).
Staff members: MAKSUT COSKUN, 1951 (Dryopteris, Asplenium).
SEMRA KURUCU, 1952 (Cytology and chemotaxonomy of Allium).
GÜLDEN SEZIK, 1945 (Helichrysum).
Specialization in research: Systematics of medicinal plants, floristic research.
Loans: To recognized botanical institutions.
Periodical and serial works: Journal of Faculty of Pharmacy of Ankara University.
Exchange: Some duplicates available.

ANKARA: *Ankara Üniversitesi, Fen Fakültesi Herbaryumu,* (**ANK**), Sistematik Botanik Kürsüsü, Beşevler-Ankara, **Turkey.**
Telephone: 236550 or 232105.
Status: University.
Foundation: 1935. Number of specimens: 70.000.
Herbarium: Mostly Turkish plants.
Important collections: Part of P. H. Davis' collection, P. Sintenis, J. F. N. Bornmüller, Kotte, J. G. Gassner, Markgraf, H. Birand, K. Krause.
Director: YILDIRIM AKMAN, 1932 (Phytosociology, ecology).
Curator: TUNA EKIM, 1940; 236550/0189 (Taxonomy).
Staff members: OLCAY ABALI (Algology).
MUSTAFA AYDOGDU (Ecology).
GÜLER AYKULU, 1940 (Algology).
MEHMET DEMIRÖRS (Ecology).
ATABAY DUZENLI (Ecology).
ARIZ GÖNÜLOL (Algology).
RESIT ILARSLAN (Taxonomy).
OSMAN KETENOGLU (Ecology).
MAHMUT KILING (Ecology).
TURHAN USLU (Ecology).
ENDER YURAKULOL, 1940 (Ecology).
Specialization in research: Floristics, ecology and phytosociology.
Periodical and serial works: Communication of Faculty of Science, University of Ankara.

ANKARA: *Forest Research Institute Herbarium,* (**ANKO**), P.K. 24, Bahçelievler, Ankara, **Turkey.**

Telephone: 131734.
Status: Adherence to General Directorate of Forestry under Ministry of Forestry.
Foundation: 1959. Number of specimens: 1.015.
Herbarium: Trees and shrubs in forest regions of Turkey.
Important collections: Gymnosperms and angiosperms of Turkey.
Specialization in research: Forest research.

ANKARA: *Herbarium, British Institute of Archaeology,* (**BIA**), Tahran Caddesi 21, Kavaklidere, Ankara, **Turkey.** (Information 1974)
Foundation: 1970. Number of specimens: 4.500.
Herbarium: Plants of Konya and Elâziğ Provinces.
Specialization in research: Identification of plant remains from archaeological excavations.

ANKARA: *Herbarium, Department of Botany, Hacettepe University,* (**HUB**), Beytepe Campus, Ankara, **Turkey.**
Telephone: 235130-1373; 235164-1373; 236730-1373.
Status: University.
Foundation: 1973. Number of specimens: 15.000.
Herbarium: Specimens from various parts of Anatolia and Russian Armenia.
Director: HASAN PEŞMEN, 1939 (Flowering plants of Turkey).
Staff members: SADIK ERIK, 1948.
ADIL GÜNER, 1950 (Iris of Turkey).
ŞINASI YILDIRIMLI, 1949.
BAYRAM YILDIZ, 1947.
Specialization in research: Flora of Turkey.
Loans: Available to well-known herbaria.
Exchange: Available: Plants of Turkey. Desired: Specimens from neighboring countries.

ANKARA: *Hacettepe Üniversitesi Eczacilik Fakültesi Herbaryumu,* (**HUEF**), Farmakognozi ve Farmasötik Botanik Bölümü, Hacettepe – Ankara, **Turkey.**
Status: Hacettepe University, Ankara.
Foundation: 1969. Number of specimens: 2.300.
Herbarium: Turkey.
Important collections: E. Sezik (Orchidaceae).
Director: EKREM SEZIK (Orchidaceae and Caryophyllaceae of Turkey).
Curator: GÜLENDAM TÜMEN (Labiatae, especially Ziziphora).
Staff members: ZELIHA AKDEMIR (Helichrysum).
AHMET BAŞARAN (Labiatae, especially Stachys).
IHSAN ÇALIŞ (Saponaria, Primula).
AKIN ÇUBUKÇU (Hypericaceae, Labiatae).
NURTEN EZER (Sideritis).
SEDEF HAKCI.
YAVUZ BORA ÖZER (Orchidaceae).
ICLAL SARAÇOĞLU.
ERDEM YEŞILADA (Polygala, Bolanthus).
Specialization in research: Medicinal plants of

Turkey, especially flavonoid, saponin, volatile oil containing plants.

Exchange: Some duplicates of Turkish plants.

ANN ARBOR: *Herbarium of the American Fern Society, University of Michigan,* **(AFS)**, North University Building, Ann Arbor, Michigan 48109, **U.S.A.**

Status: Society Herbarium.

Foundation: 1900. *Number of specimens:* 10.000.

Herbarium: Pteridophytes, mainly North America, scattered worldwide representation.

Remarks: AFS incorporated in MICH.

ANN ARBOR: *Herbarium of the University of Michigan,* **(MICH)**, North University Building, Ann Arbor, Michigan 48109, **U.S.A.**

Telephone: 313/764-2407.

Status: A department of the College of Literature, Science, and the Arts of the University of Michigan.

Foundation: First collections received in 1837; present organization established in 1921. *Number of specimens:* 1.420.000.

Herbarium: Worldwide, specializing in plants of temperate North America, especially the Great Lakes region (all groups), eastern North America, the West Indies, and the Pacific Islands (marine algae), tropical America (bryophytes), Mexico, the southwestern Pacific region, and southeastern Asia (vascular plants).

Important collections: W. R. Taylor (marine algae), D. V. Baxter (polypores), C. H. Kauffman (agarics), E. B. Mains (rusts and insecticolous fungi), R. L. Shaffer (agarics), A. H. Smith (agarics, boletes, gastromycetes), B. Fink (lichens), H. A. Crum (bryophytes), W. C. Steere (bryophytes), herbarium of Parke, Davis & Co. (vascular plants), Douglass Houghton (vascular plants of the eastern U.S.), Adams Jewett (vascular plants of France and the eastern U.S.), R. R. Dreisbach (vascular plants), F. J. Hermann (Cyperaceae, Juncaceae), K. Lems (vascular plants of the Canary Islands), R. McVaugh (vascular plants of Mexico), H. H. Bartlett (vascular plants of the southwestern Pacific region), W. N. Koelz (vascular plants of southeastern Asia), E. G. Voss (vascular plants of Michigan); herbarium of the American Fern Society (AFS).

Director: ROBERT L. SHAFFER, Curator of Fungi, 1929 (Higher fungi).

Staff members: CHRISTIANE ANDERSON, 1944 (Malpighiaceae).

WILLIAM R. ANDERSON, Associate Curator of Vascular Plants, 1942 (Malpighiaceae; *Elaphoglossum*).

HOWARD A. CRUM, Curator of Bryophytes and Lichens, 1922 (Moss flora of eastern North America; *Sphagnum*).

GEORGE F. ESTABROOK, 1942 (Estimation of evolutionary relationships among organisms).

ROBERT FOGEL, 1947 (Hypogeous fungi).

ROGERS MCVAUGH, 1909 (Vascular plant flora of Mexico; Myrtaceae).

ANTON A. REZNICEK, 1950 (*Carex;* prairie floras).

ALEXANDER H. SMITH, 1904 (Higher fungi).

WM. RANDOLPH TAYLOR, 1895 (Marine algae).

EDWARD G. VOSS, 1929 (Vascular plant flora of the upper Great Lakes region; botanical nomenclature).

WARREN H. WAGNER JR., 1920 (Pteridophytes; evolution of vascular plants).

MICHAEL J. WYNNE, Associate Curator of Algae, 1940 (Marine algae).

Specialization in research: Systematics, floristics, and ecology of higher fungi and mosses, especially of North America, and vascular plants of northeastern North America, Mexico, and northern South America.

Associated botanic garden: Matthaei Botanical Gardens of the University of Michigan, 1800 N. Dixboro Rd., Ann Arbor, Michigan 48109, U.S.A.

Loans: To recognized botanical institutions.

Periodical and serial works: Contributions from the University of Michigan Herbarium (issued irregularly); The Michigan Botanist, with 4 issues per year, is edited at the Herbarium for the Michigan Botanical Club.

Exchange: Desired from all parts of the world, by arrangement with the Curators only.

ANTIOQUIA: *Department of Biology, University of Antioquia,* **(HUA)** -- *see* MEDELLIN.

ANTWERPEN: *Dr. Henri Van Heurck Museum,* **(AWH)**, Royal Zoological Society of Antwerp, Koningin Astridplein 26, B-2000 Antwerpen, **Belgium**.

Telephone: 31 – 31.16.40.

Status: Collections Van Heurck property of the City of Antwerp.

Foundation: 1867 (Acquisition of herb. Sieber- von Reichenbach by Dr. H. Van Heurck). *Number of specimens:* 250.000; 20.000 slides (Diatomeae).

Herbarium: Worldwide.

Important collections: F. W. Sieber, von Reichenbach, H. F. Van Heurck, C. L. P. Zeyher, Spruce, J. W. Horneman, P. Salzmann, T. Kotschy, G. H. W. Schimper. Diatomeae: W. Arnott, P. T. Cleve and J. D. Möller, T. Eulenstein, Janisch, Klävsen, F. T. Kützing (tubes), J. D. Möller, W. Smith, J. A. Tempère et H. Peragallo, Van Heurck, A. W. H. Weissflog.

Director: J. F. GEERAERTS, 1931.

Curator: G. VAN STEENBERGEN, 1937.

Staff member: C. KRUYFHOOFT, 1950 (Diatomeae).

Loans: To be addressed to the Municipality of Antwerp, Town Hall, B-2000 Antwerpen, Belgium.

L'AQUILA: *Herbarium Aquilanum,* **(AQUI)**, Istituto Botanico dell'Università, Piazza Annunziata 1, 67100 L'Aquila, **Italy**.

Telephone: 0864-20029.

Status: Adherence to University.

Foundation: 1966. *Number of specimens:* 28.000 (25.000 spermatophyta, 3.000 fungi).

Herbarium: Mainly Cormophyta from Central and Southern Italy, Italian macrofungi.

Director and Curator: Professor of Botany or Professor of Geobotany of the University.

Staff members: ARISTIDE CARILLI (Industrial microfungi).

GIUSEPPE CHICHIRICCO (Cytotaxonomy).

GIULIANO FRIZZI (Plant geography).

FRANCO DEL GROSSO (Cytotaxonomy, freshwater algae).

GIOVANNI PACIONI (Macrofungi, entopathogenic fungi).

MARINO POGLIANI (Cytotaxonomy).

GABRIELE SEBASTIANI (Floristics).

FERNANDO TAMMARO (Floristics, plant geography, medicinal plants).

LUIGI VERI (Floristics, vegetation).

Research associates: NICOLA CAPORALE (Vegetation of grasslands).

ANNABELLA PACE (Vegetation of grasslands).

GIANFRANCO PIRONE (Flora and vegetation of Lucania, Southern Italy).

Specialization in research: Flora and vegetation of Italy and mediterranean area; plant geography and ecology; biosystematics; mycology.

Associated botanic garden: Giardino Alpino del Gran Sasso d'Italia (founded 1955).

Loans: To recognized botanical institutions.

Periodical and serial works: Raccolta di lavori botanici dell'Istituto Botanico Università l'Aquila, Index seminum Horti Botanici Aquilani.

Exchange: Yes.

ARACAJU: *Herbário, Departamento de Biologia, Universidade Federal de Sergipe,* **(ASE),** Rua Vila Cristina, 1051, 49.000 Aracaju, Sergipe, **Brazil.**

Telephone: (55)079/222-3121.

Foundation: 1975. *Number of specimens:* 1.100.

Herbarium: Flora of the state of Sergipe and of the sandstone table mountains of Pirambu, Sergipe.

Curator: MARCELO RAMOS DA FONSECA, 1948; 222–9404.

Staff members: ANTÔNIO CARLOS CARVALHO BARRETO, 1950.

GILVANE VIANA SOUZA, 1951.

Loans: To specialists for 3 months; extensions upon request.

Exchange: Yes.

ARCADIA: *Herbarium, Los Angeles State and County Arboretum,* **(LASCA),** 301 North Baldwin Avenue, Arcadia, California 91006, **U.S.A.**

Telephone: 213/446-8251.

Status: Associated with Los Angeles County Department of Arboreta and Botanic Gardens.

Foundation: 1960. *Number of specimens:* 50.000.

Herbarium: Exotic woody flora; vouchers of plants at Los Angeles State and County Arboretum.

Director: GARY D. WALLACE, 1946 (Ericaceae; flora of southern California, especially off-shore islands).

Curator: JEANETTE HUBER, 1922 (Myrtaceae; *Acacia*).

Specialization in research: Exotic flora of southern California.

Associated botanic garden: Los Angeles State and County Arboretum.

Loans: Short term, to recognized institutions.

Exchange: Available: Cultivated exotic flora; limited number of weeds and native flora. Wanted: Woody material suitable for cultivation; economic plants.

ARCATA: *Herbarium, Department of Biology, Humboldt State University,* **(HSC),** Arcata, California 95521, **U.S.A.**

Telephone: 707/826-4801.

Foundation: 1960. *Number of specimens:* 140.000.

Herbarium: Vascular plants of northwestern California and southwestern Oregon; regional, Mexican, Caribbean, tropical South Pacific bryophytes; regional algae, fungi, and lichens; desmids of North America.

Director: JAMES PAYNE SMITH, JR., 1941 (Flora of northwest California; Gramineae).

Staff members: DAVID LARGENT, Curator of Fungi, 1937 (Agaricologist; Rhodophyllaceae).

MICHAEL MESLER, Curator of Pteridophytes, 1947 (Systematics of vascular plants).

THOMAS NELSON, 1928 (Systematics of ultramafics; distribution of rare plants; flora of northwest California).

DANIEL NORRIS, Curator of Bryophytes, 1933 (Mosses of western North America and tropical South Pacific).

ROBERT RASMUSSEN, Curator of Marine Algae, 1933 (Morphology of Rhodophyta, marine macroalgae of northern California; limiting factors of species distribution).

J. O. SAWYER, 1939 (Vegetation of northern California).

WILLIAM VINYARD, Curator of Freshwater Algae, 1922 (Desmids of North America; freshwater algae).

Specialization in research: Flora of northwest California; regional, tropical South Pacific mosses; regional fungi, mycorrhiza of northern California, *Leptonia* of North America; regional algae, desmids of North America: vegetation of northern California.

Loans: No special restrictions.

Exchange: Vascular plants of western North America; bryophytes worldwide, preferably extra-North America; fungi of western North America.

AREIA: *Herbário Jayme Coelho de Moraes, Centro de Ciências Agrárias, Universidade Federal da Paraíba,* **(EAN),** Campus III, 58.397 Areia, Paraíba, **Brazil.**

Telephone: (55)083/362-2259.
Foundation: 1938. *Number of specimens:* 2.000.
Herbarium: Mainly species of "brejo" and semi-arid regions of Paraíba State.
Important collections: Jayme Coelho de Moraes, B. Pickel, L. Smith, Rizzini.
    Director: NORMANDO MELQUÍADES DE ARAÚJO, 1946 (Genetics).
    Curator: VANIA PERAZZO BARBOSA FEVEREIRO, 1948 (Leguminosae; flora of "brejo").
    Staff members: PAULO CÉSAR AYRES FEVEREIRO, 1942 (Brazilian *Vigna*, Leguminosae).
        ANTÔNIO DE OLIVEIRA GALVÃO, 1941 (Physiology of *Spondias*, Anacardiaceae).
    Specialization in research: Flora of "brejo" of Paraíba State; Leguminosae (Phaseolae) of northeastern Brazil; physiology of *Spondias*.
    Loans: Temporarily suspended while herbarium is being organized.

ARMIDALE: *Herbarium, Department of Botany, University of New England*, (**NE**), Armidale, New South Wales 2351, **Australia.** (Information 1974)
Status: University.
Foundation: 1938; re-established after fire in 1958.
Number of specimens: 30.000.
Herbarium: Australia, mainly NE New South Wales.
    Specialization in research: Autochthonous flora of Australia.
    Loans: To recognized botanical institutions.

ASHKHABAD: *Herbarium, Botanical Institute of the Turkmenia Academy of Sciences, Laboratory of Flora and Systematics of Vascular Plants*, (**ASH**), Srobody prospect 81, 744000 Ashkhabad, **U.S.S.R.**
Status: Directed by Academy of Sciences of the Turkmen S.S.R.
Foundation: 1930. *Number of specimens:* 145.000.
    Director: P. CHOPANOV.
    Specialization in research: Local flora.
    Associated botanic garden: Turkmen Botanic Garden of the Academy of Sciences.
    Periodical and serial works: Flora of Turkmenistan.

ASHLAND: *Herbarium, Department of Biology, Southern Oregon State College*, (**SOC**), Ashland, Oregon 97520, **U.S.A.**
Telephone: 503/482-6341.
Status: Administered by Oregon State System of Higher Education.
Foundation: 1967. *Number of specimens:* 5.000.
Herbarium: Vascular plants of southern Oregon.
    Director: FRANK A. LANG, 1937 (Biosystematics of Pteridophytes; flora of southern Oregon).
    Specialization in research: Flora of southern Oregon.
    Loans: To recognized botanists and institutions.
    Exchange: Only in special arranged cases.

ASUNCIÓN: *Jardin Botánico*, (**AS**), Asunción, **Paraguay.**

ATCHISON: *Herbarium, Biology Department, Benedictine College*, (**HWBA**), North Campus, Atchison, Kansas 66002, **U.S.A.**
Telephone: 913/367-5340, ext. 526.
Foundation: 1950. *Number of specimens:* 850.
Herbarium: Specimens from Atchison County, Kansas.
Important collections: Hubert W. Blocker.
    Curator: EUGENE W. DEHNER, 1914.
    Loans: Usual regulations.
    Exchange: Yes.

ATHENS: *Agricultural College of Athens, Institute of Systematic Botany*, (**ACA**), Botanikos Kipos, Iera Odos 75, Athens 301, **Greece.**
Telephone: 3466153.
Status: College Institute.
Foundation: 1921. *Number of specimens:* 12.000.
Herbarium: Mainly flowering plants of the Greek flora.
Important collections: Many old specimens collected by Orphanides, Tountas, Halacsy, Dimadis, Malakates.
    Director: CONSTANTIN ZERLENTIS.
    Curator: MARIA STEFANAKI (Agronomist).
    Staff members: VASO BRATZI (Laboratory preparator).
        JANNIS CHRONOPOULOS (Agronomist).
        GEORGE SARLIS (Agronomist).
    Specialization in research: Applied agricultural botany and plant geography.
    Loans: To recognized botanical institutions.
    Exchange: Available: Flowering plants of the Greek flora. Desired: Poisonous and pharmaceutical plants, algae, lichens, bryophyta.

ATHENS: *Herbarium, The Goulandris Natural History Museum*, (**ATH**), 13 Levidou Str., Kifissia, Athens, **Greece.**
Telephone: 8015 870, 8080254.
Status: Private foundation.
Foundation: 1964. *Number of specimens:* 170.000.
Herbarium: Vascular plants of Greece and Balkan Peninsula.
Important collections: Goulandris Herbarium, Goulimis collection.
    Curator: KIKI DIMAS.
    Staff members: ELLI STAMADIADOU.
        C. ZAHARIADI.
    Specialization in research: Flora of Greece: Paeoniaceae, Liliaceae, Amaryllidaceae, Iridaceae, alpine plants.
    Loans: To recognized botanical institutions.
    Periodical and serial works: Annales Musei Goulandris.
    Exchange: Available: Plants of Greece. Desired: Plants of palaeomediterranean zone.

ATHENS: *Botanical Museum and Herbarium, University of Athens,* (**ATHU**), Panepistimiopolis, Athens 621, **Greece.**
Telephone: 743-396.
Status: University.
Foundation: 1850. *Number of specimens:* 114.000 (110.000 phanerogams, 4.000 cryptogams).
Herbarium: Worldwide collection, especially Greece.
Important collections: Orphanides, T. Heldreich, Tuntas.
  Director: CONSTANTINOS TH. ANAGNOSTIDIS, 1924 (Algae, Cyanophyta, bacteria).
  Curator: ARTEMIOS G. YANNITSAROS, 1938 (Spermatophytes).
  Staff members: PAULINE H. HARITONIDOU, 1920 (Spermatophytes).
    EVANGELIA KAPSANAKI-GOTSI, 1950 (Fungi).
  Staff of Institute of Systematic Botany and Botanical Garden of University who collect and identify plant specimens for the herbarium:
    IOANNIS BITIS, 1947 (Algae); LEMONIA I. KOUMPLI-SOVANTZI, 1945 (Spermatophytes); TATIANA I. KYRIACOPOULOS, 1951 (Algae); ATHENA V. OECONOMOU-AMILLI, 1947 (Algae); MARIA E. PANTIDOU, 1918 (Fungi); MARIA N. ROUSSO-MOUSTAKAKI-THEODORAKI, 1949 (Cyanophytes); PANAGIOTIS N. TSOUKATOS, 1929 (Algae).
  Specialization in research: Flora of Greece.
  Associated botanic garden: Botanical Garden of the University of Athens.
  Loans: To recognized botanical institutions; types usually not loaned.
  Remarks: Facilities for visiting botanists.

ATHENS: *Bartley Herbarium, Department of Botany, Ohio University,* (**BHO**), Athens, Ohio 45701, **U.S.A.**
Telephone: 614/595-6012; 594-5821.
Foundation: 1934. *Number of specimens:* 35.000.
Herbarium: Flora of southeastern Ohio and adjacent states.
Important collections: Floyd Bartley (southeastern Ohio), Charles Goslin (Fairfield County, Ohio).
  Curators: ROBERT M. LLOYD, 1938 (Systematics and evolutionary biology of Pteridophytes).
    WARREN A. WISTENDAHL, 1920; 614/594-5860 (Plant ecology).
  Loans: Yes.
  Exchange: No.

ATHENS: *Herbarium, Botany Department, University of Georgia,* (**GA**), Plant Sciences Building, Athens, Georgia 30602, **U.S.A.**
Telephone: 404/542-3732.
Foundation: 1920. *Number of specimens:* 140.000.
Herbarium: Vascular plants of southeastern U.S., especially Alabama, Georgia, Louisiana, and Mississippi.
Important collections: Vernonieae (Compositae).
  Curator: SAMUEL B. JONES, 1933 (*Vernonia*, tribe Vernonieae, Compositae; southeastern U.S. flora).
  Staff members: NANCY C. COILE, 1940 (Flora of Georgia).
    DAVID E. GIANNASI, 1943 (Biochemical systematics of *Dahlia, Cassia,* ferns).
  Specialization in research: Systematics of Vernonieae; floristics of Georgia; flavonoid biochemical systematics.
  Associated botanic garden: University of Georgia Botanical Garden, Athens, Georgia 30602, U.S.A.; 404/542-1244.
  Loans: To recognized institutions.
  Exchange: Available: Southeastern U.S. Desired: Economic plants, tropical material, Vernonieae, Compositae.

ATHENS: *Julian H. Miller Mycological Herbarium, Department of Plant Pathology, University of Georgia,* (**GAM**), Athens, Georgia 30602, **U.S.A.**.
Telephone: 404/542-2571.
Status: Part of the Department of Plant Pathology, University of Georgia, and a unit of the University of Georgia Natural History Museum.
Foundation: 1950 (J. H. Miller's personal herbarium begun in 1930's). *Number of specimens:* 20.000.
Herbarium: Fungi of southeastern U.S., with emphasis on ascomycetes and deuteromycetes; worldwide collections of *Xylaria* and *Hypoxylon.*
Important collections: Types of ascomycetes described by J. H. Miller and G. E. Thompson; *Hypoxylon* specimens examined in J. H. Miller's monograph.
  Curator: RICHARD T. HANLIN, 1931 (Pyrenomycetes and conidial states).
  Staff member: E. S. LUTTRELL, 1919 (Loculoascomycetes; pyrenomycetes and deuteromycetes).
  Specialization in research: Morphology and taxonomy of perithecial ascomycetes and their conidial states; economically important ascomycetes.
  Associated botanic garden: University of Georgia Botanic Garden.
  Loans: Available to qualified researchers on an individual basis.
  Exchange: Limited to individual requests at present.

ATHERTON: *Herbarium, Queensland Regional Station, C.S.I.R.O., Division of Forest Research,* (**QRS**), P.O. Box 273, Atherton, Queensland 4883, **Australia.**
Telephone: (070) 911 755.
Status: Commonwealth of Australia.
Foundation: 1971. *Number of specimens:* 60.000.
Important collections: H. Flecker collection (Tropical Queensland).
  Director: B. P. M. HYLAND, 1937 (Trees of Australian tropical rain forest).
  Curator: S. E. BARBAGALLO, 1959.
  Staff member: B. GRAY, 1939 (Rain forest vines, ferns, orchids).

Specialization in research: Rain forests of North Queensland.

Loans: To recognized institutions.

Exchange: Available: Rain forest plants of North Queensland. Desired: Collections from Malesia.

ATLANTA: *Range, Timber & Wildlife, Southern Region, U.S. Forest Service,* **(FSSR),** 1720 Peachtree Road, N.W., Atlanta, Georgia 30309, **U.S.A.**

Status: U.S. Department of Agriculture, Forest Service.

Foundation: 1962. *Number of specimens:* 10.000.

Herbarium: Mainly southeastern grasses, forbs, and shrubs.

Important collections: J. H. Buel, A. W. Johnson, E. H. Bomberger, E. E. Ripper.

    Director: LEVESTER PENDERGRASS, 1946.

    Specialization in research: Mycology; systematic study of myxomycete occurrence on bark of living trees.

Loans: To recognized botanical institutions.

ATLANTA: *Herbarium, Biology Department, Emory University,* **(GEO),** Atlanta, Georgia 30322, **U.S.A.**

Telephone: 404/329-4211.

Foundation: 1949. *Number of specimens:* 18.575.

Herbarium: Flora of Georgia.

Important collections: R. Thorne (southwestern Georgia), Don Eyles (aquatic plants of the Southeast).

    Director and Curator: WILLIAM H. MURDY, 1928 (Granite outcrops communities).

Loans: To professional botanists.

AUBURN: *Herbarium, Department of Botany, Plant Pathology, and Microbiology, Auburn University,* **(AUA),** Auburn, Alabama 36849, **U.S.A.**

Telephone: 205/826-4830.

Foundation: 1856 (university); 1950 (herbarium). *Number of specimens:* 39.100.

Herbarium: Vascular flora of Alabama, with secondary emphasis on other southeastern states.

Important collections: E. F. Andrews (2.500), A. W. Chapman (1.000).

    Curator: JOHN D. FREEMAN, 1941 (Vascular plant systematics; endangered species; *Trillium;* floristics).

    Staff member: GARETH MORGAN-JONES, 1940 (Taxonomic mycology; fungi imperfecti; ascomycetes; pyrenocarpous lichens).

    Specialization in research: Flora of Alabama (in general); poisonous plants and endangered species of the state and region.

    Associated botanic garden: Auburn University Arboretum.

Loans: Usual regulations to recognized botanical institutions.

    Periodical and serial works: Departmental and Agricultural Experiment Station Bulletins.

    Exchange: Available: General collections from Alabama, Georgia, Florida, and Tennessee.

    Remarks: Original herbarium at Auburn University was destroyed by fire in 1920's.

AUCKLAND: *Auckland Institute and Museum (Cheeseman Herbarium),* **(AK),** Private Bag, Auckland, **New Zealand.**

Telephone: 30443.

Status: A public museum of research and education.

Foundation: Museum 1852, Cheeseman Herbarium 1870. *Number of specimens:* 152.000.

Herbarium: General collections of New Zealand plants (except fungi), emphasis on vascular flora; worldwide collections, emphasis on adventives.

Important collections: J. Banks and Solander (New Zealand), T. F. Cheeseman (New Zealand, Kermadec Islands, Raratonga), E. D. Hatch (Orchids), A. K. Lindauer (Algae), F. L. Harvey (Algae), E. Craig (Ferns), I. C. Martindale (U.S.A.), W. M. Canby (U.S.A.), Bennett (England).

    Director of Museum: G. S. PARK (Anthropology).

    Curator: JEANNE H. GOULDING, 1915 (Maori fibre plants, history of AK herbarium).

    Staff member: E. B. BANGERTER (Adventives).

    Specialization in research: New Zealand and related flora.

    Associated botanic garden: Auckland Regional Botanic Garden, Hill Road, R.D., Manurewa, Auckland.

Loans: No restrictions, but approval of Government needed for export of type specimens.

    Periodical and serial works: Annual Records of the Auckland Institute and Museum, Occasional Bulletins.

    Exchange: Available: Native and introduced plants of New Zealand. Desired: General collections, especially from countries bordering the Pacific.

AUCKLAND: *Herbarium, Botany Department, University of Auckland,* **(AKU),** Private Bag, Auckland, **New Zealand.**

Telephone: 792-300.

Status: State University.

Foundation: 1883. *Number of specimens:* 24.000 (12.000 algae, 6.000 bryophytes).

Herbarium: General with emphasis on New Zealand.

Important collections: V. W. Lindauer (Algae), J. E. Braggins (3.000 Bryophytes).

    Director: P. H. LOVELL, 1938 (Weed ecophysiology).

    Curator: J. E. BRAGGINS, 1944 (Pteridophytes, bryophytes).

    Staff member: J. A. RATTENBURY, 1918 (Genetics, taxonomy).

    Specialization in research: New Zealand and related flora.

Loans: To recognized botanical institutions.

13

AUCKLAND: *Herbarium, Plant Diseases Division, Department of Scientific and Industrial Research,* (**PDD**), Mt. Albert Research Centre, Private Bag, Auckland, **New Zealand.**
Telephone: 893-660.
Status: State.
Foundation: 1936. *Number of specimens:* 40.000.
Herbarium: Fungi only.
Important collections: W. Colenso (duplicates of many fungal specimens held at K), G. H. Cunningham, R. F. R. McNabb, Reliquiae Petrakianae; UNDP/FAO Survey of Plant Pests and Diseases in the South Pacific (fungi).
   Director: P. J. Brook, 1926 (Plant pathology).
   Curator: E. H. C. McKenzie, 1946 (Taxonomy of fungi imperfecti).
   Staff members: P. K. Buchanan, 1957 (Taxonomy of Coelomycetes).
   G. J. Samuels, 1944 (Taxonomy of Ascomycetes and fungi imperfecti).
Specialization in research: Taxonomy of fungi of N.Z. and the South Pacific.
Loans: To recognized botanical institutions for a period of six months, consent of Government required for export of types.
   Periodical and serial works: Occasional Bulletins N.Z., D.S.I.R.
   Exchange: Available on a limited basis.

AUSTIN: *Austin High School Herbarium,* (**AHS**), Austin, Texas 78712, **U.S.A.** – – discontinued.

AUSTIN: *University of Texas Herbarium,* (**TEX**), *C. L. Lundell Herbarium,* (**LL**), Department of Botany, Plant Resources Center, University of Texas, Austin, Texas 78712, **U.S.A.**
Telephone: 512/471-5262; 471-5904.
Foundation: 1900. *Number of specimens:* 900.000.
Herbarium: Primarily vascular plants, with emphasis on Texas and Latin America, especially Mexico; combined herbaria of the University of Texas (TEX) and the Lundell Herbarium (LL).
Important collections: S. F. Blake, E. Contreras, D. S. Correll, P. H. Gentle, J. Henrickson, G. B. Hinton, I. M. Johnston, M. C. Johnston, C. L. Lundell, E. Matuda, R. McVaugh, H. N. Moldenke, C. H. Muller, C. G. Pringle, R. Runyon, W. A. Silveus (grasses), B. H. Warnock.
   Director: B. L. Turner, 1925 (Compositae).
   Associate Director: M. C. Johnston, 1930 (Rhamnaceae, Euphorbiaceae; North American, including Mexican, floristics).
   Curator: Jackie M. Poole, 1950 (Nyctaginaceae; Mexican floristics).
   Staff members: C. J. Alexopoulos, 1907 (Mycology).
   H. C. Bold, 1909 (Algae; cryptogams).
   T. Delevoryas, 1929 (Paleobotany).
   C. L. Lundell, 1907 (Myrsinaceae, Sapotaceae, Lauraceae, Celastraceae).
   T. J. Mabry, 1932 (Phytochemistry).

C. H. Muller, 1909 (*Quercus*).
   Beryl Simpson, 1942 (Andean biogeography, Krameriaceae).
   Specialization in research: Monographic studies; flora of Latin America; Compositae; comparative phytochemistry.
   Loans: To recognized institutions; specimens to be annotated.
   Exchange: Available: U.S. and Latin America. Desired: Southwestern U.S. and Latin America; Asteraceae, Poaceae, Fabaceae worldwide.

AUTUN: *Herbarium, Société d'Histoire Naturelle et des Amis du Muséum d'Autun,* (**AUT**), 19 rue Saint Antoine, 71400 Autun, **France.** (Information 1974)
Status: Private foundation.
Foundation: 1886. *Number of specimens:* 500.000.
Herbarium: General and regional collections.
Important collections: F. X. Gillot (European phanerogams), H. Philibert (mosses), J. L. Lucand (fungi), J. E. Carion, C. Grognot (regional phanerogams).
   Specialization in research: Flora of Bourgogne.
   Periodical and serial works: Quarterly Bulletin.

AVIGNON: *Herbarium, Museum Requien,* (**AV**), 67 rue Joseph-Vernet, 84000 Avignon, **France.**
Telephone: 16(90)82.43.51.
Status: Natural history museum.
Foundation: 1840. *Number of specimens:* 250.000.
Herbarium: Plants of Vaucluse, France and worldwide; large number of specimens sent to Requien and annotated by well-known botanists of 19th C.
Important collections: Herbaria of E. Requien, J. L. A. Loiseleur-Deslongchamps, Gimet, Georgel, M. Palun, Veilex.
   Director: J. Granier, 1930, Conservator of Muséum Requien.
   Staff members: E. Bonnoure, 1953.
   P. Moulet, 1955.
   Loans: To recognized botanical institutions.

AVON: *Herbarium, Laboratoire de Botanique Tropicale,* (**ABT**), Avon, Seine et Marne, **France.** (Information 1974)
Status: Faculté des Sciences, Université de Paris (Adresse postale: 1 rue Guy de la Brosse, 75005 Paris).
Foundation: 1958. *Number of specimens:* 20.000.
Herbarium: West Africa, Brazil, Guyana, Indochina.
Specialization in research: Tropical flora and phytogeography, morphology and anatomy of tropical plants.

AYLESBURY: *Herbarium, Building Research Establishment, Princes Risborough Laboratory,* (**FPRL**), Princess Risborough, Aylesbury, Buckinghamshire HP17 9PX, England, **Great Britain.**
Telephone: (08444) 3101.
Status: Directed by the Government.

Foundation: 1927. *Number of specimens:* Herbarium 1: Timber species, 30.000, including native and exotic species; Herbarium 2: Fungi, 1.000 dried fruit bodies of wood inhabiting macro-fungi, 500 live cultures of wood-inhabiting fungi, including wood-staining fungi.

Director: E. J. GIBSON.

Curator: Herbarium 1 (Timber species): Section leader – Properties of Materials Section; Herbarium 2 (Fungi): Section leader – Biodeterioration Section.

Staff member: Herb. 2: JANICE CAREY (Mycologist).

Specialization in research: Timber research, research on light-weight building components.

Loans: Herb. 1: Samples available for viewing but not usually for loan. Herb. 2: Cultures are for sale, fruit bodies normally viewing only.

Periodical and serial works: Information Papers, Technical Notes and miscellaneous publications.

Exchange: Wanted: Specimens of timbers, especially from tropical areas.

AZUSA: *Herbarium, Department of Biological Sciences, Citrus College,* (**AZUS**), 18824 E. Foothill Blvd., Azusa, California 91702, **U.S.A.**

Telephone: 213/335-0521.

Foundation: 1930. *Number of specimens:* 1.800.

Herbarium: Mostly vascular plants from southern California chaparral and desert regions.

Director and Curator: MARSCHALL C. STEVENS, 1937.

B

BAARN: *Herbarium, Centraalbureau voor Schimmelcultures*, **(CBS)**, Oosterstraat 1, P.O. Box 273, 3740 AG Baarn, **Netherlands.**
Telephone: 02154-11841.
Status: Institute of the Royal Netherlands Academy of Sciences.
Foundation: CBS 1907, herbarium 1965. *Number of specimens:* 20.000 plus 25.000 living strains of fungi, yeasts and Actinomycetes.
Herbarium: Fungi.
Important collections: R. A. Samson and H. C. Evans, entomogenous fungi (2.000 including types).
Director: J. A. VON ARX, 1922 (Ascomycetes, general mycology).
Curator of Herbarium: H. A. VAN DER AA, 1935 (Sphaeropsidales).
Curator of Culture Collection: M. A. A. SCHIPPER, 1923 (Mucorales).
Staff members: G. W. VAN EIJK, 1932 (Biochemistry).
K. W. GAMS, 1934 (*Verticillium, Acremonium* and related genera).
E. J. HERMANIDES-NIJHOF, 1934 (*Fusarium, Aureobasidium*).
G. S. DE HOOG, 1948 (Dematiaceae).
R. P. W. M. JACOBS, 1948 (Oomycetes).
C. A. N. VAN OORSCHOT, 1951 (*Chrysosporium, Geotrichum* and related genera).
L. RODRIGUES DE MIRANDA, 1925 (Basidiomycetous yeasts).
R. A. SAMSON, 1946 (Paecilomyces, *Penicillium* and related genera, entomogenous fungi).
M. T. SMITH, 1940 (Ascomycetous yeasts).
J. A. STALPERS, 1947 (Basidiomycetes).
G. A. DE VRIES, 1919 (Human and animal ecology).
A. C. M. WEIJMAN, 1947 (Biochemistry, physiology).
D. YARROW, 1935 (Saccharomyces and related genera).
Specialization in research: Mycology, taxonomy and biochemistry.
Loans: 6–12 months to approved institutions.
Periodical and serial works: List of Cultures, Studies in Mycology.
Exchange: Living cultures of species not already in collection are accepted.

BAD GODESBERG: *Bundesanstalt für Vegetationskunde, Naturschutz und Landschaftspflege*, **(ZVS)**, Heerstrasse 110, 532 Bad Godesberg, **Federal Republic of Germany**, BRD. (Information 1974)
Status: Federal institute.
Foundation: 1939. *Number of specimens:* 85.000 (60.000 phanerogams, 25.000 cryptogams).
Herbarium: Europe.

BAGHDAD: *National Herbarium of Iraq*, **(BAG)**, Ministry of Agriculture and Agrarian Reform, Abu-Ghraib, Baghdad, **Iraq.**
Telephone: 009641-5550200.
Status: State directed.
Foundation: 1946. *Number of specimens:* 50.000.
Herbarium: Wild and cultivated plants of Iraq.
Director: SABAH A. OMAR, 1937.
Curator: SHUKUR T. AL-KAISI, 1946.
Staff members: SAHIRA A. R. AL-ABDULLY, 1943.
WEDAD H. AL-AZZAWI, 1954.
A. H. AL-KHAYAT, 1932.
JINAN AL-MUCHTAR, 1938.
THAMER J. RIDHA, 1953.
SALAH T. SALIH, 1951.
Specialization in research: Flora of Iraq.
Associated botanic garden: Botanical Garden Za'afaraniya.
Loans: To recognized botanical institutions.
Exchange: Available: Plants of Iraq. Desired: Specimens or publications.

BAGHDAD: *Herbarium, College of Agriculture, University of Baghdad*, **(BUA)**, Abu Ghraib, Baghdad, **Iraq.** (Information 1974)
Foundation: 1962. *Number of specimens:* 5.000.
Specialization in research: Flora of Iraq, economic plants.

BAGHDAD: *Herbarium, College of Education, University of Baghdad*, **(BUE)**, Baghdad, **Iraq.**

BAGHDAD: *The University Herbarium, College of Science*, **(BUH)**, Baghdad, **Iraq.**

BAGHDAD: *Iraq Natural History Research Centre and Museum, University of Baghdad*, **(BUNH)**, Bab Al-Muadham, Baghdad, **Iraq.**
Telephone: 68361, 68362, 65790.
Status: University of Baghdad.
Foundation: 1946. *Number of specimens:* 10.000.
Herbarium: Mostly flora of Iraq.
Director: MUNIR K. BUNNI.
Curator: M. F. KARAM, 1950.
Staff member: N. Y. OTHMAN, 1940.
Specialization in research: Flora of Iraq.
Loans: To recognized institutions.
Periodical and serial works: Bulletin of Natural History Research Centre and Museum, Publication of Natural History Research Centre and Museum.
Exchange: Yes, specimens or periodicals.

BAGNÈRES-DE-LUCHON: *Société Julien Sacaze, Société Pyrénéiste d'Etudes Historiques, Archéologiques et Scientifiques du pays de Luchon, Musée du*

Pays de Luchon, (**LUCH**), Château Lafont, 18 Allées d'Etigny, Bagnères-de-Luchon, Haute garonne, **France.** (Information 1974)
Status: Municipal.
Foundation: 1916. *Number of specimens:* 1.600.
Herbarium: Collections of Abbé Jourtau.

BAHÍA BLANCA: *Herbario, Departamento Ciencias Agrarias, Universidad Nacional de Sur,* (**BB**), Rondeau 29, 8000 Bahía Blanca, Buenos Aires, **Argentina.**
Telephone: (54)091/21-233; 30-024.
Foundation: 1950. *Number of specimens:* 4.000.
Herbarium: Vascular plants of area surrounding Bahía Blanca, especially Gramineae, Leguminosae, and Compositae.
  Director: HAYDÉE NORA VERETTONI, 1923 (Systematics).
  Staff members: ESTELA ARAMAYO, 1946.
    ANA ANDRADA DE GALAN, 1956 (Taxonomy).
    SERGIO LAMBERTO, 1941.
    ALDA VALLE DE FIGGINI, 1944.
  Specialization in research: Flora of Bahía Blanca.
  Loans: Usual regulations.
  Exchange: Yes.

BAKU: *Herbarium, Botanical Institute of the Academy of Sciences of Azerbaijan SSR,* (**BAK**), Potamdarskoye Avenue 40, 370073 Baku, **U.S.S.R.**
Telephone: 37-32-30.
Status: State institute.
Foundation: 1931. *Number of specimens:* 600.000.
Herbarium: Plants of Azerbaijan, Caucasus and Eastern Europe.
  Director: ALEKPEROV URHAN KYASIMOVICH, 1943.
  Curator: KH. PH. ACHUNDOV, 1914 (Flora of Azerbaijan).
  Staff member: E. CH. KHALILOV, 1913 (Flora of Azerbaijan, *Trifolium*).
  Specialization in research: Azerbaijanian flora.
  Associated botanic garden: Botanical Garden of the Botanical Institute.
  Exchange: Available: Plants of Azerbaijan.

BALBOA: *Summit Herbarium,* (**SCZ**), Apartado 2072, Balboa, **Panama.**
Telephone: 52-5539.
Status: Jointly governed by the Missouri Botanical Garden and Smithsonian Tropical Research Institute.
Foundation: 1968. *Number of specimens:* 12.000 (10 types).
Herbarium: Plants of Panama.
Important collections: U.S. Army Tropic Test Center Herbarium.
  Director: W. G. D'ARCY, 1931, Missouri Botanical Garden (MO), St. Louis (Flora of Panama).
  Curator: THOMAS M. ANTONIO (Flora of Panama).
  Specialization in research: Flora of Panama.
  Loans: Usual conditions.

Exchange: Through Missouri Botanical Garden (MO).
Remarks: Formerly listed under Canal Zone Summit Herbarium (SCZ); most collections are duplicated at MO.

BALBOA: *Barro Colorado Island Herbarium, Smithsonian Tropical Research Institute,* (**STRI**), Apartado 2072, Balboa, **Panama.**
Telephone: 52-2124.
Foundation: 1923. *Number of specimens:* 2.000.
Herbarium: Plants of Barro Colorado Nature Monument.
  Director: IRA RUBINOFF (Marine biology).
  Staff members: ROBERT L. DRESSLER (Orchids).
    ROBIN B. FOSTER.
  Loans: Generally not desired.
  Remarks: All collections of historic interest (Paul C. Standley, etc.) have been transferred to the Missouri Botanical Garden (MO). A synoptic herbarium of the flora of Barro Colorado Island is maintained here for the convenience of those working on the Island. Many of the collections of Dressler are deposited in the University of Panama herbarium (PMA). Other extensive collections from Barro Colorado Island and other parts of Panama are to be found at MO, US, and DUKE.

BALCARCE: *Herbario, Estación Experimental Regional Agropecuaria, Instituto Nacional de Tecnologia Agropecuaria,* (**BAL**), Correo Central 276, 7620 Balcarce, Buenos Aires, **Argentina.**
Telephone: Balcarce 2148.
Foundation: 1970. *Number of specimens:* 2.000.
Herbarium: Flora of southeastern Buenos Aires Province; wild species of tuber-bearing Solanums of Argentina.
Important collections: J. G. Hawkes, J. Hermsen, W. Hoffmann, K. A. Okada, H. Ross.
  Curator: K. A. OKADA, 1935 (Exploration, maintenance, and evaluation of tuber-bearing *Solanum* germplasm).
  Staff member: ANDREA CLAUSEN, 1949 (Tuber-bearing Solanums).
  Specialization in research: Biosystematic studies of wild tuber-bearing Solanums.
  Loans: To institutions or individual research workers.
  Exchange: Can be arranged on request.

BALTIMORE: *Herbarium, Department of Biological Sciences, Towson State University,* (**BALT**), 8000 York Road, Baltimore, Maryland 21204, **U.S.A.**
Telephone: 301/321-3042.
Foundation: 1967. *Number of specimens:* 41-46.000 (35-40.000 vascular plants, 4.000 lichens, 2.000 algae and bryophytes).
Herbarium: North American collection, with emphasis on the middle Atlantic states.
Important collections: Skorepa and Norden

(Maryland lichens); New World *Crotalaria*, including some isotypes, many type photographs and original description sheets.

Director and Curator: DONALD R. WINDLER, 1940 (Taxonomy of Leguminosae –– *Crotalaria, Neptunia*).

Staff members: MAURITZ G. ANDERSON, 1918 (Mycology; Phycomycetes).

RICHARD L. HILTON, JR. (Phycology).

JAMES C. HULL, 1945 (Ecology).

FREDERICK MORSINK, 1931 (Plant pathology; plant physiology).

LOIS ODELL, 1915 (Horticulture).

ERIK P. SCULLY, 1949 (Evolution).

ROBERT E. SHOEMAKER, 1939 (Paleobotany).

Specialization in research: Flora of Maryland; taxonomy of legume genera.

Loans: To recognized botanical institutions.

Exchange: Wanted: Tropical New World legumes, marine algae, lichens.

Remarks: Interested in receiving unidentified New World *Crotalaria* in exchange for identifications.

BANARAS: *Herbarium, Department of Botany, Banaras Hindu University,* (**BAN**), Banaras 5, **India.** (Information 1974)

Status: University.

Foundation: 1918.

Herbarium: Angiosperms from Indo-Gangetic Plains, Vindhyan Hills and Himalayas.

Specialization in research: Flora of Gangetic Valley and Eastern Uttar Pradesh, ecology.

Associated botanic garden: Banaras Hindu University Botanic Garden.

BANDUNG: *Herbarium Bandungense, Department Biologi, Fakultas Matematika + Ilmu Pasti Alam, Institut Teknologi Bandung,* (**FIPIA**), Jl. Ganeca 10, Bandung, **Indonesia.**

Telephone: 84252-84258, ext. 325.

Status: University.

Foundation: 1949. *Number of specimens:* 10.000.

Herbarium: Plants of Indonesia, especially Java.

Director: R. E. SOERIAATMADJA, 1936 (Plant ecology).

Curator: SRI HAJATI WIDODO, 1936 (Plant systematics).

Staff members: INGE BIRSJAM, 1931 (Cryptogamic botany).

UNDANG A. DASUKI, 1943 (Cryptogamic botany).

R. G. DIDIH, 1935 (Plant systematics).

Specialization in research: Flora of Java.

Loans: To recognized botanical institutions.

Exchange: Desired: Tropical plants.

BANGALORE: *Herbarium, Centre for Taxonomic Studies, St. Joseph's College,* (**JCB**), P.B. 5031, Bangalore 560001, **India.**

Telephone: 579380.

Status: Constituent College of Bangalore University.

Foundation: 1964. *Number of specimens:* 50.000.

Herbarium: Angiosperms, ferns and fern allies of Western Peninsular India.

Important collections: Types of species described or collected by C. Saldanka, Hassan Flora Project collections, Karnataka State flora collections.

Director: CECIL J. SALDANHA, 1926 (Floristics of Western India, Scrophulariaceae, Orchidaceae).

Staff members. S. B. MANOHAR, 1955 (Euphorbiaceae, Convolvulaceae).

B. R. RAMESH, 1956 (Rubiaceae, Asteraceae).

S. R. RAMESH, 1955 (Poaceae, Lamiaceae).

R. GURUDEVA SINGH, 1956 (Fabaceae).

K. P. SREENATH, 1955 (Acanthaceae, Amaranthaceae).

BANGALORE: *Herbarium, Regional Research Centre (Ay.),* (**RRCBI**), Government Central Pharmacy Annexe, Jayanagar, Bangalore 560011, **India.**

Telephone: 607919.

Status: Affiliated with Mysore University.

Foundation: 1971. *Number of specimens:* 6.000.

Herbarium: Plants of Karnataka, especially those used in Ayurvedic system of medicine.

Director: B. V. HOLLA, 1940 (Ayurveda plants).

Curator: S. N. YOGANARASIMHAN, 1944 (Taxonomy, floristics, pharmacognosy and phytochemistry).

Staff members: MR. GOVINDAIAH, 1955 (Taxonomy).

Z. MARY, 1948 (Pharmacognosy).

V. S. TOGUNASHI, 1941 (Ayurvedic botany).

Specialization in research: Plants of Karnataka, especially medicinal plants of Ayurveda; pharmacognosy and phytochemistry of medicinal plants.

Loans: Short term to recognized institutions.

Exchange: Exchange of specimens can be arranged in return for reprints, books or specimens.

BANGI: *Herbarium, Botany Department, Universiti Kebangsaan Malaysia,* (**UKMB**), Bangi, Selangor, **Malaysia.**

Status: National university.

Foundation: 1970. *Number of specimens:* 9.000.

Herbarium: Fungi, bryophytes, pteridophytes and higher plants of Malaysia; ecological and phytochemical collections.

Important collections: W. Littke (bryophytes), A. L. Mohamed (Vitaceae, Rhamnaceae), N. Tamin (*Burmannia*), Farah D. Ghani (Araceae), plants of Bangi Forest Reserve.

Director (Biological Sciences): B. S. JALANI, 1946 (Applied genetics).

Curator: ABDUL LATIFF MOHAMED, 1948 (Vitaceae, Rhamnaceae).

Staff members: SHAFIE AHMED, 1944 (Plant ecology).

AZIZ BIDIN, 1948 (Fern chemistry).
FARAH D. GHANI, 1950 (Araceae, economic botany).
KHATIJAH HUSSIN, 1949 (Anatomy, *Eugenia*).
DAVID T. JONES, 1950 (Bryophytes).
MOHAMED OMAR, 1945 (Fungi).
ISMAIL SAHID, 1950 (Ferns).
NORAINI M. TAMIN, 1949 (*Burmannia*, montane ecology).
Specialization in research: Malesian flora, especially Vitaceae, Malayan montane ecology.
Loans: To recognized botanical institutions.
Exchange: Available: Plants of Peninsular Malaysia. Desired: Worldwide plants for teaching.

BANGKOK: *Botanical Section, Technical Division, Department of Agriculture,* (**BK**), Bangkok, **Thailand.** (Information 1974)
Status: State institute.
Foundation: 1921. *Number of specimens:* 55.000.
Herbarium: Spermatophyta, pteridophyta.
Loans: By special arrangement.

BANGKOK: *The Forest Herbarium, Royal Forest Department,* (**BKF**), Bangkok 9, **Thailand.** (Information 1974)
Status: Official bureau directed by the Royal Forest Department, Ministry of Agriculture and Cooperative.
Foundation: 1905. *Number of specimens:* 60.000.
Herbarium: Worldwide, Thailand and adjacent countries.
Specialization in research: Flora of Thailand, medicinal plants.
Associated botanic garden: Phu Khae Botanic Gardens, Saraburi; Khao Chong Botanic Gardens, Trang.
Loans: To recognized botanical institutions.

BANGOR: *Herbarium, School of Plant Biology, University College of North Wales,* (**UCNW**), Bangor LL57 2UW, Wales, **Great Britain.** (Information 1974)
Status: University.
Foundation: About 1890. *Number of specimens:* 25.000.
Herbarium: Flowering plants, bryophytes, ferns, lichens and algae (chiefly British Isles and Europe).
Loans: To recognized botanical institutions.

BANYULS-SUR-MER: *Laboratoire Arago de la Faculté des Sciences de Paris,* (**ARAGO**), Banyuls-sur-Mer, **France.**

BARCELONA: *Institut Botànic de Barcelona,* (**BC**), Av. dels Muntanyans, Parc de Montjuïc, Barcelona-4, Catalonia, **Spain.**
Telephone: 34-3-3258050; 34-3-3258104.
Status: Municipal.
Foundation: 1917. *Number of specimens:* 600.000.
Herbarium: Worldwide herbarium, mainly Europe,

Mediterranean region and Ibero-Magrebine flora.
Important collections: P. Font Quer, Fr. Sennen.
Director: O. DE BOLÓS, 1924 (Geobotany, floristics).
Staff members: F. MASCLANS, 1905 (Floristics).
J. M. MONTSERRAT, 1955 (Taxonomy and floristics of higher plants).
A. ROMO, 1955 (Floristics and geobotany).
E. SIERRA, 1919 (Floristics of higher plants).
Specialization in research: Ibero-Magrebine flora and vegetation.
Associated botanic garden: Jardí Botànic de Barcelona.
Loans: To recognized botanical institutions.
Periodical and serial works: Collectanea Botanica, Treballs de l'Institut Botànic de Barcelona.
Exchange: Yes.

BARCELONA: *Departament de Botánica, Facultad de Biologia, Universidad de Barcelona,* (**BCC**), Gran Via, 585 Barcelona-7, **Spain.**
Telephone: 34-3-3026524.
Status: University.
Foundation: 1920. *Number of specimens:* 20.000.
Herbarium: Worldwide.
Important collections: Planelles (Flora of Galicia).
Director: ORIO DE BOLÓS, 1924 (Geobotany, floristics).
Staff members: I. ALVARO, 1955 (Bryology).
M. A. CARDONA, 1940 (Cytotaxonomy of plants).
A. CARRILLO, 1954 (Geobotany, floristics).
A. FARRAS, 1949 (Geobotany, floristics).
E. GRACIA, 1952 (Cryptogamy, mycology).
N. HLADUN, 1951 (Lichenology).
R. M. MASALLES, 1948 (Geobotany, floristics).
J. M. NINOT, 1955 (Geobotany, floristics).
M. T. PERDIGÓ, 1925 (Geobotany, floristics).
E. VELASCO, 1948 (Geobotany, floristics).
J. VIGO, 1937 (Geobotany, floristics).
Specialization in research: Flora and vegetation of the Catalan Countries (Catalonia, Balearic Islands and Valencia); cytotaxonomy of plants; lichenology; mycology, including myxomycetes.
Periodical and serial works: Acta Botanica Barcinonensia, Folia Botanica Miscellanea.
Exchange: Yes.

BARCELONA: *Departamento de Botánica, Facultad de Farmacia,* (**BCF**), Núcleo Universitario de Pedralbes. Diagonal, s/n–Barcelona, **Spain.**
Telephone: 93/330-91-03.
Foundation: 1943. *Number of specimens:* 70.000.
Herbarium: Specimens of Catalunya, Pyrenées, Northern Spain, Baleares, Aragón, Castilla, Valencia and Andalucía.
Important collections: Fr. Sennen, Font Quer, Rothmaler, T. M. Losa España.
Director: J. SEOANE-CAMBA, 1933 (Phycology).
Curator: J. MOLERO-BRIONES, 1946 (Floristics and systematics of vascular plants).

Specialization in research: Systematic botany in general.

BARI: *Herbarium, Istituto di Botanica dell'Università,* **(BI)**, Via Amendola 175, 70126 Bari, **Italy.**
Telephone: 339549.
Status: University.
Foundation: 1940. *Number of specimens:* 40.000.
Herbarium: Mediterranean flora.
Director: ORESTE ARRIGONI, 1928.
Curator: VITTORIO LA SELVA, 1926.
Specialization in research: Mediterranean flora, especially Puglia.
Associated botanic garden: Yes.
Loans: To recognized botanical institutions.
Exchange: Available: Specimens from Puglia.
Desired: Specimens from everywhere, especially the Mediterranean Region.

BARODA: *Herbarium, University of Baroda,* **(BARO)**, Baroda, **India.**

BARQUISIMETO: *Herbario, Escuela Agronomia, Universidad Centro Occidental "Lisandro Alvarado,"* **(UCOB)**, Barquisimeto, Lara, **Venezuela.**
Foundation: 1974. *Number of specimens:* 1.500.
Herbarium: Regional herbarium for the states of Lara, Falcon, Yaracuy, Portuguesa (Region Centro Occidental) of Venezuela.
Curator: CHARLES L. BURANDT, JR., 1950.
Specialization in research: Flora of region.
Loans: Yes.
Exchange: Available: Grasses of South America.
Desired: Literature.

BASEL: *Botanisches Institut der Universität,* **(BAS)**, Schönbeinstrasse 6, CH-4056 Basel, **Switzerland.**
Telephone: 061/25 69 15.
Status: University.
Foundation: 1588-89. *Number of specimens:* 200.000; seedling collection 5.000 and seed collection 25.000.
Herbarium: General herbarium, Swiss herbarium, historical collections.
Important collections: C. Bauhin, W. de Lachenal, F. Sarasin, A. Thellung, H. Zoller.
Director: HEINRICH ZOLLER, 1923 (Palaeobotany, phytosociology, bryophytes and phanerogams).
Curator: CLAUDE FARRON, 1933, Curator of the Botanical Garden (Tropical phanerogams, seed collecting and seed morphology).
Associated botanic garden: Yes.
Loans: To recognized botanical institutions.
Exchange: Limited.

BASEL: *Basler Botanische Gesellschaft,* **(BASBG)**, Postfach 63, CH-4020 Basel, **Switzerland.**
Telephone: 061-494090, 061-256915.
Status: Private.
Foundation: 1958. *Number of specimens:* 150.000.

Herbarium: Phanerogams and pteridophytes of Switzerland, Central Europe, Mittelmeergebiet, Turkey.
Important collections: Herbaria of H. Reese, A. Huber-Morath, E. Issler, C. Simon, M. Nydegger, Ed. Berger.
Curator: CHRISTIAN HEITZ, 1942; 061-385611 (*Diphasiastrum*).
Staff members: MAX NYDEGGER.
CHARLES SIMON.
Loans: To recognized botanical institutions for one year at most.
Periodical and serial works: Bauhinia.
Exchange: Available: Central and southern Europe. Desired: Plants from other lake areas.

BASEL: *Stiftung Herbarium Paul Aellen,* **(PAE)** – incorporated in G as G-PAE.

BASSANO DEL GRAPPA: *Museo-Biblioteca-Archivio (Sezione Erbario),* **(BASSA)**, Via Museo, 12-36061 Bassano del Grappa (Vicenza), **Italy.**
Telephone: 0424-22235.
Status: Civic property.
Foundation: 1828. *Number of specimens:* 17.000 (9.000 damaged by acts of war).
Director: FERNANDO RIGON, 1944 (History of art).
Curator: GIUSEPPE MARCHENTE, 1910 (Voluntary collaborator).
Staff members: Staff of the Civico Museo e Biblioteca.
Loans and exchange: Not possible.

BATON ROUGE: *Herbarium, Department of Botany, Louisiana State University,* **(LSU)**, Baton Rouge, Louisiana 70803, **U.S.A.**
Telephone: 504/388-8485.
Foundation: 1869. *Number of specimens:* 100.000.
Herbarium: Louisiana and neotropical flora; Piperaceae; Asteraceae.
Important collections: Americus Featherman (ca. 1870); E. C. Wurzlow (ca. 1915).
Director: LOWELL E. URBATSCH, 1942 (Asteraceae, biochemical systematics and monographs).
Staff members: CLAIR A. BROWN (Wildflowers; wood, pollen, and fossil samples).
GARRIE P. LANDRY, 1951 (Pteridophytes; Cycads).
MEREDITH H. LIEUX, 1939 (Pollen morphol.).
SHIRLEY C. TUCKER, 1927 (Piperaceae; primitive angiosperms; lichens; anatomy and morphology).
STEPHEN WHIPPLE, 1944 (Forest ecology, population dynamics).
Specialization in research: According to the interests of staff members and institutional specialization given above.
Loans: To recognized botanists and botanical institutions.

Exchange: Available: Mostly southern North American, general, staff research vouchers. Desired: Specimens from all groups, especially Asteraceae, Piperaceae, Magnoliales.
Remarks: Pollen collection of 3.500 slides, mostly southeastern U.S. species.

BATON ROUGE: *Mycological Herbarium, Botany Department, Louisiana State University,* (**LSUM**), Baton Rouge, Louisiana 70803, **U.S.A.**
Telephone: 504/388-8485.
Foundation: 1954. *Number of specimens:* 18.000.
Herbarium: Higher fungi and bryophyta of tropical America and U.S.
Important collections: B. Lowy (Tremellales of American tropics).
Director and Curator: B. Lowy, 1916 (Neotropical Tremellales).
Specialization in research: Taxonomy and phylogeny of Tremellales; ethnomycology.
Loans: To recognized botanists and botanical institutions.
Exchange: Available: Mostly neotropical Tremellales. Desired: Worldwide collections of Tremellales.

BATON ROUGE: *Herbarium of Parasitic Seed Plants,* (**PSP**) – – *see* WATERVILLE.

BATUMI: *Herbarium, Botanical Garden of Batumi, Academy of Sciences of Georgian S.S.R.,* (**BATU**), Post Office Machindzauri, 384533 Batumi, **U.S.S.R.**
Telephone: 94444.
Status: Directed by Academy of Sciences.
Foundation: 1912. *Number of specimens:* 45.000.
Herbarium: Mainly wild plants of Adjaria and cultivated plants of the botanical garden, some collections from U.S.A., Bulgaria, Romania.
Director: NODARI M. SHARASHIDZE, 1925 (Physiology).
Curator: ALEXANDRA A. DMITRIEVA, 1905 (Horticulture).
Staff members: MURAN J. DAVITADZE, 1943 (Morphology).
MERI A. DJICURIDZE, 1929 (Technician).
ISOLDA M. LOMATADZE, 1948 (Technician).
VAJA M. MEMIADZE, 1936 (Horticulture).
Specialization in research: Flora of Adjaria.
Associated botanic garden: The Botanical Garden of Batumi.
Periodical and serial works: Isvestia of the Botanical Garden of Batumi.

BAUTZEN: *Herbarium, Arbeitsgemeinschaft Isis,* (**ISIS**), Bautzen, Sachsen, **German Democratic Republic,** DDR – – transferred to GLM.

BAYONNE: *Muséum d'Histoire Naturelle de Bayonne,* (**BAY**), Rue Jacques Lafitte 7, Bayonne (Bas-Pyr.), **France.**

BEDFORD: *Concord Field Station Herbarium of the Museum of Comparative Zoology of Harvard University,* (**BEDF**), Old Causeway Road, Bedford, Massachusetts 01730, **U.S.A.**
Telephone: 617/275-1725.
Status: Private institution.
Foundation: 1972. *Number of specimens:* 3.640.
Herbarium: Synoptic collection of vascular plants of New England.
Director: C. RICHARD TAYLOR, 1939.
Staff members: RAY ANGELO, 1948 (Woody plants of New England).
JEAN BAXTER, 1911 (Vascular plants of New England).
MARY WALKER, 1923 (Mountain plants of New England).
Specialization in research: Flora of Concord, Massachusetts.
Exchange: Available: Assorted material from North America, mostly New England. Wanted: New England material.
Remarks: Herbarium is card-indexed.

BEIJING: *see* PEKING.

BEIRUT: *Post Herbarium, Faculty of Agricultural Sciences, American University of Beirut,* (**BEI**), Beirut, **Lebanon.** (Information 1974)
Status: Independent university.
Number of specimens: 68.000.
Important collections: G. E. Post and J. E. Dinsmore (southern Turkey, Syria, Lebanon, Jordan, Palestine and Sinai), W. S. Edgecombe (Lebanon), S. A. Chaudhary (*Iris* of Lebanon and Syria).

BELÉM: *Faculdade de Farmacia, Universidade Federal de Pará,* (**HF**), Avenida Generalissimo Deodoro 1562, 66.000 Belém, Pará, **Brazil** – – discontinued.

BELÉM: *Herbário, Centro de Pesquisa Agropecuária do Trópico Úmido, EMBRAPA,* (**IAN**), Trav. Enéas Pinheiro, Caixa Postal 48, 66.000 Belém, Pará, **Brazil.**
Telephone: (55)091/226-1941; 226-1741; 226-1541.
Status: Federal government, Ministério da Agricultura.
Foundation: 1940 (as Instituto Agronômico do Norte; later changed to Instituto de Pesquisa Agropecuária do Norte; changed in 1975 to CPATU/EMBRAPA). *Number of specimens:* 170.000; 15.000 wood samples.
Herbarium: Mainly Amazonian flora.
Important collections: G. A. Black, A. Ducke, R. L. Fróes, J. M. Pires.
Director: CRISTO NAZARÉ BARBOSA DO NASCIMENTO.
Curator: IRENICE ALVES RODRIGUES, 1935; 091/226-1541 (Taxonomy; forestry).
Staff members: OSMAR JOSÉ ROMEIRO DE AGUIAR, 1948 (Forest exploitation).

FERNANDO CARNEIRO DE ALBUQUERQUE, 1932 (Plant pathology; mycology).

SILVIO BRIENZA, JR., 1955 (Pasture agriculture; silviculture).

ANTÓNIO APARECIDO CARPANEZZI, 1950 (Ecology; silviculture).

JOÃO OLEGÁRIO PEREIRA DE CARVALHO, 1949 (Forest management).

MARIA CARMELITA A. CONCEIÇÃO, 1952 (Taxonomy).

HAROLDO BASTOS DA COSTA, 1949 (Forest exploitation).

PERMÍNIO PASCOAL COSTA FILHO, 1945 (Forest exploitation).

MÁRIO DANTAS, 1944 (Ecology).

MARIA DE LOURDES REIS DUARTE, 1944 (Plant pathology; mycology).

JOAQUIM IVANIR GOMES, 1945; 091/226-1541 (Wood anatomy; identification).

MILTON KANASHIRO, 1954 (Genetics; crop improvement).

JOSÉ DO CARMO ALVES LOPES, 1953 (Forest management).

LUCIANO CARLOS TAVARES MARQUES, 1949 (Silviculture).

JOSÉ NATALINO MACEDO SILVA, 1946 (Forest inventory).

NOEMI GERALDES VIANNA, 1956 (Seed technology).

JORGE ALBERTO GAZEL YARED, 1949 (Silviculture).

Specialization in research: Amazonian flora; forestry; forest inventory.

Associated botanic garden: Forest reserve in Belém, 400 hectares; reserves in the state of Pará: Altamira, Capitão Poço.

Loans: In general to recognized botanical institutions.

Periodical and serial works: Boletim; Pesquisa Agropecuária.

Exchange: Available: Amazonian plants. Desired: Specimens from Latin America, especially Brazil.

Remarks: It is anticipated that the IAN and MG herbaria will be united in the coming year.

BELÉM: *Herbário, Museu Paraense Emílio Goeldi,* **(MG),** Avenida Magalhães Barata 376, Caixa Postal 399, 66.000 Belém, Pará, **Brazil.**

Telephone: (55)091/222-1722.

Status: Federal government.

Foundation: 1866 (Museum), 1895 (Herbarium).

Number of specimens: 75.000.

Herbarium: Flora of Amazonian region.

Important collections: A. Ducke, J. Huber, J. M. Pires, G. T. Prance, R. Spruce, E. Ule.

Director: JOÃO MURÇA PIRES, 1917 (Quiinaceae and Sapotaceae of the Amazonian flora; plant ecology).

Curator: PAULO B. CAVALCANTE, 1922 (*Diospy-*

ros, Ebenaceae, Gnetaceae, *Simaba,* Simarubaceae of the Amazonian flora).

Staff members: MARIA NAZARÉ C. BASTOS, 1953 (Grasses of the Amazon).

MARIA ELISABETH VAN DEN BERG (Guttiferae of Brazil; medicinal plants).

JACQUES IVAN G. JANGOUX, 1938 (Monimiaceae; ethnobotany).

PEDRO LUIZ B. LISBÔA (Anatomy of Amazonian woods).

MARIA GRAÇA A. LOBO, 1949 (*Eperua,* Leguminosae).

ANTONIO SÉRGIO L. DA SILVA, 1953 (*Inga,* Leguminosae).

RAIMUNDA CONCEIÇÃO QUEIROZ DE VILHENA (Anatomy and morphology of Amazonian plants).

Specialization in research: Taxonomy and ecology of the Amazonian flora; forestry inventory; studies of economic resources.

Associated botanic garden: Horto Botânico do Museu Goeldi.

Loans: In general to recognized botanical institutions.

Periodical and serial works: Boletim do Museu Paraense Emílio Goeldi, nova série, Botânica.

Exchange: Available: Amazonian plants. Desired: Specimens from South America, especially from the Hylaea.

BELFAST: *Herbarium, Ulster Museum,* **(BEL),** Botanic Gardens, Belfast BT9 5AB, Northern Ireland, **Great Britain.**

Telephone: 0232-668251 (-2, -3, -4, -5).

Status: National Museum of Northern Ireland.

Foundation: 1905. *Number of specimens:* 60.000.

Herbarium: All groups, mainly NE Ireland, also rest of Ireland and Great Britain.

Important collections: J. Templeton, S. A. Stewart, S. Wear, C. H. Waddell, C. Bailey, Richard Spruce (Duplicates?), W. H. Harvey, A. W. Stelfox (Myxomycetes).

Curator: PAUL HACKNEY, 1945 (Vascular plants of NE Ireland).

Staff member: OSBORNE MORTON (Marine algae of Ireland).

Specialization in research: Floristic studies of Northern Ireland.

Associated botanic garden: None (adjacent Botanic Garden is non-functioning).

Loans: Considered individually.

Exchange: Inquiries welcome.

BELFAST: *Herbarium, Department of Botany, The Queen's University,* **(BFT)** – transferred to BEL.

BELLINGHAM: *Herbarium, Biology Department, Western Washington University,* **(WWB),** Bellingham, Washington 98225, **U.S.A.**

Telephone: 206/676-3649.

Foundation: 1945. *Number of specimens:* 22.000.

Herbarium: Local vascular plants, few mosses and fungi; plants of the North Cascades of Washington.

Director and Curator: RONALD J. TAYLOR, 1932 (Vascular plant systematics).

Staff member: FRED RHOADES (Algae, mosses, and fungi).

Specialization in research: Flora and ecology of North Cascades.

Loans: Normal regulations.

Exchange: On request.

Remarks: Collections are computerized for convenient use.

BELLVILLE: *Herbarium, University of the Western Cape,* (**UWC**), Modderdam Road, Private Bag X17, Bellville 7530, **South Africa.**

Telephone: 021-976161.

Status: Department of Botany of the University.

Foundation: 1962. *Number of specimens:* 6.000.

Herbarium: General teaching herbarium, Coastal forelands of the Western Cape.

Important collections: Cape Flat Nature Reserve; Tygerberg Nature Reserve.

Curator: R. O. MOFFETT, 1937 (Anacardiaceae in Southern Africa).

Staff members: A. B. LOW, 1952 (Curator of Cape Flats Nature Reserve).

F. M. WEITZ, 1954 (*Corymbium*).

Specialization in research: Taxonomy of *Rhus* and *Corymbium*, ecology of Cape Flats.

Associated botanic garden: Cape Flats Nature Reserve of the University of the Western Cape.

Loans: To recognized institutions.

BELMOPAN: *Herbarium, Forestry Department, Ministry of Natural Resources,* (**BRH**), Belmopan, **Belize.**

Telephone: (501)08/2166.

Status: Government department.

Foundation: 1940. *Number of specimens:* 4.000.

Herbarium: Flora of Belize.

Director: Chief Forest Officer.

BELO HORIZONTE: *Herbário, Departamento de Botânica, Instituto de Ciências Biológicas, Universidade Federal de Minas Gerais,* (**BHCB**), Avenida Antônio Carlos 6627, 30.000 Belo Horizonte, Minas Gerais, **Brazil.**

Telephone: (55)031/441-0066, ramal 271.

Foundation: 1968. *Number of specimens:* 3.000.

Herbarium: Plants of the cerrado of Minas Gerais; medicinal plants.

Important collections: José Maurício Ferrari, Telma S. M. Grandi, José A. de Oliveira, Maria Raimunda Rodrigues, Claudio A. da Silva, José M. Pinheiro Sobrinho, Maria Madalena P. de Souza.

Director and Curator: JOSÉ MAURÍCIO FERRARI, 1925; 031/461-3917 (Brazilian medicinal plants).

Staff members: TELMA S. M. GRANDI, 1943 (Brazilian medicinal plants).

JOSÉ LUIZ PEDERSOLI (Plants of the cerrado of Minas Gerais).

JOSÉ MARTINS PINHEIRO SOBRINHO, 1922 (Brazilian medicinal plants).

Specialization in research: Brazilian medicinal plants; plants of the cerrado of Minas Gerais.

Associated botanic garden: Museu de História Natural, Rua Gustavo da Silveira, 1035 Horto, Belo Horizonte, Minas Gerais, Brazil.

Periodical and serial works: Oreades.

Exchange: Wanted: Medicinal plants.

BELO HORIZONTE: *Instituto Agronômico,* (**BHMG**), Belo Horizonte, Minas Gerais, **Brazil** -- incorporated in BHMH.

BELO HORIZONTE: *Herbário, Museu de História Natural, Universidade Federal de Minas Gerais,* (**BHMH**), Rua Gustavo da Silveira, 1035 Horto, Caixa Postal 2475, 30.000 Belo Horizonte, Minas Gerais, **Brazil.**

Telephone: (55)031/461-7666; 461-7830.

Foundation: 1970. *Number of specimens:* 6.000.

Herbarium: Phanerogams of Minas Gerais.

Curator: JOSÉ LUIZ PEDERSOLI (Plants of the cerrado of Minas Gerais).

BELO HORIZONTE: *Herbário e Xiloteca, Fundação Centro Tecnológico de Minas Gerais,* (**HXBH**), Avenida José Cândido da Silveira, 2000 Horto, Caixa Postal 2306, 30.000 Belo Horizonte, Minas Gerais, **Brazil.**

Telephone: (55)031/461-7933; 461-0117.

Foundation: 1978. *Number of specimens:* 4.600.

Herbarium: Brazilian plants; woods, fruits, and seeds.

Important collections: Edir Carvalho Tenório (Pernambuco and Minas Gerais, Brazil), L. C. de Freitas (Minas Gerais, Brazil), J. C. Badini (Ouro Preto and Minas Gerais states, Brazil), M. B. Ferreira, L. Krieger, W. N. Vidal.

Director: JOSÉ ROOSEVELT PEREIRA, 1938 (Engineering).

Curator: E. C. TENÓRIO, 1942 (Plant taxonomy; vegetation mapping).

Staff members: DULCE HELENA S. ÁSSIMOS, 1956 (Plant taxonomy; vegetation mapping).

CLAUDETTE BRERA, 1957 (Plant taxonomy; vegetation mapping).

MARLENE DE LIMA DELGADO, 1957 (Vegetation mapping).

ZULMA FLORES, 1953 (Plant taxonomy; vegetation mapping).

LUIZ CARLOS DE FREITAS, 1935 (Plant anatomy).

DENISE VIANNA, 1957 (Vegetation mapping).

Specialization in research: Flora of Minas Gerais; taxonomy of grasses and other flowering plants of Brazil; cerrado and caatinga vegetation; woods and wood technology.

23

Loans: To institutions under special agreement.
Exchange: Yes.

BELO HORIZONTE: *Empresa de Pesquisa Agropecuária de Minas Gerais,* (**PAMG**), Avenida Amazonas 115, Caixa Postal 515, 30.000 Belo Horizonte, Minas Gerais, **Brazil.**
Telephone: (55)031/222-6544, ramal 42, 43, or 45.
Foundation: 1974. *Number of specimens:* 15.000.
Herbarium: Minas Gerais; cerrado, caatinga vegetation; native Leguminosae, especially *Stylosanthes, Zornia,* and *Desmodium.*
   Director: HELIO ANDRADE ALVES, 1937 (Pastures: cattle).
   Curator: MITZI BRANDÃO FERREIRA, 1933; 031/222-6544, ramal 45 (Plant taxonomy; Leguminosae, especially *Stylosanthes* and *Zornia;* poisonous plants; weeds; cerrado vegetation).
   Staff members: LUCÍA HELENA DE SOUSA CUNHA, 1954 (Physiology; cerrado seeds; poisonous plants; weeds).
   MARIA TEREZA COIMBRA PRATES (Dendrology).
   Specialization in research: Native forage, especially Leguminosae; toxic plants for cattle; seeds of cerrado plants and native trees.
   Associated botanic garden: Jardim Botânico de Belo Horizonte, Museu de História Natural, UFMG, Hôrto, 30.000 Belo Horizonte.
   Loans: To institutions, for 6 months.
   Exchange: Yes, plants of the cerrado.

BELOIT: *Herbarium, Biology Department, Beloit College,* (**BELC**), Beloit, Wisconsin 53511, **U.S.A.**
Telephone: 608/365-3391, ext. 287.
Foundation: 1890. *Number of specimens:* 18.000.
Herbarium: Regional, with emphasis on Wisconsin.
   Director and Curator: RICHARD D. NEWSOME, 1931 (Plant ecology).
   Specialization in research: Prairie ecology.
   Loans: Usual regulations.
   Exchange: Yes.

BELTON: *Herbarium, Department of Biology, University of Mary Hardin-Baylor,* (**HABAYC**), Belton, Texas 76513, **U.S.A.**
Telephone: 817/939-5811, ext. 246.
Foundation: Early 1900s. *Number of specimens:* 2.249.
Herbarium: Emphasis on Texas flora.
   Director and Curator: STANLEY D. CASTO, 1940 (Central Texas flora).
   Loans: Yes.
   Exchange: Yes.

BELTSVILLE: *U.S. National Seed Herbarium, Plant Taxonomy Laboratory,* (**BARC**), Room 238, Building 001, BARC-West, Beltsville, Maryland 20705, **U.S.A.**
Telephone: 301/344-2612.
Status: Seed-fruit collection of U.S. Department of Agriculture, Science and Education Administration.
Foundation: 1908. *Number of specimens:* 100.000.
Herbarium: Seed-fruit collection.
   Director and Curator: CHARLES R. GUNN, 1927 (Seeds and fruits of all families, especially Fabaceae; tropical drift disseminules; exotic weeds; Fabaceae supraspecific nomenclature; Vicieae).
   Staff members: LYDIA R. POOLE (Exotic weeds).
   CAROLE A. RITCHIE (Exotic weeds).
   Specialization in research: Isolated seed-fruit morphology and taxonomy; exotic weeds.
   Associated botanic garden: U.S. National Arboretum.
   Loans: To recognized researchers.
   Periodical and serial works: Technical USDA Bulletins, Agricultural Handbooks, Yearbooks of Agriculture.

BELTSVILLE: *U.S. National Fungus Collections,* (**BPI**), Building 011A, BARC-West, Beltsville, Maryland 20705, **U.S.A.**
Telephone: 301/344-3365.
Status: U.S. Department of Agriculture.
Foundation: Established in 1869 as the Pathological Collections. *Number of specimens:* 825.000.
Herbarium: General collection of fungi; all groups, excluding lichens.
Important collections: Fungus collections of the Smithsonian Institution (US), Missouri Botanical Garden (MO), Stanford University (DS), Brooklyn Botanic Garden (BKL); G. Bresadola, Travis Brooks, F. Bubak, George W. Carver, C. E. Chardon, R. Ciferri, Esther Dick (Snell), E. F. Guba, George G. Hedgcock, Anna E. Jenkins, A. B. Langlois, Curtis G. Lloyd, W. H. Long, T. H. Macbride, George W. Martin, O. A. Reinking, L. D. von Schweinitz, C. L. Shear, Walter Snell, P. C. Standley, John A. Stevenson, James R. Weir, George L. Zundel.
   Director: PAUL L. LENTZ, 1918; 301/344-3365; 344-3366 (Aphyllophorales, Polyporales; taxonomy and morphology of phytopathogens).
   Curator: DAVID F. FARR, 1941; 301/344-2274 (Aquatic Phycomycetes; Agaricales).
   Staff members: LEKH R. BATRA, 1929 (Hemiascomycetes, Plectomycetes, Discomycetes, Sclerotiniaceae; phytopathogens; insect-fungus relationships).
   MARIE L. FARR, 1927 (Myxomycetes, Pyrenomycetes; black mildews).
   KENT H. MCKNIGHT, 1921 (Agaricales, Boletales, Gasteromycetes, Discomycetes).
   FRANCIS A. VECKER, 1930 (Pyrenomycetes; cytology and development morphology of phytopathogens).
   Specialization in research: Taxonomy, morphology, cytology, life history, and biology of selected plant-pathogenic fungi, noncultivated mushrooms, and fungi in other major groups, also including myxomycetes.
   Loans: For research study by qualified scientists

for 6 months.

Exchange: Available and Desired: Fungi and publication reprints.

BEOGRAD: *Botaničko odeljenje, Prirodnjački muzej (Botanical Department, Natural History Museum),* **(BEO),** Njegoševa 51, Yu-11000 Beograd, **Yugoslavia.**
Telephone: 011-442-259.
Status: Independent institution.
Foundation: 1895. *Number of specimens:* 102.000.
Herbarium: Plants of Balkan Peninsula, mushrooms.
   Director: VOJISLAV NIKOLIĆ, 1925 (Flora, Taxonomy).
   Curator: NIKOLA DIKLIĆ, 1925 (Flora, taxonomy).
   Staff member: ALEKSANDER SIGUNOV, 1922 (Forest botany).
   Specialization in research: Flora of Balkan Peninsula.
   Periodical and serial works: Glasnik Prirodnjačkog muzeja (Bulletin of the Natural History Museum, Ser. B and C).
   Exchange: Yes.

BERGEN: *Herbariet, Botanisk Institutt, Universitetet i Bergen,* **(BG),** Postbox 12, N-5014 Bergen Universitetet, **Norway.**
Telephone: 05-212040, ext. 3345, 3339, 3340.
Status: University.
Foundation: 1825 (Museum), 1948 (University).
Number of specimens: 500.000.
Herbarium: West Norwegian phanerogams, worldwide (general); cryptogams, especially lichens, mosses.
Important collections: J. J. Havaas (lichens), P. Wendelbo (Iran/Afghanistan phanerogams), J. Naustdal (Norwegian vascular plants), E. Jørgensen (algae, liverworts, *Euphrasia*), B. Kaalaas (liverworts), J. M. Norman (lichens).
   Assistant Director and Curator: DAGFINN MOE, 1939 (Palynology, Norwegian vascular plants).
   Staff members: KNUT FAEGRI, 1909 (Palynology).
      PER M. JØRGENSEN, 1944 (Lichenology, alien phanerogams).
      ARNFINN SKOGEN, 1933 (*Sphagnum,* Scandinavian vascular plants).
   Specialization in research: Norwegian flora and vegetation including the historical aspect.
   Associated botanic garden: Botanisk hage (Botanical garden) Universitetet i Bergen.
   Loans: To recognized scientific institutions, generally on a reciprocal basis.
   Exchange: Especially phanerogams.

BERKELEY: *Jepson Herbarium and Library, Department of Botany, University of California,* **(JEPS),** Berkeley, California 94720, **U.S.A.**
Telephone: 415/642-2465.

Status: Privately endowed unit within the university of California, a state university.
Foundation: 1950. *Number of specimens:* 80.000.
Herbarium: Vascular plants of California.
Important collections: W. L. Jepson, Rimo Bacigalupi.
   Director: ROBERT ORNDUFF, 1932 (Population biology).
   Curator: LAWRENCE R. HECKARD, 1923 (Flora of California, especially Orobanchaceae and Scrophulariaceae).
   Staff members: RIMO BACIGALUPI, 1901 (Flora of California).
      LAURAMAY T. DEMPSTER, 1905 (*Galium* of the New World).
   Specialization in research: California flora (vascular plants).
   Associated botanic garden: University of California Botanical Garden.
   Loans: To recognized scientific institutions.
   Periodical and serial works: W. L. Jepson's Flora of California.
   Exchange: None.

BERKELEY: *Forest Disease Herbarium, Pacific Southwest Forest and Range Experiment Station,* **(PFRS),** P.O. Box 245, Berkeley, California 94701, **U.S.A.**
Telephone: 415/486-3156.
Status: U.S. Department of Agriculture, Forest Service.
Foundation: Early 1900's. *Number of specimens:* 5.100 (5.000 fungi, 100 vascular plants).
Herbarium: Mainly forest diseases of California.
   Curator: ROBERT F. SCHARPF.
   Specialization in research: Forest pathology.
   Loans: To recognized institutions.

BERKELEY: *Herbarium, Department of Botany, University of California,* **(UC),** Berkeley, California 94720, **U.S.A.**
Telephone: 415/642-2465.
Status: An instructional and research unit of the University of California, a state university governed by a Board of Regents.
Foundation: 1872. *Number of specimens:* 1.500.000.
Herbarium: Worldwide with specialization in the Americas and the Pacific Basin, covering the plant kingdom; strong in marine algae.
Important collections: Phycological collections of W. A. Setchell, Setchell & N. L. Gardner, California Academy of Sciences (CAS), Dudley Herbarium (DS), Missouri Botanical Garden (MO), G. F. Papenfuss, P. C. Silva, S. Earle; fungal and lichen collections of L. Bonar, H. E. Parks, J. P. Tracy, T. T. McCabe, W. Blasdale, E. Morse; bryological collections of J. Proskauer, M. A. Howe; pteridological collections of E. B. Copeland, E. Rosenstock, Y. Mexia; vascular plant collections of A. M. Alexander & A. Kellogg, E. B. Babcock & G. L. Stebbins, M. Baker, C. R. Ball,

25

T. S. & K. Brandegee, W. Brewer, A. M. Carter, I. Clokey, L. Constance, V. Duran, C. Epling (transferred from LA), H. M. Hall, R. F. Hoover, J. G. Lemmon, H. L. Mason, T. T. McCabe, H. E. McMinn, E. D. Merrill, Y. Mexia, C. A. Purpus, C. W. Sharsmith, H. K. Sharsmith, J. P. Tracy; UC Botanical Garden Latin American expeditions: P. C. Hutchison, A. A. Beetle, W. Eyerdam, T. H. Goodspeed, O.B. Horton, J. L. Morrison, H. Stork, J. West, F. Woytkowski; Vegetative Type Map Survey, USFS.

Director: ROBERT ORNDUFF, 1932 (Population biology).

Curator: THOMAS DUNCAN, 1948 (Seed plants).

Staff members: ANNETTA CARTER, 1907 (Flora of the Sierra de la Giganta, Baja California).

LINCOLN CONSTANCE, 1909 (Hydrophyllaceae, Umbelliferae).

GEORGE PAPENFUSS, 1903 (Phycology).

PAUL C. SILVA, 1922 (In charge of phycological collections; marine algae, especially of the Pacific Coast; *Codium*; botanical nomenclature; phycological bibliography).

ALAN R. SMITH, 1943 (In charge of pteridophytes and grasses; fern systematics; *Thelypteris*; Latin American ferns).

JOHN L. STROTHER, 1941 (In charge of exchange; Compositae).

ISABELLE TAVARES, 1921 (In charge of mycological and bryological collections; Laboulbeniales; *Usnea*).

Specialization in research: According to interests of staff members and institutional specialization given previously.

Associated botanic garden: University of California Botanical Garden.

Loans: To recognized scientific institutions.

Periodical and serial works: University of California Publications in Botany.

Exchange: Available, in limited amount: Mostly western North America, general; staff research vouchers. Desired: Specimens from all groups, especially from the Americas and the Pacific Basin.

BERLIN: *Botanischer Garten und Botanisches Museum Berlin-Dahlem,* (**B**), Königin-Luise-Strasse 6-8, D-1000 Berlin 33, **Federal Republic of Germany,** BRD.

Telephone: (030)-831 40 41.

Status: Land of Berlin.

Foundation: Garden 1679, herbarium 1815. *Number of specimens:* 2.000.000.

Herbarium: World-wide, especially Central Europe, SW. Asia, Togo, Hawaii.

Important collections: Historical collection: C. L. Willdenow (B-W). Other important collections: Angiosperms: J. F. N. Bornmüller (Balcan Pen., Near East), J. & M. S. Clemens (New Guinea), K. Dinter (SW. Africa), A. Peter (Africa), G. Kükenthal (Cyperaceae). Pteridophytes (mostly preserved): A. Braun, G. Forster, G. Hieronymus, J. F. Klotzsch, M. Kuhn, G. Kunze, H. F. Link, G. H. Mettenius, J.

Milde, K. Sprengel. Mosses: S. E. de Bridel, C. Warnstorf. Fungi: E. Jahn (Myxomycetes), P. Hennings, W. Kirschstein, A. Ludwig, Th. Nitschke, C. G. T. Preuss, L. Rabenhorst, G. Winter. Lichens: O. Behr, J. G. Lahm, G. Lettau, W. Zopf (Lichen substances). Special collections (mostly preserved): Fruits and seeds (palm fruits separate), gymnosperm cones, spirit collection, wood collection, fossils, vegetal remains from Egyptian tombs (G. Schweinfurth).

Director: WERNER GREUTER, 1938 (Mediterranean flora, nomenclature).

Curator of Phanerogams: PAUL HIEPKO, 1932 (Flora of Togo, nomenclature).

Curator of Cryptogams: WOLFRAM SCHULTZE-MOTEL, 1934 (Musci).

Staff members: FRIEDHELM BUTZIN, 1936 (Orchidaceae, Gramineae).

HARTMUT ERN, 1935, Head of the Garden Dept. (Phytogeography, conservation, Leguminosae).

ISOLDE HAGEMANN, 1944 (*Hypericum*, flora of Greece).

MADJIT HAKKI, 1934 (Scrophulariaceae).

BURGHARD HEIN, 1944 (Fungi, especially Ascomycetes).

H. WALTER LACK, 1949 (Compositae, bibliography).

BEAT ERNST LEUENBERGER, 1946 (Cactaceae, especially *Pereskia*).

ANICK MATHEY, 1940 (Lichens).

DIETER E. MEYER, 1926 (Pteridophyta).

HEIDEMARIE NOWAK-KRAWIETZ, 1944 (Algae, tropical Musci).

EVA POTZTAL, 1924, Head of the Public Museum Dept. (Gramineae, Palmae).

THOMAS RAUS, 1949 (Flora of Greece, phytogeography).

HILDEMAR SCHOLZ, 1928, Head of the Publications and Library Dept. (Gramineae, flora of Togo).

BERNHARD ZEPERNICK, 1926 (Ethnobotany, public relations).

Honorary staff members: WALTER DOMKE, 1899 (Conservation).

JOHANNES GERLOFF, 1915 (Algae).

FRITZ MATTICK, 1901 (Lichens, phytogeography).

EDITH RAADTS, 1914 (*Kalanchoë, Sansevieria*).

GEORG M. SCHULZE, 1909 (African Balsaminaceae).

ADOLF STRAUS, 1904 (Palaeobotany).

FRIEDRICH TIMLER, 1914 (Bibliography).

Specialization in research: Flora of Togo; flora of the Mediterranean, especially Greece; conservation.

Associated botanic garden: Yes.

Loans: To recognized botanical institutions; only photographs of B-W loaned.

Periodical and serial works: Willdenowia, Englera, OPTIMA-Newsletter.

Exchange: On request. Worldwide, excl. Central and North Europe.

Remarks: Herbarium destroyed by fire in 1943 except B-W, type material of selected Angiosperm groups; Pteridophytes, Fungi p.p. (Uredineae and Fungi imperfecti), and special collections (cf. De Herbario Berolinensi Notulae 1-..., Willdenowia 8.1978 seqq.).

BERLIN: *Bereich Botanik und Arboretum des Museums für Naturkunde der Humboldt-Universität zu Berlin,* **(BHU),** Späthstrasse 80/81, DDR-1195 Berlin-Baumschulenweg, **German Democratic Republic, DDR.**
Telephone: 6329941.
Status: Directed by the Humboldt University.
Foundation: 1960. *Number of specimens:* 220.000.
Herbarium: Worldwide, mainly phanerogams, bryophyta and fungi; associated collections of pollen slides and seeds.
Important collections: Th. Nees von Esenbeck (in part), L. C. Treviranus.
Director: W. VENT, 1920 (Systematics of spermatophytes, phytogeography, dendrobiology).
Curator: M. BÄSSLER, 1935 (Fabaceae, Mimosaceae, nomenclature, floristics).
Staff members: D. BENKERT, 1933 (Fungi, floristics).
 CHRISTA BEURTON, 1945 (*Achillea,* Rutaceae).
 P. BRÜCKNER, 1946 (Buxaceae, palynology).
 CLAUDIA GONNERMANN, 1952 (Papaveraceae, fruit and seed morphology).
 K.-H. HOEPFNER, 1930 (Arboretum).
 E. KÖHLER, 1932 (Buxaceae, Euphorbiaceae, palynology).
 BIRGIT MORY, 1944 (*Glaucium,* Celastraceae).
 G. NATHO, 1930 (Betulaceae, anatomy, morphology, history).
 GISELA NOACK, 1928 (Arboretum, history).
 INGELORE QUASDORF, 1932 (Arboretum).
 URSULA RÄNDEL, 1941 (Papaveraceae, Malvaceae; dendrology).
 BÄRBEL SCHMIDT, 1949 (*Coronilla*).
 H. SCHMIDT, 1929 (*Viburnum,* history).
 G. STOHR, 1928 (*Festuca, Rubus,* floristics).
Specialization in research: Taxonomy of the Eurasian flora, flora of the DDR, Cuban flora, palynology.
Associated botanic garden: Arboretum.
Loans: To recognized botanical institutions.
Periodical and serial works: Feddes Repertorium, Zeitschrift für botanische Taxonomie und Geobotanik; Gleditschia, Beiträge zur botanischen Taxonomie und deren Grenzgebiete; Annual seed-lists; Guidebooks to the Arboretum.

BERLIN: *Institut für Systematische Botanik und Pflanzengeographie der Freien Universität Berlin,* **(BSB),** Altensteinstr. 6, 1000 Berlin 33, (Dahlem), **Federal Republic of Germany,** BRD.

Telephone: 030/838 3149.
Status: Directed by the Free University of Berlin.
Foundation: 1955. *Number of specimens:* 8.600.
Herbarium: Flora of Central Europe, morphological and teratological collections.
Staff members: URSULA GEISSLER, 1931 (Algae, especially diatoms and ultrastructure).
 WERNER GREUTER, 1938 (Mediterranean flora, nomenclature).
 CHRISTIAN LEUCKERT, 1930 (Lichens and chemotaxonomy).
 GERNOT LYSEK, 1937 (Fungi).
 BODO SCHICK, 1944 (Comparative ecology and morphology of Spermatophyta, floral ecology).
Loans: To recognized botanical institutions.

BERN: *Systematisch-Geobotanisches Institut der Universität Bern,* **(BERN),** Altenbergrain 21, CH-3013 Bern, **Switzerland.**
Telephone: 031/42 20 58.
Status: Directed by State and University of Bern.
Foundation: 1861. *Number of specimens:* 360.000.
Herbarium: Flora of Switzerland (especially Kanton Bern), Alps, Mediterranean, parasitic fungi, macrolichens of the Alps.
Important collections: Eduard Fischer (Parasitic fungi), F. von Tavel (Ferns), Eduard Frey (Lichens), Felix Platter.
Director and Curator: GERHARD LANG, 1924 (Vegetation ecology, paleoecology).
Staff members: KLAUS AMMANN, 1940 (Taxonomy of lichens).
 OTTO HEGG, 1930 (Vegetation ecology).
Specialization in research: Vegetation ecology, palaeoecology, pollen analysis.
Associated botanic garden: Botanischer Garten.
Loans: On request.
Periodical and serial works: Jahresbericht Systematisch-Geobotanisches Institut der Universität Bern.
Exchange: Lichens, mosses, liverworts.

BERRIEN SPRINGS: *Herbarium, Museum of Natural History, Biology Department, Andrews University,* **(AUB),** Berrien Springs, Michigan 49104, **U.S.A.**
Telephone: 616/471-7404.
Status: Private university.
Foundation: 1960. *Number of specimens:* 10.000.
Herbarium: Southwestern Michigan and northwestern Indiana; Urticaceae; arctic and alpine flora of North America.
Curator: DENNIS W. WOODLAND, 1940; 616/471-3240 (Urticaceae of North America; alpine flora; flora of southwestern Michigan).
Staff members: LEONARD HARE, 1921 (Arctic flora and ecology).
 CLIFTON KELLER, 1937 (Phytogeography; computerized information retrieval; local flora).
Specialization in research: Biosystematics; computerized information retrieval; local flora.

Loans: To recognized institutions, normal regulations.

Exchange: Available: Vascular plants of central U.S. and alpine. Desired: Central U.S.; arctic and alpine; Urticaceae.

Remarks: Facilities for visiting scientists.

BHAVNAGAR: *Herbarium, Central Salt and Marine Chemicals Research Institute,* (**BHAV**), Bhavnagar, 364002, **India.** (Information 1974)

Status: Government of India.

Foundation: 1961. *Number of specimens:* 2.500.

Herbarium: Indian marine algae.

Loans: On special request only.

BINGHAMTON: *Herbarium, Department of Biological Sciences, State University of New York,* (**BING**), Binghamton, New York 13901, **U.S.A.**

Telephone: 607/798-2160.

Foundation: 1953. *Number of specimens:* 8.000.

Herbarium: North American algae and bryophytes; New York vascular plants.

Important collections: R. E. Andrus (bryophytes), E. F. Schumacher (algae).

Curator of Vascular Plants and Algae: GEORGE F. SCHUMACHER, 1924; 607/798-2445.

Curator of Bryophytes: RICHARD E. ANDRUS, 1941; 607/798-2160.

Specialization in research: Algal ecology and distribution; *Sphagnum* taxonomy, distribution and ecology.

Loans: To recognized institutions.

Exchange: Available: Bryophytes, especially *Sphagnum.*

BIRMINGHAM: *British Antarctic Survey Herbarium,* (**AAS**) – see CAMBRIDGE.

BIRMINGHAM: *Herbarium, City of Birmingham Museums and Art Gallery,* (**BIRA**), Chamberlain Square, Birmingham B3 3DH, England, **Great Britain.**

Telephone: 021-235-2838.

Status: Municipal.

Foundation: 1885. *Number of specimens:* 60.000.

Herbarium: Representative British flora, also European and N. American.

Important collections: J. E. Bagnall (including *Rubus, Rosa,* Bryophyta); E. M. Reynolds, W. Whitwell, P. G. M. Rhodes (Lichens).

Director: Keeper of Natural History.

Curator: B. ABELL SEDDON, 1933 (Aquatic vascular plants, palynology, vegetation history).

Staff members: None exclusively for herbarium.

Loans: To recognized botanists and institutions.

Remarks: The herbarium is part of a general Natural History Department.

BIRMINGHAM: *Herbarium, Department of Botany, The University,* (**BIRM**), Edgbaston, Birmingham B15 2TT, England, **Great Britain.** (Information 1976)

Status: University.

Foundation: 1882. *Number of specimens:* 150.000.

Herbarium: British and European plants, ferns and mosses, British fungi; Solanaceae; *Beta* from Asia Minor.

Important collections: R. C. L. Burgess, herb. J. G. Hawkes (*Solanum* sect. *Tuberarium*), W. Hillhouse, L. Kitching, A. Ley (*Rubus, Rosa, Hieracium*), H. S. Thompson, G. S. and W. West; voucher specimens for A Computer Mapped Flora (County of Warwickshire).

Specialization in research: Floristic surveys of Warwickshire, vascular flora of Wyre Forest, Worcestershire, experimental taxonomy of Solanaceae, bipolar vegetation studies.

Associated botanic garden: University Botanic Garden.

Loans: To recognized botanical institutions.

BLACKSBURG: *Massey Herbarium, Department of Biology, Virginia Polytechnic Institute and State University,* (**VPI**), Blacksburg, Virginia 24061, **U.S.A.**

Telephone: 703/961-5746.

Foundation: 1935. *Number of specimens:* 86.000 (70.000 vascular plants, 16.000 fungi).

Herbarium: Emphasis on flowering plants of Virginia and the Appalachian Region; boreal and arctic fungi.

Important collections: J. C. Benedict, O. K. Miller, L. J. Uttal.

Director: R. BAMBACH, 1934 (Paleoecology).

Curator: D. M. PORTER, 1937 (Systematics of Burseraceae, Rutaceae, Zygophyllaceae; island phytogeography; Charles Darwin's botanical work).

Staff members: G. P. FRANK, 1953 (Systematics of Apiaceae).

O. K. MILLER, 1930 (Basidiomycetes; fungi of North America, especially boreal and arctic regions).

M. L. SMYTH, 1904 (Field collecting of vascular plants; herbarium practice).

Specialization in research: Flora of Virginia and the Appalachian Region (especially rare or endangered species; aquatics); systematics and fruiting of Homobasidiomycetes; fungi of arctic and boreal regions.

Associated botanic garden: Virginia Polytechnic Institute and State University Botanic Garden.

Loans: To recognized botanical institutions.

Periodical and serial works: The Distributional History of the Biota of the Southern Appalachians: Research Division Monographs, Virginia Polytechnic Institute and State University.

Exchange: Virginia, Florida, Alaskan arctic, Pacific Northwest; limited exchanges in vascular plants and fungi encouraged.

BLOEMFONTEIN: *Geo Potts Herbarium, Depart-*

ment of Botany, University of the Orange Free State, (**BLFU**), P.O. Box 339, Bloemfontein 9300, **South Africa.**
Telephone: 051-70711, ext. 316 or 338.
Status: University.
Foundation: 1905. *Number of specimens:* 13.000.
Herbarium: Southern Africa and Marion Island in the South Atlantic.
Important collections: The Geo Potts collection.
Director: J. N. ELOFF, 1939 (Biochemistry, *Microcystis*).
Curator: H. J. T. VENTER, 1938 (Taxonomy, *Monsonia, Erodium*, Periplocaceae).
Staff members: J. A. COETZEE, 1921 (Palynology).
A. M. JOUBERT, 1952 (Taxonomy, *Lycium*).
R. L. VERHOEVEN, 1945 (Anatomy and cytology, *Monsonia, Raphionacme, Lycium*).
E. M. VAN ZINDEREN BAKKER, 1907 (Palynology).
Specialization in research: Palynology (Tertiary vegetation of the Cape Region, present and quaternary vegetation of East and Southern Africa, especially Namib); taxonomy (Geraniaceae, Periplocaceae, Solanaceae of Southern Africa); phytosociology (Province Orange Free State and Marion Island in the South Atlantic).
Associated botanic garden: Yes.
Loans: To recognized botanical institutions.
Periodical and serial works: Biennial reports on palynology in Africa.
Exchange: Available: Limited number of Southern African plants.

BLOOMFIELD HILLS: *Billington Herbarium, Cranbrook Institute of Science,* (**BLH**), Box 801, Bloomfield Hills, Michigan 48013, **U.S.A.**
Telephone: 313/645-3223.
Status: Private foundation.
Foundation: 1947. *Number of specimens:* 48.000.
Herbarium: Principally Michigan vascular plants.
Important collections: O. A. Farwell.
Director and Curator: JAMES R. WELLS, 1932 (Taxonomy; floristics of vascular plants; ecology).
Loans: To qualified institutions.

BLOOMINGTON: *Herbarium, Department of Biology, Indiana University,* (**IND**), Bloomington, Indiana 47401, **U.S.A.**
Telephone: 812/337-5007.
Foundation: 1885. *Number of specimens:* 140.000 vascular plants.
Herbarium: Primarily flora of Indiana.
Important collections: Charles C. Deam.
Director: CHARLES B. HEISER, 1920 (*Helianthus, Capsicum;* domesticated plants).
Curator: LEWIS JOHNSON, 1947.
Staff members: DONALD BURTON, 1936 (*Solanum nigrum* group).
DAVID DILCHER, 1936 (Paleobotany).

GERALD GASTONY, 1940 (Biosystematics of ferns).
RICHARD MAXWELL, 1926 (Leguminosae).
Specialization in research: Biosystematics.
Loans: To recognized institutions.

BOCA RATON: *Herbarium, Department of Biological Sciences, Florida Atlantic University,* (**FAU**), Boca Raton, Florida 33431, **U.S.A.**
Telephone: 305/395-5100, ext. 2729.
Status: State university.
Foundation: 1969. *Number of specimens:* 23.000.
Herbarium: Specialization in flora of southeastern Florida, especially Broward, Dade, Palm Beach, Martin, and St. Lucie counties.
Director: DANIEL F. AUSTIN, 1943 (Convolvulaceae; southern Florida ecology).
Staff members: ROBERT B. GRIMM (Marine algae).
CLIFTON E. NAUMAN (Pteridophytes).
GEORGE W. STAPLES, III, 1953 (Convolvulaceae).
Specialization in research: Floristics of southeastern Florida; monographic studies of Convolvulaceae.
Loans: To recognized institutions.
Exchange: Particular interest in Convolvulaceae, but tropical plants generally.

BOGOR: *Herbarium Bogoriense,* (**BO**), Jalan Raya Juanda 22-24, Bogor, **Indonesia.**
Telephone: (0251)22035.
Status: Research center of Lembaga Biologi Nasional, Lembaga Ilmu Pengetahuan Indonesia.
Foundation: 1817. *Number of specimens:* 1.600.000.
Herbarium: Phanerogams and some cryptogams, emphasizing Malesia.
Important collections: C. L. von Blume, J. K. Hasskarl, J. E. Teijsmann, S. H. Koorders, C. A. Backer (Malesian phanerogams), A. G. O. Penzig, K. B. Boedijn (fungi).
Director and Curator: KUSWATA KARTAWINATA, 1936 (Forest botany and ecology).
Staff members: ROCHADI ABDULHADI, 1950 (Ecology).
A. LATIEF BURHAN, 1953 (Araceae).
DEDDY DARNAEDY, 1952 (Pteridophytes).
GREGORI G. HAMBALI, 1949 (Biology of Loranthaceae and Araceae, economic botany).
KARTINI KRAMADIBRATA, 1952 (Autecology).
JOHANIS P. MOGEA, 1947 (Palmae).
TUKIRIN PARTOMIHARDJO, 1952 (Ecology, vascular epiphytes).
SUHARDJONO PRAWIROATMODJO, 1952 (Morphology, forest trees).
M. A. RIFAI (Discomycetes, Hyphomycetes).
SOEDARSONO RISWAN, 1945 (Ecology).
HARINI M. SANGAT, 1950 (Ethnobotany).
HERWASONO SOEDJITO, 1952 (Ecology).
NINIEK W. SOETJIPTO, 1941 (Economic botany).
SUKRISTIJONO SUKARDJO, 1950 (Ecology).

HARI SUDEWO, 1950 (Autecology).
EKO B. WALUYO, 1951 (Ethnobotany).
HARRY WIRIADINATA, 1949 (Forest trees, Leguminosae).
Specialization in research: Flora of Malesia and forest ecology.
Associated botanic garden: Kebun Raya Bogor, Jalan Raya Juanda 11.
Loans: To recognized botanical institutions.
Periodical and serial works: Reinwardtia.
Exchange: Available: Specimens from Indonesia. Desired: Specimens from Southeast Asia and surrounding areas.
Remarks: Facilities for visiting botanists, preparation of and administrative support to botanical exploration inside Indonesia.

BOGOR: *Lembaga Pusat Penjelidikan Kehutanan (Forest Research Institute)*, **(BZF)**, Bogor, **Indonesia.** (Information 1964)
Status: Division of Forest Service of Indonesia.
Foundation: 1917. *Number of specimens:* 45.000.
Herbarium: Trees of Indonesia.
Specialization in research: Indonesian tree flora.
Associated botanic garden: Arboretum and Experimental Gardens of Silviculture Division.
Loans: On request.
Periodical and serial works: Pengumuman (Communications) and Reports.

BOGOTÁ: *Herbario, Museo del Instituto de La Salle,* **(BOG)**, Calle 11 No. 1-47, Apartado Aéreo 27389, Bogotá, **Colombia.**
Telephone: (57)234-61-89; 243-06-50.
Status: Universidad Social Católica de La Salle, a private institution.
Foundation: 1913. *Number of specimens:* 11.200.
Herbarium: Emphasis on flora of Colombia.
Director: DANIEL J. GONZÁLEZ, 1909.
Curator: RAMÓN GUEVARA, 1920; 243-06-50.
Specialization in research: Flora of Colombia; *Lupinus* (Leguminosae).
Periodical and serial works: Occasional papers in Boletín del Instituto de La Salle.
Exchange: Occasional.
Remarks: Herbarium was destroyed by fire on 10 April 1948; rebuilding began soon thereafter.

BOGOTÁ: *Herbario Nacional Colombiano, Instituto de Ciencias Naturales, Museo de Historia Natural, Universidad Nacional,* **(COL),** Apartado 7495, Bogotá, **Colombia.**
Telephone: (57)2442387; 2444403.
Foundation: 1931. *Number of specimens:* 200.000.
Herbarium: Colombia and adjacent countries.
Important collections: F. A. Barkley, H. Bischler, A. M. Cleef, J. Cuatrecasas, S. Díaz P., A. Dugand, K. P. Dumont, J. M. Duque-Jaramillo, A. Fernández P., E. Forero, H. García-Barriga, A. Gentry, O. Haught, G. Huertas, J. M. Idrobo, H. S. Irwin, R. Jaramillo, E. P.

Killip, E. L. Little, G. Lozano, L. E. Mora, M. T. Murillo, E. Pérez-Arbeláez, P. Pinto E., G. T. Prance, R. Romero-Castañeda, C. Saravia, R. E. Schultes, J. Schunke V., J. J. Triana, L. Uribe U., L. A. Camargo, J. H. Torres, J. C. Mutis.
Director: POLIDORO PINTO E., 1926 (Gramineae).
Curator: GUSTAVO LOZANO-CONTRERAS, 1938 (Magnoliaceae; ecology).
Staff members: JAIME AGUIRRE, 1951 (Hepaticae).
LUIS ENRIQUE AGUIRRE G., 1944 (Chemical systematics).
LUIS ALFREDO CAMARGO G., 1920 (*Berberis*).
SANTIAGO DIAZ-PIEDRAHITA, 1944 (Compositae).
ALVARO FERNÁNDEZ-PÉREZ, 1920 (Violaceae, Orchidaceae, Lentibulariaceae).
ENRIQUE FORERO, 1942 (Neotropical Connaraceae; flora of Chocó; *Calliandra*).
HERNANDO GARCÍA-BARRIGA, 1913 (Medicinal plants).
JESUS M. IDROBO M., 1917 (Marantaceae).
ROBERTO JARAMILLO-MEJÍA, 1919 (Compositae; flora of Colombia).
LUIS EDUARDO MORA O., 1931 (Cyperaceae, Gunneraceae).
MARÍA TERESA MURILLO P., 1929 (Colombian pteridophytes).
ORLANDO RANGEL CH., 1950 (*Draba:* taxonomy and ecology).
JORGE HERNÁN TORRES R., 1935 (Economic botany).
Specialization in research: Flora of Colombia.
Loans: To recognized botanical institutions, by application to the Curator.
Periodical and serial works: Caldasia (botany, zoology, geology, anthropology); Mutisia (botany); Catálogo Illustrado de las Plantas de Cundinamarca.
Exchange: Available: Specimens from Colombia. Desired: Mainly from Neotropical regions; photographs of types; reprints of works on tropical plants.
Remarks: Label data on all 200.000 specimens are available in a computer data bank (see Taxon 25: 85-94. 1976).
The Director should be contacted regarding field work to be carried out by foreigners in Colombia.

BOGOTÁ: *Herbario Fitopatológico Colombiano, Instituto Colombiano Agropecuario,* **(ICA),** Tibaitatá, Apartado Aéreo 151123, El Dorado, 6420 Bogotá, **Colombia.**
Status: Government institution.
Foundation: 1930. *Number of specimens:* 3.500.
Herbarium: Pathogenic fungi.
Important collections: C. Garcés-Orejuela.
Remarks: The ICA herbarium has been incorporated in COL.

BOGOTÁ: *Herbario Forestal, Facultad de Ingeniería Forestal, Universidad Distrital,* (**UDBC**), Carrera 8a, No. 40-78, Bogotá, **Colombia.** (Information 1977)
Status: Directed by the University's Instituto de Investigaciones y Proyectos Forestales y Madereros.
Foundation: 1960. *Number of specimens:* 12.000.
Herbarium: Regional.

BOISE: *Herbarium, Intermountain Forest and Range Experiment Station,* (**BOIS**), 316 East Myrtle Street, Boise, Idaho 83706, **U.S.A.**
Telephone: 208/334-1457.
Status: U.S. Department of Agriculture, Forest Service.
Foundation: 1940. *Number of specimens:* 3.050.
Herbarium: Flora of central and southern Idaho.
Important collections: Shantz and Pigmigsel (early 1900's range survey of the Snake River Plains and Great Basin).
Curator: ROBERT STEELE (Forest ecology).
Specialization in research: Forest and range research.
Loans: Usual regulations.
Exchange: Occasional.

BOISE: *Herbarium, Idaho Department of Fish and Game,* (**IFGH**), 109 W. 44th Street, Boise, Idaho 83704, **U.S.A.**
Telephone: 208/384-3969.
Status: Supported by Pitman-Robertson funds and Idaho Department of Fish and Game.
Foundation: 1973. *Number of specimens:* 3.000.
Herbarium: Flora of Idaho.
Important collections: Barbara Ertter, James W. Grimes.
Director and Curator: CAROL A. MOLSEE PRENTICE, 1948 (Range plant systematics).
Specialization in research: Wildlife food habits.

BOLOGNA: *Herbarium, Istituto Botanico dell'Università,* (**BOLO**), Via Irnerio 42, Bologna, **Italy.** (Information 1974)
Status: University.
Foundation: 1568 (as Botanic Garden).
Herbarium: Flora of Italy.
Important collections: A. Bertoloni herbarium.

BOMBAY: *Blatter Herbarium, St. Xavier's College,* (**BLAT**), Bombay 400 001, **India.** (Information 1974)
Status: Private college directed by the Society of Jesus, affiliated to University of Bombay.
Foundation: About 1918. *Number of specimens:* 100.000.
Important collections: L. J. Sedgwick and Bell, E. Blatter and associates, Father Santapau, C. McCann, B. Mundkur and E. Gonzalves.
Specialization in research: Phanerogamic flora of India.
Loans: To recognized botanical institutions.

BONN: *Bundesforschungsanstalt für Naturschutz und Landschaftsökologie,* (**BNL**), Konstantinstrasse 110, 5300 Bonn 2, **Federal Republic of Germany,** BRD.
Telephone: 0228/330041-44.
Status: Federal institute.
Foundation: 1939. *Number of specimens:* 9.500 (7.500 phanerogams, 2.000 cryptogams).
Director: WERNER TRAUTMANN, 1924 (Plant ecology, conservation).
Curator: HANS G. FINK, 1945.
Staff member: BEATE SPHAN, 1956.
Loans: Possible on request.

BONN: *Botanisches Institut der Universität Bonn, Abt. für Morphologie und Systematik,* (**BONN**), Meckenheimer Allee 170, D-53 Bonn 1, **Federal Republic of Germany,** BRD.
Status: Institute of the University of Bonn.
Important collections: Herbarium Hermann Nessel (5.500 Pteridophyta).
Head of the Division: PETER LEINS.
Curator: KLAUS KRAMER.
Associated botanic garden: Botanischer Garten der Universität Bonn.
Remarks: The herbarium was destroyed in 1944 with the exception of the Nessel collection.

BOONE: *Herbarium, Department of Biology, Appalachian State University,* (**BOON**), Rankin Science Building, Boone, North Carolina 28608, **U.S.A.**
Telephone: 704/262-3025.
Foundation: 1953. *Number of specimens:* 16.000.
Herbarium: Good local herbarium of the southern Appalachians.
Director and Curator: I. W. CARPENTER, JR. 1923 (Vascular plants of southern Appalachians).
Staff members: JOHN J. BOND, 1939 (Fungi).
MARIE L. HICKS, 1928 (Bryophytes).
Specialization in research: Local floras with emphasis on distribution of liverworts.
Loans: Usual regulations, for 6 months.
Exchange: Southern Appalachian plants.

BORDEAUX: *Herbier du Jardin Botanique,* (**BORD**), Terrasse du Jardin Public, Place Bardineau, 33000 – Bordeaux, **France.**
Telephone: (56)52-18-77.
Status: Municipal.
Foundation: 1850. *Number of specimens:* 85.000.
Important collections: Herbiers J. M. G. Lespinasse, L. Motelay, Charles Desmoulins, A. F. Jeanjean, E. H. Brochon, J. M. L. Dufour, Clavaud.
Director: JEAN EYMÉ, 1921, Professor at Faculty of Sciences (Cytology).
Curator: HENRI BESANÇON, 1929 (Flora of SW France and the Languedoc).
Staff members: MARCEL BESSE, 1920.
JEAN CASSE, 1917.
Associated botanic garden: Jardin Botanique de Bordeaux.

BORREGO SPRINGS: *Herbarium, Anza-Borrego Desert State Park,* **(BSCA),** Box 428, Borrego Springs, California 92004, **U.S.A.**
Telephone: 714/767-5311.
Status: State park.
Foundation: 1960. *Number of specimens:* 2.000.
Herbarium: Desert plants of Anza-Borrego State Park.
Director: PAUL R. JOHNSON.

BOSTON: *Herbarium, Department of Biology, Boston State College,* **(BOSC),** 625 Huntington Avenue, Boston, Massachusetts 02115, **U.S.A.**
Telephone: 617/731-3300, ext. 280.
Foundation: 1970. *Number of specimens:* 16.500.
Herbarium: Vascular flora of U.S., especially aquatics of New England.
Director and Curator: C. BARRE HELLQUIST, 1940 (Vascular aquatic plants).
Specialization in research: Aquatic flora of New England.
Loans: No special restrictions.
Exchange: Available: Aquatics, especially *Potamogeton.* Desired: Aquatics from the world.

BOSTON: *Stuart K. Harris Herbarium, Biological Science Center, Boston University,* **(BSN),** 2 Cummington Street, Boston, Massachusetts 02215, **U.S.A.**
Telephone: 617/353-2432; 353-2433.
Foundation: 1939. *Number of specimens:* 3.800.
Important collections: Stuart K. Harris; Natural History Society of Boston.
Director and Curator: RICHARD PRIMACK (Population genetics; times of pollination and flowering).
Remarks: Part of this collection has been incorporated in the Gray Herbarium (GH), Cambridge, Massachusetts.

BOSTON: *Husky Herbarium, Department of Biology, Northeastern University,* **(HNUB),** 360 Huntington Avenue, Boston, Massachusetts 02115, **U.S.A.**
Telephone: 617/437-2260.
Status: Private university.
Foundation: 1965. *Number of specimens:* 15.500.
Herbarium: Local vascular plants.
Important collections: Begoniaceae, Lycopodiaceae.
Director: DANIEL C. SCHEIRER, 1946; 617/437-2256.
Curator: DONALD CHENEY; 617/437-2260.
Associated botanic garden: Northeastern University Botanical Station and Greenhouses, Woburn, Massachusetts.
Loans: No restrictions.
Exchange: When material is available.

BOSTON: *Herbarium, Massachusetts College of Pharmacy and Allied Health Sciences,* **(MCP),** 179 Longwood Avenue, Boston, Massachusetts 02115, **U.S.A.**

Telephone: 617/732-2960.
Status: Private college.
Foundation: 1923. *Number of specimens:* 14.000.
Herbarium: Plants with economic value, especially medicinal; spices, dyes; medicinal plants, especially *Rauwolfia;* gums, resins.
Director and Curator: JOHN D. LEARY, 1934 (Natural product chemistry; pharmacognosy).
Staff member: BENJAMIN R. HERSHENSON.
Specialization in research: Phytochemistry; poisonous plant research; plant drugs of abuse.
Loans: Handled on a case by case request.
Exchange: Case by case requests considered.
Remarks: Collection supported by library collections on medicinal plants.

BOTUCATU: *Herbário, Departamento de Botânica, Instituto Básico de Biologia Médica e Agrícola de Botucatu,* **(BOTU),** Caixa Postal 526, 18.610 Botucatu, São Paulo, **Brazil.**
Telephone: (55)0149/22-0555.
Status: Universidade Estadual Paulista "Julio de Mesquita Filho" (UNESP).
Foundation: 1966. *Number of specimens:* 10.000.
Herbarium: Emphasis on Brazil; cerrado plants; forest plants of Botucatu.
Director: WILMA PEREIRA BASTOS RAMOS, 1933 (Pharmacology).
Curator: AYRTON AMARAL, JR., 1948; 0149/22-2448 (Taxonomy of tropical Orchidaceae, Erythroxylaceae).
Staff members: GRACI M. CORSO, 1941 (Plant anatomy and physiology).
IRINA D. GENTCHUJNICOV, 1914 (Weeds; cultivated and toxic plants; ecology).
GERHARD K. GOTTSBERGER, 1940 (Flower ecology; Myxomycetes; Annonaceae).
ILSE S. GOTTSBERGER, 1940 (Cerrado plants; ecology).
CARLOS A. F. MOURA, 1929 (Turneraceae, Araliaceae; taxonomy and plant anatomy).
JOSÉ FIGUEREDO PEDRAS, 1945 (Plant physiology).
JOÃO D. RODRIGUES, 1945 (Plant physiology).
SELMA DZIMIDAS RODRIGUES, 1948 (Plant physiology).
YURIKO YANAGISAWA, 1951 (Ecology and floral biology of Bignoniaceae).
Specialization in research: Cerrado vegetation; taxonomy of Erythroxylaceae, Turneraceae, Araliaceae, Orchidaceae, Annonaceae, Myxomycetes; plant physiology, ecology, and anatomy.
Associated botanic garden: Jardim Botânico do Instituto Básico de Biologia Médica e Agrícola.
Loans: In general to recognized botanical institutions.
Exchange: Available: Cerrado and forest plants of the region of Botucatu; weeds and Brazilian plants.
Remarks: Facilities for visiting botanists.

BOUKOKO: *Herbarium, Station Centrale de Boukoko*, **(SCB)**, via M'Baiki, Boukoko, Oubangui-Chari, **Central African Republic.** (Information 1964)
Status: Directed by O.R.S.T.O.M., Paris.
Foundation: 1942. *Number of specimens:* 3.600.

BOULDER: *Herbarium, University of Colorado Museum*, **(COLO)**, Campus Box 218, Boulder, Colorado 80302, **U.S.A.**
Telephone: 303/492-6171; 492-6336.
Foundation: 1890. *Number of specimens:* 335.000.
Herbarium: All groups; western North America, Europe, Galapagos, Australia, New Guinea.
Important collections: Abbé F. Hy (lichens), Eugene Monguillon (cryptogams), Abbé Letacq; E. Ripart (algae), Seville Flowers (cryptogams), W. A. Weber, D. K. Bailey (*Pinus*), D. Wiens (*Arceuthobium*), J. A. Ewan (*Delphinium*).
Director: PETER ROBINSON (Vertebrate paleontologist).
Curator: WILLIAM A. WEBER, 1918 (Floristics; phanerogams, bryophytes, lichens).
Specialization in research: Floristics of western North America; Galapagos Islands (bryophytes, lichens).
Loans: One year renewable; only for taxonomic revisions, not for geographic searches.
Periodical and serial works: Natural History Inventory of Colorado (No. 1, Botany).
Exchange: Available: Lichenes Exsiccati distributed by the University of Colorado Museum; general exchange of vascular plants and bryophytes.

BOULDER: *Herbarium, Gesneriad Gardens*, **(GGB)**, 2945 Third Street, Boulder, Colorado 80302, **U.S.A.**
Telephone: 303/442-1020.
Status: Private, unendowed.
Foundation: 1965. *Number of specimens:* 6.500.
Herbarium: Scrophulariales, especially Gesneriaceae; Colorado local flora.
Director and Curator: DALE L. DENHAM, 1922 (Taxonomy of New World Gesneriaceae).
Staff member: MIRIAM L. DENHAM, 1921 (Taxonomic significance of trichomes).
Specialization in research: Taxonomy of New World Gesneriaceae.
Associated botanic garden: Gesneriad Gardens.
Loans: No special restrictions to recognized individuals or institutions.
Exchange: Available: Colorado plants. Desired: Neotropical Gesneriaceae.

BOWLING GREEN: *Herbarium, Department of Biological Sciences, Bowling Green State University*, **(BGSU)**, Bowling Green, Ohio 43403, **U.S.A.**
Telephone: 419/372-2434.
Foundation: 1967. *Number of specimens:* 20.000.
Herbarium: Local flora of northwestern Ohio; mainly plants of oak openings habitat.
Important collections: E. L. Moseley (1900–1928).

Director and Curator: NATHAN WILLIAM EASTERLY, 1927 (Oak openings floristics and ecology).
Specialization in research: Ecology and floristics of sand habitats, oak openings.
Loans: Usual regulations, for 6 months; request annotation labels be used.

BOZEMAN: *W. E. Booth Herbarium, Biology Department, Montana State University*, **(MONT)**, Bozeman, Montana 59715, **U.S.A.**
Telephone: 406/994-3322.
Foundation: 1892. *Number of specimens:* 75.000.
Herbarium: Primarily Montana vascular plants, lichens, and bryophytes.
Important collections: R. S. Williams, J. W. Blankinship, F. Kelsey, P. A. Rydberg and C. E. Bessey.
Director and Curator: JOHN H. RUMELY, 1926 (Montana flora).
Specialization in research: Revision of the Montana floral manuals.
Loans: Standard conditions.
Periodical and serial works: Plant series in Montana Academy of Sciences Proceedings.
Exchange: Welcome.

BRADFORD: *Herbarium, Bradford Art Galleries and Museums*, **(CMM)**, Cartwright Hall, Lister Park, Bradford, West Yorkshire BD9 4NS, England, **Great Britain**.
Telephone: 0274-493313.
Status: Municipal (directed by City of Bradford Metropolitan Council).
Foundation: 1879. *Number of specimens:* 60.000.
Herbarium: Mainly Great Britain (Phanerogams and cryptogams), some European and American material.
Important collections: F. Arnold Lees, T. Hebden, T. W. Gissing, J. W. Carter, A. Graham.
Director of Art Gallery: P. MICHAEL DIAMOND, 1942.
Curator: MARGARET M. HARTLEY, 1943.
Associated botanic garden: The Botanic Garden, Lister Park.
Remarks: CMM and KGY amalgamated in 1974, WKD received on long loan in 1976.

BRADFORD: *Herbarium, Pharmaceutical Society of Great Britain, Department of Pharmacy, University of Bradford*, **(PSGB)**, Richmond Road, Bradford, West Yorkshire BD7 1DP, England, **Great Britain.**
Telephone: 0274-33466.
Status: Donated to the university by Pharmaceutical Society.
Foundation: 1842. *Number of specimens:* 9.300.
Herbarium: Drug plants, British and foreign; over 10.000 materia medica specimens.
Director and Curator: WILLIAM EDWARD COURT, 1921 (Pharmacognosy).
Staff members: KEITH J. HARKISS (Pharmacognosy).

PETER A. LINLEY (Pharmacognosy).
JANET M. PECK (Pharmacognosy).
Specialization in research: Phytochemical studies of *Rauwolfia* and related Apocynaceae.
Loans: To recognized botanical institutions.

BRASÍLIA: *Herbário, Centro Nacional de Recursos Genéticos, Empresa Brasileira de Pesquisa Agropecuária, CENARGEN/EMBRAPA,* (**CEN**), Avenida W-5 Norte Parque Rural, Caixa Postal 10.2372, 70.000 Brasília, Distrito Federal, **Brazil.**
Telephone: (55)061/273-0100; 272-4203.
Status: Directed by the Federal Government, Brazilian Enterprise for Agriculture Research (Ministério da Agricultura).
Foundation: 1976. *Number of specimens:* 10.000.
Herbarium: Economic plants, especially grasses, legumes, cassava, Annonas, pineapple and their wild progenitors; ornamental plants.
Director: DALMO CATAULI GIACOMETTI, 1921 (Germplasm of tropical fruits).
Curator: LIDIO CORADIN, 1949; 061/272-4203 (Taxonomy of grasses; plant germplasm collecting).
Staff members: ANTONIO COSTA ALLEM, 1949 (Taxonomy of Euphorbiaceae; plant germplasm collecting).
JOSÉ FRANCISCO MONTENEGRO VALLS, 1945 (Taxonomy of grasses; plant germplasm collecting).
Specialization in research: Taxonomy of grasses of South America; taxonomy of Euphorbiaceae, with emphasis on *Manihot;* documentation of plant germplasm with emphasis on native forage crops (grasses and legumes), *Manihot,* and *Ananas.*
Loans: To recognized botanical institutions.
Exchange: Available: Brazil, mainly grasses and legumes. Desired: Brazilian economic plants, especially forage species of grasses and legumes, *Ananas, Manihot;* ornamental plants.
Remarks: Work is complemented by a network of Active Banks of Germplasm located in different regions of Brazil.

BRASÍLIA: *Herbário da Reserva Ecológica do Instituto Brasileiro de Geografia e Estatística,* (**IBGE**), Edifício Venâncio II, 2nd andar Reserva Ecológica do IBGE, 70.302 Brasília, Distrito Federal, **Brazil.**
Telephone: (55)061/562-6800.
Foundation: 1977. *Number of specimens:* 5.000.
Herbarium: Central Plateau of Brazil (tropical dry vegetation), especially grasses, legumes, and trees.
Important collections: Ezechias Paulo Heringer, George Eiten, William Rodrigues, Tarciso Sousa Filgueiras, Francisco das Chagas e Silva, Roberta Cunha de Mendonça, Benedito Alício da Silva Pereira, Anajulia Elizabete Heringer Salles, Geraldo Ismael da Rocha.
Director: MAURÍCIO RANGEL REIS.
Curator: EZECHIAS PAULO HERINGER (Dendr.).
Staff members: TARCISO SOUSA FILGUEIRAS (Grasses).

ROBERTA CUNHA DE MENDONÇA, 1952 (Anatomy).
BENEDITO A. DA SILVA PEREIRA, 1948 (Culture of plant tissues).
GERALDO ISMAEL ROCHA, 1950 (Propagation of wild species).
ANAJULIA ELIZABETE HERINGER SALLES, 1953 (Phytogeography).
FRANCISCO DAS CHAGAS E SILVA, 1948 (Propagation of wild trees).
Specialization in research: Autecology; wild plants for pasture; species of the natural flora for wood, for food for wild animals, and for gardens; grasses and Leguminosae.
Loans: To recognized herbaria for six months.
Periodical and serial works: Bulletin of Geography; Revista Brasileira de Geografia; Anuário de Geografia e Estatística.
Exchange: Mainly for tree specimens.

BRASÍLIA: *Herbário, Departamento de Biologia Vegetal, Fundação Universidade de Brasilia,* (**UB**), Caixa Postal 153081, 70.910 Brasília, Distrito Federal, **Brazil.**
Telephone: (55)061/272-0000, ramal 2282.
Foundation: 1963. *Number of specimens:* 80.000.
Herbarium: Mainly flora of central Brazil.
Important collections: H. S. Irwin (central Brazil), J. A. Ratter (central Brazil), G. Eiten and L. T. Eiten (Brazil), W. R. Anderson (central Brazil), J. M. Pires (central Brazil, Amazonia), R. P. Belém (Bahia), S. G. Fonseca (central Brazil), E. Onishi (central Brazil), E. P. Heringer (central Brazil), Royal Society Expedition to Mato Grosso (1967-1969).
Director: THEREZINHA ISAIA PAVIANI, 1929 (Anatomy of Cerrado species).
Curator: JOSEPH H. KIRKBRIDE, JR., 1943 (Neotropical Rubiaceae).
Staff members: MARILUSA ARAÚJO GRANJA E BARROS, 1945 (Phenology of Cerrado species).
HASAN BOLKAN, 1939 (Mycology).
LINDA STYER CALDAS, 1945 (Physiology of Cerrado species).
GEORGE EITEN, 1923 (Phytosociology of Cerrado).
DAVID ROS GIFFORD, 1924 (Ecology).
M. CRISTINA GARCÍA DE KIRKBRIDE, 1945 (Neotropical Rubiaceae; phytosociology).
JOSÉ ELIAS DE PAULA, 1934 (Anatomy of wood).
Specialization in research: Flora and ecology of Brazil with emphasis on the Cerrados.
Associated botanic garden: Estação Experimental de Biologia (50 ha); Fazenda Agua Limpia, Campo Experimental (4.000 ha).
Loans: To recognized institutions.
Exchange: Available: Specimens from central Brazil. Desired: Specimens from the Neotropics.

BRATISLAVA: *Slovenské národné múzeum,* (**BRA**), 885 36 Vajanského nábr. 2, Bratislava, **Czechoslovakia.**

Telephone: 336551.
Status: Directed by state.
Foundation: 1924. *Number of specimens:* 390.000
(150.000 cryptogams, 240.000 phanerogams).
Herbarium: Worldwide, especially Central Europe.
Important collections: A. Kmeť (phanerogams: *Rosa,* fungi), K. Kalchbrenner (phanerogams, fungi), Nádvorník (lichens).
   Director: ALOJZ HABOVŠTIAK, 1932 (Archaeology).
      Curators: JURAJ HAJDÚK, 1928 (Phanerogams).
      ŠTEFAN JURIŠ, 1928 (Algae).
      PAVOL LIZOŇ, 1945 (Fungi).
      IVAN PIŠÚT, 1935 (Lichens).
   Specialization in research: Flora of Slovakia.
   Loans: To recognized botanical institutions.
   Periodical and serial works: Acta rerum naturalium Musei Nationalis slovaci, Bratislava; Annotatiònes zoologicae et botanicae.
   Exchange: Available: Lichens from Slovakia.

BRATISLAVA: *Botanický ústav Slovenskej akadémie vied,* **(SAV),** Dúbravská cesta 26, 80900 Bratislava, **Czechoslovakia.** (Information 1974)
Foundation: 1953. *Number of specimens:* 85.000.
Herbarium: Tracheophyta of Europe, Czechoslovakia, especially Slovakia, Asia Minor.
Loans: To recognized botanical institutions.

BRATISLAVA: *Department of Systematic Botany of Faculty of Natural Sciences, Comenius University,* **(SLO),** Révová 39, 80100 Bratislava, **Czechoslovakia.**
Telephone: 334745.
Status: Adherent to university.
Foundation: 1940. *Number of specimens:* 153.000
(138.000 phanerogams, 15.000 cryptogams).
Herbarium: Slovak flora.
   Director: JOZEF MÁJOVSKÝ, 1920 (Taxonomy of higher plants, cytotaxonomy).
   Curator: JÁN ZÁBORSKÝ, 1928 (Taxonomy, morphology of Spermatophyta).
   Specialization in research: Cytotaxonomy of the Slovak flora.
   Associated botanic garden: Botanic Garden of Comenius University.
   Loans: To recognized institutions.
   Periodical and serial works: Acta facultatis rerum naturalium Universitatis Comenianae, Botanica.

BRAZZAVILLE: *Herbarium, Centre ORSTOM,* **(IEC),** B.P. 181, Brazzaville, **People's Republic of the Congo.** (Information 1974)
Status: Local centre of O.R.S.T.O.M., Paris.
Foundation: 1949. *Number of specimens:* 30.000.
Herbarium: République du Congo, République Gabonaise, République Centrafricaine.

BRAZZAVILLE: *Institut de Recherches Scientifiques au Congo,* **(IRSC)** – – *see* IEC.

BREMEN: *Herbarium, Übersee-Museum,* **(BREM),** Bahnhofsplatz 13, D-2800 Bremen 1, **Federal Republic of Germany,** BRD.
Telephone: 0421/397-8357.
Status: Public Museum, directed by the town.
Foundation: Herbarium generale 1830; herbarium communale 1865. *Number of specimens:* 350.000 (phanerogams 250.000, cryptogams 100.000).
Herbarium: Herbarium generale: worldwide; Herbarium communale: Flora Bremensis, Northwestern Germany, including North Sea Islands.
Important collections: H. Farenholtz (Venezuela), W. O. Focke (Rubi authentici), Koldewey-expedition 1869/70 (Lichens from Greenland), H. Sandstede (Lichens, excl. *Cladonia*), W. Bertram (Mosses), C. A. Weber (especially *Sphagnum*),· E. Lemmermann.
   Director: HERBERT GANSLMAYR, 1937 (Ethnology).
   Curator: HEINRICH KUHBIER, 0421/352430 (Flora of the German North Sea Islands, West Mediterranean flora).
   Specialization in research: Flora Bremensis, Flora of the North Sea Islands, Cyperaceae of South America, Mediterranean flora.
   Loans: In general to all recognized institutions.
   Periodical and serial works: Veröffentlichungen aus dem Übersee-Museum Bremen, Reihe A, Naturwissenschaften.
   Exchange: Available: Plants from Northwestern Germany and a restricted number of duplicates from Venezuela, Cameroun; Hawaiian ferns. Desired: African and Mediterranean plants from all groups, Monocotyledons from South America, ferns, *Carex,* marine algae of the Northern Hemisphere.
   Remarks: Facilities for visiting botanists.

BREST: *Herbarium, Faculté des Sciences,* **(BRE),** Brest, **France.** (Information 1974)
Status: Faculté des Sciences de Brest.
Foundation: 1959.
Important collections: Herbier M. Perrault.

BRIDGETOWN: *The Barbados Herbarium, Department of Biology, University of the West Indies,* **(BAR),** Cave Hill Campus, P.O. Box 64, Bridgetown, **Barbados.**
Telephone: 809/42-02191, ext. 337.
Foundation: 1935. *Number of specimens:* 4.000.
Herbarium: Mainly flora of Barbados.
Important collections: J. A. Allan (grasses of Barbados), J. Browne, L. E. Chinnery, E. G. B. Gooding, A. E. S. McIntosh.
   Curator: L. E. CHINNERY, 1950 (Plant taxonomy and ecology).
   Specialization in research: Revision of "Flora of Barbados."
   Associated botanic garden: None at this date, but one is planned on the campus.
   Loans: Acknowledgment of receipt, speedy re-

turn, reprints of works citing specimens.

Periodical and serial works: Barbados Herbarium Publications (irregular).

Exchange: Desired: Especially pantropical weeds and Lesser Antillean material.

BRIDGEWATER: *Herbarium, Department of Biology, Bridgewater College,* (**BDWR**), Bridgewater, Virginia 22812, **U.S.A.**

Telephone: 703/828-2501.

Foundation: 1880. *Number of specimens:* 3.000.

Herbarium: Emphasis on the Shenandoah Valley and Blue Ridge Mountains.

Director and Curator: L. MICHAEL HILL, 1941 (Botany, genetics).

Specialization in research: Vascular flora of Virginia; biosystematics of higher plants with emphasis on interspecific hybridization and cytogenetics.

Loans: For periods of 1 year.

BRIGNOLES: *Salgues Foundation of Brignoles for the Development of Biological Sciences,* (**SFB**), Brignoles, **France.** (Information 1974)

Remarks: Activities limited; R. Salgues is a collaborator at MTU.

BRISBANE: *Queensland Herbarium,* (**BRI**), Meiers Road, Indooroopilly, Queensland 4068, **Australia.**

Telephone: (07)-371 3511.

Status: Founded by the Queensland Government: Botany Branch, Department of Primary Industries.

Foundation: 1880. *Number of specimens:* 400.000.

Herbarium: Chiefly Australia, New Guinea, Solomon Islands, some worldwide collections.

Important collections: F. M. Bailey, J. F. Bailey, C. T. White, S. T. Blake, L. S. Smith, S. L. Everist, L. J. Webb & J. G. Tracey.

Director: R. W. JOHNSON, 1930 (Herbarium organization, computerization of herbarium records, ecology, numerical taxonomy, Convolvulaceae).

Assistant Director: L. PEDLEY, 1930 (*Acacia, Tephrosia,* Polygalaceae, phytogeography).

Staff members: N. B. BYRNES, 1922 (Myrtaceae, Combretaceae).

J. R. CLARKSON, 1950 (Flora and vegetation of North Queensland).

R. DOWLING, 1949 (Vegetation survey and mapping, mangrove ecology, revegetation).

J. A. ELSOL, 1954 (Cyperaceae, vegetation survey and mapping).

R. J. HENDERSON, 1938 (Queensland angiosperms, cytotaxonomy, nomenclature).

L. JESSUP, 1947 (Flora of Queensland, taxonomy of rainforest species).

H. E. KLEINSCHMIDT, 1925 (Weeds, ornamental plants, Queensland flora).

T. J. McDONALD, 1935 (Vegetation mapping, rehabilitation of mined areas, ecology of Queensland sand dune vegetation).

W. J. F. McDONALD, 1946 (Vegetation survey and mapping).

S. T. REYNOLDS, 1932 (Sapindaceae, Anacardiaceae, *Sida,* rainforest species).

E. M. ROSS, 1952 (Flora of Queensland).

B. K. SIMON, 1943 (Gramineae).

T. D. STANDLEY, 1952 (Aquatic plants, flora of Queensland).

Specialization in research: Flora of Queensland, rainforest taxonomy, vegetation mapping.

Loans: To recognized botanical institutions.

Periodical and serial works: Austrobaileya, Technical Bulletins.

Exchange: Available: Miscellaneous Queensland plants.

BRISBANE: *Herbarium, Plant Pathology Branch, Department of Primary Industries,* (**BRIP**), Meiers Road, Indooroopilly, Queensland 4068, **Australia.**

Telephone: (07) 3713511.

Status: State government.

Foundation: About 1900. *Number of specimens:* 14.000.

Herbarium: Plant parasitic and plant-associated microfungi, mainly from Queensland.

Important collections: F. M. Bailey (formerly in BRI).

Director: R. C. COLBRAN, 1926 (Nematology).

Curator: J. L. ALCORN, 1937 (Taxonomy of plant parasitic fungi).

Specialization in research: Plant parasitic fungi.

Loans: To recognized botanical institutions.

BRISBANE: *Herbarium of the University of Queensland,* (**BRIU**), St. Lucia, Queensland 4067, **Australia.**

Telephone: 07 - 377111.

Status: University.

Foundation: Circa 1940. *Number of specimens:* 40.000 (Embryophyta 10.000, lichens 15.000, algae 15.000).

Herbarium: Queensland algae and embryophyta, Australian lichens.

Important collections: A. B. Cribb (algae, including types), R. W. Rogers (lichens).

Director: A. B. CRIBB, 1925 (Algae).

Curator: R. W. ROGERS, 1944; 07-3772790 (Australian lichen taxonomy and ecology).

Staff member: L. G. JESSUP, 1954 (Embryophyte determination).

Specialization in research: Taxonomy and ecology of Australian and South Pacific algae and lichens.

Loans: To recognized institutions.

Exchange: Limited.

Remarks: R. F. N. Langdon fungal types have been dispersed to BRIP and DAR. Embryophyta are for teaching only.

BRISTOL: *Herbarium, Department of Botany, University of Bristol,* (**BRIST**), Woodland Road, Bristol

BS8 1UG, England, **Great Britain.**
Telephone: (0272)-24161.
Status: University.
Foundation: 1909. *Number of specimens:* 90.000
(80.000 vascular, 10.000 non-vascular).
Herbarium: Mainly European, especially S.W.
England, including aliens; ferns of China and other
worldwide material.
Important collections: C. Bucknall (British and
European), E. Armitage (Bryophytes), O. V. Dar-
bishire (Lichens and algae), G. W. Garlick (British),
W. Hancock (Chinese ferns etc.), Father Reader (Bri-
tish, incl. mosses and lichens), C. I. & N. Y. Sandwith
(British adventives), J. W. White (British and
European).
   Director: The Melville Wills Professor of Botany
(not known for 1980-).
   Curator: D. GLEDHILL, 1929 (Experimental tax-
onomy and conservation of endangered plants of
SW England).
   Specialization in research: Botanical histories of
the Avon Gorge and Lizard Peninsula; biological
field studies, garden culture and propagation of
endangered plants of SW England.
   Associated botanic garden: University Botanic
Gardens, Bracken Hill, North Road, Leigh Wood,
Bristol.

BRISTOL: *Herbarium, City of Bristol Museum and
Art Gallery,* (**BRISTM**), Queen's Road, Bristol BS8
1RL, England, **Great Britain.**
Telephone: (0272) 299771.
Status: Museum herbarium.
Foundation: Includes collections of Bristol Institution founded 1823. *Number of specimens:* 30.000.
Herbarium: A general herbarium with specimens
dated late 18th century to present day, including im-
portant local material, i.e. Avon Gorge, Leigh
woods, etc.
Important collections: Glennis Smith (foreign:
European and Alpine, 3.254 species), Ivor Evans (Bri-
tish, mostly local, many rarities, 2.200 sheets); Mu-
seum Herb. "A" (10 vols, 1.500 sheets, Mid 19th cen-
tury); Main Mus. Herb. (includes H. Thomas herb.,
Sandwith, Dr. J. L. Knapp, Thwaites and Old Bristol
Naturalists Soc. Herb., about 4.000); J. L. Knapp
Grasses (British, 1824, 118 spec.); A. Broughton herb.
(Jamaican plants, 1786-96, includes type specimens);
R. Braithwaite herb. (British Sphagnaceae, 53 species,
1877); J. E. Leefe herb. (British Salicaceae,
1842-1844, 49 species).
   Director of Museum: NICHOLAS THOMAS (Arche-
ology).
   Curator of Natural History Section: ANNE J.
HOLLOWELL.
   Assistant Curator: CHARLES J. T. COPP.
   Staff members: JANET RATCLIFFE (Botanical and
biological records).
     SUSAN SWANSBOROUGH (Museum).
   Specialization in research: No taxonomic re-

search; herbarium subject of a computer documentation project, local collection for Biological Record Centre.
Loans: For scientific purposes only.
Remarks: The Museum suffered extensive loss
and damage to its herbaria in 1940, including loss of
most of foreign material, Old Bristol Institution
collections and cryptogams.

BRNO: *Herbarium, Botanical Department of the Mo-
ravian Museum,* (**BRNM**), Preslova 1, 602 00 Brno,
Czechoslovakia.
Status: Directed by the state.
Foundation: 1818. *Number of specimens:* 650.000.
Herbarium: Worldwide, emphasizing Moravian
flora.
Important collections: Herbarium J. F. Freyn, her-
barium E. Formánek, herbarium J. Podpěra (*Bryum*),
herbarium R. Picbauer (fungi).
   Director and Curator: KAREL SUTORÝ, 1947 (Tax-
onomy of flowering plants, plant geography).
   Staff member: VALENTIN POSPÍŠIL, 1912 (Bryo-
phytes).
   Specialization in research: Flora of Czechoslo-
vakia.
Loans: To recognized botanical institutions.
Periodical and serial works: Acta Musei Mo-
raviae, Sci. Nat.

BRNO: *Herbarium, Institute of Plant Biology, Uni-
versity of J. E. Purkyně,* (**BRNU**), Kotlářská 2, 611 37
Brno, **Czechoslovakia.**
Status: State university.
Foundation: 1921. *Number of specimens:* 480.000.
Herbarium: Worldwide, especially Europe, Near
East, West Asia and Balkan Peninsula.
   Director: ZDENĚK LAŠTŮVKA, 1923 (Anatomy,
plant physiology).
   Curator: MARIE DVOŘÁKOVÁ, 1940 (Taxonomy
of vascular plants).
   Staff members: JAROSLAVA DUBOVÁ, 1953 (Plant
sociology).
     FRANTŠEK DVOŘÁK, 1921 (Taxonomy of vas-
cular plants, caryology).
     ZDENĚK ŠEDA, 1930 (Ecology, conservation).
     ZDENĚK SLADÝ, 1930 (Experimental mor-
phology, anatomy).
     MIROSLAV SMEJKAL, 1927 (Taxonomy of vas-
cular plants, phytogeography, flora of Czechoslovakia).
     JAN ŠPAČEK, 1927 (Mycology, phytopatholo-
gy).
     JIŘÍ UNAR, 1938 (Plant sociology, ecology).
   Specialization in research: Czechoslovak flora
and vegetation.
Loans: To recognized botanical institutions.
Periodical and serial works: Folia Facultatis
Scientiarum Naturalium Universitatis Purkynianae Brunensis, Biologia; Scripta Facultatis Scientiarum Naturalium Universitatis Purkynianae Bru-

nensis, Biologia.

Exchange: Available: Flora exsiccata Reipublicae Socialisticae Čechoslovacae, Centur. XVII (vascular plants). Desired: Specimens of all groups, especially vascular plants.

BROCKPORT: *Herbarium, Department of Biological Sciences, State University of New York, College at Brockport,* (**BROC**), Brockport, New York 14420 **U.S.A.**

Telephone: 716/395-2729 (herbarium); 395-2193 (department).

Foundation: 1968. *Number of specimens:* 16.346.

Herbarium: General collection, emphasizing western New York, with specimens from U.S., Canada, Central America.

Director and Curator: H. DAVID HAMMOND, 1924 (Floristics).

Specialization in research: Flora of the Genesee Region.

Associated botanic garden: Arboretum on Fancher Campus (Orleans County, New York).

Loans: No special conditions.

Exchange: Available: General assortment. Desired: Aquatics, Compositae, Gramineae, Cyperaceae.

BRONX: *Herbarium, New York Botanical Garden,* (**NY**) – – *see* NEW YORK.

BROOKINGS: *Herbarium, Department of Biology, South Dakota State University,* (**SDC**), Brookings, South Dakota 57007, **U.S.A.**

Telephone: 605/688-6141.

Foundation: 1891. *Number of specimens:* 30.000.

Herbarium: Vascular plants of South Dakota and eastern U.S.; fungi and lichens of U.S.

Important collections: Edward C. Berry (lichens).

Director and Curator: GARY E. LARSON, 1950 (Taxonomy and ecology of aquatic vascular plants).

Specialization in research: Vascular flora of South Dakota.

Loans: Upon request to qualified investigators and institutions.

Exchange: Available: South Dakota flowering plants and vascular aquatics. Desired: Aquatic vascular plants from other parts of North America.

BROOKLYN: *Herbarium, Brooklyn Botanic Garden,* (**BKL**), 1000 Washington Avenue, Brooklyn, New York 11225, **U.S.A.**

Telephone: 212/622-4433.

Foundation: 1910. *Number of specimens:* 200.000.

Herbarium: Long Island and North America in general; good representation of Philippines and South China specimens.

Important collections: Incorporates collections of Brooklyn Lyceum, Brooklyn Institute of Arts & Sciences, and Long Island (N.Y.) Historical Society; A.

A. Heller, H. K. Svenson (*Eleocharis:* Galapagos Islands; U.S.), R. C. Benedict (*Nephrolepis*), W. H. Harvey (Australian algae), C. Schneider (Arnold Arboretum), E. L. Miller herbarium, A. Gray (North American Gramineae and Cyperaceae).

Director: DONALD E. MOORE, 1928.

Curator: STEPHEN K-M. TIM, 1937 (Ascomycetes).

Staff members: THOMAS J. DELENDICK, 1947 (Biochemical systematics of Aceraceae; ferns; hardy plants).

BRENDA WEISMAN, 1932 (Microbial genetics).

Specialization in research: Long Island flora; chemical systematics of Aceraceae.

Associated botanic garden: Brooklyn Botanic Garden.

Loans: No special restrictions, but loans of types at discretion of Curator.

Exchange: Limited at present.

BROWNSVILLE: *Robert Runyon Herbarium,* (**RUNYON**), P.O. Box 3311, Brownsville, Texas 78520, **U.S.A.**

Number of specimens: 5.000.

Herbarium: Flora of the Lower Rio Grande Valley of Texas, and northern Mexico.

Remarks: Entire herbarium was given to the University of Texas (TEX), Austin, in 1968.

BROWNWOOD: *Herbarium, Biology Department, Howard Payne University,* (**HPC**), Brownwood, Texas 76801, **U.S.A.**

Telephone: 915/646-2502, ext. 243.

Foundation: 1965. *Number of specimens:* 30.000.

Herbarium: Flora of central Texas, especially Edward's Plateau; ferns of Texas.

Important collections: Wm. L. McCart, Jack W. Stanford, U. T. Waterfall, Jimmy L. Blassingame, Chester M. Rowell.

Director and Curator: JACK W. STANFORD, 1935 (Flora of central Texas; vegetation of Texas Edward's Plateau).

Specialization in research: Floristics.

Loans: Available for 6 months to recognized institutions; postage paid by the borrower.

Exchange: Desired: Mexico, Texas, other southwestern states; also foreign inquiries solicited.

BRUNEI: *Herbarium, Office of the Conservator of Forests,* (**BRUN**), Brunei, **Brunei.** (Information 1974)

Status: Directed by state.

Foundation: 1935. *Number of specimens:* 7.000.

Herbarium: Woody plants of Borneo.

BRUXELLES: *Jardin Botanique National de Belgique – Nationale Plantentuin van België,* (**BR**) – see MEISE.

BRUXELLES: *Laboratoire de Génétique des Plantes Supérieures,* (**BRGE**), 1850 Chaussée de Wavre, Bruxelles 16, **Belgium.** (Information 1974)

Status: Université Libre de Belgium.
Foundation: 1961. *Number of specimens:* 3.000.
Associated botanic garden: Jardin Expérimental Jean Massart.
Periodical and serial works: Travaux du Laboratoire de Botanique Systématique et d'Ecologie de l'Université Libre de Bruxelles.

BRUXELLES: *Laboratoire de Botanique Systématique et d'Ecologie,* (**BRLU**), 28 Avenue Paul Heger, 1050 Bruxelles, **Belgium.**
Telephone: 02-6490030, ext. 2137.
Status: Université Libre de Bruxelles.
Foundation: 1948. *Number of specimens:* 150.000.
Herbarium: Africa, W. Europe, Mediterranean, lichens.
Important collections: Herb. L. Hauman (Argentina, Ruwenzori); Herb. P. Duvigneaud (Zaïre).
Director: PAUL DUVIGNEAUD, 1913 (Systematics, ecology, phytogeography).
Staff members: SIMONE DENAEYER, 1930 (Ecology).
 CLAUDE LEFEBVRE, 1941 (Genetics, biosystematics).
 JEAN LEJOLY, 1945 (Ecology of Tropical Africa).
 MARTIN TANGHE, 1936 (Ecology, plant sociology).
Specialization in research: Flora and vegetation of tropical Africa; ecology.
Associated botanic garden: Jardin experimental Jean Massart, 1850 Chaussée de Wavre, 1160 Bruxelles, Belgique.
Exchange: Available: African flora.

BRUXELLES: *Laboratorium voor Algemene Plantkunde en Natuurbeheer,* (**BRVU**), Pleinlaan 2, B-1050 Bruxelles, **Belgium.**
Telephone: (02) 648.55.40.
Status: Vrije Universiteit Brussel (Free University of Bruxelles).
Foundation: 1970. *Number of specimens:* 35.000.
Herbarium: Belgium; Africa, S. of Sahara; general herbarium.
Important collections: Lisowski, Malaisse & Symoens (high plateau of Shaba); Symoens (Central Africa).
Director: JEAN-JACQUES SYMOENS, 1927 (Ecology, limnology, freshwater algae and macrophytes).
Curator: NICO KOEDAM, 1957 (European ferns).
Staff members: PHILIPPE BÜSCHER, 1956 (European mosses).
 LUK DERONDE, 1948 (Freshwater biology).
 DIRK VAN SPEYBROECK, 1958 (Phytosociology and nature management).
Specialization in research: Limnology, freshwater algae and macrophytes.
Associated botanic garden: Small arboretum.
Loans: To scientific institutions and recognized specialists.

Exchange: Available: Specimens from W. Europe and Central Africa. Desired: Aquatic plants and halophytes.

BUCARAMANGA: *Herbario, Departamento de Biología, Universidad Industrial de Santander,* (**UIS**), Apartado Aéreo 678, Bucaramanga, Santander, **Colombia.**
Telephone: (57)71/56141, 57131, ext. 169.
Foundation: 1975. *Number of specimens:* 2.500.
Herbarium: Flora of Santander.
Director: RAMIRO ALVAREZ SIERRA, 1942.
Curator: NESTOR RAUL SIERRA DUEÑEZ, 1954; 71/55052.
Exchange: Yes.

BUCKHANNON: *George B. Rossbach Herbarium, West Virginia Wesleyan College,* (**WVW**), Buckhannon, West Virginia 26201, **U.S.A.**
Telephone: 304/473-8064.
Status: Private college.
Foundation: 1949. *Number of specimens:* 23.000.
Herbarium: Emphasis on collections from northeastern U.S.; good representation from West Virginia, Maine, Canada, Northwest Territories, Puerto Rico, Galapagos Islands.
Important collections: George B. Rossbach, Joseph F. Glencoe, Katharine B. Gregg.
Director and Curator: JOSEPH F. GLENCOE, 1936 (Systematic botany; seed plants).
Exchange: Yes, limited.

BUCUREŞTI: *Herbarium, University of Bucureşti,* (**BUC**), Soseaua Cotroceni 32, 76258 Bucureşti, **Romania.**
Telephone: 49.41.25 and 49.76.95.
Status: University.
Foundation: 1882. *Number of specimens:* 500.000.
Herbarium: General collection and flora of Romania.
Important collections: T. Săvulescu (Pucciniaceae, Ustilaginaceae, Tilletiaceae).
Director: VASILE DIACONESCU, 1927 (Dendrology).
Curator: GEORGE NEDELCU, 1938 (Ecology, phytosociology).
Staff member: GHEORGHE MOHAN, 1943 (Bryology).
Specialization in research: Romanian flora.
Associated botanic garden: Botanic Garden of Bucurest.
Loans: No; specimens must be consulted in the herbarium.
Exchange: Yes.

BUCUREŞTI: *Herbarium, Institutul de Biologie "Tr. Savulescu" al Academici R.P.R.,* (**BUCA**), Spl. Independenţei 296, Bucureşti 17, **Romania.** (Information 1974)
Status: State institute.

Foundation: 1960. *Number of specimens:* 160.000.
Herbarium: Plants of Romania.
Important collections: Tr. Săvulescu, Gh. P. Grinţescu, I. Prodan, C. Zahariadi.
  Specialization in research: Romanian flora.
  Loans: To recognized institutions, for six months.
  Periodical and serial works: Revue Roumaine de Biologie, Série de Botanique; Studi și cercetări de biologie, seria Botanică.

BUCUREȘTI: *Herbarium, Institutul de Cercetari Forestiere,* (**BUCF**), Sos. Pipera 46, București, **Romania.** (Information 1974)
Status: Ministry of Forestry.
Foundation: 1929. *Number of specimens:* 70.000.
Herbarium: Plants of Romania.

BUCUREȘTI: *Institutul de Stiințe Biologice Herbarul Micologic,* (**BUCM**), Spl. Independenței 296, R-77748 București 17, **Romania.**
Telephone: 492335 or 492830.
Status: State foundation.
Foundation: 1928. *Number of specimens:* 65.000.
Herbarium: Fungi of Romania and world, mainly plant parasitic.
Important collections: T. Săvulescu, I. C. Constantineanu, C. Sandu-Ville.
  Curator: O. CONSTANTINESCU, 1933 (Taxonomy of microfungi, Hyphomycetes, and Peronosporales).
  Staff member: G. NEGREAN, 1932 (Flora of Romania, fungi, and flowering plants).
  Specialization in research: Mycoflora of Romania, taxonomy of microfungi, especially plant parasitic.
  Loans: To recognized botanical institutions for six months.
  Exchange: Available: Microfungi of Romania. Desired: Microfungi, especially from temperate zones.
  Remarks: The herbarium includes living cultures of 450 strains of fungi and 2600 microscope slides.

BUDAPEST: *Botanical Department of the Hungarian History Museum,* (**BP**), Könyveškálmán krt. 40, Pf. 22, H-1476 Budapest VIII, **Hungary.**
Telephone: 137-220.
Foundation: 1870. *Number of specimens:* 1.500.000.
Herbarium: Herbarium Generale, Herbarium Carpato-Pannonicum, pteridophytes and cryptogams.
  Director: JULIA SZUJKÓ-LACZA (Cytology, histology, morphology, ecology of flowering plants).
  Curators: M. BABOS, Macrofungi (Mycology).
  Zs. DEBRECZY, Herbarium Generale (Flowering plants).
  J. GÖNCZÖL, Microfungi (Mycology).
  L. HABLY, Paleobotanical Collection (Paleobotany).

L. HAJDU, Algae (Algology).
P. KOMÁROMY, Algal Culture Collection (Soil algology).
D. KOVÁTS, Herbarium Carpato-Pannonicum (Flowering plants).
I. RÁCZ, Fruit and Seed Collection (Flowering plants).
M. RAJCZY, Bryophytes (Bryology).
T. SZERDAHELYI, Pteridophytes (Vascular plants, pteridophytes).
  Staff members: G. BOHUS (Mycology).
  Z. K. DOBOLYI (Flowering plants).
  F. RADICS (Flowering plants).
  GY. SZOLLÁT (Flowering plants).
  L. VAJDA (Bryology).
  K. VERSEGHY (Lichens).
  Specialization in research: Flora of Hungary and part of Central Europe: taxonomy, floristics and ecology.
  Loans: To recognized botanical institutions, specimens and algal cultures.
  Periodical and serial works: Studia Botanica Hungarica.
  Exchange: Available: Specimens from Hungary. Desired: Worldwide, flowering plants and cryptogams.

BUDAPEST: *Herbarium, Institute of Plant Taxonomy and Ecology of the Eötvös L. University,* (**BPU**), 1088, Muzeum körut 4A, Budapest, **Hungary.** (Information 1974)
Status: University.
Foundation: 1912. *Number of specimens:* 245.000.
Herbarium: Worldwide.
  Specialization in research: Flora and phytogeography of Hungary, grassland and forest steppe ecology, conservation, bryoecology.
  Associated botanic garden: Botanic Garden of the University, Illés utca 25, 1083 Budapest.
  Loans: With permission of Ministry of Public Education and the Hungarian Academy of Sciences.
  Periodical and serial works: Index Horti Botanici Univ. Budapestinensis; Annales Universitatis Scientiarum Budapestinensis, Sectio Biologica; Abstracta Botanica.

BUENOS AIRES: *Herbario, Museo Argentino de Ciencias Naturales "Bernardino Rivadavia" e Instituto Nacional de Investigación de las Ciencias Naturales,* (**BA**), Avenida Angel Gallardo 470, Casilla de Correo 10, Sucursal 5, 1405 Buenos Aires, **Argentina.**
Telephone: (54)812-1561.
Status: Ministerio de Cultura y Educación.
Foundation: 1823. *Number of specimens:* 102.000.
Herbarium: Mainly Argentina and surrounding countries.
Important collections: A. Castellanos (Cactaceae), L. Hauman, G. Niederlein, C. Skottsberg.
  Director: JOSE MARIA GALLARDO, 1925 (Herpet.).

Curator: VICENTE R. PERRONE, 1917 (Vascular plants).

Division of Phanerogams: EVANGELINA SANCHEZ DE GARCIA, 1934 (Anatomy of Gramineae).

MIRTA ARRIAGA, 1950 (Anatomy of Gramineae).

MARTHA CARTAGINESE, 1940 (Phanerogams).

M. ISABEL CASABONA DE DRISALDI, 1950 (Anatomy of phanerogams).

MIRTA LOPEZ, 1944 (Phanerogams).

JUAN CARLOS MONTIEL, 1920 (Phanerogams).

ENRIQUE RATERA, 1920 (Phanerogams).

Division of Cryptogams: BEATRIZ CALVIELLO DE ROLDAN, 1934 (Fungi).

CARLOTA CARL DE DONTERBERG, 1907 (Charophyta).

CELINA MATTERI, 1943 (Musci).

GABRIELA H. DE MENÉNDEZ, 1927 (Hepaticae).

CARMEN PUJALS, 1916 (Rhodophyta).

DELIA I. DE ROTSCHILD, 1915 (*Rhizobium*).

SILVIA SOLARI, 1944 (Hepaticae).

Division of Paleobotany: WOLFGANG VOLKHEIMER, 1928 (Palynology; paleoclimatology).

OSCAR GONZÁLEZ AMICON, 1939 (Palynology).

MARTA CACCAVARI DE FILICE, 1943 (Palynology).

Division of Plankton: ESTEBAN BOLTOVSKOY, 1912 (Zooplankton).

CARLOS MARTÍNEZ MACCHIAVELLO (Diatoms; botanist of the Instituto Antártico Argentino).

Estaciòn Hidrobiológica de Puerto Quequén: ENRIQUE BALECH, 1912 (Phytoplankton).

Specialization in research: Flora of Argentina; taxonomy of South American bryophytes; bacteriology of Argentina seas; recent and fossil (neogene) marine diatoms; palynology of Argentina sediments; taxonomy and morphology of fossil plants; anatomy of fossil and recent woods and cuticles.

Loans: To recognized institutions.

Periodical and serial works: Revista, Comunicaciones, Miscelánea and Extras del Museo Argentina de Ciencias Naturales "Bernardino Rivadavia."

Exchange: Available: Algae, bryophytes, pteridophytes, and phanerogams of Argentina. Wanted: Specimens from North and South America, South Africa, Southern Islands, Australia, New Zealand, Tasmania.

BUENOS AIRES: *Herbario "Gaspar Xuárez," Facultad de Agronomía, Universidad de Buenos Aires,* (**BAA**), Avenida San Martín 4453, 1417 Buenos Aires, **Argentina.**

Telephone: (54)52-0903.

Foundation: 1962. *Number of specimens:* 150.000.

Herbarium: Phanerogams of Austral America; rich in grasses, economic plants, and weeds.

Important collections: Lorenzo R. Parodi.

Director: JULIÁN ALBERTO CÁMARA-HERNÁNDEZ,

1932 (*Zea mays* and relatives; taxonomy and evolution; genetic resources conservation).

Curator: ROBERTO D. TORTOSA, 1946 (Rhamnaceae).

Staff members: LEONOR CUSATO, 1945 (Taxonomy of *Lupinus*).

ANA D'AMBROGIO, 1941 (Anatomy of Spermatophyta).

SARA MALDONADO, 1944 (Embryology and anatomy of angiosperms).

DIEGO MEDAN, 1951 (Anatomy of Spermatophyta).

MARÍA DEL C. MENENDEZ SEVILLANO, 1947 (Ethnobotany on native forms of *Phaseolus vulgaris*).

ANA M. MIANTE ALZOGARAY, 1941 (*Zea mays* taxonomy).

MÓNICA TOURN, 1950 (Anatomy of Spermatophyta).

JUAN J. VALLA, 1929 (Floral biology).

Specialization in research: Taxonomy and anatomy of Gramineae, Rhamnaceae, economic plants, and weeds.

Associated botanic garden: Jardín Botánico de la Facultad de Agronomía de la Universidad de Buenos Aires.

Loans: To recognized botanical institutions.

Exchange: Available: Phanerogams from Argentina.

BUENOS AIRES: *Unidad Botánica Agrícola del I.N.T.A.*, (**BAB**) -- *see* CASTELAR.

BUENOS AIRES: *Herbario, Centro de Estudios Farmacologicos y de Principios Naturales,* (**BACP**), Serrano 661, 1414 Buenos Aires, **Argentina.**

Telephone: (54)854-6490/5602.

Status: Consejo Nacional de Investigaciones Científicas y Técnicas (CONICET).

Foundation: 1975. *Number of specimens:* 4.000.

Herbarium: Economic plants and some vascular plants from specific studies (Cruciferae, Commelinaceae, Oxalidaceae).

Director: OSVALDO BOELCKE (Cruciferae; flora of Patagonia).

Curator: PASTOR ARENAS (Ethnobotany).

Staff members: DANIEL DE AZKUE (Cytogenetics).

ANA DELL'ARCIPRETE (Ethnobotany).

GUSTAVO GIBERTI (Anatomy).

ARTURO MARTÍNEZ (Cytogenetics).

JUAN B. MARTÍNEZ (Cruciferae).

MARÍA A. MARTÍNEZ (Chemotaxonomy).

CRISTINA ROMANCZUK (Anatomy).

Specialization in research: Taxonomy of Cruciferae; ethnobotany of the Chaco Region and northwestern Argentina; cytogenetics and chemotaxonomic research in Commelinaceae, Cruciferae, and Oxalidaceae; anatomy of economic plants.

Loans: To recognized scientific institutions and,

in some instances, to individuals.

Periodical and serial works: Parodiana (to appear soon).

Exchange: Available: Plants of Paraguay and northwestern Argentina; economic plants. Desired: Economic and medicinal plants of the world.

BUENOS AIRES: *Herbario, Museo de Botánica y Farmacología Juan A. Domínguez,* **(BAF)**, Junín 954, ler. Piso, 1113 Buenos Aires, **Argentina.**

Telephone: (54)84-9569.

Status: Facultad de Farmacia y Bioquímica, Universidad de Buenos Aires.

Foundation: 1900. *Number of specimens:* 750.000.

Herbarium: Worldwide, emphasis on Argentina and neighboring countries.

Important collections: B. Balansa, O. Boelcke, A. Buchtien, A. L. Cabrera, J. A. Caro, J. A. Domínguez, A. Flossdorf, E. Hassler, G. H. E. W. Hieronymus, N. Illin, P. Jörgensen, J. Koslowsky, F. Kurtz, M. Lillo, A. de Llamas, P. G. Lorentz, J. F. Molfino, G. Niederlein, L. R. Parodi, M. S. Pennington, Philippi, M. Rodríguez, C. Spegazzini, J. Steinbach, S. Venturi.

Director: José Alfredo Caro, 1919 (Gramineae).

Curator: María Rosa Calarco, 1951 (Plant microtechnique).

Staff members: Alberto Gurni, 1947 (Chemotaxonomy).

María Dolores Montero, 1951 (Plant microtechnique).

Specialization in research: Systematics and chemotaxonomy of phanerogams.

Loans: Upon request to the Director.

Periodical and serial works: Dominguezia.

Remarks: Included here are 4.000 jars of medicinal plant derivatives, a collection of woods, and the Bonpland archives.

BUENOS AIRES: *Herbario, Departamento de Ciencias Biológicas, Facultad de Ciencias Exactas y Naturales, Universidad de Buenos Aires,* **(BAFC)**, II Pabellón, 4to piso, Ciudad Universitaria (Núñez), 1428 Buenos Aires, **Argentina.**

Telephone: (54)782-5020/29, ext. 202.

Foundation: 1955. *Number of specimens:* 30.000, mostly fungi.

Herbarium: Phanerogams and cryptogams of Argentina and other S. American countries; bryophyta from Patagonia; continental algae, Basidiomycetes, and Discomycetes (mostly Andean and wood-rotting fungi).

Important collections: R. Singer (types of Agaricales).

Curator of the Cryptogamic Herbarium: Jorge E. Wright, 1922 (Basidiomycetes, Aphyllophorales, Gasteromycetes; *Tulostoma*).

Curator of the Phanerogamic Herbarium: Ramón A. Palacios, 1941 (Biosystematics of *Prosopis*).

Staff members: Juan Accorinti, 1931 (Plant physiology; physiology of *Scenedesmus*).

Elena Ancíbor, 1932 (Plant anatomy of high altitude plants).

María Delia Bertoni, 1945 (Mycology; biology of Nectriaceae).

Lilia Bravo, 1945 (Taxonomy of phanerogams; *Cassia*).

Daniel Cabral, 1946 (Mycology; fungi of the phylloplane).

Miguel A. Galvagno, 1946 (Mycology; biochemistry of cell walls).

Alicia M. Godeas de Liberman, 1943 (Ecology of soil fungi; Fungi Imperfecti).

Juan H. Hunziker, 1926 (Genetics of *Prosopis* and *Bulnesia;* biosystematics).

Elsa N. Lacoste de Diaz, 1923 (Continental algae; Desmidiaceae).

Silvia E. López, 1949 (Mycology; wood-rotting fungi).

Lucila de Miguel, 1936 (Plant physiology; germination of seeds).

Carlos A. Naranjo, 1941 (Genetics of Amaryllidaceae).

Lidia Poggio, 1944 (Genetics of *Prosopis*).

María E. Ranalli de Cinto, 1940 (Biology and systematics of Ascobolaceae).

Edgardo Romero, 1936 (Paleobotany).

Cristina Zaccaro de Mule, 1945 (Plant physiology; physiology of Nostocaccae).

Gloria Zupla, 1945 (Plant physiology; physiology of Cyanophyta).

Specialization in research: Biosystematics, mycology and phycology; physiology of algae; genetics of several groups of higher plants; flora of southern South America; cryptogamic flora of Tierra del Fuego and southern Andes; mycological flora of national parks (Argentina); soil fungi (ecology and taxonomy); wood-rotting fungi.

Loans: To responsible individuals and institutions.

Periodical and serial works: Publications de la Facultad de Ciencias Exactas y Naturales (discontinued).

Exchange: Available: Limited numbers of fungi, particularly Aphyllophorales. Wanted: Determined material of Gastromycetes and Aphyllophorales.

BUENOS AIRES: *Dirección de Investigaciones Forestales,* **(BAI)** –– *see* CASTELAR.

BUENOS AIRES: *Herbario, Dirección de Mantenimiento y Preservación de la Flora, Instituto Municipal de Botánica,* **(BAJ)**, Parque Pte. Dr. Nicolás Avellaneda, Lacarra y Directorio, 1407 Buenos Aires, **Argentina.**

Telephone: (54)69-3954.

Status: Municipalidad de la Ciudad de Buenos Aires.

Foundation: 1898. *Number of specimens:* 10.020.

Herbarium: Emphasis on central and northern Argentina; cultivated plants; samples of species grown in the Jardín Botánico "Carlos Thays"; austral Africa, Bulgaria, Rumania.

Important collections: R. Schlechter (austral Africa; 1892–1895), N. Vihodcevsky (Bulgaria; 1952–1956); G. Malos, M. Olaru, M. Paum, and Albuia (Rumania; 1960).

Director: ANTONIO AMADO GARCIA, 1926 (Taxonomy).

Curator: JULIO SOLANO, 1927.

Staff members: FERNANDO R. FRADUSCO, 1926. ROQUE GARONE, 1921.

EUGENIO J. PINGITORE, 1948 (Taxonomy).

Associated botanic garden: Jardín Botánico "Carlos Thays," Avenida Santa Fe 3951, 1425 Buenos Aires, Argentina.

Loans: In very special cases.

Periodical and serial works: Revista del Instituto Municipal de Botánica; Index Seminum.

Exchange: Yes.

BUENOS AIRES: *Herbario, Proteccion de la Naturaleza,* **(BUEN),** Santa Fe 690, Buenos Aires, **Argentina** – – incorporated in BA.

BUENOS AIRES: *Dirección Nacional del Antártico,* **(IAA),** Cerrito 1248, Buenos Aires, **Argentina** – – discontinued.

BUENOS AIRES: *Herbario, Instituto Nacional de Farmacología y Bromatología,* **(INFYB),** Caseros 2161, 1264 Capital Federal, Buenos Aires, **Argentina.**

Telephone: (54)27-9191; 26-2510.

Status: Subsecretary of Public Health.

Foundation: 1966. *Number of specimens:* 6.500.

Herbarium: Vascular plants of pharmacological value.

Important collections: Toxic and medicinal plants; José Laureano Amorín, Luis Q. Cristiani, Susana Michans, Edgardo N. Orfila, Cecilia Xiffreda, Rosario Sorbello, María C. Bogado.

Director: JOSÉ LAUREANO AMORÍN, 1918 (Taxonomy).

Curator: ROSARIO SORBELLO, 1920; 50-6075.

Specialization in research: Medicinal plants.

Loans: Usual regulations.

Exchange: Reprints.

BUENOS AIRES: *División de Fitopatología, Instituto de Sanidad Vegetal,* **(LCF)** – – see CASTELAR.

BUFFALO: *Clinton Herbarium, Buffalo Museum of Science,* **(BUF),** Humboldt Parkway, Buffalo, New York 14211, **U.S.A.**

Telephone: 716/896-5200.

Status: Owned and administered by Buffalo Society of Natural Sciences.

Foundation: 1861. *Number of specimens:* 60.000.

Herbarium: Flora of the Niagara Frontier Region;

major portion of general herbarium obtained through exchange during latter part of last century.

Important collections: J. L. Berlandier (Texas, Mexico), M. N. Blytt (Scandinavia), H. N. Bolander (California), A. W. Chapman (Florida), J. P. Couthouy (Ecuador), H. K. D. Eggert (Missouri, Illinois), A. Fendler (Trinidad), A. B. Ghiesbrecht (Mexico), E. Hall (Oregon, Texas), J. P. Harbour (Rocky Mountains), A. Kellogg and W. G. W. Hartford (California), L. Lesquereux (mosses), J. Macoun (Canada), P. MacOwan (Africa), Mexican Boundary Survey, C. T. Mohr (Alabama), F. von Mueller (Australia), E. Palmer (California), C. H. Peck (North American fungi, many isotypes), G. H. W. Schimper (European mosses), Wolle (algae), C. Wright (Cuba).

Curator: RICHARD H. ZANDER, 1941 (Bryology).

Specialization in research: Bryology.

Loans: No unusual restrictions.

Periodical and serial works: Notes from the Clinton Herbarium.

Exchange: None at present.

BUFFALO: *Herbarium, Department of Biology, Canisius College,* **(CANI),** 2001 Main Street, Buffalo, New York 14208, **U.S.A.**

Telephone: 716/883-7000, ext. 870.

Foundation: 1870. *Number of specimens:* 4.350.

Herbarium: Pteridophytes; western New York vascular plants; marine algae; some older European collections.

Important collections: J. H. Wibbe, Bro. Peter, Fr. Casimir Joseph, F. James Dorst, Hannah T. Croasdale, Clifford J. Awald, John L. Blum, Robert F. Blasdell, E. H. Ketchledge, W. Herbst, Frühling.

Director and Curator: ROBERT F. BLASDELL, 1929 (Ferns).

Specialization in research: Anatomy and taxonomy of ferns.

Loans: To recognized institutions.

BULAWAYO: *Herbarium, National Museum of Rhodesia,* **(BUL),** 8th Avenue, Bulawayo, **Zimbabwe.** (Information 1974)

Status: State museum.

Foundation: 1901. *Number of specimens:* 10.000.

Herbarium: Rhodesia and adjacent areas.

Specialization in research: Local flora and dendrochronology.

Periodical and serial works: Occasional Papers of the National Museums of Rhodesia.

BURLINGTON: *Pringle Herbarium, Department of Botany, University of Vermont,* **(VT),** Burlington, Vermont 05405, **U.S.A.**

Telephone: 802/656-3221.

Status: State university.

Foundation: 1870. *Number of specimens:* 337.000.

Herbarium: Worldwide, with emphasis on U.S., Mexico, New England, and Vermont.

Important collections: C. G. Pringle (Mexico), Mrs.

Nellie F. Flynn (Vermont), Ezra Brainerd (*Viola, Rubus*), Dana S. Carpenter (Vermont), D. Lewis Dutton (Vermont), A. J. Grout (mosses), Sidney F. Blake (northwestern Vermont), Leopold A. Charette (Vermont), herbarium of Ernest L. Smith (Vermont), J. W. Congdon (Rhode Island), Arthur E. Blewitt (Connecticut), E. H. Eames (Connecticut), D. C. Eaton (Connecticut), F. F. Forbes (Massachusetts), Steven R. Hill (New World), Thomas Morong (Massachusetts), A. S. Pease (New Hampshire), F. C. Seymour (Nicaragua), F. Sellow (Brazil), R. K. F. Pilger (Brazil), O. Buchtein (Chile), C. M. Belshaw (Peru), some duplicates of numbers destroyed at Berlin.

Curator: DAVID S. BARRINGTON, 1948 (Pteridophyta).

Specialization in research: Systematics and population biology of New World vascular plants.

Loans: To recognized institutions and qualified individuals from the region.

Exchange: Available: Plants of Vermont and New World tropics. Desired: Plants from New World.

BURNABY: *Herbarium, Department of Biological Sciences, Simon Fraser University,* (**SFUV**), Burnaby, British Columbia, **Canada** V5A 1S6.

Telephone: 604/291-4475.

Foundation: 1965. *Number of specimens:* 10.000.

Herbarium: Arctic and Rocky Mountains of British Columbia, Yukon, and Canada; mass collections of *Ranunculus eschscholtzii* complex.

Staff members: R. BROOK, 1939 (Ecology).

F. FISHER, 1926 (Biosystematics).

R. MATHEWES, 1948 (Palaeoecology).

Specialization in research: Arctic ecology; British Columbia forest vegetation/ecology; evolutionary ecology; alpine biosystematics.

Associated botanic garden: Simon Fraser University Arboretum.

BURNLEY: *Plant Research Institute,* (**VPRI**), Swan St., Burnley, Victoria 3121, **Australia.**

Telephone: (03) 810 1511.

Status: State Government, Department of Agriculture.

Foundation: 1890. *Number of specimens:* 11.000.

Herbarium: Plant pathogens, especially plant pathogenic fungi of Victoria.

Important collections: Daniel McAlpine.

Director and Curator: IAN G. PASCOE, 1949 (Plant pathogenic fungi).

Specialization in research: Taxonomy of plant pathogenic fungi, especially Coelomycetes.

Loans: Six month limit.

Exchange: Not available.

C

CAEN: *Laboratoire d'Algologie fondamentale et appliquée,* **(CN),** 39 rue Desmoueux, 14000-Caen, **France.**
Telephone: (16-31) 76.01-41.
Status: University of Caen.
Number of specimens: 4.000.
Herbarium: Marine algae with some freshwater specimens.
Important collections: J. V. F. Lamouroux (complete coll.), F. J. Chauvin (complete coll.), Lenormand (algae only), F. A. Pelvet (complete coll.).
Director and Curator: P. GAYRAL, 1921 (Algal taxonomy).
Staff member: C. BILLARD, 1947 (Algal taxonomy).
Specialization in research: Taxonomy of marine algae: marine plankton especially Chrysophyceae and Prymnesiophyceae, Laminariales, Ulvales.
Loans: No loans, photographs of specimens, eventually gift of fragments.
Remarks: The phanerogam collection (except Corbier's herbarium) is now kept and curated by the Museum d'Histoire Naturelle in Paris.

CAGLIARI: *Istituto Botanico della Università,* **(CAG),** Viale Fra Ignazio da Laconi 13, Cagliari, Sardinia, **Italy.** (Information 1974)
Status: University.
Foundation: 1855 (Botanic Garden). *Number of specimens:* 40.000.
Herbarium: Mediterranean flora, especially Sardinian endemic plants.
Specialization in research: Mediterranean flora, endemic taxa, cytotaxonomy, ecology.
Associated botanic garden: Orto Botanico della Università di Cagliari.
Loans: To recognized botanical institutions.
Periodical and serial works: Lavori dell'Istituto Botanico dell'Università di Cagliari.

CAIRNS: *Flecker Herbarium,* **(CAIRNS),** c/o North Queensland Naturalists' Club, P.O. Box 991, Cairns, Queensland 4870, **Australia** – – incorporated in QRS.

CAIRO: *Herbarium, Department of Botany, Faculty of Science, Cairo University,* **(CAI),** Giza, Cairo, **Egypt.** (Information 1974)
Status: University.
Foundation: 1925. *Number of specimens:* 200.000.
Herbarium: Worldwide, especially Egypt.
Specialization in research: Flora and vegetation of Egypt.
Associated botanic garden: Botanic Gardens of Qubba, Orman and Zohria, belonging to the Ministry of Agriculture.
Periodical and serial works: Bulletin of the Faculty of Science, Cairo University (including Flora of Egypt); Publications from the Cairo University Herbarium.

CAIRO: *Herbarium, Department of Botany, Faculty of Science, A'in Shams University,* **(CAIA),** Abbassia, Cairo, **Egypt.** (Information 1974)
Status: University.
Foundation: 1950. *Number of specimens:* 1.300.
Herbarium: Egyptian desert plants.
Specialization in research: Ecology, taxonomy, mycology, physiology of fungi, phytopathology, microbiology, cytology, cytogenetics, plant breeding, palaeobotany.
Periodical and serial works: A'in Shams Science Bulletin.

CAIRO: *Herbarium, The Desert Institute,* **(CAIH),** Mataria, Cairo, **Egypt.** (Information 1964)
Status: State institution.
Foundation: 1951. *Number of specimens:* 16.000.
Herbarium: Arid and semi-arid regions of the Nile Basin and Middle East.
Associated botanic garden: Private garden of native and exotic plants of the arid zone.
Periodical and serial works: Bulletin de l'Institut du Désert d'Egypte, Publications de l'Institut du Désert d'Egypte.

CAIRO: *The Herbarium, Flora and Phytotaxonomy Researches,* **(CAIM),** P.O. Box, Ministry of Agriculture, Dokki, Cairo, A.R., **Egypt.**
Telephone: 702687, 702879.
Status: Agricultural Research Centre.
Foundation: 1918. *Number of specimens:* 200.000.
Herbarium: Flora of Egypt; plants of the Sudan, Arabia, the Mediterranean and temperate regions.
Important collections: N. D. Simpson, J. R. Shabotai, M. Drar, A. I. Ramis, A. Khattab, M. Abdallah & F. Sa'ad; p.p.: P. Ascherson, G. Schweinfurth, E. Sickenberger, Letourneau, Bolland, G. Maire, A. Kaiser (Egypt) and M. Zohary (Palestine).
Director: FATIMA M. SA'AD, 1925 (Flora of Egypt, *Convolvulus*).
Curator: ABBAS ABD EL-SALAM, 1932 (Flora of Egypt and Arabia).
Staff members: NADIA ANWER, 1946 (Cultivated plants).
MONA ATTA, 1945 (Flora of Egypt, identification of prohibited plants).
MAGIDA COSTANIN, 1942 (Flora of Egypt, identification of prohibited plants).
ALY ABD EL-ATY, 1950 (Exchange).
MOHAMED ABD EL-FATTAH, 1950 (Documentation of Flora of Egypt).
SAMIR ABD EL-GAFFAR, 1951 (Librarian).

45

SIHAM EL-NOKRASHY, 1943 (Botanical artist).
AHMED ABD EL-RAZIK, 1948 (Documentation of general collections).
HOSSEIN HILMY, 1958 (Flora of Egypt).
'AIDA SAKR, 1936 (Botanical artist).
SHERIF SHOKRY, 1948 (Flora of Egypt).
Research associate: MOUSTAFA S. ABDALLAH, 1918 (Flora of Egypt; Resedaceae).
Specialization in research: Flora of Egypt.
Loans: In general to recognized botanical institutions.
Periodical and serial works: Notes from the Agricultural Research Centre Herbarium, Egypt.
Exchange: Available: Specimens from Egypt. Desired: Worldwide.

CAJAMARCA: *Herbario, Departamento de Biología, Sección de Botánica, Universidad Nacional Técnica de Cajamarca,* **(CPUN),** Ciudad Universitaria, Apartado 16, Cajamarca, **Peru.**
Telephone: 2555.
Foundation: 1966. *Number of specimens:* 3.000.
Herbarium: Flora of Peru, especially Department of Cajamarca and Amazonas.
Important collections: Isidoro M. Sanchez Vega.
Director: ISIDORO M. SANCHEZ VEGA, 1938 (Flora of Peru).
Staff members: WILMAN RUIZ VIGO, 1943.
JOSE SANCHEZ VEGA, 1940.
JOSE CABANILLAS SORIANO, 1951.
Specialization in research: Taxonomy and morphology of phanerogams, especially Leguminosae, Compositae, Cruciferae, Gramineae; flora of Cajamarca.
Loans: To recognized institutions.
Exchange: Yes.

CALCUTTA: *Economic Herbarium, Industrial Section, Indian Museum, Botanical Survey of India,* **(BSIS),** 1 Sudder Street, Calcutta – 700016, **India.**
Telephone: 23-3579, 23-6703.
Status: Government of India.
Foundation: 1896–97. *Number of specimens:* 50.000.
Herbarium: Phanerogams, ferns, marine algae, mainly Indian.
Important collections: Sir George Watt (economic plants), I. H. Burkill (*Dioscorea* of India), C. A. Barber (Sorghum), K. S. Srinivasan (algae).
Director: S. K. JAIN, 1926 (Taxonomy, floristics, economic botany, ethnobotany, conservation).
Curator: K. P. JANARDHANAN, 1933 (Taxonomy, floristics, ecology).
Staff members: D. K. BANERJEE, 1940 (Taxonomy of grasses, ethnobotany, economic botany).
B. N. CHAKRAVORTY, 1938 (Horticulture, plant introduction).
R. V. KAMMATHY, 1932 (Taxonomy, floristics, cytotaxonomy, Commelinaceae).
Specialization in research: Revision of families of economic plants for the Flora of India project, stud-

ies of economic plants.
Associated botanic garden: Indian Botanic Garden, Howrah-3.
Loans: With permission of the director.
Periodical and serial works: Bulletin of the Botanical Survey of India, Records of the Botanical Survey of India, Flora of India.

CALCUTTA: *Central National Herbarium, Botanical Survey of India,* **(CAL),** P.O. Botanic Garden, Howrah-711103, **India.**
Telephone: 67-3231.
Status: Government of India, Department of Science and Technology.
Foundation: 1793. *Number of specimens:* 1.250.000.
Herbarium: Worldwide, mainly phanerogams and ferns of India, south and southeast Asia; some mosses, lichens and algae.
Important collections: W. Roxburgh, N. Wallich, W. Griffith, R. Wight, M. P. Edgeworth, J. D. Hooker and T. Thomson, R. H. Beddome, G. H. K. Thwaites, W. S. Kurz, C. B. Clarke, G. King, J. S. Gamble, R. Pantling, D. Prain, C. A, Barber, G. Forrest, A. Henry, Rev. B. Scortechini, E. D. Merrill, K. P. Biswas, S. K. Mukherjee, V. Narayanaswami.
Director: S. K. JAIN (Poaceae, endangered taxa and conservation, ethnobotany).
Deputy Director (Herbarium): K. THOTHATHRI, 1929 (Leguminosae, flora of Andaman and Nicobar Islands, phytogeography).
Staff members: R. K. BASAK (Brassicaceae, Simaroubaceae).
D. B. DEB (Rubiaceae, Liliaceae).
G. SEN GUPTA (Solanaceae, flora of Bhutan).
M. P. NAYAR (Melastomataceae, phytogeography).
G. PANIGRAHI (Rosaceae, pteridophytes).
A. S. RAO (Orchidaceae, flora of eastern Himalaya).
J. N. VOHRA (Mosses).
Specialization in research: Flora of India, Flora of the Plains of Bengal.
Associated botanic garden: Indian Botanic Garden.
Loans: To heads of botanical institutions; types and rare specimens usually not loaned.
Periodical and serial works: Fascicles of Flora of India, Bulletin of the Botanical Survey of India, Records of the Botanical Survey of India.
Exchange: Available: Indian phanerogams. Desired: Phanerogams and ferns of Asia, Malesian Islands, tropical America, Africa and Australia.

CALCUTTA: *Botany Department of R. G. Kar Medical College,* **(CMY),** Calcutta, **India** –– discontinued.

CALCUTTA: *Herbarium, Department of Botany, Calcutta University,* **(CUH),** 35 Ballygunge Circular Road, Calcutta – 700019, **India.** (Information 1974)

Status: University.
Foundation: 1921. *Number of specimens:* 25.000.
Herbarium: India, Eastern Himalayas, Assam, West Bengal, Sunderbans.

CALDAS DA SAÚDE: *Instituto Nun'Alvres*, **(INA)**, 4780 Caldas da Saúde, **Portugal.**
Telephone: Vila Nova Famalicão: 53072.
Foundation: 1932.
Herbarium: Bryophyta.
Important collections: Musci, Hepaticae.
    Curator: JOSÉ G. CARVALHAIS, 1912 (Bryology).
    Loans: Depending on availability of specimens.
    Exchange: Eventually.

CALDWELL: *Harold M. Tucker Herbarium, College of Idaho*, **(CIC)**, Caldwell, Idaho 83605, **U.S.A.**
Telephone: 208/459-5232.
Status: Private college.
Foundation: 1891. *Number of specimens:* 18.000.
Herbarium: Flora of the Owyhee Uplift, Snake River Plains and northwestern Great Basin.
    Curator: PATRICIA L. PACKARD.
    Specialization in research: Correlation of geologic history with evolutionary history, especially cytogenetic evolution and types and rate of evolution.
    Loans: To recognized herbaria.
    Exchange: Owyhee Uplift, Snake River Plains, northwestern Great Basin and Idaho Batholith.

CALGARY: *Herbarium, Department of Biology, University of Calgary*, **(UAC)**, Calgary, Alberta, **Canada** T2N 1N4.
Telephone: 403/284-5262.
Foundation: 1962. *Number of specimens:* 100.000.
Herbarium: Mainly Alberta, British Columbia, and Northwest Territories; vascular and non-vascular, especially mosses and lichens.
Important collections: C. Bird (lichens and mosses), B. M. Hallworth, R. T. Ogilvie, A. R. Prince; Sanson collection from Banff, Alberta, including collection by John Macoun.
    Curator: C. C. CHINNAPPA, 1939 (Biosystematics).
    Staff member: PATRICIA DICKSON, 1955.
    Specialization in research: Evolutionary strategies and patterns of variation; *Erigeron, Allium, Smilacina,* and *Stellaria longipes* complex.
    Loans: 6 months to 1 year.
    Exchange: Available: Lichens and mosses.

CALI: *Herbario, Departamento de Biología, Universidad del Valle*, **(CUVC)**, Apartado Aéreo 2188, Cali, Valle, **Colombia.**
Telephone: (57)393041.
Foundation: 1966. *Number of specimens:* 13.500.
Herbarium: Flora of Valle.
    Director: NANCY BASTIDAS DE PASCUAS, 1951.
    Curator: ISIDORO CABRERA R., 1922.

Staff member: NESTOR PAZ, 1954.

CAMBRIDGE: *Herbarium, Arnold Arboretum of Harvard University,* **(A)**, 22 Divinity Avenue, Cambridge, Massachusetts 02138, **U.S.A.**
Telephone: 617/495-2363.
Status: Affiliated institution of the Faculty of Arts and Sciences of Harvard University.
Foundation: 1872. *Number of specimens:* 1.091.886.
Herbarium: Eastern Asia, Malesia; ornamental plants under cultivation.
Important collections: Chinese and Philippine collections, especially since 1900, E. H. Wilson, J. F. Rock, G. Forrest; L. J. Brass (New Guinea).
    Director: PETER S. ASHTON, 1934 (Systematics, evolutionary biology, and ecology of the Dipterocarpaceae and their forests).
    Supervisor: PETER F. STEVENS, 1944 (Systematics of Ericaceae; Old World Guttiferae; flora of New Guinea).
    Staff members: RICHARD A. HOWARD, 1917 (Systematics and anatomy of Icacinaceae and *Coccoloba;* floristics of West Indies).
    BERNICE G. SCHUBERT, 1913 (Systematics of *Begonia, Desmodium, Dioscorea*).
    STEPHEN A. SPONGBERG, 1942 (Systematics of woody plants).
    RICHARD WEAVER, 1943 (Systematics of Gentianaceae).
    CARROLL E. WOOD, JR., 1921 (Systematics; plant geography; flora of southeastern U.S.).
    Specialization in research: As listed above.
    Associated botanic garden: Arnold Arboretum, Jamaica Plain, Massachusetts 02130; Case Estates of the Arnold Arboretum, Weston, Massachusetts 02193.
    Loans: Usual regulations.
    Periodical and serial works: Journal of the Arnold Arboretum; Arnoldia.
    Exchange: Eastern Asia, Malesia, tropical America, southeastern U.S., cultivated from many areas.
    Remarks: Specimens of cultivated plants are kept in Jamaica Plain (AAH).

CAMBRIDGE: *British Antarctic Survey Herbarium,* **(AAS)**, British Antarctic Survey Life Sciences Division, Plant Biology Section, Madingley Road, Cambridge CB3 0ET, England, **Great Britain.**
Telephone: 0223-61188.
Status: Sponsored by a Research Council.
Foundation: 1969. *Number of specimens:* 25.650 (Lichens 5.000, vascular plants 500, macrofungi 150, bryophytes 20.000). Bryophytes on loan to ACHE, Austral Cryptogamic Herbarium, Institute of Terrestrial Ecology, Bush Estate, Penicuik, Midlothian EH26 0QB, Scotland.
Herbarium: Cryptogams and phanerogams from Antarctic and Subantarctic regions.
Important collections: Lichens of South Georgia and maritime Antarctic (South Orkney, South Shet-

land, South Sandwich Islands; Antarctic Peninsula), including some type specimens. Vascular plants of the Subantarctic island, especially South Georgia and maritime Antarctic region (also Falkland Islands, Tierra del Fuego). Macrofungi of South Georgia and maritime Antarctic. Mosses and liverworts of South Georgia and maritime Antarctic (+ continental Antarctic, other Subantarctic islands, Falkland Islands).

Director and Curator: R. I. Lewis Smith, 1942, Head of Plant Biology Section, British Antarctic Survey (Ecology of Antarctic and Subantarctic cryptogams and phanerogams).

Staff member: D. W. H. Walton, 1945 (Taxonomy of *Acaena*, ecology of Subantarctic phanerogams).

Specialization in research: Antarctic and Subantarctic cryptogamic and phanerogamic floras.

Loans: To recognized botanical institutions.

Periodical and serial works: British Antarctic Survey Bulletin, British Antarctic Survey Scientific Reports.

Exchange: Available: Lichens, vascular plants, macrofungi from Antarctic and Subantarctic regions. Desired: All terrestrial groups from high southern latitudes.

Remarks: A computer based data bank is used by ACHE for retrieval and sorting of records of all terrestrial plant groups in AAS and ACHE. A collection of live maritime Antarctic and South Georgian plants is maintained and seed may be obtained on request.

CAMBRIDGE: *Orchid Herbarium of Oakes Ames, Botanical Museum of Harvard University,* **(AMES),** 22 Divinity Avenue, Cambridge, Massachusetts 02138, **U.S.A.**

Telephone: 617/495-2360.

Foundation: 1899. *Number of specimens:* 125.000.

Herbarium: Orchidaceae.

Important collections: Over 10.000 type specimens of species described by O. Ames, G. A. Schweinfurth, J. J. Smith, F. R. R. Schlechter, F. W. L. Kraenzlin, J. Lindley, H. G. Reichenbach, L. O. Williams, L. A. Garay.

Director: Richard Evans Schultes, 1915 (Economic botany).

Curator: Leslie A. Garay, 1924 (Systematics and evolution of the entire orchid family).

Staff members: G. C. K. Dunsterville, 1905 (Venezuelan orchids).

Gunnar Seidenfaden, 1908 (Asiatic orchids).

John E. Stacy, 1918 (*Oncidium* and related genera).

Herman R. Sweet, 1909 (Orchidaceae).

Specialization in research: Systematics of Orchidaceae; monographic and floristic studies.

Loans: On a limited basis; types for monographic studies only.

Periodical and serial works: Botanical Museum Leaflets, Harvard University.

Exchange: Orchids.

Remarks: All orchids from the herbaria of the Arnold Arboretum (A) and Gray Herbarium (GH) are on indefinite deposit in AMES. Their availability for loan is governed by the terms of the parent institutions.

CAMBRIDGE: *Herbarium, Botany School, University of Cambridge,* **(CGE),** Downing Street, Cambridge CB2 3EA, England, **Great Britain.**

Telephone: 0223-61414.

Status: University.

Foundation: 1761. *Number of specimens:* 550.000 (130.000 British).

Herbarium: World herbarium, particularly rich in historical collections; additions mainly restricted to specimens from western Palearctic Region.

Important collections: C. C. Babington, (CGE-B, c. 55.000 British Isles, incl. types of *Rubus*; Iceland); S. H. Bickham (British Isles, 24.000); M. Botteri (Mexico); T. Bridges (S. America); C. J. F. Bunbury (6.000, especially S. America, incl. types); E. J. H. Corner (*Ficus*, Basidiomycetes); H. Cuming (S. America, Pacific, Philippines, several sets); A. Cunningham (New Zealand); C. Darwin (S. America, Galápagos, numerous types); D. Douglas (N. America, Pacific, numerous types, his own and J. Lindley's, and 31 *Lupinus* types by himself, Lindley, Bentham and Agardh); H. J. Elwes & A. Henry (Trees of Great Britain and Ireland, incl. types); G. Gardner (3 sets, incl. fern lectotypes and his own herbarium of Pteridophyta); G. Genevier (incl. large *Rubus* collection with many types); W. Griffith (Asia, very good set); T. Hartweg (C. & S. America); G. D. Haviland & C. Hose (Borneo); W. P. Hiern (mainly India); W. Houstoun (Mexico, Jamaica); A. Jordan (France, type gatherings); J. Laflin (Bryophytes, 20–30.000 packets); C. M. Lemann (over 50.000 sheets worldwide, mostly not his own collecting, named by G. Bentham); J. J. Linden (C. & S. America); J. Lindley (58.000 sheets incl. a large number of types, especially Australian, orchids at K); T. Lobb (Asia); R. T. Lowe (Madeira, types); E. S. Marshall (23.000 British Isles, types); A. Mathews (S. America, Pacific); A. Menzies (S. America, Pacific); J. Miers (Brazil); T. Mitchell (Australia, many Lindley types); W. E. Nicholson (Large collection of Bryophytes, mainly British and European); R. Spruce (S. America, Pyrenees); G. H. K. Thwaites (Ceylon); N. Wallich (India, S. Africa); C. Wright (Cuba).

Director: R. G. West, Professor in charge of the Botany School.

Curator: D. Briggs, 1936 (Genecology and experimental taxonomy).

Assistant Curator: P. D. Sell, 1929 (Taxonomy of British and European flora, especially *Cerastium*, Compositae tribe Cichorieae incl. *Hieracium* and *Pilosella, Fumaria, Scleranthus*; nomenclature, bibliography, typification).

Staff member: B. S. Parris, 1945 (Pteridophyta

of the world, especially Grammitidaceae).

Specialization in research: Flora of the western Palearctic region.

Associated botanic garden: University Botanic Garden, Cambridge.

Loans: To botanical institutions.

CAMBRIDGE: *Herbarium, University Botanic Garden,* **(CGG),** 1Brookside, Cambridge CB2 1JF, England, **Great Britain.**

Telephone: 0223 350101.

Status: Sub-department of the Department of Botany, Cambridge University.

Foundation: Garden founded 1762; moved to present site 1846 (earliest herbarium specimens c. 1820).

Number of specimens: 13.000–14.000.

Herbarium: Mostly cultivated plants of Cambridge Botanic Garden, including cultivars.

Important collections: Collections arising from recent taxonomic studies on *Acaena, Bergenia, Geranium, Ruscus.*

Director: S. M. WALTERS, 1920 (Taxonomy of European flora, especially *Alchemilla, Eleocharis, Silene*).

Curator: P. F. YEO, 1929 (Taxonomy of cultivated plants, especially *Geranium*; taxonomy of *Euphrasia*; pollination).

Staff member: C. J. KING, 1926.

Specialization in research: Taxonomy and nomenclature of ornamental plants.

Loans: To botanical institutions.

Periodical and serial works: Annual seed exchange list.

Exchange: Available: Limited number of cultivated plants.

CAMBRIDGE: *Economic Herbarium of Oakes Ames, Botanical Museum of Harvard University,* **(ECON),** Cambridge, Massachusetts 02138, **U.S.A.**

Telephone: 617/495-2326.

Status: Private institution.

Foundation: 1858. *Number of specimens:* 36.600.

Herbarium: Plants useful or harmful to man; cultivated plants; wild plants involved in origin of cultivated plants; chemical voucher specimens.

Important collections: W. H. Hodge (*Cinchona*), R. E. Schultes (*Hevea* and related genera), R. E. Schultes and T. Plowman (*Cannabis*), P. C. Mangelsdorf (*Maize*).

Director and Curator: RICHARD EVANS SCHULTES, 1915 (Biodynamic plants of American tropics, primarily Amazonia; rubber-yielding plants).

Staff members: SCOTT E. WILDER, 1953.

JAMES L. ZARUCCHI, 1953.

Specialization in research: Teaching and research in economic botany, ethnobotany, and phytochemistry.

Loans: To specialists.

Periodical and serial works: Botanical Museum Leaflets.

Exchange: Available: Tropical American economic specimens. Desired: Economic material.

CAMBRIDGE: *Farlow Reference Library and Herbarium of Cryptogamic Botany, Harvard University,* **(FH),** 20 Divinity Avenue, Cambridge, Massachusetts 02138, **U.S.A.**

Telephone: 617/495-2368; 495-2369.

Status: Private institution.

Foundation: 1919. *Number of specimens:* 1.206.037.

Herbarium: Worldwide collections of non-vascular cryptogamic plants, especially original reference herbaria of authors of names and undistributed exsiccatae.

Important collections: Fungi: Bucholz, E. A. Burt, M. A. Curtis, J. B. Ellis, W. G. Farlow, J. H. Faull, F. X. R. von Höhnel, D. H. Linder, N. T. Patouillard, J. Rick, T. Taylor, R. Thaxter, Thiessen, White. Algae: Agardh, J. W. Bailey, Bornet, F. S. Collins, W. G. Farlow, Harvey, Hauck, I. M. Lamb, S. R. Lenormand, Rabenhorst. Lichens: H. E. Hasse, R. H. Howe, E. D. Merrill, L. W. Riddle, Robbins, C. J. Sprague, T. Taylor, E. Tuckerman. Bryophytes: E. B. Bartram, F. S. Collins, M. Fleischer, C. C. Haynes, T. P. James, V. F. Schiffner, W. S. Sullivant, T. Taylor, F. Verdoorn.

Director: OTTO T. SOLBRIG, 1930 (Biosystematics; population biology).

Curator: DONALD H. PFISTER, 1945 (Discomycetes).

Staff members: TIMOTHY BARONI, 1949 (Agaricales).

GERALDINE C. KAYE, 1935 (Librarian).

Honorary research associates: SYLVIA EARLE, 1935 (Phycology).

ROBERT K. EDGAR, 1943 (Diatoms).

GENEVA SAYRE, 1911 (Bryology).

Specialization in research: Systematics of cryptogams; bibliography and documentation.

Associated botanic garden: Arnold Arboretum.

Loans: To recognized institutions under normal regulations.

Periodical and serial works: Occasional Papers of the Farlow Herbarium.

Exchange: Available: Sets of Reliqueae Farloweana; bryophytes from the E. B. Bartram herbarium; other bryophytes. Desired: Published exsiccatae, reference specimens.

Remarks: Indexes to various separately housed herbaria are published as available: Bartram moss, Fleischer moss, Schiffner moss, Schiffner hepatic, Patouillard fungus, Bailey diatoms, Cheever diatoms, Taylor moss, Sullivant hepatics.

CAMBRIDGE: *Gray Herbarium of Harvard University,* **(GH),** 22 Divinity Avenue, Cambridge, Massachusetts 02138, **U.S.A.**

Telephone: 617/495-2365.

Status: Private institution.

Foundation: 1864. *Number of specimens:* 1.790.928.

Herbarium: Worldwide collection of vascular plants with greatest strength in western hemisphere material, especially North America, including Mexico and the West Indies.

Important collections: Early collections of western and southwestern United States and Mexico including many of the important exploring expeditions of the 19th century. Types and collections of Asa Gray, Sereno Watson, B. L. Robinson, M. L. Fernald, Ivan Johnston, Lyman Smith, R. C. Rollins. Collections of W. H. Brewer, W. J. Burchell, W. C. Cusick, T. Drummond, A. Fendler, C. V. Hartman, E. Langlassé, F. J. Lindheimer, G. Mandon, T. Nuttall, W. N. Suksdorf.

Director: OTTO T. SOLBRIG, 1930 (Biosystematics; population biology).

Staff members: REED C. ROLLINS, 1911 (Systematics and evolutionary biology; Cruciferae and *Parthenium*).

ELIZABETH A. SHAW, 1938 (Cruciferae; history of botany in the U.S. in the 19th century).

ALICE F. TRYON, 1920 (Biosystematics; palynology; cytology).

ROLLA M. TRYON, 1916 (Biogeography of tropical America; pteridophyte systematics).

Specialization in research: Monographic studies of various genera and families, especially Pteridophyta and Cruciferae; biosystematic and chemosystematic approaches are utilized in studying problems in systematics and evolution; floristic studies of eastern North America, southeastern United States and northeastern Mexico.

Associated botanic garden: Arnold Arboretum.

Loans: Normal loan regulations.

Periodical and serial works: Contributions from the Gray Herbarium of Harvard University; Memoirs of the Gray Herbarium of Harvard University; Gray Herbarium Card Index of New Species and Varieties of Plants of North and South America (issued quarterly).

Exchange: Available: North America including Mexico. Wanted: Western Hemisphere.

CAMBRIDGE: *Herbarium, New England Botanical Club,* **(NEBC),** 22 Divinity Avenue, Cambridge, Massachusetts 02138, **U.S.A.**

Telephone: 617/495-1000.

Foundation: 1895. *Number of specimens:* 243.000.

Herbarium: Flora of New England.

Curator: C. BARRE HELLQUIST, 1940; 617/331-3300, ext. 280 (Aquatic flora of New England).

Staff members: RAYMOND ANGELO, 1948 (New England woody plants).

DONOVAN BOWLEY, 1945 (Non-vascular plants).

Specialization in research: Flora of New England.

Loans: Usual conditions.

Periodical and serial works: Rhodora.

Exchange: Available: Some New England material.

CAMERINO: *Erbario dell' Istituto di Botanica dell'Università di Camerino,* **(CAME),** Via Pontoni 5, 62032 Camerino (Macerata), **Italy.**

Telephone: 0737-2527.

Status: University.

Foundation: 1920. *Number of specimens:* 20.000.

Herbarium: Flora of Italy and Central Apennines.

Important collections: V. Marchesoni (Flora of Sibillini Mountains).

Director: FRANCO PEDROTTI, 1934 (Plant sociology, vegetation mapping, flora of Central Alps).

Staff members: SANDRO BALLELLI, 1944 (Italian flora).

EDOARDO BIONDI, 1944 (Paleobotany).

CARMELA CORTINI PEDROTTI, 1931 (Bryology).

ANTONIO DELL'UOMO, 1944 (Algology).

CARLO FRANCALANCIA, 1942 (Vegetation mapping).

ETTORE ORSOMANDO, 1940 (Plant sociology).

Specialization in research: Bryology of Italy, plant sociology of Apennines and Central Alps, vegetation mapping, conservation, paleobotany.

Associated botanic garden: Orto Botanica dell' Università di Camerino.

Periodical and serial works: Pubblicazioni dell' Istituto di Botanica dell' Università di Camerino, La Riserva Naturale di Torricchio.

Exchange: Yes.

Remarks: In 1970 the Botanical Institute of Camerino acquired the Natural Reserve of Torricchio, an area of 317 hectares.

CAMPINAS: *Phanerogamic Herbarium, Instituto Agronômico de Campinas,* **(IAC),** Avenida Barão de Itapura 1481, Caixa Postal 28, 13.100 Campinas, São Paulo, **Brazil.**

Telephone: (55)0192/31-5422, ramal 155.

Status: Secretaria da Agricultura do Estado de São Paulo.

Foundation: 1969. *Number of specimens:* 28.000.

Herbarium: Mainly Brazil.

Important collections: Gramineae, Compositae.

Director: CONDORCET ARANHA.

Staff members: ANNUNCIATA BROLEZE.

MARCIA ATAURI CARDELLI.

ROSE MARY PIO.

ELDO ANTONIO MONTEIRO DA SILVA.

Specialization in research: Economic botany; taxonomy, systematics, and anatomy; plants of agronomic interest.

Loans: For 90 days.

Periodical and serial works: Revista Bragantia.

Exchange: Yes.

CAMPINAS: *Mycological Herbarium, Instituto Agronômico de Campinas,* **(IACM),** Avenida Barão de Itapura 1481, Caixa Postal 28, 13.100 Campinas, São Paulo, **Brazil.**

Telephone: (55)0192/31-5422, ramal 177.

Status: State institution.
Foundation: 1932. *Number of specimens:* 8.000.
Herbarium: Brazilian mycological flora.
Important collections: A. S. Costa, H. P. Krug, J. Rick, A. P. Viégas.
    Director: FRANCISCO DA COSTA VERDADE, 1921 (Soils specialization).
    Curator: OSVALDO PARADELA FILHO, 1938 (General plant pathology).
    Staff members: MARIA ANGÉLICA PIZZINATTO GERALDI, 1954 (Plant pathology).
    MARGARIDA FUMIKO ITO, 1949 (Plant pathology).
        SÉRGIO ALMEIDA DE MORAES, 1950 (Plant pathology).
        ADHAIR RICCI JUNIOR, 1950 (Plant pathology).
        JACIRO SOAVE, 1942 (Plant and seed pathologist: cotton and rice).
        MAURO HIDEO SUGIMORI, 1945 (Plant pathology).
Specialization in research: Plant diseases caused by fungi bacteria and nematodes; plant breeding for disease resistance; seed pathology.
Loans: Usual regulations.
Periodical and serial works: Bragantia.
Exchange: Yes.

CAMPINAS: *Herbário, Departamento de Morfologia e Sistemática Vegetais, Instituto de Biologia, Universidade Estadual de Campinas (UNICAMP),* **(UEC),** Caixa Postal 1170, 13.100 Campinas, São Paulo, **Brazil.**
Telephone: (55)0192/39-1301, ramal 309.
Foundation: 1974. *Number of specimens:* 25.000.
Herbarium: Plants of Brazil; flora of Serra do Cipó; forage legumes.
    Director: HERMÓGENES DE FREITAS LEITÃO FILHO, 1944 (Phytosociological studies in forests and cerrado vegetation of Brazil; taxonomy of Compositae).
    Curator: MARINA BRAGATTO VASCONCELLOS, 1955.
    Staff members: ANTONIO CARLOS GABRIELLI, 1941 (Anatomy of Bignoniaceae).
        CARLOS A. JOLY, 1955 (Ecology).
        LUIZA S. KINOSHITA GOUVÊA, 1947 (Ericaceae).
        FERNANDO R. MARTINS, 1949 (Forest phytosociology).
        MARIA ELIZABETH M. RAMOS, 1951 (Leguminosae, Lotoideae).
        MARLIES SAZIMA, 1944 (Floral biology).
        JOÃO SEMIR, 1937 (Compositae, Vernonieae, Melastomataceae).
        GEORGE J. SHEPHERD, 1949 (Cyperaceae, experimental taxonomy).
        WILLIAM H. STUBBLEBINE, 1947 (Chemical and plant ecology).
        JORGE Y. TAMASHIRO, 1949 (Leguminosae, Caesalpinioideae, Mimosoideae).
        NEUSA TARODA, 1952 (Sterculiaceae).

Specialization in research: Taxonomy of vascular plants of Brazil; ecology studies in forest and cerrado vegetation of Brazil.
Loans: No special conditions.
Exchange: Available: Forest and cerrado plants of Brazil.

CANAL ZONE: *Summit Herbarium,* **(SCZ)** – – *see* BALBOA.

CANBERRA: *Herbarium Australiense,* **(CANB),** P.O. Box 1600, Canberra City, A.C.T. 2601, **Australia.**
Telephone: 062-465904.
Status: Administered by the Commonwealth Scientific and Industrial Research Organization (CSIRO), Australia.
Foundation: 1930. *Number of specimens:* 350.000.
Herbarium: Worldwide, with specialization in Australia, New Guinea, and the south-western Pacific islands.
Important collections: L. J. Brass (NE Australia and New Guinea, mostly from 1948 onwards), N. T. Burbidge (Australia), R. Brown (Australia), C. E. Carr (SE New Guinea); CSIRO Div. of Land Research (Papua New Guinea and Northern Australia): L. A. Craven, R. D. Hoogland, M. Lazarides, R. Schodde; A. Dietrich (Queensland), A. H. S. Lucas (Australian algae, at present on loan to NSW).
    Curator: H. EICHLER, 1916 (Australian Hydrocotyloideae, Australian and Malesian Ranunculaceae, Australian Zygophyllaceae, nomenclature).
    Staff members: L. G. ADAMS, 1929 (*Solenogyne,* Australian *Gentiana*).
        L. A. CRAVEN, 1945 (Australian *Calytrix* and allied genera, *Syzygium, Acmena,* Papuasian *Homalium,* New Guinean Plantaginaceae).
        M. GRAY, 1929 (Australian alpine and subalpine flora, naturalized weeds, flora of Australian Capital Territory).
        T. G. HARTLEY, 1931 (Australian, SE Asian and SW Pacific Rutaceae, New Guinean *Syzygium, Acmena*).
        A. KANIS, 1934 (Australian and New Guinean Amaranthaceae, except *Ptilotus,* Australian and Malesian Mimosaceae, except *Acacia,* Indo-pacific Ochnaceae).
        M. LAZARIDES, 1928 (Poaceae of tropical and arid Australia).
        J. G. WEST, 1949 (Australian *Dodonaea,* Australian Portulacaceae).
Specialization in research: Taxonomic revisions and floristic studies concerning the Australasian region.
Associated botanic garden: See International Directory of Botanical Gardens: CSIRO, Division of Plant Industry, Genetic Resources section.
Loans: To approved institutions.
Periodical and serial works: Contributions from Herbarium Australiense 1-26 (discontinued); Brunonia.

Exchange: Available: Specimens from Australia (limited number). Desired: Specimens from all parts of the world, but particularly Australasian, Pacific and SE. Asian regions.

Remarks: See also Atherton (QRS) and Canberra (FRI) which are part of Herbarium Australiense located separately. Cooperating institutions: Research Schools of Biological Sciences and Pacific Studies, Australian National University, Canberra. Australian Biological Resources Study: Flora of Australia Project (Dept. of Science, Bureau of Flora and Fauna).

CANBERRA: *Herbarium, National Botanic Gardens,* **(CBG),** Department of the Capital Territory, P.O. Box 158, Canberra City, A.C.T. 2601, **Australia.**

Telephone: 062 473822 (Switchboard).

Status: Commonwealth Government.

Foundation: 1945. *Number of specimens:* 100.000 (90.000 vascular plants, 10.000 non-vascular plants).

Herbarium: General herbarium, relating principally to the Australian and South West Pacific floras.

Director: ROBERT W. BODEN, 1935 (Conservation).

Curator: ARTHUR B. COURT; (062) 496460 (Taxonomy and phylogeny of *Acacia*, nomenclature, history of Australian taxonomy).

Staff members: ESTELLE M. CANNING (Taxonomy of Rhamnaceae, particularly *Cryptandra* and *Spyridium*).

MICHAEL D. CRISP (Taxonomy of Fabaceae, especially *Daviesia*, *Brachysema* and related genera).

HEINAR STREIMANN, 1938 (Taxonomy of Musci of Australia and New Guinea).

IAN R. H. TELFORD, 1941 (Taxonomy of Australian Cucurbitaceae, *Epacris* and *Rupicola*).

DOUGLAS VERDON (Taxonomy of Australian lichens, especially *Leptogium*; hepaticae).

Specialization in research: Australian flora.

Associated botanic garden: National Botanic Gardens.

Loans: To recognized botanical institutions.

Exchange: Australian vascular plants and bryophytes.

Remarks: Vouchered collection of more than 2.500 taxa of living indigenous Australian plants established in the National Botanic Gardens for scientific research with expansion continuing.

CANBERRA: *Herbarium of the Division of Forest Research, CSIRO,* **(FRI),** Banks St., Yarralumla, Canberra, A.C.T. 2600, **Australia.**

Telephone: (062) 818208.

Status: Part of the Herbarium Australiense.

Foundation: 1927. *Number of specimens:* 25.000.

Herbarium: Mainly the *Eucalyptus* collection of the Herbarium Australiense.

Important collections: M. R. Jacobs, M. I. H. Brooker, G. M. Chippendale.

Curator: G. M. CHIPPENDALE, 1921 (*Eucalyptus* taxonomy, nomenclature, distribution, data banking).

Staff members: M. I. H. BROOKER, 1934 (*Eucalyptus* taxonomy, phyllotaxis, seed morphology).

R. D. JOHNSTON, 1922 (Forest ecology, *Eucalyptus* card key).

Specialization in research: Eucalyptus species, forest ecology.

Loans: On request to research institutions.

Periodical and serial works: Australian Forest Research.

Exchange: Eucalyptus species.

CANBERRA: *Gauba Herbarium, Department of Botany, Faculty of Science, Australian National University,* **(GAUBA),** Canberra, A.C.T. 2600, **Australia.**

Telephone: 062/493255 or 492882.

Status: University.

Foundation: 1958. *Number of specimens:* 20.000.

Herbarium: Flora of the Australian Capital Territory and adjoining regions, Australia, especially *Eucalyptus.*

Director: Head of the Department of Botany ex officio.

Staff member: J. A. CARNAHAN, 1926 (Plant ecology).

Loans: To approved institutions.

CANOAS: *Instituto Geobiológico La Salle,* **(SALLE),** Canoas, Rio Grande do Sul, **Brazil** – – incorporated in ICN.

CANTON: – – *see* GUANGZHOU.

CANYON: *Herbarium, Biology Department, West Texas State University,* **(WTS),** Canyon, Texas 79016, **U.S.A.**

Telephone: 806/656-2262.

Foundation: 1970. *Number of specimens:* 50.000.

Herbarium: Mainly plants of western U.S. and Alaska.

Important collections: S. Welsh (Alaska, Utah), L. C. Higgins (Boraginaceae).

Director and Curator: LARRY C. HIGGINS, 1936 (Boraginaceae of U.S. and Mexico).

Specialization in research: Flora of Texas panhandle and Utah; Boraginaceae of U.S. and Mexico.

Loans: Usual regulations, 1 year period.

Exchange: Welcome all exchanges.

CAPE COAST: *Department of Botany, University of Cape Coast,* **(CCG),** Cape Coast, **Ghana.** (Information 1974)

Status: University.

Foundation: 1963. *Number of specimens:* 4.000.

Herbarium: Worldwide, gymnosperms and angiosperms.

Specialization in research: Flora of West Tropical Africa.

CAPE TOWN: *Bolus Herbarium, University of Cape Town,* **(BOL)**, Rondebosch 7700, **South Africa.**
Telephone: 021-69-8531.
Status: Research Institute of the University.
Foundation: 1867. *Number of specimens:* 240.000.
Herbarium: Extra-tropical South Africa (angiosperms, gymnosperms, pteridophyta, bryophyta, lichens, fungi, algae).
Important collections: H. Bolus, L. Bolus, N. S. Pillans, E. Esterhuysen, R. S. Adamson, T. M. Salter, H. G. Fourcade.
Director and Curator: E. A. C. L. E. SCHELPE, 1924 (Orchidaceae, Pteridophyta, Musci).
Staff members: P. A. BEAN, 1930 (Rutaceae).
E. E. ESTERHUYSEN, 1912 (Restionaceae).
A. V. HALL, 1936 (Orchidaceae).
Specialization in research: South African angiospermic and cryptogamic flora.
Associated botanic garden: University of Cape Town Botanical Collection.
Loans: To approved institutions for periods of up to six months.
Periodical and serial works: Contributions from the Bolus Herbarium.
Exchange: Available: Specimens of South African flora. Desired: Tropical African Bryophyta, Pteridophyta and Orchidaceae.

CAPE TOWN: *Guthrie Herbarium, Department of Botany, University of Cape Town,* **(CT)**, Rondebosch 7700, **South Africa.** (Information 1974)
Status: University.
Foundation: About 1920. *Number of specimens:* 10.000.
Herbarium: Cape Peninsula flora, mainly phanerogams.
Specialization in research: The Cape Peninsula flora.
Loans: To recognized botanical institutions.

CAPE TOWN: *Compton Herbarium,* **(NBG)**, and *South African Museum Herbarium,* **(SAM)**, National Botanic Gardens of South Africa, Kirstenbosch, Private Bag X7, Claremont 7735, **South Africa.**
Telephone: (021) - 771166.
Status: Declared cultural institution, Dept. of Agricultural Technical Services. Governed by a special Board of Trustees. The Director is also Harold Person, Prof. of Botany in the University of Cape Town.
Foundation: 1855 (SAM), 1937 (NBG). *Number of specimens:* 250.000.
Herbarium: Principally phanerogams and cryptogams of Southern Africa; also small worldwide collection.
Important collections: NBG: T. M. Salter, R. H. Compton, W. F. Barker. SAM: K. Dinter & P. Range (South West Africa), C. W. L. Pappe, C. F. Ecklon, K. L. Zeyher, P. MacOwan, T. P. Stokoe (For detailed list of collectors see: Index herbariorum Austro-Africanarum p. 5–10 (1971), publ. S.A. Assoc. of Botanists).

Director: H. B. RYCROFT, 1918.
Curator: J. P. ROURKE, 1942 (African Proteaceae, Stilbaceae, pollination biology).
Staff members: P. FAIRALL, 1917 (Asteraceae, Poaceae).
C. E. LABUSCHAGNE, 1942 (Ethnobotany).
D. A. SNIJMAN, 1949 (*Haemanthus*).
Honorary research workers: W. F. BARKER (*Lachenalia*).
T. T. BARNARD (Botanical bibliography).
I. J. M. WILLIAMS (Rutaceae).
Specialization in research: Taxonomy of South African flora, especially the Namaqualand area and Cape Floristic Kingdom.
Associated botanic garden: National Botanic Gardens of South Africa, Kirstenbosch; Karoo Botanic Garden, Worcester.
Loans: For periods of six months to recognized botanical institutions.
Periodical and serial works: Journal of South African Botany.
Remarks: Small working herbaria (between 500 and 1.500 sheets), representative of the local flora of regional gardens under the control of the National Botanic Gardens of South Africa, are maintained at the Lowveld Botanic Garden, Nelspruit, the Orange Free State Botanic Garden, Bloemfontein, the Drakensberg Botanic Garden, Harrismith and the Harold Porter Botanic Garden, Betty's Bay. No loans are made from these herbaria as they are formed from duplicates, the main set being housed in NBG.

CARACAS: *Herbario Dr. Victor Manuel Ovalles, Facultad de Farmacia, Universidad Central de Venezuela,* **(MYF)**, Apartado 40.109, Caracas 1040A, **Venezuela.**
Telephone: (58)02/61-98-11, ext. 3303; 62-15-43.
Foundation: 1974. *Number of specimens:* 1.500.
Herbarium: Dependency of the Pharmacy Faculty for its Natural Products Laboratory; vouchers for screening program in search for medicinal plants; ethnobotanical material.
Director and Curator: STEPHEN S. TILLETT, 1930 (*Passiflora*).
Specialization in research: Ethnobotany of Venezuela; collection, identification, and voucher for major program in a search for new medicinal plants.
Associated botanic garden: Medicinal plant garden.
Loans: Usual regulations.
Periodical and serial works: El Noticiero Botánico.
Exchange: Desired: *Passiflora*; ethnobotanical and medicinal plants.

CARACAS: *Instituto Botánico,* **(VEN)**, Apartado 2156, Caracas, **Venezuela.**
Telephone: (58)02/62-61-91.
Status: Herbario Nacional, Ministerio del Am-

biente y de los Recursos Naturales Renovables.

Foundation: 1920. *Number of specimens:* 140.000.

Herbarium: Mainly flora of Venezuela and adjacent countries.

Important collections: L. Aristeguieta, F. Cardona, A. Ernst, O. Huber, A. Jahn, T. Lasser, B. Maguire, G. Morillo, H. Pittier, L. Ruiz-Terán, J. A. Steyermark, F. Tamayo, V. Vareschi, Ll. Williams.

Director: TOBIAS LASSER, 1911.

Curator: JULIAN A. STEYERMARK, 1909 (Flora and plant geography of Venezuela; Piperaceae, Sabiaceae, Rubiaceae).

Staff members: FRANCISCO DELASCIO (Flora of Venezuela; Vitaceae).

ZORAIDA L. DE FEBRES (Gramineae).

BEATRIZ GARÓFALO (Gramineae).

ANGEL GONZALEZ (Macroscopic algae).

RUBÉN MONTES (Ecology).

GILBERTO MORILLO (Asclepiadaceae, Apocynaceae; flora of Venezuela).

Specialization in research: Flora of Venezuela (16 volumes have been published, 4 in press).

Associated botanic garden: Jardin Botánico.

Loans: For one year to recognized botanical institutions.

Periodical and serial works: Acta Botanica Venezuelica; Flora of Venezuela.

Exchange: Available: Specimens from Venezuela. Desired: Specimens from Costa Rica, Panama, Colombia, the Guianas, Amazonian Brazil, Venezuela, Trinidad.

CARBONDALE: *The Hepatic Herbarium, The American Bryological and Lichenological Society, Department of Botany, Southern Illinois University,* (**ABSH**), Carbondale, Illinois 62901, **U.S.A.**

Telephone: 618/536-2331.

Status: The Society Hepatic Herbarium.

Foundation: 1902. *Number of specimens:* 29.000.

Herbarium: Hepatophyta and Anthocerotophyta, primarily of the U.S.

Important collections: Mary S. Taylor herbarium (8.000).

Director and Curator: RAYMOND STOTLER, 1940 (Taxonomy, biosystematics, and ecology of bryophytes).

Staff member: BARBARA CRANDALL STOTLER, 1942 (Anatomy and morphogenesis of bryophytes; director of the hepatic exchange).

Specialization in research: Floristics, classification, and developmental morphology of bryophytes.

Loans: Standard regulations.

Periodical and serial works: The Bryologist, published by the Society.

Exchange: Available: Worldwide via the Society Hepatic exchange.

CARBONDALE: *Herbarium, Department of Botany, Southern Illinois University,* (**SIU**), Carbondale, Il-

linois 62901, **U.S.A.**

Telephone: 618/536-2331.

Foundation: 1878 by George Hazel French. *Number of specimens:* 150.000.

Herbarium: Flora of southern Illinois and tropical America; emphasis on Leguminosae, *Solanum,* liverworts.

Important collections: George Hazel French (5.000); herbarium of the American Bryological and Lichenological Society; *Solanum* sect. *Tuberarium.*

Curator: DONALD UGENT, 1933 (Biosystematics; Solanaceae sect. *Tuberarium*).

Staff members: LAWRENCE MATTEN, 1938 (Fossils).

MICHAEL MIBB, 1950 (Forestry).

ROBERT MOHLENBROCK, 1931 (Leguminosae; flora of Illinois).

BARBARA STOTLER, 1942 (Liverworts).

RAYMOND STOTLER, 1940 (Liverworts).

WALTER SUNDBERG, 1939 (Fungi).

Specialization in research: Flora of Illinois; *Solanum;* Leguminosae; liverworts; fungi.

Associated botanic garden: Department of Botany botanical garden.

Loans: To institutions only.

Exchange: Available: Southern Illinois and adjacent states. Wanted: Good collections from any area.

CÁRDENAS: *Herbario, Departamento de Ecología, Colegio Superior de Agricultura Tropical,* (**CSAT**), Apartado postal 24, Cárdenas, Tabasco, **Mexico.**

Telephone: 20460.

Status: Under the Secretary of Agriculture and Hydraulic Resources.

Foundation: 1969. *Number of specimens:* 3.000.

Herbarium: Primarily flora of Tabasco, with adjacent states also represented.

Important collections: R. Almeida (53), A. Beetle (53), J. Cantú (95), C. Cowan (2.000), H. Puig (600).

Director: STEPHEN R. GLIESSMAN, 1946 (Tropical agroecology; allelopathy).

Curator: CLARK P. COWAN, 1951.

Staff member: MIGUEL ALBERTO MAGAÑA A., 1956.

Specialization in research: Flora of Tabasco; weeds of major crops systems of the region; grasses of Tabasco.

Associated botanic garden: Jardín Botánico Colegio Superior de Agricultura Tropical.

Loans: To recognized institutions and individuals.

Exchange: Available: Vascular plants of Tabasco. Wanted: Plants from adjacent states and Tabasco, copies or reprints of relevant literature.

Remarks: Recently reactivated in 1977 after a period of inactivity. Active exchange program and emphasis on establishing a basis for the flora project.

CARDIFF: *Herbarium, British Bryological Society, Department of Botany, National Museum of Wales,* **(BBSUK)**, Cardiff CF1 3NP, Wales, **Great Britain.**
Telephone: 0222-397951.
Status: Society herbarium.
Foundation: 1924. *Number of specimens:* 28.000.
Herbarium: Musci and hepaticae, mainly British Isles.
Important collections: Voucher specimens for national and vice-county or otherwise interesting records, many of them from leading British bryologists.
Curator: S. G. HARRISON, 1924.
Loans: To recognized botanical institutions.
Periodical and serial works: The Journal of Bryology, Bulletin of the British Bryological Society.

CARDIFF: *Herbarium, Department of Botany, National Museum of Wales,* **(NMW)**, Cardiff CF1 3NP, Wales, **Great Britain.**
Telephone: 0222 397951.
Status: A state-supported institution administered under a Royal Charter by an independent Court of Governors.
Foundation: 1912. *Number of specimens:* 253.000.
Herbarium: Worldwide, mainly British and Welsh flora (all groups including cultivated plants).
Important collections: J. E. Griffith, A. R. Horwood, D. A. Jones, H. H. Knight, P. W. Richards, J. H. Salter, W. A. Shoolbred, C. T. & E. Vachell, A. E. Wade, J. H. Wheldon.
Curator: S. G. HARRISON, 1924 (Cultivated and economic plants, Pteridophyta, Coniferae, collectors).
Staff members: R. G. ELLIS, 1942 (Welsh flowering plants, distribution, history of Welsh botany; *Oenothera* in Britain, Flora of Glamorgan).
A. R. PERRY, 1938 (Systematics and geography of fungi, lichens and bryophytes; Flora of Oxfordshire).
Specialization in research: Flora of Wales.
Loans: To recognized institutions and accredited research workers.
Exchange: Available: Specimens from Great Britain (especially Wales). Desired: Specimens (all taxonomic groups) from north temperate zone.
Remarks: Facilities for visiting botanists.

CARDIFF: *Herbarium, Department of Botany, University College,* **(UCSW)**, P.O. Box 78, Cardiff CF1 1XL Wales, **Great Britain.** (Information 1974)
Status: University.
Foundation: 1883. *Number of specimens:* 10.000.
Herbarium: British flora.
Important collections: Herbarium of the late Prof. A. H. Trow, used in compiling his Flora of Glamorgan.
Associated botanic garden: Departmental Experimental Station, Leckwith.

CARMEL VALLEY: *Herbarium, Hastings Natural History Reservation, University of California,* **(CAVA)**, Star Route Box 80, Carmel Valley, California 93924, **U.S.A.**
Foundation: 1937. *Number of specimens:* 4.000.
Herbarium: Flora of the 2000 acre reservation.
Staff member: JAMES R. GRIFFIN (Ecology).

CARROLLTON: *Herbarium, Department of Biology, West Georgia College,* **(WGC)**, Carrollton, Georgia 30118, **U.S.A.**
Telephone: 404/834-1314.
Foundation: 1963. *Number of specimens:* 6.000.
Herbarium: Vascular plants and bryophytes of Georgia and surrounding areas.
Important collections: Robert Lampton.
Curator: DEXTER BYRD.
Specialization in research: Bidens of Georgia.
Loans: To recognized institutions.
Exchange: Yes.

CARSON CITY: *Herbarium, Nevada State Museum,* **(NSMC)**, Capitol Complex, Carson City, Nevada 89710, **U.S.A.**
Telephone: 702/885-4810.
Foundation: 1973. *Number of specimens:* 6.000.
Herbarium: Mainly flora of Nevada.
Curator: ANN PINZL, 1946.
Loans: Can be arranged.
Exchange: Can be arranged.

CALAV: *Herbarium, Městské muzeum Čáslav,* **(CVM)**, Čáslav, **Czechoslovakia.** (Information 1974)
Foundation: 1864. *Number of specimens:* 3.000.
Herbarium: Cryptogams and phanerogams; Czechoslovakia, central and eastern Europe.

CASTELAR: *Herbario, Departamento de Botánica Agrícola, Instituto Nacional de Tecnología Agropecuaria,* **(BAB)**, 1712 Castelar, Buenos Aires, **Argentina.**
Telephone: (54)621-1819; 621-0840.
Status: Unit of the Centro de Investigaciones de Recursos Naturales del Instituto Nacional de Tecnología Agropecuaria (I.N.T.A.).
Foundation: 1899. *Number of specimens:* 500.000.
Herbarium: Plants of South America, especially Argentina.
Important collections: O. Boelcke, E. C. Clos, J. Hunziker, A. Soriano, C. Spegazzini.
Director: VICTOR MILANO, 1921 (Plant introduction).
Curator: MAEVIA N. CORREA, 1914 (Flora Patagónica; Orchidaceae).
Herbarium assistant: ROBERTO GÓMEZ CADRET, 1941.
Staff members: B. AARON DE EILBERG, 1935 (Ecophysiology of weeds).
E. BONAVÍA DE GUTH, 1918 (Quality of wood).
M. A. CAIROLI, 1944 (Physiology of herbicides).

S. Crespo, 1928 (Flora Patagónica; Typhaceae; Labiatae).

M. Elechosa, 1948 (Aromatic plants).

H. Lafourcade, 1931 (Aromatic plants).

M. C. Marcavillaca, 1927 (Tissue culture).

H. Maroder, 1935 (Physiology of herbicides).

L. Mendoza, 1930 (Forestry).

I. Mizrahi, 1931 (Aromatic plants).

A. M. Molina de Riera, 1947 (Taxonomy).

E. Molinari, 1921 (Cultivated plants).

R. L. Pérez-Moreau, 1931 (Flora Patagónica; Boraginaceae; Typhaceae).

I. Prego de Maroder, 1944 (Physiology of herbicides).

A. Ragonese, 1909 (Phytogeography).

M. Rubió de Pol, 1950 (Taxonomy).

Specialization in research: Flora Patagónica; Flora Chaqueña; aromatic plants; Orchidaceae, Labiatae, Boraginaceae.

Associated botanic garden: Hortus Botanicus Castelarensis.

Loans: To recognized botanical institutions.

Periodical and serial works: Serie Fitogeográfica; Flora Patagónica; Notas preliminares para la Flora Chaqueña; Index Seminum; Las Plantas Cultivadas en la República Argentina.

Exchange: Desired: Worldwide.

Remarks: Formerly listed under Buenos Aires.

CASTELAR: *Herbario, Bosques Argentina Investigación, Instituto Forestal Nacional,* (**BAI**), Correo Central 42, 1708 Moron, Castelar, Buenos Aires, **Argentina.**

Telephone: (54)665-3362/0068.

Status: Servicio Forestal.

Foundation: 1948. *Number of specimens:* 1.500.

Herbarium: Mainly Apocynaceae, Anacardiaceae, Bignoniaceae, Lauraceae, Meliaceae, Sapindaceae, Leguminosae, Fagaceae, Rutaceae.

Important collections: J. A. Castiglioni, Carmelich, Devoto, R. Falcone, Buchinger, A. Ragonese, Rial Alberti, Castellanos, E. M. Rodriguez, D. Yacubson, Tortorelli, Yacobi, Mangieri, Táccari, J. R. Ottone, Mutarelli, Valente, Cersósimo, Lugea, A. Burkart.

Director: Julio A. Castiglioni, 1920 (Dendrology).

Curator: Nélida J. Mateo, 1925.

Staff member: Elvira M. Rodriguez (Wood anatomy).

Specialization in research: Forest botany, wood structure.

Exchange: Yes.

Remarks: Formerly listed under Buenos Aires.

CASTELAR: *Herbario, Departamento de Patología Vegetal, Instituto Nacional de Tecnología Agropecuaria,* (**LCF**), Correo Central 25, 1712 Castelar, Buenos Aires, **Argentina.**

Telephone: (54)621-1683; 621-1534.

Status: Department of the Centro Nacional de Investigaciones Agropecuarias, Instituto Nacional de Tecnología Agropecuaria (I.N.T.A.).

Foundation: 1958. *Number of specimens:* 3.212.

Herbarium: Diseases caused mainly by fungi of wild and cultivated plants of Argentina and other countries.

Director: Horacio F. Rizzo, 1932 (Plant pathology).

Staff members: Dora Elsa Barreto, 1944 (Seed pathology).

Alicia Edith de Biasi, 1941 (Virology).

Delia Norma Erbaggi, 1946 (Bacteriology).

Corvalio Fortugno, 1929 (Virology).

Emilia Teresa Rivero, 1945 (Diseases).

María Amalia Rocca de Sarasola, 1919 (Predisposition of plants to diseases; allelopathy).

Lidia Angélica Rossi, 1927 (General plant pathology; bacteriology).

Beatriz Stegman de Gurfinkel, 1939 (Virology).

Specialization in research: Plant pathology, mycology, bacteriology, virology.

Loans: To recognized institutions and individual workers.

Periodical and serial works: Contributions to the Revista de Investigaciones Agropecuarias (RIA).

Remarks: Specimens housed in the División de Fitopatología, Instituto de Sanidad Vegetal, Ministerio de Agricultura y Ganadería, Paseo Colón 922, Buenos Aires until 1958 when transferred to present address.

CASTLEGAR: *Herbarium, Department of Environmental Sciences, Selkirk College,* (**SCCBC**), P.O. Box 1200, Castlegar, British Columbia, **Canada** V1N 3J1.

Telephone: 604/365-7292.

Number of specimens: 5.000.

Herbarium: Mainly flora of British Columbia; includes Notre Dame University (NLSN) collections.

CATANIA: *Istituto di Botanica, Orto Botanico, Università di Catania,* (**CAT**), Via Antonio Longo 19, Catania, Sicilia, **Italy.** (Information 1964)

Status: University.

Foundation: 1858. *Number of specimens:* 15.000 (10.000 herbarium generale, 5.000 herbarium Siculum).

Loans: To recognized botanical institutions.

Periodical and serial works: Bollettino dell'Istituto di Botanica della Università di Catania.

CAYENNE: *Herbier, Centre O.R.S.T.O.M.,* (**CAY**), Route de Montabo, B.P. 165, 97301 Cayenne Cedex, **French Guiana.**

Telephone: 594/31 27 85.

Status: Office de la Recherche Scientifique et Technique Outre-Mer (Gouvernmental Service).

Foundation: 1956. *Number of specimens:* 25.000.

Herbarium: Flora of French Guiana (angiosperms,

ferns, bryophytes).

Important collections: G. Cremers, J. J. de Granville, P. Grenand, R. A. A. Oldeman, R. Bena, J. Hoock, H. Jacquemin, J. P. Lescure, C. Moretti, A. Raynal-Roques, Y. Veyret.

Director: J. J. DE GRANVILLE, 1943 (Forest flora, especially monocotylédons and understory species; phytogeography).

Curator: G. CREMERS, 1936 (Plant architecture; forest inventory).

Staff members: P. GRENAND, 1944 (Ethnobotany of Indian tribes; vernacular names).

H. JACQUEMIN, 1924 (Phytochemistry).

J. P. LESCURE, 1945 (Forest architecture and ecology).

C. MORETTI, 1947 (Phytochemistry).

M. F. PREVOST, 1941 (Forest dynamics and regeneration).

Specialization in research: Forest flora, plant biology, and ecology.

Loans: To recognized botanical institutions; air mail only.

Exchange: Desired: Plants of adjacent countries (northern Brazil, southern Venezuela, Suriname, Guyana).

Remarks: Facilities for visiting botanists if announced in time; no permit required and no restrictions to collect and carry out herbarium specimens from French Guiana.

CEDAR FALLS: *Herbarium, Department of Biology, University of Northern Iowa,* (ISTC), Cedar Falls, Iowa 50613, **U.S.A.**

Telephone: 319/273-2456.

Foundation: 1900. *Number of specimens:* 20.000.

Herbarium: Iowa, Iran, Honduras.

Important collections: Martin L. Grant (Iran).

Curator: LAWRENCE J. EILERS, 1927; 319/273-2218 (Taxonomy and floristics of Iowa vascular plants).

Specialization in research: Vascular plants of Iowa.

Associated botanic garden: Biological Preserve System, University of Northern Iowa.

Loans: To recognized institutions.

Exchange: Iowa and midwestern U.S. plants.

CERNǍUTI: *Botanical Institute of the University,* (CERN), Cernǎuti (Czernowitz), Bessarabia, **U.S.S.R.** (Information 1974)

Herbarium: Bucovina, Boraginaceae.

Important collections: F. Herbich, P. Gusuleac.

ČESKÉ BUDĚJOVICE: *Herbarium, Jihočeské Muzeum,* (CB), Dukelská 1, 37000 České Budějovice, **Czechoslovakia.**

Telephone: 37461, ext. 26 or 27.

Status: Regional museum.

Foundation: 1961. *Number of specimens:* 50.000 (44.800 vascular plants, 3.200 bryophytes, 2.000 fungi).

Herbarium: Plants of South Bohemia.

Important collections: Z. Kluzák (fungi), M. Rivola (bryophytes), D. Blažková, A. Čábera, S. Kučera, J. Vaněček, A. Veselý (vascular plants).

Director: ZDENĚK KLUZÁK, 1926 (Boletaceae).

Curator: MIROSLAV VANSA, 1952 (Vascular plants).

Specialization in research: Regional flora.

Periodical and serial works: Sborník Jihočeského muzea v. Českých Budějovicích-Přírodní vědy.

CHACRAS DE CORIA: *Herbario, Facultad de Ciencias Agrarias, Universidad Nacional de Cuyo,* (MEN), Almirante Brown 500, Luján de Cuyo, 5505 Chacras de Coria, Mendoza, **Argentina.**

Telephone: (54)960004; 960396; 960469.

Foundation: 1940. *Number of specimens:* 3.500.

Director: CARLOS CHERUBINI, 1921.

Staff member: SUSANA LUISA ARNO, 1942.

Specialization in research: Morphology and systematics of spermatophytes.

Remarks: Formerly listed under Mendoza.

CHADRON: *Herbarium, Department of Biology, Chadron State College,* (CSCN), Science Building, Chadron, Nebraska 69337, **U.S.A.**

Telephone: 308/432-9955; 432-6385.

Foundation: 1911. *Number of specimens:* 14.467.

Herbarium: Flora of western Nebraska and the central Great Plains.

Important collections: Bidens of North America.

Director and Curator: RONALD R. WEEDON, 1939 (*Bidens*; flora of the central Great Plains).

Specialization in research: Vegetation and flora of the Pine Ridge of northwestern Nebraska and adjacent environs; flora of the central Great Plains; taxonomy and distribution of *Bidens* (Asteraceae) and *Triodanis* (Campanulaceae).

Loans: No special restrictions.

Exchange: Available: Central Great Plains. Desired: Material from anywhere, especially from the prairies and plains of central North America or thᵣ Intermountain Region; *Bidens.*

CHALK RIVER: *Herbarium, Petawawa National Forestry Institute, Canadian Forestry Service, Environment Canada,* (PFES), Chalk River, Ontario, **Canada** KOJ 1JO.

Telephone: 613/589-2880.

Status: Federal government.

Foundation: 1921. *Number of specimens:* 8.200, including 1.200 bryophytes, lichens, and mosses.

Herbarium: Native and foreign trees; county wide forest flora; OTF herbarium of 5.200 specimens is housed here.

Director: R. M. NEWNHAM.

Curator: M. L. ANDERSON.

Specialization in research: Local forest flora.

Loans: To recognized botanical institutions.

Exchange: Canadian flora.

CHAMICAL: *Herbario de la Sub-estación Experimental Agropecuaria La Rioja, Instituto Nacional de Tecnologia Agropecuaria,* (**CHAM**), Casilla de Correo 6, 5380 Chamical, La Rioja, **Argentina.**

Status: Estación Experimental Agropecuaria San Luis del Instituto Nacional de Tecnologia Agropecuaria.

Foundation: 1978. *Number of specimens:* 1.100.

Herbarium: Regional vascular plants, especially Provincia de La Rioja, región de Los Llanos.

Important collections: Eduardo Aguirre, Fernando Biurrun, Salvador Rosas, Pedro Namur, Graciela Fernandez, Roberto Gonzalez, Felipe Salinas.

   Director: FERNANDO BIURRUN (Phytoecology).

   Curator: EDUARDO AGUIRRE (Malvaceae, Leguminosae).

   Staff members: GRACIELA FERNANDEZ.

   CARLOS SOTO.

Specialization in research: Arid zone plants; preparation of field keys; species lists by habitat.

Loans: Yes.

Exchange: Especially arid and semiarid zone specimens.

CHAMICAL: *Herbario, Instituto de Zonas Aridas, Universidad Provincial de La Rioja,* (**IZAC**), San Martin 250, 5380 Chamical, La Rioja, **Argentina.**

Foundation: 1976. *Number of specimens:* 5.500.

Herbarium: Regional vascular plants.

Important collections: Fernando N. Biurrun.

   Director: ELIZABETH PAGLIARI.

   Curator: RAÚL CORZO, 1954 (Cactaceae, Leguminosae).

   Staff member: FRANCISCO FERREYRA, 1955.

   Collaborators: CARMEN AGUERO.

   EDUARDO AGUIRRE.

   JUAN NIEVAS.

   AMERICO OYOLA.

Exchange: Available: Specimens from arid and semi-arid areas.

CHANDIGARH: *Herbarium, Department of Botany, Panjab University,* (**PAN**), Sector-14, Chandigarh, PIN-160014, **India.**

Telephone: 22960.

Status: University.

Foundation: 1947. *Number of specimens:* 35.000.

Herbarium: All groups, especially fungi, ferns and fern allies of Northwestern and Eastern Himalayas, mosses, grasses, orchids and trees of Himalayas.

   Director: H. S. SOHI, 1930 (Mycology and plant pathology).

   Curator: M. P. SHARMA (Mycology, taxonomy).

   Staff members: R. K. BHANWRA (Embryology).

   H. K. CHEEMA (Tissue culture).

   S. P. CHODA (Embryology).

   K. K. DHIR (Pteridology, physiology).

   P. S. KAUSHAL (Radiation botany).

   S. C. KAUSHAL (Mycology).

   S. P. KHULLAR (Cytology).

   S. S. KUMAR (Bryology).

   D. S. LOYAL (Morphogenesis).

   C. L. MANDHAR (Plant pathology).

   K. K. NANDA (Plant physiology).

   A. M. NARULA (Mycology, gymnosperms).

   R. S. PATHANIA (Gymnosperms).

   G. S. RAWLA (Mycology, plant pathology).

   T. S. SAREEN (Forest genetics).

   B. R. SHARMA (Horticulture, Angiosperms).

   M. L. SHARMA (Cytology).

   K. S. THIND (Mycology, plant pathology).

   S. C. VERMA (Cytogenetics).

   S. P. VIJ (Orchidaceae).

Specialization in research: Mycology and plant pathology, physiology, cytogenetics, Pteridophytes.

Associated botanic garden: Botanic Garden of Panjab University.

Loans: With permission of director for a period of 90 days; type specimens loaned for 30 days.

Exchange: May be arranged with permission of director.

CHAPEL HILL: *Herbarium, Department of Botany, The University of North Carolina,* (**NCU**), Coker Hall 010A, Chapel Hill, North Carolina 27514, **U.S.A.**

Telephone: 919/933-6931.

Foundation: 1903. *Number of specimens:* 561.005.

Herbarium: Vascular plants of southeastern U.S.; flora of Carolinas; marine algae; bryophytes of North Carolina and southeastern U.S.; fungi (*Septobasidium, Coelomomyces,* Actinoplanaceae).

Important collections: W. W. Ashe (vascular plants); W. C. Coker and J. N. Couch (fungi); southeastern U.S. by physiographic province and Carolinas by county.

   Director: ALBERT E. RADFORD, 1918 (Flora of the Carolinas).

   Administrator and Curator: JIMMY R. MASSEY, 1940 (Vascular plants).

   Staff members: WILLIAM C. DICKISON, Curator of Wood Collections, 1941.

   PATRICIA GENSEL, Curator of Fossil Plants and Pollen Reference Slides, 1944.

   MAX HOMMERSAND, Curator of Algae, 1930.

   LINDSAY OLIVE, Curator of Fungi, 1917.

Specialization in research: Flora of southeastern U.S.; Sphagnums of North Carolina; sub-fossil moss assemblages; wood anatomy of Dilleniales and related groups; taxonomic and phytogeographic relationships of marine algae of California, Pacific, Mexico, and Japan; systematic and phytogenetic studies of the Mycelozoa; natural areas and threatened and endangered species of the Southeast.

Associated botanic garden: North Carolina Botanical Garden.

Loans: To recognized institutions.

Periodical and serial works: Journal of Elisha Mitchell Scientific Society.

Exchange: Southeastern U.S. material.

CHAPINGO: *Herbario, Departamento de Bosques, Universidad Autónoma Chapingo,* (**CHAP**), Apartado postal 37, Chapingo, México, **Mexico.**
Telephone: 5-85-45-55, ext. 5342.
Foundation: 1965. *Number of specimens:* 3.250.
Herbarium: Mainly woody plants of Mexico, with emphasis on species of economic importance.
Important collections: T. D. Pennington and J. Sarukhán.
> *Director:* ENRIQUE GUÍZAR NOLAZCO, 1954.
> *Curator:* FERNANDO ZAVALA CHÁVEZ, 1953.
> *Staff members:* EMMA ESTRADA MARTÍNEZ, 1950.
>> FRANCISCO RAMOS MARCHENA, 1925 (Identification).
> *Specialization in research:* Floristics and ecology of México.
> *Loans:* To recognized botanical institutions.
> *Exchange:* Available and Wanted: Woody plants of Mexico.

CHAPINGO: *Herbario-Hortorio, Rama de Botánica, Colegio de Postgraduados,* (**CHAPA**), Chapingo, México, **Mexico.**
Telephone: 5/585-45-55.
Status: Colegio de Postgraduados, Escuela Nacional de Agricultura.
Foundation: 1973. *Number of specimens:* 30.000.
Herbarium: Plants of Mexico and adjacent areas.
Important collections: Efraím Hernández Xolocotzi.
> *Director and Curator:* STEPHEN D. KOCH, 1940 (Gramineae).
> *Staff members:* JOSÉ D. GARCÍA PÉREZ, 1945 (Compositae of Mexico).
>> THOMAS L. WENDT, 1950 (Trees of Mexico; Polygalaceae).
> *Specialization in research:* Flora of Mexico, with special emphasis on the Gramineae, trees, and other economically important groups.
> *Loans:* No special restrictions.
> *Periodical and serial works:* Agrociencia.
> *Exchange:* Available: Plants of Mexico. Desired: Plants of tropical regions of the world, especially trees; Gramineae of the world.

CHARDJOW: *Herbarium of the Repetek Sandy Desert Reserve, Desert Institute of the Turkmen Academy of Sciences,* (**RSDR**), Chardjow Region, Turkmen S.S.R., 746060 **U.S.S.R.**
Telephone: 44-70.
Status: Subdivision of Desert Institute of the Turkmen Academy of Sciences in Ashkhabad.
Foundation: 1912. *Number of specimens:* 684.
Herbarium: Plants of Karakum Desert and western U.S.A.
Important collections: E. B. Bartram, D. Demaree, W. W. Eggleston, J. Ewan, M. E. Jones, T. H. Kearney, D. T. MacDougal, E. J. Palmer, C. A. Purpus, I. L. Wiggins.

CHARKOW: *Herbarium of the Ukrainian Institute for Scientific Research of Socialist Agriculture,* (**CW**), Chajkovskaja 4, Charkow, Ukraine, **U.S.S.R.** (Information 1974)
Number of specimens: 800.000.
Herbarium: Worldwide.
Important collections: Herbarium Turczaninov.

CHARKOW: *Charkowskij Botanitscheskij Sad,* (**CWB**), Klotschkowskaja 52, Charkow, **U.S.S.R.**

CHARKOW: *University Herbarium,* (**CWU**), Charkow, **U.S.S.R.**

CHARLESTON: *Herbarium, The Charleston Museum,* (**CHARL**), 360 Meeting Street, Charleston, South Carolina 29403, **U.S.A.**
Telephone: 803/722-2996.
Status: Independent public museum.
Foundation: 1773. *Number of specimens:* 25.000.
Herbarium: South Carolina, especially Charleston area.
Important collections: Herbaria of Stephen Elliott, Henry W. Ravenel, Lewis Gibbes, Cranmore Wallace, Kenneth Hunt, Francis Porcher.
> *Director:* DONALD G. HEROLD.
> *Curator:* ALBERT E. SANDERS.
> *Staff member:* JANET PEARLMAN.
> *Specialization in research:* Botanical survey of South Carolina, especially the Lower Coastal Plain.
> *Loans:* For 6 months, renewable upon request; Elliott herbarium no longer sent on loan but available for on-site study.
> *Exchange:* Yes.

CHARLESTON: *Forest Service Herbarium, Southeastern Forest Experiment Station, Forestry Sciences Laboratory,* (**CHAS**), 2730 Savannah Highway, Charleston, South Carolina 29407, **U.S.A.**
Telephone: 803/556-4860.
Status: U.S. Department of Agriculture, Forest Service.
Foundation: 1951. *Number of specimens:* 1.000.
Herbarium: Mainly trees, forbs, and shrubs of the Francis Marion National Forest.
Important collections: E. L. Little, Jr. (*Quercus*), D. S. Priester (*Nyssa*).
> *Curator:* DAVID S. PRIESTER, 1943.
> *Specialization in research:* Regeneration of wetland hardwoods in the Southeastern Coastal Plain.
> *Loans:* To recognized botanical institutions.
> *Exchange:* Available: Specimens from the Francis Marion National Forest, South Carolina. Desired: Asian varieties of *Nyssa*.

CHARLESTON: *Herbarium, Biology Department, The Citadel,* (**CITA**), Charleston, South Carolina 29409, **U.S.A.**
Telephone: 803/792-7877.
Foundation: 1970. *Number of specimens:* 7.000.

Herbarium: Regional herbarium with emphasis on vascular plants of South Carolina Coastal Plain; endangered and threatened vascular plants of South Carolina Coastal Plain.

Director and Curator: RICHARD D. PORCHER, 1939 (Plant taxonomy; plant ecology).

Loans: No special restrictions.

CHARLESTON: *Stover Herbarium, Botany Department, Eastern Illinois University,* **(EIU),** Charleston, Illinois 61920, **U.S.A.**

Telephone: 217/581-3525.

Foundation: 1961. *Number of specimens:* 40.000.

Herbarium: Flora of central Illinois.

Director: TERRY WEIDNER (Plant physiologist).

Curator: JOHN E. EBINGER, 1933 (Flora of central Illinois).

Loans: No restrictions; to any recognized botanical institution.

Exchange: Available: Central Illinois. Desired: Material from eastern U.S.

CHARLESTON: *Herbarium, Department of Natural Sciences, Morris Harvey College of Arts and Sciences, University of Charleston,* **(MVC),** 2300 MacCorkle Avenue S.E., Charleston, West Virginia 25304, **U.S.A.**

Telephone: 304/346-9471, ext. 235, 262.

Foundation: 1888. *Number of specimens:* 3.990.

Herbarium: Mainly West Virginia, some shale barren and bog species.

Important collections: Fred Coffindaffer (Tennessee, West Virginia), Margaret Denison, C. J. Harris (algae; 1875–1880).

Director: ROBERT G. NUNLEY (Aquatic plants; algae).

Curator: MEREWYN D. MEADORS (Dendrology).

Staff members: CARL T. MEADORS (Entomology; plant galls).

PATRICIA SHEETS.

GLENN E. SMITH (Higher fungi; diseases of plants).

Specialization in research: Anatomical comparisons of Betulaceae; horned oak gall.

Loans: To recognized botanical institutions.

Exchange: Desired: Woody plants, including horticultural varieties.

CHARLOTTE: *Herbarium, Department of Biology, University of North Carolina,* **(UNCC),** Charlotte, North Carolina 28223, **U.S.A.**

Telephone: 704/597-2315.

Foundation: 1966. *Number of specimens:* 15.000.

Herbarium: Floristics of Mecklenburg County and the two Carolinas.

Director: JAMES F. MATTHEWS, 1935 (Floristics, endangered and threatened species).

Curator: T. LAWRENCE MELLICHAMP, 1948 (Vascular plant systematics).

Specialization in research: Floristics and species biology.

Associated botanic garden: Van Landingham Glen, University of North Carolina at Charlotte.

Loans: Upon arrangement.

Exchange: Limited.

Remarks: Herbarium is computerized with search capability on geographic, collectors, dates, and taxonomic levels.

CHARLOTTESVILLE: *University of Virginia Herbarium,* **(VA),** Charlottesville, Virginia 22904, **U.S.A.**

Foundation: 1923. *Number of specimens:* 3.000.

Remarks: This herbarium was transferred to Mountain Lake Biological Station at Pembroke, Virginia 24136 several years ago.

CHARLOTTETOWN: *Laboratory of Plant Pathology,* **(PEI),** P.O. Box 220, Charlottetown, Prince Edward Island, **Canada.**

Number of sheets: 600.

Remarks: Original herbarium destroyed by fire in 1951.

CHARLOTTETOWN: *Herbarium, Biology Department, University of Prince Edward Island,* **(UPEI),** Charlottetown, Prince Edward Island, **Canada** C1A 4P3.

Telephone: 902/892-4121, loc. 168.

Foundation: 1969. *Number of specimens:* 2.000.

Herbarium: Local collections.

Director: I. G. MACQUARRIE, 1933 (Ecology).

Staff member: L. A. HANIC, 1930 (Algology).

CHATTANOOGA: *Herbarium, Department of Biology, University of Tennessee,* **(UCHT),** Chattanooga, Tennessee 37402, **U.S.A.**

Telephone: 615/755-4341.

Foundation: 1886. *Number of specimens:* 7.000.

Herbarium: Mainly southeastern Tennessee and northern Georgia.

Director and Curator: GENE S. VAN HORN, 1940 (Floristics; Asteraceae, Ranunculaceae).

Specialization in research: Floristics of southeastern U.S.

Loans: Various conditions can be arranged; prefer 6 month terms.

Exchange: Available: Tennessee and northern Georgia. Desired: Practically any vascular plant material.

CHEB: *Herbarium, Oblastní vlastivědné muzeum,* **(CHEB),** Náměstí krále Jiřího z Poděbrad č. 3, Cheb, **Czechoslovakia.** (Information 1974)

Number of specimens: 7.000.

Herbarium: Tracheophyta and cryptogams of western Bohemia.

Loans: To recognized botanical institutions.

CHENGDU: *Herbarium, Department of Biology, National Sichuan University,* **(SZ),** Chengdu, Sichuan, **People's Republic of China.** (Information 1964)

Status: University.
Foundation: 1935. *Number of specimens:* 35.000.
Herbarium: Worldwide herbarium, mainly phanerogams of Sichuan and Sikang provinces.
Associated botanic garden: Botanic Garden of the University.
Periodical and serial works: Icones Plantarum Omeiensium.

CHENGDU: *Herbarium, West China University,* **(WCU),** Chengdu, Sichuan, **People's Republic of China.**

CHERBOURG: *Herbarium, Société Nationale des Sciences Naturelles et Mathématiques,* **(CHE),** 21 Rue Bonhomme, 50100 Cherbourg, **France.**
Telephone: 16 (33) 532806.
Status: Société nationale.
Foundation: 1851. *Number of specimens:* 30.000.
Herbarium: Vascular plants, algae, lichens, mosses, hepatics, fungi.
Important collections: Herb. A. F. Le Jolis (Algae in bound volumes), herb. L. Corbière (lichens, mosses, hepatics, fungi).
Director: M. DURCHON, Professeur d'Université (Lille), 82 Rue Colbert S. 13, 59000 Lille.
Assistant Director: M. ANCELLIN, Veterinary surgeon, 4 Impasse Balmont, Rue de la Duché, 50100 Cherbourg.
Président: M. P. GERMAIN, 9 Rue de Lorraine, 50100 Cherbourg.
Staff members: No special staff for the herbarium. Connections with Museum National d'Histoire Naturelle de Paris.
Periodical and serial works: Mémoires.
Remarks: Very old herbarium, partly deteriorated. The Society possesses a library with 80.000 volumes.

CHERNOVZY: *Herbarium, Department of Botany, Chernovzy University,* **(CHER),** Fedkovicha St. 11, 274022 Chernovzy, **U.S.S.R.**
Status: University.
Foundation: 1918. *Number of specimens:* 150.000.
Director: L. S. SERPOKRYLOVA.

CHIAPAS: *Instituto Botánico de Chiapas,* **(CHIP)** – – *see* TUXTLA GUTIÉRREZ.

CHICAGO: *Herbarium, Department of Biological Sciences, University of Illinois at Chicago Circle,* **(CHI),** Box 4348, Chicago, Illinois 60680, **U.S.A.**
Telephone: 312/966-2993.
Foundation: 1955. *Number of specimens:* 25.000.
Herbarium: Flora of Chicago region; emphasis on Gramineae and Palmae.
Important collections: S. F. Glassman (Chicago region grass collections during 1950's; Cocosoid palms from Brazil); types of *Syagrus* and *Butia;* Bro. Leon (*Copernicia* types from Cuba in 1930's).

Director and Curator: SIDNEY F. GLASSMAN, 1919 (Cocosoid palms; systematics).
Staff members: STEVEN WELLER, 1950 (Breeding systems and population studies).
GEORGE WILDER, 1948 (Developmental anatomy of Cyclanthaceae).
Specialization in research: Systematics of Palmae; leaf anatomy of Cocosoid palms.
Loans: No restrictions.
Exchange: Available: Vascular plants of Chicago region.

CHICAGO: *John G. Searle Herbarium, Field Museum of Natural History,* **(F),** Roosevelt Road at Lake Shore Drive, Chicago, Illinois 60605, **U.S.A.**
Telephone: 312/922-9410.
Status: Private institution.
Foundation: 1893. *Number of specimens:* 2.358.300.
Herbarium: Cryptogamic herbarium worldwide; phanerogamic herbarium worldwide with emphasis on tropical America and North America, especially rich in collections from Guatemala, Honduras, Costa Rica, Colombia, Ecuador, and Peru.
Important collections: About 50.000 photographs of types of South and Central America taken prior to World War II at the larger European institutions; P. C. Standley (Central America), J. Steyermark (Missouri, Guatemala, Venezuela, Ecuador), J. Cuatrecasas (Colombia), F. Solis (Ecuador), R. Spruce (Peru, Brazil, Ecuador), J. F. Macbride (Peru), Ll. Williams (Peru), L. O. Williams (Central America); duplicates from the de Candolle-Delessert herbaria.
Director: LORIN I. NEVLING, JR., 1930 (Flora of Veracruz; systematics of American Thymelaeaceae).
Chairman, Department of Botany: WILLIAM C. BURGER, 1932 (Flora of Costa Rica; *Ficus;* Piperaceae; angiosperm phylogeny).
Staff members: MICHAEL O. DILLON, 1947 (Flora of Peru; Compositae).
JOHN J. ENGEL, 1941 (Austral and Tasmanian Hepaticae).
SYLVIA M. FEUER, 1950 (Palynology and ultrastructure of Santalales).
WILLIAM E. GRIMÉ, 1940 (Ethnobotany).
MICHAEL NEE, 1947 (Solanaceae; New World Tropics).
CHRISTINE J. NIEZGODA, 1950 (Palynology; Mimosoid legumes; Myoporaceae).
TIMOTHY C. PLOWMAN, 1944 (Flora of Peru; systematics of *Brunfelsia* and Erythroxylaceae; ethnobotany).
PATRICIO P. PONCE DE LEÓN, 1915 (Gasteromycetes).
ROBERT G. STOLZE, 1927 (Neotropical ferns; ferns of Guatemala).
Research associates: ROBERT F. BETZ.
MARGERY CARLSON.
ROBIN FOSTER.
SIDNEY GLASSMAN.

61

ROLF SINGER.

D. DOEL SOEJARTO.

Specialization in research: Neotropics; North America and western South America.

Loans: To recognized botanical institutions.

Periodical and serial works: Fieldiana, Botany; Field Museum Publications in Botany; Publications of the Field Columbian Museum, Botanical Series. These are considered to be a continuing series with Fieldiana, Botany being the title currently used.

Exchange: Available: Tropical American material. Desired: Vascular plants of the tropics, especially neotropics; non-vascular plants on a worldwide basis.

CHICKASHA: *Herbarium, Department of Mathematics and Natural Science, University of Science & Arts of Oklahoma,* **(OCLA),** 17th Street and Grand Avenue, Chickasha, Oklahoma 73018, **U.S.A.**

Telephone: 405/224-3140.

Foundation: 1971. *Number of specimens:* 6.000.

Herbarium: Emphasis on local collections, North American Orchidaceae, and rare plants from Oklahoma.

Important collections: Orchidaceae of the central plains region of North America.

Director: LAWRENCE K. MAGRATH, 1943 (Orchidaceae).

Specialization in research: North American Orchidaceae (central plains region) distribution, ecology, and systematics.

Loans: No restrictions to qualified investigators.

Exchange: Available: Vascular plants of Oklahoma and adjacent areas (including some Orchidaceae). Desired: Any Orchidaceae, general vascular plants from North or Central America.

CHICO: *Herbarium, Department of Biological Sciences, California State University,* **(CHSC),** Chico, California 95929, **U.S.A.**

Telephone: 916/895-5381.

Foundation: 1930's. *Number of specimens:* 29.000.

Herbarium: Vascular plants and myxomycete flora, primarily of northern California.

Director and Curator: KINGSLEY R. STERN, 1927 (*Dicentra*).

Staff members: ROBERT I. EDIGER, 1937 (Senecioneae).

DONALD T. KOWALSKI, 1938 (Myxomycetes of the world).

ROBERT A. SCHLISING, 1937 (*Calystegia*).

Specialization in research: Fumariaceae, Convolvulaceae; flora of northern California; Myxomycetes; Senecioneae; rare and endangered species of California.

Loans: For six months, to institutions.

Exchange: Available: Limited material of northern California.

Remarks: Herbarium includes seed collection;

some seeds available for exchange.

CHIHUAHUA: *Herbario, Rancho Experimental La Campana, Instituto Nacional de Pecuarias,* **(RELC),** Apartado postal 682, Chihuahua, Chihuahua, **Mexico.**

Telephone: 141/2-56-55.

Foundation: 1973. *Number of specimens:* 4.100.

Herbarium: Flora of the state of Chihuahua, especially grasses.

Director: LUIS CARLOS FIERRO, 1951 (Range management).

Curator: ALICIA MELGOZA, 1956.

Specialization in research: Range management.

Loans: No.

Periodical and serial works: Pastizales (Bulletin).

Exchange: Yes.

CHILANGA: *Herbarium, Mount Makulu Research Station,* **(MRSC),** P/Bag 7, Chilanga, **Zambia.**

Telephone: Chilanga 312.

Status: Central agricultural research station.

Number of specimens: 20.000.

Herbarium: Emphasis on grasses, legumes and weeds.

Staff member: R. VERNON (agricultural weeds of Zambia).

Remarks: The herbarium is in a poor state, reflecting the low priority given it by Government.

CHOMUTOV: *Vlastivědné muzeum Chomutov,* **(CHOM),** Náměsti 1. máje 1, Chomutov, **Czechoslovakia.** (Information 1974)

Number of specimens: 5.000.

Herbarium: Regional Cormophyta.

Specialization in research: Regional botany.

Loans: To recognized botanical institutions.

CHRISTCHURCH: *Canterbury Museum,* **(CANTY)** – incorporated in CHR.

CHRISTCHURCH: *Herbarium, Botany Department, University of Christchurch,* **(CANU),** Private Bag, Christchurch, **New Zealand.**

Telephone: 482009, ext. 515.

Status: University.

Foundation: 1958. *Number of specimens:* 35.000.

Herbarium: Algae, bryophytes, endemic and introduced flora of New Zealand.

Important collections: Laing Algal Herbarium.

Director: JOSEPHINE WARD HAMMOND, 1939; 482009, ext. 537 (Compositae).

Staff member: MARY C. BARKER, 1927.

Specialization in research: Arthurs Pass Flora, algae of Ellesmere, revision of *Raoulia*, intergeneric relationships in Gnaphalionae.

Loans: With permission of director.

CHRISTCHURCH: *J. B. Armstrong Herbarium, Christchurch Botanic Gardens,* **(CHBG),** Parks and

Recreation Department, Christchurch City Council, P.O. Box 237, Christchurch, **New Zealand.**
Telephone: 61-701.
Foundation: 1863. *Number of specimens:* 2.500.
Herbarium: New Zealand flowering plants, ferns, mosses, lichens and algae.
Important collections: J. B. Armstrong, J. F. Armstrong.
    Director: N. W. DRAIN, 1932 (Ornamental horticulture).
    Curator: A. G. JOLLIFFE, 1950 (Ornamental horticulture, education).

CHRISTCHURCH: *Botany Division, Department of Scientific and Industrial Research,* **(CHR)**, Private Bag, Christchurch, **New Zealand.**
Telephone: (3)22-8019.
Status: Government department.
Foundation: 1928. *Number of specimens:* 320.000.
Herbarium: Worldwide especially New Zealand region and tropical Pacific flora; all groups except fungi.
Important collections: H. H. Allan, K. W. Allison, T. W. N. Beckett, H. Carse, A. J. Healy, R. Mason, L. B. Moore, G. Simpson.
    Director: H. E. CONNOR, 1922 (Taxonomy and reproductive systems of grasses).
    Curator: D. R. GIVEN, 1943 (Taxonomy of Pteridophyta, Compositae and naturalized Rosaceae, studies of subantarctic floras).
    Assistant Curator: B. H. MACMILLAN, 1933.
    Staff members: U. V. CASSIE, 1926 (Taxonomy of N.Z. fresh water algae.
    E. EDGAR, 1929 (Taxonomy of monocotyledonous flora of N.Z. especially Juncaceae, Cyperaceae, Gramineae).
    D. J. GALLOWAY, 1942 (Taxonomy of N.Z. lichens).
    P. J. GARNOCK-JONES, 1950 (Taxonomy of N.Z. Brassicaceae).
    E. J. GODLEY, 1919 (Flower biology of N.Z. plants, subantarctic floras).
    M. J. PARSONS, 1941 (Taxonomy of N.Z. marine algae).
    W. R. SYKES, 1927 (Taxonomy of N.Z. cultivated and naturalized plants, studies of Pacific Island floras).
    C. J. WEBB, 1949 (Reproductive biology of N.Z. plants, taxonomy of Umbelliferae and Leguminosae).
Specialization in research: Indigenous, naturalized and cultivated flora of the New Zealand botanical region.
Associated botanic garden: Divisional garden of 9.25 hectares.
Loans: To recognized botanical or academic institutions, normally short term.
Periodical and serial works: Triennial Report.
Exchange: Available: Indigenous, naturalized and cultivated New Zealand specimens. Desired: Specimens of all groups of temperate and subtropical regions and tropical Pacific.

CHUR: *Herbarium, Bündner Natur-Museum,* **(CHUR)**, Masanserstrasse 31, 7000 Chur, **Switzerland.**
Telephone: 081 22 15 58.
Status: Directed by Kanton Graubünden.
Foundation: 1929.
Herbarium: Rhaetic Alps.
Important collections: Favre (Swiss National Park, fungi).
    Director: JUERG MUELLER, 1945 (Ecology).
    Curator: PAUL MUELLER, 1906 (Seed dispersal, floristics).
    Specialization in research: Flora Rhaetica.
    Associated botanic garden: Alpengarten Alp Grüm.
    Loans: Yes.
    Periodical and serial works: Jahresberichte der Naturforschenden Gesellschaft Graubünden.
    Exchange: Not possible.

CINCINNATI: *Herbarium, Department of Biological Sciences, University of Cincinnati,* **(CINC)**, Cincinnati, Ohio 45221, **U.S.A.**
Telephone: 513/475-3741.
Foundation: ca. 1925. *Number of specimens:* 125.000.
Herbarium: Vascular plants, especially from the Cincinnati region; bryophytes and lichens more general.
Important collections: Curtis Gates Lloyd, E. Lucy Braun, Margaret Fulford, Jerry A. Snider, Janice Beatley, Howard A. Crum, Dale H. Vitt, Ann E. Rushing, Theodore Esslinger.
    Director and Curator: JERRY A. SNIDER, 1937 (Bryophytes).
    Specialization in research: Cytology and taxonomy of bryophytes.
    Loans: To recognized botanical institutions.
    Remarks: The Curtis Gates Lloyd collection of phanerogams is on permanent loan from LLO; since fall 1978, duplicate specimens of all materials placed on the American Bryological and Lichenological Society's moss exchange have been deposited at CINC.

CINCINNATI: *Lloyd Library and Museum,* **(LLO)**, 309 West Court Street, Cincinnati, Ohio 45221, **U.S.A.**
Status: Private institution founded by John Uri Lloyd, Curtis Gates Lloyd, and Nelson Ashley Lloyd (brothers).
Foundation: 1864. *Number of specimens:* Phanerogams: 29.000; fungi: 59.000, see below.
Herbarium: Worldwide; the phanerogamic collection (collected by C. G. Lloyd) is on loan at CINC; the collection of fungi is on loan at BPI.
    Staff member: JOHN GRIGGS, Librarian.
    Associated botanic garden: Lloyd Arboretum, Crittenden, Kentucky.

63

Periodical and serial works: Lloydia, a quarterly journal of biological science; formerly: Bulletins, Mycological Writings, Bibliographical Contributions, and Pharmacy Reprints.

Remarks: Book collection on botany, pharmacy, eclectic medicine, natural sciences and allied biological sciences, 150.000 volumes and about 100.000 pamphlets, 4.000 periodical titles.

CINCO SALTOS: *Herbario, Facultad de Ciencias Agrarias, Universidad Nacional del Comahue,* **(ARC),** Cátedra de Botánica, Casilla de Correo 60, 8303 Cinco Saltos, Río Negro, **Argentina.**
Telephone: (54)0943/8204; 8005.
Foundation: 1979. *Number of specimens:* 500.
Herbarium: Vascular plants of southern Argentina.
Director: LUISA A. CONTICELLO, 1947 (Gramineae).
Curator: LILIANA A. DE DONNARI, 1950; 0943/5780 (Malvaceae).
Staff members: MIRTA M. DE CUCULICH (Anatomy, morphology).

LUIS GARCÍA, 1950 (Cactaceae).

CARLOS E. PÉREZ, 1948 (Coniferae).

Specialization in research: Study of the regional vegetation.
Loans: Usual regulations.
Exchange: Available and Desired: Specimens, especially weeds, from southern Argentina.

CLAREMONT: *Herbaria of Rancho Santa Ana Botanic Garden* **(RSA)** *and Pomona College* **(POM),** *Rancho Santa Ana Botanic Garden,* 1500 N. College Avenue, Claremont, California 91711, **U.S.A.**
Telephone: 714/626-3922.
Status: Private foundation (RSA); privately endowed liberal arts college (POM).
Foundation: 1927 (RSA); 1864 (POM). *Number of specimens:* 281.000 (RSA); 325.000 (POM); total 606.000 sheets and packets and 100.000 ancillary collections (wood blocks, pollen, and wood anatomy slides).
Herbarium: Flora of California, but emphasis also on western U.S., Mexico, Pacific Basin, islands of world, and groups of phyletic and phytogeographic significance; *Astragalus, Ranunculus;* Cactaceae, Onagraceae.
Important collections: POM: M. E. Jones (Great Basin, western North America; *Astragalus*), C. F. Baker (Central America, Cuba, western North America), P. A. Munz (California, New York; Onagraceae; *Delphinium*), L. Benson (North American *Ranunculus* and Cactaceae), F. R. Fosberg (Pacific, Ceylon, world). RSA: R. F. Thorne (California, midwestern and southeastern U.S., Mexico, Australasia; aquatics), P. A. Munz (California, New York; Onagraceae; *Delphinium*), C. B. Wolf (California; *Rhamnus* and *Cupressus* of North America), R. C. Barneby (*Astragalus* of North America), F. W. Peirson (California), S. Carlquist (California, Australasia, Pacific.

South Africa, Malaya, Macaronesia; Stylidiaceae, Goodeniaceae, Asteraceae, Bruniineae, Penaeaceae), V. and A. Grant (Polemoniaceae), P. H. Raven (Onagraceae; California), L. Lenz (*Iris, Brodiaea-Tritelea* complex), J. Henrickson (*Fouquieria;* Mexico), R. K. Benjamin (Laboulbeniales, Mucorales).
Director: RSA: LEE W. LENZ, 1915 (Cytology; taxonomy of *Iris, Brodiaea* complex).

POM: WALTER BERTSCH, 1934; 714/621-8000 (Plant physiology; Orchidaceae).
Curator: ROBERT F. THORNE, 1920 (Angiosperm phylogeny and geography; aquatic angiosperms; floristics).
Staff members: RICHARD K. BENJAMIN, 1922 (Mycology; Laboulbeniales, Mucorales).

LYMAN BENSON, 1909 (*Ranunculus, Pleuropogon, Prosopis;* Cactaceae; natural floras of North America; desert floras).

SHERWIN CARLQUIST, 1930 (Plant anatomy; palynology; insular biology).

JAMES HENRICKSON, 1940 (Fouquieriaceae; desert floras).

REID MORAN, 1916 (Baja California).

RON LYNN SCOGIN, 1941 (Biochemical systematics).
Specialization in research: Systematic botany; phylogeny and geography of angiosperms; floristics, especially of California, Mexico, and Australasia; taxonomy of Laboulbeniales, Mucorales, Celastraceae, Crossosomataceae, *Iris, Brodiaea* complex, *Ranunculus,* Cactaceae, Balanopaceae, Stylidiaceae, Goodeniaceae, Pittosporales, Restionaceae, Simmondsiaceae; aquatic phanerogams; plant anatomy; palynology; angiosperm biochemistry.
Associated botanic garden: Rancho Santa Ana Botanic Garden.
Loans: To recognized botanical institutions.
Periodical and serial works: Aliso.
Exchange: Available: Vascular plants of California, Australasia, Mexico, South Africa, islands of world. Desired: Australasia, California, Mexico, Pacific, western North America, islands generally; aquatics, parasites, and other plants of phylogenetic or phytogeographic significance.
Remarks: Since 1951 the herbaria of Pomona College (POM) and Rancho Santa Ana Botanic Garden (RSA) have been housed in the same building at RSA; since 1966 the two collections have been fully integrated. A loan request to either institution is considered also as a request to the other.

CLARKSVILLE: *Herbarium, Department of Biology, Austin Peay State University,* **(APSC),** Clarksville, Tennessee 37040, **U.S.A.**
Telephone: 615/648-7781.
Foundation: 1948. *Number of specimens:* 17.000.
Herbarium: Tennessee and Kentucky.
Important collections: Alfred Clebsch (middle Tennessee).

Director and Curator: EDWARD W. CHESTER, 1939 (Flora of Tennessee and Kentucky).
Specialization in research: Floristics of Tennessee and Kentucky.
Loans: Standard regulations.
Exchange: Vascular plants of Tennessee and Kentucky.

CLEMSON: Herbarium, Department of Botany, Clemson University, **(CLEMS)**, Clemson, South Carolina 29631, **U.S.A.**
Telephone: 803/656-3452; 656-3456.
Foundation: 1927 (first herbarium destroyed by fire in 1926). Number of specimens: 16.000 (15.000 vascular plants, 1.000 bryophytes); beginning fungus collection.
Herbarium: Flora of southeastern U.S.
Director: JOHN E. FAIREY, III, 1940 (Scleria, Cyperaceae; flora of South Carolina).
Curator: CAROLINE C. DOUGLASS, 1946 (Bryology; flora of South Carolina).
Specialization in research: State and regional floristics; rare and endangered species of South Carolina.
Associated botanic garden: Clemson University Horticultural Gardens, Department of Horticulture, Clemson University, Clemson, North Carolina 29631.
Loans: To qualified institutions.
Exchange: Available: Vascular plants and bryophytes from South Carolina. Desired: Vascular plants and bryophytes from southeastern U.S.

CLERMONT-FERRAND: Herbier de l'Université de Clermont II, Laboratoire de Botanique, **(CLF)**, 4 rue Ledru, 63038 Clermont-Ferrand Cedex, **France.**
Telephone: 16 (73) 93-35-71.
Status: Property of the University on deposit at Lab. de Botanique.
Foundation: 1925. Number of specimens: 250.000.
Important collections: Herb. Martial Lamotte, herb. Maurice Chassagne, herb. Ch.d' Alleizette, General herbarium, Cryptogamic herb. (Lamy de la Chapelle, Husnot, Roumeguere, Heribaud); herb. Le Grand (France et Europe), herb. S. E. Lassimonne, herb. Dumas-Damont (Spermatophytes and bryophytes of Auvergne), herb. Lavarenne (Auvergne).
Director: J.-E. LOISEAU, 1921 (Flora and vegetation of Central France).
Curator: N. BAUMGARTNER, 1939 (Mediterranean flora).
Loans: 6 months.
Exchange: Not at present.

CLEVELAND: Herbarium, Cleveland Museum of Natural History, **(CLM)**, Wade Oval, University Circle, Cleveland, Ohio 44106, **U.S.A.**
Telephone: 216/231-4600.
Foundation: 1920; organized for accessibility during early 1970's. Number of specimens: 40.000.

Herbarium: Vascular plants, mostly from four northeastern counties of Ohio.
Curator: JAMES K. BISSELL, 1947 (Local flora).
Loans: One year.

CLEVELAND: Herbarium, Department of Biological Sciences, Delta State University, **(DSC)**, P.O. Box 3262, Cleveland, Mississippi 38733, **U.S.A.**
Telephone: 601/843-5521.
Foundation: 1927. Number of specimens: 6.000.
Herbarium: Emphasis on trees of North America and flora of Mississippi.
Director and Curator: ROBERT A. STEWART, 1942.
Loans: Yes.
Exchange: Yes.

CLUJ: see CLUJ-NAPOCA.

CLUJ-NAPOCA: Herbarium Universitatis Napocensis (Herbarul Universității), **(CL)**, Str. Republicii nr. 42, 3400 Cluj-Napoca, **Romania.**
Telephone: 24060.
Status: University.
Foundation: 1872. Number of specimens: 620.000.
Herbarium: General collection, mainly temperate boreal plants.
Director: ONORIU RAȚIU, 1927 (Phytosociology).
Curator: FĂRCAȘIU VOICHIȚA, 1931 (Agronomy).
Staff member: GERGELY IOAN, 1928 (Phytosociology).
Specialization in research: Taxonomic research on Romanian flora.
Loans: Arranged on reciprocal basis.
Periodical and serial works: Flora Romaniae Exsiccata.

CLUJ-NAPOCA: Herbarium, Institutul Agronomic "Dr. Petru Groza," **(CLA)**, Str. Mănăștur 3, 3400 Cluj-Napoca, **Romania.**
Telephone: 951-12440/191.
Status: Agronomical Institute.
Foundation: 1905. Number of specimens: 30.000.
Herbarium: Spontaneous and cultivated plants of Romania.
Important collections: Iuliu Prodan, Bela Páter, Alexandru Buia, Anton Nyárády.
Director: IOAN PUIA, 1923 (Ecology).
Curator: ATTILA T. SZABÓ, 1941 (Applied botany).
Staff members: EUGENIA CHIRCĂ, 1940 (General botany, allelopathy).
IOAN MOLDOVAN, 1934 (Geobotany, floristics).
DIONISIE PÁZMÁNY, 1932 (Mycology, plant systematics).
DOINA STANA, 1947 (Agricultural botany).
Specialization in research: Floristics, plant ecology, studies of economically important spontaneous higher plants and fungi.

Associated botanic garden: Gradina Agrobotanică.

Loans: Limited.

Periodical and serial works: Index Seminum; Notulae Botanicae Horti Agrobotanici Cluj-Napoca.

Exchange: Yes.

CLUJ-NAPOCA: *Centrul de Cercetări Biologice, Laboratorul de ecologie,* (**CLCB**), Str. Republicii 48, Cluj-Napoca, **Romania.** (Information 1974)

Status: Ministry of Education.

Foundation: 1960. *Number of specimens:* 30.000.

Herbarium: Flora of Romania.

Loans: To recognized botanical institutions.

COCHABAMBA: *Herbario Forestal Nacional "M. Cárdenas," Centro Desarrollo Forestal, Ministerio de A.A.C.C. Agropecuarias,* (**BOLV**), Casilla Correo 895, Cochabamba, **Bolivia.**

Telephone: 2-5322 - 22225.

Status: Supported by the municipality of Cochabamba and the National Forestry Development Center, a dependency of the Bolivian Ministry of Agriculture; herbarium located on the grounds of the "Jardín Botánico Martin Cárdenas."

Foundation: Botanical garden 1973; national forestry herbarium 1976, as a cooperative project between FAO/CDF. *Number of specimens:* 2.000.

Herbarium: Emphasis on forests of Pacto Andino, especially trees of Bolivia.

Important collections: H. H. Rusby, E. K. Balls, M. Cárdenas, J. G. Hawkes and J. P. Hjerting (*Solanum*).

Staff members: ESTEBAN CARDONA MONTENEGRO, 1947 (Dendrology).

ASENCIÓN GONZALES ESCOBAR, 1934 (Silviculture).

WALDO A. TERCEROS GOITIA, 1954.

Specialization in research: Trees of Bolivia; also Cactaceae, *Amaryllis*, and *Solanum*.

Associated botanic garden: Jardín Botánico "M. Cárdenas," Casilla 538, Cochabamba, Bolivia.

Loans: To recognized herbaria on request.

Exchange: Yes, particularly interested in exchanging new material for collections made by earlier expeditions to Bolivia.

Remarks: Through the FAO forestry project, G. Hartshorn serves as a dendrology consultant to the BOLV herbarium.

COCHABAMBA: *Herbario, Departamento de Botánica, Universidad Mayor de San Simón,* (**COCH**), Cochabamba, **Bolivia** – – discontinued.

COIMBATORE: *Herbarium, Forest Research Centre,* (**FRC**), R. S. Puram P.O., Coimbatore 641 002, Tamil Nadu, **India.**

Telephone: 24550.

Status: A regional centre of Forest Research Institute and Colleges, Dehra Dun; Ministry of Agriculture and Irrigation.

Foundation: 1962. *Number of specimens:* 15.000.

Herbarium: Angiosperms, gymnosperms and pteridophytes of South India, mainly forests of Tamil Nadu, Kerala, Karnataka and Andhra states.

Important collections: T. F. Bourdillon, C. E. C. Fischer and Rama Rao.

Director: K. SHANMUGANATHAN.

Curator: K. N. SUBRAMANIAN (Taxonomy, forest flora of South India).

Staff members: C. K. JAYACHANDRAN.

N. P. MAHADEVAN.

Specialization in research: Forest flora of South India.

Associated botanic garden: Arboretum and Botanical Garden of Forest Research Centre.

Loans: To recognized botanical institutions.

Exchange: Available: Angiosperms, gymnosperms and pteridophytes of South India. Desired: Phanerogams from tropics of world; seeds or cuttings of ornamental plants.

Remarks: The collections of Fischer, Bourdillon and Rama Rao were originally in Gass Forest Museum, Coimbatore, established in 1901, and were transferred to this herbarium in 1962.

COIMBATORE: *Herbarium, Botanical Survey of India, Southern Circle,* (**MH**), Tamil Nadu Agricultural University, Lawley Road (P.O.), Coimbatore-641003, **India.**

Telephone: 36467.

Status: Government institution, Department of Science and Technology.

Foundation: 1853, as Madras Herbarium; 1957 taken over by B.S.I. *Number of specimens:* 200.000.

Herbarium: Worldwide collection, especially South India.

Important collections: C. A. Barber, R. H. Beddome, T. F. Bourdillon, Fischer, J. S. Gamble, J. D. Hooker and T. Thomson, M. A. Lawson, G. H. K. Thwaites, R. Wight.

Deputy Director: N. C. NAIR, 1927 (Flora of India, taxonomy and morphology, angiosperms, ferns).

Staff members: M. CHANDRABOSE, 1940 (Polygalaceae, Combretaceae of South India).

A. N. HENRY, 1936 (Burseraceae of South India, nomenclature).

G. R. KUMARI, 1929 (Flora of South India).

V. J. NAIR, 1940 (Gramineae of South India).

K. RAMAMURTHY, 1933 (Celastraceae of South India).

N. C. RATHAKRISHNAN, 1939 (Orchidaceae of South India).

G. V. SUBBA RAO, 1928 (Flora of Andhra Pradesh, Leguminosae).

K. VIVEKANANTHAN, 1938 (Compositae of South India).

Specialization in research: State floras of Tamil Nadu, Kerala and Andhra Pradesh; revisionary studies for Flora of India Project.

Associated botanic garden: Experimental Garden and National Orchidarium, Botanical Survey of India, Yercaud, Salem Dt., Tamil Nadu.

Loans: With permission of director.

Periodical and serial works: Bulletin of Botanical Survey of India.

Exchange: Available: Plants of Kerala, Tamil Nadu and Andhra Pradesh.

COIMBRA: *Botanical Institute of the University of Coimbra,* **(COI),** 3049 Coimbra, **Portugal.**

Telephone: 039 - 22897 or 25221.

Status: University.

Foundation: 1772. *Number of specimens:* 760.000.

Herbarium: Worldwide, mainly phanerogams. Spec.: Mediterranean region, Portugal, tropical Africa and Macaronesia.

Important collections: Herb. H. M. Willkomm.

Director: J. BARROS NEVES (Liliaceae, cytotaxonomy).

Curator: JORGE A. R. PAIVA (Polygalaceae, Flora of Portugal, Macaronesia and tropical Africa).

Staff members: MARIA TERESA DE ALMEIDA (Numerical taxonomy, flora of Portugal).

MARIA DE FÁTIMA ALMEIDA SANTOS (Taxonomy and cytotaxonomy of algae).

A. FERNANDES (Retired; Amaryllidaceae, flora of Portugal, Macaronesia and tropical Africa).

ROSETTE FERNANDES (Flora of Portugal, Macaronesia and tropical Africa).

MARIA TERESA LEITÃO PINTO (Cytotaxonomy).

ISABEL NOGUEIRA (Flora of Portugal, Macaronesia and tropical Africa).

J. E. ORMONDE (Flora of Portugal and Macaronesia).

MARGARIDA QUEIRÓS (Cytotaxonomy).

A. QUEIROZ-LOPES (Flora of Portugal).

Specialization in research: Flora of Portugal, Macaronesia and tropical Africa; caryosystematics.

Associated botanic garden: Botanic Garden of the University of Coimbra.

Loans: In general to recognized botanical institutions.

Periodical and serial works: Iconographya Selecta Florae Azoricae; Boletim da Sociedade Broteriana; Memorias da Sociedade Broteriana, Anuário da Sociedade Broteriana; Conspectus Florae Angolensis; Index Seminum.

Exchange: Available: Specimens from Portugal, Macaronesia, flora of tropical Angola and Mozambique. Desired: Specimens of all groups from all regions.

Remarks: Facilities for visiting botanists.

COLLEGE PARK: *Herbarium, Department of Botany, University of Maryland,* **(MARY),** College Park, Maryland 20742, **U.S.A.**

Telephone: 301/454-3812.

Status: Public institution.

Foundation: 1901. *Number of specimens:* 40.000.

Herbarium: Plants of Maryland and the Chesapeake Bay Region, Middle Atlantic states, and Intermountain Region (western U.S.); mainly vascular plants.

Important collections: J. B. S. Norton (Maryland; Gramineae), S. R. Hill (Maryland, Connecticut, Texas), R. G. Brown (Maryland), J. L. Reveal (western plants, including types), E. A. Higgins (Assateague Island).

Curator: STEVEN R. HILL, 1950 (Malvaceae; Bahama flora; *Anemia, Malvastrum*).

Staff members: PAUL BARRETT, 1941 (Arctic ecology; seed bank studies; ecological studies of Maryland plants).

RUSSELL G. BROWN, 1905 (Plants of Maryland and West Virginia).

ELIZABETH A. HIGGINS, 1927 (Plants of Maryland).

JAMES L. REVEAL, 1941 (Floristic studies on vascular plants of western U.S.; monographic studies of *Eriogonum* and *Salvia*).

SHIRLEY D. VAN VALKENBURG, 1925 (Nannoplankton of Chesapeake Bay; algae of Maryland and the Chesapeake Bay region).

Specialization in research: Plants and plant ecology of Maryland and the Middle Atlantic states; floristics of the Intermountain Region.

Loans: To all recognized institutions.

Periodical and serial works: Chesapeake Science (Published by the Natural Resources Institute of the University of Maryland).

Exchange: Available: Plants of Maryland, northeastern U.S., and Intermountain Region. Desired: Plants from the neotropics and Old World tropics.

COLLEGE PLACE: *Walla Walla College Natural History Herbarium, Department of Biological Sciences, Walla Walla College,* **(WCP),** Life Science Building 226, West Whitman Drive, College Place, Washington 99324, **U.S.A.**

Telephone: 509/527-2483 (director's office); 527-2602 (department office).

Foundation: 1940. *Number of specimens:* 20.000.

Herbarium: Primarily Pacific Northwest, but good general representation of North America.

Director and Curator: ALBERT E. GRABLE, 1939 (Vascular plants).

Specialization in research: Flora of southeastern Washington and northeastern Oregon.

Loans: Usual regulations.

Exchange: Yes.

Remarks: Computer listing of available records in progress.

COLLEGE STATION: *S. M. Tracy Herbarium, Department of Range Science, Texas A&M University,* **(TAES),** College Station, Texas 77843, **U.S.A.**

Telephone: 713/845-4328.

Foundation: 1930. *Number of specimens:* 130.000.

Herbarium: Grasses (Poaceae).

Important collections: S. M. Tracy (Gulf Coast), C. G. Pringle (Mexico), F. W. Gould (Mexico, southwestern U.S., Sri Lanka grasses), Jimenez (Dominican Republic), S. L. Hatch (New Mexico).

Curator: STEPHAN L. HATCH, 1945 (Grass systematics).

Staff member: CLIFFORD L. MORDEN, 1955 (Grass systematics).

Specialization in research: Biosystematic research on grasses.

Loans: Period of 6 months; returned by insured parcel post or prepaid express; all material returned at the same time.

Periodical and serial works: Texas Agricultural Experiment Station bulletins.

Exchange: Available: Texas, general, mostly grasses. Desired: Grasses of the world.

COLLEGE STATION: *Herbarium, Department of Biology, Texas A&M University,* (**TAMU**), College Station, Texas 77843, **U.S.A.**

Telephone: 713/845-3346; 845-3347.

Foundation: 1975. *Number of specimens:* 10.000.

Herbarium: Vascular plants, bryophytes, and lichens of Texas, especially eastern Texas; domesticated plants; macroalgae of the Texas gulf coast.

Curator: HUGH D. WILSON, 1943 (Systematics and evolution of domesticated plants; floristics).

Staff members: ELENOR R. COX (Phycology).

DALE M. J. MUELLER, 1939 (Bryology).

Specialization in research: Floristics of eastern Texas; biosystematics of domesticated taxa.

Loans: In general to recognized botanical institutions.

Exchange: Available: General collections from eastern Texas. Desired: Material from Texas and southeastern U.S.; domesticated plants.

COLORADO SPRINGS: *Herbarium, Department of Biology, Colorado College,* (**COCO**), Colorado Springs, Colorado 80903, **U.S.A.**

Telephone: 303/473-2233, ext. 317.

Foundation: 1874. *Number of specimens:* 11.000.

Herbarium: Flora of Pikes Peak area.

Important collections: Penstemon.

Curator: JACK L. CARTER, 1929.

COLUMBIA: *Herbarium, Division of Biological Sciences, University of Missouri,* (**UMO**), 201 Tucker Hall, Columbia, Missouri 65211, **U.S.A.**

Telephone: 314/882-6519.

Foundation: 1856. *Number of specimens:* 250.000.

Herbarium: Flora of Missouri; *Lupinus* of world; grasses; Compositae; Mexico and Central America (ca 25.000).

Important collections: W. E. Maneval (Mycology), E. J. Palmer (*Crataegus, Quercus*), D. B. Dunn (*Lu-*

pinus; Atomic Test Site vouchers), J. A. Steyermark (Missouri), F. Daniels, W. E. Harmon (Guatemala), D. LeDoux (Cretaceous; Missouri), J. M. Wood (Devonian, Pennsylvanian).

Curator: DAVID B. DUNN, 1917 (*Lupinus*; flora of southwestern U.S. and Mexico).

Staff members: OSCAR H. CALVERT, 1918 (Mycology; plant pathology).

BILLY G. CUMBIE, 1930 (Comparative plant anatomy).

CHARLES S. GOWANS, 1923 (Phycology; genetics and systematics).

CLAIR L. KUCERA, 1922 (Agrostology; prairie ecology).

JOSEPH M. WOOD, 1921 (Paleobotany; micropaleontology).

Specialization in research: Epidermal studies of Commelinaceae and 200 other families; biosystematic and monographic studies of *Lupinus*; prairie ecological studies; comparative plant anatomy studies of herbaceous and woody dicots; paleobotanical studies of Devonian, Pennsylvanian, and Cretaceous of Missouri, macro and microfossils.

Loans: To any recognized individual or institution.

Periodical and serial works: Museum monographs; Transactions of Missouri Academy of Science; University Press.

Exchange: Available: U.S., Mexico, Central America. Desired: Will exchange U.S. material for U.S. or foreign; will exchange Mexican and Central American only for foreign specimens.

Remarks: Voucher specimens for the tropical woods of India; Syracuse wood samples of North American trees; 6.000 megafossils, 2.000 microfossils, 1.900 Devonian and Pennsylvanian, 2.000 Cretaceous of Missouri.

COLUMBIA: *Herbarium, Department of Biology, University of South Carolina,* (**USCH**), Columbia, South Carolina 29208, **U.S.A.**

Telephone: 803/777-8196; 777-4141.

Foundation: 1950. *Number of specimens:* 30.000.

Herbarium: Mainly a collection of representative South Carolina flora and the southeastern U.S. in general.

Director: WADE T. BATSON, JR., 1912 (South Carolina flora).

Specialization in research: South Carolina inventory studies.

Loans: One year.

Exchange: Yes, southeastern U.S. in particular.

COLUMBUS: *Herbarium, Department of Science/Mathematics, Columbus College,* (**COLG**), Columbus, Georgia 31906, **U.S.A.**

Telephone: 404/568-2069.

Foundation: 1971. *Number of specimens:* 3.000.

Herbarium: Local flora.

Curator: ZACK FAUST, 1939 (Systematics of *Vernonia*).

Specialization in research: Systematics of *Vernonia*; ferns of southeastern U.S.

COLUMBUS: *Herbarium, Department of Biological Sciences, Mississippi University for Women,* (**MSCW**), Columbus, Mississippi 39701, **U.S.A.**
Telephone: 601/328-0812.
Foundation: 1938. *Number of specimens:* 2.600.
Herbarium: Local flora.
Director and Curator: HARRY L. SHERMAN, 1927 (Vascular plants of Mississippi and Alabama).
Specialization in research: Biosystematics of *Schoenolirion* and other native lilies.
Loans: To any recognized individual or institution.

COLUMBUS: *Herbarium, Department of Botany, The Ohio State University,* (**OS**), 1735 Neil Avenue, Columbus, Ohio 43210, **U.S.A.**
Telephone: 614/422-3296.
Foundation: 1891. *Number of specimens:* 260.000.
Herbarium: Flora of Ohio; vascular plants with particular strength in aquatic groups and in the Compositae; mosses, lichens, and diatoms.
Important collections: Type specimens of vascular plants: T. H. Kearney, W. A. Kellerman, L. M. Underwood and A. D. Selby. Vascular plants: W. A. Kellerman (Guatemala), W. S. Sullivan (Ohio), A. Gray (Gramineae and Cyperaceae), J. H. Schaffner (*Equisetum*), L. S. Hopkins (pteridophytes), J. A. Duke (Panama), Herbarium of the Ohio Agricultural Experiment Station of Wooster, Ohio, The North American Appalachian Experimental Herbarium prepared by H. N. Moldenke, F. Bartley, and L. L. Pontius. Non-vascular plants: Fletcher and Edward Hodge (diatoms), H. Van Heurck (diatoms), H. L. Smith (diatoms), W. S. Sullivant (Musci Alleghaniensis), W. S. Sullivant and L. Lesquereux (Musci Boreali — Americani sive Specimina Exsiccata Muscorum).
Director: TOD F. STUESSY, 1943 (Compositae of the world).
Herbarium Supervisor: JOHN J. FURLOW, 1942 (Betulaceae).
Curators: DANIEL J. CRAWFORD, 1942 (Chemosystematics; *Coreopsis, Chenopodium*).
EMANUEL D. RUDOLPH, 1927 (Lichens).
RONALD L. STUCKEY, 1938 (Flowering aquatic plants; vascular plants of Ohio).
Specialization in research: Ohio floristics and plant geography; monographic and revisionary studies in vascular aquatic plants, the Compositae, and the Betulaceae; taxonomic, ecological, and physiological studies of lichens.
Loans: To recognized institutions without restriction (usually for a period of one year with the opportunity for renewal).
Periodical and serial works: The Ohio Journal of Science; Bulletins of the Ohio Biological Survey, note series, informative circulars.

Exchange: Available: Latin American Compositae; Ohio vascular plants. Desired: Latin American Compositae; aquatic vascular plants.

COMMERCE: *Herbarium, Biology Department, East Texas State University,* (**ETST**), Commerce, Texas 75428, **U.S.A.**
Telephone: 214/886-5889; 886-5366.
Foundation: 1930. *Number of specimens:* 2.500.
Herbarium: Vascular plants and mosses of east Texas.
Director and Curator: EVAN PAUL ROBERTS, 1914 (Taxonomy of Texas vascular plants).
Specialization in research: Texas flora.
Loans: To recognized botanical institutions.
Exchange: Local flora.

CONCARNEAU: *Herbier Crouan, College de France, Laboratoire de Biologie Marine,* (**CO**), B.P. 11, F.29181 Concarneau, **France.**
Telephone: 16 (98) 97 12 32.
Status: Educational.
Foundation: 1856. *Number of specimens:* 4.000.
Herbarium: Algae, fungi, higher plants.
Important collections: Algae of Western Europe.
Director: YVES LE GAL, 1939 (Biochemist).
Curator: MARIE LOUISE LE GAL, 1939 (Botanist).
Specialization in research: Marine biochemistry, ecology.
Loans: On request.

CONCEPCIÓN: *Herbario, Departamento de Botánica, Instituto de Biología, Universidad de Concepción,* (**CONC**), Casilla 1367, Barrio Universitario, Concepción, **Chile.**
Telephone: 24985.
Foundation: 1918. *Number of specimens:* 65.000.
Herbarium: Chilean plants; other collections: Sporotheca, 6.500 slides; xylotheca, 500 samples of Chilean woody plants.
Director: CLODOMIRO MARTICORENA, 1929 (Palynology; taxonomy of vascular plants).
Curator: MAX QUEZADA, 1936 (Taxonomy of vascular plants).
Staff members: JORGE ARRIAGADA, 1947 (Taxonomy; plant sociology).
MARIELA GONZÁLEZ, 1947 (Micro-algae).
OSCAR MATTHEI, 1935 (Gramineae; weeds).
OSCAR PARRA, 1944 (Micro-algae).
PATRICIO RIVERA, 1942 (Diatoms).
ROBERTO RODRÍQUEZ, 1944 (Pteridophyta; plant anatomy).
EDUARDO UGARTE, 1946 (Taxonomy; plant sociology).
Specialization in research: Chilean flora.
Associated botanic garden: Parque Botánica Hualpén.
Loans: To recognized botanical institutes.
Periodical and serial works: Gayana.
Exchange: Available: Plants of Chile. Wanted:

Plants of Argentina, Bolivia, and Peru; Compositae.

COPENHAGEN: *Botanical Museum and Herbarium,* **(C)**, Gothersgade 130, DK-1123 Copenhagen K., **Denmark.**
Telephone: 01-111744.
Status: University of Copenhagen.
Foundation: 1759. *Number of specimens:* 2.000.000.
Herbarium: Worldwide herbarium, especially Denmark, Faroe Islands, Greenland and Iceland.
Important collections: P. Forskål (Arabia), M. Vahl, J. Lange (Spain), Liebmann (Mexico), Ørsted, (Central America), E. Warming (Brazil), F. C. E. Børgesen (Algae), O. Rostrup (Fungi).
Director: No director, Keeper, elected for 3 year-periods.
Staff members: ROLF DAHLGREN, 1932 (Taxonomy of Angiosperms, flora of South Africa).
ANNE FOX MAULE, 1917 (Botanical history, registration of type-specimens).
BENT FREDSKILD, 1929 (History of the Greenland flora, Arctic vascular plants).
ALFRED HANSEN, 1925 (Flora of Denmark, adventives; *Agropyron*; Mediterranean and Makaronesian flora, bibliography).
BERTEL HANSEN, 1932 (Phanerogams, Balanophoraceae, Acanthaceae, Rutaceae and Xyridaceae of S.E. Asia, flora of Thailand).
CARLO HANSEN, 1932 (Phanerogams, Melastomataceae).
ERIC STEEN HANSEN, 1943 (Lichens, especially arctic).
JØRGEN BENTH HANSEN, 1917 (Algae, especially marine).
HENNING KNUDSEN, 1948 (Fungi, Agaricales, Agaricaceae).
JETTE LEWINSKY, 1948 (Bryophytes, *Orthotrichum*).
GERT STEEN MOGENSEN, 1944 (Bryophytes, especially arctic).
KNUD RAHN, 1928 (Plantaginaceae).
Specialization in research: Flora of Denmark, Greenland, the Arctic, South Africa, South America, South East Asia, Thailand.
Associated botanic garden: The Botanic Garden of the University of Copenhagen, Øster Farimagsgade 2B.
Loans: In general to recognized botanical institutions.
Exchange: Available: Specimens from Denmark, the Arctic, South America, Thailand. Desired: Specimens from all groups and countries.

COPENHAGEN: *Herbarium, Department of Plant Pathology,* **(CP)**, Thorvaldsensvej 40, Entrance no. 8, DK-1871 Copenhagen V, **Denmark.** (Information 1974)
Status: Royal Veterinary and Agricultural University.

Foundation: 1883. *Number of specimens:* 22.000.
Herbarium: Fungi of Scandinavia, especially Denmark.
Important collections: E. Rostrup, O. Rostrup, C. Ferdinandsen, N. F. Buchwald.

CORAL GABLES: *Buswell Herbarium, Department of Biology, University of Miami,* **(BUS)**, P.O. Box 249118, Coral Gables, Florida 33124, **U.S.A.**
Telephone: 305/284-4272.
Number of specimens: 12.000–15.000.
Herbarium: Strong in Ecuadorian (Rio Palenque) and South Florida material.
Important collections: W. M. Buswell.
Staff member: DAVID P. JANOS, 1947 (Tropical mycorrhizal fungi).
Loans: Inactive but may inquire concerning types.
Exchange: None at present.

CÓRDOBA: *Herbario, Museo Botánico, Facultad de Ciencias Exactas, Físicas y Naturales,* **(CORD)**, Casilla de Correo 495, Avda. Vélez Sarsfield 299, 5000 Córdoba, Córdoba, **Argentina.**
Telephone: (54)22284, 44126, 27814, ext. 54.
Status: Universidad Nacional de Córdoba.
Foundation: 1870. *Number of specimens:* 300.000.
Herbarium: Worldwide, mainly phanerogams; emphasis on southern part of South America, mainly the mediterranean and western region of Argentina.
Important collections: G. Hieronymus, C. Hosseus, F. Kurtz, P. Lorentz, G. Niederlein, F. Schickendantz, T. Stuckert.
Director: ARMANDO TEODORO HUNZIKER, 1919 (Solanaceae, *Amaranthus*, Amaryllidaceae, Cactaceae; flora of central Argentina).
Curator: ESTHER G. DE MAUTINO, 1938.
Staff members: ANA MARÍA ANTON, 1942 (Poaceae).
LUIS ARIZA ESPINAR, 1933 (Asteraceae; flora of central Argentina).
MARTA E. ASTEGIANO, 1944 (Poaceae).
LUIS M. BERNARDELLO, 1953 (*Lycium*).
ALFREDO E. COCUCCI, 1926 (*Ruprechtia*; Orchidaceae, Hydnoraceae; embryology).
MARÍA TERESA COSA, 1946 (Acanthaceae; *Nierembergia*; embryology).
MARÍA CRISTINA COSTA, 1955 (Melliferous plants of Córdoba).
TERESA EMIL DI FULVIO, 1930 (*Azolla, Sclerophylax*; Boraginaceae; embryology; karyology).
LAURA S. DOMINGUEZ, 1952 (Mycology).
NILDA DOTTORI, 1944 (Ulmaceae).
CARLOS PROSPERI, 1954 (Phycology).
ROSA SUBILS, 1929 (*Euphorbia*; Caryophyllaceae; flora of central Argentina).
Specialization in research: Taxonomy and morphology of Solanaceae, Asteraceae, Cactaceae, Amaryllidaceae, Poaceae; flora of central Argentina; embryology; karyology.

Loans: To recognized botanical institutions.

Periodical and serial works: Kurtziana (annual); Lorentzia (irregular); Trabajos del Museo Botanico (reprints).

Exchange: Available: Argentina specimens. Wanted: Specimens of Solanaceae, Hydnoraceae, *Ruprechtia*, Orchidaceae (South America), Boraginaceae, and Asteraceae.

CORRIENTES: *Herbario, Instituto de Botánica del Nordeste*, **(CTES)**, Sargento Cabral 2139, Casilla de Correo 209, 3400 Corrientes, Corrientes, **Argentina.**

Telephone: (54)27309.

Status: Universidad Nacional del Nordeste, Consejo Nacional de Investigaciones Científicas y Técnicas.

Foundation: 1965. *Number of specimens:* 120.000.

Herbarium: Vascular plants and lichens of northern Argentina and neighboring countries (Bolivia, Brazil, Paraguay); Malvaceae.

Important collections: Antonio Krapovickas, Augusto G. Schulz.

Director: ANTONIO KRAPOVICKAS, 1921 (Malvaceae, Leguminosae; *Arachis*).

Curator: CARMEN L. CRISTÓBAL, 1932 (Sterculiaceae).

Staff members: MARÍA MERCEDES ARBO, 1945 (Turneraceae; local flora).

AVELIANO FERNÁNDEZ, 1943 (Cytology).

LIDIA ITATI FERRARO, 1951 (Lichens).

LUIS AMADO MROGINSKI, 1946 (Physiology).

STELLA MARIS PIRE, 1943 (Local flora).

CAMILO LUIS QUARIN, 1943 (Cytotaxonomy; Gramineae).

AURELIO SCHININI, 1943 (Local flora).

SARA GRACIELA TRESSENS, 1944 (Local flora).

Scientific collaborators: RAUL N. MARTINEZ CROVETTO, 1921 (Cucurbitaceae; ethnobotany).

TROELS MYNDEL PEDERSEN, 1916 (Amaranthaceae, Caryophyllaceae, Cyperaceae).

Loans: To recognized botanical institutions.

Periodical and serial works: Bonplandia.

Exchange: Available.

CORRIENTES: *Herbarium Humboldtianum, Facultad de Ciencias Exactas y Naturales y Agrimensura, Universidad Nacional del Nordeste*, **(CTESN)**, Casilla 326, San Lorenzo 690, 3400 Corrientes, **Argentina.**

Telephone: (54)23126; 24055; 24638.

Foundation: 1968. *Number of specimens:* 21.500.

Herbarium: Floristic inventory of plant communities from Argentina and adjacent countries; South American Aristolochiaceae.

Important collections: L. Zulema Ahumada, Ulrich G. Eskuche.

Director: ULRICH G. ESKUCHE, 1926 (Phytosociology).

Curator: L. ZULEMA AHUMADA, 1930 (Aristolochiaceae).

Specialization in research: Aristolochiaceae,

Scrophulariaceae (Gratioleae), Euphorbiaceae (Crotoneae, Acalypheae); phytosociology of Argentina and adjacent countries.

Loans: Usual regulations.

Exchange: Yes.

CORVALLIS: *Herbarium, Department of Botany and Plant Pathology, Oregon State University*, **(OSC, WILLU)**, Corvallis, Oregon 97331, **U.S.A.**

Telephone: 503/754-4106.

Status: Public, state-supported university, administered by Oregon State System of Higher Education.

Foundation: 1886. *Number of specimens:* 230.000.

Herbarium: Vascular plants, with emphasis on Pacific Northwest region; fungi, including pathogenic; bryophytes.

Important collections: Repository for Morton E. Peck Herbarium (WILLU) of Willamette University (32.000 Oregon specimens, included in total, above); Albert N. Steward (Oregon), Helen M. Gilkey (Tuberales), James M. Trappe, Thomas Howell, Lewis Henderson, Wm. Cusick, Georgia Mason (Wallowa Mountains), E. I. Sanborn (Hepaticae), H. C. Gilbert (Myxomycetes); major holdings of Endogonaceae.

Chairman of Department: THOMAS C. MOORE, 1936.

Curator: KENTON L. CHAMBERS, 1929 (Biosystematics of Compositae; floristics of Pacific Northwest).

Staff members: WILLIAM C. DENISON, 1928 (Mycological Curator; taxonomy of Pezizales; ecology of forest lichens).

LAREA D. JOHNSTON, 1935 (Aquatic plants; weeds of Oregon; flora of Oregon).

JAMES M. TRAPPE, 1931 (Taxonomic mycology; mycorrhizae; forest pathology).

Specialization in research: Biosystematics of vascular plants; flora of Oregon; taxonomy and ecology of fungi and lichens.

Loans: No restrictions.

Exchange: By arrangement only. Available: Vascular plants of Pacific Northwest region.

Remarks: The Morton E. Peck Herbarium (WILLU) of Willamette University is now housed at OSC. Both OSC and WILLU specimens are sent on all loan requests.

CORVALLIS: *Herbarium, Forest Products Collection, Department of Forest Products, School of Forestry, Oregon State University*, **(OSUF)**, Corvallis, Oregon 97331, **U.S.A.**

Telephone: 503/754-3154.

Foundation: 1950. *Number of specimens:* 2.500.

Herbarium: Collection of wood samples and identification literature.

Director: HELMUTH RESCH, 1933 (Wood physics).

Curator: ROBERT KRAHMER, 1932 (Wood anatomy).

Specialization in research: Anatomical, physical, and chemical properties of wood and wood-based products, their manufacture and use.

Exchange: Informal exchange with other wood collections of universities.

COTONOU: *Herbier National du Bénin, Université Nationale du Bénin,* **(BENIN),** Campus Universitaire d'Abomey-Calavi, BP. 526 – Cotonou (R.P.B.), **Bénin.**
Telephone: 36.00.74, 36.01.05, 36.01.22, 36.01.26.
Status: University.
Foundation: 1970. *Number of specimens:* 1.500.
Herbarium: Angiosperms.
Director: PAUL HOUNGNON, 1943 (Forest ranger, systematics).
Staff members: NESTOR HOUEDJISSI, 1953.
 SIMONE DE SOUZA.
Specialization in research: Floristics, phenology, ethnobotany, medicinal plants.
Associated botanic garden: A small botanical garden.
Exchange: Yes.

COVENTRY: *Herbarium, Herbert Art Gallery and Museum,* **(COV),** Jordon Well, Coventry CV1 5QP, Warwickshire, England, **Great Britain.** (Information 1974)
Status: Local museum.
Foundation: About 1950. *Number of specimens:* 1.500.
Herbarium: Warwickshire, especially Coventry area.

COYOACÁN: *Instituto Nacional de Investigaciones Forestales,* **(ICF)** – – *see* MEXICO (INIF).

CRAIOVA: *Herbarium, Catedra de Fitopatologie a Universității,* **(CRAF),** str. Libertății 15, Craiova, **Romania.** (Information 1974)
Status: University.
Foundation: 1950. *Number of specimens:* 1.500.
Herbarium: Fungi, worldwide and Europe.
Periodical and serial works: Schedae ad Fl. Olteniae Exsiccatam.
Loans: To recognized phytopathological and botanical institutions.

CRAIOVA: *Herbarium, Botany Department, University of Craiova,* **(CRAI),** Libertății 15, 1100 Craiova, **Romania.**
Telephone: 941/16595-154.
Status: University.
Foundation: 1951. *Number of specimens:* 4.500.
Herbarium: Flowering plants of Europe, Asia, America and Australia.
Director: MARIN PĂUN, 1924.
Staff members: DUMITRU CA'RȚU, 1933 (Taxonomy).
 MARIANA CA'RȚU, 1926 (Taxonomy).
 CONSTANTIN MALOS, 1933 (Taxonomy).
 GHEORGHE POPESCU, 1939 (Taxonomy).

Specialization in research: Taxonomy, ecology, phytocenology; Fabaceae.
Periodical and serial works: Flora Olteniae Exsiccata.
Exchange: Yes.

CRAWFORDSVILLE: *Herbarium, Biology Department, Wabash College,* **(WAB),** Crawfordsville, Indiana 47933, **U.S.A.**
Telephone: 317/362-1400.
Foundation: 1879. *Number of specimens:* 19.954.
Herbarium: Indiana, U.S., Hawaii, Greenland, Mexico, Lebanon; voucher specimens for Allee Memorial Forest research tract.
Important collections: Hayden Expedition of 1872 to Yellowstone in the John M. Coulter collection, R. S. Cowan (Hawaii), A. Clapp, C. C. Deam, Alida M. Cunningham, D. Bodine, A. R. Bechtel, R. A. Laubengayer, William Leavenworth, Daniel B. Ward.
Director: AUSTIN BROOKS, 1938 (Algology).
Curator: ROBERT O. PETTY, 1933.
Loans: To recognized scientific institutions.
Exchange: Limited basis only.

CRUZ DAS ALMAS: *Herbário, Centro Nacional de Pesquisa de Mandioca e Fruticultura, Empresa Brasileira de Pesquisa Agropecuária,* **(IAL),** Caixa Postal 007, 44.380 Cruz das Almas, Bahia, **Brazil.**
Status: Brazilian Agricultural Research Institution.
Foundation: 1952 (Instituto Agronômico do Leste until 1975). *Number of specimens:* 8.000.
Herbarium: Eastern Brazil, with emphasis on cassava and fruit crops.
Director: MARIO AUGUSTO PINTO DA CUNHA.
Specialization in research: Coordination of research concerning cassava, citrus fruits, pineapple, banana, and mango, with the objective of increasing production, improving the quality of products, and exploiting underutilized areas for the development of crops.

CUIABÁ: *Herbário, Universidade Federal de Mato Grosso,* **(UFMT),** Avenida Fernando Corrêa da Costa, 78.000 Cuiabá, Mato Crosso, **Brazil.**
Telephone: (55)065/321-4010.
Foundation: 1979. *Number of specimens:* 3.000.
Herbarium: Flora of central Brazil.
Important collections: G. Guarim Neto, G. T. Prance.
Curator: GERMANO GUARIM NETO, 1950 (Sapindaceae).
Staff members: MARIA SALETTI FERRAZ (Ecology).
 ERMELINDA M. D. L. FREIRE (Fungi).
 VERA L. M. DOS S. GUARIM (General ecology).
 ANTÔNIO A. A. MACIEL (Palynology).
 EDSON C. DE C. MORAES (Fungi).
 ANAJDE L. PRADO (Malpighiaceae).
 NAGIB SADDI (Clusiaceae).
 CAROLINA J. DA SILVA (General ecology).

Specialization in research: Flora of Cerrado and Pantanal.
Loans: No restrictions.
Exchange: Brazilian flora.

CULLOWHEE: Herbarium, Department of Biology, Western Carolina University, (**WCUH**), Cullowhee, North Carolina 28723, **U.S.A.**
Telephone: 704/227-7244.
Foundation: 1961. Number of specimens: 18.000.
Herbarium: Flora of southwestern North Carolina mountainous region; vascular plants of the Southern Highland rock outcrops.
Curator: JAMES H. HORTON.
Specialization in research: Southern Appalachian mountain floristics.
Loans: Usual regulations.
Exchange: With NCU.

CURITIBA: Herbário, Escola de Florestas, (**EFC**), Caixa Postal 2959, 80.000 Curitiba, Paraná, **Brazil.**

CURITIBA: Instituto de Biologia do Paraná, (**IBP**), Curitiba, Paraná, **Brazil** — incorporated in herb. Hatschbach (private).

CURITIBA: Herbário, Instituto Paranaense de Botânica, (**IPB**), Caixa Postal 1362, 80.000 Curitiba, Paraná, **Brazil.**
Status: Private foundation.
Foundation: 1952. Number of specimens: 6.300.
Herbarium: Flora of Paraná.
Other activities: Estatistica Botânica Fanerogamica; Catalogue of Phanerogamic Genera; Bibliography of Flora of Paraná, 2.000 volumes; Dictionary of technical botanical terms (17.000) for the Portuguese language.
Director: JOÃO ANGELY (Phanerogams of Paraná).

CURITIBA: Herbário, Museu Botânico Municipal, (**MBM**), Caixa Postal 1142, 80.000 Curitiba, Paraná, **Brazil.**
Telephone: (55)041/276-5615.
Status: Prefeitura Municipal de Curitiba.
Foundation: 1965. Number of specimens: 65.000.
Herbarium: General southern and central Brazil collection.
Important collections: Gert Hatschbach (43.000 numbers).
Director: GERT HATSCHBACH, 1923 (Flora of Paraná).
Curator: RONALDO KUMMROV, 1947.
Specialization in research: Flora of Paraná.
Associated botanic garden: Reserva Biologica de Sapitanduva.
Loans: Upon request, for determination.
Periodical and serial works: Boletim do Museu Botânico Municipal.
Exchange: Available: Southern and central Bra-

zil. Desired: Latin American specimens.

CURITIBA: Herbário Per Karl Dusén, Fundação Instituto Agronômico do Paraná, (**PKDC**), Rua Nivaldo Braga 1225, Capão da Imbuia, Caixa Postal 1493, 80.000 Curitiba, Paraná, **Brazil.**
Telephone: (55)041/262-7362; 262-1362.
Status: Secretaria da Agricultura.
Foundation: 1939. Number of specimens: 20.800.
Herbarium: Flora of Paraná.
Important collections: P. K. Dusén.
Director: RAUL JULIATO.
Curator: LUIZA THEREZA DECONTO DOMBROWSKI (Plant taxonomy).
Staff members: YOSHIKO SAITO KUNIYOSHI (Silviculture).
ADSON RAMOS (Silviculture).
Specialization in research: Flora of Paraná.
Loans: Yes.
Periodical and serial works: Informe da Pesquisa.
Exchange: Available: Duplicates from Paraná.

CURITIBA: Herbário, Departamento de Botânica, Universidade Federal do Paraná, (**UPCB**), Centro Politécnico, 80.000 Curitiba, Paraná, **Brazil.**
Telephone: (55)041/263-3234.
Foundation: 1952. Number of specimens: 10.800.
Herbarium: Phanerogams and algae of Paraná.
Director: PAULO K. C. CARNEIRO MONTEIRO, 1930 (Ecology).
Curator: OLAVO ARAUJO GUIMARÃES, 1937 (Phanerogams of Paraná).
Staff members: ADRIANO BIDÁ, 1942 (Phanerogams).
NOBOR IMAGUIRE, 1928 (Plant ecology).
AYRTON DE MATTOS, 1924 (Algae).
HERMES MOREIRA FILHO, 1929 (Diatoms).
Specialization in research: Diatoms and phanerogams of Paraná.
Loans: Usual regulations.
Periodical and serial works: Acta Biologica Paranaense.
Exchange: Available: Plants of Paraná. Desired: Plants of South America.

CUZCO: Herbario Vargas, Facultad de Ciencias, Universidad Nacional de San Antonio Abad del Cuzco, (**CUZ**), Avenida de la Cultura, Apartado 367, Cuzco, **Peru.**
Telephone: 2440, anexo 62.
Status: Departamento Academico de Ciencias Biológicas de la Universidad Nacional del Cuzco.
Foundation: 1935. Number of specimens: 22.000.
Herbarium: Flora of southern Peru.
Important collections: G. Bües (ferns, lichens); Solanum (2.000).
Director: EFRAÍN CARRILLO PEZO (Gramineae).
Staff members: RENE CHÁVEZ (Genetic resources and phytogeography).
FELIPE MARÍN MORENO (Phytogeography).

73

EFRAÍN MOLLEAPAZA ARISPE (Ecology).
FRANCISCO PÉREZ BARREDA (Ferns).
HORACIO ZAMALLOA DIAZ (Physiology).
Specialization in research: Southern Andean plants; phytogeography; ecology.

Periodical and serial works: Cantua.

Exchange: Available: Plants of southern Peru.

D

DAKAR: *Herbarium, Département de Biologie Végétale,* **(DAKAR)**, Faculté des Sciences, Dakar, **Senegal.**
Telephone: 22.04.43.
Status: Department of the Faculty of Sciences.
Foundation: 1960. *Number of specimens:* 8.000.
Herbarium: Plants of the various regions of Senegal.
Important collections: Herb. J. Berhaut (Senegal), Miège (Senegal, Côte d'Ivoire, Congo), Doumbia (Casamance), Oumar E. Kane (North Senegal).
  Director: GUY KAHLEM (Plant physiology).
  Staff members: AMADOU TIDIANE BA.
  OUMAR E. KANE.
  ABDOULAYE SANOKHO.
Specialization in research: Ecophysiology, parasitic plants.
Periodical and serial works: Index Seminum.
Exchange: Grains, seeds.

DAKAR: *Herbarium, Institut Fondamental d'Afrique Noire,* **(IFAN)**, B.P. 206, Dakar, **Senegal.** (Information 1974)
Status: Institute of University of Dakar.
Foundation: 1942. *Number of specimens:* 110.000.
Herbarium: Tropical West Africa.
Specialization in research: West African flora.
Associated botanic garden: Jardin Botanique de l'IFAN.
Loans: To recognized botanical institutions or specialists.
Periodical and serial works: Notes Africaines; Bulletin de l'IFAN, Série A; Icones Plantarum Africanum; Mémoires et Notes Diverses.

DALLAS: *Herbarium, Southern Methodist University,* **(SMU)**, Dallas, Texas 75275, **U.S.A.**
Telephone: 214/692-2257.
Status: Private institution.
Foundation: 1944. *Number of specimens:* 372.000.
Herbarium: Vascular plants: Fabaceae, Asteraceae, weeds, cultivated; bryophytes; lichens.
Important collections: Herbaria of D. S. Correll, Delzie Demaree, P. O. Schallert, Lloyd Shinners, Eula Whitehouse; collections of Robert Kral, C. G. Pringle, F. J. Lindheimer, A. Ruth, J. Reverchon; A. J. Grout's North American Musci Exsiccatae, T. Drummond's Musci Americani, P. T. Husnot's Musc. Gall.
  Curator: WM. F. MAHLER, 1930 (Leguminosae pollen morphology; bryophyte and vascular plant floristics).
  Staff member: BARNEY L. LIPSCOMB, 1950 (Cyperaceae; general vascular plant floristics).
Specialization in research: Floristics.
Loans: No special restrictions.

Periodical and serial works: Sida, Contributions to Botany (privately published and edited by Wm. F. Mahler).
Exchange: Available: Mostly Texas, Arkansas, Oklahoma. Desired: General collections from all parts of the world.

DALLAS: *Lundell Herbarium, Plant Sciences Laboratory, University of Texas at Dallas,* **(UTD)** – – *see* RICHARDSON.

DAMIEN: *Ekman Herbarium, University of Haiti,* **(EHH)**, Damien, **Haiti.** (see addenda)

DANVILLE: *Bryophyte Herbarium, Centre College of Kentucky,* **(KBRYO)**, Walnut Street, Danville, Kentucky 40422, **U.S.A.**
Telephone: 606/236-5211.
Foundation: 1974. *Number of specimens:* 1.000.
Herbarium: Mainly Virginia and Kentucky bryophytes.
  Director and Curator: SUSAN MOYLE STUDLAR, 1944 (Bryology).
Specialization in research: Bryophyte ecology: factors controlling distribution; trampling stress on trail species.
Loans: Negotiable.
Exchange: Yes.

DARBHANGA: *Herbarium, Department of Botany, Mithila University,* **(DMU)**, Darbhanga 846004, **India.** (Information 1974)
Foundation: 1970. *Number of specimens:* 5.000.
Herbarium: All groups; mainly from Mithila, North Bihar.
Periodical and serial works: Videha, Planto, Vanaspati, Flora of Mithila.

DAR ES SALAAM: *Herbarium, Botany Department, University of Dar es Salaam,* **(DSM)**, Dar es Salaam, **Tanzania.** (Information 1974)
Status: University.
Foundation: 1965. *Number of specimens:* 22.000.
Herbarium: Tropical Africa, mainly Tanzania.
Specialization in research: Tanzanian plants, wild and cultivated and macroscopic marine algae.
Loans: To recognized botanical institutions.

DARWIN: *Herbarium of the Northern Territory,* **(DNA)**, Division of Agriculture and Stock, Department of Primary Production, P.O. Box 5160, Darwin, N.T. 5794, **Australia.**
Telephone: 089/220318.
Status: Under Northern Territory Government.
Foundation: 1967. *Number of specimens:* 15.000.
Herbarium: Angiosperms, mainly from Northern

Territory, N. of 15° S latitude.
Director and Curator: CLYDE ROBERT DUNLOP, 1946 (Compositae).
Staff member: MADELEINE O. RANKIN (Australian Moraceae).
Specialization in research: Taxonomy of Australian Compositae.
Loans: To reputable institutions, 6 months duration.
Exchange: Tropical Compositae (Old World).

DAVENPORT: *Herbarium, Putnam Museum,* (**BDI**), 1717 West 12th Street, Davenport, Iowa 52804, **U.S.A.**
Telephone: 319/324-1933.
Status: Private institution.
Foundation: 1867. *Number of specimens:* 10.000.
Herbarium: Flora of Scott, Muscatine and surrounding counties in Iowa and Rock Island and Whiteside counties in Illinois.
Important collections: W. D. Barnes (9.500), L. F. Guldner (5.000), N. Melville, E. Ross (1.000).
Director: JOSEPH L. CARTWRIGHT.
Curator: JANICE A. HALL (Anthropology).
Loans: To recognized institutions.
Periodical and serial works: Proceedings of the Davenport Academy of Natural Sciences (ceased in 1914).
Remarks: Formerly Davenport Public Museum.

DAVIS: *Herbarium, Department of Agronomy and Range Science, University of California,* (**AHUC**), Davis, California 95616, **U.S.A.**
Telephone: 916/752-1701.
Foundation: 1913. *Number of specimens:* 37.606.
Herbarium: Specialty in grasses, especially *Orcuttia, Neostapfia, Agrostis,* and *Stipa,* and legumes of California; general collections of other plant families.
Director and Curator: BEECHER CRAMPTON, 1918 (Grasses).
Specialization in research: Taxonomy of grasses of California.
Loans: Usual conditions.
Periodical and serial works: Contributions to the Flora of the Sacramento Valley.
Exchange: Limited, usually grasses.
Remarks: Seed collection of 11.375 lots.

DAVIS: *Herbarium, Department of Botany, University of California,* (**DAV**), Davis, California 95616, **U.S.A.**
Telephone: 916/752-1091.
Foundation: 1922. *Number of specimens:* 85.000.
Herbarium: California flora; weedy species of Mediterranean-type climate regions; *Quercus* of the New World; Euphorbiaceae; neotropical material; alpine flora of western North America.
Important collections: Euphorbiaceae, especially neotropical material; *Quercus* of the New World.
Director: JOHN M. TUCKER, 1916 (Biosystematic

studies in New World *Quercus*).
Curator: B. JUNE MCCASKILL, 1930 (Plant identification, taxonomy and geographic distribution of weeds).
Staff members: DONALD W. KYHOS, 1929 (Biosystematic studies in Compositae).
GRADY L. WEBSTER, 1927 (Monographic studies in the Euphorbiaceae).
Specialization in research: As above.
Associated botanic garden: University of California Arboretum, Davis, California.
Loans: To all recognized botanical institutions; no special restrictions.
Exchange: Available: Natives, weedy and poisonous species mainly of California; cultivated ornamentals; neotropical flora. Desired: Weedy and poisonous species, especially from regions of Mediterranean-type climate; Euphorbiaceae, Fagaceae, Compositae of world.

DAVIS: *Herbarium, Department of Environmental Horticulture, University of California,* (**DAVH**), Davis, California 95616, **U.S.A.**
Telephone: 916/752-0379; 752-0130.
Foundation: 1952. *Number of specimens:* 5.000.
Herbarium: Woody cultivated plants primarily.
Director: ANDREW T. LEISER, 1923 (Taxonomy of woody ornamental plants).
Loans: No special conditions.
Exchange: Limited.
Remarks: Primarily for departmental teaching and research. Facilitates public service requests for plant identification.

DAYTON: *Herbarium, Dayton Museum of Natural History,* (**DMNH**), 2629 Ridge Avenue, Dayton, Ohio 45415, **U.S.A.**
Telephone: 513/275-7432.
Foundation: 1893. *Number of specimens:* 8.500.
Herbarium: Mainly southwestern Ohio.
Important collections: John W. Van Cleve (Ohio; mid-1800s), William B. Werther (woody plants).
Director: E. J. KOESTNER, 1916.
Curator: GARY A. COOVERT, 1950 (Flora of southwestern Ohio).
Specialization in research: Vascular plants of southwestern Ohio.
Loans: Usual conditions; generally for 1 year.
Exchange: Possible.

DEBRECEN: *Herbarium, Botanical Institute of L. Kossuth University,* (**DE**), Debrecen 4010, **Hungary.**
Telephone: 52 16666/155.
Status: University.
Foundation: 1924. *Number of specimens:* 4.200.
Herbarium: Plants of Hungary, for teaching.
Director: ISTVÁN PRÉCSÉNYI, 1924 (Ecology).
Associated botanic garden: Botanical Garden of L. Kossuth University.

DEDZA: *Herbarium, Silvicultural Research Station,* **(NYAS)** – – incorporated in MAL.

DECATUR: *Herbarium, Department of Biology, Agnes Scott College,* **(DECA)**, Room 100-A, Campbell Hall, Decatur, Georgia 30030, **U.S.A.**

Telephone: 404/373-2571, ext. 376.
Status: Private institution.
Foundation: 1906. *Number of specimens:* 2.500.
Herbarium: Regional flora.
    Curator: M. ELOISE BROWN CARTER, 1950.
    Loans: No special restrictions.

DECORAH: *Herbarium, Department of Biology, Luther College,* **(LCDI)**, Decorah, Iowa 52101, **U.S.A.**

Telephone: 319/387-1117.
Foundation: 1968. *Number of specimens:* 1.000.
Herbarium: Local collections.
Important collections: Alois F. Kovarik (1899–1901).
    Director and Curator: ROGER M. KNUTSON, 1933 (Plant pathology).
    Loans: Usual regulations.

DEGANYA ALEPH: *Herbarium of "Beth Gordon," The A. D. Gordon Agriculture, Nature and Kinnereth Valley Study Institute,* **(BEGO)**, Deganya Aleph 15 120, D.N. Emeq Ha Yarden, **Israel.**

Telephone: 067-50040.
Status: Regional study institute.
Foundation: 1936. *Number of specimens:* 7.000.
Herbarium: Plants of Israel; plants of the Kinnereth Region; ornamental plants of Israel; plant diseases.
    Director and Curator: SAMUEL LULAV, 1911.
    Staff member: DINA ILAN, 1915.
    Specialization in research: Local flora and fauna.

DEHRA DUN: *Northern Circle, Botanical Survey of India,* **(BSD)**, Dehra Dun, **India.** (Information 1974)

Status: Government of India.
Foundation: 1956. *Number of specimens:* 42.000.
Herbarium: Plants of Western Uttar Pradesh, Punjab, Haryana, Himachal Pradesh, Jammu, Kashmir and Northwest Himalaya.
    Specialization in research: Flora of India.
    Loans: With permission of the director.
    Periodical and serial works: Bulletin of the Botanical Survey of India, Records of the Botanical Survey of India.

DEHRA DUN: *Herbarium, Forest Research Institute and College,* **(DD)**, P.O. New Forest, Dehra Dun 248006, U.P. **India.**

Telephone: 7021-28/67, 86.
Status: Government of India, Ministry of Agriculture and Irrigation.
Foundation: 1890. *Number of specimens:* 325.000.
Herbarium: Phanerogams and ferns of world, mainly India and adjacent countries, carpological collections.

Important collections: J. E. T. Aitchison, N. L. Bor, D. Brandis, J. F. Dulhie, J. S. Gamble, G. Govan, Gustav Mann, H. H. Haines, W. Jameson, U. N. Kanjilal, A. E. Lowrie, H. F. Mooney, A. E. Osmaston, R. N. Parker, C. E. Parkinson, M. B. Raizada, J. R. Royle, K. C. Sahni, R. R. Stewart.
    Director: K. M. VAID, 1923 (Himalayan flora).
    Curator: K. N. BAHADUR, 1935 (Meliaceae, bamboos, nomenclature).
    Staff members: S. S. R. BENNET, 1940 (Floristics, nomenclature).
    R. C. GAUR, 1933 (Nomenclature).
    S. S. JAIN, 1952 (Floristics).
    H. B. NAITHANI, 1944 (Gramineae, Cyperaceae).
    Specialization in research: Taxonomy and nomenclature of Indian forest flora, floras of Goa and Arunachal Pradesh.
    Associated botanic garden: Arboretum and Botanical Garden of the Forest Research Institute and College.
    Loans: With permission of Director.
    Periodical and serial works: Indian Forest Records, Forest Bulletin, Forest Leaflets, Annual Report.
    Exchange: Desired: Worldwide, especially plants of tropics.

DEKALB: *Herbarium, Department of Biological Sciences, Northern Illinois University,* **(DEK)**, DeKalb, Illinois 60115, **U.S.A.**

Telephone: 815/753-0433.
Foundation: 1962. *Number of specimens:* 17.800 (9.500 vascular plants, 8.300 bryophytes).
Herbarium: Local coverage of wild and cultivated vascular plants plus selected taxa representative of world flora; North American bryophytes.
    Director and Curator: PAUL D. SØRENSEN, 1934 (Systematics of flowering plants; *Dahlia, Arbutus*; floristics of upper midwestern U.S.).
    Specialization in research: Mainly teaching; ecological and systematic research on a preliminary level only.
    Loans: Yes, encouraged, to responsible individuals and institutions.
    Exchange: Yes.

DELAND: *Herbarium, Department of Biology, Stetson University,* **(DLF)**, DeLand, Florida 32720, **U.S.A.**

Telephone: 904/734-4121, ext. 233, 235.
Status: Private university.
Foundation: 1950. *Number of specimens:* 10.000.
Herbarium: Mostly local flora of central Florida; some specimens from Ecuador, Galapagos Islands, Kenya, Hawaii.
Important collections: C. Darling, W. F. Harkness, B. Hart Wright, J. Bennett, E. M. Norman, E. Pritchard, E. P. St. John.
    Curator: ELIANE M. NORMAN, 1931 (New World

Buddleja; Florida flora).
   Specialization in research: Central Florida; pollination studies.
   Loans: No special regulations.
   Exchange: On a small scale.

DELAWARE: *Herbarium, Ohio Wesleyan University,* **(OWU)**, Delaware, Ohio 43015, **U.S.A.**
   Telephone: 614/369-4431, ext. 400.
   Foundation: 1870. *Number of specimens:* 12.000.
   Herbarium: Vascular plants of central Ohio.
   Director and Curator: JANE M. DECKER, 1935 (Pteridophytes).
   Loans: Usual regulations.
   Exchange: Limited.

DELHI: – – *see* NEW DELHI.

DELTA: *Herbarium, Delta Waterfowl Research Station,* **(DELTA)** – – *see* PORTAGE LA PRAIRIE.

DENTON: *Benjamin B. Harris Herbarium, Department of Biological Sciences, North Texas State University,* **(NTSC)**, Denton, Texas 76203, **U.S.A.**
   Telephone: 817/788-2011.
   Foundation: 1914. *Number of specimens:* 16.000.
   Herbarium: Mainly Texas plants; emphasis on allergenic plants, weeds, and grasses.
   Curator: U. C. BANERJEE, 1937 (Allergenic plants; *Parthenium, Psophocarpus*).
   Loans: No special restrictions.
   Exchange: Available: Local plants. Desired: Grasses of the world.

DENTON: *Herbarium, Texas Women's University,* **(TCSW)**, Denton, Texas 76204, **U.S.A.**
   Telephone: 817/566-6400.

DENVER: *Herbarium of Colorado State Museum,* **(COLOM)**, Denver, Colorado 80201, **U.S.A.**
   Remarks: Herbarium was dispersed several years ago. The Alice Eastwood collections went to the University of Colorado (COLO). The Bethel collections were divided between Fort Collins (CS) and the University of Colorado (COLO). See Ewan, Rocky Mountain Naturalists, pp. 164 and 300. The remainder of the specimens are deposited at the Denver Botanic Gardens (KHD).

DENVER: *Herbarium of Fungi, Denver Botanic Gardens,* **(DBG)**, 909 York Street, Denver, Colorado 80206, **U.S.A.**
   Telephone: 303/575-3059; 575-2547.
   Status: Administered jointly by the City and County of Denver and the Denver Botanic Gardens, Inc., a private foundation.
   Foundation: 1951. *Number of specimens:* 12.000.
   Herbarium: Fleshy fungi and Myxomycetes, mostly of Colorado.
   Director: WILLIAM G. GAMBILL, JR., 1915.

   Curator: D. H. MITCHEL, 1917 (Myxomycetes).
   Staff member: S. W. CHAPMAN, 1926 (Myxomycetes).
   Associated botanic garden: Denver Botanic Gardens.
   Loans: Usual restrictions.
   Exchange: Available.
   Remarks: Herbarium housed in same building as the Kathryn Kalmbach Herbarium (KHD) of vascular flora.

DENVER: *Division of Range and Wildlife Management, U.S. Forest Service, Rocky Mountain Region,* **(DENF)** – – *see* LAKEWOOD.

DENVER: *Kathryn Kalmbach Herbarium, Denver Botanic Gardens,* **(KHD)**, 909 York Street, Denver, Colorado 80206, **U.S.A.**
   Telephone: 303/575-2547.
   Foundation: 1946. *Number of specimens:* 15.000.
   Herbarium: Colorado native and cultivated plants.
   Director: WILLIAM G. GAMBILL.
   Curator: HELEN M. ZEINER.
   Associated botanic garden: Denver Botanic Gardens.

DE PERE: *The Heraly MacDonald Herbarium, Division of Natural Sciences, Saint Norbert College,* **(SNC)**, De Pere, Wisconsin 54115, **U.S.A.**
   Telephone: 414/337-3200.
   Status: Private college.
   Foundation: 1926. *Number of specimens:* 10.000.
   Herbarium: Vascular plants of Wisconsin and the world.
   Curator: JOHN PHYTHYON (Plant physiology).
   Loans: To recognized botanical institutions or specialists.

DETROIT: *Herbarium, Department of Biology, Wayne State University,* **(WUD)**, Detroit, Michigan 48202, **U.S.A.**
   Telephone: 313/577-2873, 2874, or 2875.
   Foundation: 1950. *Number of specimens:* 17.000.
   Herbarium: Regional, mainly Michigan.
   Curator: C. M. ROGERS, 1919.
   Specialization in research: Systematics of *Linum* and segregate genera.
   Loans: No restrictions.
   Exchange: Available: Some Great Lakes region plants.

DIJON: *Laboratoire de Botanique, Faculté des Sciences de la Vie et de l'Environnement,* **(DI)**, Bâtiment Mirande, 6 Bd Gabriel, F 21.000 Dijon, **France.** (Information 1974)
   Status: University.
   Number of specimens: 5.000.
   Periodical and serial works: Bulletin Scientifique de Bourgogne, Travaux des Laboratoires de Biologie Végétale de la Faculté des Sciences de Dijon.

DILLON BEACH: *Herbarium, Pacific Marine Station,* **(PMS),** Dillon Beach, Marin Co., California 94929, **U.S.A.** – – discontinued.

DINARD: *Laboratoire Maritime du Muséum National d'Histoire Naturelle,* **(DIN),** 17 Avenue George V, Dinard (Ille-et-Vilaine), **France.** (Information 1974)
Status: Directed by the Muséum d'Histoire Naturelle de Paris.
Foundation: 1882, transferred to Dinard in 1935.
Number of specimens: 6.500.
   Herbarium: Local and Atlantic flora.
   Specialization in research: Ecology of man-made lakes.
   Loans: To recognized scientists and institutions.
   Periodical and serial works: Bulletin du Laboratoire Maritime de Dinard.

DIRE DAWA: *Herbarium, Agricultural College of the Haile Selassi 1st University,* **(ACD),** c/o Agricultural College, Box 138, Dire Dawa, **Ethiopia.** (Information 1974)
   Number of specimens: 6.000.
   Herbarium: Plants of Harar Highlands.

DISKO: *Herbarium, Danish Arctic Station,* **(DISKO),** Disko, 3953 Godhavn, **Greenland.**
Status: Institute at the University of Copenhagen.
Foundation: 1906.
   Specialization in research: Local flora and fauna and their biology.
   Periodical and serial works: Publications from the Danish Arctic Station on Disko Island, Greenland.
   Remarks: The herbarium of the Arctic Station has been removed except for a small collection of local flora, all duplicates from the Botanical Museum of Copenhagen.

DIYARBAKIR: *Diyarbakir Üniversitesi Herbaryumu,* **(DUF),** Diyarbakir Üniversitesi, Fen Fakültesi, Botanik Bölümü, Diyarbakir, **Turkey.**
Telephone: 3585.
Status: University of Diyarbakir.
Foundation: 1974. *Number of specimens:* 2.500.
Herbarium: South-East Anatolia.
Important collections: H. Demiriz, Ö. Saya, H. Misirdali, H. Malyer, G. Kaynak (1974–79).
   Director: HÜSEYIN ŞAHINKAYA, 1921 (Microbiology).
   Curator: HÜSEYIN MISIRDALI, 1946 (*Consolida* and *Delphinium*).
   Staff members: DAVUT BAŞARAN, 1946 (Tissue culture).
      GÖNÜL KAYNAK, 1950 (Pteridophytes of Diyarbakir area).
      NAZMI KILIÇ, 1943 (Ecophysiology).
      HULUSI MALYER, 1954 (Geophytes of Karacadağ).
      ÖMER SAYA, 1952 (*Bunium* and *Carum*).

Specialization in research: Flora and vegetation of South-East Anatolia.
   Loans: In general to recognized institutions and herbaria.
   Exchange: Available: Some duplicates of South-East Anatolian plants.

DNEPROPETROVSK: *Herbarium, Department of Botany, Dnepropetrovsk State University,* **(DSU),** Gagarina Prospect 72, 320625 Dnepropetrovsk, **U.S.S.R.**
   Foundation: 1918. *Number of specimens:* 80.000.
   Director: A. L. BELGARD.

DOMODOSSOLA: *Herbarium, Collegio Rosmini,* **(DOMO),** Domodossola, **Italy.** (Information 1964)
Status: Private foundation directed by Rosminian religious order.
   Foundation: 1874. *Number of specimens:* 13.500.
   Herbarium: Flora Oscellana, flora Italica, flora Formazzensis.

DONSKOYE: *Herbarium, Galichya Gora Reserve of Voronezh University,* **(VU),** Zadonsk Region, Lipetsk Oblast, 399020 S. Donskoye, **U.S.S.R.**
   Number of specimens: 40.000.
   Director of Reserve: A. J. GRIGORJEVSKAJA.
   Director of Herbarium: L. N. KRASNOSHTANOVA.

DORNBIRN: *Herbarium, Vorarlberger Naturschau,* **(BREG),** Marktstrasse 33, A-6850 Dornbirn, **Austria.** (Information 1974)
   Foundation: 1959.
   Herbarium: Flora of Vorarlberg.
   Important collections: Herb. A. Krafft, J. Blumrich, A. Ender, T. von A. Bruhin, Schwimmer.

DORTMUND: *Herbarium dendrologicum tremoniense, Botanischer Garten Rombergpark der Stadt Dortmund,* **(DORT),** Am Rombergpark 49, D-46 Dortmund 50, **Federal Republic of Germany,** BRD.
Telephone: 0231/54224164.
Status: City owned, belonging to the community of Dortmund.
   Foundation: 1951. *Number of specimens:* 8.000.
   Herbarium: Woody plants, mainly from temperate zones, also some subtropical.
   Important collections: Cultivars from deciduous and evergreen trees and shrubs of the temperate zones.
   Director: OTTO BÜNEMANN, 1929 (General dendrology, extension).
   Curator: HERIBERT REIF, 1949 (Dendrology: conifers).
   Staff members: GÜNTER BEIER, 1930 (Dendrology; horticultural cultivars).
      MANFRED KLOSE, 1926 (Dendrology; roses).
   Specialization in research: Horticultural dendrology.
   Exchange: None, impossible because of lack of staff.
   Remarks: Nearly all specimens were collected by

79

G. Krüssmann, the former Director of the herbarium.

DOUAI: *Société Nationale d'Agriculture, Sciences et Arts,* (**DO**), Douai, **France.**

DOVER: *Claude E. Phillips Herbarium, Department of Agriculture and Natural Resources, Delaware State College,* (**DOV**), Dover, Delaware 19901, **U.S.A.**
Telephone: 302/736-5120; 736-5195.
Foundation: 1977. *Number of specimens:* 60.500.
Herbarium: Plants of the Del-Mar-Va Peninsula; University of Delaware (DELS).
Important collections: H. R. Baker, William Canby, Claude E. Phillips, Edward Tatnall, Robert Tatnall.
   Co-Curators: NORMAN H. DILL, 1938 (Flora of Del-Mar-Va).
   THOMPSON D. PIZZOLATO, 1943 (Floral anatomy of Poaceae).
   ARTHUR O. TUCKER, 1945 (*Mentha;* flora of Del-Mar-Va).
Specialization in research: Flora of Del-Mar-Va; cultivated herbs and essential oil plants.
Loans: To recognized botanical institutions.
Exchange: Available: Material from Del-Mar-Va.
Remarks: DELS herbarium was merged with DOV in 1980.

DRESDEN: *Herbarium des Botanischen Gartens der Technischen Universität Dresden,* (**DR**), Stübelallee 2, DDR-8019 Dresden, **German Democratic Republic, DDR.**
Status: University.
Foundation: 1879. *Number of specimens:* 300.000.
Herbarium: Worldwide phanerogams and cryptogams, especially Europe and Mittelmeergebiet.
Important collections: Th. Wolf (*Potentilla*).
Director: HARALD LINKE, 1928 (Garden and landscape development).
Curator: WOLFRAM SPANOWSKY, 1929 (Palynology, Primulaceae, succulents).
Associated botanic garden: Botanischer Garten der Technischen Universität Dresden.
Loans: To recognized botanical institutions.
Periodical and serial works: Berichte der Arbeitsgemeinschaft sächsischer Botaniker.
Exchange: Possible and desired, on a small scale.

DUBLIN: *National Museum of Ireland,* (**DBN**), Kildare Street, Dublin, **Ireland** –– *see* DUBLIN: *National Botanic Gardens* (formerly DUB).

DUBLIN: *Herbarium, National Botanic Gardens,* (**DBN**), Glasnevin, Dublin 9, **Ireland.**
Telephone: 377596, 374388.
Status: State directed (Department of Agriculture).
Foundation: 1795 (Botanic Gardens). *Number of specimens:* 600.000.
Herbarium: Irish, British and worldwide phanero-

gams and cryptogams.
Important collections: W. R. McNab (incl. Robert Brown, Australia), J. A. L. Preiss (Australia), J. McNab (N. America), C. E. H. Ostenfeld (Australia), Augustine Henry (China, Forestry herb.), W. H. Harvey (Australia, S. Africa), J. Niven (S. Africa), V. Ball (India), H. C. Hart (Br. Polar Expedition, Arctic), R. Praeger, H. W. Lett, Th. Jones, M. C. Knowles, A. Ball, David Moore, T. Johnson, Baron de Tabley (all British Isles); Hort. Siccus Leydenensis (c. 1660).
Director: AIDAN BRADY.
Curator: MARY J. P. SCANNELL (Flora of Ireland; *Erica, Juncus, Hydrilla, Rumex,* mycological flora of Ireland, freshwater and marine algae, Quaternary macrofossils, biohistory).
Staff members: E. CHARLES NELSON, 1951 (*Erica* in Ireland, Australian Proteaceae, biohistory and bibliography).
   DONAL M. SYNNOTT (Irish bryophytes and pteridophytes).
Specialization in research: Flora of Ireland.
Associated botanic garden: National Botanic Gardens.
Loans: To recognized botanical institutions.
Periodical and serial works: Glasra (Contrib. Nat. Bot. Gard., Glasnevin); Index Seminum.
Exchange: Worldwide, especially Europe.

DUBLIN: *Herbarium, School of Botany, Trinity College,* (**TCD**), Dublin 2, **Ireland.**
Telephone: 772941.
Status: University.
Foundation: 1834. *Number of specimens:* 225.000.
Herbarium: Mainly angiosperms and algae, smaller collections of other groups.
Important collections: W. H. Harvey (algae and South African angiosperms; many types), A. F. G. Kerr (Thailand; many isotypes), J. D. Hooker (Himalaya; many isotypes).
Curator: D. A. WEBB, 1912 (Flora of Ireland and Europe, *Saxifraga*).
Specialization in research: Flora of western Ireland, taxonomy of European *Saxifraga*.
Associated botanic garden: Trinity College Botanic Garden, Palmerston Park, Dublin 6.
Loans: To recognized botanical institutions, for 6 months to one year.
Exchange: Limited.

DUISBURG: *Fach Botanik, Gesamthochschule Duisburg,* (**DUIS**), Fachbereich 6, Lotharstrasse 65, Postfach 101629, D4100 Duisburg 1, **Federal Republic of Germany,** BRD.
Telephone: 0203/3051.
Status: Gesamthochschule (University) Duisburg.
Foundation: 1972. *Number of specimens:* 40.000 (Bryophyta 30.000, phanerogams 10.000).
Herbarium: Most species from Germany, especially of Nordrhein-Westfalen.
Director and *Head Curator:* RUPRECHT DÜLL,

1931 (Bryophyta).
Curator: HERFRIED KUTZELNIGG, 1941 (Phanero-gamae).

DULUTH: *Olga Lakela Herbarium, Department of Biology, University of Minnesota,* (**DUL**), Duluth, Minnesota 55812, **U.S.A.**
Telephone: 218/726-8110; 726-7264.
Foundation: 1935. *Number of specimens:* 35.500.
Herbarium: Primarily flora of northern Minnesota; representatives of most U.S. genera, especially south Florida.
Important collections: Olga Lakela.
Director and Curator: PAUL H. MONSON, 1925 (Marsh and aquatic flowering plants; local flora).
Specialization in research: Flora of northern Minnesota, especially marsh and aquatic flowering plants.
Loans: No special restrictions.
Exchange: Available: Local material. Desired: Limited amounts of general U.S. and Canadian material.

DUNDO: *Herbarium, Museu do Dundo,* (**DIA**), Dundo, Lunda District, **Angola.** (Information 1974)
Status: Private foundation.
Foundation: 1947. *Number of specimens:* 1.200.
Herbarium: Plants of Angola.

DUNEDIN: *Herbarium, Botany Department, University of Otago,* (**OTA**), P.O. Box 56, Dunedin, **New Zealand.**
Telephone: 771-640, ext. 8894/5.
Status: University.
Foundation: 1946. *Number of specimens:* 25.000.
Herbarium: Mainly New Zealand native vascular plants, some bryophytes and lichens.
Head of Botany Department: P. BANNISTER, 1939 (Physiological ecology).
Specialization in research: Montane and alpine species.
Loans: Available, if sent at own expense.

DUNEDIN: *Herbarium, Otago Museum,* (**OTM**), Dunedin, **New Zealand.**

DURANT: *Herbarium, Department of Biology, Southeastern Oklahoma State University,* (**DUR**), Durant, Oklahoma 74701, **U.S.A.**
Telephone: 405/924-0121, ext. 209.
Foundation: 1969. *Number of specimens:* 52.000.
Herbarium: One-third Oklahoma, one-third other states of U.S., one-third foreign.
Important collections: John and Connie Taylor, G. W. Stevens (early Oklahoma), E. J. Palmer (early woody Oklahoma), Lindheimer (early Texas); more than 2.500 sheets of *Solidago*; extensive collections of Alaska and Dauphin Island, Alabama.
Director and Curator: R. JOHN TAYLOR, 1930 (Oklahoma flora; rarely collected and endangered

species; aquatic and woody species).
Staff member: CONSTANCE S. TAYLOR, 1937 (Oklahoma flora; *Euthamia, Solidago*).
Specialization in research: Oklahoma, Alaska, and Dauphin Island floras; rare species; *Solidago, Euthamia,* and *Aster.*
Loans: For 6 months.
Periodical and serial works: Publication of the Herbarium of Southeastern Oklahoma State University (published irregularly).
Exchange: Available: General material. Wanted: General material, especially *Solidago* and *Euthamia.*

DURBAN: *Natal Herbarium,* (**NH**), Botanical Research Unit, Botanic Gardens Road, Durban, 4001 **South Africa.**
Telephone: 031-216441.
Status: State owned regional herbarium of Botanical Research Institute, Pretoria (PRE).
Foundation: 1882. *Number of specimens:* 50.000 (c. 50.000 extra-African and tropical African specimens now housed in PRE).
Herbarium: Southern Africa mainly Natal.
Important collections: J. Buchanan (ferns and grasses), M. S. Evans, H. Forbes, A. P. D. McClean, E. J. Moll, J. H. Ross, R. G. Strey, J. M. Wood.
Director: B. DE WINTER, Botanical Research Institute, Pretoria (PRE).
Curator: Vacant.
Staff members: L. MACKENSIE.
B. J. PIENAAR (General identifications).
B. M. SASSEN.
Herbarium: Flora of Natal.
Loans: To recognized botanical institutions.
Periodical and serial works: see PRE: Flora of Southern Africa; Flowering Plants of Africa; Bothalia.
Exchange: Through PRE.

DURHAM: *Moss Herbarium, American Bryological Society, Department of Botany, Duke University,* (**ABSM**), Durham, North Carolina 27706, **U.S.A.**
Remarks: This herbarium has been intercalated into the Duke University Herbarium (DUKE). The ABSM packets are so noted.

DURHAM: *Herbarium, Department of Botany, University of Durham,* (**DHM**), South Road, Durham, England, **Great Britain.**
Telephone: (0385) 64971.
Status: University.
Foundation: c. 1948. *Number of specimens:* 20.000.
Herbarium: Mainly British vascular plants, some European and N. American.
Director: DONALD BOULTER, 1926 (Molecular biologist).
Loans: On request.

DURHAM: *Herbarium, Department of Botany, Duke*

University, (**DUKE**), Durham, North Carolina 27706, **U.S.A.**

Telephone: 919/684-3056 (vascular plants); 684-3375 (algae); 684-3603 (bryophytes, lichens).

Status: Privately endowed university.

Foundation: 1932. *Number of specimens:* 555.000 (275.000 vascular plants; 280.000 algae, bryophytes, lichens).

Herbarium: Southeastern U.S.; Central America.

Important collections: Herbaria of A. J. Grout, Johan Havaas, F. J. Harmand, American Bryological Society.

Curators: ROBERT L. WILBUR, 1925 (Systematics of vascular plants, especially of eastern North America and Central America).

LEWIS E. ANDERSON, 1912 (Bryophytes of eastern North America; cytobryology, ecology, and systematics).

WILLIAM LOUIS CULBERSON, 1929 (Lichenology; chemosystematics and niche characteristics).

TERRY W. JOHNSON, JR., 1923 (Mycology; systematics of marine and freshwater fungi; myxomycetes).

RICHARD B. SEARLES, 1936 (Phycology; systematics and ecology of benthic marine algae, especially western North Atlantic and southern South America).

Staff member: DONALD E. STONE, 1930 (Biosystematics; Juglandaceae; pollination biology).

Loans: Usual conditions.

Exchange: Desired: Vascular plants from Mexico, Central America, and West Indies.

Remarks: Excellent bryological and lichenological herbaria.

DURHAM: *Albion R. Hodgdon Herbarium, Department of Botany and Plant Pathology, University of New Hampshire*, (**NHA**), Nesmith Hall, Durham, New Hampshire 03824, **U.S.A.**

Telephone: 603/862-2060.

Foundation: 1892. *Number of specimens:* 130.000.

Herbarium: New Hampshire vascular and marine algal floras; Maine; coastal New England; Bay of Fundy (Canada).

Important collections: W. Boott, W. M. Canby, A. A. Eaton, A. Fendler (New Mexico), K. Furbish, A. R. Hodgdon (New England), M. E. Jones, F. Lindheimer (Texas), T. C. Porter, G. Vasey; Bowdoin College herbarium (Parker Cleaveland); Portland Society of Natural History herbarium.

Director and Curator of Vascular Plants: GAR-

RETT E. CROW, 1942 (Vascular plants; Caryophyllaceae, *Sagina*).

Curator of Marine Algae: ARTHUR C. MATHIESON, 1937 (Ecology and floristics of marine algae).

Staff members: ROBERT O. BLANCHARD, 1939 (Mycology).

A. LINN BOGLE, 1931 (Hamamelidaceae; vascular plants).

Specialization in research: Floristics and endangered species of New Hampshire/New England; aquatic flora of New England; systematics of vascular plants; ecology and floristics of North Atlantic marine algae; systematics of marine algae.

Loans: To recognized institutions.

Periodical and serial works: New Hampshire Agricultural Experiment Station (Bulletins and Research Reports).

Exchange: Especially aquatic and alpine plants.

Remarks: Historical ties with the Dartmouth College herbarium, Hanover (HNH). The collection at Dartmouth was divided, and the NHA collection was then founded with a nucleus of 1.500 specimens in 1892 when the Agricultural College moved to Durham from the Dartmouth Campus it had shared.

DUSHAMBE: *Department of Flora and Systematics of Higher Plants, Botanical Institute of the Tadzhikistan Academy of Sciences*, (**TAD**), Karamova St. 27, 734017 Dushambe, **U.S.S.R.**

Foundation: 1932. *Number of specimens:* 145.000.

Herbarium: Flora of Tadzhikistan.

Director: P. N. OVCZINNIKOV.

DÜSSELDORF: *Botanisches Institut der Universität*, (**DUSS**), Universitätstrasse 1, 4000 Düsseldorf 1, **Federal Republic of Germany,** BRD.

Telephone: 0211/3111.

Status: University of Düsseldorf.

Foundation: 1967. *Number of specimens:* 6.000.

Herbarium: Cultivated *Oenothera*.

Important collections: Oenothera.

Director: WILFRIED STUBBE, 1920 (Cytogenetics of *Oenothera*).

Curator: WERNER DIETRICH, 1938 (Taxonomy of *Oenothera*).

Specialization in research: Cytogenetics and taxonomy of *Oenothera*.

Associated botanic garden: Yes.

Loans: To recognized institutions and individuals.

E

EAST LANSING: *Herbarium, Department of Botany and Plant Pathology, Michigan State University,* (**MSC**), East Lansing, Michigan 48824, **U.S.A.**

Telephone: 517/355-4696 (Beal-Darlington herbarium); 355-4580 (Cryptogamic herbarium); 355-4630 (Paleobotanical-palynological collections).

Status: Under Department of Botany and Plant Pathology, Michigan State University, a land-grant state university governed by a Board of Trustees.

Foundation: 1863. *Number of specimens:* 426.304 (255.243 Beal-Darlington herbarium; 142.261 cryptogams; 28.800 paleobotanical-palynological collections).

Herbarium: Comprised of the Beal-Darlington herbarium (vacular plants), the Cryptogamic herbarium (non-vascular plants), and the Paleobotanical-palynological collections. Worldwide collections with specialization in vascular plants of North America, Mexico, Guatemala, and the Bahamas; lichens and some bryophytes of North America, the West Indies, south temperate and subantarctic regions; paleobotany and palynology of North America.

Important collections: Vascular plants: W. J. Beal (Gramineae), W. T. Gillis (Anacardiaceae; Bahamas), J. A. Churchill (especially Cyperaceae), J. H. Beaman (alpine areas of Mexico and Guatemala, tropics of Veracruz; Compositae of Mexico and Central America); holotypes of J. W. Andresen, W. Beal, J. H. Beaman, G. E. Crow, D. C. D. DeJong, J. J. Furlow, W. T. Gillis, J. L. Grashoff, E. K. Longpre, I. W. Knobloch, E. P. Roberts, W. D. Stevens, P. Van Faasen, E. E. Watson. Lichens: I. M. Brodo (Long Island, New York), R. C. Harris (especially pyrenocarpous lichens), H. A. Imshaug (alpine western America, West Indies, Tenerife, south temperate/subantarctic regions), R. M. Taylor (littoral northeastern America), C. M. Wetmore (Black Hills of South Dakota, Wyoming). Bryophytes: H. T. Darlington (Michigan), J. J. Engel (Falkland Islands, Patagonia, Kerguelen, New Zealand), D. Vitt (Auckland and Campbell Islands), M. Ostafichuk (Tierra del Fuego). Fungi: Myxomycete collections of C. J. Alexopoulos and E. S. Beneke. Paleobotany-palynology: The Michigan Basin, Upper Cretaceous of the Rocky Mountain area, Miocene of Oregon and western Idaho, Pennsylvanian of the Central Appalachians, modern sediments of the Gulf of California and western Mexico.

Curator of the Beal-Darlington Herbarium: JOHN H. BEAMAN, 1929 (Alpine areas of Mexico and Guatemala; tropics of Veracruz; Compositae of Mexico and Central America).

Acting Curator of the Beal-Darlington Herbarium: SUSAN R. KEPHART, 1952 (Evolutionary ecology and systematics).

Curator of the Paleobotanical-Palynological Collections: AUREAL CROSS, 1916 (Paleobotany, palynology).

Curator of the Cryptogamic Herbarium: HENRY A. IMSHAUG, 1925 (Lichens).

Staff members: RAYMOND H. HOLLENSEN, 1931 (Hepatics).

CAROL JONES, 1926 (Bibliographic materials).

IRVING W. KNOBLOCH, 1907 (Pteridophytes).

STEPHEN N. STEPHENSON, 1933 (Ecology; agrostology).

RALPH E. TAGGART, 1941 (Paleobotany; angiosperm leaf morphology).

WILLIAM TAI, 1934 (Cytogenetics and cytotaxonomy).

WAYNE H. WEIDLICH, 1943 (Plant anatomy and morphology).

Specialization in research: Biosystematics of Compositae; alpine flora of Mexico and Guatemala; cytotaxonomic studies of cheilanthoid ferns; temperate forest, prairie and Sonoran desert ecosystems; palynology of ancient and modern sediments; evaluation of the taxonomic value of fine venation features in angiosperm leaves; developmental organization of vascular systems in the Nymphaeaceae and ferns; cytotaxonomic and cytogenetic studies in the Gramineae, Onagraceae, Cyperaceae, and *Mimulus;* lichen taxonomy and phytogeography; speciation and floral biology of vascular plants, especially *Asclepias.*

Associated botanic garden: W. J. Beal Botanical Garden, 310 Manly Miles Building, Michigan State University.

Loans: In general, to recognized scientific institutions made through the Curators of the Beal-Darlington Herbarium, the Cryptogamic Herbarium, and the Paleobotanical-Palynological Collections.

Periodical and serial works: Publications of the Museum, Michigan State University, Biological Series, published at irregular intervals by the Museum.

Exchange; Available: Vascular plants of Michigan, Mexico, Guatemala, and Nicaragua; lichens and bryophytes. Desired: Vascular plants of all areas, especially Compositae and tropical plants; lichens and bryophytes.

EAST ORANGE: *Herbarium, Department of Biology, Upsala College,* (**EONJ**), East Orange, New Jersey 07019, **U.S.A.**

Telephone: 201/266-7207.

Number of specimens: 1.000.

Herbarium: Mainly local plants.

Curator: EDWARD S. KUBERSKY.

EDINBURG: *Herbarium, Department of Biology, Pan American University,* (**PAUH**), Edinburg, Texas 78539, **U.S.A.**

Telephone: 512/381-3537.
Foundation: 1970. *Number of specimens:* 7.000.
Herbarium: Flora of southern Texas.
Director: ROBERT LONARD, 1942 (Plant taxonomy and ecology).
Specialization in research: Floristics of the region.
Loans: For 6 months.
Exchange: Yes.

EDINBURGH: *Austral Cryptogamic Herbarium, Institute of Terrestrial Ecology,* **(ACHE),** Bush Estate, Penicuik, Midlothian EH26 OQB, Scotland, **Great Britain.**
Telephone: 031-445-4343.
Status: Sponsored by a Research Council.
Foundation: 1975. *Number of specimens:* 20.000.
Herbarium: Bryophytes of Antarctic regions and southern South America, New Zealand and Arctic material of bi-polar species.
Important collections: British Antarctic Survey Bryophyte Herbarium (AAS), on permanent loan; bryophytes of sub-Antarctic islands particularly South Georgia and Iles Crozet.
Director: S. W. GREENE, 1928, Head of Sub-Division of Plant Biology (Austral bryophytes, bibliographic documentation of bryophytes).
Curator: B. G. BELL, 1942 (Taxonomy of Antarctic mosses).
Staff members: A. HALCROW, 1936 (Data banking).
G. G. HÄSSEL DE MENENDEZ, 1927, Honorary member (Taxonomy of Patagonian and Antarctic liverworts).
P. J. LIGHTOWLERS, 1955 (Taxonomy of Antarctic mosses, especially *Tortula*).
T. D. MURRAY, 1944 (Cultivation of bryophytes).
Specialization in research: Antarctic, sub-Antarctic and southern South America, bryophyte flora.
Loans: To recognized botanical institutions.
Periodical and serial works: Bryophyte flora of South Georgia and Antarctica appearing in British Antarctic Survey Bulletin; British Antarctic Survey Scientific Reports.
Exchange: Available and desired: Bryophytes from Antarctic regions and neighboring continental areas.

EDINBURGH: *Herbarium, Royal Botanic Garden,* **(E),** Inverleith Row, Edinburgh EH3 5LR, Scotland, **Great Britain.**
Telephone: 031/552 7171.
Status: Directed by the Government.
Foundation: 1670. *Number of specimens:* 1.700.000.
Herbarium: Worldwide phanerogams and cryptogams.
Important collections: G. Forrest (China: Phanerogam herbarium of A. A. H. Leveillé (includes Maire, Esquirol, Faurie, Taquet specimens from China);

P. H. Davis (Turkey, SW. Asia, N. Africa); B. L. Burtt (S. Africa); R. K. Greville (Cryptogams); Phanerogams (except British) of Glasgow University on permanent loan (E-GL).
Director: D. M. HENDERSON, 1927 (Uredinales).
Curator: I. C. HEDGE, 1928 (Flora of SW. Asia, *Salvia* of Old World).
Assistant Keeper: J. CULLEN, 1936 (Cultivated plants, *Rhododendron*).
Staff members: G. C. ARGENT, 1941 (Tropical plants, especially Ericaceae, Musaceae).
D. F. CHAMBERLAIN, 1941 (*Rhododendron,* bryophytes).
B. COPPINS, 1949 (Ascomycetes, lichens).
A. J. C. GRIERSON, 1929 (Compositae, flora of Bhutan).
J. M. LAMOND, 1936 (SW. Asian Umbelliferae).
L. A. LAUENER, 1918 (Leveillé herbarium, Sino-Himalayan Ranunculaceae).
D. G. LONG, 1948 (Flora of Bhutan, bryophytes).
D. McKEAN, 1948 (British herbarium).
V. MATTHEWS, 1941 (Cultivated plants).
A. G. MILLER, 1951 (Cruciferae, flora of Arabia).
C. N. PAGE, 1942 (Coniferae, pteridophytes).
J. A. RATTER, 1934 (Brazilian vegetation, cytogenetics).
R. M. SMITH, 1953 (SE. Asian Zingiberaceae).
R. WATLING, 1938 (Agaricales, especially Bolbitiaceae and Boletaceae).
P. J. B. WOODS, 1932 (Orchidaceae SE. Asia, *Aeschynanthus,* Gesneriaceae).
Associates: J. C. M. ALEXANDER, 1944 (Taxonomy of cultivated plants).
B. L. BURTT, 1913 (Gesneriaceae, Zingiberaceae; S. Africa).
H. H. DAVIDIAN, 1907 (*Rhododendron*).
P. D. ORTON (Agaricales).

Education and Museum
G. ANDERSON, 1944 (Horticultural training).
R. B. BURBIDGE, 1943 (Exhibition Hall).
C. C. WOOD, 1945 (Education).

Library
M. V. MATHEW, 1928 (Librarian).

University of Edinburgh/SRC Flora of Turkey Unit
P. H. DAVIS, 1918 (Flora of Turkey).
J. R. EDMONDSON, 1948 (Flora of Turkey).
R. R. MILL, 1950 (Flora of Turkey).
Specialization in research: Taxonomy of plants in cultivation: Ericaceae, Coniferae, Gesneriaceae, Labiatae, Zingiberaceae; Floras of SW. Asia, Bhutan: Uredinales and Agaricales.
Associated botanic garden: Royal Botanic Garden, Edinburgh. Outstations: Younger Botanic Garden, Benmore, by Dunoon, Argyll; Logan Bo-

tanic Garden, by Ardwell, Wigtown; Dawyck Arboretum, Stobo, Peebleshire.

Loans: To recognized institutions.

Periodical and serial works: Notes Royal Botanic Garden Edinburgh, Catalogue of Living Plants.

Exchange: Available: Mostly SW. Asia.

EDMOND: *Herbarium, Biology Department, Central State University,* (**CSU**), 100 North University Drive, Edmond, Oklahoma 73034, **U.S.A.**

Telephone: 405/341-2980.

Foundation: 1940. *Number of specimens:* 8.700.

Herbarium: Emphasis on Oklahoma, some Mexico and southwestern U.S.

Important collections: Viola, Desmanthus.

Director and Curator: JOE E. VAUGHAN, 1932 (Taxonomy of legumes; flora of Oklahoma and Mexico).

Staff members: THIERON HARRISON, 1943 (Flora of Oklahoma).

NORMAN RUSSELL, 1924 (*Viola;* flora of Oklahoma).

Loans: No special restrictions.

Exchange: Available: Oklahoma; violets of North America; *Desmanthus.*

EDMONTON: *Herbarium, Department of Botany, University of Alberta,* (**ALTA**), Edmonton, Alberta, **Canada** T6G 2E9.

Telephone: 403/432-5518 (paleobotany); 432-5523 (vascular plants, bryophytes, lichens); 432-3410 (fungi).

Foundation: 1916. *Number of specimens:* 203.000 (83.000 vascular plants; 12.000 lichens; 85.000 bryophytes; 15.000 fossils, including 7.200 compressions, 6.000 slides).

Herbarium: Vascular plants and lichens of arctic and cordilleran Canada; bryophytes of the New World and Australasia; wood-decay fungi; Tertiary and carboniferous plant fossils.

Important collections: W. C. McCalla (vascular plants of Alberta), E. H. Moss (Vascular plants of Alberta), J. G. Packer (vascular plants of Alberta), W. N. Stewart (fossils), G. H. Turner (vascular plants of Alberta), D. H. Vitt (bryophytes); ca. 40 vascular plant, 60 bryophyte, 35 fossil, and 10 lichen type specimens.

Curators: LORENE L. KENNEDY, 1921 (Mycology; biosystematics of Polyporaceae).

JOHN G. PACKER, 1929; 403/432-3627 (Vascular plants; vascular plant flora of Alberta; taxonomy of arctic and alpine plants).

RUTH A. STOCKEY, 1950 (Paleobotany; conifer evolution).

DALE H. VITT, 1944; 403/432-3380 (Bryophytes and lichens; bryophyte systematics and evolution; ecology of wetlands).

Staff members: LOUISE ABELE, 1952 (Mycology).

MIKE OSTAFICHUK, 1929 (Bryophytes).

GORDON RINGIUS, 1949 (Vascular plant taxonomy).

Associated staff: K. E. DENFORD (Chemosystematics).

M. HICKMAN (Algal culture collection).

C. SCHWEGER (Pollen collection; Department of Anthropology).

Specialization in research: Arctic and alpine taxonomy; paleobotany of western North America; wood-decay fungal research; systematics of polar and temperate bryophytes and lichens.

Associated botanic garden: Devonian Botanic Garden.

Loans: Six months to one year, from individual curators, renewal upon request.

Exchange: Bryophytes, lichens, Polyporales, vascular plants, available from individual curators.

EDMONTON: *Herbarium, Northern Forest Research Centre, Canadian Forestry Service, Environment Canada,* (**CAFB**), 5320 122 Street, Edmonton, Alberta, **Canada** T6H 3S5.

Telephone: 403/435-7210.

Status: Government of Canada.

Foundation: CAFB (1929) –– Calgary (vascular plants); WINF (1930) –– Winnipeg; amalgamated and re-established in Edmonton in 1971. *Number of specimens:* 17.000 (13.000 vascular plants, 4.000 bryophytes and lichens).

Herbarium: Forest flora (including bryophytes and lichens) of Manitoba, Saskatchewan, Alberta, Northwest and Yukon Territories.

Important collections: S. C. Zoltai, G. W. Scotter, and J. D. Johnson (vascular plants of Northwest Territories); I. G. Corns, P. Achuff, S. Kojima, and J. R. Dyck (vascular plants from Banff and Jasper National Parks, Alberta).

Director: G. T. SILVER (Entomology).

Curator: J. D. JOHNSON, 1951 (Floristic ecology, taxonomy).

Staff members: I. G. CORNS, 1948 (Forest soil relationships; land classification; ecology).

Y. HIRATSUKA, 1933 (Taxonomy and biology of forest tree rusts; tree disease identification).

W. D. HOLLAND, 1923 (Forest soils; land classification).

S. S. MALHOTRA (Air pollution impact; physiology).

S. C. ZOLTAI, 1928 (Soils, ecology, and vegetation of forested and northern communities).

Specialization in research: Plant ecology; silviculture research; environmental impact; land classification.

Loans: Courtesy exchange.

Exchange: Limited selection of vascular plants.

Remarks: The herbarium is maintained primarily to facilitate research in forest communities in central and northern Canada.

EDMONTON: *Mycological Herbarium, Northern*

Forest Research Centre, Canadian Forestry Service, (**CFB**), 5320 122 Street, Edmonton, Alberta, **Canada** T6H 3S5.
Telephone: 403/435-7210.
Status: Government of Canada.
Foundation: CFB (1952) and WINFM (1965) amalgamated and re-established in Edmonton in 1970.
Number of specimens: 25.000 fungi.
Herbarium: Forest fungi of Alberta, Saskatchewan, Manitoba, and the Northwest Territories.
Important collections: B. C. Sutton (forest microfungi; Manitoba, Saskatchewan).
Director: G. T. SILVER (Entomology).
Curator: Y. HIRATSUKA, 1933 (Taxonomy and biology of rust fungi; tree disease identification).
Staff members: J. EMOND, 1928 (Tree pest extension service).
P. J. MARUYAMA, 1929 (Tree disease identification).
J. PETTY, 1926 (Field survey of forest pests).
J. M. POWELL, 1933 (Serobiology of tree diseases; bioclimatology).
H. ZALASKY, 1924 (Canker diseases; frost injury of trees).
Specialization in research: Detection and identification of forest diseases of Alberta, Saskatchewan, Manitoba, and the Northwest Territories; taxonomy and biology of forest tree rusts of western North America.
Loans: Courtesy exchange.
Exchange: Available: Forest tree rusts of western Canada; forest fungi of Alberta, Saskatchewan, and Northwest Territories.
Remarks: All specimens formerly in CFB (Calgary), WINFM (Winnipeg), and SAFB (Saskatoon) are now included in this herbarium.

EDMONTON: *Herbarium, Provincial Museum of Alberta,* (**PMAE**), 12845 102nd Avenue, Edmonton, Alberta, **Canada** T5N OM6.
Telephone: 403/427-1734.
Status: Government of Alberta.
Foundation: 1967. *Number of specimens:* 9.000.
Herbarium: Chiefly vascular plants of the province of Alberta; beginning ethnobotanical collections pertaining to Indian people of Alberta.
Curator: JULIA O. HRAPKO (Alpine plant ecology; ethnobotany).
Specialization in research: Flora and ethnobotany of Alberta; vegetation of Alberta Rocky Mountains.

EGER: *Herbarium, Department of Botany, Ho Si Minh Teacher's College,* (**EGR**), H-3301, Eger, pf. 43, **Hungary**. (Information 1974)
Status: Directed by Hungarian Ministry of Education.
Foundation: 1948. *Number of specimens:* 27.000.
Herbarium: Worldwide bryophytes, especially North Vietnam, India and East Africa; lichens and

phanerogams from Europe.
Specialization in research: Bryoflora of North Vietnam and East Africa, lichens of North Hungary, phanerogam flora of SW Hungary.
Loans: To recognized botanical institutions.
Periodical and serial works: Acta Academiae Paedagogicae.
Remarks: Foreign bryophytes on long-term loan to VBI.

ELISABETHVILLE: *Laboratoire de Biologie Générale et de Botanique,* (**EBV**) – – *see* LUBUMBASHI.

ELLENSBURG: *Herbarium, Biology Department, Central Washington University,* (**ELRG**), Ellensburg, Washington 98926, **U.S.A.**
Telephone: 509/963-3370.
Foundation: 1920. *Number of specimens:* 17.500.
Herbarium: Regional flora, including 8.500 fossil wood and 5.000 fossil leaf specimens.
Director and Curator: WILLIAM W. BARKER, 1930 (Vascular plants).
Staff members: DAVID HOSFORD, 1941 (Fungi).
EDWARD KLUCKING, 1929 (Fossil plants).
Specialization in research: Flora of central Washington; Miocene flora of northwest North America.
Loans: To recognized botanical institutions.

ELVAS: *Herbarium, Estação de Melhoramento de Plantas,* (**ELVE**), Elvas, **Portugal.** (Information 1974)
Status: Department of Agriculture.
Foundation: 1946. *Number of specimens:* 50.000.
Herbarium: Vascular plants of Portugal, Madeira, Portuguese Guinea, Cap Vert Islands, Portuguese Timor; cultivated plants of Macau.
Specialization in research: Taxonomy of cultivated plants; flora and vegetation of Portugal, Madeira, Cap Vert Islands and Portuguese Guinea; ecology of native pastures in dry regions.
Loans: To recognized botanical institutions.
Periodical and serial works: Melhoramento.

EMORY: *Herbarium, Biology Department, Emory and Henry College,* (**EHCV**), P.O. Drawer DDD, Emory, Virginia 24327, **U.S.A.**
Telephone: 703/944-3121.
Foundation: 1960. *Number of specimens:* 2.362 vascular plants, 320 bryophytes.
Herbarium: Vascular plants and bryophytes of southwestern Virginia, mainly Washington County.
Director and Curator: GEORGE E. TREADWELL, JR., 1941 (Woody plants endemic to southeastern U.S.).

EMPANGENI: *Herbarium, University of Zululand,* (**ZULU**), Private Bag Kwa-Dlangezwa, via Empangeni, Zululand, **South Africa.** (Information 1974)
Status: University.
Foundation: 1961. *Number of specimens:* 6.000.

Herbarium: Flora of Zululand.
Specialization in research: Flora of Zululand.

EMPORIA: *Herbarium, Department of Biology, Emporia State University,* (**KSTC**), Emporia, Kansas 66801, **U.S.A.**
Telephone: 316/343-1200.
Foundation: 1863. *Number of specimens:* 70.000.
Herbarium: Vascular plants of midwestern U.S.
Important collections: Frank Ulysses Grant Agrelius.
    Director: JAMES S. WILSON.
    Specialization in research: Weed populations.
    Loans: For up to 2 years.
    Exchange: Yes.

ENTEBBE: *Herbarium, Ministry of Agriculture, Forestry and Cooperatives, Forest Department,* (**ENT**), P.O. Box 31, Entebbe, **Uganda.** (Information 1974)
Status: Directed by state.
Foundation: 1900. *Number of specimens:* 10.000.
Herbarium: Woody plants mainly from Uganda.
    Specialization in research: Woody flora of Uganda.
    Associated botanic garden: Entebbe Botanic Garden.
    Loans: To recognized botanical institutions.
    Periodical and serial works: Amendment Lists to Indigenous Trees of Uganda.

ENUGU: *Enugu Forest Herbarium,* (**EFH**), Forestry Commission, P.M.B. 1028, Enugu, **Nigeria.**
Status: Ministry of Agriculture and Food Production, Anambra State.
Foundation: 1970. *Number of specimens:* 10.000.
Herbarium: Flora of Nigeria with emphasis on Eastern states; edible wild woody plants.
Important collections: Collections from the Milliken Hill, Enugu.
    Director: JONATHAN C. OKAFOR, 1934 (*Combretum*, intraspecific variation of edible woody plants, vegetative propagation).
    Curator: VICTOR U. AMAZU, 1945.
    Staff member: GODFREY AMAZIGO, 1939.
    Specialization in research: Taxonomy of Nigerian climbers and edible woody plants; ecological distribution of plants in traditional farming systems of humid tropical areas of Nigeria.
    Associated botanic garden: Biological Garden Enugu.
    Loans: Duration 3 months.
    Exchange: With other African or West African herbaria.

EPHRAIM: *Herbarium, Snow College,* (**EPHR**), Ephraim, Utah 84627, **U.S.A.**
Telephone: 801/283-4021, ext. 294.
Foundation: 1940. *Number of specimens:* 3.000.
Herbarium: Mainly flowering plants of central and southern Utah.

Director and Curator: A. CLYDE BLAUER, 1939 (Taxonomy of browse shrubs of the Great Basin with emphasis on *Artemisia, Chrysothamnus,* and *Atriplex*).

EREVAN: – – *see* YEREVAN.

ERLANGEN: *Botanisches Institut der Universität Erlangen,* (**ER**), Schlossgarten 4, Erlangen, **Federal Republic of Germany,** BRD. (Information 1964)
Status: University.
Foundation: 1825. *Number of specimens:* 25.000.
Herbarium: Flora of Central Europe.
Important collections: Herb. Joachim Camerarius (1534-98).
    Specialization in research: Phytogeography of Central Europe.
    Loans: To recognized botanical institutions.

ERZURUM: *Atatürk Üniversitesi Herbaryumu,* (**ATA**), Fen Fakültesi, Atatürk Üniversitesi, Erzurum, **Turkey.** (Information 1974)
Status: University.
Foundation: 1969. *Number of specimens:* 3.000.
Herbarium: East Anatolia.
    Specialization in research: Flora of East Anatolia.
    Loans: To recognized botanical institutions.

ESKISEHIR: *Türkiye Sekerfabrikalari Zirai Arastirma Enstitüsü,* (**ESK**) – – *see* ETIMESGUT.

ETIMESGUT: *Türkiye Seker Fabrikalari A. S. Seker Enstitüsü,* (**ESK**), (Institute for Agricultural and Technological Sugar Beet Research), Etimesgut, Ankara, **Turkey.** (Information 1974)
Status: Turkish Sugar Factories Co.
Foundation: 1932. *Number of specimens:* 725.
Herbarium: Flora of Central Anatolia.

EUGENE: *Herbarium, Science Department, Lane Community College,* (**LCEU**), 4000 East 30th Avenue, Eugene, Oregon 97405, **U.S.A.**
Telephone: 503/747-4501.
Foundation: 1967. *Number of specimens:* 2.500.
Herbarium: Mainly local plants.
    Staff member: FREEMAN ROWE, 1930 (Teaching botany).

EUGENE: *Herbarium, Department of Biology, University of Oregon,* (**ORE**), Eugene, Oregon 97403, **U.S.A.**
Telephone: 503/686-3033.
Foundation: 1903. *Number of specimens:* 103.000.
Herbarium: Oregon and Pacific Northwest; vascular plants, bryophytes, lichens.
Important collections: Lichens: Y. Asahina, M. Fomin, L. H. Pike, F. P. Sipe. Bryophytes: M. A. Flinn, A. S. Foster, T. C. Frye, L. F. Henderson, F. A. MacFadden. Vascular plants: W. C. Cusick, L. E.

Detling, M. W. Gorman, L. F. Henderson, T. J. Howell, O. L. Ireland, L. Leach, J. B. Leiberg, G. Mason, W. N. Suksdorf, C. D. White.

Director and Curator: DAVID H. WAGNER, 1945 (Flora of Oregon; bryophytes, pteridophytes).

Specialization in research: Biosystematics, ecology; floristics of region.

Loans: To recognized institutions under usual conditions.

Exchange: By arrangement; regional emphasis (vascular plants), boreal and temperate (bryophytes, lichens).

Remarks: All fungi were transferred on permanent loan to OSC in 1977.

EVANSTON: *Botany Department, Northwestern University,* **(NWU)**, Evanston, Illinois, **U.S.A.** – – incorporated in F.

EXETER: *Herbarium, Department of Biological Sciences, University of Exeter,* **(EXR)**, Hatherly Biological Laboratories, Prince of Wales Road, Exeter EX4 4PS, England, **Great Britain.**

Telephone: 0392/77911.

Status: University.

Foundation: 1953. *Number of specimens:* 26.000.

Herbarium: British Isles, especially S.W. England; some European.

Director: J. WEBSTER, 1925 (Mycology).

Curator: R. B. IVIMEY-COOK, 1932 (*Ononis, Mammillaria*).

Specialization in research: Flora of Devon.

Associated botanic garden: Garden of the University of Exeter.

Loans: To bona fide teaching institutions and research workers.

Exchange: Would be considered, but no real facilites exist.

EXETER: *Herbarium, Royal Albert Memorial Museum,* **(RAMM)**, Queen Street, Exeter, Devon EX4 3RX, England, **Great Britain.**

Telephone: 0392-56724.

Status: Exeter City Council.

Foundation: 1868. *Number of specimens:* 36.000.

Herbarium: Representative collections of British spermatophyta, pteridophyta and lichens, with emphasis on Devon specimens; musci, Sphagnaceae, hepaticae and fungi predominantly from Devon; some foreign material.

Important collections: No known types. General colls. by Rev. H. Boyden, W. P. Hiern; F. J. Smith (spermatophyta and pteridophyta); W. S. M. d'Urban (including S. African and N. American colls.) and C. H. Wright; G. B. Savery (Musci, Sphagnaceae and hepaticae), A. Griffiths and Rev. R. Cresswell (Algae).

Director: STEPHEN LOCKE.

Curator: DAVID BOLTON, 1947 (Plant ecology).

Loans: Occasional (Under exceptional conditions for bona fide research. Material can be studied on the premises).

Remarks: Herbarium undergoing re-storage and consolidation at present. Documentation to be completed and catalogue to be published at a later date.

EXPERIMENT: *Georgia Agricultural Experiment Station,* **(GAES)**, Georgia, **U.S.A.** – – incorporated in GA.

F

FAIRBANKS: *Herbarium, University of Alaska Museum*, **(ALA)**, Fairbanks, Alaska 99701, **U.S.A.**
Telephone: 907/479-7108; 479-7109.
Foundation: 1915. *Number of specimens:* 90.000.
Herbarium: Alaska and other circumpolar areas.
Important collections: A. E. Porsild, L. A. Viereck, G. W. Argus, D. F. Murray, J. P. Anderson, W. C. Steere, H. Krog, B. M. Murray; herbaria of Institute of Northern Forestry (U.S. Forest Service) and the Naval Arctic Research Laboratory, Barrow.
Curator: DAVID F. MURRAY, 1937 (Arctic and alpine flora; systematics).
Museum affiliates: BARBARA M. MURRAY, 1938 (Alaskan bryophytes and lichens; systematics of Andreaeopsida).
LESLIE A. VIERECK, 1930 (Alaska trees and shrubs).
Specialization in research: Floristics of Alaska.
Associated botanic garden: Boreal Arboretum (inactive).
Loans: No special restrictions.
Periodical and serial works: University of Alaska Biological Papers (issued irregularly).
Exchange: Available: Alaskan material. Desired: Circumpolar, arctic-alpine material.

FAIRFAX: *Herbarium, Biology Department, George Mason University*, **(GMUF)**, 4400 University Drive, Fairfax, Virginia 22030, **U.S.A.**
Telephone: 703/323-2182.
Foundation: 1967. *Number of specimens:* 17.000.
Herbarium: Mostly northern Virginia; some from Puerto Rico, North Carolina, south-central Missouri, Florida, Jamaica.
Curator: TED BRADLEY, 1940 (General flora; *Triodanis*).
Exchange: Yes.

FAIRMONT: *Herbarium, Department of Biology, Fairmont State College*, **(FWVA)**, Locust Avenue, Fairmont, West Virginia 26554, **U.S.A.**
Telephone: 304/367-4269.
Foundation: 1976. *Number of specimens:* 2.100 (1.600 vascular plants, 500 fungi).
Herbarium: Primarily specimens from northern West Virginia, western Montana, and southwestern Virginia.
Curator: STEVEN L. STEPHENSON, 1943; 304/367-4158 (Plant ecology; flora and vegetation of the central Appalachians).
Specialization in research: Distributional relationships of taxa in the central Appalachians.
Loans: Up to 6 months; borrower must pay postage.
Exchange: Yes, with WVA.

FARGO: *Herbarium, Botany Department, North Dakota State University*, **(NDA)**, Fargo, North Dakota 58105, **U.S.A.**
Telephone: 701/237-7222.
Status: State university and State Experiment Station.
Foundation: 1890. *Number of specimens:* 165.000 (145.000 vascular plants; 20.000 non-vascular plants).
Herbarium: Chiefly North Dakota vascular plants with a good representation of Northern Great Plains plants; chiefly North Dakota and Minnesota lichens and bryophytes.
Important collections: H. L. Bolley, O. A. Stevens, C. B. Waldron.
Director and Curator: WILLIAM T. BARKER, 1941 (Floristics of the Great Plains).
Staff members: GARY CLAMBEY, 1945 (Forest-prairie ecotone ecology).
TED ESSLINGER, 1944 (Lichens and mosses of U.S.).
HAROLD GOETZ, 1932 (Grassland ecology; Gramineae).
DON KIRBY, 1948 (Range ecology).
WARREN WHITMAN, 1911 (Range ecology; Gramineae).
Specialization in research: Aquatic vascular plants; floristics of the prairies and plains.
Loans: To institutions.
Periodical and serial works: Agricultural Experiment Station Bulletins; Bimonthly Bulletin of the Agricultural Experiment Station.
Exchange: Available: North Dakota vascular plants. Desired: Vascular plants of the U.S.

FARMVILLE: *Herbarium, Longwood College*, **(FARM)**, Farmville, Virginia 23901, **U.S.A.**
Telephone: 804/392-9351.
Foundation: 1963. *Number of specimens:* 65.000.
Herbarium: Mostly Virginia.
Important collections: Charles E. Stevens, Bernard Mikula, Henry K. Svenson, A. M. Harvill, Jr.
Director and Curator: A. M. HARVILL, JR., 1916 (Phytogeography).
Specialization in research: Phytogeography of the Middle Atlantic States; flora of Virginia.
Loans: Arranged.

FAYETTEVILLE: *Herbarium, Department of Botany and Bacteriology, University of Arkansas*, **(UARK)**, Fayetteville, Arkansas 72701, **U.S.A.**
Telephone: 501/575-4901.
Status: Public institution.
Foundation: 1876. *Number of specimens:* 63.000.
Herbarium: Plants of Arkansas and the general area; *Coreopsis* of North America.
Important collections: F. L. Harvey, D. M. Moore.

Director: EDWIN B. SMITH, 1936 (Biosystematics of *Coreopsis;* floristics of Arkansas).
Specialization in research: Floristics of Arkansas.
Loans: To recognized institutions and herbaria.
Exchange: Limited to small agreements from the general area.

FERRARA: *Istituto di Botanica Università,* (**FER**), Corso Porta Mare 2, 44100 Ferrara, **Italy.**
Telephone: (0532) 33161/21151.
Status: University.
Foundation: 1771. *Number of specimens:* 11.000.
Herbarium: Vascular plants.
Director: GIUSEPPE DALL'OLIO, 1924 (Pharmaceutical botany).
Staff members: MARIA BASSI, 1924 (Systematic botany).
DONATELLA MARES, 1946.
FILIPPO PICCOLI, 1940 (Systematic botany).
GIAN LUIGI VANNINI, 1938 (General botany).
Specialization in research: Cell biology, medicinal plants, phytogeography.
Loans: To recognized botanical institutions.
Exchange: Yes.

FIRENZE: *Herbarium Universitatis Florentinae, Museo Botanico,* (**FI**), Via Giorgio La Pira 4, I-50121 Firenze, **Italy.**
Telephone: 055/284411.
Status: University.
Foundation: 1842. *Number of specimens:* 3.500.000.
Herbarium: Worldwide herbarium, all groups, Italy, Mediterranean, Pandanaceae, Palmae.
Important collections: A. Baldacci, O. Beccari, A. Biondi, E. Bourgeau, A. C. Chabert, R. Corti, De Notaris, C. F. Ecklon, A. Figari, A. Fiori, O. Gavioli, G. Giraldi, H. Groves, E. Levier, Marchesetti, Marchesoni, U. Martelli, Micheli, Moretti, R. Pampanini, F. Parlatore, R. A. Philippi, G. Raddi, G. H. W. Schimper, Silvestri, C. P. S. Sommier, Vaccari. Herbarium Webbianum (FI-W) with coll. of P. M. A. Broussonet, R. Desfontaines, G. Gardner, C. Gaudichaud, J. J. H. Labillardière, Mercier, C. H. B. A. Moquin-Tandon, H. Ruiz & Pavon, M. Sessé & J. M. Moçiño, Soleirol, P. B. Webb and many others (see Webbia 32(1). 1977) founded in 1832; herbarium of O. Beccari, world-wide emphasis on Macaronesia, South America, Australia, Mediterranean area.
Director: GUIDO MOGGI, 1927 (Flora of Southern Italy, flora of N.E. tropical Africa, *Eucalyptus).*
Staff members: PIER VIRGILIO ARRIGONI, 1932 (Flora of Sardinia and Italy pro parte).
ENIO NARDI, 1942 (Pteridophyta, *Aquilegia).*
PAOLO PAOLI, 1938 (Palynology, flora of mediterranean Italy).
MAURO RAFFAELLI, 1944 (Bryophyta, *Polygonum).*

CARLO RICCERI, 1933 (*Eragrostis).*
MILENA RIZZOTTO, 1936 (Endemic plants of Italy).
GIANFRANCO SARTONI, 1943 (Algae).
Specialization in research: Flora and vegetation of Italy and Mediterranean area; plant geography and ecology, biosystematics.
Associated botanic garden: Orto Botanico dell'Università di Firenze (Giardino dei Semplici), Via Micheli 3, Firenze.
Loans: To recognized institutions, but with restrictions and with the exception of rare and type material.
Periodical and serial works: Webbia, Pubblicazioni della Fondazione F. Parlatore, Pubblicazioni del Museo Botanico.
Exchange: Available: Specimens from Italy. Desired: Worldwide.
Remarks: The Herbarium Universitatis Florentinae includes the following herbaria: the General Herbarium which incorporates the Herbarium Centrale Italicum (3.000.000 specimens) and to which belong the Herbarium Libycum (15.000 specimens) and the Herbarium Cryptogamicum (150.000 specimens); separate historical herbaria: Herbarium Webbianum (FI-W), 300.000 specimens, see important collections, Herbarium Beccarianum – Malesia (FI-B), 15.000 specimens, Herbarium Michelianum (FI-M), 18.000 specimens.

FIRENZE: *Erbario dell'Istituto di Botanica della Facoltà di Agraria,* (**FIAF**), Piazzale delle Cascine 18-50144, Firenze, **Italy.**
Telephone: 055-365798.
Status: University.
Foundation: 1880. *Number of specimens:* 45.000.
Herbarium: Pteridophyta Gymnospermae, Angiospermae; Italy, especially Toscana.
Curator: Vacant.

FIRENZE: *Istituto di Patologia Forestale dell'Università,* (**FIPF**), Piazzale delle Cascine 28, 50144 Firenze, **Italy.** (Information 1974)
Status: University.
Herbarium: Plants of Italy.

FIRENZE: *Erbario Tropicale di Firenze,* (**FT**), Via Giorgio La Pira 4, I-50121 Firenze, **Italy.**
Telephone: 055/284411.
Status: Directed by the State.
Foundation: 1904. *Number of specimens:* 300.000.
Herbarium: Mainly tropical Africa, especially Eritrea, Ethiopia, Somalia, including wood collections of East African trees.
Important collections: I. Baldrati, Bavazzano, O. Beccari, Chedeville, E. Chiovenda, R. Corradi, G. Cufodontis, Fiori, Moggi, Negri, G. Paoli & Stefanini, Pappi, R. E. G. Pichi-Sermolli, Puccioni, Robecchi-Bricchetti, Ruspoli & Riva, G. H. W. Schimper, Schweinfurth & D. Riva, A. Terracciano.

Director: GUIDO MOGGI, 1927 (Flora of Somalia).

Staff members: GIANFRANCO SARTONI, 1943 (Algae).

MARCELLO TARDELLI, 1944.

Specialization in research: Flora of North East Tropical Africa.

Loans: To recognized institutions, with numerous restrictions.

Periodical and serial works: Adumbratio Florae Aethiopicae, Pubblicazioni dell'Erbario Tropicale, Atlante Micrografico dei Legni dell' Africa Orientale.

Exchange: Available: North-East tropical Africa. Desired: Tropical Africa.

Remarks: The Herbarium Aethiopicum (formerly Herbarium Coloniale Florentinum) is included in and constitutes the main part of the "Erbario Tropicale di Firenze."

FLAGSTAFF: *Deaver Herbarium, Department of Biology, Box 5640, Northern Arizona University,* (**ASC**), Flagstaff, Arizona 86001, **U.S.A.**

Telephone: 602/523-4225; 523-2381.

Status: State university.

Foundation: 1930. *Number of specimens:* 35.000.

Herbarium: Flora of northern Arizona, especially San Francisco Peaks, Walnut Canyon, Wapatki and Sunset Crater, Grand Canyon, Petrified Forest, Oak Creek Canyon.

Important collections: C. F. Deaver, D. Demaree, L. N. Goodding, R. Gierisch, M. E. Jones, T. H. Kearney, E. L. Little, J. M. Rominger, J. J. Thornber.

Director and Curator: JAMES M. ROMINGER, 1928; 602/523-4225; 774-3544 (Agrostology; *Setaria*).

Staff members: DEAN BLINN, 1941 (Diatoms; algae).

RICHARD H. HEVLY, 1934 (Martyniaceae; cheilanthoid ferns, especially *Notholaena*).

JACK S. STATES, 1941 (*Aspergillus*).

Specialization in research: Floristics of northern Arizona; grasses of Arizona.

Loans: For 6 months to recognized scientific institutions.

Exchange: Yes.

Remarks: Name for Arizona State College changed to Northern Arizona University in 1966.

FLAGSTAFF: *Herbarium, Forestry Sciences Laboratory, Rocky Mountain Forest and Range Experiment Station, Northern Arizona University,* (**FSLF**), Flagstaff, Arizona 86001, **U.S.A.**

Telephone: 602/779-3311, ext. 1521.

Status: U.S. Department of Agriculture, Forest Service.

Number of specimens: 1.000.

Herbarium: Plants of Coconino County, Arizona.

Director: LAWRENCE D. GARRETT.

Curator: WILLIAM H. KRUSE, 1938.

Specialization in research: Forest, range, and wildlife.

FLAGSTAFF: *Herbarium, Museum of Northern Arizona,* (**MNA**), Route 4, Box 720, Flagstaff, Arizona 86001, **U.S.A.**

Telephone: 602/774-5211, ext. 68 or 20.

Status: Private research institution.

Foundation: 1934. *Number of specimens:* 28.000.

Herbarium: Bryophytes and vascular plants of southwestern U.S. with strong concentration on northern Arizona.

Important collections: A. and B. Phillips (Arizona Strip), A. Phillips, B. Phillips, and M. Theroux (Grand Canyon), A. Johnson (Bryophytes).

Curator: ARTHUR M. PHILLIPS, III, 1947 (Flora of southwestern U.S. deserts; endangered species).

Staff members: L. T. GREEN, III, 1947 (Field specialist; endangered species).

JILL MAZZONI, 1953 (Field specialist; endangered species).

BARBARA G. PHILLIPS, 1945 (Flora of Arizona; anatomy and morphology of Nyctaginaceae).

Specialization in research: Endangered species status; ecological research in southwestern U.S.

Loans: Available for 6 month period to qualified individuals associated with other herbaria in academic or research institutions.

Periodical and serial works: Plateau.

Exchange: For plants of southwestern U.S. only.

FLORIANA: *Herbarium, Argotti Botanic Garden,* (**ARG**), Floriana, **Malta.** (Information 1974)

Status: Royal University of Malta.

Foundation: 1675 by Dr. Joseph Zammit. *Number of specimens:* 10.000.

Herbarium: Worldwide.

Specialization in research: Mediterranean flora.

Associated botanic garden: Argotti Botanic Garden.

FLORIANÓPOLIS: *Herbário do Hôrto Botânico, Departamento de Biologia, Universidade Federal de Santa Catarina,* (**FLOR**), Campus Universitário, Trindade, Caixa Postal 476, 88.000 Florianópolis, Santa Catarina, **Brazil.**

Telephone: (55)0482/33-1000, ramal 242.

Foundation: 1964. *Number of specimens:* 13.000.

Herbarium: Southern Brazil, especially Ilha de Santa Catarina.

Director: ANTÔNIO BRESOLIN, 1919 (Taxonomy).

Curator: ADEMIR REIS, 1951 (Annonaceae).

Staff members: ROBERTO M. KLEIN, 1923 (Taxonomy; plant ecology).

ROSELI MARIA DE S. MOSIMANN, 1945 (Taxonomy of Bacillariophyceae, Chrysophyta, diatoms).

MARIA TEREZINHA PAULILO, 1954 (Plant physiology).

MARIA LEONOR DEL REI SOUZA, 1955 (Taxonomy).

ANA MARIA VIANNA, 1954 (Plant physiology).

Specialization in research: Medicinal plants; research on reforestation using native plants; inventory of the flora of Ilha de Santa Catarina; inventory of diatoms of continental waters; Bacillariophyceae.

Loans: Usual regulations.

Periodical and serial works: Insula, Boletim do Horto Botanico da UFSC; Florula da Ilha de Santa Catarina.

Exchange: Worldwide.

FOND DU LAC: *Herbarium, Department of Biology, University of Wisconsin Center,* (**FDLW**), Prairie Road, Fond du Lac, Wisconsin 54935, **U.S.A.**

Telephone: 414/922-8440, ext. 32.

Foundation: 1968. *Number of specimens:* 200.

Herbarium: Local flora.

Director and Curator: ELIZABETH LAMB HAYES.

FOOCHOW: *Herbarium, Fukien Christian University,* (**FCU**), Foochow, Fukien, **People's Republic of China.** (Information 1974)

Herbarium: Plants of Fukien province.

Important collections: F. P. Metcalf (15.000).

FORSSA: *Herbarium, Forssa Museum of Natural History,* (**FOR**), Vapaudenkatu 5B17, Forssa, **Finland.** (Information 1974)

Status: Owned by Nature Conservation Society of Southwest Häme, subsidized by city.

Foundation: 1957. *Number of specimens:* 11.000.

Specialization in research: Flora of Southwest Häme.

Loans: To recognized botanical institutions.

Periodical and serial works: Lounais-Hämeen Luonto.

FORTALEZA: *Herbário Prisco Bezerra, Departamento de Biologia, Centro de Ciências, Universidade Federal do Ceará,* (**EAC**), Caixa Postal D-141, 60.000 Fortaleza, Ceará, **Brazil.**

Telephone: (55)85/223-2521.

Foundation: 1939 as Herbário da Escola de Agronomia do Ceará; transferred to Departamento de Biologia in 1970. *Number of specimens:* 8.000.

Curator: AFRANIO GOMES FERNANDES, 1927 (Taxonomy of vascular plants, especially Leguminosae).

Staff members: PRISCO BEZERRA, 1913 (Taxonomy of vascular plants, especially Leguminosae).

JOSÉ DE RIBAMAR PINTO SOARES, 1940 (Taxonomy of vascular plants).

Specialization in research: Regional flora of northeastern Brazil.

Loans: To recognized botanical institutions.

Exchange: Mostly Leguminosae.

Remarks: The herbarium is contributing to the "Programa Flora" of the Brazilian National Research Council.

FORT COLLINS: *Herbarium, Department of Botany, Colorado State University,* (**CS**), Fort Collins, Colorado 80523, **U.S.A.**

Telephone: 303/491-6036.

Foundation: 1881. *Number of specimens:* 60.000.

Herbarium: Principally of Colorado, adjacent Wyoming and Utah; includes 78 types.

Important collections: James Cassidy, C. Crandall, Harold Harrington, J. Cowan, J. Christ.

Curator: DIETER H. WILKEN, 1944 (Floristics of Colorado; systematics of Polemoniaceae).

Specialization in research: Integrated with systematic botany program in the Department of Botany and floristic inventory of Colorado.

Loans: Not to exceed 6 months.

Exchange: With herbaria specializing in western North American flora.

FORT COLLINS: *Forest Pathology Herbarium, U.S. Forest Service, Rocky Mountain Forest and Range Experiment Station,* (**FPF**), 240 West Prospect Street, Fort Collins, Colorado 80526, **U.S.A.**

Telephone: 303/221-4390.

Status: U.S. Department of Agriculture, Forest Service.

Foundation: 1952. *Number of specimens:* 12.000.

Herbarium: Forest disease organisms of the Rocky Mountains and the southwestern U.S.

Important collections: Foliage diseases (Hypodermataceae) and rust fungi; major collections of dwarf mistletoes (*Arceuthobium*) and *Phoradendron.*

Curator: F. G. HAWKSWORTH, 1926 (Mistletoes, especially *Arceuthobium* of the world).

Staff members: T. E. HINDS, 1923 (Tree canker and decay fungi).

J. M. STALEY, 1929 (Foliage diseases, especially Hypodermataceae).

Specialization in research: Forest disease fungi and mistletoes.

Loans: No special restrictions.

Exchange: Yes.

FORT COLLINS: *Forest Service Herbarium, Rocky Mountain Forest and Range Experiment Station,* (**USFS**), 3825 East Mulberry, Fort Collins, Colorado 80524, **U.S.A.**

Telephone: 303/221-4390.

Status: U.S. Department of Agriculture, Forest Service.

Foundation: 1911. *Number of specimens:* 150.000.

Herbarium: Specimens documenting research and management of plants in National Forests; western U.S. plants of interest in range, wildlife habitat and watershed studies.

Curator: CHARLES FEDDEMA, 1920.

Specialization in research: Plants of importance

to National Forest management.

Loans: To recognized botanical institutions.

Remarks: Types of new taxa described by the staff are deposited in the U.S. National Herbarium (US). This Forest Service Herbarium was transferred from Washington, D.C. to Fort Collins a few years ago. The main collections of the Costa Rica and Ecuador forest survey parties are deposited in F.

FORT PIERCE: *Herbarium, Harbor Branch Foundation,* **(HBFH),** R.R. 1, Box 196, Fort Pierce, Florida 33450, **U.S.A.**

Telephone: 305/465-2400.

Status: Private foundation.

Foundation: 1975. *Number of specimens:* 10.000.

Herbarium: Marine algae and vascular plants, including Chlorophyta, Phaeophyta, Rhodophyta, Bacillariophyceae, seagrasses, mangrove marsh and salt zone plants with special reference to Florida.

Important collections: M. Charner Benz, Stephen M. Blair, Nathaniel J. Eiseman, Robert A. Gibson, Margaret O. Hall, F. Carol Stephens; Florida seagrasses, algae of the east Florida continental shelf and the Indian river; diatoms of the east Florida continental shelf, the western Bahamas continental shelf, and the Indian River; Epizoic diatoms.

Director: ROBERT S. JONES, 1936 (Ichthyology).

Curators: NATHANIEL J. EISEMAN, 1943 (Systematics and ecology of marine macroalgae and marine vascular plants).

ROBERT A. GIBSON, 1946 (Marine diatom biology).

Specialization in research: Systematics and ecology of benthic marine macroalgae, vascular plants, and diatoms.

Loans: No restrictions on macrophytes, 90 day maximum on diatoms.

Exchange: Desired.

Remarks: Visitors welcome.

FORT QU'APPELLE: *Fort Qu'Appelle Herbarium,* **(FQH),** Central Avenue, P.O. Box 1043, Fort Qu'Appelle, Saskatchewan, **Canada** SOG 1SO.

Telephone: 306/332-4322.

Status: Administered by Fort Qu'Appelle Naturalists Society.

Foundation: 1959 (vascular); 1961 (cryptogamic). *Number of specimens:* 9.500 (8.000 vascular plants, 1.500 cryptogams).

Herbarium: Vascular plants from Saskatchewan, northwestern Ontario. Lesser collections from western Manitoba, western and southern Alberta, eastern British Columbia, Canadian arctic Victoria and Devon islands, U.S.A., northwestern and west-central Europe. Cryptogamic collections from northwestern Ontario, Saskatchewan, Alberta, Finland, West-central Europe.

Director and Curator: BERNARD DE VRIES, 1921 (Range extension and taxonomy of vascular flora

of east-central Saskatchewan).

Specialization in research: Taxonomy of Saskatchewan plants.

Loans: For a period of 2 months to recognized botanical institutions, herbaria, and specialists.

Exchange: Available: Saskatchewan and Ontario. Desired: All vascular plant groups, especially from the Great Plains. Prefer Orchidaceae, Leguminosae, and medicinal plants (worldwide).

Remarks: Plantae Medica Herbarium founded in 1978; these specimens will not be sent on loan.

FORT WORTH: *Albert Ruth Herbarium, Department of Biology, Texas Christian University,* **(FW),** Fort Worth, Texas 76129, **U.S.A.** ‒‒ incorporated in FWM.

Foundation: 1873. *Number of specimens:* 8.500.

Herbarium: Bolivia, France, Italy, Switzerland, Alaska, U.S., Canada.

FORT WORTH: *Herbarium, Fort Worth Museum of Science and History,* **(FWM),** 1501 Montgomery Street, Fort Worth, Texas 76107, **U.S.A.**

Telephone: 817/732-1631.

Foundation: 1940. *Number of specimens:* 12.000.

Herbarium: Mainly local, some from southwestern U.S. and Central America.

Important collections: Albert Ruth herbarium of Texas Christian University (FW) received in 1971.

Director: DON R. OTTO, 1943 (Historian).

Curator: WILLIAM J. VOSS, 1934 (Local southwestern angiosperms).

Staff member: JAMES P. DIFFILY, 1953.

Loans: To qualified researchers for a reasonable period of time.

Exchange: Yes.

FRANKFURT: *Forschungsinstitut und Naturmuseum Senckenberg,* **(FR),** Senckenberg-Anlage 25, Frankfurt a. M., **Federal Republic of Germany,** BRD. (Information 1974)

Status: Supported by government.

Foundation: 1817. *Number of specimens:* 450.000.

Important collections: W. P. E. S. Ruepell (Abyssinia), herb. J. B. C. W. Fresenius.

Loans: To recognized botanical institutions.

Periodical and serial works: Natur & Museum, Senckenbergiana Biologica, Senckenbergiana Lethaea, Abhandl. Senckenbergischen Naturforschenden Gesellschaft. Senckenberg-Bücher, Aufsätze und Reden der Senckenbergischen Naturforschenden Gesellschaft.

FREDERICKSBURG: *Herbarium, Department of Biological Sciences, Mary Washington College,* **(MWCF),** Fredericksburg, Virginia 22401, **U.S.A.**

Telephone: 703/899-4689.

Foundation: 1972. *Number of specimens:* 4.000.

Herbarium: Many specimens from Jamaica.

Important collections: I. Cornman, Stephen W. Fuller.

Director and Curator: STEPHEN W. FULLER, 1945 (Phycology).

FREDERICTON: *Environmental Management, Maritimes Forest Research Centre,* (**AFES**), P.O. Box 4000, Fredericton, New Brunswick, **Canada** E3B 5P7 — — incorporated in UNB in 1980.
Status: Canadian Forestry Service.
Foundation: 1940. *Number of specimens:* 4.000.
Herbarium: Vascular plants of the Maritime Provinces.
Important collections: G. C. Cunningham.

FREDERICTON: *Mycological Herbarium, Forest Insect and Disease Survey, Maritimes Forest Research Centre,* (**FFB**), College Hill, P.O. Box 4000, Fredericton, New Brunswick, **Canada** E3B 5P7.
Telephone: 506/452-3500; 452-3516.
Status: Federal government research establishment.
Foundation: 1954. *Number of specimens:* 7.000.
Herbarium: Mostly forest fungi representing the mycoflora of the Maritime Provinces of Canada.
Director: MURRAY M. NEILSON, 1930 (Insect pathology).
Curator: LASZLO P. MAGASI, 1935 (Mycology).
Staff member: KENNETH J. HARRISON, 1947 (Mushrooms).
Specialization in research: Diseases of forest and shade trees.
Loans: Usual regulations.
Exchange: Yes.

FREDERICTON: *Connell Memorial Herbarium, Biology Department, University of New Brunswick,* (**UNB**), College Hill, P.O. Box 4400, Fredericton, New Brunswick, **Canada** E3B 5A3.
Telephone: 506/453-4583 (curator). *Telex:* 014-46202.
Foundation: 1839 by James Robb. *Number of specimens:* 40.800 (30.000 New Brunswick; 3.000 sheets, 2.000 slides, 800 liquid algae).
Herbarium: Mainly New Brunswick; large collections of *Rubus, Amelanchier,* and *Betula* of Maritime Canada; marine algae from the Canadian Maritime Provinces, United Kingdom, Pacific North America, South Australia; vascular plants of the Maritimes Forest Research Centre (AFES).
Important collections: James Robb, fasc. Carices Boreali-Americanae of S. T. Olney.
Curators: HAROLD R. HINDS, 1937; 506/453-4583 (Vascular flora, macrolichens, and macrofungi of New Brunswick).
A. R. A. TAYLOR, 1921 (Algae).
Specialization in research: Distribution of vascular plants of New Brunswick; documentation of rare and endangered plants of New Brunswick; plant resources of the Malaseet and Micmac Amerindians of New Brunswick as identified from flotation samples; marine algal flora of Maritime Can-

ada; taxonomy and ecology of *Polysiphonia* and *Chondrus.*
Loans: To recognized institutions, usual conditions.
Exchange: Available: New Brunswick vascular plants, macro-lichens, marine algae. Desired: Eastern Canada, northeastern U.S.A., and arctic vascular plants and macro-lichens; marine algae of the North Atlantic; worldwide *Chondrus* and Rhodomelaceae.

FREETOWN: *Herbarium, Department of Botany, Fourah Bay College,* (**FBC**), University of Sierra Leone, Freetown, **Sierra Leone,** West Africa. (Information 1974)
Status: University.
Foundation: 1964. *Number of specimens:* 12.000.
Herbarium: All groups, mainly West Africa; montane flora of Loma Mountains and Tingi Hills.
Specialization in research: Flora of West Tropical Africa.
Associated botanic garden: Fourah Bay College Botanic Garden.
Loans: To recognized botanical institutions.

FREETOWN: *National Herbarium, Department of Biological Sciences, Njala University College,* (**SL**), University of Sierra Leone, P.M.B., Freetown, **Sierra Leone,** West Africa.
Status: University.
Foundation: 1906. *Number of specimens:* 21.000.
Herbarium: Plants of West Tropical Africa, including carpological collection.
Director and Curator: B. M. S. TURAY, 1950 (Anatomy and systematic botany).
Staff members: J. L. BOBOR, 1936.
P. J. C. HARRIS (Ecology).
A. JOHNSON.
H. M. LOMBIE, 1960.
K. T. SEBASTIAN (Anatomy).
ABU SESSAY (Physiology and taxonomy).
Specialization in research: Flora of Sierra Leone: grasses, savanna trees, weeds, medicinal plants and poisonous plants.
Loans: With permission of director.
Exchange: Yes.

FREIBURG: *Herbarium, Institut für Biologie II, Lehrstuhl für Geobotanik,* (**FB**), Albert-Ludwigs Universität, Schänzlestrasse 1, D 7800 Freiburg, **Federal Republic of Germany,** BRD.
Remarks: Herbarium discontinued, greater part to Landessammlungen für Naturkunde, Karlsruhe (KR).

FRESNO: *Fresno Herbarium, Department of Biology, California State University,* (**FSC**), Fresno, California 93740, **U.S.A.**
Telephone: 209/487-2001.
Status: State University.

Foundation: 1925. *Number of specimens:* 34.000.
Herbarium: Central California from Sierra Nevada to coastal areas to Mojave Desert.
Important collections: Charles Quibell, John Weiler, Jack Springer, John Stebbins, P. A. Munz, Jack Rockwell.
> *Director and Curator:* JOHN STEBBINS, 1951 (Central Sierra Nevada flora).
> *Loans:* No restrictions.
> *Exchange:* Available: San Joaquin Valley species.

FRIDAY HARBOR: *Herbarium, Friday Harbor Laboratories, University of Washington,* (**FHL**), Friday Harbor, Washington 98250, **U.S.A.**
Telephone: 206/543-1484.
Status: University of Washington.
Foundation: 1904. *Number of specimens:* 3.200.
Herbarium: Marine benthic algae of the Pacific Northwest.
> *Director:* A. O. DENNIS WILLOWS, 1941 (Neurophysiology).
> *Curator:* DAVID DUGGINS (Marine benthic ecology).
> *Specialization in research:* Algal flora of San Juan Archipelago and adjacent regions of Washington and British Columbia.

FRUNZE: *Herbarium, Laboratory of Flora, Biological Institute of Academy of Sciences of Kirghiz S.S.R.,* (**FRU**), XXII Partsezda St., 265, 720071 Frunze, **U.S.S.R.**
Status: Directed by Academy of Science.
Foundation: 1941. *Number of specimens:* 100.000.
Herbarium: Plants of Kirghiz Republic.
> *Director:* R. A. AIDAROVA.

FUKUOKA: *Herbarium, Laboratory of Wood Science, Faculty of Agriculture, Kyushu University,* (**FU**), 6-10-1 Hakozaki, Higashi-ku, Fukuoka 812, **Japan.**
Telephone: (092) 641-1101, ext. 6351-3.
Status: University.
Foundation: 1920's. *Number of specimens:* 14.264 (233 types) and 5630 wood samples.
Herbarium: Plants of Micronesia and New Guinea; wood samples from Asia, Europe and North America.
Important collections: R. Kanehira.
> *Director:* TSUTOMU MATSUMOTO, 1920 (Wood science).
> *Curator:* JUICHI TSUTSUMI, 1932 (Wood science).
> *Specialization in research:* Study of wood formation and quality, identification of wood by microscopic structure.
> *Remarks:* The loan service of this herbarium has been suspended, but exchange of tropical wood samples is encouraged.

FULLERTON: *Faye A. MacFadden Herbarium, Department of Biology, California State University,* (**MACF**), Fullerton, California 92634, **U.S.A.**
Telephone: 714/773-2556.
Foundation: 1962. *Number of specimens:* 40.650 (23.500 vascular plants, 15.000 bryophytes, 1.000 algae, 150 fungi, 1.000 lichens).
Herbarium: Emphasis on northwestern U.S. and southwestern Canada; floras of the Southwest and southern California.
Important collections: Faye MacFadden.
> *Director:* C. EUGENE JONES, 1942.
> *Curator:* TRUDY R. ERICSON, 1925.

FUNCHAL: *Herbario do Jardim Botânico da Madeira,* (**MADJ**), Quinta do Bom Sucesso- Caminho do Meio, 9000 Funchal, **Madeira.**
Telephone: 20519.
Status: Direcção dos Serviços Agrícolas.
Foundation: 1960. *Number of specimens:* 2.500.
Herbarium: Spontaneous and sub-spontaneous species, some cultivated species.
> *Director:* RUI MANUEL DA SILVA VIEIRA, 1926 (Agronomist).
> *Curator:* FILIPA MARIA MIRA, 1949 (Technical agrarian engineer).
> *Staff members:* DOMINGOS NÓIA, 1949 (Agricultural techniques).
> RUI SANTOS, 1943 (Agricultural techniques).
> *Specialization in research:* Various studies on the indigenous and cultivated plants of Madeira Islands.
> *Associated botanic garden:* Jardim Botanico da Madeira.
> *Loans:* Always possible for study material.
> *Exchange:* Available: Seeds and duplicates.

FUNCHAL: *Herbarium, Museu Municipal do Funchal,* (**MADM**), 9000 Funchal, **Madeira.**
Telephone: 29761.
Status: Municipality (Independent).
Foundation: 1932. *Number of specimens:* 3.000.
Herbarium: Vascular plants of the Archipelago of Madeira.
> *Director and Curator:* G. E. MAUL, 1909 (Ichthyology).
> *Specialization in research:* Ichthyology.
> *Periodical and serial works:* Boletim do Museum Municipal do Funchal, Bocagiana.

FUNCHAL: *Herbarium, Museu de História Natural do Seminário do Funchal,* (**MADS**), Funchal, **Madeira.** (Information 1974)
Status: Directed by Funchal Seminary.
Foundation: 1882. Number of specimens: 3.700.
Herbarium: Flora of Madeira Archipelago and Salvage Islands.

G

GABORONE: *The National Herbarium,* **(GAB),** P.O. Box 114, Gaborone, **Botswana.**
Telephone: 53792.
Status: A branch of the National Museum and Art Gallery.
Foundation: 1978. *Number of specimens:* 4.000.
Herbarium: Plants of Botswana (formerly housed in Agriculture and Forestry Department herbaria).
Director of Museum: D. A. N. NTETA, 1939.

GABORONE: *Herbarium, Department of Biology, University College of Botswana,* **(UCBG),** Private Bag 0022, Gaborone, **Botswana.**
Telephone: 51155 ext. 268.
Status: University.
Foundation: 1974. *Number of specimens:* 4.000.
Herbarium: Plants of Botswana.
Director, Department of Biology: R. HARTLAND-ROWE, 1927.
Specialization in research: Local flora.
Loans: To local institutions only.
Exchange: With other institutions in Botswana.

GAINESVILLE: *Herbarium, Department of Botany, University of Florida,* **(FLAS),** Gainesville, Florida 32611, **U.S.A.**
Telephone: 904/392-1767 (vascular plant herbarium); 392-6577 (bryophyte and lichen herbarium); 392-2158 (mycological herbarium).
Status: State university; herbarium is also affiliated with the Institute of Food and Agricultural Sciences and the Florida State Museum.
Foundation: 1925. *Number of specimens:* 290.000.
Herbarium: Vascular flora of Florida, the southeastern U.S. coastal plain, and the New World Tropics; tropical and southeastern bryophytes; agarics, polypores, and other fungi.
Important collections: W. A. Murrill (fungi), Servin Rapp (lichens).
Director: WILLIAM LOUIS STERN, 1926 (Comparative anatomy of vascular plants).
Curators: JOSEPH S. DAVIS, 1929 (Algae; ecology of hypersaline systems).
DANA G. GRIFFIN, III, 1938 (Bryophytes and lichens).
WALTER S. JUDD, 1951 (Vascular plants; systematics of angiosperms).
JAMES W. KIMBROUGH, 1934 (Fungi; cytology, morphology, and taxonomy of Ascomycetes).
Staff members: GERALD L. BENNY, 1942 (Zygomycete and Plectomycete development and taxonomy).
DAVID W. HALL, 1940 (Flora of Florida; Gramineae).
LYNN M. HODGSON, 1948 (Algae).
KENT D. PERKINS, 1953 (Economic botany; endangered species).
FRANK C. SEYMOUR, 1895 (Flora of Nicaragua).
DANIEL B. WARD, 1928 (Vascular plants; flora of Florida).
Specialization in research: As above.
Loans: No special restrictions.
Exchange: Available: Vascular plants from Florida and adjacent tropical and subtropical areas; tropical and subtropical bryophytes and fungi. Desired: Vascular plants, bryophytes, and fungi from tropical and subtropical areas.

GAINESVILLE: *Herbarium, Division of Plant Industry,* **(PIHG),** P.O. Box 1269, Gainesville, Florida 32602, **U.S.A.**
Telephone: 904/372-3505, ext. 115.
Status: Florida Department of Agriculture and Consumer Services.
Foundation: 1964. *Number of specimens:* 4.600.
Herbarium: General collection of native and introduced plants, especially cultivated ornamental plants.
Curator: K. R. LANGDON, 1928 (Taxonomy).
Staff member: C. R. ARTAUD, 1940.

GALÁPAGOS: *Herbario, Estación Científica Charles Darwin,* **(CDS)** – – *see* PUERTO AYORA.

GALESBURG: *Herbarium, Department of Biology, Knox College,* **(KNOX),** Galesburg, Illinois 61401, **U.S.A.**
Telephone: 309/343-0112, ext. 305.
Foundation: 1882. *Number of specimens:* 20.000.
Herbarium: Primarily western Illinois, but many from other parts of U.S., some from Europe and Latin America.
Important collections: S. B. Mead (western Illinois; 1833–1870), G. Engelmann, G. B. Purdy, C. W. Short, T. J. Hale, A. H. Curtiss, M. Tommasini, E. Hall and J. P. Harbour.
Director and Curator: GEORGE H. WARD, 1916 (Biosystematics; *Artemisia*).
Specialization in research: Artemisia.
Loans: To be returned in good condition in reasonable time; to other herbaria.

GALWAY: *Herbarium, University College,* **(GALW),** Galway, **Ireland.**

GATERSLEBEN: *Herbarium, Zentralinstitut für Genetik und Kulturpflanzenforschung,* **(GAT),** Corrensstr. 3, DDR 4325 Gatersleben, Kreis Aschersleben, **German Democratic Republic,** DDR.
Telephone: Gatersleben 50.
Status: Akademie der Wissenschaften der DDR.

Foundation: 1946. *Number of specimens:* 270.000.
Herbarium: Europe, East Asia, Mongolia, Cuba; cultivated plants (temperate zones).
Important collections: F. Hermann.
Director: H. Böhme, 1928 (General and microbial genetics).
Curator: P. Hanelt, 1930 (Systematics of cultivated plants, Leguminosae, *Carthamus,* cultivated Cruciferae).
Staff members: R. Fritsch, 1944 (Anatomy and taxonomy of cultivated plants).
K. Hammer, 1944 (*Aegilops, Hordeum, Papaver, Linum,* pollination biology).
J. Kruse, 1936 (*Aegilops, Avena, Setaria,* Compositae-Cynareae).
Chr. O. Lehmann, 1926 (Cereals, *Lycopersicon, Pisum, Glycine,* genetic resources).
H. Maass, 1940 (*Vicia* agg. *narbonensis*).
D. Meyer, 1951 (Numerical taxonomy, *Pisum*).
H. Ohle, 1937 (*Calendula,* anatomy and cytology of cultivated plants).
K. Pistrick, 1954 (*Raphanus*).
J. Schultze-Motel, 1930 (Gramineae, forest plants, palaeoethnobotany, numerical taxonomy of cultivated plants).
Specialization in research: Systematics of cultivated plants.
Associated botanic garden: Kulturpflanzenweltsortiment Gatersleben.
Loans: To recognized botanical institutions.
Periodical and serial works: Die Kulturpflanze.
Exchange: Available: Cultivated plants of temperate zones, wild plants from Europe, Mongolia, China, Cuba. Wanted: Cultivated plants from the tropics; wild plants from extra-European regions.

GATLINBURG: *Herbarium, Uplands Field Research Lab, Great Smoky Mountains National Park,* (**GS-MNP**), Gatlinburg, Tennessee 37738, **U.S.A.**
Telephone: 615/436-7120.
Status: U.S. Department of the Interior, National Park Service.
Foundation: 1934. *Number of specimens:* 7.000.
Herbarium: Vascular plant collection of Great Smoky Mountains National Park.
Curator: Peter S. White, 1948 (Vascular plant floristics; rare species; monitoring; plant ecology).
Specialization in research: Floristics; rare and endangered documentation; vegetation mapping and survey; monitoring.
Loans: For short periods.
Exchange: For regional materials.

GEMBLOUX: *Herbarium, Laboratoire Forestier de l'Etat,* (**LFG**), Gembloux, **Belgium.**

GENESEO: *Herbarium, Biology Department, College of Arts and Sciences, State University of New York,* (**GESU**), Geneseo, New York 14454, **U.S.A.**
Telephone: 716/245-5301; 245-5279.

Foundation: 1965. *Number of specimens:* 12.500.
Herbarium: Mainly Genesee Valley region of western New York.
Important collections: E. B. Ehrle, H. S. Forest, William R. Horsey (cultivated woody plants from the Rochester Parks collection), James Kelly (New York), Lawrence J. King (local weeds), W. A. Mathews, Seanna R. Rugenstein; aquatic vascular plants of western Finger Lakes area.
Director: Lawrence J. King, 1915 (Vascular plants, especially weeds).
Curator of Aquatic Plants: Herman S. Forest, 1921 (Aquatic plants; American chestnut).
Curator of Bryophytes: Richard Reilly.
Curator of Paleobotany: David Brauer.
Staff member: Archibald Reid (Ecological surveys).
Specialization in research: Floristics of Genesee River drainage basin; western New York.
Loans: Usual conditions.
Exchange: Made on a mutually agreed basis.

GENEVA: *Herbarium, Department of Biology, Hobart & William Smith Colleges,* (**DH**), Geneva, New York 14456, **U.S.A.**
Telephone: 315/789-5500.
Status: Private college.
Foundation: 1910. *Number of specimens:* 5.000.
Herbarium: Local flora.
Director: Craig Smith, 1951 (Ecology of submersed aquatics).

GENÈVE: *Herbarium, Conservatoire et Jardin botaniques de la Ville de Genève,* (**G**), Case postale 60, CH-1292 Chambésy/GE, **Switzerland.**
Telephone: (022) 32.69.69.
Status: Municipal, associated with the Genevese University (Center of Botany).
Foundation: 1817. *Number of specimens:* 5.000.000.
Herbarium: Worldwide.
Important collections: Herb. Aellen (G-PAE), W. Barbey–E. Boissier, P. E. Boissier (G-BOIS), J. J. Brun (Diatoms), J. & N. L. Burmann, E. Burnat (G-BU), A. P. Alph., Cos. de Candolle (G-DC), B. Delessert (G-DEL), Favre, V. Fayod, K. W. G. L. Fuckel, E. Hassler, Hedwig-Schwaegrichen, W. G. Herter, Kunkel, Looser, Mouterde, Müller Argoviensis, Pabot, Rechinger, G. F. Reuter, F. Stephani.
Director: G. Bocquet, 1927 (Systematics, biosystematics, especially *Silene, Digitalis, Liquidambar,* morphology).
Curator of Phanerogams: A. Charpin, 1937 (Chorology, regional and mediterranean flora).
Curator of Cryptogams: P. Geissler, 1947 (Hepaticae, Index Hepaticarum).
Staff members: L. Bernardi, 1920 (Tropical flora).
H. M. Burdet, 1939 (Biosystematics, bibliography, botanical history).
M. Dittrich, 1934 (Compositae, exchange program).

P. Hainard, 1936 (Vegetation mapping and plant ecology).

F. Jacquemoud, 1946 (Cruciferae: *Sterigmostemon*).

O. Monthoux, 1932 (Mycophyta: Agaricales).

R. Spichiger, 1946 (Tropical flora).

Adélaïde Stork, 1937 (Cruciferae, seed-coat morphology, African botany).

M.-A. Thiebaud, 1943 (Iridaceae, Cyperaceae, floristics of West-Mediterranean islands).

Research associates: D. Aeschimann, 1956 (Biosystematics, especially *Silene vulgaris*).

D. Jeanmonod, 1953 (Numerical taxonomy, genus *Silene*).

J.-M. Mascherpa, 1942 (Numerical taxonomy, taxonomy of Phaseolinae, computer specimen identification).

Specialization in research: Floristics, biosystematics, systematics, morphology, nomenclature, history of botany, numerical taxonomy).

Associated botanic garden: Yes.

Loans: To botanical institutions only; G-DC and G-BU excluded, G-BOIS (Flora orientalis) on a restricted basis.

Periodical and serial works: Candollea, Boissiera, Publications hors-série, Série documentaire.

Exchange: Various duplicates upon request.

GENOVA: *Herbarium, Museo Civico di Storia Naturale "Giacomo Doria,"* (**GDOR**), Via Brigata Liguria 9, I-16121 Genova, **Italy.**

Telephone: 010/564567.

Status: Civic Museum.

Foundation: 1867.

Important collections: Herb. M. G. Doria (see Gestro, 1925, Ann. Mus. Civ. St. Nat. Genova, vol. 50, pp. 363–383); herb. F. Baglietto (excl. lichens); herb. G. Durazzo Grimaldi; herb. M. Mazzantini; herb. C. Sbarbaro (only lichens).

Director: Lilia Capocaccia, 1931 (Herpetology).

Loans: Not provided. It is possible to study the material in the Museum.

Remarks: In future a comprehensive list of all herbaria present in our Museum will be published.

GENOVA: *Erbario dell'Istituto Botanico "Hanbury" e Orto Botanico dell' Università di Genova,* (**GE**), Corso Dogali 1/C, 16136 Genova, **Italy.**

Telephone: 010/280903-294691.

Status: University.

Foundation: 1803 (Botanical garden). *Number of specimens:* 70.000.

Herbarium: Mainly Europe.

Important collections: E. Bicknell, A. G. O. Penzig, P. Bubani.

Director: Salvatore Gentile, 1934 (Flora and vegetation of Europe, plant sociology, forest ecosystem, vegetation mapping).

Curator: Fabrizia Fossati Sanviti, 1938 (Flora and vegetation of the Mediterranean and Apennines).

Specialization in research: Flora and vegetation of Italy; plant ecology, vegetation mapping.

Associated botanic garden: Orto Botanico dell'Università di Genova.

Loans: Yes.

Periodical and serial works: Pubblicazioni dell'Istituto Botanico "Hanbury" dell'Università di Genova.

Exchange: Not possible.

GENT: *Herbarium van de Rijksuniversiteit,* (**GENT**), K. L. Ledeganckstraat 35, B 9000 Gent, **Belgium.**

Telephone: 091/22.78.21.

Status: University.

Foundation: 1837. *Number of specimens:* 150.000.

Herbarium: General collection.

Director: P. Van Der Veken, 1928 (Cyperaceae, Poaceae, Myxomycetes, African flora).

Staff members: E. Coppejans, 1948 (Marine algae).

P. Goetghebeur, 1952 (Cyperaceae, *Digitaria*).

W. Van Cotthem, 1934 (Pteridophyta, systematic anatomy).

Associated botanic garden: Plantentuin van de Rijksuniversiteit.

Loans: To recognized botanical institutions.

Exchange: Limited.

GEORGE: *Herbarium, Saasveld Forest Research Station,* (**SAAS**), Private Bag X6531, George 6530, **South Africa.**

Telephone: 0441-2059 or 0441-2065.

Status: Department of Forestry.

Foundation: 1920. *Number of specimens:* 9.300.

Herbarium: Mainly voucher specimens collected during ecological studies.

Important collections: Southern Cape Flora, with special reference to indigenous rain forests (Knysna forest) and sclerophyllous shrublands (Mountain fynbos).

Director: P. W. Lange, Officer in Charge, Saasveld Forestry Station.

Curator: C. J. Geldenhuys, 1946, Forest ecologist.

Specialization in research: Regional forest flora, and local shrubland floras.

Loans: To South African institutions or on ad hoc basis.

Exchange: Can be arranged.

GEORGETOWN: *Herbarium, Department of Biology, University of Guyana,* (**BRG**), Turkeyen, Greater Georgetown, **Guyana.**

Telephone: 69201.

Foundation: 1879. *Number of specimens:* 25.000.

Herbarium: Flora of Guyana.

Important collections: G. S. Jenman.

Director: TEJ B. SINGH (Fisheries biologist).
Staff member: HARRY LALL (Weed flora).
Specialization in research: Flora of Guyana; ethnobotany; economic plants.
Associated botanic garden: Georgetown Botanic Gardens, Ministry of Agriculture.
Loans: No special regulations for recognized institutions.
Exchange: Available: Flora of Guyana. Desired: Economic species.
Remarks: Duplicates of most of the collections may be found at K, NY, and U.

GEORGETOWN: *Herbarium, Guyana Forestry Commission,* **(FDG)**, Water Street, Georgetown, **Guyana.**
Telephone: 02-53894.
Status: Directed by the Conservator of Forests.
Foundation: 1926. *Number of specimens:* 8.017; also 2.701 wood specimens. .
Herbarium: Flora of Guyana.
Important collections: W. M. C. Bagshawe, Jonah Boyan, Rufus Boyan, T. A. W. Davis, D. B. Fanshawe, J. C. Fredericks, N. G. L. Guppy, Kenneth King, B. Maguire, C. A. Persaud, N. Y. Sandwith, I. A. Welch.
Director: DAVID H. PERSRAM, 1931 (Forestry).
Curator: RAMNARINE PERSAUD, 1941 (Flora of Guyana).
Associated botanic garden: Botanical Gardens, Georgetown.
Remarks: Herbarium is used by visiting botanists, institutions, and the public.

GEZIRA: *Wad Medani Herbarium,* **(WM)**, Ministry of Agriculture, Gezira, **Sudan.**

GLASGOW: *Herbarium, Department of Botany, University of Glasgow,* **(GL)**, Glasgow G12 8QQ, Scotland, **Great Britain.** (Information 1974)
Status: University.
Foundation: About 1780. *Number of specimens:* 200.000.
Herbarium: Worldwide.
Important collections: W. J. Hooker (1820–40, worldwide, especially Chile), Walker Arnott (1820–67, worldwide), R. Wight (India), J. Drummond (Australia), F. W. Beechey and J. Gillies (Peru).
Loans: To recognized botanical institutions. Requests for non-British spermatophytes should be addressed to Royal Botanical Garden, Edinburgh (E), to whom these specimens are on permanent loan.

GLASGOW: *Department of Natural History, Museum and Art Gallery,* **(GLAM)**, Kelvin Grove, Glasgow G3 8AG, Scotland, **Great Britain.**
Telephone: 041-334-1134.
Status: Local Government (City of Glasgow District Council).
Foundation: 1870. *Number of specimens:* 30.000.

Herbarium: Mainly collections of local societies and amateurs, from 2nd half of the 19th century, all plant groups, mostly British.
Important collections: Dr. James Stirtọn (1833–1917) collections of lichens (2000) and mosses (7000). Type specimens of Scottish interest: Philosophical Society of Glasgow. Flowering plants: Rev. John Fleming (1785–1857), contains material from George Don Snr.
Director: ALASDAIR A. AULD (Fine art).
Curator: All enquiries to the Keeper, Dept. of Natural History.
Loans: For up to one year, unless renewed in writing.
Exchange: Possible.

GLENNS: *Herbarium, Middle Peninsula and Northern Neck Plant Classification Depository, Rappahannock Community College,* **(GLEN)**, South Campus, Glenns, Virginia 23149, **U.S.A.** (Information 1974).
Telephone: 804/758-5324.
Foundation: 1971. *Number of specimens:* 1.080.
Herbarium: Flora of Virginia.
Important collections: Topotypes of species described from John Clayton's material.

GOIÂNIA: *Herbário, Departamento de Botânica, Universidade Federal de Goiás,* **(UFG)**, 74.000 Goiânia, Goiás, **Brazil.**
Telephone: (55)062/261-0143; 261-3088.
Foundation: 1968. *Number of specimens:* 8.004.
Herbarium: State of Goiás.
Director: JOSÉ ÂNGELO RIZZO, 1931 (Systematics; floristics).
Curator: ANA BARBOSA FERRO PEIXOTO, 1927 (Systematics).
Staff members: LEILA DA GRAÇA AMARAL, 1950 (Systematics).
HELENO DIAS FERREIRA, 1948 (Systematics).
Specialization in research: Flora of Goiás.
Associated botanic garden: Jardim Botânico da Prefeitura de Goiânia, Setor Pedro Ludovico, 74.000 Goiânia, Goiás, Brazil.
Exchange: Yes.

GÖRLITZ: *Herbarium, Staatliches Museum für Naturkunde Görlitz, Forschungsstelle,* **(GLM)**, Am Museum 1, DDR-8900 Görlitz, **German Democratic Republic,** DDR.
Telephone: Görlitz 5864, 4444.
Status: State Government of Universities.
Foundation: 1811. *Number of specimens:* 85.000.
Herbarium: Herb. Flora Lusatica; herb. Generale, mainly Central Europe.
Important collections: Flora Lusatica (Barber, G. Feurich, M. Militzer); lichens (A. Schade).
Director: WOLFRAM DUNGER, 1929 (Soil arthropods, ecology).
Curator: INGRID DUNGER, 1932 (Polyporaceae s.l.).

Staff member: PETRA GIRG, 1956.
Specialization in research: Flora Lusatica (S.E.
German Dem. Rep.); ecology of wood fungi.
· Loans: In general to recognized botanical
institutes.
Periodical and serial works: Abhandlungen und
Berichte des Naturkundemuseums Görlitz.
Exchange: Restricted, information on request.

GÖTEBORG: Herbarium, Botanical Museum, **(GB)**,
Carl Skottsbergs Gata 22, S-413 10 Göteborg, **Sweden.**
Telephone: 031-418700 (411891).
Status: Department of the Royal University of
Göteborg.
Foundation: 1926 (as the Herbarium of the Botanic
Garden of Göteborg, taken over by the State in
1962). Number of specimens: 1.250.000.
Herbarium: Worldwide.
Important collections: J. Eriksson (Aphyllophorales),· G. Harling et al. (Ecuador), A. Hayek (C.
Europe, the Balkan States, 90.000 sheets), F. Kingdon-Ward (India), A. H. Magnusson (Lichens), C.
Skottsberg (Hawaii, Juan Fernandez), H. Smith
(China).
Director: GUNNAR HARLING, 1920 (Cyclanthaceae, flora of Tropical South America, especially Ecuador; embryology of Angiospermae,
especially Compositae).
Head Curator: BO PETERSON, 1918 (Thymelaeaceae, botanical bibliography).
Staff member: DAN NILSON, 1947 (Lichens, especially Erioderma).
Research associates: LENNART ANDERSSON, 1948
(Marantaceae, Musaceae).
LARS ARVIDSSON, 1949 (Lichens, especially
Coccocarpia).
GUNNAR DEGELIUS, 1939 (Taxonomy and ecology of lichens).
UNO ELIASSON, 1939 (Flora of the Galápagos
Islands, Myxomycetes).
JOHN ERIKSSON, 1921 (Corticiaceae).
SVEN FRANSÉN, 1949 (Neotropical bryophytes,
especially Bartramia).
NILS HALLENBERG, 1947 (Aphyllophorales, N.
Iran, N. Europe).
STIG JACOBSSON, 1938 (Agaricales).
MAGNUS LIDÈN, 1951 (Fumariaceae).
ULF MOLAU, 1951 (Calceolaria).
MAGNUS NEUENDORF, 1942 (Alstroemeriaceae,
especially Bomarea).
KARIN PERSSON, 1938 (Cytotaxonomy of Colchicum and Scilloideae).
SVEN-OLOF STRANDHEDE, 1930 (Eleocharis,
hay-fever and dispersal of airborne pollen grains,
chromosome studies in flowering plants of S.
Spain).
STELLAN SUNHEDE, 1942 (Gasteromycetes,
Aphyllophorales, wood and bark inhabiting fungi
on Quercus in North Europe).

PER WENDELBO, 1927 (Flora of Afghanistan
and Iran, Liliiflorae, especially Allium).
Specialization in research: Flora of Tropical
South America, plant morphology.
Associated botanic garden: Botanic Garden of
Göteborg.
Loans: In general to recognized botanical
institutions.
Periodical and serial works: Flora of Ecuador.
Exchange: Available: Mainly specimens from
Scandinavia. Desired: Specimens from all parts of
the world, especially South America.

GÖTTINGEN: Systematisch-Geobotanisches Institut
der Universität Göttingen, **(GOET)**, Untere Karspüle
2, D-3400 Göttingen, **Federal Republic of Germany,**
BRD.
Telephone: 0551-395731.
Status: University.
Foundation: 1832. Number of specimens: 750.000.
Herbarium: Worldwide herbarium, mainly vascular plants, bryophytes and lichens.
Important collections: Herbaria of F. G. Bartling,
F. Ehrhart (p.p.), G. Forster (p.p.), A. Grisebach, A.
von Haller (p.p.), G. F. W. Meyer, J. Ch., H. L. and H.
Wendland (cf. Taxon 21:287–289). Few types of
H. A. Schrader (his herbarium is at LE).
Director: GERHARD WAGENITZ, 1927 (Compositae, especially Centaurea, general taxonomy of
angiosperms).
Curator: KLAUS LEWEJOHANN, 1937 (Gramineae,
Cyperaceae, floristics of Central Europe and
Macaronesia).
Staff members: URSULA HOFMANN, 1941 (Morphology and anatomy of angiosperms).
FRED-GÜNTER SCHROEDER, 1930 (Plant geography of holarctic).
Specialization in research: Taxonomy of Compositae (Asteraceae), floristics of Central and
Southern Europe and the Near East.
Associated botanic garden: Neuer Botanischer
Garten der Universität, Grisebachstr. 1a.
Loans: To recognized botanical institutions
(Forster-types, photographs only).
Exchange: Available: Limited vascular plants
from Central Europe.

GOTTWALDOV: Herbarium, Oblastní Muzeum
Jihovýchodní Moravy, **(GM)**, Lešná u Gottwaldova,
763 14 Gottwaldov, **Czechoslovakia.**
Telephone: 91 244.
Foundation: 1956. Number of specimens: 21.000.
Herbarium: Cryptogams and phanerogams of the
region.
Director: MILAN SMÝKAL, 1925.
Curator: MARIE ELSNEROVÁ, 1942.
Specialization in research: Systematics.

GRAHAMSTOWN: Herbarium, Albany Museum,
(GRA), Botanical Research Unit, P.O. Box 101,

Grahamstown, **South Africa.** (Information 1974)
Status: Provincial museum.
Foundation: 1855 (museum), 1889 (herbarium).
Number of specimens: 125.000.
Herbarium: Worldwide, cryptogams and phanerogams.
Important collections: African phanerogams (MacOwan herbarium in part): L. L. Britten, H. G. Flanagan, T. V. Paterson, A. Pegler, S. Schonland (all first sets); W. J. Burchell, K. Dinter, R. A. Dyer, C. F. Ecklon and C. L. P. Zeyher, F. Eyles and W. J. P. Johnson, H. G. Fourcode, E. E. Galpin, J. Medley-Wood, E. J., C. E. and F. Lugard, M. Rautanen, A. Rehmann, F. A. Rogers, A. F. W. Schimper, H. Schintz, R. Schlechter, A. Schenck, T. R. Sim, R. Story, F. L. Stuhlmann, A. J. Teague, A. Whyte, H. Wild, M. Wilman, C. Zeyher. Extra-African (MacOwen Herbarium): H. F. Hance, R. Wright, F. von Müller, J. C. Meliss, W. J. Burchell, H. N. Bolander, W. M. Canby, A. Eaton, E. Hall. Worldwide cryptogams: M. A. Pocock Herbarium, including Baird, Bourelli, G. F. Papenfuss.
Specialization in research: Eastern Cape Province flora and marine algae.

GRAHAMSTOWN: *Rhodes University Herbarium, Department of Plant Sciences, Rhodes University,* (**RUH**), P.O. Box 94, Grahamstown 6140, **South Africa.**
Telephone: (0461)2443.
Status: University.
Foundation: 1942. *Number of specimens:* 25.000.
Herbarium: General, mainly Eastern Cape and South African.
Important collections: Tyson collection of marine algae.
Director: S. C. SEAGRIEF, 1927, Head of the Department of Plant Sciences (Algology).
Curator: R. A. LUBKE, 1940 (Numerical taxonomy).
Specialization in research: Marine and freshwater S. African algae, numerical taxonomy of selected taxa.
Loans: On application to recognized taxonomists.
Exchange: Available: Limited number of Eastern Cape specimens.

GRANADA: *Facultad de Farmacia,* (**GDA**), Catedra de Botánica, c/ Rector Lopez Argüeta s/n, Granada, **Spain.**
Telephone: 958/23-16-65.
Status: University of Granada.
Foundation: 1870. *Number of specimens:* 50.000.
Important collections: General herbarium, consisting of Herb. de Amo y Mora, Academia Malaguena de Ciencias, herb. de Modesto Laza Palacios, herb. de J. M. Muñoz Medina, herb. of duplicates of Miguel Ladero (greater part of this coll. in MAF).

Director: MIGUEL LADERO ALVAREZ, 1939 (Taxonomy and phytosociology).
Curator: OSWALDO SOCORRO ABREU, 1949; 28-49-05 (Taxonomy and phytosociology).
Staff members: JESUS HURTADO MORALES, 1919 (Collecting).
MANUEL LOPEZ GUADALUPE, 1933 (Taxonomy).
JOAQUIN MOLERO MESA, 1952 (Taxonomy).
LUISA ZAFRA VALVERDE, 1942 (Taxonomy).
Periodical and serial works: Trabajos del Departamento de Botánica de la Universidad de Granada.
Exchange: Possible.

GRAND CANYON: *Herbarium, Grand Canyon National Park,* (**GCNP**), Box 129, Grand Canyon, Arizona 86023, **U.S.A.**
Telephone: 602/638-2411, ext. 261.
Status: U.S. Department of the Interior, National Park Service.
Foundation: 1929. *Number of specimens:* 7.000.
Herbarium: Plants of Grand Canyon National Park.
Director: JOHN C. O'BRIEN.
Curator: KAREN BRANTLEY, 1949.
Staff members: DIANE L. SHARP, 1956.
STARR SWEENY, 1955.
PAT ZUCCARO, 1952.
Specialization in research: Inventory of Grand Canyon National Park flora.
Loans: No special regulations.
Exchange: Must first be made available to other government agencies.

GRANDE PRAIRIE: *Herbarium, Grande Prairie Regional College,* (**GPA**), Grande Prairie, Alberta, **Canada.**
Telephone: 403/532-3766.
Foundation: 1966. *Number of specimens:* 1.500.
Herbarium: Used primarily for teaching; primarily a collection of plants native to the Peace River Region.
Director: PAUL LEMAY, 1942 (Plant anatomy).
Curator: STUART MCGREGOR; 403/532-8830, ext. 358.
Specialization in research: Calcium translocation in plant roots.

GRAND FORKS: *Herbarium, Biology Department, University of North Dakota,* (**GFND**), Starcher Hall, Grand Forks, North Dakota 58202, **U.S.A.**
Telephone: 701/777-2621.
Foundation: 1948. *Number of specimens:* 25.000.
Herbarium: Flora of North Dakota.
Curator: JOHN C. LA DUKE, 1950 (Chemosystematics and evolutionary botany; systematics of *Tithonia*).
Specialization in research: Flora of North Dakota; biosystematic and chemosystematic approaches are utilized in studying problems in sys-

tematics and evolution.

Loans: To recognized botanical institutions.

Exchange: Available: North Dakota vascular plants. Desired: U.S. vascular plants, especially prairie species.

GRAND RAPIDS: *Herbarium, Aquinas College,* (AQC), 1607 Robinson Road, Grand Rapids, Michigan 49506, **U.S.A.**

Telephone: 616/459-8281.

Status: Private institution.

Foundation: 1931. *Number of specimens:* 5.500.

Herbarium: Flora of Michigan and New Mexico.

Curator: EUGENE SMITH (Michigan flora).

Staff member: Sister ALICE WITTENBACH, 1937 (Palynology of Inuleae; Michigan flora).

GRAND RAPIDS: *Herbarium, Department of Botany, Life Science Division, Grand Rapids Junior College,* (**GRJC**), 143 Bostwick Avenue N.E., Grand Rapids, Michigan 49503, **U.S.A.**

Telephone: 616/456-4847.

Status: Administered by the Grand Rapids Board of Administration.

Foundation: 1921. *Number of specimens:* 2.500.

Herbarium: Plants growing in the vicinity of Grand Rapids, Michigan.

Director: ARTHUR JACK HEYDENBURG, 1930.

Specialization in research: Fine structure of white oak (*Quercus alba*) mycorrhizae.

GRANVILLE: *Herbarium, Biology Department, Denison University,* (**DEN**), Granville, Ohio 43023, **U.S.A.**

Telephone: 614/587-0810.

Status: Privately endowed college.

Foundation: 1885. *Number of specimens:* 25.000.

Herbarium: Ohio; general U.S. and worldwide ferns.

Important collections: Cathcart (ferns).

Director and Curator: JULIANA C. MULROY, 1948 (*Saxifraga, Arenaria*).

Loans: Usual regulations.

GRAZ: *Abteilung für Botanik, Steiermärkisches Landesmuseum Joanneum,* (**GJO**), Raubergasse 10, A-8010 Graz, Styria, **Austria.**

Telephone: 0316/831-2803.

Status: Provincial government museum.

Foundation: 1811, founded by Johann v. Habsburg, Archduke of Austria. *Number of specimens:* 300.000.

Herbarium: Mainly vascular plants and mosses of Europe, particularly of the Eastern Alps.

Important collections: Herbarium C. v. Attems, W. Becker (*Viola* exsicc.), J. Breidler (p. maj. p.), J. Brunnthaler (p.p.), J. Döller-Wolframsberg (Algae), I. Dörfler (herb. norm.), M. v. Eichenfeld, J. Ernst (Algae), B. Fest (p.p.), S. Garovaglio (Brioteca austriaca, Muschi Austria inf., Muschi rari Prov. Como), J. Glowacki (p. maj. p.), C. M. Gottsche & Rabenhorst

(Hepat. europ.), J. v. Habsburg, A. v. Hayek (Fl. exsicc. styriace), S. V. Hohenwarth, J. M. Holzinger (p.p.), D. H. Hoppe (? Herb. vivum pl. gramin.), J. W. Hübner & F. F. Genth (Deutschl. Lebermoose), A. J. v. Kerner-Marilaun (Fl. exsicc. austro-hung.), K. Koegeler, T. Kotschy (Egypt, Syria etc.), L. Kristof, F. Lindheimer (Fl. Texana exsicc. p.p. ?), J. Maly, G. v. Marktanner-Turneretscher, W. Migula (Cryptog. Germ., Austr. Helv. exsicc.), F. Müllner, Museum Pal. Vindob. (Kryptog. exsicc.), G. de Notaris (mosses of Haly), P. S. Pallas (Siberia), A. Paulin (Fl. exsicc. carniol.), F. v. Portenschlag (p.p.), K. Prohaska, L. Rabenhorst (Lich. europ. exsicc.), M. v. Rainer-Haarbach, A. Rochel (*Salix* of Hungary), M. Sadler (p.p.), L. E. Schaerer (Lich. helv. exsicc.), J. Schefczik, J. C. Schleicher (*Salix* of Switzerland), V. Schiffner (Hepat. europ. exsicc.), A. Schnitzlein (p.p.), F. W. Sieber (Crete, Egypt, West Indies, Australia, etc.), G. Strobl (p.p.), F. v. Thümen (Mycotheca univ.), J. Traunsteiner (p.p.), F. Unger, F. Verbniak, L. C. v. Vest, P. Wierzbicki, F. X. v. Wulffen (p. maj. p.?), Zool. Station Triest (Algae adriat. exsicc., p.p.?); G. Strobl (Herb. univ. Fl. Ital.) is in care of GJO, but belongs to ADMONT.

Head of Department of Botany: DETLEF ERNET, 1941 (Systematics of Valerianaceae especially *Valerianella, Fedia;* karyosystematics, systematic morphology, dispersal biology).

Specialization in research: Systematics and evolution of various angiosperms, flora of Styria.

Associated botanic garden: Alpengarten Rannach, Rannach 15, A-8046 St. Veit b. Graz, Styria.

Loans: In general to recognized botanical institutions.

Periodical and serial works: Mitteilungen der Abteilung für Botanik am Landesmuseum Joanneum in Graz.

Remarks: The restoration of the cryptogamcollections, started in 1979, may cause some restrictions to loans.

GRAZ: *Herbarium, Institut für Botanik* (**GZU**), Holteigasse 6, A-8010 Graz, **Austria.**

Telephone: 0316/31581/537.

Status: Institute of the University of Graz.

Foundation: About 1900. *Number of specimens:* 550.000.

Herbarium: Mainly Cormophyta from Central and Southern Europe, Eastern Alps; lichens of Europe.

Important collections: C. F. Ecklon & C. L. P. Zeyher (p.p.), K. Fritsch, D. H. Hoppe, Nees v. Esenbeck (p.p.), C. Schmarda (Ceylon).

Director: J. POELT, 1924 (Systematics and biology of lichens, mainly from Europe and the Himalayas; Lecanoraceae, Teloschistaceae, Physciaceae).

Staff members: J. HAFELLNER, 1951 (Systematics of Patellariaceae, lichenicolous fungi, various groups of lichens).

H. MAYRHOFER, 1953 (Various groups of lichens esp. Physciaceae).

H. Pittoni-Dannenfeldt, 1924 (*Leontodon*).

P. Remler, 1953 (Ascomycetes).

H. Teppner, 1941 (Karyosystematics; *Waldsteinia, Onosma, Mentha, Anthoxanthum* and other grasses).

Specialization in research: Karyosystematics and evolution of various angiosperms (worldwide), flora and vegetation of Central and Southern Europe, Eastern Alps, systematics of lichenized and non-lichenized Ascomycetes.

Associated botanic garden: Botanischer Garten der Universität.

Loans: To recognized institutions on a mutual basis.

Periodical and serial works: Phyton, Annales Rei Botanicae, Plantae Graecenses (Exsicc.).

Exchange: European spermatophyta, lichens.

GREAT FALLS: *Herbarium, Department of Biology, College of Great Falls,* (**GFC**), 1301 20th Street South, Great Falls, Montana 59405, **U.S.A.**

Telephone: 406/761-8210.

Foundation: 1932. *Number of specimens:* 7.000 (2.000 vascular plants, 5.000 bryophytes).

Herbarium: Local flora; Hepaticae of northwestern N. America.

Director and Curator: Won S. Hong.

Specialization in research: Hepaticae of northwestern N. America.

GREELEY: *Herbarium, Department of Biological Sciences, University of Northern Colorado,* (**GREE**), Ross Hall, Greeley, Colorado 80639, **U.S.A.**

Telephone: 303/351-2532.

Number of specimens: 10.000.

Herbarium: Vascular plants of eastern Colorado and adjacent regions.

Director and Curator: William E. Harmon, 1941 (*Lupinus*).

Specialization in research: Taxonomy of vascular plants; flora of Rocky Mountains, Mexico, and Central America.

Loans: Usual regulations.

Exchange: Plants of Rocky Mountain region and some from Central America.

GREENCASTLE: *Truman G. Yuncker Herbarium, Department of Botany and Bacteriology, De Pauw University,* (**DPU**), 7 Harrison Hall, Greencastle, Indiana 46135, **U.S.A.**

Telephone: 317/653-9721, ext. 2858, 2859.

Status: Private, endowed Methodist University.

Foundation: 1870. *Number of specimens:* 133.500.

Herbarium: All groups of fungi, especially Indiana Myxomycetes; all groups of algae; possibly largest collections of Indiana hepatics and lichens; large collection of mosses, especially Fontinalaceae and Hookeriaceae of North and Central America and West Indies; Cuscutaceae and Piperaceae.

Important collections: T. G. Yuncker (Piperaceae, Cuscutaceae), W. H. Welch (mosses).

Director and Curator: Richard Alan Mayes, 1948 (Plant taxonomy and biochemical systematics, especially Poaceae of Indiana, Virginia, and mid-Appalachians; Asteraceae, especially Astereae).

Curator Emeritus: Winona H. Welch, 1896 (Plant taxonomy, especially mosses; Fontinalaceae, Hookeriaceae).

Specialization in research: Fontinalaceae of the world; Hookeriaceae of North and Central America and West Indies; mosses of Indiana; Poaceae of Indiana, Virginia, and mid-Appalachians.

Loans: To authorized persons.

Exchange: Limited.

GREENSBORO: *Herbarium, Department of Biology, North Carolina A & T State University,* (**NCATG**), Greensboro, North Carolina 27411, **U.S.A.**

Telephone: 919/379-7907.

Foundation: 1977. *Number of specimens:* 5.000.

Herbarium: Mainly plants of Piedmont North Carolina.

Curator: A. James Hicks, 1938 (Systematics of Compositae; flora of Piedmont North Carolina).

Assistant Curator: Lonnette Edwards.

Loans: Usual regulations.

Exchange: Available: Flora of Piedmont North Carolina. Desired: Flora of Piedmont North Carolina; poisonous plants of world.

GREENVILLE: *Ives Herbarium, Department of Biology, Furman University,* (**FUGR**), Poinsett Highway, Greenville, South Carolina 29613, **U.S.A.**

Telephone: 803/294-2085.

Foundation: 1930's. *Number of specimens:* 19.000.

Herbarium: Mainly southeastern U.S.

Director and Curator: C. Leland Rodgers (Plant taxonomy, ecology).

Loans: Within U.S.; prompt return expected.

Exchange: As time allows.

GREIFSWALD: *Herbarium, Sektion Biologie der Ernst-Moritz-Arndt-Universität Greifswald,* (**GFW**), Grimmer Strasse 88, DDR-22 Greifswald, **German Democratic Republic**, DDR. (Information 1974)

Status: University.

Foundation: 1763. *Number of specimens:* 100.000.

Herbarium: Worldwide, especially Middle Europe, Northeastern Germany.

Associated botanic garden: Botanic Garden of the University of Greifswald.

Loans: To recognized botanical institutions.

GRENOBLE: *Laboratoire de Botanique et Biologie végétale de l'Université Scientifique et Médicale,* (**GR**), Domaine Universitaire, B.P. 53X, 38041 Grenoble Cedex, **France**.

Telephone: (76)44-82-72.

Status: State University of Grenoble.
Number of specimens: 150.000.
Herbarium: Western Alps (Dauphiné), Tunisia, Sahara, Népal; lichens.
  Director: P. OZENDA, 1920 (Phytogeography, desert flora, lichens, radiobiology).
  Curator: A. TONNEL, 1935 (Cartography).
  Specialization in research: Vegetation mapping; phytogeography and ecology of the mountains of the world.
  Associated botanic garden: Jardin botanique de l'Institut alpin du Lautaret (Hautes-Alpes).
  Loans: Normal regulations.
  Periodical and serial works: Index seminum of the Jardin alpin du Lautaret, Documents de Cartographie écologique.
  Exchange: Available: Dried specimens, seeds and living plants from the French Alps. Desired: Mountain plants, desert plants.

GRENOBLE: *Herbarium, Museum d'Histoire Naturelle,* **(GRM),** 1 Rue Dolomieu, 38000 Grenoble, **France.**
Telephone: 16-(76)-44-05-35.
Status: Municipal.
Foundation: 1851. *Number of specimens:* 500.000–1.000.000.
Herbarium: 10 important herbaria in good condition.
Important collections: Herbarium Villars, XVIIIth century; herbarium Mutel, XIXth century; herbarium Révil, XIXth century.
  Director: ARMAND FAYARD, 1946 (Animal ecology).

GRINNELL: *Herbarium, Biology Department, Grinnell College,* **(GRI),** Grinnell, Iowa 50112, **U.S.A.**
Telephone: 515/236-6181, ext. 490.
Status: Private institution.
Foundation: 1900. *Number of specimens:* 16.000.
Herbarium: Flora of central Iowa.
  Director and Curator: L. H. DURKEE, 1927 (Acanthaceae of Central America).
  Specialization in research: Flora of Jasper and Poweshiek counties, Iowa.
  Loans: No special restrictions.
  Exchange: Available: Prairie and oak-hickory forest. Desired: General material from anywhere.

GRONINGEN: *Herbarium, Department for Systematic Botany of the Botanical Laboratory,* **(GRO)** -- *see* Haren.

GRUVER: *Herbarium, Science Research Center,* **(SRCG),** 112 Main, Box 1095, Gruver, Texas 79040, **U.S.A.**
Telephone: 806/733-2202.
Status: Affiliated with Hardin-Simmons University, Abilene, Texas.
Foundation: 1977. *Number of specimens:* 4.000.

Herbarium: Juniperus of North America and Caribbean; specimens documenting chemosystematic and evolutionary systematics of North American *Juniperus.*
Important collections: Robert P. Adams, Walter A. Kelley, James Kistler, Thomas A. Zanoni.
  Director: ROBERT P. ADAMS, 1939 (*Juniperus*).
  Specialization in research: Systematics and chemosystematics of *Juniperus;* multivariate data analysis; analysis of hydrocarbons from plants.

GUADALAJARA: *Herbario, Departamento de Pulpa y Papel, Centro Regional de Enseñanza Técnica Industrial de Guadalajara,* **(CREG),** Calle El Chaco 3223, Fraccionamiento Providencia, Apartado Postal 6-725, Guadalajara, Jalisco, **Mexico.**
Telephone: 9136-15-69-87.
Foundation: 1975. *Number of specimens:* 7.000; wood collection of 500 specimens.
Herbarium: Forest flora of México.
Important collections: Luz María González Villarreal, Servando Carvajal Hernández, Sergio Martínez Esquivel, Román Lamas Robles, Luz María Villarreal de Puga, Rafael Guzmán Mejía, Gustavo Mancinas Zaldivar.
  Director: LUZ MARÍA GONZÁLEZ VILLARREAL, 1954 (Wood anatomy; Fagaceae).
  Curator: SERVANDO CARVAJAL HERNÁNDEZ, 1955 (Taxonomy of vascular plants; floristics and ecology of weeds).
  Staff members: ROMÁN LAMAS ROBLES, 1943 (Chemistry of natural products).
  MARÍA DE JESÚS FLORES MORENO, 1958 (Chemistry and physics of wood).
  GUSTAVO MANCINAS ZALDIVAR, 1958 (Cellulosic survey).
  Specialization in research: Forest flora of México with special emphasis on species for pulp and paper making.
  Loans: To scientific institutions, by arrangement with the curator.
  Exchange: Available: Mexican flora, especially of Jalisco; wood specimens and herbarium vouchers of tropical and temperate woody plants.

GUADALAJARA: *Herbario, Escuela de Biología, Universidad Autonoma de Guadalajara,* **(GUADA),** Lomas del Valle, Guadalajara, Jalisco, **Mexico.**
Telephone: 15-88-02.
Foundation: 1967. *Number of specimens:* 26.000.
Herbarium: Plants of the State of Jalisco; emphasis on Leguminosae, Compositae, and weedy plants.
  Director: CARLOS LUIS DIAZ LUNA, 1936 (Weedy plants of Jalisco).
  Curator: BLANCA CORRES ZEPEDA, 1947 (Ferns of Jalisco).
  Specialization in research: Weedy plants.
  Associated botanic garden: Jardin Botanico Universidad Autonoma de Guadalajara.
  Exchange: Yes, all groups of plants.

GUADALAJARA: *Herbario, Instituto de Botánica, Universidad de Guadalajara,* **(IBUG)** –– *see* ZAPOPAN.

GUANARE: *Herbario Universitario, School of Natural Resources, Universidad Nacional Experimental de los Llanos Occidentales "Ezequiel Zamora,"* **(PORT),** Guanare, Portuguesa, **Venezuela.**
Telephone: (58)057/53328.
Status: Part of the School of Natural Resources, Vice-rectorado Produccion Agricola, UNELLEZ.
Foundation: 1980. *Number of specimens:* 1.000.
Herbarium: Flora of the western savanna region of Venezuela.
Director: BASIL STERGIOS, 1940 (Floristics; population ecology; aquatic plants; *Campsiandra,* Leguminosae; *Gnaphalium,* Compositae).
Curator: FRANCISCO ORTEGA, 1952 (Floristics; ferns and fern allies; seedling morphology).
Staff member: CARLOS RAMIREZ, 1935 (Nonvascular cryptogams).
Specialization in research: Flora of Portuguesa State, including pteridophytes, lichens, hepatics, and bryophytes; aquatic plants of Apure State; manual of tree seedlings for the western savanna of Venezuela.
Loans: Within the coming two years.
Exchange: Available and Desired: Venezuela specimens.

GUANGZHOU: *Herbarium, Department of Forestry, College of Agriculture of South China,* **(CANT),** Shek-p' ai, Guangzhou, Guangdong, **People's Republic of China.**
Director: TSIANG YING (Apocynaceae, Asclepiadaceae).

GUANGZHOU: *Herbarium, Botanical Institute, Academia Sinica,* **(IBSC),** Guangzhou, Guangdong, **People's Republic of China.**
Telephone: 78464.
Status: Directed by Academia Sinica.
Foundation: 1928 (Transfer of part of herbarium of Sun Yatsen University, originally herbarium of Lingnan University, LU). *Number of specimens:* 520.000.
Herbarium: Bryophytes, pteridophytes and spermatophytes of China, especially South China.
Important collections: Collections of South China.
Director and Curator: CHEN FENG-HWAI, 1900 (Taxonomy of Compositae and Primulaceae, landscape gardening).
Assistant Curators: HUANG CHENG-CHIU, 1922 (Fagaceae, Rutaceae, Geraniaceae).
LING YEOU-RUENN, 1937 (Araliaceae, Compositae, Olacaceae).
Keeper of Herbarium: CHOW HAN-CHUAN, 1919.
Staff members: CHEN PANG-YÜ, 1936 (Leguminosae, Simaroubaceae, Meliaceae, Opiliaceae).
CHEN SEN-JEN, 1933 (Botanical Garden, Zingiberaceae).

CHEN TE-CHAO, 1926 (Leguminosae, Lardizabalaceae, Sapindaceae, Meliaceae).
CHEN WEI-CU'IU, 1934 (Cucurbitaceae, Rubiaceae).
CHENG SI-JÜNG, 1934 (Botanical Garden, Orchidaceae).
CHIA LIANG-CHI, 1921 (Gramineae, Oleaceae).
HU CH'I-MING, 1934 (Compositae, Primulaceae).
HWANG SHU-MEI, 1933 (Aristolochiaceae, Cyperaceae, Euphorbiaceae, Saxifragaceae, Styracaceae).
KIU HUA-SHING, 1929 (Convolvulaceae, Euphorbiaceae, Loranthaceae, Proteaceae).
KO WAN-CHEUNG, 1916 (Rhizophoraceae, Rubiaceae, Sonneratiaceae).
LIN PAN-JUAN, 1936 (Bryophyta).
LAW YUH-WU, 1917 (Magnoliaceae, Sabiaceae, Pinaceae).
LO HSIEN-SHUI, 1927 (Acanthaceae, Menispermaceae, Rubiaceae, Sapindaceae).
TAM PUI-CHEUNG, 1921 (Ericaceae, Santalaceae, Orchidaceae, Balanophoraceae).
TANG' CHEN-ZHI, 1934 (Botanical Garden, Orchidaceae, Palmae).
TSENG YUNG-CH'IEN, 1930 (Compositae, Euphorbiaceae, Piperaceae).
WANG CHU-HAO, 1923 (Pteridophyta).
WEI CHAO-FEN, 1934 (Leguminosae, Palmae, Saxifragaceae).
WU CHAO-HUNG, 1934 (Pteridophyta).
WU TE-LING, 1934 (Leguminosae, Lowiaceae, Zingiberaceae).
WU YIN-CH'AN (Pteridophyta, Lardizabalaceae, Menispermaceae).
WU YUNG-FEN, 1924 (Sabiaceae, Symplocaceae).
YUAN YUN-CHENG, 1936 (Droseraceae, Nepenthaceae, Rubiaceae).
Specialization in research: Chinese medicinal herbs, chemotaxonomy, woody flora of China, flora of Xizang.
Associated botanic garden: South China Botanical Garden, Longdong, Guangzhou; Ding-Hu-Shan Arboretum, Ding-Hu-Shan, Kwangtung.
Loans: Short-term loans for Flora of China.
Periodical and serial works: Flora Reipublicae Popularis Sinicae, Flora of Hainan, Flora of Guangdong, Colored Icones of Chinese Common Medicinal Herbs.
Exchange: Available: Specimens of South China. Desired: Tropical and subtropical plants of the world.

GUANGZHOU: *Herbarium, Lingnan University,* **(LU),** Guangzhou, Guangdong, **People's Republic of China** –– *see* IBSC and SYS.

GUANGZHOU: *Herbarium, Department of Biology, Sun Yatsen University,* **(SYS),** Guangzhou, Guang-

dong, **People's Republic of China.**
Telephone: 51710-278.
Status: University.
Foundation: 1916. *Number of specimens:* 160.000.
Herbarium: Plants of Hainan, Guangdong, Guangxi, Fukien and Chiangxi provinces; Vietnam, Malaya.
  Director: CHANG HUNG-TA, 1914 (Hamamelidaceae, Theaceae, Pittosporaceae, Myrtaceae, Tiliaceae, Elaeocarpaceae).
  Curator: YEN SHEN-SHIANG, 1920; 51710-583 (Flora of South China).
  Staff members: HUANG YUN-FEE, 1937 (*Albizzia*, Ranunculaceae).
    LI ZHI-FA, 1936 (Mosses).
    LIU LAN-FAN, 1935 (Lythraceae).
    MIAU RU-FUAI, 1942 (Ferns, *Syzygium*).
    WANG BA-SUNG, 1933 (Ferns; Gramineae, especially bamboos).
    ZHONG HEN, 1937 (Fresh-water Chlorophyceae).
    ZHU WAN-CHIA, 1924 (Fresh-water Chlorophyceae and Cyanophyceae).
  Specialization in research: Origin and development of Chinese flora, karst (limestone) flora of South China.
  Remarks: Herbarium founded by Canton Christian College, transferred to Lingnan University (LU) in 1920; part of collections went to Botanical Institute (IBSC) in 1928 and the rest to Sun Yatsen University.

GUANTÁNAMO: *Colegio del Sagrado Corazón,* (CSC), Guantánamo, **Cuba** –– incorporated in HAC.

GUATEMALA: *Herbario "Ulises Rojas," Museo Nacional de Historia Natural,* (GUAT), Apartado postal 987, Guatemala, **Guatemala.**
Telephone: (502)2/310406.
Foundation: 1972. *Number of specimens:* 5.000.
Herbarium: Flora of Guatemala.

GUATEMALA: *Herbario, Escuela de Biología, Museo de Historia Natural y Jardín Botánico, Universidad de San Carlos de Guatemala,* (USCG), Avenida de la Reforma 0-43, Zona 10, Guatemala, **Guatemala.**
Foundation: 1922. *Number of specimens:* 31.253.
Herbarium: Flora of Guatemala.
Important collections: Ferns.
  Director: MARIO DARY (Ferns).
  Staff members: JOSÉ MARÍA AGUILAR (Conifers).
    ELFRIEDE DE POLL (Orchidaceae).
  Specialization in research: Ferns, Loranthaceae, *Eryngium* in Guatemala.

GUATEMALA: *Herbario, Universidad del Valle de Guatemala,* (UVAL), Apartado Postal 82, Guatemala, **Guatemala.**
Telephone: (502)2/690791; 690792; 690793; 692563; 692776; 692827.
Status: Serves biology and agriculture departments.

Foundation: 1974. *Number of specimens:* 5.000.
Herbarium: Flora of Guatemala, with emphasis on Orchidaceae, Bromeliaceae, conifers, and marine algae.
  Director and Curator: MARGARET DIX, 1939 (Orchidaceae; epiphyte ecology).
  Staff members: MICHAEL DIX, 1938 (Ecology, especially cloud forest).
    KAREN LIND, 1947 (Pines).
    LAURA SCHUSTER, 1941 (Commelinaceae).
  Specialization in research: Distribution and taxonomy of plants of Guatemala; Orchidaceae; pollination biology of Orchidaceae and Commelinaceae; cloud forest ecology.
  Associated botanic garden: University Arboretum.
  Loans: Costs paid by institution requesting loan.
  Exchange: Especially Orchidaceae, Bromeliaceae, ferns, mosses, lichens.

GUAYAQUIL: *Herbario, Facultad de Ciencias Naturales, Universidad Estatal de Guayaquil,* (GUAY), Avenida 25 de Julio-El Guaamo, Apartado Aereo 471, Guayaquil, **Ecuador.**
Foundation: 1969. *Number of specimens:* 8.000.
Herbarium: Flora of Ecuador.
Important collections: C. Dodson, A. Gentry, Amy Gilmartin, Florinda Trivivño V., Flor Maria Valverde Badillo.
  Director: FLORINDA TRIVIVÑO (Economic plants).
  Director, Departamento de Botánica: FLOR MARIA VALVERDE (Flora of Ecuador).
  Staff members: CARLOTA BECERRA (Forestry).
    JOSÉ MIÑO (Poaceae).
    CARLOS GARCIA RIZZO (Morphology).
    FIDEL SOLANO.
    GLADYS DE TAZÁN (Ecology).
    PILAR DE VELEZ (Pteridology).
  Exchange: Available: Flora of Ecuador.

GUAYAQUIL: *Rio Palenque Science Center,* (RPSC) –– see Santo Domingo de los Colorados.

GUELPH: *Herbarium, Department of Botany and Genetics, University of Guelph,* (OAC), Guelph, Ontario, **Canada** N1G 2W1.
Telephone: 519/824-4120.
Foundation: 1869. *Number of specimens:* 57.000.
Herbarium: Native and introduced plants of Ontario and Canada.
Important collections: Newton Tripp, J. Macoun.
  Curator of Phanerogamic Section: JACK F. ALEX, 1928 (Weedy and introduced species).
  Curator of Mycological Section: GEORGE L. BARRON.
  Staff members: DONALD M. BRITTON, 1923 (Pteridophytes).
    JUDITH M. CANNE (Compositae, Scrophulariaceae).

HUGH M. DALE, 1919 (Aquatics).
JOSEPH F. GERRATH (Algae, Musci).
DOUGLAS W. LARSON (Lichens).

Specialization in research: Flora of Ontario; monographic studies in selected groups in Compositae, Scrophulariaceae, Berberidaceae, pteridophytes, and soil inhabiting fungi; taxonomic and ecological studies on weedy species.

Associated botanic garden: University of Guelph Arboretum.

Loans: To recognized botanical institutions.

Exchange: Available: Plants of Ontario and Canada. Desired: Plants from other temperate areas of the world; genera with counterparts in Canada.

GUILIN: *Herbarium, Guangxi Institute of Botany,* **(IBK),** Yenshan, Guilin, Guangxi, **People's Republic of China.**

Status: Directed by Guangxi Committee of Science and Technology.

Foundation: 1935. *Number of specimens:* 250.000.

Herbarium: Plants of China, especially Guangxi, Guangdong, Sichuan and Yunnan Provinces.

Important collections: Liang H. Y., Ko S. P., Chung Z. S., Lau S. K., Longzheng Expedition.

Deputy Director: CHUNG Z. S.

Curator: LEE S. K., 1915 (Lauraceae, Ebenaceae, Lythraceae).

Staff member: LIANG C. F. (Actinidiaceae).

Specialization in research: Flora of China, flora of Guangxi, plant geography.

Associated botanic garden: Hortus Guilinensis.

Loans: To recognized botanical institutions.

Exchange: Available: Specimens from Guangxi. Desired: Old collections from China, important economic plants, publications concerning Chinese flora, monographs.

H

HABANA: *Herbario, Academia de Ciencias Medicas, Fisicas y Naturales de La Habana,* (**HABA**), Calle Cuba 460, Habana, **Cuba** – – incorporated in HAC.
Number of specimens: 6.000.
Herbarium: Flora of Cuba.

HABANA: *Herbario, Instituto de Biologia, Departamento de Ecologia Forestal, Academia de Ciencias de Cuba,* (**HABE**), Capitolio Nacional, Habana, **Cuba.** (Information 1974)
Foundation: 1964. *Number of specimens:* 8.000.

HABANA: *Herbario, Academia de Ciencias de Cuba, Instituto de Botánica,* (**HAC**), Calzada del Cerro 1257, Habana 6, **Cuba.**
Telephone: 79-8329; 79-8343.
Status: Academia de Ciencias de Cuba.
Foundation: 1959. *Number of specimens:* 134.600.
Herbarium: Primarily flora of Cuba.
Important collections: Herbaria HABA, LS, SV, and Colegio de La Salle, Santiago de Cuba, incorporated here; Julián Acuña, Brother Alain, C. F. Baker, A. H. Curtiss, A. S. Hitchcock, E. P. Killip, Brother León, G. Proctor, J. T. Roig, J. A. Shafer, P. Sintenis, Urban, Charles Wright.
    Director: MAYRA FERNÁNDEZ Z., 1948 (Rubiaceae).
    Curator: PEDRO HERRERA O., 1941 (Compositae).
    Staff members: A. BARRETO, 1945 (Caesalpiniaceae).
    L. CATASÚS, 1939 (Gramineae).
    A. COMAS, 1949 (Freshwater algae; Chlorophyceae).
    P. DUARTE, 1922 (Taxonomy of mosses).
    M. C. FERNÁNDEZ, 1954 (Cariosystematics).
    S. HERRERA, 1945 (Fungi; Aphilophorales).
    A. LOBAINA, 1950 (Fabaceae).
    A. MERCADO, 1937 (Fungi).
    M. MONCADA, 1937 (Palynology).
    O. MUÑIZ, 1937 (Palmae).
    D. REYES, 1941 (Hepaticae).
    E. SOSA, 1933 (Marine algae).
    M. I. TORRES, 1943 (Lichens).
    M. A. VALES, 1950 (Systematic wood anatomy).
Specialization in research: Flora of Cuba.
Associated botanic garden: Jardín Botánico de La Habana, Calle 26 e/C. Puentes Grandes y Ave. Boyeros; Jardín Botánico Cienfuegos, Soledad, Cienfuegos.
Loans: In general to recognized herbaria.
Periodical and serial works: Acta Botánica Cubana.
Exchange: Available: Cuban plants. Wanted: Exotic plants, preferably families represented in the Cuban and Caribbean region.
Remarks: By decision of the Academia de Ciencias de Cuba the old herbaria HABA, LS, and SV have been incorporated in the Herbarium of the Instituto de Botánica (HAC).

HABANA: *Herbario, Jardín Botánico Nacional, Universidad de La Habana,* (**HAJB**), Carretera del Rocío Km. 3 1/2, Calabazar, Habana, **Cuba.**
Telephone: 44-5525.
Foundation: 1902. *Number of specimens:* 50.000.
Herbarium: Mainly Cuban flora.
Important collections: Herbarium of the Universidad de Oriente, Santiago de Cuba; E. L. Ekman (300), M. López Figueiras (3.500), Herbario Micológico (3.000), Meyer, Köhler, Dietrich, Lepper, Manitz, Lippold, Kreisel, Bassler, Mory, Catasús, López, Herrera, Duharte, Ortega, Brother León, Brother Alain, J. B. Acuña, J. T. Roig, Rändel, Stohr, García.
    Director: ANGELA LEIVA, 1948 (Plant physiology).
    Curator: LUTGARDA GONZÁLEZ, 1948 (Plant taxonomy, ecology).
    Staff members: ALBERTO ALVAREZ, 1949 (Plant taxonomy).
    ALBERTO ARECES, 1947 (Plant taxonomy).
    ROSALINA BERAZAÍN, 1946 (Phytogeography).
    JOHANNES BISSE, 1935 (Plant taxonomy).
    MARTA DÍAZ, 1950 (Plant taxonomy).
    JORGE GUTIERREZ, 1950 (Plant taxonomy).
    GLORIA RECIO, 1944 (Mycology).
    MIGUEL RODRÍGUEZ, 1949 (Mycology).
    CARLOS SÁNCHÉZ, 1953 (Plant taxonomy).
    HILDELISA SARALEGUI, 1950 (Plant taxonomy).
Specialization in research: Flora of Cuba.
Associated botanic garden: Jardín Botánico Nacional.
Loans: Usual regulations.
Periodical and serial works: Serie Botánica, Revista Ciencias (before 1979); Revista del Jardín Botánico Nacional (from 1980).

HABANA: *Herbario, Instituto de Segunda Enseñanza de La Habana,* (**IH**), Agramonte y San Martín, Habana, **Cuba.** (Information 1964)
Foundation: 1864. *Number of specimens:* 4.000.

HABANA: *Herbario de La Salle, Colegio de La Salle,* (**LS**), Calle 13 n. 608, Vedado, Habana, **Cuba** – – incorporated in HAC.
Foundation: 1906. *Number of specimens:* 50.000.
Herbarium: Cuba and Antilles.

HABANA: *Herbario, Instituto de Agronomía,* (**SV**), Santiago de las Vegas, Habana, **Cuba** – – housed at HAC.

Foundation: 1904. *Number of specimens:* 50.000.
Herbarium: Worldwide, especially Cuba and plants of economic importance.
Important collections: Charles Wright, Brother León, Brother Alain.

HACHIOJI: *Asakawa Herbarium of Forestry and Forest Products Research Institute,* (**TFA**), 1833 Nagafusa-cho, Hachioji, Tokyo 193, **Japan.**
Telephone: 0426-61-1121.
Status: National Institute under Ministry of Agriculture, Forestry and Fisheries.
Foundation: 1922. *Number of specimens:* 55.000.
Herbarium: Plants of Japan, trees and shrubs of the world.
> *Director:* M. HOSOI, 1921 (Forest management).
> *Curator:* Y. KOBAYASHI, 1924 (Dendrology).
> *Staff member:* H. TAODA, 1945 (Forest botany, bryology).
> *Specialization in research:* Forest flora of Japan and adjacent regions, flowering cherries of Japan.
> *Associated botanic garden:* Asakawa Arboretum.
Loans: To recognized institutions.
Exchange: Available: Plants of Japan, including cultivated plants. Desired: Woody plants.
Remarks: The Arboretum has good collections of Japanese trees, especially flowering cherry races and conifers.

HAKGALA: *Herbarium, Hakgala Botanic Garden,* (**HAKS**), Hakgala, **Sri Lanka.**

HALIFAX: *Herbarium, Department of Biology, Dalhousie University,* (**DAL**), Halifax, Nova Scotia, **Canada** B3H 4J1.
Telephone: 902/424-2042.
Foundation: ca. 1930 (Lawson Herbarium was deposited at CAN in 1950). *Number of specimens:* 10.000.
Herbarium: General teaching collection, mainly eastern Canada.
> *Curator:* M. J. HARVEY, 1935 (Grasses of North America).
Loans: Yes.

HALIFAX: *Herbarium, Atlantic Regional Laboratory, National Research Council of Canada,* (**NRCC**), 1411 Oxford Street, Halifax, Nova Scotia, **Canada** B3H 3Z1.
Telephone: 902/429-6450.
Status: Government.
Foundation: 1952. *Number of specimens:* 20.000.
Herbarium: Marine algae of eastern Canada (and smaller collections from New England, Bermuda, Bahamas, British Isles, Pacific North America, Chile, Japan, and Australia).
Important collections: Major regional collection of marine algae from Maritime Provinces of Canada.
> *Curator:* C. J. BIRD, 1947 (Marine phycology systematics and floristics).

> *Staff member:* J. MCLACHLAN, 1930 (Marine phycology culture and life histories).
> *Specialization in research:* Systematics and floristics of north Atlantic marine algae; culture and life histories of marine Rhodophyceae, especially Carrageenophytes, *Gracilaria.*
Loans: No special conditions.
Exchange: Eastern Canadian marine algae.

HALIFAX: *Herbarium, Nova Scotia Museum,* (**NSPM**), 1747 Summer Street, Halifax, Nova Scotia, **Canada** B3H 3A6.
Telephone: 902/429-4610.
Status: Provincial museum.
Foundation: 1867. *Number of specimens:* 24.000.
Herbarium: Flora of Nova Scotia.
Important collections: C. MacFarlane (marine algae), A. H. Mackay (lichens), several collections from mid to late 19th century Nova Scotia collectors.
> *Director:* J. L. MARTIN, 1922.
> *Curator:* ALEX A. WILSON, 1948.
Loans: All requests considered.

HALIFAX: *Seaweeds Division, Nova Scotia Research Foundation,* (**NSRF**), P.O. Box 1027, Halifax, Nova Scotia, **Canada** – – incorporated in NSPM.

HALLE: *Martin-Luther-Universität, Sektion Biowissenschaften, Wissenschaftsbereich Geobotanik und Botanischer Garten,* (**HAL**), Neuwerk 21, DDR-402 Halle (Saale), **German Democratic Republic,** DDR.
Telephone: 23867.
Status: University.
Foundation: 1817. *Number of specimens:* 380.000.
Herbarium: Historically valuable worldwide herbarium (especially Mexico, Brasilia, S. Africa, Australia).
Important collections: Herb. D. F. L. von Schlechtendal, including the original coll. of C. J. W. Schiede (Mexico), O. Behr (Australia), C. G. Ehrenberg (West Indies, Mexico), F. Pabst (Brasilia), and several duplicates from the herb. Willdenow; herb. C. Schkuhr (especially *Carex*); K. Kerstan (Afghanistan); K. Koppe (Bryophytes).
> *Director:* RUDOLF SCHUBERT, 1927 (Ecology, geobotany, lichens, bryophytes).
> *Curator:* KLAUS WERNER, 1928 (Systematics, nomenclature, morphology).
> *Staff members:* UWE BRAUN, 1953 (Microfungi, especially Uredinales, Erisyphales).
> HEINRICH DÖRFELT, 1940 (Mycogeography, macrofungi, especially Agaricales).
> FRIEDRICH EBEL, 1934 (Custodian of the Botanic Garden, morphology).
> ECKEHART JÄGER, 1934 (Regional geobotany, eco-morphology).
> HERMANN MEUSEL, Emeritus, 1909 (Chorology, morphology, systematics, especially *Carlina*).
> HELMUT MÜHLBERG, 1932 (Morphology, lifeforms of Poaceae, aquatic plants).

STEPHAN RAUSCHERT, 1931 (Floristics, taxonomy, nomenclature).

Specialization in research: Flora and geobotany of southern part of GDR, ecology, taxonomy and life-forms of Mediterranean and C. European flora.

Associated botanic garden: Botanischer Garten der Universität Halle, Am Kirchtor 3.

Loans: In general to recognized botanical institutions (excl. bound exsiccatae).

Periodical and serial works: Mitteilungen aus dem Wissenschaftsbereich Geobotanik und Botanischer Garten der Martin-Luther-Universität Halle-Wittenberg; *Hercynia.*

Exchange: Available: Specimens from Central Germany. Desired: Specimens from Mediterranean Region and Asia.

Remarks: The herbarium of K. Sprengel is *not* at Halle.

HALLSTATT: *Botanische Station,* **(HALLST),** Hallstatt, **Austria** –– discontinued.

HAMBURG: *Herbarium, Institut für Allgemeine Botanik und Botanischer Garten,* **(HBG),** Jungiusstrasse 6-8, D-2000 Hamburg 13, **Federal Republic of Germany,** BRD.

Telephone: 040-41232318-41232301.

Status: Part of University Department.

Foundation: 1879. *Number of specimens:* 800.000.

Herbarium: Worldwide, including rich collections of algae and fungi.

Important collections: R. E. B. Sadebeck (Pteridophyta), H. W. Buek (Europe), E. Brandis, Clemens, J. G. Hallier, Hans Winkler, Wissmann (Asia), M. J. Dinklage, K. Dinter, G. W. J. Mildbraed (2. voyage), J. A. Schmidt, G. A. Zenker (Africa), O. Buchtien, E. H. G. Ule (America, Brazil: fungi, bryophytes), A. Dietrich, E. O. Gräffe, J. A. L. Preiss (Australia), F. Binder, C. W. von Nägeli, Richter (Algae), P. W. Magnus, C. F. E. Erichsen (Lichens), W. Moenkemeyer.

Director: The acting director of the institute.

Curator: KLAUS KUBITZKI, 1933, ad interim (Flora of South America, chemosystematics, Lauraceae, Guttiferae).

Staff members: INGEBORG FRIEDERICHSEN, 1916 (Fungi).

PAULA WIEMANN, 1917 (Phanerogams, ecology).

Research associates: HANS-DIETER IHLENFELDT, 1932 (Mesembryanthemaceae, Pedaliaceae, morphology).

HEIDRUN HARTMANN, 1942 (Mesembryanthemaceae; Pedaliaceae, morphology).

HANS-HELMUT POPPENDIECK, 1948 (Mesembryanthemaceae, Cochlospermaceae, Leg.-Lonchocarpinae).

ALEXANDER SCHMIDT, 1931 (Ascomycetes, *Viola*).

Associated botanic garden: New botanic garden,

belonging to the Institute, Hesten 10, D-2000 Hamburg 52.

Loans: Usual conditions.

Periodical and serial works: Mitteil. Inst. Allg. Bot. Hamburg.

Exchange: Bryophytes: W. Anatolia; Angiosperms: Germany, Australia (coll. A. Dietrich).

HAMILTON: *George R. Cooley Herbarium, Department of Biology, Colgate University,* **(GRCH),** Hamilton, New York 13346, **U.S.A.**

Telephone: 315/824-1000, ext. 347.

Foundation: 1971. *Number of specimens:* 15.000.

Herbarium: Vascular flora of northeastern U.S., especially Madison County, New York; vascular plants of Jamaica, West Indies, Europe, southern Asia, Melanesia, southern Florida.

Director and Curator: ROBERT E. GOODWIN, 1926 (Vertebrate ecology).

Loans: No special restrictions.

HAMILTON: *Herbarium, Royal Botanical Gardens,* **(HAM),** Box 399, Hamilton, Ontario, **Canada** L8N 3H8.

Telephone: 416/527-1158.

Status: Independent institution, supported by municipal, provincial and private funds.

Foundation: Royal Botanical Gardens 1941; Herbarium 1950. *Number of specimens:* 65.000.

Herbarium: Vascular plants: wild plants from all regions with emphasis on southern Ontario; cultivated plants from Royal Botanical Gardens collections and elsewhere.

Director: LESLIE LAKING, 1916.

Curator: JAMES S. PRINGLE, 1937 (Taxonomy of Gentianaceae, *Clematis, Syringa;* flora of the Great Lakes region).

Staff member: FREEK VRUGTMAN, 1927 (Taxonomy of cultivated woody plants; nomenclature of cultivated plants).

Specialization in research: Taxonomy of vascular plants; plant breeding; plant pathology; aquatic biology; studies in Canadian horticultural history.

Associated botanic garden: Royal Botanical Gardens.

Loans: No special regulations.

Periodical and serial works: The Gardens' Bulletin (3 to 6 per year); Royal Botanical Gardens' Technical Bulletin (irregular).

Exchange: Yes.

HAMILTON: *Herbarium, Biology Department, Hamilton College, McMaster University,* **(MCM),** Hamilton, Ontario, **Canada** –– incorporated in HAM.

HANGCHOW: *see* HANGZHOU.

HANGZHOU: *Herbarium, Hangchow Christian College,* **(HC),** Hangzhou, Zhejiang, **People's Republic of China.**

HANGZHOU: *Herbarium, Hangzhou Botanic Garden,* **(HHBG)**, Hangzhou, Zhejiang, **People's Republic of China.**

HANGZHOU: *Herbarium, University of Zhejiang,* **(HU)**, Hangzhou, Zhejiang, **People's Republic of China.**

HANNOVER: *Herbarium, Institut für Vegetationskunde,* **(HAN)**, Nienburgerstrasse 17, 3 Hannover, **Federal Republic of Germany,** BRD.
Telephone: 0511/762/4701; 0511/762/3632.
Status: Institute of the University of Hannover.
Foundation: 1965. *Number of specimens:* 50.000.
Herbarium: Niedersachsen herbarium (Lower Saxonia); Mitteleuropa-Herbarium (Middle Europe); Welt Herbarium (Worldwide).
  Director: HANS ZEIDLER, 1915 (Plant ecology).
  Curator: HANS MÖLLER, 1937 (Plant ecology).
  Specialization in research: Ecology (no systematics).

HANOVER: *Jesup Herbarium, Department of Biological Sciences, Dartmouth College,* **(HNH)**, Hanover, New Hampshire 03755, **U.S.A.**
Telephone: 603/646-2314.
Status: Private institution.
Foundation: 1880. *Number of specimens:* 60.000.
Herbarium: Predominantly northeastern U.S.; some from Alaska, Northwest Territories, Ungava, Newfoundland, Greenland, Australia, Turkey; collections of many early American botanists.
  Curator: JAMES P. POOLE, 1889.
  Staff member: ROBERT M. DOWNS.
  Loans: To recognized institutions.
  Exchange: Yes.

HAREN: *Herbarium, Biological Centre, Department of Systematic Botany,* **(GRO)**, Kerklaan 30, P.O. Box 14, Haren (Groningen), **Netherlands.** (Information 1974)
Status: University.
Foundation: 1890. *Number of specimens:* 150.000.
Herbarium: Mainly European plants and bryophytes.
Important collections: R. van der Wijk and van Zanten (Musci, especially Malaysia and Australia); duplicates from African collections: K. Dinter, H. Rudatis, G. Scheffler, G. H. W. Schimper, F. R. R. Schlechter, A. F. Stolz, G. A. Zenker and Pitard; herbarium University of Franeker.
  Specialization in research: Taxonomy of bryophytes, biosystematics and morphology of phanerogams, taxonomy and life-histories of algae.
  Associated botanic garden: Hortus de Wolf.
  Loans: To recognized botanical institutions.

HARPENDEN: *Harpenden Laboratory, Ministry of Agriculture, Fish·ries and Food, Agricultural Development and Advis(·y Service,* **(PPL)**, Hatching Green, Harpenden, Hertfordshire, AL5 2BD, England, **Great Britain.**
Telephone: 058 27 5241.
Status: Ministry of Agriculture, Fisheries and Food Laboratory.
Foundation: 1947. *Number of specimens:* 2.400.
Herbarium: Plant pathogenic fungi on British and imported plant material.
  Curator: P. W. SELLAR, 1942.
  Specialization in research: Plant pathology.
  Loans: None (but special arrangements could be made on request).
  Exchange: Yes.

HARRISBURG: *Herbarium, Bureau of Plant Industry, Pennsylvania Department of Agriculture,* **(PAM)**, 2301 North Cameron Street, Harrisburg, Pennsylvania 17110, **U.S.A.**
Telephone: 717/787-4843.
Status: Commonwealth of Pennsylvania.
Foundation: Early 1900's. *Number of specimens:* 26.000.
Herbarium: Mainly Pennsylvania.
  Director: WENDELL P. DITMER, 1922.
  Exchange: If requested.
  Remarks: Used chiefly as a reference collection for identification of plants or seeds.

HARRISONBURG: *Herbarium, Department of Biology, Eastern Mennonite College,* **(HAVI)**, Harrisonburg, Virginia 22801, **U.S.A.**
Telephone: 703/433-2771.
Foundation: 1930's. *Number of specimens:* 3.000.
Herbarium: Mainly local vascular plants; some plants from North Carolina, West Virginia, and Pennsylvania.
  Curator: A. CLAIR MELLINGER, 1942 (Plant ecology, systematics).
  Loans: Usual regulations.

HARRISONBURG: *Herbarium, Department of Biology, James Madison University,* **(JMUH)**, Burruss Hall Rm. 303, Harrisonburg, Virginia 22807, **U.S.A.**
Telephone: 703/433-6340; 433-6225.
Foundation: 1972. *Number of specimens:* 7.000 vascular plants.
Herbarium: Vascular plants of western Virginia.
  Director and Curator: NORLYN L. BODKIN, 1937 (Plant systematics).
  Staff member: EMILY E. BAXTER, 1935.
  Specialization in research: North American *Melanthium*; floristics of western Virginia; shale barren species.
  Loans: For 6 months to recognized botanical institutions; proper storage required.
  Exchange: Yes.

HAYS: *Elam Bartholomew Herbarium, Fort Hays State University,* **(FHKSC)**, Hays, Kansas 67601, **U.S.A.**

Foundation: 1929. *Number of specimens:* 20.500.
Herbarium: Mixed prairie floristics.
Important collections: Elam Bartholomew (rusts; 5.000).
Curator: HOWARD C. REYNOLDS (Agrostology; dendrology).
Specialization in research: Flora of Ellis County, Kansas.
Loans: To recognized specialists.
Periodical and serial works: The Fort Hays State Studies.
Exchange: Available: Flora of the mixed prairie. Desired: Grasses and tree specimens.

HAYWARD: *Herbarium, Department of Biological Sciences, California State University,* (**HAY**), Hayward, California 94542, **U.S.A.**
Telephone: 415/881-3460; 881-3471.
Foundation: 1957. *Number of specimens:* 7.000.
Herbarium: California and adjacent states.
Director: ROBERT J. BAALMAN, 1939 (Plant ecology).
Curator: MARY LOU WILCOX.
Staff members: ROLF W. BENSELER.
DENNIS R. PARNELL.
Specialization in research: Systematics of local populations; hybridization.
Loans: Usual regulations.
Exchange: North American collections.

HEIDELBERG: *Institut für Systematische Botanik der Universität Heidelberg,* (**HEID**), Im Neuenheimer Feld 280, D-6900 Heidelberg, **Federal Republic of Germany, BRD.**
Telephone: 06221/4655 or 4675.
Status: University institute.
Foundation: 1960. *Number of specimens:* 20.000.
Herbarium: Plants of South Africa, South America, Madagascar and Europe.
Director: WERNER RAUH, 1913 (Bromeliads, cacti, succulents).
Curator: PETER WERTAL, 1938 (Flora of the mediterranean region).
Staff members: WILHELM BARTLLOH, 1946 (Epiphytic cacti).
WOLFGANG HAGEMANN, 1929 (Ferns).
HANS FRIEDRICH SCHOLCH, 1934 (Flora of Germany).
KARL-HEINZ WILLER, 1933 (Cryptogams).
Specialization in research: Bromeliads, cacti and succulents, ferns, mosses.
Associated botanic garden: Botanical Garden of the University.
Loans: To recognized botanical institutions.
Periodical and serial works: Tropische und subtropische Pflanzenwelt.

HELSINKI: *Herbarium, Botanical Museum, University of Helsinki,* (**H**), Unioninkatu 44, SF-00170 Helsinki 17, **Finland.**

Telephone: 90-650 188.
Status: A state university.
Foundation: ca. 1750 (most of the early collections destroyed by fire in 1827). *Number of specimens:* 2.370.000 (Vascular plants 1.400.000, bryophytes 470.000, lichens 280.000, fungi 200.000, algae 20.000).
Herbarium: Worldwide, especially Finland, NW Russia, Scandinavia, Estonia, Macaronesia, Mediterranean countries, Middle East, Caucasia, Central Asia, Japan, Canada, Namibia, Fuego-Patagonia; all groups. Rich bryophyte collections also from other regions, incl. India, Australia, New Zealand, Brazil.
Important collections: Vascular plants: M. Brenner, S. E. Bridel, V. F. Brotherus, A. K. Cajander, C. N. Hellenius, A. Kalela (Cajander), E. Kausel (Myrtaceae), A. O. Kihlman (Kairamo), H. Lindberg, C. Linnaeus (ca. 80 specimens), G. Marklund, A. v. Nordmann, J. P. Norrlin, A. Palmgren, M. Rautanen, B. Saarsoo (*Taraxacum*), C. R. Sahlberg, Chr. Steven. Bryophytes: V. F. Brotherus (H-BR), H. Buch, J. J. Dillenius (Duplicates), S. O. Lindberg (H-SOL), C. Müller (in H-BR). Lichens: E. Acharius (H-ACH), G. Lång (Deposition from HSI), W. Nylander (H-NYL), V. Räsänen. Fungi: P. A. Karsten, M. Laurila (Deposition from HPP), J. I. Liro. Algae: C. Cedercreutz, R. Grönblad, K. E. Hirn. Especially the collections Bridel, Sahlberg, Steven, H-ACH, H-BR, H-SOL, and H-NYL contain numerous specimens of other important foreign authors. The oldest collections include many 18th century specimens of Swedish and Finnish authors.
Director: JAAKKO JALAS, 1920 (Biosystematics and plant geography, mapping the distribution of vascular plants of Europe; *Thymus*).
Head Curator Phanerogamic Herbarium: ILKKA KUKKONEN, 1926 (Cyperaceae, especially Cariceae group, Ustilaginales, plant anatomy, chemotaxonomy).
Head Curator Cryptogamic Herbarium: TIMO KOPONEN (acting), 1939 (Bryophytes, especially N. Europe, East Asia, Canada, Mniaceae, Amblystegiaceae).
Curators: HARRI HARMAJA (acting), 1944 (Macromycetes, Tricholomataceae, especially *Clitocybe*, Pezizales, especially *Gyromitra, Helvella, Otidea*).
PEKKA ISOVIITA, 1931 (Peatland flora, especially *Sphagnum*, nomenclature).
PERTTI UOTILA, 1943 (Flora of Finland and E. Mediterranean area, *Chenopodium;* aquatic plants).
Staff members: MAURI KORHONEN, 1927 (Macromycetes).
JUHA SUOMINEN, 1936 (Flora of Finland, adventive flora, mapping the distribution of vascular plants of Europe).
HEIKKI TOIVONEN, 1947 (Taxonomy of *Carex*, aquatic flora and vegetation of Fennoscandia).
ORVO VITIKAINEN, 1940 (Lichens, especially *Peltigera, Lecanora subfusca* group).
Retired staff: LARS FAGERSTRÖM, 1914 (Flora of Finland, especially *Ranunculus auricomus* group,

Hieracium, Carex sect. *Extensae*).

ILMARI HIITONEN, 1898 (Flora of Finland, especially *Salix*).

BROR PETTERSSON, 1895 (Flora of Canary Is.).

HEIKKI ROIVAINEN, 1900 (Bryophytes, micromycetes, vascular plants, especially Fuego-Patagonia, Finnish Lappland).

Associated staff: MARJATTA AALTO, 1939 (Subfossils, fruit morphology of *Potamogeton*, palaeoethnobotany).

TEUVO AHTI, 1934 (Boreal lichens, especially Finland, Newfoundland, Mongolia, Cladoniaceae).

PENTTI ALANKO, 1936 (Garden plants, micromycetes).

LEENA HÄMET-AHTI, 1931 (Plant geography and flora of boreal zone, *Luzula, Juncus*, dendrology).

MARJA HÄRKÖNEN, 1939 (Ecology and taxonomy of Myxomycetes).

ARTO KURTTO, 1951 (Biosystematics of *Symphytum*).

ILKKA KYTÖVUORI, 1941 (Flora of northern Fennoscandia, taxonomy of *Epilobium; Lactarius*).

HANS LUTHER, 1915 (Ecology and taxonomy of aquatic plants and anthropocores, algae, environmental conservation).

TUOMO NIEMELÄ, 1940 (Experimental taxonomy of Aphyllophorales, Polypores, stereoid and hydnaceous fungi).

JARI OKSANEN, 1954 (Phytosociology).

ANNIKKI PALMEN, 1929 (Hemerochorous and garden plants, *Salix repens* group).

PENTTI SORSA, 1929 (Palynology, spore morphology, especially Bryales; aeropalynology).

TUULI TIMONEN, 1946 (Morphology and anatomy of Cyperaceae).

RISTO TUOMIKOSKI, 1911 (Agaricales, bryophytes; entomology).

HEINO VÄNSKÄ, 1943 (Saxicolous lichens, especially *Lecanora polytropa* group).

SEPPO VUOKKO, 1946 (Flora of Northern Finland, especially serpentinicolous plants).

Honorary research associates: GUSTAV KVIST, 1909 (*Ranunculus auricomus* group).

ERKKI REINIKKA, 1954 (*Taraxacum*).

JAAKKO SARVELA, 1914 (Pteridophyta).

CARL ERIC SONCK, 1905 (Flora of Finland, *Taraxacum*).

AKSELI VALTA, 1911 (*Rumex*).

Associated botanic garden: Botanical Garden of the University of Helsinki.

Loans: In general to recognized scientific institutions (except the lichen collection of Acharius).

Exchange: Available: Mainly plants of Finland (all groups), Canada (mosses and lichens), East Asia (mosses), Africa, Fuego-Patagonia, Mediterranean and South west Asia (vascular plants). Desired: All groups from any region, especially from holarctic areas.

Periodical and serial works: Helsingin yliopiston kasvimuseon monisteita (Pamphlets issued by the Botanical Museum, University of Helsinki).

Remarks: See also KYM, which is deposited in H as a separate collection. Secretariat of the committee for mapping the flora of Europe (Atlas Florae Europaeae) in H.

HELSINKI: *Herbarium, Institute of General Botany, University of Helsinki,* (**HEL**), Viikki, 00710 Helsinki 71, **Finland.**

Telephone: 90-378011/340.
Status: State University.
Foundation: 1934. *Number of specimens:* 49.800.
Herbarium: Europe, especially Finland.
Director: VEIKKO HINTIKKA, 1931 (*Mycena*).
Staff members: RIITTA GRÖNROOS, 1943 (*Salix*).

IRMA JÄRVINEN, 1947 (Hepaticae).
Loans: To recognized scientific institutions.
Remarks: The herbarium has no staff of its own. It is managed by university teachers.

HELSINKI: *Herbarium, Finnish Forest Research Institute (Herbarium Instituti Forestalis Fenniae),* (**HFR**), Unioninkatu 40A, SF-00170 Helsinki 17, **Finland.**

Telephone: (90) 661 401.
Status: State institute.
Foundation: 1925. *Number of specimens:* 60.000 (Part of earlier material transferred to H).
Herbarium: Finnish forest plants and fungi.
Important collections: Viljo Kujala (Fungi and vascular plants); dendrological collections, mainly by Sakari Saarnijoki.

Director: TAUNO KALLIO, 1923 (Forest pathology, root rot fungi of trees).
Staff members: TIMO KURKELA, 1937 (Uredinales and other microfungi).

LALLI LAINE, 1930 (Aphyllophorales fungi, vascular plants).
Specialization in research: Forest research, forest pathology, dendrology.
Associated botanic garden: Dendrological Parks in the Research Forests of the Institute (Solböle, Ruotsinkylä and Punkaharju).
Loans: In general to recognized scientific institutions.
Periodical and serial works: Communicationes Instituti Forestalis Fenniae, Folia Forestalia.
Exchange: Available: Fungi, mainly parasitic, from Finland.

HELSINKI: *Herbarium, Institute of Horticulture,* (**HHC**), Viikki, 00710 Helsinki 71, **Finland.**

Telephone: 90-378011.
Status: University of Helsinki.
Foundation: 1962. *Number of specimens:* 3.000.
Herbarium: For student use.
Director and Curator: ERKKI KAUKOVIRTA, 1934 (Floriculture).

Associated botanic garden: Botanic Garden of the University of Helsinki, Unionink. 44, Helsinki 17.

HELSINKI: *Herbarium, Department of Plant Pathology, University of Helsinki,* **(HPP)**, Helsinki 71, **Finland.** (Information 1974)
Status: University.
Foundation: 1920. *Number of specimens:* 45.000.
Herbarium: Parasitic fungi.
Important collections: J. I. Liro (Mycotheca fennica), Matti Laurila (Herb. instituti phytopathologici universitatis Helsinki).
Loans: To recognized botanical institutions.

HELSINKI: *Department of Silviculture Herbarium, Helsinki University,* **(HSI)**, Unioninkatu 40 B, SF-00170 Helsinki 17, **Finland.**
Telephone: 90-19241.
Status: University.
Foundation: 1908. *Number of specimens:* 100.000.
Herbarium: Vascular plants, bryophytes, lichens, fungi, algae, Finnish and foreign.
Important collections: Cone herbarium (collected by A. K. Cajander and Risto Sarvas).
Director: MATTI LEIKOLA, 1935 (Forestry).
Curator: AUNE KOPONEN, 1938, 90-1924310 (Bryophyte taxonomy, Splachnaceae).
Specialization in research: Forestry, dendrology.
Loans: On request.

HELSINKI: *Herbarium of Kymenlaakso,* **(KYM)**, Botanical Museum, Unioninkatu 44, SF-00170 Helsinki 17, **Finland.**
Telephone: 90-650188.
Status: Kymenlaakson Luonnon Ystävät (Kymenlaakso Society of Naturalists).
Foundation: 1959. *Number of specimens:* 10.000.
Herbarium: Kymenlaakso district (SE Finland).
Curator: ARVI ULVINEN, 1897; 90-687538.
Staff member: KALEVI VILJAMAA, 1920.
Specialization in research: Flora of Kymenlaakso district.
Loans: In general to recognized scientific institutions, through H.
Periodical and serial works: Kymenlaakson Luonto, Kymenlaakson Luonnon Ystävien julkaisuja.
Remarks: Permanently deposited in H as a separate herbarium.

HEVERLEE: *Carnoy Instituut, Laboratorium voor beschrijvende plantkunde,* **(LV)**, Kardinaal Mercierlaan 92, B-3030 Heverlee, **Belgium.**
Status: Catholic University Leuven.
Foundation: 1890. *Number of specimens:* 100.000.
Herbarium: Worldwide.
Important collections: de Bullemont, J. H. Wibbe, Baguet, Giltay.
Curator: E. PETIT (Systematics, phytogeography).
Loans: To recognized institutions.

HICKORY CORNERS: *Herbarium, Kellogg Biological Station, Michigan State University,* **(KBSMS)**, 3700 East Gull Lake Drive, Hickory Corners, Michigan 49060, **U.S.A.**
Telephone: 616/671-5117.
Foundation: 1956. *Number of specimens:* 6.000.
Herbarium: Mainly Michigan flora.
Important collections: J. C. Elliott, W. T. Gillis (Anacardiaceae), R. S. Gross, B. G. Stergios (southwestern Michigan).
Director and Curator: PATRICIA A. WERNER, 1941 (Flora of midwestern U.S.).
Specialization in research: Population biology; pollination; *Solidago,* especially *S. canadensis* complex.
Loans: To recognized botanical institutions.
Periodical and serial works: Kellogg Biological Station Contribution Series (ecology, evolution).
Exchange: Available: Southwestern Michigan flora, including vegetative life stages. Desired: Great Lakes flora; tall grass prairie.

HIGHLAND HEIGHTS: *Herbarium, Northern Kentucky University,* **(KNK)**, Highland Heights, Kentucky 41076, **U.S.A.**
Telephone: 606/292-5300.
Status: State university.
Foundation: 1973. *Number of specimens:* 20.000.
Herbarium: Kentucky; central U.S.
Director: JOHN W. THIERET, 1926 (Gramineae; Scrophulariaceae, *Cyperus*; vascular flora of central U.S.).
Specialization in research: Kentucky flora.
Loans: To scientific institutes.
Exchange: Available: Mainly plants of Kentucky.

HILLSBORO: *Herbarium, Fox Research Forest,* **(SPH)**, Center Road, Hillsboro, New Hampshire 03244, **U.S.A.**
Telephone: 603/464-3453.
Status: New Hampshire Department of Resources and Economic Development.
Foundation: 1932. *Number of specimens:* 500.
Herbarium: Local.
Director and Curator: PHILIP VERRIER, 1941 (Forestry).
Specialization in research: Forestry.
Periodical and serial works: Fox Forest Notes; Fox Forest Bulletin.

HIROSHIMA: *Herbarium, Botanical Institute, Hiroshima University,* **(HIRO)**, Higashisenda-machi 1-1-89, Naka-ku, Hiroshima 730, **Japan.**
Telephone: 0822-41-1221, ext. 298 and 711.
Status: University.
Foundation: 1929. *Number of specimens:* 710.000.
Herbarium: Worldwide collection, mainly bryophytes and lichens of Japan, Korea and Formosa.
Important collections: Y. Horikawa (bryophytes),

H. Suzuki (*Sphagnum*), H. Ando (*Hypnum*), S. Inumaru (lichens), T. Seki and T. Nakano (bryophytes and vascular plants of Patagonia).

Director: HISATSUGU ANDO, 1922 (Taxonomy and ecology of bryophytes, especially Hypnaceae).

Curator: TAROW SEKI, 1934 (Taxonomy and ecology of bryophytes, especially Sematophyllaceae).

Staff members: NOBORU ISHIHASHI, 1946 (Phytosociology).

MINORU NAKANISHI, 1937 (Lichens).

TAKETO NAKANO, 1943 (Freshwater and soil algae).

KUNITO NEHIRA, 1936 (Bryophytes, ecology).

MASAYOSHI OSHIO, 1937 (Lichens).

GENTARO TOYOHARA, 1942 (Phytosociology).

Specialization in research: Freshwater algae, lichens and bryophytes of Asia, southern South America and Antarctic region; phytosociology.

Associated botanic garden: Miyajima Natural Botanical Garden, Miyajima-cho, Saiki-gun.

Loans: To recognized botanical institutions.

Periodical and serial works: Journal of Science of the Hiroshima University, Ser. B, Div. 2 (Botany), Hikobia.

Exchange: Available: Japanese lichens, bryophytes and higher plants. Desired: Algae, lichens, bryophytes and higher plants of world.

HLOHOVEC: *Herbarium, Okresné muzeum,* (**HLO**), Hlohovec, **Czechoslovakia.** (Information 1974)

Number of specimens: 7.500.

Herbarium: Regionae Tracheophyta.

Specialization in research: Systematics and regional flora.

Loans: To recognized botanical institutions.

HLUBOKÁ: *Herbarium, Agricultural Museum of Praha, Hunting Lodge, Ohrada,* (**OH**), 373 41 Hluboká n. Vltavou, České Budějovice, **Czechoslovakia.**

Telephone: 965340.

Status: Affiliated with Institute of Scientific Technical Information of Agriculture, Praha.

Foundation: 1959.

Herbarium: Plants of Bohemia.

Director: MIROSLAV LANDA, 1926 (Forest management).

Curator: MARCELA ANDRESKOVÁ, 1936 (Forest management).

Staff member: VLASTA ŠVEJDOVÁ, 1936.

Specialization in research: Forest management.

HOBART: *Tasmanian Herbarium, University of Tasmania,* (**HO**), GPO Box 252c, Hobart, Tasmania 7001, **Australia.**

Telephone: (002) 230561, ext. 253.

Status: Department of the Tasmanian Museum and Art Gallery.

Foundation: 1928. *Number of specimens:* 85.000.

Herbarium: Phanerogams and cryptogams, mainly Tasmanian.

Important collections: R. C. Gunn, J. Milligan, L. A. Meredith (Algae), W. Archer, L. Rodway, F. Perrin (Algae), W. M. Curtis, G. C. Bratt (Lichens), W. A. Weymouth (Cryptogams).

Director Tasmanian Museum and Art Gallery: D. R. GREGG (Geology).

Curator: A. E. ORCHARD, 1946 (Haloragaceae).

Staff members: A. BROWN, 1952.

W. M. CURTIS, 1905 (Honorary Botanist, Students' Flora of Tasmania).

D. I. MORRIS, 1924 (Honorary Botanist, Students' Flora of Tasmania).

Specialization in research: Flora of Tasmania.

Loans: To recognized herbaria only. Requests to be made through the Director of the requesting institution.

Exchange: Available: Limited quantities of Tasmanian plants, mainly phanerogams. Desired: Reference collections worldwide, especially from southern hemisphere.

HOLLAND: *Herbarium, Biology Department, Hope College,* (**HCHM**), Holland, Michigan 49423, **U.S.A.**

Telephone: 616/392-5111.

Foundation: 1965. *Number of specimens:* 6.500.

Herbarium: Michigan flora.

Director and Curator: PAUL VAN FAASEN, 1934 (*Aster*, Compositae).

Staff member: MEREDITH BLACKWELL (Slime molds).

Specialization in research: Compositae.

Loans: Usual regulations.

Exchange: Yes.

HONG KONG: *Herbarium, Agriculture and Fisheries Department,* (**HK**), 393 Canton Road, 14/F Kowloon, **Hong Kong.**

Telephone: 688111.

Status: Hong Kong Government.

Foundation: 1878. *Number of specimens:* 33.300.

Herbarium: China, mainly phanerogams.

Important collections: A. Henry, E. H. Wilson, G. Forrest, S. T. Dunn, W. J. Tutcher.

Director: J. M. RIDDELL-SWAN, 1926.

Curator: S. P. LAU, 1948 (Flora and vegetation of Hong Kong).

Staff member: T. P. WONG SIU, 1947 (Flora of Hong Kong).

Specialization in research: Flora of Hong Kong; nomenclature; ecology.

Associated botanic garden: Hong Kong Zoological and Botanic Gardens.

Loans: By permission of the Director.

Periodical and serial works: Checklist of Hong Kong Plants.

Exchange: Available: Local collections. Desired: Subtropical plants.

Remarks: International seed exchange service.

HONIARA: *Forestry Division Herbarium,* (**BSIP**),

Ministry of Natural Resources, Honiara, **Solomon Islands.**

Telephone: 370.

Status: Administered by Forestry Division.

Foundation: 1965. *Number of specimens:* 20.000.

Herbarium: Mainly trees and some ferns and herbaceous species of Solomon Islands.

Director: RODERICK TERRY KERA, 1938.

Staff members: EDMOND INIMUA, 1939.

BARABAS SIRUTEE, 1942.

Specialization in research: Herbarium used mainly for identification.

Associated botanic garden: Honiara Botanical Garden.

Remarks: Herbarium is closed due to lack of funds, but is still used by Forestry Division.

HONOLULU: *Herbarium Pacificum, Department of Botany, Bernice P. Bishop Museum,* **(BISH),** P.O. Box 19000-A, Honolulu, Hawaii 96819, **U.S.A.**

Telephone: 808/847-3511.

Status: Independent private museum.

Foundation: 1889. *Number of specimens:* 450.000.

Herbarium: Pacific wide representation with large collections from the Hawaiian Islands, Polynesia, Micronesia, and New Guinea.

Important collections: W. Hillebrand (Hawaii), J. F. Rock (Hawaii, southeast China, Tibet), H. St. John (Hawaii, Pacific), O. Degener (Hawaii), F. R. Fosberg (Hawaii, Pacific), C. N. Forbes (Hawaii), L. J. Brass (New Guinea), R. Kanehira (Micronesia), F. McClure (China), M. L. Grant (Tahiti), A. C. Smith (Fiji), E. Christophersen (Samoa), A. D. E. Elmer (Philippines), E. D. Merrill (Philippines), S. F. Kajewski (New Hebrides), P. van Royen (New Guinea).

Director: E. CREUTZ, 1913 (Nuclear physicist).

Senior Botanist: P. VAN ROYEN, 1923 (Alpine flora of New Guinea; general tropical families; Gentianaceae, Podostemaceae, Sapotaceae).

Chairman: S. H. SOHMER, 1941 (Vascular plant systematics, particularly of Amaranthaceae and *Psychotria*, Rubiaceae).

Staff members: G. BUELOW (Tongan flora).

W. GEYER, 1955 (Hawaiian flora).

Research associates: I. A. ABBOTT, 1919 (Algae).

E. D. CARR, 1945 (Biosystematics of Hawaiian flora).

M. DOTY, 1916 (Algae).

F. R. FOSBERG, 1913 (Tropical floras).

D. HERBST, 1934 (Hawaiian flora).

C. LAMOUREUX, 1933 (Wood anatomy).

J. A. MEDLER, 1912 (Tropical floras).

D. MUELLER-DOMBOIS, 1925 (Ecology).

R. E. RINTZ, 1932 (Tropical floras).

A. C. SMITH, 1906 (Flora of Fiji).

C. W. SMITH, 1938 (Hawaiian lichens).

H. ST. JOHN, 1892 (Tropical and Hawaiian floras).

W. THEOBALD, 1936 (Horticulture).

Field Associates: C. CHRISTENSEN, 1940 (Hawaiian flora).

B. GAGNE-HARRISON, 1947 (Tropical floras).

W. J. HOE, 1941 (Pacific mosses).

J. D. JACOBI, 1942 (Hawaiian flora).

K. M. NAGATA, 1945 (Tropical flora).

J. K. OBATA, 1925 (Hawaiian flora).

S. P. PERLMAN, 1956 (Hawaiian flora).

G. E. SPENCE, 1956 (Hawaiian flora).

R. L. STEMMERMAN, 1952 (Tropical floras).

F. L. WARSCHAUER, 1950 (Hawaiian flora).

A. WHISTLER, 1944 (Flora of Samoa).

Specialization in research: Plant geography of the Pacific Basin; taxonomy of floras of the Pacific Basin; flora of the Hawaiian Islands; biosystematics of the Hawaiian flora.

Loans: To qualified scientists; if large quantities only part will be sent at a time; Hawaiian types usually only isotypes.

Periodical and serial works: Bulletin of the Bernice P. Bishop Museum.

Exchange: Available: Hawaiian and Pacific material. Desired: Pacific and Asian tropical material.

HONOLULU: *Herbarium, Department of Botany, University of Hawaii,* **(HAW),** 3190 Maile Way, Honolulu, Hawaii 96822, **U.S.A.**

Telephone: 808/948-8369.

Number of specimens: 20.000, including 4.000 lichens.

Curator: GERALD D. CARR, 1945; 808/948-8304 (Biosystematics; chromosome evolution; Pacific Coast and Hawaiian Madiinae-Heliantheae, Asteraceae; *Pedicularis*).

Specialization in research: Systematics of Hawaiian flora.

Loans: By arrangement with the curators.

Exchange: No aggressive program.

Remarks: Harold St. John Library is associated with the herbarium. The private collections of Maxwell S. Doty (50.000 algae) and William J. Hoe (15.000 bryophytes) are currently housed here.

HONOLULU: *Herbarium, Harold L. Lyon Arboretum,* **(HLA),** 3860 Manoa Road, Honolulu, Hawaii 96822, **U.S.A.**

Telephone: 808/988-3177.

Status: A research facility of the University of Hawaii at Manoa.

Foundation: 1918. *Number of specimens:* 5.000.

Herbarium: Native and adventive plants in Hawaii; vouchers of plants cultivated in the arboretum.

Director: YONEO SAGAWA, 1926 (Cytology; cytogenetics).

Staff members: PATRICIA AVERY, 1932.

ROBERT T. HIRANO, 1939 (Ornamental and economic plants; tropical botany; horticulture).

KENNETH M. NAGATA, 1945 (Hawaiian plants).

WESLEY TERAOKA, 1950 (Economic geography).

LOUIS WITAKER, 1949 (Ecology).

Specialization in research: Native and adventive flora of Hawaii.

Associated botanic garden: Harold L. Lyon Arboretum.

Loans: To recognized institutions.

Periodical and serial works: Lyonia; Lyon Arboretum Lecture Series.

Exchange: Yes, for specimens which come within the interests of the Arboretum's collections.

HOUGHTON: *Isle Royale National Park,* **(IRP),** 87 North Ripley Street, Houghton, Michigan 49931, **U.S.A.**

Telephone: 906/482-3310.

Status: U.S. Department of Interior, National Park Service.

Foundation: 1940. *Number of specimens:* 500.

Herbarium: Flora of Isle Royale National Park with specimens collected from a transitional (hardwood/boreal) community.

Director and Curator: ROBERT A. HUGGINS, 1944 (Field ecology).

Specialization in research: Close relationship with moose/timber wolf research.

Loans: To recognized institutions (summer only).

Remarks: Herbarium is located at the Mott Island Headquarters which is closed from 15 October through 15 May.

HOUGHTON: *Herbarium, Department of Biological Sciences, Michigan Technological University,* **(MCT),** Houghton, Michigan 49931, **U.S.A.**

Foundation: 1937. *Number of specimens:* 400.

Herbarium: Local flora.

Remarks: Many specimens previously in this collection are now deposited in the Ford Forestry Center Herbarium (MCTF), Michigan Technological University, L'Anse, Michigan 49946.

HOUGHTON: *Cryptogamic Herbarium, Department of Biological Sciences, Michigan Technological University,* **(MCTC),** Houghton, Michigan 49931, **U.S.A.**

Telephone: 906/487-2011.

Foundation: 1968. *Number of specimens:* 5.000.

Herbarium: Emphasis on Michigan mosses and lichens.

Important collections: Lichens (Caliciales), mosses (*Fontinalis*).

Director and Curator: FREDERIC H. ERBISCH, 1937 (Lichenology).

Staff member: JANICE M. GLIME, 1941 (Bryology).

Specialization in research: Effects of gamma radiation on lichens; biology of *Fontinalis*.

Exchange: Available: Michigan mosses and lichens.

HOUGHTON LAKE HEIGHTS: *Herbarium, Department of Natural Resources, Houghton Lake Wild-*

life Research Station, **(HL),** Box 158, Houghton Lake Heights, Michigan 48630, **U.S.A.**

Telephone: 517/422-5191.

Status: State of Michigan.

Foundation: 1952. *Number of specimens:* 500.

Herbarium: Plants of northern Lower Michigan.

Director and Curator: JERRY P. DUVENDECK.

Staff members: H. ROBERT GRAY.

    RICHARD J. MORAN.

    JAMES R. TERRY.

    LARRY G. VISSER.

Specialization in research: Forest wildlife research.

Loans: Examination at the station only.

HOUSTON: *Herbarium, University of Houston,* **(HOU),** Houston, Texas, **U.S.A.** – – discontinued.

HOUSTON: *Herbarium, Museum of Natural History of Houston,* **(HPM),** P.O. Box 8175, 5555 Montrose Boulevard, Houston, Texas 77030, **U.S.A.**

Status: Private non-profit corporation.

Foundation: 1947. *Number of specimens:* 5.000.

Herbarium: General Texas flora, especially in the Galveston Bay area.

Important collections: Alfred Traverse (watershed of Galveston Bay).

Director: T. E. PULLEY.

Loans: No.

Remarks: Collections are available for study by qualified persons who come to the Museum.

HRADEC KRÁLOVÉ: *Herbarium, Krajské muzeum Hradec Králové,* **(HR),** Přírodovědné oddělení, Husovo nám. 124, Hradec Králové, **Czechoslovakia.** (Information 1974)

Foundation: 1938. *Number of specimens:* 17.800.

Herbarium: Tracheophyta, bryophytes and lichens of Czechoslovakia and central Europe.

Specialization in research: Floristics, systematics.

Loans: To recognized botanical institutions.

Periodical and serial works: Fontes Musei Reginaehradecensis, Acta Museu Reginaehradecensis Seria A.

HSINING: *Northwest Plateau Institute of Biology, Academia Sinica,* **(HNWP)** – – see XINING.

HUANCAYO: *Herbario Huancayo, Universidad Nacional del Centro del Perú,* **(HCEN),** Calle Real 160, Apartado 138, Huancayo, **Peru.**

Telephone: 235341.

Foundation: 1977. *Number of specimens:* 3.500.

Herbarium: Flora of central Peru.

Staff members: DANIEL BARRÓN DOLORIER, 1932 (Plant geography).

    PEDRO SEDANO PALOMINO (Forestry).

Specialization in research: Flora of central Peru.

HUÁNUCO: *Herbario, Universidad Nacional de Huánuco "Hermilio Valdizán,"* (**HHUA**), Jirón Dos de Mayo 680, Huánuco, **Peru.**

Telephone: 2340; 2341.

Status: Sociedad Peruana de Botánica.

Foundation: 1971. *Number of specimens:* 4.580.

Herbarium: Flora de Huánuco.

Important collections: Daniel Barron Dolorier, Carlos Espinoza Fernandez, Luis A. Jump Saldivar, Dora Elena Rivera Lopez, Ruddy N. Minaya Cruz, Juan M. Apac Yabar.

  Director and Curator: JUAN P. HUAPALLA YÁBAR, 1933.

  Specialization in research: Flora de Huánuco.

  Associated botanic garden: Jardín Botánico de la Universidad Nacional de Huánuco "Hermilio Valdizán," Ciudad Universitaria, Cayhuayna.

  Periodical and serial works: Boletín Informativo.

HUHEHOT: *Herbarium, Department of Biology, University of Inner Mongolia,* (**HIMC**), Huhehot, Inner Mongolia, **People's Republic of China.**

Status: University.

Foundation: 1958. *Number of specimens:* 40.000.

Herbarium: Plants of Inner Mongolia.

Director: MA Y. C. (Gentianaceae, Cruciferae, Umbelliferae, Orobanchaceae).

Staff members: LI P. (Ecology, geobotany).

  LIU S. R. (Taxonomy).

  LIU Z. L. (Plant geography).

  SUN H. L. (Grassland ecology).

  WU C. J. (Taxonomy).

  YONG S. P. (Geobotany).

  ZENG S. T. (Ecology).

  ZHAO Z. Y. (Taxonomy).

Specialization in research: Flora and vegetation of Inner Mongolia, taxonomy, geobotany.

HUMPOLEC: *Herbarium, Muzeum v Humpolci,* (**HUMP**), okr. Havlíčkův Brod, Humpolec, **Czechoslovakia.** (Information 1974).

Foundation: 1895. *Number of specimens:* 4.700.

Herbarium: Tracheophyta of Czechoslovakia.

Specialization in research: Systematics.

Loans: To recognized botanical institutions.

HUNTINGTON: *Herbarium, Department of Biological Sciences, Marshall University,* (**MUHW**), Huntington, West Virginia 25701, **U.S.A.**

Telephone: 304/696-6467; 696-3148.

Foundation: 1930. *Number of specimens:* 30.000, including 3.000 bryophytes.

Herbarium: Mostly West Virginia plants.

Important collections: F. A. Gilbert; collections of Harvard botanists of the 1920's and 1930's; Cyperaceae and *Carex.*

  Director and Curator: DAN K. EVANS, 1938 (Systematics of flowering plants, especially *Carex*; flora of West Virginia).

  Specialization in research: Systematics of flowering plants, especially *Carex* (Cyperaceae); flora of West Virginia, including floristic studies of extreme areas (sand and mud flats, rock outcrops, aquatic areas); rare and endangered species of West Virginia.

  Loans: For six months.

  Exchange: Yes, with six eastern and midwestern universities.

HUNTINGTON BEACH: *Herbarium, Biology Department, Golden West College,* (**HUBE**), 15744 Golden West Street, Huntington Beach, California 92647, **U.S.A.**

Telephone: 714/892-7711.

Foundation: 1966. *Number of specimens:* 600.

Herbarium: California flora, including aliens, cultivated, and some marine species.

Important collections: Hayden Williams.

  Director and Curator: SHARRON A. CLARK, 1944 (Taxonomy; cytogenetics; tomato genetics).

  Staff members: CANDACE DONELLEY.

  HAROLD FITZWATER.

  Specialization in research: Algae of the Channel Islands, including Catalina.

  Associated botanic garden: Small arboretum.

HUNTSVILLE: *Herbarium, Department of Biology, University of Alabama,* (**HALA**), P.O. Box 1247, Huntsville, Alabama 35807, **U.S.A.**

Telephone: 205/895-6094; 895-6260.

Foundation: 1976. *Number of specimens:* 1.000.

Herbarium: Northern Alabama, Tennessee Valley, Cumberland Plateau.

  Director: ROBERT O. LAWTON, 1950 (Tropical montane rain forest trees).

  Loans: To professional biologists at recognized institutions.

HUNTSVILLE: *Herbarium, Department of Life Sciences, Sam Houston State University,* (**SHST**), Huntsville, Texas 77341, **U.S.A.**

Telephone: 713/295-6211, ext. 1594 and 1556.

Foundation: 1899 (15.000 specimens destroyed by fire 3 February 1978; rebuilding began shortly thereafter). *Number of specimens:* 4.000.

Herbarium: East Texas flora.

  Director: SUSAN C. BARBER, 1952 (Plant taxonomy; *Verbena*).

  Specialization in research: Numerical and breeding studies in *Verbena.*

  Loans: Usual regulations.

HYDERABAD: *Herbarium and Botanical Museum, Osmania University,* (**HY**), Hyderabad 7, **India.** (Information 1964)

Status: University.

Foundation: 1933. *Number of specimens:* 5.000.

Herbarium: Mainly angiosperms of Hyderabad.

  Associated botanic garden: Botanic Garden of Osmania University.

I

IAŞI: *Herbarium, Facultatea de Biologie-Geografie-Geologie, Universitatea "Al. I. Cuza,"* **(I),** Strada 23 August nr. 11 6600 Iaşi, **Romania.**
Telephone: 981-11720, 981-41320.
Status: University.
Foundation: 1867. *Number of specimens:* 200.000.
Herbarium: Worldwide collection, especially Romania.
Important collections: Ion C. Constantineanu (micromycetes), C. Roumequère (Fungi Selecti Galici Exsiccati), Sydon (*Ustilago*).
Director: CONSTANTIN TOMA, 1935 (Morphology).
Curator: ION SÂRBU, 1933 (Flora and vegetation of Romania).
Specialization in research: Flora of Romania.
Loans: With permission of director.
Exchange: Yes.

IAŞI: *Herbarium, Grădina botanică,* **(IAGB),** Str. Dumbrava Roşie 9, Iaşi, **Romania.** (Information 1974)
Status: University.
Foundation: 1963. *Number of specimens:* 25.000.
Herbarium: Romanian plants.
Periodical and serial works: Delectus seminum, Flora Moldaviae et Dodrogeae Exsiccata.
Loans: To recognized botanical institutions.

IAŞI: *Institutul Agronomic,* (IASI), Aleea Sadoveanu 3, 6600 Iaşi, **Romania.**
Telephone: 981/40820.
Status: Agronomical Institute.
Foundation: 1952. *Number of specimens:* 30.000.
Herbarium: Plants of Romania.
Important collections: M. Răvărut.
Director: E. TURENSCHI, 1922 (Taxonomy of angiosperms, geobotany).
Curator: M. TOMA, 1934 (Macromycetes of Romania).
Staff members: LUCIA IFTENI, 1927 (Anatomy of angiosperms).
P. PASCAL, 1934 (Bryophytes of Romania, geobotany).
V. ZANOSCHI, 1934 (Algology of Romania, geobotany).
Specialization in research: Flora of Romania.
Loans: To recognized institutions.
Exchange: Available: Angiosperms of Romania. Desired: Plants of Europe.

IAŞI: *Herbarium "S. Sandu-Ville," Institutul Agronomic "Ion Ionescu de la Brad,"* **(IBIR),** M. Madoveanu 3, 6600 Iaşi, **Romania.**
Telephone: 980/40801, 980/40802, 980/40820.
Status: Agronomical Institute.

Foundation: 1930. *Number of specimens:* 12.900.
Herbarium: Saprophytic and parasitic micromycetes.
Important collections: Oescu and Rădulescu (Erysiphaceae), C. Sandu-Ville (Erysiphaceae, Pyrenomycetales), Lazăr (micromycetes of Leguminosae), Hatman, micromycetes of Gramineae), Viorica (soil micromycetes).
Director and Curator: IACOB VIORICA, 1940.
Staff members: TEODOR GEORGESCU, 1942.
MIRCEA HATMAN, 1927.
ALEXANDRU LAZĂR, 1927.
Specialization in research: Saprophytic and parasitic micromycetes on cultivated and spontaneous plants.

IBADAN: *Forest Herbarium, Forestry Research Institute of Nigeria,* **(FHI),** P.M.B. 5054, Ibadan, **Nigeria.**
Telephone: 414441.
Status: Adherence to Forestry Research Institute of Nigeria.
Foundation: 1942. *Number of specimens:* 100.000.
Herbarium: Mostly tropical species.
Director: O. A. ATANDA (Plant breeding).
Curator: ZAC. O. GBILE, 1937.
Staff member: M. O. SOLADOYE, 1945.
Specialization in research: Flora of Nigeria.
Loans: For a maximum of 6 months.
Exchange: Yes.

IBADAN: *Herbarium, Department of Botany, University of Ibadan,* **(UCI),** Ibadan, Oyo State, **Nigeria.**
Telephone: 462550, ext. 1403.
Status: University.
Foundation: 1948. *Number of specimens:* 17.000.
Herbarium: Mainly vascular plants of Nigeria and Cameroon.
Director (Head, Department of Botany): M. B. SCOTT-EMUAKPOR, 1936 (Genetics).
Curator: JOYCE LOWE, 1933 (Cyperaceae, Nigerian herbaceous plants).
Associated botanic garden: Botanical Garden of University of Ibadan.
Loans: To recognized botanical institutions, for six months.
Exchange: Yes.

IBAGUÉ: *Herbario, Departamento de Biología, Universidad del Tolima,* **(TOLI),** Ibagué, Tolima, **Colombia.**
Telephone: (57)82/34219.
Foundation: 1959. *Number of specimens:* 4.500.
Herbarium: Mainly flora of Colombia; some Peru, Brazil, Spain, and U.S.A.
Important collections: Raúl Echeverry E., José

Cuatrecasas, Claude Sastre.
Director: RAÚL ECHEVERRY E.
Curator: JORGE PUERTA.
Staff members: ROBERTO JARAMILLO M.
MARÍA TERESA MURILLO.
Collaborators: LUIS ALEJANDRO VIDAL C.
MARÍA MAGDALENA ECHEVERRY DE POLANCO.
FERNANDO ALI HUERTOS.
SANTIAGO LÓPEZ-PALACIOS.
Specialization in research: Weeds of cultivated areas; ornamental and useful plants.
Associated botanic garden: Jardín Botánico Alejandro von Humboldt de la Universidad del Tolima.

ILE-IFE: *Herbarium, Department of Botany, University of Ife,* **(IFE)**, Ile-Ife, **Nigeria.**
Status: University.
Foundation: 1962. *Number of specimens:* 25.000.
Herbarium: Plants of Nigeria, Orchidaceae of West Africa.
Director and Curator: WILLIAM W. SANFORD, 1924 (Ecology, orchid taxonomy).
Staff members: E. ODU (Bryophytes).
A. O. OLATUNJI (Plant anatomy).
O. OLORODE (Cytogenetics, grass taxonomy).
Specialization in research: Orchidaceae, savanna ecology.
Periodical and serial works: Ife Herbarium Bulletins.

ILLMITZ: *Herbarium, Biologische Station Neusiedlersee,* **(NBSI)**, Biologische Forschungsinstitut für Burgenland, A 7142 Illmitz, Burgenland, **Austria.**

INDIANA: *Arthur G. Shields Herbarium, Biology Department, Indiana University of Pennsylvania,* **(IUP)**, Indiana, Pennsylvania 15705, **U.S.A.**
Telephone: 412/357-2356.
Foundation: 1966. *Number of specimens:* 10.000.
Herbarium: Floristics of eastern U.S., with emphasis on western Pennsylvania flora.
Director and Curator: JERRY L. PICKERING, 1942 (Local floristics; chemotaxonomy; protein chemistry; Umbelliferae).
Specialization in research: Local flora; flora of the mid-Atlantic states; comparative protein chemistry.
Loans: In general to recognized botanical institutions and departments.
Exchange: Available: General collections from western Pennsylvania. Desired: U.S. and Canada.

INDIANAPOLIS: *Friesner Herbarium, Department of Botany, Butler University,* **(BUT)**, Indianapolis, Indiana 46208, **U.S.A.**
Status: Private university.
Foundation: 1919. *Number of specimens:* 100.000.
Herbarium: Plants of Indiana.
Important collections: Extensive collections of *Sol-*

idago, Charophyceae, and Cyanophyceae; special collections in grasses and algae.
Curator: WILLARD F. YATES, JR. (Compositae, Solanaceae).
Staff members: F. A. DAILY (Phycology; Charophyceae).
W. A. DAILY (Phycology; Myxophyceae).
JOHN F. PELTON (Ecology).
REX N. WEBSTER (Mycology; Rhodophyceae).
Loans: Suspended due to inadequate funds for herbarium assistants.
Periodical and serial works: Butler University Botanical Studies (suspended).
Remarks: Botanists are invited to visit the herbarium and examine specimens.

INDIANAPOLIS: *Department of Biology, Crispus Attucks High School,* **(CAHS)**, Indianapolis, Indiana 46200, **U.S.A.** -- discontinued.

INDIANOLA: *Herbarium, Department of Biology, Simpson College,* **(SICH)**, Indianola, Iowa 50125, **U.S.A.**
Telephone: 515/961-6251, ext. 698.
Status: Private college.
Foundation: 1956. *Number of specimens:* 500.
Herbarium: Primarily grasses of midwestern U.S.
Director: Chairman of Biology Department.
Remarks: Collections used for teaching.

INNSBRUCK: *Herbarium, Institut für Botanik der Universität Innsbruck,* **(IB)**, Sternwartestrasse 15, A-6020 Innsbruck, **Austria.**
Telephone: 05222/336019731.
Status: University.
Foundation: Before 1850. *Number of specimens:* 100.000.
Herbarium: Alpine flora of Tyrol and adjacent areas.
Director: H. PITSCHMANN, 1922 (Plant geography).
Curator of Phanerogams: G. GRABHERR, 1946 (Flora and vegetation of Tyrol).
Curator of Cryptogams: G. GÄRTNER, 1946 (Phycology).
Staff members: S. BORTENSCHLAGER, 1940 (Palynology).
H. REISIGL, 1929 (Phycology, plant geography).
E. ROTT, 1951 (Phycology, Limnology).
Specialization in research: Southern alpine flora.
Associated botanic garden: Botanischer Garten der Universität Innsbruck.
Loans: To recognized botanical institutions.
Exchange: Oreophytes, algae.

INNSBRUCK: *Herbarium, Tiroler Landesmuseum Ferdinandeum,* **(IBF)**, Zeughaus, Zeughausgasse 1, A-6020 Innsbruck, **Austria.**
Telephone: 5222/27 4 39.

Status: Private.

Foundation: 1824. *Number of specimens:* 250.000.

Herbarium: Plants from Tyrol in its former borders (= North Tyrol/Austria, South Tyrol and Trentino/Italy), Vorarlberg and Austria general.

Important collections: Murr (Tyrol, Vorarlberg), Sarnthein (Tyrol, Vorarlberg), Tappeiner (Tyrol), Zimmeter (Tyrol, mainly southern), A. Heimerl (Tyrol, mainly southern), Valde Lievre (Tyrol – Trentino), Giovanni (Trentino), Lanser (Tyrol [Osttirol]), herb. Stift Wilten (Tyrol), herb. Stift Fiecht (Tyrol), Traunsteiner (Tyrol), and some famous historical herbaria (H. Guarinoni, ca. 1680).

Director of Museum: ERICH EGG, 1920 (Historical science).

Curator: GERHARD TARMANN, 1950; 34 26 64 (private) (Entomologist).

Specialization in research: Floristic Tyrol (incl. Trentino), Vorarlberg and surrounding areas.

Loans: With permission of director.

Periodical and serial works: Veröffentlichungen des Tiroler Landesmuseum Ferdinandeum.

Exchange: Yes.

Remarks: A group of interested amateur botanists take care of the collections.

IOWA CITY: *Herbarium, Department of Botany, University of Iowa,* (**IA**), Iowa City, Iowa 52242, **U.S.A.**

Telephone: 319/353-5790.

Foundation: 1870. *Number of specimens:* 325.200.

Herbarium: Emphasis on midwestern U.S., especially Iowa.

Important collections: G. W. Martin (fungi), A. P. Morgan (fungi), J. M. Holzinger (bryophytes), W. S. Sullivant (bryophytes); fossil cycads from South Dakota; Compositae (Coreopsidineae), Iridaceae, and Liliaceae from Mexico.

Director and Curator: ROBERT L. HULBARY, 1917 (Plant morphology, anatomy; reproductive biology of mosses and liverworts).

Staff members: ROBERT W. CRUDEN, 1936 (Pollination biology; biosystematics of Iridaceae and Liliaceae of Mexico and Central America).

THOMAS E. MELCHERT, Curator of Phanerogams, 1936 (Chemotaxonomy and cytotaxonomy of Compositae, Coreopsidineae of Mexico and Central America).

JEFFERY T. SCHABILION, Curator of Fossil Plants, 1942 (Morphology and systematics of Paleozoic ferns, sphenophylls, lycopods, and Cordaites).

Specialization in research: Systematics and evolution of Coreopsidineae, Iridaceae, and Liliaceae of Mexico and Central America; systematics and reproductive biology of bryophytes; chemotaxonomy; cytotaxonomy; genecology; pollination biology; floristics of Iowa and midwestern U.S.

Loans: Usual regulations.

Periodical and serial works: University of Iowa Studies in Natural History (irregular).

Exchange: Bryophytes only.

IPSWICH: *Ipswich Museum Herbarium,* (**IPS**), The Museum, High Street, Ipswich, Suffolk IP1 3QH, England, **Great Britain.**

Telephone: 0473-213761/2.

Foundation: 1846. *Number of specimens:* 15.000.

Herbarium: Mainly 19th and early 20th century British material with a strong emphasis on Suffolk.

Important collections: Herb. of Rev. W. M. Hind, including collections of voucher material for his publication "The Flora of Suffolk," 1889.

Director: A. G. HATTON, 1950 (Material culture of China).

Curator: C. A. GREEN, 1951.

Specialization in research: Flora of Suffolk.

Loans: With permission of the director and the consent of Committee.

IQUITOS: *Herbarium Amazonense, Universidad Nacional de la Amazonía Peruana,* (**AMAZ**), Jirón Próspero No. 584, Apartado 421, Iquitos, **Peru.**

Telephone: 23-53-51.

Foundation: 1972. *Number of specimens:* 10.000.

Herbarium: Flora of Peruvian Amazonia.

Important collections: Alwyn Gentry, Sidney McDaniel, Juan Revilla, Franklin Ayala (medicinal plants), Jose Schunke, Manuel Rimachi.

Director: FRANKLIN AYALA FLORES, 1941 (Dioscoreaceae; medical tropical plants).

Honorary Curator: ALWYN GENTRY, 1946 (Bignoniaceae; tropical taxonomy and floristics; flora of Peru).

Staff members: ELIAS ANDRADE CORTEZ, 1953 (Fungi).

MARINA BENDAYÁN ACOSTA, 1950 (General botany).

PEDRO CAREY SOLIS, 1946 (Tropical fresh water algae; desmids).

SIDNEY MCDANIEL, 1940 (Flora of Amazonian Peru; Ericaceae, Piperaceae).

SEGUNDO PASCUAL CAMACHO, 1940 (Plant physiology).

PEDRO SUAREZ MERA, 1947 (Aquatic plants).

Specialization in research: Flora of Peru; Flora Desmidiológica de Loreto.

Loans: To recognized botanical institutions.

Periodical and serial works: Conocimiento, yearly bulletin.

Exchange: Available: Plants from Loreto Department. Wanted: Vascular plants from Amazonia.

Remarks: The herbarium is growing rapidly as a result of convenio among Universidad Nacional de la Amazonía Peruana, Missouri Botanical Garden, and Institute for Botanical Exploration.

IRKUTSK: *Popov Herbarium, Physiological and Biochemical Institute of the Siberian Section of Academy of Sciences of U.S.S.R.,* (**IRK**), Ab. Yashch.

1243, 664039 Irkutsk, **U.S.S.R.**
Status: Directed by Academy of Sciences.
Foundation: 1951.
Director: V. V. BUSSIK.
Remarks: Most specimens have been transferred to the Central Siberian Botanical Garden, Novosibirsk (NS); only duplicates, many unmounted, remain at IRK.

IRVINE: *Herbarium, Museum of Systematic Biology, School of Biological Sciences, University of California,* **(IRVC),** Irvine, California 92664, **U.S.A.** (Information 1974)
Foundation: 1965. *Number of specimens:* 8.000.
Herbarium: Regional southern California, southwestern U.S. and adjacent Mexico.

ISLAMABAD: *Herbarium, Quaid-I-Azam University,* **(ISL),** Islamabad, **Pakistan.**
Telephone: 23328.
Status: University.
Foundation: 1974. *Number of specimens:* 165.000.
Herbarium: Mainly flowering plants and ferns of northern and northwestern Pakistan.
Important collections: Numerous types of new taxa of angiosperms of Pakistan.
Director: MOHAMMAD NAZEER CHAUDHRI, 1932 (Polygonaceae, Centrospermae and Euphorbiaceae of Pakistan, Paronychiinae of the world).
Curator: RIZWANA ALEEM QURESHI, 1950 (Ranales, Rhoeadales, Rosales of Pakistan).
Staff members: MOHAMMAD BASHIR AHMAD, 1955 (Solanaceae and Scrophulariaceae of Pakistan).
TANWEER AKHTAR, 1949 (Compositae and Gramineae of Pakistan).
FARHAT BANO, 1953 (Taxonomic documentation).
MOHAMMAD ASLAM MIRZA, 1955 (Illustrator).
S. MUQARRAB SHAH, 1946 (Monocotyledons, except grasses, of Pakistan).
MOHAMMAD ZUBAIR, 1954 (Rubiales and Campanulaceae of Pakistan).
Specialization in research: Flora of Pothohar Region, taxonomic studies on flora of Pakistan, useful plants and wildflowers of Pakistan.
Loans: To recognized botanical institutions.
Periodical and serial works: Pakistan Systematics.
Exchange: Available: Plants of Pakistan.

ISTANBUL: *Istanbul Üniversitesi Eczacilik Fakültesi Herbaryumu (Herbarium of the Faculty of Pharmacy of Istanbul University),* **(ISTE),** Eczacilik Fakültesi Farmasötik Botanik Kürsüsü Üniversite, Istanbul, **Turkey.**
Telephone: 224200/673 or 224200/674.
Status: University.
Foundation: 1945. *Number of specimens:* 43.930.
Herbarium: Mainly Turkey (Pteridophyta, Gymnospermae, Monocotyledonae, Dicotyledonae).

Important collections: T. Baytop (Turkish bulbous plants, including 8 types), P. H. Davis (650 Turkish specimens).
Director and Curator: ASUMAN BAYTOP, 1920 (Medicinal plants, Turkish Solanaceae, Arundinae, *Nonea, Typha, Phalaris*).
Staff members: KERIM ALPINAR, 1954 (Flora of Akdağ).
GÜLDAN ÇAKIRER, 1952 (Flora of Sultan Dağlari).
NERIMAN ÖZHATAY, 1947 (Orobanchaceae of European Turkey, cytotaxonomy of Turkish Alliaceae).
MUSTAFA SARAÇOĞLU, 1956 (Annual *Papaver* of Turkey).
ERTAN TUZLACI, 1949 (Flora of Honaz Daği and Marmara Adasi, *Asphodeline* of Turkey).
Specialization in research: Systematic and cytotaxonomic research on Turkish plants.
Loans: By arrangement.
Periodical and serial works: Istanbul Üniversitesi Eczacilik Fakültesi Mecmuasi (Journal of Faculty of Pharmacy of Istanbul University).
Exchange: Yes.

ISTANBUL: *Istanbul Üniversitesi Fen Fakültesi Herbaryumu,* **(ISTF),** Istanbul Üniversitesi, Botanik ve Genetik Kürsüsü, Süleymaniye – Istanbul, **Turkey.**
Telephone: 22 21 78, 26 45 46.
Status: University of Istanbul.
Foundation: 1936. *Number of specimens:* 35.000.
Herbarium: Turkey and some Near East countries.
Important collections: A. Heilbronn, M. Heilbronn (Başarman), A. Attila, H. Demiriz, B. Tutel, A. Aydin, A. Çirpici and G. Sünter.
Director: HÜSNÜ DEMIRIZ, 1920 (Taxonomy, flora of Turkey, Pteridophyta, Caryophyllaceae, Ranunculaceae).
Curator: BETÛL TUTEL, 1929 (Taxonomy, flora and endemics of Turkey, Pteridophyta, *Plantago*).
Staff members: AYTEN AYDIN, 1930 (Taxonomy, flora of Turkey, Pteridophyta, Labiatae).
SABAHAT BAYKAL, 1942 (Ecophysiology, salt and drought resistance, pollution).
TÜLAY ÇELEBIOĞLU, 1943 (Taxonomy, *Lotus* and *Dorycnium*).
ERGÜL ÇETIN, 1947 (Ecology).
ALI ÇIRPICI, 1947 (Taxonomy, flora of Murat Daği, *Ranunculus*).
KADRIYE ERTAN, 1932 (Paleobotany, fossil gymnospermous woods).
NEBAHAT GENÇ, 1935 (Cytology and embryology of *Isatis*).
NERMIN GÖZÜKIRMIZI, 1951 (Genetics, effects of mutagens).
PIRAYE KOKTAY, 1941 (Cytology, *Papaver* and *Verbascum*).
ORHAN KÜÇÜKER, 1954 (Morphology and cytology of *Colchicum*).
SEMRA KUŞ, 1951 (Taxonomy and cytology

of *Ranunculus*).
ATOK OLGUN, 1944 (Cytogenetics, population genetics).
GÖKSEL OLGUN, 1938 (Ultrastructure, cytology and embryology of Scrophulariaceae).
MUAZZEZ ÖNAL, 1928 (Ecophysiology, salt tolerance).
GÜLER ORALER, 1943 (Genetics, especially yeasts).
RECEP ÖZTÜRK, 1944 (Cytology and embryology of *Paeonia*).
GANIMET SÜNTER, 1943 (Taxonomy, *Dianthus*, flora of Kapidag peninsula).
MEHMET TOPAKTAS, 1951 (Cytogenetics, plant amelioration).
JALE TÖREN, 1919 (Cytoembryology, Berberidaceae).
BILGIN TÖZÜN, 1932 (Taxonomy and cytology of algae).
MERAL ÜNAL, 1950 (Embryology of Ranunculaceae).
NEBAHAT YAKAR-TAN, 1915 (Morphology, cytology, *Digitalis* of Turkey).
Specialization in research: Flora and vegetation of Turkey.
Associated botanic garden: Istanbul Üniversitesi Botanik Bahçesi (Hortus Botanicus Universitatis Istanbulensis).
Loans: To recognized institutions and herbaria.
Periodical and serial works: Istanbul Üniversitesi Fen Fakültesi Mecmuasi Seri B.
Exchange: Available: Turkish plants. Desired: Plants of Near East, floristic literature relating to Oriental flora, especially Turkey.

ISTANBUL: *Herbarium, Istanbul Üniversitesi Orman Fakültesi, Orman botanigi kürsüsü,* (**ISTO**), Büyükdere-Istanbul, **Turkey.** (Information 1974)
Status: University of Istanbul.
Foundation: 1952. *Number of specimens:* 6.400.
Herbarium: Woody and herbaceous plants of Turkey, some fungi; collection of gymnosperm pollen grains.
Specialization in research: Flora of Turkey.
Associated botanic garden: Bahçeköy Arboretum.
Loans: To recognized botanical institutions.
Periodical and serial works: Revue de la Faculté des Sciences Forestières de l'Université d'Istanbul.

ITABUNA: *Herbário do Centro de Pesquisas do Cacau, CEPEC,* (**CEPEC**), Caixa Postal 7, 45.600 Itabuna, Bahia, **Brazil.**
Telephone: (55)211-2211, ramal 131.
Status: Federal government.
Foundation: 1965. *Number of specimens:* 20.000.
Herbarium: Plants of the cocoa producing regions of Bahia and Espírito Santo; 100 marked types of Bahian plants.
Important collections: R. P. Belém, T. S. dos Santos,

S. A. Mori, R. M. Harley.
Director: ROBERTO J. PEREIRA, 1939 (Ecology of weedy plants; control of weeds).
Curator: ANDRÉ M. DE CARVALHO, 1951 (Flora of the cocoa region).
Staff members: GILDRO LISBOA, 1939 (Taxonomy and ecology of weedy plants; economic plants of the cocoa region).
LUIZ A. MATTOS SILVA, 1949 (Flora of the cocoa region).
SÉRGIO DA VINHA (Flora and ecology of the cocoa region).
Specialization in research: Preparation of a flora of the cocoa producing region of Bahia; studies of the taxonomy and ecology of the weeds of the region; studies of the taxonomy and ecology of the economic plants of the region.
Associated botanic garden: A botanical reserve of 43 hectares on the grounds of the cocoa research center.
Loans: To recognized botanical institutions.
Periodical and serial works: Revista Theobroma (Journal of the Cocoa Research Center); Boletins Técnicos.
Exchange: Desired: Plants of Bahia.
Remarks: Revisions of plant families for the cocoa producing region of Bahia by outside specialists are welcomed.

ITAJAÍ: *Herbário "Barbosa Rodrigues,"* (**HBR**), Avenida Marcos Konder 800, 88.300 Itajaí, Santa Catarina, **Brazil.**
Telephone: (55)0473/44-2725.
Status: Private foundation.
Foundation: 1942. *Number of specimens:* 66.000.
Herbarium: South Brazil, chiefly states of Santa Catarina, Paraná, and Rio Grande do Sul.
Important collections: R. Reitz, R. M. Klein, B. Rambo, G. Hatschbach, L. B. Smith.
Director: RAULINO REITZ, 1919 (Bromeliaceae; taxonomy).
Curator: ROBERTO MIGUEL KLEIN (Phytosociology).
Specialization in research: General flora of the states of Santa Catarina, Paraná, and Rio Grande do Sul; Bromeliaceae of Brazil.
Associated botanic garden: Parque Botânico do Morro Baú (Atlantic coast rain forest).
Loans: Normal regulations, but types and very fragile specimens may be withheld.
Periodical and serial works: Sellowia, formerly Anais Botânicos do Herbário "Barbosa Rodriques"; Bromelia (Boletim da Sociedade Brasileira de Bromélias); Flora Ilustrada Catarinense (7.006 pages published covering 102 families).

ITHACA: *Liberty Hyde Bailey Hortorium, Cornell University,* (**BH**), 467 Mann Library Building, Ithaca, New York 14853, **U.S.A.**
Telephone: 607/256-2131.

Status: A unit of the Division of Biological Sciences and the New York State College of Agriculture and Life Sciences.

Foundation: 1935. *Number of specimens:* 388.671.

Herbarium: Worldwide with emphasis on cultivated plants and their wild counterparts, economically and ethnobotanically important plants, and the family Palmae.

Important collections: Brassica, N. Amer. *Carex, Cucurbita,* Palmae, *Rubus, Vitis;* cultivated plants; Japan; photos of palm types of R. Spruce and J. W. H. Trail, C. F. P. von Martius, O. Beccari; L. H. Bailey.

Director: DAVID M. BATES, 1935 (Malvales; cultivated plants; ethnobotany).

Curator: PETER A. HYYPIO, 1921 (Cyperaceae, Gramineae; weeds; cultivated plants).

Staff members: ETHEL Z. BAILEY, 1889 (Cultivated plants).

ROBERT T. CLAUSEN, 1911 (Crassulaceae, *Sedum* and related genera; Ophioglossaceae; vascular plants of the glaciated Allegheny Plateau).

WILLIAM J. DRESS, 1918 (Compositae; cultivated plants).

JOHN W. INGRAM, JR., 1924 (Ericaceae, Euphorbiaceae; cultivated plants).

NATALIE W. UHL, 1919 (Anatomy of palms).

MICHAEL D. WHALEN, 1950 (Solanaceae).

Specialization in research: Systematics of cultivated and economically and ethnobotanically important plants; Palmae, Malvaceae, Euphorbiaceae, Gesneriaceae, Solanaceae.

Associated botanic garden: The Cornell Plantations, 100 Judd Falls Road, Ithaca, New York 14850.

Loans: To recognized institutions, normally for a period of one year; loans include specimens from the Wiegand Herbarium (CU).

Periodical and serial works: Baileya, a journal of horticultural taxonomy; Gentes Herbarum.

Exchange: Available: Cultivated plants; native flora of North America. Wanted: Cultivated material, especially of subtropical, tropical, and Mediterranean regions; general collections from the southern hemisphere and temperate Asia; Palmae, Malvales, Solanaceae.

Remarks: A large collection of preserved palm material (fruits, flowers, and woody parts), miscellaneous preserved material, and a seed reference collection of northeastern U.S.

ITHACA: *Wiegand Herbarium, Cornell University,* (CU), 467 Mann Library Building, Ithaca, New York 14853, **U.S.A.**

Telephone: 607/256-2131.

Status: Since 1977, an integrated part of the herbarium of the L. H. Bailey Hortorium (BH).

Foundation: 1871. *Number of specimens:* 323.852.

Herbarium: Flora of North America, especially eastern regions, glaciated Allegheny Plateau; Ophioglossaceae, Leguminosa, crassulaceae (*Sedum*), *Amelanchier, Aster;* flora of Cayuga Lake Basin.

Important collections: Horace Mann (Hawaii); bryophyte collections of John K. Small, Albert L. Andrews; K. M. Wiegand, W. C. Muenscher.

Loans: Requests should be made to the L. H. Bailey Hortorium.

Remarks: In 1977, the Wiegand Herbarium (CU) was integrated with the L. H. Bailey Hortorium Herbarium (BH).

ITHACA: *Plant Pathology Herbarium, Cornell University,* (**CUP**), Ithaca, New York 14853, **U.S.A.**

Telephone: 607/256-3292; 256-3293.

Status: Part of the New York State College of Agriculture and Life Sciences and of the New York State Agricultural Experiment Station.

Foundation: 1907. *Number of specimens:* 300.000.

Herbarium: Fungi, particularly of the Americas, neotropics, Macronesia, China, Japan, and southeastern Asia.

Important collections: G. F. Atkinson, A. H. Chivers, C. Chupp, E. J. Durand, C. E. Fairman, H. M. Fitzpatrick, J. Gremmen, E. E. Honey, H. H. Whetzel, W. L. White, C. Chardon, A. P. Viégas, S. C. Teng; undestroyed portion of Chinese National Fungus Collection (Peking).

Director: RICHARD P. KORF, 1925 (Taxonomy and nomenclature of Discomycetes).

Curator: SUSAN C. GRUFF, 1953 (Taxonomy of Discomycetes).

Staff members: FRANÇOISE CANDOUSSAU, 1934 (Taxonomy of Pyrenomycetes).

JAMES W. LORBEER, 1931 (*Botrytis;* genetics of *Botryotinia*).

LINDA J. SPIELMAN, 1946 (Taxonomy and biology of Valsaceae).

Specialization in research: Discomycetes; plant pathogens.

Loans: In general for 6 months.

Periodical and serial works: Discomycetes Exsiccati.

Exchange: Fungi of all groups.

Remarks: Some of the CUP set of the Chinese National Fungus Collection (Peking) is also duplicated in BPI, but many are unitunicates at CUP.

IZMIR: *Botanik Bahçesi ve Herbaryum Merkezi, Ege University, Faculty of Science,* (**EGE**), Bornova-Izmir, **Turkey.**

Telephone: 180110/2838.

Status: University.

Foundation: 1964. *Number of specimens:* 30.000.

Herbarium: Gymnospermae, angiospermae, cryptogamae.

Important collections: Geraniaceae, Leguminosae, Compositae, Labiatae, aquatic plants; part of the collections of Post and Schwarz; Gökçeada (Imbroz) and Bozcaada (Tenedos).

Director: ÖZCAN SEÇMEN, 1947 (Taxonomy, sociology).

Curator: ERKUTER LEBLEBICI, 1939 (Labiatae, Primulaceae).

Staff members: VEYSEL AYSEL, 1950 (Algology, Rhodophyta).

GÜVAN GÖRK, 1951 (Plant sociology).

AHMET YAYINTAŞ, 1950 (Plant sociology).

Specialization in research: Flora and vegetation of West Anatolia.

Associated botanic garden: Ege Botanical Garden.

Loans: West Anatolian specimens for a short period.

Periodical and serial works: Journal of Faculty of Science, Ege University.

Exchange: Available: Aquatic plants of West Anatolia.

IZMIR: *Herbarium, Zirai Araştirma ve Introdüksiyon Merkezi (Agricultural Research and Introduction Center),* **(IZ),** Posta kutusu 25, Karşiyaka, Izmir, **Turkey.** (Information 1974)

Status: Ministry of Agriculture.

Foundation: 1964. *Number of specimens:* 4.000.

Herbarium: Economic plants of Turkey.

Specialization in research: Taxonomy of economic plants and their wild relatives of Turkey.

IZMIR: *Herbaryumu, Eczacilik Fakültesi, Ege Üniversitesi,* **(IZEF),** Farmasötik Botanik Kürsüsü, Inciralti-Izmir, **Turkey.**

Foundation: 1979. *Number of specimens:* 1.000.

Herbarium: West Anatolia.

Director: NECMETTIN ZEYBEK (Taxonomy, marine algae, halophytic Chenopodiaceae, *Galanthus*).

Staff members: ISMET AKBULUT (*Origanum, Thymus*).

FERIHA ŞEKERCI (*Viola*).

Specialization in research: Medicinal plants of Turkey.

Loans: In general to recognized institutes and herbaria.

Exchange: Some duplicates of Turkish plants.

J

JACKSON: *Herbarium, Bridger-Teton National Forest,* **(BTJW),** P.O. Box 1888, Jackson, Wyoming 83001, **U.S.A.**
Telephone: 307/733-2752.
Status: U.S. Department of Agriculture, Forest Service.
Foundation: 1976. *Number of specimens:* 5.000.
Herbarium: Early range conditions and forest sites; plants of Bridger-Teton National Forest and associated lands.
Important collections: John and Leila Shultz (Wyoming and Salt River ranges, Wyoming).
Curator: ANDREW P. YOUNGBLOOD, 1954 (Forest ecology).
Specialization in research: Local flora.

JAIPUR: *Herbarium, Department of Botany, University of Rajasthan,* **(RUBL),** Jaipur 302004, **India.**
Telephone: 75765.
Status: University.
Foundation: 1963. *Number of specimens:* 14.000.
Herbarium: Flora of Rajasthan, especially Jaipur and Jhalawar districts, flora of Aravallis and Himalayan hills stations, Nilgiris, Krusaddi Islands.
Director: B. TIAGI, 1922 (Parasitic angiosperms, Gramineae, Tubiflorae, nematode-induced abnormalities in plants, floristics).
Curator: SHIVA SHARMA, 1931 (Flora of arid regions of Aravallis, ethnobotany, medicinal plants).
Staff members: S. MISRA (Compositae, plant mycoplasma diseases).
    K. K. SHARMA (Gramineae).
    P. D. SHARMA (Mosses).
    D. SINGH (Cucurbitaceae).
Specialization in research: Floristics, floras and monographs.
Loans: To recognized botanical institutions.
Exchange: Available: Plants of Jaipur. Desired: Cryptogams.

JAMAICA PLAIN: *Herbarium, Arnold Arboretum, Harvard University,* **(AAH),** The Arborway, Jamaica Plain, Massachusetts 02130, **U.S.A.**
Foundation: 1872.
Remarks: All data concerning this herbarium of cultivated plants are presented with those of the Arnold Arboretum (A), Harvard University, Cambridge, Massachusetts 02138.

JAMESTOWN: *Herbarium, Northern Prairie Wildlife Research Center,* **(NPWRC),** P.O. Box 1747, Jamestown, North Dakota 58401, **U.S.A.**
Telephone: 701/252-5639.
Status: U.S. Department of the Interior, Fish and Wildlife Service.
Foundation: 1965. *Number of specimens:* 5.000.

Herbarium: Vascular plants of the wetlands and upland grasslands of the northern Great Plains.
Director: REX STENDELL, 1941 (Pesticide research).
Curator: HAROLD A. KANTRUD, 1937 (Grassland ecologist).
Specialization in research: Prairie wetland and grassland wildlife research; emphasis on waterfowl, mammals, and migratory birds.
Loans: Yes, for 6 months.
Remarks: Data from herbarium collections available in computer compatible format.

JANESVILLE: *Herbarium, University of Wisconsin,* **(UWJ),** Rock County Campus, Kellogg Avenue, Janesville, Wisconsin 53545, **U.S.A.**
Telephone: 608/755-2853.
Foundation: 1966. *Number of specimens:* 3.900.
Herbarium: Rock and Green counties, Wisconsin; Yates County, New York.
Staff member: MARION M. RICE, 1923.
Specialization in research: Rock and Green counties, Wisconsin; Yates County, New York.
Exchange: Available: Material from counties listed above. Desired: Finger Lakes region and Costa Rica.

JENA: *Herbarium Haussknecht, Sektion Biologie der Friedrich-Schiller-Universität,* **(JE),** Schlossgasse, DDR-69 Jena, **German Democratic Republic,** DDR.
Telephone: 8222184.
Status: Institution of the University of Jena.
Foundation: 1895 (private, at Weimar; since 1949 associated with University of Jena). *Number of specimens:* 2.500.000.
Herbarium: Worldwide herbarium of all groups, mainly phanerogams of Europe and the Near East, bryophytes worldwide, many types and isotypes.
Important collections: Phanerogams: C. Haussknecht, J. F. N. Bornmüller, Ch. Gaillardot, Ch. I. Blanche, Th. Strauss, O. Schwarz, W. Rothmaler, Ch. E. Weigel, M. J. Schleiden, T. Ph. Ekart, Th. Irmisch, E. Haeckel, W. Vatke, E. Torges, E. Sagorski, Sporleder. Cryptogams: Th. Herzog, K. Schliephacke, H. Winter, W. Migula, H. Diedicke, P. Dietel.
Director: GERHARD KLOTZ, 1928 (*Echium, Cotoneaster*; dendrology).
Curator: FRIEDRICH KARL MEYER, 1926; 8222183 (Flora of Balcan Peninsula, Brassicaceae, nomenclature).
Staff members: JOHANNES BISSE, 1935 (Flora of Cuba, Pinaceae, Myrtaceae).
    RICLEF GROLLE, 1934 (Hepaticae).
    KARL-FRIEDRICH GÜNTHER, 1941 (Morphology, Papaveraceae).
    GERALD HIRSCH, 1953 (Pezizales).

HANS LIPPOLD, 1932 (Flora of Cuba, Aceraceae, Sapindaceae, Apocynaceae).

HERMANN MANITZ, 1941 (Palynology, Convolvulaceae, nomenclature, bibliography).

Specialization in research: Flora of Europe, especially Mediterranean, the Near East; flora of Cuba.

Associated botanic garden: Botanischer Garten der Friedrich-Schiller Universität, Goetheallee 26.

Loans: In general to recognized botanical institutions.

Periodical and serial works: Beiträge zur Phytotaxonomie (in Wissenschaftl. Zeitschr. der Friedrich-Schiller Univ.); in collaboration with Thüringische Botanische Gesellschaft: Mitteilungen der Thüringischen Botanischen Gesellschaft.

Exchange: Available: Specimens from Europe and the Mediterranean. Desired: Specimens from all groups and regions.

Remarks: Botanical library of over 70.000 volumes, incorporated in the library of Thür. Bot. Ges.

JENA: *Schiller University,* (**SUJ**) – – discontinued.

JERUSALEM: *Herbarium, Department of Botany, The Hebrew University,* (**HUJ**), Givath Ram, Jerusalem, **Israel.**

Telephone: 972-2-584316.

Status: Unit of Division of Plant Systematics.

Foundation: 1928. *Number of specimens:* 600.000.

Herbarium: Mainly floras of the Middle East, with emphasis on Israel, Jordan, Sinai, Turkey, Iran and the Mediterranean.

Important collections: A. Eig, M. Zohary, N. Feinbrun (Middle Eastern collections from 1920 onwards).

Curator: CHAIA C. HEYN, 1924 (Biosystematics, Leguminosae, mosses of Israel).

Deputy curator: D. HELLER, 1936 (*Trifolium,* bibliography of Middle Eastern floras).

Staff members: A. DANIN, 1938 (Desert floras and vegetation).

NAOMI FEINBRUN, 1900 (Retired; cytotaxonomy, flora of Israel and Jordan).

ILANA HERRNSTADT, 1940 (Mosses of Israel).

FANIA KOLLMANN, 1916 (Retired; *Allium*).

J. LORCH, 1924 (Palaeobotany).

U. PLITMANN, 1936 (Biosystematics, Leguminosae, weeds).

A. SHMIDA, 1945 (Mountain floras, Cruciferae).

M. ZOHARY, 1898 (Retired; flora and vegetation of the Middle East).

Specialization in research: Flora of the Middle East, mosses of Israel, Leguminosae, Liliaceae, wild relatives of cultivated plants, biosystematics, chemo- and cytotaxonomy.

Associated botanic garden: The Botanic Garden of the Hebrew University.

Loans: To recognized botanical institutions.

Periodical and serial works: Flora Palaestina, Conspectus Florae Orientalis.

Exchange: Available: Mainly plants of Israel and Sinai. Desired: Plants of the Middle East, the Mediterranean and Central Asia.

JIHLAVA: *Herbarium, Muzeum Vysočiny,* (**MJ**), Nám. Míru 58, Jihlava, **Czechoslovakia.** (Information 1974).

Foundation: 1892. *Number of specimens:* 15.000.

Herbarium: Phanerogams and cryptogams of Czechoslovakia.

Specialization in research: Phytogeography, floristics.

Loans: To recognized botanical institutions.

Periodical and serial works: Vlasticědný sborník Vysočiny, oddíl věd přírodních.

JINAN: *Herbarium, Department of Biology, University of Shandong,* (**JSPC**), Jinan, Shandong, **People's Republic of China.**

Telephone: 43861.

Status: University.

Foundation: 1946. *Number of specimens:* 10.000.

Herbarium: Plants of Yunnan, Guangdong, Jiangxi, Zhejiang and Shandong Provinces.

Director: ZHOU GUANG-YU, 1924 (Ecology).

Curator: ZHENG YI-JIN, 1931 (Taxonomy).

Staff members: TANG PAN-CHANG, 1938 (Taxonomy).

ZHANG DE-SHAN, 1942 (Taxonomy).

Exchange: Yes.

JINAN: *Herbarium, Shantung Christian University,* (**SCU**), Jinan, Shandong, **People's Republic of China.**

Remarks: Present location unknown.

JOÃO PESSOA: *Herbário Lauro Pires Xavier, Departamento de Biologia, Centro de Ciências Exatas e da Natureza, Universidade Federal da Paraíba,* (**JPB**), Campus Universitário, 58.000 João Pessoa, Paraíba, **Brazil.**

Telephone: (55)224-7200.

Foundation: 1938. *Number of specimens:* 3.133.

Herbarium: Flora of Brazil, especially Paraíba.

Important collections: Lauro Pires Xavier.

Curator: ADERALDO LEOCÁDIO DA SILVA; 224-7200, ramal 2436 (Taxonomy of phanerogams).

Staff members: SEVERINA ACIOLI F. DE GOIS (Algae of freshwater).

CARLOS ALBERTO BELTRÃO DE MIRANDA (Taxonomy of phanerogams).

MARIA ALVES DE SOUSA (Fungi, especially Hymenochaetaceae).

Loans: To recognized botanical institutions.

JODHPUR: *Herbarium, Botanical Survey of India, Arid Zone Circle,* (**BSJO**), D-7 Shastri Nagar, Jodhpur-342003, Rajasthan, **India.**

Telephone: 22742.

Status: Government, Department of Science and Technology.

Foundation: 1972. *Number of specimens:* 10.000.

Herbarium: Plants of Northwestern India, especially Rajasthan and Gujarat.

Deputy Director: B. V. SHETTY, 1931 (Flora of South Indian hilltops and Western Rajasthan, cytotaxonomy, Vitaceae, Tamaricaceae).

Curator: V. SINGH, 1947 (Flora of Eastern Rajasthan, Zygophyllaceae).

Staff members: S. K. MALHOTRA, 1929 (Floristics).

R. P. PANDEY, 1952 (Flora of Western Rajasthan, ecology).

Specialization in research: Flora of Rajasthan, revision of Tamaricaceae and Zygophyllaceae for Flora of India.

Loans: By permission of director of Botanical Survey of India (CAL).

Exchange: Available: Plants of Rajasthan.

JODHPUR: *Herbarium, Department of Botany, University of Jodhpur,* **(JAC),** Jodhpur, **India.** (Information 1974)

Status: University.

Foundation: 1953. *Number of specimens:* 5.000.

Herbarium: Mostly desert plants of Rajasthan.

Important collections: Santisarup, M. M. Bhandri.

Specialization in research: Rajasthan flora, cytotaxonomy, biosystematics of desert plants.

Associated botanic garden: Botanical Gardens of the University of Jodhpur.

Loans: To recognized botanical institutions.

JOHANNESBURG: *Moss Herbarium, Department of Botany, University of the Witwatersrand,* **(J),** 1 Jan Smuts Avenue, Johannesburg 2001, **South Africa.**

Telephone: 011 39-4011 Ext. 401.

Status: Unit within Department of Botany.

Foundation: 1917. *Number of specimens:* 53.000.

Herbarium: South Africa, specializing in the flora of the Witwatersrand.

Important collections: C. E. Moss (S. Africa), H. B. Gilliland (Zimbabwe), A. O. D. Mogg (Inhaca Island), O. Kerfoot (Southern Africa), L. E. Davidson (S. Africa), K. A. Dahlstrand (S. Africa).

Director: C. F. CRESSWELL, 1933 (Head, Department of Botany, physiology).

Curator: L. E. DAVIDSON, 1916 (Flora of Blydepoort Nature Reserve).

Staff members: P. L. FORBES, 1925 (Cyperaceae). J. MUNDAY, 1928 (Poaceae and *Monechma*).

Specialization in research: Witwatersrand Flora.

Loans: In general to recognized botanical institutions.

Exchange: Available: Witwatersrand and other Southern African plants.

JOHNSON CITY: *Herbarium, Department of Biological Science, East Tennessee State University,* **(ETSU),** Johnson City, Tennessee 37614, **U.S.A.**

Telephone: 615/929-4350.

Number of specimens: 12.737.

Herbarium: Emphasis on flora of Tennessee.

Important collections: D. M. Brown (Roan Mountain), J. H. B. Garner (Indonesia), Frank Barclay (western North America and Canada).

Curator: JOHN C. WARDEN, 1930 (Systematics, ecology).

Specialization in research: Fungi, bryophytes, and vascular plants of the southern Appalachians.

Exchange: Yes.

JONESBORO: *Herbarium, Department of Biological Science, Arkansas State University,* **(STAR),** State University, Arkansas 72467, **U.S.A.**

Telephone: 501/972-3082.

Foundation: 1946. *Number of specimens:* 20.000.

Herbarium: General collections, especially from Arkansas and southeastern U.S.; comprehensive collections of Crowley's Ridge, Arkansas.

Important collections: Edward L. Richards, Delzie Demaree.

Director and Curator: EDWARD L. RICHARDS, 1927 (Compositae, flora of Arkansas).

Specialization in research: Compositae (*Ratibida*) and floristics of Arkansas.

Loans: Reputable herbarium requests, with reasonable time limit.

Exchange: Available: Arkansas specimens. Desired: Material from anywhere in the U.S. and New World tropics.

Remarks: Formerly listed under State University.

JOPLIN: *Herbarium, Biology Department, Missouri Southern State College,* **(MCJ),** Joplin, Missouri 64836, **U.S.A.**

Telephone: 417/624-8100.

Foundation: 1968. *Number of specimens:* 17.000.

Herbarium: Local flora; all groups.

Important collections: F. C. Seymour fungi exsiccati.

Co-Directors: JAMES R. JACKSON, 1947 (Ecological distribution and environmental variations; local flora).

E. SAM GIBSON, 1938 (Local flora; Colorado mountain flora; *Senecio* of North and Central America).

Staff member: L. J. GIER, 1904 (Bryophytes; Thuidiaceae of Latin America).

Specialization in research: Botanical survey of Center Creek drainage area (Jasper County, Missouri) pre-empoundment study; Thuidiaceae of Latin America; handbook of lichens, hepatics, and mosses of Missouri.

Associated botanic garden: Missouri Southern State College Wildlife Area and Outdoor Laboratory.

Loans: All groups except fungi exsiccati.

Exchange: Vascular plants of Missouri, Kansas,

Colorado, Central America.

JUIZ DE FORA: *Herbário, Centro de Ensino Superior de Juiz de Fora,* (**CESJ**), Caixa Postal 668, 36.100 Juiz de Fora, Minas Gerais, **Brazil.**
Telephone: (55)032/211-0255.
Foundation: 1969. *Number of specimens:* 18.000.
Herbarium: Flora of Minas Gerais.
Director and Curator: LEOPOLDO KRIEGER.
Loans: Yes.
Exchange: Yes.

JYVÄSKYLÄ: *Natural Science Collections, University of Jyväskylä,* (**JYV**), SF-40100 Jyväskylä 10, **Finland.**
Telephone: 358/41/291211.
Status: A division of the Museum, University of Jyväskylä.
Foundation: 1863. *Number of specimens:* 14.900 (Vascular plants 10.000, bryophytes 2.000, lichens 1.300, fungi 1.600).

Herbarium: Finnish, especially central Finnish flora.
Important collections: L. L. Laestadius, E. W. Blom.
Director: TERTTU RAATIKAINEN, 1934 (*Sorbus,* ecology and distribution of weeds).
Curator: VELI SAARI, 1944 (Vascular plants, bryophytes, macrofungi, flora of nature reserves).
Staff members: PERTTI ELORANTA, 1943 (Ecology of freshwater algae).
   VARPU ELORANTA, 1942 (Experimental algae study, algal tests).
   MIKKO RAATIKAINEN, 1932 (Ecology, distribution and sociology of weeds).
Specialization in research: Flora of central Finland; environmental conservation.
Loans: In general to recognized scientific institutions.
Periodical and serial works: Biol. Res. Rep. Univ. Jyväskylä, Jyväskylän yliopiston Biologian laitoksen Tiedonantoja.

K

KABUL: *Herbarium, University of Kabul,* (**KABA**), Kabul, **Afghanistan.**

KAGOSHIMA: *Herbarium, Kagoshima University,* (**KAG**), Kagoshima, **Japan.**

KALAMAZOO: *Clarence R. Hanes Herbarium, Department of Biology, Western Michigan University,* (**WMU**), Kalamazoo, Michigan 49008, **U.S.A.**
Telephone: 616/383-1674.
Status: State university.
Foundation: 1917. *Number of specimens:* 26.000.
Herbarium: General collections of worldwide distribution but emphasis on flora of southwestern Michigan and on local rare, threatened, and endangered species.
Important collections: C. R. and F. N. Hanes (Kalamazoo County, Michigan: 3.500), F. W. Rapp (Kalamazoo County, Michigan: 6.000), L. H. Harvey (Maine), L. Kenoyer, Upjohn medicinal plants.
  Director: RICHARD W. PIPPEN, 1935 (Systematics of Cacalioid genera, Asteraceae; rare and endangered species of southwestern Michigan).
  Specialization in research: Systematic and ecological studies of rare plants and habitats in southwestern Michigan.
  Loans: No special restrictions.
  Exchange: Available: Vascular plants of southwestern Michigan, some from Mexico and Belize. Desired: All groups of vascular plants from anywhere.

KAMAKURA: *Herbarium, Biological Institute, Yokohama University,* (**KAMA**), Kamakura, Kanagawa, **Japan.**

KAMLOOPS: *Herbarium, Agriculture Canada Research Station,* (**ACK**), 3015 Ord Road, Kamloops, British Columbia, **Canada** V2B 8A9.
Telephone: 604/376-5565.
Foundation: 1936. *Number of specimens:* 3.000.
Herbarium: Grasslands and forested rangelands of the British Columbia interior.
  Staff member: ALASTAIR MCLEAN.
  Specialization in research: Range ecology, management, soils and physiology.
  Loans: Usual regulations.
  Exchange: Limited.

KAMPALA: *Kawanda Herbarium,* (**KAW**), Kawanda Research Station, P.O. Box 7065, Kampala, **Uganda.**
Telephone: 67621/2/3.
Status: Agricultural research station.
Foundation: 1904. *Number of specimens:* 2.535.
Herbarium: Local herbarium with Uganda collection and limited collections from Kenya and Tanzania.

Important collections: Gramineae, Compositae, Papilionaceae, Rubiaceae, Polypodiaceae, Euphorbiaceae, Orchidaceae, Asclepiadaceae, Scrophulariaceae, Acanthaceae, Labiatae.
  Director: DEBORAH KYOBE, 1954 (Banana taxonomy).
  Curator: E. K. DDAMULIRA, 1921.
  Staff members: JANE NAKASINGA, 1959.
    JOHN WANAGALYA, 1956.
  Specialization in research: Research programs have just been initiated in crop taxonomy (bananas, sweet potatoes and cassava).
  Associated botanic garden: Entebbe Botanic Gardens, P.O. Box 40, Entebbe.
  Loans: Materials can be loaned for 12 months after which application has to be renewed by the user.
  Exchange: Hope to start as soon as possible.
  Remarks: Herbarium work has been pending for 9 years due to lack of taxonomists in the country, but some are being trained now.

KAMPALA: *Makerere Herbarium, Makerere University,* (**MHU**), P.O. Box 7062, Kampala, **Uganda.**
Telephone: 42 471-385.
Status: University.
Foundation: 1946. *Number of specimens:* 3.400.
Herbarium: Spermatophytes and thallophytes.
  Assistant Curator: A. B. KATENDE, 1926 (Trees and shrubs of East Africa).
  Staff members: E. Z. BUKENYA (*Solanum*).
    E. K. Z. KAKUDIDI, 1955 (Curatorial trainee).
    E. N. OGWAL, 1949 (*Commelina*).
  Specialization in research: East African vascular plants.
  Associated botanic garden: Makerere University Botanic Garden.

KANAZAWA: *Herbarium, Faculty of Science, University of Kanazawa,* (**KANA**), 1-1 Marunouchi, Kanazawa 920, Ishikawa, **Japan.**
Telephone: 0762-62-4281.
Status: University.
Foundation: 1950. *Number of specimens:* 100.000.
Herbarium: Bryophytes and spermatophytes of Japan.
  Director and Curator of Spermatophytes: NOBUO SATOMI, 1922 (Geobotany of spermatophytes).
  Curator of Bryophytes: ISAWO KAWAI, 1926 (Phylogeny of bryophytes).
  Staff member: SADAKO YOSHITAKE, 1926 (Systematic botany).
  Specialization in research: Geobotany of spermatophytes and phylogeny of bryophytes.
  Associated botanic garden: Botanic Garden of Kanazawa University.

Loans: With permission of director.
Exchange: Can be arranged.
Periodical and serial works: Science Reports of Kanazawa University.

KARACHI: *Herbarium, Department of Botany, University of Karachi,* (**KUH**), Karachi - 32, **Pakistan.**
Telephone: 418920.
Status: University.
Foundation: 1953. *Number of specimens:* 65.000.
Herbarium: General collection vascular plants.
  Director: S. I. ALI, 1930 (Legumes, flora of Pakistan, flora of Libya).
  Curator: SAEEDA QAISER (Ornamental trees and shrubs of Pakistan).
  Staff members: KHADIJA AZIZ (Aquatic plants of Pakistan).
    KAMAL AKHTAN MALIK, 1950 (Palmae, Acanthaceae of Pakistan).
    SYED NAZIMUDDUI, 1948 (Rubiaceae, Rhamnaceae of Pakistan).
    M. QAISER, 1946 (Flora of Pakistan, Tamaricaceae).
Specialization in research: Flora of Pakistan.
Loans: To recognized botanical institutions.
Periodical and serial works: Flora of Pakistan.
Exchange: Yes.

KARIYA: *Herbarium, Department of Biology, Aichi Kyoiku University,* (**AICH**), Igaya-cho, Kariya-shi, Aichi-ken 448, **Japan.**
Telephone: 0566-36-3111.
Status: University.
Foundation: 1977. *Number of specimens:* 10.000.
Herbarium: Vascular plants of Japan and Ryuku Islands.
  Director: Head of Department of Biology.
  Curator: SHUNSUKE SERIZAWA, 1948 (Taxonomy of pteridophytes).
Specialization in research: Pteridophytes of Japan and Ryuku Islands, flora of Aichi Prefecture.
Loans: To recognized botanical institutions.
Exchange: Available: Pteridophytes of Japan and Ryuku Islands. Desired: Pteridophytes of the world.

KARLSRUHE: *Herbarium, Landessammlungen f. Naturkunde,* (**KR**), Erbprinzenstrasse 13, D-7500 Karlsruhe 1, **Federal Republic of Germany,** BRD.
Telephone: 0721-21931.
Status: Museum of Natural History.
Foundation: 1780. *Number of specimens:* 260.000.
Herbarium: Phanerogams, ferns, musci, hepaticae, lichens, especially S.W. Germany.
Important collections: C. C. Gmelin, C. Doell, A. Kneucker, K. Mueller (Hepatics from S.W. Germany).
  Curator: GEORG PHILIPPI, 1936 (Hepaticae, musci).
  Staff member: ADAM HOELZER, 1946 (*Sphagnum*).

Specialization in research: SW. Germany, especially ecology.
Loans: Possible.
Periodical and serial works: Beiträge zur naturkundlichen Forschung in Südwest-deutschland.

KAŠPERSKÉ HORY: *Herbarium, Muzeum Šumavy,* (**KHMS**), přírodoveděcké pracov., Kašperské Hory, **Czechoslovakia.** (Information 1974)
Foundation: 1951. *Number of specimens:* 7.000.
Herbarium: Tracheophyta, bryophytes and lichens of Czechoslovakia, especially eastern and central Bohemia, Mount Šumava.

KASSEL: *Herbarium, Phytowissenschaftliche Abteilung, Naturkundemuseum im Ottoneum,* (**KASSEL**), Steinweg 2, BRD-3500 Kassel 1, **Federal Republic of Germany,** BRD.
Telephone: 05 61/7 87 40 14.
Status: Institute of the Community (Stadt Kassel).
Foundation: 1569. *Number of specimens:* 400.000.
Herbarium: Hesse, Germany, Mediterranean, Europe; Macaronesia; Chile, South America; Antarctica.
Important collections: Gerhard Follmann (Lichens), Arnold Grimme (Mosses), Georg Krasske (Diatoms), Caspar Ratzenberger (Oldest German plant collection), Carl Schildbach (Woods), Hermann Schulz (Galls, mines, phytopathogenic fungi).
  Director: GERHARD FOLLMANN, 1930 (Chemotaxonomy, phytosociology, lichenology).
  Curator: HANS WITZEL, 1928 (Mycology).
  Staff members: KARLHEINZ FINGERLE, 1935 (Bryology).
    HANNA MÜLLER, 1899 (Morphology).
    HEINZ WIEDEMANN, 1920 (Phytogeography, phytosociology).
Specialization in research: Floristics and vegetation of Hesse; chemotaxonomy, especially of lichens; world monograph of Roccellaceae; cryptogamic flora of Macaronesia.
Associated botanic garden: Botanischer Garten der Stadt Kassel, Park Schönfeld.
Loans: To recognized botanical institutions.
Periodical and serial works: Philippia. Abhandlungen und Berichte aus dem Naturkunde-museum im Ottoneum zu Kassel.
Exchange: Available: Lichenes Exsiccati Selecti a Museo Historiae Naturalis Casselensi Editi; vascular plants of Hesse.

KATOWICE: *Herbarium, Department of Plant Systematics, Silesian University,* (**KTU**), Jagiellońska 28, 40-032 Katowice, **Poland.**
Telephone: 518-811.
Status: Directed by Silesian University.
Foundation: 1972. *Number of specimens:* 25.000.
Herbarium: Vascular plants of Upper Silesia.
Important collections: Oenothera of Europe.
  Director: KRZYSZTOF ROSTAŃSKI, 1930 (Tax-

onomy of *Oenothera, Euphorbia* and *Valeriana*).
Curator: ANDRZEJ SENDEK, 1933 (Floristics, vascular plants of Silesia).
Staff members: ELŻBIETA KRAWCZYK, 1948.
FRANCISZEK LUDERS, 1904.
ROMUALDA SUMARA, 1952.
Specialization in research: Flora of Upper Silesia, influence of industrial air pollution on forests.
Loans: To recognized institutions.
Periodical and serial works: Acta Biologica Katowice.
Exchange: Available: Silesian vascular plants. Desired: Vascular plants, especially Eurasia.

KAUNAS: *Vytauto Didžiojo Universiteto Augalu Sistematikos Kabineta,* **(KA)**, Kaunas, Freda, Lithuania, **U.S.S.R.** (Information 1974)
Herbarium: Plants of Lithuania.
Important collections: C. Regel.

KAZAN: *Herbarium, Department of Botany, Lenin University of Kazan,* **(KAZ)**, Lenin St. 18, 420008 Kazan, **U.S.S.R.**
Status: University.
Foundation: 1830. *Number of specimens:* 77.000 (50.000 vascular plants, 27.000 non-vascular plants, mainly lichens).
Curator: A. G. SMIRNOV.

KEELE: *E. S. Edees Herbarium, Department of Biological Sciences, University of Keele,* **(KLE)**, Keele, Staffs. ST5 5BG, England, **Great Britain.**
Telephone: 0782/621111, Ext. 512.
Status: University.
Foundation: 1955. *Number of specimens:* 12.000.
Herbarium: British flora.
Director: K. M. GOODWAY, 1930 (Evolutionary genetics).
Associated botanic garden: Yes.
Loans: To recognized botanical institutions.

KEENE: *Herbarium, Biology Department, Keene State College,* **(KESC)**, 229 Main Street, Keene, New Hampshire 03431, **U.S.A.**
Telephone: 603/352-1909.
Foundation: 1969. *Number of specimens:* 15.000.
Herbarium: Mainly vascular plants.
Curator: DAVID GREGORY.
Exchange: Available.

KEFAR MALAL: *Herbarium, Independent Biological Laboratories,* **(IBL)**, P.O.B. Ramatayin, Kefar Malal, **Israel.** (Information 1974)
Status: Private foundation.
Foundation: 1929.
Herbarium: Algae of Palestine and Transjordan.
Specialization in research: Ecology and industrial uses of algae.
Periodical and serial works: Bulletin.

KEIGHELY: *Borough Museum,* **(KGY)** – *see* BRADFORD (CMM).

KENEMA: *Kenema Forestry Herbarium, Forestry Research Office,* **(FHK)**, c/o Divisional Forest Office, Bambawo via Kenema, **Sierra Leone,** West Africa.
Status: Department of Forestry.
Foundation: 1964. *Number of specimens:* 2.857.
Herbarium: A small collection used for identification; duplicates at Fourah Bay College, University of Sierra Leone.
Director of Forest Research Branch: HASSAN R. S. MOHAMMED, 1947 (Silviculture).
Curator: SOSO K. SAMAI, 1943.
Staff members: S. D. BOCKARI, 1950.
A. M. KAMARA, 1949.
SHARKA KOROMA, 1954.
ERNEST NEGBEMA.
Specialization in research: Silviculture, especially provenance trials of indigenous and exotic species.
Associated botanic garden: Kenema Nursery Arboretum.
Exchange: Available: Specimens of forest trees.

KENNETT SQUARE: *Longwood Gardens,* **(KEN)**, Kennett Square, Pennsylvania 19348, **U.S.A.**
Telephone: 215/388-6741.
Status: Private foundation.
Foundation: 1955. *Number of specimens:* 6.500.
Herbarium: Cultivated ornamentals, temperate and tropical.
Director: EVERITT L. MILLER, 1918.
Curator: DONALD G. HUTTLESTON, 1920 (Cultivated ornamentals).
Staff member: FREDERICK P. DARKE, 1952.
Associated botanic garden: Longwood Gardens.
Loans: Normal regulations.
Exchange: None.

KENOSHA: *Herbarium, Department of Biology, Carthage College,* **(CART)**, 2001 Alford Drive, Kenosha, Wisconsin 53141, **U.S.A.**
Telephone: 414/551-8500.
Foundation: 1921. *Number of specimens:* 13.000.
Herbarium: Flora of Hancock County, Illinois.
Important collections: Alice L. Kibbe.
Director: R. M. TIEFEL, 1928 (Plant morphology).

KENT: *Herbarium, Department of Biological Sciences, Kent State University,* **(KE)**, Kent, Ohio 44242, **U.S.A.**
Telephone: 216/672-2266.
Foundation: 1921. *Number of specimens:* 60.000.
Herbarium: Vascular plants of eastern U.S., especially Ohio; mycoflora of Great Lakes region.
Important collections: Ohio vascular plant collections of Tom S. Cooperrider, Allison W. Cusick, and Almon N. Rood; eastern North American mycological collections of Samuel J. Mazzer.

Curator of Phanerogamic Collections: TOM S. COOPERRIDER, 1927 (Ohio flora; *Chelone, Lysimachia*).

Curator of Cryptogamic Collections: SAMUEL J. MAZZER, 1934 (Mycoflora of Great Lakes region; mycogeographic relationships between eastern Asia and North America).

Staff members: MIWAKO K. COOPERRIDER (Hybridization in *Quercus*).

ALAN K. GRAHAM, 1934 (Vegetational history; Lythraceae, with Shirley A. Graham).

Associated botanic garden: University Arboretum and Botanical Gardens.

Loans: To recognized institutions.

Exchange: Available: Vascular plants of Ohio. Desired: Vascular plants and fungi of eastern North America and eastern Asia.

KEPONG: *Forest Research Institute,* (**KEP**), Kepong, Selangor, **Malaysia.**

Telephone: 03-662633.

Status: Government, Forest Department.

Foundation: 1918. *Number of specimens:* 115.000.

Herbarium: Trees of Malaya, Sabah and Sarawak, especially Dipterocarpaceae and Palmae.

Director: SALLEH MOHD NOR, 1940 (Forest inventory).

Curator: K. M. KOCHUMMEN (Tree flora of Malay Peninsula).

Staff members: CHAN YEE CHONG.

MAT ASRI BIN NGAH.

Specialization in research: Tree flora of Malaya.

Associated botanic garden: Arboretum of native species, especially Dipterocarpaceae.

Loans: To recognized institutions.

Periodical and serial works: The Malaysian Forester, Research Pamphlets and Malaya Forest Record (private circulation).

Exchange: Available: Tree specimens from Malay Peninsula. Desired: Tree specimens from all groups in S.E. Asia.

KEW: *Herbarium, Commonwealth Mycological Institute,* (**IMI**), Ferry Lane, Kew, Richmond, Surrey TW9 3AF, England, **Great Britain.**

Telephone: 01-940-4086 or 4087.

Status: A unit of the Commonwealth Agricultural Bureaux organization.

Foundation: 1921. *Number of specimens:* 250.000.

Herbarium: Microfungi, worldwide, including many plant pathogens from Commonwealth countries; also fungi of importance in industry, soil and forestry.

Director: A. JOHNSTON.

Assistant director: C. BOOTH (Pyrenomycetes, especially Hypocreales incl. anamorphs *Fusarium, Cylindrocarpon*).

Principal mycologist: B. C. SUTTON (Deuteromycetes, especially Coelomycetes, *Eucalyptus* microfungi).

Staff members: J. F. BRADBURY (Plant pathogenic bacteria).

B. KITTY BRADY (Hyphomycetes-Moniliaceae, *Vertillium, Trichoderma*).

SHIELA M. FRANCIS (*Alternaria*, Peronosporales).

D. L. HAWKSWORTH (Ascomycetes, lichens).

P. M. KIRK (Hyphomycetes-Dematiaceae, Zygomycetes).

D. W. MINTER (Hyphomycetes-Moniliales, Lophodermataceae, Pine microfungi).

J. ELIZABETH M. MORDUE (*Colletotrichum, Pestalotiopsis*, Uredinales, Ustilaginales).

AGNES H. S. ONIONS (Culture collection, *Penicillium, Aspergillus,* Paecilomyces).

E. PUNITHALINGAM (Sphaeropsidales).

A. SIVANESAN (Ascomycetes).

D. JEAN STAMPS (Phycomycetes, especially *Phytophthora, Pythium*).

PHYLLIS M. STOCKDALE (Medical fungi, Gymnoascaceae).

Specialization in research: The taxonomy and nomenclature of micro-fungi, especially groups including economically important plant pathogens.

Loans: In general to recognized mycological institutions.

Periodical and serial works: Review of Plant Pathology; Review of Medical and Vet. Mycology; Mycological Papers; Index of Fungi; Bibliography of Systematic Mycology; Phytopathological Papers; CMI Descriptions of Pathogenic Fungi and Bacteria; CMI/AAB Descriptions of Plant Viruses; CMI Distribution Maps of Plant Diseases.

Exchange: Microfungi.

Remarks: A large culture collection forms an integral part of the Herbarium.

KEW: *The Herbarium, Royal Botanic Gardens,* (**K**), Kew, Richmond, Surrey TW9 3AB, England, **Great Britain.**

Telephone: 01-940 1171/4.

Status: State institution.

Foundation: 1841 (RBG, Kew, as government institution), 1853 herbarium and library. *Number of specimens:* over 5.000.000.

Herbarium: Worldwide herbarium specially rich in types and in collections from tropical Africa, tropical Asia, Australasia and in specimens of Orchidaceae, Gramineae and larger fungi.

· *Important collections:* E. F. André, R. Baron, G. Bentham, M. J. Berkeley (fungi), W. Borrer, W. J. Burchell, G. C. Churchill, C. B. Clarke, M. C. Cooke (fungi), A. Cunningham, J. F. Duthie, J. R. & G. Forster, J. S. Gamble, G. Gardner, J. Gay, A. Gonan, W. Hancock, G. B. Hinton, H. J. Howard (Myxomycetes), A. Henry, J. D. & W. J. Hooker, A. F. G. Kerr, F. C. Lehmann, J. Lightfoot, J. Lindley (K-L, orchids), J. T. Moggridge, T. Moore (Ferns), R. C. A. Prior, J. P. Rottler, R. Spruce, N. Wallich (K-W), H. C. Watson (K-WA), E. A. Willmott, E. H. Wilson.

Director: J. P. M. BRENAN, 1917 (Tropical Africa, Chenopodiaceae, Old World Commelinaceae, Leguminosae, Mimosoideae).

Deputy Director and Keeper: P. S. GREEN, 1920 (SW. Pacific, Oleaceae).

Deputy Keeper: G. LL. LUCAS, 1935 (Conservation).

Assistant keepers: W. D. CLAYTON, 1926 (Gramineae).

L. L. FORMAN, 1929 (Tropical eastern Asia, Menispermaceae, Fagaceae).

F. N. HEPPER, 1929 (Tropical Africa, Scrophulariaceae, Lemnaceae).

D. A. REID, 1927 (Fungi, temperate and tropical basidiomycetes).

C. C. TOWNSEND, 1926 (Eastern Mediterranean region and SW. Asia, especially Iraq, *Haplophyllum*, Amaranthaceae).

Staff members: A. G. BAILEY, 1933 (Plant quarantine, Gasteromycetes).

THALIA A. BENCE, 1938 (Index Kewensis).

IRENE BLEWETT, 1922 (General Service Unit).

JEAN K. BOWDEN, 1930 (Biographical studies, Kew Bulletin).

DIANE M. BRIDSON, 1942 (African Rubiaceae).

GAIL L. R. BROMLEY, 1950 (Verbenaceae).

R. K. BRUMMITT, 1937 (Flora Zambesiaca, African Leguminosae and Acanthaceae, *Calystegia*; nomenclature).

VERA CHIDZEY, 1939 (Kew Bulletin).

M. J. E. COODE, 1937 (Elaeocarpaceae; Kew Bulletin).

T. A. COPE, 1949 (Gramineae).

E. JILL COWLEY, 1940 (*Roscoea, Cautleya*).

P. J. CRIBB, 1946 (Orchidaceae).

FRANCES G. DAVIES, 1944 (Compositae).

J. DRANSFIELD, 1945 (Palmae).

I. K. FERGUSON, 1938 (Palynology).

D. V. FIELD, 1937 (Asclepiadaceae, *Gloriosa*).

C. GREY-WILSON, 1944 (Temperate Asia, *Impatiens, Dionysia*, Magnoliaceae).

J. W. GRIMES, 1950 (Pteridophyta).

PATRICIA HALLIDAY, 1930 (SW. Asian Compositae).

R. M. HARLEY, 1936 (Neotropics, Labiatae).

SUSAN HOLMES, 1933 (Succulent *Euphorbia*).

E. R. HOLTTUM, Honorary Associate, 1895 (Pteridophyta).

SHEILA S. HOOPER, 1925 (Cyperaceae, especially Africa).

D. R. HUNT, 1938 (New World Commelinaceae, Cactaceae, cultivated plants).

FRANCES M. JARRETT, 1931 (Pteridophyta, *Artocarpus*).

C. JEFFREY, 1934 (Temperate Asia, Compositae, Cucurbitaceae).

G. P. LEWIS, 1952 (Neotropical Leguminosae).

W. MARAIS, 1929 (Mascarene Is., petaloid monocots).

B. F. MATHEW, 1936 (*Crocus*, petaloid monocots).

S. J. MAYO, 1949 (Araceae).

R. D. MEIKLE, 1923 (Eastern Mediterranean, Cyprus, Salicaceae).

SARAH F. OLDFIELD, 1955 (Conservation).

D. N. PEGLER, 1938 (Fungi, tropical Agaricales).

D. PHILCOX, 1926 (Neotropics, tropical Scrophulariaceae).

J. LESLEY M. PINNER, 1932 (Index Kewensis).

DIANA M. POLHILL, 1934 (Flora of Tropical Africa).

R. M. POLHILL, 1937 (Flora of Tropical Africa, Leguminosae).

MADELINE M. POOLE, 1945 (Palynology).

A. RADCLIFFE-SMITH, 1938 (Euphorbiaceae).

S. A. RENVOIZE, 1944 (Gramineae).

M. J. S. SANDS, 1938 (*Balanites, Begonia*).

B. M. SPOONER, 1951 (Ascomycetes).

B. L. STANNARD, 1944 (African Simaroubaceae).

N. P. TAYLOR, 1956 (Cultivated plants, Cactaceae).

P. G. TAYLOR, 1926 (Orchidaceae, *Utricularia*).

B. VERDCOURT, 1925 (Tropical Africa, African Papilionaceae and Rubiaceae, Convolvulaceae).

G. E. WICKENS, 1927 (NE. Africa, Arabia).

J. J. WOOD, 1952 (Orchidaceae).

Stationed at the British Museum (Natural History), BM:

E. LAUNERT, 1926 (Flora Zambesiaca, African Gramineae, *Marsilea*).

Jodrell Laboratory

Keeper: K. JONES, 1926 (Chromosome evolution and cytotaxonomy of angiosperms, Commelinaceae).

Staff members: P. E. BRANDHAM, 1937 (Chromosomes and evolution in Aloineae).

CHRISTINE A. BRIGHTON, 1945 (Chromosomes of *Crocus*).

D. F. CUTLER, 1939 (Experimental and comparative anatomy, particularly in Liliales).

J. DICKIE, 1952 (Physiology of seed germination in Leguminosae).

LINDA FELLOWS, 1943 (Biochemistry of Tephrosieae and Dalbergieae).

D. J. C. FOX, 1937 (Design of apparatus, mathematic modes of seed germination, computerization of seed bank).

ROWENA M. O. GALE, 1944 (Plant anatomy, enquiry service).

MARY GREGORY, 1932 (Literature of anatomy and experimental taxonomy).

MARGARET A. T. JOHNSON, 1946 (Chromosomes of Liliaceae and some Cactaceae, *Mamillaria*).

ANN Y. KENTON, 1951 (Chromosome evolution, Commelinaceae).

C. R. METCALFE, Honorary Associate, 1904 (Systematic anatomy).

S. J. Owens, 1947 (Breeding systems in Commelinaceae).

T. Reynolds, 1933 (Biochemistry, secondary metabolites, especially those showing growth-regulating properties, isoenzymes).

P. Rudall, 1954 (Systematic anatomy, Labiatae).

R. D. Smith, 1945 (Seed storage and collection).

Margaret Y. Stant, 1926 (Comparative and developmental anatomy, seed micro-morphology, Caryophyllaceae, Commelinaceae).

Museums: Rosemary C. R. Angel, 1925 (Economic botany).

Bentham-Moxon staff: H. K. Airy Shaw, 1902 (Plant classification, Euphorbiaceae of tropical Asia).

Government of Iraq: Evan Guest, 1902 (Flora of Iraq).

Specialization in research: Floras of tropical Africa, Australia, Cyprus, Iraq, Mascarenes; Orchidaceae, Gramineae, fungi, pteridophyta. No official research is now carried out on algae, bryophyta, and lichens. Kew collections of these groups are on permanent loan to British Museum (Natural History).

Associated botanic garden: Royal Botanic Gardens, Kew (Kew and Wakehurst Place).

Loans: Loans may be made at the Director's discretion when these do not interfere with the work of the Institution, except from the original Wallich Herbarium (K-W). A copy of the regulations concerning loans can be supplied on application to the Director, to whom all requests for loans must be made.

Periodical and serial works: Index Kewensis; Kew Bulletin: Icones Plantarum; Botanical Magazine; Kew Record of Taxonomic Literature.

Exchange: Worldwide, but especially from the tropics.

Remarks: Botanical Library of over 120.000 bound volumes, about 2.000 current periodicals and serials, about 140.000 separates and reprints, over 175.000 paintings, drawings and photographs of plants, 250.000 letters, manuscripts etc., and 10.000 sheet maps.

KHARTOUM: *Herbarium, Forest Research and Education Institute,* **(KHF)**, Soba, Khartoum, **Sudan.** (Information 1974)
Status: Directed by state.
Foundation: 1962. *Number of specimens:* 4.500.
Herbarium: Plants of Sudan, especially forest timber trees and economic plants.
Specialization in research: African flora, especially Sudan.
Associated botanic garden: Khartoum Botanic Garden and Forest Arboreta.
Loans: With permission of director.
Periodical and serial works: Forests Research Institute Pamphlets, Soba; F. R. I. Bulletin.

KHARTOUM: *Herbarium, University of Khartoum,* **(KHU)**, Khartoum, **Sudan.**

KIEL: *Botanisches Institut der Universität Kiel,* **(KIEL)**, Biologiezentrum Olshausenstrasse 40-60, D-2300 Kiel, **Federal Republic of Germany,** BRD.
Telephone: 0431/880-4285, -4286, -4300.
Status: Department of the University of Kiel.
Foundation: 1875. *Number of specimens:* 65.000.
Important collections: Phanerogams worldwide, especially Schleswig-Holstein (Northern Germany), bryophytes, lichens.
Director: Klaus Dierssen, 1948 (Phytosociology, bryophytes).
Staff members: Ernst-Wilhelm Raabe, 1913 (Phanerogams).
Hartmut Usinger, 1938 (Palynology, bryophytes).
Specialization in research: Phytosociology, palynology, floristics of Central Europe.
Associated botanic garden: Botanical Garden of the Botanical Department.
Loans: To all recognized botanical institutions.

KIEV: *N. G. Kholodny Institute of Botany of the Academy of Sciences of the Ukrainian SSR,* **(KW)**, Repin Street 2, Kiev 252601, **U.S.S.R.**
Telephone: 24-40-41.
Status: State institute.
Foundation: 1931. *Number of specimens:* 1.000.000.
Herbarium: General collections, mainly Ukrainian plants.
Important collections: W. G. Besser, W. M. Czernjaew, J. E. Gilibert, A. S. Rogowicz, I. Th. Schmalhausen, N. von Turczaninov.
Director: K. M. Sytnik, 1926 (Plant physiology).
Curators of the Vascular Plant Herbarium: T. J. Omelczuk-Mjakuschko, 1933 (Taxonomy of Alliaceae, Crassulaceae and *Stachys*).
B. V. Zarerucha, 1927 (Flora and phytogeography of western regions of Ukrainian SSR).
Curators of the Bryological Herbarium: A. Th. Baczurina, 1908 (Ukrainian bryoflora, especially peat bogs).
L. J. Partyka, 1932 (Ukrainian bryoflora, especially Crimea and Carpathian Mountains).
Curators of the Mycological Herbarium: I. A. Dudka, 1934 (Fungi, especially Hyphomycetes).
L. V. Smyk, 1937 (Fungi, especially Ascomycetes, Sphaeriales).
Curators of the Lichenological Herbarium: O. B. Blum, 1937 (Taxonomy, geography and ecology of lichens).
E. G. Kopaczevskaja, 1927 (Taxonomy and geography of lichens).
Specialization in research: Taxonomy and geography of wild plants of the Ukrainian SSR.
Loans: To recognized botanical institutions.

Periodical and serial works: Ukrainian Botanical Journal (formerly Botanical Journal of the Academy of Sciences of the Ukrainian SSR), Novitates Systematicae plantarum vascularium et non vascularium.

Exchange: Available: Plants of Ukrainian SSR. Desired: Plants of world, especially Europe.

KIEV: *Herbarium, Central Republic Botanical Garden of the Ukrainian Academy of Sciences,* (**KWHA**), Timiryazevskaya Street 1, Kiev 14, Ukraine 252014 **U.S.S.R.**

Telephone: 95-04-80.

Status: State institute.

Foundation: 1948. *Number of specimens:* 120.000.

Herbarium: Vascular plants of U.S.S.R., native and introduced.

Director: A. M. GRODZINSKY, 1926 (Plant physiology).

Head of Department of Flora: I. I. SIKURA, 1932 (Introduction of native flora, Middle Asia).

Curator: I. I. MOROZ, 1937 (Introduction of native flora, Caryophyllaceae).

Specialization in research: Flora of U.S.S.R., especially medicinal, ornamental and other groups of interest for introduction.

Associated botanic garden: Yes.

Loans: To recognized botanical institutions.

Periodical and serial works: Ukrainian Botanical Journal, Introduction and Acclimatization in Ukraine Yearbook.

Exchange: Available: Ukrainian flora, wild and cultivated. Desired: Asteraceae, Caryophyllaceae, Orchidaceae, *Gentiana*, *Campanula*, Liliaceae from any area; plants of Europe and Mediterranean Region.

KIMBERLEY: *Herbarium, Alexander McGregor Memorial Museum,* (**KMG**), P.O. Box 316, 2 Egerton Rd., Kimberley C. P. 8300, **South Africa.**

Telephone: 0531-28311; 0531-25862.

Status: Directed by a Board of Trustees.

Foundation: 1908. *Number of specimens:* 10.000.

Herbarium: Plants of Northern Cape, South Africa; some preserved and carpological collections.

Important collections: W. Wilman (Griqualand West), O. A. Leistner (Southern Kalahari).

Director: RICHARD LIVERSIDGE.

Curator: ANDREW GUBB, 1950 (Ecology, vegetation of N. Cape).

Staff member: BERNARD EVERYDAY, 1957.

Specialization in research: Synecological and syntaxonomical classification of the vegetation of the Northern Cape, identification of rumen contents of game animals.

Associated botanic garden: Alex Hall Botanic Garden.

Loans: With permission of the director.

KING'S LYNN: *Herbarium, Museum and Art Gallery,* (**KLN**), King's Lynn, England, **Great Britain** – – incorporated in NWH.

KINGSTON: *Herbarium, The Institute of Jamaica,* (**IJ**), 12-14 East Street, Kingston, **Jamaica.**

Telephone: 809/922-0620, ext. 12, 31.

Status: Part of the Natural History Division, The Institute of Jamaica, a government-supported cultural organization.

Foundation: 1879. *Number of specimens:* 107.000.

Herbarium: Regional collection containing material from nearly all the West Indian islands and most continental areas bordering the Caribbean Sea and Gulf of Mexico.

Important collections: W. Buch (Haiti), D. S. Correll (Bahamas), E. L. Ekman (Haiti), P. Gentle (Belize), G. B. Hinton (Mexico), G. R. Proctor (Jamaica, Cayman Islands, Lesser Antilles, Central America).

Curator: G. R. PROCTOR, 1920 (Flora of Jamaica and the West Indies; pteridophytes).

Staff members: L. GREEN, 1929 (Marine algae of the Caribbean).

S. C. SINHA, 1935 (Morphology of *Acacia*).

Specialization in research: Taxonomy and distribution of the Caribbean flora.

Loans: To recognized botanical institutions.

Periodical and serial works: Bulletin of the Institute of Jamaica, Science Series; Sloanea (occasional papers).

Exchange: Available: Mainly Jamaican plants. Wanted: Specimens from the Caribbean area, including Central America, etc.

KINGSTON: *Herbarium, Department of Botany, University of Rhode Island,* (**KIRI**), Kingston, Rhode Island 02881, **U.S.A.**

Telephone: 401/792-2161.

Foundation: 1892. *Number of specimens:* 15.000.

Herbarium: Mostly Rhode Island collections.

Important collections: Walter H. Snell (mycology).

Curator: RICHARD L. HAUKE, 1930 (Systematics of *Equisetum*).

Specialization in research: Local flora.

Loans: To recognized institutions.

KINGSTON: *Fowler Herbarium, Biology Department, Queen's University,* (**QK**), Kingston, Ontario, **Canada** K7L 3N6.

Telephone: 613/547-6675.

Foundation: 1860. *Number of specimens:* 120.000.

Herbarium: Mostly vascular plants; good collection of local and arctic bryophytes and lichens; very few algae or fungi.

Important collections: Old historic Canadian collections of J. Fowler, J. Macoun, R. Bell, A. Drummond, B. Billings, R. E. Beschel (Canadian and Russian arctic, Greenland, Finland), J. E. Roy.

Curator: ADÈLE CROWDER, 1926 (Ecology; *Drosera*).

Staff members: A. E. GARWOOD (Flora of eastern

Ontario and Arizona).

Specialization in research: Flora of eastern Ontario; moss flora of eastern Ontario.

Loans: Six months, except by special arrangement.

Exchange: Available: Local vascular plants and bryophytes; some arctic material.

KINGSTON: *Herbarium, Department of Botany, University of the West Indies,* (**UCWI**), Mona, Kingston 7, **Jamaica.**

Telephone: 809/927-0753.

Foundation: 1950. *Number of specimens:* 70.000.

Herbarium: West Indies, especially Jamaica.

Important collections: William Harris (Jamaica, 1890–1918), J. Campbell (Jamaica), P. Sintenis (Puerto Rico, 1884–1887), C. D. Adams, G. R. Proctor, W. R. Anderson, M. Crosby, E. B. and H. A. Hespenheide, D. Sternberg, R. A. Howard, N. L. Britton, J. Hart, D. Morris.

Curator: MERLYN ALLWOOD, 1921 (Identification of flowering plants).

Loans: None.

Exchange: None.

KINGSVILLE: *Herbarium, Biology Department, Texas Arts and Industries University,* (**TAIC**), P.O. Box 158, Kingsville, Texas 78363, **U.S.A.**

Telephone: 512/595-3803.

Status: Directed by the state.

Foundation: 1932. *Number of specimens:* 5.000.

Herbarium: Mostly southern Texas.

Director: GEORGE G. WILLIGES, 1924.

KIROVSK: *Herbarium, S. M. Kirov Polar-Alpine Botanical Garden, Kolsk Branch of USSR Academy of Science, Laboratory of Flora and Plant Resources,* (**KPABG**), Kirovsk, **U.S.S.R.**

Foundation: 1931. *Number of specimens:* 63.000. (50.000 arctic plants, 13.000 introduced plants).

Director: M. L. RAMENSKAJA.

KISHINEV: *Herbarium, Botanical Garden of the Academy of Sciences of the Moldavian SSR,* (**CHIS**), 18 Lesnaja Street, 277018 Kishinev, **U.S.S.R.**

Telephone: 55-61-69.

Status: State institute.

Foundation: 1948. *Number of specimens:* 160.000.

Herbarium: All groups of plants from Moldavian SSR, some from other areas of U.S.S.R. and West Europe.

Director: A. A. CHEBOTARU, 1932 (Embryology).

Curator: T. S. HEIDEMAN, 1903 (Floristics, geobotany).

Staff members: S. I. MANIK, 1947 (Fungi).

L. P. NICOLAJEVA, 1925 (Floristics, geobotany).

A. F. RAILJAN, 1946 (Systematics).

G. P. SIMONOV, 1924 (Mosses, lichens).

C. R. VITKO, 1934 (Floristics, geobotany).

Specialization in research: Flora of the Moldavian SSR.

Associated botanic garden: Botanical Garden of the Academy of Sciences of the Moldavian SSR.

KISHINEV: *Herbarium, Faculty of Agriculture,* (**CHISA**), Kishinev, **U.S.S.R.**

KITWE: *Herbarium, Forest Department, Ministry of Lands and Natural Resources,* (**NDO**), P.O. Box 2099, Kitwe, **Zambia.**

Telephone: 210456.

Status: Government Department.

Foundation: 1931. *Number of specimens:* 40.000.

Herbarium: Woody and herbaceous plants, including grasses, of Zambia.

Curator: S. M. CHISUMPA, 1948 (Forest ecology).

Specialization in research: Vegetation and plant distribution; identification.

Loans: For one year only.

Periodical and serial works: Forest Research Pamphlets, Bulletins, Notes.

Exchange: Yes.

KLAGENFURT: *Landesherbar, Landesmuseum für Kärnten,* (**KL**), Museumgasse 2, A-9010 Klagenfurt, **Austria.**

Telephone: 04222-33603.

Status: Department of Amt der Kärntner Landesregierung.

Foundation: 1848. *Number of specimens:* 100.000.

Herbarium: Alpine and European plants, especially plants of Carinthia.

Important collections: Herbaria of A. Traunfellner, D. Pacher, Benz, Sabidussi, Glantschnig, A. Neumann (*Rubus* of Carinthia), Tobisch (fungi), J. Steiner (lichens of Carinthia).

Director of Museum: GERNOF PICCOTTINI.

Curator: GERFRIED H. LEUTE, 1941; ext. 636.

Staff member: ISOLDE E. MÜLLER, 1953 (Flora Mitteleuropas).

Specialization in research: Flora of Carinthia, taxonomy of Apiaceae.

Associated botanic garden: Botanischer Garten des Landes Kärnten, Kinkstrasse 6, A-9020 Klagenfurt.

Loans: To recognized botanical institutions.

Periodical and serial works: Carinthia II.

Exchange: Available: Plants of Carinthia and eastern Alps. Desired: European plants, Apiaceae from all parts of world.

KNOXVILLE: *Herbarium, Department of Botany, University of Tennessee,* (**TENN**), Knoxville, Tennessee 37916, **U.S.A.**

Telephone: 615/974-2256.

Foundation: 1888, destroyed by fire in 1934 and immediately re-established. *Number of specimens:* 400.000.

Herbarium: Vascular plants of Tennessee, southern Appalachians, Great Smoky Mountain National

Park, Mexico, Guatemala; fungi chiefly of southeastern U.S.; bryophytes and pteridophytes of the world.
Important collections: Zodda (bryophytes), A. J. Sharp (bryophytes and vascular plants of southern Appalachians, Mexico, and Guatemala), L. R. Hesler (fungi of southern Appalachians; many types).

Director: A. MURRAY EVANS, 1932 (Pteridophytes and flowering plants).

Curator: B. EUGENE WOFFORD, 1943 (Flowering plants).

Staff members: R. H. PETERSEN, 1934 (Fungi).
    E. E. SCHILLING, JR., 1953 (Flowering plants).
    A. J. SHARP, 1904, Emeritus Curator of Bryophytes.
    D. K. SMITH, 1946 (Bryophytes).

Specialization in research: Tennessee flora; mosses of Mexico; pteridophytes of southeastern U.S.; tropical polypodioid ferns; bryophytes of Tennessee, Alaska, and the Aleutians; *Solanum, Helianthus*; flavonoid systematics; taxonomy of Basidiomycetes.

Associated botanic garden: University of Tennessee Arboretum, Department of Forestry, University of Tennessee.

Loans: To any accredited institution.

Periodical and serial works: Contributions from the Botanical Laboratory, The University of Tennessee, New Series.

Exchange: Available: Tennessee and southeastern U.S. plants. Desired: Latin American and Old World plants.

KÓRNIK: *Herbarium, Institute of Dendrology,* **(KOR),** ul. Parkowa 5, 62-035 Kórnik (near Poznań), **Poland.**

Telephone: 165.

Status: Polish Academy of Sciences.

Foundation: 1952. *Number of specimens:* 50.000.

Herbarium: Trees and shrubs, especially Poland, eastern Mediterranean region and southwest Asia.

Director: WŁADYSŁAW BUGAŁA, 1924 (Dendrology).

Curator: KAZIMIERZ BROWICZ, 1925 (Taxonomy and geography of woody plants: *Colutea, Periploca,* W. Asiatic Prunoideae and Pomoideae).

Staff members: ADAM BORATYŃSKI, 1948 (Geobotany).

    JERZY ZIELINSKI, 1943 (Taxonomy and geography of *Rosa*).

Specialization in research: Taxonomy and geography of woody plants of southwest Asia and eastern Mediterranean region.

Associated botanic garden: Kórnik Arboretum.

Loans: To recognized botanical institutions.

Periodical and serial works: Arboretum Kórnickie, Atlas of Distribution of Trees and Shrubs in Poland.

Exchange: Available: Polish trees and shrubs, cultivated plants. Desired: W. Asiatic and Mediterranean woody plants.

KOŠICE: *Katedra biológie Prírodovedeckej fakulty Univerzity P. J. Safárika,* **(KO),** Kuzmanyho 12, Košice, **Czechoslovakia.**

KRAKÓW: *Herbarium Universitatis Jagellonicae Cracoviensis,* **(KRA),** ul. Lubicz, 31-512 Kraków, **Poland.**

Telephone: 210-33 (ext. 421), 161-44 (ext. 52).

Status: Department of Plant Taxonomy and Phytogeography of the Institute of Botany at the Jagellonian University.

Foundation: 1780. *Number of specimens:* 226.900 (180.000 phanerogams, 13.600 bryophytes, 16.800 fungi, 15.000 lichens, 1.500 myxophytes).

Herbarium: Holarctic; Europe, especially Poland; tropical Africa.

Important collections: K. Jelski, M. Raciborski (Pteridophytes of Java), J. Kornaś (Pteridophytes of tropical Africa).

Director: JAN KORNAŚ, 1923 (Pteridophytes, phytogeography, plant sociology).

Curator: ZBIGNIEW DZWONKO, 1947 (Plant sociology).

Staff members: ANNA DZWONKO, 1943 (Phanerogams).

    BARBARA GUMIŃSKA, 1924 (Fungi).
    MARIA OLECH, 1941 (Lichens).
    ANNA PACYNA, 1940 (Phanerogams).
    HELENA TRZCIŃSKA-TACIK, 1936 (Phanerogams).
    EUGENIA URSZULA ZAJĄC, 1941 (Phanerogams).
    ADAM ZAJĄC, 1940 (Phanerogams).

Specialization in research: Flora of Poland (Phanerogams, fungi, lichens), pteridophytes of tropical Africa, phanerogams of Mongolia.

Associated botanic garden: Botanic Garden of the Jagellonian University, ul. Kopernika 27, 31-501 Kraków.

Loans: To recognized institutions.

Periodical and serial works: Zeszyty Naukowe Uniwersytetu Jagiellońskiego, Prace Botaniczne; Plantae Poloniae Exsiccatae.

Exchange: Available: European plants, especially Poland. Desired: Plants from the Holarctic and tropical Africa, especially Pteridophytes.

KRAKÓW: *Herbarium of the Botanical Institute of the Polish Academy of Sciences,* **(KRAM),** ul. Lubicz 46, 31-512 Kraków, **Poland.**

Telephone: 16144.

Status: Polish Academy of Sciences.

Foundation: About 1850. *Number of specimens:* 370.000 (270.000 vascular plants, 44.000 bryophytes, 38.000 lichens, 18.000 fungi).

Herbarium: Plants of Central Europe, Balkan Peninsula.

Important collections: E. Janczewski, A. Jasiewicz, J. Nowak, B. Kotula, B. Pawłowski, E. Wołoszczak, H. Zapałowicz, A. Zmuda.

Director and Curator: A. Jasiewicz, 1928 (Taxonomy of *Scabiosa*, Scrophulariaceae of Europe, Balkan Peninsula flora).
Staff members: M. Gostyńska-Jakuszewska, 1933 (*Crataegus*).
J. Nowak, 1931 (Lichens, especially *Verrucaria*).
R. Ochyra, 1949 (Bryophytes).
A. Pałkowa, 1927.
M. Pawlus, 1954 (*Festuca*).
M. Sychowa, 1927 (*Myosotis*).
T. Tacik, 1926 (*Taraxacum, Epilobium*).
W. Wojewoda, 1932 (Fungi).
Specialization in research: Flora of Poland and Balkan Peninsula.
Loans: To recognized botanical institutions.
Periodical and serial works: Fragmenta Floristica et Geobotanica.
Exchange: Available: Plants of Poland. Desired: Plants of Europe, Asia and North America.

KRASNODAR: *Herbarium, Department of Botany, Kubansk Agricultural Institute,* (**KBAI**), Kalinina St. 13, 350044 Krasnodar, **U.S.S.R.**
Foundation: 1958. *Number of specimens:* 40.000.
Herbarium: Flora of NW Caucasus.
Director: A. A. Dorovskaja.

KRASNOJARSK: *Herbarium, Krasnojarsk Pedagogical Institute,* (**KRAS**), Prospect Mira 83, 660607 Krasnojarsk, **U.S.S.R.**
Foundation: 1939. *Number of specimens:* 50.000.
Herbarium: Flora of Central Siberia.
Director: L. I. Kashina.
Curator of Cryptogams: M. I. Beglyanova.

KUALA LUMPUR: *Herbarium, Department of Agriculture,* (**KLA**), Swettenham Road, Kuala Lumpur, **Malaysia.** (Information 1974)
Status: Federal.
Foundation: 1904.
Herbarium: Tropical flora and fungi.
Specialization in research: Tropical plants.
Periodical and serial works: Malaysian Agricultural Journal.

KUALA LUMPUR: *Herbarium, Department of Botany, University of Malaya,* (**KLU**), Pantai Valley, Kuala Lumpur, **Malaysia.**
Telephone: 54631.
Status: University.
Foundation: 1960. *Number of specimens:* 30.000.
Herbarium: All groups, with emphasis on Old World Tropics, especially Malesia.
Important collections: E. Soepadmo, M. E. D. Poore (Fagaceae), B. C. Stone (Pandanaceae, Rutaceae), S. C. Chin (limestone flora of Malaya), plants of Malaysian National Parks, vouchers for ecological and ethnobotanical studies.
Director and Curator: Benjamin C. Stone, 1933

(Flora of Malaysia, biogeography, Rutaceae, Pandanaceae).
Staff members: Chin See Chung (Limestone flora, ethnobotany).
A. Kuthubutheen (Mycology).
M. G. Manuel (Bryology, pteridology).
Haji Mohamed (Bryology).
A. Nawawi (Mycology).
M. Ratna Sabapathy (Freshwater algae).
Mahmud Sider (Field investigator).
E. Soepadmo (Fagaceae, Ulmaceae, Malaysian flora, ecology).
Specialization in research: Malesian flora.
Associated botanic garden: University of Malaya Botanical Garden.
Loans: By permission of the Curator.
Exchange: Desired: Publications and specimens from Asian and Pacific countries.

KUCHING: *Sarawak Herbarium,* (**SAR**), Forest Department Headquarters, Jalan Badruddin, Kuching, Sarawak, **E. Malaysia.**
Telephone: 082/22161.
Status: Forest Department.
Foundation: 1961. *Number of specimens:* 73.000.
Herbarium: Gymnosperms and phanerogams of Malaysia.
Director: Joseph K. K. Yong, 1930.
Curator: Paul P. K. Chai, 1941.
Staff members: Mohamad Akip, 1946.
Rena George, 1955.
Othman Ismawi, 1940.
Bernard M. H. Lee, 1953.
James Mamit, 1948.
Ilias Paie, 1934.
Peter P. K. Sie, 1947.
Yii Puan Ching, 1951.
Specialization in research: Sarawak flora, ecology, ethnobotany and phenology.
Associated botanic garden: Biological Centre, Semengoh.
Loans: To recognized botanical institutions for 1 year.
Exchange: Yes, mainly with tropical herbaria.

KUKIZAKI: *Herbarium, Silviculture Division, Forestry and Forest Products Research Institute,* (**TF**), P.O. Box 2, Ushiku, Ibaraki 300-12, **Japan.**
Status: National institution.
Foundation: 1878. *Number of specimens:* 10.000.
Herbarium: Flora of Japan.
Director of Silviculture Division: K. Hatiya (Synecology).
Staff members: T. Maeda (Synecology).
N. Karizumi (Synecology).
Associated botanic garden: Tsukuba Arboretum.
Periodical and serial works: Bulletin of the Forestry and Forest Products Research Institute.
Remarks: Formerly listed under Tokyo; the complete set of specimens (ca. 90.000) is kept in the

Asakawa Herbarium (TFA). Requests for loans and exchange should be addressed to the Curator, Asakawa Herbarium, 1833 Nagafusa-cho, Hachioji, Tokyo 193, Japan.

KUMASI: *Forest Herbarium, Ministry of Forestry,* **(KUM)**, Kumasi, **Ghana.** (Information 1974)
Status: Directed by state.
Foundation: 1923. *Number of specimens:* 8.600.
Herbarium: Mainly flora of Ghana.

KUMASI: *Herbarium, University of Science and Technology,* **(KUU)**, Kumasi, **Ghana.**

KUNMING: *Herbarium of Kunming Institute of Botany, Academia Sinica,* **(KUN)**, Helongtan, Kunming, Yunnan, **People's Republic of China.**
Telephone: 4053 or 4197.
Status: Directed by Academia Sinica.
Foundation: 1930. *Number of specimens:* 692.000 (650.000 phanerogams, 30.000 bryophytes, 6.000 fungi, 5.000 pteridophytes, 1.000 lichens).
Herbarium: All groups.
Important collections: Plants of Yunnan, Szechwan and Tibet.
  Director: WU CHENG-YIH (Phytotaxonomy, floistics).
  Vice Directors: CAI XI-TAO (Phytotaxonomy, natural resources of tropical and subtropical plants).
  CHANG AO-LO (Director of Botanical Garden; cultivated *Camellia, Rhododendron*).
  Curator of Phanerogamic Herbarium: LI XI-WEN (Phytotaxonomy).
  Curator of Cryptogamic Herbarium: ZANG MU (Mycology, bryology).
  Head, Laboratory of Wood Anatomy and Wood Herbarium: TANG YEO.
  Staff member: LI XIN-JIANG (Bryology).
Specialization in research: Utilization of tropical, subtropical and alpine plants of Yunnan and Tibet.
Associated botanic garden: Botanical Garden of Kunming Institute of Botany.
Loans: With permission of the Director.
Periodical and serial works: Acta Botanica Yunnanica, Flora Yunnanica.
Exchange: Available: Chinese plants of all groups.

KUNMING: *Herbarium, Yunnan University,* **(YUKU)**, Kunming, Yunnan, **People's Republic of China.**
Status: University.
Foundation: 1922. *Number of specimens:* 60.000.
Herbarium: Plants of Yunnan and adjacent provinces.
  Curator: SUN PI-HSING (Taxonomy).
  Staff members: HSU WEN-HSUAN (Bryophytes).
  T'ANG T'ING-KUEI (Medicinal plants).
  Specialization in research: Local flora and teaching.

Remarks: The herbarium includes a special collection of seeds and roots of medicinal plants.

KUOPIO: *Herbarium, Department of Natural History, Kuopio Museum,* **(KUO)**, Kuopio, **Finland.** (Information 1974)
Status: Owned by Kuopio Naturalist's Society, maintained by city; used by Kuopio University.
Foundation: 1897. *Number of specimens:* 140.000.
Herbarium: Vascular plants, bryophytes, lichens and fungi from NW Europe, Siberia and North America; phanerogams from South America, Africa and Australia.
Important collections: J. Pekkarinen (Finnish *Hieracium*), A. J. Mela (Finnish vascular plants), O. A. F. Lönnbohm (vascular plants and fungi of Siberia).
Loans: To recognized botanical institutions.
Periodical and serial works: Savonia, Savon Luonto.

KUTNÁ HORA: *Herbarium, Oblastní muzeum Kutna Hora,* **(OMKH)**, Kutná Hora, **Czechoslovakia.** (Information 1974)
Foundation: 1877. *Number of specimens:* 3.500.
Herbarium: Plants of Czechoslovakia.
Loans: To recognized botanical institutions.

KWEILIN: *Institute of Economic Botany,* **(IBK)** -- see GUILIN: *Guangxi Institute of Botany.*

KYOTO: *Herbarium, Department of Botany, Faculty of Science, Kyoto University,* **(KYO)**, Sakyo-ku, Kyoto 606, **Japan.**
Telephone: 075-751-2111, ext. 4131-3.
Status: Department of National University.
Foundation: 1921. *Number of specimens:* 950.000.
Herbarium: Mainly East and Southeast Asia.
Important collections: U. Faurie, G. Koidzumi, Z. Tashiro, S. Kitamura, J. Ohwi, M. Tagawa, R. Toyama, G. Murata, T. Kaneshiro, K. Mayebara.
  Director: K. IWATSUKI, 1934 (Pteridophytes, Southeast Asian flora).
  Staff members: M. KATO, 1946 (Pteridophytes, comparative morphology).
  H. KOYAMA, 1937 (Compositae).
  G. MURATA, 1927 (Labiatae, floristics).
  Research associate: M. HOTTA, 1935 (Araceae).
  Honorary research associate: S. KITAMURA, 1906 (Compositae, flora of Japan and Himalayas).
  Specialization in research: Taxonomy of vascular plants and bryophytes; flora of East and Southeast Asia.
Associated botanic garden: Botanic Garden of Faculty of Science, Kyoto University.
Loans: To recognized botanical institutions.
Periodical and serial works: Memoirs of the Faculty of Science, Kyoto University, Biology Series.
Exchange: Available: Vascular plants of Japan. Desired: Worldwide collections.

L

LACEY: *Herbarium, Department of Biology, Saint Martin's College,* **(OSMC),** Lacey, Washington 98503, **U.S.A.**
Telephone: 206/491-4700.
Status: Private college.
Foundation: 1895. *Number of specimens:* 13.000.
Herbarium: General, with good representation of Pacific Northwest vascular plants, some local marine algae.
    Curator: CHRISTOPHER E. ABAIR, 1924.
    Specialization in research: Native plants of the Pacific Northwest.
    Loans: Usual regulations.
    Exchange: Available: Specimens from the Pacific Northwest. Desired: Specimens from any part of the world; marine algae welcome.
    Remarks: Formerly listed under Olympia.

LA CROSSE: *Herbarium, Department of Biology, University of Wisconsin-La Crosse,* **(UWL),** La Crosse, Wisconsin 54601, **U.S.A.**
Telephone: 608/785-8251.
Foundation: 1968. *Number of specimens:* 35.000.
Herbarium: Emphasis on vascular plants of Wisconsin.
Important collections: Oren Frazee (midwestern U.S.), Alvin M. Peterson (southwestern Wisconsin); plants of the Upper Mississippi River Floodplain.
    Specialization in research: Floristics of local flora, vegetation of floodplain of Upper Mississippi River, and systematic studies of various angiosperm genera.
    Loans: To any qualified worker.
    Periodical and serial works: Contributions from University of Wisconsin–La Crosse Herbarium (irregular).
    Exchange: General exchange sought to increase representation for teaching and research purposes.

LAE: *Herbarium, Division of Botany, Department of Forests,* **(LAE),** P.O. Box 314, Lae, **Papua New Guinea.** (Information 1974)
Status: Directed by state.
Foundation: 1944. *Number of specimens:* 200.000.
Herbarium: Plants of New Guinea and SW Pacific.
    Specialization in research: New Guinea flora.
    Associated botanic garden: Botanic Garden, Lae; Kauli Botanic Reserve, Wau.
    Loans: To recognized botanical institutions.
    Periodical and serial works: Forest Manuals, Botany Bulletins, Timber Species Leaflets, Flora Handbooks.

LAFAYETTE: *Herbarium, Department of Biology, University of Southwestern Louisiana,* **(LAF),** Lafayette, Louisiana 70504, **U.S.A.**

Telephone: 318/264-6748; 264-6749; 264-6750.
Status: State university.
Foundation: ca. 1940. *Number of specimens:* 82.000 (22.000 bryophytes, 60.000 vascular plants).
Herbarium: Musci of U.S. Gulf Coastal Plain; vascular plants, especially Poaceae, of Louisiana.
Important collections: Charles M. Allen (Poaceae of Louisiana), William D. Reese (Bryophytes), John W. Thieret (Vascular plants of Louisiana).
    Director: WILLIAM D. REESE, 1928 (Systematics of Musci; Musci of U.S. Gulf Coastal Plain; New World Calymperaceae).
    Curator: ROY C. BROWN, 1947 (Biosystematics of Compositae; fine structure of meiosis).
    Staff members: CHARLES M. ALLEN, 1945 (Poaceae and Euphorbiaceae of Louisiana).
        VICTORIA I. SULLIVAN, 1941 (Biology of aquatic vascular plants).
    Specialization in research: Louisiana flora; Musci of the U.S. Gulf Coastal Plain; Calymperaceae of the Western Hemisphere.
    Loans: No special restrictions.
    Exchange: Available: Vascular plants of Louisiana; Musci of the U.S. Gulf Coastal Plain. Desired: Musci and vascular plants of the Gulf Coastal Plain.

LAFAYETTE: *Kriebel Herbarium, Department of Biological Sciences, Purdue University,* **(PUL)** – – *see* WEST LAFAYETTE.

LAFAYETTE: *Arthur Herbarium, Department of Botany and Plant Pathology, Purdue University,* **(PUR)** – – *see* WEST LAFAYETTE.

LAFAYETTE: *Ornamental Horticulture Herbarium, Department of Plant Industry and General Agriculture, University of Southwestern Louisiana,* **(USLH),** P.O. Box 44433, Lafayette, Louisiana 70504, **U.S.A.**
Telephone: 318/264-6064.
Foundation: 1958. *Number of specimens:* 12.500.
Herbarium: Primarily cultivated species from Louisiana.
    Director: J. A. FORET.
    Loans: Usual regulations.

LAGOS: *Lagos University Herbarium,* **(LUH),** Department of Biological Sciences, University of Lagos, Akoka, Lagos, **Nigeria.**
Telephone: 841361, ext. 516.
Status: University.
Foundation: 1971. *Number of specimens:* 2.500.
Important collections: *Sida* species (Malvaceae).
    Curator: REGINALD E. UGBOROGHO, 1934 (Cytogenetics, taxonomy).
    Staff member: BEN ALEAGBU.

Specialization in research: Cytogenetics, ecology, taxonomy, biosystematics.

LAGRANDE: *Range and Wildlife Habitat Laboratory, Pacific Northwest Forest and Range Experiment Station, U.S. Forest Service,* (**LAGO**), Route 2, Box 2315, LaGrande, Oregon 97850, **U.S.A.**
Telephone: 503/963-7122.
Status: U.S. Department of Agriculture, Forest Service.
Foundation: 1911. *Number of specimens:* 8.000.
Herbarium: Mostly flowering plants from the Pacific Northwest; emphasis on grasses, sedges, forbs, and shrubs of value as ungulate forage; flora of the Starkey Experimental Forest and Range.
Curator: GERALD STRICKLER, 1928 (Plant ecology).
Specialization in research: Range management and ecology: from grass, forb, shrub autecology to community structure, function, and classification to ungulate management systems on forested lands.
Remarks: Includes specimens formerly deposited at the U.S. Forest Service, Portland (POFS).

LAGUNA: *Department of Plant Pathology, Central Experiment Station, College of Agriculture, University of the Philippines,* (**CALP**) –– see LOS BAÑOS: *Mycological Herbarium, University of the Philippines Museum of Natural History.*

LAGUNA: *Herbarium of the College of Forestry,* (**LBC**) –– see LOS BAÑOS.

LAHORE: *Herbarium, Panjab University,* (**LAH**), Lahore, **Pakistan.** (Information 1974, present address unknown)
Status: University.
Number of specimens: 50.000.
Herbarium: Flora of Tibet, bryophytes, lichens, fungi.

LAHTI: *Herbarium of Lahden Luonnonystävät,* (**LHT**), Savonkatu 1 A 50, Lahti, **Finland.** (Information 1974)
Status: Owned by Friends of Nature of Lahti, subsidized by city.
Foundation: 1966. *Number of specimens:* 4.250.
Herbarium: Mainly microfungi and vascular plants of Finland.
Specialization in research: Flora of Päijät-Häme and North Uusimaa, microfungi of Finland.
Loans: To recognized botanical institutions.
Periodical and serial works: Lahden Luonnonystäväin julkaisuja.

LA JOLLA: *Scripps Institution of Oceanography, University of California,* (**SCR**), La Jolla, California 92093, **U.S.A.**
Telephone: 714/452-4836.
Foundation: 1962. *Number of specimens:* 1.600.

Herbarium: Small collection of marine benthic algae, with specimens from the U.S. Pacific Coast, or collected during Scripps expeditions in the Pacific Ocean.
Important collections: Mary S. Snyder.
Director: RALPH A. LEWIN (Experimental phycology).
Curator: JOAN G. STEWART (Marine algal morphology and ecology). 619-534-4295

LA JOLLA: *The Traub Herbarium of the American Plant Life Society,* (**TRA**), 2678 Prestwick Court, La Jolla, California 92037, **U.S.A.**
Status: American Plant Life Society.
Foundation: 1942. *Number of specimens:* 3.000.
Herbarium: Includes many type specimens of Amaryllidaceae.
Director: HAMILTON P. TRAUB (Amaryllidaceae).
Specialization in research: Amaryllidaceae.
Periodical and serial works: Experimental work published in Plant Life, including the Year Book of the Amaryllidaceae, since 1932.
Remarks: Formerly listed under San Diego.

LA JUNTA: *Herbarium, Biology Department, Otero Junior College,* (**LAJC**), La Junta, Colorado 81050, **U.S.A.**
Telephone: 303/384-4443.
Foundation: 1941. *Number of specimens:* 1.200.
Herbarium: Local flora of southeastern Colorado.
Director and Curator: DEXTER W. HESS.

LAKELAND: *Herbarium, Biology Department, Florida Southern College,* (**FSCL**), MacDonald and Johnson streets, Lakeland, Florida 33802, **U.S.A.**
Telephone: 813/683-5521, ext. 472.
Foundation: 1930. *Number of specimens:* 10.000.
Herbarium: Local flora.
Curator: MARGARET L. GILBERT, 1928 (Plant ecology).
Specialization in research: Central Florida flora.

LAKEVIEW: *Herbarium, Bureau of Land Management,* (**BLMLK**), Box 151, 1000 South Ninth Street, Lakeview, Oregon 97630, **U.S.A.**
Telephone: 503/947-2177.
Status: U.S. Department of the Interior.
Foundation: 1977. *Number of specimens:* 3.700.
Herbarium: Southcentral Oregon and northwest Nevada.
Curator: VIRGINIA LEE CROSBY, 1950.

LAKEVIEW: *Herbarium, Fremont National Forest,* (**FNLO**), 34 North D Street, P.O. Box 551, Lakeview, Oregon 97630, **U.S.A.**
Status: U.S. Department of Agriculture, Forest Service.
Foundation: 1910. *Number of specimens:* 2.000.
Herbarium: Range plants.
Remarks: In 1981 these collections will be trans-

ferred to BLMLK.

LAKEWOOD: *Herbarium, Range and Wildlife Management, Rocky Mountain Region, U.S. Forest Service,* **(DENF)**, P.O. Box 25127, 11177 West 8th Avenue, Lakewood, Colorado 80225, **U.S.A.**
  Telephone: 303/234-4011.
  Status: U.S. Department of Agriculture, Forest Service.
  Foundation: 1910. *Number of specimens:* 1.500.
  Herbarium: Specimens for plant identification needs in National Forest management.
    Director: WALLACE B. GALLAHER, 1926 (Range management).
    Curator: ROBERT F. BUTTERY, 1929 (Ecology).
    Remarks: Formerly listed under Denver.

LA LAGUNA: *Departamento de Botanica, Facultad de Biologia, Universidad de La Laguna,* **(TFC)**, La Laguna, Tenerife, Canary Islands, **Spain.**
  Telephone: 922-253343.
  Status: University.
  Foundation: 1969. *Number of specimens:* 14.000.
    Director: WOLFREDO WILDFRET DE LA TORRE (Phanerogams, phytosociology).
    Staff members: ESPERANZA BELFRAN TEJERA (Mycology, phanerogams, taxonomy).
      PEDRO PEREZ DE PAZ (Phanerogams, taxonomy).

LALITPUR: *Botanical Survey and Herbarium Section,* **(KATH)**, Godawary, Lalitpur, **Nepal.**
  Telephone: 15217.
  Status: Department of Medicinal Plants, Ministry of Forests.
  Foundation: 1960. *Number of specimens:* 75.000.
  Herbarium: Flora of Nepal.
    Director: S. B. MALLA (Flora of Nepal).
    Specialization in research: Survey of the Flora of Nepal and adjoining areas.
    Associated botanic garden: Royal Botanical Garden.
    Loans: To institutions.
    Periodical and serial works: Bulletin of the Department of Medicinal Plants (irregular).

LAMBAYEQUE: *Herbario Lambayeque, Universidad Nacional Pedro Ruiz Gallo,* **(PRG)**, Plaza Principal, Apartado 48, Lambayeque, **Peru.**
  Foundation: 1970. *Number of specimens:* 4.450.
  Herbarium: Northern Peru.
    Director: ANGEL DIAZ CELIS, 1922 (Malvaceae; ecology of weeds).
    Staff members: GUILLERMO DELGADO.
      JUAN LAOS (Algae).
      LEOPOLDO VASQUEZ NUÑEZ (Taxonomy).
    Specialization in research: Ecology of weeds; flora of northern Peru.
    Periodical and serial works: Revista Cientifica, Universidad Nacional Pedro Ruiz Gallo, Lambayeque.

Exchange: Yes.

LANCASTER: *Herbarium, North Museum, Franklin and Marshall College,* **(FMC)**, P.O. Box 3003, Lancaster, Pennsylvania 17604, **U.S.A.**
  Telephone: 717/291-3941.
  Foundation: 1952. *Number of specimens:* 13.000.
  Herbarium: Flora of the northeastern U.S. (75%), southeastern U.S. (25%); contains specimens dating back to mid-19th century.
  Important collections: G. H. E. Muhlenberg, T. C. Porter, J. K. Small, A. A. Heller, J. J. Carter, A. P. Garber, W. Auxer, Mrs. C. Y. Tanger, Miss E. Groff, H. K. Groff; 5.000 species represented in the Groff seed collection.
    Director: W. FRED KINSEY, III (New World Archeology).
    Curator: JANE GRUSHOW, 1941 (Plant physiology).
    Staff members: PAUL EYLER.
      RALPH MILLER.

LANCASTER: *Lancaster University, Department of Biological Sciences,* **(LANC)**, Lancaster LA1 4YQ, England, **Great Britain.**
  Telephone: (0524)65201.
  Status: University.
  Foundation: 1965. *Number of specimens:* 46.000.
  Herbarium: Divided into European herbarium 31.000, Arctic herbarium 15.000.
    Curator: GEOFFREY HALLIDAY, 1933 (Arctic vascular plants, especially east Greenland).
    Specialization in research: The vascular flora of the arctic, particularly east Greenland; vascular flora of north-west England.
    Loans: To recognized institutions.
    Exchange: Available: British and Arctic material. Desired: European and Arctic.

L'ANSE: *Herbarium, Ford Forestry Center, Michigan Technological University,* **(MCTF)**, L'Anse, Michigan 49946, **U.S.A.**
  Telephone: 906/524-6181; 450-2450.
  Status: Department of the School of Forestry and Wood Products, Michigan Technological University.
  Foundation: 1960. *Number of specimens:* 40.000.
  Herbarium: Specializes in plants of the Upper Great Lakes Region; interested in woody plants (especially trees) of the world.
  Important collections: O. A. Farwell.
    Director: ERIC A. BOURDO, JR. (Forestry, ecology).
    Specialization in research: Forestry and ecology research on northern forest types.
    Loans: Usual regulations.
    Exchange: Special interest is in woody plants; willing to exchange with any other herbaria.

LA PAZ: *Herbario Nacional de Bolivia, Universidad Mayor de San Andres, Campus Universitario Cota*

Cota, **(LPB)**, Casilla 20127, La Paz, **Bolivia.**
Telephone: 376818.
Status: Institute of Ecology and Ministry of Agriculture.
Foundation: 1974. *Number of specimens:* 9.000.
Herbarium: Bolivian plants.
Important collections: Roy F. Steinbach, Raúl R. Lara, Stephan G. Beck.
Staff members: STEPHAN G. BECK, 1944 (Bolivian flora, ecology).
RAÚL R. LARA, 1934 (Gramineae).
ROBERTO CH. VASQUEZ, 1942 (Orchidaceae).
Specialization in research: Bolivian flora and vegetation; study of eco-regions.
Loans: To all recognized institutions and monographers.
Exchange: Available: Bolivian plants for identification. Desired: Determined plants of Bolivia and neighboring countries.
Remarks: Visitors are welcome.

LA PLATA: *Herbario, División Plantas Vasculares del Museo de La Plata,* **(LP)**, Paseo del Bosque, 1900 La Plata, Buenos Aires, **Argentina.**
Telephone: (54)021/3-9125.
Status: Universidad Nacional de La Plata.
Foundation: 1884. *Number of specimens:* 300.000.
Herbarium: Vascular plants, especially Gramineae, Compositae, and Pteridophyta.
Important collections: C. Spegazzini (vascular plants), N. Alboff, C. Berg, A. L. Cabrera, H. Fabris, E. R. de la Sota.
Director: ELÍAS R. DE LA SOTA, 1932 (Pteridophyta).
Curator: MARÍA AMELIA TORRES, 1934 (Gramineae).
Staff members: JORGE V. CRISCI, 1945 (Compositae; numerical taxonomy).
MARÍA CRISTINA P. ORSI, 1947 (Berberidaceae).
AÍDA PONTIROLI, 1919 (Umbelliferae, Campanulaceae, Calyceraceae, Asclepiadaceae).
DELIA C. AÑÓN SUÁREZ, 1917 (Portulacaceae).
CAROLA R. VOLPONI, 1947 (Caryophyllaceae).
ELSA M. ZARDINI, 1949 (Compositae; useful plants).
Specialization in research: South American Compositae, Argentina Gramineae, Pteridophyta from the Neotropics; flora of Argentina; flora and phytogeography of Ventania and Tandilia mountains.
Loans: To botanical institutions.
Periodical and serial works: Revista Museo de La Plata, sec. Botánica.
Exchange: Available: Plants from Argentina and neighboring countries. Wanted: Compositae, Gramineae, and Pteridophyta of the world.

LA PLATA: *Herbario, Facultad de Agronomía, Universidad Nacional de La Plata,* **(LPAG)**, Calle 60 y 117, 1900 La Plata, Buenos Aires, **Argentina.**

Number of specimens: 2.500.
Herbarium: Vascular plants of Patagonia and southern Andes, Parque Nacional Iguazú and Islas Malvinas; mainly Misodendraceae, Fagaceae, and Coniferales.
Director: EDGARDO N. ORFILA.
Staff members: ISMAEL ANDÍA.
CARLOS H. FERNÁNDEZ.
MARÍA CRISTINA FLOREZ.
SUSANA FREIRE.
OSCAR GONZALEZ.
IDA R. VOLKART.
Loans: Usual conditions.
Exchange: Available and Desired: Argentina.

LA PLATA: *Herbario, Laboratorio de Botánica de la Dirección de Agricultura,* **(LPD)**, Paseo del Bosque, 1900 La Plata, Buenos Aires, **Argentina.**
Status: Directed by the state.
Foundation: 1938. *Number of specimens:* 8.000.
Herbarium: Indigenous and cultivated flora of the Buenos Aires Province.
Curator: DECIO PIERGENTILI.

LA PLATA: *Herbario, Instituto de Botánica "C. Spegazzini,"* **(LPS)**, Calle 53 No. 477, La Plata, Buenos Aires, **Argentina.**
Telephone: (54)021/2-9845.
Status: Museo de La Plata.
Foundation: 1935. *Number of specimens:* 45.000.
Herbarium: Fungi, mainly from Argentina, Paraguay, and southern Brazil; ca. 4.000 types.
Important collections: Irma J. Gamundi, E. Horak, Juan Carlos Lindquist, F. Petrak's Mycotheca Generalis, R. Singer, W. G. Solheim's Mycoflora Saximontanensis, C. Spegazzini, J. Wright.
Director: IRMA GAMUNDI DE AMOS, 1927 (Taxonomy and biology of Discomycetes; ecology of leaf-inhabiting fungi).
Curator: HECTOR MANUEL GOROSTIAGA, 1919.
Staff members: ALICIA SUSANA AMBROSIO, 1953 (Biology of Hyphomycetes).
ANGELICA MARGARITA ARAMBARRI, 1945 (Myxomycetes, Hyphomycetes).
ANA MARIA BUCSINSZKY, 1950 (Hyphomycetes).
CRISTINA ALICIA CORDO, 1951 (Biology of *Septoria* and *Pyricularia*).
LORENZO FRANCISCO CUOMO, 1927.
JUAN CARLOS LINDQUIST, 1899 (Uredinales).
HORACIO SPINEDI, 1951 (Ecology of Hyphomycetes).
Specialization in research: Taxonomy of fungi: Uredinales, Discomycetes, Hyphomycetes, and Myxomycetes.
Loans: To recognized institutions and specialists.
Exchange: Fungi; reprints.

LA POCATIÈRE: *Herbier, Institut de technologie*

agricole, **(QSA)**, La Pocatière, Québec, **Canada**. (Information 1974).

Foundation: 1859. *Number of specimens:* 33.000.

Herbarium: Pathology, taxonomy, mycology.

Remarks: Formerly listed as Sainte-Anne-de-la-Pocatière.

LARAMIE: *Rocky Mountain Herbarium, University of Wyoming,* **(RM)**, Laramie, Wyoming 82071, **U.S.A.**

Telephone: 307/766-2236; 766-2380.

Foundation: 1894. *Number of specimens:* 340.000 (4.000 types).

Herbarium: Flora of Wyoming, the Rocky Mountains, and western U.S.; arctic and alpine plants.

Important collections: C. F. Baker, I. W. Clokey, W. C. Cusick, L. N. Goodding, H. Hapeman, A. A. Heller, M. E. Jones, J. F. Macbride (western U.S.), A. Nelson, E. Nelson, G. E. Osterhout, E. B. Payson, C. L. Porter, C. G. Pringle, P. A. Rydberg, L. O. Williams (western U.S.), E. O. Wooton.

Director and Curator: RONALD L. HARTMAN, 1945 (Compositae, Caryophyllaceae, Umbelliferae; systematics; floristics).

Staff members: B. E. NELSON, 1947 (Floristics).

RAY UMBER, 1948 (Scrophulariaceae, Verbenaceae; biochemical systematics).

Specialization in research: Floristics of Wyoming and Rocky Mountains.

Loans: To recognized institutions for 1 year, extension if requested.

Periodical and serial works: University of Wyoming Publications.

Exchange: Available: Rocky Mountain region. Desired: Alpine and arctic plants; western North America and Mexico.

LARAMIE: *Wilhelm G. Solheim Mycological Herbarium, University of Wyoming,* **(RMS)**, Laramie, Wyoming 82071, **U.S.A.**

Telephone: 307/766-2236; 766-2380.

Foundation: 1929. *Number of specimens:* 50.000.

Herbarium: Worldwide; emphasis on Rocky Mountains, especially plant pathogens.

Important collections: J. F. Brenckle, R. Ciferri, W. B. Cooke, J. B. Ellis and B. M. Everhart, W. Krieger, F. Petrak, H. Sydow, L. Theissen, F. E. and E. S. Clements.

Director and Curator: RONALD L. HARTMAN, 1945 (Vascular plants).

Staff members: M. CHRISTENSEN, 1932 (Soil fungi).

P. M. FAZIO, 1942.

B. E. NELSON, 1947.

J. A. FERNANDEZ, 1947 (Soil pathogenic fungi).

Specialization in research: Rocky Mountain fungi; plant pathogens.

Loans: To recognized institutions for 1 year, extension if requested.

Periodical and serial works: University of Wyoming Publications.

Exchange: Mycoflora Saximontanensis Exsiccata duplicate material.

Remarks: Associated with the Rocky Mountain Herbarium (RM).

LARAMIE: *Range Management Herbarium, College of Agriculture, University of Wyoming,* **(WYAC)**, Laramie, Wyoming 82071, **U.S.A.**

Telephone: 307/766-4236.

Foundation: 1946. *Number of specimens:* 60.000.

Herbarium: Grasses (6.000 Wyoming, 4.000 Mexico, 50.000 world, especially Iran).

Important collections: A. A. Beetle.

Director and Curator: ALAN ACKERMAN BEETLE, 1913 (*Artemisia;* grasses of the world).

Specialization in research: World grasses, origin and distribution.

Loans: Usual conditions.

Exchange: Yes.

LA ROCHELLE: *Herbarium, Muséum d'Histoire Naturelle et d'Ethnographie de la Rochelle,* **(LR)**, 28 Rue Albert Ier, 17000 La Rochelle, **France.**

Telephone: 46. 41 18 25.

Foundation: 1770.

Important collections: Guiguet-Rochelaise and Savatier-Fouillade (more than 10.000 spec., mostly from France), L. Faye and Ayraud-Dreuilh (3.000–5.000 spec.), herb. A. J. A. Bonpland, herb. d'Orbigny (historical value).

Curator: R. DUGUY.

LAS CRUCES: *Herbarium, Biology Department, New Mexico State University,* **(NMC)**, Las Cruces, New Mexico 88003, **U.S.A.**

Telephone: 505/646-3611 (department); 646-3732 (curator).

Foundation: 1890. *Number of specimens:* 50.000.

Herbarium: Emphasis on New Mexico and northern Mexico; some western U.S. and worldwide.

Important collections: E. O. Wooton, P. C. Standley, R. W. Spellenberg, C. G. Pringle, O. B. Metcalf, M. E. Jones.

Director and Curator: RICHARD W. SPELLENBERG, 1940 (Southwest U.S. flora; Nyctaginaceae of North America).

Specialization in research: Floristics of southwestern U.S. and northern Mexico; cytotaxonomy.

Loans: To any recognized research institution for research purposes.

Exchange: Limited, from areas of specialization.

LAS CRUCES: *Range Science Herbarium, Department of Animal and Range Sciences, New Mexico State University,* **(NMCR)**, Box 31, Las Cruces, New Mexico 88003, **U.S.A.**

Telephone: 505/646-2514.

Number of specimens: 6.000.

Herbarium: Important range and poisonous plants

of New Mexico.
Director and Curator: KELLY W. ALLRED, 1949
(Grass systematics).
Specialization in research: Range ecology; grass
systematics.
Exchange: Range plants of North America.

LAS PALMAS: *Herbarium Las Palmas, El Museo
Canario,* (**LPA**), 33 Dr Chil, Las Palmas, Canary Is-
lands, **Spain.** (Information 1974)
Status: Private foundation.
Foundation: 1965. *Number of specimens:* 2.500.
Herbarium: Flora of Canary Islands.
Specialization in research: Flora of Gran Ca-
naria, cultivated plants.
Loans: To recognized botanical institutions.
Periodical and serial works: Cuadernos de
Botánica.

LAS VEGAS: *Herbarium, Department of Biological
Sciences, University of Nevada,* (**UNLV**), Las Vegas,
Nevada 89154, **U.S.A.**
Telephone: 702/739-3251.
Foundation: 1969. *Number of specimens:* 17.000.
Herbarium: Vascular plants of the Mojave Desert,
Great Basin, Nevada and contiguous areas.
Director: WESLEY E. NILES, 1932 (Flora of the
Mojave Desert; taxonomy of Asteraceae).
Specialization in research: Floristics of the Mo-
jave Desert, Great Basin, Nevada and contiguous
areas; floristics and phytogeography of alpine vas-
cular plants of the Intermountain Region; flora of
the Death Valley area.
Loans: Usual regulations.
Exchange: Yes.

LA TRAPPE: *Laboratoire de l'Institut Agronomique
d'Oka, Université de Montréal,* (**LT**) – – incorporated
in QFA.

LATROBE: *Herbarium, Department of Biology, Saint
Vincent College,* (**LAT**), Latrobe, Pennsylvania 15650,
U.S.A.
Telephone: 412/539-9761, ext. 361.
Status: Private institution.
Foundation: 1875. *Number of specimens:* 10.000.
Herbarium: Local and northern Canada.
Director and Curator: MAXIMILIAN G. DUMAN,
1906 (Systematics and distribution of northern Ca-
nadian *Carex*).
Loans: Normal regulations.
Exchange: Limited exchange of northern *Carex*.
Remarks: Original herbarium burned in 1963.

LAURINBURG: *Herbarium, Department of Biology,
St. Andrews Presbyterian College,* (**SAPCL**), Laurin-
burg, North Carolina 28352, **U.S.A.**
Telephone: 919/276-3652.
Status: Private institution.
Foundation: 1960. *Number of specimens:* 5.000.

Herbarium: Mainly local flora, especially of the
sandhills and coastal areas of the Carolinas.
Curator: NORMAN C. MELVIN, III, 1950 (System-
atics of Ericaceae).
Specialization in research: Numerical taxonomy
and phytogeography of Ericaceae.
Loans: To established institutions for 1 year.
Exchange: Welcome.

LAUSANNE: *Herbarium, Musée botanique cantonal,*
(**LAU**), Avenue de Cour 14bis, CH-1007 Lausanne,
Switzerland.
Telephone: (021)26.24.09.
Status: Dependent on the State (Department of
public instruction).
Foundation: 1924. *Number of specimens:* 600.000.
Herbarium: Worldwide, especially phanerogams of
Europe, Northern Africa, Swiss Mosses, Myxomy-
cetes.
Important collections: Swiss herbarium, especially
Vaudois; herb. J. C. Schleicher, J. Muret, E. Wilczek;
herb. of Mosses and Myxomycetes of Charles Mey-
lan; herb. J. F. A. T. Gaudin.
Director: PIERRE VILLARET, 1918 (Research of
local floristics, geobotany, quaternary flora of
Switzerland.
Curator: GINO MÜLLER (Cytotaxonomy).
Collaborator: HEINZ CLÉMENÇON, 1935 (Agar-
icales – taxonomy, cytology).
Specialization in research: Local floristics and
geobotany; palynology; quaternary flora of C.
Europe; mycology (Agaricales); algology.
Associated botanic garden: Jardin botanique de la
Ville et de l'Université de Lausanne; Jardin alpin
de Pont de Nant s/Bex.
Loans: To all monographers and recognized
institutions.
Exchange: Available: Specimens of Switzerland.
Desired: Worldwide.

LAVRAS: *Herbário, Departamento de Biologia, Es-
cola Superior de Agricultura de Lavras,* (**ESAL**), Caixa
Postal 37, 37.200 Lavras, Minas Gerais, **Brazil.**
Status: Ministério da Educação e Cultura.
Number of specimens: 5.000.
Herbarium: Flora of Minas Gerais.
Director: MANUEL LOSADA GAVILANES.
Staff members: DOUGLAS ANTONIO DE CARVAL-
HO.
  SILAS COSTA PEREIRA.
  JOSÉ CARDOSO PINTO.
Collaborator: MITZI BRANDÃO FERREIRA.
Specialization in research: Flora of Minas Ge-
rais; Gramineae, Leguminosae.
Loans: Yes.
Exchange: Yes.

LAWAI: *Herbarium, Pacific Tropical Botanical Garden,* (**PTBG**), P.O. Box 340, Lawai, Kauai, Hawaii
96765, **U.S.A.**

Telephone: 808/332-8131; 332-8901.
Status: Private, nonprofit organization.
Foundation: 1971. *Number of specimens:* 2.500.
Herbarium: Hawaiian flora; Garden voucher specimens; general reference collection of tropical floras.
Director: WILLIAM L. THEOBALD, 1936 (Flora of Hawaiian Islands, Pacific Islands, Sri Lanka).
Staff member: ALBERT C. SMITH, Editorial consultant, 1906 (Flora of Fiji).
Specialization in research: Flora of Hawaiian Islands, Fiji; living collections of tropical plants of value to man (nutrition, medicine, conservation, ethnobotany, basic botanical value).
Loans: No special restrictions.
Periodical and serial works: Allertonia (series of occasional papers); Bulletin; Memoirs series; Flora of Fiji; A New Flora of the Hawaiian Islands.
Exchange: Available: Plants of Hawaii. Desired: General tropical collections (including living material).

LAWRENCE: *Herbarium, University of Kansas,* **(KANU),** 2045 Avenue A, Campus West, Lawrence, Kansas 66044, **U.S.A.**
Telephone: 913/864-4493; 864-4505.
Foundation: 1873. *Number of specimens:* 250.000.
Herbarium: Primarily devoted to plants of the Great Plains, with special emphasis on Kansas.
Director: RONALD L. MCGREGOR, 1919 (Vascular flora of the Great Plains, especially Kansas).
Curator: RALPH E. BROOKS, 1950 (Vascular flora of the Great Plains, especially Kansas).
Specialization in research: Flora of the Great Plains, especially Kansas.
Loans: Made for one year upon request to Curator.
Exchange: Desired: Specimens from North America north of Mexico.

LEEDS: *Herbarium, Department of Plant Sciences, University of Leeds,* **(LDS),** Leeds, West Yorkshire LS2 9JT, England, **Great Britain.**
Telephone: Leeds 31751.
Status: University.
Foundation: 1904. *Number of specimens:* 35.000.
Herbarium: Mainly British.
Director: D. J. HARBERD (Crop plants, biosystematics of Gramineae, Cruciferae, Orchidaceae).
Staff members: T. S. CROSBY (Biosystematics of *Lachenalia*).
    W. A. SLEDGE (Ferns of Ceylon and Samoa).
    A. SLEEP (Biosystematics of *Asplenium* and *Polystichum*, ferns of Japan).
Associated botanic garden: University of Leeds, Dept. of Plant Sciences, Botany Experimental Gardens (Curator: T. S. Crosby).
Loans: To all qualified institutions and individuals.

LEERSUM: *Herbarium Rijksinstituut voor Natuur-*

beheer (Research Institute for Nature Management), **(RIN),** Kasteel Broekhuizen, Broekhuizerlaan 2, 3956 ZR Leersum, **Netherlands.**
Telephone: 03434-2941.
Status: Department of the Rijksherbarium, Leiden.
Foundation: 1957. *Number of specimens:* 2.369.
Herbarium: Spermatophyta and pteridophyta of Netherlands and adjacent countries.
Curator: G. LONDO, 1935.

LEEUWARDEN: *Herbarium, Fries Natuurhistorisch Museum,* **(FNM),** Heerestraat 13, 8911 LC Leeuwarden, **Netherlands.**
Telephone: 05100-29085.
Status: Private society.
Foundation: 1923. *Number of specimens:* 2.000.
Herbarium: Netherlands.
Director and Curator: G. STOBBE, 1924 (Entomology).
Loans: On request.
Exchange: Not possible.

LEGON: *Ghana Herbarium, Department of Botany, University of Ghana,* **(GC),** Box 55, **Ghana,** West Africa.
Status: University.
Foundation: 1948. *Number of specimens:* 70.000.
Herbarium: Angiosperms, pteridophytes, bryophytes, algae and fungi, mainly of Ghana.
Important collections: G. W. Lawson and John (W. African marine algae), Jones (W. African hepatics), C.D. Adams (pteridophytes), J. K. Morton, J. B. Hall, A. A. Enti and Abbiw (angiosperms).
Director: E. LAING, 1931 (Genetics).
Curator: Vacant.
Staff members: D. K. ABBIW, 1939 (Forest trees of Ghana).
Specialization in research: Flora of Ghana; floristics and identification service.
Associated botanic garden: University Botanic Garden, Legon.
Loans: To recognized botanical institutions.
Periodical and serial works: Index Seminum.
Exchange: Specimens from Ghana in exchange for specimens from elsewhere in Africa, or herbarium materials.

LEGON: *Ghana Mycological Herbarium, University College of Ghana,* **(GCM),** Legon, **Ghana** — incorporated in GC.

LEICESTER: *Herbarium, University of Leicester,* **(LTR),** Leicester, LE1 7RH, England, **Great Britain.**
Telephone: 0533-554455.
Status: University.
Foundation: 1945. *Number of specimens:* 102.000.
Herbarium: Europe and Mediterranean Basin; vascular plants.
Important collections: T. G. Tutin, E. K. Horwood, B. M. Allen, B. L. Smythies, O. Polunin, A. O. Chater.

Director: H. Smith, 1935 (Plant physiology).
Curator: C. A. Stace, 1938 (Biosystematics and taxonomy of European angiosperms, especially Gramineae; flora of Great Britain and Ireland).
Staff members: T. G. Tutin, 1908 (Flora Europaea, flora of the British Isles).
Specialization in research: Floristic and biosystematic work on British and European vascular plants.
Associated botanic garden: University of Leicester Botanic Garden, Stoughton Drive South, Leicester LE2 2NA.
Loans: To recognized botanical institutions.
Periodical and serial works: Index Seminun.
Exchange: Available: European vascular plants. Desired: European and Mediterranean taxa.

LEIDEN: *Rijksherbarium*, (L), Schelpenkade 6, 2313 ZT Leiden, **Netherlands.**
Telephone: 071-130541.
Status: State University.
Foundation: Herbarium of Leiden University from c. 1575 onward; founded as State herbarium 1829.
Number of specimens: 2.500.000.
Herbarium: Worldwide phanerogams and cryptogams with emphasis on tropical Asia, Malesia, Australia, Pacific and Europe.
Important collections: Rich 19th century collections of phanerogams from Malesia (C. L. von Blume, H. Kuhl & J. C. A. van Hasselt, A. Zippel, C. G. C. Reinwardt, W. H. de Vriese, J. K. Hasskarl, P. W. Korthals, F. W. Junghuhn); Japan (P. F. Von Siebold); the Netherlands: bryophytes (F. Dozy & J. H. Molkenboer, Van der Sande Lacoste); fungi (Persoon); lichens (G. W. Körber), algae (F. T. Kützing, F. Hauck, W. F. R. Suringar, A. A. Weber-Van Bosse).
Director: C. Kalkman, 1928 (Malesian Rosaceae).
Staff members: F. A. C. B. Adema, 1939 (Flora of the Netherlands, Compositae).
P. Baas, 1944 (Systematic anatomy).
M. M. J. van Balgooy, 1932 (Plant geography, Pacific flora).
C. Bas, 1928 (Fungi: Agaricales).
J. van Brummelen, 1932 (Fungi: Discomycetes).
R. Geesink, 1945 (Malesian Papilionaceae).
W. A. van Heel, 1928 (Flora and fruit morphology).
Ding Hou, 1921 (Malesian Anacardiaceae, Aristolochiaceae, Celastraceae, Centrolepidaceae, Rhizophoraceae, Thymelaeaceae).
M. Jacobs, 1929 (Capparaceae, Fagaceae, Juglandaceae, Malpighiaceae, Violaceae, history of botany, nature conservation in Malesia).
W. F. B. Jülich, 1942 (Fungi: Aphyllophorales).
P. W. Leenhouts, 1926 (Malesian Burseraceae, Connaraceae, Dichapetalaceae, Goodeniaceae, Loganiaceae, Sapindaceae, bot. illustr.).

G. M. Lokhorst, 1943 (Chlorophyta).
R. van der Meijden, 1945 (Malesian Haloragaceae, Polygalaceae, flora of the Netherlands).
J. Mennema, 1930 (Labiatae, flora of the Netherlands).
J. Muller, 1921 (Palynology).
H. P. Nooteboom, 1934 (Malesian Magnoliaceae, Simaroubaceae, Symplocaceae).
W. F. Prud'homme van Reine, 1941 (Phaeophyta).
A. Touw, 1935 (Musci).
J. F. Veldkamp, 1941 (Malesian Gramineae, Oxalidaceae).
W. Vink, 1931 (Malesian Sapotaceae, Winteraceae).
E. F. de Vogel, 1942 (Malesian Orchidaceae, tree seedlings).
W. J. J. O. de Wilde, 1936 (Malesian Myristicaceae, Najadaceae, Passifloraceae).
Research associates: A. M. Brand, 1948 (Fungi: *Agaricus*).
R. W. J. M. van der Ham, 1951 (Flora of the Netherlands).
P. Heukels, 1948 (Flora of the Netherlands).
G. J. de Joncheère, 1909 (Pteridophytes).
E. Kits van Waveren, 1906 (Fungi: Agaricales).
R. A. Maas Geesteranus, 1911 (Fungi: Agaricales).
S. J. van Oostsroom, 1906 (Flora of the Netherlands).
Mrs. A. J. Quené-Boterenbrood, 1930 (Flora of the Netherlands).
C. E. Ridsdale, 1944 (Rubiaceae).
W. V. Rubers, 1944 (Musci of the Netherlands).
H. O. Sleumer, 1906 (Ericaceae, Flacourtiaceae, Olacaceae).
J. L. van Soest, 1908 (*Taraxacum*).
C. G. G. J. van Steenis, 1901 (General editor of Flora Malesiana, Malesian Bignoniaceae, *Nothofagus*, etc.).
E. J. Weeda, 1952 (Flora of the Netherlands).
Specialization in research: Flora of Malesia and the Asian-Pacific area in general; flora of the Netherlands, cryptogams and phanerogams; algae and fungi of Europe; systematic anatomy and palynology.
Loans: To recognized botanical institutions.
Periodical and serial works: Blumea; Persoonia; Gorteria; Pacific Plant Areas; Flora Malesiana Bulletin; Identification lists of Malesian specimens.
Exchange: Available: specimens from Malesia, the Netherlands and Western Europe. Desired: Specimens of all groups, especially from E. Asia to the Pacific and from Europe.
Remarks: Center of the activities of Flora Malesiana Foundation.

LEIDEN: *Koninklijke Nederlandse Botanische Ver-*

eniging *(Royal Botanical Society of the Netherlands)*, (**NBV**), c/o Schelpenkade 6, 2313 ZT Leiden, **Netherlands.**

Telephone: 071-130541.
Status: Independent society, the herbarium of which is deposited in the building of the Rijksherbarium, Leiden.
Foundation: 1845. *Number of specimens:* 150.000.
Herbarium: Plants of the Netherlands.
Loans: To recognized botanical institutions and botanists.
Periodical and serial works: Acta Botanica Neerlandica; Flora Neerlandica.
Remarks: The society has no scientific staff. The herbarium is directed by a committee, c/o Rijksherbarium, Leiden.

LEIPZIG: *Herbarium universitatis Lipsiensis, WB Taxonomie/Ökologie und Botanischer Garten der Sektion Biowissenschaften der KMU,* (**LZ**), Talstrasse 33, DDR-701 Leipzig, **German Democratic Republic, DDR.**

Telephone: 7165 437 and 7165 342.
Status: University.
Foundation: 1806. *Number of specimens:* 40.000.
Herbarium: The old herbarium was destroyed during World War II. It contained collections from all over the world, e.g. the Herbaria of Kunze, Drege, Mettenius, Römer, Schenk, Czapek and many others. A new collection is now being established.
Important collections: Since 1966 herb. Otto Fiedler (mainly adventive plants of Germany); since 1972 Herb. Peruvianum collections G. et C. Müller and P. Gutte et al 8.000 specimens, duplicates from the Herbarium San Marcos, Lima.
Director: G. K. MÜLLER, 1929 (Geobotany and taxonomy of Peruvian plants).
Curator: P. GUTTE, 1939 (Geobotany of Peruvian plants, ruderal plant communities).
Staff members: C. MÜLLER, 1928 (Poaceae: *Chloris, Polypogon*).
  D. SCHULZ, 1931 (Asteraceae: *Galinsoga, Tridax*).
Specialization in research: Weedy plants of South America; Loma- and Puna vegetation of Peru.
Associated botanic garden: Botanischer Garten der Karl-Marx-Universität, Linnéstr. 1, 701 Leipzig.
Loans: To recognized botanical institutions.
Exchange: Available: Specimens from the DDR. Desired: Weedy plants from tropical and subtropical regions.

LE MANS: *Herbarium, Academie de Caen, Centre Universitaire du Mans,* (**LEMA**), C.S.U., Route de Laval, Le Mans, **France.**

LENINGRAD: *Herbarium, Department of Botany and Dendrology, S. M. Kirov Forest Technology Academy,* (**KFTA**), Institutskii Per. 5, 194018 Leningrad, **U.S.S.R.**

Number of specimens: 300.000.
Director: N. Y. BULYGIN.

LENINGRAD: *Herbarium of the Department of Higher Plants, V. L. Komarov Botanical Institute of the Academy of Sciences of the U.S.S.R.,* (**LE**), Prof. Popov Street 2, 197022 Leningrad, **U.S.S.R.**

Telephone: 234-12-37.
Status: Directed by Academy of Sciences of U.S.S.R.
Foundation: 1714 (as medical garden), 1823 (herbarium and library). *Number of specimens:* Over 5.000.000.
Herbarium: Worldwide herbarium especially rich in types of the flora of the U.S.S.R. and Northern and Central Asia.
Important collections: F. A. M. von Bieberstein, A. A. von Bunge, L. A. von Chamisso, O. and B. Fedtschenko, F. E. L. Fischer, G. S. Karelin, Klementz, V. L. Komarov, S. I. Korshinsky, G. H. von Langsdorff, C. F. von Ledebour, V. I. Lipsky, K. I. Maximovicz, G. F. W. Meyer, G. N. Potanin, N. M. Prshewalski, C. Regel, L. Riedel, F. J. Ruprecht, A. G. von Schrenk, C. B. von Trinius, N. von Turczaninov.
Director: A. L. TAKHTAJAN, 1910 (Macrophylogeny and evolution of angiosperms, Armenian flora, *Paris*).
Head Curator: V. I. GRUBOV, 1917, 234-84-65 (Rhamnaceae, Chenopodiaceae of Asia, Valerianaceae, *Leontopodium*, flora and phytogeography of Central Asia).

Sectio Foreign Countries
(excluding East and Central Asia)
Curator: N. S. FILATOVA, 1930 (Asteraceae, especially *Artemisia*).
Staff members: N. N. IMKHANITSKAYA, 1935 (Lauraceae, Magnoliaceae).
  M. E. KIRPICZNIKOV, 1913 (Asteraceae systematics, botanical terminology).

Sectio East and Central Asia
Curator: V. I. GRUBOV.
Staff members: A. E. BORODINA, 1953 (Polygonaceae of temperate Asia).
  G. P. YAKOVLEV, 1938 (Fabaceae).
  O. I. STARIKOVA, 1929 (Chinese and Korean texts).

Sectio European U.S.S.R
Curator: N. N. TZVELEV, 1925 (Poaceae, Orobanchaceae, Asteraceae).
Staff members: T. G. LEONOVA, 1930 (*Euonymus, Artemisia*).
  V. M. VINOGRADOVA, 1937 (Apiaceae of U.R.S.S).

Sectio Caucasus
Curator: T. N. POPOVA, 1940 (Boraginaceae: *Onosma, Heliotropium, Myosotis*; Scrophulariaceae: *Pedicularis, Melampyrum*, of Caucasus).

Sectio Middle Asia
Curator: V. P. BOTSCHANTZEV, 1910 (Chenopo-

diaceae, subfamily Salsoloideae of Asia, Africa; *Erigeron*, Brassicaceae).

Staff members: O. V. TSCHERNEVA, 1929 (Asteraceae: Cynareae, especially *Cousinia;* Lamiaceae of Central and Middle Asia).

I. T. VASSILCZENKO, 1903 (*Medicago, Trigonella, Oxytropis, Vitis,* Prunoideae, Brassicaceae of Middle Asia, Iran, Afghanistan, Pakistan).

Sectio Siberia and Far East

Curator: S. JU. LIPSCHITZ, 1905 (*Scorzonera, Saussurea,* botanical bibliography).

Staff member: YU. P. KOSHEVNIKOV, 1942 (Caryophyllaceae, *Montia, Dryas* of Central Asia and Far East).

Sectio Duplicate Collections (Exchange)

Curator: L. I. IVANINA, 1917 (Scrophulariaceae of U.S.S.R. and Central Asia, Gesneriaceae).

Laboratory of Taxonomy and Geography of Higher Plants

Head Manager: AN. A. FEDOROV, 1908 (Taxonomy of higher plants, phytogeography, Campanulaceae, Primulaceae, Dipterocarpaceae, *Pyrus*).

Staff members: T. V. EGOROVA, 1930 (Cyperaceae).

V. N. GLADKOVA, 1936 (Cytotaxonomy of Rosaceae: Maloideae, Lamiaceae).

A. R. GRINTAL, 1937 (Aquatic plants).

I. A. GRUDZINSKAJA, 1920 (Ulmaceae, morphology of woody plants).

YU. D. GUSEV, 1922 (Chenopodiaceae of Europe, adventive flora of U.S.S.R.).

S. S. IKONNIKOV, 1931 (Caryophyllaceae, flora of Pamir, Badakhshan and Alaj).

R. V. KAMELIN, 1938 (Flora and phytogeography of Middle Asia, *Allium, Potentilla*).

G. YU. KONETSCHNAJA, 1951 (Asteraceae: *Senecio*).

I. A. LINCZEVSKY, 1908 (Plumbaginaceae, history of Mediterranean flora, nomenclature).

M. I. MAXIMOVA, 1938 (Arctic flora).

G. L. MENITSKY, 1937 (Fagaceae, Lamiaceae).

E. V. MORDAK, 1934 (Liliaceae: *Scilla*).

S. K. TSCHEREPANOV, 1921 (Betulaceae: *Alnus;* Asteraceae: Cynareae; nomenclature).

L. I. VASSILIEVA, 1923 (Fabaceae: Hedysareae of Middle Asia).

T. I. ZAIKONNIKOVA, 1929 (Saxifragaceae, *Deutzia, Sorbus, Aster, Erigeron*).

Specialization in research: Flora of U.S.S.R., North, West and Central Asia, Mediterranean flora.

Associated botanic garden: Yes.

Loans: To recognized botanical institutions.

Periodical and serial works: Novitates systematicae plantarum vascularium, Schedae ad Herb. Florae Rossicae (U.R.S.S.), Flora of the European part of the U.S.S.R.

Exchange: Available: Plants of Soviet Union, Eurasia. Desired: Plants of Asia and East, tropical plants of both hemispheres.

LENINGRAD: *Herbarium of the Cathedra Botanica, Leningrad University,* (**LECB**), V. O. Quay of University 7/9, 199164 Leningrad, **U.S.S.R.**

Telephone: 218-94-00.

Status: State university.

Foundation: 1920's. *Number of specimens:* 685.000.

Herbarium: Worldwide, especially plants of northern U.S.S.R.

Important collections: G. Bongard, E. Lindemann, O. A. Muraviova (Gymnosperms).

Director: V. M. SHMIDT, 1927 (Systematics and geography of plants).

Curator: M. A. VASILIUCHINA, 1936 (Systematics and geography of plants).

Staff member: E. Y. YEREMEYEVA, 1960 (Systematics and geography of plants).

Specialization in research: Plant geography and floristics.

Exchange: Within U.S.S.R.

LENINGRAD: *The All-Union Institute for Plant Protection,* (**LEP**), Herzen Street 42, Leningrad, **U.S.S.R.** – – *see* WIR.

LENINGRAD: *Herbarium, The All-Union Institute of Plant Industry,* (**WIR**), Herzen Street 44, 190000 Leningrad, **U.S.S.R.** (Information 1974)

Status: Belonging to All-Union Academy of Agricultural Sciences.

Foundation: 1923. *Number of specimens:* 225.000.

Herbarium: Cultivated and weedy plants of U.S.S.R. and other countries.

Important collections: S. M. Bukasov, K. F. Kostina, N. V. Kovalev, A. I. Mal'tsev, V. V. Nikitin, K. I. Pangalo, M. G. Popov, Y. I. Prokhanov, E. N. Sinskaya, A. K. Stankevich, T. N. Ul'yanova, N. I. Vavilov, E. V. Wulf, S. V. Yuzepchuk, P. M. Zhukovsky.

Specialization in research: Taxonomy and geography of cultivated plants, geography of weedy plants of U.S.S.R.

Loans: To recognized botanical institutions.

Periodical and serial works: Bulletin of Applied Botany, Genetics and Plant Breeding; Delectus plantarum.

LENNOXVILLE: *Herbarium, Bishop's University,* (**BULQ**), Johnson Science Building, Lennoxville, Québec, **Canada** J1M 1Z7.

Telephone: 819/569-9551.

Number of specimens: 10.000.

Herbarium: Mostly vascular plants of the Eastern Townships, Québec.

Director and Curator: R. VAN HULST, 1947 (Ecology).

Specialization in research: Forest ecology.

Exchange: Welcome.

LETHBRIDGE: *Herbarium, Department of Biological Sciences, University of Lethbridge,* (**LEA**), 4401 University Drive, Lethbridge, Alberta, **Canada** T1K 3M4.

Telephone: 403/329-2246.
Foundation: 1968. *Number of specimens:* 10.000.
Herbarium: Southern Alberta, especially Waterton Lakes National Park.
   Curator: JOB KUIJT, 1930 (Flora of southern Alberta; structure and affinities of parasitic flowering plants).
   Specialization in research: Flora of southern Alberta Rocky Mountains.
   Loans: Standard conditions.
   Exchange: Limited material available.

LETHBRIDGE: *Herbarium, Research Station, Agriculture Canada,* (**LRS**), Lethbridge, Alberta, **Canada** TıJ 4Bı.
   Telephone: 403/327-4561.
   Foundation: 1917. *Number of specimens:* 8.722.
Herbarium: Primarily native and introduced plants of mixed prairie range areas.
   Director: J. E. ANDREWS, 1922.
   Curator: S. SMOLIAK, 1926.
   Staff member: R. G. GSCHAID, 1941.
   Specialization in research: Range management, ecology, and forage crops.

LEUVEN: *Carnoy Instituut, Laboratorium voor beschrijvende plantkunde,* (**LV**) *-- see* HEVERLEE.

LEVELLAND: *Herbarium, Science Department, South Plains College,* (**SPLT**), Levelland, Texas 79336, **U.S.A.**
   Telephone: 806/894-9611, ext. 285.
   Foundation: 1968. *Number of specimens:* 20.000.
Herbarium: Local flora and ferns of the southwestern U.S.A.
   Director: JIM BLASSINGAME, 1938 (Southwestern U.S. ferns).
   Loans: In general to recognized botanical institutions.
   Exchange: Available: Specimens from Texas. Desired: Specimens of *Cheilanthes, Pellaea, Notholaena;* Chihuahuan Desert.

LEVIN: *Plant Health and Diagnostic Station, Horticultural Research Centre,* (**LEV**), Kimberley Road, Levin, **New Zealand.**
   Telephone: Levin 87059.
   Status: State Institution (Ministry of Agriculture and Fisheries).
   Foundation: 1951. *Number of specimens:* 12.000.
Herbarium: Horticultural plants, weeds, seeds, plant products, plant pathogenic fungi; mainly New Zealand collections and quarantine interceptions.
   Curator of Botany: MYRA HAMPTON, 1942 (Plant and seed identification).
   Curator of Mycology: GILLIAN LAUNDON, 1938 (Identification, taxonomy and nomenclature of fungi).
   Loans: To recognized botanical institutions.
   Remarks: The Station holds a culture collection

of fungi and a catalogue of New Zealand plant disease records.

LEWISBURG: *Wayne E. Manning Herbarium, Department of Biology, Bucknell University,* (**BUPL**), Lewisburg, Pennsylvania 17837, **U.S.A.**
   Telephone: 717/524-1155.
   Status: Private university.
   Foundation: 1945. *Number of specimens:* 20.000.
Herbarium: Vascular plants of Pennsylvania, New England, New Jersey, West Virginia, Georgia, South Carolina, Florida, and Mexico.
Important collections: Wayne E. Manning (Juglandaceae from U.S., Guatemala, Costa Rica, Peru, China, India, Philippines, and Mexico; includes Juglandaceae fruit collections), Frances Sargent, 700 sheets of Exsiccati Grayanae.
   Director and Curator: WARREN G. ABRAHAMSON, 1947 (Evolutionary plant ecology, coevolution).
   Specialization in research: Local flora; plant population biology; Juglandaceae.
   Loans: In general to recognized botanical institutions.
   Exchange: Can be arranged.

LEWISTON: *Herbarium, Department of Biology, Bates College,* (**BCL**), Lewiston, Maine 04240, **U.S.A.**
   Telephone: 207/784-8333.
   Foundation: 1880. *Number of specimens:* 4.000.
Herbarium: Plants of New England; some collections from the late 1800's.
   Director: ROBERT M. CHUTE.
   Loans: Yes.

LEXINGTON: *Herbarium, Thomas Hunt Morgan School of Biological Sciences, University of Kentucky,* (**KY**), Lexington, Kentucky 40506, **U.S.A.**
   Telephone: 606/257-2740.
   Foundation: 1949 (original herbarium of 30.000 specimens destroyed by fire in 1948). *Number of specimens:* 50.000.
Herbarium: Flora of Kentucky, including bryophytes and lichens; flora of Ceylon and southeast Asia.
Important collections: Charles W. Short (several hundred survived the 1948 fire), Mary Wharton (Black shale region of Kentucky).
   Curator: WILLEM MEIJER, 1923 (Flora of Kentucky; several families for flora of Ceylon; systematics of neotropical Tiliaceae and Dipterocarpaceae).
   Specialization in research: Flora of Kentucky, including bryophytes and lichens.
   Loans: To any recognized botanical institution.
   Exchange: Plants of Kentucky and Ceylon.

LEXINGTON: *Herbarium, Virginia Military Institute,* (**VMIL**), Lexington, Virginia 24450, **U.S.A.**
   Telephone: 703/463-6247; 463-6248.
   Foundation: 1839. *Number of specimens:* 20.000.

Herbarium: Primarily local collections, with some from North Carolina, West Virginia, and a few other states.

Director: ALAN G. C. WHITE, 1915 (General interest and biochemistry).

Curator: OSCAR W. GUPTON, 1924.

Specialization in research: General interest in vascular taxonomy and ecology.

Loans: Usual care, 6 months, annotations.

Exchange: Sporadic.

LIBEREC: *Herbarium, Severočeské Muzeum,* **(LIM),** Leninova II, 460 01 Liberec I, **Czechoslovakia.**

Telephone: 237 65-6.

Status: Regional museum.

Foundation: 1873. *Number of specimens:* 25.000.

Herbarium: Plants of Czechoslovakia, especially Bohemia, Sudety massif and Slovakia.

Director, Natural History Department: MILOSLAV NEVRLÝ, 1937 (Zoology).

Curator: ALOIS ČVANČARA, 1945 (Taxonomy of higher plants).

Staff member: MILOSLAV STUDNIČKA, 1949 (Geobotany, ecology).

Specialization in research: Taxonomy of Gentianaceae (*Centaurium, Blackstonia, Swertia*), Empetraceae, Droseraceae, *Crocus, Polypodium.*

Loans: To recognized botanical institutions.

Periodical and serial works: Sborník Severočeského Muzea, Ser. Natur.

Exchange: Yes.

LIBERTY: *Herbarium, Department of Biology, William Jewell College,* **(WJC),** College Hill, Liberty, Missouri 64068, **U.S.A.**

Telephone: 816/781-3806, ext. 229.

Status: Private institution.

Foundation: 1877. *Number of specimens:* 15.000.

Herbarium: Local collections.

Director and Curator: BURDETTE L. WAGENKNECHT, 1925 (Cultivated woody plants; local flora).

Specialization in research: Local flora.

Loans: Standard conditions, to recognized institutions.

Exchange: Welcome.

LIÈGE: *Herbarium et Jardin Botanique de l'Université,* **(LG),** Département de Botanique, Sart Tilman, B-4000 Liège, **Belgium.**

Telephone: 041/56.18.50 (Director), 56.18.54 (Phanerogamic herbarium), 56.18.53 (Cryptogamic herbarium).

Status: Botany Department of the University of Liège.

Foundation: 1819. *Number of specimens:* 200.000.

Herbarium: Worldwide, chiefly Europe and Central Africa, important cryptogamic collections.

Important collections: R. J. Courtois, C. J. E. Morren, A. F. Spring, including valuable material of con-

temporary botanists (A. L. S. Lejeune, M. A. Libert, Persoon); many published exsiccata, including rare sets and Belgian herbaria; Gasteromycetes; African lichens.

Director: J. LAMBINON, 1936 (Floristics of Western Europe and East Central Africa, terrestrial cryptogams, zoocecidia, nature conservation, bibliography of natural history).

Curators: P. AUQUIER, 1939, Vascular plants onomy and biosystematics of Poaceae, especially *Festuca, Vulpia;* floristics of Europe).

V. DEMOULIN, 1946, Thallophytes except lichens (Taxonomy of Gasteromycetes, macromycetes of Europe, phylogeny of cryptogams).

J. RAMAUT, 1924, Museum (Chemotaxonomy, especially lichens, pharmaceutical botany).

R. SCHUMACKER, 1937, Bryophytes (Bryophyta of W. Europe, floristics of Belgium, phytosociology, nature conservation).

E. SÉRUSIAUX, 1953, Lichens (Lichens, especially Africa and foliicolous species; nature conservation).

Laboratory of Systematics, Phytogeography and Ecology

Staff members: J. P. DESCY, 1949 (Freshwater algae in relation to pollution).

A. EMPAIN, 1949 (Aquatic mosses, ecology and relation to pollution).

R. FABRI, 1954 (Freshwater algae, ecology applied to nature management).

A. FROMENT, 1935 (Ecology of forests and heaths, nature management, conservation).

C. JOYE, 1956 (Phytosociology of terrestrial bryophytes).

J. REMACLE, 1936 (Soil and freshwater microbiology).

Botanic Garden

Staff members: J. BEAUJEAN, 1947 (Rock garden plants).

W. BELLOTTE, 1936 (Floristics of Europe, management seed exchange).

W. DEBAISIEUX, 1936 (Macaronesian succulents).

R. RENARD, 1944 (Cytotaxonomy).

J. ROUSSELLE, 1946 (Cactaceae, succulents).

Associate staff members: J. DAMBLON, 1913 (Floristics of Belgium, especially Macromycetes).

PH. DESTINAY, 1946 (Management, education in nature conservation).

G. TROUPIN, 1923 (Flora and vegetation of tropical Africa, numerical taxonomy).

Specialization in research: Flora and vegetation of Western and South Europe and East Central Africa, taxonomy and ecology of cryptogams, chemotaxonomy, nature conservation and management, biological indicators of water pollution.

Associated botanic garden: Jardin Botanique de l'Université de Liège.

Loans: To all qualified institutions and individuals.

Periodical and serial works: Lejeunia, Revue de Botanique. Société pour l'Echange des Plantes Vasculaires de l'Europe occidentale et du Bassin méditerranéen (Secr. P. Auquier).

Exchange: Available: Vascular plants and terrestrial cryptogams, especially from Europe and Central Africa, zoocecidia. Desired: The same, worldwide (especially Europe, Mediterranean area and Africa).

Remarks: Associated field laboratories: Station Scientifique des Hautes Fagnes (cf. LGHF), Station de Recherches sous-marines et océanographiques ("Stareso"), La Revellata, B.P. 33, F-20260 Calvi, Corse, France.

LIÈGE [WAISMES-ROBERTVILLE]: *Station Scientifique des Hautes Fagnes (Université de Liège),* **(LGHF),** Mont Rigi, B-4898 Waismes-Robertville, **Belgium.**
Telephone: 80/446182.
Status: Université de Liège.
Foundation: 1924 (reconstructed in 1975). *Number of specimens:* 14.000.
Herbarium: Phanerogams, pteridophytes, bryophytes, lichens, some Macromycetes of the Ardennes.
Important collections: M. A. Libert (Cryptogamae Arduennae).
Director and Curator: RENÉ SCHUMACKER, 1937 (Floristics and phytosociology).
Specialization in research: Interdisciplinary Station for ecological research on the Ardennes massif, in particular Les Hautes Fagnes.
Loans: On request.
Exchange: On request.

LILLE: *Fédération Universitaire et Polytechnique (Association d'Ecoles Supérieures et de Facultés Catholiques),* **(LILLE),** 60 Boulevard Vauban, 59046 Lille Cédex, **France.** (Information 1974)
Status: Free university.
Foundation: 1877.
Associated botanic garden: Jardin Botanique "Boulay."

LIMA: *Herbario, Departamento de Biología, Sección Botánica, Universidad Nacional Agraria,* **(MOL),** Apartado 456, La Molina, Lima, **Peru.**
Telephone: 35-20-35.
Foundation: 1905. *Number of specimens:* 12.000.
Herbarium: Peruvian and neotropical flora; economic and drug plants.
Important collections: A. Weberbauer.
Director: EDGARDO MACHADO CAZORLA, 1938 (Economic botany; Erythroxylaceae).
Curator: OSCAR VILCHEZ LARA, 1933 (Leguminosae).
Staff members: JORGE DE ALBERTIS (Cactaceae). LUIS DELGADO (*Capsicum;* Chenopodiaceae). CARLOS LOPEZ OCAÑA (Ecology). JUAN TORRES (Morphology).

JORGE YON KON (Fungi).
Specialization in research: Peruvian flora, chiefly economic and narcotic plants.
Associated botanic garden: Jardín Botánico de la Universidad Nacional Agraria, La Molina.
Loans: Normal regulations.
Periodical and serial works: Anales Cientificos de la Universidad Nacional Agraria.
Exchange: Available: Gramineae, Erythroxylaceae, Solanaceae, Leguminosae.

LIMA: *Herbario, Instituto de Botánica y Recursos Vegetales Terapéuticos, Universidad Nacional Mayor de San Marcos,* **(SMF),** Casilla 3551, Lima 1, **Peru.**
Telephone: 27-59-35.
Foundation: 1966. *Number of specimens:* 27.482..
Herbarium: Flora of Peru and neotropics; economic plants.
Important collections: Octavio Velarde Nuñez, Jaroslav Souckup, Peter Gutte, Gerd. Muller, Julio Lopez Guillen, Juana Infantes.
Director: JULIO LOPEZ GUILLEN, 1914 (Scrophulariaceae).
Curator: JAROSLAV SOUCKUP, 1902 (Ferns).
Staff members: ALFONSO DEL CASTILLO ICAZA. IRMA KIYAN DE CORNELIO (Compositae). LIDIA MOYA ARRIOLA. VICTORIA PALOMINO (Gramineae). ROSA ZARATE.
Specialization in research: Peruvian flora; medicinal plants.
Associated botanic garden: Jardin Botánico de la Universidad Nacional Mayor de San Marcos, Jirón Puno 1002.

LIMA: *Herbario San Marcos, Museo de Historia Natural, Universidad Nacional Mayor de San Marcos de Lima,* **(USM),** Avenida Arenales 1256, Apartado 1109, Lima, **Peru.**
Telephone: 71-01-17.
Foundation: 1918. *Number of specimens:* 250.000.
Herbarium: Peru, mostly Amazon Basin.
Important collections: César Acleto, Elida Carrillo, Emma Cerrate, Ramón Ferreyra, Alwyn Gentry, José Gómez, Paul Hutchison, Antonio Raimondi, Juan Revilla, Oscar Tovar, Augusto Weberbauer, Félix Woytkowski.
Director: RAMÓN FERREYRA, 1912 (Compositae, Polygalaceae, Nolanaceae).
Curator: EMMA CERRATE, 1920 (Economic botany; floristic studies of the Department of Ancash in central Peru).
Staff members: CÉSAR ACLETO, 1937 (Phycology). JUAN ACOSTA, 1941 (Marine algae). ELIDA CARRILLO, 1940 (Legum, *Phaseolus*). MAGDA CHANCO, 1941 (Malvaceae, *Nototriche, Palaua*). JOSÉ GÓMEZ, 1932 *(Rhizobium).* BERTA HERRERA, 1930 (Compositae, *Trixis, Gynoxys*).

153

OSCAR TOVAR, 1923 (Gramineae).
GRACIELA VILCAPOMA, 1941 (Solanaceae).
Specialization in research: Revision of Peruvian taxa; floristic studies of some Peruvian ecosystems (flora of the Coast, Sierra, and Humid tropics).
Loans: Usual regulations.
Periodical and serial works: Publicaciones Serie B, Botanica Memorias, Revista de Divulgación.
Exchange: Yes.

LINCOLN: *C. E. Bessey Herbarium, University of Nebraska State Museum,* (**NEB**), W-532 Nebraska Hall 5U, Lincoln, Nebraska 68588, **U.S.A.**
Telephone: 402/472-2613.
Status: An administrative unit of the University of Nebraska.
Foundation: 1871. *Number of specimens:* 250.000.
Herbarium: Emphasis on vascular flora of the Great Plains; collection of lichens is fairly large.
Important collections: C. E. Bessey, J. M. Bates, J. G. Smith, F. E. Clements (fungal types), W. Kiener (lichens); duplicates of many early collectors in the central U.S. (often including isotypes) as: P. A. Rydberg, A. Nelson, C. Parry, A. Heller, G. Vasey.
Curator: MARGARET R. BOLICK, 1950 (Asteraceae; pollen).
Staff member: ROBERT B. KAUL; 402/472-2715 (Aquatic plants).
Specialization in research: Flora of Nebraska and the Great Plains.
Loans: Usual terms.
Exchange: Currently only to a limited extent. Available: Specimens from Nebraska. Desired: Specimens from North America.

LINDICH: *Fürstin-Eugenie-Institut für Arzneipflanzenforschung,* (**ERZ**), Schloss Lindich, **Federal Republic of Germany,** BRD – – discontinued.

LINHARES: *Herbário, Companhia Vale do Rio Doce, Reserva Florestal da Cia. Vale do Rio Doce,* (**CVRD**), Km 118 da BR 101 Norte, P.O. Box 91, 22.900 Linhares, Espírito Santo, **Brazil.**
Telephone: (55)027/264-2214.
Status: Private institution.
Foundation: 1963. *Number of specimens:* 2.000.
Herbarium: Vascular plants of the Linhares Forest Reservation.
Important collections: A. M. Lino, J. Spada, D. A. Folli, I. A. Silva, D. Sucre, A. L. Peixoto, H. S. Lima.
Director: RENATO MORAES DE JESUS, 1951 (Forest engineer).
Curator: ARIANE LUNA PEIXOTO, 1947; 021-767-3134, ramal 286 (Monimiaceae, Mollinedieae, and woody plants of Espírito Santo).
Staff members: MERCEDES T. ROSA, 1957 (Woody plants of Espírito Santo).
INES M. SILVA, 1957 (Woody plants of Espírito Santo).
Contributors: GRAZIELA M. BARROSO, 1912

(Compositae, Araceae, and Leguminosae).
HAROLDO S. LIMA, 1956 (Leguminosae, Faboideae).
Specialization in research: Vascular flora of northern Espírito Santo (Linhares Forest Reservation); forest survey and improvement; enrichment with valuable native stands; sustained yield; mixed stands; storage and germination of seeds of native trees.
Associated botanic garden: Linhares Forest Reservation.
Loans: To recognized botanical institutions.
Exchange: Available: Seeds from tropical trees native to Espírito Santo. Wanted: Seeds of trees from other parts of the world.

LINZ: *Botanische Abteilung am Oberösterreichischen Landesmuseum,* (**LI**), Museumstrasse 14, A-4010 Linz, **Austria.** (Information 1974)
Status: Directed by O. Ö. Landesregierung.
Foundation: 1833. *Number of specimens:* 400.000.
Herbarium: Mainly collections of 19th century from Upper Austria, central and southern Europe.
Specialization in research: Caryology, chorology, systematics and taxonomy of *Scilla* and Antirrhineae; Upper Austrian flora.
Periodical and serial works: Jahrbuch des O. Ö. Musealvereins, Mitteilungen der Botanischen Arbeitsgemeinschaft am O. Ö. Landesmuseum.

LISBOA: *Herbarium, Instituto Dos Cereais,* (**CRCA**) – – transferred to LISI.

LISBOA: *Herbarium, Sociedade de Geografia de Lisboa,* (**LIG**), Portas de Santo Antão, Lisboa – 2, **Portugal.**

LISBOA: *Herbarium, Centro de Botânica da Junta de Investigaçoes Científicas do Ultramar,* (**LISC**), Rua da Junqueira 86, P-1300 Lisboa, **Portugal.**
Telephone: 64 55 18.
Status: Directed by the State (Ministry of Education and Science).
Foundation: 1948. *Number of specimens:* 200.000.
Herbarium: Tropical Africa (mainly Mozambique, Angola, Guiné-Bissau and Cabo Verde).
Important collections: J. M. Antunes, E. Dekindt, J. V. G. Espírito Santo, J. Gossweiler, G. le Testu, E. J. S. M. Mendes, F. A. Mendonça, H. J. E. Schlieben, A. R. Torre.
Director: E. J. MENDES, 1924 (*Commiphora*, Rosales, flora and phytogeography of Angola).
Staff members: A. E. GONÇALVES, 1939 (Flora of Mozambique).
M. L. GONÇALVES, 1934 (Aizoaceae s.l., Malvales, flora of Mozambique).
E. S. MARTINS, 1944 (Rubiaceae of Angola).
M. P. VIDIGAL, 1935 (Flora of Mozambique).
Specialization in research: Taxonomy and phytogeography, mainly Flora Zambesiaca area,

Angola, Guiné-Bissau and Cabo Verde.

Associated botanic garden: Jardim e Museu agrícola do Ultramar, Calçada do Galvão, P-1300 Lisboa.

Loans: In general to recognized institutions.

Periodical and serial works: Conspectus Florae Angolensis (in collab. with BM and COI); Flora Zambesiaca (in collab. with BM, K and SRGH); Flora de Moçambique (in collab. with COI and LMU); Garcia de Orta, Sér. Bot.

Exchange: Available: Specimens from Mozambique and Angola. Desired: Africa, mainly South of Sahara.

LISBOA: *Herbarium, Estação de Biologia Florestal,* (**LISFA**), Avenida João Crisóstomo 26-28, Lisboa, **Portugal.** (Information 1974)

Status: Directed by Ministry of Economy.

Foundation: 1916. *Number of specimens:* 30.000.

Herbarium: Mainly vascular plants, some bryophytes and fungi; Portugal, Madeira and Azores.

Specialization in research: Native flora and vegetation, forest and pasture seeds.

Loans: To recognized botanical institutions.

Periodical and serial works: Publicações da Direcção Geral dos Serviços Florestais e Aquicolas, Estudos e Divulgação Técnica, Estudos e Informações.

LISBOA: *Herbarium, Instituto Superior de Agronomia,* (**LISI**), Tapada da Ajuda, 1300 Lisboa, **Portugal.** (Information 1974)

Status: Universidade Técnica.

Foundation: 1917. *Number of specimens:* 55.000.

Herbarium: Portugal, Azores and Madeira.

Specialization in research: Portuguese, European and Macronesian floras, Portuguese trees, economic plants.

Associated botanic garden: Jardim Botanico da Ajuda.

Loans: To recognized botanical institutions.

Periodical and serial works: Anais do Instituto Superior de Agronomia.

LISBOA: *Herbarium, Jardim e Museum Agrícola do Ultramar,* (**LISJC**), Calçada do Galvão, 1400 Lisboa, **Portugal.**

Telephone: 637023.

Status: Junta de Investigações científicas do Ultramar.

Foundation: 1906. *Number of specimens:* 52.500.

Herbarium: Plants of Portugal and Portuguese-speaking countries.

Important collections: J. Gossweiler, J. V. G. Espírito Santo, J. B. Teixeira.

Director: CLÁUDIO MANUEL BUGALHO SEMEDO, 1922 (Agriculture).

Curator: MARIA CÁNDIDA LIBERATO, 1944 (Taxonomy).

Associated botanic garden: Yes.

Loans: In general to recognized institutions.

Periodical and serial works: Flora da Guiné Portuguesa, Flora de S. Tomé e Principe.

Exchange: Available: Specimens from continental Portugal and cultivated plants. Desired: Specimens from tropical Africa, America and Macaronesia.

LISBOA: *Herbarium, Missão de Estudos Agronómicos do Ultramar,* (**LISM**), Lisboa, **Portugal.**

LISBOA: *Museu, Laboratório e Jardim Botanico,* (**LISU**), Rua da Escola Politécnica, 1294 Lisboa, **Portugal.**

Telephone: 661521 × 20.

Status: University of Lisbon.

Foundation: 1839. *Number of specimens:* 500.000.

Herbarium: Mainly phanerogams, worldwide, Portugal and Angola.

Important collections: F. Welwitsch (phanerogams and cryptogams), A. Pereira Coutinho (phanerogams), J. Daveau (phanerogams), C. N. Tavares (lichens), J. Pinto-Lopes (fungi, Polyporaceae).

Director: J. PINTO-LOPES, 1915 (Polyporaceae).

Curator: C. SÉRGIO, 1942 (Bryophyta of Portugal, including Azores and Madeira).

Staff members: I. MELO, 1947 (Polyporaceae).

A. L. BELO CORREIA, 1930 (Phanerogams).

Associated botanic garden: Botanic Garden of the University of Lisbon.

Loans: To recognized botanical institutions.

Periodical and serial works: Portugaliae Acta Biologica, Series B; Revista de Biologia; Delectus Sporarum et Seminum.

Exchange: Yes.

LISBOA: *Herbarium, Laboratório de Patologia Vegetal "Veríssimo de Almeida,"* (**LISVA**), Lisboa, **Portugal.**

LISLE: *Herbarium, Morton Arboretum,* (**MOR**), Lisle, Illinois 60532, **U.S.A.**

Telephone: 312/968-0074.

Status: Private institution.

Foundation: 1922. *Number of specimens:* 40.000.

Herbarium: Vascular plants of the Chicago region, woody cultivated and spontaneous plants.

Important collections: E. J. Palmer (southeastern U.S.).

Director: MARION T. HALL, 1920 (Cytotaxonomy of Cupressaceae).

Curator: WILLIAM J. HESS, 1934 (Taxonomy of Rosaceae and Cornaceae).

Staff members: FLOYD SWINK, 1920 (Flora of Chicago region; cultivated plant identification).

GERALD WILHELM, 1948 (Flora of Chicago region; vegetation of natural lands).

Specialization in research: Taxonomy of cultivated and wild plants; flora of Chicago region; natural areas survey.

Loans: Available to recognized botanical institutions.
Periodical and serial works: Arboretum Quarterly; Plant Information Bulletin.
Exchange: Primarily woody plants either cultivated or spontaneous anywhere in the world.

LITOMĚŘICE: *Herbarium, Okresní Museum Litoměřice,* (**LIT**), Mírové nam., 412 01 Litoměřice, **Czechoslovakia.**
Telephone: 2019.
Status: Museum.
Foundation: 1965. *Number of specimens:* 45.000.
Herbarium: Tracheophyta of Czechoslovakia, especially NW Bohemia.
Important collections: W. Karl.
Director: EVA ŠTÍBROVÁ, 1950 (History).
Curator: K. KUBÁT, 1941 (Plant taxonomy and phytogeography).
Specialization in research: Flora of NW Bohemia, taxonomy of *Papaver* and *Rumex.*
Loans: Yes.
Exchange: Yes.

LITTLE ROCK: *Herbarium, Biology Department, University of Arkansas at Little Rock,* (**LRU**), 33rd and University Avenue, Little Rock, Arkansas 72204, **U.S.A.**
Telephone: 501/569-3247.
Foundation: 1965. *Number of specimens:* 6.000.
Herbarium: Teaching herbarium.
Director: CLARENCE B. SINCLAIR, 1924 (Commelinaceae).
Specialization in research: Surface characteristics of leaves by peels and SEM studies.
Loans: Normal regulations.
Exchange: Available: Central Arkansas.

LIVERPOOL: *Herbarium, Merseyside County Museums,* (**LIV**), William Brown Street, Liverpool L3 8EN, England, **Great Britain.**
Telephone: 051-207 0001.
Status: Municipal.
Foundation: 1851. *Number of specimens:* 160.000.
Herbarium: Worldwide.
Important collections: Herbaria of: J. F. Royle (Himalayas), Liverpool Botanic Garden (including duplicates from J. E. Smith), University of Liverpool's British Herbarium (on permanent loan from LIVU); collections of: J. Banks, J. Bradbury, F. Buchanan-Hamilton, P. Forskål, J. R. and G. Forster, B. Heyne, T. von Heldreich, J. G. Klein, C. Linnaeus, W. R. Linton, A. Menzies, H. Muhlenberg, T. Nuttall, P. S. Pallas, W. Roscoe, J. P. Rottler, J. E. Stocks, T. Velley, N. Wallich, and J. R. Wellsted.
Director of Museums: RICHARD A. FOSTER.
Curator: JOHN R. EDMONDSON, 1948 (Taxonomy of Mediterranean and Arabian floras; plant geography).

Staff member: ANGUS S. GUNN, 1953 (History of Velley material from French Guiana).
Specialization in research: British flora; documentation of types in historic collections.
Loans: To recognized botanical institutes.
Exchange: Available: British flowering plants and ferns.

LIVERPOOL: *Herbarium, The Hartley Botanical Laboratories,* (**LIVU**), Liverpool 3, England, **Great Britain.** (Information 1974)
Status: University.
Foundation: 1889. *Number of specimens:* 150.000.
Herbarium: Worldwide, especially Europe and Mediterranean area.
Important collections: W. R. Linton (Great Britain).
Specialization in research: Preparation and editing of the Flora Europaea, preparation of the Flora of British Marine Algae.
Associated botanic garden: University of Liverpool Botanic Gardens, Ness, Neston, Wirral, Cheshire.
Loans: To recognized botanical institutions.

LJUBLJANA: *Herbarium, Prirodoslovni Muzej Slovenije,* (**LJM**), Prešernova 20, p.p. 290, 61000 Ljubljana, **Yugoslavia.**
Telephone: 061-22-451.
Status: State institution.
Foundation: 1821. *Number of specimens:* 50.000.
Herbarium: Ferns and flowering plants of Europe (especially Slovenia).
Important collections: Flysser (1696), C. Hacquet, Zois, Freyer, Hladnik, Flora exsiccata Carniolica, Flora exsiccata Austro-Hungarica, Flora exsiccata Germanica, Herbarium Mycologicum Voss.
Director: MARKO ALJANČIČ, 1933 (General biology).
Curator: NADA PRAPROTNIK, 1951 (Alpine flora).
Specialization in research: Slovenian and Yugoslav flora.
Associated botanic garden: Alpinum Juliana, Trenta, 65232 Soča, Slovenija.
Loans: To recognized botanical institutions.
Periodical and serial works: Scopolia.

LJUBLJANA: *Botanični Inštitut, Univerza v Ljubljana,* (**LJU**), Ljubljana, **Yugoslavia.** (Information 1974)
Status: University.
Foundation: 1920. *Number of specimens:* 100.000.
Herbarium: Phanerogams, ferns and mosses of Europe, especially Alps and Balkan, and Nepal.
Specialization in research: Flora of the Alps, Mediterranean flora, flora of Central Balkan, flora of Nepal.
Associated botanic garden: Botanični vrt Univerze v Ljubljani.
Loans: To recognized botanical institutions.

ŁÓDŹ: *Herbarium, Institute of Environmental Biology, Łódź University,* (**LOD**), Banacha 12/16, PL-90-237 Łódź, **Poland.**
Telephone: 842/813-14.
Status: University.
Foundation: 1945. *Number of specimens:* 220.000.
Herbarium: Phanerogams, lichens and fungi of Europe, especially Central Poland.
Director: ROMUALD OLACZEK, 1934 (Geobotany).
Curators: LUCYNA FAGASIEWICZ, 1920 (Phanerogams).
MARIA ŁAWRYNOWICZ, 1943 (Hypogeous fungi).
Staff members: KRYSTYNA CZYŻEWSKA, 1938 (Lichens).
JANUSZ HEREŹNIAK, 1935 (Dendrology).
RYSZARD SOWA, 1927 (Synantropic flora).
AURELIA URSZULA WARCHOLIŃSKA, 1932 (Ecology and phytosociology of weeds).
Specialization in research: Flora, vegetation mapping and conservation in Central Poland; taxonomy and geography of fungi.
Loans: By application to the curators.
Exchange: Yes, especially hypogeous fungi.

LOGAN: *Intermountain Herbarium, Department of Biology, UMC 45, Utah State University,* (**UTC**), Logan, Utah 84322, **U.S.A.**
Telephone: 801/750-1586 (herbarium).
Foundation: 1931. *Number of specimens:* 166.500 (165.000 phanerogams, 1.500 cryptogams).
Herbarium: Flora of the Intermountain Region, including Utah, Nevada, southern Idaho, and southeastern Oregon.
Important collections: B. Maguire, A. H. Holmgren, N. H. Holmgren, J. L. Reveal, A. Cronquist, M. E. Jones, C. P. Smith.
Director: MARY E. BARKWORTH, 1941; 801/750-1584 (Poaceae, especially Stipeae of North America).
Curator: LEILA M. SHULTZ, 1946; 801/750-1586 (Floristics of the Intermountain West; *Artemisia;* bryophytes).
Staff member: ARTHUR H. HOLMGREN, 1912 (Flora of the Intermountain Region; Poaceae).
Specialization in research: Flora of the Intermountain Region.
Loans: To botanical institutions.
Exchange: Available: Plants of the Intermountain West, especially Great Basin and Wasatch Mountains. Desired: Vascular plants and bryophytes.

LOJA: *Herbarium Universitatis Loxensis "Reinaldo Espinosa," Facultad de Ciencias Agrícolas, Universidad Nacional de Loja,* (**LOJA**), Casilla letra B, Loja, **Ecuador.**
Telephone: 961730.
Foundation: 1946. *Number of specimens:* 3.500.

Herbarium: Flora of southern Ecuador; medicinal plants; trees of southern Ecuador; weeds of Ecuador.
Important collections: Reinaldo Espinosa.
Director: FRANCISCO A. VIVAR C. (General botany; plant physiology).
Staff member: KLEVER A. POMA VALVERDE (General botany).
Specialization in research: Medicinal plants; trees; flora of Amazonian Ecuador.

LOMA LINDA: *Herbarium, Department of Biology, Loma Linda University,* (**LOMA**), 24971 Stewart Street, Loma Linda, California 92354, **U.S.A.**
Telephone: 714/824-0800, ext. 2976.
Foundation: 1964. *Number of specimens:* 3.000.
Herbarium: Local flora, especially Santa Ana Mountain.
Director and Curator: EARL W. LATHROP, 1924 (Floristics; plant ecology).
Specialization in research: Vernal pool floristics; plant response to utility corridors, off-road vehicles, prescribed burns.
Associated botanic garden: Loma Linda University campus arboretum, Riverside, California 92505, U.S.A.

LOMÉ: *Herbier de l'Université du Bénin, Laboratoire de Biologie Végétale, Université du Bénin,* (**TOGO**), B.P. 1515, Lomé, **Togo.**
Status: University.
Foundation: 1977. *Number of specimens:* 7.000.
Herbarium: Flora of Togo and adjacent countries.
Important collections: Phyllanthoideae of Africa and Madagascar (Coll. Brunel), duplicates of types at Paris, Berlin-Dahlem, Strasbourg.
Director and Curator: JEAN FREDERIC BRUNEL, 1945 (Taxonomy of Phyllanthoideae, Euphorbiaceae; useful plants of Togo).
Staff members: M. GUMEDZOE, 1947 (Phytopathology, useful plants).
M. KPAKOTE, 1944 (Ecology, useful plants).
Specialization in research: Flora of Togo.
Associated botanic garden: Jardin d'Essais du Laboratoire de Biologie Végétale; Ferme expérimentale de l'Ecole supérieure d'Agronomie.
Loans: On request.
Periodical and serial works: Semina Togoensia, in Index Seminum Université L. Pasteur, Strasbourg (France); Annales de l'Université du Bénin, Lomé.
Exchange: On request.
Remarks: Numerous duplicates at B.

LONDON: *Herbarium, British Museum (Natural History),* (**BM**), Cromwell Road, London SW7 5BD, England, **Great Britain.**
Telephone: 01-589-6323.
Status: Financed from public funds but administered by a body of Trustees.
Foundation: 1753. *Number of specimens:* 4.000.000.
Herbarium: Worldwide herbarium with collections

of all groups except fungi, historical collections include many Linnaean types.

Important collections: Enumerated in "The history of the collections contained in the Natural History Departments of the British Museum." Since then acquired valuable collections of Phanerogamae from Europe (incl. Herb. F. G. Guiol, Greece and Herb. Joseph Héribaud, France), Angola, Tropical Africa (incl. Herb. G. le Testu), the Himalaya and S. E. Tibet (incl. collections by F. Ludlow, G. Sherriff, Stainton, G. Taylor and L. H. J. Williams), Siam (A. F. G. Kerr), New Guinea (C. E. Carr), W. Indies; the Pteridophyta of C. Christensen and collections from Indonesia (H. Alston), New Guinea (C. Jermy), S. America (H. Alston); the Musci of H. N. Dixon; the Algae of W. & G. S. West and F. E. Fritsch; the Charophyta of G. O. Allen; the Diatomeae of W. E. Baxter, E. Grove, F. Kitton, F. W. Payne. The bryophyta, lichenes and algae previously at K were transferred to BM on permanent loan in 1969, and the fungi from BM to K at the same time.

Director of Museum: R. H. HEDLEY, 1928 (Protozoa).

Keeper of the Department of Botany: J. F. M. CANNON, 1930 (Umbelliferae).

Deputy keeper: P. W. JAMES, 1930 (Lichens).

Flowering Plants

Staff members: S. BLACKMORE, 1952 (Palynology).

A. O. CHATER, 1933 (Curation of extra-European phanerogams, flora of Nepal, *Carex*).

G. C. S. CLARKE, 1944 (Palynology, pollen flora of NW Europe).

E. W. GROVES, 1923 (Southern cool–temperate and Indian Ocean islands, history of early collections).

J. O. DOROTHY HILLCOAT, 1904 (Retired; flora of Arabia).

C. J. HUMPHRIES, 1947 (Curation of European phanerogams, Compositae: Anthemideae, Gramineae).

FRANCES K. KUPICHA, 1947 (Krukoff Curator of African botany, Flora Zambesiaca; African phanerogams).

E. LAUNERT, 1926 (Flora Zambesiaca, African Gramineae, Malpighiaceae, *Marsilea*).

J. LEWIS, 1921 (*Xyris*, cultivated gymnosperms, theory of systematics).

J. B. MARSHALL, 1913 (Retired; Compositae: *Crepis, Conyza*, history of early collections).

G. A. MATTHEWS, 1924 (Curation of British phanerogams).

R. J. PANKHURST, 1940 (Curation of British phanerogams, computer-based methods for identification).

N. K. B. ROBSON, 1928 (Guttiferae, especially *Hypericum*, Celastraceae, angiosperms).

W. T. STEARN, 1911 (Retired; taxonomy and nomenclature especially cultivated plants, Linnaean typification, bibliography, hist. bot.).

D. A. SUTTON, 1952 (Scrophulariaceae: Antirrhineae, seed morphology).

A. R. VICKERY, 1947 (Curation of extra-European phanerogams, plant folklore).

CAROLINE WHITEFORD, 1933 (Cultivated plants, flora of Belize).

Cryptogamic Plants

Staff members: A. EDDY, 1937 (Musci, especially Tropical Asian and African *Sphagnum*).

C. R. FRASER-JENKINS, 1948 (Research fellow; European pteridophytes, Aspidiaceae of Asia, especially Nepal).

A. J. HARRINGTON, 1942 (Hepaticae, especially of Tropical Africa).

LINDA M. IRVINE, 1928 (British marine algae, especially Rhodophyta).

P. W. JAMES, 1930 (Lichens, especially of Europe and temperate Southern Hemisphere).

A. C. JERMY, 1932 (Pteridophytes, especially *Selaginella, Isoetes* and Tropical Asia, Athyriaceae, Malesia; phytogeography, conservation).

D. W. JOHN, 1942 (Freshwater algae).

J. R. LAUNDON, 1934 (Lichens, especially sterile crustose species).

T. B. B. PADDOCK, 1942 (Diatoms).

J. H. PRICE, 1932 (Marine algae, taxonomy and ecology of macroalgae, especially Ceramiaceae, South Atlantic, historical studies).

R. ROSS, 1912 (Retired; diatoms, Ericoideae excluding S. Africa).

PATRICIA A. SIMS, 1932 (Diatoms).

Cytology Laboratory

Staff member: MARY GIBBY, 1949 (Cytogenetics, angiosperms and pteridophytes, especially *Dryopteris*).

Fine Structure and Histochemistry

Staff member: J. M. PETTITT, 1937 (Reproductive processes, especially Cycads and seagrasses).

Library

Librarian: JUDITH A. DIMENT, 1946 (History of botany, botanical bibliography).

Specialization in research: Flora of British Isles and Europe; Angiospermae of Nepal, Flora Zambesiaca area, Arabia, Central America; pteridophyta, especially of Malaysia, bryophyta, especially Africa and S. E. Asia; lichens; algae (all groups).

Associated botanic garden: Chelsea Physic Garden, 66 Royal Hospital Road, London SW3 4HS.

Loans: To recognized botanical institutions, loans of types limited to six months.

Periodical and serial works: Bulletin of the British Museum (Natural History), Botany Series.

Exchange: Available: All groups except fungi. Desired: Vascular plants from Europe, N. Africa, N. & Central America, Caribbean, Arctic, Antarctic; other groups except fungi, worldwide.

Remarks: The Sloane Herbarium can be referred to as BM-SL.

LONDON: *Herbarium, Department of Botany and Plant Technology, Imperial College of Science and Technology,* **(ICST),** Prince Consort Road, London S.W. 7, England, **Great Britain.** (Information 1974)
Status: College of London University.
Foundation: 1907. *Number of specimens:* 1.000.
Herbarium: Mainly European plants, for teaching purposes.

LONDON: *Herbarium, The Linnean Society of London,* **(LINN),** Burlington House, Piccadilly, London W1V OLQ, England, **Great Britain.**
Telephone: 01-734-1040.
Status: Private.
Foundation: 1788. *Number of specimens:* 33.800 (Herb. Linn. 13.800, herb. Smith 20.000).
Herbarium: Worldwide.
Important collections: Carolus Linnaeus; Sir James Edward Smith (separately stored herbaria).
Director and Curator: WILLIAM T. STEARN, President.
Staff member: L. L. FORMAN (vide K).
Loans: Specimens loaned only to BM and K.
Periodical and serial works: Botanical Journal of the Linnean Society; Biological Journal of the Linnean Society; Linnean Society Symposium Series.
Remarks: The Society's "British Herbarium" [cf. J. Linn. Soc. (Bot.) 4: 194. 1860] is now owned by the British Museum (Natural History). Microfiche editions of the Linnaean and Smithian herbaria are available from: Inter Documentation Company AG, Poststrasse 14, 6300 Zug, Switzerland.

LONDON: *Herbarium, South London Botanical Institute,* **(SLBI),** 323 Norwood Road, London S.E. 24, England, **Great Britain.** (Information 1974)
Status: Private foundation.
Foundation: 1911. *Number of specimens:* 150.000.
Herbarium: Phanerogams and vascular cryptogams of British Isles and Europe, bryophytes and algae of British Isles, plants of Shetland Islands.

LONDON: *Herbarium, Department of Plant Sciences, University of Western Ontario,* **(UWO),** London, Ontario, **Canada** N6A 5B5.
Telephone: 519/679-3108.
Foundation: 1916. *Number of specimens:* 30.000.
Herbarium: North America, mainly Ontario.
Important collections: Worldwide Arundinelleae (Gramineae); Ontario *Crataegus* (Rosaceae).
Director and Curator: J. B. PHIPPS (Worldwide Arundinelleae; North American *Crataegus*).
Staff members: P. B. CAVEN (Weeds; Ontario).
F. S. COOK (Bryophytes; Ontario).
D. M. FAHSELT (Lichens; Ontario).
R. C. JANCEY (Podalyriae, Leguminosae of Australia; *Pinus* of North America).
A. MAUS (General; Great Lakes sand dunes).
Specialization in research: As above.
Associated botanic garden: The University of

Western Ontario Arboretum; Plant Sciences Department Field Station.
Loans: To recognized botanical institutions.
Exchange: Available: Ontario flora, especially *Crataegus.* Desired: General flora; *Crataegus* of northeastern North America.

LONG BEACH: *Herbarium, Biology Department, California State University,* **(LOB),** 1250 Bellflower Boulevard, Long Beach, California 90840, **U.S.A.**
Telephone: 213/498-4917.
Foundation: 1949. *Number of specimens:* 19.500.
Herbarium: Flora of southern California; vascular plants of southern California and southeastern U.S.; marine algae of southern California coast and southern South America.
Co-Directors: PHILIP C. BAKER, Curator of Vascular Plants (Angiosperm systematics).
GEOFFREY L. LEISTER, Curator of Marine Algae.
Staff member: JAMES BOURRET (Mycology).
Specialization in research: Biosystematics of desert vascular plants; taxonomy of Gigartinaceae (Rhodophycophyta).
Exchange: Available: Local southern California vascular plants and marine algae.

LOS ANGELES: *Herbarium, Allan Hancock Foundation, University of Southern California,* **(AHFH),** Los Angeles, California 90007, **U.S.A.**
Telephone: 213/741-7535; 741-7069.
Status: Foundation, directed by the University of Southern California, a private university.
Foundation: 1946. *Number of specimens:* 60.000.
Herbarium: Exclusively marine plants, primarily benthic algae; worldwide representation with emphasis on eastern Pacific.
Important collections: W. R. Taylor (Galapagos; Caribbean), E. Y. Dawson (Mexico, Central America, Peru, Vietnam), Nina Loomis herbarium, R. B. Setzer (U.S. Pacific coast), Los Angeles County Museum (LAM) algae, University of Southern California (USC) marine algae (Southern California 1920's and 1930's).
Director: DAVID N. YOUNG, 1947 (Ultrastructure, ecology, systematics of benthic marine algae).
Curator: ROBERT B. SETZER, 1944 (Systematics, phycogeography, and ecology of benthic marine algae).
Specialization in research: Benthic marine algal systematics, distribution, ecology, ultrastructure.
Loans: In general to recognized institutions.
Periodical and serial works: Several series of the Allan Hancock Foundation Publications. Current series is Allan Hancock Monographs in Marine Biology.
Exchange: Available: California marine algae. Desired: Worldwide marine algae.
Remarks: Land plants of AHFH, previously housed at USC, transferred to LAM in 1976. Ma-

rine algae of LAM transferred to AHFH in 1976.

LOS ANGELES: *Herbarium, Department of Biology, California State University,* **(CSLA),** Los Angeles, California 90032, **U.S.A.**
Telephone: 213/224-3518; 224-3258.
Foundation: ca. 1956. *Number of specimens:* 30.000.
Herbarium: Southern California, Mojave Desert, Chihuahuan Desert, Baja California, Mexico.
Important collections: James Henrickson, Barry Prigge, Richard Straw.
    Director: JAMES HENRICKSON, 1940 (Flora of Chihuahuan Desert, Sierra Madre Occidental, Mojave Desert; Fouquieriaceae).
    Staff member: RICHARD M. STRAW, 1926 (*Penstemon*).
    Specialization in research: Floristics of Chihuahuan Desert, Sierra Madre Occidental, Mexico, Mojave Desert.
    Loans: Usual conditions.
    Exchange: Available: Southern California, Mojave Desert. Desired: Northern Mexico, western North America.

LOS ANGELES: *Herbarium, University of California,* **(LA),** 405 Hilgard Avenue, Los Angeles, California 90024, **U.S.A.**
Telephone: 213/825-3620.
Foundation: 1925. *Number of specimens:* 250.000.
Herbarium: Flora of southern California and adjacent regions; other Mediterranean climatic regions; subtropical ornamentals.
Important collections: Research collections of Onagraceae and Loasaceae; Epling collection of American Lamiaceae transferred to Berkeley (UC) in 1977.
    Director and Curator: ARTHUR C. GIBSON, 1947 (Cactaceae, Burseraceae).
    Staff members: BARBARA JOE HOSHIZAKI, 1928 (Pteridophyta).
    F. HARLAN LEWIS, 1919 (Onagraceae).
    MILDRED E. MATHIAS, 1906 (Apiaceae).
    JONATHAN D. SAUER, 1918 (*Amaranthus, Canavalia, Stenotaphrum*).
    HENRY J. THOMPSON, 1921 (Loasaceae).
    DAVID S. VERITY, 1930 (*Dudleya*; flora of southern California).
    Associated botanic garden: Mildred E. Mathias Botanical Garden.
    Loans: To recognized institutions.
    Exchange: For plants of arid and semiarid vegetation.

LOS ANGELES: *Natural History Museum of Los Angeles County,* **(LAM),** 900 Exposition Boulevard, Los Angeles, California 90007, **U.S.A.**
Telephone: 213/744-3379.
Status: Operating foundation and local government support.
Foundation: Museum: 1913; Herbarium: 1927.

Number of specimens: 250.000.
Herbarium: Ascomycete fungi of tropical Pacific basin and neotropics; fungi, ferns, mosses of southern California; flowering plants of southwestern U.S., especially California, Mexico, neotropics, and Pacific basin.
Important collections: A. Davidson (southern California), Wm. A. Bryan (Juan Fernandez), H. E. Hasse (lichens), L. C. Wheeler; herbaria (excluding algae) of University of Southern California (USC) and Allan Hancock Foundation (AHFH).
    Director: DON R. REYNOLDS, 1938 (Mycology).
    Staff members: C. DAVIDSON, 1944 (Flora of Bolivia; evolutionary plant anatomy).
    R. GUSTAFSON, 1939 (Flora of Hawaii).
    Research Associates: S. KEELEY, 1948 (*Vernonia*).
    FRITS ZEYLEMAKER, 1915 (Cactaceae).
    Specialization in research: Taxonomy and developmental studies of foliicolous Ascomycetes; flora of neotropics, Hawaii, and southern California; plant anatomy of tropical buttress trees.
    Associated botanic garden: Los Angeles State and County Arboretum, 301 N. Baldwin Ave., Arcadia, California 91006, U.S.A.
    Loans: In general to recognized botanical institutions.
    Periodical and serial works: Natural History Museum Contributions in Science (technical papers published at irregular intervals).
    Exchange: Neotropical, southern California, Mexico.
    Remarks: Herbaria (excluding algae) of USC and AHFH incorporated with LAM in 1976. Marine algae of LAM transferred to AHFH in 1976.

LOS ANGELES: *Herbarium, Department of Biology, Occidental College,* **(LOC),** 1600 Campus Road, Los Angeles, California 90041, **U.S.A.**
Telephone: 213/259-2898.
Foundation: 1905. *Number of specimens:* 15.000.
Herbarium: Southern California vascular plants.
    Director: JON E. KEELEY, 1949 (*Arctostaphylos*).
    Loans: Yes.
    Exchange: Yes.

LOS ANGELES: *Herbarium, Department of Biological Sciences, University of Southern California,* **(USC),** University Park, Los Angeles, California 90007, **U.S.A.** – – integrated with LAM.
Foundation: 1923. *Number of specimens:* 23.000.
Herbarium: Southern California regional flora.

LOS BAÑOS: *Herbarium, College of Agriculture, University of the Philippines,* **(CAHUP),** Los Baños, College, Laguna, **Philippines.** (Information 1974)
Status: University.
Foundation: 1909. *Number of specimens:* 22.000.
Herbarium: Philippine plants.
    Specialization in research: Mt. Makiling flora, morphology and anatomy of major Philippine

economic plants.

Associated botanic garden: Los Baños College of Agriculture Arboretum.

Loans: To recognized botanical institutions.

Periodical and serial works: Philippine Agriculturist.

LOS BAÑOS: *Mycological Herbarium, University of the Philippines Museum of Natural History,* (**CALP**), Los Baños, College, Laguna, **Philippines.**

Telephone: 26-17.

Status: University.

Foundation: 1966. *Number of specimens:* 10.000.

Herbarium: Fungi.

Important collections: Jenkins and Bitancourt Exsiccatae, Ocfemia collection, T. H. Quimio (Agaricales of Mt. Maquiling), D. Reynolds (Philippine Myxomycetes), I. J. Dogma (Clavariales).

Director of Museum: JUAN PANCHO, 1929 (Taxonomy).

Curators: IRENEO J. DOGMA, JR., 1942 (Lower fungi).

TRICITA H. QUIMIO, 1939 (Higher fungi).

Specialization in research: Plant pathogenic fungi, Agaricales of Mt. Maquiling.

Exchange: Yes.

LOS BAÑOS: *Herbarium, Forest Products Research and Industries Development Commission,* (**CLP**), National Sciences Development Board, Los Baños, College, Laguna, **Philippines.** (Information 1974)

Status: Government agency.

Foundation: 1954. *Number of specimens:* 2.300.

Herbarium: Philippine woody plants and spermatophytes.

Specialization in research: Philippine woody plants.

Loans: To recognized botanical institutions.

LOS BAÑOS: *Herbarium, College of Forestry, University of the Philippines,* (**LBC**), Los Baños, College, Laguna 3720, **Philippines.**

Telephone: 35-32.

Status: State university.

Foundation: 1910. *Number of specimens:* 12.000.

Herbarium: Mainly Philippine trees, voucher specimens and spirit collections of tree seedlings, carpological collection and wood specimens of commercial trees and other forest plants.

Director: CELSO B. LANTICAN, 1941 (Wood anatomy).

Curator: EDWIN S. FERNANDO, 1953 (Tree seedling morphology, plant taxonomy).

Staff members: LUCIO L. QUIMBO, 1923 (Dendrology, botanical microtechnique).

ENRIQUITO D. DE GUZMAN, 1940 (Forest pathology and mycology).

Specialization in research: Tree flora of the Philippines, forest flora of Mt. Makiling.

Associated garden: Makiling Botanic Garden.

Loans: To recognized botanical institutions.

Periodical and serial works: Pterocarpus, Philipp. Sci. J. Forestry.

Exchange: Available: Philippine forest plants. Desired: Forest plants of other regions, especially Malesia, Polynesia and tropics.

Remarks: Most early collections were destroyed by fire in 1940.

LOUISVILLE: *Davies Herbarium, Department of Biology, University of Louisville,* (**DHL**), Louisville, Kentucky 40208, **U.S.A.**

Telephone: 502/588-6771.

Foundation: 1953. *Number of specimens:* 28.500.

Herbarium: Vascular plants of Kentucky and surrounding states.

Director and Curator: W. S. DAVIS, 1930 (Systematics of *Malacothrix,* Asteraceae).

Specialization in research: Floristic work in Kentucky.

Loans: Usual regulations.

Exchange: Available: Plants of Kentucky.

LOURENÇO MARQUES: – – *see* MAPUTO.

LOUVAIN-LA-NEUVE: *Mycothèque de l'Université Catholique de Louvain,* (**MUCL**), Place Croix du Sud 3, B-1348 Louvain-la-Neuve, **Belgium.**

Telephone: (0)10-418181, ext. 3742.

Status: Belongs to Laboratoire de Mycologie systématique et appliquée, Fac. Sciences Agronomiques, Université Catholique de Louvain.

Foundation: 1894, by Prof. Ph. Biourge, later preserved as "Mycothèque Biourge" (1938-1968), fused with coll. G. L. Hennebert in 1968 as MUCL. *Number of specimens:* 12.000, living and dried cultures.

Herbarium: Fungi: Hyphomycetes, flora of Belgium, Europe, North America, Congo.

Important collections: Ph. Biourge (*Penicillium*), J. A. Meyer, G. L. Hennebert.

Director and Curator: GRÉGOIRE L. HENNEBERT, 1929 (Taxonomy and nomenclature of fungi).

Specialization in research: Taxonomy and nomenclature of fungi; applied mycology.

Periodical and serial works: Mycotaxon.

Exchange: Yes.

LUANDA: (**LUA**) – – *see* NOVA LISBOA.

LUANDA: *Herbarium, Instituto de Investigação Científica de Angola,* (**LUAI**), Centro de Estudos de Sá da Bandeira, P.O. Box 485, Sá da Bandeira, Luanda, **Angola.** (Information 1974)

Status: Directed by state.

Foundation: 1958. *Number of specimens:* 30.000.

Herbarium: Flora of Africa south of the Sahara, especially Angola.

Important collections: L. Grandvaux Barbosa, O. Azancot de Menezes, R. Santos.

Specialization in research: Vegetation mapping.

Loans: To recognized botanical institutions.
Periodical and serial works: Publicações do Instituto de Investigação Cientifica de Angola.

LUBBOCK: *E. L. Reed Herbarium, Department of Biological Sciences, Texas Tech University,* **(TTC),** Box 4149, Lubbock, Texas 79409, **U.S.A.**
Telephone: 806/742-2722.
Foundation: 1925. *Number of specimens:* 20.000.
Herbarium: Arid lands collections, especially southwestern U.S. and Chihuahuan portion of Mexico.
  Curator: DAVID K. NORTHINGTON, 1944 (Systematics and chemosystematics of phanerogams).
  Staff member: RAYMOND C. JACKSON (Cytogenetics of *Haplopappus*).
  Specialization in research: Arid and semi-arid land vascular plant systematics; phylogeny as determined by chemosystematics and cytogenetics.
  Loans: To recognized institutions or individuals.
  Periodical and serial works: Texas Tech University Museum Series.
  Exchange: Available: Plants from west Texas, especially the high plains and panhandle. Desired: Sophoreae and arid land plants in general.

LÜBECK: *Herbarium, Naturhistorisches Museum zu Lübeck,* **(LUB),** Mühlendamm 1-3, 2400 Lübeck, **Federal Republic of Germany,** BRD. (Information 1974)
Status: Municipal.
Foundation: 1945. *Number of specimens:* 4.500.
Herbarium: Plants of Schleswig-Holstein.
  Periodical and serial works: Berichte des Vereins Natur und Heimat und des Natuurhistorischen Museums zu Lübeck.
  Loans: To recognized botanical institutions.

LUBLIN: *Department of Plant Systematics and Geography of the University,* **(LBL),** ul. Glowackiego 2, Lublin, **Poland.** (Information 1964)
Foundation: 1945. *Number of specimens:* 114.000.

LUBLIN: *Cryptogamic Herbarium (Herbarium Muscorum), Institute of Biology, University of M. Curie-Skłodowska,* **(LBLC),** ul. Akademicka 19, 20-033 Lublin, **Poland.**
Telephone: 382-71.
Status: Institute of University.
Foundation: 1947. *Number of specimens:* 13.750.
Herbarium: Mosses and hepatics, general collections, Mongolian and Philippine collections.
  Director and Curator: KAZIMIERZ KARCZMARZ, 1933 (Bryology, palaeobotany).
  Staff members: MAREK BLOCH, 1946 (Bryology).
  MIROSŁAWA BLOCH, 1945 (Bryology).
  ANNA KORNIJÓW, 1955 (Bryology).
  ALEKSANDER W. SOKOŁOWSKI, 1930 (Floristics, phytocenology).
  FLORIAN ŚWIĘS, 1939 (Floristics, geobotany).

Specialization in research: Floristics, ecology, taxonomy, palaeobotany; flora of Mongolia and Philippines; hepatics of Carpathian Mts.; bryocenology of Polish National Parks.
  Associated botanic garden: Botanic Garden of M. Curie-Skłodowska University.
  Loans: At present only to Polish institutions.
  Periodical and serial works: Hepaticae Exsiccatae Palotinatus Lublinensis, Hepaticae Europae Orientalis Exsiccatae, Musci et Hepaticae Mongoliae.
  Exchange: Yes.

LUBUMBASHI: *Laboratoire de Biologie générale et de Botanique,* **(EBV)** – – incorporated in LSHI.

LUBUMBASHI: *Service de Botanique Systématique et Ecologie Tropicales, Université Nationale du Zaïre,* **(LSHI),** B.P. 1825, Lubumbashi, **Zaïre.** (Information 1974)
Status: University.
Foundation: 1968. *Number of specimens:* 25.000.
Herbarium: Plants of Zaïre and Zambia.
  Specialization in research: Flora and vegetation of Shaba highlands, forest ecology.
  Loans: To recognized botanical institutions.
  Periodical and serial works: Travaux du Service de Botanique Systématique et Ecologie Tropicales.

LUCCA: *Herbarium Horti Lucensi,* **(LUCCA),** Via S. Micheletto n. 5, 55 100 Lucca, **Italy.**
Telephone: 0583/46665.
Status: Adherence to Botanical Garden of Lucca municipality.
Foundation: ca. 1830. *Number of specimens:* 25.000.
Important collections: "H. Bicchianum" (Lucca Bic.): Flora of Italy, especially of Lucca District (Tuscany, Cesare Bicchi); "Plantae Lucenses" (Lucca Puc.): Typical flora of Lucca District (Tuscany, Puccinelli).
  Director: Vacant.
  Curator: PAOLO EMILIO TOMEI, 1947 (Phytogeography, mainly of marshes and bogs).
  Staff members: ANGELO LIPPI, 1946.
  DANILO DONNINI, 1929.
  Specialization in research: Taxonomy and chorology of vascular plants of humid zones of Italy.
  Associated botanic garden: Orto Botanico del Comune di Lucca.
  Loans: No loans until herbarium rearrangement has been finished.

LUCKNOW: *Herbarium, Central Institute of Medicinal and Aromatic Plants,* **(CIMAP),** Faridinagar (near Kukrail Picnic Spot), Lucknow 226010, **India.**
Telephone: 81170.
Status: Scientific institution under Council of Scientific and Industrial Research.
Foundation: 1978. *Number of specimens:* 1.500.
Herbarium: Medicinal and aromatic plants of India.
  Director: AKHTAR HUSAIN, 1928 (Plant pathol-

ogy; medicinal and aromatic plants).

Curator: N. C. SHAH, 1936 (Ethnobotany; survey of medicinal and aromatic plants).

Specialization in research: Study of medicinal and aromatic plants.

Associated botanic garden: Arboretum and herbal garden.

Loans: Yes.

Exchange: Medicinal and aromatic plants.

LUCKNOW: *Herbarium of National Botanical Research Institute,* **(LWG)**, Lucknow 226001, **India.**

Status: Council of Scientific and Industrial Research, New Delhi.

Foundation: 1948 (taken over by Council in 1953). *Number of specimens:* 110.000.

Herbarium: Lichens, ferns and angiosperms of India; carpological collections.

Important collections: Gills (Kumaon), Wing-field Dudgeon (lichens of Mussourie).

Director: T. N. KHOSHOO, 1927 (Biosystematics).

Head of Taxonomy and Herbarium: S. L. KAPOOR, 1931 (Floristics, taxonomy of *Clematis*, Oleaceae, cuticular studies of Apocynaceae, economic botany).

Curator: S. R. PAUL, 1933 (Floristics, phytogeography, taxonomy Indian Nyctaginaceae).

Staff members: P. H. S. KHAN, 1931 (Seed morphology).

V. S. SHARMA, 1931 (Floristics, taxonomy of angiosperms).

AJAY SINGH, 1926 (Indian lichens).

K. P. SRIVASTAVA, 1920 (Indian bryophytes).

Specialization in research: Taxonomic studies of ornamental and economic plants.

Associated botanic garden: Botanical Garden of National Botanical Research Institute.

Loans: To recognized botanical institutions.

Periodical and serial works: National Botanical Research Institute Newsletter, New Botanist, Annual Report.

Exchange: Available: Indian plants. Desired: Specimens of cultivated, ornamental and economic plants.

LUCKNOW: *University Herbarium,* **(LWU)**, Lucknow, **India.**

LUDWIGSBURG: *Staatliches Museum für Naturkunde Stuttgart, Abteilung für Botanik,* **(STU)**, Arsenalplatz 3, D-7140 Ludwigsburg, **Federal Republic of Germany,** BRD.

Telephone: 07141/1412545,-46,-47.

Status: Directed by the State.

Foundation: 1791. *Number of specimens:* 400.000.

Herbarium: General herbarium, especially South Germany.

Important collections: F. Fleischer (*Carex*), J. F. N. Bornmüller (Turkey, Iran), W. Schimper (Ethiopia), Th. Kotschy (Sudan), F. Hegelmaier (*Callitriche,*

Lemnaceae), K. Bertsch and K. Müller (SW Germany), V. Wirth (Lichenes), A. Vezda (Lich. sel. exs.), F. Arnold (Lich. exs.), Chr. F. Hochstetter (Lichenes).

Director: BERNHARD ZIEGLER, 1929 (Palaeontology).

Curator: OSKAR SEBALD, 1929 (Lamiaceae of tropical Africa, especially *Leucas, Otostegia;* flora of Ethiopia; vegetation mapping SW Germany).

Staff members: SIEGMUND SEYBOLD, 1939 (*Marrubium,* flora of SW Germany).

VOLKMAR WIRTH, 1943 (Ecology of lichens, especially Lecideaceae).

Specialization in research: Flora and vegetation of south-western Germany.

Loans: To botanists and botanical institutions.

Periodical and serial works: Stuttgarter Beiträge zur Naturkunde Serie A (Biologie).

Exchange: Available: Plants of Southern Germany. Desired: Labiatae, especially *Leucas, Marrubium.*

LUND: *Botanical Museum,* **(LD)**, Ö. Vallgatan 18, S-223 61 Lund, **Sweden.**

Telephone: 046-124 100 ext. 715.

Status: Division of the Department of Systematic Botany, State University of Lund.

Foundation: Teaching in botany started 1668, herbarium about 1770. *Number of specimens:* 2.300.000.

Herbarium: Worldwide herbarium, all groups, especially Scandinavia, Mediterranean region, South Africa.

Important collections: C. A. and J. G. Agardh (Algae), S. Berggren (Bryophytes, esp. New Zealand), R. Dahlgren (*Aspalathus,* Penaeaceae), Th. C. E. Fries, T. Norlindh and H. Weimarck (Rhodesia, S. Africa), C. E. Gustafsson (*Rubus*), J. O. Hagström (*Potamogeton*), K. Th. Hartweg (S. America), O. J. Hasslow (Characeae), H. Kylin (Algae), R. Matsson (*Rosa*), S. Murbeck (N. Africa, *Verbascum, Celsia*), L. M. Neuman (Scandinavia), O. Nordstedt (Freshwater algae), L. Preiss (Australia), K. Rechinger (Central Europe), A. J. Retzius (incl. herb. E. Acharius, Phanerogams and several isotypes from O. Swartz and C. P. Thunberg), H. Runemark et al. (Greece), P. Sintenis (Central and Southern Europe, Southwestern Asia, Puerto Rico), R. Spruce (S. America, Mexico), L. J. Wahlstedt (Characeae).

Director: H. RUNEMARK, 1927 (Flora of Greece). [Correspondence concerning the Museum and Herbarium should be addressed to the Curator].

Curator: S. SNOGERUP, 1929.

Staff members and Research associates: O. ALMBORN, 1914 (Lichens, esp. South Africa, history of botany, botanical bibliography).

I. BJÖRKQVIST, 1931 (Alismataceae).

R. VON BOTHMER, 1943 (*Hordeum, Scutellaria* subsect. *Peregrinae*).

GERTRUD DAHLGREN, 1931 (*Sanguisorba, Erodium* of the East Mediterranean).

MARIE ELLMER, 1949 (*Glechoma*).

L. Engstrand, 1942 (Umbelliferae).

R. Franzén, 1957 (Alpine flora of central Greece).

L. Å. Gustavsson, 1946 (Alpine flora of central Greece).

H. Hjelmqvist, 1905 (Fagaceae, especially S.E. Asia; archaeological botany).

J. Th. Johansson (Flora of Indonesia).

T. Karlèn, 1953 (*Muscari*).

T. Karlsson, 1945 (*Euphrasia*).

M. Knutsson, 1952 (*Aconitum*).

I. Kärnefelt, 1944 (Lichens, especially *Cetraria* and *Cornicularia*).

T. Landström, 1944 (*Ornithogalum*).

P. Lassen, 1942 (Leguminosae, especially Trifolieae and Loteae; flora of Northern Morocco).

Hilde Nybom, 1951 (*Rubus*).

A. Oredsson, 1938 (*Rubus, Epilobium* of Southern Sweden; frequency mapping).

Dagmar Persson, 1930 (*Stachys swansonii* group in Greece).

Zandra Persson, 1951 (*Hordeum* of South America).

Susanna Riebe, 1953 (Flora of Indonesia).

A. Schmitt, 1951 (*Carex*).

Britt Snogerup, 1934 (*Odontites*).

S. Snogerup, 1929 (*Juncus, Brassica oleracea* group, *Bupleurum* especially annual species, floras of Greece and Egypt).

Kristina Sundbäck, 1949 (Marine diatoms).

B. Sundström, 1944 (Marine diatoms, especially *Chaetoceras*).

T. von Wachenfeldt, 1934 (Marine algae, especially in Oresund).

G. Weimarck, 1936 (*Hierochloe, Heracleum sphondylium* group; chemotaxonomy).

B. Widén, 1944 (*Helianthemum oelandicum* group).

Specialization in research: Experimental taxonomy, especially of the Mediterranean and Scandinavian flora.

Associated botanic garden: Botanic Garden of the University of Lund.

Loans: In general to recognized botanical institutes. Specimens of Agardh's herbarium are not sent on loan.

Periodical and serial works: Botaniska Notiser (issued at Lund from 1839 to 1980, with some interruptions) will be amalgamated with the Nordic Journal of Botany (to be issued at Copenhagen from 1981 onwards). Botaniska Notiser, Supplement (1947-1954) is being continued by Opera Botanica (from 1953 onwards). Svensk Botanisk Tidskrift (edited at Stockholm from 1907-1975) is edited at Lund since 1976.

Exchange: Available: Mainly specimens from Europe, especially Scandinavia and the Mediterranean; Bryophytes, Lichens. Desired: Specimens of all groups, especially from the Mediterranean and Africa. A "Catalogue of specimens available for exchange" is issued annually.

LUSAKA: *Mount Makulu Pasture Research Station,* **(MPR)**, Lusaka, **Zambia.**

LUSAKA: *Herbarium, Biology Department, University of Zambia,* **(UZL)**, P.O. Box 32379, Lusaka, **Zambia.**

Telephone: 54755, ext. 495.

Status: University.

Foundation: 1966. *Number of specimens:* 17.500.

Herbarium: Plants of Zambia and adjacent countries of East and Central Africa.

   Director: Head of Biology Department.

   Curators: P. S. M. Phiri, 1940.

      J. N. Zulu, 1949.

   Assistant Curator: T. K. Lungu, 1941.

   Specialization in research: Flora of Zambia.

   Loans: To recognized botanical institutions.

   Exchange: Yes.

   Remarks: The herbarium of International Red Locust Control Organisation of Central and Southern Africa (LCO) is incorporated in UZL.

LUSAN: *Herbarium, Botanic Garden, Academia Sinica,* **(LUS)**, Lusan, Gansu, **People's Republic of China.**

LUSHAN: *Herbarium, Lushan Botanical Garden,* **(LBG)**, P.O. Box 4, Lushan, Jiangxi, **People's Republic of China.**

Telephone: 2223.

Foundation: 1934. *Number of specimens:* 140.000.

Herbarium: All groups Chinese plants, especially Jiangxi Province.

   Director: Chin Chih-Ping, 1920.

   Vice Director: Mu Tsung-Shan, 1925.

   Curator: Lai Shu-Sheng, 1930; 4245 (Systematics of higher plants).

   Vice Curator: Wang Kiang-Lin, 1938 (Ecological geobotany).

   Staff members: Neih Ming-Hsang, 1932 (Systematics).

      Shan Han-Jung, 1938 (Phytology).

      Sheng Shau-Chin, 1930 (Systematics).

      Yang Kien-Kuo, 1938 (Ecological geobotany).

   Specialization in research: Vegetation of Jiangxi Province, utilizing wild plants, compiling Flora of China, and List of Medicinal Plants of China.

LUSHOTO: *Forest Division Herbarium, Silviculture Research Station,* **(TFD)**, P.O. Box 95, Lushoto, **Tanzania.**

Telephone: Lushoto 32.

Status: Silviculture Research.

Foundation: 1948. *Number of specimens:* 20.000.

Herbarium: Angiospermae-Dicotyledonae: Acanthaceae, Zygophyllaceae; Angiospermae-Monocotyledonae: Agavaceae, Zingiberaceae; Gymnospermae, ferns and few mosses.

Curator: C. K. RUFFO, 1935 (General forestry, systematic botany).

Staff members: S. CHILONGOLA, 1949 (Forestry). N. MAGOGO, 1951 (Forestry). S. SHABANI, 1932 (Mounting and identification). T. SIGARA, 1948 (Mounting and identification).

Specialization in research: Silviculture research.

Loans: For research purposes and scientific studies.

Periodical and serial works: Flora of Tropical East Africa (Royal Botanic Gardens, Kew).

Exchange: Yes.

LUXEMBOURG: *Musée d'Histoire naturelle,* (**LUX**), Luxembourg, **Luxembourg.** (Information 1974)

Status: Directed by the state.

Foundation: 1850. *Number of specimens:* 30.000.

Herbarium: Flora of Luxembourg.

Periodical and serial works: Publications du Musée d'Histoire naturelle.

LWOW: *Zielnik ogrodu Botanicznego Universitetu J.K.,* (**LW**), sw. Mikolaja 4, Lwow, Ukraine, **U.S.S.R.** (Information 1974)

Herbarium: Flora of Poland, especially Siebenbürgen.

LWOW: *Agricultural Experiment Station,* (**LWA**), Zyblikiewicza 40, Lwow, Ukraine, **U.S.S.R.**

LWOW: *Museum Dzieduszykich,* (**LWD**), Rutowskiega 18, Lwow, Ukraine, **U.S.S.R.**

LWOW: *Musée des Sciences Naturelles de la Société Scientifique de Chevtchenko,* (**LWS**), Léopol, 42/II Rue Czarniecki, Lwow, Ukraine, **U.S.S.R.**

Herbarium: Plants of Ukraine.

LYNCHBURG: *Herbarium, Lynchburg College,* (**LYN**), Lynchburg, Virginia 24501, **U.S.A.**

Telephone: 804/845-9071, ext. 365.

Status: Private, church related.

Foundation: 1927. *Number of specimens:* 35.000.

Herbarium: Vascular flora of the southern Piedmont and the central Blue Ridge Mountains of Virginia; many state of Virginia records in this collection; Virginia Ranunculaceae.

Director and Curator: GWYNN W. RAMSEY, 1931 (Biosystematics of *Cimicifuga;* Virginia flora).

Specialization in research: Ecological-floristic research in Virginia, mainly in the southern Piedmont and the central Blue Ridge Mountains; Ranunculaceae of Virginia.

Associated botanic garden: Lynchburg College Arboretum.

Loans: Annotations requested; to other institutions and researchers for three month periods or longer by arrangement.

Exchange: Yes.

Remarks: More than 4.000 slides document representatives of plant families.

LYNCHBURG: *Herbarium, Biology Department, Randolph-Macon Woman's College,* (**RMWC**), Lynchburg, Virginia 24503, **U.S.A.**

Telephone: 804/846-7392, ext. 321.

Foundation: 1924. *Number of specimens:* 12.000.

Herbarium: Mainly plants of central Virginia, with emphasis on Piedmont and Blue Ridge Mountain flora; ferns of Rhode Island.

Director and Curator: DOROTHY C. BLISS, 1916 (Ferns; Liliaceae).

Specialization in research: Liliaceae of Virginia; research for anticipated Flora of Virginia.

Loans: Normal regulations.

Exchange: Available: Blue Ridge Mountain plants.

LYON: *Herbiers de l'Université de Lyon,* (**LY**) *--see* VILLEURBANNE.

M

MAASTRICHT: *Herbarium, Natuurhistorisch Museum,* **(MAAS),** Bosquetplein 6-7, 6211 KJ Maastricht, **Netherlands.**
Telephone: 043-13671.
Status: Municipal institution.
Foundation: 1912. *Number of specimens:* 30.000.
Herbarium: South Limburg (Netherlands), mainly phanerogams.
Important collections: De Wever, Rieter, Grégoire.
Director: Vacant.
Curator: D. TH. DE GRAAF, 1953 (Phanerogams).
Staff member: A. A. VAN HEURN, 1924.
Specialization in research: Flora of Limburg (Netherlands).
Associated botanic garden: De Wever Tuin.
Loans: In general to recognized botanical institutions.
Periodical and serial works: Natuurhistorisch Maandblad, Publicaties van het Natuurhistorisch Genootschap.
Exchange: Available: Flora of Limburg.

MACAPÁ: *Herbário Amapaense, Museu Ângelo Moreira da Costa Lima,* **(HAMAB),** Avenida Feliciano Coelho 1509, Macapá, Amapá, **Brazil.**
Telephone: (55)621-3214.
Number of specimens: 1.800.
Herbarium: Flora of Amapá.
Head of Botany Department: BENEDITO VITOR RABELO.
Curator: ANTÔNIA NAZARÉ VAZ VIDAL.
Staff members: RAIMUNDO NONATO DO NASCIMENTO.
CÍCERO PENAFORT.
Exchange: Available: Flora of Amapá. Desired: Literature.

MACOMB: *R. M. Myers Herbarium, Department of Biological Sciences, Western Illinois University,* **(MWI),** Macomb, Illinois 61455, **U.S.A.**
Telephone: 309/298-1472.
Status: State institution.
Foundation: 1945. *Number of specimens:* 26.000.
Herbarium: Flora of Illinois, especially the west-central part; useful plants of the world; some tropical plants.
Important collections: A Eads (Massachusetts vascular plants), R. M. Myers (west-central Illinois vascular plants), R. T. Rexroat (west-central Illinois vascular plants).
Director and Curator: R. D. HENRY, 1927 (Vascular flora of west-central Illinois).
Staff members: R. V. GESSNER, 1948 (Mycology).
L. M. O'FLAHERTY, 1941 (Phycology and bryology).
B.M. STIDD, 1936 (Carboniferous paleobotany).

Specialization in research: Flora of west-central Illinois and Illinois.
Loans: To approved individuals and institutions.
Periodical and serial works: Western Illinois University Series in the Biological Sciences.
Exchange: Available: Flora of Illinois. Desired: Midwestern U.S.
Remarks: Type and figured specimens of Carboniferous Coal-Ball plants.

MADISON: *Herbarium, Forest Products Laboratory, Center for Forest Mycology Research,* **(CFMR),** P.O. Box 5130, Madison, Wisconsin 53705, **U.S.A.** (formerly Laurel, Forest Disease Laboratory, BFDL).
Telephone: 608/264-5600.
Status: U.S. Department of Agriculture, Forest Service.
Foundation: ca. 1910. *Number of specimens:* 18.600.
Herbarium: Holobasidiomycetidae, especially wood-inhabiting species.
Director: ROBERT L. YOUNGS (Forest Products Technologist).
Curator: FRANCES F. LOMBARD, 1915; 608/264-5614 (Aphyllophorales, cultural identification).
Staff members: HAROLD H. BURDSALL, JR., 1940 (Aphyllophorales).
MICHAEL J. LARSEN, 1938 (Aphyllophorales).
KAREN K. NAKASONE, 1953 (Aphyllophorales, cultural identifications).
JOHN G. PALMER, 1924 (Physiology of Holobasidiomycetidae, especially ectomycorrhizal and wood-destroying isolates).
Specialization in research: Taxonomy, ecology, physiology, and culture preservation of Holobasidiomycetidae associated with forests and wood products.
Loans: 90 days to qualified institutions.
Remarks: 10.000 living isolates in aseptic agar culture.

MADISON: *Herbarium, Forest Products Laboratory, Center for Wood Anatomy Research,* **(MAD),** P.O. Box 5130, Madison, Wisconsin 53705, **U.S.A.**
Telephone: 608/264-5742.
Status: U.S. Department of Agriculture, Forest Service.
Foundation: 1931. *Number of specimens:* 30.000 herbarium sheets; 96.000 wood samples.
Herbarium: Woody plants of the world.
Important collections: Samuel James Record collection from the School of Forestry at Yale (Y); P. C. Standley, A. Ducke, H. M. Curran, Schlieben, Stahl, E. L. Little, Stern et al., B. A. Krukoff, A. C. Smith.
Director: ROBERT L. YOUNGS, 1924 (Wood utilization).
Staff members: DONNA J. CHRISTENSEN, 1945

(Identification of North American woods).

REGIS B. MILLER, 1943 (Wood anatomy of Flacourtiaceae and Juglandaceae; identification of woods of the world).

J. THOMAS QUIRK, 1933 (Wood anatomy of Vochysiaceae).

Specialization in research: Systematic wood anatomy and identification.

Loans: To qualified institutions (herbarium or wood samples).

Periodical and serial works: Forest Products Laboratory technical notes and reports.

Exchange: Available: Primarily wood specimens. Desired: Vouchered wood samples.

MADISON: *Herbarium, Department of Botany, University of Wisconsin,* (**WIS**), Birge Hall, 430 Lincoln Drive, Madison, Wisconsin 53706, **U.S.A.**

Telephone: 608/262-2792.

Foundation: 1849. *Number of specimens:* 735.000.

Herbarium: Wisconsin, central U.S. and Ozarks, southern U.S., Mexico, some Caribbean, tropical American, and Russian plants; worldwide representation: aquatic plants, parasitic fungi, arctic lichens, mosses, *Zea, Solanum.*

Important collections: I. A. Lapham (with collections made by C. S. Rafinesque, C. W. Short, and others), S. H. Watson, T. J. Hale, L. M. Umbach, J. J. Davis, L. S. Cheney, N. C. Fassett, F. C. Seymour, P. L. Ricker and H. Greene (parasitic fungi), G. B. Van Schaack (grasses), J. W. Thomson (lichens), H. H. Iltis (Arkansas, Wisconsin, Peru, Ecuador, U.S.S.R., Mexico), D. Ugent (Peru, Bolivia), F. S. Crosswhite (*Penstemon*).

Director: HUGH H. ILTIS, 1925 (Taxonomy of higher plants; Capparidaceae; *Zea, Solanum*; flora of Wisconsin; plant geography; evolution; preservation of biota; human ecology).

Curator: THEODORE S. COCHRANE, 1942 (Taxonomy of higher plants; Capparidaceae; flora of Wisconsin).

Staff members: ROBERT R. KOWAL, 1939 (*Senecio* sect. *Aurei*; numerical taxonomy).

JOHN W. THOMSON, 1913 (Lichens of North America, especially the Arctic; higher plant taxonomy).

Honorary associates: MICHAEL NEE, 1947 (Solanaceae; flora of Veracruz, Mexico and Richland County, Wisconsin).

JAMES H. ZIMMERMAN, 1924 (Veratrae, Liliaceae of the world; *Carex* of midwestern U.S.).

Specialization in research: Flora and ecology of Wisconsin; lichens of North America and Arctic; parasitic fungi of Wisconsin; mosses of the world; Capparidaceae, Solanaceae, neotropical Ericaceae; *Senecio* of eastern North America; taxonomy and evolution of *Zea.*

Associated botanic garden: Botany Garden, Department of Botany, University of Wisconsin; University of Wisconsin Arboretum, 1207 Seminole

Highway, Madison, Wisconsin 53711.

Loans: To recognized botanists or botanical institutions; no special regulations.

Periodical and serial works: Transactions of the Wisconsin Academy of Sciences, Arts, and Letters.

Exchange: Available: Specimens from Wisconsin and central U.S., Mexico, Russia. Desired: Specimens from central and southern U.S., Great Plains, eastern Asia, Latin America; any Capparidaceae, *Solanum,* and *Zea.*

Remarks: Extensive taxonomic/cytotaxonomic reprint collection, including libraries of D. C. Cooper, F. J. Hermann, H. A. Senn; collection of 850 pollen slides of north temperate and boreal North America.

MADRAS: *Herbarium, Department of Botany, Presidency College,* (**PCM**), Madras 600005, (Tamil Nadu), **India.** (Information 1976)

Status: Government.

Foundation: 1901. *Number of specimens:* 100.000.

Herbarium: Angiosperms, Cyperaceae and medicinal plants.

Specialization in research: Flora of Tamil Nadu, especially Cyperaceae, Elatinaceae, Oxalidaceae.

Loans: To recognized botanical institutions.

MADRID: *Herbarium, Jardín Botánico,* (**MA**), Plaza de Murillo 2, Madrid 14, **Spain.**

Status: Directed by the Consejo Superior de Investigaciones Científicas.

Foundation: 1781. *Number of specimens:* 500.000.

Herbarium: Phanerogams and cryptogams, especially Mediterranean region.

Important collections: A. J. Cavanilles herbarium, H. Ruiz et J. A. Pavón, Mutis, M. Sessé et J. M. Moçino, Pau, R. González Fragoso (Fungi), P. Unamuno (Fungi), Jordán de Urries (Fungi), A. Casares-Gil (Bryophyta).

Director: F. D. CALONGE (Mycology).

Curators: PALOMA BLANCO FDEZ. DE CALEYA.

ANTONIO REGUEIRO Y GLEZ.-BARROS.

Staff members: SANTIAGO CASTROVIEJO BOLIBAR (Taxonomy of vascular plants).

GINEZ LOPEZ GONZALEZ (Taxonomy of vascular plants).

CONCEPCION SAENZ LAIN (Palynology, taxonomy).

ENRIQUE VALDES BERMEJO (Taxonomy of vascular plants).

Specialization in research: Mediterranean flora.

Associated botanic garden: Jardín Botánico de Madrid.

Loans: In general to recognized botanical institutions.

Periodical and serial works: Anales del Jardín Botánico.

Exchange: Specimens from Mediterranean region. Desired: All regions of the world, especially the Mediterranean.

MADRID: *Herbario de la Facultad de Farmacia de Madrid*, (**MAF**), Departamento de Botánica, Facultad de Farmacia, Universidad Complutense, Madrid-3, **Spain.**
Telephone: 449 15 45.
Status: University.
Foundation: 1890. *Number of specimens:* 150.000.
Herbarium: Mediterranean and Canary Island flora.
Important collections: P. A. Pourret, Pérez-Lara, P. Font Quer, Huguet del Villar, Lázaro e Ibiza, Rivas Goday, Borja, J. Cuatrecasas.
Director: S. RIVAS-MARTÍNEZ, 1935 (Phanerogams, phytosociology, geographic botany).
Curator: E. BARRENO RODRÍGUEZ, 1950.
Staff members: C. ARNAIZ (Taxonomy, phytosociology).
E. BARRENO (Lichenology, phytosociology of lichens).
R. CARBALLAL (Cryptogamy).
A. CRESPO (Lichenology, phytosociology of lichens).
M. GUTIÉRREZ-BUSTILLO (Taxonomy, palynology, cytotaxonomy).
C. NAVARRO (Phanerogams, phytosociology north of Spain).
C. PARDO (Palynology, taxonomy of Umbelliferae).
J. L. PÉREZ-CIRERA (Algology, phytosociology of algae).
Specialization in research: Taxonomy of Iberian flora; phytosociology of Iberian Peninsula and North Africa; lichenology and air pollution; algology.
Loans: For three months, to recognized botanical institutions or researchers.
Periodical and serial works: Lazaroa (from 1980).
Exchange: Available: Specimens from Spain. Desired: Eurasiatic and North African flora (phanerogams, algae, lichens).

MADRID: *Instituto Forestal de la Moncloa*, (**MA-FST**), Burjasot, Madrid, **Spain** -- discontinued.

MAHALAPYE: *Herbarium, Department of Agriculture*, (**MAH**), Box 10, Mahalapye, **Botswana.** (Information 1974)
Foundation: 1951. *Number of specimens:* 1.350.
Herbarium: Indigenous grasses, shrubs and trees.

MAIKOP: *Herbarium, Caucasus State Reserve*, (**CSR**), Sovetskaya St. 187, Krasnodarsk Region, 352700 Maikop, **U.S.S.R.**
Foundation: 1928. *Number of specimens:* 80.000.
Director: M. D. ALTUCHOV.

MAINZ: *Institut für Spezielle Botanik und Botanischer Garten der Johannes Gutenberg-Universität*, (**MJG**), Saarstr. 21, P.O. Box 3980, D- 6500 Mainz, **Federal Republic of Germany, BRD.**

Telephone: 06131/392533.
Status: University of Mainz.
Foundation: 1946 (Institute), 1964 (Herbarium).
Herbarium: Worldwide, Europe.
Important collections: Coll. H. Weber (Páramovegetation).
Director: DIMITRI HARTL, 1926 (Morphology and systematics, Scrophulariaceae).
Curator: ULRICH HECKER, 1936; 06131/392628 (Dendrology, dispersal).
Staff members: DIETER LÜPNITZ, 1940 (Plant geography).
ALBRECHT SIEGERT, 1934 (Plant morphology).
Associated botanic garden: Botanischer Garten der Johannes Gutenberg-Universität Mainz.
Loans: In general to recognized botanical institutions.
Exchange: Yes.

MAISONS ALFORT: *Herbarium, Institut d'Elevage et de Médecine vétérinaire des Pays Tropicaux*, (**ALF**), 10 Rue Curie, 94700 Maisons Alfort, **France.**
Telephone: 368-88-73.
Status: Public.
Foundation: 1920. *Number of specimens:* 25.000.
Herbarium: Arid areas of Africa and Arabia.
Director: A. PROVOST, 1930 (Veterinary science).
Curator: J. P. LEBRUN, 1932 (Floristics and phytogeography of dry zones of Africa).
Loans: Yes.
Periodical and serial works: Revue d'Elevage et de Médecine Vétérinaire des Pays Tropicaux, Nouvelle série.

MAKARSKA: *Herbar Biokovskog Područja*, (**MA-KAR**), Žrtava Fašizma 1, YU-58300 Makarska, **Yugoslavia.**
Telephone: 058-611-256.
Status: Adherence to Institut "Planina i More."
Foundation: 1963. *Number of specimens:* 1.900.
Herbarium: Mountain and coastal flora.
Director: JURE RADIĆ, 1920 (Malacology and botany).
Curator: EDITH SOLIĆ, 1946.
Staff members: NADA BRBOLEŽA, 1962 (Physiology).
BRANKA ČEBIN, 1960 (Marine biology).
Specialization in research: Mountain and coastal flora.
Associated botanic garden: Botanical Garden of VRT Institut "Planina i More."

MAKHACHKALA: *Herbarium, Department of Botany, Lenin University of Dagestan*, (**LENUD**), Dzerzhinskovo St. 12, 367025 Makhachkala, **U.S.S.R.**
Foundation: 1943. *Number of specimens:* 50.000.
Director: A. D. RADZHI.

MÁLAGA: *Herbario de la Facultad de Ciencias de la Universidad de Málaga*, (**MGC**), Departamento de

Botánica, Camino de la Misericordia s/n, Málaga-4, **Spain.**
 Telephone: 952/328607.
 Status: University.
 Foundation: 1972. *Number of specimens:* 10.000.
 Herbarium: Mainly phanerogams, also algae and bryophytes.
 Director: ALFREDO ASENSI MARFIL, 1949 (Phytosociology).
 Curator: BLANCA DIEZ GARRETAS, 1950 (Phytosociology).
 Staff members: FRANCISCO CONDE POYALES, 1948 (Algology).
 JUAN GUERRA MONTES, 1952 (Bryosociology).
 ENRIQUE SALVO TIERRA, 1957 (Pteridology).
 Specialization in research: Algology, bryosociology, pteridology, phytosociology, taxonomy.
 Loans: 3 months.
 Periodical and serial works: Acta Botanica Malacitana.
 Exchange: Yes.

MANAGUA: *Herbario, Facultad de Ciencias Agropecuarias, Universidad Nacional Autonoma de Nicaragua,* (**ENAG**), KM 12$^1/_2$ Carretera Norte, Managua, **Nicaragua.**
 Telephone: 31930.
 Foundation: 1956. *Number of specimens:* 2.000.
 Director and Curator: ALAIN MEIRAT GNUYEN (Agronomy).
 Loans: Yes.

MANAGUA: *Herbario Nacional de Nicaragua,* (**HNMN**), Apartado 4271, Managua, D.N. **Nicaragua.**
 Telephone: 72247.
 Status: Centro Investigaciones Geográficas, Ministerio de Cultura.
 Foundation: 1977. *Number of specimens:* 30.000.
 Herbarium: Flora of Nicaragua and Central America.
 Director: WARREN DOUGLAS STEVENS, 1944 (Flora of Nicaragua; Asclepiadaceae, Apocynaceae).
 Curator: ALFREDO GRIJALVA P., 1946 (Flora of Nicaragua).
 Specialization in research: Flora of Nicaragua.
 Loans: To recognized botanical institutions.

MANAGUA: *Herbario, Instituto Pedagógico de Varones,* (**MGA**), Managua, **Nicaragua** – – discontinued.

MANAUS: *Herbário, Instituto Nacional de Pesquisas da Amazônia,* (**INPA**), Estrada do Aleixo 1756, Coroado, Caixa Postal 478, 69.000 Manaus, Amazonas, **Brazil.**
 Telephone: (55)092/236-5700; 236-5765; 236-5450,· ramal 120, 121.
 Status: Affiliated with Conselho Nacional de Desenvolvimento Científico e Tecnológico (CNPq).

Foundation: 1954. *Number of specimens:* 100.000; 7.000 wood samples.
 Herbarium: Flora of Brazilian Amazon.
 Important collections: G. T. Prance.
 Director: WILLIAM ANTONIO RODRIGUES, 1928 (Neotropical Myristicaceae; Amazon flora).
 Curator: MARLENE FREITAS DA SILVA, 1937 (Caryocaraceae; *Peltogyne, Dimorphandra*; Amazon flora).
 Staff members: MARIA LÚCIA ABSY (Palynology of the Quaternary).
 BYRON WILSON PEREIRA DE ALBUQUERQUE, 1932 (Rutaceae of the Amazon).
 ANTHONY B. ANDERSON, 1950 (Plant ecology).
 IZONETE DE JESUS ARAUJO, 1947 (Basidiomycetes, Cortinariaceae).
 MARILENE MARINHO NOGUEIRA BRAGA, 1949 (Plant anatomy).
 PEDRO IVO SOARES BRAGA, 1950 (Orchidaceae).
 LÉA MARIA MEDEIROS CARREIRA, 1949 (Palynology).
 ANGELA CONTE LEITE, 1953 (Plant ecology).
 EDUARDO LLERAS PEREZ, 1944 (Trigoniaceae; ecophysiology; morphogenesis).
 ARTHUR ARAUJO LOUREIRO, 1932 (Wood anatomy).
 Specialization in research: Flora of Brazilian Amazonia; taxonomy, morphology, palynology, and ecology.
 Associated botanic garden: Reserva Florestal Ducke; Reserva Biológica Walter Egler; Reserva Biológica de Campina; Tropical Silviculture Experimental Station.
 Loans: To recognized botanical institutions; requests should be addressed to the Curator.
 Periodical and serial works: Acta Amazonica.
 Exchange: Available: Vascular plants, bryophytes, fungi of Brazilian Amazonia. Desired: Neotropical material, especially of areas adjacent to Brazilian Amazonia.
 Remarks: Will send herbarium specimens to specialists for revision and identification.

MANCHESTER: *Herbarium, The Manchester Museum, The University,* (**MANCH**), Manchester 13, England, **Great Britain.** (Information 1974)
 Status: Directed by a joint committee responsible to the University Council.
 Foundation: 1821. *Number of specimens:* 3.000.000.
 Herbarium: General worldwide collections, bryophytes; also thin sections of fossil plants, especially Carboniferous.
 Important collections: C. Bailey (British and European plants), herb. J. C. Melvill, R. Spruce (bryophytes of Andes and Amazon), W. H. Pearson (hepatics).
 Loans: To recognized botanical institutions.
 Periodical and serial works: Guide to Collections.

MANDALAY: *Herbarium, Arts and Science Univer-*

sity, (**ASM**), Mandalay, **Burma.** (Information 1974)
Status: University.
Foundation: 1965. *Number of specimens:* 2.000.
Herbarium: Spermatophytes of Central and Upper
Burma.
Loans: To recognized botanical institutions.

MANDALAY: *Herbarium, Agricultural College and
Research Institute*, (**MAND**), Mandalay, **Burma** – –
discontinued.

MANGILAO: *Herbarium, Department of Biology,
University of Guam*, (**GUAM**), UOG Station, Mang-
ilao, **Guam** 96913.
Telephone: 671/734-2921, ext. 361.
Foundation: 1961. *Number of specimens:* 6.000.
Herbarium: Floras of Guam, Micronesia, and
Northern Mariana Islands; benthic algae of the Pacific.
Important collections: P. H. Moore, D. R. Smith, B.
C. Stone, and R. T. Tsuda.
   Director and Curator: DOUGLAS R. SMITH, 1930
(Mosses of Micronesia).
   Staff members: PHILIP H. MOORE, 1919 (Vascular
plants of Micronesia).
      ROY T. TSUDA, 1939 (Pacific algae).
   Specialization in research: Floristics of mosses
and vascular plants of Guam and Micronesia.
Loans: To specialists at recognized institutions.
Periodical and serial works: Micronesica, Journal
of the University of Guam.
Exchange: Available: Micronesia flora. Desired:
Specimens from other tropical Pacific areas.

MANHATTAN: *Herbarium, Division of Biology, Kan-
sas State University*, (**KSC**), Manhattan, Kansas
66506, **U.S.A.**
Telephone: 913/532-6619.
Foundation: About 1877. *Number of specimens:*
216.000.
Herbarium: Flora of Kansas and the Great Plains;
fungi of the Great Plains; fungus parasites on grasses;
aeromycology.
Important collections: A. S. Hitchcock (grasses); P.
A. Rydberg and R. H. Imler (Great Plains); Elam
Bartholomew (fungi); W. A. Kellerman.
   Curator: T. M. BARKLEY, 1934 (New World *Senecio*; flora of the Great Plains).
   Staff members: C. L. KRAMER, 1928 (Mycology;
systematics of *Taphrina*; aeromycology; spore-
dispersal).
      A. SPENCER TOMB, 1943 (Systematics of Lac-
tuceae, Asteraceae; palynology; chemosystemat-
ics).
   Specialization in research: Flora of Great Plains
project; applied research in connection with the
Kansas Agricultural Station.
   Associated botanic garden: Arboretum, Department of Horticulture, Kansas State University.
Loans: Normal regulations.
Exchange: Available: Great Plains plants. De-

sired: Collections relevant to the Great Plains;
weeds; *Senecio*.

MANILA: *Philippine National Herbarium*, (**PNH**),
Old Congress Building, P. Burgos Street, P.O. Box
2659, Manila, **Philippines.**
Telephone: 47-68-87.
Status: State institution.
Foundation: 1901. *Number of specimens:* 160.000.
Herbarium: Worldwide herbarium, especially all
groups of plants of the Philippines.
Important collections: E. D. Merrill, A. D. E. Elmer,
Ramos and G. E. Edaño.
   Director: GODOFREDO L. ALCASID, 1909 (Zoolo-
gy).
   Curator: ROMUALDO M. DEL ROSARIO, 1939
(Phytogeography, Philippine hepatics, mosses and
liverworts).
   Staff members: PACIENTE A. CORDERO, JR., 1941
(Algae, marine biology).
      FRANCISCO R. DELA CRUZ, 1926.
      LUISITO T. EVANGELISTA, 1956 (Fungi).
      ODILON B. FERNANDO, 1935.
      DOMINGO A. MADULID, 1946 (Phanerogams,
especially palms, historical botany, ethnobotany).
      RUBEN B. MANALANG, 1947.
      CARMEN R. NAVA, 1952.
      ERNESTO J. REYNOSO, 1934 (Herbarium tech-
niques, field collection).
      CENON V. SAN JUAN, 1956 (Fern and fern allies).
      REYNALDA L. VARILLA, 1933 (Economic
botany).
      WILFREDO F. VENDIVIL, 1949 (Flowering
plants).
   Specialization in research: Flora of the Philippines, ethnobotany, marine biology, economic botany, historical botany.
   Associated botanic garden: Philippine National
Botanic Garden, Real, Quezon and Botanical Garden, Mt. Makiling, Los Baños, Laguna.
Loans: To recognized botanical institutions and
specialists.
Periodical and serial works: Philippine National
Museum Botanical Publication.
Exchange: Available: Philippine specimens. De-
sired: Specimens from all groups, especially from
Indo-Malesia.

MANIZALES: *Herbario, Facultad de Agronomía,
Universidad de Caldas*, (**FAUC**), Apartado Aéreo
275, Manizales, Caldas, **Colombia.**
Telephone: (57)69/54-599.
Foundation: 1954. *Number of specimens:* 6.500.
Herbarium: Includes native, economically impor-
tant, and weedy plants of Colombia.
Important collections: J. M. Duque Jaramillo.
   Director: ZULMA PIÑEROS DE SANTANA, 1952.
   Curator: DAVID MANZUR MACIAS, 1949; 229-36
(Agronomy).
   Staff member: ALBERTO LONDOÑO ZAPATA, 1945.

Associated botanic garden: Jardín Botánico, Universidad de Caldas.

MANKATO: *Herbarium, Biology Department, Mankato State University,* (**MANK**), Mankato, Minnesota 56001, **U.S.A.**
Telephone: 507/389-2780.
Foundation: 1895. *Number of specimens:* 4.000.
Herbarium: Regional flora; ferns and fern allies of Minnesota; depository for Department of Natural Resources in southern Minnesota; Kasota Prairie vouchers.
Director: DON GORDON, 1939 (Angiosperms).
Associated botanic garden: Mankato State University Arboretum.
Loans: To recognized institutions.
Exchange: Yes.

MANOKWARI: *Section of Forest Botany, Forestry Division,* (**MAN**), Manokwari, **Indonesia.**

MAPLE: *Forest Pathology Laboratory, Southern Research Station,* (**MFB**) – – see SAULT STE. MARIE (SSMF).

MAPUTO: *Direcção de Agricultura e Florestas, Secção de Botânica e Ecologia,* (**LM**) – – incorporated in LMA.

MAPUTO: *Instituto de Investigação Agronómica de Moçambique, Divisão de Botânica Sistemática e Geobotânica,* (**LMA**), P.O. Box 3658, Maputo, **Mozambique.** (Information 1974)
Status: Directed by state.
Foundation: 1965 (incorporating LM and LMJ).
Number of specimens: 41.000.
Herbarium: Phanerogams and vascular cryptogams of Mozambique.
Specialization in research: Flora and vegetation of Mozambique.
Periodical and serial works: Comunicações, Agronomia Moçambicana.
Loans: To recognized botanical institutions, for four months; types are not loaned.

MAPUTO: *Instituto de Investigaçao Científica de Mozambique,* (**LMC**) – – incorporated in LMU.

MAPUTO: *Botanical Department of the Cotton Research Centre (Centro de Investigação Científica Algodoeira),* (**LMJ**) – – incorporated in LMA.

MAPUTO: *Herbário, Faculdade de Biologia, Universidade da Eduardo Mondlane,* (**LMU**), C.P. 257, Maputo, **Mozambique.**
Telephone: 743009 (91).
Status: University.
Foundation: 1963. *Number of specimens:* 20.000.
Herbarium: Mainly phanerogams, pteridophytes and algae of Mozambique and adjacent areas.

Director: JAR DE KONING, 1943 (Flora of Mozambique, especially Liliaceae).
Staff members: PAUL C. M. JANSEN, 1943 (Medicinal plants).
PETER A. SCHÄFER, 1944 (Flora of Mozambique, ecology).
Specialization in research: Flora of Mozambique.
Loans: To recognized botanical institutions.
Periodical and serial works: Index Seminum.
Exchange: Available: Specimens from Mozambique and adjacent areas. Desired: African specimens.

MARACAIBO: *Herbario Zulia, Facultad de Agronomía, Universidad del Zulia,* (**HERZU**), Apartado 526, Maracaibo, Zulia, **Venezuela.**
Telephone: 061/51-22-08; 51-22-48; 51-21-97, ext. 291 and 271.
Foundation: 1975. *Number of specimens:* 8.000.
Herbarium: Venezuelan flora, especially of the state of Zulia; Sierra de Perijá; aquatic plants of Zulia.
Important collections: Dana Griffin (bryophytes).
Director: JOSÉ OMAR ZAMBRANO C., 1940 (Aquatic plants).
Staff members: ROBINSON CARVAJAL, 1955.
NORA FARÍA SÁNCHEZ, 1941 (Weeds of cultivated areas; forage grasses).
RENATO PEÑA LEÓN, 1931 (Leguminosae).
Specialization in research: Regional flora; weeds of cultivated areas.
Loans: Yes.
Periodical and serial works: Revista de la Facultad de Agronomía.
Exchange: Yes.

MARACAY: *Herbarium, Instituto Universitario Pedagógico Experimental "Rafael Alberto Escobar Lara,"* (**IPMY**), Apartado 288, Maracay, Aragua, **Venezuela.**
Foundation: 1976. *Number of specimens:* 3.500.
Herbarium: Flora of Aragua.
Curator: MARIO JOSÉ LOBO D.
Exchange: Available: Venezuela. Desired: All groups.

MARACAY: *Herbario, Facultad de Agronomía, Instituto de Botánica Agrícola, Universidad Central de Venezuela,* (**MY**), Maracay, Aragua, **Venezuela.**
Telephone: (58)043/24126; 27101; 28996.
Foundation: 1949. *Number of specimens:* 56.000.
Herbarium: Emphasis on central and Andean region of Venezuela; Caricaceae of the world.
Important collections: Victor M. Badillo, Lourdes C. de Guevara, Carmen E. Benítez de Rojas, Baltasar Trujillo, Giovanna Ferrari, H. Rodriguez, Ludwig Schnee, Mauricio Ramia, Patricio Montaldo, Elod Ijjasz, Félix Cardona, Antonio Fernández.
Director: JESUS R. BOLÍVAR (Plant physiology).
Curator: CARMEN E. BENÍTEZ DE ROJAS, 1937 (Solanaceae of Venezuela).

Staff members: V. M. BADILLO, 1920 (Caricaceae; Compositae of Venezuela).

GIOVANNA FERRARI, 1925 (Loranthaceae of Venezuela; palynology).

LOURDES C. DE GUEVARA, 1933 (Leguminosae of Venezuela).

HECTOR RODRIGUEZ, 1948.

BALTASAR TRUJILLO, 1927 (Cucurbitaceae and Cactaceae of Venezuela).

Specialization in research: Flora of Venezuela.

Associated botanic garden: Jardín Botánico.

Loans: Usual regulations.

Exchange: Yes, especially in specialties of staff.

MARBURG: *Fachbereich Biologie der Philipps-Universität, Botanik,* (**MB**), Lahnberge, D-355 Marburg (Lahn), **Federal Republic of Germany, BRD.** (Information 1974)

Status: University.

Foundation: 1880. *Number of specimens:* 300.000.

Specialization in research: Lichenology, cytotaxonomy.

Associated botanic garden: Botanischer Garten der Universität Marburg.

Loans: To recognized botanical institutions.

MARLBOROUGH: *Herbarium, Marlborough College,* (**MACO**), Marlborough, England, **Great Britain.** (Information 1974)

Status: Public school.

Foundation: 1915.

Herbarium: British flowering plants.

MARQUETTE: *Herbarium, Biology Department, Northern Michigan University,* (**NM**), Marquette, Michigan 49855, **U.S.A.**

Telephone: 906/227-2443; 227-2310.

Status: Directed by the state.

Foundation: 1950. *Number of specimens:* 5.000.

Herbarium: Upper Peninsula of Michigan.

Director: MAYNARD C. BOWERS, 1930 (Biosystematics, bryology).

Staff member: SAMUEL L. HESS, 1942; 906/227-2183; 227-2310 (Fleshy fungi).

Specialization in research: Upper Peninsula, Michigan.

Loans: To any qualified institution or individual.

MARSEILLE: *Laboratoire de Botanique, Université de Provence (U.1),* (**MARS**), Place Victor-Hugo, Centre St. Charles, F.13331 Marseille Cedex 3, **France.**

Telephone: (91) 959071.

Status: University.

Herbarium: General herbarium, Mediterranean region, some former French colonies.

Director: President of the University.

Curator: PIERRE DONADILLE, 1936 (Systematics, Armeria).

Staff members: J. CONTANDRIOPOULOS (Cytotaxonomy).

C. LUCIANI (Umbelliferae).

C. VIGNAL (Gramineae).

Specialization in research: Systematics and cytotaxonomy, Mediterranean region.

Exchange: Specimens of the Mediterranean region.

MARSEILLE: *Laboratoire de Botanique, Faculté des Sciences St. Jerôme,* (**MARSSJ**), Laboratoire de Botanique et Ecologie Méditerranéen, F-13397 Marseille Cedex 4, **France.**

Telephone: (91) 989010 poste 535.

Status: Université d'Aix-Marseille III.

Foundation: 1964. *Number of specimens:* 200.000.

Important collections: Herb. P. Cousturier, Herb. E. Jahandiez, herb. Quézel, herb. Gamisans, herb. Gruber.

Director: P. QUÉZEL, 1926 (Phytosociology, ecology and floristics of the Bassin Méditerranéen).

Curator: J. GAMISANS, 1944 (Floristics and phytosociology; Corsica).

M. GRUBER, 1943 (Floristics and phytosociology; Pyrenees).

Staff members: G. AUBERT (Ecology, Ericaceae).

M. BARBERO (Ecology; Alps, Bassin Médit.).

G. BONIN (Ecology, numerical techniques; Italy).

J. P. HEBRARD (Bryophytes; Alps, Bassin Médit.).

R. LOISEL (Floristics and phytosociology; Provence, North Africa).

H. SANDOZ (Ecology; Alps).

C. ZEVACO-SCHMITZ (Phytosociology; Corsica).

Specialization in research: Floristics, phytosociology, ecology of the Alps (South), Pyrenees, Corsica, Bassin Méditerranéen.

Associated botanic garden: Yes, very small.

Loans: Very restricted (caused by absence of technical staff).

Periodical and serial works: Ecologia Mediterranea.

MARYLHURST: *Herbarium, Marylhurst College,* (**MARO**), Marylhurst, Oregon 97036, **U.S.A.** (Information 1974)

Number of specimens: 2.081.

Herbarium: Vascular plants of Washington and Oregon, especially eastern Washington and southwestern Oregon, collected mainly in the 1930's.

MARYVILLE: *Herbarium, Department of Biology, Northwest Missouri State University,* (**NMSU**), Garrett-Strong Science Building, Maryville, Missouri 64468, **U.S.A.**

Telephone: 816/582-7141, ext. 1203.

Foundation: Pre-1930. *Number of specimens:* 8.000.

Herbarium: Concentration on northwestern Missouri, especially Nodaway County.

Director: B. D. SCOTT, 1931 (Biosystematics).

Loans: Usual regulations.
Exchange: Available: Specimens from Nodaway County, Missouri.

MASERU: *Maseru Herbarium, Maseru Experiment Station,* (**MASE**), P.O. Box 24, Maseru, **Lesotho.** (Information 1974)
Status: Government.
Foundation: 1950. *Number of specimens:* 4.000.
Herbarium: Mainly phanerogams of Lesotho.

MATANZAS: *Herbario, Instituto de Segunda, Enseñanza de Matanzas,* (**IM**), Matanzas, **Cuba** – – incorporated in HAC.
Number of specimens: 2.000.

MATSUMOTO: *Herbarium and Biological Institute, Faculty of Liberal Arts, Shinshu University,* (**SHIN**), 3-1-1 Asahi, Matsumoto, **Japan.** (Information 1974)
Status: University.
Foundation: 1960. *Number of specimens:* 35.000.
Herbarium: Vascular plants of Eastern Asia, especially Japan.
Specialization in research: Asiatic plants, especially of limestone areas.
Loans: To recognized botanical institutions.

MATSUYAMA: *Forestry Department, Matsuyama Agricultural College,* (**MATSU**), Matsuyama, Ehime-Ken, **Japan.**

MAYAGUEZ: *Herbario, Ficoteca Puertorriqueña, Departamento de Ciencias Marinas, Universidad de Puerto Rico, Recinto Universitario de Mayaguez,* (**FPDB**), Mayaguez, **Puerto Rico** 00708.
Telephone: 305/832-4040, ext. 2579.
Foundation: 1958. *Number of specimens:* 20.000.
Herbarium: Marine algae of the Caribbean.
Important collections: M. Díaz-Piferrer, Lucy M. de Díaz-Piferrer, Harold J. Humm, Hans G. Schweiger, G. Robin South, Josephine Tilden.
Director: M. DÍAZ-PIFERRER, 1919 (Marine phycology; benthic Caribbean marine algae).
Curator: LUCY M. DE DÍAZ-PIFERRER.
Specialization in research: Taxonomy, ecology, biogeography, and ecology of benthic marine algae in the Caribbean.
Loans: To recognized institutions, not to private individuals.
Periodical and serial works: Caribbean Journal of Science.
Exchange: Specimens and reprints.

MAYAGUEZ: *Herbario, Departamento de Biología, Universidad de Puerto Rico, Recinto Universitario de Mayaguez,* (**MAPR**), Mayaguez, **Puerto Rico** 00708.
Telephone: 809/832-4040, ext. 2405.
Foundation: 1958. *Number of specimens:* 9.000.
Herbarium: Mostly plants from Puerto Rico and neighboring islands.

Director and Curator: GARY L. BRECKON, 1940 (Euphorbiaceae, Ericaceae).
Staff member: CARLOS BETANCOURT, 1936 (Mycology).
Specialization in research: Taxonomy of fungi, ferns, Cyperaceae, Euphorbiaceae.
Associated botanic garden: Agricultural Experiment Station Botanical Garden, Rio Piedras.
Loans: 3 month basis.
Periodical and serial works: Caribbean Journal of Science.
Exchange: Ferns, sedges.

MAYAGUEZ: *Herbarium, Department of Marine Sciences, University of Puerto Rico,* (**MSM**), Mayaguez, **Puerto Rico** 00708.
Telephone: 809/832-4040, ext. 3447.
Foundation: 1958. *Number of specimens:* 14.000.
Herbarium: Caribbean marine algae; some collections from Japan, Australia, Europe.
Important collections: M. A. Howe (Puerto Rico; especially red algae).
Director: MANUEL HERNANDEZ-AVILA (Physical oceanography).
Curator: LUIS R. ALMODOVAR, 1930 (Deep water algae; coral reef algae).
Staff members: ALIDA ORTIZ (*Gracilaria* in Puerto Rico).
DAVID BALLANTINE (Algal epiphytes).
Specialization in research: Collections of epiphytic algae from 50–100 feet; *Gracilaria* from Puerto Rico and the West Indies; marine flora of Puerto Rico.
Loans: For 3 months to recognized institutions and individuals.
Exchange: Available upon request.

MBALA: *Herbarium, International Red Locust Control Organisation for Central and Southern Africa,* (**LCO**) – – incorporated in UZL.

MEDELLÍN: *Herbario, Departamento de Biología, Universidad de Antioquia,* (**HUA**), Apartado Aéreo 1226, Medellín, Antioquia, **Colombia.**
Telephone: (57)33-05-99, ext. 253.
Foundation: 1969. *Number of specimens:* 12.000.
Herbarium: Flora of Antioquia and the region surrounding the Chocó.
Important collections: Linda Albert de E., Lucía Atehortúa, Yuly Denslow, Sigifredo Espinal, Ramiro Fonnegra G., D. B. Lellinger, Timothy Plowman, Enrique Renteria A., José I. Santa, D. D. Soejarto, E. R. de la Sota.
Director and Curator: RAMIRO FONNEGRA G., 1947 (Plant taxonomy).
Staff members: LUCÍA ATEHORTÚA (Taxonomy of ferns).
ENRIQUE RENTERIA A., 1950 (Plant taxonomy).
JOSÉ I. SANTA S., 1942 (Plant morphology).
Specialization in research: Flora of Antioquia.

Loans: Institution to institution.
Exchange: Yes.
Remarks: Formerly listed under Antioquia.

MEDELLÍN: *Herbario, Fundacion Jardin Botanico "Joaquin Antonio Uribe,"* (**JAUM**), Carrera 52 No. 73-298, Apartado Aéro 51-407, Medellín, Antioquia, **Colombia.**
Telephone: (57)33-70-25, ext. 28; 44-79-11.
Status: Private foundation.
Foundation: 1973. *Number of specimens:* 2.500.
Herbarium: Flora of Magdalena Medio; flora of Urabá; economic plants; Orchidaceae; Pteridophyta.
Director: ALVARO ARANGO M. (Orchidaceae).
Curator: ENRIQUE RENTERIA ARRIAGA (Flora of Santander y Magdalena Medio; Anacardiaceae).
Staff member: CECILIA GOMEZ MONDRAGÓN (Flora of Urabá).
Specialization in research: Floras of Antioquia, of the Urabá Región, of the Magdalena Medio Región; Orchidaceae of Colombia.
Loans: Usual regulations.
Periodical and serial works: Closely related to the publication of Orquideología, the journal of the Colombian Orchid Society.
Exchange: Flora of the Magdalena Medio Región.

MEDELLÍN: *Herbario "Gabriel Gutierrez V.," Facultad de Ciencias, Universidad Nacional de Colombia, Seccional Medellín,* (**MEDEL**), Apartado 568, Medellín, Antioquia, **Colombia.**
Telephone: (57)30-02-80.
Foundation: 1927. *Number of specimens:* 24.231.
Herbarium: Flora of Colombia, especially Antioquia; about 150 types.
Director and Curator: JAIME RIVERA-CASTRO, 1936 (Flora of Antioquia).
Staff members: SIGIFREDO ESPINAL-T. (Ecology). DARIO SANCHEZ-S. (Biology).
Loans: Yes.
Exchange: Yes.
Remarks: Herbarium previously known as "Herbario, Facultad Nacional de Agronomía."

MEDFORD: *Phippen-LaCroix Herbarium, Department of Biology, Tufts University,* (**TUFT**), Medford, Massachusetts 02155, **U.S.A.**
Telephone: 617/628-5000, ext. 421.
Foundation: 1963 (restarted 1975 after fire). *Number of specimens:* 12.000.
Herbarium: Plants of eastern U.S., Bahamas, New Zealand.
Important collections: New Zealand North Island; *Hudsonia* from U.S.
Director and Curator: NORTON H. NICKERSON, 1926 (Coastal and inland wetlands ecology; conservation of ecosystems).
Specialization in research: Coastal plants of eastern U.S.; mangroves, wetlands, swamps, marshes,

in study of usefulness of these land forms to man as functioning ecosystems; medicinal plants of the Bahamas.
Exchange: Available: Bahamas, New Zealand, eastern U.S. material.
Remarks: Herbarium has been augmented by gifts of superfluous material since its complete destruction in 1975.

MEISE: *Herbarium, Jardin Botanique National de Belgique – Nationale Plantentuin van België,* (**BR**), Domein van Bouchout, B-1860 Meise, **Belgium.**
Telephone: 02/269 39 05.
Status: State institution under the Ministry of Agriculture.
Foundation: 1870. *Number of specimens:* Over 2.000.000.
Herbarium: Worldwide, especially Belgium, Tropical Africa and the genus *Rosa.*
Important collections: Spermatophyta and Pteridophyta: coll. of Rosae of F. Crépin and G. A. Boulenger; herb. A. Cogniaux (Cucurbitaceae, Melastomataceae, Orchidaceae); coll. R. Schlechter; Africa: herb. of Zaïre, Rwanda and Burundi, important collections from other countries, H. Baum, T. Kassner, T. Lécard, Rehmann, H. J. E. Schlieben, etc.; America: C. F. P. von Martius (private herbarium incl. W. J. Burchell, A. F. M. Glaziou, R. Spruce, etc.), H. G. Galeotti, L. Hauman, J. J. Linden, H. F. Pittier, H. R. Wullschlägel; Asia: Clemens, W. Griffith, W. Roxburgh, Thwaites, N. Wallich; Australia: F. von Müller; Europe: R. B. C. Dumortier, Félix, A. L. S. Lejeune, Libert, R. Mosseray, and many collections from Belgium. Bryophyta and Thallophyta. Bryophyta: Bequaert, Demaret, F. Lebrun, A. Louis, Dumortier; Algae: Chalon, G. Westendorp & Wallays, C. H. Delogne, H. F. Van Heurck & A. Grunow; Fungi: Beeli, J. E. Bommer & M. Rousseau, M. Goossens-Fontana, M. A. Libert, Mouton (list of types published in Bull. Jard. Bot. Nat. Belg., 48: 221–230. 1978), H. Vanderyst, Westendorp & Wallays; Lichens: Delogne, L. Giltay, Libert, H. E. L. G. Coemans.
Director: E. PETIT, 1927 (Rubiaceae and Musci of tropical Africa).
Département Spermatophytes et Ptéridophytes
Curator: A. LAWALREE, 1921 (Vascular plants of Western Europe, Pteridophyta of Central Africa).
Staff members: PAUL BAMPS, 1932 (Flora of tropical Africa, editor of Flore d'Afrique Centrale and Distributiones Plantarum Africanarum).
JEAN LEONARD, 1920 (Flora of north-african and asiatic deserts, especially Iran).
LOUIS LIBEN, 1926 (Flora of central Africa).
ELMAR ROBBRECHT, 1946 (Taxonomy of African Rubiaceae; classification of Rubiaceae).
ANDRÉ ROBYNS, 1935 (Flora of central Africa; Bombacaceae, worldwide, including palynology; editor of Bulletin du Jardin Botanique National de Belgique).

LEO VANHECKE, 1947 (Flora and vegetation of western Europe, Hydrophytes, editor of Dumortiera).

Département Bryophytes et Thallophytes

Curator: A. BIENFAIT, 1927 (Cytology and morphology in relation to systematics).

Staff members: PIERRE COMPÈRE, 1934 (Algae of Belgium and tropical Africa).

JAN RAMMELOO, 1946 (Myxomycetes, Fungi of Belgium and tropical Africa).

Service de la Documentation (Library)

RAYMOND CLARYSSE, 1943.

Service des Collections Vivantes (Botanical Garden)

FRIEDA BILLIET, 1943.

EDMOND LAMMENS, 1928.

Specialization in research: Flora and vegetation of Belgium and western Europe; flora and phytogeography of Central Africa (Zaïre, Rwanda, Burundi); conservation of nature.

Associated botanic garden: Jardin Botanique National de Belgique.

Loans: To recognized scientific institutions, on written application to the director.

Periodical and serial works: Bulletin du Jardin botanique national de Belgique / Bulletin van de nationale Plantentuin van België; Dumortiera; Flore générale de Belgique (Bryophyta, Pteridophyta, Spermatophyta); Flore d'Afrique centrale (Pteridophyta and Spermatophyta of Zaïre, Rwanda and Burundi); Distributiones plantarum africanarum; Flore illustrée des champignons d'Afrique centrale.

Exchange: Available: specimens from Belgium, western Europe and central Africa. Desired: all groups, especially phanerogams and cryptogams of central Africa, worldwide Bombacaceae and Rubiaceae.

MELBOURNE: *Herbarium, Department of Botany, La Trobe University,* (**LTB**), Bundoora, Melbourne, Victoria 3083, **Australia.** (Information 1977)

Status: University.

Foundation: 1970. *Number of specimens:* 15.000.

Herbarium: Vascular plants and algae of southern and eastern Australia.

Specialization in research: Flora of tropical and temperate eastern Australia, chemical and numerical taxonomy, marine algae.

Loans: To recognized botanical institutions.

MELBOURNE: *National Herbarium of Victoria,* (**MEL**), Royal Botanic Gardens, Birdwood Avenue, South Yarra, Victoria 3141, **Australia.**

Telephone: 03-737030, 03-638935.

Status: State Government of Victoria.

Foundation: 1857. *Number of specimens:* 1.000.000.

Herbarium: Australian and worldwide.

Important collections: Australian collections since 1788 include many duplicates from Robert Brown and full representation of F. v. Mueller's collections, Ra-

leigh Black's herbarium of Tasmanian plants, most of J. Drummond's Western Australian plants and the larger part of O. Sonder's herbarium (including many numbers from the F. W. Sieber, J. G. Lehmann and J. A. L. Preiss herbaria), Norman A. Wakefield Victorian collections, including many types, James H. Willis Australian collections, including types.

Director: D. M. CHURCHILL, 1933 (Geobotany).

Curator: J. H. ROSS, 1941 (Fabaceae).

Staff members: H. I. ASTON, 1934 (Menyanthaceae; aquatic vascular plants).

R. B. FILSON, 1930 (Lichens).

P. K. GULLAN, 1950 (Victorian vegetation studies).

P. F. LUMLEY, 1938 (Horticultural botany, *Callistemon*),

T. B. MUIR, 1929 (Orchidaceae of Australia).

P. S. SHORT, 1955 (Compositae).

R. V. SMITH, 1923 (Naturalized alien plants; Compositae, holly-leaved Grevilleas).

M. A. TODD, 1922 (Victorian vascular plants).

Associated botanic garden: Royal Botanic Gardens, Melbourne; Cranbourne Annexe, Cranbourne; Werribee Park Annexe.

Loans: In general to recognized botanical institutions.

Periodical and serial works: Muelleria.

Exchange: Available: Australian vascular plants especially of Victoria.

Remarks: Facilities extended to visiting botanists. A new herbarium is planned, with enlarged staff and facilities.

MELBOURNE: *Botany School Herbarium, University of Melbourne,* (**MELU**), Parkville, Victoria 3052, **Australia.**

Telephone: (03) 3415040.

Status: University.

Foundation: 1929. *Number of specimens:* 120.000.

Herbarium: Predominantly plants of Victoria.

Important collections: G. Beaton (Fungi), H. J. Swart (Fungi), Sophie C. Ducker (Algae), G. T. Kraft (Algae), Ilma G. Stone (Mosses).

Director: Chairman of the Botany School.

Curator: Tutor in systematics.

Staff members: DONALD MALCOLM CALDER, 1933 (General; Loranthaceae, *Viola*).

THOMAS CARRICK CHAMBERS, 1930 (Blechnaceae).

I. CLARKE, 1950 (Angiosperms).

SOPHIE CHARLOTTE DUCKER, 1909 (Algae).

SUZANNE LAWLESS DUIGAN, 1924 (Angiosperms).

GERALD THOMPSON KRAFT, 1939 (Algae).

PAULINE YVONNE LADIGES, 1948 (*Eucalyptus*).

ILMA GRACE STONE, 1913 (Musci).

HARING JOHANNES SWART, 1922 (Leaf parasitizing fungi).

GRETNA MARGARET WESTE, 1917 (Fungi, Discomycetes).

Specialization in research: Particularly algal, fungal and bryophyte taxonomy.
Loans: To recognized institutions; initially for 6 months, but extensions can be arranged.
Exchange: Not generally available.

MELBOURNE: *Herbarium, Department of Botany, Monash University,* (**MUCV**), Clayton, Victoria 3168, **Australia.**
Telephone: (03) 541-3810.
Status: University.
Foundation: 1973. *Number of specimens:* 11.000 (5.000 vascular plants, 6.000 bryophytes, marine algae, fungi).
Herbarium: Teaching and research herbarium, predominantly State of Victoria.
Curator: ANNE DE CORONA, 1929.
Specialization in research: Taxonomy of Victorian cryptogams.
Loans: Available.
Exchange: By private arrangement only.

MEMPHIS: *Herbarium, Department of Biology, Memphis State University,* (**MEM**), Memphis, Tennessee 38152, **U.S.A.**
Telephone: 901/454-2971.
Foundation: 1952. *Number of specimens:* 16.686 (14.640 vascular plants, 2.000 fungi, 46 algae).
Herbarium: Emphasis on plants of Kentucky and the Mid-Mississippi basin.
Important collections: Raymond Athey (Kentucky, other U.S., Canada, Europe), E. T. Browne, Jr. (Kentucky, Tennessee, Arkansas), T. N. McCoy (Kentucky ferns and fern-allies), H. P. Riley (South Africa).
Director and Curator: EDWARD T. BROWNE, JR., 1926 (Vascular flora of Kentucky and the Mid-Mississippi basin).
Staff members: H. DELANO BLACK, 1937 (Mycology of western Tennessee).
G. L. HOWELL, 1928 (Plant physiology).
R. W. McGOWAN, 1922 (General botany; field botany; ecology).
N. A. MILLER, 1932 (General plant ecology; plant autecology).
F. P. OTT (Phycology; taxonomy).
B. H. WISE, 1925 (Plant physiology; Asclepiadaceae of Florida).
Research associate: RAYMOND ATHEY, 1914 (Kentucky flora).
Specialization in research: Floristic studies of vascular plant species of Kentucky and Mid-Mississippi basin.
Associated botanic garden: Curator is member, Board of Directors, Memphis Botanic Garden Foundation.
Loans: For 6-month period, but longer periods may be negotiated upon request. Available on loan September-April.
Exchange: Available: Mostly Kentucky, western

Tennessee, Arkansas. Desired: Preferably Kentucky and Liliaceae.

MEMPHIS: *Herbarium, Department of Biology, Southwestern at Memphis,* (**SWMT**), 2000 N. Parkway, Memphis, Tennessee 38112, **U.S.A.**
Telephone: 901/274-1800.
Foundation: 1925. *Number of specimens:* 5.000.
Herbarium: General vascular plants, especially western Tennessee; Asteraceae.
Director: JOHN OLSEN, 1950; 901/274-1800, ext. 218 (Asteraceae, especially Heliantheae).
Specialization in research: Systematics of Heliantheae, *Verbesina.*
Associated botanic garden: Southwestern at Memphis Arboretum.
Loans: No special restrictions.
Exchange: Available: Plants of western Tennessee. Desired: Asteraceae from any locality.

MENDOZA: *Facultad de Ciencias Agrarias,* (**MEN**) – – *see* CHACRAS DE CORIA.

MENDOZA: *Herbario Ruiz Leal, Instituto Argentino de Investigaciones de las Zonas Aridas,* (**MERL**), Consejo Nacional de Investigaciones Cientificas y Técnicas, Casilla de Correo 507, Correo Central, 5500 Mendoza, Mendoza, **Argentina.**
Telephone: (54)061/241995; 241797.
Foundation: 1916. *Number of specimens:* 29.900.
Herbarium: Primarily flora of the Province of Mendoza.
Important collections: Fungi; Gramineae, Leguminosae, Compositae; Adrián Ruiz Leal, Fidel A. Roig, Juan Semper, José A. Ambrosetti, Luis A. Del Vitto, Eduardo Mendez.
Curator: JOSÉ ARTURO AMBROSETTI, 1939 (Plant taxonomy).
Staff members: MARGARITA CABRERA, 1925.
ADRIANA LUISA CICCARELLI, 1959 (Plant taxonomy).
LUIS A. DEL VITTO, 1954 (Plant taxonomy).
Specialization in research: Flora of arid lands in western Argentina.
Loans: For 6 months.
Periodical and serial works: Deserta.
Exchange: Yes.

MENGLA: *Herbarium of Yunnan Institute of Tropical Botany, Academia Sinica,* (**HITBC**), Mengla County, Yunnan, **People's Republic of China.**
Telephone: Jinghong 905.
Status: Directed by Academia Sinica.
Foundation: 1964. *Number of specimens:* 50.000.
Herbarium: Tropical plants of China.
Important collections: Pei Sheng-ji, Li Yan-hui, Tao Guo-da.
Director: TSAI HSI-TAO, 1910 (Taxonomy of higher plants, plant resources).
Curator: PEI SHENG-JI, 1938 (Taxonomy of high-

er plants, plant resources).

Staff members: CHAO SHI-WANG, 1936 (Medicinal plants of south Yunnan).

CHEN PEI-SHAN, 1938 (Piperaceae and Zingiberaceae of China).

CHEN SAN-YANG, 1937 (Palmae of China).

LI YAN-HUI, 1930 (Taxonomy of tropical plants, Myristicaceae and Guttiferae of China).

PEI SHENG-JI (Palmae of China).

SUN JI-LIANG, 1952 (*Bambusa* of China).

TAO GUO-DA, 1939 (Dipterocarpaceae of China).

TONG SHAO-QUAN, 1935 (Dipterocarpaceae and Zingiberaceae of China).

Specialization in research: Tropical flora of south Yunnan, classification of tropical plants of China, tropical plant resources and utilization.

Associated botanic garden: Botanical Garden of Yunnan Institute of Tropical Botany.

Loans: To recognized botanical institutions.

Periodical and serial works: Tropical Plant Bulletin.

Exchange: Yes.

MERCURY: *Herbarium, Nevada Test Site,* (**NTS**), Mercury, Nevada 89023, U.S.A. (Mailing address: Janice C. Beatley, Department of Biological Sciences, University of Cincinnati, Cincinnati, Ohio 45223.)

Status: Atomic Energy Commission.

Foundation: 1959. *Number of specimens:* 14.000 (5.000 of these have been transferred to US).

Herbarium: Vascular plants of central-southern Nevada, especially southern part of Nye County.

Important collections: Janice C. Beatley (Nevada Test Site, Nellis Air Force Range; Ash Meadows, Nevada).

Curator: JANICE C. BEATLEY (Flora of southern Nevada).

Loans: No special restrictions; permission granted through Curator.

Remarks: Duplicates have been deposited at DS, NY, RENO, RSA.

MÉRIDA: *Herbario, Facultad de Ciencias Forestales, Universidad de Los Andes,* (**MER**), Mérida, **Venezuela.** (Information 1974)

Status: Under Departamento de Botánica.

Foundation: 1951. *Number of specimens:* 30.000.

Herbarium: Venezuelan plants.

MÉRIDA: *Herbario, Departamento de Botanica y Farmacognosia, Facultad de Farmacia, Universidad de Los Andes,* (**MERF**), Mérida 5101, **Venezuela.**

Director and Curator: DAVID DIAZ-MIRANDA.

Staff member: MANUAL LOPEZ-FIGUEIRAS (Lichens). (See addenda)

MERION: *Herbarium, Arboretum of the Barnes Foundation,* (**ABFM**), Box 128, Merion, Pennsylvania 19066, U.S.A.

Telephone: 215/664-8880.

Status: Private.

Foundation: 1922. *Number of specimens:* 9.000.

Herbarium: Woody plants, both native and cultivated.

Director: JOHN S. PENNY, 1914 (Palynology).

Curator: JOHN M. FOGG, JR., 1898.

Specialization in research: Hardiness of woody ornamental plants.

Associated botanic garden: Arboretum of the Barnes Foundation.

Loans: No special conditions.

Exchange: With 8 other American herbaria.

MESSINA: *Istituto ed Orto Botanico,* (**MS**), Piazza XX Settembre, Messina, **Italy.** (Information 1964)

Status: University.

Foundation: 1894. *Number of specimens:* 20.000.

Herbarium: General herbarium, herbarium siculum.

Important collections: Herb. Giuseppe Sequenza.

METEPEC: *Herbario, Comision Coordinadora para el Desarrollo Agricola y Ganadero del Estado de México,* (**CODAGEM**), Conjunto CODAGEM, Metepec, México, **Mexico.**

Telephone: 91721-6-02-68, 6-08-65, 6-09-99.

Status: Government of the state of Mexico.

Foundation: 1952. *Number of specimens:* 20.451.

Herbarium: Vascular plants of the state of Mexico.

Important collections: Maximino Martinez, Eizi Matuda, Hernando Sanchez Mejorada, Fernando Castañeda Bringas.

Director: SALVADOR SANCHEZ COLIN, 1912 (Agronomist).

Curator: FERNANDO CASTAÑEDA BRINGAS, 1931 (Biology).

Staff member: LUZ MARIA TORRES ZEPEDA.

Specialization in research: Vascular plant flora of the state of Mexico.

Exchange: Yes.

Remarks: This herbarium was originally founded by Dr. Matuda in Toluca.

MÉXICO: *Herbario, Asociacion Méxicana de Orquideologia,* (**AMO**), Apartado postal 53-123, México 17, Distrito Federal, **Mexico.** Street address: Cerrada de Moctezuma 16, La Herradura, México, 10, Distrito Federal, Huixquilucan, Mexico.

Telephone: (5) 589-58-49.

Foundation: 1976. *Number of specimens:* 2.000.

Herbarium: Orchidaceae only, mainly neotropical and especially Mexico.

Important collections: Eric Hagsater, Ed. W. Greenwood, Roberto Gonzalez Tamayo (western Mexico).

Director: ERIC HAGSATER, 1945 (Orchidaceae of Mexico; *Epidendrum* and *Notylia* sec. *Macroclinium; Oncidium* from Mexico and Central America).

Research Associates: ERNESTO AGUIRRE LEON (Orchidaceae ecology and pollination; *Clowesia*).

ROBERT L. DRESSLER (Orchidaceae, especially of America; pollination; *Encyclia*).

ROBERTO GONZALEZ TAMAYO (Orchidaceae, especially of western Mexico).

ED. W. GREENWOOD (Orchidaceae, especially from Oaxaca; *Govenia, Spiranthes, Malaxis, Habenaria, Arpophyllum*).

FEDERICO HALBINGER (Orchidaceae; *Barkeria, Odontoglossum*, and allied genera from Mexico and Central America).

ARIEL V. NAVARRO (Orchidaceae; *Bletia, Laelia* of Mexico).

OCTAVIO SUAREZ (Orchidaceae; *Lepanthes* of Mexico).

Specialization in research: Taxonomy of the Orchidaceae, including chemotaxonomy, pollination, and ecology; propagation and conservation of native species.

Associated botanic garden: Jardin Botanico de Chapultepec.

Loans: To recognized institutions.

Periodical and serial works: Orquidea (Méx.), founded 1971 (series 2), specialized in the Orchidaceae of Mexico and Central America, illustrated.

Exchange: Available: Orchidaceae of Mexico. Desired: Orchidaceae of Neotropics, especially Mexico and Central America.

Remarks: Additional collections: Flowers preserved in liquid: 600; library (books and journals): 2.000; photographs and transparencies: 18.000; phototypes and photographs of important specimens: 1.500.

MÉXICO: *Herbario, Escuela Nacional de Ciencias Biológicas, Instituto Politécnico Nacional,* (**ENCB**), Carpio y Plan de Ayala, Apartado postal 17-564, México 17, Distrito Federal, **Mexico.**

Telephone: (905)5/47-28-29.

Status: Supported by the Federal Government of Mexico.

Foundation: 1943. *Number of specimens:* 220.000 (6.000 algae, 42.000 fungi and lichens, 2.000 bryophytes, 5.000 pteridophytes, 165.000 phanerogams).

Herbarium: Vascular plants, macromycetes and marine algae of Mexico and neighboring areas form the bulk of the collection; special regional interest in the flora of the Valley of Mexico; *Bursera, Psilocybe,* and *Scleroderma* are well represented.

Important collections: D. Breedlove (mostly Chiapas), L. González Q. (mainly Hidalgo), G. Guzmán (fungi, lichens, and myxomycetes), G. B. Hinton (southwest Mexico), L. Huerta (marine algae), R. McVaugh (mostly western Mexico), A. Molina R. (Central America), L. Paray (Mexico), J. Rzedowski (Mexico), M. Sousa (Leguminosae), A. Ventura (Valley of Mexico), F. Ventura (mostly Veracruz and Puebla).

Head, Department of Botany: MARÍA DE LA LUZ ARREGUÍN, 1950 (Pteridophytes; flora of the Valley

of Mexico).

Curators: MARÍA DE LOS ANGELES CÁRDENAS, Curator of Bryophytes, 1949 (Bryophytes of Mexico).

GASTÓN GUZMÁN, Curator of Mycology, 1932 (Macromycetes).

JERZY RZEDOWSKI, Curator of Vascular Plants, 1926 (Flora and plant geography of Mexico).

MARÍA ELENA SÁNCHEZ, Curator of Algae, 1929 (Algae of Mexico).

Staff members: GRACIELA CALDERÓN, 1931 (Flora of the Valley of Mexico).

LAURA DÁVALOS, 1934 (Lichens and macromycetes).

JUDITH ESPINOSA, 1935 (In charge of seed and fossil plant collections; paleobotany; flora of the Valley of Mexico).

LAURA HUERTA, 1913 (Marine algae).

JOSÉ MIGUEL MEDINA, 1952.

RODOLFO PALACIOS, 1929 (In charge of pollen collection; palynology).

CONCEPCIÓN RODRÍGUEZ, 1941 (Flora of the Valley of Mexico; weeds).

MARINA VILLEGAS, 1940 (In charge of collection of useful plants).

Specialization in research: Taxonomy, floristics, geography, ecology, and uses of Mexican vascular plants, fungi, and algae; paleobotany; pollen morphology.

Loans: Without special restrictions.

Periodical and serial works: Anales de la Escuela Nacional de Ciencias Biológicas.

Exchange: Available: Vascular plants, fungi, and other cryptogams from Mexico. Wanted: Flowering plants and cryptogams from any part of the world, but preferably from Mexico and neighboring areas.

MÉXICO: *Herbario, Departamento de Biología, Facultad de Ciencias, Universidad Nacional Autónoma de México,* (**FCME**), Apartado postal 70-399, México 20, Distrito Federal, **Mexico.**

Telephone: (905)5/50-52-15, ext. 3944.

Foundation: 1940. *Number of specimens:* 11.250.

Herbarium: Flora of México, mainly of the Valley of México and the state of Veracruz.

Important collections: C. G. Pringle, E. Matuda, Ramírez-Cantú, and Riba and Nava.

Director: NELLY DIEGO PÉREZ, 1943 (Cyperaceae).

Curator: JAIME JIMÉNEZ RAMÍREZ, 1952 (Plant taxonomy).

Staff members: JOAQUÍN CIFUENTES BLANCO, 1953 (Fungi).

FRANCISCO G. LOREA HERNÁNDEZ, 1956 (Rubiaceae, Pteridophyta).

MARÍA JULIA CARABIAS LILLO, 1954 (Seeds).

JORGE GONZÁLEZ GONZÁLEZ, 1945 (Algae).

Specialization in research: Flora of Mexico.

Loans: Available on request.

Exchange: Available: Mainly specimens from

the Valley of México. Wanted: Neotropical specimens of plants and seeds.

MÉXICO: *Herbario, Instituto Nacional de Investigaciones Forestales, Secretaría de Agricultura y Ganadería,* (**INIF**), Progreso 5, Coyoacán, México 21, Distrito Federal, **Mexico.** (Information 1976)
Foundation: 1958. *Number of specimens:* 33.150.
Herbarium: Mexican plants, especially phanerogams of the coniferous and tropical forests.
Important collections: D. Breedlove, J. Chavelas, H. S. Gentry, X. Madrigal, A. May Nah, R. Moran, L. Vela.
   Curator: DALILA ORTIZ CISNEROS (Tropical plants).
   Staff members: XAVIER MADRIGAL SÁNCHEZ (Conifers).
   LUCIANO VELA GÁLVEZ (Conifers).
Specialization in research: Flora and ecology of coniferous forests.
Loans: To recognized institutions.
Exchange: Available: Woody plants of temperate and tropical zones. Desired: Plants of economic importance.

MÉXICO: *Museo de Historia Natural de la Ciudad de México,* (**MEX**), México, Distrito Federal, **Mexico** – – discontinued.

MÉXICO: *Herbario Nacional de México, Departamento de Botánica, Instituto de Biología, Universidad Nacional Autónoma de México,* (**MEXU**), Apartado postal 70-367, México 20, Distrito Federal, **Mexico.**
Telephone: (905)550-52-15, ext. 4880, 4881, 4882.
Foundation: 1881. *Number of specimens:* 310.000.
Herbarium: Mainly México and Central America; also collections of fruits, seeds, wood, pollen, and photographs.
Important collections: 2.360 types; F. Altamirano (2.018), G. Arsène (1.883), W. Boege (3.800), D. Breedlove (10.890), C. Conzatti (2.323), H. S. Gentry (3.960), J. González Ortega (3.600), G. B. Hinton (3.506), E. Langlassé, E. Lyonnet (6.000), E. Matuda (20.500), M. Martínez, T. MacDougall (1.100), R. McVaugh (2.622), F. Miranda (10.002), E. Palmer (2579), C. G. Pringle (22.000), J. G. Schaffner, A. J. Sharp (7.692), M. Sousa S. (10.300), J. Trappe, J. Vázquez Sánchez (7.500).
   Director and Curator: MARIO SOUSA SÁNCHEZ, 1940 (Taxonomy of Mexican Leguminosae; ecology, pollination, and dispersal of seeds; floristics; history of botany).
   Staff members: C. ELVIRA AGUIRRE ACOSTA, 1954 (Taxonomy of macro-fungi).
   GLORIA ANDRADE MUNGUÍA, 1949 (History of botany).
   HELIA BRAVO HOLLIS, 1901 (Taxonomy of Cactaceae).
   ARMANDO BUTANDA CERVERA, 1942 (Botanical bibliography).

Head of herbarium - 1990
Dra. Patricia Dávila Aranda

MA. DE LOS ANGELES CÁRDENAS, 1949 (Taxonomy of bryophytes).
   FERNANDO CHIANG CABRERA, 1943 (Taxonomy of Celastraceae and Solanaceae).
   ALFONSO DELGADO SALINAS, 1950 (Taxonomy of the tribe Phaseolinae and the genus *Cassia*, Leguminosae).
   CLAUDIO DELGADILLO MOYA, 1945 (Phytogeography and taxonomy of mosses of Mexico).
   FRANCISCO ESPINOZA, 1954 (Weedy plants).
   HILDA FLORES OLVERA, 1953 (History of botany; halophytes).
   MARÍA TERESA GERMÁN RAMÍREZ, 1946 (Taxonomy of Meliaceae and the genus *Galactia*, Leguminosae).
   FRANCISCO GONZÁLEZ MEDRANO, 1939 (Woody flora of Tamaulipas).
   ANTONIO LOT HELGUERAS, 1945 (Aquatic plants; taxonomy and floristics).
   MIGUEL ANGEL MARTÍNEZ ALFARO, 1942 (Ethnobotany).
   ALEJANDRO NOVELO RETANA, 1951 (Aquatic plants; taxonomy and floristics).
   MARTHA ORTEGA GONZÁLEZ, 1933 (Freshwater algae).
   MARISELA PARDAVÉ DÍAZ, 1949 (Phytopathology).
   MAGDALENA PEÑA, 1939 (Taxonomy and floristics of Orchidaceae).
   LUIS ALFREDO PÉREZ JIMÉNEZ, 1943 (Tropical trees).
   EVANGELINA PÉREZ-SILVA, 1931 (Taxonomy of macro-fungi).
   HERMILO QUERO RICO (Taxonomy and floristics of Palmae).
   MA. DE LOURDES RICO ARCE, 1955 (Taxonomy of *Acacia*, Leguminosae).
   HERNANDO SÁNCHEZ MEJORADA, 1926 (Taxonomy of Cactaceae).
   LEIA SCHEINVAR (Taxonomy of *Opuntia*, Cactaceae).
   JAVIER VALDÉS GUTIÉRREZ, 1931 (Halophytes and gypsophiles).
   MARTHA ZENTENO ZEVADA, 1920 (Phytopathology).
Specialization in research: Flora of México.
Associated botanic garden: Jardín Botánico del Instituto de Biología, Universidad Nacional Autónoma de México.
Loans: To scientific institutions only.
Periodical and serial works: Anales del Instituto de Biología, Universidad Nacional Autónoma de México, Ser. Botánica (since 1929).
Exchange: General collections of Mexico, especially of the states of Oaxaca, Hidalgo, Querétaro, Quintana Roo, and Michoacán.

MIAMI: *Herbarium, Fairchild Tropical Garden,* (**FTG**), 10901 Old Cutler Road, Miami, Florida 33156, **U.S.A.** (Herbarium: 11035 Old Cutler Road).

Telephone: 305/665-2844.
Status: Private institution.
Foundation: 1967. *Number of specimens:* 40.000.
Herbarium: Native plants of Florida and the West Indies, with emphasis on the Bahama Archipelago; vouchers of cultivated plants of South Florida.
Important collections: Vascular plant collections of G. Avery, W. M. Buswell, D. S. and H. B. Correll, F. Craighead, W. T. Gillis, S. R. Hill, J. Popenoe, R. P. Sauleda.
    Director: JOHN POPENOE, 1929 (Horticulture).
    Curator: D. S. CORRELL, 1908 (Floras and monographs).
    Staff member: HELEN B. CORRELL, 1907 (Floras and monographs).
    Specialization in research: Preparation of a *Flora of the Bahama Archipelago*; research toward a *Flora of Florida*; *Tripsacum* (Gramineae).
    Associated botanic garden: Fairchild Tropical Garden.
    Loans: No special restrictions.
    Periodical and serial works: Fairchild Tropical Garden Bulletin.
    Exchange: Available: Florida, West Indies (especially Bahamas); cultivated plants of Fairchild Tropical Garden. Desired: Florida, West Indies.
    Remarks: 2132 seed collections; wood collection.

MIDDLEBURY: *Herbarium, Biology Department, Middlebury College,* **(MID)**, Middlebury, Vermont 05753, **U.S.A.**
Telephone: 802/388-2802.
Status: Private college.
Foundation: 1800. *Number of specimens:* 500.
Herbarium: Vermont flora.
Important collections: Ezra Brainerd, Henry M. Seeley.
    Director and Curator: C. R. LANDGREN (Plant physiology).
    Remarks: Important collections have been transferred to the University of Vermont (VT); remaining collections are used for teaching purposes.

MIDDLETOWN: *Herbarium, Department of Natural Resources, Lord Fairfax Community College,* **(LFCC)**, P.O. Box 47, Middletown, Virginia 22645, **U.S.A.**
Telephone: 703/869-1120.
Status: State institution.
Foundation: 1974. *Number of specimens:* 10.000.
Herbarium: General collection from Virginia and Ontario; many aquatics and Mexican ferns.
    Director: ROBERT C. SIMPSON, 1948 (Orchidaceae, aquatics, flora of northwestern Virginia).
    Specialization in research: Flora of northwestern Virginia; systematics of Orchidaceae.
    Loans: Must be annotated.

MIDDLETOWN: *Herbarium, Department of Biology, Wesleyan University,* **(WECO)**, Middletown, Connecticut 06457, **U.S.A.** -- Now in NY.

Telephone: 203/347-9411.
Foundation: 1850. *Number of specimens:* 7.500.
Herbarium: Native flora, temperate zone, mountainous regions of U.S.

MILANO: *Herbarium, Istituto di Scienze Botaniche,* **(MI)**, Via Giuseppe Colombo 60, 20133 Milano, **Italy**.
Telephone: 292161-296967.
Status: Università degli Studi di Milano.
Foundation: 1925.
Herbarium: Mainly phanerogams of Italy.
    Remarks: The herbarium is soon to be moved to a new location.

MILANO: *Istituto di Patalogia Vegetale dell'Università,* **(MIPV)**, Via Celoria 2, 20133 Milano, **Italy**. (Information 1974)
Foundation: 1870.
Important collections: G. B. Traverso (fungi).

MILFORD: *Herbarium, Desert Experimental Range, Intermountain Experiment Station,* **(DERM)**, Milford, Utah 84751, **U.S.A.** (Information 1974)
Status: U.S. Department of Agriculture.
Foundation: 1934. *Number of specimens:* 2.014.
Herbarium: Great Basin desert, Utah.

MILFORD: *Herbarium, Iowa Lakeside Laboratory,* **(ILH)**, Milford, Iowa 51351, **U.S.A.**
Telephone: 712/337-3669.
Status: Directed by the Iowa Board of Regents.
Foundation: 1909. *Number of specimens:* 6.000.
Herbarium: Plants of Iowa.
    Curator: LAWRENCE J. EILERS, 1927 (Taxonomy and floristics of Iowa vascular plants).
    Staff members: DONALD R. FARRAR (Bryophytes, pteridophytes).
        CHARLES W. REIMER (Diatoms).
    Specialization in research: Northwest Iowa.
    Associated botanic garden: Iowa Lakeside Laboratory (140 acres).
    Loans: Available only in summer (June-August).
    Exchange: Northwestern Iowa and adjacent areas.
    Remarks: A biological field station, open during the summer.

MILLERSVILLE: *Herbarium, Department of Biology, Millersville State College,* **(MVSC)**, Millersville, Pennsylvania 17551, **U.S.A.**
Telephone: 717/872-5411.
Foundation: 1968. *Number of specimens:* 5.500.
Herbarium: Flora of lower Susquehanna River valley.
Important collections: Thomas C. Porter.
    Curator: JAMES C. PARKS, 1942 (Floristics; Synantherology).
    Specialization in research: Floristics of lower Susquehanna River valley and Pennsylvania.
    Loans: 6 months to recognized herbaria.

Exchange: Available: General collections from eastern U.S., including some from the New Jersey Pine Barrens.

MILTON: *Herbarium, Biology Department, Milton College,* **(MCW),** College Street, Milton, Wisconsin 53563, **U.S.A.**
Telephone: 608/868-2928.
Foundation: 1848. *Number of specimens:* 2.000.
Herbarium: Southern Wisconsin.
Important collections: S. H. Wilson, Wm. M. Canby.
  Director and Curator: L. M. VAN HORN, 1911 (Bird adrenal physiology).

MILWAUKEE: *Herbarium, Milwaukee Public Museum,* **(MIL),** 800 West Wells Street, Milwaukee, Wisconsin 53233, **U.S.A.**
Telephone: 414/278-2711.
Status: County Museum.
Foundation: 1852. *Number of specimens:* 130.000.
Herbarium: Vascular and non-vascular plants of Wisconsin, North America, and the Neotropics.
Important collections: Albert M. Fuller (*Rubus*), Emil P. Kruschke (*Crataegus*), Huron H. Smith (ethnobotanical collection).
  Director and Curator of Non-vascular Plants: MARTYN J. DIBBEN, 1943 (Lichens, bryophytes, fleshy fungi).
  Curator of Vascular Plants: W. CARL TAYLOR, 1946 (Ferns, gymnosperms, flowering plants).
  Curatorial Assistants: TRUDY R. BERTRAM, 1949 (Non-vascular plants).
    NEIL T. LUEBKE, 1950 (Vascular plants).
  Specialization in research: Metropolitan Milwaukee flora; cryptogams of Wisconsin; ferns and fern allies of Wisconsin; chemosystematics of lichens; biosystematics of Isoëtaceae; New World tropical lichens.
  Associated botanic garden: Boerner Botanical Garden and Mitchell Park Conservatory, Milwaukee, Wisconsin.
  Loans: To recognized botanists and botanical institutions.
  Periodical and serial works: Contributions, Publications, and Special Publications in Biology and Geology, Milwaukee Public Museum Press.
  Exchange: Available: Specimens from Wisconsin, North America, and the Neotropics. Wanted: Specimens from Europe, North America, and the tropics.

MILWAUKEE: *Herbarium, Department of Botany, University of Wisconsin,* **(UWM),** P.O. Box 413, Milwaukee, Wisconsin 53201, **U.S.A.**
Telephone: 414/963-4298.
Foundation: 1956. *Number of specimens:* 85.000.
Herbarium: Wisconsin and North American vascular plants; North American rust fungi; Wisconsin lichens and mosses.

Important collections: Hainer (Wisconsin fleshy fungi), Torres (Zinnias, including several types), Hatcher (South American leafy liverworts).
  Director: PETER J. SALAMUN, 1919 (Taxonomy of vascular plants of Wisconsin; vascular aquatic plants of fresh waters).
  Staff members: JOHN W. BAXTER, 1918 (Fungi; Uredinales).
    JOHN L. BLUM, 1917 (Phycology).
    ROBERT ROBBINS, 1946 (Anatomy of vascular plants; gymnosperms and pteridophytes).
    FOREST W. STEARNS, 1918 (Plant, forest, and urban ecology).
    PHILIP B. WHITFORD, 1920 (Plant and prairie ecology).
  Adjunct staff members: MARTYN DIBBEN, 1943 (Lichenology).
    CARL TAYLOR, 1946 (Pteridophytes).
  Specialization in research: Flora and ecology of Wisconsin and midwestern U.S.; algae of the Great Lakes region; rust fungi of North America; lake shore vegetation of Lake Michigan and Lake Superior.
  Associated botanic garden: University of Wisconsin-Milwaukee field stations.
  Loans: To recognized botanists or botanical institutions, under usual herbarium procedures, for period up to one year.
  Exchange: Available: Plants from Wisconsin and limited numbers from Mexico and western U.S. Desired: Plants from all regions.

MINERAL: *Herbarium, Lassen Volcanic National Park,* **(LVNP),** Mineral, California 96063, **U.S.A.**
Telephone: 916/595-4441.
Status: U.S. Department of the Interior, National Park Service.
Foundation: 1916. *Number of specimens:* 3.000.
Herbarium: Flora of the southern Cascade Range.
  Director and Curator: RICHARD L. VANCE.

MINSK: *Herbarium, Biological Institute of Academy of Sciences of the Belorussya S.S.R.,* **(MSK),** Stalin Street 108, Minsk, **U.S.S.R.** (Information 1964)
Foundation: 1945. *Number of specimens:* 23.000.
Herbarium: Vascular plants and lichens of Belorussya.

MISENHEIMER: *Herbarium, Division of Natural and Health Sciences, Pfeiffer College,* **(PFC),** Misenheimer, North Carolina 28109, **U.S.A.**
  Remarks: Collections no longer available for public use.

MISSISSAUGA: *Herbarium, Erindale College, University of Toronto,* **(TRTE),** 3359 Mississauga Road, Mississauga, Ontario, **Canada** L5L 1C6.
Telephone: 416/828-5379.
Foundation: 1968. *Number of specimens:* 15.000.
Herbarium: Mainly vascular plants from central

and southern Ontario.

Curator: P. W. BALL, 1932 (Cyperaceae of eastern Canada; *Salicornia* and *Arthrocnemum*).

Loans: For up to 1 year; to recognized institutions.

Exchange: Available: Southern Ontario.

Remarks: Formerly listed under Toronto.

MISSISSIPPI STATE: *Herbarium, Institute for Botanical Exploration,* (**IBE**), Box EN, Mississippi State, Mississippi 39762, **U.S.A.**

Telephone: 601/325-3120.

Status: Non-profit research institute.

Foundation: 1975. *Number of specimens:* 72.500.

Herbarium: Worldwide with emphasis on southeastern U.S. and tropical America.

Director and Curator: SIDNEY MCDANIEL, 1940 (Floras of southeastern U.S., Amazonian Peru, and Alaska; Cyperaceae, Compositae).

Staff members: CHARLES T. BRYSON, 1950 (Cyperaceae, especially *Carex*).

ROBIN B. FOSTER, 1945 (Tropical ecology; flora of Madre de Dios, Peru).

W. C. HOLMES, 1945 (Tropical Compositae; flora of Louisiana).

GWEN K. PERKINS, 1920 (Flora of Prince of Wales Island, Alaska).

MANUEL RIMACHI Y., 1955 (Flora of Amazonian Peru).

Specialization in research: Floras of southeastern U.S., Amazonian Peru, and Prince of Wales Island, Alaska.

Associated botanic garden: Crosby Memorial Arboretum, Picayune, Mississippi (in development).

Loans: Normal regulations.

Exchange: Available: Southeastern U.S., Alaska, tropical America. Desired: Worldwide.

Remarks: Duplicates of some tropical material available for determination by specialists.

MISSISSIPPI STATE: *Herbarium, Department of Biological Sciences, Mississippi State University,* (**MISSA**), Drawer GY, Mississippi State, Mississippi 39762, **U.S.A.**

Telephone: 601/325-3120.

Foundation: 1890. *Number of specimens:* 40.000.

Herbarium: Mainly vascular plants of Mississippi.

Director and Curator: SIDNEY MCDANIEL, 1940 (Flora of Amazonian Peru and southern U.S.; Ericaceae, Piperaceae; *Carex*).

Staff member: J. RAY WATSON, 1935 (Vascular flora of Mississippi).

Specialization in research: Flora of Mississippi.

Loans: To recognized institutions and individuals.

Exchange: Available: Mississippi material.

MISSOULA: *Herbarium, Botany Department, University of Montana,* (**MONTU**), Missoula, Montana 59812, **U.S.A.**

Telephone: 406/243-5222.

Foundation: 1909. *Number of specimens:* 100.000.

Herbarium: Regional herbarium specializing in vascular flora of northern Rocky Mountain region.

Important collections: J. E. Kirkwood (Rocky Mountain trees and shrubs), C. Leo Hitchcock, P. A. Rydberg and C. E. Bessey, M. J. Elrod, J. W. Blankinship, L. H. Harvey (New World *Eragrostis*), F. Rose (Montana), Klaus Lackschewitz (Montana).

Curator: SHERMAN J. PREECE, 1923; 406/243-5182 (*Zigadenus*; Montana trees and shrubs; Montana aquatic vascular plants).

Staff members: KLAUS LACKSCHEWITZ, 1911 (Flora of Montana, especially the alpine).

CHARLES N. MILLER, 1938 (Paleobotany; Osmundaceae).

KATHLEEN M. PETERSON, 1948 (Lamiaceae, *Salvia* subgenus *Calosphace* section *Farinaceae*).

MELVIN THORNTON, 1928 (Fungi).

Specialization in research: As above.

Loans: Usual regulations.

Exchange: Limited.

MISSOULA: *Herbarium, Forestry Sciences Laboratory, Intermountain Forest and Range Experiment Station, Forest Service, U.S. Department of Agriculture,* (**MRC**), Drawer G, Missoula, Montana 59806, **U.S.A.**

Telephone: 406/329-3533.

Status: U.S. Department of Agriculture, Forest Service.

Foundation: 1932. *Number of specimens:* 8.000.

Herbarium: Flora of the National Forests and adjacent areas of Montana and northern Idaho (principally northern Rocky Mountains, U.S.A.).

Curator: PETER F. STICKNEY, 1929 (Northern Rocky Mountain flora and its distribution; secondary forest succession; Pacific Northwest tussock *Festuca*).

Specialization in research: Flora of northern Rocky Mountains (U.S.A.); composition of forest communities and changes associated with wildfire and management treatments.

Loans: Of limited duration to recognized institutions.

Remarks: Formerly Missoula Research Center; established and maintained primarily for reference and documentation of basic and applied research conducted for the management of wildlands.

MODENA: *Herbarium, Istituto Botanica dell' Università,* (**MOD**), Modena, **Italy.** (Information 1974)

Status: University.

Foundation: 1772. *Number of specimens:* 18.000.

Herbarium: Worldwide collections especially Italy, including cryptogams.

MOGADISHU: *National Herbarium, National Range Agency,* (**MOG**), P.O. Box 1759, Mogadishu, **Somalia,** East Africa.

Status: National Range Agency, an autonomous agency under the Ministry of Livestock, Forestry and Range Management, Government of Somalia.

Foundation: 1978. *Number of specimens:* 10.000.

Herbarium: Plants of Somalia and other parts of the world.

Important collections: Glover, Gillet, Bally.

General Manager: ABDULLAHI AHMED KARANI, Chief of National Range Agency.

Director: S. M. A. KAZMI (Plant taxonomy, phytogeography).

Staff member: O. J. HANSEN (Scrophulariaceae, Labiatae, Gramineae).

Specialization in research: Flora of Somalia.

Loans: Yes.

Periodical and serial works: Somali Range Bulletin; proposed to publish Flora of Somalia in series in 1984.

Exchange: Available: Specimens from Somalia. Desired: Specimens from East Africa, Africa, any subtropical, arid and semi-arid areas.

Remarks: Newly established herbarium; any help in the form of literature, specimens and scientific cooperation in naming the plants by specialists will be greatly appreciated.

MONMOUTH: *Herbarium, Oregon College of Education,* (**MOC**), 345 N. Monmouth Avenue, Monmouth, Oregon 97361, **U.S.A.**

Telephone: 503/838-1220, ext. 491.

Foundation: 1950. *Number of specimens:* 2.000.

Herbarium: Local collections.

Director and Curator: J. MORRIS JOHNSON, 1937 (General vascular plant taxonomy; field botany of threatened and endangered species).

Loans: Usual regulations.

MONROE: *Herbarium, Biology Department, Northeast Louisiana University,* (**NLU**), Monroe, Louisiana 71209, **U.S.A.**

Telephone: 318/342-3108.

Status: State university.

Foundation: 1966. *Number of specimens:* 186.241.

Herbarium: General vascular plants of Gulf South and eastern U.S.; most extensive collection of Louisiana plants; over 5.000 sheets of *Ophioglossum*; surveys for several Louisiana parishes.

Director and Curator: R. DALE THOMAS, 1936 (Field botany and floristic studies; taxonomy and distribution of *Ophioglossum*; Louisiana flora).

Specialization in research: Flora of Louisiana, including atlas and checklist; studying distribution of *Ophioglossum* in the Gulf South.

Loans: To other herbaria; no special conditions.

Exchange: Desired: General exchange with any herbarium from any area of the world. Gift of specimens in any family for their determinations.

Remarks: Will collect material for anyone in exchange for expenses in field.

MONROVIA: *Harley Herbarium, College of Agriculture and Forestry, University of Liberia,* (**LIB**), Monrovia, **Liberia.** (Information 1974)

Status: University.

Foundation: 1960. *Number of specimens:* 7.000.

Herbarium: West African flora, especially Liberia.

Loans: To recognized botanical institutions for one year; types are not loaned.

MONTERÍA: *Herbario, Departamento de Biología, Universidad Nacional de Córdoba,* (**HUC**), Apartado Aéreo 354, Montería, Córdoba, **Colombia.** (Information 1977)

Foundation: 1976. *Number of specimens:* 1.000.

Herbarium: Weeds and cultivated plants of Córdoba.

MONTERREY: *Herbario, Departamento de Biología, Instituto Tecnológico y de Estudios Superiores de Monterrey,* (**MEMO**), Avenida Eugenio Garza Sada 2501, Sucursal de Correos "J", Monterrey, Nuevo León, **Mexico.**

Telephone: 9183/58-20-00, ext. 454.

Foundation: 1948. *Number of specimens:* 5.000.

Herbarium: Mexican vascular plants; Gramineae, Leguminosae; desert and semi-desert plants.

Director: LEONEL ROBLES G. (Phytopathology).

Curator: RAUL A. GARZA-CUEVAS (Biology).

Specialization in research: Flora and ecology of northeastern Mexico.

Loans: Usual regulations to recognized institutions.

Exchange: Available: Semi-desert plants. Desired: Plants of tropical and temperate regions.

MONTERREY: *Herbario, Facultad de Ciencias Biológicas, Universidad Autónoma de Nuevo León,* (**UNL**), Ciudad Universitaria, Apartado postal 2790, Monterrey, Nuevo León, **Mexico.**

Telephone: 52-39-06; 52-39-05.

Foundation: 1957. *Number of specimens:* 11.000.

Herbarium: Especially Sierra Madre Oriental of Tamaulipas and Nuevo León; deserts of Coahuila, Nuevo León, and Tamaulipas.

Important collections: F. A. Barkley, A. Hernandez Corzo, B. C. Tharp, B. H. Warnock, J. Marroquin, P. Rojas M., J. Rzedowski, J. L. Gutierres Lobatos, G. Alanis, H. Sanchez.

Director: J. LUIS GUTIERRES LOBATOS.

Curator: MAURICIO GONZÁLEZ FERRARA, 1956.

Staff members: GLAFIRO ALANIS FLORES.

JORGE ELIZONDO ELIZONDO, 1958 (Cactaceae).

RAUL FLORES OLVERA, 1956.

ROSA ELIA HERNANDEZ VALENCIA, 1958 (Cactaceae).

J. JAVIER ORTIZ, 1957 (Gramineae).

ERNESTO RAMIREZ ALVAREZ, 1958.

HUMBERTO SANCHEZ VEGA.

EDUARDO VILLANUEVA MONTEMAYOR, 1958 (Leguminosae).

Specialization in research: Flora of Nuevo León and adjacent states; general floristics; ethnobotany; weeds of the citrus region; forest trees.
Exchange: Desired: Vascular plants, especially pteridophytes.

MONTEVIDEO: *Dirección de Agronomia, Ministerio de Ganaderia y Agricultura,* (**MVDA**), Calle Uruguay, Montevideo, **Uruguay** –– discontinued.

MONTEVIDEO: *Herbario, Laboratorio de Botánica, Facultad de Agronomia,* (**MVFA**), Casilla de Correo 1238, Avenida Garzón 780, Montevideo, **Uruguay.**
Telephone: 39-71-91.
Status: Universidad de la República.
Foundation: 1907. *Number of specimens:* 60.000.
Herbarium: Vascular plants of Uruguay.
Important collections: M. B. Berro, E. Marchesi, A. Lombardo, B. Rosengurtt.
Director: B. ROSENGURTT, 1916 (Gramineae).
Curator: E. MARCHESI, 1943 (Compositae).
Staff members: R. BRESCIA, 1930 (Chief of the garden).
P. FERRÉS, 1950 (Anatomy of Gramineae).
P. IZAGUIRRE DE ARTUCIO, 1932 (Orchidaceae; embryology of Gramineae).
A. LAGUARDIA, 1937 (Anatomy, cytology, and embryology of Gramineae).
A. LOMBARDO, 1902 (Flora montevidensis).
O. DEL PUERTO, 1931 (Weeds; Gramineae).
G. ZILIANI, 1946 (Anatomy and embryology of Gramineae).
Specialization in research: Flora of Uruguay.
Associated botanic garden: Yes.
Loans: No special conditions.
Exchange: Irregular.

MONTEVIDEO: *Herbario, Laboratorio de Botánica, Facultad de Hum. y Ciencias,* (**MVHC**), Cerrito 73, Montevideo, **Uruguay.** (Information 1974)
Status: State university.
Foundation: 1955. *Number of specimens:* 4.000.
Herbarium: Vascular plants of Uruguay.

MONTEVIDEO: *Herbario, Museo Nacional de Historia Natural de Montevideo,* (**MVM**), Casilla de Correo 399, Montevideo, **Uruguay.**
Telephone: 90-41-14.
Status: State institution.
Foundation: 1890. *Number of specimens:* 85.000.
Herbarium: Vascular plants from Uruguay, Argentina, and Paraguay; lichens from Uruguay and Argentina.
Important collections: J. Arechavaleta, E. Gibert, C. Osten, D. Legrand.
Director and Curator: HÉCTOR S. OSORIO, 1928 (Lichens from Uruguay, Argentina, and southern Brazil).
Staff members: J. CHEBATAROFF (Cyperaceae, Compositae).

D. LEGRAND (Myrtaceae; *Portulaca*).
A. LOMBARDO (Pteridophytes; cultivated plants).
E. MARCHESI (Compositae).
B. ROSENGURTT (Gramineae).
Specialization in research: Taxonomy of vascular plants of Uruguay and lichens of Uruguay, Argentina, and southern Brazil.
Loans: Restricted.
Periodical and serial works: Comunicaciones Botanicas del Museo Nacional de Historia Natural; Anales del Museo Nacional de Historia Natural.
Exchange: With institutions with similar interests.

MONTGOMERY: *Herbarium, West Virginia Institute of Technology,* (**WVIT**), Montgomery, West Virginia 25136, **U.S.A.**
Telephone: 304/442-3236.
Number of specimens: 2.000.
Herbarium: Local flora.
Director and Curator: VIOLET S. PHILLIPS, 1918.
Specialization in research: Economic importance of local flora.
Exchange: Limited.

MONTPELLIER: *École Nationale Superieure Agronomique Botanique,* (**MPA**), Laboratoire de Botanique, 34060 Montpellier Cedex, **France.**
Telephone: (67) 63 19 15.
Status: Ministry of Agriculture.
Foundation: 1900. *Number of specimens:* 75.000 (50.000 phanerogams, 25.000 cryptogams).
Herbarium: Phanerogams (France), cryptogams (France and worldwide).
Important collections: Phanerogams: E. Durand, Perris, Le Sourd, Gonod d'Artemard, L. Barrandon, G. Mandon, G. Kuhnholtz-Lordat; Cryptogams: G. Boyer, V. Ducomet, G. Arnaud, E. Foex, G. Kuhnholtz-Lordat, P. Renaud, P. Bernaux.
Director: P. SIGNORET, 1931 (Virology).
Curators: P. BERNAUX, 1919 (Phytopathology).
CL. LECOT, 1931 (Wood inhabiting fungi).
J. MAILLET, 1951 (Weeds).
Specialization in research: Weeds; evolution of the vineyard flora; pathology: phytopathology of cereal grains and Soja; wood inhabiting fungi.
Loans: To recognized institutions.
Exchange: Available: Phanerogams (France); cryptogams (worldwide).

MONTPELLIER: *Institut de Botanique,* (**MPU**), 163 rue Auguste Broussonnet, 34000 Montpellier, **France.**
Telephone: (67) 63.17.93.
Status: State university.
Foundation: 1890. *Number of specimens:* 4.000.000.
Herbarium: Phanerogams and cryptogams, Mediterranean collections.
Important collections: (see "Les Herbiers de l'Institut de Botanique de Montpellier." *Naturalia*

Monspeliensia, Sér. Bot., fasc. 18, 1967. "Les Herbiers de l'Institut de Botanique de Montpellier. Nouvelles acquisitions depuis 1967." *Naturalia Monspeliensia*, Sér. Bot., fasc. 23–24, 1972–1973. "L'Herbier de l'Abbé H. Coste à Montpellier." *Naturalia Monspeliensia*, Sér. Bot., fasc. 23–24, 1972–1973. "L'Herbier Jean de Vichet, témoin de la flore ancienne de Montpellier et de ses environs." *Naturalia Monspeliensia*, Sér. Bot., fasc. 26, 1976).

Director: M. DENIZOT, 1931 (Algology).
Curator: L. GRANEL DE SOLIGNAC.

Institut de Botanique
Staff members: L. BERTRAND.
J. L. BOMPAR.
J. J. CORRE.
A. DUBOIS.
B. GARRONE.
M. GODRON.
F. HALLÉ.
M. LAURET.
J. MATHEZ.
P. MONNIER.
L. PASSAMA.
S. PUECH.
C. RAYNAUD.
R. RIOUALL.
CH. SAUVAGE.
B. THIEBAUT.

Faculté des Sciences
Staff members: A. L. M. BONNET.
N. GRAMBAST.
CH. HÉBANT.
J. L. VERNET.
PH. VERNET.

Faculté de Médecine
Staff members: J. A. RIOUX, Chef de Service du Laboratoire d'Ecologie Médicale et Pathologie Parasitaire, Directeur du Jardin des Plantes.
H. HARANT, Ancien Directeur du Jardin des Plantes.
D. T. JARRY, Chef de Travaux.
Other staff:
C. BILLOT.
D. M. JARRY.
F. PRATLONG.

Faculté de Pharmacie
Staff members: G. PRIVAT, Chef de Service.
CL. ANDARY.
F. ENJALBERT.
M. E. MOTTE.
J. PELLECUER.
J. RASCOL.
J. L. ROUSSEL.
Specialization in research: Mediterranean flora.
Associated botanic garden: Jardin des Plantes.
Loans: To recognized institutions.
Periodical and serial works: Naturalia Monspeliensia.
Exchange: Yes.

MONTPELLIER: *Herbarium, Station Internationale de Géobotanique Méditerranéne et Alpine*, (**SIGMA**), Rue du Pioch de Boutonnet, Montpellier (Hérault), **France.** (Information 1974)
Status: Private foundation.
Foundation: 1930. *Number of specimens:* 60.000.
Herbarium: Phanerogams of Europe and Northern Africa.
Specialization in research: Mediterranean, alpine and Pyrenean flora and vegetation.
Periodical and serial works: Communications of the S.I.G.M.A., Vegetatio, Acta Geobotanica.

MONTRÉAL: *Herbier Marie-Victorin, Institut Botanique, Université de Montréal*, (**MT**), 4101 est, rue Sherbrooke, Montréal, Québec, **Canada** H1X 2B2.
Telephone: 514/872-2680.
Foundation: 1920. *Number of specimens:* 630.000 (600.000 vascular plants, 30.000 bryophytes).
Herbarium: Worldwide, mainly pteridophytes and phanerogams; emphasis on Québec and Newfoundland.
Important collections: Fr. Marie-Victorin collections from eastern Canada and Cuba; custody of F. H. Dupret moss collection.
Director: ERNEST ROULEAU, 1916 (Taxonomy, nomenclature; Canadian flora).
Curator: LOUIS-PHILIPPE HÉBERT, 1947 (Cytotaxonomy; Canadian flora).
Staff members: ANDRÉ BOUCHARD, 1946 (Ecology).
MICHEL FAMELART, 1937 (Morphology).
STUART HAY, 1946.
JOACHIM VIETH, 1925 (Morphology, anatomy).
Specialization in research: Flora of eastern Canada.
Associated botanic garden: Jardin Botanique de Montréal.
Loans: To recognized botanical institutions upon receipt of request by curator.
Periodical and serial works: Contributions de l'Institut Botanique de l'Université de Montréal (1922–1969).
Exchange: Available: Eastern Canada. Wanted: From all parts of the world.

MONTRÉAL: *Herbarium, Jardin Botanique de Montréal*, (**MTJB**), 4101 est, rue Sherbrooke, Montréal, Québec, **Canada** H1X 2B2.
Telephone: 514/872-4543.
Status: A municipal botanical garden.
Foundation: 1936. *Number of specimens:* 50.000 vascular plants.
Herbarium: Worldwide, pteridophytes and phanerogams; mainly North America.
Important collections: Marcel Raymond worldwide Cyperaceae collection.
Director: PIERRE BOURQUE, 1942.
Curator: LOUIS-PHILIPPE HÉBERT, 1947 (Cytotaxonomy; Canadian flora).

Staff members: JENO ARROS, 1916 (Succulent plants).

DENIS BARABÉ, 1951 (Morphology; theoretical systematics).

ANDRÉ BOUCHARD, 1946 (Ecology).

NORMAND CORNELLIER, 1934 (Araceae; Canadian flora).

Loans: To recognized botanical institutions upon receipt of request by curator.

Periodical and serial works: Mémoires du Jardin Botanique de Montréal (1940–1966).

Exchange: Available: Eastern Canada. Wanted: From all parts of the world.

MONTRÉAL: *McGill University Herbarium, Department of Plant Science, Box 4000, Macdonald College P.O.,* (**MTMG**), Ste-Anne-de-Bellevue, Québec, **Canada** H9X ICO.

Telephone: 514/457-2000.

Foundation: 1820. *Number of specimens:* 110.000.

Herbarium: Québec and eastern Canada; North America; alpine, arctic, and boreal regions.

Important collections: W. H. Brittain (*Betula;* North America), T. J. W. Burgess (eastern Canada), E.O. Callen (*Euphrasia, Lotus*), R. R. Campbell (Canada), W. F. Grant (*Lotus*), A. A. Heller (U.S., Hawaii), A. F. Holmes (Montreal area), J. M. Macoun (early Canadian collections), R. M. Middleton (Britain, North America), C. G. Pringle (Central America), D. E. Swales (Quebec; arctic), D. W. Woodland (*Urtica*).

Director: LUC BROUILLET, 1954 (Biosystematics of *Aster*).

Curator: MARCIA J. WATERWAY, 1951 (Biosystematics of *Lycopodium, Carex*; subarctic flora).

Staff members: WILLIAM F. GRANT, 1924 (Cytogenetics and chemotaxonomy of *Lotus*).

DOROTHY E. SWALES, 1901 (Arctic plants; pollination).

Specialization in research: Biosystematics; eastern Canadian flora; arctic flora of North America.

Associated botanic garden: Morgan Arboretum.

Loans: To recognized botanical institutions; normal regulations.

Exchange: Available: North American arctic and subarctic; eastern Canadian; eastern North American *Carex*. Desired: Arctic circumpolar; North America; North American *Carex*.

Remarks: The herbarium contains some of the earliest collections made in Canada. Since 1972 the herbaria of Macdonald College and McGill University have been combined as one collection on the Macdonald campus.

MONTRÉAL: *Herbier, Laboratoire de Recherches, Service de la Faune, Ministère du Tourisme, de la Chasse et de la Pêche du Québec,* (**QPAR**), 5075 rue Fullum, Montréal 178, Québec, **Canada.** (Information 1974)

Status: Government institution.

Foundation: 1963. *Number of specimens:* 20.000.

Herbarium: Aquatic and riparian plants of Quebec.

MONTRÉAL: *Herbier, Département des Sciences Biologiques, Université du Québec à Montréal,* (**UQAM**), Case postale 8888, Montréal, Québec, **Canada** H3C 3P8.

Telephone: 514/282-3350.

Foundation: 1970. *Number of specimens:* 10.000.

Herbarium: Vascular hydrophytes of the province of Québec, Canada.

Director and Curator: CLAUDE HAMEL, 1942 (Floristics and ecology of vascular hydrophytes).

Specialization in research: Floristics and ecology of vascular hydrophytes; research on weedy aquatic plants, in particular *Myriophyllum spicatum.*

Loans: Three months.

Exchange: Vascular hydrophytes.

MOORHEAD: *Herbarium, Department of Biology, Moorhead State University,* (**MRD**), Moorhead, Minnesota 56560, **U.S.A.**

Telephone: 218/236-2572.

Foundation: 1890's. *Number of specimens:* 8.000–10.000.

Herbarium: Emphasis on vascular flora of the Red River Drainage Basin (eastern North Dakota and northwestern Minnesota).

Director and Curator: R. H. PEMBLE, 1941 (Phytogeography and plant ecology of the Drainage Basin of the Red River of the North).

Specialization in research: Phytogeography of the Red River Drainage Basin (eastern North Dakota and northwestern Minnesota).

Loans: Standard conditions.

Exchange: Limited, but interested parties may inquire.

MOREHEAD CITY: *Mycological Herbarium, Institute of Marine Sciences, University of North Carolina,* (**IMS**), Morehead City, North Carolina 28557, **U.S.A.**

Telephone: 919/726-6841.

Status: Associated with the University of North Carolina at Chapel Hill.

Foundation: 1964. *Number of specimens:* 8.000.

Herbarium: Marine fungi (parasites, symbionts, saprobes, occurring in marine and estuarine habitats).

Important collections: J. and E. Kohlmeyer (especially permanent slides).

Director: DIRK FRANKENBERG, 1937 (Marine ecology).

Curator: JAN J. KOHLMEYER, 1928 (Marine mycology).

Specialization in research: Taxonomy, morphology, ecology of marine fungi.

Loans: Usual regulations.

Exchange: Available and desired: Fungi from marine habitats.

MORELIA: *Herbario, Escuela de Biología, Universidad Michoacana de San Nicolás de Hidalgo,* **(EBUM)**, Edificio "L", Ciudad Universitaria, Santiago Tapia 403, Morelia, Michoacán, **Mexico.**
Telephone: 91451 3-21-81.
Foundation: 1977. *Number of specimens:* 3.500.
Herbarium: Vascular plants of Michoacán.
Important collections: Martínez Solorzano, G. Arsène.
    Director and Curator: JOSÉ L. MAGAÑA MENDOZA, 1947 (Gymnosperms).
    Staff members: LUZ DEL SOCORRO RODRÍGUEZ J., 1948 (Vascular plants).
    FERNANDO GUEVARA F., 1953 (*Bursera* of Michoacán).
    MARTHA BUSTOS ZAGAL, 1955 (Ecology).
Specialization in research: Flora of Michoacán.
Loans: To recognized institutions.
Exchange: Primarily plants of Mexico.
Remarks: Facilities for visiting botanists.

MORGANTOWN: *Herbarium, West Virginia University,* **(WVA)**, Morgantown, West Virginia 26505, **U.S.A.**
Telephone: 304/293-3979.
Status: State university.
Foundation: 1893. *Number of specimens:* 150.000.
Herbarium: Concentration on vascular plants of the Mid-Appalachians.
Important collections: Hannibal Davis (*Rubus*), Ward Sharp (*Crataegus*).
    Curator: ROY B. CLARKSON, 1926 (Mid-Appalachian species distribution).
    Staff members: HOMER DUPPSTADT, 1923 (Mid-Appalachian grasses, sedges, composites).
    LINDA RADER, 1950.
Specialization in research: Distribution of Mid-Appalachian vascular plants.
Associated botanic garden: Earl L. Core Arboretum.
Loans: To institutions for 1 year.
Periodical and serial works: Contributions of the Herbarium of West Virginia University; Castanea (Journal of the Southern Appalachian Botanical Club).
Exchange: With foreign and western herbaria.

MORIOKA: *Herbarium, Department of Biology, Faculty of Education, Iwate University,* **(IUM)**, 18-33 Ueda 3-chome, Morioka 020, **Japan.**
Telephone: 0196-23-5171, ext. 2291.
Status: University.
Foundation: 1949. *Number of specimens:* 60.000.
Herbarium: Ferns and flowering plants of Japan, mainly Iwate Prefecture, Tohoku District.
    Curator: YUTAKA SUDA, 1935 (Cytotaxonomy of Ranunculaceae).
Loans: No.
Exchange: Available: Plants of Japan.

MOSCOW: *Herbarium, Department of Biological Sciences, University of Idaho,* **(ID)**, Moscow, Idaho 83843, **U.S.A.**
Telephone: 208/885-6798; 885-6280.
Foundation: 1906 (L. F. Henderson herbarium destroyed by fire in 1906). *Number of specimens:* 86.000.
Herbarium: Flora of Idaho and the Pacific Northwest.
Important collections: J. H. Christ, H. J. Rust, C. R. Stillinger, W. H. Baker.
    Director and Curator: DOUGLASS M. HENDERSON, 1938; 208/885-6798 (Vascular plants; *Sisyrinchium*).
    Staff members: DOYLE E. ANDEREGG, 1930; 208/885-6737 (Bryophytes).
    EDMUND E. TYLUTKI, 1926; 208/885-6349 (Mycology; Agaricales, *Cystoderma*).
Specialization in research: Flora of east-central Idaho; alpine flora of Idaho; rare plants of Idaho; biosystematics of Pacific Northwest vascular plants; floristic studies of the higher fungi of the Pacific Northwest and of the bryophytes of Idaho.
Loans: To recognized scientific institutions.
Exchange: Available: Vascular plants of the Northern Rockies, many alpine. Desired: Plants from Idaho and the Northern Rockies, the American Arctic.

MOSCOW: *Research Herbarium, Forest, Wildlife, and Range Experiment Station, College of Forestry, University of Idaho,* **(IDF)**, Moscow, Idaho 83843, **U.S.A.**
Telephone: 208/885-6444.
Foundation: 1909. *Number of specimens:* 11.000.
Herbarium: Wildlands flora of northern Rocky Mountains, especially native and introduced woody plants.
    Director: FREDERIC D. JOHNSON, 1925 (Woody plants).
    Curator: STEVEN J. BRUNSFELD, 1953 (Alpine flora; *Salix*).
    Staff members: C. MICHAEL FALTER, 1941 (Aquatic plants).
    ARTHUR P. PARTRIDGE, 1927 (Wood decay fungi and disease organisms).
    JAMES M. PEEK, 1936 (Wildlife forage plants).
    EDWIN W. TISDALE, 1910 (Range plants).
Specialization in research: Wildland communities classification and dynamics; phytogeography and taxonomy of disjunct and endemic plants; rare plants; naturalized plants.
Associated botanic garden: Shattuck Arboretum.
Loans: Usual conditions.
Exchange: Possible.

MOSCOW: *Herbarium, Main Botanic Garden, Academy of Sciences of the USSR,* **(MHA)**, Botanicheskaya Street 4, 127276 Moscow, **U.S.S.R.**
Telephone: Moscow 4821373.
Status: State institute.

Foundation: 1960. *Number of specimens:* 220.000.

Herbarium: Vascular plants only; indigenous flora of the USSR; introduced (cultivated) plants (not commercial agricultural cultivars); worldwide collection started.

Important collections: V. N. Voroshilov et al. (Soviet Far East, ca. 15.000 sheets), E. E. Gogina (Caucasus, ca. 15.000 sheets), M. V. Kultiassov, G. M. Proscuriakova (Turkmenia, ca. 10.000 sheets), A. K. Skvortsov (*Salix*, ca. 10.000 sheets), V. N. Sukachev and A. K. Skvortsov (*Betula*, ca. 5.000 sheets).

Director of the Garden: N. V. TSITSIN (Remote hybridization, cereal crops breeding).

Director of the Department of Flora (which includes the herbarium): A. K. SKVORTSOV (Flora of Central Russia, Salicaceae, *Betula*, Onagraceae).

Curator: G. M. PROSCURIAKOVA (Flora of Turkmenia).

Staff members: N. B. BELYANINA (Flora of Crimea).

E. E. GOGINA (Flora of the Caucasus).

V. N. VOROSHILOV (Flora of Soviet Far East, *Aconitum, Valeriana*).

Specialization in research: Chiefly groups of interest for introduction (ligneous, medicinal, ornamental); flora of the central region of the European part of USSR; flora of Turkmenia; flora of the Soviet Far East.

Loans: Usual regulations.

Periodical and serial works: Bulletin of the Main Botanic Garden (Bulletin Glavnogo Botanicheskogo sada).

Exchange: Available: Ligneous plants wild and cultivated, from various regions of USSR. Desired: Vascular plants from Southern Europe and Mediterranean, temperate Asia and Americas, other regions by arrangement.

MOSCOW: *Herbarium, All-Union Scientific Investigation Institute of Medicinal Plants, Ministry of Medical Industry,* (**MOSM**), P/o Vilar, Lenin Region, 142790 Moscow Oblast, **U.S.S.R.**

Foundation: 1949. *Number of specimens:* 90.000.

Director of Laboratory: A. I. SHRETER.

MOSCOW: *Herbarium, Lenin State Pedagogical Institute,* (**MOSP**), Kibaltschitsch str. 6, Moscow 129243, **U.S.S.R.**

Telephone: 283-15-73.

Status: State institute.

Foundation: 1936. *Number of specimens:* 85.000.

Herbarium: Flora of U.S.S.R., especially *Salix, Veronica,* plants of Zangezur and Zheguli mountains.

Curator: ANDREJ G. ELENEVSKY, 1928 (*Veronica,* Ranunculaceae).

Staff member: TATJANA G. DERVIS-SOKOLOVA, 1928 (*Salix, Stachys, Ranunculus*).

MOSCOW: *Herbarium, Biology – Soils Department, M. V. Lomonosov State University of Moscow,* (**MW**),

Lenin Hills, MGU, 117234 Moscow B-234, **U.S.S.R.**

Status: University.

Foundation: 1780. *Number of specimens:* 600.000.

Herbarium: Plants of European U.S.S.R., Caucasus, Kazakhstan, Middle Asia, Siberia, Far East and foreign collections.

Important collections: F. Ehrhart, herb. G. F. Hoffmann, C. B. von Trinius, A. V. Haller, C. P. Thunberg, Jr. and G. Forster, Hugo Dickson, Murrahi, Brown.

Director: V. N. PAVLOV.

MOSKVA – – *see* MOSCOW.

MOSUL: *Herbarium, College of Agriculture and Forestry,* (**MOS**), Mosul, **Iraq.**

MOUNT PLEASANT: *Herbarium, Department of Biology, Central Michigan University,* (**CMC**), Mount Pleasant, Michigan 48859, **U.S.A.**

Telephone: 517/774-3626; 774-3227.

Status: State university.

Foundation: 1955. *Number of specimens:* 20.000.

Herbarium: Local flora; Beaver Island flora.

Director: DANIEL E. WUJEK, 1939 (Aquatic plants).

Staff member: GILBERT STARKS, 1934 (Compositae).

Specialization in research: Local flora; Beaver Island flora; emphasis on aquatic plants.

Loans: No special restrictions.

MOUNT VERNON: *Herbarium, Biology Department, Cornell College,* (**MOVC**), Mount Vernon, Iowa 52314, **U.S.A.**

Telephone: 319/895-8811.

Foundation: 1967. *Number of specimens:* 1.000.

Herbarium: Mainly local flora.

Important collections: Robert Hellwig (ferns of Oaxaca, Mexico), Paul Christiansen (vascular flora of Howard County, Iowa).

Director and Curator: PAUL A. CHRISTIANSEN, 1932 (Plant ecology).

MTUBATUBA: *Herbarium, Hluhluwe Game Reserve Research Centre,* (**NPB**), P.O. Box 25, Mtubatuba, 3935 **South Africa.**

Telephone: Hluhluwe Game Reserve no. 8, via Mtubatuba.

Status: Natal Parks Game and Fish Preservation Board.

Foundation: 1953. *Number of specimens:* 8.706.

Important collections: C. J. Ward's collection from Zululand.

Director and Curator: I. A. W. MACDONALD, 1949 (Ecology).

Staff member: A. WHATELEY, 1945 (Ecology).

Specialization in research: Ecology.

Loans: Yes.

Periodical and serial works: Lammergeyer, Journal of the Natal Parks, Game and Fish Preservation Board.

MÜNCHEN: *Herbarium, Botanische Staatssammlung*, **(M)**, Menzinger Strasse 67, D-8000 München 19, **Federal Republic of Germany,** BRD.
Telephone: 089/1792 257.
Status: Forms part of the Collections (Natural Sciences) of the Free State of Bavaria.
Foundation: 1813. *Number of specimens:* 2.000.000 (1.200.000 vascular plants, 85.000 algae, 260.000 fungi, 180.000 lichens, 230.000 bryophytes, c. 100.000 special collections, cecidia etc.).
Herbarium: Worldwide.
Important collections: J. C. D. Schreber, J. A. & J. H. Schultes, J. G. Zuccarini, C. F. P. von Martius (Brazil), W. F. Karwinski (Mexico), E. Rosenstock (Pteridophytes), A. von Krempelhuber (Lichens), F. C. G. Arnold (Lichens), Poelt (Lichens), A. Allescher (Fungi), Killermann (higher fungi), A. G. Soehner (Fungi hypogaei), Niessl von Mayendorf (Fungi), Reinbold (Marine algae), Weinzierl (Diatoms).
Director: H. MERXMÜLLER, 1920 (Flora of S.W. Africa and Europe; African Compositae; biosystematics; Professor of Systematic Botany at the University of Munich).
Deputy Director, Head of Cryptogamic Herbarium: H. HERTEL, 1939 (Lichenology).
Staff members: W. LIPPERT, 1937 (Flora of Europe).
H. ROESSLER, 1926 (Flora of S.W. Africa).
A. SCHREIBER, 1927 (Flora of S.W. Africa).
Research associates: G. BENL, 1910 (*Ptilotus,* ferns).
J. BOGNER, 1939 (Araceae, aquatic plants).
P. DÖBBELER, 1946 (Bryophilous fungi).
H.-CHR. FRIEDRICH, 1925 (Crassulaceae, Aizoaceae).
J. GRAU, 1937 (Asteraceae-Astereae, cytotaxonomy of Boraginaceae, flora of Chile).
A. KRESS, 1932 (Primulaceae).
K. MÄGDEFRAU, 1907 (History of botany, bryology).
D. PODLECH, 1931 (Flora of Afghanistan, *Astragalus*).
W. SAUER, 1935 (Caryosystematics of *Avena* s. lat., *Pulmonaria, Iris*).
Specialization in research: S.W. Africa, Europe, Afghanistan; cytotaxonomy; lichenology.
Associated botanic garden: Botanic Garden, Munich.
Loans: In general to recognized botanical institutions.
Periodical and serial works: Mitteilungen der Botanischen Staatssammlung München, Berichte der Bayerischen Botanischen Gesellschaft.
Exchange: Available: Central and Southern European plants; lichens. Desired: Specimens from all groups.
Remarks: Associated: Library of the Bavarian

Botanical Society, Munich.

MUNCIE: *Herbarium, Department of Biology, Ball State University,* **(BSUH)**, Muncie, Indiana 47306, U.S.A.
Telephone: 317/285-6877.
Foundation: 1897. *Number of specimens:* 12.000.
Herbarium: Midwestern U.S. flora, especially east central Indiana; flora of Belize.
Director and Curator: WM. BLISS CRANKSHAW, 1925; 317/285-4329 (Plant ecology; Indiana flora).
Staff members: A. EISER (Ornamental plants).
D. HENDRICKSON (Thermophilic fungi).
T. R. MERTENS (*Polygonum, Tragopogon*).
J. NISBET (Ultramicroscopic morphology).
N. NORTON (Stratigraphic palynology).
H. SENFT (Aquatic macrophytes).
F. STEVENSON (Bryophytes).
C. WARNES (Aquatic microbiology).
Specialization in research: Tall grass prairie; Indiana flora; bryophytes.
Loans: 3 months.
Exchange: Indiana flora.

MÜNSTER: *Herbarium, Westfälisches Landesmuseum für Naturkunde,* **(MSTR)**, Himmelreichallee 50 (from 1982 Sentrupen Strasse), D-4400 Münster, **Federal Republic of Germany,** BRD.
Telephone: 0251-82011.
Status: Administered by the Landschaftsverband Westfalen-Lippe.
Foundation: 1830. *Number of specimens:* 300.000.
Herbarium: Westfalen.
Important collections: Gottlieb Lahm (1811–1888), Carl Ernst August Weihe (1779–1834).
Director: LUDWIG FRANZISKET, 1917 (Zoology).
Curator: BRUNHILD GRIES, 1937.
Specialization in research: Flora of Westfalen.
Loans: 3 month loans to recognized botanical institutions.
Periodical and serial works: Abhandlungen aus dem Landesmuseum für Naturkunde zu Münster in Westfalen; Natur und Heimat.

MURRAY: *Herbarium, Department of Biology, Murray State University,* **(MUR)**, Murray, Kentucky 42071, U.S.A.
Telephone: 502/762-2786.
Foundation: 1967. *Number of specimens:* 17.000.
Herbarium: Primarily Kentucky, especially the flora of the Jackson Purchase Region.
Important collections: Thomas McCoy (ferns).
Curator: MARIAN JANE FULLER.
Specialization in research: Floristics of the Jackson Purchase Region of Kentucky.
Loans: 6 months.
Exchange: Yes.

MUSKEGON: *Herbarium, Life Science Department, Muskegon Community College,* **(MUSK)**, 221 S. Quar-

terline Road, Muskegon, Michigan 49442, **U.S.A.**
  Telephone: 616/773-9131.
  Foundation: 1978. *Number of specimens:* 600.

Herbarium: Local plants.
  Curator: ROY STRUVEN, 1925; 616/893-4115.

N

NACOGDOCHES: *Herbarium, Department of Biology, Stephen F. Austin State University,* (**ASTC**), P.O. Box 13003, Nacogdoches, Texas 75962, **U.S.A.**
Telephone: 713/569-3601.
Foundation: 1949. *Number of specimens:* 50.000.
Herbarium: Emphasis on flora of eastern Texas.
Director and Curator: ELRAY S. NIXON, 1931 (Floristic ecology).
Loans: Yes; must be returned within reasonable time.
Exchange: Yes.

NAIROBI: *East African Herbarium,* (**EA**), Museum Hill, P.O. Box 45166, Nairobi, **Kenya,** East Africa.
Telephone: 743513.
Status: At present under Kenya Agriculture Research Institute.
Foundation: 1902, as the "Herbarium des Biologisch-Landwirtschaftlichen Institutes, Amani, D.O.A." *Number of specimens:* 344.000.
Herbarium: Vascular and non-vascular plants of Kenya, Tanzania and Uganda, other Eastern Africa Countries and Tropical Arabia, incorporating National (Coryndon) Musem Herbarium.
Important collections: Over 500 types of taxa described by Berlin botanists before 1920: Busse, Uhlig, Warnecke, Hansford.
Director and Curator: C. H. S. KABUYE, 1938 (East African Gramineae, Cyperaceae and Malvaceae, taxonomy).
Staff members: M. G. GILBERT, 1943 (Flora of eastern Africa, especially arid areas; Asclepiadaceae, especially stapeliads; *Vernonia* and allied genera; *Euphorbia*.
G. W. GATHERI, 1953 (Flora of Tropical East Africa; Nyctaginaceae).
J. B. GILLETT, 1911 (National Museum Botanist; tropical African Papilionaceae and Burseraceae).
Specialization in research: East African flora and its economic significance; services in identification of plants to other researchers.
Loans: To recognized botanical institutions.
Exchange: Duplicates, as they become available, are distributed to Kew and other institutions where the taxonomy of Tropical African plants is studied. Desired: Specimens from Tropical Africa south of the Sahara.
Remarks: Facilities for visiting botanists and expeditions.

NAIROBI: *Nairobi University Herbarium,* (**NAI**), Department of Botany, University of Nairobi, P.O. Box 30197, Nairobi, **Kenya.**
Telephone: 43185 or 43553.
Status: University.

Foundation: 1957. *Number of specimens:* 30.000.
Herbarium: Mainly Kenyan flora, and some collections from other African countries south of the Sahara.
Important collections: W. E. Isaac (Marine algae of Kenya), A. Agnew (Upland Kenya flora), J. O. Kokwaro (East African flora).
Director: J. O. KOKWARO (East African Anacardiaceae, Geraniaceae, Rutaceae, Valerianaceae, medicinal plants of East Africa, wild economic plants, vegetation and land use).
Staff members: M. N. BAIG (Terrestrial ecology).
S. F. DOSSAJI (Phytochemistry).
J. J. GAUDET (Aquatic botany, especially tropical swamps, weed biology).
H. N. B. GOPALAN (Genetics).
S. K. IMBAMBA (Physiology).
T. K. MUKIAMA (Genetics).
S. G. NJUGUNA (Aquatic botany).
T. S. RANGAN (Morphogenesis in tissue culture of angiosperms).
R. E. ROWLAND (Cytogenetics).
SUBRAMONIAN (Mycology).
A. R. D. TAYLOR (Physiology).
D. WIDDOWSON (Microbiology).
Specialization in research: Flora of Upland Kenya, flora of tropical East Africa, medicinal plants of East Africa, wild economic plants of East Africa.
Associated botanic garden: The University Botanic Garden.
Loans: To recognized botanical institutions.
Exchange: Available: Mostly Kenyan flora from marine to alpine plants. Desired: Tropical and subtropical specimens.

NALCHIK: *Herbarium, Kabargin-Balkarsk Section of the All-Union Botanical Society,* (**AUBSN**), Chernyshevskoya St. 173, 360017 Nalchik, **U.S.S.R.**
Foundation: 1970. *Number of specimens:* 10.000.
Director: E. N. PETROV.

NAMUR: *Laboratoire de Botanique, Facultés Universitaires Notre-Dame de la Paix,* (**NAM**), 61, rue de Bruxelles, B-5000 Namur, **Belgium.**
Telephone: 081/229061, 229062.
Status: Université libre.
Foundation: 1831. *Number of specimens:* 52.000 (vascular plants 20.000, bryophytes and lichens 32.000).
Herbarium: General herbarium, chiefly Belgium and Central Africa.
Director and Curator: JEAN LOUIS DE SLOOVER, 1936 (Bryology).
Staff members: JEAN MARGOT, 1939 (Lichens, air pollution).
LOUIS LECLERCQ, 1952 (Algology).

Specialization in research: Taxonomy of bryophytes, lichens and algae; pollution.
Loans: For 12 months.
Exchange: Available: Bryophytes.

NANCY: *Laboratoire de Botanique, Université de Nancy I*, (**NCY**), C.O. 140, 54037 Nancy Cedex, **France**.
Telephone: (83.)28.93.93.
Status: University.
Foundation: ca. 1850. *Number of specimens:* 33.000.
Herbarium: General herbarium consisting of herbaria of Soyer-Willemetz, Godron and others.
Important collections: A. Coppey (Bryophytes, lichens), F. Fautrey (Lichens), C. Flagey (Lichens), Harmand (Lichens), Wirtgen *(Rubus)*.
Director: F. MANGENOT, 1913.

NANJING: *Herbarium, Department of Biology, Nanjing University*, (**N**), Ling-Hai-Rou, Nanjing, Jiangsu, **People's Republic of China.**
Status: University.
Foundation: 1902. *Number of specimens:* 100.000.
Herbarium: Plants of Sichuan, Yunnan, Guizhou and Guangxi Provinces; includes old Nanking University and Central University herbaria.
Staff member: WANG C. P. (Gramineae).
Specialization in research: Bamboo and general Gramineae for Flora of China.

NANJING: *Herbarium, Jiangsu Botanical Institute*, (**NAS**), 210014 Nanjing, Jiangsu, **People's Republic of China.**
Status: Provincial Academy of Sciences.
Foundation: 1929. *Number of specimens:* 500.000.
Herbarium: Plants of eastern China.
Important collections: Ching R. C. (Pteridophytes of Kwangsi province), Ching R. C. and Tsiang T. (Spermatophytes from Guangxi, Guizhou, Yunnan and Jiangxi provinces).
Director: SHAN REN-HWA (Umbelliferae).
Deputy Director: SHEN CHEN-KWEI (Plant introduction, economic plants).
Curator: FANG WEN-CHIEN (Myrsinaceae, Verbenaceae).
Staff members: CHEN SHOU-LIANG (Gramineae).
CHOO TAI-YIEN (Cruciferae).
LU LIEN-LEE (Cruciferae).
SHEH MENG-LAN (Umbelliferae).
Specialization in research: Flora of Jiangsu and adjacent provinces.
Associated botanic garden: Hortus Botanicus Nanjingensis Mem. Sun Yat-Sen.
Exchange: Yes.

NANJING: *Dendrological Herbarium, Nanjing Technological College of Forest Products*, (**NF**), Shaoshan Road, 210037 Nanjing, Jiangsu, **People's Republic of China.**
Telephone: 43161.
Status: College.

Foundation: 1923. *Number of specimens:* 70.000.
Herbarium: Woody plants of China.
Important collections: Collections from Hubei, Jiangsu, Anhui and Yunnan provinces, including types of *Metasequoia glyptostroboides* and *Calycanthus chinensis*.
Director and Curator: CHAO CHI-SON, 1936 (Conifers, Fagaceae, Bambusoideae).
Staff members: CHU CHENG-DE, 1928 (Conifers, Fagaceae, Bambusoideae).
HUANG PENG-CHENG, 1932 (Leguminosae).
SHANG CHI-BEI, 1935 (Araliaceae).
Specialization in research: Chinese trees, especially conifers, Chinese bamboo.
Associated botanic garden: Arboretum of Nanjing Technological College of Forest Products.
Periodical and serial works: Journal of Nanjing Technological College of Forest Products.
Exchange: International exchange of specimens is planned.

NANJING: *Herbarium, Institute of Geology and Paleontology, Academia Sinica*, (**NPA**), Nanjing, Jiangsu, **People's Republic of China** – – discontinued.

NANJING: *Herbarium, Botanical Garden of Sun Yatsen Tomb and Memorial Park Commission*, (**NSM**), Nanjing, Jiangsu, **People's Republic of China.**

NANKING: – – *see* NANJING.

NANKING: *Botanical Research Station and Garden of the Academia Sinica*, (**NAS**) – – *see* NANJING: *Herbarium, Jiangsu Botanical Institute*.

NANKING: *The Herbarium, College of Agriculture and Forestry*, (**NF**) – – *see* NANJING: *Dendrological Herbarium, Nanjing Technological College of Forest Products*.

NANTES: *Herbarium, Muséum d'Histoire Naturelle de Nantes*, (**NTM**), Place de la Monnaie, Nantes, **France.** (Information 1964)
Status: Municipal institution.
Foundation: 1799. *Number of specimens:* 100.000.
Herbarium: Worldwide and regional flora.
Specialization in research: Flora of Bretagne and Vendée.
Associated botanic garden: Jardin Botanique de la Ville de Nantes.
Periodical and serial works: Bulletin de la Société des Sciences Naturelles de l'Ouest de la France.

NAPOLI: *Instituto Botanico della Università di Napoli*, (**NAP**), Via Foria 223, Napoli, **Italy.** (Information 1974)
Status: University.
Foundation: 1796.
Herbarium: Flora of Mediterranean region.
Specialization in research: Mediterranean flora,

especially S. Italy, Sicily and Alps.
Periodical and serial works: Delpinoa.

NASHVILLE: *Herbarium, Department of Botany and Zoology, Vanderbilt University,* (**VDB**), Box 1705, Station B, Nashville, Tennessee 37235, **U.S.A.**
Telephone: 615/322-6676.
Status: Private institution.
Foundation: 1935. *Number of specimens:* 170.000.
Herbarium: General U.S. collection, with concentration on southeastern U.S., especially Alabama and Tennessee; small Mexican collection; North American Cyperaceae and Xyridaceae; *Rhexia* (Melastomataceae); *Trillium* (Liliaceae).
Important collections: Jesse Shaver (ferns), Delzie Demaree, Robert Kral, R. K. Godfrey, S. McDaniel.
Director and Curator: ROBERT KRAL, 1926 (Xyridaceae, Cyperaceae; flora of southeastern U.S.).
Associate Curator: R. BEN CHANNELL, 1924; 615/322-2961 (Biosystematics).
Specialization in research: Flora of southeastern U.S.
Loans: For reasonable periods to recognized institutions.
Exchange: Available: Southeastern U.S. Desired: General collections, especially Cyperaceae, Xyridaceae.

NATCHITOCHES: *Herbarium, Department of Biological Sciences, Northwestern State University,* (**NATC**), Natchitoches, Louisiana 71457, **U.S.A.**
Telephone: 318/357-4485.
Foundation: 1937. *Number of specimens:* 18.450.
Herbarium: Plants of west central Louisiana.
Important collections: Sidney McDaniel and Manual Rimachi types of *Mikania*.
Director and Curator: WALTER C. HOLMES, 1944 (*Mikania;* flora of Louisiana; southeastern Louisiana French ethnobotany).
Specialization in research: Floristics of Louisiana.
Loans: Normal regulations.
Exchange: Available: Louisiana plants. Desired: *Mikania;* Compositae.

NATICK: *Mycology Laboratory (Culture Collection), Pioneering Research Laboratory, U.S. Army Natick Laboratories,* (**QM**), Natick, Massachusetts 01760, **U.S.A.**
Status: A research unit of the U.S. Army.
Foundation: 1943. *Number of specimens:* 6.000 fungi.
Herbarium: Fungi associated with degradation phenomena, pollution control, waste conversion; isolation of fungi in Pacific Islands, New Guinea, Thailand, Java.
Remarks: Living and dried collections have been transferred to the Agriculture Research Culture Collection, Northern Regional Research Center, U.S. Department of Agriculture, 1815 North University Street, Peoria, Illinois 61604. As soon as arrangements can be made, the QM herbarium specimens will be transferred to an appropriate facility. The living collections will be maintained at the Northern Regional Research Center.

NDOLA: (**NDO**) –– *see* KITWE.

NEDLANDS: *Botany Department Herbarium, University of Australia,* (**UWA**), Nedlands, Western Australia 6009, **Australia.**
Telephone: 380 2201 or 380 2212.
Status: University.
Foundation: 1914. *Number of specimens:* 30.000.
Herbarium: 30.000 (19.500 Western Australian angiosperms, 4.000 marine algae, 2.500 fungi, 4.000 lichens, bryophytes, pteridophytes and gymnosperms).
Important collections: Marine algae, fungi and lichens of Southwestern Australia, *Stylidium, Thysanotus,* seagrasses, native ferns. No types are held (these are sent to WA).
Director and Head of Department: J. PATE (Plant physiology of legumes and native tuberous plants).
Curator: G. G. SMITH (Morphology of marine algae, pteridophytes).
Staff members: C. A. ATKINS (Plant biochemistry).
D. BELL (Terrestrial ecology).
N. H. BRITTAN (Experimental taxonomy of Liliaceae).
R. N. HILTON (Mycology).
S. H. JAMES (Cyto-evolution of *Stylidium, Isotoma, Anigozanthos, Dampiera, Laxmaunia* and Myrtaceae).
W. A. LONERAGAN (Terrestrial ecology).
A. J. McCOMB (Nutrient cycling and productivity in wetlands).
Loans: Available worldwide to researchers, initially for 6 months but with extensions on request.

NELSON: *Herbarium, Department of Biological Sciences, Notre Dame University,* (**NLSN**), Nelson, British Columbia, **Canada** V1L 3C7 –– transferred to Castlegar (SCCBC).
Foundation: 1964. *Number of specimens:* 8.000.

NEUCHÂTEL: *Institut de Botanique de l'Université,* (**NEU**), 22 rue de Chantemerle, CH- 2007 Neuchâtel, **Switzerland.**
Telephone: CH 038/25 64 34.
Status: Université de Neuchâtel.
Foundation: During the XIX Century as part of the Musée d'Histoire naturelle de la ville de Neuchâtel; in 1918 the collections were transferred to the University; the Botanical Institute was founded in 1946.
Number of specimens: 450.000.
Herbarium: Cryptogamic herbarium, general phanerogamic herbarium, phanerogamic herbarium of Switzerland.
Important collections: Cryptogams: Herb. P. Morthier (Micromycetes of Europe), E. Mayor (Micro-

mycetes of the world), L. Lesquereux (mosses of Europe and North America). Phanerogams: Herb. L'Héritier (p.p.), herb. La Trobe (Australia, p.p.).

Director: CLAUDE FAVARGER, 1913 (Cytotaxonomy, cytogeography, phanerogams).

Curator: CHARLES TERRIER, 1912 (Micromycetes).

Staff members: K.-L. HUYNH (Palynology and anatomy for taxonomic purposes).

PH. KÜPFER, 1942 (Cytotaxonomy, mountain floras of W. Mediterranean region).

J.-L. RICHARD, 1921 (Phytosociology, ecology) *Specialization in research:* Cytotaxonomy of mountain floras, especially Alps, Pyrenees, Atlas; taxonomy of the Alsinoideae and Paronychioideae, *Sempervivum, Hormatophylla, Aethionema, Jasione, Pandanus.*

Associated botanic garden: Yes.

Loans: Yes.

Periodical and serial works: Travaux de l'Institut de Botanique de l'Université.

Exchange: Will be possible as soon as all specimens are mounted.

NEW ALBANY: *Herbarium, Indiana University Southeast,* (**JEF**), 4201 Grant Line Road, New Albany, Indiana 47150, **U.S.A.**

Telephone: 812/945-2731, ext. 377.

Foundation: 1971. *Number of specimens:* 3.000.

Herbarium: Local flora, including Kentucky.

Important collections: Richard H. Maxwell (Ceylon Phaseoleae).

Curator: RICHARD H. MAXWELL, 1926 (*Dioclea,* Leguminosae).

Specialization in research: Leguminosae.

Loans: Usual regulations.

Remarks: Formerly listed under Jeffersonville.

NEWARK: *Herbarium, Society of Natural History of Delaware, Department of Plant Science, University of Delaware,* (**DELS**), Newark, Delaware 19711, **U.S.A.** – – incorporated in DOV in 1980.

NEWARK: *Herbarium, Botany Department, Newark College of Arts and Sciences of Rutgers University,* (**NCAS**), 195 University Avenue, Newark, New Jersey 07102, **U.S.A.**

Telephone: 201/648-5131.

Status: State university.

Foundation: 1974. *Number of specimens:* 3.000.

Herbarium: General collection of vascular plants of northeastern U.S.

Curator: CHRISTOPHER S. CAMPBELL, 1946 (Gramineae).

Loans: To recognized botanists or botanical institutions.

Exchange: Available: Vascular plants of northeastern U.S. Desired: Vascular plants of North America.

NEWARK: *Herbarium, Newark Museum,* (**NEMU**), P.O. Box 540, 43 Washington Street, Newark, New Jersey 07101, **U.S.A.**

Telephone: 201/733-6590.

Foundation: 1925. *Number of specimens:* 3.000.

Herbarium: Local.

Important collections: William S. Disbrow, Vernon Frazee.

Director: IRVING H. BLACK, 1918.

NEW BRUNSWICK: *Chrysler Herbarium, Department of Botany, Rutgers University,* (**CHRB**), Nelson Biological Labs, Busch Campus, New Brunswick, New Jersey 08903, **U.S.A.**

Telephone: 201/932-2843.

Foundation: 1925. *Number of specimens:* 110.100 (106.000 vascular plants, 1.600 bryophytes, 2.500 algae).

Herbarium: Emphasis on New Jersey flora.

Important collections: Repository for endangered species and voucher specimens for botanical research conducted in New Jersey; important historical specimens of New Jersey flora dating from 1850.

Director: DAVID E. FAIRBROTHERS, 1925 (Chemosystematics).

Curator: NICHOLAS CAIAZZA, 1952 (Plant ecology).

Specialization in research: New Jersey flora; threatened and endangered species; voucher specimens from ecological and taxonomic research.

Loans: Available to any recognized botanical department or institution.

Remarks: The Douglass College Herbarium (RUT) of Rutgers University has been closed, and the specimens contained there are being incorporated into CHRB.

NEW BRUNSWICK: *Department of Biological Sciences, Douglass College, Rutgers University,* (**RUT**), New Brunswick, New Jersey 08903, **U.S.A.** – – incorporated in CHRB.

Foundation: 1926. *Number of specimens:* 10.500.

NEW BRUNSWICK: *Herbarium, Department of Plant Pathology, Cook College, Rutgers University,* (**RUTPP**), New Brunswick, New Jersey 08903, **U.S.A.**

Telephone: 201/932-9375.

NEWCASTLE UPON TYNE: *Herbarium, Natural History Society of Northumbria, Hancock Museum,* (**HAMU**), Barras Bridge, Newcastle upon Tyne NE2 4PT, England, **Great Britain.**

Telephone: 0632-22359.

Status: University of Newcastle upon Tyne.

Foundation: 1829. *Number of specimens:* 16.257.

Herbarium: Vascular plants, majority 19th century, British.

Important collections: J. Adamson, T. Belt, J. F. Bigge, R. B. Bowman, W. McLean Brown, R. B. Cooke, M. A. Dickinson, R. E. Embleton, M. Han-

cock, B. King, T. Pigg, W. Robertson, J. Storey, J. Thornhill, W. C. Trevelyan, N. J. Winch.
  Curator of Museum: A. M. TYNAN.
  Deputy Curator: A. G. LONG, 1915 (Palaeobotany).
  Loans: On application.

NEW CONCORD: *Herbarium, Biology Department, Muskingum College,* (**MUS**), Science Center, New Concord, Ohio 43762, **U.S.A.**
  Telephone: 614/826-8224.
  Foundation: 1950. *Number of specimens:* 23.000.
  Herbarium: Emphasis on Pteridophyta and Ohio specimens.
  Important collections: W. Adams Pteridophyta collection.
    Director and Curator: CLEMENT E. DASCH, 1925.
    Loans: For 1 year.
    Exchange: Yes, on a one for one basis.

NEW DELHI: *Herbarium, Department of Botany, University of Delhi,* (**DUH**), New Delhi 7, **India.** (Information 1974)
  Status: University.
  Foundation: 1947. *Number of specimens:* 15.000.
  Herbarium: Mainly vascular plants and some cryptogams of Delhi, adjacent areas and Himalayas.
    Specialization in research: Floristic survey and ecological studies of Delhi; cytotaxonomy, chemotaxonomy and biosystematics of Indian plants.
    Loans: Available on a small scale only.

NEW DELHI: *Herbarium Cryptogamiae Indiae Orientalis, Division of Mycology and Plant Pathology,* (**HCIO**), Indian Agricultural Research Institute, New Delhi – 110012, **India.**
  Telephone: 582438.
  Status: Part of Agricultural Research Institute.
  Foundation: 1905. *Number of specimens:* 34.000.
  Herbarium: Fungi of India, including 2.500 type specimens.
    Important collections: M. J. Berkeley, A. A. Bitancourt and F. Jenkins, E. J. Butler, Dastur, W. G. Farlow, Fischer, S. N. Mitra, Padwick, T. S. Ramakrishnan, Solheim, Walker.
    Director: H. K. JAIN (Cytogenetics).
    Curator: A. K. SARBHOY, 1939 (Soil fungi, Mucorales, Aspergilli and Dematiaceous Hyphomycetes).
    Staff members: D. K. AGARWAL, 1945 (Dematiaceous Hyphomycetes, Sphaeriales).
    D. S. MANN, 1936 (Technician).
    Specialization in research: Dematiaceous Hyphomycetes of Northern India.
    Loans: To recognized botanical institutions.
    Periodical and serial works: Fungi of India Supplements.
    Exchange: Yes.

NEW DELHI: *Herbarium, Division of Plant Introduc-*tion, *Indian Agricultural Research Institute,* (**IARI**), New Delhi 12, **India.** (Information 1974)
  Status: Indian Council of Agricultural Research.
  Foundation: 1940. *Number of specimens:* 5.500.
  Herbarium: Indian plants, introduced plants of economic value and wild relatives of crop plants.
    Specialization in research: Classification of crop plants, nomenclature of economic plants.
    Loans: To recognized botanical institutions.
    Periodical and serial works: Plant Introduction Reports.

NEW HAVEN: *Herbarium, Connecticut Botanical Society, Osborn Memorial Laboratories, Yale University,* (**NCBS**), New Haven, Connecticut 06520, **U.S.A.**
  Telephone: 203/432-4484.
  Status: Activity of an incorporated society.
  Foundation: 1903. *Number of specimens:* 30.500.
  Herbarium: Vascular flora of Connecticut.
    Important collections: C. B. Graves, E. H. Eames, C. H. Bissell, L. Andrews, E. B. Harger, C. A, Weatherby.
    Curator: DONALD M. SWAN.
    Specialization in research: Floristics and geography of the vascular flora of Connecticut.
    Loans: Usual restrictions.
    Remarks: Herbarium housed with Yale University Herbarium (YU), New Haven.

NEW HAVEN: *Herbarium, Connecticut Agricultural Experiment Station,* (**NHES**), P.O. Box 1106, New Haven, Connecticut 06504, **U.S.A.**
  Telephone: 203/789-7261.
  Foundation: 1900. *Number of specimens:* 16.000.
  Herbarium: Mainly Basidiomycetes, some seed specimens.
    Important collections: G. P. Clinton collection of smut fungi now on permanent loan to Beltsville (BPI).
    Director: SAUL RICH.

NEW HAVEN: *Samuel Jones Record Memorial Collection, School of Forestry, Yale University,* (**Y**), New Haven, Connecticut 06511, **U.S.A.** –– transferred to MAD in 1969.
  Foundation: 1900. *Number of specimens:* 17.000.
  Herbarium: Principally Tropical American but woody plants from all over the world are represented; herbarium is primarily a collection of voucher specimens for the wood collection.

NEW HAVEN: *Herbarium, Osborn Memorial Laboratories, Yale University,* (**YU**), 167 Prospect Street, New Haven, Connecticut 06520, **U.S.A.**
  Telephone: 203/432-4484.
  Status: Private institution; a division of the Peabody Museum of Natural History of Yale University.
  Foundation: 1864 by D. C. Eaton; institutionalized in 1895. *Number of specimens:* 220.000.
  Herbarium: Flora worldwide but especially of Connecticut and New England and generally North

America; rich in ferns and bryophytes.

Important collections: Herbaria of Daniel Cady Eaton and Alexander William Evans; duplicates of H. N. Bolander, F. J. Lindheimer, C. R. Orcutt, E. Palmer, C. C. Parry, C. G. Pringle, S. Watson, and C. Wright.

Curator: JAMES ERIC RODMAN, 1945 (Systematics, especially chemotaxonomy, of Cruciferae).

Staff members: LAUREN BROWN, 1947 (Gramineae, Cyperaceae).

STEVEN N. HANDEL, 1945 (Plant ecology, pollination biology, *Carex*).

BRUCE H. TIFFNEY, 1949 (Angiosperm fruits and seeds, paleobotany).

Specialization in research: Floristics of Connecticut and New England; systematics of Cruciferae, especially chemosystematics and biosystematics.

Associated botanic garden: Marsh Botanical Garden, Department of Biology, Yale University, P.O. Box 2169, New Haven, Connecticut 06520, U.S.A.

Loans: In general to recognized botanical institutions.

Periodical and serial works: Publications (Bulletin, Postilla, and Discovery) of the Peabody Museum of Natural History of Yale University.

Exchange: Available: Specimens from North America. Desired: Cruciferae of the world.

NEW ORLEANS: *Herbarium, Department of Biology, Tulane University,* (**NO**), New Orleans, Louisiana 70118, **U.S.A.**

Telephone: 504/865-5191.

Status: Private university.

Foundation: 1895. *Number of specimens:* 88.000.

Herbarium: Worldwide, but especially Louisiana and southeastern U.S., Colorado (Rocky Mts.), southern California, Yucatan; neotropical fungi; ferns of Colombia and Brazil.

Important collections: Joseph A. Ewan herbarium, including L. M. Booth (s. California), I. Clokey (Colorado), D. Keck (*Penstemon*), J. G. Lemmon (California and Arizona ferns), F. W. Peirson (California), Y. Mexia, Gray Herbarium exsiccatae of Fernald period; New Orleans Academy of Science herbarium, including J. Riddell, J. Hale, J. Joor; R. S. Cocks, D. Demaree, E. P. Killip (Florida), D. Stone (*Carya*), A. L. Welden (fungi), A. Gray (North American Gramineae and Cyperaceae).

Director and Curator: STEVEN P. DARWIN, 1949 (Tropical Rubiaceae; flora of Louisiana).

Staff members: ANNE S. BRADBURN, 1933 (Barrier island vegetation of the Mississippi Gulf Coast).

JOSEPH A. EWAN, 1909 (Biobibliography of American natural history).

LEONARD B. THIEN, 1938 (Pollination biology of primitive angiosperms and orchids).

ARTHUR L. WELDEN, 1927 (Neotropical fungi, especially Thelephoraceae).

Specialization in research: Flora of Louisiana and southern Mississippi; monographic studies as listed above; flora of Yucatan, Mexico; biographical studies of American naturalists.

Associated botanic garden: Audubon Park (City of New Orleans).

Loans: In general to recognized botanical institutions.

Periodical and serial works: Tulane Studies in Zoology and Botany.

Exchange: Available: Louisiana, western North America. Desired: Southeastern U.S., Mexico, and northern Latin America.

Remarks: Minna F. Koch Memorial Library of Botany.

NEW ORLEANS: *Herbarium, Department of Biological Sciences, University of New Orleans,* (**NOLS**), Lakefront, New Orleans, Louisiana 70122, **U.S.A.**

Telephone: 504/283-0307; 283-0589.

Foundation: 1970. *Number of specimens:* 8.000.

Herbarium: Louisiana.

Director and Curator: JOHN F. UTLEY, 1944 (Bromeliaceae, Marcgraviaceae; epiphytes).

Staff member: KATHLEEN BURT-UTLEY, 1944 (Begoniaceae, Orchidaceae).

Specialization in research: Local floristics; neotropical epiphytes.

NEW YORK: *Herbarium, New York Botanical Garden,* (**NY**), Bronx, New York 10458, **U.S.A.**

Telephone: 212/220-8700 (institution); 220-8626 (herbarium); see numbers for staff members below.

Status: A private institution governed by its own Board of Managers; receives some financial support from the City and State of New York; joint graduate student program with City University of New York.

Foundation: 1891; opened in 1900. *Number of specimens:* 4.300.000, including 14.000 fossils; also 3.700 pollen slides.

Herbarium: Worldwide herbarium in all groups with greatest strength in tropical America and the United States.

Important collections: Herbaria of: Columbia College and Barnard College, Columbia University, New York College of Pharmacy, Princeton University, Torrey Botanical Club. Vascular plant collections of: E. J. Alexander, C. F. Baker, R. C. Barneby, J. H. Barnhart, E. P. Bicknell, N. L. Britton, W. H. Camp, W. M. Canby, J. H. Christ, F. E. Clements, A. Cronquist, O. Degener, A. Ducke, W. W. Eggleston, J. C. Fremont, H. A. Gleason, H. E. Hasse, A. A. Heller, G. B. Hinton, N. H. Holmgren, H. S. Irwin, E. P. James, G. S. Jenman (ferns), D. D. Keck, B. A. Krukoff, O. Kuntze, W. H. Leggett, L. Lesquereux, A. Liogier, D. T. MacDougal, K. K. Mackenzie, B. Maguire, K. I. Maximovicz, C. F. Meisner, J. T. Mickel (ferns), H. Moldenke, T. Morong, G. V. Nash, F. W. Pennell, G. T. Prance, C. G. Pringle, J. F. Rock, H. H. Rusby, P. A. Rydberg, J. A. Shafer, C. L. Shear, J. K. Small, A. C. Smith, Richard Spruce, G. Tessman, J. Torrey, F. Tweedy, L. M. Underwood (ferns), A. M. Vail, P.

Wilson, A. Wood. Bryophyte herbaria of: Dudley Herbarium, Stanford University (arctic bryophytes and Dudley's New York State collection), Florida State University, University of Kansas. Bryophyte collections of: C. F. Austin, G. N. Best, A. O. Black, Ruth Schornherst Breen, E. G. Britton, W. R. Buck, L. J. Gier, I. M. Haring, C. C. Haynes, M. A. Howe, A. Jaeger, W. Mitten, P. Patterson, G. L. Smith, W. C. Steere, W. Uggla, L. M. Underwood, R. S. Williams. Mycological collections of: H. J. Banker, G. S. Burlingham, A. Chivers, S. Damon, F. S. Earle, J. B. Ellis, R. Hagelstein, R. A. Harper, G. Massee, W. A. Murrill, C. T. Rogerson, F. J. Seaver, W. C. Sturgis, S. M. Zeller. Algal collections of: J. A. Allen, F. S. Collins, R. Hagelstein, M. A. Howe, L. M. Underwood, R. D. Wood. Lichenological collections of: G.P. Anderson, W. W. Calkins (ex herb. H. J. Banker), H. and M. Fleming, H. E. Hasse, W. A. Leighton, P. V. LeRoy, A. Schneider, R. Torrey, A. Vigener.

President: JAMES M. HESTER, 1924; 212/220-8722.

Vice President and Director of Botanical Research: GHILLEAN T. PRANCE, 1937; 212/220-8628 (Amazon Basin flora; Chrysobalanaceae, Dichapetalaceae, Lecythidaceae).

Head Curator: PATRICIA K. HOLMGREN, 1940; 212/220-8626 (Floristics of western U.S.; Cruciferae).

Staff members: MICHAEL J. BALICK, 1952; 212/220-8763 (Neotropical Palmae; economic botany of food plants and ethnobotany of the Amazon Valley).

RUPERT C. BARNEBY, 1911; 212/220-8648 (Leguminosae, especially *Astragalus, Dalea, Cassia;* Menispermaceae).

WILLIAM R. BUCK, 1950; 212/220-8624 (Pleurocarpous mosses).

ARTHUR CRONQUIST, 1919; 212/220-8631 (Floristics of the U.S.; general classification systems; Asteraceae).

KENT P. DUMONT, 1941; 212/220-8613 (Fungi; Discomycetes, Helotiales, Sclerotiniaceae).

THOMAS S. ELIAS, 1942; 914/677-5343 (Relationships of the woody flora of North America and Eurasia; structure, evolution, and distribution of secretory tissues; systematics of mimosoid legumes).

NOEL H. HOLMGREN, 1937; 212/220-8638 (Floristics of western U.S.; Scrophulariaceae).

JACQUELYN A. KALLUNKI, 1948; 212/220-8639 (Neotropical plant identification; population biology of *Goodyera*).

TETSUO KOYAMA, 1935; 212/220-8647; 220-8742 (Cyperaceae of the world; Smilacaceae; flora of Asia; economic botany).

LESLIE LANDRUM, 1946; 212/220-8651 (B. A. Krukoff Research Associate; Myrtaceae).

JAMES L. LUTEYN, 1948; 212/220-8645 (Neotropical floristics; Ericaceae).

BASSETT MAGUIRE, 1904; 212/220-8632 (Floristics and phytogeography of the neotropics; neotropical Clusiaceae).

JOHN T. MICKEL, 1934; 212/220-8636 (Pteridophytes; fern flora of Oaxaca, Mexico; fern phylogeny; *Elaphoglossum*).

SCOTT A. MORI, 1941; 212/220-8625 (Lecythidaceae; floristics of central and eastern Brazil).

CLARK T. ROGERSON, 1918; 212/220-8612 (Fungi; Pyrenomycetes, Sphaeriales, Hypocreales).

FREDERICK C. SEAMAN, 1948; 212/220-8667 (Biochemical systematics).

WILLIAM C. STEERE, 1907; 212/220-8727 (Bryophytes; moss flora of arctic America).

Honorary curators and collaborators: SIRI VON REIS ALTSCHUL (Ethnobotany).

HERMAN F. BECKER (Paleobotany; Tertiary fossil floras of western U.S.).

OTTO and ISA DEGENER (Hawaiian flora).

RICHARD C. HARRIS (Lichens).

B. A. KRUKOFF (*Erythrina, Strychnos;* Menispermaceae).

ALAIN LIOGIER (Flora of the West Indies, especially Puerto Rico).

HAROLD N. MOLDENKE (Verbenaceae, Eriocaulaceae).

DENNIS WM. STEVENSON, 1942: 212/280-5454 (Morphology and systematics of Cycadales, Commelinales, and Lycopodiophyta).

Specialization in research: Floras of tropical America, United States, Arctic regions; monographic studies in several families as listed above.

Associated botanic garden: New York Botanical Garden, Bronx, New York 10458, U.S.A.: *President:* JAMES M. HESTER, 212/220-8722; Cary Arboretum, Millbrook, New York 12545, U.S.A.: *Director:* WILLARD W. PAYNE, 914/677-5343.

Loans: To institutions, by request to the Head Curator.

Periodical and serial works: Botanical Review; Brittonia; Economic Botany (published for the Society for Economic Botany); Flora Neotropica (published for the Organization for Flora Neotropica); Memoirs of the New York Botanical Garden; Mycologia (published for the Mycological Society of America); North American Flora. For information on above publications, write or phone MARÍA L. LEBRÓN-LUTEYN, Scientific Publications Office, 212/220-8721.

Exchange: In all plant groups; emphasis on tropical America and western United States.

Remarks: A full service botanical library is available to all researchers. The collections include 195.000 bound volumes, 275.000 pamphlets, 3.000 serial titles, manuscripts, correspondence, photographs, botanical art. Services include xerography, photography, on-line data base searches, literature searches, loans. CHARLES R. LONG, 212/220-8750, is the Director of Library and Plant Information Services.

NIAGARA FALLS: *Herbarium, Niagara Parks Com-*

mission School of Horticulture, (**NFO**), Box 150, Niagara Falls, Ontario, **Canada** L2E 6T2.
Telephone: 416/356-8554.
Status: Autonomous but responsible to Province of Ontario.
Foundation: 1936. *Number of specimens:* 2.200.
Herbarium: Mainly ornamental herbaceous and woody materials with specialization in native materials of southern Ontario.
Important collections: Some specimens collected by Niagara Parks botanist in the 1890's.
Director: R. H. BARNSLEY, 1923 (Administration and horticultural organization).
Curator: M. H. DELL, 1946 (Botany; plant classification).
Staff members: W. SNOWDEN, 1933 (Floriculture).
J. WHITE, 1952 (Soils).
Specialization in research: Cultivated ornamentals.
Loans: No.

NIAMEY: *Herbier, Ecole des Sciences de Niamey,* (**ESN**), Laboratoire de Biologie Végétale, BP 91, Niamey, **Niger.**

NICE: *Herbarium, Muséum d'Histoire Naturelle (= Musée Barla),* (**NICE**), 6obis Bd. Risso, 06300 Nice, **France.**
Telephone: 93/55.15.24.
Status: Municipal museum.
Foundation: 1824.
Herbarium: Old herbaria, regional and Mediterranean region.
Important collections: Herb. J. B. J. J. Barla.
Director: GÉRARD THOMEL (Paleontology).
Staff member: GABRIEL ALZIAR (Systematic botany).
Associated botanic garden: Jardins botaniques de la ville de Nice.
Loans: Possible.
Exchange: Exchange of cereal grains possible.
Remarks: Herbarium being reorganized.

NICHINAN: *Herbarium, Hattori Botanical Laboratory,* (**NICH**), 3888 Hon-machi, Nichinan-shi, Miyazaki-ken 889-25, **Japan.**
Telephone: 09872-5-0110.
Status: Private foundation.
Foundation: 1946. *Number of specimens:* 350.000.
Herbarium: Bryophytes and lichens of the world.
Important collections: Sh. Okamura (Bryophytes), A. Noguchi (Mosses), S. Hattori (Hepatics), Z. Iwatsuki (Mosses), M. Mizutani (Hepatics).
Director and Curator: ZENNOSKE IWATSUKI, 1929 (Bryology).
Staff members: SINSKE HATTORI, 1915 (Bryology).
MASAMI MIZUTANI, 1930 (Bryology).
AKIRA NOGUCHI, 1907 (Bryology).

Research associates: TAIROKU AMAKAWA, 1917, Nakamuragakuen College (Bryology).
HIROSHI INOUE, 1932, National Science Museum, Tokyo (Bryology).
NAOFUMI KITAGAWA, 1935, Nara Kyoiku Univ. (Bryology).
URARA MIZUSHIMA, 1927, Tokyo (Bryology).
NORIWO TAKAKI, 1915, Aichi Gakuin Univ. (Bryology).
ISAO YOSHIMURA, 1933, Kochigakuen College (Lichenology).
Specialization in research: Bryophytes of Asia (taxonomy, geography, ecology).
Loans: To recognized botanical institutions.
Periodical and serial works: Journal of Hattori Botanical Laboratory, Miscellanea Bryologica et Lichenologica.
Exchange: Available: Sets of Japanese Bryophytes (Musci Japonici Exsiccati, Hepaticae Japonicae Exsiccatae). Desired: Bryophytes, particularly from Asia and Oceania.

NICOSIA: *Cyprus Herbarium, Department of Agriculture,* (**CYP**), Nicosia, **Cyprus.** (Information 1964)
Status: Government.
Foundation: 1933. *Number of specimens:* 4.000.
Herbarium: Mainly plants of Cyprus.

NITERÓI: *Herbário, Jardim Botânico de Niterói,* (**NIT**), Alameda São Boaventura 770, Fonseca, 24.000 Niterói, Rio de Janeiro, **Brazil.** (Information 1978)
Status: Secretaria de Agricultura e Abastecimento.
Foundation: 1975. *Number of specimens:* 1.400.

NITRA: *Katedra rastlinnej biológie, Agronomická fakulta, Vysoká skola pol'nohospodárska, (Department of Plant Biology, College of Agronomy, Institute of Agriculture),* (**NI**), Nitra, **Czechoslovakia.** (Information 1974)
Foundation: 1946. *Number of specimens:* 30.000.
Herbarium: Czechoslovakia, especially western and eastern Slovakia.
Specialization in research: Systematics, geobotany, agrobotany.
Loans: To recognized botanical institutions.

NJALA: *Njala University College,* (**NJ**) – – incorporated in SL.

NORFOLK: *Herbarium, Department of Biological Sciences, Old Dominion University* (**ODU**), Hampton Boulevard, Norfolk, Virginia 23508, **U.S.A.**
Telephone: 804/440-3595.
Foundation: 1950. *Number of specimens:* 15.000 vascular plants; separate algal collection.
Herbarium: Used mainly as a teaching collection and for floristic studies.
Important collections: L. Rabenhorst (Die Algen Europas: 6 volumes), F. S. Collins (Phycotheca

Boreali- America: 55 volumes).

Director and Curator: LYTTON J. MUSSELMAN, 1943; 804/440-3610 (Parasitic angiosperms, especially Scrophulariaceae).

Specialization in research: Floristics of southeastern Virginia and adjacent North Carolina; systematics of *Dryopteris;* biology of parasitic angiosperms.

Associated botanic garden: Norfolk Botanical Gardens.

Loans: Usual regulations; no loan of algal specimens.

Exchange: Available: Plants of the Great Dismal Swamp, root parasites of southern U.S. Desired: Parasitic angiosperms, worldwide.

NORMAL: *Herbarium, Department of Biological Sciences, Illinois State University,* (**ISU**), Normal, Illinois 61761, **U.S.A.**

Telephone: 309/438-7351.

Foundation: 1857. *Number of specimens:* 15.000.

Herbarium: Plants of Illinois; Umbelliferae, especially *Perideridia;* Scrophulariaceae, especially *Cordylanthus, Castilleja,* and *Orthocarpus;* Basidiomycetes.

Curator of Vascular Plants: T. I. CHUANG, 1933 (*Cordylanthus, Castilleja, Orthocarpus,* Scrophulariaceae; flora of Illinois).

Curator of Mycological Collections: A. E. LIBERTA (Lower Basidiomycetes).

Specialization in research: Cytotaxonomy of Umbelliferae; biosystematics of genera *Cordylanthus, Castilleja,* and *Orthocarpus* (Scrophulariaceae); palynology of Hydrophyllaceae; seed morphology of Scrophulariaceae and Hydrophyllaceae; taxonomy of lower Basidiomycetes; flora of Illinois.

Loans: In general to botanical institutions.

Exchange: Available: Plants of Illinois; *Cordylanthus, Castilleja,* and *Orthocarpus* (Scrophulariaceae). Desired: *Castilleja;* plants of midwestern U.S.

NORMAN: *Robert Bebb Herbarium, Department of Botany and Microbiology, Oklahoma Biological Survey, University of Oklahoma,* (**OKL**), 770 Van Vleet Oval, Norman, Oklahoma 73019, **U.S.A.**

Telephone: 405/325-6443.

Foundation: 1920. *Number of specimens:* 180.000.

Herbarium: Flora of Oklahoma; southern prairie and southcentral U.S.; northcentral Mexico.

Important collections: George J. Goodman, U. T. Waterfall, G. W. Stevens, James Reveal, Milton Hopkins.

Director: JAMES R. ESTES, 1937 (Poaceae of North America; cytotaxonomy, biosystematics, pollination ecology).

Associates: CHARLES P. DAGHLIAN, 1950 (Paleobotany: angiosperm paleobotany with emphasis on the monocotyledons to include fossil flowers and pollen).

RAYMOND B. PHILLIPS, 1949 (Systematics: computer-assisted methods in systematics with emphasis on the Saxifragaceae and Scrophulariaceae).

JOHN J. SKVARLA, 1935 (Palynology: comparative pollen morphology with emphasis on the Myrtales and Asterales).

Specialization in research: Flora of Oklahoma, southwestern U.S., and North American grasslands; polyploidy; coevolution of plants and pollinators; cluster analysis; cladistics; phylogeny.

Loans: Reasonable period of time.

Exchange: Available: Plants of Oklahoma and adjacent areas. Desired: New World flora.

NORTHAMPTON: *Herbarium, Department of Biological Sciences, Smith College,* (**SCHN**), Clark Science Center, Northampton, Massachusetts 01063, **U.S.A.**

Telephone: 413/584-2700.

Status: Private institution.

Foundation: 1875. *Number of specimens:* 53.000.

Herbarium: New England and general eastern North American vascular flora.

Director: C. JOHN BURK, 1935 (Ecology and floristics of wetlands and coastal areas).

Specialization in research: New England flora; marsh and coastal vegetation.

Associated botanic garden: Smith College Botanic Gardens.

Loans: Usual conditions.

NORTH DARTMOUTH: *Hellerman Diatom Herbarium, Department of Biology, Southeastern Massachusetts University,* (**HDSM**), North Dartmouth, Massachusetts 02747, **U.S.A.**

Telephone: 617/999-8225.

Foundation: 1975. *Number of determinations:* 60.000. *Number of collections:* 3.000.

Herbarium: Freshwater diatoms of the eastern and northcentral U.S. and estuarine and coastal diatoms of New England.

Important collections: J. Hellerman, R. K. Edgar.

Curator: ROBERT K. EDGAR, 1943 (Diatom systematics and ecology).

Specialization in research: Systematics and ecology of benthic marine diatoms of New England.

Loans: No restrictions.

NORTHFIELD: *Herbarium, Biology Department, Carleton College,* (**CARL**), Olin Hall, Northfield, Minnesota 55057, **U.S.A.**

Telephone: 507/663-4392.

Status: Private college.

Foundation: 1880. *Number of specimens:* 20.000.

Herbarium: Plants from Minnesota, Costa Rica.

Director: WILLIAM H. MUIR, 1928 (Vascular cryptogams).

Specialization in research: Vascular cryptogam distribution in Minnesota.

Associated botanic garden: Carleton College Arboretum.

Loans: Normal regulations.

Exchange: Negotiable.

Remarks: Herbarium serves mainly teaching purpose.

NORTHFIELD: *Herbarium, Norwich University,* **(NUV),** Cabot Science Building, Northfield, Vermont 05663, **U.S.A.**

Telephone: 802/485-5011, ext. 243.

Foundation: 1974. *Number of specimens:* 2.500.

Herbarium: Teaching herbarium containing collections from northeastern U.S., especially Vermont.

Director: LAUREN D. HOWARD, 1950 (Phytosociology and plant taxonomy).

Specialization in research: Plant ecology and succession in the New England area.

Exchange: With VT and HHH.

NORTHRIDGE: *Herbarium, Department of Biology, California State University,* **(SFV),** 18111 Nordhoff Street, Northridge, California 91330, **U.S.A.**

Telephone: 213/885-3310; 885-3356.

Foundation: 1958. *Number of specimens:* 11.000.

Herbarium: Vascular plants of southern California and southeastern U.S.

Director: KENNETH A. WILSON, 1928 (Systematic morphology of pteridophytes).

Staff members: WILLIAM A. EMBODEN, 1935 (Narcotic plants; introgression in *Salvia*).

VELVA E. RUDD, 1910 (Leguminosae).

JOHN E. SWANSON, 1928 (*Claytonia;* numerical taxonomy).

MARY JANE TEIMAN, 1953 (Systematic anatomy of Grammitidaceae).

Specialization in research: Leguminosae systematics; narcotic plants; *Salvia, Claytonia,* Grammitidaceae.

Associated botanic garden: Botanic Garden, Department of Biology, California State University, Northridge.

Loans: To recognized botanical institutions.

Exchange: Available: Southern California vascular plants. Desired: Pteridophytes, Leguminosae, vascular plants from southwestern U.S. and Mexico.

NORWICH: *Herbarium, Norwich Castle Museum (Norfolk Museums Service),* **(NWH),** Norwich NR1 3JU, England, **Great Britain.**

Telephone: 22233 ext. 649.

Status: Norfolk County Council.

Foundation: 1825. *Number of specimens:* 35.000 (26.000 vascular plants, 9.000 non-vascular plants).

Herbarium: Mainly British vascular plants with particular emphasis on the County of Norfolk (some foreign material).

Important collections: F. H. Barclay, E. Davie, H. D. Geldart, H. Glasspoole, F. Long, Norwich Botanic

Society, W. L. Notcutt, Sir J. Paget, A. W. Preston, F. Robinson (part), P. E. Rumbelow, A. Bull, H. J. Howard (Myxomycetes), S. A. Manning (Lichens), D. Turner (Algae).

Director Norfolk Museums Service: F. W. CHEETHAM.

Curator: P. W. LAMBLEY, 1946 (Lichens; the East Anglian flora).

Specialization in research: The flora of Eastern England.

Loans: Normally 3 months to recognized institutions.

Exchange: Exchange of British material.

Remarks: TRD (Thetford) and KLN (King's Lynn) now in NWH.

NOTRE DAME: *The Edward Lee Greene Herbarium,* **(NDG),** *and the Julius A. Nieuwland Herbarium,* **(ND),** *Department of Biology, University of Notre Dame,* Notre Dame, Indiana 46556, **U.S.A.**

Telephone: 219/283-6684; 283-7496.

Status: Private university.

Foundation: 1860. *Number of specimens:* 210.000 (ND) 65.000 (NDG).

Herbarium: ND: an open collection of midwestern U.S. material, plus considerable amount western U.S. and Europe; NDG: a closed collection of pre-1915 material, mostly from western and mid-Atlantic U.S.

Important collections: ND: Julius A. Nieuwland (midwestern U.S.), Raymond F. Potzger (midwestern U.S.); NDG: E. L. Greene (9.000), 56.000 specimens of other collectors made before 1915.

Curator: THEODORE J. CROVELLO, 1940 (Brassicaceae; biogeography; flora of Indiana; computers in systematics).

Staff member: BARBARA HELLENTHAL (Trees of Indiana; weed seed identification).

Specialization in research: State of Indiana; rare plants of Indiana; use of computers to: a) help reconstruct itineraries of Greene and other American collectors, b) help inventory and determine location of type specimens of Greene and others.

Loans: To established herbaria and museums, usually for one year; types included.

Periodical and serial works: American Midland Naturalist.

Exchange: Brassicaceae only.

Remarks: NDG: a) for all 65.000 specimens, label, annotation, accession, and state of specimen data have been computerized, and can be searched and sorted in many ways, b) an index of over 3.500 pre-1915 botanical books (including herbals) constituting Greene's library is available, c) a computerized, annotated catalog of over 4.400 new taxa or combinations by Greene is available. ND: Location of BRASSBAND, the Brassicaceae computerized data bank at Notre Dame; currently contains data on 35.000 specimens of the genera *Streptanthus* and *Cardamine* from about 75 herbaria.

NOTTINGHAM: *Herbarium, Department of Botany, University of Nottingham,* **(NHM),** Nottingham, England, **Great Britain.** (Information 1974)
Status: University.
Foundation: 1948. *Number of specimens:* 2.000.
Herbarium: Flowering plants of United Kingdom.

NOTTINGHAM: *Herbarium, Natural History Museum,* **(NOT),** Wollaton Hall, Wollaton, Nottingham NG8 2AE, England, **Great Britain.**
Telephone: 0602 281333.
Status: Local government.
Foundation: ca. 1867. *Number of specimens:* 80.000.
Herbarium: British and worldwide.
Important collections: G. L. Fisher series (*Rosa, Rubus*), Fisher Arctic collection, E. M. Holmes (Lichens), W. J. Carr herbarium (British plants, with a local bias).
 Director: B. LOUGHBROUGH.
 Curator: B. PLAYLE.
 Staff members: W. HEYES.
  G. WALLEY.
Loans: By arrangement.
Exchange: In general, no.
Remarks: Currently being computerized.

NOUMÉA: *Herbarium, Centre O.R.S.T.O.M. de Nouméa,* **(NOU),** B.P. A5 Cedex, Nouméa, **New Caledonia.** (Information 1974)
Status: Office of O.R.S.T.O.M., Paris.
Foundation: 1964. *Number of specimens:* 20.000.
Herbarium: Vascular cryptogams and phanerogams of New Caledonia and New Hebrides.
Specialization in research: Plants of New Caledonia, New Hebrides.

NOVA FRIBURGO: *Herbarium Friburgense Colégio Anchieta,* **(FCAB),** Rua General Osório 180, 28.600 Nova Friburgo, Rio de Janeiro, **Brazil.**
Telephone: (55)0245/225769; 220940.
Status: Private institution of the Society of Jesus – – Jesuits.
Foundation: 1940. *Number of specimens:* 3.000.
Herbarium: Phanerogams and cryptogams of Brazil.
Important collections: 15 types; José Eugênio Leite, Jayme Capell, Emmanuel C. R. do Amarante, João Dornstauder, Josafá Carlos de Siqueira, Aloysio Sehnem.
 Director: ESTANISLAU KOSTKA E SILVA, 1929.
 Curator: JOSAFÁ CARLOS DE SIQUEIRA, 1951 (Amaranthaceae).
Specialization in research: Systematics; economic botany; phytochemistry.
Periodical and serial works: Eugeniana (founded in 1980 to publish research results from the herbarium).
Exchange: Available: Brazilian material.
Remarks: Herbarium became active in 1978 after 26 years of inactivity.

NOVA LISBOA: *Herbarium, Instituto de Investigação Agronómica de Angola,* **(LUA),** C.P. 406, Nova Lisboa, **Angola.** (Information 1974)
Status: Government.
Foundation: 1941. *Number of specimens:* 35.000.
Herbarium: Vascular plants of Angola and Africa south of the Sahara.
Important collections: J. Grossweiler, J. Brito Teixeira.
 Associated botanic garden: Botanic Garden of Salazar and Floristic Reserve No. 1, Chianga.
Loans: To recognized botanical institutions.
Periodical and serial works: Annual Report, Index Seminum.

NOVO-ALEKSANDROVSK: *Herbarium, Sakhalin Complex Institute for Scientific Investigation, Botanical Garden,* **(NABG),** 694050 Novo-Aleksandrovsk, Sakhalin Oblast, **U.S.S.R.**
Number of specimens: 15.000.
 Director: Y. D. ISHIN.

NOVOSIBIRSK: *Herbarium, Siberian Central Botanical Garden,* **(NS),** 101 Zolotodolinskaya Ul., Novosibirsk 90, **U.S.S.R.**
Telephone: 6-41-02.
Status: Siberian Branch of USSR Academy of Sciences.
Foundation: 1945–1950. *Number of specimens:* 350.000.
Herbarium: Plants of Siberia and neighboring areas, most from Popov Herbarium transferred from Urkutsk in 1978.
Important collections: Lichens; mosses of Siberia and Soviet Far East; vascular plants of Central Siberia (Irkutsk and Czita districts, Buryatia), Sayan Mts., Stanovoye Nagorye Highlands, the plateau of Putorana, northern Mongolia, Tuva, Altai Mts. and Khakassia.
 Director: LEONID I. MALYSHEV, 1931 (Floristics, systematics, phytogeography).
 Curators: LEONID V. BARDUNOV, 1932, Div. of Mosses (Bryology).
  IVAN M. KRASNOBOROV, 1931, Div. of West and Middle Siberia (Floristics, systematics).
  GALINA A. PESHKOVA, 1930, Div. of East Siberia (Floristics, systematics, phytogeography).
Specialization in research: Floristics and taxonomy of Siberian plants, bryology, lichenology.
Loans: One month term within USSR, six months abroad.
Exchange: Yes.

NSUKKA: *Herbarium, University of Nigeria,* **(UNN),** Nsukka, **Nigeria.** (Information 1974)
Status: University.
Foundation: 1962.

NUEVA SAN SALVADOR: *Herbario, Centro Nacional de Tecnologia Agropecuaria,* **(TECLA),** Apar-

tado postal 885, Nueva San Salvador, **El Salvador.**
Telephone: (503)28-20-66.
Status: Ministerio de Agricultura y Ganaderia.
Curator: ANA MORGOTH CHÁVEZ.
Remarks: Plan to reactivate herbarium in the area of weeds of EL Salvador; formerly listed under Santa Tecla.

NYABYEYA: *Herbarium, Uganda Forest School,* **(UFS),** P.O. Masindi, Nyabyeya, **Uganda.** (Information 1974)
Status: Directed by state.
Foundation: 1934. *Number of specimens:* 750.
Herbarium: Uganda forest species.

O

OAKLAND: *Herbarium, Natural Sciences Department, Oakland Museum,* **(OAKL)**, 1000 Oak Street, Oakland, California 94607, **U.S.A.**
Telephone: 415/273-3884.
Foundation: 1969. *Number of specimens:* 1.200.
Herbarium: California plants.
  Director: JOHN E. PEETZ.
  Curator: DONALD D. LINSDALE.
  Staff members: C. DON MACNEILL (Ferns).
    GENEVIEVE PRLAIN (General botany).
    JULIE STOLL (Marine algae).
  Loans: Usual regulations.

OAKLAND: *Herbarium, Biology Department, Mills College,* **(OMC)**, Oakland, California 94613, **U.S.A.**
Telephone: 415/632-2700, ext. 304.
Status: Private college.
Foundation: 1919. *Number of specimens:* 7.500.
Herbarium: Native and introduced woody plants of California; Lauraceae, *Quercus* and *Corylus* worldwide; Tertiary fossils of Asia Minor, Turkey; Liliaceae of California.
  Director and Curator: B. KASAPLIGIL, 1918 (*Pinus, Corylus, Quercus,* Lauraceae, Tertiary floras of Asia Minor).
  Specialization in research: Quercus, Corylus, Liliaceae, Lauraceae morphology and ontogeny.
  Associated botanic garden: William Joseph McInnes Memorial Botanic Garden of Mills College, Oakland, California 94613, U.S.A.
  Loans: To recognized institutions.
  Exchange: Reprints.
  Remarks: Approximately 4.000 Howard E. McMinn collections of native California plants have been transferred to UC.

OBERLIN: *Herbarium, Department of Biology, Kettering Hall of Science, Oberlin College,* **(OC)**, West Lotain Street, Oberlin, Ohio 44074, **U.S.A.**
Telephone: 216/775-8315.
Foundation: 1889. *Number of specimens:* 34.046.
Herbarium: Plants of Ohio.
Important collections: Henry C. Beardslee, Mary E. Day, Frederick O. Grover, George T. Jones, Herbert L. Jones, W. Preston Smith, E. Wilkinson.
  Director: GEORGE TALLMON JONES, 1897.
  Specialization in research: Distribution of plants of northern Ohio.
  Loans: To recognized institutions.
  Exchange: Ohio plants.
  Remarks: All non-Ohio specimens (ca. 170.000) were sold to Miami University, (MU), Oxford, Ohio, in 1967.

ODESSA: *Herbarium, Department of Morphology and Systematics of Plants, I.I. Mecynikov State University of Odessa,* **(MSUD)**, Shampanskii per. 2, 270015 Odessa, **U.S.S.R.**
Foundation: 1865. *Number of specimens:* 50.000.
Director: N. M. PASHKOVSKAJA.

OEIRAS: *Herbarium, Estação Agronómica Nacional,* **(LISE)**, Oeiras, **Portugal.** (Information 1974)
Status: Ministry of Economy.
Foundation: 1937. *Number of specimens:* 80.000.
Herbarium: Vascular plants, fungi and cultivated plants of Portugal.
  Specialization in research: Flora and vegetation of Portugal, atmospheric pollen, paleoethnobotany.
  Loans: To recognized botanical institutions.
  Periodical and serial works: Agronomia Lusitana, De Flora Lusitana Commentarii, Index Seminum.

OGDEN: *Herbarium, U.S. Forest Service, Intermountain Region,* **(OGDF)**, Federal Office Building, 324 25th Street, Ogden, Utah 84401, **U.S.A.**
Telephone: 801/626-3444.
Status: U.S. Department of Agriculture, Forest Service.
Foundation: 1905. *Number of specimens:* 18.200.
Herbarium: Emphasis on the mountain flora of the Intermountain Region.
Important collections: I. Tidestrom, I. W. Clokey.
  Director: HALLIE L. COX.
  Curator: MONT E. LEWIS, 1906 (*Carex*).
  Loans: Usual regulations.
  Exchange: Yes.

OGDEN: *Herbarium, Weber State College,* **(WSCO)**, Ogden, Utah 84408, **U.S.A.**
Telephone: 801/626-6179.
Foundation: 1967. *Number of specimens:* 15.800.
Herbarium: Flora of north central Utah and the islands of the Great Salt Lake, Utah; *Penstemon* of Utah.
  Director and Curator: STEPHEN L. CLARK (*Penstemon;* marsh and aquatic plants of Utah).
  Loans: Normal regulations.
  Exchange: Available: *Penstemon;* marsh flora; flora of north central Utah. Desired: *Penstemon,* ferns, bryophytes.

OLDHAM: *Herbarium, Werneth Park Study Centre and Natural History Museum,* **(WERN)**, Frederick Street, Oldham, Lancashire, England, **Great Britain.** (Information 1974)
Status: Branch of Public Libraries.
Foundation: 1938. *Number of specimens:* 6.000.
Herbarium: Phanerogams and bryophytes of the British Isles.

OLDS: *Herbarium, Horticultural Programs, Olds College,* **(OLDS),** Olds, Alberta, **Canada** TOM 1PO.
Telephone: 304/556-8253.
Foundation: 1963. *Number of specimens:* 18.000.
Herbarium: Woody species of importance to horticulture on the northern Great Plains; weedy plants in agriculture; range species.
Curator: B. J. GODWIN, 1928 (Horticulture; entomology).
Loans: For 6 months.
Exchange: Willing to consider.

OLIVET: *Herbarium, Biology Department, Olivet College,* **(OLV),** Olivet, Michigan 49076, **U.S.A.**
Telephone: 616/749-7000.
Foundation: 1890. *Number of specimens:* 1.500.
Herbarium: Mosses of Canada; local collections from Michigan, especially Olivet.
Director: EDWARD P. SPEARE.

OLOMOUC: *Katedra botaniky, přírod. fakulty University Palackého,* **(OL),** Leninstr. 26, Olomouc, **Czechoslovakia.** (Information 1974)
Status: University.
Foundation: 1946. *Number of specimens:* 37.000.
Herbarium: Pteridophytes and phanerogams of Europe.
Specialization in research: Taxonomy of Central-European higher plants.
Associated botanic garden: Botanic Garden of Palacký University.
Loans: To recognized botanical institutions.
Periodical and serial works: Acta Universitatis Palackyanae, series Biologica.

OLOMOUC: *Herbarium, Vlastivědny ustav-muzeum,* **(OLM),** Nám. Republiky 5, Olomouc, **Czechoslovakia.** (Information 1974)
Foundation: 1918. *Number of specimens:* 140.000.
Herbarium: All groups, worldwide and Czechoslovakia.
Specialization in research: Geobotany, floristics and conservation.
Loans: To recognized botanical institutions.
Periodical and serial works: Zprávy Vlastivědného ústavu, Malá řada (Práce odboru přirodních věd).

OLOMOUC: *Herbarium, Katedra příodopisu pedagogické fakulty Univerzity Palackého,* **(OLP),** Zerotínovo nám. 2, 771 40 Olomouc, **Czechoslovakia.**
Telephone: 229 51.
Status: University.
Foundation: 1964. *Number of specimens:* 3.000.
Herbarium: Cryptogams and phanerogams of Czechoslovakia.
Curator: BRONISLAV HLŮZA, 1929 (Mycology).
Specialization in research: Mycoecology of *Amanita.*

OLYMPIA: *Herbarium, Department of Biology, Saint Martin's College,* **(OSMC)** – – *see* LACEY.

OMAHA: *Herbarium, Department of Biology, University of Nebraska at Omaha,* **(OMA),** Omaha, Nebraska 68182, **U.S.A.**
Telephone: 402/554-2641.
Foundation: 1968. *Number of specimens:* 20.500 (6.500 vascular plants, 11.000 lichens, 3.000 bryophytes).
Herbarium: Primarily vascular plants of Great Plains; U.S. bryophytes; worldwide lichens.
Important collections: R. S. Egan (10.000 lichens).
Curators: R. S. EGAN, 1945 (Lichens).
P. V. PRIOR, 1921 (Bryophytes).
D. M. SUTHERLAND, 1940 (Vascular plants).
Staff member: R. S. IRVING, 1942 (Systematics of *Hedeoma,* Labiatae).
Specialization in research: Great Plains floristics, especially grasses.
Loans: No special restrictions.
Exchange: Available and desired.

ONEONTA: *Hoysradt Herbarium, Hartwick College,* **(HHH),** Oneonta, New York 13820, **U.S.A.**
Telephone: 607/432-4200.
Foundation: 1968. *Number of specimens:* 20.000.
Herbarium: Local; San Salvador Island; Bahamas.
Important collections: Lyman H. Hoysradt.
Curator: ROBERT R. SMITH, 1934 (Taxonomy of vascular plants).
Specialization in research: Flora of Otsego County, San Salvador Island, and the Bahamas.
Loans: To recognized botanical institutes.
Exchange: Available.

OPAVA: *Slezské Muzeum, Botanical Department,* **(OP),** Vítězného února 35, 746 46 Opava, **Czechoslovakia.**
Telephone: 2535.
Status: State institution.
Foundation: 1814. *Number of specimens:* 157.000.
Herbarium: Tracheophyta, Bryophyta and lichens.
Important collections: E. Bauer bryophytes.
Curator: JOSEF DUDA, 1925 (Hepaticae).
Specialization in research: Czechoslovakia, especially Hepaticae.
Associated botanic garden: Arboretum, Nový Dvůr v Opavy (Director, FRANTIŠEK KRKAVEC).
Loans: To recognized botanical institutes.
Periodical and serial works: Časopis Slezského muzea, ser. A (Acta Musei Silesiae).
Exchange: Available: Hepaticae of Czechoslovakia. Desired: Bryophytes, especially Hepaticae.

ÖREBRO: *Karolinska Högre Allmänna Läroverket,* **(OREB),** Örebro, **Sweden.** (Information 1974)
Status: State school.
Herbarium: Plants of Sweden.

ORLANDO: *Herbarium, Department of Biological Sciences, University of Central Florida,* (**FTU**), Orlando, Florida 32816, **U.S.A.**

Telephone: 305/275-2148.

Status: Formerly Florida Technological University.

Foundation: 1968. *Number of specimens:* 19.000 (16.000 vascular plants, 1.500 bryophytes, 500 lichens, 500 fungi, 500 algae).

Herbarium: Worldwide , especially tropical floras and bryophytes.

    Director: HARVEY A. MILLER, 1928 (Bryology; phytogeography).

    Curator: HENRY O. WHITTIER, 1937 (Tropical Pacific mosses; Florida floristics).

    Collaborators: ROBIN B. HUCK, 1935 (Labiatae; subtropical scrub floras).

        ELIANE M. NORMAN, 1931 (Buddleiaceae).

    Specialization in research: Florida floristics; tropical bryophytes.

Loans: Normal regulations.

Exchange: By prior arrangement. Available: Florida vascular plants; tropical bryophytes. Desired: Tropical and subtropical specimens.

Remarks: Collections of Harvey A. Miller (ca. 60.000 bryophytes) and Henry O. Whittier (ca. 10.000 bryophytes) are maintained as private collections separate from each other and from FTU. Facilities are available for visiting investigators.

ORLÉANS: *Herbarium, Musée des Sciences Naturelles,* (**ORM**), 2 rue Marcel Proust, Orléans, Loiret, **France.** (Information 1974)

Status: Municipal institution.

Foundation: 1823. *Number of specimens:* 100.000.

Herbarium: Plants of France, mainly Dept. Loiret.

Important collections: Aug. Prouvençal de St. Hilaire (France).

ORONO: *Herbarium, Department of Botany and Plant Pathology, University of Maine,* (**MAINE**), Folger Library, Orono, Maine 04473, **U.S.A.**

Telephone: 207/581-7861.

Foundation: 1890. *Number of specimens:* 66.000.

Herbarium: Largest part of collection from Maine.

Important collections: Joseph Blake, Mrs. F. Hinckley, H. P. Scoullar, C. Curtis, H. W. Merrill, M. Quimby, L. Coburn, S. Gordon, R. C. Bean, O. Neal, G. B. Rossbach, K. P. Jansson, G. D. Chamberlain, E. Bicknell, C. D. Richards, F. S. Collins (algae), J. B. Ellis and B. M. Everhart (fungi), A. Cook (fungi), L. M. Underwood (Hepaticae), C. E. Cummings and F. C. Seymour (lichens), E. Bartholomew (fungi), R. Homola (fungi).

    Director and Curator: CHARLES D. RICHARDS, 1920 (Vascular plants of Maine).

    Staff member: RICHARD HOMOLA, 1934 (Fungi).

    Specialization in research: Flora of Maine.

    Associated botanic garden: Fay Hyland Botanical Plantation.

Loans: Yes.

Exchange: Yes.

ORSAY: *Laboratoire de Biologie Végétale, Faculté des Sciences,* (**VIL**), 91405 Orsay, **France.** (Information 1974)

Status: Directed by Faculté des Sciences.

Foundation: Transferred to Orsay in 1968. *Number of specimens:* 70.000.

Herbarium: Flora of France.

OSAKA: *Herbarium, Osaka Museum of Natural History,* (**OSA**), Nagai Park, Higashi-Sumiyoshi-ku, Osaka 546, **Japan.**

Telephone: 06-697-6221.

Status: Municipal.

Foundation: 1950. *Number of specimens:* 150.000.

Herbarium: Marine algae, bryophytes and vascular plants of Japan and adjacent region.

Important collections: S. Miki, water plants of Japan; pollen and spores of Japanese vascular plants.

    Director: MANZO CHIJI, 1927 (Geology and paleontology).

    Curator: KO SETO, 1930 (Pteridophyta).

    Staff members: TAKAYOSHI NASU, 1941 (Palynology).

        TOMOO NUNOTANI, 1948 (Forest ecology).

        MOTOHARU OKAMOTO, 1947 (Fagaceae).

    Specialization in research: Flora of Japan.

    Associated botanic garden: Nagai Botanical Garden.

Loans: To recognized botanical institutions.

Periodical and serial works: Bulletin, Occasional Papers, Special Publications.

Exchange: Available: Vascular plants of Japan and their pollen and spores. Desired: Worldwide specimens.

OSHKOSH: *Herbarium, Biology Department, University of Wisconsin – Oshkosh,* (**OSH**), Oshkosh, Wisconsin 54901, **U.S.A.**

Telephone: 414/424-1108.

Foundation: 1964. *Number of specimens:* 56.000.

Herbarium: Wisconsin primarily; midwestern U.S., Mexico, and Central America.

Important collections: Buckstaff.

    Director and Curator: NEIL A. HARRIMAN, 1938 (Juncaceae).

    Specialization in research: Cytotaxonomy in Juncaceae; floristics.

Loans: Usual conditions.

Exchange: Available: General collections, midwestern U.S., Mexico, and Central America. Desired: General collections from anywhere in the world.

Remarks: The Buckstaff Herbarium of the Oshkosh Public Museum became part of OSH in 1976.

OSLO: *Botanical Garden and Museum,* (**O**), Trondheimsvn. 23B, Oslo 5, **Norway.**

Telephone: 02-686960.
Status: University of Oslo.
Foundation: 1812. *Number of specimens:* 1.250.000 (vascular plants 850.000, cryptogams 400.000).
Herbarium: Worldwide.
Important collections: Many Norwegians, including B.A. Lynge, Norman, S. C. Sommerfelt (Norway, the Arctic), H. F. A. von Eggers (Ecuador), C. Bock, von Rosthorn (China), H. C. Printz (Siberia), E. Christophersen, E. Baardseth (Tristan da Cunha), Wendelbo (Chitral), G. Borgen, Krog, Lid, Sunding (Canary Islands, Cape Verde Islands), C. A. Berg, H. Krog (U.S.A.), C. A. Berg, O. C. Dahl (Australia), A. & I. N. Bjørnstad, H. Krog, Nordal, Ryvarden (East Africa).
Director: Elected among permanent staff members for 2 year period.
Curators: ANDERS DANIELSEN, 1919 (Vascular plants, palynology).
GRO GULDEN, 1939 (Taxonomy and ecology, Agaricales).
JON KAASA, 1918 (Scandinavian vascular plants).
HILDUR KROG, 1922 (Taxonomy and distribution of arctic and tropical lichens).
Staff members: ROLF Y. BERG, 1925 (Embryology, taxonomy and myrmecochory of vascular plants).
LIV BORGEN, 1943 (Cytotaxonomy of Macaronesian vascular plants).
KLAUS HØILAND, 1948 (Taxonomy and distribution, Agaricales).
GUNVOR S. KNABEN, 1911 (Cytotaxonomy and phytogeography of arctic vascular plants).
ELMAR MARKER, 1939 (Phytosociology, vegetation mapping).
HAAVARD ØSTHAGEN, 1945 (Taxonomy and floristics of lichens).
PER SUNDING, 1937 (Phytosociology, ecology and taxonomy of Macaronesian vascular plants).
ROLF WAHLSTRØM, 1945 (Cytotaxonomy, Liliales).
Loans: In general to recognized botanical institutions.
Periodical and serial works: Seed exchange catalogue of the Botanical Garden.
Exchange: Available: Norwegian, Arctic and Tristan vascular plants; bryophytes, lichens and fungi.

OSNABRÜCK: *Herbarium, Naturwissenschaftliches Museum der Stadt Osnabrück,* (**OSN**), Heger-Tor-Wall 28, D-4500 Osnabrück, **Federal Republic of Germany,** BRD.
Telephone: 0541-3234441.
Status: Public Museum, directed by the town.
Foundation: 1870. *Number of specimens:* 11.000.
Herbarium: Central Europe, particularly Lower Saxony.
Important collections: K. Koch, H. Buschbaum.
Director: HORST KLASSEN, 1932 (Geology).

Curator: RAINER EHRNSBERGER, 1944; 0541-3234442 (Zoology).
Specialization in research: No floristic research (at the moment).
Associated botanic garden: Botanic Garden of Osnabrück is planned.
Loans: In general to recognized botanical institutions.
Periodical and serial works: Osnabrücker Naturwissenschaftliche Mitteilungen (together with the Naturwissenschaftliche Verein Osnabrück).

OTTAWA: *National Herbarium of Canada, Botany Division, National Museum of Natural Sciences, National Museums of Canada,* (**CAN, CANA, CANL, CANM**), Ottawa, Ontario, **Canada** K1A OM8.
Telephone: 613/995-9252.
Status: Part of a Canadian government corporation: The National Museums of Canada.
Foundation: 1842 (foundation of the National Museum); 1882 (formal foundation of Herbarium).
Number of specimens: Vascular plants (CAN) 440.392; algae (CANA) 20.452; lichens (CANL) 72.125; mosses and liverworts (CANM) 183.622.
Herbarium: Vascular plants: mainly Canada, good circumpolar representation, many types; algae mainly North American marine algae, especially the Canadian Arctic; lichens: mainly Canadian, but coverage is worldwide; mosses and liverworts: mainly North American.
Important collections: Vascular plants: John Macoun, James M. Macoun, M. O. Malte, A. E. Porsild, collections by current staff, numerous exsiccatae; algae: John Macoun (Canada), R. K. S. Lee (Canadian Arctic), Phycotheca Boreali-Americana; lichens: I. M. Lamb; mosses and liverworts: John Macoun, James M. Macoun, Howard A. Crum.
Director: LOUIS LEMIEUX, 1925.
Chief Botanist: JAMES H. SOPER, 1916 (Flora of Ontario).
Staff within Sections:
1. *Vascular Plant Section* (CAN):
Curator: JOHN M. GILLETT, 1918 (Leguminosae, *Trifolium*).
Staff members: GEORGE W. ARGUS, 1929 (*Salix;* rare plants of Canada).
ALBERT W. DUGAL, 1942 (Exhibit planner).
MARCELLA A. DUMAS, 1919 (Preparator).
ERICH HABER, 1943 (*Pyrola,* Pyrolaceae).
MICHAEL J. SHCHEPANEK, 1940 (Conservator).
JAMES H. SOPER, 1916 (Flora of Ontario).
DAVID J. WHITE, 1947.
2. *Phycology Section* (CANA):
Acting Curator: JAMES H. SOPER, 1916.
3. *Lichenology Section* (CANL):
Curator: IRWIN M. BRODO, 1935 (*Lecanora subfusca* group; floristic studies on parts of Canada, especially the Queen Charlotte Islands, B.C.; catalogue of Canadian lichens).
Staff member: PAK YAU WONG, 1939 (Lichen

flora of southern Ontario).

4. *Bryophyte Section* (CANM):
   Curator: ROBERT R. IRELAND, 1932 (Moss flora of the Maritime Provinces).
   Staff member: LINDA M. LEY, 1947.
   Specialization in research: Flora of Canada; systematics, floristics, and phytogeography of vascular plants, algae, lichens, and mosses.
   Loans: In general to recognized botanical institutions.
   Periodical and serial works: Museum Bulletins (from 1913); Contributions to Botany (after 1958); National Museum of Natural Sciences, Publications in Botany (from 1969); SYLLOGEUS (after 1972).
   Exchange: Available: Chiefly Canadian material. Wanted: Specimens from all parts of the world.
   Remarks: Working space is available for visiting scientists; the library has a long series of botanical publications. In 1968 the herbarium was divided into four sections (see Taxon 17: 335. 1968) coded CAN (as before), CANA, CANL, and CANM (as detailed above).

OTTAWA: *Herbarium, Department of Biology, Carleton University,* (**CCO**), Ottawa, Ontario, **Canada** K1S 5B6.
Telephone: 613/231-3871.
Foundation: 1952. *Number of specimens:* 30.000.
Herbarium: Mainly Canada.
Important collections: John Bell (Newfoundland and Lake Huron; used for Macoun's *Flora of Canada*).
   Director and Curator of Vascular Plants: I. L. BAYLY, 1929 (Aquatic macrophytes).
   Curator of Non-vascular Plants: W. I. ILLMAN, 1920 (Mycology).
   Staff members: G. REEDER, 1920.
   J. VAN ENGEN, 1931.
   Specialization in research: Introgression in macrophytes and tree species.
   Loans: To accredited institutions.
   Exchange: Eagerly solicited.

OTTAWA: *Vascular Plant Herbarium, Biosystematics Research Institute, Agriculture Canada,* (**DAO**), Central Experimental Farm, Ottawa, Ontario, **Canada** K1A OC6.
Telephone: 613/995-9461.
Status: Government department.
Foundation: 1886. *Number of specimens:* 675.000.
Herbarium: Worldwide, mainly north temperate, especially Canada (native, weedy, and cultivated).
Important collections: Types for 5.000-6.000 taxa; main collectors: J. F. Alex, I. J. Bassett, B. Boivin (18.000), W. M. Bowden, P. F. Bruggemann, J. A. Calder (40.000), W. J. Cody (23.000), J. Dearness (2.500), W. G. Dore (25.000), M. G. Dudley (850), J. W. Eastham, D. Erskine, J. Fletcher (3.000), C. Frankton, L. O. Gaiser (5.000), J. M. Gillett, H. Groh,

L. Jenkins (9.500), W. Krivda, D. R. Lindsay, J. Macoun (2.000), W. H. Minshall, R. J. Moore, T. Mosquin (7.500), G. A. Mulligan, J. A. Parmelee, Mrs. Perceval, A. Saunders, H. A. Senn, J. Woodruff; also large sets from G. W. Argus, R. E. Beschel, T. J. W. Burgess, L. Cinq-Mars.(1.900), A. Dutilly, C. E. Garton, J. H. Hudson, L. E. James, G. F. Ledingham, A. Legault, M. Lettors, E. Lepage, A. Löve, D. Löve, E. H. Moss, P. Roberts, A. E. Roland, Rolland-Germain, E. Rouleau, J. Rousseau, R. C. Russell, G. W. Scotter (7.000), E. C. Smith, J. H. Soper, T. M. C. Taylor, G. H. Turner (5.000), Marie-Victorin; cultivated plants collected by: J. M. Gillett, H. L. Rhodes, L. C. Sherk. This is the basic herbarium for the Canadian Weed Survey, Weeds of Canada, Flora of the Prairie Provinces, Flora of the Queen Charlotte Islands, Catalogue of Saskatchewan, Check-list of Plants of the Ottawa District and Prince Edward Isl.
   Director (Acting): G. A. MULLIGAN, 1928 (Weeds; Cruciferae).
   Curator: W. J. CODY, 1922 (Flora of northern Canada; Canadian ferns).
   Staff members: S. G. AIKEN, 1938 (Gramineae; *Myriophyllum*).
   I. J. BASSETT, 1921 (Anemophilous groups; palynology).
   B. R. BAUM, 1937 (*Tamarix;* Aveneae, Triticeae).
   B. BOIVIN, 1916 (Canadian flora).
   F. W. COLLINS, 1945 *(Brassica).*
   J. MCNEILL, 1933 (Weeds; Caryophyllaceae; *Polygonum).*
   E. SMALL, 1940 *(Daucus, Cannabis, Medicago, Melilotus).*
   S. WARWICK, 1954 (Variation in eastern Canadian weeds).
   Specialization in research: Cultivated plants; noxious plants; Canadian flora.
   Associated botanic garden: Botanic Garden and Arboretum, Central Experimental Farm.
   Loans: To recognized institutions.
   Exchange: Available: Canada. Desired: North temperate cultivated plants and weeds; Canadian native and related floras.

OTTAWA: *National Mycological Herbarium, Biosystematics Research Institute, Agriculture Canada,* (**DAOM**), Central Experimental Farm, Ottawa, Ontario, **Canada** K1A OC6.
Telephone: 613/995-9461.
Status: Government department.
Foundation: 1909. *Number of specimens:* 225.000.
Herbarium: Fungi, all major groups mainly from north temperate and arctic-alpine regions.
Important collections: Roy F. Cain, G. D. Darker (Hypodermataceae), John Dearness (on loan from Montreal Botanic Garden, MTJB), W. L. Gordon (especially *Fusarium*), J. W. Groves (Helotiales), J. Macoun (Thelephoraceae, Polyporaceae), L. E. Wehmeyer.

Director: G. A. MULLIGAN.

Curator: J. A. PARMELEE, 1924 (Uredinales; parasitic fungi).

Staff members: D. J. S. BARR, 1937 (Mastigomycotina).

J. D. BISSETT, 1948 (Coelomycetes).
M. P. CORLETT, 1937 (Pyrenomycetes).
J. H. GINNS, 1938 (Aphyllophorales).
S. J. HUGHES, 1918 (Hyphomycetes).
G. A. NEISH, 1949 (Plectomycetes, Hyphomycetes).
S. A. REDHEAD, 1950 (Agaricales).
R. A. SHOEMAKER, 1928 (Pyrenomycetes).

Research Associates: R. MACRAE *(Poria).*
M. K. NOBLES (Aphyllophorales).
D. B. O. SAVILE (Uredinales; phylogeny).

Specialization in research: Taxonomic, cultural and life history studies; identification service; maintenance of a National Herbarium and Culture Collection.

Associated botanic garden: Arboretum and Botanic Garden, Ottawa Research Station, Agriculture Canada, Central Experimental Farm, Ottawa, Ontario, Canada K1A OC6.

Loans: To recognized institutions; apply to curator.

Periodical and serial works: Fungi Canadenses (introduced, 1973).

Exchange: Available: Canadian fungi. Desired: Representative fungi from other regions.

OTTAWA: *Dominion Forest Service,* **(OTF),** Ottawa, Ontario, **Canada** -- housed in Chalk River with PFES.

OTTAWA: *Herbarium, Département de Biologie, Université d'Ottawa,* **(OTT),** 30 Somerset Street, Ottawa, Ontario, **Canada** K1N 6N5.

Telephone: 613/231-2332; 231-2954; 231-2336.
Foundation: 1966. *Number of specimens:* 5.000.
Herbarium: Plants of Ontario; *Vicia, Pisum.*
Important collections: C. Nozzolillo.
Directors: J. T. ARNASON.
C. NOZZOLILLO, 1926.
Specialization in research: Chemotaxonomic studies of legumes, *Impatiens,* and Compositae.

OULU: *Botanical Museum, University of Oulu,* **(OULU),** P.O. Box 191, SF-00101 Oulu 10, **Finland.**

Telephone: 981-17960, Internat. 358-81-17960 (from 1983: 345411).

Status: University of Oulu.

Foundation: 1959 (The herbarium is based on the collections of Oulun Luonnonystäväin Yhdistys [Society of the Friends of Nature of Oulu] founded 1927).

Number of specimens: 250.000 (vascular plants 190.000, mosses, lichens and fungi 60.000).

Herbarium: Fennoscandian, especially northern Finnish, and arctic and boreal flora of Northern Hemisphere.

Important collections: L. Heikkinen (especially apogamous groups), P. S. Jokela (Finnish), E. & M. Ohenoja (Fennoscandian, Svalbard, N. Canadian); A. Railonsala (*Taraxacum,* including types), T. Ulvinen (Fennoscandian).

Director: SIRKKA KUPILA-AHVENNIEMI, 1927; 981 – 332005; from 1983: 345411. (Plant physiology).

Curator: TAUNO ULVINEN, 1930 (Taxonomy, ecology and distribution of Finnish Vascular plants, mosses, and fungi).

Staff members: SEPPO EUROLA, 1930 (Sociology, ecology and distribution of Finnish vascular plants, alluvial meadows and arctic heaths; snow-algae).

PAAVO HAVAS, 1929 (Ecology, esp. production of northern plant communities).

EERO KAAKINEN, 1947 (Sociology and ecology of grass-herb forest and bog vegetation; floristics).

UHRO MÄKIRINTA, 1934 (Sociology, ecology and taxonomy of aquatic plants).

ESTERI OHENOJA, 1937 (Taxonomy, ecology and production of larger fungi; arctic fungi).

MARTTI OHENOJA, 1933 (Taxonomy and distribution of mosses).

YRJÖ VASARI, 1930 (Quaternary palaeoecology, floristics and history of flora, taxonomy of vascular plants).

Specialization in research: Taxonomy, distribution and ecology of vascular plants and cryptogams, esp. mosses and fungi, of the arctic and boreal zones.

Associated botanic garden: Botanical Garden, University of Oulu.

Loans: To recognized botanical institutes and specialists.

Periodical and serial works: Aquilo, Ser. Botanica (Editor: Societas Amicorum Naturae Ouluensis).

Exchange: Available: Vascular plants and cryptogams mainly from Northern Finland. Desired: Specimens of all groups mainly of the arctic and boreal flora.

Remarks: Present address: Kajaanintie 42. From 1983: Linnanmaa, SF-90570 Oulu 57, Finland.

OURO PRÊTO: *Herbário, Escola de Minas, Universidade Federal de Ouro Prêto,* **(EM),** Praça Tiradentes 20, 35.400 Ouro Prêto, Minas Gerais, **Brazil.**

Telephone: (55)031/551-1119.
Foundation: 1900. *Number of specimens:* 5.020.
Herbarium: Mainly vascular plants from Ouro Prêto.

Director and Curator: CARLOS EDUARDO LISBOA, 1945 (Pharmacology).

OURO PRÊTO: *Escola de Farmácia, Universidade Federal de Ouro Prêto,* **(OUPR),** Rua Costa Sena 171, 35.400 Ouro Prêto, Minas Gerais, **Brazil.**

Telephone: (55)031/551-1154, ramal 25.
Status: Ministério da Educação e Cultura.

Foundation: 1892. *Number of specimens:* 26.000.
Herbarium: Mainly flora of Minas Gerais.
Director: José Badini.
Curators: Amélia Kassis de Oliveira Santos, 1947 (Systematics).
　Maria Aparecida Zurlo, 1948 (Systematics).
Exchange: Yes.

OVIEDO: *Departamento de Botánica, Universidad de Oviedo, Facultad de Ciencias (Sección Biológicas),* **(FCO),** Jesus Arias de Velasco s/n, Oviedo, **Spain.**
Telephone: 985-233200 ext. 152.
Status: University.
Foundation: 1968. *Number of specimens:* 5.000.
Herbarium: Vascular plants, bryophytes.
Important collections: "Bryotheca Iberica" de P. Allorge.
Director: Matias Mayor Lopez, 1939 (Phytogeography).
Curator: Tomas E. Diaz Gonzalez, 1949 (Taxonomy and phytogeography of vascular plants).
Staff members: Carmen Fernandez Ordoñez, 1949 (Bryophytes).
　Rosa M. Simó Martinez (Bryophytes).
　Esther Vignón Arvizu, 1950 (Bryosociology).
Specialization in research: Flora and vegetation of vascular plants and bryophytes.
Periodical and serial works: Trabajos del Departamento de Botánica; Notas floristicas y ecológicas.
Exchange: Periodicals.

OXFORD: *Forest Herbarium, Department of Forestry, University of Oxford,* **(FHO),** South Parks Road, Oxford OX1 3RA, England, **Great Britain.**
Status: University.
Foundation: 1924. *Number of specimens:* 155.000.
Herbarium: Worldwide, mostly woody genera.
Director: The Professor of Forest Science (ex officio).
Curator: F. White (Ebenaceae, worldwide; flora and vegetation of Africa).
Staff members: B. T. Styles (Meliaceae, tropical Pines).
Specialization in research: Monographic work on tropical woody groups; nomenclature of timber-producing species.
Associated botanic garden: Oxford Botanic Garden, High Street, Oxford.
Exchange: Available: Mainly woody plants from tropical Africa, fewer from elsewhere. Desired: Good material of genera of importance in forestry.
Remarks: Visitors should make arrangements in advance, preferably in writing.

OXFORD: *Willard Sherman Turrell Herbarium, Department of Botany, Miami University,* **(MU),** Oxford, Ohio 45056, **U.S.A.**
Telephone: 513/529-2755; 529-5321.
Foundation: 1906. *Number of specimens:* 275.000.

Herbarium: General and worldwide.
Important collections: Oberlin College herbarium (140.000; non-Ohio specimens) which includes collections of Mary Fiske Spencer (Europe), Percy Train (California, Nevada), C. G. Pringle (Mexico), F. O. Grover (New England; oaks). Collections of William Bridge Cooke (fungi), Bruce Fink (lichens and fungi), Natalie Goodall (Tierra del Fuego), George T. Jones (Ohio), Harvey A. Miller (bryophytes of Micronesia, Hawaii, Puerto Rico).
Curator: W. Hardy Eshbaugh, 1936 (Solanaceae, especially *Capsicum;* experimental plant systematics; ethnobotany).
Staff members: Will H. Blackwell, Jr., 1939 (Classical taxonomy; North American Chenopodiaceae).
　Charles Heimsch, 1914 (Systematic plant anatomy).
　Gene P. Williamson, 1915 (Field mycology).
　Thomas K. Wilson, 1931 (Comparative and systematic plant morphology; Canellaceae, Myristicaceae, and families with Ranalean affinities).
Specialization in research: Solanaceae, *Capsicum;* North American Chenopodiaceae; Canellaceae, Myristicaceae, and Ranalian families; Ohio flora; Bahamas flora.
Loans: No restrictions.
Exchange: Programs already established.

OXFORD: *Fielding-Druce Herbarium, Department of Botany, University of Oxford,* **(OXF),** Botany School, South Parks Road, Oxford OX1 3RA, England, **Great Britain.**
Status: University.
Foundation: Ancient herbaria 1621, Fielding Herbarium 1852, Druce Herbarium 1932. *Number of specimens:* 375.000 (Fielding Herbarium 250.000, Druce Herbarium 125.000).
Herbarium: Worldwide, especially British Isles, the Arctic and South America.
Important collections: Historical collections include the herbaria of: R. Morison, A. Dubois, J. Bobart, W. Sherard, J. Dillenius, J. Sibthorp. The Fielding Herbarium contains collections of J. D. Prescott, E. G. von Steudel (1836), A. H. Haworth, H. Cuming, Lobb, Heudelot, T. Kotschy, D. Douglas, T. Drummond, J. M. Moçino and M. Sessé, J. Gillies, L. Riedel, H. Ruiz & J. A. Pavon, R. Spruce (1st set), C. Sandeman (see Clokie, Herbaria in the University of Oxford, 1964).
Director: The Sherardian Professor of Botany, ex officio.
Curator: F. White (Ebenaceae, worldwide; flora and vegetation of Africa).
Staff member: C. M. Pannell (*Aglaia,* Meliaceae).
Honorary staff members: D. J. Mabberley (Meliaceae, history of taxonomy).
　R. C. Palmer (British flora).
Specialization in research: Varies according to

interests of research students.

Associated botanic garden: Oxford Botanic Garden, High Street, Oxford.

Loans: To bona fide investigators, but historic specimens (mostly pre-1800) are not normally lent.

Exchange: Programs already established.

Remarks: Visitors should make arrangements in advance, preferably in writing.

OYSTER BAY: *Herbarium, Planting Fields Arboretum,* **(OBPF),** Box 58, Oyster Bay, New York 11771, **U.S.A.**

Telephone: 516/922-9200.

Status: Administered by the Long Island State Park and Recreation Commission.

Foundation: 1960. *Number of specimens:* 9.500.

Herbarium: Vascular plants of Long Island, including native and ornamental woody plants, native and naturalized herbaceous plants.

Director: GORDON E. JONES, 1921 (Horticulture).

Curator: GRACE E. LOTOWYCZ, 1916 (Field botany of Long Island).

Staff member: CAROL JOHNSTON (Ferns, fern allies).

Associated botanic garden: Planting Fields Arboretum.

P

PACIFIC GROVE: *Gilbert M. Smith Herbarium, Hopkins Marine Station, Stanford University,* **(GMS),** Pacific Grove, California 93950, **U.S.A.**
Telephone: 408/373-0464.
Status: Part of the Department of Biological Sciences, Stanford University, a private institution.
Foundation: 1940. *Number of specimens:* 13.000.
Herbarium: Marine algae of central California.
Important collections: G. M. Smith (collections from which illustrations for "Marine Algae of the Monterey Peninsula, California" were prepared), B. M. Davis and C. P. Nott (early California collectors of algae), G. J. Hollenberg and I. A. Abbott (California algae), J. N. Norris, N. L. Nicholson.
Curator: ISABELLA A. ABBOTT.
Specialization in research: Marine biology.
Loans: Limited numbers for limited times.
Exchange: Whenever material is in excess.

PACIFIC GROVE: *Herbarium, Museum of Natural History,* **(PGM),** 165 Forest Avenue, Pacific Grove, California 93950, **U.S.A.**
Telephone: 408/372-4212.
Status: City-owned museum.
Foundation: 1881. *Number of specimens:* 2.000.
Herbarium: Taxa of Monterey County, California, and nearby areas.
Director: VERNAL L. YADON, 1930.
Loans: To qualified researchers for specified periods of time.

PADOVA: *Istituto di Botanica e Fisiologia Vegetale,* **(PAD),** Via Orto Botanico 15, 35100 Padova, **Italy.**
Telephone: 049/26922-656684.
Status: State institution.
Foundation: 1837 (General herbarium). *Number of specimens:* 218.100 (General herb.).
Herbarium: Erb. generale: Higher plants (Phanerogams and cryptogams), Italy and foreign; Erb. Mycologico "P. A. Saccardo": microscopic and macroscopic fungi, founded in 1874, 18.500 spec.; Erb. Lichenologico Zahlbruckner: coll. of lichens, donated in 1940, 3.000 spec.; Erb. Algologico of Prof. A. Forti, donated in 1937, 11.000 spec.; Cecidotheca "A. Trotter," donated by Prof. Trotter in 1910, coll. of galls, 14520 exsiccata; Erb. Fenologico "A. Marcello," donated in 1965 by Prof. A. Marcello, 4.800 exsiccata, phenological coll. (Italy and England); Coll. Muschi, 2.600 spec.; Erb. De Visiani, founded 1876, higher plants and cryptogams, plants of Dalmatia; Erb. Veneto, founded 1850, higher plants (Phanerogams and cryptogams; Venetia).
Important collections: Erb. Gen.: R. Pampanini, A. Béguinot, Fiori, F. Pfaff; erb. Myc. Baker, B. Balansa, Brenkle, G. Briosi, F. Cavara, Cooke, De Notaris, F. Petrak, E. Rehm, Rommel, P. A. Saccardo, G. Speg-

azzini, P. Sydow, Thümen; erb. Lich.: A. Zahlbruckner, C. B. Massalongo, P. Bolzon, G. Pfaff, I. Nievo, R. Solla, B. Balansa; erb. Alg.: Ardissone, Reichelet, M. G. Doria, E. Levier, Pantocsek, Orsini, N. A. Pedicino; Cecidotheca Trotter, Schutz, Dittrich, Lingelsheiù, Mülner, G. B. Traverso, Hieronymus; erb. Fen.: Marcello; coll. Muschi G. Pfaff, H. V. Harnell, R. Sterner (Scandinavian musci), Berenger, Rabenhorst (Bryotheca europaea), De Notaris; erb. De Visiani: Páncic, Freyn, Pichler, Pantocsek; erb. Veneto: Gola, Tonzig, A. G. O. Penzig, G. Pfaff, Chiamenti, Pampanini, Zenari.
Director: NELLO BAGNI.
Staff members: SERGIO CHIESA, 1930 (Systematics).
 ELISABETTA DAL COL, 1929 (Erb. De Visiani; systematics).
Specialization in research: Floristics, phenology.
Associated botanic garden: Orto Botanico.
Loans: For a short period only.
Exchange: Possible.

PALERMO: *Erbario Siculo and Erbario Generale,* **(PAL),** Via Archirafi 38 (Erb. Siculo), 90125 Palermo; Via Lincoln 2 (Erb. Gen.), 90133 Palermo, **Italy.**
Telephone: 091-236940-230493-231472.
Status: University of Palermo.
Foundation: Ca. 1860. *Number of specimens:* 82.300 (Erb. Siculo 2.300, Erb. Gen. 80.000).
Important collections: Tineo, Todaro, Macaluso, G. E. Mattei, Lanza.
Director: ANDREA DI MARTINO, 1926 (Floristics).
Curator: COSIMO MARCENO, 1939; 447206 (Geobotany, phytosociology, biosystematics).
Staff members: R. BARONE, 1950 (Diatomeae).
 SEBASTIANO CALVO, 1950 (Hydrobiology of plants).
 G. GIACCONE, 1936 (Aquatic phytobiology).
 F. MARIA RAIMONDO, 1944 (Geobotany and biosystematics).
 M. SORTINO, 1936 (Hydrobiology of plants).
Specialization in research: Geobotany, biosystematics, algology.
Associated botanic garden: Yes.
Loans: To recognized botanical institutions.
Exchange: Yes.

PALISADES: *Herbarium, Lamont-Doherty Geological Observatory of Columbia University,* **(LGO),** Palisades, New York 10964, **U.S.A.**
Telephone: 914/359-2900, ext. 229.
Status: Private institution.
Foundation: 1949. *Number of specimens:* 20.000.
Herbarium: Worldwide collection of marine plankton.
Director: MANIK TALWANI.

Curator: ALLAN BÉ (Micropaleontology).

PALMER: *Herbarium, University of Alaska Agricultural Experiment Station,* (**AES**), Box AE, Palmer, Alaska 99645, **U.S.A.**
Telephone: 907/745-3257.
Foundation: 1948. *Number of specimens:* 4.800.
Herbarium: Alaska and neighboring regions.
Director: J. V. DREW (Soil science).
Curator: WM. W. MITCHELL, 1923 (Taxonomic and ecologic research on grasses and grasslands).
Staff members: L. J. KLEBESADEL, 1928 (Taxonomy of Alaskan legumes).
J. D. MCKENDRICK, 1939 (Range plants).
R. L. TAYLOR, 1923 (Cereals and turf-grasses).
Specialization in research: Alaskan agronomy.
Loans: No special regulations.
Exchange: Available: Alaska. Desired: Boreal, subarctic, and arctic grasses.

PALMERSTON NORTH: *Herbarium, Botany and Zoology Department, Massey University,* (**MPN**), Palmerston North, **New Zealand.**
Telephone: 69-099.
Status: University.
Foundation: 1945. *Number of specimens:* 12.000.
Herbarium: New Zealand native, adventive and cultivated flora.
Important collections: E. A. Hodgson (liverworts), B. E. Molesworth (native plants).
Curator: MARGOT B. FORDE, 1935; 68-019 (Biosystematics of native flora and forage plants, plant introduction).
Staff member: ELLA CAMPBELL (Bryophytes, orchids, swamp vegetation).
Specialization in research: Ecology and taxonomy of New Zealand flora, bryophyte systematics.
Associated botanic garden: Massey University Botanic Garden.
Loans: To recognized botanical institutions.

PALMIRA: *Herbario, Facultad de Ciencias Agropecuarias, Universidad Nacional, Seccional Palmira,* (**VALLE**), Apartado Aéreo 237, Palmira, Valle, **Colombia.**
Telephone: (57)31/28121, 28122, 28123.
Foundation: 1942. *Number of specimens:* 12.671.
Herbarium: Flora del Valle del Cauca; mainly Compositae, Ericaceae, Melastomataceae, Guttiferae, Solanaceae, Moraceae, Piperaceae, Mimosaceae.
Important collections: José Cuatrecasas.
Director: EUGENIO ESCOBAR MANRIQUE, 1943.
Staff members: JAIRO ARANGO B.
GABRIEL DE LA CRUZ.
Specialization in research: Economic botany; geobotany.
Loans: Usual regulations.
Periodical and serial works: Acta Agronómica.

PANAMÁ: *Herbario, Escuela de Biología, Universidad de Panamá,* (**PMA**), Estafeta Universitaria, Panamá, **Panama.**
Telephone: 64-0582.
Foundation: 1968. *Number of specimens:* 20.000.
Herbarium: Plants of Panama, mainly angiosperms and ferns, more recently bryophytes and lichens.
Director and Curator: MIREYA D. CORREA A., 1940; 60-2605 (Taxonomy, mainly angiosperms and ferns).
Staff members: LUIS CARRASQUILLA, 1944 (Taxonomy of angiosperms).
NOVENCIDO ESCOBAR, 1917 (Taxonomy of economic plants).
CLAUDIA DE PERALTA, 1943 (Wood anatomy).
NORIS SALAZAR, 1947 (Taxonomy of bryophytes and lichens).
ALBERTO TAYLOR, 1932 (Morphology and genetics; taxonomy of Ranales, Papilionoideae, Cyperaceae, Gramineae, Palmae).
Specialization in research: Flora of Panama.
Loans: To recognized botanical institutes.
Exchange: Available: Panama. Desired: Neotropics, especially Central America and Colombia.
Remarks: Botanists collecting in Panama must leave or send duplicates of each collection made in Panama to the University of Panama.

PARAMARIBO: *National Herbarium of Suriname, Faculty of Natural Resources, University of Suriname,* (**BBS**), P.O. Box 9212, Paramaribo, **Suriname.**
Telephone: 61070.
Foundation: 1946. *Number of specimens:* 19.000.
Herbarium: Flora of Suriname; wood collection of 8.000 specimens.
Curator: MARGA C. M. WERKHOVEN, 1946.
Staff member: CORNELLY I. I. VREDEN, 1949.
Associated botanic garden: An experimental garden is being constructed for ecological and taxonomic purposes.
Loans: Usual terms, to authorized institutions.
Exchange: Duplicates sent for identification.
Remarks: Formerly Herbarium Suriname Forest Service; as of 1 January 1980, National Herbarium of Suriname.

PARANÁ: *Herbario, Museo de Ciencias Naturales y Antropológicas de Entre Ríos,* (**PAR**), Rivadavia 462, Casilla de Correo 71, 3100 Paraná, Entre Ríos, **Argentina.**
Status: Dirección de Cultura de la Secretaría de Cultura y Educación.
Foundation: 1916. *Number of specimens:* 5.500.
Herbarium: Vascular plants of Entre Ríos, San Luis, Paraguay, and France; mainly Compositae, Leguminosae, and Gramineae.
Director: OLGA J. DE BELTRÁN.
Curator: LUCÍA E. ALTAMIRANO (Leguminosae).
Staff member: JUAN M. JOZAMI (Woody plants).
Periodical and serial works: Memorias del Museo

de Entre Ríos.
Exchange: Available: Unidentified Argentina plants. Desired: Woody plants from Argentina.

PARAOPEBA: *Horto Florestal,* **(PMG)**, 35.774 Paraopeba, Minas Gerais, **Brazil.** (Information 1974)
Status: Belonging to the Department of Agriculture.
Foundation: 1951. *Number of specimens:* 6.500.
Herbarium: Flora of Minas Gerais.

PARDUBICE: *Herbarium, Východočeské museum,* **(MP)**, 531 34 Pardubice, **Czechoslovakia.** (Information 1974)
Foundation: 1927. *Number of specimens:* 55.300.
Herbarium: Plants of Czechoslovakia, especially Northeast Bohemia.
Specialization in research: Orchidaceae.
Loans: To recognized botanical institutions.

PARIS: *Muséum National d'Histoire Naturelle, Laboratoire de Phanérogamie,* **(P)**, 16 Rue de Buffon, 75005 Paris, **France.**
Telephone: 16(1) 336.47.25.
Status: Ministère des Universités.
Foundation: 1635. *Number of specimens:* 6.500.000.
Herbarium: Worldwide collection of phanerogams and vascular cryptogams, especially from Africa (N, W and equatorial), SE Asia, Europe, Guyana, Madagascar and Mascarene Islands, New Caledonia.
Important collections: J. G. Adam, M. Adanson, d'Alleizette, J. Arènes, J. M. Arvet-Touvet, E. Aubert de la Rüe, F. Aublet, H. E. Baillon, B. Balansa, T. N. Baudin, C. P. Bélanger, R. Benoist, J. Berhaut, P. Boccone, L. H. Boivin, Bon, Roland Bonaparte (pteridophytes including H. Christ), H. Bordère, J. B. G. M. Bory de St. Vincent, Bouby, E. Bourgeau, E. G. & F. A. Camus, R. Capuron, J. Cavalerie, Aug. Chevalier (P-CHEV), L. Chevallier, E. S. C. Cosson (P-CO), A. T. Danty d'Isnard, A. David, R. Decary, Delacour, P. J. M. Delavay, E. F. Deplanche, R. Desfontaines (Flora Atlantica), A. N. Desvaux, E. Didier, E. Drake del Castillo, J. F. Drège, F. Ducloux, J. S. C. Dumont d'Urville, Elias Durand (P-DU), P. A. Eberhardt, F. Evrard, P. G. Farges, U. J. Faurie, A. L. A. Fée, J. R. & G. Forster, I. Franc, A. R. Franchet, C. Gaudichaud, C. Gay, A. F. M. Glaziou, J. Goudot, R. Gombault, J. C. M. Grenier, A. Haller (P-HA), H. Humbert, F. W. H. A. Humboldt and Bonpland, G. de l'Isle, H. Jacques-Félix, V. Jacquemont, H. E. Jeanpert, A., A. L. & B. de Jussieu (P-JU), T. J. Klaine, J. B. A. P. M. de Lamarck (P-LA), A. J. Le Rat, G. M. P. C. Le Testu, Letouzey, F. L. l'Herminier, Lenormand, Leschenault, A. A. H. Léveillé, Frère Louis, J. Loureiro, MacKee, A. & F. A. Michaux, C. H. B. A. Moquin-Tandon, J. A. I. Pancher, P. E. Perrier de la Bâthie, Pételot, du Petit-Thouars, J. B. L. Pierre, Plumier, Pobéguin, Poilane, J. L. M. Poiret, F. A. Pourret, T. Puel, R. Quartin Dillon, Raynal, E. J. Rémy, A. Richard, A. Risso, J. J. Rousseau, A. de St. Hilaire, C.

Sacleux, P. A. Sagot, R. Schnell, Sonnerat, Soulier, H. Soyaux, E. Spach, J. D. Surian, L. E. Tisserant, J. P. de Tournefort, J. M. C. de Tristan, J. L. Trochain, S. Vaillant, E. Vieillard, H. A. Weddell, Zenker, H. Zollinger.
Director: Jean-F. Leroy (Flora of Madagascar, Rubiaceae, Meliaceae, primitive families, morphology and history of botany).
Honorary Director: A. Aubréville (Membre de l'Institut).
Curator: N. Hallé (Sub-director, Maître de Conférences; Orchidaceae of Pacific area, Rubiaceae of Gabon, Hippocrateaceae, botanical illustration).
Sub-director, Maître de Conférence: G. Aymonin (Thymelaeaceae, flora of Europe, history of French botany, conservation).
Staff members: F. Badré (Pteridophyta of Mascarene Islands, France).
S. Barrier (Plants of Peru).
C. Cusset (Podostemaceae, aquatic plants).
J. J. Floret (Rhizophoraceae, plants of Cameroun, Gabon, Comores).
M. Guédés (Morphology).
J. Jérémie (Monimiaceae, plants of West Indies).
M. Keddam (Palynology of Rubiaceae, Pteridophyta).
A. Raynal-Roques (Gamopetala, aquatic plants).
C. Sastre (Ochnaceae, plants of South America).
C. Tirel (Elaeocarpaceae).
J. F. Villiers (Plants of Cameroun and Gabon).
Principal Technician: J. C. Jolinon (Herbarium).
Technician: M. Chalopin (Anatomy).
Voluntary staff: L. Allorge (Apocynaceae).
P. Boiteau (Apocynaceae).
B. de Retz (*Hieracium*).
H. Jacques-Felix (Gramineae, Melastomataceae of Cameroun).
M. Kerguelen (Gramineae).
J. P. Lebrun (Dry zone of Africa, distribution maps).
O. Poncy (Leguminosae: *Inga,* Aristolochiaceae).
Honorary staff: P. Jovet.
J. Leandri.
R. Letouzey.
A. Lourteig.
H. S. Mackee.
M. L. Tardieu-Blot.
J. Vidal.

Centre National de la Recherche Scientifique (C.N.R.S.)
Maître de Recherche: H. Heine (Acanthaceae, Solanaceae, Convolvulaceae, cultivated plants).

Staff members: M. Lescot (Flacourtiaceae of New Caledonia).

D. Lobreau-Callen (Palynology, especially Celastrales).

G. Maury-Lechon (Dipterocarpaceae).

H. D. Schotsman (*Callitriche*).

Ecole Pratique des Hautes Etudes (E.P.H.E.)
Directeur-Adjoint: A. le Thomas (Annonaceae, palynology).

Office de la Recherche Scientifique et Technique d'Outre Mer (O.R.S.T.O.M.)
Directeur de Recherche: J. Bosser (Gramineae, Orchidaceae of Madagascar and Mascarene Islands).

Staff members: F. Friedmann (Plants of Mascarene Islands).

J. Mouton (Documentation, flora of Guyana).

M. Peltier (Leguminosae of Madagascar).

M. Schmid (Inspecteur; plants of New Caledonia and New Hebrides).

Y. Veyret (Orchidaceae of Guyana).

Loans: To recognized botanical institutions.

Periodical and serial works: Adansonia, ser. 2 (since 1961), Flore du Cambodge, Laos, Vietnam (1960), Flore du Cameroun (1963), Flore du Gabon (1961), Flore de Madagascar et des Comores (1936), Flore de la Nouvelle-Calédonie et Dépendances (1967).

Exchange: Limited.

PARIS: *Laboratoire d'Ethnobotanique, Museum National d'Histoire Naturelle,* (**PAT**), 57 Rue Cuvier, 75005 Paris, **France.**

PARIS: *Muséum National d'Histoire Naturelle, Laboratoire de Cryptogamie,* (**PC**), 12 Rue de Buffon, 75005 Paris, **France.**
Telephone: 331 3521; 331 9511.
Status: Ministère de l'Education Nationale.
Foundation: 1904. *Number of specimens:* 4.000.000.
Herbarium: Cryptogams: Algae, lichens, bryophytes; living cultures of Desmidiaceae, Chlorophyceae and *Penicillium.*
Important collections: M. Bizot, R. Bonaparte, J. B. E. Bornet, E. G. & F. A. Camus, J. Cardot, P. A. Hariot, A. M. Hue, J. P. F. C. Montagne, R. Potier de la Várde, L. Quélet, C. F. Sauvageau, M. H. I. Thériot, G. A. Thuret, C. & E. L. R. Tulasne.
Director: Suzanne Jovet, 1914 (Bryology).
Staff members: Françoise Ardre, 1931 (Algology).

Raymond Baudoin, 1947 (Bryology).
Roger Cailleux, 1929 (Mycology).
Alain Coute, 1939 (Algology).
Pierre Fusey, 1921 (Protection of materials).
Jean Mouchacca, 1939 (Mycology).
Jacqueline Nicot, 1916 (Mycology).
Michel Ricard, 1943 (Diatoms).
Marie-France Roquebert, 1940 (Mycology).

Specialization in research: Taxonomy systematics, ecology, cytology, ultrastructure; biodegradation of carbohydrates; phytopathology.
Loans: To recognized institutions and specialists, except specimens of herb. Montagne and herb. Thuret-Bornet.
Periodical and serial works: Revue Bryologique et Lichénologique, Revue de Mycologie, Revue Algologique.
Exchange: Yes, especially those groups studied by the members of the institute.

PARIS: *Muséum National d'Histoire Naturelle, Laboratoire de Biologie Végétale Appliquée,* (**PCU**), 61 Rue de Buffon, 75005 Paris, **France.**
Telephone: 331 52 71.
Status: Ministère des Universités (Educ. Nat.).
Foundation: 1793. *Number of specimens:* 9.000.
Herbarium: Cultivated vascular plants.
Director: J. L. Hamel, 1916 (Caryology).
Staff members: M. T. Cerceau, 1930 (Palynology).

C. Fuchs, 1932 (Morphology).
B. Moussel, 1933 (Cytology of sexual reproduction).
J. M. Turmel, 1920 (Ecology).

PARMA: *Herbarium, Istituto Botanico dell'Università,* (**PARMA**), Parma, **Italy.** (Information 1974)
Foundation: 1770.
Herbarium: General, including cryptogams.
Important collections: Herb. G. Passerini.

PASADENA: *Herbarium, Department of Life Sciences, Pasadena City College,* (**PASA**), 1570 East Colorado Boulevard, Pasadena, California 91106, **U.S.A.**
Telephone: 213/578-7461.
Number of specimens: 2.700.
Herbarium: Vascular plants of southern California; algae from Monterey southward.
Staff member: Ila M. Dennis.

PASTO: *Herbario, Facultad de Ciencias Agricolas, Universidad de Nariño,* (**PSO**), Ciudad Universitaria Torobajo, Apartado Aéreo 505, Pasto, Nariño, **Colombia.**
Telephone: (57)58-50; 22-89.
Foundation: 1962. *Number of specimens:* 9.300.
Herbarium: Flora of Colombia, especially Nariño, Putumayo, bajo Magdalena.
Important collections: Luis Eduardo Mora O.; Rubiaceae, Ericaceae, Leguminosae, Gramineae, Gesneriaceae, Melastomataceae, Compositae, Clusiaceae.
Director: Olga Salazar de Benavides, 1944 (Flora of Nariño; *Lupinus*).
Curator: Jorge Riascos, 1932 (Solanaceae).
Staff members: Jaime Rosero, 1943 (Flora of Colombia).

Gerardo López J., 1943 (Weeds from warm and cold areas).

Specialization in research: Study of the flora of the Costa Pacífica in relation to the flora of the Chocó; dispersal of *Bombacopsis.*
   Associated botanic garden: Yes.
   Loans: Usual regulations.
   Exchange: Yes.

PASURUAN: *Java Sugar Experimental Station,* **(PAS)**, Pasuruan, Java, **Indonesia** – – deposited on permanent loan at BO.

PATIALA: *Herbarium, Department of Botany, Punjabi University,* **(PUN)**, Patiala – 147002, **India.**
   Telephone: 3261, 3262, 3263, 3264, Ext. 22.
   Status: University.
   Foundation: 1967. *Number of specimens:* 28.500 (25.000 phanerogams, 3.500 pteridophytes).
   Herbarium: Flowering plants of Punjab Plains and Western Himalayas, pteridophytes of India.
   Important collections: Types of *Lepisorus* and voucher specimens for chromosome counts.
   Director: S. S. BIR, 1929 (Cytogenetics, morphology, anatomy, ecology, biosystematics, floristics and taxonomy of pteridophytes and flowering plants).
   Curator: M. SHARMA, 1940 (Taxonomy of angiosperms).
   Specialization in research: Morphological and cytotaxonomical studies in ferns, fern allies and angiosperms.
   Associated botanic garden: Botanic Gardens, Punjabi University.
   Loans: To recognized institutions.
   Exchange: Yes.

PATRAS: *Botanical Institute and Botanical Museum of the University of Patras,* **(UPA)**, Patras, **Greece.** (Information 1974)
   Status: University.
   Foundation: 1967. *Number of specimens:* 40.000.
   Herbarium: Mainly Mediterranean plants.
   Specialization in research: Flora of Greece.
   Loans: To recognized botanical institutions.

PAVIA: *Botanical Institute, The University,* **(PAV)**, P.O. Box 99, 27100 – Pavia, **Italy.** (Information 1974)
   Status: Government institute.
   Foundation: 1780. *Number of specimens:* 160.000.
   Herbarium: General herbarium phanerogams and fungi, mosses and lichens of Europe, plants of Italy, especially Lombardy.
   Specialization in research: Phytosociology, phytopathology, mycology, histochemistry.
   Associated botanic garden: Orto Botanico Università di Pavia.
   Loans: To recognized botanical institutions.
   Periodical and serial works: Atti Istituto Botanico Laboratorio Crittogamico Università Pavia, Archivo Botanico e Biogeografico Italiano.

PÉCS: *Department of Botany, Museum of Natural History,* **(PECS)**, Rák-czi ut 34, Pécs, **Hungary.** (Information 1974).
   Status: Directed by Comitat Baranya.
   Foundation: 1947. *Number of specimens:* 20.000.
   Herbarium: Flora of mountain Mecsek (South Hungary); anthophyta, fungi, musci.
   Specialization in research: Flora of mountain Mecsek.
   Loans: To recognized botanical institutions.
   Periodical and serial works: Yearbook.

PEKING (Beijing): *Herbarium, Fan Memorial Institute of Biology,* **(FM)**, Beijing, **People's Republic of China** – – *see* PE.

PEKING (Beijing): *Herbarium, Institute of Botany, Academia Sinica,* **(PE)**, Beijing, **People's Republic of China.**
   Status: Directed by Academia Sinica.
   Foundation: 1950, by the amalgamation of the Institute of Botany, Academy of Peking, the Fan Memorial Institute of Biology and the Institute of Botany, Academia Sinica of old China. *Number of specimens:* 1.200.000.
   Herbarium: Mainly Chinese flora.
   Director of Institute: TANG B. S.
   Staff members: CHEN SING-CHI (Liliaceae, Orchidaceae).
      CHEN T. R. (Urticaceae).
      CHEN YI-LING (Balsaminaceae, Compositae).
      CHIANG WAN-FU (Rosaceae).
      CHING REN-CHANG (Pteridophytes).
      DAI LUN-KAI (Cyperaceae).
      FU LI-KUO (Gymnosperms).
      HONG DE-YUANG (Commelinaceae, Compositae).
      KU TSUE-CHIH (Rosaceae).
      KUAN K'E-CHIEN (Rosaceae, Cruciferae).
      KUANG KO-ZEN (Solanaceae).
      LANG KAI-YUNG (Liliaceae).
      LI AN-JEN (Polygalaceae).
      LI P. C. (Juglandaceae).
      LING YONG (Compositae).
      LU AN-MING (Juglandaceae, Solanaceae).
      LU LING-TI (Rosaceae).
      SHIH CHU (Compositae).
      TANG TSIN (Cyperaceae, Liliaceae, Orchidaceae).
      TSI ZHAN-HUO (Stemonaceae).
      TSIEN CHO-PO (Polygonaceae).
      TSOONG PU-CHIU (Scrophulariaceae).
      WANG FA-TSUAN (Cyperaceae, Smilacaceae, Liliaceae, Orchidaceae).
      WANG WEN-TS'AI (Ranunculaceae, Labiatae, Urticaceae).
      WU PAN-CHEN (Bryophytes).
      YING TSUN-SHEN (Berberidaceae).
      YÜ TE-TSUN (Rosaceae).
   Specialization in research: Flora of China, plant

resources of China.

Associated botanic gardens: The Botanic Garden of Beijing; Sun Yatsen Botanic Garden, Nanjing; Lushan Botanic Garden, Jiangxi; Botanic Garden of Kunming, Yunnan.

Loans: To recognized botanical institutions.

Periodical and serial works: Acta Phytotaxonomica Sinica, Handbook of Chinese Flora, Manual of Economic Plants.

Exchange: Available: Chinese plants. Desired: Specimens from all over the world.

PEKING (BEIJING): *Herbarium, Department of Botany, Beijing Medical College,* **(PEM),** Beijing, **People's Republic of China.**

Telephone: 277-601, ext. 559.

Status: College.

Foundation: 1943. *Number of specimens:* 15.000.

Herbarium: Seed plants of China.

Director: CHING-YUNG JOYCE CHENG, 1919 (Taxonomy of Celastraceae and traditional Chinese drug plants).

Curator: TSUO-CHING KAO, 1926 (Taxonomy of *Rheum, Celastrus, Microtropis*).

Staff member: DUO-XIAN TIAN, 1935 (cytogenetics, especially *Asarum*).

Specialization in research: Taxonomy and cytology of seed plants, drug plants.

Associated botanic garden: Botanic Garden of Beijing Medical College (for teaching).

Loans: To recognized botanical institutions.

Exchange: Available: Chinese phanerogams. Desired: Ephedraceae, Aristolochiaceae, Celastraceae, Valerianaceae and *Rheum; Trichosanthes,* especially from India and Indochina.

PEKING (Beijing): *Herbarium, National University of Peking Teachers College,* **(PET),** Beijing, **People's Republic of China** -- *see* PE.

PEKING (Beijing): *Herbarium, Yenching University,* **(PEY),** Beijing, **People's Republic of China** -- *see* PE.

PELLSTON: *Herbarium, University of Michigan Biological Station,* **(UMBS),** Pellston, Michigan 49769, **U.S.A.** (Postal address formerly Cheboygan).

Telephone: 616/539-8406 (summer only).

Status: The Biological Station is a department of the University of Michigan.

Foundation: 1909. *Number of specimens:* 16.500 (9.935 vascular plants; 6.500 bryophytes, lichens).

Herbarium: Flora of northern Michigan (bryophytes, lichens, and vascular plants only).

Director: DAVID M. GATES, 1921.

Curators: HOWARD CRUM, 1922 (Bryophytes, lichens).

EDWARD G. VOSS, 1929 (Vascular plants).

Specialization in research: Taxonomic, phytogeographical, and ecological problems in the Great Lakes region.

Loans: By special arrangement; normally only in the summer.

Remarks: Consultation possible mid-June to mid-August; at other times only by special arrangement.

PELOTAS: *Herbário, Departamento de Botânica, Instituto de Biologia, Universidade Federal de Pelotas,* **(PEL),** 96.100 Pelotas, Rio Grande do Sul, **Brazil.**

Telephone: (55)0532/210933, ramal 280.

Status: Convênio EMBRAPA/Universidade Federal de Pelotas.

Foundation: 1946. *Number of specimens:* 12.000.

Herbarium: Southern Brazil.

Important collections: Irmão Teodoro Luiz, Jason R. Swallen, Emilia Santos, Elza Fromm Trinta; Passifloraceae, Gramineae.

Director: JOSÉ DA COSTA SACCO, 1930 (Passifloraceae).

Curator: EDEGAR CARDOSO DOS SANTOS, 1933 (Southern Brazil weeds).

Staff members: CELSO MAIA CARVALHAL, 1953 (Southern Brazil forests).

ZULMAR MORAES, 1930 (Southern Brazil weeds).

Specialization in research: Taxonomy of Passifloraceae; weeds; southern Brazil flora.

Associated botanic garden: Horto Botânico Irmão Teodoro Luiz.

Loans: In general to recognized botanical institutes.

Exchange: Available: Southern Brazil flora. Desired: Weeds in general; Passifloraceae.

PENSACOLA: *Herbarium, Building 58, Department of Biology, University of West Florida,* **(UWFP),** Pensacola, Florida 32504, **U.S.A.**

Telephone: 904/476-9500, ext. 283.

Status: State university.

Foundation: 1974. *Number of specimens:* 5.000.

Herbarium: Vascular plants of Escambia County, Florida, and contiguous counties; small collections of bryophytes and macroscopic algae; excellent collections of ferns and fern allies.

Important collections: James R. Burkhalter, Bruce Hansen, John B. Nelson.

Director: MICHAEL I. COUSENS, 1943 (Pteridology, bryology).

Specialization in research: Vascular flora of local geographic area.

Loans: Usual regulations.

Exchange: No active program at this time.

PENZA: *Herbarium, V. G. Belinsk Pedagogical Institute of Penza,* **(PKM),** Lermontova St. 37, 440602 Penza, **U.S.S.R.**

Foundation: 1894. *Number of specimens:* 85.000.

Herbarium: Mainly plants of the middle Volga, Penza and adjacent areas.

Director and Curator: A. A. SOLYANOV.

PERADENIYA: *National Herbarium, Division of Systematic Botany, Royal Botanic Gardens,* **(PDA),** Peradeniya, **Sri Lanka.**
Telephone: 08/8053.
Status: Department of Agriculture.
Foundation: 1817. *Number of specimens:* 100.000.
Herbarium: Mainly plants of Ceylon.
Important collections: Thwaites, Trimen, Willis, Amaratunga, Smithsonian collection (1968–1979).
Keeper: K. D. L. AMARATUNGA (Marsh flora, weeds).
Staff member: A. H. M. JAYASURIYA (Ecology, Begoniaceae).
Specialization in research: Flora of Ceylon.
Associated botanic garden: Royal Botanic Gardens.
Loans: No.

PERM: *Department of Botany, A. M. Gorky University of Perm,* **(PERM),** Bukireva 15, Building 2, 614005 Perm, **U.S.S.R.**
Foundation: 1927. *Number of specimens:* 50.000.
Director: A. N. PONOMAREV.

PERTH: *Herbarium, City Museum,* **(PER),** Perth, Scotland, **Great Britain.**

PERTH: *Western Australian Herbarium,* **(PERTH),** Department of Agriculture, George Street, South Perth, Western Australia 6151, **Australia.**
Telephone: (09) 3670111.
Status: Branch of Western Australian State Department of Agriculture.
Foundation: 1929. *Number of specimens:* 200.000.
Herbarium: Vascular plants, algae, bryophytes and lichens of Western Australia.
Important collections: C. A. Gardner, R. D. Royce, C. R. P. Andrews, W. E. Blackall, W. V. Fitzgerald, B. T. Goadby (Orchids), A. Morrison.
Director and Curator: JOHN W. GREEN, 1930 (Myrtaceae).
Staff members: THEODORE E. H. APLIN, 1927 (Economic botany, toxic plants).
ALEX S. GEORGE, 1939 (Orchidaceae, Proteaceae, arid flora).
ROGER J. HNATIUK, 1946 (Ecology, *Eremaea, Melaleuca*).
KEVIN F. KENNEALLY, 1945 (Tropical flora, mangroves).
NICHOLAS S. LANDER, 1948 (General flora, Asteraceae).
NEVILLE G. MARCHANT, 1939 (Myrtaceae, *Drosera, Xyris*).
BRUCE R. MASLIN, 1946 (*Acacia*).
GILLIAN PERRY, 1943 (*Logania*, naturalized flora).
PAUL G. WILSON, 1928 (Chenopodiaceae, Asteraceae, Rutaceae).
Specialization in research: Taxonomy, floristics, phytogeography and ecology of Western Aus-

tralian flora.
Loans: In general to recognized taxonomic institutions.
Periodical and serial works: Nuytsia; Western Australian Herbarium Research Notes.
Exchange: Western Australian flora.

PERTH: *Herbarium, Perth Museum and Art Gallery,* **(PTH),** George Street, Perth, Tayside, Scotland, **Great Britain.**
Telephone: 0738/32488.
Status: Financed by District Council.
Foundation: Links with 1784, first Natural History Museum 1881, present site 1934. *Number of specimens:* 25.000.
Herbarium: Mainly Perthshire and Scotland, smaller European and worldwide collections of flowering plants, also mosses, lichens, ferns and fungi.
Important collections: Perthshire herbarium (ex Perthshire Society of Natural Sciences), Francis Buchanan White, John Hutton Balfour, H. M. Drummond-Hay, A. Sturrock, Wm. Barclay, A. W. Brown, Francis Isaiah White, R. H. Meldrum.
Director: J. A. BLAIR.
Curator: M. A. TAYLOR, 1953.
Loans: By application to the Keeper of Natural Sciences.

PERTH: *Herbarium, University of Western Australia,* **(UWA)** – – *see* NEDLANDS.

PERUGIA: *Herbarium, Istituto Interfacoltà di Botanica dell'Università,* **(PERU),** 74 Borgo XX Giugno, 06100 Perugia, **Italy.**
Telephone: 075-30628.
Status: University of Perugia.
Foundation: 1896. *Number of specimens:* 25.000.
Herbarium: Vascular plants, mainly Umbria.
Important collections: Herbarium Andrea Batelli.
Director of Institute: LUIGI DE CAPITE, 1921 (Plant anatomy, physiology).
Curator: RODOLFO E. G. PICHI SERMOLLI, 1912 (Phylogeny and taxonomy of Pteridophyta, especially tropical Africa, flora and vegetation of Ethiopia and Somalia, plant geography).
Staff members: MARIO PAOLA BIZZARRI, 1937 (Taxonomy of African *Selaginella*).
MAURO ROBERTO CAGIOTTI, 1946 (Flora of Umbria).
PAOLA GAUDENZIO, 1947 (Flora of Ethiopia and Somalia).
ALESSANDRO MENGHINI, 1941 (Flora of Umbria, medicinal plants).
GIANFRANCO MINCIGRUCCI, 1945 (Flora of Umbria).
Specialization in research: Flora of Umbria and contiguous regions, taxonomy and nomenclature of Pteridophyta.
Associated botanic garden: Orto Botanico dell'Università, San Costanzo, 06100 Perugia.

Loans: To recognized botanical institutions.

PESHAWAR: *Herbarium, Islamia College,* (**ICP**), Peshawar, **Pakistan.**

PESHAWAR: *Herbarium, Pakistan Council of Scientific and Industrial Research,* (**PES**), P.O. Peshawar University, Peshawar, **Pakistan.** (Information 1974)
Status: Government.
Foundation: 1958. *Number of specimens:* 25.000.
Herbarium: Vascular plants of Pakistan.
Specialization in research: Flora of Pakistan, Kashmir and Western Himalayas.
Loans: To recognized botanical institutions.
Periodical and serial works: Sultania.

PESHAWAR: *Herbarium, Pakistan Forest Institute,* (**PPFI**), Peshawar, **Pakistan.** (Information 1974)
Status: Forest Institute.
Foundation: 1947. *Number of specimens:* 20.000.
Herbarium: Pakistan and adjacent areas.
Specialization in research: Phytosociology and taxonomy of higher plants.
Loans: To recognized botanical institutions.
Periodical and serial works: Pakistan Journal of Forestry, Flora of Peshawar District and Khyber Agency, Flora of Malakand Division.

PESHAWAR: *Herbarium, Botany Department, Peshawar University,* (**PUP**), Peshawar, **Pakistan.**
Telephone: 8318.
Status: University.
Foundation: 1952. *Number of specimens:* 40.000.
Herbarium: Plants of Pakistan.
Director: ISLAM M. KHAN, 1935.
Curator: GHAZALA ANJUM.
Specialization in research: Flora of Pakistan.
Associated botanic garden: University Garden.

PETERBOROUGH: *Herbarium, Biology Department, Trent University,* (**TUP**), Peterborough, Ontario, **Canada** K9J 7B8.
Telephone: 705/748-1424.
Foundation: 1966. *Number of specimens:* 2.000.
Herbarium: Plants of Ontario.
Curator: ROGER JONES, 1940; 705/748-1556.

PETERSBURG: *Herbarium, Department of Life Sciences, Virginia State University,* (**VSUH**), Petersburg, Virginia 23803, **U.S.A.**
Telephone: 804/520-6122.
Foundation: 1980. *Number of specimens:* 4.300.
Herbarium: Mostly Virginia plants, especially from the surrounding counties.
Director and Curator: SHAUKAT M. SIDDIQI, 1936 (North American *Juncus*).
Specialization in research: Local floristics; *Juncus* in North America.

PETROZAVODSK: *Herbarium, O. V. Kuusinen*

State University, (**PZV**), Lenin Street 39, Petrozavodsk, **U.S.S.R.** (Information 1974)
Status: Directed by the state.
Foundation: 1947. *Number of specimens:* 800.
Herbarium: Local flora.
Associated botanic garden: Botanical Garden of O. V. Kuusinen State University.

PHILADELPHIA: *Herbarium, Morris Arboretum, University of Pennsylvania,* (**MOAR**), 9414 Meadowbrook Avenue, Philadelphia, Pennsylvania 19118, **U.S.A.**
Foundation: 1933. *Number of specimens:* 45.000.
Herbarium: Woody plants of northern temperate regions.
Director: WILLIAM M. KLEIN.
Staff member: ANN F. RHOADS (Plant pathology).
Specialization in research: Woody flora of temperate regions.
Loans: Standard regulations.
Periodical and serial works: Morris Arboretum Newsletter.
Exchange: Yes.

PHILADELPHIA: *Herbarium, University of Pennsylvania,* (**PENN**), Philadelphia, Pennsylvania 19118, **U.S.A.** -- incorporated in PH.
Foundation: 1892. *Number of specimens:* 250.000.
Herbarium: State of Pennsylvania and Atlantic Coastal Plain of North America.

PHILADELPHIA: *Herbarium, Academy of Natural Sciences of Philadelphia,* (**PH**), 19th and the Parkway, Philadelphia, Pennsylvania 19103, **U.S.A.**
Telephone: 215/299-1192; 299-1193.
Status: Private museum.
Foundation: 1812. *Number of specimens:* 2.000.000, including diatoms.
Herbarium: Earliest major herbarium in North America, with major strength from 1780, worldwide collections as early as 1689.
Important collections: General worldwide; herbaria of Henry Muhlenberg (1753–1815), Benjamin Smith Barton (1766–1815), Thomas Nuttall (deposited before 1835), Louis David von Schweinitz (1780–1834), William Baldwin (1779–1819), Charles W. Short (1794–1863), T. C. Porter, A. B. Lambert (fragment, including F. Pursh types), Edgar T. Wherry (*Phlox*), Philadelphia Botanical Club (1780-present), Vascular Flora of Pennsylvania, University of Pennsylvania (PENN), Francis Wolle (cryptogams), T. Eckfeldt (lichens).
Director and Curator: JAMES A. MEARS, 1944 (*Parthenium* [Asteraceae], Amaranthaceae; taxonomy, chemotaxonomy).
Staff members: FRANCIS DROUET, 1907 (Blue-green algae).
HEINZ KOERNER, 1942 (Diatoms).
RUTH PATRICK, 1907 (Diatoms; aquatic ecol.).

CHARLES REIMER, 1926 (Diatoms).
ALFRED E. SCHUYLER, 1935 (Cyperaceae).
Specialization in research: Plant systematics and ecology.

Loans: To recognized institutional herbaria; inquire regarding diatoms.

Periodical and serial works: Proceedings of the Academy of Natural Sciences; Bartonia; Notulae Naturae.

Exchange: Generally limited to regions of special interest (Pennsylvania, New Jersey, Mexico, western South America) and families of interest (Amaranthaceae, Cyperaceae, Polemoniaceae, Scrophulariaceae, pteridophytes).

Remarks: Limited funds available to bring qualified students to Philadelphia to study specific collections.

PHILADELPHIA: *Herbarium, Department of Biology, Philadelphia College of Pharmacy and Science,* (**PHIL**), 43rd Street, and Kingsessing and Woodland avenues, Philadelphia, Pennsylvania 19104, **U.S.A.** – – transferred to NA.

Foundation: 1821; Martindale herbarium presented 1894.

Herbarium: Worldwide, with emphasis on local and U.S. flora.

Important collections: I. C. Martindale herbarium.

PHOENIX: *Herbarium, Desert Botanical Garden,* (**DES**), Papago Park, P.O. Box 5415, Phoenix, Arizona 85010, **U.S.A.**

Telephone: 602/941-1217.

Status: Private institution.

Foundation: 1937; 1950 (Herbarium). *Number of specimens:* 38.000.

Herbarium: Desert vegetation of southwestern U.S. and Mexico.

Important collections: H. S. Gentry (Mexico, southwestern U.S.; Agavaceae; 200 types), G. B. Hinton (Mexico; 12 types), R. E. Collom (Arizona), J. H. Lehr (Arizona; *Carex*).

Director: CHARLES A. HUCKINS, 1941 (Systematics of Maloideae).

Curator: J. HARRY LEHR, 1901 (*Carex*).

Staff member: HOWARD SCOTT GENTRY, 1903 (Systematics of *Agave*; economic plants).

Specialization in research: Desert vegetation; cacti and other succulents; economic plants for arid regions.

Loans: To recognized botanical institutions.

Periodical and serial works: Saguaroland Bulletin.

Exchange: Available: Desert specimens from Arizona; *Carex* from U.S. Desired: Specimens from desert regions of the world; *Carex* (cosmopolitan).

PIETERMARITZBURG: *Herbarium, Department of Botany, University of Natal,* (**NU**), P.O. Box 375,

Pietermaritzburg 3200, Natal, **South Africa.**

Telephone: 0331-63320.

Status: University.

Foundation: 1910. *Number of specimens:* 77.000.

Herbarium: Mainly flora of Natal and nearby.

Director: R. N. PIENAAR, 1942 (Phytoplankton and nanoplankton taxonomy; developmental studies on scale-bearing nanoplankton).

Curator: O. M. HILLIARD, 1925 (Flora of Natal, flowering plants).

Staff member: J. STEWART (Orchidaceae, Asclepiadaceae).

Specialization in research: Flora of Natal.

Loans: To recognized botanical institutions.

PINAWA: *Herbarium, Whiteshell Nuclear Research Establishment,* (**WNRE**), Pinawa, Manitoba, **Canada** ROE 1Lo.

Telephone: 204/753-2311.

Status: Atomic Energy of Canada, Ltd., Crown corporation, research establishment.

Foundation: 1967. *Number of specimens:* 17.000.

Important collections: Worldwide *Betula*; irradiated plants (from FIG area).

Director and Curator: JANET R. DUGLE, 1934 (*Betula, Picea, Rosa;* radiation ecology, especially of trees and shrubs).

Staff member: P. ANNE SMITH.

PINCKNEY: *Herbarium, Edwin S. George Reserve, University of Michigan,* (**MGR**), 9250 Kelly Road, Pinckney, Michigan 48169, **U.S.A.**

Telephone: 313/878-6643.

Status: Administered by the Museum of Zoology, University of Michigan, Ann Arbor.

Foundation: 1946. *Number of specimens:* 1.000.

Herbarium: Restricted to local flora.

Loans: No.

Remarks: Used for reference by local research workers in natural history and ecology.

PINEVILLE: *Herbarium, Range Management Research, Southern Forest Experiment Station, U.S. Forest Service,* (**SFRP**), 2500 Shreveport Highway, Pineville, Louisiana 71360, **U.S.A.**

Telephone: 318/445-6511, ext. 373.

Status: U.S. Department of Agriculture, Forest Service.

Foundation: 1955. *Number of specimens:* 3.600.

Herbarium: Flowering plants, especially Gramineae, Cyperaceae, and Juncaceae, of southeastern U.S.

Director: HAROLD E. GRELEN, 1929 (Applied range management research).

Specialization in research: Primarily forage value, phenology, and botanical composition as related to range research.

Loans: Normal regulations.

Exchange: Within the southeastern region.

PIRACICABA: Herbário, Escola Superior de Agricultura "Luiz de Queiroz," Departamento de Botânica, Universidade de São Paulo, **(ESA)**, Caixa Postal 9, 13.400 Piracicaba, São Paulo, **Brazil.**

Telephone: (55)33-0011.

Foundation: 1922. Number of specimens: 2.500.

Herbarium: Flora of Piracicaba.

Director and Curator: LUIZ ANTONIO ROCHELLE, 1935 (Systematics).

Specialization in research: Cucurbitaceae; systematics and biology.

Exchange: Yes.

PISA: Herbarium Horti Pisani, **(PI)**, Via L. Ghini 5, I-56100 Pisa, **Italy.**

Telephone: 050/23027 or 050/500825.

Status: Adherence to Botanical Institute and Garden, University of Pisa.

Foundation: Circa 1840. Number of specimens: 300.000.

Herbarium: Separate collections of flowering plants and cryptogamic plants, worldwide, especially Italy.

Important collections: Flowering plants: General herbarium (Flora of the world with collections of C. F. P. von Martius, Mendon, P. E. Boissier (Spain), P. Savi, etc.); H. T. Caruel PI-CAR (mainly flora of Tuscany); H. G. Arcangeli PI-ARC (Flora of Italy); H. G. Passerini PI-PASS (Flora of Tuscany); H. Pellegrini PI-PELL (Flora of Italy, mainly of Apuan Alps); H. Cittadella PI-CITT (Flora of Lucca's country – Tuscany); H. M. Guadagno PI-GUAD (Flora of Southern Italy and Mediterranean countries, many specimens exchanged from Northern and Central Europe). Cryptogamic plants: General herbarium (with G. Raddi's types); H. A. Bottini PI-BOTT (Musci from Italy; types of Bottini, Röell, Warnstorff); H. F. A. Artaria PI-ART (Musci from Italy).

Director: PAOLO MELETTI, 1927 (Seed physiology, ecophysiology).

Curator: CARLO DEL PRETE, 1949 (European and Mediterranean Orchids, orophylous plants from Europe).

Staff members: G. CELA, 1931 (Cytotaxonomy of Centaurea, aliens).

G. CORSI, 1936 (Experimental embryology, pharmaceutical plants).

F. GARBARI, 1937 (Biosystematics of Liliales, cytotaxonomy of endemics).

G. MONTI, 1941 (Mycology, Italian mushrooms).

P. E. TOMEI, 1947 (Phytogeography, especially marshes and bogs).

Specialization in research: Taxonomy, cytotaxonomy and chorology of Orchidaceae, Liliales, Asteraceae; Italian endemics; Mediterranean entities and Apennines vegetation.

Associated botanic garden: Orto Botanico dell'Università di Pisa.

Loans: To official institutions for three months.

Periodical and serial works: Acta Horti Pisani (a collection of reprints, published by staff of the Botanical Institute).

Exchange: Only "Acta Horti Pisani," on request from official institutions.

PITTSBURG: Theodore M. Sperry Herbarium, Department of Biology, Pittsburg State University, **(KSP)**, 1701 S. Broadway, Pittsburg, Kansas 66762, **U.S.A.**

Telephone: 316/231-7000, ext. 253 or 221.

Foundation: 1946. Number of specimens: 25.000.

Herbarium: Primarily vascular plants of southeastern Kansas; comparative specimens from central Africa, Europe, and South America.

Director: RALPH W. KELTING, 1918 (General taxonomy of vascular plants; histology).

Curator: THEODORE M. SPERRY, 1907 (General taxonomy of vascular plants; ecology).

Loans: Upon request for three months.

PITTSBURGH: Herbarium, Carnegie Museum of Natural History, **(CM)**, 4400 Forbes Avenue, Pittsburgh, Pennsylvania 15213, **U.S.A.**

Telephone: 412/622-3253.

Status: Carnegie Institute, a private foundation.

Foundation: 1895. Number of specimens: 567.000 (500.000 vascular plants; 18.000 bryophytes; 35.000 fungi; 14.000 lichens).

Herbarium: Worldwide, with greatest strength in eastern North America.

Important collections: I. W. Clokey, A. H. Curtiss, J. Drummond, A. D. E. Elmer (Borneo), E. H. Graham (Uinta Basin, U.S.A.; British Guiana), H. M. Hall, O. E. Jennings (Ontario; Cuba), J. G. Lemmon (southwestern U.S.A.), E. Palmer (southwestern U.S.A.; Mexico), S. B. Parish, C. C. Parry, C. G. Pringle (southwestern U.S.A.; Mexico), H. H. Rusby, J. A. Shafer (Cuba), C. W. Short, H. H. Smith (Colombia), J. Wolle (herbarium), C. Wright, C. B. S. Zeyher.

Director: CRAIG C. BLACK, 1932 (Vertebrate paleontology; museology).

Curator: FREDERICK H. UTECH, 1943; 412/622-3246 (Angiosperm taxonomy; Liliaceae).

Staff members: DAVID E. BOUFFORD, 1941 (Angiosperm taxonomy).

EMILY W. WOOD, 1949 (Angiosperm taxonomy).

Adjunct staff (from Hunt Institute): A. F. GÜNTHER BUCHHEIM, 1924 (Botanical nomenclature and bibliography).

T. D. JACOBSEN, 1950 (Angiosperm taxonomy; Allium).

ROBERT W. KIGER, 1940 (Angiosperm taxonomy; Flacourtiaceae; Talinum; history of botany).

MICHAEL T. STIEBER, 1943 (Angiosperm taxonomy; Agrostology; Ichnanthus; botanical biography).

JAMES J. WHITE, 1941 (Botanical art and illustration).
Specialization in research: Floristics and biosystematics of Appalachian and related floras -- eastern Asia, Europe and western North America.
Associated botanic garden: Powdermill Nature Reserve, Star Route South, Rector, Pennsylvania 15677, **U.S.A.**
Loans: To recognized botanical institutions.
Periodical and serial works: Annals of Carnegie Museum of Natural History; Bulletin of Carnegie Museum of Natural History.
Exchange: Available: Eastern North America and Appalachian region. Desired: All North Temperate.
Remarks: Cooperative affiliation with Hunt Institute for Botanical Documentation, Carnegie-Mellon University, Pittsburgh, Pennsylvania 15213, U.S.A.

PLACERVILLE: *Herbarium, Institute of Forest Genetics, Pacific Southwest Forest and Range Experiment Station,* **(IFGP)**, 2480 Carson Road, Placerville, California 95667, **U.S.A.**
Status: U.S. Department of Agriculture, Forest Service.
Foundation: 1925. *Number of specimens:* 10.000.
Herbarium: Emphasis on *Pinus* and *Abies.*
Curator: W. B. CRITCHFIELD.
Specialization in research: Species hybridization in *Pinus* and *Abies.*
Associated botanic garden: Eddy Arboretum (collection of pine species).
Loans: Usual regulations.
Remarks: The herbarium is used occasionally by six scientists in this research group. F. T. LEDIG is Project Leader of the research group titled Genetics of Western Conifers.

PLAINFIELD: *Herbarium, Goddard College,* **(FMH)**, Plainfield, Vermont 05667, **U.S.A.**
Telephone: 802/454-8311, ext. 254.
Foundation: 1945. *Number of specimens:* 3.300.
Herbarium: New England in general, with emphasis on Washington County, Vermont.
Director and Curator: ROBERT A. JERVIS, 1938 (Ecology and biogeography).
Remarks: This herbarium was previously called the N. F. Flynn Memorial Herbarium, Natural History Museum. The collection of 5.000 specimens listed in edition 5 is now a permanent part of the University of Vermont herbarium, **(VT)**, Burlington. The present collection of 3.300 was begun in 1970.

PLEASANT HILL: *Herbarium, Diablo Valley College Museum,* **(DVM)**, 321 Golf Club Road, Pleasant Hill, California 94523, **U.S.A.**
Telephone: 415/685-1230.

Status: Community college.
Foundation: 1960. *Number of specimens:* 2.500.
Herbarium: Primarily native and naturalized California specimens.
Director: J. S. BYRNE, 1932.
Associated botanic garden: California Native Plants.
Loans: Yes.
Exchange: Yes.

PLZEŇ: *Herbarium, Západočeské Muzeum (West Bohemian Museum),* **(PL)**, Kopeckého sady 2, 301 50 Plzeň, **Czechoslovakia.**
Telephone: 398 67, 343 61.
Foundation: About 1910. *Number of specimens:* 50.000.
Herbarium: Central Europe and Czechoslovakia, especially Western Bohemia.
Important collections: Celakovský collection (1850–1905).
Director: JIŘÍ MELŠA, 1929.
Curators: JAROMÍR SOFRON, 1932 (Geobotany).
MIROSLAVA ŠANDOVÁ, 1947 (Geobotany).
Staff members: ELIŠKA KUHNOVÁ, 1929.
ILA ŠEDO, 1951.
Specialization in research: Floristic and geobotanical research in Western Bohemia.
Loans: Short term to recognized botanical institutions.
Periodical and serial works: Zprávy muzeí Západočeského Kraje, ser. natur.; Sborník Západočeského muzea, ser. natur.; Folia musei rerum naturalium Bohemiae occidentalis, ser. Botanica.

POCATELLO: *Ray J. Davis Herbarium, Idaho State University,* **(IDS)**, P.O. Box 8096, Pocatello, Idaho 83209, **U.S.A.**
Telephone: 208/236-2200; 236-3530.
Status: Idaho Museum of Natural History; state university.
Foundation: 1931. *Number of specimens:* 55.000.
Herbarium: Flora of Idaho; northwest and cold desert plants; some foreign representation: Taiwan, Russia, Japan; includes Caribou National Forest herbarium.
Important collections: Ray J. Davis.
Director: KARL E. HOLTE, 1931 (Floristic studies; rare and endangered plant searches).
Specialization in research: Identification and collection of plants on the Targhee and Caribou national forests, Idaho Nuclear Engineering Laboratory, various strip mine sites, and all of Idaho.
Loans: No special restrictions.
Exchange: Available: Material from southeastern Idaho and southeastern Oregon. Desired: Especially trees, grasses, and sedges; foreign material willingly received.
Remarks: Herbarium served as basis for the *Flora of Idaho.*

PODĚBRADY: *Polabské muzeum v Podĕbradech,* (**OMP**), Podĕbrady, **Czechoslovakia.** (Information 1974)
Foundation: 1903. *Number of specimens:* 11.000.
Herbarium: Plants of Europe and Czechoslovakia.
Specialization in research: Gasteromycetes and hallucinogenic mushrooms, ethnomycology, conservation.
Loans: To recognized botanical institutions.
Periodical and serial works: Vlastivĕdný zpravodaj Polabí.

POINT LOOKOUT: *Herbarium, Biology Department, School of the Ozarks,* (**SOTO**), Point Lookout, Missouri 65726, **U.S.A.**
Telephone: 417/334-6411.
Foundation: 1956. *Number of specimens:* 8.410.
Herbarium: Mainly southwestern Missouri, especially the White River Ozark area.
Director and Curator: ALICE ALLEN NIGHTINGALE, 1896; 417/334-6411, ext. 229 (Compositae of White River Ozark area).
Staff member: KENTON C. OLSON, 1939; 417/334-6411, ext. 235 (Plant anatomy).
Specialization in research: Flora of the Ozark glades.

POINT REYES: *Herbarium, Point Reyes National Seashore,* (**PORE**), Point Reyes, California 94956, **U.S.A.**
Telephone: 415/663-8522; 663-8523; 663-8524.
Status: U.S. Department of the Interior, National Park Service.
Foundation: 1962. *Number of specimens:* 1.096.
Herbarium: Plants of Point Reyes National Seashore.
Director: JOHN L. SANSING.
Specialization in research: Range trend transit study experimental prescribed burn.

POMONA: *Herbarium, Botany Department, California State Polytechnic University,* (**CSPU**), 3801 West Temple Avenue, Pomona, California 91711, **U.S.A.**
Telephone: 714/598-4419.
Foundation: 1969. *Number of specimens:* 26.000 mosses, 6.000 vascular plants.
Important collections: Moss collections of Faye MacFadden (MACF), UCLA herbarium (LA), and Los Angeles County Museum (LAM); Cynthia M. Galloway, Marion P. Harthill, David M. Long, Brent D. Mishler, Marcus E. Jones, Philip A. Munz.
Director and Curator: MARION P. HARTHILL, 1909 (Mosses).
Specialization in research: Mosses of southern California.
Loans: Standard regulations.
Exchange: Yes.
Remarks: Lichen herbarium being started.

PONDICHERRY: *Herbarium, Institut Français,* (**HIFP**), 10 Saint Louis Street, Pondicherry 605001, **India.**
Telephone: 170.
Status: Affiliated to Ministry of Foreign Affairs and University Paul Sabatier, France.
Foundation: 1956. *Number of specimens:* 7.000.
Herbarium: Flora of South India, especially mangroves, palms of Western Ghats and dry areas.
Director: P. LEGRIS, 1921 (Tropical ecology, forestry, bioclimatology).
Curator: G. THANIKAIMONI, 1938 (Palynology, taxonomy of Palmae, Araceae, Menispermaceae).
Staff members: V. M. MEHER-HOMJI, 1932 (Phytogeography, bioclimatology, tropical ecology).
J. P. PASCAL, 1944 (Tropical ecology).
Y. N. SEETARAM, 1949 (Palynology).
G. VASANTHY, 1945 (Palynology, plants of South Indian Hills).
Specialization in research: Tropical palynology, vegetation mapping, ecological studies of forests.
Loans: No.
Periodical and serial works: Travaux de la Section Scientifique et Technique de l'Institut Français de Pondichéry.

PONTA DELGADA: *Herbarium, Museu Distrital de Ponta Delgada,* (**AZ**), Ponta Delgada, **Azores.**

POONA: *Ajrekar Mycological Herbarium,* (**AMH**) – – *see* PUNE.

POPAYÁN: *Herbario, Museo de Historia Natural, Universidad del Cauca,* (**CAUP**), Apartado Aéreo 1113, Popayán, Cauca, **Colombia.** (Information 1977)
Foundation: 1936. *Number of specimens:* 3.400.

POPRAD: *Tatranské múzeum v Poprade,* (**POP**) – – incorporated in TNP.

PORTAGE LA PRAIRIE: *Herbarium, Delta Waterfowl Research Station,* (**DELTA**), R.R. 1, Portage la Prairie, Manitoba, **Canada** R1N 3A1 – – incorporated in WINDM.
Telephone: 204/857-9125; 857-9872.
Remarks: Formerly listed under Delta.

PORTAGE LA PRAIRIE: *Herbarium, Delta Marsh, University of Manitoba Field Station,* (**WINDM**), Box 8, Site 2, R.R. 1, Portage la Prairie, Manitoba, **Canada** RIN 3A1.
Telephone: 204/274-2106 (Delta); 474-9297 (University of Manitoba).
Foundation: 1967. *Number of specimens:* 2.250.
Herbarium: Delta Marsh and adjacent areas.
Director and Curator: JENNIFER M. SHAY (Wetland ecologist).
Specialization in research: Wetland ecology and productivity.

Loans: As required by recognized institutions.

PORT BLAIR: *Regional Herbarium, Andaman-Nicobar Circle, Botanical Survey of India,* (**PBL**), Horticultural Road, Port Blair 744102, **India.**
Telephone: 637.
Status: Government, Department of Science and Technology.
Foundation: 1972. *Number of specimens:* 20.000.
Herbarium: Mainly plants of Andaman and Nicobar Islands.
Important collections: N. P. Balakrishnan, K. Thothathri, J. L. Ellis and K. Ramamurthy, N. C. Nair, N. Bhargava, P. Chakra, P. Chakralonty.
  Director: N. P. BALAKRISHNAN, 1935 (Systematics of angiosperms, Euphorbiaceae).
  Curator: M. K. VASUDEVA RAO, 1941 (Systematics of angiosperms).
  Staff members: P. BASU, 1940 (Floristics).
  R. K. PREMANATH, 1952 (Floristics).
  Specialization in research: Flora of Andaman and Nicobar Islands (phytogeography, ecology and conservation).
Loans: To recognized botanical institutions.
Exchange: Available: Plants of Andaman and Nicobar Islands. Desired: Plants of southeast Asia.

PORT ELIZABETH: *F. R. Long Herbarium,* (**MPE**) – housed in PEU.

PORT ELIZABETH: *Herbarium of the University of Port Elizabeth,* (**PEU**), P.O. Box 1600, Port Elizabeth 6000, **South Africa.**
Telephone: 041-5311320.
Status: Botany Department of the University.
Foundation: 1970. *Number of specimens:* 10.000.
Herbarium: Plants of the Eastern Cape.
Important collections: F. R. Long herbarium, L. N. Prosser herbarium.
  Specialization in research: Eastern Cape Province flora.
Loans: To recognized botanical institutions.
  Exchange: Available: Duplicates of varied local collections.
  Remarks: The F. R. Long Herbarium (MPE) is now housed in PEU.

PORTICI: *Istituto di Patologia Vegetale dell'Università,* (**POR**), Portici (Napoli), **Italy.** (Information 1974)
Herbarium: Pathological fungi.

PORTLAND: *U.S. Forest Service, R-10, Division of Range Management,* (**POFS**), Portland, Oregon 97208, **U.S.A.** – – incorporated in LAGO.

PORT MORESBY: *Herbarium, Department of Primary Industry, Plant Pathology Branch,* (**PNG**), P.O. Box 2417, Konedobu, Port Moresby, **Papua New Guinea.**
Telephone: 214699.
Status: Government.
Foundation: 1955. *Number of specimens:* 10.000.
Herbarium: Mainly pathogenic fungi of Papua New Guinea, some other fungi, algae, and lichens; microscope slides and liquid preparations.
Important collections: Pathogenic fungi, *Rhizobium* nodule bacteria.
  Director: J. NATERA.
  Curator: G. R. KULA,
  Associate: DOROTHY R. SHAW (Former curator).
  Specialization in research: Checklist of pathogenic fungi in Papua New Guinea.
  Periodical and serial works: P.N.G. Agricultural Journal, Harvest Research Bulletin.
  Exchange: Material is sent to Commonwealth Mycological Institute, Kew.
  Remarks: The checklist of pathogenic fungi in Papua New Guinea, originally published in 1963, is currently under revision in Australia.

PORT MORESBY: *University Herbarium, Department of Biology, University of Papua New Guinea,* (**UPNG**), P.O. Box 4820, University, N.C.D., **Papua New Guinea.**
Telephone: 253900 ext. 2210.
Status: University.
Foundation: 1969. *Number of specimens:* 10.000.
Herbarium: Teaching and reference collection, mainly vascular plants of Papua New Guinea with emphasis on Port Moresby region.
Important collections: Seagrasses of Papua New Guinea; *Schefflera* (Araliaceae), mainly of New Guinea; locality record file of the Port Moresby region vascular flora.
  Director: Vacant.
  Curator: D. G. FRODIN, 1940 (Araliaceae, Lauraceae, flora and vegetation of Papuasia, especially Port Moresby region; history of botanical work in New Guinea, bibliography).
  Staff members: G. J. LEACH, 1952 (Myrtaceae, Ebenaceae, chemosystematics).
  K. NAONI (Technical work).
  A. VINAS, 1950 (Technical work).
  Specialization in research: Annotated checklist of the flora of the Port Moresby region; mangrove taxonomy and distribution; floristic handbooks.
  Associated botanic garden: None. The former University Botanic Garden (est. 1971) was at the end of 1976 transferred to the government as the National Capital Botanic Garden.
Loans: To recognized institutions under special circumstances.
  Periodical and serial works: Occasional Papers in Biology, Science in New Guinea.
  Exchange: Yes, but irregularly.
  Remarks: Serious damage was sustained in a fire in 1978, with up to 20% of the general collection lost (mainly Leguminosae, Moraceae, and monocotyledons).

PORTO: *Instituto de Botânica "Dr. Gonçalo Sampaio," Faculdade de Ciências da Universidade do Porto,* **(PO),** Rua do Campo Alegre 1191, 4100 Porto, **Portugal.**
Telephone: 62153.
Status: University.
Foundation: 1892. *Number of specimens:* 50.000.
Herbarium: Mainly plants of Portugal.
Important collections: Herbarium Gonçalo Sampaio.
Director: ROBERTO SALEMA DE MAGALHÃES FARIA VIEIRA RIBEIRO, 1932 (Cell biology).
Curator: MARIA FERNANDA LIXA FILGUEIRAS, 1924.
Staff members: MARIA ALICE DE ALMEIDA CORREIA DE SOUSA, 1922.
ANDRÉ DOS ANJOS DE SERRA, 1930.
ANA FERNANDA RODRÍGUES, 1954.
Associated botanic garden: Botanic Garden of Instituto de Botânica "Dr. Gonçalo Sampaio."
Loans: To recognized botanical institutions.
Periodical and serial works: Index Seminum.
Exchange: Yes, specimens and seeds.

PORTO ALEGRE: *Herbário, Departamento de Pesquisa, Instituto de Pesquisas Zootécnicas "Francisco Osório,"* **(BLA),** Rua Gonçalves Dias 570, 90.000 Porto Alegre, Rio Grande do Sul, **Brazil.**
Telephone: (55) 0512/33-5411, ramal 65.
Status: Secretary of Agriculture of the state of Rio Grande do Sul.
Foundation: 1954. *Number of specimens:* 13.700.
Herbarium: Gramineae, Leguminosae, and other forage plants of Rio Grande do Sul.
Important collections: A. A. Araújo, I. Barreto, I. Boldrini, E. M. Cavalheiro, W. D. Clayton, V. Froner, A. Kappel, H. Longhi, A. Normann-Kämpf, A. Pott, J. Valls.
Curator: ANA M. BARCELLOS-HERVÉ, 1951 (Gramineae).
Staff member: CICILIA R. DILLENBURG, 1928 (Gramineae).
Specialization in research: Systematics of Gramineae of Rio Grande do Sul.
Loans: To institutions and specialists; usual regulations.
Periodical and serial works: Anuário Técnico do Instituto de Pesquisas Zootécnicas "Francisco Osório."
Exchange: Gramineae and Leguminosae from temperate and subtropical regions.

PORTO ALEGRE: *Herbário "Prof. Dr. Alarich R. H. Schultz," Museu de Ciências Naturais da Fundação Zoobotânica do Rio Grande do Sul,* **(HAS),** Avenida Salvador França 1427, Caixa Postal Box 1188, 90.000 Porto Alegre, Rio Grande do Sul, **Brazil.**
Telephone: (55)0512/31-5915; 31-7018.
Foundation: 1975. *Number of specimens:* 14.180, including 2.500 lots in liquid (algae).

Herbarium: Flora of Rio Grande do Sul.
Director: HERACLIDES SANTA HELENA, 1919.
Curator: OLINDA LEITES BUENO, 1943 (Taxonomy, ecology of phanerogams, especially Malvaceae).
Staff members: LUCIA WILHELMS AGUIAR, 1938 (Taxonomy, ecology of phanerogams).
ALBANO BACKS, 1933 (Synecology).
TANIA CAROLINA BUSELATO, 1955 (Taxonomy of marine algae; fresh-water phytoplankton; diatoms).
VERA LUCIA M. CALLEGARO, 1948 (Taxonomy, ecology of marine algae).
GILBERTO C. FERRAZ, 1941 (Limnology).
LIZETE MARIA KREMER, 1954 (Taxonomy of dinoflagellates).
JORGE E. MARIATH, 1953 (Taxonomy, morphology, anatomy of Rubiaceae; numerical taxonomy).
LIA MARTAU, 1933 (Taxonomy, ecology of phanerogams).
SUZANA MARIA DE A. MARTINS, 1955 (Taxonomy of lichens).
ZULANIRA MEYER ROSA, 1950 (Taxonomy of microscopic algae, especially marine diatoms).
SANDRA MARIA A. DA SILVA, 1953 (Taxonomy of fresh-water algae).
ZILDA FERNANDES SOARES, 1930 (Taxonomy, ecology of phanerogams).
LEZILDA C. TORGAN, 1951 (Taxonomy, ecology of fresh-water algae).
IETI UNGARETTI, 1933 (Taxonomy of fresh-water algae, especially desmids).
VERA REGINA WERNER, 1955 (Taxonomy of fresh-water algae).
Specialization in research: Flora of Rio Grande do Sul.
Associated botanic garden: Jardim Botânico da Fundação Zoobotânica do Rio Grande do Sul.
Loans: Usual regulations.
Periodical and serial works: Iheringia: Botanica.
Exchange: Plants of Rio Grande do Sul.

PORTO ALEGRE: *Herbário, Departamento de Botânica, Universidade Federal do Rio Grande do Sul,* **(ICN),** Avenida Paulo Gama, 90.000 Porto Alegre, Rio Grande do Sul, **Brazil.**
Telephone: (55)0512/25-4676.
Foundation: 1937. *Number of specimens:* 50.000.
Herbarium: Flora of Rio Grande do Sul.
Curator: BRUNO E. IRGANG, 1941 (Local flora; angiosperms; aquatic plants).
Staff members: LUIS R. M. BAPTISTA (Algae; Leguminosae; vegetation).
MARIA L. L. BAPTISTA (Hepaticae; Annonaceae).
ILSI J. BOLDRINI (Gramineae).
ZORAIDO S. V. CERONI (Caryophyllaceae).
ROSA M. GUERRERO (Fungi; Tremellales).
MARIA H. HOMRICH (Fungi; Gasteromycetes).

ATELENE N. KÄMPF (Gramineae).
MARIAL L. PORTO (Rubiaceae; local flora).
ENY C. VIANNA (Hepaticae).
HILDA M. L. WAGNER (Gramineae).
Specialization in research: All plant groups; flora of Rio Grande do Sul.
Loans: Usual regulations.
Periodical and serial works: Flora Ilustrada do Rio Grande do Sul.

PORTO ALEGRE: *Herbário, Museu de Ciências da Pontifícia Universidade Católica do Rio Grande do Sul,* **(MPUC),** Avenida Ipiranga 6681, Prédio 10, Caixa Postal 1429, 90.000 Porto Alegre, Rio Grande do Sul, **Brazil.**
Telephone: (55)0512/23-9400, ramal 138.
Foundation: 1967. *Number of specimens:* 3.500.
Herbarium: Flora of Rio Grande do Sul.
Important collections: Gramineae, Compositae, pteridophytes, and algae.
  Director: JETER JORGE BERTOLETTI, 1939 (Biogeography; aquaculture).
  Curator: GISLAINE CARDOSO HILTL, 1954; 0512/41-6496 (Ecology).
  Staff members: MÁRCIA THEREZINHA MENNA BARRETO DAS NEVES, 1953 (Biology).
    SELVA MARIZA NUNES, 1944 (Naturalist).
Specialization in research: Inventory of the native flora of the state of Rio Grande do Sul.
Loans: No; gifts and exchanges only.
Periodical and serial works: Comunicações do Museu de Ciências da PUCRGS.
Exchange: Yes, where there is mutual interest.

PORTO ALEGRE: *Herbário, Seção de Fitopatologia, Divisão de Pesquisas Agrícolas, Instituto de Pesquisas Agronômicas,* **(SFPA),** Rua Gonçalves Dias 570, 90.000 Porto Alegre, Rio Grande do Sul, **Brazil.**
Status: Secretaria da Agricultura.
Foundation: 1943. *Number of specimens:* 4.478 phytopathogenic fungi.
Herbarium: Plant pathogenic fungi and bacteria.
  Staff members: JOÃO A. M. AMADO (Plant pathology; wheat fungus diseases).
    RALPH W. BAUMGART (Plant pathology; wheat fungus diseases).
    W. S. FULCO.
    NEY KREMER LUZ (Plant pathology, wheat fungus diseases).

PORT VICTORIA: *Herbarium, Department of Agriculture,* **(SEY),** Mont Fleuri, Mahe, **Seychelles.** (Information 1974)
Status: Government.
Foundation: 1962. *Number of specimens:* 500.
Herbarium: Endemic and exotic plants of the Seychelles.
  Associated botanic garden: Seychelles Botanic Garden.
Loans: To recognized botanical institutions.

PORT VILA: *Herbarium, Forestry Section, Department of Agriculture,* **(PVNH),** Port Vila, **New Hebrides.**
Telephone: 2525.
Status: Government department.
Foundation: 1974. *Number of specimens:* 2.000.
Herbarium: Plants of New Hebrides.
Important collections: Royal Society Expedition to New Hebrides, 1971.
  Director and Curator: R. M. BENNETT, 1939.

PORVOO: *Herbarium, Porvoo Museum of Natural History,* **(PRV),** Papinkatu 18, Porvoo, **Finland.** (Information 1974)
Status: City of Porvoo in cooperation with a society of natural sciences.
Foundation: 1957. *Number of specimens:* 4.000.
Herbarium: Flowering plants, mosses and lichens of East Fennoscandia.
  Specialization in research: Flora of eastern Uusimaa.
Loans: To recognized botanical institutions.

POTCHEFSTROOM: *Herbarium, Potchefstroom University for C.H.E.,* **(PUC),** Potchefstroom 2520, **South Africa.**
Telephone: 22112.
Status: University.
Foundation: 1932. *Number of specimens:* 20.000.
Herbarium: Mainly flowering plants of Western Transvaal.
Important collections: H. G. Schweickerdt, W. J. Louw.
  Director and Curator: D. J. BOTHA, 1939 (South African Menispermaceae, *Pterocelastrus*).
  Staff members: M. C. PAPENDORF, 1917 (Fungi).
    W. J. JOOSTE, 1933 (Fungi imperfecti).
    B. UBBINK, 1932 (Angiospermae).
    P. D. DE VILLIERS, 1942 (Angiospermae).
  Specialization in research: External morphology, pollen morphology, anatomy.
  Associated botanic garden: Wynand Louw Botanic Garden, Potchefstroom University.
Loans: On request to recognized institutions.
Exchange: Available: Transvaal flowering plants.

POUGHKEEPSIE: *Herbarium, Department of Biology, Vassar College,* **(VAS),** Poughkeepsie, New York 12601, **U.S.A.**
Telephone: 914/452-7000, ext. 2067.
Foundation: 1861. *Number of specimens:* 18.500.
Herbarium: Local.
  Curator: MARK A. SCHLESSMAN, 1952 (Vascular plant systematics).
  Specialization in research: Systematics of *Lomatium*, North American Umbelliferae.
Loans: To recognized institutions.

POZNAŃ: *Herbarium of the Department of Plant*

Taxonomy, Adam Mickiewicz University, (POZ), Stalingradzka 14, 61-713 Poznań, Poland.
Telephone: 505-18.
Status: University.
Foundation: 1925. Number of specimens: 180.000 (150.000 phanerogams, 30.000 lichens).
Herbarium: Phanerogams of Poland and Europe, lichens of Europe.
Important collections: Zukowski (Cyperaceae), Latowski (Lepidium).
Director: WALDEMAR ZUKOWSKI, 1935 (Taxonomy and chorology of phanerogams).
Curator: KAROL LATOWSKI, 1939 (Taxonomy and chorology of phanerogams).
Staff members: IWONA ANDERS, 1954 (Cytotaxonomy).
BOGDAN JACKOWIAK, 1954 (Chorology of phanerogams).
MAŁGORZATA KLIMO, 1947 (Numerical taxonomy).
ZYGMUNT TOBOLEWSKI, 1927 (Taxonomy and ecology of lichens).
Specialization in research: Experimental and numerical taxonomy, flora of Poland and Europe, ruderal and segetal flora of Poland.
Associated botanic garden: Botanic Garden of the Adam Mickiewicz University, Dąbrowskiego 165, 60-594 Poznań.
Loans: To recognized botanical institutions.
Periodical and serial works: Lichenotheca Polonica, taxonomic publications by Poznań Society of Friends of Science.
Exchange: Available: Plants of Poland and Europe. Desired: Holarctic phanerogams.
Remarks: The herbarium is interested in sending material to specialists for revision.

POZNAŃ: Herbarium of the Department of Geobotany, Adam Mickiewicz University, (POZG), Stalingradzka 14, 61-713 Poznań, Poland.
Telephone: 500-01.
Status: University.
Foundation: 1925. Number of specimens: 160.000 (60.000 bryophytes, 100.000 phanerogams).
Herbarium: Bryophytes of world, phanerogams of tropics, mainly Central Africa.
Important collections: Lisowski (Central Africa, Guinea, Zaire).
Director: STANISŁAW LISOWSKI, 1924 (Bryology, taxonomy tropical phanerogams).
Curator: PIOTR SZMAJDA, 1945 (Taxonomy and chorology of mosses).
Staff member: ANNA RUSIŃSKA, 1947 (Taxonomy and ecology of mosses).
Specialization in research: Bryophytes; tropical vascular plants, mainly Africa; geobotany.
Associated botanic garden: Botanic Garden of the Adam Mickiewicz University, Dąbrowskiego 165, 60-594 Poznań.
Loans: To recognized botanical institutions.

Periodical and serial works: Bryotheca Polonica.
Exchange: Available: Bryophytes, phanerogams from Africa. Desired: Mosses and tropical phanerogams.
Remarks: The herbarium is interested in sending material to specialists for revision.

PRAHA: Botanické oddělení Přírodověd. muzea Národního muzea v Praze (Department of Botany, National Museum in Prague), (PR), 252 43 Průhonice near Praha, Czechoslovakia.
Telephone: 759531, 759621.
Status: Directed by state.
Foundation: 1818. Number of specimens: 1.500.000.
Herbarium: Worldwide, mostly phanerogams, also algae, bryophytes, pteridophytes.
Important collections: T. Haenke, J. S. and K. B. Presl, F. Waldstein, P. Kitaibel, K. F. Wallroth (Thuringia), J. E. Pohl (Brasilia), F. W. Sieber, J. F. Drège, J. G. Lehmann (Potentilla), R. Schlechter (Africa, New Caledonia), I. F. Tausch, H. Cuming (Philippines), N. Wallich (India), J. Lhotsky, C. F. Ecklon, C. L. P. Zeyher, J. M. Hildebrandt (Madagascar), P. Sintenis, T. Kotschy, J. S. Pringle, K. Sprengel, E. H. G. Ule, G. A. Zenker (Cameroons), F. Petrak (Cirsium), K. Vandas (Balcan), K. Domin (Australia).
Director: JIŘÍ SOJÁK, 1936 (Taxonomy of Potentilla, flora of Czechoslovakia).
Curator: BLANKA DEYLOVÁ-SKOČDOPOLOVÁ, 1944 (Flora of Czechoslovakia).
Staff members: JINDŘICH CHRTEK, 1930 (Taxonomy of phanerogams).
HANA FRANKLOVÁ, 1946 (Bryophytes).
Specialization in research: Flora of Czechoslovakia.
Loans: To recognized botanical institutions.
Periodical and serial works: Acta Musei Nationalis Pragae-Řada B, Časopis Národního muzea-Odd. Přír.
Exchange: Available: Specimens from all groups. Desired: Specimens from all groups.

PRAHA: Herbarium, Universitatis Carolinae Facultatis Scientiae Naturalis, Institutum Botanicum, (PRC), Benátská 2, 128 01 Praha 2, Czechoslovakia.
Telephone: 29 79 41-49.
Status: University.
Foundation: 1775. Number of specimens: 2.000.000.
Herbarium: Worldwide, especially Central Europe, Carpathians and Balkan Peninsula.
Important collections: Presl, P. M. Opiz, Tausch, J. E. Holuby, Oborny, J. Velenovský, Sterneck, Beck, Vilhelm, Cejp, J. E. Kabát, Rohlena, K. Domin, J. Dostál.
Director of Cryptogamic Section: ZDENĚK URBAN, 1923 (Taxonomy of Uredinales and Ustilaginales, wood microfungi).
Director of Vascular Plant Section: RADOVAN HENDRYCH, 1926 (Taxonomy and phytogeography of Trifolium and Thesium, flora of Carpathians).

Curator of Cryptogamic Section: JIŘÍ VÁŇA, 1940 (Hepaticae).
Curator of Vascular Plant Section: BOHDAN KŘISA, 1936 (Taxonomy, flora of Czechoslovakia).
Staff members: JAN ČABART, 1931 (Ecology).
OLGA FASSATIOVÁ, 1924 (Hyphomycetes, entomogenous fungi).
HELENA HENDRYCHOVÁ, 1948 (Phytogeography).
TOMÁŠ KALINA, 1935 (Cytology and taxonomy of algae).
JAROSLAVA MARKOVÁ, 1947 (Mycology, Uredinales).
JANA OSBORNOVÁ, 1937 (Geobotany, ecology).
KAREL PRÁŠIL, 1949 (Mycology, Deuteromycetes).
MARCELA PUNČOCHÁŘOVÁ, 1941 (Phycology).
VĚNCESLAVA REJZLOVÁ, 1946 (Anatomy).
ANTONÍN ROUBAL, 1925 (Taxonomy, *Crataegus*).
ANNA SKALICKÁ, 1932 (Taxonomy, dendrology).
VLADIMÍR SKALICKÝ, 1930 (Mycology, taxonomy, phytogeography of Czechoslovakia).
JIŘINA SLAVÍKOVÁ, 1926 (Geobotany, ecology).
ZDEŇKA SCAVÍKOVÁ, 1935 (Morphology, floral biology).
MICHAELA ŠOURKOVÁ, 1944 (Taxonomy).
MARIE VÁŇOVÁ, 1943 (Mycology, Mucorales).
HELENA WUDYOVÁ, 1940 (Phycology, lichenology).
Specialization in research: Flora and vegetation of Czechoslovakia: taxonomy, morphology, phytogeography, geobotany, ecology.
Associated botanic garden: Hortus Botanicus Universitatis Carolinae.
Loans: To recognized botanical institutions.

PRAHA: *Mycological Department of the National Museum,* (**PRM**), Tř. Vítězného února 74, 115 79 Praha--1, **Czechoslovakia.**
Telephone: 269451.
Status: Directed by state.
Foundation: 1818. *Number of specimens:* 300.000.
Herbarium: Worldwide collection fungi and lichens, especially Europe and northern Asia.
Important collections: Herbarium A. K. J. Corda (Deuteromycetes), herb. I. A. Pilat (mainly Polyporaceae), herb. J. Velenovský (Hymenomycetes, Discomycetes), herb. M. Svrček (mainly Ascomycetes), herb. M. Servít (lichens), herb. J. Suza (lichens), herb. J. Anders (lichens, mainly *Cladonia*), herb. A. Hilitzer (fungi, lichens), herb. F. Bubák (in part).
Director: ZDENĚK POUZAR, 1932 (Taxonomic mycology, Aphyllophorales, *Hypoxylon*).
Curator: M. SVRČEK, 1925 (Taxonomic mycology, Discomycetes, Agaricales, Aphyllophorales).
Specialization in research: Discomycetes, Polyporaceae and *Hypoxylon*.

Loans: To recognized botanical institutions.
Periodical and serial works: Acta Musei Nationalis Pragae, Časopis Národního muzea.
Exchange: Available: Fungi. Desired: All groups of fungi.

PRAIRIE VIEW: *Herbarium, Department of Biology, Prairie View A & M University,* (**TPV**), Prairie View, Texas 77445, **U.S.A.** -- discontinued.

PRETORIA: *National Herbarium, Botanical Research Institute,* (**PRE**), 2 Cussonia Ave., P. Bag X101, Pretoria, 0001 **South Africa.**
Telephone: 012 861164.
Status: Department of Agriculture and Fisheries of the Government of the Republic.
Foundation: 1903. *Number of specimens:* 800.000 (520.000 from Southern Africa are recorded in a data bank served by E. D. P. programme, PRECIS).
Herbarium: Mainly African phanerogams and cryptogams excluding fungi, Poaceae of the world.
Important collections: E. E. Galpin, R. Marloth, R. H. Compton (Swaziland collections), H. G. Flanagan, Transvaal museum. Also: J. P. H. Acocks, L. E. Codd, R. A. Dyer, I. B. Pole Evans, A. Dieterlen, R. Schlechter, A. Pegler, G. W. Reynolds, H. J. E. Schlieben, B. de Winter, D. J. B. Killick, D. Edwards, J. Hutchinson, J. Burtt Davy, J. C. Smuts. Bryophytes: T. R. Sim, H. A. Wager, Rehmann, R. E. Magill, J. van Rooy, F. Eyles & R. Dümmer (cf. Index Herb. Aust. Afr. for more details).
Director: B. DE WINTER (Poaceae, general systematics).
Deputy Director: D. J. B. KILLICK (General systematics and nomenclature).
Assistant Director: D. EDWARDS (Vegetation studies).
Curator: E. G. H. OLIVER (Ericoideae, Cape flora).
Assistant Curator: E. VAN HOEPEN (Information and identification service).
Staff members: T. H. ARNOLD (Cyperaceae, origin and evolution of crop plants).
F. BRUSSE (Lichens).
R. P. ELLIS (Anatomy of Poaceae).
G. GERMISHUIZEN (General systematics).
P. P. J. HERMAN (General systematics).
R. E. MAGILL (Bryophytes).
E. RETIEF (Campanulaceae).
J. VAN ROOY (Bryophytes).
S. SMITHIES (General systematics).
L. SMOOK (Poaceae).
C. H. STIRTON (Fabaceae, biosystematics of *Lantana* and *Rubus*).
W. G. WELMAN (General systematics).
Flora of South Africa Research Team
Head: O. A. LEISTNER (General systematics).
Staff members: H. ANDERSON (Triassic floras of Gondwanaland).

J. ANDERSON (Triassic floras of Gondwanaland).

L. E. W. CODD (Reappointed after retirement;
Lamiaceae).

G. E. GIBBS RUSSELL (Poaceae).

H. F. GLEN (Liaison officer at Kew, 1980/82;
Mesembryanthemaceae, E. D. P.).

K. IMMELMAN (General systematics).

A. A. OBERMEYER-MAUVE (Reappointed after
retirement; monocots).

Loans: To recognized botanical institutions.

Periodical and serial works: Bothalia, Memoirs of
the Botanical Survey of Southern Africa, Flowering
Plants of Africa (miscellaneous coloured plates
with text), Flora of Southern Africa.

Exchange: Available: South African plants. Desired: African duplicates and world grasses.

Remarks: Herbarium staff includes 12 tech-
nicians, 2 artists and 1 photographer. Additional
sections in the Institute with 14 botanists and 6
technical staff deal with vegetation analysis, production studies, ecosystem research, plant utilization, ethnobotany, cyto-genetics, poisonous &
medical plants and weed research (cf. Bothalia 13, 1
& 2, 1980). The E. D. P. Section has been transferred to the central department's computer division.

PRETORIA: *National Mycological Herbarium,*
(PREM), Private Bag X134, 590 Vermeulen St., Pretoria 0001 **South Africa.**

Telephone: 012 28-5140.

Status: Government, Department of Agriculture
and Fisheries.

Foundation: 1908. *Number of specimens:* 46.000.

Important collections: A.M. Bottomley, E. M. Doidge, C. G. Hansford, P. MacOwan, A. Pegler, W. G.
Rump, J. M. Wood.

Curator: G. C. A. VAN DER WESTHUIZEN, 1923
(Wood-rotting fungi, plant pathogenic fungi).

Staff members: ALICE P. BAXTER, 1954 (*Collecto-
trichum,* Coelomycetes).

CECILIA ROUX, 1946 (Mycotoxigenic fungi).

D. B. SCOTT, 1936 (Root and stalk-rot
pathogens).

A. H. THOMPSON, 1950 (*Phytophthora,
Pythium*).

Specialization in research: Identification and
classification of crop plant pathogens; identity and
ecology of toxigenic fungi of pasture and stock
feeds.

Loans: To recognized botanical institutions, for
three months.

PRETORIA: *Forestry Herbarium, South African
Forestry Research Institute,* **(PRF)**, Ketjen St., P.O.
Box 727, Pretoria 0001, **South Africa.**

Telephone: 012 487120.

Status: Department of Forestry, Research Division.

Foundation: 1912. *Number of specimens.* 16.000.

Herbarium: Trees and shrubs of South Africa, na-

tive and cultivated; some foreign collections, especially *Pinus* and *Eucalyptus.*

Curator: R. J. POYNTON, 1925 (Cultivated trees,
especially South African timber species).

Staff members: P. J. BROWN, 1949 (Identification).

K. S. MARAIS, 1937 (Herbarium maintenance).

Specialization in research: Taxonomy and nomenclature of trees, especially timber trees and
cultivated.

Associated botanic garden: Arboreta of Department of Forestry.

Loans: On special request only.

Exchange: Limited.

Remarks: The herbarium is housed in cabinets
constructed of South African timbers.

PRETORIA: *H. G. W. J. Schweickerdt Herbarium,
Department of Botany, University of Pretoria,* **(PRU)**,
Pretoria 0002, **South Africa.**

Telephone: 012 746051 x 543.

Status: University.

Foundation: 1924. *Number of specimens:* 45.000.

Herbarium: Phanerogams and cryptogams of
Southern Africa.

Director: N. GROBBELAAR, 1928 (Physiology of
nitrogen metabolism, especially nitrogen fixation,
Leguminosae).

Curator: A. E. VAN WYK, 1952 (Taxonomy of
phanerogams, Myrtaceae).

Staff members: M. I. CLAASSEN, 1931 (Algae,
Desmidiaceae).

L. A. COETZER, 1942 (Morphology, Leguminosae).

A. EICKER, 1935 (Mycology, microfungi,
mushroom cultivation).

J. V. VAN GREUNING, 1940 (Morphology, Restionaceae, *Ficus, Pavetta*).

P. D. F. KOK, 1944 (Taxonomy of phanerogams, Poaceae, *Pavetta*).

W. F. REYNEKE, 1945 (Morphology, Araliaceae, Liliaceae, *Pavetta*).

P. J. ROBBERTSE, 1932 (Morphology/anatomy,
Acacia, Pavetta).

Specialization in research: Taxonomy of Southern Africa flora.

Associated botanic garden: University of Pretoria
Botanic Garden.

Loans: To recognized botanical institutions.

Exchange: Available: Specimens from Southern
Africa. Desired: African plants.

PRETORIA: *Transvaal Museum,* **(TRV)** -- incorporated in PRE.

PRICE: *Herbarium, Manti-LaSal National Forest,*
(MALS), 350 East Main Street, Price, Utah 84501,
U.S.A.

Telephone: 801/637-2817.

Status: U.S.D.A., Forest Service.

Foundation: 1910. *Number of specimens:* 1.800.
Herbarium: Vascular plants of southeastern Utah.
Important collections: Plants of the Wasatch Plateau, LaSal and Abajo mountains.
Director and Curator: ROBERT M. THOMPSON, 1929.

PRICE: *Herbarium, College of Eastern Utah,* (**PRI**), 450 East 4th North, Price, Utah 84501, **U.S.A.**
Telephone: 801/637-2120.
Foundation: 1938. *Number of specimens:* 7.500.
Herbarium: Vascular plants primarily of southeastern Utah.
Director and Curator: LAMONT ARNOLD.
Loans: Can be arranged.
Exchange: Yes.

PRINEVILLE: *Ochoco National Forest,* (**OCNF**), Box 490, Prineville, Oregon 97754, **U.S.A.** – – incorporated in LAGO.

PROVIDENCE: *Herbarium, Division of Biological and Medical Sciences, Brown University,* (**BRU**), Waterman Street, Providence, Rhode Island 02912, **U.S.A.**
Telephone: 401/863-3281.
Foundation: 1878 (the year of the death of S. T. Olney, an amateur who collaborated considerably with Asa Gray. Olney's original herbarium formed the nucleus of the Brown herbarium). *Number of specimens:* 100.000 vascular plants, bryophytes, lichens, algae; fungi in the Walter H. Snell Fungus Herbarium which is housed in the same building.
Herbarium: Mainly North America, especially Rhode Island flora; some Old World; voucher specimens of cytogenetic research in the Gramineae.
Important collections: Early American Railroad and Boundary Survey Expeditions; F. S. Collins, M. L. Fernald, S. T. Olney.
Curator: GEORGE L. CHURCH, 1903 (Cytogenetics of Gramineae).
Specialization in research: Genetics of speciation in the Hordeae.
Loans: To recognized institutions.

PROVO: *Herbarium, Room 375, Monte L. Bean Life Science Museum, Brigham Young University,* (**BRY**), Provo, Utah 84602, **U.S.A.**
Telephone: 801/374-1211, ext. 2289.
Status: Private, supported by the Church of Jesus Christ of Latter-day Saints.
Foundation: 1923. *Number of specimens:* 208.000.
Herbarium: Mainly phanerogams of western North America.
Important collections: B. F. Harrison, W. P. Cottam, Maxcine M. Williams, W. D. Stanton, I. E. Diehl, L. C. Higgins, N. D. Atwood, S. L. Welsh, Elizabeth Neese, F. H. Sargent.
Director: STANLEY L. WELSH, 1928 (Arctic flora; Leguminosae).

Curator: KAYE H. THORNE, 1939 (Utah flora).
Staff members: SHEREL GOODRICH, 1943 (Floras of central Nevada and Uinta Basin, Utah; Apiaceae of Utah; *Cymopterus*).
ELIZABETH NEESE, 1934 (Floras of Henry Mountains and Uinta Basin, Utah; threatened and endangered species of Utah).
Specialization in research: Flora of Utah; Leguminosae.
Loans: To responsible institutions.
Periodical and serial works: Great Basin Naturalist.
Exchange: General North America; Leguminosae and Poaceae worldwide.

PROVO: *Herbarium, Shrub Sciences Laboratory, U.S. Forest Service, Intermountain Forest and Range Experiment Station,* (**SSLP**), 735 N. 500 E., Provo, Utah 84601, **U.S.A.**
Telephone: 801/377-5717.
Status: U.S. Department of Agriculture, Forest Service.
Foundation: 1975. *Number of specimens:* 2.000.
Herbarium: Intermountain shrubs, particularly *Artemisia* (560), *Chrysothamnus* (700), and *Atriplex*.
Curator: E. D. McARTHUR, 1941 (Cytogenetics and evolution).
Specialization in research: Wildland shrub taxonomy, selection, breeding, nutritive quality, insect and disease problems, ecology, and establishment techniques.

PUEBLO: *Herbarium, Biology Department, University of Southern Colorado,* (**PUSC**), 2200 Bonforte Boulevard, Pueblo, Colorado 81001, **U.S.A.**
Telephone: 303/549-2270.
Foundation: 1962. *Number of specimens:* 3.500.
Herbarium: Regional flora of southern Colorado.
Important collections: H. D. Harrington, N. L. Osborn, W. C. Martin.
Director and Curator: NEAL L. OSBORN, 1936 (Montane flora of northern New Mexico and southern Colorado).
Loans: Usual regulations.
Exchange: Yes.

PUERTO AYORA: *Herbario, Estación Biológica Charles Darwin,* (**CDS**), Puerto Ayora, Isla Santa Cruz, Galápagos Islands, **Ecuador** (Mailing address: Casilla 58-39, Guayaquil, Ecuador).
Foundation: 1964. *Number of specimens:* 3.000.
Herbarium: Flora of the Galápagos Islands.
Important collections: D. M. Porter, I. L. Wiggins; Darwin Station staff.

PUERTO DE LA CRUZ: *Jardín de Aclimatación de Plantas de La Orotava,* (**ORT**), Puerto de la Cruz, Tenerife, Canary Islands, **Spain.**
Telephone: 922-371172.
Status: Instituto Nacional Invest. Agrarias.

Foundation: 1788 (Jardín de Aclimatación), 1943 (Herbarium). *Number of specimens:* 26.000.
Herbarium: Flora of Canary Islands, Sweden, Cataluña.
Important collections: E. R. Sventenius (Flora Canaria).
Director: ALONSO ARROYO, 1945 (Horticulture).
Curator: ARNOLDO SANTOS GUERRA, 1948; 922-540154 (Phanerogams, algae).
Staff members: MANUEL FERNÁNDEZ GALVAN, 1947 (Flora Canaria, Phanerogams).
CARMEN LUISA MARTINEZ ESTEVEZ, 1953.
Specialization in research: Phytosociology, cartography, taxonomy of phanerogams of the Canary Islands.
Associated botanic garden: Jardín de Aclimatación de Plantas de la Orotava.
Periodical and serial works: Index Seminum.
Exchange: Flora of Macaronesia, Mediterranean flora.
Remarks: Formerly listed under Tenerife.

PULLMAN: *Marion Ownbey Herbarium, Washington State University,* **(WS),** Pullman, Washington 99164, **U.S.A.**
Telephone: 509/335-3250.
Foundation: 1890. *Number of specimens:* 285.000.
Herbarium: Vascular plants of the Pacific Northwest and related flora; all groups except fungi.
Important collections: R. K. Beattie, W. C. Cusick, R. F. Daubenmire, M. Ownbey, C. V. Piper, H. St. John, W. N. Suksdorf; *Allium, Calochortus, Tragopogon.*
Director: AMY JEAN GILMARTIN, 1932 (Umbelliferae, Bromeliaceae).
Assistant Curator: JOY MASTROGIUSEPPE (*Pinus, Carex*).
Staff members: BEVERLY HUNTER (*Rhacomitrium*).
SUSAN SKILLMAN (Cactaceae).
Specialization in research: Pacific Northwest flora; multivariate analysis and numerical taxonomy.
Associated botanic garden: Experimental garden only.
Loans: Available under usual restrictions.
Exchange: Available: Plants of western North America. Desired: Umbelliferae of the world; plants of temperate northern hemisphere.

PULLMAN: *Mycological Herbarium, Department of Plant Pathology, Washington State University,* **(WSP),** Pullman, Washington 99164, **U.S.A.**
Telephone: 509/335-1086; 335-9541.
Foundation: 1915. *Number of specimens:* 64.000.
Herbarium: Mainly a collection of mycological specimens with all major groups of fungi represented; emphasis on parasitic members from northwestern U.S.
Important collections: William B. Cooke, Ruben

Duran, George W. Fischer, F. D. Heald, Jack D. Rogers, Charles Gardner Shaw, Wilhelm G. Solheim, Roderick Sprague, Wilhelm N. Suksdorf.
Director: CHARLES GARDNER SHAW, 1917 (Downy mildews).
Curator: ROSY J. CHACKO (Wood decay fungi).
Staff members: RUBEN DURAN, 1924 (Ustilaginales).
JACK D. ROGERS, 1937 (Ascomycetes).
Specialization in research: Emphasis on plant pathology, especially forest and cereal pathology.
Loans: To individuals associated with educational or research institutions for a period of three months.
Periodical and serial works: Washington Research Studies; Bulletins of Washington Agricultural Research Center.
Exchange: Yes.

PUNE: *Ajrekar Mycological Herbarium,* **(AMH),** Maharashtra Association for the Cultivation of Science -- Research Institute, Law College Road, Pune 411 003, **India.**
Telephone: 56357.
Status: Affiliated with University of Pune and Mahatma Phule Agricultural University.
Foundation: 1968. *Number of specimens:* 155.000 (10.000 lichens, 4.500 general fungi, 1.000 mushrooms).
Herbarium: General collection Ascomycetes, lichens of India, mushrooms of S.W. India.
Director: G. B. DEODIKAR, 1915 (Plant breeding and genetics).
Curator: V. P. BHIDE, 1915.
Staff members: ALAKA PANDE, 1943 (Ascomycetes, Deuteromycetes).
P. G. PATWARDHAN, 1935 (Lichens).
V. G. RAO, 1937 (Ascomycetes, Deuteromycetes).
A. V. SATHE, 1935 (Agaricales, Uredinales).
Specialization in research: General taxonomy of fungi and applied mycology.
Loans: Short term to recognized institutions.
Exchange: Yes.
Remarks: Formerly listed under Poona.

PUNE: *Botanical Survey of India, Western Circle,* **(BSI),** 7-Koregaon Road, Pune 411 001, Maharashtra, **India.**
Telephone: 22125, 28679.
Status: Government of India, Department of Science and Technology.
Foundation: 1898. *Number of specimens:* 138.000.
Herbarium: Plants of Maharashtra and Karnataka states and union territories of Goa, Daman, Diu and Nagar-Haweli.
Important collections: R. K. Bhide, T. Cooke, W. A. Talbot, Indraji Thaker, G. M. Woodrow.
Deputy Director: B. D. SHARMA, 1935 (Palynology, taxonomy).

Staff members: M. Y. Ansari, 1929 (Taxonomy, ecology).

U. R. Deshpande, 1930 (Taxonomy).

S. Y. Kamble, 1940 (Taxonomy, cytology).

S. Karthikeyan, 1940 (Taxonomy, bibliography, history of botany).

M. J. Kothari, 1943 (Taxonomy).

S. K. Mudaliar, 1933 (Taxonomy).

V. V. Nisal, 1942 (Horticulture).

N. P. Singh, 1941 (Taxonomy, phytogeography, flora of Eastern Karnataka).

Specialization in research: Taxonomy, cytology, palynology, ecology and phytogeography.

Associated botanic garden: Experimental Botanical Garden and Arboretum, Survey No. 88, Mundhwa, Pune 411 036.

Loans: By application to the Director, Botanical Survey of India, CAL.

Periodical and serial works: Bulletin of the Botanical Survey of India, Records of the Botanical Survey of India, Fascicles of Flora of India.

Exchange: Available: Cryptogams and phanerogams of Western India. Desired: Cryptogams and phanerogams of tropical and sub-tropical areas.

Remarks: Formerly listed under Calcutta (CAL).

PUNTA ARENAS: *Herbario, Instituto de la Pata-* *gonia,* **(HIP),** Casilla 102-D, Punta Arenas, Magallanes, **Chile.**

Telephone: 23039.

Status: Non-profit, private research foundation.

Foundation: 1970. *Number of specimens:* 8.500.

Herbarium: Mainly vascular plants; Patagonia and Tierra del Fuego.

Important collections: Edmundo Pisano V., Orlando Dollenz A., David M. Moore, R. Natalie P. Goodall, Transecta Botánica de Patagonia Austral, G. D. McSweeney, Jenny Davidson.

Director: Edmundo Pisano-Valdés, 1919 (Phytogeography; ecology).

Staff member: Orlando Dollenz-Alvarez, 1947 (Phytosociology).

Specialization in research: Phytogeography, distribution, and systematics of Fuego-Patagonian plants.

Associated botanic garden: Jardín Botánico "Carl Skottsberg."

Loans: Three months, only to herbaria included in Index Herbariorum or adhered to universities.

Periodical and serial works: Anales del Instituto de la Patagonia.

Exchange: Interested in exchange of Fuego-Patagonian plants.

Q

QINGDAO: *Herbarium, Department of Biology, National University of Shandong,* **(TS),** Qingdao, Shandong, **People's Republic of China.**

QUÉBEC: *Herbier du Laboratoire d'ecologie forestière, Ecologie forestière, Université Laval,* **(QEF),** Québec, Québec, **Canada** G1K 7P4.
Telephone: 418/656-2838; 656-4190.
Foundation: 1975. *Number of specimens:* 6.100 (2.000 vascular plants, 3.500 bryophytes, 600 lichens).
Herbarium: Flora of Quebec.
Director and Curator: MIROSLAV M. GRANDTNER, 1928 (Plant ecology).
Specialization in research: Ecology and phytogeography.
Loans: No general policy.
Periodical and serial works: Etudes écologiques (series of monographs).
Exchange: Available: Etudes écologiques. Wanted: Similar publications.

QUÉBEC: *Herbier Louis-Marie, Faculté des Sciences de l'agriculture et de l'alimentation, Université Laval,* **(QFA),** Sainte-Foy, Québec, **Canada** G1K 7P4.
Telephone: 418/656-2613.
Foundation: Founded in 1962 with the transfer of LT (founded in 1923). *Number of specimens:* 213.200 (180.000 vascular plants, 23.000 bryophytes, 1.300 fungi, 5.300 algae, 3.600 lichens).
Herbarium: Mostly North American material, especially Canadian and Québec.
Important collections: Père Louis-Marie (100.000; formerly LT), Père A. Dutilly (12.000), L. Cinq-Mars (9.000), Leblanc (28.000), André Cardinal (5.000; formerly QUC), J. P. Bernard (6.500); incorporated herbaria: QFS (15.000), part of ULF (15.000), QPH (extended loan) about 15.000).
Curator: ROBERT GAUTHIER, 1941; 418/656-2741 (Mosses; *Sphagnum*).
Staff members: JEAN-PAUL BERNARD, 1921 (Flora of Manitoba and Québec).
BERNARD BOIVIN, 1916 (Flora of Canada; biography; bibliography; history; nomenclature; *Thalictrum, Westringia*).
Specialization in research: Phytogeography, floristics, and taxonomy of Canadian plants.
Loans: To recognized institutions.
Periodical and serial works: Provancheria; Ludoviciana.
Exchange: Available: Plants from Québec. Wanted: Plants from the northern hemisphere.
Remarks: ULF has been incorporated in QFA, not in QUC as indicated in edition 6.

QUÉBEC: *Herbier, Centre de Recherches Forestières des Laurentides, Environnement Canada,* **(QFB),** P.O. Box 3800, Sainte-Foy, Québec, **Canada** G1V 4C7.
Telephone: 418/694-3922.
Status: Canadian Forestry Service, Department of Environment, Ottawa.
Foundation: 1952. *Number of specimens:* 19.000.
Herbarium: Mainly fungi.
Director: CARL WINGET, 1938.
Head Forest Disease Survey: DENIS LACHANCE, 1939.
Curator: RENÉ N. CAUCHON (Mycology; forest pathology and biology).
Staff members: G. B. OUELLETTE, 1932 (Mycology).
EDGAR SMERLIS, 1922 (Ascomycetes).
Specialization in research: Organisms related to forest and ornamental tree diseases.
Loans: Usual regulations.

QUÉBEC: *Environnement Canada Land Directorate Québec Region,* **(QFBE),** C. P. 10100, Sainte-Foy, Québec, **Canada** G1V 4H5.
Telephone: 418/694-3244.
Foundation: 1967. *Number of specimens:* 16.250 (vascular plants 9.600, mosses 4.500, lichens 1.500, hepatics 350, other 300).
Herbarium: Québec.
Curator: JEAN-LOUIS LETHIECQ, 1934; 418/694-3244; 694-3964 (Taxonomy of bryophytes, lichens, and vascular plants).
Specialization in research: Ecological land classification.

QUÉBEC: *Faculté des Sciences, Université Laval,* **(QFS),** Québec, Québec, **Canada** — incorporated in QFA.

QUÉBEC: *Musée du Québec, Section des sciences naturelles,* **(QMP)** – incorporated in QUE.

QUÉBEC: *Herbier Provancher, Département de biologie, Faculté des Sciences, Université Laval,* **(QPH),** Québec, Québec, **Canada** G1K 7P4.
Telephone: 418/656-3594.
Foundation: 1854. *Number of specimens:* 15.000.
Herbarium: Flora of Quebec.
Important collections: L. Provancher herbarium (800).
Remarks: On extended loan to QFA, except for Provancher herbarium.

QUÉBEC: *Herbier Cardinal, Département de biologie, Faculté des Sciences, Université Laval,* **(QUC),** Québec, Québec, **Canada** G1K 7P4 — incorporated in QFA.
Foundation: 1938. *Number of specimens:* 6.000.
Herbarium: Marine algae, Golfe Saint Laurent, es-

pecially Quebec coasts.

QUÉBEC: *Herbier du Québec,* **(QUE),** Complexe scientifique, 2700 rue Einstein, Sainte-Foy, Québec, **Canada** GIP 3W8.
Telephone: 418/643-2348.
Status: Gouvernement du Québec, Ministère de l'Agriculture.
Foundation: 1972. *Number of specimens:* 90.000 (80.000 vascular plants, 6.000 bryophytes, 2.000 lichens, 2.000 fungi).
Herbarium: Flora of northern hemisphere (cryptogams and phanerogams).
Important collections: Herbarium of the Laboratoire de botanique, Division des mauvaises herbes (41.000); herbarium of the Musée du Québec (formerly QMP, 35.000); herbarium of the ministère des terres et forêts du Québec; herbaria D.-N. St-Cyr, J. W. Marr, P. Dansereau, J. Rousseau.
Director: ANDRÉ VÉZINA, 1947 (Chef de la division botanique, écologie et malherbologie).
Curators: PIERRE MASSON, 1919 (Cryptogamic herbarium).
ANDRÉ VÉZINA, 1947 (Phanerogamic herbarium).
Staff members: CLAUDE-J. BOUCHARD, 1944 (Plant ecology).
DOMINIQUE DOYON, 1932 (Plant ecology).
CAMILLE GERVAIS, 1933 (Cytogenetics and cytotaxonomy).
LOUISE GUAY, 1951.
Specialization in research: Québec flora; weed taxonomy; weed seedling identification.
Loans: To recognized institutions.
Exchange: Available: Vascular plants and bryophytes from Québec. Wanted: Vascular plants and bryophytes of the northern hemisphere.

QUÉBEC: *Herbier, Service Canadien de la Faune, Région du Québec,* **(SCFQ),** 2700 Blvd. Laurier, C.P. 10.100, Sainte-Foy, Québec, **Canada** GIV 4H5.
Telephone: 418/694-3914.
Status: Ministère de l'Environnement Canada.
Foundation: 1972. *Number of specimens:* 6.000.
Herbarium: Maìnly aquatic and riparian vegetation.
Curator: LÉO-GUY DE REPENTIGNY, 1942.

QUÉBEC: *Herbier, Département d'écologie et de pédologie, Faculté de foresterie et géodésie, Université Laval,* **(ULF),** Québec, Québec, **Canada** GIK 7P4 -- incorporated in part in QFA.

QUEZON: *Herbarium, National Botanic Garden,* **(PNBG)** -- *see* SINILOAN.

QUEZON CITY: *Herbarium, Department of Botany, College of Arts and Sciences, University of Philippines,* **(PUH),** Quezon City, **Philippines.** (Information 1974)
Status: University.

Foundation: 1908 (destroyed during World War II, rehabilitated in 1946). *Number of specimens:* 6.000.
Herbarium: Flowering plants, especially grasses, algae, fungi and mosses of Pacific and Eastern Asia.
Specialization in research: Philippine flora.
Associated botanic garden: U.P. Experiment Garden.
Periodical and serial works: Natural and Applied Science Bulletin of the University of the Philippines.

QUITO: *Herbario del Instituto de Ciencias Naturales, Universidad Central,* **(Q),** Casilla 633, Quito, **Ecuador.**
Foundation: 1850. *Number of specimens:* 25.300.
Herbarium: Flora of Ecuador.
Important collections: G. Jameson, L. Sodiro S. J., I. Padilla, A. Ortega.
Director: FRANCISCO LATORRE (Pharmacology).
Staff members: JESUS INCA (Systematic botany).
ALBERTO ORTEGA (Anatomy).
INEZ PADILLA (Systematic botany).
Periodical and serial works: Ciencia y Naturaleza, journal of the department.
Exchange: Available: Ecuadorean plants.

QUITO: *Herbario "Luciano Andrade Marin," Centro Forestal de Conocoto, Dirección de Desarrollo Forestal, Ministerio de Agricultura y Ganadería,* **(QAME),** Casilla 099-B, Quito, **Ecuador.**
Telephone: 311092; 513808.
Foundation: 1968. *Number of specimens:* 3.500.
Herbarium: Plants of Ecuador.
Important collections: Campuzano, R. G. Dixon, E. L. Little.
Director: EDGAR VASQUEZ, 1947 (Forestry).
Staff member: ALFREDO FLORES, 1939.
Specialization in research: Technology of wood.
Exchange: Available: Plants of Ecuador.

QUITO: *Herbario, Instituto de Cienciäs, Pontificia Universidad Catolica del Ecuador,* **(QCA),** Avenida 12 de Octubre, Apartado 2184, Quito, **Ecuador.**
Telephone: 239149.
Foundation: 1970. *Number of specimens:* 15.000.
Herbarium: Flora of Ecuador and South America.
Important collections: J. Boeke, T. Croat, C. Dodson, A. Gentry, L. Holm-Nielsen, J. Jaramillo, M. Madison, B. MacBryde, L. Mille, B. Øllgaard.
Director: HENRIK BALSLEV, 1951 (Juncaceae; floristics).
Curator: JAIME JARAMILLO, 1944 (Ceja Andina; use of plants; floristics).
Staff members: ROCIO ALARCON, 1957 (Medicinal plants).
RAMON ANDRADE, 1959 (Phytogeography).
JUDITH AYALA, 1946 (Fungi).
ELIZABETH BRAVO, 1956 (Alismataceae).
Specialization in research: Flora of Ecuador; phytogeography; ethnobotany.
Periodical and serial works: Revista de la Uni-

versidad Catolica, occasional.

Exchange: Available: Plants of Ecuador.

QUITO: *Herbario, Museo Nacional de Ciencias Naturales,* (**QCNE**), Apartado 67, Calle Tamayo, Quito, **Ecuador.**

Telephone: 235176.

Status: New branch of the National Museum of Natural History.

Foundation: 1979. *Number of specimens:* 2.000.

Herbarium: Flora of Ecuador.

Important collections: L. Holm-Nielsen.

   Director: MIGUEL MORENO, 1919.

   Advisor: LAURITZ B. HOLM-NIELSEN (Helobiales; *Passiflora, Phyllanthus;* phytogeography).

   Periodical and serial works: Revista de la Museo Nacional de Ciencias Naturales.

   Remarks: This collection is proposed to be the national herbarium.

QUITO: *Herbario "P. Luis Sodiro," Bibloteca Ecuatoriana "Aurelio Espinosa Pólit,"* (**QPLS**), Apartado 160, Quito, **Ecuador.**

Telephone: 530420.

Foundation: 1868. *Number of specimens:* 29.000, including Sodiro types.

Herbarium: Flora of Ecuador.

Important collections: P. Luis Sodiro.

   Director: JULIÁN G. BRAVO.

   Remarks: This collection contains a very good set of Sodiro's specimens; Padre Bravo has made it possible to use the collections even though they have not been given much botanical care since the death of Sodiro.

QUITO: *Herbario, Departamento de Ecologia, Programa Nacional de Regionalización, Ministerio de Agricultura y Ganadería,* (**QPNRA**), Casilla 099-B, Edif. La Filantrópica, Quito, **Ecuador.**

Telephone: 510200.

Foundation: 1975. *Number of specimens:* 3.000.

Herbarium: Flora of Ecuador.

Important collections: A. Arévalo, J. Boeke, L. Cañadas, T. Croat, L. Dávolos, W. Estrada, J. Luteyn, G. Morales, R. Oldeman, R. Padilla, A. Temple.

   Director: LUIS CAÑADAS CRUZ, 1933 (Forestry).

   Staff member: LUPE DÁVALOS N., 1953; 215555 (Flora of Ecuador).

   Specialization in research: Ecological mapping; flora in relation to the ecosystem.

   Exchange: Available: Plants of Ecuador.

R

RABAT: *Institut Scientifique Chérifien, Laboratoire de Taxonomie et Ecologie des Végétaux Supérieurs,* (**RAB**), Avenue Moulay Chérif, Rabat, **Morocco.** (Information 1974)
Status: Government institute.
Foundation: 1921. *Number of specimens:* 100.000.
Herbarium: Flora of Morocco and the Sahara, including cryptogams.
Specialization in research: Flora of Morocco (phanerogams and vascular cryptogams), phytosociology.
Loans: To recognized botanical institutions.
Periodical and serial works: Travaux de l'Institut scientifique chérifien, série botanique; Publications de la Société des sciences naturelles et physiques du Maroc: Comptes rendus, Bulletin, Mémoires et Variétés.

RABAT: *Herbarium, Laboratoire de Biologie Végétale,* (**RAU**), Faculté des Sciences, Avenue Moulay Chérif, Rabat, **Morocco.** (Information 1974)
Status: University.
Foundation: 1957.
Herbarium: Marine algae of Morocco.

RADFORD: *Herbarium, Biology Department, Box 5792, Radford University,* (**RUHV**), Radford, Virginia 24142, **U.S.A.**
Telephone: 703/731-5129.
Foundation: 1913. *Number of specimens:* 5.000.
Herbarium: Emphasis on Virginia, especially southwestern part (Montgomery and Pulaski counties).
Director and Curator: PATRICK B. MIKESELL, 1940 (*Calystegia*, Convolvulaceae; flora of southwestern Virginia).
Loans: Upon request.
Exchange: Available: Southwestern Virginia specimens.

RALEIGH: *Herbarium, Department of Botany, North Carolina State University,* (**NCSC**), Raleigh, North Carolina 27650, **U.S.A.**
Telephone: 919/737-2700.
Foundation: 1947. *Number of specimens:* 98.000.
Herbarium: Plants of North Carolina and southeastern U.S.
Important collections: Voucher specimens for cytogenetic studies on crop plants (peanuts, cotton, tobacco, pine, blueberries); woody plants, legumes, composites, grasses, aquatics; fleshy fungi, mycorrhizae.
Curator: JAMES W. HARDIN, 1929 (Woody plants; flora of southeastern U.S.).
Staff members: ROBERT L. BECKMANN, 1945 (Chemotaxonomy of weeds and woody plants).
PAUL R. FANTZ, 1941 (*Clitoria;* cultivated ornamentals).

LARRY F. GRAND, 1940 (Forest pathology; fleshy fungi).
JON M. STUCKY, 1945 (Biosystematics of weeds).
DAVID H. TIMOTHY, 1928 (Agrostology).
Specialization in research: Flora of southeastern U.S.; variation in woody plants; biosystematics of weeds; forest pathology; cytotaxonomy of grasses.
Loans: To curators of recognized herbaria.
Exchange: Southeastern U.S. material.

RANGOON: *Forest Department Herbarium,* (**RAF**), 526 Merchant Street, Rangoon, **Burma.** (Information 1974)
Foundation: 1925 (at Maymyo, moved to Rangoon 1932). *Number of specimens:* 17.000.

RANGOON: *Herbarium, Rangoon University,* (**RANG**), Rangoon, **Burma.** (Information 1974)
Status: University.
Foundation: 1947. *Number of specimens:* 15.000.
Herbarium: Flora of Burma, mainly pteridophytes.

RANGOON: *Herbarium, Union of Burma Applied Research Institute,* (**RAS**), Pharmaceutical Department, Rangoon, **Burma.** (Information 1974)
Status: Directed by state.
Foundation: 1953. *Number of specimens:* 1.500.
Herbarium: Medicinal plants.

RAWALPINDI: *Stewart Herbarium, Gordon College,* (**RAW**), Rawalpindi, **Pakistan.** (Information 1974)
Status: Private foundation (American United Presbyterian Mission).
Foundation: 1893. *Number of specimens:* 60.000.
Herbarium: Ferns and flowering plants from Burma, Nepal, Kashmir, Pakistan and Afghanistan.
Specialization in research: Flora of Pakistan.
Loans: To recognized botanical institutions.

READING: *Herbarium, Plant Science Laboratories, University of Reading,* (**RNG**), Whiteknights, Reading RG6 2AS, England, **Great Britain.**
Telephone: (0734) 85123 ext. 7912.
Status: University.
Foundation: About 1900. *Number of specimens:* 104.000 (including 5.500 bryophytes).
Herbarium: Europe, especially Great Britain and Iberian Peninsula, N. Africa and Macaronesia; Tierra del Fuego and cool temperate South America; Pteridophytes, worldwide; Bryophytes, British and Arctic.
Important collections: J. E. Lousley (GB), P. H. Davis (N. Africa), K. M. Lyell (Pteridophytes).
Director: V. H. HEYWOOD, 1927 (Umbelliferae, Compositae, Mediterranean flora, conservation and resources especially in S. America).

Deputy Director: D. M. MOORE, 1933 (Flora of temperate S. America, phytogeography, flora of Macaronesia, biosystematics).

Curator: S. L. JURY, 1949 (Umbelliferae, Flora of Spain and Mediterranean region).

Staff members: P. D. W. BARNARD, 1932 (Trinidad pteridophytes).

R. E. LONGTON, 1939 (Biosystematics of bryophytes).

B. PICKERSGILL, 1940 (Origin and evolution of cultivated plants, identification of archaeobotanical material from the New World tropics).

G. D. ROWLEY, 1921 (Succulents, history and taxonomy of cultivated ornamentals).

Specialization in research: Flora of Europe, Mediterranean region, Macaronesia, temperate S. America, succulents, Umbelliferae, Compositae, *Fragaria, Potentilla, Aegilops, Triticum, Fuchsia,* British Aliens, biosystematic studies on bryophytes.

Associated botanic garden: Plant Science Botanic Garden.

Loans: In general to recognized botanical institutions.

Exchange: Available: Great Britain, Southern Europe and North Africa, temperate South America, including bruophytes. Desired: European, Mediterranean and temperate South American material.

READING: *Herbarium, Reading Public Museum and Art Gallery,* **(RPM),** 500 Museum Road, Reading, Pennsylvania 19611, **U.S.A.**

Telephone: 215/371-5837; 371-5838.

Foundation: 1930. *Number of specimens:* 2.000.

Herbarium: Mainly local vascular plants.

Important collections: Thomas J. Oberlin.

Remarks: Herbarium inactive.

READING: *Department of Agricultural Botany, The University,* **(RU)** – – incorporated in RNG.

RECIFE: *Herbário, Empresa Pernambucana de Pesquisa Agropecuária,* **(IPA),** Avenida General San Martin 1371, Caixa Postal 1022, Bonji, 50.000 Recife, Pernambuco, **Brazil.**

Telephone: (55)081/227-0500.

Status: Secretaria da Agricultura.

Foundation: 1935. *Number of specimens:* 24.920.

Herbarium: Chiefly northeastern Brazil but also from Amazonas and Minas Gerais.

Important collections: D. Andrade Lima (6.350), Bento Pickel (6.000).

Director: FERNANDO CHAVES LINS, 1932 (Agronomist).

Curator: DÁRDANO DE ANDRADE LIMA, 1919; 231-30-92 (Leguminosae; phytogeography).

Staff members: JÚLIO ZOÉ DE BRITO, 1953 (Taxonomy).

FERNANDO ANTÔNIO TÁVORA GALINDO, 1955 (Taxonomy).

VALDELICE CORREIA LIMA, 1943 (Taxonomy).

MÁRIO ALBERTO MAIA FILHO, 1955 (Taxonomy).

ANA LUIZA DÚ BOCAGE NETA, 1956 (Taxonomy).

RITA DE CASSIA ARÁUJO PEREIRA, 1953 (Taxonomy).

ANA CLÁUDIA PASCHOAL PERRUCI, 1952.

MARCELO DE ATAIDE SILVA, 1946 (Taxonomy).

MARIA FERNANDA FERREIRA DA SILVA, 1953 (Taxonomy).

Specialization in research: Flora of northeastern Brazil; Brazilian Leguminosae.

Loans: To qualified institutions and specialists, for 6 months.

Exchange: Yes.

Remarks: Formerly Instituto de Pesquisas Agronômicas.

RECIFE: *Herbário, Departamento de Botânica, Centro de Ciências Biológicas, Universidade Federal de Pernambuco,* **(UFP),** Cidade Universitária, Avenida Artur de Sá, 50.000 Recife, Pernambuco, **Brazil.**

Telephone: (55)081/227-2466.

Foundation: 1968. *Number of specimens:* 8.000.

Herbarium: General herbarium, especially northeastern Brazil.

Important collections: G. Mariz (Clusiaceae), Lauro Xavier Filho (lichens), Laise Cavalcanti-Andrade (Myxomycetes).

Curators: LAISE DE HOLLANDA CAVALCANTI-ANDRADE, 1947 (Myxomycetes).

GERALDO MARIZ, 1923 (Clusiaceae of Brazil; fresh-water algae).

Staff members: JOSÉ LUIZ DE HAMBURGO ALVES, 1937 (Palynology).

DILOSA C. ALENCAR BARBOSA, 1947 (Seeds).

MARIA S. BARROS, 1947 (*Tovomita,* Clusiaceae).

IVA C. LEÃO-BARROS, 1947 (Schizaeaceae, Solanaceae).

LAURO XAVIER FILHO, 1939 (Lichenology).

Specialization in research: Flora of Pernambuco.

Loans: In general to recognized individuals and botanical institutions.

Periodical and serial works: Estudos e Pesquisas, Série B, Universidade Federal de Pernambuco.

RECIFE: *Herbário, Departamento de Micologia, Centro de Ciências Biológicas, Universidade Federal de Pernambuco,* **(URM),** Cidade Universitária, Avenida Prof. Artur de Sá, 50.000 Recife, Pernambuco, **Brazil.**

Foundation: 1954. *Number of specimens:* 72.800.

Herbarium: Tropical and temperate fungi.

Important collections: J. A. von Arx, Augusto Chaves Batista, José Luiz Bezerra, Lee Bonar, Ana Amélia Salgado Alves da Silva Cavalcanti, Maria Auxiliadora de Queiroz Cavalcanti, Wlandemir de Albuquerque Cavalcanti, R. Ciferri, William Bridge Cooke, Ezequias P. Henninger, Dárdano de Andrade Lima, T. H. Macbride, G. W. Martin, Franz Petrak,

Bento Pickel, Danuza José Muniz Poroca, Rolf Singer, Osvaldo Soares, Camille Torrend, Albino Vital.
Curator: DANUZA JOSÉ MUNIZ POROCA (Ascomycetes, Xylariaceae).
Staff members: WILMA THEREZINHA GADELHA DE ASSUNÇÃO (Soil Deuteromycetes).
JOSÉ LUIZ BEZERRA (Discomycetes).
ANA AMÉLIA SALGADO ALVES DA SILVA CAVALCANTI (Deuterolichens).
MARIA AUXILIADORA DE QUEIROZ CAVALCANTI (Basidiomycetes, Polyporaceae).
MARIA DULCINÉIA CAVALCANTI (Yeasts; medical mycology; dermatophytes).
WLANDEMIR DE ALBUQUERQUE CAVALCANTI (Ascomycetes, Deuteromycetes; Ascolichens, Deuterolichens).
RUTH GARNIER DE SOUZA FALCÃO (Ascomycetes).
MARIA JOSÉ DOS SANTOS FERNANDES (Ascomycetes, Deuteromycetes).
MARIA INAIÁ IVO (Yeasts; medical mycology; dermatophytes).
DÉBORA MARIA MASSA LIMA (Phytopathology; sugar cane fungus diseases).
JOSÉ AMÉRICO DE LIMA (Aerial Deuteromycetes).
ELZA AUREA DE LUNA (Fungal cytology).
NELLY PACHECO DE LYRA (Aquatic fungi).
MARIA JOSÉ PEREZ MACIEL (Aspergillales).
HERALDO DA SILVA MAIA (Ascomycetes, Deuteromycetes: phytopathology; fungus diseases of ornamental plants).
FRANCISCO CORDEIRO NETO (Fungus biochemistry).
GENEROSA EMILIA PONTUAL PERES (Ascomycetes, Deuteromycetes).
LUZINETE ACIOLE DE QUEIROZ (Pathogenic yeasts).
THEREZINHA TAVARES DE BARROS SOUZA (Ascomycetes).
HARBANSH PRASAL UPADHYAY (Aquatic fungi; Ascomycetes).
Specialization in research: Tropical mycology.
Exchange: Worldwide fungi.

REDDING: *Herbarium, Agriculture and Natural Resources Division, Shasta College,* (**RESC**), 1065 North Old Oregon Trail, Redding, California 96001, **U.S.A.**
Telephone: 916/241-3523.
Foundation: 1965. *Number of specimens:* 600.
Herbarium: Agronomic crops, forest, and range weeds; range grasses, browse, and forest plants.

REDLANDS: *Herbarium, University of Redlands,* (**RED**), Redlands, California 92373, **U.S.A.** (Information 1974)
Number of specimens: 5.000.
Herbarium: California chaparral.

RÉDUIT: *The Mauritius Herbarium,* (**MAU**), Mauritius Sugar Industry Research Institute, Réduit, **Mauritius.**
Telephone: 54-1061/62/63/64.
Status: A public herbarium dedicated to education and research.
Foundation: 1960. *Number of specimens:* 25.000.
Herbarium: Comprises the combined herbaria of the Mauritius Institutes and Public Museum, the Department of Agriculture and the Mauritius Sugar Industry Research Institute.
Important collections: Type specimens – endemic species Mascarene Islands.
Director: J. D. DE R. DE SAINT ANTOINE, 1923 (Sugar technology).
Curator: R. JULIEN, 1939 (Pteridophyta, Sugar cane physiology).
Staff members: J. GUÉHO, 1937.
G. LECORDIER, 1956.
Specialization in research: Flora of Mascarene Islands.
Loans: To recognized institutions and to individuals in certain circumstances.
Periodical and serial works: Weed flora leaflets and Flora of Mascarene Islands.

REGENSBURG: *Regensburgische Botanische Gesellschaft,* (**REG**), Postfach Universität, 8400 Regensburg, **Federal Republic of Germany,** BRD.
Telephone: 0941-9433108.
Status: Private, on loan to the university.
Foundation: 1804. *Number of specimens:* 40.000.
Herbarium: Local flora of Regensburg, Germany, Europe.
Important collections: Mayr (Bacillariophyceae), Familler (Bryophytes), Wirtgen (Vascular plants), v. Welden (Vascular plants).
Director: A. BRESINSKY, 1935 (Mycology, geobotany).
Specialization in research: Mycology, geobotany.
Associated botanic garden: Botanischer Versuchs- und Lehrgarten.
Loans: On request.
Periodical and serial works: Hoppea, Denkschriften Regensburgischen Botanische Gesellschaft.
Exchange: Yes (Periodicals).
Remarks: Regensburgische Botanische Gesellschaft is the oldest still existing botanical society in the world (year of foundation 1790).

REGGIO EMILIA: *Herbarium, Civici Musei e Gallerie,* (**SPAL**), Via Spallanzani I, 42100 Reggio Emilia, **Italy** (Information 1974)
Status: Municipal museum.
Foundation: 1799. *Number of specimens:* 7.000.
Herbarium: Local flora.
Important collections: Herbarium of Lazzaro Spallanzani, Filippo Re, Giovanni Fabriani.

REGINA: *Herbarium, Agriculture Canada, Regina Research Station,* (**DAS**), Box 440, Regina, Saskatchewan, **Canada** S4P 3A2.

Telephone: 306/585-0255.

Status: Agriculture Canada.

Foundation: 1964. *Number of specimens:* 4.000.

Herbarium: Mainly weedy vascular plants of western Canada.

  Director: J. R. HAY, 1925 (Weed control).

  Curator: A. G. THOMAS, 1943 (Weed ecology).

  Specialization in research: Weed species of agricultural land in the prairie region.

REGINA: *Herbarium, Biology Department, University of Regina,* (**USAS**), Regina, Saskatchewan, **Canada** S4S OA2.

Telephone: 306/584-4254.

Status: University of Regina and Museum of Natural History (Provincial Government).

Foundation: 1945. *Number of specimens:* 25.000.

Herbarium: Vascular plants of Saskatchewan, with emphasis on grasses and sedges; *Astragalus* worldwide.

  Curator: GEORGE F. LEDINGHAM, 1911 (Saskatchewan flora; *Astragalus, Carex*).

  Specialization in research: Distribution of Saskatchewan vascular plant species; identification of rare and endangered vascular plants of southern Saskatchewan.

  Loans: Usual conditions.

  Exchange: Yes, by arrangement.

  Remarks: Bard Herbarium of the Provincial Government included here.

RENNER: *Lundell Herbarium, Texas Research Foundation,* (**LL**), Renner, Texas 75079, **U.S.A.** – – housed at TEX.

Foundation: 1943. *Number of specimens:* 65.000.

Herbarium: Grasses of the world; phanerogams of Texas, Mexico, Central America; Yucatan Peninsula, British Honduras, Texas.

RENNES: *Laboratoire de Botanique de la Faculté des Sciences,* (**REN**), Avenue du Général Leclerc, 35 Rennes, **France.** (Information 1974)

Status: University.

Foundation: 1840. *Number of specimens:* 100.000.

Herbarium: Phanerogams of France, Europe, Africa and Asia; bryophytes of Southern Hemisphere.

  Specialization in research: Armorican flora.

  Associated botanic garden: Jardin Botanique de la Faculté des Sciences de Rennes.

  Loans: To recognized botanical institutions.

  Periodical and serial works: Botanical Rhedonica (Bulletin des Laboratoires de Botanique de la Faculté des Sciences de Rennes).

RENO: *Herbarium, Nevada State Department of Agriculture,* (**NSDA**), P.O. Box 11100, 350 Capitol Hill Avenue, Reno, Nevada 89510, **U.S.A.**

Telephone: 702/784-6401.

Foundation: 1962. *Number of specimens:* 1.070.

Herbarium: Vascular plants, many noxious weeds, numerous range plants from throughout Nevada.

  Director: PHILIP C. MARTINELLI, 1924.

  Curator: ROBERT C. BECHTEL, 1924 (Entomologist).

RENO: *University of Nevada Herbarium,* (**RENO**), *and Nevada Agricultural Experiment Station Herbarium,* (**NESH**), Renewable Natural Resources Division, University of Nevada, Reno, Nevada 89557, **U.S.A.**

Telephone: 702/784-6188.

Foundation: 1890. *Number of specimens:* 67.000.

Herbarium: Mainly Nevada and adjacent states; vascular plants, mosses.

Important collections: Endangered plants of Nevada; isotypes from the Mt. Rose area; Sheldon Antelope Refuge collection; George Whittell Forest and Wildlife Area collection; duplicate collection from Nevada Test Site; Percy Train (Nevada), F. J. Lindheimer (Flora Texana), A. A. Heller, I. W. Clokey, A. Nelson, P. B. Kennedy.

  Curator: HUGH N. MOZINGO, 1925 (Bryology, grasses, cacti).

  Specialization in research: Mosses of Nevada; aquatic plants; ferns and fern allies; cacti; grasses of Nevada.

  Loans: To any recognized institution, 6 month loan period with renewal.

  Exchange: Limited by available personnel, but have exchange programs for western species, aquatic plants generally, and some southeastern U.S. plants.

REPETEK: *Herbarium of the Desert Experiment Station of the W.I.R.,* (**REP**), Repetek, **U.S.S.R.**

RÉUNION: *Herbier de la Réunion,* (**STCR**) – – *see* SAINT CLOTHILDE.

REXBURG: *Herbarium, Ricks College,* (**RICK**), Rexburg, Idaho 83440, **U.S.A.**

Telephone: 208/356-2536.

Status: Private institution.

Foundation: 1957. *Number of specimens:* 12.000.

Herbarium: Eastern Idaho, mostly Madison, Teton, and Jefferson counties.

  Director and Curator: DELBERT W. LINDSAY, 1924 (Flora of eastern Idaho).

  Specialization in research: Flora of eastern Idaho.

  Loans: Yes.

  Exchange: Yes.

REYKJAVIK: *Herbarium, Department of Botany, Museum of Natural History,* (**ICEL**), P.O. Box 5320, 125 Reykjavik, **Iceland.**

Telephone: 91-15487, 91-12728.

Status: State institution.

Foundation: 1889. *Number of specimens:* 120.000.

Herbarium: Arctic and boreal plants, especially Icelandic vascular plants and mosses.

Director and Curator: EYTHOR EINARSSON, 1929 (Icelandic vascular plants, especially alpine vegetation, plant succession).

Staff member: BERGTHOR JOHANNSSON, 1933 (Icelandic bryophytes).

Specialization in research: Taxonomy and distribution of Icelandic vascular plants and mosses; alpine vegetation of Iceland and plant succession.

Loans: To recognized botanical institutions.

Periodical and serial works: Acta Naturalia Islandicae.

Exchange: Available: Limited number Icelandic vascular plants and mosses. Desired: Arctic and boreal plants.

RICHARDSON: *Lundell Herbarium, Plant Sciences Laboratory, University of Texas at Dallas,* (**UTD**), Box 688, Richardson, Texas 75080, **U.S.A.**

Telephone: 214/690-2279.

Foundation: 1972 at UTD. *Number of specimens:* 250.000.

Herbarium: Neotropics, Texas, worldwide.

Important collections: C. L. Lundell, Percy H. Gentle, Elias Contreras, C. G. Pringle, E. Matuda, George B. Hinton.

Director: CYRUS LONGWORTH LUNDELL, 1907 (Plants of southwestern U.S. and the neotropics; neotropical Myrsinaceae; Celastraceae of Mexico and Central America).

Staff member: BETTY G. HAYGOOD, 1935.

Specialization in research: Floristics and monographic studies of Texas and the neotropics.

Loans: Restricted.

Periodical and serial works: Wrightia.

Exchange: Neotropical, Texas specimens.

Remarks: Formerly listed under Dallas.

RICHFIELD: *Herbarium, Fishlake National Forest,* (**FNFR**), P.O. Box 628, 170 North Main Street, Richfield, Utah 84701, **U.S.A.**

Telephone: 801/584-8241; 896-4491.

Status: U.S.D.A., Forest Service.

Foundation: 1925. *Number of specimens:* 2.500.

Herbarium: Mainly from Fishlake National Forest.

Curator: JAMES L. MOWER.

RICHMOND: *Herbarium, Department of Biology, Earlham College,* (**EAR**), Richmond, Indiana 47374. **U.S.A.**

Telephone: 317/962-6561.

Status: Private school, under the direction of the Society of Friends (Quakers).

Foundation: College founded in 1847. Herbarium destroyed by fire in 1924; present collection accumulated since then. *Number of specimens:* 15.000-16.000.

Herbarium: Local flora.

Curator: DOROTHY ANN DOUGLAS, 1951 (Plant ecology).

Loans: Usual regulations.

RICHMOND: *Herbarium, Department of Biological Sciences, Eastern Kentucky University,* (**EKY**), Richmond, Kentucky 40475, **U.S.A.**

Telephone: 606/622-2212 (Department); 622-2271 (Curator's office).

Foundation: 1974. *Number of specimens:* 8.600.

Herbarium: Flora of Kentucky and southeastern U.S.

Curator: J. STUART LASSETTER, 1944 (*Vicia*, Leguminosae, biosystematics).

Specialization in research: *Vicia* biosystematics; local Kentucky flora.

Loans: Usual conditions.

Exchange: Available: Limited numbers of Kentucky and southeastern U.S. plants.

RICHMOND: *Herbarium, Department of Biology, Virginia Commonwealth University,* (**VCU**), 816 Park Avenue, Richmond, Virginia 23284, **U.S.A.**

Telephone: 804/257-1562.

Foundation: 1968. *Number of specimens:* 15.000.

Herbarium: Vascular plants from central Virginia.

Director and Curator: MILES F. JOHNSON 1936 (Virginia flora; *Ageratum*, Asteraceae).

Specialization in research: Floristics, especially in Virginia flora.

Loans: Loans to institutions for up to a year, can be extended.

Exchange: Can be arranged for Virginia flora.

RICHMOND: *Herbarium, Virginia Department of Agriculture and Consumer Services,* (**VDAC**), Room 238, Consolidated Laboratories Building, 1 North 14th Street, Richmond, Virginia 23219, **U.S.A.**

Telephone: 804/786-8795.

Status: Adjunct to the Virginia State Seed Laboratory.

Foundation: 1912. *Number of specimens:* 3.300.

Herbarium: Mainly plants of Virginia; crop and weed species.

Curator: HARRY L. SMITH, 1922.

RIGA: *Herbarium, Department of Botany, Latvian State University,* (**RIG**), Fr. Gaila Street 10, 226200 Riga, **U.S.S.R.**

Telephone: 332566.

Status: University.

Foundation: 1919. *Number of specimens:* 100.000.

Herbarium: Higher plants of Latvian and Estonian S.S.R., lichens and fungi of Latvian S.S.R.

Important collections: K. R. Kupffer (Herbarium Balticum, general herbarium), J. Mikutowicz (Bryotheca Baltica), J. Smarods (fungi latvici exsiccati).

Director: A. MAURINŠ, 1924 (Dendrology).

Curator: E. VIMBA, 1930 (Mycology).

Staff members: G. ĀBELE, 1931 (Higher plants, conservation).

V. LANGENFELDS, 1923 (Higher plants, *Malus*).

A. Piterāns, 1930 (Systematics and ecology of lichens).
Specialization in research: Flora and vegetation of Latvian S.S.R. (mycology, lichenology, dendrology and conservation).
Associated botanic garden: Botanic Garden of Latvian State University.
Loans: To recognized botanical institutions.
Periodical and serial works: Scientific Works of Latvian State University: Vols. 49 and 74, Botany.
Exchange: Available: Higher plants, fungi and lichens of Latvian S.S.R.

RIJSWIJK: *Koninklijke Shell (Shell Research N.V.),* **(SRR)** – discontinued.

RIMOUSKI: *Herbier, L'Ecole d'Agriculture,* **(RIM),** Rimouski, Québec, **Canada.**
Foundation: 1926. *Number of specimens:* 30.000.
Herbarium: Mainly Quebec, Labrador, and northern Canada.
Remarks: According to Boivin, this is the private herbarium of E. Lepage, which is now housed at 83 ouest, St-Jean-Baptiste, Rimouski, Québec, Canada.

RIMOUSKI: *Herbier, Département de Biologie, Université du Québec à Rimouski,* **(UQAR),** 300 avenue des Ursulines, Rimouski, Québec, **Canada** G5L 3A1.
Telephone: 418/724-1610.
Foundation: 1970. *Number of specimens:* 10.000.
Herbarium: Flora of eastern Québec.
Important collections: Herbier A. A. DeChamplain; herbier du Bureau d'Aménagement de l'Est du Québec.
Curator: Paul Demalsy, 1928 (Flora of eastern Quebec).
Specialization in research: General flora of eastern Quebec.
Loans: Usual conditions.

RIO CLARO: *Herbarium Rioclarense, Instituto de Biociências, Universidade Estadual Paulista "Julio de Mesquita Filho,"* **(HRCB),** Avenida 24-A, Caixa Postal 178, 13.500 Rio Claro, São Paulo, **Brazil.**
Telephone: (55)0195/34-7354.
Foundation: 1977. *Number of specimens:* 5.000.
Herbarium: Flora of the State of São Paulo.
Director: Sergio Nereu Pagano (Ecophysiology of native forests).
Curator: Giorgio de Marinis (Taxonomy and ecology of weeds).
Staff members: Célia Massa Beltrati (Plant anatomy).
Oswaldo Cesar (Taxonomy and ecophysiology of native forests).
Reinaldo Monteiro (Plants of cerrado).
Antonia Lélia G. Piccolo (Ecophysiology).
Osvaldo Aulino da Silva (Plants of cerrado).
Paulo Günther Windisch (Neotrop. pter.).

Specialization in research: Weeds and flora of southeastern Brazil.
Loans: Yes, upon request to Curator.
Periodical and serial works: Naturalia, review of biosciences of UNESP.
Exchange: Available: Plants from southeastern Brazil. Desired: Neotropical plants and weeds.

RIO DE JANEIRO: *Herbário Alberto Castellanos, FEEMA, DECAM,* **(GUA),** Estrada da Vista Chinesa 741, Alto da Boa Vista, 20.531 Rio de Janeiro, Rio de Janeiro, **Brazil.**
Telephone: (55)021/268-8849.
Status: Servico de Botânica Aplicada, Departamento de Conservacão Ambien tal, Fund. Est. Enga. Meio Ambiente (Applied Botany Serv., Environ. Conserv. Dept., State Found. of Environ. Engineering).
Foundation: 1955. *Number of specimens:* 15.000.
Herbarium: Flora of Rio de Janeiro State; Tijuca National Park (tropical rain forest), Restinga, and Mangroves.
Important collections: Alberto Castellanos (4.000), especially Cactaceae and Bromeliaceae; types of Polypodiaceae, Gramineae, Musaceae, Vochysiaceae, Melastomataceae, Rubiaceae, and Verbenaceae.
Director: Benito Piropo Da-Rin.
Curator: Maria Célia Vianna (Vochysiaceae).
Staff members: Dorothy Sue Dunn de Araujo (Ecology, mangroves).
Jorge Pedro Pereira Carauta (Taxonomy of Moraceae, *Dorstenia* and *Ficus;* endangered and rare species of Rio de Janeiro state).
Matilde Bucci Casari (Endangered species of *Anthurium* and *Halophila*).
Henrique Ferreira Martins (Vochysiaceae, *Callisthene;* phytogeography).
Ronaldo Fernandes de Oliveira (Ecology, succession).
Aparecida Maria Neiva Vilaça (Using plants to combat noise pollution).
Specialization in research: Nature conservation.
Loans: By special request only.
Periodical and serial works: Vellozia, Arboreto Carioca.
Exchange: Available: Specimens from Rio de Janeiro State. Desired: Specimens from Brazil, especially Moraceae, Vochysiaceae, aquatic and mangrove plants; phototypes of tropical American plants.
Remarks: The Herbarium will be moved to a new building in Jacarepaguá, a suburb of Rio de Janeiro, at the end of 1981.

RIO DE JANEIRO: *Herbarium Bradeanum,* **(HB),** Caixa Postal 15.005, ZC-06 20.000 Rio de Janeiro, Rio de Janeiro, **Brazil.**
Telephone: None.
Foundation: 1958. *Number of specimens:* 71.000.
Herbarium: Flora of Brazil.

Important collections: Alexander Curt Brade (orchids, ferns from Costa Rica, São Paulo), A. Duarte, G. Pabst, E. Pereira.
Director: MARGARETE EMMERICH, 1933 (Euphorbiaceae; ethnobotany).
Curator of Phanerogams: EDMUNDO PEREIRA, 1914 (Bromeliaceae).
Curator of Ferns: PAULO GÜNTHER WINDISCH, 1948 (Ferns).
Staff members: GRAZIELA BARROSO, 1912 (Compositae).
JOSÉ DA COSTA SACCO, 1930 (Passifloraceae).
LÉLIA DUARTE, 1933 (Paleobotany).
E. P. HERINGER, 1905 (Forestry).
DARDANO DE A. LIMA, 1919 (Flora of northeastern Brazil, especially Leguminosae).
J. FONTELLA PEREIRA, 1936 (Asclepiadaceae).
EMILIA SANTOS, 1936 (*Heliconia;* Bombacaceae).
ELZA FROMM TRINTA, 1934 (Lentibulariaceae).
DIMITRI Sucre (Rubiaceae).
IDA DE VATTIMO (Lauraceae).
Specialization in research: Flora of Brazil.
Loans: Normal conditions.
Periodical and serial works: Bradea; Boletim do Herbarium Bradeanum.
Exchange: Available: Southeastern Brazil and Central Plateau. Desired: Orchidaceae and ferns from Latin America; Bromeliaceae from Brazil.

RIO DE JANEIRO: *Herbário, Departamento de Botânica, Museu Nacional,* (**R**), Quinta da Boa Vista, São Cristovão, 20.942 Rio de Janeiro, Rio de Janeiro, **Brazil.**
Telephone: (55)021/228-7010.
Status: Universidade Federal do Rio de Janeiro.
Foundation: 1842. *Number of specimens:* 450.000.
Herbarium: Tropical phanerogams and cryptogams, mainly Brazil.
Important collections: P. K. H. Dusén, A. F. M. Glaziou, P. von Luetzelburg, Regnell, Commissão Rondon, A. J. Sampaio, C. A. W. Schwacke, Álvaro Silveira, E. H. G. Ule, José Vidal.
Director: LUIZ EMYGDIO DE MELLO FILHO, 1913 (*Heliconia, Ficus*).
Curator: WILMA T. ORMOND, 1928 (Biosystematics).
Staff members: AYDIL GRAVE DE ANDRADE, 1930 (Taxonomy, anatomy).
JESUS CARLOS COUTINHO BARCIA, 1938 (Pteridophytes).
ALICIA RITA CORTELLA DE CASTELLS, 1939 (Biosystematics, anatomy).
LEDA DAU, 1924 (Germination of seeds).
MARGARETE EMMERICH, 1933 (General taxonomy, especially Euphorbiaceae; ethnobotany).
CARMEN LUCIA DE ALMEIDA FERRAZ, 1946 (Anatomy).
BERNARDO FLASTER, 1934 (General taxonomy, especially Gesneriaceae).

VERA LUCIA DE MORAES HUSZAR, 1951 (Freshwater algae).
ALVARO XAVIER MOREIRA, 1920 (Palynology).
LÉA DE JESUS NEVES, 1939 (Anatomy).
ARLINE SOUZA DE OLIVEIRA, 1941 (Euphorbiaceae).
MARIA CÉLIA BEZERRA PINHEIRO, 1941 (Biosystematics).
AUGUSTO RUSCHI, 1915 (Orchidaceae).
HELIANE GENOFRE SALLES, 1949 (Physiology and germination of seeds).
EMILIA A. A. DOS SANTOS, 1936 *(Heliconia).*
ELZA FROMM TRINTA, 1934 (Lentibulariaceae).
Specialization in research: Flora of Brazil, especially the eastern and southern parts; ecology, biosystematics, and flora of the sand plains and high mountains of southeastern Brazil.
Associated botanic garden: 2 hectares of experimental gardens for ecological and biosystematic purposes.
Loans: For six months, only to institutions; types are sent only under special agreement.
Periodical and serial works: Boletim do Museu Nacional, n.s., Botânica; Arquivos do Museu Nacional; Publicações avulsas do Museu Nacional.
Exchange: Available: Flora of Brazil, especially local areas. Desired: Tropical plants from any part of the world; plants from arid zones.
Remarks: The Department of Botany is divided into 7 sections: morphology, physiology, palynology, tracheophytes, non-tracheophytes, forest botany, and ecology.

RIO DE JANEIRO: *Herbário, Jardim Botânico do Rio de Janeiro,* (**RB**), Rua Pacheco Leão 915, 20.000 Rio de Janeiro, Rio de Janeiro, **Brazil.**
Telephone: (55)021/274-4847; 266-2038; 246-6908.
Status: Directed by the Federal Government through the Instituto Brasileiro de Desenvolvimento Florestal (IBDF), Ministério da Agricultura.
Foundation: 1808. *Number of specimens:* 199.925; 5.300 dry fruits, 6.307 wood samples, 7.000 living plants, 18.000 microscope plates.
Herbarium: Emphasis on flora of Brazil.
Important collections: A. Brade, L. B. Damazio, A. P. Duarte, A. Ducke, P. Campos Porto, J. G. Kuhlmann, G. Martinelli, C. A. W. Schwacke, R. Spruce, D. Sucre.
Director: FERNANDO DE TASSO FRAGOSO PIRES.
Curator: ELSIE FRANKLIM GUIMARÃES, 1935; 021/266-2038; 246-9708 (Piperaceae, Gentianaceae, Trigoniaceae, Loganiaceae, Boraginaceae).
Staff members: PAULO AGOSTINHO DE MATTOS ARAUJO (Wood anatomy).
HUMBERTO DE SOUZA BARREIRO (Heliconiaceae, Meliaceae).
GRAZIELA MACIEL BARROSO (Compositae, Araceae, Myrtaceae, Dioscoreaceae, Leguminosae).
ANTONIA RANGEL BASTOS (Olacaceae).

241

LÚCIA D'AVILA FREIRE DE CARVALHO (Solanaceae, Rhamnaceae).

CECÍLIA GONÇALVES COSTA (Anatomy).

JOAQUIM IGNÁCIO DE ALMEIDA FALCÃO (Convolvulaceae).

WANDETTE FRAGA DE ALMEIDA FALCÃO (Anatomy).

FÁTIMA SÉRGIO GIL (Cytomorphology).

IDA DE VATTIMO GIL (Lauraceae).

DELPHOS JOSÉ GUIMARÃES (Cytomorphology).

CARMEN LÚCIA FALCÃO ICHASO (Scrophulariaceae).

MARIA DO CARMO MENDES MARQUES (Polygalaceae).

OSNIR MARQUETE (Cytomorphology).

ARMANDO DE MATTOS FILHO (Wood anatomy).

HONÓRIO MONTEIRO NETTO (Cytomorphology).

CARLOS TOLEDO RIZZINI (Loranthaceae; phytogeography).

NILDA MARQUETE FERREIRA DA SILVA (Combretaceae, Violaceae, Asclepiadaceae).

ABIGAIL FREIRE RIBEIRO DE SOUZA (Fungi).

ODETTE PEREIRA TRAVASSOS (Pteridophytes).

MARIA DA CONCEIÇÃO VALENTE (Anatomy).

ÍTALO DE VATTIMO (Bignoniaceae).

Research associates: ELENICE DE LIMA COSTA (Anatomy).

VALÉRIO FLECHTMANN FERREIRA (Apocynaceae, Orchidaceae).

HAROLDO CAVALCANTE DE LIMA (Leguminosae).

GUSTAVO MARTINELLI (Bromeliaceae).

LUCIANA MAUTONE (Boraginaceae).

Specialization in research: Taxonomy, anatomy, floral biology, cytomorphology.

Associated botanic garden: Jardim Botânico do Rio de Janeiro.

Loans: Usual regulations, for 6 months.

Periodical and serial works: Rodriguésia; Arquivos do Jardim Botânico.

Exchange: In all groups.

RIO DE JANEIRO: *Herbário, Instituto de Ecologia e Exp. Agricolas,* (**RBE**), Caixa Postal 1620, Rio de Janeiro, Rio de Janeiro, **Brazil.** (Information 1974)
Status: Government institute.
Foundation: 1938. *Number of specimens:* 5.000.

RIO DE JANEIRO: *Herbário, Laboratório de Botânica, Escola Nacional de Agronômia, Universidade Rural,* (**RBR**), Caixa Postal 25, Rio de Janeiro, Rio de Janeiro, **Brazil.** (Information 1974)
Foundation: 1916. *Number of specimens:* 12.000.
Herbarium: Brazilian plants; Malvaceae of the world.

RIO DE JANEIRO: *Herbário, Departamento de Botânica, Instituto de Biologia, Universidade Federal do Rio de Janeiro,* (**RFA**), Cidade Universitária, Ilha do

Fundão, ZC-32 Rio de Janeiro, Rio de Janeiro, **Brazil.**
Telephone: (55)021/280-7893.
Foundation: 1953. *Number of specimens:* 38.000.
Herbarium: Mainly Brazilian specimens, all groups.
Director and Curator: PAULO OCCHIONI, 1915 (Chloranthaceae, Symplocaceae, Canellaceae, Asclepiadaceae; *Oxypetalum*).
Staff members: GERUSA BRUNOW FONTENELLE, 1940 (Anatomy; floral biology).

ELENA MARIA OCCHIONI MARTINS, 1948 (Mimosaceae, *Stryphnodendron*).

GILBERTO JOSÉ PEREIRA MITCHELL, 1951 (Phaeophyta, Rhodophyta).

MAGDA REGINA DA SILVA PADILHA, 1949 (Theophrastaceae).

CECILIA MARIA RIZZINI, 1955 (Taxonomy of *Coccoloba*, Polygonaceae).

VERLANDE DUARTE DA SILVEIRA, 1909 (Ascomycetes, Basidiomycetes).

VERA REGINA CAMPOS VIANA, 1949 (Anatomy).
Loans: Usual regulations.
Periodical and serial works: Leandra.
Exchange: Yes.
Remarks: Formerly listed as Herbario da Faculdade Nacional de Farmácia da Universidade do Brasil, Rio de Janeiro.

RIO DE JANEIRO: *Herbário, Seção Experimental de Agrostologia, Instituto de Zootecnia,* (**RIZ**), Km 47, Rio de Janeiro, Rio de Janeiro, **Brazil.** (Information 1974)
Foundation: 1921. *Number of specimens:* 3.900.
Herbarium: Brazilian Gramineae.

RIO DE JANEIRO: *Herbário, Departamento de Fitopatologia, Universidade Federal Rural do Rio de Janeiro,* (**UFRJ**), Antiga Rodovia Rio-São Paulo, Km 47, Via Campo Grande, 20.000 Rio de Janeiro, Rio de Janeiro, **Brazil.**
Status: Ministry of Agriculture.
Number of specimens: 7.000 fungi.
Important collections: Arsene Puttemans.

RÍO PIEDRAS: *Herbarium, Institute of Tropical Forestry,* (**RPPR**), P.O. Box AQ, Río Piedras, **Puerto Rico** 00928.
Telephone: 809/753-4335.
Status: U.S. Department of Agriculture, Forest Service.
Foundation: 1939. *Number of specimens:* 3.000.
Herbarium: Arborescent species of Puerto Rico.
Director: ARIEL E. LUGO (Ecology).
Curator: P. L. WEAVER (Forest ecology).

RÍO PIEDRAS: *Herbario, Jardin Botánico, Administracion Central, Universidad de Puerto Rico,* (**UPR**), G.P.O. Box 4984-G, San Juan, **Puerto Rico** 00936.
Telephone: 809/751-6815; 763-4408.
Foundation: 1976. *Number of specimens:* 6.000.
Herbarium: Plants of the Caribbean, especially

Puerto Rico and the Virgin Islands.
Important collections: Roy O. Woodbury, Alain H. Liogier.

 Director: ALAIN H. LIOGIER, 1916 (Floras of Cuba, Hispaniola, Puerto Rico).
 Curator: MARÍA P. MEJIA, 1932 (Ferns of Puerto Rico).
 Staff members: LUIS F. MARTORELL, 1910.
  EDWIN SOLANO, 1958.
 Specialization in research: Flora of Puerto Rico and Hispaniola.
 Associated botanic garden: Jardin Botánico, Universidad de Puerto Rico.
 Loans: 6 months.
 Exchange: Caribbean plants.

RIVER FALLS: *Herbarium, Department of Biology, University of Wisconsin,* (**RIVE**), River Falls, Wisconsin 54022, **U.S.A.**
 Telephone: 715/425-3362.
 Number of specimens: 8.500.
 Herbarium: Emphasis on flora of west-central Wisconsin; rare and endangered species of west-central Wisconsin.
 Curator: JAMES W. RICHARDSON, 1937 (Euphorbiaceae of central U.S. and the Great Plains.
 Specialization in research: Euphorbiaceae of central U.S. and the Great Plains; flora of western Wisconsin.
 Loans: No restrictions.
 Exchange: Yes.

RIVERSIDE: *Herbarium, Department of Botany and Plant Sciences, University of California,* (**UCR**), Riverside, California 92521, **U.S.A.**
 Telephone: 714/787-3601.
 Foundation: 1956. *Number of specimens:* 20.000.
 Herbarium: Regional flora.
 Director: FRANK C. VASEK, 1927 (Vegetation of California; *Clarkia; Juniperus*).
 Curator: ANDREW SANDERS, 1950.
 Staff members: NORMAN C. ELLSTRAND, 1952 (Population ecology; *Oenothera*).
  RAINER W. SCORA, 1928 (Chemosystematics; *Monarda;* Rutaceae).
  J. G. WAINES, 1940 (Crop evolution; Triticeae; *Phaseolus*).
 Specialization in research: Regional flora; vegetation dynamics; evolution; population ecology.
 Associated botanic garden: University of California, Riverside, Botanic Gardens.
 Loans: No special conditions.
 Exchange: Available: Local and regional species.

ROANOKE: *Herbarium, Department of Biology, Virginia Western Community College,* (**ROAN**), P.O. Box 4195, Roanoke, Virginia 24015, **U.S.A.**
 Telephone: 703/982-7326.
 Foundation: 1968. *Number of specimens:* 1.200.
 Herbarium: Local flora.

 Director and Curator: RICHARD W. CRITES, 1944 (Plant ecology).
 Staff members: LOUIS BASS *(Trillium).*
  LYNNE KOUR (Spring wildflowers).
  MIKE SLAUGHTER, 1951 (Lichens).

ROCHESTER: *Monroe County Parks Department Herbarium,* (**HPH**), 375 Westfall Road, Rochester, New York 14620, **U.S.A.**
 Foundation: 716/244-4640, ext. 36.
 Status: County institution.
 Foundation: 1888. *Number of specimens:* 15.200; 780 fruit and seed collections.
 Herbarium: Chiefly woody plants of the North Temperate climate.
 Important collections: Magnolia, Rhododendron, hybrid *Salix;* Ezra Brainerd, C. A. Purpus, E. J. Palmer, Joseph Rock (China); type specimens of B. H. Slavin hybrids.
 Director: CALVIN REYNOLDS.
 Curator: JAMES W. KELLY, 1939 (Temperate woody plants; New York vascular flora).
 Staff member: NOELLE GIBBS (Plant taxonomy, horticulture).
 Specialization in research: Seed hardiness and germination research; woody plant hardiness.
 Associated botanic garden: Monroe County Parks Department.
 Loans: None.
 Exchange: Seeds.

ROCHESTER: *Herbarium of the University of Rochester and the Rochester Academy of Science, Department of Biology, University of Rochester,* (**ROCH**), Rochester, New York 14627, **U.S.A.**
 Foundation: 1930 (collections of local plants in the Academy Herbarium date back to 1865). *Number of specimens:* 35.000–40.000.
 Remarks: Herbarium no longer maintained.

ROCKVILLE: *Herbarium, American Type Culture Collection,* (**ATCC**), 12301 Parklawn Drive, Rockville, Maryland 20852, **U.S.A.**
 Telephone: 301/881-2600.
 Status: Private non-profit corporation.
 Foundation: 1925. *Number of specimens:* 27.000.
 Herbarium: Private national resource for the collection, preservation, and distribution of authentic cultures of living microorganisms.
 Director: RICHARD DONOVICK, 1911 (Microbiology).
 Curators: PIERRE-MARC DAGGETT, 1948 (Protistology).
  ROBERT GHERNA, 1937 (Bacteriology).
  ROBERT HAY, 1938 (Cell culture).
  SHUNG-CHANG JONG, 1936 (Mycology).
  DAVID A. STEVENS, 1916 (Virology).
 Staff members: CHARLES D. ALDRICH, 1939 (Virology).
  E. L. HALK, 1948 (Virology).

ANNE V. HAMBURGER, 1947 (Cell culture).
HAROLD D. HATT, 1939.
HEI-TI HSU, 1939 (Virology).
JEROME KERN, 1927 (Virology).
MARVIN L. MACY, 1934 (Cell culture).
PHYLLIS A. PIENTA, 1933 (Bacteriology).
J. E. SHANNON, 1919 (Cells).
FRANK P. SIMIONE, 1946 (Microbiology).
CAROLYN D. WILLIAMS, 1939 (Cell culture).
Specialization in research: Comparative micro-
biology; microbial systematics; computer assisted
identification analyses; improved methods of char-
acterization and preservation of cultures.
Periodical and serial works: Catalogues pub-
lished every two years.

ROCKY HARBOUR: *Herbarium, Gros Morne Na-
tional Park,* (**GMNP**), Box 130, Rocky Harbour,
Newfoundland, **Canada** AOK 4NO.
Telephone: 709/458-2418; 458-2417.
Status: Government of Canada, Department of the
Environment Parks Canada.
Foundation: 1973. *Number of specimens:* 1.516.
Herbarium: Vascular plants of Gros Morne Na-
tional Park.
   Director: MALCOLM ESTABROOKS.
   Curator: ROBERT WALKER.
   Staff members: ROGER EDDY.
      DAVID HUDDLESTONE.
Specialization in research: Protection of rare,
threatened, and endangered species.

ROHNERT PARK: *Herbarium, Department of Biol-
ogy, Sonoma State University,* (**ROPA**), Rohnert Park,
California 94928, **U.S.A.**
Telephone: 707/664-2189 (Department).
Foundation: 1935. *Number of specimens:* 22.000.
Herbarium: Principally north coast counties of
California.
Important collections: North Coast Herbarium of
California (NCC) incorporated in ROPA, including
Milo S. Baker collections (1890-1960; *Viola*); J. W.
Blankinship (Lake County).
   Director and Curator: CHARLES F. QUIBELL, 1936
(Systematic anatomy of woody Saxifragaceae; flo-
ristics of north coast counties of California).
   Specialization in research: Floristics of northwest-
ern California.
   Associated botanic garden: Campus Arboretum
and Native Plant Garden.
   Loans: Usual conditions.
   Exchange: Available: Some Milo Baker speci-
mens.

ROMA: *Erbario dell'Istituto Botanico dell'Univer-
sità di Roma,* (**RO**), Città Universitaria, 00100 Roma,
Italy.
Telephone: 06-4952237.
Status: State University.
Foundation: 1872. *Number of specimens:* 420.000.

Herbarium: Two worldwide sections and one
regional.
Important collections: De Notaris, V. Cesati, E.
Fiorini-Mazzanti, Sanguinetti, Rolli, N. A. Pedicino,
P.R. Pirotta, Lusina, Cacciato, the Anzalone collec-
tion of plants from the Parco Nazionale d'Abruzzo.
   Director: The Director of the Istituto Botanico
dell'Università di Roma, ex officio.
   Curator: IGNAZIO RICCI, 1922 (Cytotaxonomy).
   Specialization in research: Italian flora.
   Loans: To recognized botanical institutions.
   Remarks: African plant specimens of the Pirotta
and Chiovenda collections have been transferred to
FT in 1915.

ROMA: *Roma Herbarium, National University of
Lesotho,* (**ROML**), Roma, **Lesotho.**
Telephone: 05021-201.
Status: University.
Foundation: 1956. *Number of specimens:* 10.000.
Herbarium: Mainly Angiosperms of Lesotho.
Important collections: Laydevant duplicates, A. F.
M. G. Jacot Guillarmod duplicates, M. Schmitz
collection.
   Director and Honorary Curator: M. SCHMITZ,
1935 (Flowering plants of Lesotho).
   Specialization in research: Flowering plants of
Lesotho (preparation of the first illustrated flora
of Lesotho).
   Remarks: Two other collections in Lesotho, Ma-
seru Agric. College Herbarium and Sehlahathebe
Herbarium, soon to form together with Roma
Herb. the National Herbarium of Lesotho.

ROMA: *Herbarium, Stazione di Patologia Vegetale,*
(**ROPV**), Via Casal de' Pazzi 250, 00156 Roma, **Italy.**
(Information 1974)
Foundation: 1897. *Number of specimens:* 1.700.
Herbarium: Fungi.
   Specialization in research: Plant pathology.
   Periodical and serial works: Bolletino della Sta-
zione di Patologia vegetale.

ROSTOCK: *Herbarium der Sektion Biologie, Botan-
ischer Garten der Wilhelm-Pieck-Universität,*
(**ROST**), Doberaner Strasse 143, DDR 25 Rostock,
German Democratic Republic, DDR.
Telephone: 0081 – 3950, App. 333 or 332.
Status: University.
Foundation: Middle of 19th century. *Number of
specimens:* 16.800.
Herbarium: Worldwide collection from the 19th
century.
   Important collections: Herb. E. H. L. Krause (Flora
Megapol.).
   Director: HELMUT PANKOW, 1929 (Algology).
   Curator: ISOLDE GEISSLER, 1932; 395 284.

ROSTOV ON DON: *Herbarium, Department of Botany, Molotov State University of Rostov,* (**RV**), Engels

Street 105, 344006 Rostov on Don, **U.S.S.R.**
Status: University.
Foundation: 1936. *Number of specimens:* 300.000.
Herbarium: Plants of Rostov District, north of Caucasus, Lower Volga and Middle Asia.
Curator: D. K. DUGUJAN.

ROTORUA: *Herbarium, Forest Research Institute,* (**NZFRI**), Private Bag, Whakarewarewa, Rotorua, **New Zealand.**
Telephone: 82179 Rotorua.
Status: Government department.
Foundation: 1945. *Number of specimens:* 14.000.
Herbarium: Plants of New Zealand, especially Pinaceae, *Eucalyptus.*
Director: E. H. BUNN, 1924, Director of Production Forestry Division, Forest Research Institute.
Curator: C. E. ECROYD, 1950.
Specialization in research: General research on all aspects of forestry, including forest products.
Associated botanic garden: A small arboretum.
Loans: Six months, may be extended on application.
Periodical and serial works: New Zealand Journal of Forestry Science.
Exchange: Available: Indigenous trees. Desired: *Eucalyptus,* Cupressaceae, Pinaceae.

ROVINJ: *Centar za istraživanje mora, Institut "Rudjer Bošković,"* (**RI**), 52 210 Rovinj, **Yugoslavia.**
Status: Self-governing.
Foundation: 1891 (demolished during World War II, renewed in 1951, reorganized in 1969). *Number of specimens:* 2.000.
Herbarium: Northern Adriatic algae.
Director: DR. OZRETIĆ.
Curator: NEVENKA ZAVODNIC (Benthic algae).
Specialization in research: Ecophysiology and biochemistry of algae.
Associated botanic garden: A small botanic garden and aquarium.
Periodical and serial works: Thalassia Jugoslavica.

RUSSELLVILLE: *Herbarium, School of Physical and Life Sciences, Arkansas Tech University,* (**APCR**), Russellville, Arkansas 72801, **U.S.A.**
Telephone: 501/968-0312.
Foundation: 1967. *Number of specimens:* 25.000.
Herbarium: Southeastern U.S., with emphasis on Arkansas.
Director and Curator: GARY TUCKER (Woody flora of Arkansas).
Specialization in research: Woody flora of Arkansas; endangered and threatened flora of southeastern U.S.
Loans: No special requirements.

RUSTON: *Herbarium, Department of Botany and Bacteriology, Louisiana Tech University,* (**LTU**), Ruston, Louisiana 71272, **U.S.A.**
Telephone: 318/257-3204.
Foundation: 1952. *Number of specimens:* 125.000.
Herbarium: Primarily vascular plants and mosses of Lousiana, Arkansas, Mississippi, and Texas.
Important collections: John Moore, Donald Rhodes; repository for Waterways Experiment Station, Corps of Engineers, National Basis and Vicksburg District, Corps of Engineers.
Director: DONALD G. RHODES, 1933 (Flora of Louisiana; Menispermaceae; bottomland hardwood ecology).
Specialization in research: Flora of Louisiana.
Loans: Require annotation for all specimens; 60 day period.
Exchange: Any vascular plants, any region.

RYDALMERE: *Biology Branch Herbarium, Biological and Chemical Research Institute, N.S.W. Department of Agriculture,* (**DAR**), Private Mailbag no. 10, Rydalmere, N.S.W. 2116, **Australia.**
Telephone: (02) 630-0251.
Status: State government.
Foundation: 1890 (N.S.W. Dept. of Agriculture).
Number of specimens: 50.000.
Herbarium: Mycology and plant pathology.
Important collections: L. R. Fraser (Capnodiales, incl. types); H. Sydow (Australian fungi, incl. types); C. G. Hawsford (Australian fungi, incl. types); J. B. Cleland and E. Cheel (Agaricales and Aphyllophorales); Includes all fungi (except lichens) formerly in herb. NSW and many duplicates from BRIU; Plant parasitic fungi of N.S.W., Tasmania, Northern Territory and Norfolk Island; H. A. Dade (Australian Dung fungi).
Director and Curator: JOHN WALKER, 1930 (Plant parasitic fungi, scolecospored Ascomycetes, Uredinales and Ustilaginales; check lists).
Staff members: P. BEEDELL, 1930 (Herbarium techniques and records).
D. CROMPTON, 1936 (Herbarium records and computer indexing input).
C. H. CURNOW, 1926 (Herbarium techniques and records).
Specialization in research: Taxonomy of Australian plant parasitic fungi.
Loans: Yes, for 6 month period.
Exchange: Available: Australian micro-fungi (especially plant parasites). Desired: Any fungi, especially parasites and sets of exsiccati, from any country.
Remarks: DAR is the largest mycological herbarium in Australia; proposed as part of the Australian National Plant Disease Collection and Fungus Herbarium; Computer index and recall system being developed.

S

SACRAMENTO: *Herbarium, California Department of Food and Agriculture,* **(CDA),** 1220 N Street, Sacramento, California 95814, **U.S.A.**
Telephone: 916/445-4521.
Foundation: 1920. *Number of specimens:* 20.000.
Herbarium: Taxonomy of weeds, especially California weeds, and their distribution.
    Director: THOMAS C. FULLER, 1918.
    Curator: G. DOUGLAS BARBE, 1929.
    Staff members: JACQUELYN J. CHESI, 1942 (Seed taxonomy and seed physiology).
    SHARON M. DOBBINS, 1942 (Seed taxonomy and seed physiology).
    BARBARA J. HASS, 1947 (Seed taxonomy and seed physiology).
    WILLA MAY LOWARY, 1917 (Seed taxonomy and seed physiology).
    DEBORAH L. MEYER, 1957 (Seed taxonomy and seed physiology).
    PAUL S. PETERSON, 1946 (Seed taxonomy and seed physiology).
    Specialization in research: California weeds and their distribution.
    Loans: On special request.
    Periodical and serial works: Bulletin, California Department of Agriculture; publication discontinued in 1966.
    Remarks: Seed herbarium of 15.000 collections.

SACRAMENTO: *Herbarium, Department of Biological Sciences, California State University,* **(SACT),** 6000 J Street, Sacramento, California 95819, **U.S.A.**
Telephone: 916/454-6535.
Foundation: 1955. *Number of specimens:* 11.000.
Herbarium: Central California.
Important collections: Michael F. Baad (Placer County, California), Josephine Van Ess (Placer County, California).
    Director and Curator: MICHAEL F. BAAD, 1941 (Floristics of Placer County, California; Caryophyllaceae).
    Staff member: JOSEPHINE VAN ESS, 1909 (Floristics of Placer County, California).
    Specialization in research: Floristics of western Sierra Nevada; ordination studies of California vegetation.
    Associated botanic garden: C. M. Goethe Arboretum, California State University, Sacramento.
    Loans: 6 months to 1 year.
    Exchange: Inactive.

SAINT ANDREWS: *Herbarium of the Department of Botany, The University,* **(STA),** St. Andrews, Fife KY16 9AL, **Scotland.**
Telephone: 0334 76161, ext. 7112.
Status: University.

Foundation: 1888. *Number of specimens:* 43.000.
Herbarium: British flora (all groups), small European collection, algae worldwide.
Important collections: G. T. West (aquatic macrophytes), W. Young (Fife), R. and M. Corstorphine (Angus).
    Director: D. H. N. SPENCE.
    Curator: A. ANGUS (Fungi of Zambia, *Phomopsis*).
    Staff members: HELEN BLACKLER (Phaeophyceae).
    E. DUNCAN (Basidiomycetes).
    P. GIBBS (Genisteae, *Echium, Chorisia*).
    R. INGRAM (Cytotaxonomy of *Ranunculus,* sect. *Ranunculus*).
    Specialization in research: European marine algae, cytotaxonomy, taxonomy of Brazilian *Chorisia, Ceiba* and *Cordia*.
    Associated botanic garden: University Botanic Garden.
    Loans: To recognized botanical institutions.
    Exchange: Available: Limited numbers of British phanerogams, fungi, algae and local flora.

SAINT AUGUSTINE: *National Herbarium of Trinidad and Tobago, Department of Biological Sciences, University of the West Indies,* **(TRIN),** St. Augustine, **Trinidad.**
Telephone: 662-5511, ext. 5.
Status: State supported.
Foundation: 1887. *Number of specimens:* 40.000.
Herbarium: Angiosperms, including cultivated plants, pteridophytes, bryophytes, fungi, and algae of Trinidad and Tobago; small number of vascular plants from other parts of the Caribbean; oldest specimens 1846.
    Curator: YASMIN S. BAKSH, 1953 (Tropical American pteridophytes).
    Staff members: C. DENNIS ADAMS, 1920 (Caribbean vascular plant flora; ecology and phytogeography).
    E. JULIAN DUNCAN, 1934 (Algae and ferns of Trinidad).
    M. BHORAI KALLOO, 1932 (Native and cultivated phanerogams; ethnobotany).
    Specialization in research: Flora of Trinidad and Tobago.
    Associated botanic garden: Royal Botanic Gardens, Port of Spain.
    Loans: To recognized botanical institutions.
    Periodical and serial works: Flora of Trinidad and Tobago, published in parts at irregular intervals.
    Exchange: Available: Duplicates of vascular plants of Trinidad and Tobago. Desired: Plants of the Caribbean region, including mainland tropical America.

Remarks: Formerly listed under Trinidad.

SAINT BERNARD: *Herbarium, Saint Bernard College,* **(SB)**, Saint Bernard, Alabama 35138, **U.S.A.** (Information 1974)
Status: Private; conducted by the Benedictine Society of Alabama.
Foundation: 1923. *Number of specimens:* 4.500.
Herbarium: Alabama.

SAINT BONAVENTURE: *Herbarium, Department of Biology, Saint Bonaventure University,* **(SBU)**, Saint Bonaventure, New York 14778, **U.S.A.**
Telephone: 716/375-2118.
Foundation: 1930. *Number of specimens:* 8.300 (6.000 vascular plants; 2.300 liverworts and mosses).
Herbarium: Vascular plants and bryophytes of Cattaraugus County, New York.
Important collections: P. Boehner (bryophytes), C. Guenther, D. Krieg, E. E. Cook.
Director and Curator: S. W. EATON, 1918 (Plant distribution).
Staff member: A. F. FINOCCHIO, 1930 (Plant anatomy).
Specialization in research: Plant distribution of Cattaraugus County, New York; plant anatomy.
Loans: Yes; please pay postage both ways.
Periodical and serial works: Science Studies (St. Bonaventure University).
Exchange: Yes.

SAINT CLOTHILDE: *Herbier de la Réunion,* **(STCR)**, Saint Clothilde, **Réunion.** –– complete address unknown.

SAINT CLOUD: *Herbarium, Department of Biological Sciences, St. Cloud State University,* **(SCL)**, St. Cloud, Minnesota 56301, **U.S.A.**
Telephone: 612/255-2036.
Foundation: 1869. *Number of specimens:* 15.000.
Herbarium: Mainly vascular plants of Minnesota; Red Lake Bog in northern Minnesota; collections representing phenological data on vascular plants of central Minnesota.
Director: WAYLAND L. EZELL, 1937 (Taxonomy and biosystematics of *Mimulus,* Scrophulariaceae).
Curator: LESTER E. LINDSTROM, 1922; 612/255-3048 (Floristics of central Minnesota).
Specialization in research: Flora and ecology of Waubun Prairie (Minnesota); floristics of granite outcrops in central Minnesota; edible wild plants of Minnesota; taxonomy and phytogeography of *Mimulus* in Minnesota and eastern U.S.
Loans: Usual regulations.
Exchange: Limited.

SAINTE-ANNE-DE-LA-POCATIÈRE: *Institut de Technologie agricole,* **(QSA)** ––*see* LA POCATIÈRE.

SAINTE-FOY: *see* Québec.

SAINT JOHN: *Herbarium, New Brunswick Museum,* **(NBM)**, 277 Douglas Avenue, Saint John, New Brunswick, **Canada** E2K 1E5.
Telephone: 506/693-1196.
Status: Provincial museum.
Foundation: 1842. *Number of specimens:* 20.000.
Herbarium: Vascular plants from New Brunswick; some local mosses; some foreign vascular plants.
Director: DAVID ROSS (Military history).
Curator: DAVID S. CHRISTIE, 1942 (General naturalist).
Specialization in research: Documentation of distribution of Provincial flora.
Loans: To recognized herbaria on short-term (up to 4 months).
Periodical and serial works: Journal of New Brunswick Museum.
Exchange: With CAN.

SAINT JOHN'S: *Herbarium, Newfoundland Forest Research Centre, Canadian Forestry Service,* **(CDFN)**, Box 6028, St. John's, Newfoundland, **Canada** A1C 5X8.
Telephone: 709/737-4862; 737-4824.
Status: Government of Canada, Environment Canada.
Foundation: 1950. *Number of specimens:* 4.500.
Herbarium: Voucher for ecological research studies in Newfoundland; Newfoundland *Carex*; mosses and lichens mainly of heathlands and peatlands; cultivated trees and shrubs in Newfoundland.
Important collections: A. W. H. Damman, Alexander Robertson, W. J. Meades, E. D. Wells, F. C. Pollett, I. J. Green.
Curator: ALEXANDER ROBERTSON, 1940; 709/737-4824 (*Carex* in Newfoundland; peatland flora; cultivated trees and shrubs).
Loans: To any herbarium for 90 days.

SAINT JOHN'S: *Herbarium, Department of Biology, Memorial University of Newfoundland,* **(NFLD)**, St. John's, Newfoundland, **Canada** A1B 3X9.
Telephone: 709/753-1200.
Foundation: Agnes Marion Ayre Herbarium (vascular plants, lichens, fungi): 1954; Phycological Herbarium: 1967; Bryophyte Herbarium: 1966. *Number of specimens:* Algae 30.000; bryophytes 30.000; vascular plants 20.000.
Herbarium: Consists of three units: Ayre Herbarium contains vascular plants, lichens, and fungi; Phycological contains mostly marine algae; Bryophyte contains mosses and liverworts.
Important collections: Agnes Marion Ayre collection of 2.440 specimens and 1.890 watercolours of Newfoundland plants, E. Rouleau (Newfoundland vascular plants), J. E. Tilden South Pacific algae (Exsiccata), freshwater algae of Newfoundland (W. R. Taylor slide collection), G. R. South (marine algae of New Zealand).
Curators: Ayre Herbarium: PETER J. SCOTT,

1948; 709/753-1200, ext. 2532 (Newfoundland vascular flora).

Phycological Herbarium: G. ROBIN SOUTH, 1940; 709/753-1200, ext. 2497 (Marine phycology).

Bryophyte Herbarium: GUY R. BRASSARD, 1943; 709/753-1200, ext. 2143 (Bryology).

Staff member: ROBERT G. HOOPER, 1946 (Marine phycology).

Specialization in research: Ayre Herbarium: flora and phytogeography of Newfoundland and Labrador; Phycological Herbarium: floristics, ecology, and life histories of marine algae of eastern Canada; Bryophyte Herbarium: bryofloristics and phytogeography of arctic and subarctic Canada.

Loans: Yes, usual conditions; correspondence or materials should be addressed to the curator of the respective section.

Exchange: Yes.

Remarks: Exsiccata issued: Algae Terrae Novae; J. E. Tilden South Pacific Plants – – Algae; Bryophyta Exsiccata Terrae-Novae et Labradoricae.

SAINT JOHNSBURY: *Herbarium, Fairbanks Museum and Planetarium,* (**SJFM**), Main and Prospect streets, St. Johnsbury, Vermont 05819, **U.S.A.**

Telephone: 802/748-2372.

Status: Private, non-profit.

Foundation: 1891. *Number of specimens:* 5.500.

Herbarium: Local flora.

Director: WILLIAM BROWN, 1942.

Curator: HOWARD B. REED, JR., 1939.

Loans: No.

SAINT JOSEPH: *Herbarium, Department of Biology, Missouri Western State College,* (**MWSJ**), St. Joseph, Missouri 64507, **U.S.A.**

Telephone: 816/271-4379; 232-8035 (curator).

Foundation: 1972. *Number of specimens:* 5.000.

Herbarium: Flora of northwest Missouri; vascular plants.

Curator: LEO A. GALLOWAY, 1921; 816/232-8035 (*Abronia,* Nyctaginaceae).

Specialization in research: Flora of northwest Missouri; Nyctaginaceae.

Loans: To recognized institutions.

Exchange: Available: Missouri specimens. Wanted: Nyctaginaceae.

SAINT LOUIS: *Herbarium, Missouri Botanical Garden,* (**MO**), P.O. Box 299, St. Louis, Missouri 63166, **U.S.A.** (Street address: 2345 Tower Grove Avenue).

Telephone: 314/577-5169.

Status: Private trust.

Foundation: 1859. *Number of specimens:* 2.850.000.

Herbarium: Worldwide, emphasis Central America, tropical South America, Africa.

Important collections: L. Abrams (southern California), J. G. Adam (Africa), P. Allen (Panama), E. Anderson (Missouri), C. F. Austin (mosses), C. F. Baker (Colorado), J. T. Baldwin (Africa), J. Ball (3.000), M. Bang (Bolivia), J. Banks and D. C. Solander (Cook's voyage), H. Barclay (Andean South America), R. D. Bayliss (Africa), J. J. Bernhardi herbarium, F. Blanchard (5.700, mainly Vermont), G. R. Boehmer and C. F. Ludwin (pre-Linnean), W. E. Broadway (West Indies), S. B. Buckley (6.000, southeastern U.S.), B. F. Bush (Missouri), J. R. Churchill (12.000–15.000, eastern U.S.), S. P. Churchill (mosses), H. S. Conard (mosses), T. B. Croat (Panama, tropical America, Middle West), M. R. Crosby (mosses), W. G. D'Arcy (Panama, tropical America, Middle West), G. Davidse (Central and South America, eastern and southern Africa), J. Davis (20.000, Missouri, Illinois, South Carolina), D. Demaree (Arkansas), R. Dressler (Panama), J. A. Drushel (10.000, eastern U.S.), J. A. Duke (Panama), J. D. Dwyer (tropical America), H. Eggert (26.704, Middle West), W. H. Emory (southwestern U.S.), G. Engelmann (97.859), A. Fendler (southwestern U.S., northwestern Mexico, Venezuela), J. C. Fremont (Western U.S.), J. Gay (600, Chile), A. H. Gentry (Central and South America, Madagascar), P. Goldblatt (Africa), A. L. Grant (Africa), A. Gray (U.S.), J. M. Greenman (Central America, Mexico; Compositae), W. E. Harmon (Guatemala), E. Hassler (Paraguay), A. A. Heller (New Mexico), A. Henry (2.163, China), G. B. Hinton (Mexico), A. S. Hitchcock (2.000, West Indies), G. Jermy (6.177, Texas, Carpathians), M. E. Jones (western U.S., northwestern Mexico), J. F. Joor (4.133, Texas), A. B. Katende (Africa), J. H. Kellogg (12.000, Missouri, Texas, Arkansas), E. P. Killip (South America), B. A. Krukoff (tropical South America), J. Lavranos (Africa), G. W. Letterman (15.000, mainly Missouri), W. H. Lewis (Panama, Bahamas), R. Liesner (Central and South America), D. H. Linder (Africa), F. J. Lindheimer (20.000, Texas), C. L. Lundell (British Honduras, Mexico), J. Macoun (Canada), G. D. McPherson (New Caledonia), W. Meijer (Malaysia), Y. Mexia (Mexico, Brazil), F. G. Meyer (Valerianaceae), V. Muehlenbach (St. Louis area), C. R. Orcutt (Mexico, southern California), E. Palmer (1.400, Mexico, Arizona), E. J. Palmer (southwestern U.S.), J. Pawek (Africa), E. Phillips (Africa), G. Pilz (Africa), H. Pittier (Venezuela), D. M. Porter (Panama, Missouri), S. F. Price (2.912), C. G. Pringle (Arizona, Mexico), P. H. Raven, P. L. Redfearn, Jr. (mosses), J. H. Redfield (16.447), M. Reekman (Africa), K. R. Robertson and D. F. Austin (Mexico, Guyana), S. A. Robertson (Africa), R. Rodin (Africa), H. H. Rusby (South America), R. W. Schery (Panama), F. C. Seymour (northeastern U.S., Nicaragua), J. D. Smith (Central America), P. C. Standley and E. O. Wooton (New Mexico), R. Steinbach (Bolivia), W. D. Stevens (Nicaragua), J. A. Steyermark (6.000, Missouri), S. M. Tracy (4.393), W. Trelease (11.000), E. F. Tyson (Panama), D. A. Watt (10.700, mainly North America), T. O. Weigel (Suriname), R. Woodson (Panama, U.S.; Apocynaceae), F. Woytkowski (4.000, Peru), C. Wright (southwestern U.S., northern Mexico), T. G. Yuncker (Belize), G. Zenker (Africa),

O. Zöllner (Chile).

Director: PETER H. RAVEN, 1936; 314/577-5110 (Onagraceae).

Director of Research: MARSHALL R. CROSBY, 1943; 314/577-5164 (Systematics and nomenclature of mosses).

Administrative Curator: NANCY R. MORIN, 1948; 314/577-5180 (Campanulaceae).

Staff members: THOMAS B. CROAT, 1938; 314/577-5163 (Araceae; Central American Sapindaceae).

WILLIAM G. D'ARCY, 1931; 314/577-5165 (Solanaceae; floristics of Panama).

GERRIT DAVIDSE, 1942; 314/577-5167 (Gramineae; floristics of Central America).

JOHN D. DWYER, 1915; 314/577-5168 (Central American Rubiaceae).

ALWYN H. GENTRY, 1945; 314/577-5171 (Bignoniaceae; flora of Chocó-Colombia; *Flora Neotropica; Flora of Peru*).

PETER GOLDBLATT, 1943; 314/577-5172 (Iridaceae; floristics of southern Africa).

RON LIESNER, 1944; 314/577-5183 (Neotropical floristics).

GORDON MCPHERSON, 1947; 314/577-5170 (Convolvulaceae, *Ipomoea;* floristics of New Caledonia).

VIKTOR MUEHLENBACH, 1898; 314/577-5176 (Adventive plants of St. Louis, Missouri).

W. DOUGLAS STEVENS, 1944; 314/577-5170 (Asclepiadaceae, Apocynaceae; *Flora de Nicaragua;* floristics of Central America).

Specialization in research: Flora de Nicaragua in conjunction with HNMN; *Flora of Peru* in conjunction with F; floristics of Central America (especially Nicaragua and Panama), tropical South America (especially Colombia, Ecuador, Peru, and Venezuela), Malagasy region, southern Africa, and New Caledonia.

Associated botanic garden: Missouri Botanical Garden; Shaw Arboretum, Gray Summit, Missouri.

Loans: Recognized botanical institutions upon receipt of written request by staff member.

Periodical and serial works: Annals of the Missouri Botanical Garden (quarterly); Monographs in Systematic Botany from the Missouri Botanical Garden (irregular).

Exchange: Worldwide, especially neotropics, Africa, and New Caledonia, including mosses.

Remarks: Teaching, in conjunction with Washington University (St. Louis), St. Louis University, University of Missouri (St. Louis), and Southern Illinois University (Edwardsville). The algal collections of MO are now at UC; fungal collections at BPI; lichen collections at US. MO's library contains over 85.000 bound volumes, about 2.000 current botanical periodicals, and additional 200.000 items including pamphlets, reprints, letters, manuscripts, paintings, drawings, photographs, and archival material.

SAINT MEINRAD: *Henrietta Herbarium, College of Liberal Arts, Saint Meinrad College,* **(SMH),** St. Meinrad, Indiana 47577, **U.S.A.**

Telephone: 812/357-6611.

Status: Private institution.

Foundation: 1950. *Number of specimens:* 2.000.

Herbarium: Local plants, mainly Indiana.

Director and Curator: RICHARD HINDEL, 1922.

SAINT PAUL: *American Bryological and Lichenological Society Herbarium, Department of Botany, University of Minnesota,* **(ABSL),** 1445 Gortner Avenue, St. Paul, Minnesota 55108, **U.S.A.**

Telephone: 612/376-7284 (curator); 373-2211 (department).

Status: Lichen herbarium of the Society; being curated with lichens at MIN.

Foundation: 1901. *Number of specimens:* 5.300.

Herbarium: Lichens, mainly North America.

Curator: CLIFFORD M. WETMORE, 1934 (Lichenology).

Specialization in research: Lichenology.

Loans: To qualified individuals and institutions.

Periodical and serial works: The Bryologist, published by the Society.

Exchange: Willing to receive gifts of lichens for the Society.

Remarks: All label data computerized.

SAINT PAUL: *Herbarium, Department of Botany, University of Minnesota,* **(MIN),** St. Paul, Minnesota 55108, **U.S.A.**

Telephone: 612/373-2227.

Foundation: 1890. *Number of specimens:* 725.000.

Herbarium: Worldwide collections, strongest for U.S. and Canada; specialization upper-midwestern plants of U.S.

Important collections: J. W. Congdon, E. W. D. Holway, J. Lunell, C. MacMillan, J. W. Moore, J. E. Tilden.

Curator: GERALD B. OWNBEY, 1916 (Systematics of seed plants).

Staff members: ERNST C. ABBE, 1905 (Morphology; arctic floristics).

JOHN W. HALL, 1918 (Paleobotany; Salviniaceae).

THOMAS MORLEY, 1917 (Melastomataceae; floristics).

CLIFFORD M. WETMORE, 1934 (Lichenology).

Specialization in research: Monographic taxonomy, floristics, floral morphology and anatomy.

Associated botanic garden: Minnesota Landscape Arboretum, 3675 Arboretum Drive, Chaska, Minnesota 55318.

Loans: To qualified institutions and individuals.

Periodical and serial works: Postelsia (1901–1906); Minnesota Botanical Studies (1894–1916); Minnesota Studies in Plant Science

(1923–1936).
Exchange: Vascular plants and lichens.

SAINT PAUL: *Department of Plant Pathology Mycological Herbarium, College of Agriculture, University of Minnesota,* (**MPPD**), 304 Stakman Hall of Plant Pathology, St. Paul, Minnesota 55108, **U.S.A.**
Telephone: 612/373-1383.
Foundation: 1910. *Number of specimens:* 45.000.
Herbarium: Fungi; Uredinales, Ustilaginales, plant pathogenic Deuteromycotina, Hypogeous Ascomycotina and Basidiomycotina; mycorrhizal Agaricales.
Important collections: J. C. Arthur, E. Bartholomew, J. F. Brenckle, W. B. Cooke, J. J. Davis, N. Ellis, E. W. D. Holway, O. Jaap, E. C. and E. L. Stakman.
Director and Curator: ELWIN L. STEWART, 1940 (Systematics of mycorrhizal fungi).
Specialization in research: Systematics and ecology of mycorrhizal fungi; taxonomy of plant pathogens and Deuteromycotina from wood.
Loans: No restrictions; generally for 6 months.
Exchange: By arrangement only. Available: Rusts, smuts, and mycorrhizal fungi from midwestern U.S. Desired: Rusts, smuts, and mycorrhizal fungi from any part of the world.
Remarks: Graduate student programs in taxonomy and ecology of mycorrhizal and plant pathogenic fungi.

SAINT PETERSBURG: *Herbarium, Department of Marine Science, University of South Florida,* (**SPMS**), 830 First Street South, St. Petersburg, Florida 33701, **U.S.A.**
Telephone: 813/893-9130.
Foundation: 1967. *Number of specimens:* Several thousand.
Curator: HAROLD J. HUMM, 1912 (Distribution, ecology, taxonomy, utilization of benthic algae of southeastern atlantic coast of U.S.A.).

SAINT PETERSBURG: *Herbarium, Marine Research Laboratory, Florida Department of Natural Resources,* (**STPE**), 100 Eighth Avenue, S.E., St. Petersburg, Florida 33731, **U.S.A.**
Telephone: 813/896-8626.
Foundation: 1959 (algae), 1972 (vascular plants).
Number of specimens: 3.500.
Herbarium: Marine and coastal species with emphasis on Florida collections.
Curator: DAVID W. CREWZ, 1947 (Mangrove and sand dune ecology).
Specialization in research: Marine algae and coastal vascular plants of Florida and the southeastern U.S.
Loans: Postage to be paid by borrower.
Periodical and serial works: Florida Marine Research Publications.
Exchange: Handled on an individual basis but chiefly coastal vascular plants (worldwide).

SAINT THOMAS: *Diagnostic Herbarium, Cooperative Extension Service, College of the Virgin Islands,* (**VIST**), St. Thomas, **U.S. Virgin Islands** 00801.
Telephone: 809/774-0210.
Status: U.S. Department of Agriculture.
Foundation: 1978. *Number of specimens:* 1.000.
Herbarium: Virgin Islands flora; cultivated and toxic plants.
Director: DARSHAN S. PADDA, 1932 (Physiological genetics).
Curator: JOHN M. MATUSZAK, 1953 (Leguminosae).
Specialization in research: Flora of Virgin Islands and Lesser Antilles; cultivated, toxic, pest host, and traditional medicinal plants.
Loans: Normal regulations.
Exchange: Desired: Tropical toxic and medicinal plants.

SALASPILS: *Herbarium, Laboratory of Botany, Institute of Biology of the Academy of Sciences of the Latvian SSR,* (**LATV**), 3 Miera Street, Salaspils, **U.S.S.R.**
Telephone: 947364.
Status: State institute.
Foundation: 1955. *Number of specimens:* 55.000.
Herbarium: Ferns and flowering plants of Latvian SSR.
Director: LAIMA TABAKA, 1924 (Floristics, systematics).
Specialization in research: Flora of Latvian SSR: floristics, systematics, phytogeography.
Periodical and serial works: Flora and Vegetation of Latvian SSR, Chorology of Flora of the Latvian SSR (rare plant species).
Exchange: Can be arranged.

SALEM: *Herbarium, Peabody Museum,* (**PM**), 161 Essex Street, Salem, Massachusetts 01970, **U.S.A.**
Status: Private foundation.
Foundation: 1875. *Number of specimens:* 7.450; 300 wood samples.
Herbarium: Flora of Essex County, Massachusetts.
Director: PETER FETCHKO (Ethnology).
Curator: JOHN NOVE.
Specialization in research: Flora of Essex County, Massachusetts.
Remarks: Collection is mostly of historical interest.

SALEM: *Herbarium, Department of Biology, Roanoke College,* (**SARC**), Salem, Virginia 24153, **U.S.A.**
Telephone: 703/389-2351.
Status: Private college.
Foundation: 1914. *Number of specimens:* 3.453.
Herbarium: Emphasis on plants of western Virginia; some from Jamaica and western U.S.; small collection of local slime molds and fungi.
Director and Curator: PHILIP C. LEE, JR. (Saprolegniaceous fungi).

Loans: Negotiable.
Exchange: Negotiable.

SALEM: *Herbarium, Department of Natural Science, Salem College,* **(SAWV),** Salem, West Virginia 26426, **U.S.A.**
Telephone: 304/782-2412.
Status: Private college.
Number of specimens: 3.600.
Herbarium: Local.
Staff member: CYNTHIA CALISE, 1952 (Bryology).

SALEM: *Peck Herbarium, Willamette University,* **(WILLU),** Salem, Oregon 97301, **U.S.A.** – – housed at OSC, Corvallis.
Foundation: 1909. *Number of specimens:* 32.000.
Herbarium: Vascular plants of Oregon.
Important collections: Morton E. Peck.

SALINA: *Herbarium, Department of Biology, Kansas Wesleyan,* **(SAL),** Salina, Kansas 67401, **U.S.A.**
Status: Private institution.
Foundation: 1955. *Number of specimens:* 1.100.
Herbarium: Central Kansas and Arkansas Ozarks.

SALISBURY: *Herbarium, University of Zimbabwe,* **(CAH),** P.O. Box MP167, Salisbury, **Zimbabwe.**
Telephone: 303211.
Status: University.
Foundation: 1955. *Number of specimens:* 12.000.
Herbarium: Plants of Southern Africa.
Director and Curator: H. WILD, 1917 (Taxonomy of Southern African Compositae, phytogeography).
Staff member: J. E. RUSHWORTH, 1944 (Cryptogams).
Specialization in research: Southern African flora, Flora Zambesiaca.
Associated botanic garden: University of Zimbabwe Botanic Garden.
Loans: To recognized botanical institutions.
Periodical and serial works: Kirkia.
Exchange: Available: Plants of Southern Africa.

SALISBURY: *National Herbarium and Botanic Garden,* **(SRGH),** P.O. Box 8100, Causeway, Salisbury, **Zimbabwe.**
Telephone: 25313/702236.
Status: Directed by State.
Foundation: 1918. *Number of specimens:* 265.000.
Herbarium: South Tropical Africa, mainly phanerogams and pteridophytes plus a small collection of bryophytes.
Important collections: N. C. Chase, F. Eyles, L. C. Leach, H. Wild.
Director: T. MÜLLER, 1932 (Woody species of Zimbabwe, ecology of rainforests, Botanic Garden).
Curator: R. B. DRUMMOND, 1924 (Taxonomy of South Tropical African plants).

Staff members: K. E. BENNETT-STURGEON, 1921 (Gramineae).
H. M. BIEGEL, 1914 (Cultivated plants).
L. C. LEACH, Hon. Botanist, 1909 (Euphorbieae, Stapelieae, *Aloe*).
S. MAVI, 1948 (Traditional uses of plants).
J. NGONI, 1943 (Flora of Zimbabwe).
G. V. POPE, 1941 (Compositae, Flora of Zimbabwe).
Specialization in research: Taxonomy of African plants, collaboration in preparation of Flora Zambesiaca.
Associated botanic garden: National Botanic Garden of Zimbabwe.
Loans: To recognized botanical institutions.
Periodical and serial works: Kirkia.
Exchange: Available: Material from Zimbabwe and neighboring countries. Desired: African material.

SALTA: *Herbario, Museo de Ciencias Naturales, Universidad Nacional de Salta,* **(MCNS),** Mendoza 2, 4400 Salta, Salta, **Argentina.**
Telephone: (54)087-21-0242.
Foundation: 1973. *Number of specimens:* 10.000.
Herbarium: Argentina, especially Andean Puna and Salta Province.
Director and Curator: LÁZARO JUAN NOVARO, 1944 (Juncaceae, Cyperaceae).
Staff members: ALICIA DE DEL CASTILLO, 1952 (Bromeliaceae).
ANTENOR ALFREDO SULECIK, 1956 (Gramineae).
FANNY J. DE VARELA, 1940 (Cruciferae).
Specialization in research: Flora del Valle Encantado, Salta Province.
Periodical and serial works: Revista de la Universidad Nacional de Salta.

SALTILLO: *Herbario, Departamento de Botánica, Universidad Autónoma Agraria "Antonio Narro,"* **(ANSM),** Buenavista, Saltillo, Coahuila, **Mexico.**
Telephone: 841/2-84-82 y 2-88-50, ext. 156.
Foundation: 1973. *Number of specimens:* 11.500.
Herbarium: Regional flora of northeastern Mexico, especially arid and subarid zones, also temperate deciduous forest, pine and oak forests, and grasslands.
Important collections: Jorge S. Marroquín (1.000), M. F. Robert, J. Valdés Reyna (1.000), Stewart, I. M. Johnston, T. Wendt.
Director: JESÚS VALDÉS REYNA, 1948 (Gramineae).
Curator: JOSÉ ANGEL VILLARREAL QUINTANILLA, 1956.
Staff members: JORGE S. MARROQUÍN, 1935 (*Berberis* of Mexico).
ROBERTO BANDA SILVA, 1948 (Fagaceae).
MIGUEL A. CAPÓ ARTEAGA, 1947 (Conifers).
Specialization in research: Types of vegetation of northern Mexico; range management; floristics of

grasslands, woodlands, and desert communities; ecological parameters; useful plants; plant geography; floristics of Coahuila.

Associated botanic garden: Jardín Botánico "Ing. Gustavo Aguirre – – Benavides."

Loans: Limited.

Periodical and serial works: Monografías Téchnico – – científicas de la Universidad Autónoma Agraria "Antonio Narro."

Exchange: Available: northeastern Mexico.

SALT LAKE CITY: *Department of Botany, East High School,* **(SLC),** Salt Lake City, Utah 84102, **U.S.A.** – – incorporated in UT.

Foundation: 1905. *Number of specimens:* 5.000.

Remarks: This herbarium which contained the collections of A. O. Garrett was incorporated in the University of Utah Herbarium (UT) at the time of Mr. Garrett's death in 1948. The University of Utah Herbarium has been known as the Garrett Herbarium since that time.

SALT LAKE CITY: *Garrett Herbarium, University of Utah,* **(UT),** Salt Lake City, Utah 84112, **U.S.A.**

Telephone: 801/581-8543; 581-6520.

Status: University of Utah Biology Department.

Foundation: 1870. *Number of specimens:* 107.586.

Herbarium: Vascular plants, mainly western North America, scattered worldwide representation; fungi, western U.S.

Important collections: A. O. Garrett, W. P. Cottam.

Director: DELBERT WIENS, 1932 (Classification, chromosome evolution, and biogeography of Viscaceae and Loranthaceae; reproductive ecology of flowering plants).

Curator: LOIS ARNOW, 1921 (Systematics of vascular flora of the Wasatch Front; grasses of Utah).

Staff member: BEVERLY ALBEE, 1922 (Systematics of vascular flora of Utah; plant macrofossils).

Specialization in research: Systematics of vascular flora of the Wasatch Front; grasses of Utah; identification of plant macrofossils.

Loans: To recognized scientific institutions.

Exchange: Available: Vascular plants of the Intermountain West. Desired: Native vascular plants of any region.

Remarks: Most of the bryophyte collections of Seville Flowers are now deposited in the Herbarium of the University of Colorado Museum, Boulder (COLO).

SALT LAKE CITY: *Herbarium, Wasatch National Forest,* **(WANF),** 8226 Federal Building, 125 South State Street, Salt Lake City, Utah 84138, **U.S.A.**

Telephone: 801/524-5107.

Status: U.S. Department of Agriculture, Forest Service.

Foundation: Mid-1940's. *Number of specimens:* 250.

Herbarium: Flora of the Wasatch National Forest.

Staff member: DON PROCTOR (Range ecology).

SALVADOR: *Herbário Alexandre Leal Costa, Instituto de Biologia, Universidade Federal da Bahia,* **(ALCB),** Campus Universitário da Federação, Ondina, 40.000 Salvador, Bahia, **Brazil.**

Telephone: (55)071/245-6909; 247-3744.

Foundation: 1950. *Number of specimens:* 7.000.

Herbarium: Flora of northeastern Bahia, including Restinga, Atlantic Coastal Forest, Caatinga, and Central highlands; Leguminosae, Euphorbiaceae, and Compositae.

Important collections: Alexandre Leal Costa.

Director and Curator: WANDA DOS REIS SANT'ANNA, 1928 (Taxonomy and anatomy; Anacardiaceae).

Staff members: ELZENI FILADELFO DE GUSMÃO, 1947 (Rubiaceae).

DAYSE VASQUES MARTINS, 1936 (Algae).

LARRY NOBLICK, 1952 (Taxonomy).

JOSÉ PEREIRA DE SOUSA, 1920 (Annonaceae).

Specialization in research: Flora of Bahia; Annonaceae, Rubiaceae; mangrove vegetation; vegetation of dry region.

Loans: Yes.

Exchange: Yes.

SALVADOR: *Herbário Antonio Nonata Marques, Empresa de Pesquisa Agropecuária da Bahia,* **(BAH),** Avenida Ademar de Barros 967, Ondina, 40.000 Salvador, Bahia, **Brazil.**

Telephone: (55)71/235-1452.

Status: State institution.

Foundation: 1952. *Number of specimens:* 2.763.

Herbarium: Mainly flora of Bahia.

Director: RENATO PINHO PEREIRA, 1934 (Agronomy).

Curator: EDNA LAUREANA P. G. DE OLIVEIRA, 1932 (Biology).

Staff members: MARTA NEVES FERRAZ DE ALMEIDA, 1951.

BERENICE CELESTE BASTOS, 1937.

MARIA DO SOCORRO GONÇALVES FERREIRA, 1953 (Forestry).

HERMÍNIA MARIA FREITAS SOUZA, 1951 (Biology).

Loans: No restrictions.

Exchange: With specialists.

SALVADOR: *Herbário, Projeto RADAMBRASIL,* **(HRB),** Rua Pernambuco 4, Pituba, Salvador, Bahia, **Brazil.**

Status: Ministério das Minas e Energia.

Foundation: 1980. *Number of specimens:* 5.000.

Herbarium: Brazilian flora.

Director of Vegetation Division: LUIZ GÓES FILHO.

Curator: HORTENSIA POUSADA BAUTISTA (Phanerogams).

Staff members: ROBERTO M. KLEIN (Ecology, taxonomy).

MARLI PIRES MORIM (Phanerogams).
ANGELA MARIA S. DA F. VAZ (Phanerogams).
HENRIQUE PIMENTA VELOSO (Ecology).
Consultants: GRAZIELA M. BARROSO (Compositae).
DÁRDANO DE ANDRADE LIMA.
GERALDO CARLOS P. PINTO (Ecology).
Specialization in research: Flora of Brazil; ecology, taxonomy, phytogeography.
Loans: To institutions, for six months.
Periodical and serial works: Levantamento de Recursos Naturais.
Exchange: Available: Brazilian flora. Desired: Tropical flora.

SALZBURG: *Herbarium, Haus der Natur,* **(SZB),** Hofstallgasse 7, Salzburg, **Austria.** (Information 1974)
Status: Private.
Foundation: About 1800. *Number of specimens:* 2.000.

SALZBURG: *Landesherbar von Salzburg,* **(SZL),** Salzburg, **Austria.** (Information 1974)
Status: Private.
Foundation: 1924.
Herbarium: Flora of Salzburg and Berchtesgaden.
Specialization in research: Mitteilungen der Naturwissenschaftlichen Arbeitsgemeinschaft am Haus der Natur.

SALZBURG: *Institut für Botanik der Universität, Abteilung f. Systematik u. Geobotanik,* **(SZU),** Freisaalweg 16, A 5020 Salzburg, **Austria.**
Telephone: 06222-44511-273, -434.
Status: Directed by Botany Department of the University.
Foundation: 1967. *Number of specimens:* 17.300 (15.000 phanerogams, 2.300 cryptogams).
Herbarium: European plants, especially central Europe, France, Mediterranean, Balkan peninsula.
Director: DIETRICH FÜRNKRANZ, 1936 (Biosystematics, flora and vegetation of the Mediterranean, ecology of fruit and seed dispersal).
Curator: HEINRICH WAGNER, 1916 (Geobotany, vegetation cartography, flora of Europe).
Staff members: PAUL HEISELMAYER, 1946 (Geobotany, micro-climatology, remote-sensing of vegetation).
THOMAS PEER, 1948 (Geobotany, vegetation cartography, soil ecology).
HANNA SCHANTL, 1949 (Palynology, history of the postglacial vegetation).
WALTER STROBL, 1944 (Geobotany, soil-biology).
ROMAN TÜRK (Dept. of Anatomy and physiology of plants), 1945 (Ecophysiology, systematics of lichens).
Specialization in research: Geobotany, mapping of Alpine vegetation (especially Salzburg, Eastern

Tyrol), micro-climatology, soil-ecology, vegetation history, biosystematics, carpo-ecology, systematics of lichens.
Associated botanic garden: Botanischer Garten der Universität Salzburg.
Loans: To recognized scientific institutions.
Periodical and serial works: Floristische Mitteilungen aus Salzburg (irregular).

SAMOËNS: *Herbarium, Laboratoire de la Jaÿsinia;* **(JAY),** 74340 Samoëns, **France.**
Status: Fondation Cognacq-Jaÿ, municipality of Samoëns (scientific address: Muséum national d'Histoire Naturelle).
Foundation: 1937. *Number of specimens:* 33.000.
Herbarium: European vascular plants, especially alpine vascular plants.
Director: J. L. HAMEL, 1916 (Caryology).
Staff member: M. FARILLE, 1945 (Systematics, ecology, floristics).
Associated botanic garden: Yes.

SAN ANGELO: *Herbarium, Department of Biology, Angelo State University,* **(SAT),** Box 10890, A.S.U. Station, San Angelo, Texas 76901, **U.S.A.**
Telephone: 915/942-2189.
Foundation: 1970. *Number of specimens:* 20.000.
Herbarium: Emphasis on southwestern Texas.
Important collections: Chester M. Rowell, Jr.
Director: CHESTER M. ROWELL, JR., 1925 (Floristics, rare and endangered species studies).
Specialization in research: Regional floristics; biology of regional rare and endangered taxa; arid land taxa.
Loans: Normal regulations.
Exchange: Limited to arid land regions.

SAN ANTONIO: *Herbarium, Our Lady of the Lake College,* **(LLC),** San Antonio, Texas 78285, **U.S.A.** (Information 1974)
Status: Private foundation, church related.
Foundation: 1932. *Number of specimens:* 10.000.
Herbarium: Worldwide with specialization in phanerogams of North America, primarily Texas.
Important collections: W. A. Silveus (grasses).

SAN CARLOS DE BARILOCHE: *Herbario Centro Regional Patagonico EERA Bariloche, Instituto Nacional de Tecnología Agropecuaria,* **(CRP),** Casilla de Correo 277, 8400 San Carlos de Bariloche, Río Negro, **Argentina.**
Telephone: (54)22731.
Status: Secretaría de Estado de Agricultura y Ganadería.
Foundation: 1966. *Number of specimens:* 6.000.
Herbarium: Vascular plants of Patagonia, especially Gramineae, Leguminosae, Compositae, Verbenaceae.
Staff member: MARÍA CLARA LATOUR, 1935 (Gramineae).

Loans: Usual regulations.
Exchange: Yes.

SANDAKAN: *Forest Department Herbarium,* **(SAN),** P.O. Box 1407, Sandakan, Sabah, **Malaysia.**
Telephone: 089 4179.
Status: Government Department.
Foundation: 1916 (herbarium completely destroyed in 1944 and nearly completely burnt in 1961). *Number of specimens:* 82.000.
Herbarium: Woody plants of Borneo, especially Sabah.
Director: None; under control of Senior Research Officer.
Curator: Forest Botanist, vacant.
Staff members: MARY P. Y. FONG, 1947 (Indexing and filing herbarium specimens).
ABAN GIBOT, 1944 (Field collecting).
Y. P. HAU, 1943 (Illustration).
LEOPOLD MADANI, 1938 (Field collecting).
DEWOL SUNDALING, 1950 (Field collecting).
Specialization in research: Woody plants of Sabah.
Exchange: Program established.

SAN DIEGO: *Herbarium, San Diego Museum of Natural History,* **(SD),** Box 1390, Balboa Park, San Diego, California 92112, **U.S.A.**
Telephone: 714/232-3821.
Status: Operated by San Diego Society of Natural History, a private corporation, but with support from the City and County of San Diego.
Foundation: 1874. *Number of specimens:* 105.000.
Herbarium: General collection, with emphasis on southern California and northern Baja California, Mexico.
Important collections: D. Cleveland, F. F. Gander, D. F. Howe (California), R. Moran (especially Baja California).
Director: ARTHUR C. ALLYN, JR., 1913 (Lepidoptera).
Curator: REID MORAN, 1916 (Crassulaceae; flora of Baja California).
Staff members: LINDA ALLEN, 1949 (Flora of San Diego County).
WILLIAM D. CLEMONS, 1920 (Local flora).
JACK L. REVEAL, 1912 (Gramineae).
Specialization in research: Vascular plants of southern California and northern Baja California, Mexico.

Loans: No special restrictions.
Periodical and serial works: Memoirs, Transactions, and Occasional Papers of the San Diego Society of Natural History; Environment Southwest.
Exchange: Available: California, Baja California. Desired: California, Mexico.

SAN DIEGO: *Herbarium, San Diego Mesa College,* **(SDM),** 7250 Mesa College Drive, San Diego, California 92111, **U.S.A.**
Telephone: 714/279-2300.
Foundation: 1960. *Number of specimens:* 2.000 vascular plants, 150 algae.
Herbarium: San Diego County.
Important collections: Albert J. Grennan, Richard Schwenkmeyer.
Director and Curator: ALBERT J. GRENNAN, 1928 (Asteraceae).
Specialization in research: Population genetics of *Isomeris arborea* (Capparidaceae).

SAN DIEGO: *Herbarium, Botany Department, San Diego State University,* **(SDSU),** College Avenue, San Diego, California 92182, **U.S.A.**
Telephone: 714/265-6529.
Foundation: 1959. *Number of specimens:* 6.000.
Herbarium: Local flora.
Director and Curator: H. L. WEDBERG, 1933.
Loans: Usual regulations.

SAN DIEGO: *The Traub Herbarium of the American Plant Life Society,* **(TRA)** — *see* LA JOLLA.

SAN FRANCISCO: *Herbarium, Department of Botany, California Academy of Sciences,* **(CAS),** Golden Gate Park, San Francisco, California 94118, **U.S.A.**
Telephone: 415/221-5100, ext. 265.
Status: Private foundation.
Foundation: 1853. *Number of specimens:* 1.400.000, including DS.
Herbarium: Worldwide (includes vascular plants, lichens, and bryophytes), especially California (including introduced weeds and ornamentals), western North America, and northern Latin America; Dudley Herbarium (DS) now integrated with CAS.
Important collections: For information on Dudley Herbarium (DS), see separate listing under San Francisco. Early California collections of H. Behr, H. Cannon (especially central California), A. Eastwood, A. Kellogg; California collections of J. T. Howell (also western North America), H. N. Pollard (Ventura and Santa Barbara counties), R. Hoover (San Luis Obispo County), P. Rubtzoff (Sonoma County marshes), E. Twisselman (Kern County and adjacent areas), L. S. Rose, E. McClintock (especially ornamentals); T. H. Kearney (Arizona), A. Stewart and J. T. Howell (Galápagos Islands), D. E. Breedlove (Mexico, California), F. Almeda (Costa Rican Melastomataceae); about 4.000 types, mostly from western North America and Latin America.
Director: GEORGE E. LINDSAY, 1916 (Cactaceae).
Chairman, Botany Department: FRANK ALMEDA, JR., 1946 (Systematics and pollination biology of neotropical Melastomataceae and Symplocaceae).
Curator: DENNIS E. BREEDLOVE, 1939 (Plants of Mexico, particularly of the states of Chiapas, Sinaloa, Durango, and Nayarit).

Staff members: ALVA DAY, 1920 (Polemoniaceae).

JOHN THOMAS HOWELL, 1903 (Plants of California, including naturalized weeds, and especially certain local areas of Marin and Monterey counties and the Sierra Nevada).

Specialization in research: Floristics and systematics.

Associated botanic garden: Strybing Arboretum and Botanical Garden of Golden Gate Park, San Francisco, California 94117, U.S.A.

Loans: In general to recognized individuals and botanical institutions.

Periodical and serial works: Occasional Papers of the California Academy of Sciences; Proceedings of the California Academy of Sciences; Pacific Discovery.

Exchange: Available and Desired: California and Latin American plants.

Remarks: The Dudley Herbarium (DS) of Stanford University has been integrated with the collections at the California Academy of Sciences (CAS). Requests for material from either of these Herbaria should be addressed to Chairman, Department of Botany, California Academy of Sciences. CAS algae collections now housed at University of California, Berkely (UC). CAS fungi, except for fleshy fungi, now housed at U.S. Department of Agriculture, Beltsville (BPI). With the exception of type specimens, most collections made before 1906 were destroyed in that year by the San Francisco earthquake and fire.

SAN FRANCISCO: *Dudley Herbarium of Stanford University,* **(DS),** Department of Botany, California Academy of Sciences, Golden Gate Park, San Francisco, California 94118, **U.S.A.**

Telephone: 415/221-5100.

Status: University; private foundation.

Foundation: 1891. *Number of specimens:* 850.000.

Herbarium: Vascular plants of western North America, including Mexico; Mediterranean plants; arctic Alaska.

Important collections: L. Abrams (western North America), C. L. Anderson, E. Applegate (northern California and Oregon), J. Beatley (southern Nevada), D. E. Breedlove (Mexico, especially Chiapas, and California), Carnegie Institution of Washington (vouchers for work of J. C. Clausen, D. D. Keck, and W. Hiesey), J. W. Congdon (Sierra Nevada foothills), W. R. Dudley (New York, California), R. S. Ferris (western North America), G. Gautier collection (includes specimens made by J. L. Berlandier, L. H. Boivin, L. A. G. Bosc, P. Commerson, H. Cuming, E. P. Duchassaing, C. F. Ecklon and C. L. P. Zeyher, J. Dombey, P. Forskål, C. Gaudichaud, G. Gautier, J. B. A. Guillemin, T. Kotschy, J. Miers, G. S. Perrottet, R. Schomburgk, R. Spruce, Verreaux, N. Wallich), W. Harvey collection (Europe, Africa, Australia, New Zealand), A. A. Heller (western North America), H.

Knoche (California, Mediterranean, Balearic Islands), C. R. Orcutt (Mexico), S. B. Parish (southern California), C. P. Smith (*Lupinus*), S. Stokes (*Eriogonum*), V. Rattan (California), P. H. Raven (Onagraceae, western North America), J. Rzedowski (Mexico), R. Taylor and J. Calder (Queen Charlotte Islands), J. H. Thomas (central California, arctic Alaska, Baja California), I. L. Wiggins (western North America, especially San Diego County, California, arctic Alaska, Baja California, Galápagos Islands), C. B. Wolf (*Cupressus,* western North America).

Director: JOHN H. THOMAS, 1928 (Flora of western North America).

Staff members: RICHARD W. Holm, 1925 (Biosystematics; Asclepiadaceae).

IRA L. WIGGINS, 1899 (Malvaceae; floras of the Sonoran Desert, Alaska, and the Galápagos Islands).

Specialization in research: As above.

Loans: To all qualified investigators, through institutions; see comments below under Remarks.

Periodical and serial works: Contributions from the Dudley Herbarium (no longer being published); Stanford University Publications University Series, Biological Sciences.

Exchange: Western North America, Mexico.

Remarks: Algae collections transferred to the University of California, Berkeley (UC); fungus collections transferred to the National Fungus Collection, Beltsville (BPI); bryophytes transferred to the New York Botanical Garden (NY) (arctic bryophytes), New York State Museum (NYS) (mainly W. R. Dudley's New York State bryophytes), Univ. of British Columbia (UBC) (various bryophytes), and the California Academy of Sciences (CAS) (the remaining collections of bryophytes). The library owns the private collection of reprints of Adolf Engler. May 15, 1976 marked the completion of the move of the Dudley Herbarium (DS) of Stanford University to the Department of Botany at the California Academy of Sciences (CAS) on long term loan. The Dudley Herbarium and the Academy Herbarium are being integrated and are being operated as a unit, even though ownership remains with their respective institutions. Please note that Dudley Herbarium specimens must be cited as DS, California Academy of Sciences Herbarium specimens as CAS. Please send all correspondence relative to loans and exchanges to: Chairman, Department of Botany, California Academy of Sciences, Golden Gate Park, San Francisco, California 94305, U.S.A., not to individual curators. Formerly listed under Stanford.

SAN FRANCISCO: *Herbarium, University of San Francisco,* **(SAFU),** San Francisco, California 94117, **U.S.A.** -- discontinued.

SAN FRANCISCO: *U.S. Forest Service Herbarium, Region Five (California), Division of Range and Wild-*

life Management, (**SFRF**), 630 Sansome Street, San Francisco, California 94111, **U.S.A.** – – deposited at CAS, San Francisco in 1980.
Status: U.S. Department of Agriculture, Forest Service.
Foundation: 1909. *Number of specimens:* 4.050.

SAN FRANCISCO: *Herbarium, Department of Biological Sciences, San Francisco State University,* (**SFSU**), 1600 Holloway Avenue, San Francisco, California 94132, **U.S.A.** ₂ᵌ₆
Telephone: 415/469-2439.
Foundation: 1959. *Number of specimens:* 68.000.
Herbarium: Specializing in cryptogamic plants; teaching collection only of vascular plants.
Important collections: Fleshy fungi of western and southeastern U.S.; lichens of California; Boletaceae of the world.
> *Director and Curator:* HARRY D. THIERS, 1919 (Fleshy fungi).
> *Staff members:* MICHAEL JOSSELYN (Algae).
> ROBERT PATTERSON (Vascular plants, especially Polemoniaceae).
> *Specialization in research:* Algal flora of San Francisco Bay area: monographic studies of Boletaceae; fleshy fungus flora of California; lichen flora of California; Polemoniaceae of U.S.
Loans: Usual restrictions.
Exchange: Fleshy fungi and lichens.

SAN ISIDRO: *Herbario, Instituto de Botánica Darwinion,* (**SI**), Labardén 200, 1640 Martínez, San Isidro, Buenos Aires, **Argentina.**
Telephone: (54)743-4800.
Status: Academia National de Ciencias Exactas, Físicas y Naturales de Buenos Aires, Consejo Nacional de Investigaciones Científicas y Técnicas (CONICET).
Foundation: 1911; national institute since 1936.
Number of specimens: 450.000.
Herbarium: Worldwide herbarium, especially vascular plants of Argentina and neighboring countries; North and South America, Europe.
Important collections: M. Barros (Cyperaceae), A. Burkart, O. Buchtien, A. L. Cabrera, F. Felippone, E. Hassler, C. M. Hicken, P. Jörgensen, Rodriguez, T. Rojas, J. Steinbach, S. Venturi.
> *Director:* ANGEL L. CABRERA, 1908 (Compositae; phytogeography).
> *Curator:* NÉLIDA M. BACIGALUPO, 1924 (Commelinaceae, Rubiaceae).
> *Staff members:* SILVIA MARGARITA BOTTA, 1942 (Verbenaceae, Scrophulariaceae).
> NORMA BEATRIZ DEGINANI, 1950 (*Viola*).
> CECILIA EZCURRA, 1954 (Compositae).
> EDITH VILMA GOMEZ, 1942 (Leguminosae).
> ENCARNACIÓN ROSA GUAGLIANONE, 1932 (Cyperaceae, Liliaceae).
> ROBERTO KIESLING, 1941 (Cactaceae).
> MARIA EMMA MULGURA, 1943 (*Atriplex, Oxa-*

lis, Malpighiaceae).
> ANA MARÍA RAGONESE, 1928 (Anatomy of phanerogams).
> ALICIA ROTMAN, 1945 (Myrtaceae).
> ALCIDES AROLDO SAENZ, 1948 (Anatomy and taxonomy of Compositae).
> MARGARITA SANCHO, 1952 (Iridaceae).
> NELIDA S. TRONCOSO, 1912 (Verbenaceae).
> EMILIO ULIBARRI, 1946 (Leguminosae).
> MARCELO VAZQUEZ, 1951 (Moraceae).
> FERNANDO OMAR ZULOAGA, 1951 (Gramineae).
> *Research associates:* OSVALDO BOELCKE, 1919 (Cruciferae).
> ELISA G. NICORA, 1912 (Gramineae).
> ZULMA RÚGOLO, 1940 (Gramineae).
> *Specialization in research:* Taxonomy and anatomy of vascular plants; regional floras of Entre Ríos, Jujuy, and San Juan.
Associated botanic garden: Pequeño Jardín Botánico.
Loans: To recognized botanical institutions for 6 to 12 months.
Periodical and serial works: Darwiniana (since 1912; now at volume 22); Hickenia (since 1976).
Exchange: Available: Vascular plants of Argentina. Desired: Vascular plants of the world.

SAN JOSÉ: *Herbario Nacional de Costa Rica, Museo Nacional,* (**CR**), P.O. Box 749, San José, **Costa Rica.**
Telephone: 21-44-29; 21-02-95.
Foundation: 1887. *Number of specimens:* 80.000.
Herbarium: General collections Costa Rican flora, Central America, worldwide; woods of Costa Rica.
Important collections: Types and isotypes of Casimir de Candolle, Christ, E. Rosenstock, Weber, P. A. Micheli, P. C. Standley, H. F. Pittier, Schlechter, Bartram, A. Engler, Pax, A. Tonduz, Wercklé; herbarium A. M. Brenes.
> *Director and Curator:* LUIS D. GÓMEZ P., 1944 (Pteridophyta; fungi).
> *Staff members:* RAFAEL A. OCAMPO (Gramineae).
> LUIS J. POVEDA (Angiosperms; trees).
> RICARDO SOTO (Phycology).
> *Honorary staff members:* WILLIAM C. BURGER (Angiosperms).
> JOSÉ CUATRECASAS (Angiosperms).
> DANIEL H. JANZEN (Ecology).
> RICHARD P. KORF (Ascomycetes).
> DAVID B. LELLINGER (Pteridophytes).
> ELKE MACKENZIE (Lichens).
> WERNER RAUH (Phytogeography).
> PETER H. RAVEN (Angiosperms).
> ROLF SINGER (Basidiomycetes).
> ROBERT G. STOLZE (Pteridophytes).
> RUGGERO TOMASELLI (Phytogeography).
> ROLLA M. TRYON (Pteridophytes).
> FLORENCE S. WAGNER (Cytology).
> WARREN H. WAGNER (Pteridophytes).
> JOHN F. UTLEY (Bromeliaceae).

ECKHARD WOLLENWEBER (Phytochemistry).
Specialization in research: Flora of Costa Rica.
Loans: To recognized botanical institutions only.
Periodical and serial works: Brenesia (biannual).
Exchange: Desired: All groups, worldwide.

SAN JOSE: *Herbarium, California State University,* (**SJSU**), San Jose, California 95192, **U.S.A.** (Information 1974)
Foundation: 1950. *Number of specimens:* 6.500.
Herbarium: California flora, especially of the Santa Cruz Mountains and Mount Hamilton ranges of the intercoastal ranges.

SAN JOSÉ: *Herbario, Escuela de Biología, Universidad de Costa Rica,* (**USJ**), Ciudad Universitaria "Rodrigo Facio," San José, **Costa Rica.**
Telephone: 25-55-55, ext. 432.
Foundation: 1940. *Number of specimens:* 20.000.
Herbarium: Flora of Costa Rica, especially trees.
⌐*Director:* JOSÉ ALBERTO SÁENZ-RENAULD, 1929 (Mycology).
Curator of Vascular Plants: LUIS A. FOURNIER O., 1935; 25-55-55, ext. 410 (Ecology; dendrology).
Curator of Nonvascular Plants: MARYSSIA NASSAR, 1939; 25-55-55, ext. 259 (Mycology).
Staff member: JORGE GÓMEZ LAURITO (Cyperaceae).
Specialization in research: Flora of Costa Rica; taxonomy, ecology, plant anatomy, phytochemistry, phytopathology, agrostology.
Associated botanic garden: Lankester Botanical Garden.
Exchange: Under restricted basis.

SAN LUIS OBISPO: *Robert F. Hoover Herbarium, Department of Biology, California Polytechnic State University,* (**OBI**), San Luis Obispo, California 93407, **U.S.A.**
Telephone: 805/546-2043.
Foundation: 1947. *Number of specimens:* 25.000.
Herbarium: Flora of San Luis Obispo.
Important collections: Robert F. Hoover (vascular plants of San Luis Obispo County), Robert Rodin (ethnobotany; Ovomboland Africa, India), Shirley Sparling (algae of San Luis Obispo County).
Director: DAVID J. KEIL (Cytotaxonomy of Asteraceae).
Staff members: MALCOLM G. MCLEOD (Local flora; *Opuntia, Dudleya*).
RHONDA RIGGINS-PIMENTEL (Local flora; *Lupinus;* Poaceae).
SHIRLEY SPARLING (Marine algae of San Luis Obispo County).
DIRK R. WALTERS (Local flora; *Schizanthus; Salpiglossidae*).
Specialization in research: Local flora.
Loans: To institutions.
Exchange: Yes.

SAN LUIS POTOSÍ: *Herbario del Instituto de Investigacion de Zonas Deserticas, Universidad Autónoma de San Luis Potosí,* (**SLPM**), Alvaro Obregon 64, San Luis Potosí, San Luis Potosí, **Mexico.**
Telephone: 2-66-04.
Foundation: 1954. *Number of specimens:* 16.000.
Herbarium: Phanerogams of the arid zones, especially Chihuahuan Desert; flora of the State of San Luis Potosí.
Important collections: J. G. Schaffner (San Luis Potosí), Antonio Gomez-Gonzalez, Fernando Gomez-Lorence, Fernando Medellin-Leal, Jerzy Rzedowski, Sonia Salas de Leon, Francisco Takaki, Julio Villa-Vega.
Director: FERNANDO MEDELLIN-LEAL, 1936 (Botanist).
Curators: FERNANDO GOMEZ-LORENCE, 1946 (Gramineae).
SONIA SALAS DE LEON, 1948 (Compositae).
Specialization in research: Flora of the arid zone of the State of San Luis Potosí.
Loans: All specimens to be returned at the same time; time can be extended upon request.
Periodical and serial works: Acta Cientifica Potosina.
Exchange: Especially plants of the arid zones.

SAN MARCOS: *Herbarium, Life Science Department, Palomar College,* (**PASM**), San Marcos, California 92069, **U.S.A.**
Telephone: 714/744-1150, ext. 263 and 293.
Foundation: 1960. *Number of specimens:* 1.800.
Herbarium: Good collection of naturalized plants of northern San Diego County, California; *Cupressus* of California and Baja; *Orobanche* of San Diego County; Martyniaceae of southwestern U.S.
Curator: WAYNE P. ARMSTRONG, 1941 (*Cupressus, Pinus, Orobanche;* Martyniaceae; naturalized weeds).

SAN MARINO: *Herbarium, Huntington Botanical Gardens,* (**HNT**), 1151 Oxford Road, San Marino, California 91108, **U.S.A.**
Telephone: 213/792-6141.
Status: Private institution.
Foundation: 1963. *Number of specimens:* 4.500.
Herbarium: Plants of Mexico; Cactaceae, Crassulaceae, Palmae, Amaryllidaceae; cultivated plants of southern California.
Important collections: Myron Kimnach (Mexico), Fredrick Boutin (Mexico, Belize).
Director: MYRON KIMNACH, 1922 (Cactaceae, Crassulaceae).
Curator: JAMES A. BAUML, 1952 (Amaryllidaceae; plants of Mexico).
Associated botanic garden: Huntington Botanical Gardens.
Loans: To recognized individuals and institutions.
Exchange: Available: Mexican specimens. De-

sired: Desert and Mexican specimens.

SAN MARTÍN DE LOS ANDES: *Herbario, Instituto Patagonico de Ciencias Naturales,* **(IPCN),** Coronel Rohde 1351, Casilla Correo 7, San Martín de los Andes, Neuquén, **Argentina.**
Telephone: (54)7208.
Status: Private institution.
Foundation: 1972. *Number of specimens:* 1.000.
Herbarium: Vascular plants from Patagonia, mainly Compositae and Leguminosae.
  Director: MARIO O. GENTILI.
  Staff member: HORACIO J. MOLINARI.
  Loans: Usual regulations.
  Exchange: Available and Desired: Vascular plants of Patagonia.

SAN MIGUEL DE TUCUMÁN: *Herbario, Instituto Miguel Lillo de la Fundación Miguel Lillo,* **(LIL),** Calle Miguel Lillo 251, Casilla de Correo 91, 4000 San Miguel de Tucumán, Tucumán, **Argentina.**
Telephone: (54)39960; 39557.
Status: Ministerio de Cultura y Educación de Argentina.
Foundation: 1931. *Number of specimens:* 700.000.
Herbarium: Worldwide, especially Argentina and neighboring countries.
Important collections: Miguel Lillo, S. Venturi, R. Schreiter, M. Cárdenas, L. Castillón.
  Director: MARTA MARÍA GRASSI, 1921 (Lichens).
  Curators: ANNA MARÍA HILDEGARD TÜRPE, 1935 (Gramineae).
    PEDRO PABLO LEGNAME, 1930 (Tubiflorae).
  Staff members: LIDIA ROSA ABADALA DE ISRAILEV, 1940 (Chemosystematics).
    MARÍA ELENA CRISTÓBAL DE HINOJO, 1945 (Cytogenetics).
    MARÍA ROSA FIGUEROA, 1945 (Solanaceae).
    ANA MARÍA FRÍAS DE FERNÁNDEZ, 1940 (Cytogenetics).
    LIONEL OSVALDO GIUSTI, 1932 (Chenopodiaceae).
    ALFREDO GRAU, 1956 (Plant anatomy).
    STEPHAN HALLOY, 1953 (Plant from high elevations).
    HILDA HERNÁNDEZ DE HOLGADO, 1925 (Lauraceae).
    BERTA ESTELA JUAREZ, 1945 (Chemosystematics).
    IRMA DOLORES LUCENA DE ROMERO, 1948 (Melastomataceae).
    BERNARDINO MATEU, 1916 (Phytochemistry).
    MARÍA ELENA MENDIONDO DE GORDILLO, 1945 (Chemosystematics).
    MARÍA EVA LOZZIA DE CANELADA, 1945 (Cytogenetics).
    MARTA QUARENGHI DE CORREA, 1950 (Chemosystematics).
    MATILDE RODRIGUEZ DE SARMIENTO, 1940 (Plant anatomy).

ELBA ROSSI DE CEBALLOS, 1945.
    MARÍA MAGDALENA SCHIAVONE, 1945 (Mosses).
    PETER SEELIGMANN, 1923 (Chemosystematics).
    MARTA DEL CARMEN SOSA, 1940 (Crassulaceae).
    BEATRIZ CONCEPCIÓN TRACANNA, 1949 (Algae).
    FEDERICO BERNARDO VERVOORST, 1923 (Floristics).
  Specialization in research: Floristic, systematic, anatomic, and cytogenetic studies with special emphasis on the northwestern Argentinian flora.
  Loans: For six months with extension upon request; types will not be sent.
  Periodical and serial works: Lilloa; Opera Lilloana; Miscelánea.
  Exchange: Desired: Identified specimens and reprints of published papers.
  Remarks: Formerly listed under Tucumán.

SAN SALVADOR: *Herbario, Departamento de Biología, Facultad de Ciencias y Humanidades, Universidad de El Salvador,* **(ITIC),** San Salvador, **El Salvador.**
Telephone: (503)25-7200, ext. 58.
Foundation: 1950. *Number of specimens:* 30.000.
Herbarium: Emphasis on vascular plants and fungi of El Salvador.
  Curator: EDY MONTALVO, 1929 (Phanerogams).
  Staff members: GUSTAVO A. ESCOBAR, 1949 (Aphyllophorales).
    JOSÉ S. FLORES, 1937 (Phanerogams).
    BESIE SIU, 1940 (Vascular cryptogams).
    JUDITH D. TOLEDO, 1944 (Gasteromycetes).
  Specialization in research: Flora of El Salvador; neotropical fungi.
  Loans: To recognized institutions.
  Periodical and serial works: Comunicaciones Biológicas.
  Exchange: Wanted: Tropical plants and fungi, especially from South America and other Central American countries.

SANTA BARBARA: *Herbarium, Santa Barbara Botanic Garden,* **(SBBG),** 1212 Mission Canyon Road, Santa Barbara, California 93105, **U.S.A.**
Telephone: 805/682-4726.
Status: Private foundation, an educational nonprofit corporation.
Foundation: 1939. *Number of specimens:* 53.000.
Herbarium: Vascular native and cultivated plants of California and adjacent areas of U.S. and Mexico; plants of the offshore islands of California and Baja California; *Ceanothus, Cryptantha.*
Important collections: Michael R. Benedict, E. R. Blakley, E. R. Chandler, Hugh and Margaret Dearing, Adolph D. E. Elmer, Steven A. Junak, Katherine K. Muller, Donald W. Myrick, Ralph N. Philbrick, H. N. Pollard, Rev. and Mrs. R. W. Summers, Maunsell

Van Rensselaer.

ETIRED → *Director and Curator:* RALPH N. PHILBRICK, 1934 (California offshore islands).

Staff members: MARY C. HOCHBERG, 1952 (Ecology).

CURATOR →STEVEN A. JUNAK, 1949 (Flora of California).

STEVEN L. TIMBROOK, 1938 (Flora of California; *Langloisia*).

Specialization in research: California offshore islands.

Associated botanic garden: Santa Barbara Botanic Garden.

Loans: To botanical institutions.

Periodical and serial works: Leaflets of the Santa Barbara Botanic Garden.

Exchange: Available: Limited number of native and cultivated California plants, especially from Santa Barbara area. Desired: Native or cultivated plants of California or adjacent areas of U.S. and Mexico.

SANTA BARBARA: *Herbarium, Santa Barbara City College,* **(SBCC)**, 721 Cliff Drive, Santa Barbara, California 93109, **U.S.A.**

Telephone: 805/965-0581, ext. 319.

Status: Community College.

Foundation: 1965. *Number of specimens:* 5.170 (2.750 vascular plants, 140 bryophytes, 1.900 algae, 380 fungi).

Herbarium: Southern California flora; *Ceanothus* of the Santa Ynez Mountains.

Director and Curator: ALLEN E. FLINCK, 1944.

Staff members: ROBERT J. CUMMINGS, 1944.

DIANE F. ELLIOTT, 1950.

MARGARET LANE, 1926.

Loans: No.

Exchange: In the future.

SANTA BARBARA: *Herbarium, Santa Barbara Museum of Natural History,* **(SBM)**, 2559 Puesta Del Sol Road, Santa Barbara, California 93105, **U.S.A.**

Telephone: 805/682-4711.

Status: Private institution.

Foundation: 1916. *Number of specimens:* 29.000.

Herbarium: Mainly southern California and Channel Islands of California; horticultural species from local gardens.

Director: DENNIS M. POWER, 1941 (Ornithology).

Curator: CLIFTON F. SMITH, 1920 (Flora of Santa Barbara region).

Loans: Usual conditions.

Exchange: With SBBG.

SANTA BARBARA: *Herbarium, Department of Biological Sciences, University of California,* **(UCSB)**, Santa Barbara, California 93106, **U.S.A.** (formerly abbreviated SBC).

Telephone: 805/961-2506.

Foundation: 1948. *Number of specimens:* 34.500.

Herbarium: Western North America, especially California and surrounding states.

Important collections: C. H. Muller (oaks).

Curator: DALE M. SMITH, 1928; 805/961-2967 (*Phlox*, Polemoniaceae; California ferns; chemotaxonomy; cytotaxonomy).

Staff members: WAYNE R. FERREN, JR., 1948 (Systematics and ecology of aquatic vascular plants).

J. ROBERT HALLER, 1930; 805/961-2552 (Yellow pine of western North America; phytogeography; plant communities of California).

Specialization in research: Flora of southern California.

Loans: To recognized botanical institutions.

Periodical and serial works: Herbarium of the University of California, Santa Barbara, Publication Series.

Exchange: Available: General southern California. Desired: Western North America; Polemoniaceae, Pinaceae, Fagaceae, Compositae, Gramineae; aquatic vascular plants.

SANTA CLARA: *Herbarium, Department of Biology, University of Santa Clara,* **(SACL)**, Santa Clara, California 95053, **U.S.A.**

Telephone: 408/984-4497.

Foundation: 1967. *Number of specimens:* 3.000.

Herbarium: Emphasis on *Chaenactis* and *Eriophyllum*; local flora.

Director and Curator: JOHN MOORING, 1926 (Biosystematics).

SANTA CLARA: *Centro Agricola Herbario, Universidad Central de Las Villas,* **(ULV)**, Seccion de Canje Internacional, Santa Clara, Las Villas, **Cuba.**

Telephone: 4581.

Foundation: 1960.

SANTA CRUZ: *Herbarium, Division of Natural Sciences, University of California,* **(UCSC)**, Santa Cruz, California 95064, **U.S.A.**

Telephone: 408/429-2918.

Foundation: 1965. *Number of specimens:* 4.050.

Herbarium: Flora of the Santa Cruz Mountains.

Staff members: WILLIAM T. DOYLE.

JEAN A. LANGENHEIM.

SANTA CRUZ DE TENERIFE: *Herbarium, Museo Insular de Ciencias Naturales de Tenerife,* **(TFMC)**, Santa Cruz de Tenerife, Tenerife, Canary Islands, **Spain.**

Remarks: Listed under Tenerife in Taxon 25: 522. 1976.

SANTA FE: *Herbario, Museo Provincial de Ciencias Naturales "Florentino Ameghino,"* **(MFA)**, Moreno 2557, 3000 Santa Fe, **Argentina.**

Telephone: (54)042/23843.

Status: Connected to the Subsecretaría de Cultura,

Ministerio de Educación y Cultura Santa Fe.

Foundation: 1951. *Number of specimens:* 2.059.

Director: CARLOS A. VIRASORO, 1948.

Curator: M. M. DE DONNET.

Specialization in research: Regional aquatic plants.

Associated botanic garden: Jardín Botánico Municipal, Municipalidad de Santa Fe, Barrio Nva. Pompeya (Camino Nogueras), 3000 Santa Fe, Argentina.

Loans: Usual regulations.

Periodical and serial works: Anales y Comunicaciones del Museo Provincial de Ciencias Naturales "Florentino Ameghino."

Exchange: Plants of Argentina.

SANTA FE: *Herbario, Dirección Ecología y Protección de la Fauna,* (**SF**), Boulevard Pellegrini 3100, Casilla de Correo 2000, Santa Fe, **Argentina.**

Telephone: 62352.

Status: Ministerio de Agricultura y Ganadería de la Provincia de Santa Fe; Facultad de Agronomia y Veterinaria de Esperanza, Universidad Nacional del Litoral.

Foundation: 1935. *Number of specimens:* 3.800.

Herbarium: Regional vascular plants, mainly Gramineae, Compositae, and Leguminosae.

Important collections: G. Covas, Al Ragonese.

SANTA MARIA: *Herbário, Departamento de Biologia, Centro de Ciências Naturais e Exatas, Universidade Federal de Santa Maria,* (**SMDB**), 97.100 Santa Maria, Rio Grande do Sul, **Brazil.**

Telephone: 055/221-1616, ramal 2339.

Foundation: 1962. *Number of specimens:* 1.570.

Herbarium: Flora of Rio Grande do Sul.

Director: ADELINO ALVAREZ FILHO, 1942 (Taxonomy).

Curator: FRANCISCA MARLENE DA SILVEIRA VIANNA, 1935 (Taxonomy).

Staff members: MARIA HELENA CECHELLA ACHUTTI (Anatomy and morphology).

ZILMA AURELIO BALDISSERA, 1936 (Taxonomy).

ISMAR BARRETO (Taxonomy).

VERA LUCIA BENDER DELLAMEA (Taxonomy).

TEREZA GRACIOLLI, 1927 (Anatomy and morphology).

AMELIA MOEMA VEIGA LOPES, 1943 (Taxonomy).

VANOLI XAVIER LOPES, 1942 (Anatomy and morphology).

JOSÉ NEWTON MARCHIORI (Wood anatomy).

SANTO MASIERO, 1922 (Taxonomy).

GILBERTO MORAES, 1952 (Plant physiology).

JOSÉ CARLOS PIGNATARO, 1933 (Plant physiology).

VICTOR HUGO SOUZA, 1931 (Plant physiology).

Specialization in research: Flora of Rio Grande do Sul.

Associated botanic garden: Jardim Botânico da Universidade Federal de Santa Maria.

Loans: Usual regulations.

Periodical and serial works: Ciência e Natura.

Exchange: Available: Plants of Rio Grande do Sul. Wanted: Duplicates sent for identification.

SANTA MARTA: *Herbario, Universidad Tecnológica del Magdalena,* (**UTMC**), Apartado Aéreo 732, Santa Marta, Magdalena, **Colombia.**

Telephone: (57)4110-4111.

Foundation: 1962. *Number of specimens:* 7.289.

Important collections: R. Romero-Castañeda, José Cuatrecasas, Lorenzo Uribe Uribe, Enrique Forero, María Teresa Murillo, Neovis de López, German Bula, Luis Eduardo Mora Osejo.

Curator: NEOVIS DE LÓPEZ, 1937.

Staff member: GERMAN BULA.

SANTA ROSA: *North Coast Herbarium of California,* (**NCC**), Santa Rosa Junior College, Santa Rosa, California 95402, **U.S.A.** -- deposited at ROPA, Rohnert Park.

Foundation: 1935. *Number of specimens:* 15.000.

Herbarium: Western U.S., Mexico.

SANTA ROSA: *Herbario, Facultad de Agronomía, Universidad Nacional de La Pampa,* (**SRFA**), Casilla de Correo 159, 6.300 Santa Rosa, La Pampa, **Argentina.**

Telephone: (54)5092; 5093; 5094.

Foundation: 1965. *Number of specimens:* 7.200.

Herbarium: Flora of La Pampa.

Important collections: Eduardo Cano, Guillermo Covas, Horacio Cunquero, Humberto Fabris, Helga Schuabe, Miguel Montes, Arnoldo Ruiz, Pedro Steibel, Héctor Troiani.

Director: HÉCTOR TROIANI, 1945 (Taxonomy of vascular plants; Compositae).

Curator: PEDRO STEIBEL, 1944 (Taxonomy of vascular plants; Gramineae).

Staff members: GUILLERMO COVAS, 1915 (Breeding of forage plants).

HORACIO CUNQUERO (Taxonomy of vascular plants).

Specialization in research: Taxonomy of grasses, Compositae, and native plants in the Province of La Pampa.

Associated botanic garden: Botanical Garden of the Faculty of Agronomy of La Pampa.

Loans: Usual regulations.

Exchange: Desired.

SANTA TECLA: *Centro Nacional de Agronómia,* (**TECLA**) -- see NUEVA SAN SALVADOR.

SANTIAGO: *Herbario, Departamento de Silvicultura, Facultad de Ciencias Forestales, Universidad de Chile,* (**EIF**), Casilla 9206, Santiago, **Chile.**

Telephone: 587042, anexo 35.

Foundation: 1966. *Number of specimens:* 10.000.
Herbarium: Chilean plants; forest trees and shrubs; Gramineae; flora of the Altiplano.
 Curator: RUDOLFO GAJARDO-MICHELL, 1947 (Phytogeography; plant ecology).
 Staff members: LEONARDO ARAYA, 1952 (Plant ecology).
 M. TERESA SERRA, 1950 (Taxonomy).

SANTIAGO: *Herbario, Seccion Botánica, Museo Nacional de Historia Natural,* (**SGO**), Casilla 787, Santiago, **Chile.**
Telephone: 90011, ext. 24 or 25.
Status: Dirección de Bibliotecas, Archivos y Museos; Ministerio de Educación.
Foundation: 1830. *Number of specimens:* 95.000 (50.000 Chilean, the remainder foreign plants).
Herbarium: Emphasis on the flora of Chile.
Important collections: R. A. Philippi (1853-1900; many types), C. G. L. Bertero (1828), C. Gay, R. Singer, K. S. Kunth, A. J. A. Bonpland, F. Sello.
 Director: GRETE MOSTNY G. (Archaeology).
 Curator: MÉLICA MUÑOZ SCHICK, 1941 (Flora of Chile).
 Staff member: ELIZABETH BARRERA M., 1947 (Cryptogamic plants; ferns).
 Specialization in research: Flora and vegetation of Chile; spores and foliar cuticle of pteridophytes.
 Loans: General collections to recognized botanical institutions.
 Periodical and serial works: Noticiario Mensual, Museo Nacional de Historia Natural; Boletín del Museo Nacional de Historia Natural.
 Exchange: Chilean plants.
 Remarks: One of the oldest herbaria in South America, containing plants collected as early as 1828.

SANTIAGO: *Herbario, Sala de Sistematica, Departamento de Biología Ambiental y de Poblaciones, Instituto de Ciencias Biológicas, Pontificia Universidad Católica de Chile,* (**SSUC**), Casilla 114-D, Santiago, **Chile.**
Telephone: 222101; 224671.
Foundation: 1960. *Number of specimens:* 2.000 algae.
Herbarium: Marine benthic algae from the Pacific coast of South America.
 Director: PATRICIO SANCHEZ, 1928 (Marine invertebrates).
 Curator: EDUARDO NEALLER.
 Staff members: BERNABÉ SANTELICES, 1945 (Marine phycology).
 M. EUGENIA VERA, 1956 (Marine phycology).
 Specialization in research: Taxonomic and population research on Chilean benthic algae.
 Loans: Yes.

SANTIAGO DE COMPOSTELA: *Herbarium, Jardín Botánico, Universidad de Santiago,* (**SANT**), Fac-

ultad de Farmacia, Avenida Las Ciencias s/n, Santiago de Compostela, La Coruña, **Spain.**
Telephone: 981/593050.
Status: University.
Foundation: 1945. *Number of specimens:* 11.000.
 Director: JESÚS IZCO, 1940 (Vegetation and plant ecology).
 Curator: ELENA GONZALEZ, 1937 (Galician flora).
 Staff members: RAMÓN ALVAREZ, 1929 (Galician flora).
 JAVIER AMIGO, 1956 (Regional flora).
 LUIS FREIRE, 1918 (Galician mycology).
 JAVIER GUITIAN, 1957 (Regional flora).
 Specialization in research: Flora of Galicia, Cistaceae.
 Loans: To recognized botanical institutions on request.
 Periodical and serial works: Trabajos Compostelanos de Biología.
 Exchange: Atlantic and subatlantic European flora.

SANTIAGO DE LOS CABALLEROS: *El Herbario "Rafael M. Moscoso," Universidad Católica Madre y Maestra,* (**UCMM**), Santiago de los Caballeros, **Dominican Republic.**
Telephone: 582-5105, ext. 277.
Foundation: 1973. *Number of specimens:* 3.000.
Herbarium: Aquatic vascular plants of Hispaniola.
 Director: RICHARD M. LOWDEN, 1943 (Aquatic vascular plant taxonomy).
 Specialization in research: Treatment of the aquatic vascular flora in the West Indies and related areas.

SANTO DOMINGO: *Herbarium, Jardín Botánico Nacional "Dr. Rafael M. Moscoso,"* (**JBSD**), Apartado 174-2, Avenida Botánica, Los Jardines, Santo Domingo, **Dominican Republic.**
Telephone: 567-6211; 567-6212; 567-6213; 567-2860.
Foundation: 1972. *Number of specimens:* 15.000.
Herbarium: Mainly angiosperms and ferns, some bryophytes and algae, of the Dominican Republic.
Important collections: A. H. Liogier, Donald D. Dod (orchids).
 Curator: IVONNE GARCIA DE LOPEZ, 1952 (Ferns of the Dominican Republic).
 Staff members: DONALD D. DOD (Orchids of the Dominican Republic).
 ADOLPHO GOTTSCHALK, 1960 (Orchids of the Dominican Republic).
 MILCÍADES MEJÍA PIMENTEL, 1952 (Flora of Hispaniola).
 THOMAS A. ZANONI, 1949 (Gymnosperms of the New World; flora of Hispaniola).
 Specialization in research: Flora of Hispaniola.
 Associated botanic garden: Jardín Botánico Nacional "Dr. Rafael M. Moscoso."

Loans: To recognized herbaria, usually for 6 months.
Periodical and serial works: Moscosoa (scientific contributions of the Jardín Botánico).
Exchange: Dominican Republic specimens for publications.

SANTO DOMINGO: *Rafael M. Moscoso Herbarium, Universidad Autónoma de Santo Domingo,* (**USD**), Santo Domingo, **Dominican Republic.**
Telephone: 533-2219.
Foundation: 1941. *Number of specimens:* 10.000.
Herbarium: Flora of the Dominican Republic.
Important collections: E. L. Ekman, M. D. Fuertes L., J. Jiménez.
Director and Curator: EUGENIO DE JESUS MARCANO F., 1923.
Specialization in research: Taxonomy, ecology.

SANTO DOMINGO DE LOS COLORADOS: *Herbarium, Rio Palenque Science Center,* (**RPSC**), Casilla 95, Santo Domingo de Los Colorados, Pichincha, **Ecuador.**
Status: Directed by a consortium of institutions including Marie Selby Botanical Gardens, University of Miami, University of South Florida, and Univ. Catolica del Ecuador.
Foundation: 1971. *Number of specimens:* 3.500.
Herbarium: Plants of western Ecuador.
Important collections: Calaway H. Dodson, A. Gentry.
Director and Curator: CALAWAY H. DODSON, 1928 (Evolution of Orchidaceae).
Specialization in research: Natural history in tropics; comparative ecology of tropical life zones.
Associated botanic garden: Marie Selby Botanical Gardens, 800 S. Palm Avenue, Sarasota, Florida 33578, U.S.A.
Loans: Duplicates available from Sarasota (SEL).
Remarks: This herbarium listed under Guayaquil in Taxon 27: 428. 1978.

SANTO TOMÉ: *Herbario, Instituto Nacional de Limnología,* (**STL**), José Macía 1933, 3016 Santo Tomé, Santa Fe, **Argentina.**
Telephone: (54)042/70723; 70152.
Status: Consejo Nacional de Investigaciones Científicas y Técnicas (CONICET).
Foundation: 1963. *Number of specimens:* 2.100.
Herbarium: Argentina, especially provinces of Córdoba and Neuquén.
Director: CLARICE PIGNALBERI DE HASSAN, 1931 (Fish biology).
Curators: MARÍA OFELIA GARCÍA DE EMILIANI, 1945 (Algae).
MARÍA CRISTINA MARTA, 1948 (Aquatic plants).
Staff member: VÍCTOR H. LALLANA, 1951 (Aquatic plants).

Specialization in research: Aquatic vegetation of the Paraná River; distribution and productivity of species.
Loans: Without restrictions.
Exchange: With other similar institutions.

SÃO LEOPOLDO: *Herbarium Anchieta, Instituto Anchietano e Unisinos,* (**PACA**), 93.000 São Leopoldo, Rio Grande do Sul, **Brazil.**
Herbarium: 15.000 fungi.
Important collections: J. Rick.

SÃO LUÍS: *Herbário Atico Seabra, Laboratório de Hidrobiologia, Universidade Federal do Maranhão,* (**UFMA**), Rua Treze de Maio 506, Caixa Postal 571, 65.000 São Luís, Maranhão, **Brazil.**
Telephone: (55)222-6371.
Foundation: 1980. *Number of specimens:* 2.777.
Herbarium: State of Maranhão, especially Leguminosae, Chlorophyta, Phaeophyta, Rhodophyta.
Directors: TEREZINHA DE JESUS ALMEIDA SILVA REGO, 1933; 222-0169.
TEREZA DE JESUS BARROS DA SILVA.
Staff members: FLORIMAR DE JESUS ARANHA, 1966 (Economic botany).
ANTONIO CARLOS LEAL DE CASTRO, 1955 (Economic botany).
MARIA JOSÉ SARAIVA LOPES, 1949 (Marine algae).
Specialization in research: Inventory of the flora of Maranhão.
Exchange: Yes.

SÃO PAULO: *Herbário, Seção de Micologia Fitopatológica, Instituto Biológico,* (**IBI**), Avenida Conselheiro Rodrigues Alves 1252, Caixa Postal 7119, 04014 São Paulo, São Paulo, **Brazil.**
Telephone: (55)011/273-0166, ramal 34.
Status: Secretaria da Agricultura.
Foundation: 1931. *Number of specimens:* 13.528.
Herbarium: Plant diseases and plant pathogens, mostly plant pathogenic fungi.
Important collections: J. Hennen and M. B. Figueiredo (Uredinales from Brazil); A. E. Jenkins and A. A. Bitancourt (Myriangiales); F. Petrak (Mycotheca generalis), A. Puttemans (rusts).
Director: MARIO BARRETO FIGUEIREDO, 1933 (Mycology; Uredinales).
Curator: MARIA DE LOURDES SILVEIRA, 1921.
Staff members: REGINA E. MELLO AMARAL, 1932 (Mycology).
ROSA MARIA G. CARDOSO, 1933 (Mycology).
MARIA IMACULADA FEITOSA, 1941 (Mycology).
CELIA DE CAMPOS LASCA, 1937 (Mycology).
VANDA MARIA A. MALAVOLTA, 1953 (Mycology).
CYBELLE PACHECO VAZ PIMENTEL, 1936 (Mycology).
GUANABARA P. BARROS PITTA, 1943 (Mycology).

Specialization in research: Mycology; plant pathogenic fungi.

SÃO PAULO: *Herbário do Estado "Maria Eneyda P. K. Fidalgo," Instituto de Botânica,* (**SP**), Caixa Postal 4005, 01000 São Paulo, São Paulo, **Brazil.**
Telephone: (55)011/275-3322.
Status: Coordenadoria da Pesquisade Recursos Naturais, Secretaria de Agricultura e Abastecimento do Estado de São Paulo, Brazil.
Foundation: 1917 (Section); 1938 (Institute). *Number of specimens:* 170.000.
Herbarium: Brazilian flora.
Director: SÔNIA MACHADO DE CAMPOS DIETRICH, 1935 (Plant physiology, biochemistry).
Curator: CARLOS EDUARDO DE MATTOS BICUDO, 1937 (Freshwater algae; Desmidiaceae).
Staff members: VERA LÚCIA RAMOS BONONI, 1944 (Higher Basidiomycetes; Hydnaceae).
SILVIA ANTÔNIA CORREA CHIEA, 1954 (Melastomataceae).
MARILZA CORDEIRO-MARINO, 1939 (Benthic marine algae).
ALCEBIADES CUSTÓDIO FILHO, 1952 (Leguminosae).
OSWALDO FIDALGO, 1928 (Polyporaceae; ethnomycology).
JOÃO SALVADOR FURTADO, 1934 (Ultrastructure; Polyporaceae).
ANTÔNIO LUIZ GONÇALVES, 1950.
DEOMAR ANTONIA DE GRANDE, 1949 (Flora of Cardoso Island).
ROSELY ANA PICCOLO GRANDI, 1949 (Soil Deuteromycetes).
SILVIA MARIA PITA DE BEAUCLAIR GUIMARAÊS, 1944 (Marine algae; Phaeophyceae).
SIGRID LUIZA JUNG, 1952 (Rubiaceae).
MIZUE KIRIZAWA, 1940 (Dioscoreaceae).
ELIZABETE APARECIDA LOPES, 1951 (Flora of Cardoso Island).
HIROKO MAKINO, 1942 (Palynology).
WALDIR MANTOVANI, 1952 (Leguminosae).
THEREZINHA SANT'ANNA MELHEM, 1936 (Palynology).
MARIA MARGARIDA DA ROCHA FIUZA DE MELO, 1945 (Sapotaceae).
ADAUTO IVO MILANEZ, 1937 (Aquatic phycomycetes).
CELI FERREIRA DA SILVA MUNIZ, 1943 (Cyperaceae).
LÚCIA JOHN BAPTISTA NOFFS, 1953.
LÚCIA CAMARGO DE ABREU OLIVEIRA, 1934 (Aquatic plants).
REINALDO ALVES DE PINHO, 1938 (Wood anatomy).
MARIA SAKANE, 1943 (Apocynaceae; Compositae).
CÉLIA LEITE SANT'ANNA, 1949 (Chlorococcales; Cyanophyceae).
TATIANA SENDULSKY, 1922 (Gramineae).

ARNALDO TOSTA SILVA, 1952 (Ferns).
THEOPHILO SALEM DA SILVA, 1940 (Gramineae).
ROSIRIS BERGEMANN DE AGUIAR SILVEIRA, 1944 (Orchidaceae).
MARIA STELLA FERNANDES SILVESTRE, 1950 (Palynology).
SANDRA FARTO BOTELHO TRUFEM, 1948 (Mucorales).
DANIEL MOREIRA VITAL, 1924 (Bryophytes).
MARIA DAS GRACAS LAPA WANDERLEY, 1947 (Xyridaceae).
NOEMY YAMAGUISHI-TOMITA, 1935 (Marine algae; Corallinaceae).
OLGA YANO, 1946 (Bryophytes).
Specialization in research: Flora of Brazil, especially of the state of São Paulo.
Associated botanic garden: Jardim Botânico de São Paulo; also three biological reserves in different climates and altitudes.
Loans: Usual regulations; requests must be made to the Curator; types are sent only under special agreement.
Periodical and serial works: Arquivos de Botânica do Estado de São Paulo (series ended in 1969); Hoehnea (phanerogams only); Rickia cryptogams only); Boletim; Flora Brasilica.
Exchange: Available: Brazilian plants. Wanted: Worldwide, mainly tropical areas.
Remarks: Facilities for visiting botanists; 560 wood samples; 4.500 pollen slides of 620 species.

SÃO PAULO: *Herbário, Faculty of Pharmacy and Biochemistry, Universidade de São Paulo,* (**SPB**) –– *see* SPF.

SÃO PAULO: *Herbário, Departamento de Botânica, Instituto de Biociências, Universidade de São Paulo,* (**SPF**), Caixa Postal 11.461, 01000 São Paulo, São Paulo, **Brazil.**
Telephone: (55)011/211-0011, branch 262, 205.
Status: State university.
Foundation: 1932. *Number of specimens:* 42.000.
Herbarium: Marine algae and angiosperms, mainly Brazilian.
Important collections: A. B. Joly, E. C. de Oliveira Filho, Y. Ugadim, E. J. de Paula, L. Sormus.
Director: ERNESTO GIESBRECHT (Organic chemistry).
Curators: E. J. DE PAULA, 1951 (Marine algae).
S. PANIZZA (Angiosperms).
Staff members: A. M. GIULIETTI, 1945 (Eriocaulaceae).
N. L. MENEZES, 1934 (Velloziaceae).
E. C. DE OLIVEIRA FILHO, 1940 (Marine algae).
A. SALATINO, 1942 (Chemosystematics).
M. L. F. SALATINO, 1948 (Annonaceae).
L. SORMUS, 1943 (Freshwater algae).
Y. UGADIM, 1939 (Marine algae).

Specialization in research: Marine algae; Desmidiaceae.
Loans: Usual conditions.
Exchange: Tropical marine algae.

SÃO PAULO: *Herbário Bento Pickel, Instituto Florestal de São Paulo,* (**SPSF**), Rua do Horto, Caixa Postal 1322, 02377 São Paulo, São Paulo, **Brazil.**
Telephone: (55)011/203-0122.
Status: Secretaria da Agricultura.
Foundation: 1896. *Number of specimens:* 6.120.
Herbarium: Brazilian trees, including wood collections.
Director: GUENJI YAMAZOE, 1935 (Silviculture).
Curator: JOÃO BATISTA BAITELLO, 1948 (Anatomy and taxonomy of trees).
Staff member: ONILDO BARBOSA, 1939 (Wood anatomy).
Specialization in research: Flora of São Paulo state.
Associated botanic garden: Instituto Florestal de São Paulo with several biological reserves in different climates and altitudes.
Loans: In general to recognized botanical institutes.
Periodical and serial works: Silvicultura em São Paulo; Boletim Técnico Instituto Florestal.
Exchange: Available: Flora of São Paulo, especially wood collections.

SAPPORO: *Laboratory of Plant Taxonomy and Ecology, Botanical Institute, Faculty of Agriculture, Hokkaido University,* (**SAP**), Sapporo, **Japan.** (Information 1974)
Status: University.
Foundation: 1876. *Number of specimens:* 130.000.
Herbarium: Bryophyta, pteridophyta and spermatophyta.
Specialization in research: Flora of boreal region.
Associated botanic garden: Botanic Garden, Hokkaido University.
Loans: To recognized botanical institutions.
Periodical and serial works: Journal of the Faculty of Agriculture.

SAPPORO: *Herbarium, Botanical Institute, Faculty of Science, Hokkaido University,* (**SAPS**), Kita 10, Nisha 8, Kitaku, Sapporo 060, **Japan.**
Telephone: (011)-711-2111, ext. 2738, 2745.
Status: Department of National University.
Foundation: 1930. *Number of specimens:* 160.000.
Herbarium: Mainly benthic marine algae, some fungi, lichens, bryophytes, pteridophytes and spermatophytes.
Important collections: Y. Yamada et al. (Algae of Micronesia, Taiwan, Japan, Kurile Islands), S. Akiyama (*Carex*).
Director and Curator: M. KUROGI, 1921 (Systematics and ecology of algae).

Staff members: M. MASUDA, 1943 (Systematics of algae).
T. YOSHIDA, 1933 (Systematics and ecology of algae).
Specialization in research: General systematics and distribution of red, brown and green algae, biosystematics of benthic marine algae in cold waters.
Loans: To recognized botanical institutions.
Periodical and serial works: Journal of the Faculty of Science, Hokkaido University, Ser. V (Botany).
Exchange: Available: Benthic marine algae.

SAPPORO: *Laboratory of Plant Virology and Mycology, Department of Botany, Faculty of Agriculture, Hokkaido University,* (**SAPA**), Kita-9, Nishi-9, Kitaku, Sapporo 060, **Japan.**
Telephone: (011)-711-2111, Ext. 2473.
Status: Department of National University.
Foundation: 1876. *Number of specimens:* 85.000.
Herbarium: Fungi (Phycomycetes, Ascomycetes, Basidiomycetes, Fungi Imperfecti).
Director: ELSHIRO SHIKATA, 1926 (Plant pathology).
Curator: ICHIRO UYEDA, 1950 (Plant pathology).
Specialization in research: Mycological flora of Japan.
Associated botanic garden: Botanical Garden, Faculty of Agriculture, Hokkaido University, Kita-3, Nishi-8, Chuo-ku.
Loans: To recognized institutions.
Periodical and serial works: Journal of the Faculty of Agriculture, Hokkaido University.

SARAJEVO: *Biološki Institut,* (**SARA**), Postfach 281, Sarajevo, **Yugoslavia.** (Information 1974)
Foundation: 1890. *Number of specimens:* 98.000.
Herbarium: Worldwide, Bosnia and Herzegovina.
Associated botanic garden: Botanički Vet.
Periodical and serial works: Godišnjak Biološkog Institut (Yearbook).

SARASOTA: *Herbarium, Mote Marine Laboratory,* (**MOT**), 1600 City Island Park, Sarasota, Florida 33577, **U.S.A.**
Telephone: 813/388-4441.
Status: Private, non-profit institution.
Foundation: 1955. *Number of specimens:* 275 species of algae.
Herbarium: West coast of Florida, including Keys; New Hampshire.
Director: WILLIAM H. TAFT, 1931 (Geologist).
Curator: SUSANNA DUDLEY.
Consultants: SYLVIA EARLE.
HAROLD HUMM.
Specialization in research: Fauna and flora of the Caribbean and Gulf of Mexico.
Loans: By special arrangement with the Director.
Periodical and serial works: Quarterly newsletters.

SARASOTA: *Herbarium, The Marie Selby Botanical Gardens,* **(SEL)**, 800 S. Palm Avenue, P.O. Box 4155, Sarasota, Florida 33577, **U.S.A.**
Telephone: 813/366-5730.
Status: Private institution.
Foundation: 1973. *Number of specimens:* 36.000.
Herbarium: Epiphytic plants; flora of Ecuador; Gesneriaceae, Orchidaceae, Araceae, Bromeliaceae.
Important collections: C. H. Dodson, C. Luer, M. Madison (Ecuador), L. O. Williams (Orchidaceae), A. Heller (Orchidaceae of Nicaragua).
Director: CALAWAY H. DODSON, 1928 (Orchidaceae; flora of western Ecuador).
Curator: MICHAEL MADISON, 1947 (Systematics of Araceae; flora of Ecuador).
Staff members: LIBBY BESSE (Palmae of Ecuador).
CARLYLE LUER, 1922 (Orchidaceae).
HARRY LUTHER (Bromeliaceae).
RUSSELL SIEBERT (Tropical ornamentals; minor tropical food plants).
KIAT TAN, 1943 (Orchidaceae).
HANS WIEHLER, 1930 (Gesneriaceae of New World).
Specialization in research: Biology and systematics of epiphytic vascular plants; flora of Ecuador.
Associated botanic garden: The Marie Selby Botanical Gardens.
Loans: To recognized institutions, for a period of one year.
Periodical and serial works: Bulletin of the Marie Selby Botanical Gardens; Aroideana; Selbyana.
Remarks: Field station: Rio Palenque Science Center, Prov. Los Rios, Ecuador.

SARATOV: *University Herbarium,* **(SARAT)**, Saratov, **U.S.S.R.**

SASKATOON: *Forest Pathology Laboratory, Department of Forestry,* **(SAFB)** –– incorporated in CFB, Edmonton.

SASKATOON: *W. P. Fraser Herbarium, Department of Plant Ecology, University of Saskatchewan,* **(SASK)**, Saskatoon, Saskatchewan, **Canada** S7N OWO.
Telephone: 306/343-3524.
Foundation: 1925. *Number of specimens:* 75.000 vascular plants.
Herbarium: Flora of Saskatchewan and western Canada; boreal and arctic flora of North America; Canadian grasslands.
Important collections: W. P. Fraser (Saskatchewan), T. N. Willing (Saskatchewan), R. T. Coupland (grasslands), G. W. Argus (*Salix*), V. L. Harms (*Heterotheca;* boreal).
Director and Curator: VERNON L. HARMS, 1930 (Flora and phytogeography of Saskatchewan; systematics of *Heterotheca* and *Sparganium;* taxonomy of northern Gramineae).
Staff members: JOHN H. HUDSON, 1923 (Tax-

onomy of Cyperaceae; flora of Saskatchewan).
ROBERT A. WRIGHT, 1955.
Specialization in research: Flora of Saskatchewan, N.W.T., and Prairie Provinces; *Sparganium, Heterotheca,* and *Carex* of western North America.
Loans: Usual regulations; 6 months unless otherwise arranged.
Exchange: Available: Flora of Saskatchewan and specialty groups. Desired: Various, especially North American boreal, arctic, cordilleran, grasslands, and lake forest; Eurasian boreal and arctic.

SASSARI: *Herbarium, Istituto Botanica Farmaceutica,* **(SASSA)**, Via Muroni 23/A, 07100 Sassari, Sardinia, **Italy.**
Telephone: 079/27.50.52.
Status: University.
Foundation: 1824. *Number of specimens:* 40.000.
Herbarium: Sardinian and Mediterranean flora, exotic medicinal plants.
Important collections: Herbarium Moris; species from India, Sarawak, Madagascar.
Director: VINCENZO PICCI, 1929 (Medical botany, morphology, phytochemistry).
Curator: ALDO DOMENICO ATZEI, 1932 (Medical botany, Sardinian flora, morphology).
Staff members: GIANUARIO MANCA, 1942 (Technician).
GAVINO MANIGA, 1936 (Technician).
ANTONIO MANUTA, 1937 (Medical botany, phytochemistry).
Specialization in research: Ethnobotany, morphology, phytochemistry, biochemistry, Sardinian medicinal plants.
Loans: No.
Periodical and serial works: Lavori Istituto Botanica Farmaceutica di Sassari.
Exchange: Yes.

SASSARI: *Erbario Istituto di Botanica, Università di Sassari,* **(SS)**, Via Muroni 25, 07100 Sassari, **Italy.**
Telephone: 079/237087.
Status: University institute.
Foundation: 1864. *Number of specimens:* 50.000.
Herbarium: General herbarium of plants of Italy and Mediterranean area, Sardinian herbarium.
Curator: BRUNO CORRIAS, 1939 (Plants of Sardinia, Orchidaceae).
Specialization in research: Flora and vegetation of Sardinia and Mediterranean area, plant geography and ecology, biosystematics.
Associated botanic garden: Orto Botanico dell'Istituto Botanica dell'Università di Sassari.
Loans: To recognized botanical institutions.
Periodical and serial works: Bullettino dell'Istituto Botanico dell'Università di Sassari.
Exchange: On request.

SAULT STE. MARIE: *Herbarium, Abitibi Woodlands Laboratory, Abitibi Paper Company,* (**AWL**), Sault Ste. Marie, Ontario, **Canada.**

Remarks: Since 1974, this herbarium has been housed at Lakehead University, Thunder Bay, Ontario, Canada P7S 5E1.

SAULT STE. MARIE: *Herbarium, Great Lakes Forest Research Centre, Canadian Forestry Service,* (**SSMF**), Box 490, Sault Ste. Marie, Ontario, **Canada** P6A 5M7.

Telephone: 705/949-9461.

Status: Government of Canada, Environment Canada.

Foundation: 1947. *Number of specimens:* 20.500 (12.000 cryptogams, 8.500 phanerogams).

Herbarium: Fungal pathogens of forest trees, particularly Ontario; phanerogams primarily from northern Ontario and the Hudson Bay Lowlands.

Director: J. H. CAYFORD, 1929.

Curator: D. T. MYREN, 1940.

Staff members: F. BRICAULT, 1918.

J. JEGLUM, 1938.

D. ROPKE, 1936.

R. SIMS, 1952.

Loans: To recognized institutions and specialists.

Exchange: Ontario specimens.

Remarks: Formerly listed as MFB (Forest Pathology Laboratory, Southern Research Station, Maple); includes Forest Pathology, Toronto.

SCHAFFHAUSEN: *Naturhistorisches Museum,* (**SCH**), Frauengasse, Schaffhausen, **Switzerland.** (Information 1974)

Herbarium: Flora of Kanton Schaffhausen and adjacent areas.

SCHENECTADY: *Herbarium, Department of Biological Sciences, Union College,* (**UCS**), Schenectady, New York 12308, **U.S.A.**

Foundation: 1840. *Number of specimens:* 6.500.

Herbarium: Mostly local flora, New York and New England.

Important collections: George R. Cooley, William Tuckerman.

Director: MICHAEL W. FROHLICH, 1947 (Systematics of *Heliotropium*).

Specialization in research: Heliotropium.

Loans: Usual regulations.

Exchange: Available: Locally collected material.

SCRANTON: *Alfred Twining Herbarium, Everhart Museum,* (**EVMU**), Nay Aug Park, Scranton, Pennsylvania 18510, **U.S.A.**

Telephone: 717/346-7186.

Foundation: 1917. *Number of specimens:* 2.000.

Herbarium: Northeastern Pennsylvania.

Important collections: Alfred Twining.

Curator: WILLIAM E. SPEARE, 1936.

SEATTLE: *Herbarium, Department of Biology, Seattle Pacific College,* (**SPC**), Seattle, Washington 98119, **U.S.A.**

Telephone: 206/281-2140.

Foundation: 1961. *Number of specimens:* 5.000.

Herbarium: Mainly algae, worldwide seagrasses, some flowering plants from Washington.

Director: RONALD C. PHILLIPS, 1932 (Distribution, ecology, and taxonomy of seagrasses).

Specialization in research: Seagrasses.

SEATTLE: *Herbarium, Department of Botany, University of Washington,* (**WTU**), Seattle, Washington 98195, **U.S.A.**

Telephone: 206/543-8850; 543-6594.

Foundation: 1880. *Number of specimens:* 500.000.

Herbarium: Worldwide, specializing in Pacific Northwest flora.

Important collections: Bryophyte collections of A. J. Grout, W. S. Sullivant, L. Lesquereux, J. Macoun, E. Bauer; vascular plant collections of C.L. Hitchcock, J. W. Thompson, W. Suksdorf, L. Abrams, J. W. Blankinship, W. C. Cusick, A. D. E. Elmer, C. S. English, W. J. Eyerdam, J. B. Flett, A. A. Heller, T. J. Howell, J. B. Leiberg, J. F. Macbride, A. Nelson, M. E. Peck, H. St. John, J. H. Sandberg.

Curator: MELINDA F. DENTON, 1944 (Systematics of vascular plants).

Staff members: JOSEPH F. AMMIRATI, 1942 (Systematics of higher fungi).

ARTHUR KRUCKEBERG, 1920 (Systematics of vascular plants and serpentine ecology).

ELVA LAWTON, 1896 (Bryology).

DANIEL E. STUNTZ, 1909 (Taxonomy of higher fungi).

Specialization in research: Systematics, floristics, and ecology of the flora of western North America.

Associated botanic garden: University of Washington Arboretum, University of Washington, Seattle, Washington 98195, U.S.A.

Loans: To recognized botanical institutions.

Exchange: From all parts of the world, but especially western North America.

SENDAI: *Herbarium, Biological Institute, Faculty of Science, Tohoku University,* (**TUS**), Aoba, Sendai 980, **Japan.**

Telephone: 0222-22-1800.

Foundation: 1924. *Number of specimens:* 250.000.

Herbarium: Vascular plants of Northern Japan, Salicaceae and Leguminosae of Asia.

Important collections: A. Kimura (Salicaceae, including 100 types).

Director: HIROYOSHI OHASHI, 1936 (Leguminosae of Asia, *Arisaema* of Japan).

Curator: CHUGAI KIMURA, 1926 (Flora of North Japan, embryology of Salicaceae and Orchidaceae).

Staff members: KANKICHI SOHMA, 1926 (Palynology).

HIROSHI TOHDA, 1933 (Embryology of Orchidaceae).
Honorary staff members: ARIKA KIMURA, 1900 (Salicaceae).
SADAO SUGAYA, 1917 (Salicaceae).
Specialization in research: Flora of Northern Japan, monographic studies in Leguminosae and Salicaceae, embryology of Orchidaceae, palynology.
Associated botanic garden: Aobayama Botanical Garden, Tohoku University, Kawauchi.
Loans: To recognized botanical institutions.
Periodical and serial works: Science Reports of the Tohoku University, Ser. 4 (Biology).
Exchange: Available: Vascular plants of Japan. Desired: Leguminosae and Salicaceae.

SENDAI: *Herbarium, Botanical Garden, Tohoku University,* **(TUSG)**, Kawauchi, Sendai 980, **Japan.**
Telephone: 0222-23-8557.
Status: University.
Foundation: 1958. *Number of specimens:* 60.000.
Herbarium: Mainly vascular plants of Japan.
Director: SIGERU IIZUMI, 1922 (Ecology).
Curator: HIROSHI TOHDA, 1933 (Morphology).
Staff member: TOSHIHIKO NAITO, 1939 (Ecology).
Honorary staff member: ARIKA KIMURA (Salicaceae).
Specialization in research: Flora of Japan.
Loans: To recognized botanical institutions.
Exchange: Available: Vascular plants of Japan.

SEOUL: *Hongnung Arboretum, Forest Research Institute,* **(KFI)**, Chongyangni, Tongdaemun-Ku, Seoul, **Korea.**

SEOUL: *Herbarium, Department of Biology, Sung Kyun Kwan University,* **(SKK)**, 3 ga 53, Meong Lyun Dong Jong Loo Gu, Seoul 110, **Korea.**
Telephone: 762-5021.
Status: University.
Foundation: 1953. *Number of specimens:* 20.000.
Herbarium: Ferns and flowering plants of North and South Korea.
Director and Curator: LEE CHAI DOO, 1926 (Morphology).
Staff members: LEE H. S., 1927 (Physiology).
PARK S. Y., 1926 (Animal physiology).
SUNG KEE C., 1928 (Genetics).

SEOUL: *The Herbarium, Seoul National University,* **(SNU)**, Seoul, **Korea.**

SEVILLA: *Departamento de Botanica, Facultad de Biologia, Universidad de Sevilla,* **(SEV)**, Avda. Reina Mercedes s/n, Sevilla, **Spain.**
Telephone: 954-61 70 11.
Status: University.
Foundation: 1965. *Number of specimens:* 50.000.
Herbarium: Spanish plants, mainly Andalusian.
Important collections: Pedro Abat, Claudio Bou-

telou and Pablo Boutelou.
Director: B. VALDES, 1942 (Plant taxonomy).
Staff members: B. CABEZUDO (Geobotany).
S. TALAVERA (Plant taxonomy).
Specialization in research: Taxonomy, caryology and palynology of Iberian and Mediterranean plants; floristics of W. Andalusia.
Loans: To recognized botanical institutions.
Periodical and serial works: Lagascalia.
Exchange: Available: Spanish plants. Desired: European & N. African plants.

SHANGHAI: *Herbarium, Department of Biology, Fudan University,* **(FUS)**, Shanghai, **People's Republic of China.**
Number of specimens: 50.000.
Staff member: HSÜ PING-SHENG (Taxonomy).

SHANGHAI: *Herbarium, Department of Biology, East China Normal University,* **(HSNU)**, 3663 North Zhong Shang Road, 200062 Shanghai, **People's Republic of China.**
Telephone: 548461-10.
Status: University.
Foundation: 1952. *Number of specimens:* 50.000.
Herbarium: Plants of Southeast China, especially Zhejiang, S. Anhui and N. Fujian Provinces.
Director: CHENG MIEN, 1898 (Flora of Southeastern China, Buxaceae).
Curator: MA WEI-LIANG, 1936 (Eriocaulaceae).
Staff members: WU GUO-FANG, 1930 (*Monotropastrum*, Chloranthaceae, Juncaceae).
LIU JIN-LIN, 1935 (Ecology).
QIEU PEI-XI, 1918 (Pteridology).
HU REN-LIANG, 1932 (Bryology).
ZHOU XIU-JIA, 1935 (Ecology).
WU YI-XIN, 1942 (Taxonomy).
SONG YONG-CHANG, 1933 (Ecology).
WANG YOU-FANG, 1956 (Bryology).
FENG ZHI-JIAN, 1932 (Taxonomy).
WU ZHI-SHEN, 1923 (Mycology).
Specialization in research: Flora (bryophytes, pteridophytes and spermatophytes) of Southeastern China, taxonomy and phytogeography.
Loans: To recognized botanical institutions.

SHANGHAI: *Herbarium, Institute of Botany, Academia Sinica,* **(SH)**, Shanghai, **People's Republic of China** –– incorporated in PE.

SHANGHAI: *Herbarium, Shanghai Baptist College,* **(SHB)**, Shanghai, **People's Republic of China** –– incorporated in NAS.

SHANGHAI: *Herbarium, St. John's University,* **(SHJ)**, Shanghai, **People's Republic of China** –– incorporated in HSNU.

SHANGHAI: *Musée Heude (Ancien, Musée de Zikawei), Université l'Aurore,* **(SHMH)**, 223 Avenue

Dubail, Shanghai, **People's Republic of China** — incorporated in NAS.

SHEFFIELD: *Herbarium, Sheffield City Museum,* **(SCM),** Weston Park, Sheffield 10, England, **Great Britain.** (Information 1974)
Status: Public museum.
Foundation: 1875. *Number of specimens:* 3.000.
Herbarium: Plants of British Isles.
Important collections: Jonathan Salt (1795–1807, local flowering plants, cultivated plants and lichens); John Smith (1830–1850, British flowering plants).

SHEFFIELD: *Herbarium, Sheffield City Museums,* **(SFD),** Weston Park, Sheffield S10 2TP, England, **Great Britain.**
Telephone: 0742 27226.
Status: Local authority museum.
Foundation: 1874. *Number of specimens:* 8.000.
Herbarium: Mainly British plants, with emphasis on South Yorkshire and Derbyshire.
Important collections: Jonathan Salt (1759–1815); Margaret Gatty (1809–1873), Algae.
Director: JOHN W. BARTLETT, 1924 (Archaeology).
Curator: TIMOTHY HOLT RILEY, 1941.
Staff members: The herbarium is staffed by the Museum's Natural Sciences Section, and has no specific personnel.
Specialization in research: Flora of the Sheffield region.
Loans: Available, conditions to be negotiated.

SHENYANG: *Cryptogamic Herbarium, Institute of Forestry and Pedology, Academia Sinica,* **(IFP),** Culture Road, Shenhe District, Shenyang, Liaoning, **People's Republic of China.**
Telephone: 82309.
Status: Directed by Academia Sinica.
Foundation: 1956. *Number of specimens:* 39.000 (28.000 bryophytes, 7.000 lichens, 4.000 fungi).
Herbarium: Cryptogams of China, especially NE provinces.
Director: GAO CHIEN, 1928 (Bryophytes).
Curators: CHEN XI-LING, 1934 (Lichens).
LIU ZHENG-NAN, 1933 (Fungi).
WANG YUN, 1941 (Fungi).
Staff members: CAO TUNG, 1946 (Bryophytes).
CHANG KUANG-CHU, 1939 (Bryophytes).
LIU SHUN, 1955 (Fungi).
XIE ZHI-XI, 1939 (Fungi).
YAN BAO-YIN, 1952 (Bryophytes).
YAN YU-XUAN, 1951 (Fungi).
ZHAO CONG-FU, 1939 (Lichens).
Specialization in research: Taxonomy of bryophytes, fungi (Agaricales and Polyporales), and lichens.
Exchange: Available: Cryptogams of China. Desired: Worldwide cryptogams.

SHERBROOKE: *Herbier Rolland-Germain, Département de Biologie, Université de Sherbrooke,* **(SFS),** Sherbrooke, Québec, **Canada** J1K 2R1.
Telephone: 819/565-3613.
Foundation: 1963. *Number of specimens:* 163.588 (158.360 vascular plants, 922 lichens, 4.306 bryophytes).
Herbarium: Mainly southeastern Quebec collection (serpentine); also arctic Ungava and Saguenay region.
Important collections: Marie-Victorin and Rolland-Germain's collection in Minganie, Anticosti Island, Gaspe Peninsula, Magdalene Islands, etc.
Director and Curator: ALBERT LEGAULT, 1919 (Floristics).
Staff member: SAMUEL BRISSON, 1918 (Floristics).
Specialization in research: Flora of southeastern Quebec.
Loans: Usual conditions.
Exchange: Available: Vascular plants mainly from southeastern Quebec. Wanted: Arctic and boreal plants.

SHILLONG: *Eastern Circle, Botanical Survey of India,* **(ASSAM),** Shillong, **India.** (Information 1974)
Status: Government of India.
Foundation: 1920. *Number of specimens:* 86.500.
Herbarium: Plants of Eastern Himalaya, Assam, Manipur, Tripura and Nefa.
Important collections: N. L. Bor, Gustav Mann, P. C. and U. N. Kanjilal.
Specialization in research: Flora of India.
Associated botanic garden: Experimental Garden, Barapani, Assam.
Loans: With permission of the director.
Periodical and serial works: Bulletin of the Botanical Survey of India, Records of the Botanical Survey of India.
Remarks: Formerly listed under Calcutta (CAL).

SHINGLETON: *Herbarium, Department of Natural Resources, Cusino Wildlife Research Station,* **(CUS),** Shingleton, Michigan 49884, **U.S.A.**
Telephone: 906/452-6226.
Status: Michigan Department of Natural Resources.
Foundation: 1936. *Number of specimens:* Several hundred.
Herbarium: General wildlife flora in central Upper Michigan.
Director and Curator: LOUIS J. VERME, 1924 (Physiology and ecology of white-tailed deer).
Staff member: JOHN J. OZOGA, 1938 (Physiology and ecology of whitetailed deer).
Specialization in research: Physiology and ecology of game wildlife, especially white-tailed deer.
Loans: To recognized scientific institutions.

SHREVEPORT: *Herbarium, Museum of Life Sciences, Department of Biological Sciences, Louisiana State University,* **(LSUS),** 8515 Youree Drive, Shreve-

port, Louisiana 71115, **U.S.A.**
Telephone: 318/797-7121.
Foundation: 1970. *Number of specimens:* 12.000.
Herbarium: Vascular flora of northwestern Louisiana; Asclepiadaceae of North America.
Important collections: S. P. Lynch (Asclepiadaceae).
Director: LAURENCE M. HARDY, 1939 (Herpetology).
Curator: STEVEN P. LYNCH, 1946 (Asclepiadaceae, Euphorbiaceae; pollination mechanisms).
Staff members: D. T. MACROBERTS, 1907 (*Tradescantia* of U.S.; vascular flora of northwestern Louisiana).
RICHARD K. SPEAIRS, 1920 (Ligneous vegetation of northwestern Louisiana and Ouachita Mountains of Arkansas and Oklahoma).
Specialization in research: Vascular plants of northwestern Louisiana and neighboring areas; Commelinaceae, especially *Tradescantia;* Asclepiadaceae, pollination mechanisms).
Loans: Normal regulations.
Periodical and serial works: Bulletin of the Museum of Life Sciences.
Exchange: Available: Northwestern Louisiana. Desired: Especially *Tradescantia* and Asclepiadaceae.

SHURI: *Herbarium of University of the Ryukyus,* (**URO**), Shuri, Okinawa, **Ryukyu Islands.**

SIBASA: *Venda Herbarium,* (**VENDA**), Private Bag X2247, Sibasa 0970, **Republic of Venda.**
Telephone: Sibasa 13.
Foundation: 1976. *Number of specimens:* 1.600.
Herbarium: Plants of Venda, including medicinal plants.
Director: N. A. MUTAKUSI, 1936.
Curator: E. N. NETSHIUNGANI, 1952.
Staff members: E. N. MUGWEDI, 1956.
P. T. NETSHISAULU, 1957.
Specialization in research: Botanical survey of Venda.

SIBIU: *Muzuel Brukenthal Sibiu, Secţia de Istorie Naturală,* (**SIB**), str. Cetăţii 1, 2400 Sibiu, **Romania.**
Telephone: 924/17873.
Status: Consiul Culturii şi Ed. Socialiste Bucureşti.
Foundation: 1849. *Number of specimens:* 147.345.
Herbarium: Plants of Europe and Romania, especially Transsylvania.
Important collections: Herbaria of Nyárády (52.500), Michael Fuss, F. Lerchenfeld (1794), F. Barth, K. Ungar.
Director: M. I. DOLTU, 1927 (Floristics).
Curator: ERIKA SCHNEIDER, 1942 (Phytocoenology, phytogeography, especially Transsylvania).
Staff member: C. DRĂGULESCU, 1949 (Floristics and phytogeography).
Specialization in research: Floristics and phyto-

coenology of Transsylvania.
Periodical and serial works: Studii şi Comunicări Şt. Naturale.

SIEDLCE: *Herbarium, Department of Botany, Wyższa Szkoła Rolnicze-Pedagogiczna,* (**WSRP**), ul. Prusa 12, 08-110 Siedlce, **Poland.**
Telephone: 5293, 5294.
Status: Agriculture and Teacher University.
Foundation: 1972. *Number of specimens:* 15.400.
Herbarium: Vascular plants and lichens of Poland, especially Central-East area.
Curator: ZYGMUNT GŁOWACKI, 1922 (Geobotany).
Specialization in research: Vascular plants of Central-East Poland.
Loans: To recognized institutions.

SIENA: *Herbarium, Accademia del Fisiocritici,* (**SIAC**), Prato S. Agostino 4, Siena, **Italy.** (Information 1974)
Status: Private foundation.
Foundation: 1691. *Number of specimens:* 500.
Herbarium: Phanerogams and cryptogams of Province of Siena.
Periodical and serial works: Atti Accademia dei Fisiocritici Siena.

SIENA: *Herbarium, Istituto di Botanica, Università di Siena,* (**SIENA**), Via Mattioli 4, 53100 Siena, **Italy.**
Telephone: 0577-281248.
Status: University.
Foundation: 1860. *Number of specimens:* 40.000.
Herbarium: Mainly regional.
Important collections: A. Nannizzi (Fungi).
Director: G. SARFATTI, 1920 (Italian flora, electron microscopy).
Curator: V. DE DOMINICIS, 1940 (Phytosociology).
Staff members: C. BARLUZZI, 1943 (Mycosociology).
A. BOSCAGLI, 1947.
S. CASINI, 1943 (Phytosociology).
E. FERRARINI, 1919 (Italian flora and vegetation, ecology, palynology).
S. FERRI, 1931 (Medicinal plants).
P. MARCHETTI, 1941.
Specialization in research: Local flora.
Associated botanic garden: Orto Botanico dell'Università di Siena.
Loans: To recognized botanical institutions.

SILVER CITY: *Herbarium, Department of Biological Science, Western New Mexico University,* (**SNM**), Silver City, New Mexico 88061, **U.S.A.**
Telephone: 505/538-6423.
Foundation: 1960. *Number of specimens:* 3.000.
Herbarium: Mainly southwestern New Mexico.
Staff member: DALE A. ZIMMERMAN.
Loans: Usual regulations.
Exchange: Hope to establish a program.

SIMFEROPOL: *Herbarium, Department of Botany of the Crimean Pedagogic Institute,* (**SIMF**), Ul. Lenina 17, Simferopol, Crimea, **U.S.S.R.**

SIMONOSEKI: *Faculty of Agriculture, Yamaguchi University,* (**YAM**) – – *see* YAMAGUCHI.

SINGAPORE: *Herbarium and Library, Botanic Gardens,* (**SING**), Cluny Road, Singapore 10, **Singapore.** (Information 1974)
Status: Government.
Foundation: 1875. *Number of specimens:* 500.000.
Herbarium: Flora of Southeast Asia, especially Malayan.
Specialization in research: Taxonomy of Malaysian plants.
Associated botanic garden: Botanic Gardens, Singapore.
Loans: To recognized botanical institutions.
Periodical and serial works: Singapore Garden Bulletin.

SINILOAN: *Philippine National Botanic Herbarium,* (**PNBG**), U.P. Quezon Land Grant, Siniloan, Laguna, **Philippines.**
Status: National Institute of Science and Technology.
Foundation: 1968. *Number of specimens:* 2.044.
Herbarium: Mosses, ferns and flowering plants of the Philippines.
Director: RONITO D. CAPIÑA, 1941 (Plant pathology).
Curator: JOSE PAULINO C. MACABENTA, 1955 (Plant anatomy).
Staff members: BELEN MERCADO, 1946 (Orchids).
EVANGELINE C. MONROYO, 1950 (Economic botany).
RHODORA PANGAN, 1955.
GLORIA I. YADAO, 1954 (Mosses).
Specialization in research: Ecology, conservation of Philippine orchids, germination of moss spores.
Remarks: Formerly listed under Quezon.

SINING: – – *see* XINING.

SINTON: *Herbarium, Welder Wildlife Foundation,* (**WWF**), P.O. Drawer 1400, Sinton, Texas 78387, **U.S.A.**
Telephone: 512/364-2643; 364-2644.
Status: Private foundation.
Foundation: 1956. *Number of specimens:* 5.600.
Herbarium: Plants of the Tamaulipan Biotic Province (south Texas).
Director: JAMES G. TEER (Game management).
Assistant Director: D. LYNN DRAWE (Range management).
Curator: GENE W. BLACKLOCK (Education).
Specialization in research: Natural history and range related subjects.
Loans: Usual regulations.

SIOUX FALLS: *Herbarium, Biology Department, Augustana College,* (**AUG**), Sioux Falls, South Dakota 57197, **U.S.A.**
Telephone: 605/336-4711.
Foundation: 1950. *Number of specimens:* 6.000.
Herbarium: Emphasis on regional flora; vouchers for ecological research; *Salix* of Black Hills and northern Great Plains.
Director and Curator: DILWYN J. ROGERS (Plant ecology).
Staff members: S. G. FROILAND (*Salix*).
L. L. TIESZEN.
Specialization in research: Ecological studies of South Dakota region.
Associated botanic garden: Augustana Prairie Garden (1 acre, on campus); Makoce Washte Prairie (40 acres; 15 miles from campus).
Loans: Normal regulations.

SITKA: *Herbarium, Tongass National Forest, R-10, U.S. Department of Agriculture,* (**TNFS**), Box 1980, Sitka, Alaska 99835, **U.S.A.**
Telephone: 907/747-6671.
Status: U.S. Department of Agriculture, Forest Service.
Foundation: 1978. *Number of specimens:* 2.000.
Herbarium: Vascular plants of southeastern Alaska.
Director and Curator: MARY CLAY MULLER, 1949.
Specialization in research: Threatened and endangered plant surveys, soil studies, wildlife studies, timber surveys.
Loans: Usual conditions.
Exchange: Yes.

SKARA: *Katedralskolan,* (**SK**), Brunsbogatan 1, S-532 00 Skara, **Sweden.**
Telephone: 0511-120 17.
Status: The Grammar School of Skara.
Number of specimens: 40.000.
Herbarium: Scandinavian vascular plants.
Director: ARNE PALMQVIST, 1933.
Curator: SVEN KILANDER, 1917 (Ecology).
Staff member: ANN NILSSON, 1942.
Specialization in research: Swedish plants.
Loans: To scientists.

SKUKUZA: *Herbarium, Kruger National Park,* (**KNP**), Research Institute, Private Bag X402, Skukuza 1350, **South Africa.**
Telephone: 0131252, 6 × 229.
Status: National Parks Board.
Foundation: 1951. *Number of specimens:* 10.000.
Herbarium: Plants of Kruger National Park.
Director: S. C. J. JOUBERT, 1941.
Curator: A. L. F. POTGIETER, 1938.
Staff members: B. J. COETZEE.
W. P. D. GERTENBACH.
F. VENTER.

Specialization in research: Ecology of Kruger National Park.

SLIPPERY ROCK: *Herbarium, Department of Biology, Slippery Rock State College,* (**SLRO**), Slippery Rock, Pennsylvania 16057, **U.S.A.**
Telephone: 412/794-7296.
Foundation: 1930. *Number of specimens:* 12.500.
Herbarium: Mainly eastern U.S.
　Director and Curator: KIMBALL S. ERDMAN, 1937 (Dendrology).
　Specialization in research: Forest composition and evolutionary theory.
　Loans: No.

SOFIA: *Herbarium, Department of Botany, University of Sofia,* (**SO**), ul. Dragan Zankov N 8, Sofia 1421, **Bulgaria.**
Telephone: 66 14 21-317.
Status: University.
Foundation: 1891. *Number of specimens:* 100.000.
Herbarium: Plants of Cuba and South Europe: Bulgaria, Greece, Macedonia.
　Director: VELTSHO VELTSHEV, 1928.
　Curator: BORIS P. KITANOV, 1912.
　Staff member: NIKOLAI VIHODCEVSKI, 1912.
　Specialization in research: Taxonomy; flora of Bulgaria, including map; Atlas of Chromosomes.
　Associated botanic garden: Botanical Garden of University, ul. Moskowska 49, Sofia 1000.
　Periodical and serial works: Flora of Bulgaria.

SOFIA: *Herbarium, College of Agriculture "Georgi Dimitroff,"* (**SOA**), Sofia, **Bulgaria.** (Information 1974)
Status: A state college.
Foundation: 1923. *Number of specimens:* 60.000.
Herbarium: Worldwide.
　Remarks: Collections moved to Herbarium of the Higher Agricultural Institute "V. Kolarov," Plovdiv, Bulgaria.

SOFIA: *Botanical Institute of the Bulgarian Academy of Sciences,* (**SOM**), Str. "Akad. G. Bontshev," Clou I, 1113 Sofia, **Bulgaria.**
Telephone: 7131/2131, 2117.
Status: Directed by Academy of Sciences.
Foundation: 1919. *Number of specimens:* 140.000.
Herbarium: Worldwide herbarium, especially Bulgaria and Balkan Peninsula, higher plants, ferns, mosses and fungi.
Important collections: B. Davidov, V. Stzbznü, I. Urumov, N. Stojanov (Greece).
　Director: VELTSHO IVANOV VELTSHEV, 1928 (Geobotany, ecology).
　Curator: NIKOLAI ANDREEV NIKOLOV, 1944; 7131/3766 (Taxonomy, chorology, floristics).
　Staff members: M. E. ANČEV (Pteridophytes, spermatophytes).
　V. FAKIZOVA.

S. I. KOŽUHAROV.
B. A. KUZMANOV.
M. L. MARKOVA.
D. R. PEEV.
S. PETROV (Bryophytes).
A. V. PETROVA.
E. SAMEVA (Fungi).
S. VANEV.
　Specialization in research: Flora of Bulgaria and Balkan Peninsula.
　Associated botanic garden: Botanic Garden of the Bulgarian Academy of Sciences.
　Periodical and serial works: Phytologia, Flora Bulgarica exsiccata.
　Exchange: Available: Bulgarian plants.

SOOCHOW: – – *see* SUZHOU.

SOUTHAMPTON: *Herbarium, Division of Natural Sciences, Southampton College, Long Island University,* (**SOUT**), Southampton, New York 11968, **U.S.A.**
Telephone: 516/283-4000.
Foundation: 1976. *Number of specimens:* 100.
Herbarium: Teaching herbarium of marine algae; specialized collection of lichens, slime molds, and bryophytes from Long Island.
Important collections: Lance Buchele.
　Director and Curator: LARRY LIDDLE, 1935 (Phycology).
　Specialization in research: Algal development.

SOUTHAMPTON: *Herbarium, Biology Department, Southampton University,* (**SPN**), Building 44, Southampton S09 5NH, England, **Great Britain.**
Telephone: 0703/559122, ext. 2444.
Status: University.
Foundation: 1960. *Number of specimens:* 10.000.
Herbarium: Worldwide collection for teaching and local flora.
　Director: M. A. SLEIGH (Flagellae).
　Curator: F. A. BISBY, 1945 (Numerical taxonomy, Leguminosae).
　Staff member: B. A. OTTO (Leguminosae).
　Specialization in research: Numerical and chemical taxonomy, Leguminosae, Vicieae Data-Base Project.
　Loans: For a period of six months.
　Remarks: Listed in Ed. 6 as SOTON.

SPEARFISH: *F. L. Bennett Herbarium, Division of Science and Mathematics, Black Hills State College,* (**BHSC**), Spearfish, South Dakota 57783, **U.S.A.**
Telephone: 605/642-6251.
Foundation: 1895. *Number of specimens:* 20.000.
Herbarium: Flora of South Dakota, especially the Black Hills.
Important collections: Black Hills orchids dating to 1890's; O. Degener (Hawaii); J. R. Thomasson (fossil grasses and other angiosperms of the Miocene-Pliocene).

Director and Curator: JOSEPH R. THOMASSON, 1946 (Fossil and living grasses; taxonomy and evolution).

Specialization in research: Taxonomy and evolution of the grasses.

Loans: To recognized institutions generally for 6-12 months (may be renewed for 6 months).

Exchange: Willing to exchange fossil or living plants, especially interested in grasses.

SPRINGFIELD: *Herbarium, Illinois State Museum,* **(ISM)**, Spring and Edwards Streets, Springfield, Illinois 62706, **U.S.A.**

Telephone: 217/782-2621.

Status: Division of Institute of Natural Resources, State of Illinois.

Foundation: 1938. *Number of specimens:* 91.000.

Herbarium: Flora of Illinois.

Curator: ALFRED C. KOELLING, 1929 (Vascular flora of Illinois).

Specialization in research: Flora of Illinois.

Loans: On approved application by recognized institutions.

Periodical and serial works: Museum Scientific Papers; Reports of Investigations; Popular Science Series.

Exchange: Available: Illinois vascular plants. Desired: Specimens from Illinois and other midwestern states.

Remarks: 500 pollen slides vouchered by specimens in herbarium; 500 collections of seeds and fruits of common midwestern species; 150 wood specimens of common midwestern species.

SPRINGFIELD: *Jacobs Herbarium, Wittenberg University,* **(JHWU)**, Springfield, Ohio 45501, **U.S.A.**

Telephone: 513/327-7719.

Status: Private institution.

Number of specimens: 10.000.

Herbarium: General Ohio, central U.S. flora; few foreign.

Important collections: J. H. W. Stuckenberg (collections from Berlin, 1894).

Director and Curator: RONALD A. DE LANGLADE, 1936 (Leaf morphogenesis).

Loans: No special restrictions.

Exchange: Yes.

SPRINGFIELD: *Ozarks Regional Herbarium, Department of Life Sciences, Southwest Missouri State University,* **(SMS)**, Springfield, Missouri 65802, **U.S.A.**

Telephone: 417/836-5882.

Status: State University.

Foundation: 1926. *Number of specimens:* 84.000 (46.000 vascular plants, 38.000 bryophytes).

Herbarium: Primarily plants of the Interior Highlands of North America.

Important collections: Bryophyte collections of Paul L. Redfearn, Jr., from the Interior Highlands of

North America; Grant Pyrah, Wallace R. Weber, J. A. Steyermark, E. J. Palmer.

Director: PAUL L. REDFEARN, JR., 1926 (Bryology).

Staff members: GRANT PYRAH, 1937 (Grasses). WALLACE R. WEBER, 1934 (Compositae).

Specialization in research: Floristics.

Loans: Usual regulations.

Exchange: Vascular plants and bryophytes from the Interior Highlands of North America.

SPRINGFIELD: *Luman Andrews Herbarium, Springfield Science Museum,* **(SPR)**, 236 State Street, Springfield, Massachusetts 01103, **U.S.A.**

Telephone: 413/733-1194.

Status: Unit of Springfield Library and Museums Association, a private non-profit organization.

Foundation: 1901. *Number of specimens:* 15.000.

Herbarium: Local flora.

Important collections: Luman Andrews.

Director: GLEN P. IVES, 1933.

Curator: EARL H. REED, 1918.

Loans: Usual regulations.

Exchange: Yes.

SRINAGAR: *Herbarium, Department of Botany, University of Kashmir,* **(KASH)**, Srinagar-190006, **India.**

Telephone: 72231-30, 72232-30, 72233-30.

Status: University.

Foundation: 1972. *Number of specimens:* 13.000.

Herbarium: Ferns and flowering plants of N. W. Himalaya and Central Asia.

Director: P. KACHROO, 1924 (Bryology, floristics, morphology).

Curator: A. R. NAQSHI, 1946 (Taxonomy).

Staff members: G. M. BHAT, 1947. G. N. DAR, 1947. N. A. SHAH, 1946.

Specialization in research: Taxonomy, ecology, morphology, cytology, physiology.

Associated botanic garden: Emporium Botanical Garden, Srinagar and Nehru Botanic Garden, Cheshmashahi.

Loans: To recognized botanical institutions.

Exchange: Available: Himalayan and Central Asian plants.

STALINABAD – – *see* DUSHAMBE.

STANFORD: *Herbarium, Department of Plant Biology, Carnegie Institution of Washington,* **(CI)**, 290 Panama Street, Stanford, California 94305, **U.S.A.**

Status: Private foundation.

Foundation: 1930. *Number of specimens:* 4.000.

Herbarium: Reference collection, mainly grass vouchers.

Remarks: Collections, including those of Clausen, Keck, and Hiesey, are permanently deposited in the Dudley Herbarium of Stanford University (DS) which is now housed at the California Academy of Sciences (CAS), San Francisco.

STANFORD: *Dudley Herbarium, Department of Biological Sciences, Stanford University,* **(DS)** -- on permanent loan to San Francisco (see separate entries for CAS and DS).

STATEN ISLAND: *Herbarium, Staten Island Museum,* **(SIM)**, 75 Stuyvesant Place, Staten Island, New York 10301, **U.S.A.**
Telephone: 212/727-1135.
Status: Division of Staten Island Institute of Arts and Sciences, privately endowed institution, but receiving support in part from the City of New York.
Foundation: 1881. *Number of specimens:* 18.000.
Herbarium: Flora of Staten Island and parts of Long Island, New York; New Jersey.
Important collections: William T. Davis herbarium; Nathaniel Lord Britton, Elizabeth G. Britton, Arthur Hollick, William H. Wiegmann, in part; hybrid violet collection of Philip Dowell.
Specialization in research: Staten Island flora.
Periodical and serial works: Proceedings in three series since 1883.

STATESBORO: *Herbarium, Department of Biology, Box 8042, Georgia Southern College,* **(GAS)**, Statesboro, Georgia 30460, **U.S.A.**
Telephone: 912/681-5494 (herbarium); 681-5487 (biology department).
Foundation: 1956. *Number of specimens:* 18.500.
Herbarium: Vascular plants, especially from Georgia and the southeastern U.S.
Important collections: Harry E. Ahles, C. Ritchie Bell, John A. Boole, Jr., John R. Bozeman, Gordon P. DeWolf, Jr., Donald J. Drapalik, Wilbur H. Duncan, Samuel B. Jones, Jr., Steven W. Leonard, Jimmy R. Massey, Albert E. Radford, Donald R. Windler.
Curator: DONALD J. DRAPALIK, 1934 (Angiosperm taxonomy).
Specialization in research: Survey of southeastern Georgia vascular vegetation; biosystematics of southeastern U.S. *Matelea* (Asclepiadaceae) and *Elliottia* (Ericaceae).
Loans: To recognized herbaria and scientific institutions.
Periodical and serial works: Elliottia, Notes from the Herbarium of Georgia Southern College.
Exchange: Flora of eastern U.S.

STATE UNIVERSITY: *Department of Biological Science, Arkansas State University,* **(STAR)** – see JONESBORO.

STAVANGER: *Herbarium, Arkeologisk Museum,* **(SVG)**, Stavanger, **Norway.**

STAVROPOL: *Herbarium of Stavropol Botanical Garden,* **(SBG)**, ab. Yashch 22, 355000 Stavropol, **U.S.S.R.**

Foundation: 1960. *Number of specimens:* 8.000.
Director: V. V. SCRIPCHINSKY.

STAVROPOL: *Herbarium of Stavropol Museum of Regional Studies,* **(SMRS)**, Dzerzhinskovo St. 135, 355000 Stavropol, **U.S.S.R.**
Foundation: 1959. *Number of specimens:* 15.000.
Director: A. K. SHVYREVA.

STAVROPOL: *Herbarium, Department of Botany, Stavropol Pedagogical Institute,* **(SPI)**, Lenina Square 1, 355009 Stavropol, **U.S.S.R.**
Foundation: 1940. *Number of specimens:* 5.000.
Director: A. I. GALUSHKO.

STELLENBOSCH: *Williams Herbarium, Faculty of Forestry, University of Stellenbosch,* **(FFS)**, Stellenbosch 7600, **South Africa.**
Telephone: 02231-71038.
Status: Faculty of Forestry.
Foundation: 1965. *Number of specimens:* 9.000.
Herbarium: Mainly indigenous and exotic trees of the different families.
Important collections: E. E. M. Loock's coll. of Mexican Pines and other Pinaceae (for provenance trials during the 1940's).
Curator: BEN-ERIK VAN WIJK, 1956 (Forest botany and taxonomy).
Specialization in research: Forest botany and taxonomy.
Associated botanic garden: 11 ha. just donated, plan to start a Eucalyptetum and Arboretum (mainly for study purposes).
Exchange: Sometimes done on special request.

STELLENBOSCH: *Wicht Herbarium, Jonkershoek Forestry Research Station,* **(JF)**, Private Bag 5011, Stellenbosch 7600, **South Africa.**
Telephone: 02231-72805.
Status: State Department of Forestry.
Foundation: c. 1935. *Number of specimens:* 10.000.
Herbarium: Collection of indigenous plants from Fynbos communities of South Western Cape Region.
Director: DONALD PATRICK BANDS, 1930 (Officer in charge of Research Station; forest hydrology and ecology).
Staff members: IRIS MARGUERITE GOUWS, 1942.
ALLAN JOHN LAMB, 1955 (Research forester).
Specialization in research: Plant communities in the Fynbos and effects of fire on vegetation.
Loans: None.

STELLENBOSCH: *Government Herbarium,* **(STE)**, Botanical Research Unit, Natuurwetenskappe Gebou, Merriman Ave., P.O. Box 471, Stellenbosch 7600, **South Africa.**
Telephone: 02231-70208.
Status: State owned regional herbarium of Botanical Research Institute, Pretoria (PRE).
Foundation: 1902. *Number of specimens:* 100.000.

273

Herbarium: Mainly flora of south-western Cape Province.

Important collections: H. Andreae, J. J. Bos, C. Boucher, M. P. de Vos, K. Dinter, A. V. Duthie, C. F. Ecklon & C. L. P. Zeyher, H. G. Fourcade, E. Galpin, J. Gillett, H. Herre, L. Hugo, P. G. Jordaan, J. D. Keet, O. Kerfoot, F. J. Kruger, E. I. Markötter, R. Marloth, E. G. H. Oliver, H. Rudatis, H. C. Taylor, J. Thode, J. C. Smuts, M. F. Thompson.

Director: B. DE WINTER, Botanical Research Institute, Pretoria (PRE).

Curator: L. HUGO (Geraniaceae; general identifications).

Staff members: D. DAVIES (General identifications).

E. PARE (Clerical).

C. M. SCHONKEN (Geraniaceae, general identifications).

R. WIKNER (Technical).

Specialization in research: Cape Flora.

Loans: To recognized botanical institutions.

Periodical and serial works: see PRE, Flora of Southern Africa; Flowering Plants of Africa; Bothalia.

Exchange: Through PRE.

Remarks: Formerly Herbarium of University of Stellenbosch.

STELLENBOSCH: *Herbarium of the Department of Botany, University of Stellenbosch,* (**STEU**), Stellenbosch 7600, **South Africa.**

Telephone: 02231-4019 or 4223.

Status: University.

Foundation: 1902. *Number of specimens:* 13.000.

Herbarium: Plants from the District of Stellenbosch.

Important collections: Geraniaceae, drift seed collection of J. Muir, herbarium P. A. van der Byl (fungi and lichens).

Director and Curator: J. J. A. VAN DER WALT, 1938 (Chairman Dept. of Botany; biosystematics of Geraniaceae).

Staff members: R. B. VAN DER MERWE, 1933 (Cryptogams).

A. D. SPREETH, 1940 (*Lachnaea*, Rutaceae).

P. VORSTER, 1945 (Biosystematics of Geraniaceae).

Specialization in research: Biosystematics of Geraniaceae.

Associated botanic garden: Botanic Garden of the University of Stellenbosch.

Loans: To recognized botanical institutions.

Exchange: Yes, especially Geraniaceae.

STEPHENVILLE: *Herbarium, Department of Biological Sciences, Tarleton State University,* (**TAC**), Box T-219, Stephenville, Texas 76402, **U.S.A.**

Telephone: 817/968-9156.

Foundation: 1899. *Number of specimens:* 500.

Herbarium: Texas and Oklahoma.

Important collections: Lula Gough (1923–24).

Curator: JOHN S. CALAHAN, JR., 1945.

STEVENS POINT: *Herbarium, Museum of Natural History, University of Wisconsin,* (**UWSP**), Stevens Point, Wisconsin 54481, **U.S.A.**

Foundation: 1968. *Number of specimens:* 102.000.

Herbarium: Vascular plants and mosses, specializing in grasses and in plants of Wisconsin; Mexican and Costa Rican mosses.

Important collections: 3.000 specimens of *Dichanthelium*, including photographs of many types; R. W. Freckmann collection of 22.000 specimens; private collection of S. K. Freckmann of 5.000 mosses is available through the UWSP herbarium.

Director: ROBERT W. FRECKMANN, 1939 (Taxonomy of grasses and Wisconsin vascular plants).

Staff members: FRANK D. BOWERS, 1937 (Taxonomy of mosses of upper Midwest, Mexico, and Costa Rica).

SALLY K. FRECKMANN, 1944 (Taxonomy of mosses of upper Midwest).

Specialization in research: Taxonomy of grasses, especially *Dichanthelium;* flora of Wisconsin; moss flora of upper Midwest, Mexico, and Costa Rica.

Loans: To recognized botanical institutions.

Periodical and serial works: Reports on the Flora and Fauna of Wisconsin, published by the Museum of Natural History, UWSP.

Exchange: Available: Wisconsin specimens and *Dichanthelium*. Desired: Vascular plants and mosses.

STILLWATER: *Herbarium, School of Biological Sciences, Oklahoma State University,* (**OKLA**), Stillwater, Oklahoma 74078, **U.S.A.**

Telephone: 405/624-5559.

Foundation: 1920. *Number of specimens:* 130.000.

Herbarium: Flora of Oklahoma.

Curator: RONALD J. TYRL, 1943 (Biosystematics; cytogenetics; taxonomy of Poaceae).

Specialization in research: As above.

Loans: Usual regulations.

Exchange: Available: Plants of Oklahoma.

STIRLING: *Herbarium, Stirling Smith Art Gallery and Museum,* (**STI**), Albert Place, Stirling, Scotland, **Great Britain.**

Telephone: 0786 2849.

Status: Local Government Authority.

Foundation: 1874. *Number of specimens:* 3.660.

Herbarium: Kidston and Stirling collection; local mosses (Mrs. Cunninghame Graham); Croal collection.

Director: JAMES K. THOMSON, 1928 (Archaeology).

Staff member: MICHAEL MCGINNES, 1954 (Geology).

Remarks: Herbarium stored at Stirling University pending reconditioning of building at Museum.

STOCKHOLM: *Herbarium, Swedish Museum of Natural History (= Naturhistoriska riksmuseet)*, **(S)**, Roslagsvägen 106, P.O. Box 50007, S-10405 Stockholm, **Sweden.**

Telephone: 08-150240.

Status: State institution.

Foundation: 1758. *Number of specimens:* 4.000.000 (Phanerogams 2.000.000, cryptogams 2.000.000).

Herbarium: Worldwide, 11 groups of plants.

Important collections: Phanerogams: Linnaean herbarium, J. G. C. Lehmann, O. W. Sonder (South Africa, incl. types of Flora Capensis), E. Asplund (South America), C. F. Ecklon, E. L. Ekman (West Indies), E. Hultén (Alaska, Kamtchatka), F. W. Klatt (Iridaceae), Regnell (Brazil), O. Swartz, A. Sparrman, C. P. Thunberg, Zeyher. Cryptogams: G. Bresadola (Fungi), J. Ångström (Bryophyta), P. T. Cleve (Diatoms), P. Dusén, G. O. A. Malme (Lichens), K. Müller (Bryophyta), J. G. C. Lehmann (Hepaticae), Roth (Bryophyta), E. Rehm (Fungi), L. Romell (Fungi), P. Sydow (Fungi, before 1919).

1. Section for Phanerogamic Botany

Director: BERTIL NORDENSTAM, 1936 (Compositae, especially Senecioneae; Liliaceae; South African flora).

Curator: KÅRE BREMER, 1948 (Melastomataceae, Compositae).

Staff members: FOLKE BJÖRKBÄCK, 1934 (Swedish mire flora, mapping methods).

BENKT SPARRE, 1918 (Flora of Ecuador, Tropaeolaceae, South American Violaceae).

Research associates: GRETA BERGGREN, 1903 (Seeds of North European plants).

TYCHO NORLINDH, 1906 (Compositae, especially South and East African; flora of Mongolia).

2. Section for Cryptogamic Botany

Director: ROLF SANTESSON, 1916 (Scandinavian and South American lichens).

Curator: ÅKE STRID, 1932 (Scandinavian lignicolous Aphyllophorales).

Staff members: THOR-BJÖRN ENGELMARK, 1947 (Dicranaceae, Scandinavian bryophytes).

GÖRAN THOR, 1953 (Lichens, especially *Chiodecton*).

Research associates: ELSA NYHOLM, 1911 (Bryophytes of Scandinavia and Asia Minor).

3. Palynological laboratory

Roslagsvägen 101, hus 8, S-10405 Stockholm

Telephone: 08-144331, 08-158414.

Foundation: In 1948 by Gunnar Erdtman as a scientific institute under the Swedish Natural Research Council. In 1975 incorporated in the Swedish Museum of Natural History. No herbarium, but a worldwide collection of 35.000–40.000 pollen slides.

Director: SIWERT NILSSON, 1933 (Apocynaceae, Oleaceae; aerobiology).

Curator: JOSEF PRAGLOWSKI, 1922 (Oenotheraceae, Fagaceae).

Staff member: BHOJ RAJ, 1925 (Verbenaceae).

4. Section for Palaeobotany (Formerly S-PA)

Until 1971 including also recent Bryophyta, Pteridophyta and Conifers. All these herbaria are now incorporated in the Sections of Cryptogamic and Phanerogamic Botany, resp. At present, exclusively paleobotanical collections.

Director: BRITTA LUNDBLAD.

Specialization in research: 1. Compositae, flora of Ecuador, South African flora and phytogeography, flora of the arctic and boreal zones. 2. Aphyllophorales, Scandinavian and South American lichens, Bryophytes from Scandinavia and Asia Minor. 3. Pollen morphology, aerobiology.

Loans: In general to recognized botanical institutions.

Periodical and serial works: Flora of Ecuador, Atlas of Seeds, Index Holmiensis, World Pollen Flora.

Exchange: Specimens mainly from Scandinavia and South America. Desired: All groups, especially South American and African.

Remarks: Section for Palaeobotany (S-PA) and Palynological Laboratory (SPL) are now incorporated in S.

STOCKHOLM: *Herbarium, Bergius Foundation,* **(SBT)**, P.O. Box 50017, S-104 05 Stockholm, **Sweden.**

Telephone: 08/15 26 24.

Status: Directed by the Royal Swedish Academy of Sciences.

Foundation: 1791. *Number of specimens:* 45.000.

Herbarium: Cultivated plants, Scandinavian phanerogams, Bergius Herbarium.

Important collections: P. J. Bergius' herbarium with plants collected by F. Hasselqvist, P. Kalm, J. G. König, Linnaeus, Löfling, P. Osbeck, S. B. T. Pallas, Sonnerat & A. Thouin, O. Swartz, C. P. Thunberg et al. (Cape Province especially well represented).

Director: MÅNS RYBERG, 1918 (Ecology, morphology).

Curator: LARS E. KERS, 1931; 08/15 26 27 (Taxonomy).

Specialization in research: Ecology, taxonomy in Capparidaceae and Fungi Hypogaei.

Associated botanic garden: Bergius Botanic Garden.

Loans: Generally not permitted.

Periodical and serial works: Seed catalogue of the botanic garden.

Exchange: Seeds and fruits.

STOCKHOLM: *Section for Palaeobotany, Naturhistoriska riksmuseet,* **(S-PA)** ‒‒ incorporated in S.

STOCKHOLM: *Palynological Laboratory,* **(SPL)** ‒‒ incorporated in S.

STOCKHOLM: *Herbarium, Institute of Botany, University of Stockholm,* **(SUNIV)**, S-106 91 Stockholm, **Sweden.**

Telephone: 08-15 01 60.
Status: University.
Foundation: 1882. *Number of specimens:* 60.000.
Herbarium: European plants.
Research associates: ARNE ANDERBERG, 1954 (Compositae).
    BARBRO AXELIUS, 1952 (Rubiaceae).
    BIRGITTA BREMER, 1950 (Rubiaceae, Grimmiaceae).
    BENGT JONSELL, 1936 (Cruciferae).
    JENS KLACKENBERG, 1951 (Gentianaceae).
    ROGER LUNDIN, 1955 (Melastomataceae).
    ANDERS TEHLER, 1947 (Roccellaceae).
    HANS-ERIK WANNTORP, 1940 (Asclepiadaceae).
    ANNETTE WIKLUND, 1953 (Compositae).
Associated botanic garden: Bergius Botanic Garden, Frescati, 104 05 Stockholm 50.
Loans: In general no loans.

STOCKTON: *Herbarium, Department of Biological Sciences, University of the Pacific,* **(CPH)**, Stockton, California 95211, **U.S.A.**
Telephone: 209/946-2181.
Status: Private institution.
Foundation: 1926. *Number of specimens:* 14.000.
Herbarium: California and western American angiosperms; Sierra Nevada serpentine soils; *Allium, Orthocarpus, Eriogonum.*
Important collections: E. E. Stanford herbarium.
Director and Curator: DALE W. MCNEAL, 1939 (Taxonomy of *Allium;* serpentine flora of the Sierra Nevada).
Specialization in research: Taxonomy of *Allium* in North America; flora of restricted habitats in California.
Loans: To accredited institutions.
Exchange: Available: *Allium* from western U.S.; general central California flora. Desired: Old World *Allium;* general western U.S.

STOCKTON: *Herbarium, San Joaquin County Department of Agriculture,* **(SSJC)**, P.O. Box 1809, 1868 E. Hazelton, Stockton, California 95201, **U.S.A.**
Telephone: 209/944-2693.
Status: County Department of Agriculture.
Foundation: 1971. *Number of specimens:* 1.450.
Herbarium: Flora of San Joaquin County, California; noxious California weeds.
Curator: JACK B. GIANELLI, 1928 (Plant taxonomy).

STOLZENAU: *Bundesanstalt für Vegetationskartierung,* **(ZVS)** *-- see* BAD GODESBERG.

STORRS: *George Safford Torrey Herbarium, Biological Sciences Group, University of Connecticut,* **(CONN)**, Life Sciences U-43, Storrs, Connecticut 06268, **U.S.A.**
Telephone: 203/486-4150.

Status: Maintained by the Biological Sciences Group, Systematic and Evolutionary Biology Section, College of Liberal Arts and Sciences of the University of Connecticut.
Foundation: 1915. *Number of specimens:* 90.000.
Herbarium: Eastern North America; neotropical flora; Devonian Tracheophytes.
Important collections: Herbaria of Edwin H. Eames, A. W. Driggs, C. C. Hanmer, Kaleb P. Jansson, Henry A. Ballou, Irving W. Patterson, A. F. Schulze, Emma J. Thompson; paleobotanical collections of H. N. Andrews, Jr.; herbaria of Connecticut Agriculture College and the Connecticut Agriculture Experiment Station (NHES), New Haven.
Director and Curator: HOWARD WM. PFEIFER (Aristolochiaceae, especially *Aristolochia;* neotropical flora).
Curator of Paleobotanical Collections: WILLIAM L. CREPET (Eocene angiosperms; Paleozoic plants -- Carboniferous).
Curator of Phycological Collections: FRANCIS R. TRAINOR (Freshwater algae).
Staff members: GREG ANDERSON (Cytotaxonomy; *Solanum*).
    KERRY A. BARRINGER (Scrophulariaceae, especially *Angelonia* and *Basistemon*).
    ERIC A. CHRISTENSON (Orchidaceae, Sarcantheae, Saccolabiinae, Sarcochilinæ).
    A. W. H. DAMMAN (Ecology; boreal flora).
    MARY M. HUBBARD (Biology).
    T. R. WEBSTER (Morphology; *Selaginella*).
Specialization in research: Monographic studies of tropical flora; physiology, morphology and anatomy of algae and vascular cryptogams; paleobotany.
Loans: In general to recognized botanical institutions.
Exchange: Available: Phanerogams of eastern U.S., Puerto Rico, northern Andes, and Mexico. Desired: Neotropical phanerogams and pteridophytes; *Aristolochia.*

STRASBOURG: *Institut de Botanique de l'Université Louis Pasteur,* **(STR)**, 28 Rue Goethe, 67083 Strasbourg Cedex, **France.** (Information 1974)
Status: University.
Foundation: About 1850. *Number of specimens:* 250.000.
Herbarium: Fungi and other cryptogams.
Important collections: Herbarium C. G. Nees (Hepaticae), herb. H. G. Mühlenbeck, herb. H. de Boissieu.
Specialization in research: Cryptogams of Alsace.
Associated botanic garden: Jardin Botanique de l'Université de Strasbourg.

STUTTGART-HOHENHEIM: *Institut für Botanik,* **(HOH)**, Garbenstrasse 30, 7000 Stuttgart 70 (Hohenheim), **Federal Republic of Germany,** BRD.
Telephone: 0711-4501 2194.

Status: University of Stuttgart-Hohenheim.
Foundation: ca. 1828. *Number of specimens:* 70.000.
Herbarium: Worldwide, especially Germany.
Director: B. FRENZEL, 1928 (History of flora and vegetation).
Curator: E. GÖTZ, 1940 (Taxonomy of vascular plants).
Specialization in research: Trees and shrubs of Europe, cultivated plants.
Associated botanic garden: Botanischer Garten der Universität Hohenheim.
Loans: To botanical institutions.
Exchange: Available: Vascular plants of the Alps and Southern Europe. Desired: Plants of Alps and Southern Europe and tropical families.

SUDBURY: *Herbarium, Department of Biology, Laurentian University,* (**SLU**), Sudbury, Ontario, **Canada** P3E 2C6.
Telephone: 705/675-1151.
Foundation: 1961. *Number of specimens:* 11.000 (10.000 vascular plants, 1.000 lichens).
Herbarium: Mainly northern Ontario and Arctic, with representation from eastern North America, Britain, Malaysia, Australia.
Important collections: Gerard Gardner.
Director and Curator: KEITH WINTERHALDER, 1935 (Plant ecology).
Staff member: GERARD M. COURTIN, 1935 (Plant ecology).
Specialization in research: Flora of northern Ontario; flora of industrially damaged sites; Arctic and sand dune flora.
Associated botanic garden: The Botanic Garden of the Biology Department, Laurentian University.
Loans: To recognized botanical institutions.
Exchange: Available: Northern Ontario vascular plants. Desired: All groups, especially Arctic and North America.

SUKHUMI: *Colchic Herbarium, Sukhumi Botanical Garden of the Georgian Academy of Sciences,* (**SUCH**), Chavchavadze Street 20, 384933 Sukhumi, Abkhaizian A.S.S.R., **U.S.S.R.**
Telephone: 2-44-58, 2-44-59.
Status: Directed by Academy of Sciences.
Foundation: 1936. *Number of specimens:* 40.000.
Herbarium: Mainly plants of Colchica, also Caucasas, Siberia, China and Asia.
Important collections: Exsiccatae of Flora U.S.S.R., types of species of North Colchica.
Director: G. G. AIBA, 1931.
Curator: A. A. KOLAKOVSKY, 1906.
Staff member: E. M. SHENGELIA, 1923.
Specialization in research: Flora and vegetation of Colchica.
Associated botanic garden: Sukhumi Botanical Garden.
Exchange: With herbaria of U.S.S.R. and Poland.

ŠUMPERK: *Vlastivědný ústav v Šumperku,* (**SUM**), Sady 1, máje 1, Šumperk, **Czechoslovakia.** (Information 1974)
Foundation: About 1850. *Number of specimens:* 12.500.
Herbarium: Tracheophyta and bryophyta, worldwide, Europe and Czechoslovakia.
Loans: To recognized botanical institutions.
Periodical and serial works: Severni Morava.

SUPERIOR: *Herbarium, Biology Department, University of Wisconsin – Superior,* (**SUWS**), 1800 Grand Avenue, Superior, Wisconsin 54880, **U.S.A.**
Telephone: 715/392-8101, ext. 408.
Foundation: 1940. *Number of specimens:* 30.000 vascular plants.
Herbarium: Flora of northern Wisconsin.
Director: RUDY G. KOCH (*Bidens;* northern Wisconsin flora).
Specialization in research: Lake Superior flora.
Loans: Loans to recognized herbaria for reasonable working times.
Exchange: Particularly Great Lakes regional flora and representative forms from other regions.

SUVA: *Fiji Herbarium, Ministry of Agriculture and Fisheries,* (**SUVA**), P.O. Box 358, Suva, **Fiji.**
Telephone: 311233 ext. 223.
Status: Ministry of Agriculture and Fisheries.
Foundation: 1933. *Number of specimens:* 18.000.
Herbarium: Plants of Fiji.
Curator: A. SUNDARESAN, 1948.
Staff members: NARAYAN SAMI NAIDU, 1955 (Economic Botany).
　　　　RAKISH PRASAD, 1960.
　　　　SAULA VODONAIVALU, 1942 (Palmae, Ferns).
Specialization in research: Flora and food crops of Fiji.
Loans: No.

SUZHOU: *Herbarium, Suzhou University,* (**SU**), Suzhou, Jiangsu, **People's Republic of China.**

SVERDLOVSK: *Herbarium of the Laboratory of Plant Ecology and Geobotany, Institute of Plant and Animal Ecology,* (**SVER**), Urals Centre Academy of Sciences, 8 Marta 202, 620008 Sverdlovsk, **U.S.S.R.**
Telephone: 220570.
Status: State Institute.
Foundation: 1945. *Number of specimens:* 105.500.
Herbarium: All groups.
Important collections: Herbarium of Urals Naturalists Association, collections of Sverdlovsk Botanical Garden, Denezhkin Kamen Reserve and Visim.
Director: PAVEL L. GORCHAKOVSKI, 1920 (Phytogeography, floristics, geobotany).
Curator: EUGENIA A. SHUROVA, 1936 (Taxonomy of higher plants).
Staff member: NINA P. SALMINA, 1946.
Specialization in research: Floristic investi-

277

gations in the Urals.

Associated botanic garden: Botanical Garden of the Institute of Plant and Animal Ecology.

Exchange: Available: Plants of Erevan, Tomsk, Irkutsk and Finland.

SWANSEA: *Herbarium, Swansea Museum,* (**SWA**), Victoria Road, Swansea 5A1 1SN, England, **Great Britain.**

Telephone: 0792 53763.

Status: University and Public Society (Jointly).

Foundation: 1838. *Number of specimens:* 1.000–1.200 vascular plants, 70 seaweeds.

Herbarium: Mostly British, collected 1798–1840.

Director: M. J. ISAAC (Marine biology).

Honorary Curator: J. HAYWARD; 0792 25678, ext. 413.

Remarks: The herbarium is in the process of being catalogued.

SWARTHMORE: *Herbarium, Biology Department, Swarthmore College,* (**SWC**), Swarthmore, Pennsylvania 19081, **U.S.A.**

Telephone: 215/447-7038.

Status: Private institution.

Foundation: 1910. *Number of specimens:* 3.300.

Director and Curator: JACOB WEINER, 1947 (Plant ecology).

Loans: Usual regulations.

SWEET BRIAR: *Herbarium, Biology Department, Sweet Briar College,* (**SWBR**), Sweet Briar, Virginia 24595, **U.S.A.** –– incorporated in LYN, Lynchburg.

Foundation: 1910. *Number of specimens:* 3.620.

SWIFT CURRENT: *Herbarium, Research Station, Agriculture Canada,* (**SCS**), Swift Current, Saskatchewan, **Canada** S9H 3X2.

Telephone: 306/773-4621.

Status: Department of Agriculture.

Foundation: 1932. *Number of specimens:* 56.000.

Herbarium: Canadian Prairie Provinces vascular plants, mosses, lichens.

Curator: JAN LOOMAN, 1919 (Range ecology, phytosociology).

Specialization in research: Ecology of the native grasslands and parklands in the Prairie Provinces.

Loans: 6 months, unless otherwise arranged.

Exchange: Available: Species from the prairies and parklands, lichens and mosses. Desired: Grassland species from the temperate regions.

SYDNEY: *National Herbarium of New South Wales,* (**NSW**), Royal Botanic Gardens, Mrs. Macquaries Road, Sydney, N.S.W. 2000, **Australia.**

Telephone: (02) 274347.

Status: State Government.

Foundation: 1896. *Number of specimens:* 1.000.000.

Herbarium: Worldwide, with emphasis on Australia, especially New South Wales.

Important collections: R. T. Baker, W. Bäurlen, E. Betche, W. F. Blakely, J. L. Boorman, E. F. Constable, R. C. Coveny, A. D. E. Elmer (Philippines), W. V. Fitzgerald, Copland King (New Guinea), A. H. S. Lucas, J. H. Maiden, E. D. Merrill (Philippines), G. I. Playfair (Algae), A. Rodway, R. Schlechter (New Guinea and Pacific), W. W. Watts (Bryophytes and pteridophytes), T. Whitelegge (Bryophytes).

Director: L. A. S. JOHNSON, 1925 (Southern hemisphere families; Myrtaceae, Proteaceae, Casuarinaceae, Restionaceae; *Eucalyptus* group, *Juncus*).

Assistant Director: BARBARA G. BRIGGS, 1934 (Restionaceae, Myrtaceae, Proteaceae; cytotaxonomy).

Staff members: JIM A. ARMSTRONG, 1950 (Rutaceae; breeding systems, pollination).

DON F. BLAXELL, 1934 (Orchidaceae, *Eucalyptus, Hoya*).

D. H. BENSON, 1949 (Vegetation survey).

MARILYN D. FOX, 1946 (Vegetation survey).

L. HAEGI, 1952 (Solanaceae, Asteraceae: Inulae, cytotaxonomy).

S. W. L. JACOBS, 1946 (Poaceae, Chenopodiaceae, photosynthetic pathways).

ALMA T. LEE, 1912 (Fabaceae, Xanthorrhoeaceae).

DON MCGILLIVRAY, 1935 (Proteaceae).

VALERIE MAY (Mrs. E. H. JONES), 1916 (Algae).

JOCELYN M. POWELL, 1939 (Epacridaceae, ethnobotany, palynology).

ANTHONY N. RODD, 1940 (Palms, ornamentals).

JOY THOMPSON, 1923 (*Leptospermum*).

MARY D. TINDALE (*Acacia*, Pteridophyta, *Glycine*).

KAREN L. WILSON, 1950 (Cyperaceae, *Juncus*).

Specialization in research: Systematics of Australian flora.

Associated botanic garden: Royal Botanic Gardens, Sydney.

Loans: To recognized botanical institutions.

Periodical and serial works: Telopea, Cunninghamia.

Exchange: Available: Australian plants (mainly from New South Wales). Desired: Most groups worldwide. Program restricted by financial constraints, and relevance to Australian region.

SYDNEY: *John Ray Herbarium, University of Sydney,* (**SYD**), Botany Building A 12, Sydney, N.S.W. 2006, **Australia.**

Telephone: 02-692-2832.

Status: Herbarium of School of Biological Sciences.

Foundation: 1914. *Number of specimens:* 40.000.

Herbarium: Flora of Australia, all plant groups.

Director: The Head of the School of Biological Sciences (changes each year or two).

Curator: R. C. CAROLIN, 1929 (Goodeniaceae, Chenopodiales).

Staff members: Various members of the School contribute to the work of the herbarium, but no staff other than the curator is assigned to it.

Specialization in research: Taxonomy of Australian plants.

Loans: To recognized botanical institutions.

SYDNEY: *The Herbarium of the University of New South Wales,* (**UNSW**), Box 1, P.O., Kensington, N.S.W. 2033, **Australia.**

Telephone: (02-) 663 0351.

Status: University.

Foundation: 1960. *Number of specimens:* 20.000, including 6.500 larger fungi.

Herbarium: Plants of Australia, mainly New South Wales and Northern Territory.

Director: JOHN T. WATERHOUSE, 1924 (Angiosperms).

Curators: PAUL ADAM, 1951 (Exotics).

ROBERT J. KING, 1945 (Algae).

CHRISTOPHER J. QUINN, 1936 (Peridophytes and gymnosperms).

HELEN P. RAMSAY, 1928 (Bryophytes).

ALEC E. WOOD, 1933 (Fungi).

Specialization in research: Agaricaceae, Myrtaceae, Podocarpaceae, moss census of New South Wales.

Loans: Available to recognized herbaria.

Exchange: Enquiries welcome; limited material available.

SYKTYVKAR: *Herbarium, Laboratory of Geobotany and Plant Systematics, Biological Institute of the Komi Section of Academy of Sciences of U.S.S.R.,* (**SYKO**), Kommunisticheskaya St. 24, 167610 Syktyvkar, Komi, **U.S.S.R.**

Status: Directed by Academy of Sciences.

Foundation: 1934. *Number of specimens:* 86.000.

Herbarium: Vascular plants, mosses and algae of European U.S.S.R.

Director: A. N. LASHCHENKOVA.

SYRACUSE: *Herbarium, Department of Plant Sciences, Syracuse University,* (**SYR**), Syracuse, New York 13210, **U.S.A.**

Foundation: 1900. *Number of specimens:* 35.000.

Remarks: Dispersal of material formerly in the SYR herbarium is as follows:

1. Specimens collected outside Onondaga County, New York, are deposited at State University, New York, College at Oswego, New York 13126.

2. Specimens collected in Onondaga County, New York, are deposited in the College of Environmental Science and Forestry, State University of New York, Syracuse (SYRF).

3. The Syracuse University Liberal Arts College collection is now at Beaver Lake Nature Center (Onondaga County facility), 3 Canton Boulevard, Baldwinsville, New York 13027.

4. Duplicate set of most species known from Onondaga County, New York, deposited in the New York State Museum, Albany (NYS).

SYRACUSE: *Herbarium, Department of Environmental and Forest Biology, College of Environmental Science and Forestry, State University of New York,* (**SYRF**), Syracuse, New York 13210, **U.S.A.**

Telephone: 315/473-8801; 473-8751.

Foundation: 1913. *Number of specimens:* 45.500.

Herbarium: Flora of central New York.

Important collections: Polyporaceae of North America (12.000), including 350 isotypes; Hyphomycetes (1.500); flora of Onondaga County, New York (Mildred E. Faust herbarium).

Curators: DUDLEY J. RAYNAL, 1947 (Flowering plants).

EDWIN H. KETCHLEDGE, 1924 (Bryophytes).

JOSIAH L. LOWE, 1905 (Polyporaceae).

CHUN J. K. WANG, 1928 (Hyphomycetes).

Specialization in research: Wood decay fungi; Homobasidiomycetes and Fungi Imperfecti.

Loans: To cooperative institutions.

Exchange: Available.

Remarks: A full set of flowering plants, ferns, and fern allies from Onondaga County previously housed in the now defunct Syracuse University Herbarium (SYR) is now located at SYRF.

SZEGED: *Herbarium, Mora Ferenc Museum,* (**SZE**), Szeged, **Hungary.** (Information 1974)

Status: Foundation of the town council.

Foundation: 1883. *Number of specimens:* 38.500.

Herbarium: All groups from Central Europe, Hungary and Austria.

Important collections: Herbarium of A. Feichtinger, A. Lányi, D. L. Galle (lichens).

Specialization in research: Hungarian lichen flora.

Periodical and serial works: Móra Ferenc Múseum Evkönyve, Jahrbuch des Móra Ferenc Museums, Annales du Musée Ferenc Móra.

T

TAHLEQUAH: *Herbarium, Division of Natural Science and Mathematics, Northeastern Oklahoma State University*, **(NOSU)**, Tahlequah, Oklahoma 74464, **U.S.A.**
Telephone: 918/456-5511, ext. 250 or 255.
Foundation: 1975. *Number of specimens:* 2.000.
Herbarium: Plants of Oklahoma.
Director and Curator: JOE M. ANDERSON, 1924 (Eastern Oklahoma flora).
Loans: Usual regulations.
Exchange: Willing to try.

TAIPEI: *The Herbarium, Department of Botany, National Taiwan University*, **(TAI)**, Taipei, **Taiwan.** (Information 1974)
Status: University.
Foundation: 1928. *Number of specimens:* 161.500.
Herbarium: Ferns and seed plants, worldwide, especially Taiwan, China, Hainan, Japan, Liukiu and Micronesia.
Specialization in research: Flora of Taiwan.
Associated botanic garden: Botanical Garden, National Taiwan University.
Loans: To recognized botanical institutions.
Periodical and serial works: Taiwania.

TAIPEI: *Herbarium, Taiwan Forestry Research Institute*, **(TAIF)**, Po-A Road Botanical Garden, Taipei, **Taiwan.** (Information 1974)
Status: Taiwan province.
Foundation: 1904. *Number of specimens:* 30.400.
Herbarium: Vascular plants of Taiwan.
Specialization in research: Flora of Taiwan.
Associated botanic garden: Taipei Botanical Garden, Taiwan Forestry Research Institute.
Loans: With permission of director.
Periodical and serial works: Bulletin of Taiwan Forestry Research Institute.

TAIPEI: *Herbarium, Taiwan Museum*, **(TAIM)**, No. 2 Siangyang Road, Taipei, **Taiwan.**

TALENCE: *Herbarium, Faculté des Sciences, Laboratoire Géologique*, **(TALE)**, Talence, **France.**

TALLAHASSEE: *Herbarium, Department of Biological Science, Unit 1, Florida State University*, **(FSU)**, Tallahassee, Florida 32306, **U.S.A.**
Telephone: 904/644-6278.
Foundation: 1940. *Number of specimens:* 160.000.
Herbarium: Southeastern U.S. and tropical America.
Director and Curator: LORAN C. ANDERSON, 1936 (Plant anatomy and systematics of *Chrysothamnus*, Compositae).
Staff members: R. K. GODFREY, 1911 (Local flora

and aquatic plants of southeastern U.S.).
NORRIS WILLIAMS, 1943 (Biosystematics and pollination biology of orchids).
Loans: Normal regulations.
Exchange: Available: Florida plants. Desired: Compositae, orchids, representative tropical material.

TAMPA: *Herbarium, Department of Biology, University of South Florida*, **(USF)**, Tampa, Florida 33620, **U.S.A.**
Telephone: 813/974-2359.
Status: State university.
Foundation: 1958. *Number of specimens:* 150.000.
Herbarium: Worldwide, with emphasis on Florida and Caribbean.
Important collections: George R. Cooley, O. Lakela, R. W. Long, James D. Ray, Jr.
Director: RICHARD P. WUNDERLIN, 1939 (Leguminosae, Cucurbitaceae; flora of Florida).
Curator: BRUCE F. HANSEN, 1944 (Apocynaceae).
Staff members: GEORGE R. COOLEY (Flora of eastern North America).
   CLINTON J. DAWES, 1935 (Algae).
   FREDERICK B. ESSIG, 1947 (Arecaceae, Zingiberaceae).
   GLENN B. FLEMING (Flora of Florida).
   DIANE T. WAGNER-MERNER, 1934 (Fungi, bryophytes).
Specialization in research: Flora of Florida; monographic studies of worldwide flora; marine algae.
Associated botanic garden: University of South Florida Botanic Garden.
Loans: To recognized scientific institutions upon receipt of request by Director.
Exchange: Worldwide, especially Neotropics.

TAMPERE: *Herbarium, Tampere Museum of Natural History*, **(TMP)**, Pirkankatu 2, SF-33210 Tampere 21, **Finland.**
Telephone: 931-29119.
Status: Municipal.
Foundation: 1961. *Number of specimens:* 28.000.
Herbarium: Vascular plants, lichenized Ascomycetes, mosses, microfungi, especially from Finland Pirkanmaa Province.
Important collections: Herb. Th. Grönblom, M. Helin, K. Holm, R. Idman (especially *Hieracium*), T. Mäkelä, I. Mäkisalo, Q. Perttulo, G. Rydmon, T. Setälä.
Director: MARTTI HELIN, 1928.
Curator: MATTI KÄÄNTÖNEN, 1944 (*Taraxacum*, adventive plants).
Staff member: TUULA KALLIO, 1940 (Salmon fishes).

Specialization in research: Flora of the Pirkanmaa Province.
Loans: To recognized institutions.
Exchange: Available: A small quantity of Finnish vascular plants.

TANANARIVE: *Institut de Recherche Scientifique de Madagascar,* (**TAN**), BP 434, Tananarive, **Madagascar.** (Information 1974)
Foundation: 1947. *Number of specimens:* 50.000.
Herbarium: Flora of Madagascar, the Comores, the Mascarenes.
  Associated botanic garden: The Botanical Garden, Tsimbazaza, Tananarive.
  Loans: To recognized botanical institutions.
  Periodical and serial works: Mémoires de l'Institut Scientifique de Madagascar, Serie B; Naturaliste Malgache.

TARANTO: *Herbarium, Istituto de Biologia Marina,* (**TAR**), Via Roma 3, Taranto, **Italy.**

TARTU: *Herbarium of the Chair of Botany, Plant Physiology and Phytopathology, Estonian Agricultural Academy,* (**EAA**), 366 Mitskurini Street, Tartu, Estonian S.S.R., **U.S.S.R.**

TARTU: *Herbarium of the Institute of Zoology and Botany of the Academy of Sciences of the E.S.S.R.,* (**TAA**), 21 Vanemuise Street, Tartu, Estonian S.S.R., **U.S.S.R.**
Status: Directed by Academy of Sciences of the Estonian S.S.R.
Foundation: 1947. *Number of specimens:* 241.000 (100.000 fungi, 141.000 higher plants).
Herbarium: Estonian vascular plants, mosses and fungi; aphyllophoraceous and heterobasidiomycetous fungi of U.S.S.R.
Important collections: Karl Ernst von Baer (6.500).
  Director: KALJU PAAVER, 1921.
  Curators: LIIVIA MARIA LAASIMER, 1918 (Systematics of vascular plants, bryology, ecology).
    AIN RAITVIIR, 1938 (Mycology).
  Specialization in research: Estonian flora, aphyllophoraceous and heterobasidiomycetous fungi of U.S.S.R.
  Loans: With permission of director (limited because of lack of staff).
  Periodical and serial works: The Flora of the Estonian S.S.R. in 11 volumes, Scripta Mycologica.
  Exchange: Limited.

TARTU: *Herbarium, State Museum of Natural Sciences,* (**TAM**), Tartu, Estonian S.S.R., **U.S.S.R.**

TARTU: *Herbarium, Department of Geobotany and Plant Systematics, Tartu State University,* (**TU**), Michurina St. 40, 202400 Tartu, Estonian S.S.R., **U.S.S.R.**
Status: University.

Foundation: 1802. *Number of specimens:* 300.000.
Herbarium: Plants of Estonia and Arctic regions, including lichens.
Director: K. EICHWALD.

TASHKENT: *Herbarium, Republic Nature Museum of Uzbekistan,* (**RNMUT**), Sagban Street 16, 700002 Tashkent, **U.S.S.R.**
Telephone: 44-33-72, 44-10-75.
Status: Ministry of Culture of Uzbek S.S.R.
Foundation: 1923. *Number of specimens:* 40.000.
Herbarium: Plants of Middle Asia, desert, foothills, mountains.
  Important collections: F. V. Androsov, M. G. Popov, M. V. Kultiassov, E. P. Korovin, T. K. Pazia, E. M. Demurina, L. L. Bulgakova.
  Director: LYDIA L. BULGAKOVA, 1929.
  Specialization in research: Nectariferous plants of the deserts and foothills.

TASHKENT: *Herbarium, Biology – Soils Faculty, Lenin State University,* (**TAK**), Karl Marx Street 35, 700047 Tashkent, **U.S.S.R.**
Status: University.
Foundation: 1920. *Number of specimens:* 500.000.
Herbarium: Mainly plants of Middle Asia, including 1.000 type specimens.
Director: T. A. ADYLOV.

TASHKENT: *Herbarium, Institute of Botany of the Uzbek Academy of Sciences,* (**TASH**), F. Khodzhaeva str. 32, 700125 Tashkent, **U.S.S.R.**
Telephone: 62-70-65, 62-73-15.
Status: Part of Laboratory of Taxonomy and Geography of Higher Plants.
Foundation: 1950. *Number of specimens:* 150.000.
Herbarium: Flora of mid-Asia, especially Uzbekistan.
  Important collections: V. I. Kudrjaschev, G. P. Sumnevitcz, Butkov, Nabiev, Pratov; 250 type specimens.
  Director: M. M. NABIEV, 1926 (Geobotany, *Calligonum, Lappula,* Cucurbitaceae).
  Staff members: M. N. ABDULLAEVA, 1923 (Malvaceae).
    S. S. KOVALEVSKAJA, 1929 (Taxonomy, Compositae: Liguliflorae).
    M. G. PACHOMOVA, 1925 (Rosaceae: *Amygdalus, Crataegus*).
    N. P. PRATOV, 1934 (Chenopodiaceae).
    M. TULAGANOVA, 1936 (Berberidaceae).
    T. I. ZUKERVANIK, 1930 (Labiatae: *Lagochilus*).
  Specialization in research: Flora of Mid-Asia.
  Associated botanic garden: Botanical Garden of the Uzbek Academy of Sciences.
  Periodical and serial works: Notulae Systematia; Critical Conspectus of Mid-Asia Flora in 10 volumes.
  Exchange: Limited.

TATRANSKÁ LOMNICA: *Herbarium, Museum of the Tatra National Park*, (**TNP**), 05960 Tatranská Lomnica, **Czechoslovakia.** (Information 1974)
Status: Directed by state.
Foundation: 1950. *Number of specimens:* 4.200.
Herbarium: Plants of Tatra National Park.

TBILISI: *Herbarium, Stalin State University of Tbilisi,* (**TB**), University Street, Tbilisi, Georgia, **U.S.S.R.** (Information 1974)
Status: University.
Foundation: 1918. *Number of specimens:* 35.500.
Herbarium: Wild and cultivated plants of Caucasus.
   Periodical and serial works: Stalinis sakhelobis Tbilisis sakhelmzipho Universitetis Shromebi.

TBILISI: *Herbarium, Botanical Institute of the Academy of Sciences of the Georgian S.S.R.,* (**TBI**), Kodjorskoje Highway, Tbilisi 380007, **U.S.S.R.**
Telephone: 99-74-48.
Status: Directed by Academy of Sciences of the Georgian S.S.R.
Foundation: 1894. *Number of specimens:* 1.000.000.
Herbarium: Mainly plants of the Caucasus, also Middle Asia, Turkey and Iran.
Important collections: A. Grossheim, D. Sosnowskyi, N. Busch.
   Director: N. KEZKHOVELI, 1897 (Geobotany).
   Curator: Z. GVINIANIDZE, 1931 (Systematics and morphology of Silenoideae, Illecebraceae and Georgian *Genista*).
   Staff members: SCH. KUTHATHELADZE, 1905 (*Pyrus*, Compositae, tribe Scorzonerinae).
      N. TSCHOLOKASCHVILI, 1932 (Alliaceae of Caucasus).
      A. AVAZNELI, 1941 (*Lathyrus* and *Orobus* of Caucasus).
   Specialization in research: Monographical study of flora of Caucasus and Georgia, plant morphology and study of old collections.
   Exchange: Available: Plants of Caucasus.

TBILISI: *Herbarium, Department of Botany, S. N. Dzhanashiya State Museum of the Georgian Academy of Sciences,* (**TGM**), Ketskhoveli St. 10, 380007 Tbilisi, Georgia, **U.S.S.R.**
Status: Directed by Academy of Sciences.
Foundation: 1852. *Number of specimens:* 112.000.
Herbarium: Flora of Caucasus, Georgia, Middle Asia, Turkey and other countries.
   Director: V. I. PAPAVA.

TEGUCIGALPA: *Herbario Paul C. Standley, Escuela Agricola Panamericana,* (**EAP**), Apartado 93, Tegucigalpa, **Honduras.**
Status: Private foundation.
Foundation: 1943. *Number of specimens:* 141.786.
Herbarium: Flora of Central America.
   Director: ANTONIO MOLINA R.

Specialization in research: Flora of Central America.
Periodical and serial works: Ceiba.
Exchange: Yes.

TEGUCIGALPA: *Herbario, Departamento de Biología, Universidad Nacional Autónoma de Honduras,* (**TEFH**), Tegucigalpa, **Honduras.**
Telephone: 504-32-2204, ext. 250.
Foundation: 1969. *Number of specimens:* 10.000.
Herbarium: Phanerogams of Honduras.
Important collections: Fred Barkley, Andre F. Clewell, Cirilo Nelson, Ernesto Vargas.
   Director and Curator: CIRILO NELSON, 1938 (Phanerogams of Honduras).
   Specialization in research: Collecting and classifying Honduras phanerogams.
   Exchange: Wanted: Tropical American specimens.

TEHRAN: *Herbarium, Plant Pests and Diseases Research Institute,* (**IRAN**), P.O. Box 3178, Tehran, **Iran.** (Information 1974)
Status: Ministry of Agriculture.
Foundation: 1948. *Number of specimens:* 62.000.

TEHRAN: *Herbarium, Faculty of Agriculture, University of Tehran,* (**KAR**), Karadj, Tehran, **Iran.** (Information 1974)
Status: University.
Foundation: 1933. *Number of specimens:* 20.000.
Herbarium: Plants of Iran.
   Associated botanic garden: Karadj College Botanic Garden.

TEHRAN: *Botanical Institute of Iran,* (**TARI**), Karaj Road, P.O. Box 8-6096, Tehran, **Iran.**
Telephone: 944198.
Status: Ministry of Agriculture.
Foundation: 1970. *Number of specimens:* 35.000.
Herbarium: Plants of Iran.
   Director: P. BABAKHANLOV, 1939.
   Curator: M. ASSADI, 1950.
   Staff members: Z. ALIZADEH FARD, 1951.
      Z. JAMZAD, 1951.
      V. MOZAFFARIAN, 1953.
      M. NOWROOZI, 1951.
      K. VOSOUGHI, 1953.
   Specialization in research: Taxonomy and exploration of flora of Iran.
   Associated botanic garden: Botanical Garden of Botanical Institute of Iran.
   Loans: To contributors to Flora Iranica and to other specialists on request.
   Periodical and serial works: Iranian Journal of Botany.
   Exchange: Local plants only.

TEHRAN: *Herbarium, Museyeh Guiah shenacy, Faculty of Pharmacy, University of Tehran,* (**TEH**), Teh-

ran, **Iran.** (Information 1974)
Status: University (since 1955).
Foundation: 1946. *Number of specimens:* 10.000.
Herbarium: Phanerogams of Iran.
Specialization in research: Persian flora.

TEL AVIV: *Herbarium, Department of Botany, Tel Aviv University,* (**TELA**), 155 Herzl St., Tel Aviv, **Israel.**

TEMPE: *Herbarium, Department of Botany and Microbiology, Arizona State University,* (**ASU**), Tempe, Arizona 85281, **U.S.A.**
Telephone: 602/965-6162.
Foundation: ca. 1910. *Number of specimens:* 150.000.
Herbarium: Flora of southwestern U.S. and northern Mexico.
Important collections: F. M. Irish, C. G. Pringle.
Director: DONALD J. PINKAVA, 1933 (Biosystematics of Cactaceae, *Opuntia,* Compositae; floristics of southwestern U.S.).
Curator: THOMAS F. DANIEL, 1954 (Flora of Arizona; floristics of Mexico; systematics of Acanthaceae).
Staff members: JAMES E. CANRIGHT, 1920 (Paleobotany; palynology of southwestern U.S.; morphology, anatomy).
W. DENNIS CLARK, 1948 (Chemosystematics of Compositae, Cactaceae; plant-animal interactions).
ELINOR LEHTO, 1915 (Flora of Arizona; cultivated plants).
THOMAS H. NASH, III, 1945 (Lichens of Arizona and southwestern U.S.).
Specialization in research: As above.
Associated botanic garden: Desert Botanical Garden of Arizona, (**DES**), Phoenix, Arizona.
Loans: No special regulations.
Exchange: Available: Plants of southwestern U.S. and Mexico. Desired: Plants of New World; cultivated plants.

TEMPE: *Herbarium, Rocky Mountain Forest and Range Experiment Station, Forest Sciences Laboratory, Arizona State University,* (**ASUF**), Tempe, Arizona 85281, **U.S.A.**
Telephone: 602/261-4365.
Status: U.S. Department of Agriculture, Forest Service.
Foundation: 1930. *Number of specimens:* 9.000.
Herbarium: Flora of southwest U.S.
Important collections: F. Shreve, S. B. Parish; *Tamarix.*
Director: DAVID R. PATTON (Flora of Southwestern U.S.).
Staff members: JOHN H. DIETERICH (Fire ecology).
O. D. KNIPE (Range ecology).
ALVIN MEDINA (Remote vegetation sensing

and classification).
ROBERT C. SZARO (Riparian flora).
Loans: No special regulations.

TEMPLE: *Herbarium, Blackland Experiment Station,* (**TEXA**), P.O. Box 414, Temple, Texas 76501, **U.S.A.** -- incorporated at TAES, College Station.
Foundation: 1928. *Number of specimens:* 5.300.
Herbarium: Central Texas flora.
Important collections: Simon Wolff.

TENERIFE: *Jardin de Aclimatación de la Orotava,* (**ORT**) -- *see* PUERTO DE LA CRUZ.
Director: MANOEL ROBERTO DEL'ARCO, 1951
TENERIFE: *Departamento de Botánica, Facultad de Ciencias, Universidad de la Laguna,* (**TFC**) -- *see* LA LAGUNA.

TENERIFE: *Museo Insular de Ciencias Naturales de Tenerife,* (**TFMC**) -- *see* SANTA CRUZ DE TENERIFE.

TERESINA: *Herbário Graziela Barroso, Departamento de Biologia, Fundação Universidade Federal do Piauí,* (**TEPB**), 64.000 Teresina, Piauí, **Brazil.**
Telephone: (55)232-1212, ramal 289.
Foundation: 1977. *Number of specimens:* 1.300.
Herbarium: Mainly flora of Piauí, especially Leguminosae, Compositae, Euphorbiaceae.
Director: MANOEL ROBERTO DEL'ARCO, 1951 (Leguminosae, Euphorbiaceae).
Curator: ANTONIO ALBERTO JORGE FARIAS CASTRO, 1954 (Leguminosae, Euphorbiaceae).
Staff members: MARIA DAS GRAÇAS MEDINA ARRAIS, 1953 (Leguminosae, Passifloraceae).
BONIFÁCIO PIRES FLANKLIM, 1936 (Leguminosae).
FRANCISCO MAURICIO TELES FREIRE, 1952 (Leguminosae, Bromeliaceae).
ADI BRITO DE SOUSA, 1942 (Leguminosae, Compositae).
Specialization in research: Leguminosae, Compositae, Euphorbiaceae, Passifloraceae, Rubiaceae.
Exchange: Leguminosae, Compositae, Euphorbiaceae.

TERMINAL ISLAND: *California Department of Fish and Game, Marine Resources Operations,* (**TIC**), 511 Tuna Street, Terminal Island California 90731, **U.S.A.** -- discontinued.

TERRE HAUTE: *Herbarium, Life Science Department, Indiana State University,* (**TER**), 279 Science Building, Terre Haute, Indiana 47808, **U.S.A.**
Telephone: 812/232-6311, ext. 2498.
Foundation: 1961. *Number of specimens:* 10.000.
Herbarium: Emphasis on midwestern natural areas and national parks floras; vascular plants of west-central Indiana, Alaska tundra, Wyoming mountains, Crater Lake, Oregon, Mammoth Cave National Park;

283

Indiana and subtropical American non-vascular plants.

Director: MARION T. JACKSON, 1933 (Plant ecology).

Staff members: SARAH CLEVENGER, 1926 (Numerical taxonomy).

JEAN D. SCHOKNECHT, 1943 (Mycology).

WILLIAM WERT, 1921 (Botany; bryophytes).

Specialization in research: Floristics of Indiana natural areas and surface disturbed lands; semitropical and Indiana fungi.

THESSALONIKI: *Herbarium Universitatis Thessalonicensis, Aristotle University of Thessaloniki, Department of Systematic Botany and Phytogeography,* (**TAU**), Thessaloniki, **Greece.**

Telephone: 991-2403 and 991-2451.

Status: Department of Faculty of Sciences, University of Thessaloniki.

Foundation: 1945. *Number of specimens:* Over 6.000.

Important collections: Herbarium Macedonicum by D. Zaganiaris, Tountas herbarium (South Greece), D. Demades (Greek forest specimens), herb. of Mt. Athos by K. Ganiatsas, Th. Heldreich, Th. Orphanides.

Director: GEORGIOS LAVRENTIADES, 1920 (Plant taxonomy and sociology).

Curator: ELISSAEOS DROSSOS, 1934; 991-2457 (Plant taxonomy and sociology).

Staff members: GREGORIOS ALEXANDRIS, 1943 (Technician).

DIMITRIOS BABALONAS, 1944 (Plant taxonomy and sociology).

NIKOLAOS CHATZIS, 1944 (Technician).

ADAMOS EVANGELOU, 1953 (Technician).

BASILIKI KARAGIANNAKIDOU, 1946 (Plant taxonomy).

STELLA KOKKINI, 1953 (Plant taxonomy and cytotaxonomy).

HERAKLES PANAGIOTIDIS, 1945 (Technician).

KONSTANTINOS PANANIKOLAOU, 1947 (Plant taxonomy and cytotaxonomy).

GEORGIOS PAVLIDES, 1928 (Plant taxonomy and sociology).

DIMITRIOS VOLIOTIS, 1933 (Plant taxonomy and geography).

EUGENIA ZACHAROFF, 1950 (Plant taxonomy and cytotaxonomy).

Specialization in research: Plant taxonomy, sociology, geography, cytotaxonomy.

Loans: On request.

Exchange: On request.

Remarks: Many specimens in private collections of staff members.

THETFORD: *Herbarium, Ancient House Museum,* (**TRD**), Thetford, England, **Great Britain** – – incorporated in NWH.

THREE RIVERS: *Herbarium, Ash Mountain, Sequoia and Kings Canyon National Parks,* (**THRI**), Three Rivers, California 93271, **U.S.A.**

Status: U.S. Department of the Interior, National Park Service.

Number of specimens: 2.200.

Herbarium: Flora of Sequoia and Kings Canyon National Parks.

Staff member: JOHN PALMER.

THUNDER BAY: *Claude E. Garton Herbarium, Department of Biology, Lakehead University,* (**LKHD**), Thunder Bay, Ontario, **Canada** P7B 5E2.

Telephone: 807/345-2121, ext. 506.

Foundation: 1957. *Number of specimens:* 60.000.

Herbarium: Emphasis on boreal plants, augmented by general U.S., Canada, and Europe.

Important collections: C. E. Garton, S. T. Losee.

Director and Curator: C. E. GARTON, 1907 (Boreal plants).

Staff member: P. BARCLAY ESTERUP.

Specialization in research: Plants of Lake Superior.

TIANJIN: *Herbarium, Musée Hoark-Ho Pai-Ho,* (**TIE**), Race Course Road, Tianjin, **People's Republic of China.** (Information 1974)

Herbarium: Plants of northern China, Manchuria, Lower Tibet and Inner Mongolia.

TIENTSIN: – – see TIANJIN.

TIKKURILA: *Herbarium, Department of Plant Pathology, Agricultural Research Centre,* (**TIK**), Tikkurila, **Finland** – – incorporated in H and HPP.

TINGO MARÍA: *Herbario Tingo María, Universidad Nacional de la Selva,* (**HTIN**), Tingo María, Huánuco, **Peru.**

Foundation: 1977. *Number of specimens:* 4.000.

Herbarium: Flora of Tingo María.

Staff members: SALVADOR CRUZ (Ecology; economic plants).

JOSÉ LOAYZA (Economic plants).

Specialization in research: Tropical plants.

TIRUCHIRAPALLI: *The Rapinat Herbarium, St. Joseph's College,* (**RHT**), Tiruchirapalli 620002, Tamilnadu, **India.**

Telephone: 24070.

Status: Private foundation, affiliated to the University of Madras.

Foundation: 1967. *Number of specimens:* 60.000.

Herbarium: Local herbarium of flowering plants, ferns and mosses, plants of Great Britain.

Important collections: K. M. Matthew (mosses of Palni hills; plants of Kurseong, E. Himalayas; flora of Carnatic, South India; plants of Great Britain), C. A. Ninan and V. S. Manickam (ferns of Palni hills).

Director: K. M. MATTHEW, 1930 (Angiosperms,

especially *Mastixia*).

Curator: S. Mukunthakumar, 1957.

Keeper: V. S. Manickam, 1941 (Ferns).

Specialization in research: Flora of Carnatic, ferns of Palni hills.

Associated botanic garden: Anglade Institute of Natural History, Sacred Heart College, Shembaganur Kodaikanal 624104, Tamilnadu.

Loans: To reputable institutions.

Exchange: Available: Flowering plants and ferns of South India. Desired: Plants of Great Britain.

TOKYO: *Makino Herbarium, Tokyo Metropolitan University,* (**MAK**), 2-1 Fukasawa, Setagaya, Tokyo 158, **Japan.**

Status: University Faculty of Science.

Foundation: 1958. *Number of specimens:* 400.000.

Herbarium: Vascular plants, bryophytes and algae, mainly of Japan Archipelago.

Important collections: Tomitaro Makino (vascular plants), Kyuichi Sakurai (bryophytes), flora of Bonin Islands.

Director: Tsunekichi Shirao, 1924.

Deputy keeper: Mikio Ono, 1932 (Cytotaxonomy of flowering plants, island biology).

Staff members: Hideo Kasaki, 1917 (Algology).

Sumiko Kobayashi, 1922 (Flora of Japan, especially Bonin Islands).

Urara Mizushima, 1927 (Bryophytes).

Yasuichi Momiyama, 1904 (Flora of Japan, dendrology).

Michio Wakabayashi, 1942 (Flora of Japan, Saxifragaceae).

Specialization in research: Taxonomy and biosystematics of vascular plants, bryophytes and algae.

Loans: To recognized botanical institutions for 6 months.

Exchange: Available: Japanese vascular plants. Desired: Vascular plants of Southern Hemisphere.

TOKYO: *Herbarium, National Institute of Polar Research,* (**NIPR**), 9-10 Kaga 1-chome, Itabashi-ku, Tokyo 173, **Japan.**

Telephone: (03)962-4711.

Status: Government institution under the Ministry of Education, Science and Culture.

Foundation: 1974. *Number of specimens:* 30.000.

Herbarium: Mainly cryptogams of Polar regions.

Important collections: Tatsuro Matsuda (Bryaceae), Hiroshi Kanda (Amblystegiaceae).

Director and Head Curator: Tatsuro Matsuda (Terrestrial ecology).

Curator: Hiroshi Kanda (Bryophytes, lichens).

Staff members: Mitsuo Fukuchi (Marine ecology).

Takao Hoshiai (Marine ecology).

Yoshikuni Ohyama (Terrestrial ecology, physiology).

Kentaro Watanabe (Phycology).

Specialization in research: Flora of Antarctic and sub-Antarctic regions.

Loans: To recognized botanical institutions.

Periodical and serial works: Antarctic Record, Memoirs of National Institute of Polar Research, Series E.

Exchange: Available: Antarctic, sub-Antarctic and Japanese bryophytes. Desired: Bryophytes, lichens, marine algae, and higher plants, especially polar areas.

TOKYO: *Herbarium, Ochanomizu University,* (**OCHA**), Tokyo, **Japan.**

TOKYO: *Government Forest Experiment Station,* (**TF**) – – *see* KUKIZAKI.

TOKYO: *Laboratory of Forest Mycology, Government Forest Experiment Station,* (**TFM**), Shimomeguro-5, Meguro, Tokyo, **Japan.** (Information 1974)

Status: Directed by Ministry of Agriculture and Forestry.

Foundation: 1878. *Number of specimens:* 15.000.

Herbarium: Fungi of Japan.

Specialization in research: Fungus flora of Asia.

Associated botanic garden: Meguro Arboretum, Asakawa Arboretum.

Loans: To recognized botanical institutions.

Periodical and serial works: Bulletin of the Government Forest Experiment Station.

TOKYO: *The Laboratory of Plant Biology, University of Tokyo,* (**TH**) – – incorporated in TI.

TOKYO: *Herbarium, Botanic Gardens Koishikawa,* (**TI**), Hakusan 3-7-1, Bunkyo-ku, Tokyo 112, **Japan.**

Telephone: 03-814-0138.

Status: University of Tokyo.

Foundation: 1877. *Number of specimens:* 1.300.000.

Herbarium: World-wide, emphasizing vascular plants of Asia.

Important collections: R. Yatabe, S. Okubo, J. Matsumura, T. Makino, M. Miyoshi (flora of Japan), B. Hayata (Formosa, Indo-China), T. Nakai (Korea, Japan), Y. Yabe, M. Kitagawa (Manchuria), G. Nakahara (Kamtchatka), G. Koidzumi, T. Tuyama (Micronesia), H. Hara, H. Kanai, H. Ohashi (East Himalaya).

Curator: Hiroyoshi Ohashi, 1936 (Leguminosae, Araceae, flora of Japan and Himalaya).

Staff members: Jin Murata, 1952 (Araceae).

Hideaki Ohba, 1943 (Crassulaceae).

Yoichi Tateishi, 1948 (Leguminosae).

Takasi Yamazaki, 1921 (Scrophulariaceae).

Honorary staff members: Hiroshi Hara, 1911 (Nomenclature, flora of Japan and Himalaya).

Sachiko Kurosawa (Cytotaxonomy).

Yasuichi Momiyama, 1908 (Lauraceae).

Specialization in research: Vascular plants of Asia, mainly eastern Asia, China and eastern Himalaya.

Associated botanic garden: Branch garden: Botanic Garden Nikko, Tochigi Prefecture.

Loans: To recognized botanical institutions.

Periodical and serial works: Journal of the Faculty of Science, University of Tokyo, Sect. III Botany.

Exchange: Available: Asian plants.

Remarks: A branch of the herbarium is located in Department of Botany, The University Museum, University of Tokyo.

TOKYO: *Tokyo Kyoiku University*, (**TKU**) – – incorporated in TKB.

TOKYO: *Herbarium, National Science Museum,* (**TNS**), Department of Botany, 3-23-1 Hyakunin-cho, Shinjuku-ku, Tokyo 160, **Japan.**

Telephone: 03-364-2311.

Status: Government Institution under the Ministry of Education.

Foundation: 1877. *Number of specimens:* 540.000.

Herbarium: Worldwide, especially of eastern Asia, all groups.

Important collections: Y. Asahina (Lichens), A. Yasuda (Lichens, fungi), Y. Emoto (Myxomycetes), H. Sasaoka (Bryophytes), H. Koidzumi (Phanerogams), J. Ohwi (Phanerogams).

Director General of the Museum: SHIGERU FUKUDA, 1910.

Director of the Department of Botany: SYO KUROKAWA, 1926 (Lichens).

Curators: HIROSHI INOUE, 1932, Div. Cryptogams (Bryophytes).

HIROO KANAI, 1930, Div. Vascular Plants (Phytogeography).

YOSIO OTANI, 1919, Div. Micro-organisms (Microfungi).

Staff members: YOSHIMICHI DOI, 1939, Div. Cryptogams (Fungi).

HIROMITSU HAGIWARA, 1945, Div. Microorganisms (Acrasiales).

HIROYUKI KASHIWADANII, 1944, Div. Cryptogams (Lichens).

YUICHI KWADOTA, 1949, Div. Experimental Botany (Phanerogams).

TOSHYUKI NAKAIKE, 1943, Div. Vascular Plants (Pteridophytes).

TUGUO TATEOKA, 1931, Div. Experimental Botany (Cytology of Gramineae).

MASAYUKI WATANABE, 1941, Div. Microorganisms (Cyanophyceae).

FUMI YAMAUCHI, 1923, Div. Vascular Plants (Wood anatomy).

Specialization in research: Floras of eastern Asia and New Guinea.

Associated botanic garden: Tsukubu Botanical Garden, 4-1-1 Amakubo, Sakura-mura, Niiharigun, Ibaraki-ken 305, Japan.

Loans: In general to recognized botanical institutions.

Periodical and serial works: Bulletin, Memoirs, Miscellaneous Reports.

Exchange: Available: Exsiccatae of phanerogams, ferns, bryophytes, lichens. Desired: Phanerogams, ferns, bryophytes, fungi and lichens of world, especially Asia and Australia.

TOKYO: *Herbarium, Section of Forest Botany, University Museum, University of Tokyo,* (**TOFO**), Yayoi 1-1, Bunkyo-Ku, Tokyo 113, **Japan.**

Telephone: 03-812-2111, ext. 5209.

Status: University.

Foundation: 1928. *Number of specimens:* 42.000.

Herbarium: Worldwide collection of woody plants, ferns and wood-rotting fungi.

Important collections: T. Inokuma (woody plants of New Guinea), S. Kurata (Japanese ferns, including 200 types).

Director: TOSHIO HAMAYA, 1928 (Dendrology, Thymelaeaceae, plant distribution, forest tree improvement).

Staff members: SHIN'ICHIRO ITO, 1948 (Mycology).

TOSHIHIKO NAKAMURA, 1954 (Bryology).

MITUSO SUZUKI, 1947 (Plant anatomy, paleobotany).

Specialization in research: Japanese forest flora.

Loans: To recognized botanical institutions; holotypes not loaned.

Exchange: Available: Woody plants.

Remarks: The Laboratory of Forest Botany, Department of Forestry, at same address has a collection of 60.000 wood samples.

TOKYO: *Tokyo University of Education,* (**TOKE**) – – incorporated in TKB.

TOMSK: *P. N. Krilov Herbarium, Kuibyshev State University of Tomsk,* (**TK**), Leninskii Prospect 36, 634010 Tomsk, **U.S.S.R.**

Status: University.

Foundation: 1885. *Number of specimens:* 260.000.

Herbarium: Mainly plants of Siberia and other parts of U.S.S.R.; Asia, Europe and America.

Director: A. V. POLOZHIY.

Specialization in research: Siberian flora.

Periodical and serial works: Flora of West Siberia, Flora provincia Krassnojarsu, Flora transbaicalia, Systematic remarks on material of the P. N. Krylov Herbarium.

TORINO: *Museum Botanicum Horti Taurinensis,* (**TO**), c/o Istituto ed Orto Botanico dell' Università, Viale Mattioli 25, 10125 Torino, **Italy.**

Telephone: 011-659884.

Status: University.

Foundation: About 1750. *Number of specimens:* 500.000.

Herbarium: Worldwide collection, Piedmont area of N. Italy, cryptogams.

Important collections: Herbaria of L. Terraneo (pre-Linnaean), Palazzi, C. Allioni, C. A. L. Bellardi, and Moris; collections of C. G. L. Bertero, J. Casaretto, D. Lisa, A. A. Carestia, M. Anzi, P. A. Saccardo, F. Cavara, O. Mattirolo, Gola, Ceruti.

Director: FRANCO MONTACCHINI, 1938 (West alpine flora).

Curator: GIULIANA FORNERIS, 1946 (West alpine flora).

Staff member: ROSANNA PIERVITTORI, 1954 (Lichens).

Specialization in research: Distribution of critical or endemic species of West alpine flora.

Associated botanic garden: Hortus Botanicus Taurinensis.

Loans: No; photographs of specimens sent on request.

Exchange: Yes.

TORINO: *Herbarium, Istituto Missioni Consolata,* (**TOM**), Corso Ferrucci 14, 10138 Torino, **Italy.**

Telephone: (011) 446446.

Status: Private.

Foundation: 1908.

Important collections: Kenya, Ethiopia, Tanzania.

Curator: Rev. Fr. C. BENINTENDE IMC.

TORONTO: *Vascular Plant Herbarium, Department of Botany, University of Toronto,* (**TRT**), Toronto, Ontario, **Canada** M5S 1A1.

Telephone: 416/978-3542.

Foundation: 1838. *Number of specimens:* 210.000.

Herbarium: North America, especially eastern Canada and adjacent U.S.; some Europe and South America.

Curator: JAMES E. ECKENWALDER, 1949 (*Populus;* gymnosperms).

Specialization in research: Flora of Ontario; systematics of various plant genera.

Associated botanic garden: Glendon Hall Laboratory and Garden.

Loans: To recognized botanical institutions.

Periodical and serial works: Index Seminum (annual).

Exchange: Available: Ontario. Desired: Holarctic.

TORONTO: *Cryptogamic Herbarium, Department of Botany, University of Toronto,* (**TRTC**), Toronto, Ontario, **Canada** M5S 1A1.

Telephone: 416/978-3543.

Foundation: 1887. *Number of specimens:* 193.000 (147.000 fungi and lichens, 41.000 bryophytes, 5.000 algae).

Herbarium: Worldwide representation with north-temperate emphasis; large collection of coprophilous fungi.

Important collections: R. F. Cain, J. H. Faull, J. W. Groves, H. S. Jackson, E. A. Moxley; several important exsiccati.

Curator: DAVID MALLOCH, 1940 (Ecology of mycorrhizae; taxonomy of higher fungi).

Staff members: R. F. CAIN, 1906 (Taxonomy of higher fungi).

R. S. KHAN, 1936 (Taxonomy of coprophilous Ascomycetes).

J. C. KRUG, 1938 (Taxonomy of Ascomycetes).

Specialization in research: Taxonomy and ecology of Agaricales and Ascomycetes.

Loans: To recognized institutions for 6 months.

Exchange: Fungi, lichens, mosses, and hepatics, mostly Canadian, but some tropical.

TORONTO: *Erindale College, University of Toronto,* (**TRTE**) – –see MISSISSAUGA.

TORONTO: *Herbarium, Botany Department, Scarborough College, University of Toronto,* (**TRTS**), West Hill, Ontario, **Canada** M1C 1A4 – – discontinued.

TORONTO: *Herbarium, Department of Biology, York University,* (**YUTO**), Toronto, Ontario, **Canada.**

TORQUAY: *Herbarium, Torquay Natural History Society,* (**TOR**), The Museum, Babbacombe Road, Torquay, Devon, **Great Britain.**

Telephone: 0803-23975.

Status: Private society.

Foundation: 1874. *Number of specimens:* 17.500.

Herbarium: County collection, other British material, predominantly Spermatophyta.

Important collections: E. Parfitt, Cunningham, Williams, G. T. Fraser, F. M. Day, C. F. Vincent, Rev. T. Stephenson (p.p.).

Director: Curator of the Torquay Natural History Museum (Non botanist).

Loans: None. Material can be studied on the premises.

Exchange: None.

Remarks: For specialist enquiries contact: D. Bolton, Asst. Curator of Natural History, RAMM, Queen Street, Exeter, Devon, England.

TORÚN: *Department of Plant Systematics and Geography, Copernicus University,* (**TRN**), Gagarina 9, 87-100 Torún, **Poland.** (Information 1974)

Status: University.

Foundation: 1946. *Number of specimens:* 180.000.

Herbarium: Flora of Poland, Europe and world.

Specialization in research: Flora of North Poland.

TOULON: *Herbarium, Musée d'Histoire Naturelle de la Ville de Toulon,* (**TLON**), Toulon (Var), **France.** (Information 1974).

Herbarium: Plants of Var.

TOULOUSE: *Laboratoire de Botanique, Université Paul Sabatier,* (**TL**), 39 Allées Jules Guesde, 31077 Toulouse Cedex, **France.**

Telephone: (61) 53-02-35 poste 26.
Status: University.
Foundation: Ca. 1850. *Number of specimens:* 270.000.
Herbarium: Angiosperms (various regions), regional angiosperms (neighboring regions of Toulouse and the Pyrenees), herbier Gaussen, gymnosperms.
Important collections: Herbier Timbal-Lagrave (France, region of Toulouse), herbier C. Duffour (France), herbier Lagrèze-Fossat (France, Switzerland), herbier Picot de Lapeyrouse (on loan in Lab. de Biologie Végétale: Prof. Leredde).
> *Director:* A. BAUDIÈRE, 1932 (Biogeography).
> *Curator:* M. SAINT-MARTIN, 1938.
> *Staff members:* M. L. ROUANE, 1936 (Lab. forestier, gymnosperm herbarium).
>> M. VASSAL, 1932 (Mimosoideae).
> *Specialization in research:* Fundamental and applied botany, morphology, anatomy, biogeography, biosystematics.
> *Loans:* For three months, except types.

TOULOUSE: *Laboratoire de Cryptogamie, Université Paul Sabatier (Sciences)*, (**TLA**), 118 route de Narbonne, 31077 Toulouse Cedex (Haute Garonne), **France.** (Information 1974)
Status: University.
Herbarium: Fungi.
Specialization in research: Southwestern France, Pyrenees.

TOULOUSE: *Laboratoire Forestier de Toulouse, Faculté des Sciences,* (**TLF**), Toulouse (Haute Garonne), **France.** (Information 1974)
Status: University.
Foundation: 1928. *Number of specimens:* 2.000.
Herbarium: Coniferae.
Specialization in research: Dendrology.
> *Associated botanic garden:* Arboretum de Jouéou, 31 Luchon.
> *Periodical and serial works:* Travaux de Laboratoire forestier de Toulouse.

TOULOUSE: *Herbarium, Jardin Botanique,* (**TLJ**), Toulouse (Haute Garonne), **France.** (Information 1974)
Status: University.
Important collections: Herbarium Picot de Lapeyrouse.

TOULOUSE: *Museum d'Histoire Naturelle de Toulouse,* (**TLM**), Toulouse (Haute Garonne), **France.** (Information 1974)
Status: Municipal museum.
Foundation: 1794. *Number of specimens:* 60.000.
Herbarium: Plants of Western Europe and North Africa.

TOULOUSE: *Chaire de Botanique, Faculté de Medecine,* (**TLP**), Toulouse (Haute Garonne), **France.**

(Information 1974)
Herbarium: Regional plants.

TOWNSVILLE: *Herbarium, Australian Institute of Marine Science,* (**AIMS**), Cape Ferguson, PMB 3, Townsville, M.S.O., Queensland, **Australia.**
Telephone: 077 789211.
Status: Australian Government Statutory Authority.
Foundation: 1974. *Number of specimens:* 2.000.
Herbarium: Specializes in tidal forest (mangrove) flora of the Australia east coast and southern New Guinea, local collections of sea grasses.
> *Director of A.I.M.S.:* J. S. BUNT (Marine productivity, ecology).
> *Curator:* N. C. DUKE, 789373 (Tidal forest flora, expecially *Rhizophora* and *Sonneratia,* ecology).
> *Staff member:* K. M. ABEL (Sea grass flora, physiology).
> *Specialization in research:* Taxonomy and ecology of the tidal forest flora.
> *Loans:* To recognized investigators by arrangement.
> *Exchange:* Available within support constraints.

TOWNSVILLE: *Botany Department, James Cook University of North Queensland,* (**JCT**), Post Office 4811, Townsville, Queensland, **Australia.**
Telephone: 077814121.
Status: University.
Foundation: 1961. *Number of specimens:* 14.000.
Herbarium: Mainly tropical Queensland.
> *Curator:* BETSY R. JACKES, 1935 (Systematics, Vitaceae).
> *Staff members:* WILLIAM R. BIRCH, 1922 (Marine angiosperms).
>> IAN R. PRICE, 1940 (Algae).
>> WARREN A. SHIPTON, 1940 (Fungi).
> *Specialization in research:* Flora of Tropical Australia.
> *Loans:* In general to recognized botanical institutions.
> *Exchange:* Available: Vascular plants and marine algae of tropical Queensland. Desired: Marine algae Indo-Pacific region.

TRABZON: *Karadeniz Teknik Üniversitesi Orman Fakültesi Herbaryumu,* (**KATO**), Karadeniz Teknik Üniversitesi, Orman Fakültesi, Orman Botaniği Kürsüsü, Trabzon, **Turkey.**
Status: Karadeniz Technical University, Trabzon.
Foundation: 1973. *Number of specimens:* 6.000.
Herbarium: North-East Anatolia.
Important collections: R. Anşin, N. Merev.
> *Curator:* RAHIM ANŞIN (Flora and vegetation of North-East Anatolia).
> *Staff members:* ZIYA GERÇEK (Anatomy of *Camellia sinensis*).
>> NESIME MEREV (Anatomy of *Alnus* and woody plants of North-East Anatolia).

Specialization in research: Flora and vegetation of North-East Anatolia; anatomy of woody plants of North-East Anatolia.

Loans: In general to recognized institutes and herbaria.

Exchange: Available: some duplicates of North-East Anatolian woody plants. Desired: Woody plants of Mediterranean area.

TŘEBÍČ: *Západomoravské muzeum v Třebíči,* (**ZMT**), Zámek 1, 674 01 Třebíč, **Czechoslovakia.**

Telephone: 2518.

Status: Directed by District National Committee.

Foundation: 1898. *Number of specimens:* 31.000 (26.900 pteridophytes and spermatophytes, 4.100 algae, fungi and lichens).

Herbarium: Plants of southwest Moravia.

Director: Jiří Uhlíř, 1932.

Curator: Svatava Ondráčková, 1936 (Floristics).

Periodical and serial works: Sborník Přírodovědeckého Klubu při Západomoravském muzeu v Třebíči.

TRENČÍN: *Herbarium Trenčianske múzeum* (**TRE**), Mierové nám. 46, Trenčín, **Czechoslovakia.**

Telephone: 4509.

Foundation: 1877. *Number of specimens:* 5.000.

Herbarium: Plants of Czechoslovakia.

Director: Pavol Moško, 1949.

Curator: Mária Mitterová, 1946 (Floristics).

Specialization in research: Floristics.

TRENTO: *Herbarium, Museo Tridentino di Scienze Naturali,* (**TR**), Trento, **Italy.** (Information 1974)

Status: Directed by Province.

Foundation: 1774. *Number of specimens:* 30.000.

Herbarium: Flora of Italy and Europe.

Important collections: Gustavo Venturi (bryophytes), F. Ambrosi, G. Bresadola, F. Facchini, E. Gelmi.

Associated botanic garden: Giardino botanico sul Monte Bondone.

Loans: To recognized botanical institutions.

Periodical and serial works: Studi Trentini di Scienze Naturali, Memorie del Museo di Storia Naturale.

TRIESTE: *Istituto ed Orto Botanico dell'Università,* (**TSB**), Via A. Valerio 30, Casella Università I-34100 Trieste, **Italy.**

Telephone: (040) 574182/574183.

Status: University.

Foundation: 1960. *Number of specimens:* 110.000.

Herbarium: Alps, Mediterranean flora, N. America, Japan; algae, musci, lichens.

Important collections: Pignatti (flora d'Italia).

Director: S. Pignatti, 1930 (Mediterranean flora, taxonomy of *Limonium*, plant sociology, data-bank of the Italian flora).

Staff members: G. Bressan, 1944 (Calcareous algae).

L. Chiapella Feoli, 1945 (Flora of the Apennines and Alps).

G. Cristofolini, 1939 (Ecology, serotaxonomy – chiefly Genisteae).

T. Cusma, 1947 (Cytotaxonomy).

E. Feoli, 1947 (Ecology, *Euphrasia*).

E. Honsell, 1921 (Chemotaxonomy of Rhodophyta).

D. Lausi, 1923 (Ecology, cytotaxonomy, flora of Yukon).

P. Nimis, 1953 (Lichens).

E. Pignatti-Wikus, 1929 (Plant sociology of the Alps).

L. Poldini, 1930 (Geobotany, flora of Southeastern Alps).

L. Rizzi Longo, 1939 (Algae).

G. Sauli, 1946 (Musci).

Specialization in research: Flora of Italy, plant sociology of phanerogams, marine algae and lichens; serotaxonomy, cytotaxonomy, chemotaxonomy, numerical taxonomy.

Associated botanic garden: Orto Botanico dell'Università.

Loans: To recognized institutions.

Periodical and serial works: Pubblicazioni dell'Istituto di Botanica di Trieste (1962), Nova Thalassia (1968).

Exchange: Available: Flora of Italy. Desired: *Limonium,* marine algae, lichens.

TRIESTE: *Herbarium, Civico Museo de Storia Naturale,* (**TSM**), Direz. Piazza Hortis 4, 34100 Trieste, **Italy.**

Status: Comune di Trieste.

Foundation: 1846. *Number of specimens:* 100.000.

Important collections: Herbaria di Tommasini, Pospichal, Zirnich; collections of Patria.

Director: Renato Mezzena, 1922 (Botany).

Staff members: Sergio Cok.

Giovanni Gerdol.

Guiseppe Gherdina.

Pietro Moratto.

TRINIDAD: *National Herbarium of Trinidad and Tobago, University of the West Indies,* (**TRIN**) – – see SAINT AUGUSTINE.

TRIPOLI: *Herbarium, Faculty of Science, Al-Faateh University,* (**ULT**), Tripoli, **Libya.**

Telephone: 39107/2489.

Status: Government.

Foundation: 1966. *Number of specimens:* 30.000.

Important collections: S. A. Alavi, S. I. Ali, L. Boulus, P. H. Davis, A. El-Gadi, S. A. Faruqi, S. M. H. Jafri, M. M. Khalifa, R. M. Labani, F. B. Rateeb, M. A. Siddiqi.

Director: A. El-Gadi (Liliaceae, Alliaceae).

Curator: M. A. Siddiqi (Cultivated plants).

Staff members: S. A. ALAVI (Compositae).
A. EL-TAIFE (Polygonaceae).
S. A. FARUQI (Gramineae).
S. M. H. JAFRI (Brassicaceae, Capparidaceae).
R. M. LABANI (Amaryllidaceae).
M. QAISER (Tamaricaceae).
F. B. RATEEB (Chenopodiaceae).
Specialization in research: Flora of Libya and N. Africa (Morocco to Egypt).
Periodical and serial works: Flora of Libya.
Exchange: Available: Plants of Libya and N. African countries. Desired: Plants of other countries and periodicals.
Remarks: Herbarium temporarily housed in Faculty of Science while a new building is under construction.

TROIS-RIVIÈRES: *Herbarium, Département Chimie-Biologie, Université du Québec à Trois-Rivières,* (**UQTR**), Case postale 500, Trois-Rivières, Québec, **Canada** G9A 5H7.
Telephone: 819/376-5641.
Number of specimens: 5.500.
Herbarium: Québec.
Director and Curator: ESTELLE LACOURSIÈRE, 1935 (Plant ecology).
Specialization in research: Aquatic and semi-aquatic habitats; plant communities.

TROMSOE: *Botanical Department of Tromsoe Museum, Institute of Museum Science, University of Tromsoe,* (**TROM**), 9000 Tromsoe, **Norway.**
Telephone: 083/86080.
Status: University.
Foundation: 1882 (Museum in 1872). *Number of specimens:* 150.000 (Phanerogams 110.000, mosses 15.000, lichens 10.000, fungi 14.000, algae 1.000).
Herbarium: Scandinavian herbarium, arctic and general herbarium, cryptogams.
Curator: OLA SKIFTE, 1923 (fungi, plant geography).
BRYNHILD VORREN, 1943 (Vascular plants, palynology, plant geography).
Staff members: ALFRED GRANMO, 1944 (Fungi, Ascomycetes).
HARALD MEHUS, 1942 (Norwegian vascular flora, teaching).
Specialization in research: Flora of Northern Norway and adjacent arctic regions.
Loans: In general to botanical institutions or to persons connected with such institutions.
Periodical and serial works: Acta borealia a. Scientia, Astarte, Tromura.
Exchange: Available: North Norwegian phanerogams, mosses, lichens, and fungi. Desired: Specimens from all groups.

TRONDHEIM: *Botanical Department, Museum of the Royal Norwegian Society for Science and Letters,* (**TRH**), Erling Skakkes gt. 47, N-7000 Trondheim, **Norway.**

Telephone: (075)92260.
Status: University of Trondheim.
Foundation: 1760. *Number of specimens:* 368.000 (vascular plants 210.000, bryophyta 120.000, lichens 20.000, fungi 10.000, algae 8.000).
Herbarium: Worldwide, emphasis on Central Norway.
Important collections: M. Foslie (Calcareous algae), I. Hagen (Bryophyta), O. Gjaerevoll (Vascular plants of Alaska), O. A. Høeg (Macrolichens and fungi of South Africa), J. E. Gunnerus (Herbarium norvegicum).
Director: O. GJAEREVOLL, 1916 (Flora of the Scandes, flora of Alaska; plant geography, plant sociology, nature conservation).
Curators: K. I. FLATBERG, 1943, *Sphagnum* and extra Nordic vascular plants (Mire vegetation; *Sphagnum* and Cyperaceae).
A. A. FRISVOLL, 1944, Bryophyta excl. *Sphagnum,* and Nordic vascular plants.
S. SIVERTSEN, 1929, Algae, fungi and lichens (Fungi, flora of the Scandes).
Staff members: E. I. AUNE, 1945 (Forest vegetation, vegetation mapping, nature conservation).
S. BRETTEN, 1940, Keeper of the alpine Kongsvoll Biological Station (*Draba,* nature conservation).
J. HOLTEN, 1946 (Plant geography).
O. KJAEREM, 1946 (Remote vegetational analysis, vegetation mapping).
A. MOEN, 1944 (Vegetation mapping, flora and vegetation of mires, nature conservation).
B. SAETHER, 1947 (Aquatic vegetation, nature conservation of river systems).
Specialization in research: Flora and vegetation of Central Norway, vegetation mapping.
Associated botanic garden: Ringve Botanical Garden, N-7000 Trondheim, Norway.
Loans: In general to recognized institutions and associated workers.
Periodical and serial works: Gunneria (formerly Miscellanea, in English or Norwegian with an English summary); Rapport, Botanisk serie (generally in Norwegian).
Exchange: Available: A limited supply of calcareous algae, and Scandinavian, especially alpine plants (including some cryptogams). Desired: Arctic and boreal vascular plants and bryophyta, Mediterranean vascular plants.

TROY: *Herbarium, Department of Biological Sciences, Troy State University,* (**TROY**), Troy, Alabama 36081, **U.S.A.**
Telephone: 205/566-3000, ext. 405.
Foundation: 1976. *Number of specimens:* 3.500.
Herbarium: Local.
Director and Curator: ROBERT A. DIETZ, 1922 (Population genetics).
Loans: Usual regulations.

TRUJILLO: *Herbarium Truxillense, Universidad Nacional de Trujillo,* (**HUT**), Calle San Martin 392, Trujillo, **Peru.**
Telephone: 23-5841.
Foundation: 1941. *Number of specimens:* 18.000.
Herbarium: Peru, especially the northern part; some specimens from Argentina and the U.S.A.
Important collections: Compositae, Gramineae, Leguminosae, Bromeliaceae, Orchidaceae, ferns.
Director: ARNALDO LÓPEZ MIRANDA, 1922 (Medicinal plants of Peru).
Curator: ABUNDIO SAGÁSTEGUI ALVA, 1932 (Peruvian Compositae; phytogeography of Peru).
Specialization in research: Flora of the northern part of Peru.
Loans: To recognized institutions and specialists.
Exchange: Compositae of South America.

TRURO: *Herbarium, Nova Scotia Agricultural College,* (**NSAC**), Box 550, Truro, Nova Scotia, **Canada** B2N 2V5.
Telephone: 902/895-1571.
Foundation: 1946. *Number of specimens:* 10.000.
Herbarium: Atlantic provinces of Canada, emphasizing Nova Scotia.
Curator: R. K. PRANGE, 1951 (Biology of *Matteuccia*).
Specialization in research: Flora of Nova Scotia.
Loans: To recognized botanical institutions.

TRUTNOV: *Herbarium, Vlastivědné muzeum Trutnov,* (**TRM**), Trutnov, **Czechoslovakia.** (Information 1974)
Foundation: 1890. *Number of specimens:* 6.000.
Herbarium: Tracheophyta of Europe and Czechoslovakia.
Specialization in research: Taxonomy and bryophytes.
Loans: To recognized botanical institutions.

TSINAN: – –*see* JINAN.

TSINGTAO: – – *see* QINGDAO.

TSUDANUMA: *Herbarium, Toho University,* (**TOHO**), Tsudanuma, Chiba, **Japan.**

TSUKABA: *Herbarium, Institute of Biological Sciences, University of Tsukuba,* (**TKB**), Sakura-mura, Niihari-gun, Ibaraki, 305 **Japan.**
Telephone: 0298(53) 4533 or 6655.
Status: University.
Foundation: 1974. *Number of specimens:* 52.000.
Herbarium: Mainly pteridophytes of Japan, some vascular plants, algae and fungi.
Director: MITSUO CHIHARA, 1927 (Taxonomy of algae).
Curator: SIGERU DAIGOBO, 1941 (Taxonomy of pteridophytes).
Staff members: YOSHIAKI HARA, 1944 (Algal ul-

trastructure and classification).
KEISUKE TUBAKI, 1924 (Taxonomy of fungi).
Loans: To recognized botanical institutions.
Exchange: Available: Algae, fungi and ferns of Japan.
Remarks: All specimens of Tokyo Kyoiku University (TKU) and Tokyo University of Education (TOKE) were incorporated into this herbarium in 1974.

TSU SHI: *Botanical Institute, Miye University,* (**TSU**), Kamihama Cho, Tsu Shi, Miye Ken, **Japan.** (Information 1974)
Status: University.
Foundation: 1921. *Number of specimens:* 5.000.
Herbarium: Trees of Japan.
Specialization in research: Subalpine forest flora of Japan, forest flora of southern Japan.
Associated botanic garden: Botanic Garden of the Miye University.
Periodical and serial works: Bulletin of the Miye University Forest, Research Data of the Miye University Forest.

TÜBINGEN: *Herbarium, Institut für Biologie I, Lehrstuhl spezielle Botanik,* (**TUB**), Auf der Morganstelle I, D-7400 Tübingen, **Federal Republic of Germany,** BRD. (Information 1974)
Status: University.
Foundation: 1847. *Number of specimens:* 97.000.
Herbarium: Bryophytes, pteridophytes and phanerogams, mainly Central Europe.
Important collections: Josef Gaertner (fruits and seeds), herbarium Karl Friedrich Gaertner, herb. C. F. Hochstetter, G. H. W. Schimper (Iter abesynicum).
Associated botanic garden: Botanischer Garten Tübingen.

TUCSON: *Herbarium, University of Arizona,* (**ARIZ**), 113 Agricultural Sciences Building, Tucson, Arizona 85721, **U.S.A.**
Telephone: 602/626-2109.
Status: University of Arizona, College of Agriculture.
Foundation: 1891. *Number of specimens:* 275.000.
Herbarium: Southwestern U.S., Arizona, Mexico mosses, ferns, seed plants; wood-rotting fungi, rusts, and Arizona fungi.
Important collections: Forrest Shreve (Mexico and southwestern deserts); herbarium of T. H. Kearney and R. H. Peebles, authors of the "Arizona Flora"; Henry Greene (midwestern parasitic fungi); George Cummins (southwestern rusts); R. L. Gilbertson (wood-rotting fungi).
Curators: CHARLES T. MASON, JR. (Limnanthaceae, Gentianaceae).
ROBERT L. GILBERTSON; 602/626-3113 (Wood-rotting fungi).
Staff members: GEORGE CUMMINS (Rust fungi).
CHARLOTTE REEDER (Grasses).

JOHN REEDER (Grasses).
Specialization in research: Flora of southwestern U.S. and adjacent Mexico.
Associated botanic garden: Boyce-Thompson Southwestern Arboretum, Superior, Arizona.
Loans: In general to recognized botanical institutions.
Exchange: Available: Specimens from Arizona. Desired: Specimens from all groups, especially from Mexico, South and Central America.

TUCSON: *Herbarium, Department of Ecology and Evolutionary Biology, University of Arizona,* (**TUC**), Tucson, Arizona 85721, **U.S.A.**
Telephone: 602/626-2364.
Foundation: 1961. *Number of specimens:* 1.500.
Herbarium: U.S. and Mexico, specializing in the Gulf of California.
Curator: ROBERT W. HOSHAW (Algae).
Specialization in research: Gulf of California algae.
Loans: Very limited.

TUCUMÁN: *Fundación e Instituto Miguel Lillo,* (**LIL**) – – *see* SAN MIGUEL DE TUCUMÁN.

TULSA: *Herbarium, Department of Natural Sciences, University of Tulsa,* (**TULS**), 600 South College, Tulsa, Oklahoma 74104, **U.S.A.**
Telephone: 918/592-6000, ext. 204.
Foundation: 1907. *Number of specimens:* 10.000.
Herbarium: Plants of Oklahoma.
Director and Curator: PAUL BUCK, 1927 (Terrestrial plant ecology).
Loans: To established herbaria.

TULUA: *Herbario Jardín Botánico "Juan María Céspedes,"* (**TULV**), Apartado Aéreo 5660, Cali, Valle, **Colombia.**
Status: Directed by Instituto Vallecaucano de Investigaciones Científicas INCIVA, Gobernación del Valle.
Foundation: 1978. *Number of specimens:* 4.000.
Director: VÍCTOR MANUEL PATIÑO (Economic botany).
Staff members: MANUEL BORRERO.
HERMES CUADROS V.
Publications: Cespedesia.

TUNIS: *Laboratoire de Biologie Végétale, Faculté des Sciences, Université de Tunis,* (**TUN**), 8 Rue de Rome, Tunis, **Tunisia.** (Information 1974)
Status: Directed by state.
Foundation: 1949. *Number of specimens:* 5.000.
Herbarium: Phanerogams of Tunis.
Specialization in research: Flora of North Africa.
Loans: To recognized botanical institutions.

TUNJA: *Herbario, Departamento de Biología, Universidad Pedagógica y Técnológica de Colombia,*

(**UPTC**), Apartado Aéreo 1069, Tunja, Boyacá, **Colombia.**
Telephone: (57)2174, ext. 57.
Foundation: 1970. *Number of specimens:* 8.000.
Herbarium: Flora of Boyacá; tropical and tropical mountain vegetation; paramo vegetation.
Director: RAFAEL GUARIN-MONTOYA, 1920 (Biology).
Curator: MARDOQUEO VILLARREAL-VELANDIA, 1926 (Botany).
Staff member: RAFAEL CASTILLO-PINILLA, 1939 (Botany).
Specialization in research: Agronomy; biochemistry.
Exchange: Yes, to institutions with similar interest.

TURKU: *Herbarium, Institute of Biology, University of Turku,* (**TUR**), SF-20500 Turku 50, **Finland.**
Telephone: SF-921/645567.
Status: Institute of the State University.
Foundation: 1919. *Number of specimens:* 500.000.
Herbarium: Worldwide, emphasis on Holarctic flora.
Important collections: Herb. Vainio: a separate worldwide lichen collection of 35.000 specimens (TUR-V).
Director: Director of the Institute.
Curator: Vacant.
Staff members: UNTO LAINE (Fennoscandian flora).
TERTTU LEMPIÄINEN (Cytogenetics and taxonomy, *Filipendula*).
Associate research workers: REINO ALAVA, Curator Emeritus (Taxonomy of Umbelliferae, Tordyliinae).
SAKARI HINNERI (Finnish archipelago flora, bryophytes).
PAAVO KALLIO, Professor Emeritus (Macrofungi, desmids).
YRJÖ MÄKINEN (Microfungi).
JAAKKO NURMI, Amanuensis of the Botanical Garden (Cytogenetics and taxonomy, *Campanula rotundifolia*-complex).
ORVOKKI RAVANKO (Cytogenetics and taxonomy, *Chara*, Dictyosiphonales s. lat., Ericaceae).
ARNE ROUSI (Cytogenetics and taxonomy, Elaeagnaceae, *Taraxacum*).
TERHO VALANNE (Cytotaxonomy, *Betula*).
MATTI YLI-REKOLA (Numerical taxonomy, variation of *Polytrichastrum alpinum*).
Specialization in research: Arctic and boreal areas.
Associated botanic garden: Botanical Garden of the University of Turku.
Loans: In general to recognized botanical institutions.
Periodical and serial works: Fungi Exsiccati Fennici.

Exchange: Available: Specimens of all groups, mainly from Fennoscandia. Desired: Vascular plants, especially from Holarctic area; other groups from any area.

TURKU (ÅBO): *Herbarium, Institute of Biology, Åbo Akademi,* (**TURA**), Porthansg. 3, SF-20500 Turku 50, **Finland.**

Telephone: 921-335133.

Status: Directed by the Åbo Akademi (a private university).

Foundation: Natural history collections 1930, Institute 1948. *Number of specimens:* 140.000.

Herbarium: Herbarium general, herbarium fennoscandicum.

Director: Bo-Jungar Wikgren, 1927 (Fish parasitology, platyhelminths).

Curator: Henrik Skult, 1923 (Plant cytology, lichenology).

Loans: For a period of 2 months.

TURLOCK: *Stanislaus Herbarium, California State College, Stanislaus,* (**SHTC**), 800 Monte Vista Avenue, Turlock, California 95380, **U.S.A.**

Telephone: 209/633-2122; 633-2489; 633-2476.

Foundation: 1965. *Number of specimens:* 1.000 (740 vascular plants, 120 algae, 140 fungi).

Director: Steve J. Grillos, 1928 (Comparative morphology of higher plants; systematics of ferns, fern allies, and flowering plants).

Staff member: David M. Gotelli (Electron microscopy; biology of lower plants).

TURRIALBA: *Herbario, Centro Agronómico Tropical de Investigación y Enseñanza,* (**CATIE**), Turrialba, **Costa Rica** – – on extended loan to CR and USJ, San José.

Telephone: 56-01-22; 56-01-69.

Number of specimens: 20.000.

Herbarium: Costa Rica phanerogams; economically important tropical crops.

TUXTLA GUTIÉRREZ: *Herbario, Instituto de Historia Natural del Estado de Chiapas,* (**CHIP**), Parque Francisco I. Madero, Apartado postal 6, Tuxtla Gutiérrez, Chiapas, **Mexico.** (Information 1976)

Foundation: 1949. *Number of specimens:* 1.000.

Herbarium: Flora of Chiapas.

Important collections: F. Miranda.

Remarks: Formerly listed as Instituto Botánico de Chiapas, Chiapas.

U

UDINE: *Herbarium, Museo Friulano di Storia Naturale,* (**MFU**), Palazzo Giacomelli, via Grazzano 1, 1-33100 Udine, **Italy.**
Telephone: 0432-293821.
Status: City of Udine.
Foundation: 1866. *Number of specimens:* 50.000.
Herbarium: Plants of Friuli-Venezia Giulia (NE Italy).
Important collections: Herbarium L. and M. Gortani.
   Director: CARLO MORANDINI, 1944.
   Curator: FABRIZIO MARTINI, 1949.
   Staff member: MERCEDES PONTONI.
   Specialization in research: Flora and vegetation of Friuli-Venezia Giulia.
   Periodical and serial works: Gortania (Atti del Museo Friulano di Storia Naturale).

UEDA: *Biological Institute and Herbarium, Shinshu University,* (**SHIN**), Ueda, Nagana Prefecture, **Japan.**
– – *see* MATSUMOTO.

ULAN-BATOR: *Herbarium, Botanical Institute of the Academy of Sciences of the M.P.R.,* (**UBA**), Marshall Zhukov Street, Ulan-Bator, **Mongolian People's Republic.**
Telephone: 51837.
Status: Directed by Academy of Sciences.
Foundation: 1974. *Number of specimens:* 100.000.
Herbarium: Flora of Mongolian People's Republic, Central Asia and South Siberia.
Important collections: Vascular plants: D. Banzragch, B. Dashnyam, T. Davazhamts, V. I. Grubov, Z. V. Karamysheva, E. I. Rachkovskaya, C. Sanchir, W. Ulziykhutag, A. A. Yunatov; fungi: T. Puntsag; algae: D. Tsetsegma; bryophytes: T. Tsegmed; lichens: U. Tsogt.
   Director: W. ULZIYKHUTAG, 1938 (Flora of Mongolia, Fabaceae: *Oxytropis, Thymus,* botanical terminology).
   Curator: C. SANCHIR, 1940 (Flora of Mongolia, Brassicaceae, *Stipa, Caragana*).
   Staff members: C. DARIYMA, 1948 (Vascular plants, especially *Artemisia*).
   B. DASHNYAM, 1929 (Flora of eastern Mongolia, geobotany).
   E. GANBOLD, 1945 (Flora of Changai mountains).
   T. TSEGMED, 1946 (Bryology).
   P. TSEPLE, 1938 (Geography).
   D. TSETSEGMA, 1953 (Algology).
   U. TSOGT, 1940 (Lichens).
   G. URANCHIMEG, 1938 (Saprophytic fungi).
   Specialization in research: Vascular flora of Mongolian People's Republic and Central Asia; systematics of algae, fungi and lichens.

Associated botanic garden: Botanic Garden of the Institute of Botany.
Loans: To recognized botanical institutions.
Periodical and serial works: Proceedings of the Institute of Botany, Flora and Vegetation of the Mongolian People's Republic.
Exchange: Available: Plants of Mongolian People's Republic and Central Asia. Desired: Specimens of *Caragana, Oxytropis* and *Astragalus.*

ULAN-BATOR: *Department of Botany, Mongolian State University,* (**UBU**), Ulan-Bator, **Mongolian People's Republic.**
   Director: T. ZHAMSRAN.

UMEÅ: *Avdelningen för ekologisk botanik, Biologiska institutionen, Umeå universitet,* (**UME**), 901 87 Umeå, **Sweden.** (Information 1974)
Status: University.
Foundation: 1967. *Number of specimens:* 50.000.
Herbarium: Vascular plants from Europe, North America and Macronesia; bryophytes, lichens and fungi from Europe.
   Specialization in research: Northern Swedish flora.
   Loans: To recognized botanical institutions.

UMTALI: *Chase Herbarium, Umtali Museum,* (**UMT**), Victory Avenue, Umtali, **Zimbabwe.**
Telephone: 63630.
Status: Small reference collection at Museum.
Foundation: 1963. *Number of specimens:* 1.200.
Herbarium: Mainly plants of the Manicaland Province, Zimbabwe.
   Director of museum: P. G. LOCKE.
   Remarks: The Chase Herbarium contains duplicates of local flora from the National Herbarium of Zimbabwe (SRGH). The Museum does not have a botanist on its staff and the collection is curated in an honorary capacity by members of the Manicaland Botanical Society.

UNIVERSITY: *Mohr Herbarium, Alabama Museum of Natural History,* (**ALU**), University, Alabama 35486, **U.S.A.** -- on permanent loan to UNA, University.
Telephone: 205/348-5960.
Status: State museum.
Foundation: Herbarium ca. 1873, Museum ca. 1926.
Number of specimens: 2.500.
Herbarium: Primarily flora of Alabama.
Important collections: Charles Mohr, T. M. Peters (fungi).
   Director and Curator: ROBERT R. HAYNES, 1945 (Systematics of aquatic vascular plants, especially the Alismatidae).

Specialization in research: Flora of Alabama.
Loans: To recognized botanical institutions.
Periodical and serial works: Bulletin of the Alabama Museum of Natural History.
Remarks: The collection is kept chiefly as a record of Dr. Mohr's work, to substantiate his *Plant Life of Alabama*, published in 1901. No specimens are being added to it.

UNIVERSITY: *Herbarium, Biology Department, University of Mississippi,* **(MISS)**, University, Mississippi 38677, **U.S.A.**
Telephone: 601/232-7203.
Foundation: 1963. *Number of specimens:* 53.000.
Herbarium: Vascular flora of Mississippi and southeastern U.S.
Important collections: E. N. Lowe (Mississippi).
Director and Curator: THOMAS M. PULLEN, 1919 (Vascular flora of Mississippi and southeastern U.S.).
Specialization in research: Vascular flora of Mississippi and southeastern U.S.
Loans: Each request considered individually.
Exchange: Available: Vascular plants of Mississippi. Desired: Vascular plants of southeastern U.S.

UNIVERSITY: *Herbarium, Department of Biology, University of Alabama,* **(UNA)**, P.O. Box 1927, University, Alabama 35486, **U.S.A.**
Telephone: 205/348-5960.
Foundation: 1950. *Number of specimens:* 40.000.
Herbarium: Vascular flora of Alabama with special emphasis on the aquatic vascular plants.
Director and Curator: ROBERT R. HAYNES, 1945 (Systematics of aquatic vascular plants, especially the Alismatidae).
Staff member: C. EARLE SMITH, JR., 1922 (Ethnobotany of several areas of Central and South America).
Specialization in research: Systematics of aquatic monocots; aquatic vascular plants of Alabama; ethnobotany of certain areas of Central and South America.
Associated botanic garden: University of Alabama Arboretum.
Loans: To recognized botanical institutions.
Exchange: Available: Alabama aquatic plants. Desired: Southeastern U.S. and Latin American flora.

UNIVERSITY PARK: *Herbarium, The Pennsylvania State University,* **(PAC)**, 202 Buckhout Laboratory, University Park, Pennsylvania 16802, **U.S.A.**
Telephone: See numbers of staff members below.
Foundation: 1872. *Number of specimens:* 170.000.
Herbarium: Flora of Pennsylvania; *Carex* of eastern North America; *Chenopodium* of North America; *Fissidens* of the Americas; rusts of the world.
Important collections: C. L. Fergus (fungi), C. J.

Hillson (algae of eastern North America), C. S. Keener (vascular flora of Pennsylvania), F. D. Kern (rusts), R. A. Pursell (bryophytes of Mexico, Venezuela, North America), vascular plants of Pennsylvania, Venezuela), L. O. Overholts (Polyporaceae of North America), H. A. Wahl (Flora of Pennsylvania; *Carex* of eastern North America; *Chenopodium* of North America), W. F. Westerfeld (Pennsylvania flora).
Staff members: C. L. FERGUS, 1917; 814/865-7861 (Mycology).
C. J. HILLSON, 1926; 814/865-6416 (Algae).
C. S. KEENER, 1931; 814/865-6201 (Angiosperms).
R. A. PURSELL, 1930; 814/865-9651 (Bryophytes).
Specialization in research: Morphology of algae; physiology of fungi; systematics of *Fissidens;* moss flora of Pennsylvania; floristics of tropical lowland bryophytes; systematics of *Carex* and North American Ranunculaceae; vascular flora of Pennsylvania.
Loans: To all recognized botanical institutions.
Exchange: Available: Pennsylvania material. Desired: Unrestricted.

UPPSALA: *The Herbarium, University of Uppsala,* **(UPS)**, P.O. Box 541, S-751 21 Uppsala, **Sweden.**
Telephone: 018-11 3418.
Status: Department of the Royal University of Uppsala.
Foundation: 1785. *Number of specimens:* 2.200.000 (including 350.000 lichens and 150.000 fungi).
Herbarium: Worldwide.
Important collections: Herb. J. Burser, herb. C. P. Thunberg, herb. E. Fries (Fungi), E. Fries (Lichens, etc.), Th. M. Fries (Lichens, etc.), C. G. Alm (*Carex*), Th. Hedlund (*Sorbus*), H. Smith (Chinese plants), A. H. Magnusson (Lichens), H. W. Arnell (Bryophytes), J. G. Åberg (Sphagna), J. A. Nannfeldt (Fungi, etc.), L. Holm (Fungi), L. Tibell (Lichens), M. Thulin (African plants), R. Santesson (Lichens p.p.), O. Hedberg (Phanerogams); K. Vanky (Ustilaginales; on deposit).
Director: R. MOBERG, 1939 (Lichens, especially Physciaceae).
Curator: S. RYMAN, 1946 (Fungi, especially Agaricales).

Institute of Systematic Botany
Telephone: 018-13 0218.
Director: O. HEDBERG, 1923 (Flora of Ethiopia, Afroalpine flora, boreal vascular plants).
Staff members: E. GUNNERBECK, 1943 (Hyphomycetes: *Ramularia*).
K. HARALDSSON, 1942 (Anatomy of Polygonaceae).
I. HEDBERG, 1927 (Cytotaxonomy, flora of Ethiopia, medicinal plants of Africa).
L. HOLM, 1921 (Pyrenomycetes, Uredinales).
K. HOLM, 1924 (Flora of Swedish Pyrenomycetes).

U.-M. HULTGÅRD, 1937 (Cytotaxonomy, *Parnassia*).

A. HUNDE, 1940 (Fabaceae, *Acacia*).

M. IWARSSON, 1948 (Labiatae).

L. JOHNSSON, 1946 (Orchidaceae, especially African aphyllous genera).

L. KÄLLSTEN, 1952 (Lichens, especially *Opegrapha*).

N. LUNDQVIST, 1930 (Coprophilous fungi).

O. LÖFGREN, 1953 (Lichens; ecology).

O. MÅRTENSSON, 1915 (Bryophytes).

J. A. NANNFELDT, 1904 (Ascomycetes, phytogeography).

A. NILSSON, 1946 (Pollination ecology, especially Orchidaceae).

O. RYDING, 1951 (Labiatae, especially *Aeollanthus*).

R. SVENSSON, 1950 (Swedish weeds).

M. THULIN, 1948 (African flora, especially Campanulaceaè, Leguminosae).

L. TIBELL, 1944 (Lichens, especially Caliciales).

K. VANKY, 1930 (Ustilaginales, sep. herb.).

M. WIGREN, 1952 (Swedish weeds).

Specialization in research: Mycology and lichenology, flora of Scandinavia, Tropical Africa.

Associated botanic garden: The Botanic Garden of the University of Uppsala.

Loans: In general to recognized botanical institutions or herbaria.

Periodical and serial works: Symbolae Botanicae Upsalienses.

Exchange: Available: Mainly Scandinavian and African plants. Wanted: All groups, especially fungi and lichens.

UPPSALA: *Herbarium, Växtbiologiska Institutionen,* **(UPSV),** Box 559, S-751 22 Uppsala, **Sweden.**

Telephone: 018/13 99 55.

Status: Department of the Royal University of Uppsala.

Foundation: 1897.

Herbarium: Scandinavian phanerogams, bryophytes and lichens.

Director: EVERT VAN DER MAAREL, 1934 (Plant ecology).

Curator: IVAR OTTOSSON, 1927.

Staff members: ERIK SJÖGREN, 1933 (Taxonomy and ecology of bryophytes).

HUGO SJÖRS, 1915 (Mire vegetation, *Sphagnum* taxonomy).

ERIK SKYE, 1927 (Lichens and air pollution).

KUNO THOMASSON, 1923 (Taxonomy and ecology of freshwater algae).

MATS WAERN, 1912 (Taxonomy and ecology of marine and brackish water algae).

EVA WILLÉN, 1940 (Ecology and taxonomy of freshwater phytoplankton).

Specialization in research: Plant ecology.

Periodical and serial works: Acta Phytogeog-

raphica Suecica, Växtekologiska Studier.

URALSK: *Herbarium, Department of Botany, A. S. Pushkin Pedagogical Institute of Uralsk,* **(PPIU),** Lenina Prospect 121, 417001 Uralsk, **U.S.S.R.**

Foundation: 1933. *Number of specimens:* 50.000.

Director: V. V. IVANOV (Flora of Kazakhstan).

URBANA: *Herbarium, Crop Evolution Laboratory, Department of Agronomy, University of Illinois,* **(CEL),** Urbana, Illinois 61801, **U.S.A.**

Telephone: 217/333-4373.

Foundation: 1967. *Number of specimens:* 50.000.

Herbarium: Gramineae, particularly Andropogoneae and genera of cereals; cultivated Fabaceae.

Important collections: Tripsacum, Bothriochloa, Cynodon, Dichanthium, Sorghum.

Curator: J. M. J. DE WET, 1927 (Gramineae).

Staff members: J. R. HARLAN, 1917 (Genetics).

K. W. HILU, 1946 (Flavonoid chemistry).

Specialization in research: Evolutionary studies in cereals and legumes; systematics of the Gramineae.

Loans: To all recognized herbaria.

Exchange: Gramineae.

URBANA: *Herbarium, Department of Botany, University of Illinois at Urbana-Champaign,* **(ILL),** Urbana, Illinois 61801, **U.S.A.**

Telephone: 217/333-2522.

Foundation: 1869. *Number of specimens:* 465.000.

Herbarium: Flora of Illinois and midwestern U.S.; increasing representation of Mexican and South American plants; fossil floras of Pennsylvanian Coal Swamps.

Important collections: V. H. Chase (40.000; mostly Illinois), G. N. Jones (40.000; Illinois and western U.S.), E. J. Hill (16.000; Illinois), W. S. Moffatt (11.000; Illinois), S. B. Mead (18.000; Illinois), L. F. Koch (9.000 bryophytes), J. T. Buchholz, T. J. Burrill, G. P. Clinton, F. Brendel, A. G. Jones (*Aster*), P. Shildneck, W. Trelease (*Piper, Quercus*), F. L. Stevens (fungi).

Curator: ALMUT G. JONES, 1923; 217/333-9357 (Biosystematics of *Aster*; flora of Illinois).

Staff members: J. LELAND CRANE, Curator of Fungi, 1935 (Pyrenomycetes, Fungi Imperfecti).

TOM L. PHILLIPS, Curator of Paleobotanical collections, 1931 (Fern evolution; analysis of coal swamp floras).

DAVID S. SEIGLER, 1940 (Chemosystematics of *Acacia*, Fabaceae, and Sapindaceae).

DAVID A. YOUNG, 1946 (Phylogeny of flowering plants; chemosystematics of Anacardiaceae, Ranunculaceae, and Rhizophoraceae).

Specialization in research: Flora of Illinois; monographic research in members of Anacardiaceae, Asteraceae, Fabaceae, Ranunculaceae, and Rhizophoraceae; monograph of *Torula* (Hyphomycetes).

Loans: To botanical institutions.

Exchange: Available: Principally modern and fossil plants of Illinois. Desired: Good material from anywhere, especially tropical regions.

Remarks: An important collection of 23.500 Pennsylvanian coal balls (vascular plants) and 4.000 plant compressions, Paleozoic algae, and vascular plants, is available.

URBANA: *Herbarium, Illinois State Natural History Survey,* **(ILLS),** 172 Natural Resources Building, Urbana, Illinois 61801, **U.S.A.**

Telephone: 217/333-6886.

Status: Illinois Institute of Natural Resources, State of Illinois.

Foundation: 1880. *Number of specimens:* 205.000 (165.000 vascular plants, 40.000 fungi).

Herbarium: Primarily vascular plants and parasitic fungi of Illinois; Hyphomycetes; fruit and seed collection.

Important collections: Vascular plants: Robert A. Evers, Charles Robertson, L. M. Umbach, Kenneth R. Robertson. Fungi: L. Tehon, J. C. Carter, J. L. Crane.

Director: GEORGE SPRUGEL, JR.

Curator of Vascular Plants: KENNETH R. ROBERTSON, 1941 (Classification of Rosaceae, Amaranthaceae, and *Jacquemontia,* Convolvulaceae).

Curator of Fungi: J. LELAND CRANE, 1935 (Classification of Hyphomycetes; aquatic Ascomycetes and Fungi Imperfecti).

Specialization in research: Plants of Illinois.

Loans: To recognized botanical institutions.

Periodical and serial works: Illinois Natural History Bulletin; Illinois Natural History Biological Notes; Illinois Natural History Survey Circular.

Exchange: Available.

UST-KAMENOGORSK: *Herbarium, Department of Botany, Ust-Kamenogorsk State Pedagogical Institute,* **(UKSPI),** 492036 Ust-Kamenogorsk, **U.S.S.R.**

Foundation: 1954. *Number of specimens:* 30.000.

Director: O. A. MICHELSON.

UTRECHT: *Institute of Systematic Botany,* **(U),** Heidelberglaan 2, P.O. Box 80.102, 3508 TC Utrecht, **Netherlands.**

Telephone: 030-531825.

Status: Department of the State University of Utrecht.

Foundation: 1816. *Number of specimens:* 600.000.

Herbarium: Worldwide herbarium of phanerogams and cryptogams, especially from Tropical America and Europe.

Important collections: The majority of collections from Suriname and the Netherlands Antilles; types of F. A. W. Miquel from tropical Asia and South America; A. M. Cleef (Colombia).

Director: A. L. STOFFERS, 1926 (Flora and vege-

tation of the Netherlands Antilles).

Curators: P. J. M. MAAS, 1939, Vascular plants, correspondence (Zingiberaceae, Cannaceae, Burmanniaceae, Triuridaceae and Gentianaceae of the New World).

L. Y. TH. WESTRA, 1932, Vascular plants, herbarium management (Nyctaginaceae: Pisonieae of the New World, Orchidaceae of the Guianas).

S. R. GRADSTEIN, 1943, Non-vascular plants (Bryophytes).

Staff members: T. BARETTA-KUIPERS, 1919 (Wood anatomy).

C. C. BERG, 1934 (Cecropiaceae, Moraceae, Urticaceae of the New World).

A. M. CLEEF, 1951 (Flora and vegetation of the Colombian Andes).

A. GÖRTS-V. RIJN, 1940 (Flora of Suriname).

W. H. A. HEKKING, 1930 (Woody Violaceae of the New World).

E. HENNIPMAN, 1937 (Pteridophytes).

M. E. E. HIJMAN, 1951 (*Dorstenia* of Africa and Asia).

M. J. JANSEN-JACOBS, 1944 (Flora of Suriname).

E. G. B. KIEFT, 1951 (*Lachemilla* of the New World).

J. KOEK-NOORMAN, 1942 (Wood anatomy).

J. C. LINDEMAN, 1921 (Flora and vegetation of Suriname and Brasil).

A. M. W. MENNEGA, 1912 (Wood anatomy; Hippocrateaceae of the New World).

E. A. MENNEGA, 1923 (Botanical gardens).

G. B. A. VAN REENEN, 1948 (Bryophytes of Colombia).

J. VAN ROODEN, 1942 (Annonaceae of the New World).

A. C. DE ROON, 1928 (Marcgraviaceae).

H. J. M. SIPMAN, 1945 (Lichens).

M. A. VAN SLAGEREN, 1955 (*Brachiolejeunea*).

S. M. C. TOPPER, 1943 (Wood anatomy of New World Moraceae).

B. TER WELLE, 1946 (Wood anatomy).

Specialization in research: Flora and vegetation of tropical America (especially Suriname, Netherlands Antilles, and Colombia); monographs for Flora Neotropica; anatomy of tropical woods.

Associated botanic garden: Hortus Botanicus, Utrecht; Cantonspark, Baarn; Fort Hoofddijk, Utrecht; Sandwijck, De Bilt; Von Gimborn Arboretum, Doorn.

Loans: In general to recognized botanical institutions.

Periodical and serial works: Flora of Suriname; Flora of the Netherlands Antilles; The Vegetation of Suriname; Mededelingen van het Botanisch Museum en Herbarium van de Rijksuniversiteit te Utrecht: Wachendorffia.

Exchange: Available: Specimens from tropical America and Europe. Desired: Specimens from all groups, especially from tropical America.

Remarks: Facilities for visiting botanists. Housed in the Institute: The International Bureau for Plant Taxonomy and Nomenclature.

Division of Biosystematics

Address: Transitorium III, Padualaan 8, Utrecht.

Head: TH. W. J. GADELLA, 1931 (*Symphytum, Ornithogalum, Hieracium pilosella* group).

Staff members: H. 'T HART, 1944 (*Sedum*).

E. KLIPHUIS, 1924 (*Galium, Symphytum*).

J. VAN LOON, 1936 (*Geranium*).

Division of Plant Ecology and Vegetation Science

Head: J. J. BARKMAN, 1922 (Vegetation structure, mycosociology).

Staff members: F. J. A. DANIËLS, 1943 (Lichen and dwarf shrub communities).

H. J. DURING, 1947 (Garovagliaceae, bryophyte communities).

J. TH. DE SMIDT, 1932 (Heathland communities, landscape ecology).

M. J. A. WERGER, 1944 (Vegetation structure, tropical vegetation, especially savannas and deserts).

J. H. WILLEMS, 1940 (Limestone grasslands).

G. ZIJLSTRA, 1941 (Autecology of limestone grassland plants).

Remarks: Several members of staff in temporary employment, specializing in grassland communities and vegetation structure.

Laboratory of Palaeobotany and Palynology

Staff members: M. BOERSMA, 1939 (Palaeozoic and Mesozoic palaeobotany).

J. VAN DER BURGH, 1937 (Mesozoic and Tertiary palaeobotany).

C. R. JANSSEN, 1930 (Quaternary palaeoecology).

W. PUNT, 1929 (Pollen morphology).

H. VISSCHER, 1937 (Pre-quaternary palynology).

Remarks: Important collection of worldwide sporotheke (pollen and spore slides), ca. 10.000 different species.

Division of Taxonomic Documentation

Head: F. A. STAFLEU, 1921 (Bibliography, history and philosophy of systematic botany).

Staff members: J. A. LEUSSINK, 1932 (Index nominum genericorum, taxonomic literature).

I. H. VEGTER, 1935 (Index herbariorum).

G. ZIJLSTRA, 1941 (Index nominum genericorum).

T. VAN INGEN (Taxonomic literature).

N. DE KWAADSTENIET (I.A.P.T.).

UTSJOKI: *The Kevo Subarctic Research Institute,* (**KEVO**), University of Turku, SF-20500 Turku 50 (winter), SF-99980 Utsjoki (summer), **Finland.**

Telephone: 921-645 932 (Turku), 997-72505 (Utsjoki).

Status: Institute of the state university.

Foundation: 1956. *Number of specimens:* 5.000.

Herbarium: Mainly vascular plants of Inari Lapland; also lichens, mosses, fungi.

Director: MATTI SULKINOJA (Cytotaxonomy of *Betula*).

Curator: SAINI HEINO (Ecophysiology of subarctic mosses).

Associate research worker: PAAVO KALLIO (Macrofungi, desmids; *Micrasterias*).

Periodical and serial works: "The Vascular Flora of Inari Lapland" published in Reports from the Kevo Subarctic Research Station.

UVALDE: *Herbarium, Biology Department, Southwest Texas Junior College,* (**UVST**), Uvalde, Texas 78801, **U.S.A.**

Telephone: 512/278-4401, ext. 225.

Foundation: 1968. *Number of specimens:* 1.438.

Herbarium: Emphasis on southwestern Texas.

Important collections: Delzie Demaree.

Director and Curator: TONEY KEENEY, 1942 (Taxonomy of flowering plants).

Loans: No restrictions.

Exchange: On request.

Remarks: Herbarium used for identifying allergenic and poisonous plants.

UZHGOROD: *Herbarium, Department of Botany, Biology Faculty, Uzhgorod University,* (**UU**), Oktyabrskaya St. 54, Uzhgorod, **U.S.S.R.**

Foundation: 1946. *Number of specimens:* 20.000.

Director: S. S. FODOR.

V

VAASA: *Herbarium of Ostrobothnia Australis,* **(VOA),** c/o M. Malmberg, Sandögatan 12, Vaasa, **Finland.** (Information 1974)
Status: Owned by Society Ostrobothnia Australis, subsidized by city.
Foundation: 1925. *Number of specimens:* 30.000.
Herbarium: Mainly vascular plants of Finland and Scandinavia, also Siberia, Madeira, Italy and Egypt.
Specialization in research: Adventive plants and *Taraxacum* of South Österbotten.
Loans: To recognized botanical institutions.
Periodical and serial works: Österbotten.

VÁCRÁTÓT: *Magyar Tudományos Akadémia Botanikai Kutatóintézete,* **(VBI),** 2163 Vácrátót, **Hungary.**
Status: Hungarian Academy of Sciences.
Foundation: 1952. *Number of specimens:* 20.000.
Herbarium: Flora of Hungary, Vietnam and Cuba.
Director: ÁRPÁD BERCZIK.
Associate Director: ATTILA BORHIDI (Flora of Cuba: Rubiaceae, Bignoniaceae, Verbenaceae, Celastraceae, Rhamnaceae, Oleaceae, Aquifoliaceae; ecology, vegetation mapping in Hungary and Cuba).

Department of Taxonomy and Botanic Garden

Head of Department: TAMÁS PÓCS (Taxonomy of tropical Hepaticae, Lepidozioideae of Africa, epiphyllous liverworts of Old World tropics, *Aphanolejeunea,* hepatic flora of Vietnam, East Africa and Cuba; bryogeography, ecology).
Emeritus Head of Department: MIKLÓS UJVÁROSI (Sociology and mapping of Hungarian weeds, horticulture).
Curator of Phanerogams: ZOLTÁN KERESZTI (Taxonomy of Hungarian *Scilla, Muscari,* Cuban Rutaceae).
Curator of Cryptogams: GABRIELLA KIS (Taxonomy of Bryaceae).

Department of Plant Ecology

Team Leaders: GÁBOR FEKETE (Plant demography, niche ecology, areal geography).
MARGIT KOVÁCS (Plant-soil relations, urban ecology).
IMRE MÁTHÉ, JR. (Phytochemistry, chemotaxonomy).
Staff members: MÁRIA DINKA (Ecology of aquatic plants).
PÁL KLINCSEK (Urban ecology, dendrology, orchids).
ERIKA MELKÓ (Numerical taxonomy of *Iris*).
EDIT MOLNÁR (Niche ecology).
JÁNOS PODANI (Cluster analysis, computer techniques).
ZOLTÁN SZÓCS (Numerical taxonomy, pattern analysis).
KATALIN TÖRÖK (Urban ecology).

ZOLTÁN TUBA (Photosynthesis ecology).
AGNES VADÁSZ (Plant chemistry).
KLÁRA VIRÁGH (Plant demography, growth analysis).
BALINT ZÓLYOMI (Director emeritus; Quaternary palynology, vegetation mapping, phytosociology).
Specialization in research: Ecology of urban ecosystems, niche ecology, mapping of Hungarian flora, flora of Cuba.
Associated botanic garden: Botanic Garden of Hungarian Academy of Sciences.
Loans: To recognized botanical institutions.
Periodical and serial works: Acta Botanica Acad. Sc. Hungaricae, Magyarország Kulturflórája.
Exchange: Available: Hungarian and Cuban vascular plants (limited); tropical Asian, African and Cuban bryophytes.
Remarks: The foreign bryophytes from EGR are on long-term loan to Vácrátót.

VALDIVIA: *Herbario, Instituto de Defensa de las Plantas, Facultad de Ciencias Agrarias, Universidad Austral de Chile,* **(HFV),** Casilla 567, Valdivia, **Chile.**
Telephone: 2681-3911-3961, ext. 236.
Foundation: 1957. *Number of specimens:* 1.600 fungi.
Herbarium: Chile; fungi, especially Uredinales.
Director: SUSANA GONZÁLEZ MACENAUER (Mycology).
Curator: JAIME MONTEALEGRE ANDRADE (Mycology).
Staff member: EDGARDO DEHRENS B. (Mycology).
Loans: To recognized institutions.
Exchange: Possible.

VALDIVIA: *Herbario, Instituto de Botánica, Facultad de Ciencias, Universidad Austral de Chile,* **(VALD),** Casilla 567, Valdivia, **Chile.**
Telephone: 3911, ext. 313.
Foundation: 1956. *Number of specimens:* 10.000.
Herbarium: Flora of southcentral Chile.
Director: MIREN ALBERDI L.
Associated botanic garden: Jardín Botánico, Instituto de Botánica.
Loans: No.
Exchange: Occasionally, on request, to a limited extent.
Remarks: Herbarium being developed.

VALDOSTA: *Herbarium, Department of Biology, Valdosta State College,* **(VSC),** Nevins Hall, Valdosta, Georgia 31601, **U.S.A.**
Telephone: 912/247-3287; 247-3288.
Foundation: 1967. *Number of specimens:* 29.500.

Herbarium: Vascular flora of the Atlantic-Gulf Coastal Plain; most complete bryological collection for Georgia.

Important collections: Robert K. Lampton (bryophytes).

Director and Curator: WAYNE R. FAIRCLOTH, 1932 (Ophioglossaceae; vascular plant systematics).

Staff member: MARY C. NORSWORTHY, 1919 (General floristics).

Specialization in research: Floristics of the Atlantic-Gulf Coastal Plain; biosystematics of Ophioglossaceae in southeastern U.S.

Loans: Interinstitutional only; small loans sent prepaid by both parties; large loans sent by express collect to borrower by prior agreement.

Exchange: Specimen-per-specimen basis with prior agreement.

VALENCIA: *Jardin Botánico de la Universidad,* **(VAL),** Valencia, **Spain.**

VALPARAÍSO: *Herbario Liquenológico, Departamento de Biología, Facultad de Matemáticas y Ciencias Naturales, Universidad de Chile Valparaíso,* **(VALPL),** Casilla 130-V, Valparaíso, **Chile.**

Telephone: 59428; 59429.

Foundation: 1964. *Number of specimens:* 21.345.

Herbarium: Mainly Chile, some Argentina, Perú, West Antarctic, Juan Fernández Islands.

Director and Curator: JORGE REDON, 1936 (Lichens).

Staff member: GERARDO GUZMÁN, 1950 (Lichens).

Specialization in research: Taxonomy and ecology of Chilean and Antarctic lichens.

Loans: Usual conditions.

Exchange: Limited.

VANCOUVER: *Herbarium, Department of Botany, University of British Columbia,* **(UBC),** 3529-6270 University Boulevard, University Campus, Vancouver, British Columbia, **Canada** V6T 2B1.

Telephone: 604/228-3344; 228-2133.

Foundation: 1920. *Number of specimens:* 446.000 (61.000 algae, 10.000 fungi, 10.000 lichens, 200.000 bryophytes, 165.000 vascular plants and ferns).

Herbarium: Main strength in native plants from British Columbia; algae collections especially well represented from adjacent areas in Washington and Alaska.

Director: R. F. SCAGEL (Phycology; marine benthic algae).

Curators: R. J. BANDONI (Mycology).

J. R. MAZE (Vascular plants).

J. OTTO (Lichens).

W. B. SCHOFIELD (Bryophytes).

Specialization in research: Marine benthic algae, bryophytes, ferns, and vascular plants.

Associated botanic garden: University of British Columbia Botanical Garden.

Loans: To recognized herbaria and/or other institutions.

Exchange: All groups, preferably by prior arrangement.

VANNES: *Herbarium, Société Polymathique du Morbihan,* **(VAN),** 2 rue Noé, Vannes, Morbihan, **France.**

VAN NUYS: *Herbarium, Department of Life Sciences, Los Angeles Valley College,* **(VNC),** 5800 Fulton Avenue, Van Nuys, California 91401, **U.S.A.**

Telephone: 213/781-1200, ext. 214; 762-4298.

Foundation: 1949. *Number of specimens:* 5.000.

Herbarium: Local flora, including algae of local beaches; allergenic plants; vacant lot and roadside introductions.

Important collections: David G. Dixon, George Hale.

Director and Curator: DAVID G. DIXON, 1924 (Cytogenetics; Onagraceae).

VARANASI: *Herbarium, Department of Mycology and Plant Pathology, Faculty of Agriculture, Banaras Hindu University,* **(BHUPP),** Varanasi – 221005, **India.**

Telephone: 54291-442.

Status: University.

Foundation: 1964. *Number of specimens:* 2.000.

Herbarium: Fungi, especially Discomycetes of Northern India.

Director: V. P. TEWARI, 1931 (Taxonomy of higher fungi).

Curator: C. C. PANT, 1941 (Taxonomy of Discomycetes).

Staff members: K. C. BASUCHAUDHORY, 1931 (Seed pathology).

R. DAYAY, 1931 (Taxonomy of Saprolegniaceae).

K. B. KHARE, 1944 (Taxonomy of Gastromycetes).

U. P. SINGH, 1942 (Taxonomy of Deuteromycetes).

Specialization in research: Taxonomy of Discomycetes.

Loans: Short term, to recognized institutions.

VEDI: *Herbarium, Khosrovsk State Reserve, State Bureau of Forestry of Armenia,* **(KSRV),** 378210 Vedi, **U.S.S.R.**

Foundation: 1958. *Number of specimens:* 15.000.

Director: M. GRIGORJAN.

VENDA: *see* SIBASA.

VERMILION: *Herbarium, Department of Biology, Lakeland College,* **(LCVA),** Vermilion Campus, Vermilion, Alberta, **Canada** TOB 4MO.

Telephone: 403/853-2971.

Foundation: 1974. *Number of specimens:* 1.800.

Herbarium: Plants of eastern Alberta from U.S.

border to North Saskatchewan River.
  Director: ANDREW KLAR, 1937.
  Staff members: CAROL KAY, 1954 (Crop science).
M. PFEFFERLE, 1946 (Crop science).
  Specialization in research: Plant geography.
  Loans: Usual regulations.
  Exchange: Requests considered individually.

VERMILLION: *Herbarium, Biology Department, University of South Dakota,* (**SDU**), Vermillion, South Dakota 57069, **U.S.A.**
  Telephone: 605/677-5211.
  Foundation: 1910. Number of specimens: 50.000.
  Herbarium: Vascular plants of South Dakota and adjoining states in north central region.
  Director and Curator: THEODORE VAN BRUGGEN, 1926 (Flora of the Great Plains).
  Specialization in research: Flora of South Dakota and upper Great Plains.
  Loans: In general to recognized botanical researchers and institutions.
  Exchange: Limited. Available: Black Hills specimens.

VERONA: *Erbario Generale del Museo Civico di Storia Naturale di Verona,* (**VER**), Sezione di Botanica, Corso Cavour 11, 37121 Verona, **Italy.**
  Telephone: 045/28157.
  Status: Municipal institution.
  Foundation: 1854. Number of specimens: 250.000.
  Herbarium: Plants of Italy, Europe, Terra del Fuoco (Argentina).
  Important collections: Lichens, hepaticae.
  Director: ALESSANDRO RUFFO, 1915 (Zoology: crustaceae, amphipoda).
  Curator: FRANCESCO BIANCHINI, 1938 (Flora of Regione Veronese).
  Staff members: MARIA VITTORIA BIANCHINI (Voluntary curator).
  FRANCESCO DI CARLO (Technician).
  AZZURRA CARRARA (Voluntary curator).
  GIUSEPPINA DE MORI (Voluntary curator).
  Specialization in research: Flora of Italy (Apennines), flora of Verona region.
  Loans: To recognized botanical institutions.
  Periodical and serial works: Bollettino del Museo Civico di Storia Naturale di Verona, Memorie.
  Exchange: Yes.

VERRIERES-LE-BUISSON: *Etablissements Vilmorin-Andrieux, Arboretum et Herbier Vilmorin,* (**VIL**) -- *see* ORSAY.

VIÇOSA: *Herbário, Departamento de Biologia Vegetal, Universidade Federal de Viçosa,* (**VIC**), 36.570 Viçosa, Minas Gerais, **Brazil.**
  Telephone: (55)031/891-1790, ramal 163.
  Foundation: 1930. Number of specimens: 10.000.
  Herbarium: Regional vascular plants, especially Minas Gerais.

  Important collections: Y. Mexia, J. G. Kuhlmann, H. S. Irwin.
  Director: J. R. P. CHAVES (Plant physiology).
  Curator: WALDOMIRO NUNES VIDAL, 1933 (Regional vascular plant flora; weeds).
  Staff members: ÉLCIO CRUZ DE ALMEIDA, 1951 (Regional vascular plant flora).
  RITA MARIA FORTUNATO DE CARVALHO.
  MARIA ROSÁRIA RODRIGUES VIDAL, 1933 (Regional vascular plant flora; weeds).
  Specialization in research: Taxonomy of vascular plants, forages, weeds.
  Loans: To recognized institutions.
  Exchange: Available: Vascular plants from Viçosa. Desired: Vascular plants from Brazil, especially from Minas Gerais.

VICTORIA: *Herbarium, Pacific Forest Research Centre, Canadian Forestry Service,* (**DAVFP**), 506 W. Burnside Road, Victoria, British Columbia, **Canada** V8Z 1M5.
  Telephone: 604/388-3811, loc. 214.
  Status: Government of Canada, Environment Canada.
  Foundation: 1940. Number of specimens: 27.000.
  Herbarium: Forest pathology, mycology, and some ecology.
  Important collections: W. G. Ziller (conifer rust collection), A. Funk (conifer stem disease collection).
  Director: T. G. HONER.
  Curator: RICHARD S. HUNT, 1944 (Survey-Extension).
  Staff members: D. CHU (Cultures; Basidiomycetes).
  AL FUNK, 1925 (Ascomycetes; fungi imperfecti).
  JOHN C. HOPKINS (Nursery storage fungi).
  D. P. LOWE (Host records).
  DUNCAN J. MORRISON (Root diseases; Basidiomycetes).
  R. B. SMITH, 1934 (Dwarf mistletoes; ecology).
  JACK R. SUTHERLAND, 1936 (Nursery and seed orchard diseases).
  G. ALLAN VAN SICKLE (Disease losses).
  ERNST VON RUDLOFF (Chemotaxonomy of conifers).
  GORDIE W. WALLIS (Root diseases; Basidiomycetes).
  H. STU WHITNEY, 1935 (Fungi; insect associations).
  Specialization in research: Diseases of forest trees.
  Associated botanic garden: Lake Cowichan Forest Experiment Station.
  Loans: To recognized botanical institutions.
  Periodical and serial works: Pest leaflets; Annual Report.
  Exchange: Available: Basidiomycetes and Ascomycetes from western Canada forests.
  Remarks: Facilities for visiting scientists, includ-

ing library (subject to prior arrangement).

VICTORIA: *Herbarium, Douglas Ecological Consultants Ltd.*, (**DECV**), 2049 Crescent Road, Victoria, British Columbia, **Canada** V8S 2G9.
Telephone: 604/592-0414.
Foundation: 1974. *Number of specimens:* 10.000 (7.000 vascular plants, 3.000 non-vascular plants).
Herbarium: Large Asteraceae collection from northwestern America; Yukon (5.000 sheets).
Important collections: George W. Douglas.
Director and Curator: GEORGE W. DOUGLAS, 1938 (Plant ecologist).
Staff member: MARILYN J. RATCLIFFE, 1956 (Plant ecologist).
Specialization in research: Synecology; systematic botany.
Loans: No special conditions other than 4 month return.
Exchange: Yes.

VICTORIA: *Herbarium, Victoria Botanic Gardens*, (**SCA**) – incorporated in YA.

VICTORIA: *Herbarium, Department of Biology, University of Victoria*, (**UVIC**), P.O. Box 1700, Victoria, British Columbia, **Canada** V8W 2Y2.
Telephone: 604/477-6911, local 4743.
Foundation: 1962. *Number of specimens:* 30.000 (22.000 vascular plants, 5.000 algae, 3.000 fungi).
Herbarium: Emphasis on Vancouver Island flora.
Curator: M. A. M. BELL, 1935 (Forest ecology; reclamation of disturbed land).
Staff members: A. P. AUSTIN, 1932 (Mitotic phenomena, phenology, and experimental ecology of marine algae).
G. GUPPY, 1950 (Systematics of the *Aster foliaceus* complex).
J. W. PADEN, 1933 (Morphology and life cycles of North American and neotropical Pezizales).
Loans: 1 or 2 years.
Exchange: Limited.

VICTORIA: *Herbarium, Botany Division, British Columbia Provincial Museum*, (**V**), Victoria, British Columbia, **Canada** V8V 1X4.
Telephone: 604/387-6513; 387-3215.
Status: Ministry of Provincial Secretary, Government of British Columbia.
Foundation: 1886. *Number of specimens:* 105.000 (95.000 vascular plants, 10.000 bryophytes and lichens).
Herbarium: Primarily from British Columbia, western Canada, and the Pacific Northwest.
Important collections: 24 type specimens.
Director: R. T. OGILVIE (Alpine and subalpine flora).
Staff members: T. C. BRAYSHAW (Amentiferae, Salicaceae, Helobiae; trees and shrubs of Canada).
L. E. PAVLICK (Gramineae).

Research associates: J. A. BAILEY (Flora of British Columbia).
A. CESKA (Cyperaceae; *Isoetes*).
G. DOUGLAS (Compositae).
M. HEIMBERGER (Ranunculaceae).
T. M. C. TAYLOR (Flora of British Columbia).
NANCY TURNER (Ethnobotany, economic botany).
Specialization in research: Flora and plant distribution of British Columbia.
Associated botanic garden: Garden of Native British Columbia Plants.
Loans: By request to Curator.
Periodical and serial works: Syesis; B. C. P. M. Occasional Papers, Handbooks, and Special Publications.
Exchange: By request.

VILA REAL: *Herbarium, Instituto Universitário de Tras-os-Montes e Alto Douro*, (**HVR**), Apart. 202, 5001 Vila Real Codex, **Portugal.**
Telephone: 22545, 24321, 24322, 24323.
Status: University.
Foundation: 1979. *Number of specimens:* 3.500.
Herbarium: General collection, mainly the Portuguese flora of Tras-os-Montes and Douro Region.
Curator: JOSÉ M. DE AGUIAR MACÉDO, 1921; 22385 (Priv.) (Floristics, vegetation mapping).
Specialization in research: Flora and vegetation of lowlands and highlands in Tras-os- Montes and Douro Region.
Loans: To botanists and recognized institutions.
Exchange: Available only in future, no stocks yet. Desired: General, especially Europe.
Remarks: Herbarium just starting, gifts very welcome.

VILLA MERCEDES: *Herbario, Instituto Nacional de Tecnología Agropecuaria, Estación Experimental Agropecuaria San Luis*, (**VMSL**), Casilla de Correo 17, 5730 Villa Mercedes, San Luis, **Argentina.**
Telephone: (54)1916.
Foundation: 1965. *Number of specimens:* 3.000.
Herbarium: Vascular plants of San Luis; range plants.
Director: DAVID LEE ANDERSON, 1938 (Ecology; range research).
Specialization in research: Description of range types and sites; flora of range areas.
Loans: Usual regulations.
Exchange: Yes.

VILLEURBANNE: *Herbiers de l'Université de Lyon, Département de Biologie Végétale*, (**LY**), 43 Bd du 11 Novembre, F-69621 Villeurbanne, **France.**
Status: University Claude Bernard-Lyon I.
Foundation: 1925. *Number of specimens:* 3.800.000.
Herbarium: General.
Important collections: Herb. Roland Bonaparte (including Herb. G. C. C. Rouy), Herb. M. Gandoger.

Director: P. BERTHET.
Associated botanic garden: Jardin Botanique de la Ville de Lyon, Parc de la Tête d'Or, Lyon.
Loans: To recognized botanical institutions.
Remarks: Formerly listed under Lyon.

VILNIUS: *Flora and Geobotanical Sector, Botanical Institute of the Lithuanian Academy of Sciences,* (**BI-LAS**), Turistu St. 47, 232021 Vilnius, **U.S.S.R.**
Foundation: 1946. *Number of specimens:* 66.000 (40.000 vascular plants, 14.000 bryophytes, 12.000 phytopathological fungi).
    Curator of Vascular Plants: A. A. LEKAVICHYUS.
    Curator of Bryophytes: I. V. MAZELAITIS.
    Curator of Phytopathological Fungi: N. STRUKCHINSKAS.

VILNIUS: *Department of Botany and Genetics, Kapsukas State University,* (**WI**), Churlionio Street 23, 232031 Vilnius, **U.S.S.R.**
Foundation: 1823. *Number of specimens:* 84.000.
Herbarium: Mainly plants of Lithuania and the Ukraine.
    Curator of Vascular Plants: M. P. NATKEVI-CHAITE.
    Curator of Cryptogams: A. I. MINKYAVICHYUS.

VISBY: *Högre Allmänna Läroverket,* (**VI**), Visby, **Sweden.**

VLADIVOSTOK: *Herbarium, Institute of Biology-Soils, Far Eastern Scientific Center of the Academy of Sciences of the U.S.S.R.,* (**VLA**), 159 G. Stoletiya Prospect, 690022 Vladivostok, **U.S.S.R.**
Status: Directed by Academy of Sciences.
Foundation: 1916. *Number of specimens:* 100.000.

Herbarium: Flora of Soviet Far East.
Important collections: I. K. Shishkin, E. N. Klobukova-Alisova, Z. I. Luchnik, T. P. Samoilov and T. V. Samoilova, Z. I. Gutnikova, B. P. Kolesnikov, G. E. Kurentsova, D. P. Vorabiev, N. E. Kabanov, Y. Y. Vasiliev, N. S. Probatova (all from Soviet Far East); D. P. Vorobiev, V. A. Nechaev, N. A. Popov, Y. A. Doronina (Kurile Isles); M. G. Popov, A. I. Tolmachev, K. D. Stepanova, E. M. Egorova, A. M. Chernyaeva (Sakhalin); D. P. Vorobiev, V. N. Voroshilov, P. T. Gorovoy, S. S. Kharkevich and T. G. Buch (Primorye, Priamurye, Okhotsk coast and Sakhalin); K. D. Stepanova (Kamchatka and Komandorskie Islands).
    Director: S. S. KHARKEVICH.
    Curator of Cryptogams: M. M. NAZAROVA.
    Specialization in research: Flora of the Soviet Far East.
    Associated botanic garden: Botanical Garden of the Far Eastern Scientific Center.

VORONEZH: *Department of Morphology, Systematics and Geography of Plants, Lenin Komsomol University of Voronezh,* (**VOR**), Universitetskaya Square, 394000 Voronezh, **U.S.S.R.**
Status: University.
Foundation: 1918. *Number of specimens:* 40.000.
    Director: N. S. KAMYSHEV.

VRCHLABI: *Herbarium, Krkonošské muzeum Vrchlabí,* (**KM**), Vrchlabi, okr. Trutnov, **Czechoslovakia.** (Information 1974)
Foundation: 1883. *Number of specimens:* 6.000.
Herbarium: Tracheophyta, bryophyta, lichens and fungi of Vrchlabi region and Krkonoše mountains.
Loans: To recognized botanical institutions.

W

WACO: *Herbarium, Department of Biology, Baylor University,* (**BAYLU**), Waco, Texas 76703, **U.S.A.**
Telephone: 817/755-2911.
Foundation: 1920. *Number of specimens:* 100.000.
Herbarium: Reference collection for central Texas.
Important collections: F. J. Lindheimer.
   Director and Curator: ROBERT C. GARDNER, 1946 (Adaptive radiation in island plants; systematics of selected central Texas groups, especially Compositae).
Loans: For 2 years.
Exchange: Limited.

WAD MEDANI: *Herbarium, Agricultural Research Division, Gezira Research Station,* (**GRS**), Wad Medani, **Sudan.**

WAGENINGEN: *Herbarium Vadense, Laboratory for Plant Taxonomy and Plant Geography,* (**WAG**), 37 Gen. Foulkesweg, P.O. Box 8010, 6700 ED Wageningen, **Netherlands.**
Telephone: 08370-83170 / 83160.
Status: Department of the Agricultural University.
Foundation: 1896. *Number of specimens:* 400.000.
Herbarium: Worldwide, mainly phanerogams, especially Tropical Africa, Mediterranean, Europe, cultivated ornamentals.
Important collections: Tropical African collections; early collections of the Netherlands and the Mediterranean area; dendrological herbarium of leading late 19th and early 20th century dendrologists.
   Curator: J. DE BRUIJN, 1935; 08370-83163.
   Staff members: J. C. ARENDS, 1940 (Cytotaxonomy of Apocynaceae, Begonia, Dichapetalum, Dracaena, Narcissus and African Orchidaceae).
   J. J. BOS, 1939 (Revision of *Dracaena*).
   F. J. BRETELER, 1932 (African Dichapetalaceae).
   A. J. M. LEEUWENBERG, 1930 (African Apocynaceae and Loganiaceae).
   J. J. F. E. DE WILDE, 1932 (African Begoniaceae).
   D. O. WIJNANDS, 1945, Keeper Botanical Gardens (Interpretation of Commelin's plates, taxonomy of ornamental plants).
   Research associates: H. J. BEENTJE, 1951 (Revision of *Strophanthus*).
   J. DE KONING, 1943 (The Banco Forest in the Ivory Coast).
   F. M. MULLER, 1907 (Identification of and research in old Mediterranean herbarium collections).
   C. J. P. SEEGELER, 1940 (Ethiopian oil crops).
   J. M. C. WESTPHAL-STEVELS, 1942 (Taxonomic and horticultural study of vegetables in Cameroon).

H. C. D. DE WIT, 1909 (Tropical aquatic plants).
Specialization in research: Taxonomy of Tropical African plants; taxonomy of cultivated plants.
Associated botanic garden: "Belmonte" and "De Dreijen."
Loans: In general to recognized botanical institutions.
Periodical and serial works: Belmontia; Bulletin van de Botanische Tuinen, Wageningen.
Exchange: Available: Specimens from tropical Africa and cultivated ornamentals. Desired: Tropical Africa, cultivated plants: ornamentals and others; general exchange.

WAGENINGEN: *Herbarium, Institute for Horticultural Plant Breeding,* (**WAHO**), Mansholtlaan 15, P.O. Box 16, 6700 AA Wageningen, **Netherlands.**
Telephone: 08370-19123.
Status: Directed by a private board; financed by the Ministry of Agriculture.
Foundation: 1943. *Number of specimens:* 2.500 sheets (plant bodies of Cactaceae mainly documented by photographs).
Herbarium: Cultivated species and cultivars of Cactaceae and other succulents.
Important collections: Conophytum, Echeveria, Gymnocalycium, Haworthia, Lobivia, Mammillaria, Neoporteria, Parodia, Rebutia, Sedum.
   Director: C. DORSMAN, Director of the Institut v. d. Veredeling v. Tuinbouwgewassen.
   Curator: H. Q. VAREKAMP, 1918 (Taxonomy of cultivated plants).
   Staff member: T. DE VRIES, 1950 (Technical assistant).
Specialization in research: No research other than the identification of taxa represented in the living collection of the IVT-Succulentarium.
Loans: In general to recognized botanical institutions.
Periodical and serial works: Occasional publications in IVT-Mededelingen.

WAGENINGEN: *Herbarium, Biological Station Wijster,* (**WBS**), Kampsweg 27, Wijster (Dr.), **Netherlands.**
Telephone: 05936-441.
Status: Landbouwhogeschool (Agricultural University), Wageningen.
Foundation: 1927. *Number of specimens:* 17.000 (fungi 10.300, bryophytes 4.000, phanerogams 1.800, lichens 800).
Herbarium: Plants of Netherlands, Scandinavia and northern Europe.
Important collections: Macrofungi (mainly Basidiomycetes) of juniper scrub, heath, grassland and

oak woods, including a number of types.

Director: J. J. BARKMAN, 1922 (Plant sociology, mycology, Galerina, microclimatology).

Curator: B. W. L. DE VRIES, 1941 (Mycology resupinate fungi on wood).

Staff member: E. ARNOLDS, 1948 (Plant sociology, grassland ecology, mycology, Hygrophorus).

Specialization in research: Ecology of larger fungi in plant communities in relation to microclimate and soil properties.

WAKEFIELD: City Art Gallery and Museum, (**WKD**) -- see BRADFORD (CMM).

WALLA WALLA: Herbarium, Department of Biology, Whitman College, (**WCW**), Walla Walla, Washington 99362, **U.S.A.**

Telephone: 509/527-5141.

Status: Private institution.

Foundation: 1963. Number of specimens: 12.000.

Herbarium: Primarily Pacific Northwest vascular plants; Cactaceae of Chihuahuan Desert; vascular plants of southeast Asia (Malaysia, Thailand).

Important collections: Pacific Northwest collections of W. Brode, P. Pope, C. V. Piper; L. Pierce (red algae); E. F. Anderson (Nepenthaceae from Malaysia).

Director and Curator: EDWARD F. ANDERSON, 1932 (Systematics of the Cactaceae).

Specialization in research: Cactaceae of the Chihuahuan Desert.

Loans: To individuals at accredited institutions for up to one year.

Exchange: Desired: From any region in the world.

WARRENSBURG: Herbarium, Biology Department, Central Missouri State University, (**WARM**), Warrensburg, Missouri 64093, **U.S.A.**

Telephone: 816/429-4933.

Foundation: 1970. Number of specimens: 12.500.

Herbarium: Carex worldwide; local flora; flora of special natural areas.

Director and Curator: DAVID CASTANER, 1934 (Carex).

Specialization in research: Carex; natural area survey.

Loans: Standard conditions.

Exchange: General, principally Carex.

WARSAW: Herbarium, A. L. Kibbe Life Science Station, Western Illinois University, (**WARK**), Warsaw, Illinois 62379, **U.S.A.**

Telephone: 217/256-4519.

Status: Field station of Western Illinois University, a state institution.

Foundation: 1965. Number of specimens: 12.000.

Herbarium: Hancock County, Illinois; flora of Mississippi River area of west-central Illinois.

Important collections: A. L. Kibbe (Hancock County, Illinois vascular plants), Earl L. Lambert (Michigan bryophytes).

Director and Curator: R. D. HENRY, 1927; 309/298-1472 (Vascular flora of west-central Illinois).

Staff members: R. V. GESSNER, 1948 (Mycology).

L. M. O'FLAHERTY, 1941 (Phycology and bryology).

Specialization in research: Flora of Hancock County, Illinois and the Central Mississippi River region.

Loans: To approved individuals and institutions.

Periodical and serial works: Western Illinois University Series in the Biological Sciences.

Exchange: Available: Some local specimens. Desired: Aquatic vascular plants and bryophytes.

WARSZAWA: Zakład Systematyki i Geografii Roślin, Uniwersytetu Warszawskiego, (**WA**), Aleje Ujazdowskie 4, 00-478 Warszawa, **Poland.**

Telephone: 28-75-15.

Status: University.

Foundation: 1917. Number of specimens: 400.000.

Herbarium: General collections, cryptogams and flora of Poland.

Director: ALINA SKIRGIEŁŁO, 1911 (Mycology).

Curator: MIROSŁAWA KOPIJ, 1934 (Phanerogams).

Specialization in research: Flora of Poland and central Asia.

Associated botanic garden: Botanic Garden of the University of Warszawa.

Loans: To recognized botanical institutions.

Exchange: Yes.

WARWICK: Herbarium, Warwickshire Museum, (**WAR**), Market Place, Warwick CV34 4SA England, **Great Britain.**

Telephone: 0926-43431 ext. 2.

Status: Local government.

Foundation: 1834. Number of specimens: 10.000.

Herbarium: Warwickshire (vice-county 38) specialization.

Important collections: Includes the herbarium of W. G. Perry (fl. 1805-35).

Director: WILLIAM C. ALLAN, 1942 (Geology).

Curator: PAMELA J. E. COPSON, 1939, Keeper of Natural History (Biology).

Specialization in research: Warwickshire flora.

Loans: Yes.

Exchange: Considered.

Remarks: Vice-county lists of non-Warwickshire British specimens available upon receipt of large prepaid envelope, stating vice-county required.

WASHINGTON: Herbarium, Catholic University of America, (**LCU**), Michigan Avenue, N.E., Washington, DC 20064, **U.S.A.**

Telephone: 202/635-5257.

Status: Private institution.

Foundation: 1930. *Number of specimens:* 150.000.

Herbarium: General, especially arctic and grasslands.

Director and Curator: CAROLYN F. C. UNZICKER, 1932 (Environmental consulting biologist).

Loans: No special restrictions.

Exchange: General.

WASHINGTON: *Herbarium, U.S. National Arboretum,* (**NA**), Washington, DC 20002, **U.S.A.**

Telephone: 202/472-9248.

Status: U.S. Department of Agriculture.

Foundation: 1934. *Number of specimens:* 450.000.

Herbarium: A worldwide herbarium devoted to cultivated plants to the cultivar level and their wild progenitors.

Important collections: I. C. Martindale herbarium (19th century U.S. and Europe; 80.000 specimens; list of collectors represented in this herbarium published in Taxon, Aug. 1973); C. R. Ball (*Salix*), Goodall (Tierra del Fuego), Furuse (Japan), T. R. Dudley (Peru); Chile, Juan Fernandez Islands; *Manihot, Pinus pungens, Juniperus virginiana.*

Director: J. R. CREECH, 1920 (Cultivated plants; *Rhododendron;* azaleas of Japan).

Curator: FREDERICK G. MEYER, 1917 (*Valeriana* of the New World; *Koelreuteria;* taxonomy of ornamentals).

Staff members: T. R. DUDLEY, 1936 (*Alyssum* and relatives; *Ilex, Viburnum;* cultivated plants).

R. M. JEFFERSON (*Malus,* ornamental crabapples; *Prunus,* ornamental cherries).

P. M. MAZZEO, 1940 (*Betula;* Virginia flora; cultivated plants).

Research collaborator: HAROLD F. WINTERS (Orchidaceae of Puerto Rico).

Specialization in research: Systematics of cultivated, economically, and ethnobotanically important plants and the cultivated woody plants of southeastern U.S.; Aquifoliaceae, Caprifoliaceae.

Associated botanic garden: U.S. National Arboretum.

Loans: To recognized botanical institutions.

Periodical and serial works: U.S. National Arboretum Contributions.

Exchange: Available: Limited number of native plants of eastern U.S. and cultivated ornamentals. Desired: General U.S. and cultivated.

Remarks: Special collection of nuts of the U.S. (cultivars).

WASHINGTON: *United States National Herbarium, Department of Botany, Smithsonian Institution,* (**US**), Washington, DC 20560, **U.S.A.**

Telephone: 202/357-2534 (main office); 357-2795 (herbarium).

Status: Independent U.S. Government Agency.

Foundation: 1868. *Number of specimens:* 4.110.000.

Herbarium: Worldwide, all groups, with emphasis on Neotropics, North America, Pacific Islands, Philippines, and Sri Lanka.

Important collections: U.S. South Pacific Exploring Expedition (1838–42), U. S. North Pacific Exploring Expedition (1853–56), Mexican Boundary Survey (1854–55), California Geological Survey (1860–67), Charles Mohr herbarium, John Donnell Smith herbarium, E. Lucy Braun herbarium, Biltmore herbarium, Colombia *Cinchona* Missions (var. coll.), A. S. Hitchcock and A. Chase (grasses), D. Griffiths (cacti), F. A. McClure (bamboo), A. Mann (diatoms), W. D. Fleming (diatoms), G. J. Hollenberg (marine algae), E. Yale Dawson (marine algae), W. R. Taylor (marine algae), H. A. Allard, M. Bang, A. D. E. Elmer, J. C. Fremont, E. P. Killip, E. D. Merrill, E. Palmer, C. C. Parry, H. Pittier, C. G. Pringle, C. A. Purpus, J. F. Rock, J. N. Rose, A. C. Smith, H. H. Smith, P. C. Standley, C. Wright.

Chairman, Department of Botany: DIETER C. WASSHAUSEN; 202/357-2534 (Neotropical Acanthaceae).

Supervisor: GEORGE F. RUSSELL; 202/357-2795 (Collections management).

Curators: EDWARD S. AYENSU; 202/357-2560 (Comparative anatomy of flowering plants).

RICHARD S. COWAN; 202/357-2568 (Neotropical Leguminosae, especially Caesalpinoideae).

RICHARD H. EYDE; 202/357-2338 (Comparative anatomy of flowering plants).

ROBERT B. FADEN; 202/357-2540 (Commelinaceae; East African flora).

MASON E. HALE, JR.; 202/357-2545 (Taxonomy and chemistry of lichens).

DAVID B. LELLINGER; 202/357-2568 (Taxonomy of neotropical pteridophyta).

DAN H. NICOLSON; 202/357-2521 (Nomenclature; Araceae; floras of Dominica and India).

JAMES N. NORRIS; 202/357-2547 (Tropical and subtropical marine algae).

JOAN W. NOWICKE; 202/357-2521 (Palynology).

ROBERT W. READ; 202/357-2540 (Systematics of neotropical monocots, especially Palmae, Bromeliaceae, Orchidaceae, Cycadales).

HAROLD E. ROBINSON; 202/357-2545 (Bryophytes; Compositae).

MARIE-HÉLÈNE SACHET; 202/357-2301 (Pacific Islands; plant ecology).

STANWYN G. SHETLER; 202/357-2521 (North American *Campanula;* flora of Alaska; biological data banking).

LAURENCE E. SKOG; 202/357-2568 (Gesneriaceae; Coriariaceae).

THOMAS R. SODERSTROM; 202/357-2795 (Systematics of Gramineae, especially Bambusoideae).

JOHN J. WURDACK; 202/357-2542 (Flora of South America; Melastomataceae).

Research associates: KATINA E. BUCHER; 202/357-2547 (Tropical and subtropical marine algae).

José Cuatrecasas; 202/357-2542 (Flora of Colombia; tropical Andean Compositae).

F. Raymond Fosberg, Botanist Emeritus; 202/357-2301 (Taxonomy and ecology of tropical islands vascular plants; Rubiaceae).

Aaron Goldberg; 202/357-2795 (Relationships and evolution of families of angiosperms).

LeRoy H. Harvey; 202/357-2795 (New World *Eragrostis*; Gramineae).

Elbert L. Little, Jr.; 202/357-2715 (Trees of the United States and tropical America; Coniferae).

Kittie F. Parker; 202/357-2542 (Compositae; southwestern U.S. flora).

Lyman B. Smith, Botanist Emeritus; 202/357-2540 (Flora of tropical America; Bromeliaceae, Begoniaceae, Velloziaceae, Brazilian Gramineae, Xyridaceae).

Specialization in research: Neotropical taxonomy; islands ecology; floral and stem anatomy; biosystematics; chemotaxonomy.

Loans: To recognized botanical institutions.

Periodical and serial works: Smithsonian Contributions to Botany; Smithsonian Contributions to Marine Science; Atoll Research Bulletin.

Exchange: Only with institutions on US exchange program. Available: Specimens from North and South America. Desired: Representative specimens of all groups and areas.

WASHINGTON: *Non-articulated Coralline Herbarium, Department of Paleobiology, U.S. National Museum of Natural History, Smithsonian Institution,* (USNC), Washington, DC 20560, U.S.A.

Telephone: 202/381-5089.

Status: Independent U.S. Government agency.

Foundation: 1960. *Number of specimens:* 8.000.

Herbarium: Worldwide herbarium, with emphasis on North Atlantic and Caribbean non-articulated coralline algae; microscope slide and paraffin blocks available for many specimens.

Important collections: Non-articulated coralline algal isotypes from the M. Foslie herbarium; type collections from the Caribbean, sub-Arctic, Hawaii, and Australia.

Director: Richard S. Fiske, 1932 (Volcanology).

Curator: Walter H. Adey, 1934 (Coralline algae).

Staff member: Patricia Adey, 1936.

Loans: M. Foslie isotypes and type specimens not loaned; all other specimens and slides are available for loan to qualified individuals or institutions.

Periodical and serial works: Smithsonian Contributions to the Marine Sciences; Smithsonian Contributions to Paleobiology.

Exchange: Considered; specimens and collections accepted.

WATERLOO: *Herbarium, Department of Biology, University of Waterloo,* (WAT), Waterloo, Ontario,

Canada N2L 3G1.

Telephone: 519/885-1211, ext. 3751.

Status: Part of Provincially funded University.

Foundation: 1968. *Number of specimens:* 43.000 (40.000 vascular plants, 3.000 fungi).

Herbarium: Mainly North American vascular plants.

Important collections: J. K. Morton and J. M. Venn (Islands of Lake Huron and Georgian Bay), J. K. Morton and L. S. Gill (Canadian Labiatae), J. K. Morton (Canadian Caryophyllaceae), W. B. Kendrick (Hyphomycetes of New Zealand), J. K. Morton and Melville (North American Compositae), J. C. Semple and L. Brouillet (North American Compositae), J. F. Calvert (eastern North America).

Director: J. K. Morton, 1928 (Biosystematics, especially Labiatae and Caryophyllaceae; phytogeography).

Curator: Joan M. Venn, 1935 (Vascular plants of Canada).

Staff members: H. C. Duthie, 1938 (Algae).

W. B. Kendrick, 1933 (Fungi).

T. NagRaj, 1929 (Fungi).

J. C. Semple, 1947 (Biosystematics, especially Compositae).

Specialization in research: Ontario and Canadian floras; flora of West Africa; montane floras of tropical Africa; biosystematics of North American Compositae, Caryophyllaceae, and Labiatae; pollen flora of North America; Hyphomycetes and Coelomycetes of the world.

Associated botanic garden: Department of Biology Arboretum, nursery, and greenhouses, ca. 25 acres.

Loans: To recognized botanical institutions.

Periodical and serial works: University of Waterloo Biology Series.

Exchange: Available: Vascular plants of North America, especially Ontario. Desired: Vascular plants of North America.

Remarks: The herbarium is growing rapidly as a result of monographic and floristic studies carried out by the staff. Limited working space is available for visitors.

WATERLOO: *Herbarium, Department of Biology, Wilfrid Laurier University,* (WLU), Waterloo, Ontario, Canada N2L 3C5.

Telephone: 519/884-1970, ext. 226.

Foundation: 1963. *Number of specimens:* 13.454 (12.284 Tracheophyta; 1.170 Bryophyta).

Herbarium: Vascular plants mainly from southern Ontario; bryophytes mainly from Ontario and Newfoundland; flora of Perth County, Ontario; plants from Pelee Island, Ontario; bryophytes of northwestern Ontario and Newfoundland.

Important collections: G. Argus, W. Baldwin, T. Beechey, C. Campbell, J. Cruise, J. Fowler, C. E. Garton, A. E. Garwood, M. Heimburger, A. Legault, D. MacLulich, T. McIntosh, L. Renecker, D. Weber,

A. Wellwood.

> *Curator:* ARNOLD A. WELLWOOD, 1914 (Floristics and genetics).
> *Specialization in research:* Floristic studies.
> *Loans:* To curators of other established herbaria.
> *Exchange:* Active program with several university herbaria.

WATERVILLE: *Herbarium of Parasitic Seed Plants,* **(PSP),** c/o Nature Center, 10045 South River Road, Waterville, Ohio 43566, **U.S.A.**

> *Telephone:* 419/878-0241.
> *Status:* Private.
> *Foundation:* 1953. *Number of specimens:* 15.000.
> *Herbarium:* Parasitic, hemi-parasitic, and saprophytic seed plants of the world, especially North America, and their hosts; woody plants of North America.

> *Director:* MARTIN A. PIEHL.
> *Staff member:* PAULA A. PIEHL, 1938 (Ultrastructure, anatomy, morphology).
> *Specialization in research:* Systematic, ecological, and evolutionary studies of parasitic and hemi-parasitic seed plants; bibliographic work on same; ecological studies of rare and endangered higher plants and habitats.
> *Loans:* To specialists for monographic work.
> *Exchange:* Available and Desired: Parasitic, hemi-parasitic, and saprophytic flowering plants; woody plants of North America. Will attempt to fill special requests for species of our area.
> *Remarks:* Formerly listed under Baton Rouge.

WATERVILLE: *Herbarium, Biology Department, Colby College,* **(WAVI),** Waterville, Maine 04901, **U.S.A.**

> *Telephone:* 207/873-1131, ext. 246.
> *Number of specimens:* 3.000.
> *Herbarium:* Emphasis on Maine and northern New England.

> *Staff members:* DAVID H. FIRMAGE, 1943 (Vascular plants).
> BRUCE E. FOWLES, 1939 (Non-vascular plants).
> *Exchange:* Available: Maine and New England specimens. Desired: New England specimens.

WAU: *Herbarium, Wau Ecology Institute,* **(WAU),** P.O. Box 77, Wau, Morobe Province, **Papua New Guinea.**

> *Telephone:* 446341.
> *Status:* Private foundation.
> *Foundation:* 1971 (1960 as Bishop Museum Field Station). *Number of specimens:* 2.000.
> *Herbarium:* Reference herbarium of plants of the Wau Valley and Mt. Kaindi, *Rhododendron* of Papua New Guinea.

> *Director:* J. L. GRESSITT (Entomology).
> *Curator:* A. ALLISON (Herpetology).
> *Associate:* D. G. FRODIN (University of Papua New Guinea).

> *Specialization in research:* None. Collections mainly support ecological studies.
> *Associated botanic garden:* Arboretum and grounds.
> *Periodical and serial works:* Wau Ecology Institute Handbooks.
> *Loans:* On application to the Director.
> *Exchange:* Most material also represented in LAE.
> *Remarks:* Not at present under regular management, although curatorial work is done from time to time.

WAVERLY: *Herbarium, Biology Department, Wartburg College,* **(WET),** Waverly, Iowa 50677, **U.S.A.**

> *Telephone:* 319/352-1200.
> *Status:* Private college.
> *Foundation:* 1930. *Number of specimens:* 2.500.
> *Herbarium:* Local plants, some Texas (inland) and Mississippi (Gulf Coast); some relict prairie species.
> *Important collections:* Bohumel Shimek.
> *Staff member:* STEPHEN MAIN.
> *Loans:* Borrower must pay costs.

WAWA: *Herbarium, Lake Superior Provincial Park,* **(LSP),** Box 1160, Wawa, Ontario, **Canada** PoS 1Ko.

> *Telephone:* 705/856-2284 (in winter, call 856-2396).
> *Status:* Directed by Ontario Ministry of Natural Resources.
> *Foundation:* 1964. *Number of specimens:* 1.200.
> *Herbarium:* Vascular plants of the eastern Lake Superior region.

> *Park Superintendent:* RAY BONENBERG.
> *Park Naturalist and Curator:* THOMAS S. H. BAXTER.
> *Loans:* Contact Park Superintendent.
> *Exchange:* Desired: Specimens from northern Michigan, Wisconsin and Minnesota.
> *Remarks:* Park open to visitors April through October.

WEATHERFORD: *Western Oklahoma Herbarium, Biology Department, Southwestern Oklahoma State University,* **(WOH),** Weatherford, Oklahoma 73096, **U.S.A.**

> *Telephone:* 405/772-6611, ext. 4301.
> *Foundation:* 1967. *Number of specimens:* 10.500.
> *Herbarium:* Western Oklahoma.
> *Director and Curator:* RONALD H. SEGAL, 1940.

WELLESLEY: *Herbarium, Department of Biological Sciences, Wellesley College,* **(WELC),** Wellesley, Massachusetts 02181, **U.S.A.**

> *Telephone:* 617/235-0320.
> *Status:* Private institution.
> *Foundation:* 1876. *Number of specimens:* 92.500.
> *Herbarium:* Lichens, mosses, and angiosperms of the U.S., especially New England.
> *Important collections:* Clara E. Cummings (li-

chens), Grace E. Howard (lichens).

Curator: Position vacant at this time.

Associated botanic garden: Alexandra Botanic Garden and the H. H. Hunnewell Arboretum.

Loans: Usual regulations.

Remarks: Herbarium relatively inactive at this time. Most of the holdings are duplicated at GH, Cambridge.

WELLINGTON: *Herbarium, National Museum of New Zealand,* (**WELT**), Private Bag, Wellington, **New Zealand.**

Telephone: 859-609.

Status: Statutory body funded by government.

Foundation: 1865. *Number of specimens:* 300.000.

Herbarium: New Zealand and related floras (mostly Australia, Pacific, Europe, N. & S. America).

Important collections: New Zealand collections, including types, of: B. C. Aston, J. Banks and D. Solander, S. Berggren, J. Buchanan, L. Cockayne, W. Colenso, A. Cunningham, W. H. Harvey (Algae), T. Kirk, C. C. Knight (Lichens), V. W. Lindauer (Algae), W. Martin, J. H. McMahon, W. R. B. Oliver, D. Petrie, G. O. K. Sainsbury (Mosses). Other important collections include herbaria of J. G. Baker, Robert Brown (Australia), William Swainson (S. America), Sylvanus Thompson. Overseas collectors: F. B. H. & E. D. W. Brown (Pacific), E. Christophersen (Pacific, Tristan da Cunha), E. B. Copeland (Ferns), A. Fendler (Ferns of Trinidad), C. N. Forbes (Pacific), F. R. Fosberg (Pacific), H. & J. Groves (Charophytes), W. F. Hillebrand (Hawaii), O. Nordstedt (Algae), J. F. Rock (Hawaii), H. St. John (Pacific), J. Tilden (Algae), T. G. Yuncker (Pacific).

Director: J. C. YALDWYN.

Curator: P. J. BROWNSEY, 1948 (Ferns of New Zealand).

Staff member: NANCY M. ADAMS (Marine algae of New Zealand, botanical illustration).

Specialization in research: Flora of New Zealand and related areas.

Loans: In general to recognized botanical institutions.

Periodical and serial works: National Museum of New Zealand records.

Exchange: Limited exchanges of N.Z. plants occasionally undertaken for plants from floras with N.Z. affinities.

WELLINGTON: *The H. D. Gordon Herbarium, Botany Department, Victoria University of Wellington,* (**WELTU**), Private Bag, Wellington, **New Zealand.**

Telephone: 04-721-000.

Status: University.

Number of specimens: 20.000.

Herbarium: Flora of New Zealand (mostly vascular plants), Myrtaceae of New Caledonia.

Director: JOHN KENNETH HEYES, 1928 (Plant physiology).

Curator: BARRY VICTOR SNEDDON, 1942 (Exper-

imental taxonomy of Australasian *Colobanthus* and *Microseris*).

Staff member: JOHN WYNDHAM DAWSON, 1928 (Taxonomy of New Zealand Umbelliferae and Pacific capsular Myrtaceae).

Specialization in research: New Zealand vascular flora; New Caledonian Myrtaceae.

Loans: To recognized botanical institutions, normally for six months but the period may be extended on request.

Exchange: Available: Limited number of New Zealand plants. Desired: Overseas plants with N.Z. affinities.

WENHAM: *Herbarium, Biology Department, Gordon College,* (**WMGC**), 255 Grapevine Road, Wenham, Massachusetts 01984, **U.S.A.**

Telephone: 617/927-2300.

Foundation: 1969. *Number of specimens:* 1.010.

Herbarium: Teaching collection of vascular plants, mosses, lichens, and algae.

Director and Curator: THOMAS C. DENT, 1928 (Taxonomy).

Specialization in research: Numerical analysis toward species separation and paleogeographic distribution of North American sugar maples.

Loans: Limited.

Exchange: Yes.

WEST CHESTER: *Darlington Herbarium, Department of Biology, West Chester State College,* (**DWC**), West Chester, Pennsylvania 19380, **U.S.A.**

Telephone: 215/436-2751.

Foundation: 1826 (second oldest institutional herbarium in U.S.A.). *Number of specimens:* 30.000.

Herbarium: Vascular plants of Europe and U.S.A.

Important collections: Historical collections of early American botanists 1820–1855; C. S. Rafinesque, Thomas Nuttall, C. W. Short, D. von Schweinitz, John Torrey, William Baldwin, John Fremont, I. A. Lapham, Asa Gray, Jacob Wolle (Jamaica), Sir William Hooker, George Engelmann, Elias Durand, E. Michener (mosses, lichens), John Bartram, H. Marshall, Franklin Expeditions, W. H. Harvey (algae; Scotland), J. Hoopes (ornamental evergreens).

Curator: WILLIAM R. OVERLEASE, 1925 (*Quercus,* red oak group).

Associated botanic garden: Robert B. Gordon Natural Area for Environmental Studies (about 60 acres on campus).

Loans: Type specimens are not sent on loan. All others are available for loan to qualified individuals or institutions.

Remarks: William Darlington's personal scientific library and personal annotated copies of most of his published books are housed here. Annotated periodical materials of the 1820-1855 period are also housed here.

WEST LAFAYETTE: *Kriebel Herbarium, Depart-*

ment of Biological Sciences, Purdue University, (**PUL**), West Lafayette, Indiana 47907, **U.S.A.**
Telephone: 317/493-1290; 493-1500.
Foundation: 1873 (dedicated Kriebel Herbarium in 1961). *Number of specimens:* 53.700.
Herbarium: Worldwide; algae, bryophytes, vascular plants.
Important collections: Ralph Kriebel (Indiana).
Director and Curator: MORRIS LEVY, 1944 (Evolutionary biology).
Specialization in research: Systematics of *Rudbeckia* and *Phlox*.
Loans: To recognized botanical institutions and researchers.
Exchange: Available: Vascular plants of Indiana and contiguous areas. Desired: *Phlox, Oenothera, Rudbeckia*.
Remarks: 50.000 slides of chytrids; formerly listed under Lafayette.

WEST LAFAYETTE: *Arthur Herbarium, Department of Botany and Plant Pathology, Purdue University*, (**PUR**), West Lafayette, Indiana 47907, **U.S.A.**
Telephone: 317/749-6511.
Foundation: 1888. *Number of specimens:* 88.000.
Herbarium: Rust fungi (Uredinales).
Important collections: Rust collections of J. C. Arthur, E. W. D. and M. M. Holway, G. R. Bisby, G. B. Cummins, H. S. Jackson, F. D. Kern, E. B. Mains, C. R. Orton, E. Bartholomew, E. Bethel, W. C. Blasdale, M. A. Carlton, C. H. Peck, J. J. Davis, J. Dearness, F. S. Earle, D. Griffiths, W. A. Kellerman, S. M. Tracy, W. H. Long, J. F. Hennen, A. P. Viegas, J. C. Lindquist, H. H. Whetzel, H. W. Thurston, J. Clemens, Stevens.
Director and Curator: JOE F. HENNEN, 1928 (Taxonomy of Uredinales).
Specialization in research: Taxonomy of Uredinales worldwide.
Loans: In general to recognized workers and institutions.
Exchange: Available: Uredinales from North America. Desired: Uredinales from any region.
Remarks: Herbarium contains most of the important rust collections from all over the world; formerly listed under Lafayette.

WHITNEY: *Herbarium, Algonquin Park Museum, Algonquin Provincial Park, Ministry of Natural Resources*, (**APM**), Box 219, Whitney, Ontario, **Canada** K0J 2M0.
Telephone: 705/633-5592; 633-5505.
Status: Associated with provincial government.
Foundation: 1969. *Number of specimens:* 3.200.
Herbarium: All specimens from within Park boundaries (3.000 square miles).
Important collections: D. F. Brunton, W. J. Crins, P. F. Maycock, P. D. Pratt, A. A. Reznicek, S. Walshe, J. G. Woods.
Director: DAN STRICKLAND, 1942 (Ornithology).

Curator: RON TOZER, 1941 (Ornithology).
Specialization in research: Floristics.
Loans: Short term to institutions only.

WIEN: *Naturhistorisches Museum, Botanische Abteilung*, (**W**), Burgring 7, Postfach 417, A-1014 Wien, **Austria.**
Telephone: 0222-934541, 932754.
Status: Directed by the state.
Foundation: 1807. *Number of specimens:* 3.500.000.
Herbarium: Worldwide, especially Central Europe, Mediterranean area, Near and Middle East, tropical lichens.
Important collections: Herbarium E. Hackel (Gramineae); herb. Reichenbach (Orchids); T. Kotschy, collections from Near East; H. Handel-Mazzetti, coll. from China; K.-H. Rechinger, coll. from Greece and SW Asia; herb. A. Zahlbruckner (lichens); herb. J. Juratzka (Bryophyta); herb. J. B. W. Lindenberg (Hepaticae); herb. A. Grunow (Algae); herb. F. Petrak (Fungi).
Director: HARALD RIEDL, 1936 (Pyrenocarpous lichens, especially from tropical areas; Boraginaceae, Araceae, mainly extratropical; *Ephedra*; Ranunculaceae; flora of SW Asia).
Staff members: FRANZ KRENDL, 1926 (Cytotaxonomy of *Galium, Asperula*; flora of the Mediterranean area).
UWE PASSAUER, 1942 (Higher fungi, especially fungus-flora of caves).
ADOLF POLATSCHEK, 1932 (Cytotaxonomy of Cruciferae, especially *Erysimum*; flora of the Austrian Alps).
Unofficial research associates: A. GILLI (*Orobanche*, flora of Papua-New Guinea, Ecuador).
K.-H. RECHINGER (Flora of SW Asia, Greece, *Rumex*, Labiatae, Compositae).
HELENE SCHIMAN-CZEIKA (Flora of SW Asia; cyanophilic lichens).
Specialization in research: Flora of Central and Southern Europe, Near and Middle East; lichens from all parts of the world with emphasis on tropical pyrenocarpous groups; vegetation and ecology of arid zones; flora of caves.
Loans: In general to recognized botanical institutions.
Periodical and serial works: Annalen des Naturhistorischen Museums in Wien.
Exchange: Available: Cryptogamae exsiccatae Musei Historico-Naturalis Vindobonensis; various phanerogams and cryptogams from Europe.
Remarks: Part of the phanerogam collection destroyed by war accidents, corresponding to nrs. 1–100, 452–1388, 1855–2828 of Dalla Torre & Harms, Genera Siphonogamarum (see Taxon vol. 1, p. 29).

WIEN: *Herbarium, Forstliche Bundesversuchsanstalt*, (**WFBVA**), Institut f. Standort der Forstlichen Bundesversuchsanstalt, A-1131 Wien, Schönbrunn, **Austria.**

Telephone: 0222-823638, 0222-842241.
Status: Federal research institute of the Ministry of Agriculture and Forestry.
Number of specimens: 50.000.
Herbarium: Forest plant communities.
Important collections: Coll. M. Onno, coll. A. Neumann.
Director: H. JELEM, forester (site classification).
Curator: A. DRESCHER, 1948 (Vegetation science).
Staff member: M. REMESCH (Vegetation science).
Specialization in research: Vegetation science in connection with site classification for forestry purposes.
Associated botanic garden: Forstliche Bundesversuchsanstalt, Versuchsgarten Tulln, A-3430 Tulln, Bildeiche (*Salix*-assortment for breeding).
Periodical and serial works: Mitteilungen der Forstlichen Bundesversuchsanstalt Wien.

WIEN: *Herbarium, Botanisches Institut der Universität für Bodenkultur,* (**WHB**), Gregor Mendel-Strasse 33, A-1180 Wien, **Austria.**
Telephone: 0222-342500/241.
Status: University.
Foundation: 1873. *Number of specimens:* 19.000.
Herbarium: Mostly plants from Austria and neighboring countries.
Director: ERICH HÜBL, 1930 (Physiographic ecology and vegetation of Eastern Austria).
Curator: WALTER FORSTNER, 1923 (Ruderal flora and vegetation of eastern Austria).
Associated botanic garden: Botanischer Garten der Universität für Bodenkultur.
Loans: No special regulations.
Exchange: With European countries.

WIEN: *Herbarium, Niederösterreichisches Landesmuseum,* (**WNLM**), Herrengasse 9, A-1014 Wien, **Austria.**
Telephone: 0222/63 57 11/3128.
Status: Directed by government of Lower Austria.
Foundation: Private foundation 1912, since 1945 directed by government. *Number of specimens:* 20.000.
Herbarium: Mainly Pteridophyta and Spermatophyta of Lower Austria, some from Burgenland.
Director: JOHANNES GRÜNDLER, 1918.
Curator: GERHARD TUISL, 1942 (Nature protection).
Specialization in research: Flora of Lower Austria.
Loans: To recognized botanical institutions.

WIEN: *Institut für Botanik und Botanischer Garten der Universität,* (**WU**), Rennweg 14, A-1030 Wien, **Austria.**
Telephone: 0222/73-12-58 and 72-68-49.
Status: State University.
Foundation: 1749; 1754 botanical garden; 1879 her-

barium. *Number of specimens:* Over 1.000.000.
Herbarium: Worldwide, particularly rich in types and collections from S.E. Europe, S.W. Asia, China, Africa.
Important collections: L. Adamovic (S.E. Europe), A. Baldacci (S.E. Europe), V. von Borbás (Hist. Hungary), Bornmüller (especially Orient), J. Breidler (C. Europe, mosses), J. Brunnthaler (especially Crypt. from Africa), C. F. Ecklon & Zeyher (Cape), K. Eggerth, orig. coll. especially Lich.), F. Ehrendorfer (especially Mediterranean, Anatolia, Tropics), De Kindt (Angola), I. Dimonic (Albania, Macedonia), I. Dörfler (especially Albania, Crete), U. J. Faurie (Japan, mosses), F. Fautrey (Crypt. Côte d'Or), A. Ginzberger (N., C. Europe, Balkan pen., Brazil with Zerny), Grimus, K. F. von Grimburg (Orig. coll. Austria, Balkan pen.), E. von Halácsy (orig. coll. incl. Herb. Graec. and Herb. Europ. with Herb. K. Richter), H. Handel-Mazzetti (Europe, S.W. Asia, China, Crypt.), A. A. von Hayek (especially Wolhynia, C. Europe), J. M. Hildebrandt (Aethiopia), D. H. Hoppe (Mosses), Karl Keck (incl. Herb. A. F. Lang with Rochel's Pl. Banat. and other orig. specim.), M. Jabornegg (Austria), Rev. Jäschke (W. Himalaya), E. Janchen (especially Balkan pen., p.p. with B. Watzl and Hand.-Mazz.), A. Kerner (orig. coll., C. Europe), J. A. Knapp (Iran), A. von Krempelhuber (Lich.), F. Luschan (orig. coll. S. Anat., Mesop.), L. Menyhárt (Sambesi), Nemetz (Eur. Turkey), Orphanides (Greece), Pichler (Greek Archip., Anat., Iran), Reuss (pat. & fil. orig. coll., Europe), Sardagna (S. Europe), V. F. Schiffner (Algae, Hepat.), Schlagintweit (Himalaya), Schweinfurth (Yemen, Sokotra), Schoch (China), O. Simony & Paulay (S. Arabia and Sokotra), Konklar (orig. coll., Austria), P. Sintenis (Cyprus, Orient, Porto Rico), G. C. Spreitzenhofer (Medit.), Stapf (Iran), J. Steiner (Lich.), Strauss (Iran), Ullepitsch (orig. coll., C. Europe), F. K. M. Vierhapper (especially C. and S.E. Europe), Vöth (Orchid. of Europe and S.W. Asia), Watanabe (Japan), Wettstein R. (Brazil, C. and S. E. Europe, Africa), Wulfen (Algae, Lich.), A. Zahlbruckner (Lich.), Zenker (Cameroun), Zederbauer (Anatolia).

Director of Botanical Garden and Institute: FRIEDRICH EHRENDORFER, 1927 (Biosystematics of Rubiaceae, Dipsacaceae, Asteraceae-Anthemideae, primitive woody angiosperms; biogeography; flora of C. Europe, Mediterranean area and S. W. Asia).
Vice Director: OTTO GSCHÖF, 1927.
Curator: EVA SCHÖNBECK-TEMESY (Floras of S.W. Asia and C. Europe, Rubiaceae).
Staff members: PETER AMBROS, 1953 (Cytology).
KARL CARNIEL, 1920 (Angiosperm embryology, cytology, electron microscopy).
MANFRED A. FISCHER, 1942 (Biosystematics of *Veronica*, flora of C. Europe, Mediterranean area, S.W. Asia).
GÜNTER GEBER, 1954 (Cytology, karyosystematics).
LOTHAR GEITLER, 1899 (Cytology, algology;

Cyanophyceae, diatoms).

HARALD GREGER, 1942 (Phytochemistry, chemosystematics of Asteraceae-Anthemideae, Valerianaceae).

JOHANN GREILHUBER, 1947 (Cytology, cytogenetics, embryology, karyosystematics).

WALTER GUTERMANN, 1935 (Systematics of *Artemisia*, flora and phytogeography of C. Europe, alpine plants, nomenclature).

MICHAEL HESSE, 1943 (Cytology, electron microscopy, micromorphology).

GERHARD KARRER, 1955 (Plant geography, floristics).

SUSANNE KLENNER (Flower ecology).

WALTER LEINFELLNER, 1910 (Morphology).

JOSEF LOIDL, 1955 (Cytology, cytogenetics).

WILFRIED MORAWETZ, 1951 (Biology of tropical plants, taxonomy of *Jacaranda*).

LISELOTTE NIKLAS (Librarian).

HERALD NIKLFELD, 1940 (Chorology, phytocoenology, mapping flora of C. Europe).

HELENE PEYER (Cytology, algology).

CHRISTIAN PUFF, 1949 (Biosystematics of Rubiaceae, mainly Africa and Madagascar).

LUISE SCHRATT (Ecology of water macrophytes, floristics).

DIETER SCHWEIZER, 1938 (Cytology, cytogenetics, cell biology).

WALTER TITZ, 1941 (Angiosperm systematics, especially numerical, biometry, biosystematics).

ELISABETH TSCHERMAK-WOESS (Cytology, cytogenetics, protistology).

KARIN VALANT (Chemosystematics of *Achillea*).

STEFAN VOGEL, 1925 (Flower ecology, plant-animal relations).

ANTON WEBER, 1947 (Morphology, systematics).

Specialization in research: Morphology, reproductive biology, distribution, systematics, cytogenetics and karyology; floristics and plant geography of C. Europe, the Mediterranean area and W. Eurasia.

Associated botanic garden: Yes.

Loans: To recognized botanical institutions.

Periodical and serial works: Plant Systematics and Evolution (in continuation of Österreichische Botanische Zeitschrift).

Exchange: On request.

WIJSTER: *Biological Station,* **(WBS)** – *see* WAGENINGEN.

WILLIAMSBURG: *Herbarium, Department of Biology, The College of William and Mary,* **(WILLI)**, Williamsburg, Virginia 23185, **U.S.A.**

Telephone: 804/253-4240.

Foundation: 1969. *Number of specimens:* 36.042.

Herbarium: Emphasis on Virginia flora.

Important collections: J. T. Baldwin, B. Speese, Ber-

nard Mikula (8.000; Virginia ca. 1949), Thomas F. Wieboldt (2.000; Virginia 1970–1980); vouchers from 16 floristic studies for areas in the coastal plain, Piedmont, or mountains; vouchers for studies of the Cichorieae, Helenieae, Heliantheae, and Senecioneae of the Asteraceae of Virginia and for the Campanulaceae and Gentianaceae of Virginia.

Director: GUSTAV W. HALL, 1934 (Biosystematics of *Bidens*, Asteraceae).

Curator: DONNA M. EGGERS WARE, 1942 (Taxonomy of North American *Valerianella;* floristics of coastal plain of Virginia).

Specialization in research: Floristics of the coastal plain of Virginia, particularly of the Peninsula of Virginia; treatments of selected tribes of the Asteraceae and miscellaneous other families as contributions toward the proposed manual of the flora of Virginia; revision of the genus *Valerianella* in North America; field research on selected endangered or threatened species.

Loans: For six months, with extensions granted when needed.

Exchange: With Virginia and other southeastern states; want to initiate exchanges with herbaria in South Carolina, Georgia, and Mississippi.

WILMINGTON: *Herbarium, Department of Biology, University of North Carolina,* **(WNC)**, Wilmington, North Carolina 28406, **U.S.A.**

Telephone: 919/791-4330, ext. 2481.

Foundation: 1965. *Number of specimens:* 16.000.

Herbarium: Marine algae of North Carolina and tropical America; fungi of Ohio and North Carolina; vascular plants of North Carolina, the southeastern coastal plain, and eastern North America.

Director and Curator: DAVID J. SIEREN, 1941 (Vascular plant taxonomy).

Curators: DONALD F. KAPRAUN, 1945; 919/791-4330, ext. 2484 (Algal ecology).

DAVID E. PADGETT, 1945; 919/791-4330, ext. 2486 (Lower aquatic fungi).

Specialization in research: Flora of eastern North Carolina.

Associated botanic garden: Herbert Bluethenthal Memorial Wildflower Preserve.

Loans: Normal regulations.

Exchange: Available: Marine algae (North Carolina and tropical America); fungi, bryophytes, and vascular plants (mostly from North Carolina). Desired: Specimens of all groups, especially from tropical and eastern North America.

WILMINGTON: *Herbarium, Department of Biology, Wilmington College,* **(WSFA)**, Kettering Hall, Room 203, Box 1301, Wilmington, Ohio 45177, **U.S.A.**

Telephone: 513/382-6661, ext. 237.

Foundation: 1935. *Number of specimens:* 2.500.

Herbarium: Local flora; bryophytes.

Director: S. F. ANLIOT, 1937 (Local flora; bryophyte communities; vegetation of Ohio and cold temperate regions, i.e., Patagonia, northern Sweden, and southeastern Alaska).

Specialization in research: Distribution and habitats of southwestern Ohio bryophytes.

Loans: Yes.

Exchange: Yes, mainly bryophytes.

WILNIUS — *see* VILNIUS.

WINCHESTER: *Herbarium, Winchester College Museum,* (**WTR**), Winchester, Hampshire, England, **Great Britain.**

WINDHOEK: *S.W.A. Herbarium,* (**WIND**), Agricultural Buildings, 83 Leutwein Street, Private Bag X13184, 9000 Windhoek, **South -West Africa.**

Telephone: 061-32041 ext. 35.

Status: State herbarium.

Foundation: 1953. *Number of specimens:* 40.000.

Herbarium: Phanerogams, mainly South West Africa, Republic of South Africa, Angola, Botswana.

Important collections: K. Dinter, W. Giess, H. Merxmüller & W. Giess, B. de Winter.

Curator and Officer-in-charge: M. A. N. MÜLLER, 1948 (Compositae).

Staff members: W. C. NEL, 1957, Professional Officer (General plant identification).

H. E. STOFFBERG, 1946 (Clerical).

Specialization in research: Flora of South West Africa.

Associated botanic garden: S.W.A. Botanic Garden.

Loans: In general to recognized botanical institutions.

Periodical and serial works: "Dinteria," contribution to the flora and vegetation of South West Africa.

Exchange: Available: South West African plants. Desired: mainly Southern African and Angola duplicates.

WINDSOR: *Herbarium, Department of Biology, University of Windsor,* (**WOCB**), 400 Sunset Avenue, Windsor, Ontario, **Canada** N9B 3P4.

Telephone: 519/253-4232.

Foundation: 1957. *Number of specimens:* 2.500.

Herbarium: Local prairie flora; Ojibway Park.

Director and Curator: W. G. BENEDICT, 1919 (Local flora).

Specialization in research: Phytopathology.

WINNEMUCCA: *Herbarium of the Winnemucca District, U.S. Department of the Interior, Bureau of Land Management,* (**WDNE**), 705 East 4th Street, Winnemucca, Nevada 89445, **U.S.A.**

Telephone: 702/623-3676.

Status: U.S. Department of the Interior, Bureau of Land Management.

Foundation: 1979. *Number of specimens:* 1.500.

Herbarium: Vascular flora of northern Nevada, especially Humboldt and Pershing counties; western Great Basin.

Important collections: M. P. Yoder-Williams.

Curator: MICHAEL P. YODER-WILLIAMS, 1953 (Nevada flora).

Staff member: MARY J. YODER-WILLIAMS, 1949 (Botanical illustration).

Specialization in research: Vascular flora of north-central Nevada, emphasizing flora of various ranges in the Winnemucca District of the Bureau of Land Management.

Loans: In general to recognized botanical institutions.

Periodical and serial works: Occasional reports published by the Bureau of Land Management for limited distribution.

Exchange: Available on request.

Remarks: Herbarium is newly established as a repository for ongoing botanical inventories of the basins and ranges of north-central Nevada.

WINNIPEG: *Herbarium, Wildlife Biological Services, Manitoba Department of Natural Resources,* (**MDNR**), Box 14, 1495 St. James Street, Winnipeg, Manitoba, **Canada** R3H 0W9.

Telephone: 204/786-9447.

Foundation: 1938. *Number of specimens:* 1.000.

Herbarium: Primarily wetland species.

Staff member: RICHARD R. P. STARDOM.

Specialization in research: Determination of muskrat habitat preferences and the effects of marsh manipulation on the preferred plant species; big game habitat studies.

Remarks: Duplicates deposited at WIN.

WINNIPEG: *Herbarium, Manitoba Museum of Man and Nature,* (**MMMN**), 190 Rupert Street, Winnipeg, Manitoba, **Canada** R3B 0N2.

Telephone: 204/956-2830, ext. 153.

Status: Private institution.

Foundation: 1932. *Number of specimens:* 10.000.

Herbarium: Mainly vascular plants of Manitoba; some bryophytes and fungi from Manitoba.

Director: H. DAVID HEMPHILL, 1933.

Curator: KAREN L. JOHNSON, 1941 (Plant ecology and geography).

Specialization in research: Occurrence and distribution of rare vascular plants of Manitoba; distribution patterns of vascular plants in the province.

Loans: To recognized botanical institutions or qualified individuals.

Exchange: Available: Limited number of Manitoba vascular plants. Desired: Arctic and alpine vascular plants.

Remarks: Most of the vascular plant specimens have been entered into the National Inventory Program Computer in Ottawa; information includes phenology.

WINNIPEG: *Herbarium, Department of Biology, University of Winnipeg,* (**UWPG**), 515 Portage Avenue, Winnipeg, Manitoba, **Canada** R3B 2E9.

Telephone: 204/786-7811, ext. 435.
Foundation: 1971. *Number of specimens:* 3.000.
Herbarium: Manitoba vascular plants.
Curator: R. STANIFORTH, 1946; 204/786-7811, ext. 433 (*Polygonum* sect. *Persicaria*).
Loans: To recognized scientific and educational institutions upon consent of the curator.

WINNIPEG: *Herbarium, Department of Botany, University of Manitoba,* (**WIN**), Winnipeg, Manitoba, **Canada** R3T 2N2.

Telephone: 204/474-9368.
Foundation: 1907. *Number of specimens:* 50.000 (40.000 vascular plants, 10.000 fungi).
Herbarium: Flora of Manitoba; worldwide representation.
Director: J. REID, 1928 (Mycology; inoperculate discomycetes; stromatic sphaeridales).
Curator: HELEN KENNEDY, 1944 (Flowering plants; Marantaceae; pollination biology).
Staff members: D. PUNTER, 1936 (Flowering plants; *Ceratophyllum;* mycology).
 JENNIFER M. SHAY, 1930 (Marsh flora; ecology).
Specialization in research: Flora of Manitoba; taxonomy of Marantaceae.
Loans: Generally to recognized botanical institutions.
Exchange: Available: Manitoba plants. Desired: Worldwide but particularly North American and boreal/arctic Eurasian material.

WINNIPEG: *Forest Research Laboratory, Department of Forestry and Rural Development,* (**WINF**) -- incorporated in CAFB and CFB, Edmonton.

WINNIPEG: *Mycological Herbarium, Forest Research Laboratory, Department of Forestry and Rural Development,* (**WINFM**) -- incorporated in CFB, Edmonton.

WINONA: *Herbarium, Biology Department, Saint Mary's College,* (**WINO**), Winona, Minnesota 55987, **U.S.A.**

Telephone: 507/452-4430, ext. 285.
Foundation: 1940. *Number of specimens:* 2.500.
Herbarium: Plants of Minnesota, especially the southeastern part; marine algae.
Director: Brother CHARLES SEVERIN.

WINOOSKI: *Herbarium, Biology Department, Saint Michael's College,* (**SMCW**), Winooski, Vermont 05404, **U.S.A.**

Telephone: 802/655-2000, ext. 2621.
Foundation: 1976. *Number of specimens:* 1.500.
Herbarium: Flora of Vermont, New York, and New England.

Director and Curator: FREDERICK H. DOBSON, III, 1941 (*Bunchosia*, Malpighiaceae).
Specialization in research: Systematics and chemistry of *Bunchosia* (Malpighiaceae).
Loans: To recognized botanical institutions.
Exchange: Available: Vermont flora. Desired: Flora of New England and New York.

WINSTON-SALEM: *Herbarium, Salem College,* (**SC**), Winston-Salem, North Carolina 27108, **U.S.A.**

Telephone: 919/721-2788.
Status: Private college.
Foundation: 1771. *Number of specimens:* 1.000.
Herbarium: Primarily southeastern U.S., especially North Carolina; some specimens from the 1800's.
Director and Curator: THOMAS B. MOWBRAY, 1940 (Plant ecology; taxonomy).
Specialization in research: Plant population/community dynamics; gradient analysis of plant communities.
Loans: To recognized herbaria.

WINSTON-SALEM: *Herbarium, Department of Biology, Wake Forest University,* (**WFU**), Winston-Salem, North Carolina 27109, **U.S.A.** (Information 1976)

Status: Private university.
Foundation: 1956. *Number of specimens:* 12.000.
Herbarium: Local vascular plants; flora of Carolinas, especially of North Piedmont and North Carolina; seedlings of woody angiosperms.

WINTERTON: *The David Killick Herbarium, Cathedral Peak Forest Research Station,* (**CPF**), Private Bag Gewaagd, P.O. Winterton, Natal, **South Africa.** (Information 1974)

Status: Established for botanical survey.
Foundation: 1951. *Number of specimens:* 3.000.
Herbarium: Flora of Cathedral Peak Forest Research Station.

WISE: *Herbarium, Biology Department, Clinch Valley College of the University of Virginia,* (**CVCW**), Wise, Virginia 24293, **U.S.A.**

Telephone: 703/328-2431.
Foundation: 1968. *Number of specimens:* 4.000.
Herbarium: Southwest Virginia, especially Wise County.
Director: J. REX BAIRD, 1932 (Myricaceae).

WOLFVILLE: *E. C. Smith Herbarium, Department of Biology, Acadia University,* (**ACAD**), Wolfville, Nova Scotia, **Canada.**

Telephone: 902/542-2201, ext. 335.
Foundation: 1910. *Number of specimens:* 128.000 (110.000 vascular plants, 15.000 fungi, 3.000 cryptogams and lichens).
Herbarium: Maritime provinces of Canada.
Important collections: M. S. Brown (bryophytes), R. H. Wetmore (*Aster, Solidago*).

Curator: S. P. VANDER KLOET, 1942 (*Vaccinium*).
Staff members: D. W. GRUND, 1938 (Boletes of Nova Scotia).
K. A. HARRISON, 1901 (Hydnaceae).
Specialization in research: Systematics of *Vaccinium, Boletum,* and *Hydnaceae.*
Loans: To recognized and reciprocating institutions, not to individuals.

WOODLAND HILLS: *Herbarium, Los Angeles Pierce College,* (**LAPC**), 6201 Winnetka Avenue, Woodland Hills, California 91371, **U.S.A.**
Telephone: 213/347-0551.
Status: Community college.
Foundation: 1948. *Number of specimens:* 6.000.
Herbarium: Local flora and exotic ornamentals.
Important collections: Ida Haines Murphy Preserve of the Nature Conservancy.
Director: A. LEE HAINES, 1912 (Agavaceae, Bromeliaceae).
Curator: P. A. MEYERS (Subalpine vegetation).
Associated botanic garden: Pierce College Arboretum.

WOODS HOLE: *Herbarium, Marine Biological Laboratory, George M. Gray Museum,* (**SPWH**), Woods Hole, Massachusetts 02543, **U.S.A.**
Telephone: 617/548-3705, ext. 531.
Foundation: 1888. *Number of specimens:* 10.000.
Herbarium: Algae (3.500); fungi; vascular plants (6.500) from the fringe of the sea, eastern North America.
Important collections: W. G. Farlow, Francis W. Pennell, John M. Fogg, Jr., Hannah Croasdale, Frank Collins (flora of Penikese Islands).
Director: PAUL R. GROSS, 1928 (Developmental biology).
Curators: LOUISE BUSH, 1907 (*Turbellaria*).
EDWIN T. MOUL, 1903 (Marine algae; lower plants).
WESLEY N. TIFFNEY, 1909 (Marine botany; vascular plants).
RUTH TURNER, 1914 (Malacology).
Staff members: EVA MONTIERO, 1928.
SUSAN WIER, 1951.
Loans: To institutions for 2–3 months.
Exchange: Yes.

WORCESTER: *Herbarium, Department of Biology, Clark University,* (**CUW**), Worcester, Massachusetts 01610, **U.S.A.**
Telephone: 617/793-7514.
Status: Private institution.
Foundation: 1929. *Number of specimens:* 70.000.
Herbarium: Vascular plants, lichens, coralline algae; teaching collection worldwide in scope; emphasis on Worcester County, Massachusetts.
Director: H. WILLIAM JOHANSEN, 1932 (Corallinaceae, Rhodophyta).
Staff member: VERNON AHMADJIAN (Lichens).

Specialization in research: Systematics of articulated Corallinaceae; lichen biology.
Loans: Usual regulations.

WROCŁAW: *Herbarium, Department of Botany, Museum of Natural History, Wrocław University,* (**WRSL**), ul. Sienkiewicza 21, 50-335 Wrocław, **Poland.**
Telephone: 22-86-14.
Status: Directed by the University.
Foundation: 1821. *Number of specimens:* 350.000.
Herbarium: Worldwide, all systematic groups.
Important collections: Herbarium K.A.G. Lauterbach (50.000 specimens).
Director: WLADYSLAW RYDZEWSKI, 1911.
Head of Botany Department: JERZY HRYNKIEWICZ, 1926 (Dendrology).
Curator: WANDA STOJANOWSKA, 1939 (Myxomycetes).
Staff members: EDWARD KOZIOŁ, 1938 (Algae).
HALINA FUGLEWICZ, 1953.
Specialization in research: Flora Silesiae.
Associated botanic garden: Ogród Botaniczny Uniwersytetu Wrocławskiego.
Loans: To recognized botanical institutes.
Periodical and serial works: Flora Silesiaca Exsiccata.
Exchange: Available: Specimens from Silesia. Desired: Specimens from all groups.

WUCHANG: *Herbarium of Wuhan University, Department of Biology,* (**WH**), Wuchang, Hubei, **People's Republic of China.**
Status: University.
Foundation: 1930. *Number of specimens:* 300.000.
Herbarium: Western and Central China, all systematic groups.
Important collections: Chou H. C., Chung H. H., Sun Hsiang-Chung, Tai Lun-Ying and Chen Chong-Hai.
Director: SUN HSIANG-CHUNG, 1908 (Taxonomy and ecology of flowering plants of Central China, especially aquatic plants).
Curator: WANG HUI-QIN, 1935 (Taxonomy and morphology of Gramineae and Hydrocharitaceae).
Staff members: CHOU LING-YUN, 1917 (Pandanaceae and Najadaceae).
CHUNG XIONG-WEN, 1936 (Bryophytes).
LI YI-JIAN, 1934 (Freshwater algae, especially Characeae).
Specialization in research: Flora of Central China.
Periodical and serial works: Journal of Natural Science of Wuhan University.
Exchange: Desired: Crop plants of worldwide economic importance.

WUCHOU: – – *see* WUZHOU.

WUGONG: *Herbarium, Northwest Botanical In-*

stitute, Academia Sinica, **(WUK)**, Wugong, Shaanxi, **People's Republic of China.**
Status: Directed by Academia Sinica.
Foundation: 1936. *Number of specimens:* 500.000.
Herbarium: Mainly plants of NW China and Tsinling floristic region.
Important collections: Type specimens of new species published in Flora Tsinlingensis and Flora Reipublicae Popularis Sinicae.

 Vice-Directors of Institute: LI CHEN-SHENG, 1931 (Plant genetics).
 YU CHAO-YING, 1934 (Taxonomy of flowering plants).
 Head, Plant Taxonomy Department: TSUI YOU-WEN, 1907 (Taxonomy of flowering plants).
 Acting Head, Plant Taxonomy Department: FU KUN-TSUN (Taxonomy of flowering plants).
 Curator: YANG JIN-XIANG, 1936 (Taxonomy of flowering plants).
 Research staff members: CHANG CHEN-WANG, 1924 (Taxonomy of flowering plants).
 CHANG MAN-HSIANG, 1934 (Bryophytes).
 CHEN YAN-SHENG, 1952 (Taxonomy of flowering plants).
 CUI XIANG-DONG, 1933 (Taxonomy of flowering plants).
 FU JING-QIU, 1934 (Taxonomy of flowering plants).
 GU YUE-PING, 1936 (Taxonomy of flowering plants).
 HO SHAN-BAO, 1930 (Taxonomy of flowering plants).
 HO YE-CHI, 1933 (Taxonomy of flowering plants).
 HSU YING-BEN, 1933 (Taxonomy of pteridophytes),
 KE PING, 1925 (Taxonomy of flowering plants).
 LU DE-QUAN, 1936 (Taxonomy of flowering plants).
 SHUI LANG-ZHAN, 1936 (Taxonomy of flowering plants).
 TANG CHANG-LIN, 1934 (Taxonomy of flowering plants).
 WANG TSO-PING, 1904 (Taxonomy of flowering plants).
 WU JIN-LING, 1937 (Lichens).
 WU SHU-YEN, 1939 (Taxonomy of flowering plants).
 YU CHAO-YING, 1934 (Taxonomy of flowering plants).
 ZHANG ZHI-YING, 1937 (Taxonomy of flowering plants).
 Supporting staff members: CHANG XIANG-MING, 1928.
 CUI JIAN-LI, 1951.
 GUO YOU-HAO, 1952.
 HU ZHI-XIN, 1953.
 LIU CHENG-SHI, 1958.

 Specialization in research: Taxonomy, mainly of NW China and Tsinling region.
 Loans: Small numbers of specimens loaned, no types.
 Periodical and serial works: Flora Tsinlingensis, Northwest Plant Survey, Flora Reipublicae Popularis Sinicae.
 Exchange: Available: Plants of Tsinling region and volumes of Flora Tsinlingensis.

WUHAN: *Herbarium, Wuhan Institute of Botany, Academia Sinica,* **(HIB)**, Wuhan, Hubei, **People's Republic of China.**
 Status: Directed by Academia Sinica.
 Foundation: 1956. *Number of specimens:* 120.000.
 Herbarium: Plants of Hubei Province.
 Director: SUN HSIANG-CHUNG.
 Staff member: FU SHU-HSIA (*Sedum*).
 Periodical and serial works: Flora Hupehensis.

WUKUNG: – – *see* WUGONG.

WÜRZBURG: *Herbarium der Universität Würzburg,* **(WB)**, Institut f. Botanik u. Pharmaz. Biologie mit Botanischem Garten, Mittlerer Dallenbergweg 64, D-8700 Würzburg, **Federal Republic of Germany,** BRD.
 Telephone: 0931/73085.
 Status: University.
 Foundation: About 1835. *Number of specimens:* 15.000.
 Herbarium: Worldwide, contains duplicates of many important collections.
 Important collections: Röll-Herbarium (Bryophytes); F. X. Heller-Herbarium; Herbarium Franconicum.
 Director: OTTO LUDWIG LANGE, 1927 (Ecophysiology).
 Curator: UW BUSCHBOM, 1939.
 Associated botanic garden: Botanischer Garten der Universität.

WÜRZBURG: *Botanisches Institut II der Universität,* **(WBM)**, Mittlerer Dallenbergweg 64, 87 Würzburg, **Federal Republic of Germany,** BRD. (Information 1974)
 Foundation: 1806.
 Herbarium: All collections destroyed in World War II, except herb. A. A. Heller and moss collections.

WUZHOU: *Herbarium, Guangxi University,* **(KU)**, Wuzhou, Guangxi, **People's Republic of China.**

WYTHEVILLE: *Herbarium, Wytheville Community College,* **(WYCO)**, Wytheville, Virginia 24382, **U.S.A.** (Information 1974)
 Telephone: 804/228-5541.
 Number of specimens: 2.500.
 Herbarium: Southwestern Virginia.

X

XALAPA: *Herbario, Instituto Nacional de Investigaciones sobre Recursos Bióticos,* (**XAL**), Apartado postal 63, Xalapa, Veracruz, **Mexico.**
Telephone: 281/525-99; 527-91; 751-02.
Status: Mexican Government Research Institute.
Foundation: 1975. *Number of specimens:* 50.000.
Herbarium: Mexican flora, including ferns and bryophytes, especially from Veracruz and southeastern México.
Important collections: D. K. Cox (*Dioscorea*); collection of photographs of the specimens in the British Museum collected by C. J. W. Schiede and F. Deppe (400) in Veracruz and W. Houstoun (200) in México; Flora of Veracruz collections and types of new taxa described in this project.
Director: ARTURO GÓMEZ-POMPA, 1934 (Flora of Mexico).
Curator: SERGIO AVENDAÑO REYES, 1952 (Useful flora of Mexico).
Assistant Curators: GONZALO CASTILLO C., 1953. JUAN I. CALZADA, 1950.
Staff members: ALICIA BÁRCENA I., 1952 (Flora Yucatanense).
ALFREDO BARRERA M., 1926 (Flora Yucatanense).
ROCIO JIMENEZ A., 1953 (Flora of Veracruz).
LUCIO GIL JUAREZ, 1948 (Bryophytes).
BEATRIZ LUDLOW-WEICHERS, 1948 (Pollen morphology of Veracruz taxa).
NANCY P. MORENO, 1953 (Flora of Veracruz).
ROBERTO ORTEGA O., 1953 (Regional floristic studies in Veracruz).
VICTORIA SOSA O., 1952 (Flora of Veracruz).
ANDREW VOVIDES, 1944 (Cycadaceae; ornamental plants).
Specialization in research: Flora of Veracruz; useful flora of Mexico; Flora Yucatanense.
Associated botanic garden: Jardin Botánico "Francisco Xavier Clavijero," Xalapa, Veracruz.
Loans: 6 months (may be extended) to recognized botanical institutions.
Periodical and serial works: Flora de Veracruz (a continuing series in fascicles describing the botanical families of Veracruz); Biótica.
Exchange: Available: Veracruz and other Mexican states. Desired: Mexico and other tropical regions of the world.
Remarks: The herbarium is 50% computerized

and will be entirely so by 1981.

XALAPA: *Herbario, Facultad de Ciencias Biológicas, Universidad Veracruzana,* (**XALU**), Apartado postal 222, Xalapa, Veracruz, **Mexico.**
Telephone: 7-92-02.
Foundation: 1975. *Number of specimens:* 29.000 (20.000 vascular plants, 9.000 fungi).
Herbarium: Regional flora.
Important collections: Jesus Dorantes, Armando Lopez Ramirez, Mario Vazques.
Director and Curator of Vascular Plants: JESUS DORANTES LOPEZ, 1949.
Curator of Fungi: ARMANDO LOPEZ RAMIREZ, 1952.
Staff members: GLORIA CARRION VILLARNABO.
MARTHA GALVÁN GUERRA.
JUVENTINO GARCÍA ALVARADO.
DANIEL MARTÍNEZ CARRERA.
MARTHA SANDOVAL PÉREZ.
ALEJANDRO SOSA MARTÍNEZ.
LUIS VILLARREAL RUIZ.
Specialization in research: Taxonomy, ecology.
Loans: Yes.
Exchange: Yes.

XIAMEN: *Herbarium, Xiamen University,* (**AU**), Xiamen, Fujian, **People's Republic of China.**
Important collections: Fujian collection of over 8.000 specimens, made under the direction of H. H. Chung in 1922-30.

XIANGGANG: – – *see* HONG KONG.

XINING: *Herbarium, Northwest Plateau Institute of Biology, Academia Sinica,* (**HNWP**), 57 Xiquan Street, Xining, Quighai, **People's Republic of China.**
Telephone: 2856.
Status: Directed by Academia Sinica.
Foundation: 1962. *Number of specimens:* 120.000.
Herbarium: Plants of Tibet Plateau, Himalaya, East Central Asia (Qinghai, Xizang and Shanxi Provinces), Southern Gansu Province, Western Sichuan and Xinjang Provinces.
Director: KUO PEN-CHAO (Gramineae).
Curator: PAN JIN-TANG (Saxifragaceae).
Staff member: GAO JIE.
Specialization in research: Flora of Tibet Plateau.
Exchange: Yes.

Y

YABA: *Herbarium, School of Biological Sciences, University of Lagos,* (**ULN**), Yaba, Lagos, **Nigeria.**

YAKUTSK: *Herbarium, Institute of Biology of the Yakutian Branch of the Siberian Academy of Sciences,* (**SASY**), Petrovskogo Street 2, Yakutsk 677891, **U.S.S.R.**
Telephone: 2-77-81.
Status: Directed by Academy of Sciences.
Foundation: 1949. *Number of specimens:* 52.000.
Herbarium: Higher plants, mosses and lichens of Yakutsk and surrounding areas.
Important collections: V. N. Andreev, M. A. Karavaev, B. V. Kuvaev, V. I. Mikhalyeva, T. F. Galationova, V. I. Perfilyeva, V. A. Sheludyakova, E. R. Trufanova.
Director: V. N. ANDREEV, 1907 (Ecology).
Staff members: E. R. TRUFANOVA, 1923 (Floristics).
V. I. ZAHAROVA, 1943 (Ecology).
Specialization in research: Flora and vegetation of Yakutsk area.
Exchange: With other herbaria in U.S.S.R.

YALTA: *Herbarium of the Nikita Botanical Gardens,* (**YALT**), 334267 Yalta, Crimea, **U.S.S.R.**
Telephone: 33-55-21.
Status: Flora and Vegetation Department, State Botanical Garden.
Foundation: 1914. *Number of specimens:* 117.000.
Herbarium: Mainly plants of Crimea, Caucasus and other regions of U.S.S.R., some world-wide collections and cultivated plants.
Director: V. N. GOLUBEV, 1926 (Geobotany, morphology).
Curator: V. M. KOSSYKH, 1931 (Systematics).
Staff members: S. V. POLUPANOVA, 1942 (Geobotany).
O. G. USACHEVA, 1956.
Specialization in research: Flora and vegetation of Crimea, morphology, population analysis of endemic, rare and threatened plants.
Loans: No.
Exchange: Yes.

YAMAGUCHI: *Herbarium, Faculty of Agriculture, Yamaguchi University,* (**YAM**), Yoshida, Yamaguchi 753, Yamaguchi Prefecture, **Japan.**
Telephone: 0893-22-6111.
Status: Associated with Laboratory of Plant Pathology.
Foundation: 1950. *Number of specimens:* 13.000.
Herbarium: Japanese vascular plants, plant parasitic fungi, especially those of bamboo.
Director: YASUMICHI NISHI, 1924 (Plant virology).

Curator: KEN KATUMOTO, 1927 (Mycology).
Loans: With permission of director.

YAMAGUTI: *Faculty of Agriculture, Yamaguti University,* (**YAM**) –– *see* YAMAGUCHI.

YANGAMBI: *Herbarium, Institut National pour l'Etude Agronomique du Congo,* (**YBI**), Yangambi, **Zaire.** (Information 1964)
Foundation: 1935. *Number of specimens:* 100.000.
Herbarium: Mainly spermatophytes and pteridophytes of Congo and Ruanda-Urundi.
Loans: To recognized botanical institutions.

YAOUNDÉ: *Herbier National du Cameroun,* (**YA**), Boîte Postale 1601, Yaoundé, **Cameroun.**
Telephone: 22-44-16.
Status: State institution: Délégation générale à la Recherche Scientifique et Technique (D.G.R.S.T.).
Foundation: 1948. *Number of specimens:* 47.500.
Herbarium: Cameroon flora, phanerogams and pteridophytes, some bryophytes.
Important collections: R. Letouzey, J. Bos, F. Breteler, W. de Wilde, A. Leeuwenberg; 1.660 pollen slides; 850 wood and liana samples; 500 fruits and seeds.
Director: B. SATABIÉ, 1942 (Irvingiaceae-Fabaceae).
Curator: M. BIHOLONG, 1938 (Asteraceae).
Staff members: J. N. ASONGANYI, 1945 (Sterculiaceae, Malvaceae).
D. DANG, 1944 (Pteridophytes; introduced and cultivated plants; aeropalynology).
Specialization in research: Taxonomy, phytogeography and ethnobotany.
Associated botanic garden: Victoria.
Loans: To recognized botanical institutions.
Exchange: Available: Limited Cameroon specimens. Desired: Cameroon specimens only.
Remarks: "Service des Eaux et Forêts du Cameroun, Section de Recherches Forestières" (YA) and "Herbarium, Victoria Botanic Gardens" (SCA) incorporated in Herbier National du Cameroun (YA).

YAROSLAVL: *Herbarium, Department of Botany, K. D. Ushinsky State Pedagogical Institute of Yaroslavl,* (**USPIY**), Kotoroslnaya Embankment 46, 150000 Yaroslavl, **U.S.S.R.**
Foundation: 1924. *Number of specimens:* 30.000.
Director: A. V. DUBROVINA.

YARRALUMA: *Forest Research Institute,* (**FRI**) –– *see* CANBERRA.

YELLOWSTONE: *Yellowstone National Park Herbarium, Mammoth Hot Springs,* (**YELLO**), P.O. Box

168, Yellowstone National Park, Wyoming 82190, **U.S.A.**

Telephone: 307/344-7381, ext. 319 or 257.

Status: U.S. Department of the Interior, National Park Service.

Foundation: 1924. *Number of specimens:* 5.633.

Herbarium: Flora of Yellowstone National Park and adjacent areas.

Director: JOHN TOWNSLEY (Superintendent).

Curator: LINDA YOUNG GREEN, 1951 (Zoology, chemistry).

Staff member: DON DESPAIN (Plant biology, ecology).

YENSHAN: *Herbarium, Botanical Institute of Guangxi,* (**IBY**), Yenshan, Guangxi, **People's Republic of China.**

YEREVAN: *Herbarium, Department of Meadows and Pastures, Armenian Institute for the Scientific Investigation of Cattle Breeding and Veterinary,* (**AISIY**), Nalbandyan St. 57, 375025 Yerevan, **U.S.S.R.**

Foundation: 1946. *Number of specimens:* 6.000.

Herbarium: Plants of meadows and pastures, especially cereals.

Director: A. K. MAGAKJAN.

YEREVAN: *Herbarium, Department of Botany, Abovjan Pedagogical Institute,* (**APIY**), Khandzhyana St. 5, 375000 Yerevan, **U.S.S.R.**

Foundation: 1947. *Number of specimens:* 7.000.

Director: D. CZATYRDSHJAN (Flora of Armenia).

YEREVAN: *Herbarium, Department of Flora and Vegetation, Botanical Garden of the Armenian Academy of Sciences,* (**BGAAS**), 375063 Yerevan, **U.S.S.R.**

Foundation: 1945. *Number of specimens:* 37.000 (30.000 vascular plants, 7.000 fungi).

Director: A. A. ACHVERDOV.

Curator, Mycological Collection: S. A. SIMONIAN.

Specialization in research: Flora of Armenia.

YEREVAN: *Phanerogamic Herbarium, Department of Botany, Yerevan State University,* (**ERCB**), Tsharenz Street 8, Yerevan 375025, **U.S.S.R.**

Telephone: 56996-300.

Status: State university.

Foundation: 1929. *Number of specimens:* 15.000.

Herbarium: Plants of Armenia.

Director: LIA LEVONOVNA OSIPIAN, 1930 (Mycology).

Curator: TAMARA GRIGOREVNA ZATURIAN, 1909 (Systematics).

Staff member: ELENA MICHAILOVNA MAMULOVA, 1947.

Specialization in research: Armenian flora, systematics and phylogeny of phanerogams.

Associated botanic garden: Botanic Garden of the Armenian Academy of Science.

Periodical and serial works: Biological Journal of Armenia, Scientific Notes of Yerevan State University.

YEREVAN: *Herbarium, Department of Plant Taxonomy and Geography, Botanical Institute of the Academy of Sciences of the Armenian S.S.R.,* (**ERE**), Yerevan 63, 375063 **U.S.S.R.**

Telephone: 24-11-02.

Status: Directed by the State.

Foundation: 1925. *Number of specimens:* 220.000.

Herbarium: Flora of Armenia and Caucasus, also Western Asia, Mediterranean, Europe and North America.

Important collections: A. G. Araratian, I. G. Arevschatian, S. G. Aslanian, V. E. Avetisian, N. S. Chandjan, An. A. Federov, E. Tz. Gabrielian, A. A. Grossheim, R. A. Karapetian, V. A. Manakian, J. I. Mulkidjanian, A. B. Schelkownicow, A. L. Takhtajan, S. G. Tamamschian.

Director: V. O. KAZARIAN, 1918 (Plant physiology).

Head of Department of Plant Taxonomy and Geography: V. E. AVETISIAN, 1928 (Caucasian Cruciferae, Armenian Valerianaceae, Onagraceae, Plantaginaceae, Lythraceae, Solanaceae, *Eryngium,* Inuleae, Astereae, Senecioneae).

Staff members: I. G. AREVSCHATIAN, 1938 (Armenian *Taraxacum, Hieracium, Echinops*).

E. M. AVETISIAN, 1923 (Palynotaxonomy of Campanulales, Loasaceae, Centaureinae, Boraginaceae and *Reseda;* palynomorphology of Armenian flora).

N. S. CHANDJAN, 1946 (Armenian Anthemideae).

E. TZ. GABRIELIAN, 1929 (W. Asian and Himalayan *Sorbus,* Armenian *Medicago, Trigonella, Tulipa, Fritillaria, Gagea,* Gramineae, Malvaceae, Santalaceae, Scrophulariaceae, Convolvulaceae).

N. G. GOCHTUNI, 1931 (Fossil flora of Sarmat, Armenia).

V. A. MANAKIAN, 1936 (Bryophytes of Armenia).

L. K. MANUKIAN, 1925 (Palynoflora of Miocene in Armenia; palynotaxonomy of *Linum, Astragalus, Sideritis, Veronica;* palynomorphology of Armenian flora).

A. K. MECHAKIAN, 1937 (Palynotaxonomy of *Reseda* and palynomorphology of Armenian flora).

E. A. NASAROVA, 1936 (Taxonomy and cytotaxonomy of Armenian Cichorioideae).

M. E. OGANESIAN, 1954 (Transcaucasian *Campanula, Symphyandra*).

G. G. OGANEZOVA, 1949 (Taxonomy and anatomy of Berberidaceae, Liliaceae).

A. I. POGOSIAN, 1935 (Cytotaxonomy of Armenian Liliaceae).

A. S. SCHCHIAN, 1905 (Caucasian Dipsacaceae, Armenian Thymelaeaceae, Urticaceae, *Helichrysum, Jurinea, Bellevalia, Muscari*).

K. G. TAMANIAN, 1946 (Caucasian *Asparagus*, Armenian *Scilla, Puschkinia, Allium*).

Tz. R. TONIAN, 1924 (Cytology of Armenian Centaureinae, Carduinae).

Specialization in research: Flora of Armenia, Caucasus and W. Asia; taxonomy, cytotaxonomy, palynotaxonomy and taxonomical anatomy of various taxa.

Associated botanic garden: Botanical Garden of Yerevan.

Loans: To recognized institutions for 6 months.

Periodical and serial works: Flora of Armenia, vol. 1–10, Acta of Botanical Institute of Academy of Sciences of the Armenian SSR, Bulletin of Botanical Garden, Bryological Journal of Armenia.

Exchange: Available: Plants of Armenia and Caucasus. Desired: Plants from all parts of world, especially W. Asian and Mediterranean.

Remarks: Formerly listed under Erevan.

YEREVAN: *Herbarium Mycologicum, Department of Dendrology, Botanical Institute of the Academy of Sciences of the Armenian S.S.R.,* (**EREM**), Yerevan 63, 375063 **U.S.S.R.**

Telephone: 24-01-40.

Status: Directed by state.

Foundation: 1957. *Number of specimens:* 7.800.

Herbarium: Fungi of Armenia (6.500 specimens) and other parts of U.S.S.R. (1.300 specimens).

Important collections: Seda A. Simonian (Erysiphales, Uredinales, Deuteromycetes).

Director: V. O. KAZARIAN, 1918 (Plant physiology).

Curator: SEDA A. SIMONIAN, 1929 (Erysiphaceae, Sphaeropsidaceae, fungi of ornamental plants).

Staff member: TAMARA H. MAMICONIAN, 1946 (Moniliales, fungi of seeds).

Specialization in research: Fungi of Armenia.

Associated botanic garden: Botanical Garden of Yerevan.

Loans: 6 months to recognized botanical institutions.

Periodical and serial works: see ERE.

Exchange: Available: Fungi of Armenia. Desired: Fungi of all parts of world, especially W. Asia and Mediterranean.

YEREVAN: *Cryptogamic Herbarium, Department of Botany, Yerevan State University,* (**ERHM**), Tsharenz Street 8, Yerevan 375025, **U.S.S.R.**

Telephone: 56996-452.

Status: State university.

Foundation: 1945. *Number of specimens:* 9.000.

Herbarium: Fungi, algae and lichens.

Director: LIA LEVONOVNA OSIPIAN, 1930 (Mycology).

Curator: DARIA NIKOLAEVNA BABAYAN, 1904, 56996-346 (Mycology).

Chief: YVETTA HAMAZASPOVNA MARTIROSSIAN,

1944 (Mycology).

Specialization in research: Study of Armenian mycoflora.

Associated botanic garden: Botanic Garden of the Armenian Academy of Science.

Periodical and serial works: Biological Journal of Armenia, Scientific Notes of Yerevan State University.

YEREVAN: *Herbarium, Department of Botany, Veterinarian Institute of Armenia,* (**VIAY**), Teryana St. 66, 375009 Yerevan, **U.S.S.R.**

Foundation: 1931. *Number of specimens:* 18.000.

Director: T. P. KOTSCHARJAN.

YEREVAN: *Herbarium, Department of Botany, Yerevan Agricultural Institute,* (**YAI**), Teryana St. 74, 375200 Yerevan, **U.S.S.R.**

Foundation: 1922. *Number of specimens:* 30.000.

Director: V. S. BADALJAN (Flora of Armenia, grasses).

YIYANG: *Herbarium, Lutheran College,* (**YH**), Yiyang, Hunan, **People's Republic of China** –– status unknown.

YOKOHAMA: *Herbarium, Agricultural Institute, Yokohama National University,* (**YNU**), 100 Gontazaka, Hodogayaku, Yokohama, **Japan.** (Information 1974)

Status: University.

Foundation: 1955. *Number of specimens:* 10.000.

Herbarium: Fungi.

YORK: *Herbarium, The Yorkshire Museum,* (**YRK**), York, Yorkshire, England, **Great Britain.** (Information 1974)

Status: City museum.

Foundation: 1823. *Number of specimens:* 45.000.

Herbarium: Cryptogams and phanerogams, mainly northern England and Yorkshire.

YOSEMITE NATIONAL PARK: *Herbarium, Yosemite Museum,* (**YM**), P.O. Box 577, Yosemite National Park, California 95389, **U.S.A.**

Telephone: 209/372-4461, ext. 261.

Status: U.S. Department of the Interior, National Park Service.

Foundation: 1924. *Number of specimens:* 4.620.

Herbarium: Plants of Yosemite National Park and vicinity.

Curator: JACK GYER, 1914.

Staff member: CRAIG D. BATES, 1952.

Specialization in research: Plants of the Yosemite region.

Remarks: Visits by appointment only.

YOUNGSTOWN: *Herbarium, Department of Biological Sciences, Youngstown State University,* (**YUO**), 410 Wick Avenue, Youngstown, Ohio 44555, **U.S.A.**

Telephone: 216/742-3601.

Foundation: 1965. *Number of specimens:* 18.989.

Herbarium: Specializing in pteridophytes; strong in flora of West Virginia and Mahoning and Trumbull counties, Ohio.

Important collections: Ernest W. Vickers (1880–1920; Ohio), John T. Laitsch (West Virginia, southeastern Ohio, western Pennsylvania), Carl F. Chuey (Ohio, Pennsylvania, West Virginia), H. E. W. N. Sturm (West Virginia, Pennsylvania), Walter Sturgeon (Ohio macrofungi), Clair L. Worley (northwestern U.S.), Almond N. Rood (Ohio), Ian A. Worley (New Zealand), G. J. de Joncheere (Europe), K. Iwatsuki (Japan), Floyd Bartley (Ohio), N. Sahashi (Japan), Edmund A. Turnan (Quebec).

Director and Curator: CARL F. CHUEY, 1944 (Pteridophytes).

Staff member: H. E. W. NICHOLAS STURM, 1931 (Lichens and pteridophytes).

Specialization in research: Geographic distribution of pteridophytes in Upper Ohio Valley; effect of time and storage conditions of spore viability gametophyte morphology; index to lichenological literature.

Loans: Six month limit.

Periodical and serial works: Laitsch.

Exchange: Duplicates of current collections in return for pteridophytes and other vascular plants.

Remarks: Collection of over 500 reprints on pteridophytes.

YPSILANTI: *Herbarium, Department of Biology, Eastern Michigan University,* (**EMC**), West Cross Street, Ypsilanti, Michigan 48197, **U.S.A.**

Telephone: 313/487-4242.

Foundation: 1880. *Number of specimens:* 20.000.

Herbarium: Regional flora.

Important collections: W. J. Beal, R. O. Belcher (Australia), D. F. M. Brown (*Woodsia*), O. A. Farwell (Michigan), E. L. Hankenson (New York; willows, *Carex*, Compositae), Ruth Hoppin (Michigan), John Macoun (Canada), G. W. Prescott (algae), C. G. Pringle, Carl Shear (fungi), C. F. Wheeler (Michigan); Phycotheca boreali-americanae.

Staff members: ROBERT O. BELCHER, 1918 (Erechthitoid *Senecio;* Australasia; aquatic Tracheophyta).

DONALD F. M. BROWN, 1920 (*Woodsia;* Michigan flora).

DENNIS G. JACKSON, 1936 (Desmids).

Specialization in research: Taxonomy of Erechthitoid Senecios of Australasia; polymorphism in Desmids; Desmids from Montana.

Loans: No special restrictions.

Exchange: Available: Southern Michigan vascular plants and algae. Desired: Vascular plants and algae from other areas.

YREKA: *Herbarium, Klamath National Forest,* (**KNFY**), 1312 Fairlane Road, Yreka, California 96097, **U.S.A.**

Telephone: 916/842-2741.

Status: U.S. Department of Agriculture, Forest Service.

Foundation: 1975. *Number of specimens:* 1.350.

Herbarium: Important range and browse species, noxious weeds; local flora; threatened and endangered species.

Director and Curator: LINDA M. BARKER, 1949 (Serpentine species; rare plants; Scrophulariaceae).

Specialization in research: Distribution and abundance of candidate threatened and endangered species in the forest; collection of major browse and range species; distribution of noxious weeds.

Loans: Not at this time.

Z

ZAGREB: *Herbarium Adriaticum, Instituti "R. Boš-kovic" Dautoniae*, (**ADRZ**), CIM Coastal Botany, POB 1016, Bijenicka 54, Zagreb, 41001 – **Yugoslavia.**
Telephone: YU-041/424.355 and 445.791.
Status: University Institute.
Foundation: 1866. *Number of specimens:* 14.000 (12.500 phanerogams, 1.500 algae).
Herbarium: Endemic, rare and endangered native plants of Adriatic Islands, Yugoslav coast, Balkans, Asia Minor and Adriatic marine flora.

> *Director of Institute:* MARKO BRANICA (Ecology).
> *Curator:* ANDRIJA-ZELIMIR LOVRIĆ, 1943 (Phyto-geography, biosystematics of *Centaurea, Drypis, Aurinia, Seseli, Phyllitis*).
> *Staff member:* B. KORICA, 1918 (Morphology, taxonomy of *Asperula, Galium, Laserpitium, Cyclamen*).
> *Specialization in research:* Endemism in Adriatic Islands and coastal ranges, conservation, floristic mapping, special floras of karst limestone, serpentine and gypsum.
> *Associated botanic garden:* Coastal Botany Experimental Grounds. Arboretum Instituti "R. Boš-kovic," Port of Rovinj, Istra Peninsula.
> *Loans:* Restricted to common taxa; photographs of rare plants and types.
> *Periodical and serial works:* Thalassia Jugoslavica, Flora Exsiccata Adriatica, Plantarum Index.
> *Exchange:* Available: Plants of Yugoslavia; specimens and seeds.
> *Remarks:* Formerly part of ZA.

ZAGREB: *Herbarium Croaticum, Department of Biology, Faculty of Science, University*, (**ZA**), Zagreb, **Yugoslavia.**
Status: Department of State University.
Foundation: 1880. *Number of specimens:* 190.000.
Herbarium: Plants of Yugoslavia, used mainly for teaching.
Exchange: Specimens and seeds of Croatia.

ZAGREB: *Herbarium "Dr. Ivo Horvat," Veterinarian Faculty, University of Zagreb*, (**ZAHO**), Heinzelova 55, YU-41000 Zagreb, **Yugoslavia.**
Telephone: YU-041/219-333.
Status: University.
Foundation: 1918. *Number of specimens:* 75.000.
Herbarium: Spermatophyta, pteridophyta and bryophyta of SE Europe, Switzerland, Polonia, Norway and Finland.
Important collections: Plants of limestone areas, endemic genera and rare mosses.

> *Curator:* MARIJA HORVAT.
> *Specialization in research:* Flora and phytocoenology of mountains and limestone karst areas in

Balkan peninsula, forestry.
> *Associated botanic garden:* National Park of Risnjak Mountain, Rijeka, West Croatia.
> *Loans:* Yes.
> *Exchange:* Yes.
> *Remarks:* Formerly part of ZA.

ZAPOPAN: *Herbario, Instituto de Botánica, Universidad de Guadalajara*, (**IBUG**), Apartado postal 139, Nextipac, Zapopan, Jalisco, **Mexico.**
Telephone: 9136-21-74-08.
Foundation: 1960. *Number of specimens:* 80.000.
Herbarium: Primarily vascular plants of Nueva Galicia; also collections of wood, pollen, seeds, mushrooms, and ferns.
Important collections: S. Carvajal H., R. Guzmán M., R. McVaugh, J. Rzedowski, L. M. Villarreal de Puga.

> *Director:* LUZ MA. VILLARREAL DE PUGA, 1913 (Taxonomy of vascular plants).
> *Curator:* RAFAEL GUZMÁN MEJÍA (Systematics of grasses).
> *Staff members:* SERVANDO CARVAJAL HERNÁNDEZ, 1955 (Weeds).
> GREGORIO NIEVES HERNÁNDEZ, 1956 (Malvaceae). *L. Guzmn - Davalos (fungi)*
> RICARDO ORNELAS URIBE, 1958 (Compositae).
> GABRIEL PÉREZ FLORES, 1958 (Cactaceae).
> CONRADO SÁNCHEZ SALAMANCA, 1956 (Solanaceae).
> JOSÉ ANTONIO VÁZQUEZ, 1959 (Leguminosae).
> *Loans:* Without special restrictions; by arrangement with Curator.
> *Periodical and serial works:* Boletín Informativo del Instituto de Botánica.
> *Exchange:* Flora of Nueva Galicia, especially grasses and weeds; by arrangement with Curator.

ZICHRON-YAAKOV: *Reliquae Aaronsohnianae*, (**AAR**), 40 Hameyasdim Street, Zichron-Yaakov 30-900, **Israel.**
Telephone: 063-90120.
Status: Hebrew University, Jerusalem.
Foundation: 1910. *Number of specimens:* 30.000.
Herbarium: Plants of Israel and Transjordan.
Important collections: Herb. A. Aaronsohn.
Remarks: For information about using herbarium, contact David Heller or Clara Chen, Faculty of Botany, Hebrew University, Jerusalem; telephone: 02-584305.

ZNOJMO: *Herbarium, Jihomoravské muzeum*, (**MZ**), Ul. Přemyslovců 6, Znojmo, **Czechoslovakia.** (Information 1974)
Number of specimens: 6.000.
Herbarium: Tracheophyta and cryptogams, world-

wide and Czechoslovakia.

Specialization in research: Systematics, cryptogams and mycology.

Loans: To recognized botanical institutions.

ZOMBA: *The National Herbarium of Malawi,* **(MAL),** Chancellor College, P.O. Box 280, Zomba, **Malawi.**

Telephone: 2791 ext. 346.

Status: University, supported by Ministry of Agriculture.

Foundation: 1966. *Number of specimens:* 40.000.

Herbarium: Fungi, bryophytes, pteridophytes and spermatophytes from Malawi and neighboring countries.

Important collections: J. D. Chapman, G. Jackson, J. Pawek, R. K. Brummitt.

Director and Curator: JAMESON H. SEYENI (Sterculiaceae, *Dombeya*; on leave until 1981).

Acting Director: BRUCE J. HARGREAVES, June–Sept. 1980.

J. D. CHAPMAN, Oct. 1980–1981.

Staff members: ELIAS A. K. BANDA, 1936 (Weeds of Malawi, vegetation surveys).

MAXWELL J. MASIYE (Herbarium assistant).

I. HASSAM PATEL (Herbarium assistant).

AUGUSTINE J. SALUBENI, 1940 (Woody plants of Malawi, vegetation surveys).

ERNEST TAWAKALI (Herbarium assistant).

Specialization in research: Weeds of Malawi, aquatic plants of Shire River, checklist of Malawi pteridophytes.

Associated botanic garden: Forestry Department Botanic Garden, Zomba.

Loans: To recognized botanical institutions for six months.

Exchange: Available: Plants of Malawi. Desired: Plants of Malawi or other countries of Flora Zambesiaca area.

ZOMBA: *Department of Agriculture,* **(ZOM)** – – incorporated in MAL.

ZÜRICH: *Geobotanisches Institut der E.T.H., Stiftung Rübel,* **(RUEB)** – – incorporated in ZT.

ZÜRICH: *Institut für Systematische Botanik der Universität Zürich,* **(Z),** Zollikerstrasse 107, CH-8008 Zürich, **Switzerland.**

Telephone: Zürich 251 3670.

Status: Department of the Cantonal University of Zürich.

Foundation: 1834. *Number of specimens:* 1.500.000.

Herbarium: Worldwide, S. Africa, New Caledonia.

Important collections: Konrad Gesser, C. Hegetschweiler; W. Becker (*Viola*); O. & R. Buser (Rosaceae, spec. *Alchemilla*); Rob. Keller (*Rosa, Rubus*); F. Käser (*Hieracium*); Al. Jordan (mostly France); W. Geilinger (N. Italy, Tanganyika); Furrer (Italy); A. Kaiser (Sinai); Bosshard (Central Asia); A. U. Däniker,

Baumann-Bodenheim, H. Hürlimann, A. Guillaumin (New Caledonia); H. Hürlimann (Tonga); H. Schinz (S.W. Africa); Rehmann, Fleck (S. and S.W. Africa); M. Rautanen (S., S.W. and trop. Africa); F. R. R. Schlechter (S. Africa); Eug. Mayor (Colombia); G. Meyer (Bolivia); d'Angremond (Suriname); Sickenberger (Malta and Egypt); A. Ernst (Indonesia and Malay Pen.); O. Appert (Madagascar). Important duplicate collections: Schlechter, F. Sarasin, Rohrdorf, I. Franc (New Caledonia); Pritzel (W. Australia); A. Henry (China); U. J. Faurie (Japan, Korea); T. Kässner (East Africa); Stolz (Tanganyika); G. A. Zenker (Trop. Africa); Soyaux (Gabon); J. Berhaut (Sénégal); H. J. E. Schlieben (E. Africa, Madagascar, Comoro Is.); Mocquerys (Sao Tomé, Madagascar); J. M. Hildebrandt (Madagascar); Clemens (New Guinea); Rudatis (S. and W. Africa); Eggers (W. Indies); P. Sintenis (Puerto Rico); W. E. Broadway (W. Indies); Pittier and Durand (Costa Rica); v. Türckheim (Guatemala); C. G. Pringle (Mexico); H. F. Pittier (Venezuela); E. Warming (S.E. Brazil); E. Heinrichs (Ecuador); Herzog (Bolivia); O. Buchtien (Bolivia); Rusby (S. America).

Director: CHRISTOPHER D. K. COOK, 1933 (Aquatic plants).

Curator: KARL U. KRAMER, 1928 (Pteridophytes).

Staff members: PETER K. ENDRESS, 1942 (Primitive angiosperms).

ILSE MENDOZA, 1919 (Canary Isles, Labiatae).

OTTO ROHWEDER, 1919 (Centrospermae).

JAKOB SCHNELLER, 1942 (Pteridophytes).

EDWIN URMI, 1944 (Bryophytes).

Associates: HANS HÜRLIMANN, 1921 (Caledonian bryophytes).

FRIEDRICH MARKGRAF, 1897 (Apocynaceae).

INGEBORG MARKGRAF, 1911 (*Festuca*).

EMIL ZOGG, 1915 (Pteridophytes).

Specialization in research: Taxonomy and morphology.

Associated botanic garden: Botanischer Garten der Universität Zürich.

Loans: To recognized botanical institutions.

Periodical and serial works: Mitteilungen aus dem Botanischen Museum der Universität Zürich.

Exchange: Yes.

ZÜRICH: *Städtische Sukkulentensammlung, I.O.S. affiliated Reserve Collection and Herbarium,* **(ZSS),** Mythenquai 88, CH 8002 Zürich, **Switzerland.**

Telephone: 01/201 45 54.

Status: Community of Zürich.

Foundation: Collection 1931, herbarium 1952. *Number of specimens:* 12.000.

Herbarium: Only succulents, worldwide.

Important collections: P. R. O. Bally, F. Ritter, W. Rauh, W. Rausch, F. Buxbaum.

Director: JOH. DIEDRICH SUPTHUT, 1935.

Specialization in research: Taxonomy.

Periodical and serial works: Index Seminum.

Remarks: Collection under protection of the International Organization of Succulent Plant Study.

ZÜRICH: *The Herbarium, Institut für Spezielle Botanik, Eidg. Technische Hochschule,* (**ZT**), Zurichbergstrasse 38, CH-8006 Zürich, **Switzerland.** (Information 1974)

Status: Federal.

Foundation: 1855. *Number of specimens:* 1.350.000 (750.000 phanerogams, 600.000 cryptogams).

Herbarium: Worldwide, especially phanerogams of Mediterranean, Switzerland and the Alps.

Important collections: J. Amann (mosses), J. Arechavaleta, E. Gäumann (rusts), A. Knapp (hypogaeic fungi), Walo Koch (Swiss flora, Alps), Fr. Meister (Diatomaceae), E. Stizenberger (lichens), E. Sulger-Büel (Swiss flora), A. Volkart (parasitic fungi). Historical collections: J. J. Scheuchzer, J. Gessner (in part).

Specialization in research: Plant pathology, fungi, Mediterranean and Swiss flora.

Loans: To recognized botanical institutions.

ZVOLEN: *Katedra botaniky a fytocenológie Vysokej školy lesníckej a drevárskej vo Zvolene,* (**ZV**), Zvolen, **Czechoslovakia.** (Information 1974)

Number of specimens: 67.000.

Herbarium: Tracheophyta of Czechoslovakia, Slovakia, Bohemia, Poland and Hungary.

Loans: To recognized botanical institutions.

I. Index to "important collections"

This is simply an index to the entries under "important collections." For further information please consult the *Collectors Index* (*Index Herbariorum*, part II, so far published A–M).

Baillon, H. E. P
Baird, GRA
Baker, C. F. HAC, MO, NY, POM, RM
Baker, H. R. DOV
Baker, J. G. (herb.) WELT
Baker, M. S. ROPA, UC
Baker, R. T. NSW
Baker, W. H. ID
Baker, PAD
Balakrishnan, N. P. PBL
Balansa, B. BAF, P, PAD
Baldacci, A. FI, WU
Baldrati, I. FT
Baldwin, J. T. MO, WILLI
Baldwin, W. DWC, PH (herb.), WLU
Balfour, J. H. PTH
Ball, A. DBN
Ball, C. R. NA, UC
Ball, J. MO
Ball, V. DBN
Ballou, H. A. CONN
Balls, E. K. BOLV
Bally, P. R. O. ZSS
Bally, MOG
Bang, M. MO, US
Banker, H. J. NY
Banks, J. AK, LIV, MO, WELT
Banzragch, D. UBA
Barber, C. A. BSIS, CAL
Barber, GLM, MH
Barbey, W.-Boissier, E. (herb.) G
Barclay, F. ETSU
Barclay, F. H. NWH
Barclay, H. MO
Barclay, W. PTH
Barker, W. F. NBG
Barkley, F. A. COL, TEFH, UNL
Barla, J. B. J. J. (herb.) NICE
Barneby, R. C. NY, RSA
Barnes, W. D. BDI
Barnhart, J. H. NY
Baron, R. K
Barrandon, L. MPA
Barreto, I. BLA
Barron Dolorier, D. HHUA
Barros, M. SI
Barth, F. (herb.) SIB
Bartholomew, E. FHKSC, KSC, MAINE, MPPD, PUR
Bartlett, H. H. MICH
Bartley, F. BHO, OS, YUO
Bartling, F. G. (herb.) GOET
Barton, B. S. (herb.) PH
Bartram, E. B. FH, RSDR
Bartram, J. DWC
Bartram, CR
Bassett, I. J. DAO
Bassler, HAJB
Batelli, A. (herb.) PERU

Bates, J. M. NEB
Batista, A. C. URM
Battandier, J. A. AL
Baudin, T. N. P
Bauer, E. OP, WTU
Bauhin, C. BAS
Baum, H. BR
Baumann-Bodenheim, Z
Bäurlen, W. NSW
Bavazzano, FT
Baxter, D. V. MICH
Baxter, W. E. BM
Bayliss, R. D. MO
Baytop, T. ISTE
Beal, W. J. EMC, MSC
Beaman, J. H. MSC
Bean, R. C. MAINE
Beardslee, H. C. OC
Beatley, J. C. CINC, DS, NTS
Beaton, G. MELU
Beattie, R. K. WS
Beccari, O. BH, FI, FT
Bechtel, A. R. WAB
Beck, S. G. LPB
Beck von Mannagetta, G. PRC
Becker, W. GJO, Z
Beckett, T. W. N. CHR
Beddome, R. H. CAL, MH
Beechey, F. W. GL
Beechey, T. WLU
Beeli, BR
Beetle, A. A. CSAT, UC, WYAC
Béguinot, A. PAD
Behr, H. CAS
Behr, O. B, HAL
Bélanger, C. P. P
Belcher, R. O. EMC
Belém, R. P. CEPEC, UB
Bell, C. R. GAS
Bell, J. CCO
Bell, R. QK
Bell, BLAT
Bellardi, C. A. L. (herb.) TO
Belshaw, C. M. VT
Belt, T. HAMU
Bena, R. CAY
Benedict, J. C. VPI
Benedict, M. R. SBBG
Benedict, R. C. BKL
Beneke, E. S. MSC
Benjamin, R. K. RSA
Bennett, J. DLF
Bennett, AK
Benoist, R. P
Benson, L. POM
Bentham, G. K
Benz, M. C. HBFH
Benz (herb.) KL
Bequaert, BR
Berenger, PAD

Berg, C. LP
Berg, C. A. O
Berger, E. (herb.) BASBG
Berggren, S. LD, WELT
Bergius, P. J. (herb.) SBT
Berhaut, J. DAKAR, P, Z
Berkeley, M. J. HCIO, K
Berlandier, J. L. BUF, DS
Bernard, J. P. QFA
Bernaux, P. MPA
Bernhardi, J. J. MO
Berro, M. B. MVFA
Berry, E. C. SDC
Bertero, C. G. L. SGO, TO
Bertoloni, A. (herb.) BOLO
Bertram, W. BREM
Bertsch, K. STU
Beschel, R. E. DAO, QK
Besser, W. G. KW
Bessey, C. E. MONT, MONTU, NEB
Best, G. N. NY
Betche, E. NSW
Bethel, E. COLOM, PUR
Bezerra, J. L. URM
Bhandari, M. M. JAC
Bhargava, N. PBL
Bhide, R. K. BSI
Bicchi, C. LUCCA
Bickham, S. H. CGE
Bicknell, E. GE, MAINE
Bicknell, E. P. NY, NYS
Bieberstein, F. A. M. VON LE
Bigge, J. F. HAMU
Billings, B. QK
Biltmore (herb.) US
Binder, A. HBG
Biondi, A. FI
Biourge, P. MUCL
Birand, H. ANK
Bird, C. UAC
Bisby, G. R. PUR
Bischler, H. COL
Bissell, C. H. NCBS
Biswas, K. P. CAL
Bitancourt, A. A. HCIO, IBI
Biurrun, F. N. CHAM, IZAC
Bizot, M. PC
Bjørnstad, A. O
Bjørnstad, I. N. O
Black, A. O. NY
Black, G. A. IAN
Black, J. M. AD
Black, R. MEL
Blackall, W. E. PERTH
Blair, S. M. HBFH
Blake, J. MAINE
Blake, S. F. TEX, VT
Blake, S. T. BRI
Blakely, W. F. NSW
Blakley, E. R. SBBG

Blanchard, F. MO
Blanche, C. I. JE
Blankinship, J. W. MONT, MONTU, ROPA, WTU
Blasdale, W. C. PUR, UC
Blasdell, R. F. CANI
Blassingame, J. L. HPC
Blatter, E. BLAT
Blažková, D. CB
Blewitt, A. E. VT
Blocker, H. W. HWBA
Blom, E. W. JYV
Blum, J. L. CANI
Blume, C. L. von BO, L
Blumrich, J. BREG
Blytt, M. N. BUF
Bobart, J. (herb.) OXF
Boccone, P. P
Bock, C. O
Bodine, D. WAB
Boedijn, K. B. BO
Boege, W. MEXU
Boehmer, G. R. MO
Boehner, P. SBU
Boeke, J. QCA, QPNRA
Boelcke, O. BAB, BAF
Bogado, M. C. INFYB
Boissier, P. E. G, PI
Boissieu, H. de (herb.) STR
Boivin, B. DAO
Boivin, L. H. DS, P
Bolander, H. N. BUF, GRA, YU
Boldrini, I. BLA
Bolland, CAIM
Bolley, H. L. NDA
Bolus, H. BOL
Bolus, L. BOL
Bolzon, P. PAD
Bomberger, E. H. FSSR
Bommer, J. E. BR
Bonaparte, R. LY, P, PC
Bonar, L. UC, URM
Bongard, G. LECB
Bonpland, A. J. A. LR (herb.), SGO
Boole, J. A. GAS
Boorman, J. L. NSW
Booth, L. M. NO
Boott, W. NHA
Bor, N. L. ASSAM, DD
Borbás, V. von WU
Bordère, H. P
Borgen, G. O
Børgesen, F. C. E. C
Borja, MAF
Bornet, J. B. E. PC
Bornet, FH
Bornmüller, J. F. N. ANK, B, JE, STU
Bornmüller, WU
Borrer, W. K
Bory de St. Vincent, J. B. G. M. P

Bos, J. STE, YA
Bosc, L. A. G. DS
Bosshard, Z
Botteri, M. CGE
Bottini, A. (herb.) PI
Bottomley, A. M. PREM
Bouby, P
Boucher, C. STE
Boulenger, G. A. BR
Boulus, L. ULT
Bourdillon, T. F. MH
Bourelli, GRA
Bourgeau, E. FI, P
Boutelou, C. SEV
Boutelou, P. SEV
Boutin, F. HNT
Bowden, W. M. DAO
Bowman, R. B. HAMU
Boyan, J. FDG
Boyan, R. FDG
Boyden, H. RAMM
Boyer, G. MPA
Bozcaada, EGE
Bozeman, J. R. GAS
Bradbury, J. LIV
Brade, A. C. HB, RB
Braggins, J. E. AKU
Brainerd, E. HPH, MID, NYS, VT
Braithwaite, R. BRISTM
Brandegee, K. UC
Brandegee, T. S. UC
Brandis, D. DD
Brandis, E. HBG
Brass, L. J. A, BISH, CANB
Bratt, G. C. HO
Braun, A. B
Braun, E. L. CINC, US (herb.)
Breedlove, D. E. CAS, DS, ENCB, INIF, MEXU
Breen, R. S. NY
Breidler, J. GJO, WU
Brenckle, J. F. MPPD, RMS
Brendel, F. ILL
Brenes, A. M. CR
Brenkle, PAD
Brenner, M. H
Bresadola, G. BPI, S, TR
Breteler, F. YA
Brewer, W. H. GH, UC
Bridel, S. E. B, H
Bridges, T. CGE
Briosi, G. PAD
Brito Teixeira, J. LUA
Brittain, W. H. MTMG
Britten, L. L. GRA
Britton, E. G. NY, SIM
Britton, N. L. NY, SIM, UCWI
Broadway, W. E. MO, Z
Brochon, E. H. (herb.) BORD
Brode, W. WCW

Brodo, I. M. MSC
Brooker, M. I. H. FRI
Brooks, T. BPI
Brotherus, V. F. H
Broughton, A. (herb.) BRISTM
Brouillet, L. WAT
Broussonet, P. M. A. FI
Brown, A. MASS
Brown, A. W. PTH
Brown, D. F. M. EMC
Brown, D. M. ETSU
Brown, E. D. W. WELT
Brown, F. B. H. WELT
Brown, M. S. ACAD
Brown, R. CANB, DBN, MEL, WELT (herb.)
Brown, R. G. MARY
Brown, W. M. HAMU
Brown, MW
Browne, E. T. MEM
Browne, J. BAR
Bruggeman, P. F. DAO
Bruhin, T. von A. BREG
Brummitt, R. K. MAL
Brun, J. J. G
Brunel, TOGO
Brunnthaler, J. GJO, WU
Brunton, D. F. APM
Bryan, W. A. LAM
Bubák, F. BPI, PRM (herb.)
Bubani, P. GE
Buch, H. H
Buch, T. G. VLA
Buch, W. IJ
Buchanan, J. NH, WELT
Buchanan-Hamilton, F. LIV
Buchele, L. SOUT
Buchholz, J. T. ILL
Buchinger, BAI
Bucholz, FH
Buchtien, O. BAF, HBG, SI, VT, Z
Buchwald, N. F. CP
Buck, W. R. NY
Buckley, S. B. MO
Bucknall, C. BRIST
Buckstaff, OSH
Buek, H. W. HBG
Buell, J. H. FSSR
Bües, G. CUZ
Buia, A. CLA
Bukasov, S. M. WIR
Bula, G. UTMC
Bulgakova, L. L. RNMUT
Bull, A. NWH
Bullemont, de LV
Bunbury, C. J. F. CGE
Bunge, A. A. von LE
Burbidge, N. T. CANB
Burchell, W. J. BR, GH, GRA, K
Burgess, R. C. L. BIRM

Burgess, T. J. W. DAO, MTMG
Burkart, A. BAI, SI
Burkhalter, J. R. UWFP
Burkill, I. H. BSIS
Burlingham, G. S. NY
Burmann, J. et N. L. G
Burnat, E. G
Burrill, T. J. ILL
Burser, J. (herb.) UPS
Burt, E. A. FH
Burtt, B. L. E
Burtt-Davy, J. PRE
Busch, N. TBI
Buschbaum, H. OSN
Buser, O. et R. Z
Bush, B. F. MO
Buswell, W. M. BUS, FTG
Butkov, TASH
Butler, E. J. HCIO
Buxbaum, F. ZSS
Byl, P. A. van der STEU

Cábera, A. CB
Cabrera, A. L. BAF, LP, SI
Cacciato, RO
Cain, R. F. DAOM, TRTC
Cajander, A. K. H, HSI
Calder, J. DS
Calder, J. A. DAO
Calkins, W. W. NY
Callen, E. O. MTMG
Calvert, J. F. WAT
Camargo, L. A. COL
Camerarius, J. ER
Camp, W. H. NY
Campbell, C. WLU
Campbell, J. UCWI
Campbell, R. R. MTMG
Campos Porto, P. RB
Campuzano, QAME
Camus, E. G. P, PC
Camus, F. A. P, PC
Cañadas, L. QPNRA
Canby, W. M. AK, DOV, GRA, MCW, NHA, NY
Candolle, A. C. P. de CR, G (herb.)
Candolle, A. L. P. P. de (herb.) G
Candolle, A. P. de (herb.) G
Cannon, E. CAS
Cano, E. ANGU, SRFA
Cantú, J. CSAT
Capell, J. FCAB
Capuron, R. P
Cárdenas, M. BOLV, LIL
Cardinal, A. QFA
Cardona, F. MY, VEN
Cardot, J. PC
Carestia, A. A. TO
Carion, J. E. AUT
Carlquist, S. RSA

Carlton, M. A. PUR
Carmelich, BAI
Caro, J. A. BAF
Carpenter, D. S. VT
Carr, C. E. BM, CANB
Carr, W. J. NOT
Carrillo, E. USM
Carse, H. CHR
Carter, A. M. UC
Carter, J. C. ILLS
Carter, J. J. FMC
Carter, J. W. CMM
Caruel, T. (herb.) PI
Carvajal H., S. CREG, IBUG
Carver, G. W. BPI
Casares-Gil, A. MA
Casaretto, J. TO
Cassidy, J. CS
Castañeda Bringas, F. CODAGEM
Castellanos, A. BA, BAI, GUA
Castiglioni, J. A. BAI
Castillón, L. LIL
Catasús, HAJB
Cathcart, DEN
Cavalcanti, A. A. S. A. da S. URM
Cavalcanti, M. A. de Q. URM
Cavalcanti, W. de A. URM
Cavalcanti-Andrade, L. UFP
Cavalerie, J. P
Cavalheiro, E. M. BLA
Cavanilles, A. J. (herb.) MA
Cavara, F. PAD, TO
Cedercreutz, C. H
Cejp, PRC
Celakovský, PL
Cerrate, E. USM
Cersósimo, BAI
Ceruti, TO
Cesati, V. RO
Chabert, A. C. FI
Chakra, P. PBL
Chakralonty, P. PBL
Chalon, BR
Chamberlain, G. D. MAINE
Chamisso, L. A. von LE
Chandjan, N. S. ERE
Chandler, E. R. SBBG
Chapman, A. W. AUA, BUF
Chapman, J. D. MAL
Chardon, C. E. BPI, CUP
Charette, L. A. VT
Chase, A. US
Chase, N. C. SRGH
Chase, V. H. ILL
Chassagne, M. (herb.) CLF
Chater, A. O. LTR
Chaudhary, S. A. BEI
Chauvin, F. J. CN
Chavelas, J. INIF
Chedeville, FT

Cheel, E. DAR
Cheeseman, T. F. AK
Chen, C. H. WII
Cheney, L. S. WIS
Chernyaeva, A. M. VLA
Chevalier, A. (herb.) P
Chevallier, L. P
Chiamenti, PAD
Chin, S. C. KLU
Chinese National Fungus Collection (Peking) CUP
Ching, R. C. NAS
Chinnery, L. E. BAR
Chiovenda, E. FT
Chippendale, G. M. FRI, NT
Chivers, A. H. CUP, NY
Chou, H. C. WH
Christ, H. P
Christ, J. CS
Christ, J. H. ID, NY
Christ, CR
Christensen, C. BM
Christiansen, P. MOVC
Christophersen, E. BISH, O, WELT
Chuey, C. F. YUO
Chung, H. H. AU, WH
Chung, Z. S. IBK
Chupp, C. D. CUP
Churchill, G. C. K
Churchill, J. A. MSC
Churchill, J. R. MO
Churchill, S. P. MO
Ciferri, R. BPI, RMS, URM
Cinq-Mars, L. DAO, QFA
Çirpici, A. ISTF
Cittadella (herb.) PI
Clapp, A. WAB
Clarke, C. B. CAL, K
Clausen, J. C. DS
Clavaud (herb.) BORD
Clayton, J. GLEN
Clayton, W. D. BLA
Cleaveland, P. NHA
Clebsch, A. APSC
Cleef, A. M. COL, U
Cleland, J. B. AD, DAR
Clemens, J. B, BR, HBG, PUR, Z
Clemens, M. S. B
Clements, E. S. RMS
Clements, F. E. NEB, NY, RMS
Cleve, P. T. AWH, S
Cleveland, D. SD
Clewell, A. F. TEFH
Clinton, G. P. ILL, NHES
Clokey, I. W. CM, NO, NYS, OGDF, RENO-NESH, RM, UC
Clos, E. C. BAB
Coburn, L. MAINE
Cockayne, L. WELT
Cocks, R. S. NO

Codd, L. E. PRE
Cody, W. J. DAO
Coemans, H. E. L. G. BR
Coffindaffer, F. MVC
Cogniaux, A. BR
Coker, W. C. NCU
Colenso, W. PDD, WELT
Collins, F. S. BRU, FH, MAINE, NY, ODU, SPWH
Collom, R. E. DES
Commerson, P. DS
Compton, R. H. NBG, PRE
Conard, H. S. MO
Congdon, J. W. DS, MIN, VT
Constable, E. F. NSW
Constance, L. UC
Constantineanu, I. C. BUCM, IASI
Contreras, E. TEX, UTD
Conzatti, C. MEXU
Cook, A. MAINE
Cook, E. E. SBU
Cooke, M. C. K
Cooke, R. B. HAMU
Cooke, T. BSI
Cooke, W. B. MPPD, MU, RMS, URM, WSP
Cooke, PAD
Cooley, G. R. UCS, USF
Cooperrider, T. S. KE
Copeland, E. B. UC, WELT
Coppey, A. NCY
Corbière, L. (herb.) CHE
Corda, A. K. J. (herb.) PRM
Corner, E. J. H. CGE
Cornman, I. MWCF
Corns, I. G. CAFB
Corradi, R. FT
Correll, D. S. FTG, IJ, SMU, TEX
Correll, H. B. FTG
Corstorphine, M. STA
Corstorphine, R. STA
Corti, R. FI
Cosson, E. S. C. (herb.) P
Costa, A. L. BAH
Costa, A. S. IACM
Coste, H. (herb.) MPU
Cottam, W. P. BRY, UT
Couch, J. N. NCU
Coulter, J. M. WAB
Coupland, R. T. SASK
Courtois, R. J. LG
Cousturier, P. (herb.) MARSSJ
Couthouy, J. P. BUF
Covas, G. ANGU, SF, SRFA
Coveny, R. C. NSW
Cowan, C. CSAT
Cowan, J. CS
Cowan, R. S. WAB
Cox, D. K. XAL
Craig, E. AK

Craighead, F. FTG
Crandall, C. CS
Crane, J. L. ILLS
Craven, L. A. CANB
Cremers, G. CAY
Crépin, F. BR
Cresswell, R. RAMM
Cribb, A. B. BRIU
Crins, W. J. APM
Cristiani, L. Q. INFYB
Croasdale, H. T. CANI, SPWH
Croat, T. B. MO, QCA, QPNRA
Cronquist, A. NY, UTC
Crosby, M. R. MO, UCWI
Crosswhite, F. S. WIS
Crow, G. E. MSC
Cruise, J. WLU
Crum, H. A. CANM, CINC, MICH
Cuatrecasas, J. COL, F, MAF, TOLI, UTMC, VALLE
Cufodontis, G. FT
Cuming, H. CGE, DS, OXF, PR
Cummings, C. E. MAINE, WELC
Cummins, G. B. ARIZ, PUR
Cunningham, A. CGE, K, WELT
Cunningham, A. M. WAB
Cunningham, G. C. AFES
Cunningham, G. H. PDD
Cunningham, TOR
Cunquero, H. SRFA
Curran, H. M. MAD
Curtis, C. MAINE
Curtis, M. A. FH, NYS
Curtis, W. M. HO
Curtiss, A. H. CM, HAC, KNOX
Cusick, A. W. KE
Cusick, W. C. GH, ORE, OSC, RM, WS, WTU
Czernjaew, W. M. KW

Dade, H. A. DAR
Dahl, O. C. O
Dahlgren, R. LD
Dahlstrand, K. A. J
Damazio, L. B. RB
Damman, A. W. H. CDFN
Damon, S. NY
Daniels, F. UMO
Däniker, A. U. Z
Dansereau, P. QUE
Danty d'Isnard, A. T. P
Darbishire, O. V. BRIST
D'Arcy, W. G. MO
Darker, G. D. DAOM
Darling, C. DLF
Darlington, H. T. MSC
Darwin, C. CGE
Dashnyam, B. UBA
Dastur, HCIO
Daubenmire, R. F. WS

Davazhamts, T. UBA
Daveau, J. LISU
David, A. P
Davidov, B. SOM
Davidse, G. MO
Davidson, A. LAM
Davidson, J. HIP
Davidson, L. E. J
Davie, E. NWH
Davis, B. M. GMS
Davis, H. WVA
Davis, J. MO
Davis, J. J. MPPD, PUR, WIS
Davis, P. H. ANK, E, ISTE, RNG, ULT
Davis, R. J. IDS
Davis, T. A. W. FDG
Davis, W. T. SIM
Dávolos, L. QPNRA
Dawson, E. Y. AHFH, US
Day, F. M. TOR
Day, M. E. OC
Deam, C. C. IND, WAB
Dearing, H. SBBG
Dearing, M. SBBG
Dearness, J. DAO, DAOM, PUR
Deaver, C. F. ASC
Decary, R. P
DeChamplain, A. A. UQAR
Degener, O. BHSC, BISH, MASS, NY
DeJong, D. C. D. MSC
De Kindt, E. LISC
De Kindt, WU
Delacour, T. A. P
Delavay, P. J. M. P
Delessert, B. G
Delogne, C. H. BR
Del Vitto, L. A. MERL
Demades, D. TAU
Demaree, D. ASC, MO, NO, RSDR, SMU, STAR, UVST, VDB
Demaret, BR
Demiriz, H. DUF, ISTF
Demurina, E. M. RNMUT
Denison, M. MVC
Denslow, W. W. MASS
Denslow, Y. HUA
Deplanche, E. F. P
Deppe, F. (photos) XAL
Desfontaines, R. FI, P
Desmoulins, C. BORD
Desvaux, A. N. P
Detling, L. E. ORE
Devoto, BAI
Dewey, C. NYS
DeWolf, G. P. GAS
Díaz P., S. COL
Díaz-Piferrer, L. M. de FPDB
Díaz-Piferrer, M. FPDB
Dick (Snell), E. BPI
Dickinson, M. A. HAMU

329

Dickson, H. MW
Didier, E. P
Diedicke, H. JE
Diehl, I. E. BRY
Dietel, P. JE
Dieterlen, A. PRE
Dietrich, A. CANB, HBG
Dietrich, HAJB
Dillenius, J. J. H, OXF
Dimadis, ACA
Dimonic, I. WU
Dinklage, M. J. HBG
Dinsmore, J. E. BEI
Dinter, K. B, GRA, GRO, HBG, SAM, STE, WIND
Disbrow, W. S. NEMU
Dittrich, PAD
Dixon, D. G. VNC
Dixon, H. N. BM
Dixon, R. G. QAME
Dod, D. D. JBSD
Dodson, C. GUAY, QCA, RPSC, SEL
Doell, C. KR
Dogma, I. J. CALP
Doidge, E. M. PREM
Dollenz A., O. HIP
Döller-Wolframsberg, J. GJO
Dombey, J. DS
Domin, K. PR, PRC
Domínguez, J. A. BAF
Don, G. GLAM
Dorantes, J. XALU
Dore, W. G. DAO
Dörfler, I. GJO, WU
Doria, M. G. GDOR (herb.), PAD
Dornstauder, J. FCAB
Doronina, Y. A. VLA
Dorst, F. J. CANI
Dostál, J. PRC
Doty, M. S. HAW
Douglas, D. CGE, OXF
Douglas, G. W. DECV
Doumbia, DAKAR
Dowell, P. SIM
Dozy, F. L
Drake del Castillo, E. P
Drapalik, D. J. GAS
Drar, M. CAIM
Drège, J. F. P, PR
Dreisbach, R. R. MICH
Dressler, R. MO
Driggs, A. W. CONN
Drummond, A. QK
Drummond, J. CM, GL, MEL
Drummond, T. GH, OXF, SMU
Drummond-Hay, H. M. PTH
Drushel, J. A. MO
Duarte, A. P. HB, RB
Dubois, A. (herb.) OXF
Duchassaing, E. P. DS

Ducke, A. IAN, MAD, MG, NY, RB
Ducker, S. C. MELU
Ducloux, F. P
Ducomet, V. MPA
Dudley, M. G. DAO
Dudley, T. R. NA
Dudley, W. R. DS
Duffour, C. (herb.) TL
Dufour, J. M. L. (herb.) BORD
Dugand, A. COL
Duharte, HAJB
Duke, J. A. MO, OS
Dulhie, J. F. DD
Dumas-Damont (herb.) CLF
Dümmer, R. PRE
Dumont, K. P. COL
Dumont d'Urville, J. S. C. P
Dumortier, R. B. C. BR
Duncan, W. H. GAS
Dunn, D. B. UMO
Dunn, S. T. HK
Dupret, F. H. MT
Duque-Jaramillo, J. M. COL, FAUC
Duran, R. WSP
Duran, V. UC
Durand, E. DWC, MPA, P (herb.)
Durand, E. J. CUP
Durand, z
Durazzo Grimaldi, G. (herb.) GDOR
Dusén, P. K. H. PKDC, R, S
Duthie, A. V. STE
Duthie, J. F. K
Dutilly, A. DAO, QFA
Dutton, D. L. VT
Duvigneaud, P. (herb.) BRLU
Dwyer, J. D. MO
Dyck, J. R. CAFB
Dyer, R. A. GRA, PRE

Eads, A. MWI
Eames, E. H. CONN, NCBS, VT
Earle, F. S. NY, PUR
Earle, S. UC
Eastham, J. W. DAO
Eastwood, A. CAS, COLOM
Eaton, A. GRA
Eaton, A. A. NHA
Eaton, D. C. VT, YU
Eberhardt, P. A. P
Echeverry E., R. TOLI
Eckfeldt, T. (herb.) PH
Ecklon, C. F. DS, FI, GRA, GZU, PR, S, SAM, STE, WU
Edaño, G. E. PNH
Edgar, R. K. HDSM
Edgecombe, W. S. BEI
Edgeworth, M. P. CAL
Edwards, D. PRE
Egan, R. S. OMA
Eggers, H. F. A. von O, Z

Eggert, H. K. D. BUF, MO
Eggerth, K. WU
Eggleston, W. W. NY, RSDR
Egorova, E. M. VLA
Ehrenberg, C. G. HAL
Ehrendorfer, F. WU
Ehrhart, F. GOET, MW
Ehrle, E. B. GESU
Eichenfeld, M. von GJO
Eig, A. HUJ
Eiseman, N. J. HBFH
Eiten, G. IBGE, UB
Eiten, L. T. UB
Ekart, T. P. JE
Ekman, E. L. EHH, HAJB, IJ, S, USD
El-Gadi, A. ULT
Elliott, J. C. KBSMS
Elliott, S. CHARL
Ellis, J. B. FH, MAINE, NY, RMS
Ellis, J. L. PBL
Ellis, N. MPPD
Elmer, A. D. E. BISH, CM, NSW, PNH, SBBG, US, WTU
Elrod, M. J. MONTU
Elwes, H. J. CGE
Embleton, R. E. HAMU
Emory, W. H. MO
Emoto, Y. TNS
Ender, A. BREG
Engel, J. J. MSC
Engelmann, G. DWC, KNOX, MO
Engler, A. CR
English, C. S. WTU
Enti, A. A. GC
Epling, C. UC
Erichsen, C. F. E. HBG
Eriksson, J. GB
Ernst, Ado. VEN
Ernst, Alf. Z
Ernst, J. GJO
Erskine, D. DAO
Ertter, B. IFGH
Eskuche, U. G. CTESN
Espinal, S. HUA
Espinosa, R. LOJA
Espinoza Fernandez, C. HHUA
Espírito Santo, J. V. G. LISC, LISJC
Esslinger, T. CINC
Esterhuysen, E. BOL
Estrada, W. QPNRA
Eulenstein, T. AWH
Evans, A. W. (herb.) YU
Evans, H. C. CBS
Evans, I. BRISTM
Evans, M. S. NH
Everhart, B. M. MAINE, RMS
Everist, S. L. BRI
Evers, R. A. ILLS
Evrard, F. P
Ewan, J. COLO, NO, RSDR

Eyerdam, W. J. UC, WTU
Eyles, D. GEO
Eyles, F. GRA, PRE, SRGH

Fabriani, G. SPAL
Fabris, H. LP, SRFA
Facchini, F. TR
Fairman, C. E. CUP
Falcone, R. BAI
Fallass, C. W. ALBC
Familler, REG
Fanshawe, D. B. FDG
Farenholtz, H. BREM
Farges, P. G. P
Farlow, W. G. FH, HCIO, SPWH
Faruqi, S. A. ULT
Farwell, O. A. BLH, EMC, MCTF
Fassett, N. C. WIS
Faull, J. H. FH, TRTC
Faurie, U. J. KYO, P, WU, Z
Faust, M. E. SYRF
Fautrey, F. NCY, WU
Favre, CHUR, G
Faye, L. LR
Fayod, V. G
Featherman, A. LSU
Federov, A. A. ERE
Fedtschenko, B. LE
Fedtschenko, O. LE
Fée, A. L. A. P
Feichtinger, A. SZE
Feinbrun, N. HUJ
Felippone, F. SI
Félix, BR
Fendler, A. BUF, GH, MO, NHA, WELT
Ferdinandsen, C. CP
Fergus, C. L. PAC
Fernald, M. L. BRU, GH
Fernández, A. MY
Fernandez, G. CHAM
Fernández P., A. COL
Ferrari, G. MY
Ferrari, J. M. BHCB
Ferreira, M. B. HXBH
Ferreyra, R. USM
Ferris, R. S. DS
Fest, B. GJO
Feurich, G. GLM
Fiedler, O. LZ
Figari, A. FI
Figueiredo, M. B. IBI
Filgueiras, T. S. IBGE
Fink, B. MICH, MU
Fiori, A. FI, FT, PAD
Fiorini-Mazzanti, E. RO
Fischer, C. E. C. FRC
Fischer, E. BERN
Fischer, F. E. L. LE
Fischer, G. W. WSP
Fischer, HCIO, MH

Fisher, G. L. NOT
Fitzgerald, W. V. NSW, PERTH
Fitzpatrick, H. M. CUP
Flagey, C. NCY
Flanagan, H. G. GRA, PRE
Fleck, Z
Flecker, H. QRS
Fleischer, F. STU
Fleischer, M. FH
Fleming, H. NY
Fleming, J. GLAM
Fleming, M. NY
Fleming, W. D. US
Fletcher, J. DAO
Fletcher, OS
Flett, J. B. WTU
Flinn, M. A. ORE
Flossdorf, A. BAF
Flowers, S. COLO
Flynn, N. F. VT
Flysser, LJM
Focke, W. O. BREM
Foex, E. MPA
Fogg, J. M. SPWH
Folli, D. A. CVRD
Follmann, G. KASSEL
Fomin, M. ORE
Fonnegra G., R. HUA
Fonseca, S. G. UB
Font Quer, P. BC, BCF, MAF
Forbes, C. N. BISH, WELT
Forbes, F. F. VT
Forbes, H. NH
Forero, E. COL, UTMC
Forest, H. S. GESU
Formánek, E. (herb.) BRNM
Forrest, G. A. CAL, E, HK
Forskål, P. C, DS, LIV
Forster, G. B, GOET, K, LIV, MW, P
Forster, J. R. K, LIV, MW, P
Fosberg, F. R. BISH, POM, WELT
Foslie, M. TRH, USNC
Foster, A. S. ORE
Fourcade, H. G. BOL, GRA, STE
Fowler, J. QK, WLU
Franc, I. P, Z
Franchet, A. R. P
Frankton, C. DAO
Fraser, G. T. TOR
Fraser, L. R. DAR
Fraser, W. P. SASK
Frazee, O. UWL
Frazee, V. NEMU
Frecentese, M. ANGU
Freckmann, R. W. UWSP
Freckmann, S. K. UWSP
Fredericks, J. C. FDG
Freitas, L. C. de HXBH
Fremont, J. C. DWC, MO, NY, US
French, G. H. SIU

Fresenius, J. B. C. W. (herb.) FR
Frey, E. BERN
Freyer, LJM
Freyn, J. F. (herb.) BRNM
Freyn, PAD
Fries, E. M. UPS
Fries, T. C. E. LD
Fries, T. M. UPS
Fritsch, F. E. BM
Fritsch, K. GZU
Fróes, R. L. IAN
Froner, V. BLA
Frühling, CANI
Frye, T. C. ORE
Fuckel, K. W. G. L. G
Fuertes L., M. D. USD
Fulford, M. CINC
Fuller, A. M. MIL
Fuller, S. W. MWCF
Funk, A. DAVFP
Furbish, K. NHA
Furlow, J. J. MSC
Furrer, Z
Furuse, NA
Fuss, M. (herb.) SIB

Gabrielian, E. T. ERE
Gaertner, J. TUB
Gaertner, K. F. TUB
Gaillardot, C. JE
Gaiser, L. O. DAO
Galationova, T. F. SASY
Galeotti, H. G. BR
Galle, D. L. SZE
Galloway, C. M. CSPU
Galpin, E. E. GRA, PRE, STE
Gamble, J. S. CAL, DD, K, MH
Gamisans (herb.) MARSSJ
Gamundi , I. J. LPS
Gander, F. F. SD
Gandoger, M. (herb.) LY
Ganiatsas, K. (herb.) TAU
Garay, L. A. AMES
Garber, A. P. FMC
Garcés-Orejuela, C. ICA
García, HAJB
García-Barriga, H. COL
Gardner, C. A. PERTH
Gardner, Geo. CGE, FI, K
Gardner, Ger. SLU
Gardner, N. L. UC
Garlick, G. W. BRIST
Garner, J. H. B. ETSU
Garovaglio, S. GJO
Garrett, A. O. UT
Garton, C. E. DAO, LKHD, WLU
Garwood, A. E. WLU
Gassner, J. G. ANK
Gatty, M. SFD
Gaudichaud, C. DS, FI, P

331

Gaudin, J. F. A. T. (herb.) LAU
Gäumann, E, ZT
Gautier, G. DS
Gavioli, O. FI
Gay, C. P, SGO
Gay, J. K, MO
Geilinger, W. Z
Gelmi, E. TR
Genevier, G. CGE
Genth, F. F. GJO
Gentle, P. H. IJ, TEX, UTD
Gentry, A. AMAZ, COL, GUAY, MO, QCA, RPSC, USM
Gentry, H. S. DES, INIF, MEXU
Georgel (herb.) AV
Gesser, K. Z
Gessner, J. ZT
Ghani, F. D. UKMB
Ghiesbrecht, A. B. BUF
Gibbes, L. CHARL
Gibert, E. J. MVM
Gibson, R. A. HBFH
Gier, L. J. NY
Gierisch, R. ASC
Giess, W. WIND
Gilbert, B. D. NYS
Gilbert, F. A. MUHW
Gilbert, H. C. OSC
Gilbert, W. J. ALBC
Gilbertson, R. L. ARIZ
Gilibert, J. E. KW
Gilkey, H. M. OSC
Gill, L. S. WAT
Gillet, MOG
Gillett, J. STE
Gillett, J. M. DAO
Gillies, J. GL, OXF
Gilliland, H. B. J
Gillis, W. T. FTG, KBSMS, MSC
Gillot, F. X. AUT
Gills, LWG
Gilmartin, A. GUAY
Giltay, L. BR
Giltay, LV
Gimet (herb.) AV
Ginzberger, A. WU
Giovanni, IBF
Giraldi, G. FI
Gissing, T. W. CMM
Glantschnig (herb.) KL
Glassman, S. F. CHI
Glasspoole, H. NWH
Glaziou, A. F. M. BR, P, R
Gleason, H. A. NY
Glencoe, J. F. WVW
Glover, P. E. MOG
Glowacki, J. GJO
Gmelin, C. C. KR
Goadby, B. T. PERTH
Godfrey, R. K. VDB

Gogina, E. E. MHA
Gökçeada, EGE
Gola, PAD, TO
Goldblatt, P. MO
Gombault, R. P
Gómez, J. USM
Gomez-Gonzalez, A. SLPM
Gomez-Lorence, F. SLPM
Gonan, A. K
Gonçalo Sampaio, PO
Gonod d'Artemard, MPA
Gonzalez, R. CHAM
González Fragoso, R. MA
González Ortega, J. MEXU
González Q., L. ENCB
Gonzalez Tamayo, R. AMO
González Villarreal, L. M. CREG
Gonzalves, E. BLAT
Goodale, A. S. MASS
Goodall, N. HIP, MU, NA
Goodding, L. N. ASC, RM
Gooding, E. G. B. BAR
Goodman, G. J. OKL
Goodspeed, T. H. UC
Goossens-Fontana, M. BR
Gordon, S. MAINE
Gordon, W. L. DAOM
Gorman, M. W. ORE
Gorovoy, P. T. VLA
Gortani, L. MFU
Gortani, M. MFU
Goslin, C. BHO
Gossweiler, J. LISC, LISJC
Gottsche, C. M. GJO
Goudot, J. P
Gough, L. TAC
Goulandris (herb.) ATH
Gould, F. W. TAES
Goulimis, ATH
Govan, G. DD
Gräffe, E. O. HBG
Graham, A. CMM
Graham, E. H. CM
Grandi, T. S. M. BHCB
Grandvaux Barbosa, L. LUAI
Grant, A. RSA
Grant, A. L. MO
Grant, M. L. BISH, ISTC
Grant, V. RSA
Grant, W. F. MTMG
Granville, J. J. de CAY
Grashoff, J. L. MSC
Graves, C. B. NCBS
Gray, A. BKL, DWC, GH, MO, NO, OS
Green, I. J. CDFN
Greene, E. L. NDG
Greene, H. ARIZ, WIS
Greenman, J. M. MO
Greenwood, E. W. AMO
Gregg, K. B. WVW

Grégoire, MAAS
Gremmen, J. CUP
Grenand, P. CAY
Grenier, J. C. M. P
Grennan, A. J. SDM
Greville, R. K. E
Griffin, D. HERZU
Griffith, J. E. NMW
Griffith, W. BR, CAL, CGE
Griffiths, A. RAMM
Griffiths, D. PUR, US
Grimes, J. W. IFGH
Grimme, A. KASSEL
Grimus, K. R. von G. WU
Grintescu, G. P. BUCA
Grisebach, A. (herb.) GOET
Groff, E. FMC
Groff, H. K. FMC
Grognot, C. AUT
Groh, H. DAO
Grönblad, R. H
Grönblom, T. (herb.) TMP
Gross, R. S. KBSMS
Grossheim, A. A. ERE, TBI
Grossweiler, J. LUA
Grout, A. J. DUKE, SMU, VT, WTU
Grove, E. BM
Grover, F. O. OC
Groves, H. FI, WELT
Groves, J. WELT
Groves, J. W. DAOM, TRTC
Gruber (herb.) MARSSJ
Grubov, V. I. UBA
Grunow, A. BR, W (herb.)
Guadagno, M. (herb.) PI
Guarinoni, H. IBF
Guba, E. F. BPI
Guenther, C. SBU
Guevara, L. C. de MY
Guiguet-Rochelaise, LR
Guillaumin, A. Z
Guillemin, J. B. A. DS
Guillemin, J. B. A. DS
Guiol, F. G. (herb.) BM
Guldner, L. F. BDI
Gunn, R. C. HO
Guppy, N. G. L. FDG
Gustafsson, C. E. LD
Gusuleac, P. CERN
Gutierres Lobatos, J. L. UNL
Gutnikova, Z. I. VLA
Gutte, P. LZ, SMF
Guzmán, G. ENCB
Guzmán M., R. CREG, IBUG

Haberer, J. V. NYS
Habsburg, J. v. GJO
Hackel, E. (herb.) W
Hacquet, C. LJM
Haeckel, E. H. JE
Haenke, T. PR

Hagelstein, R. NY
Hagen, I. TRH
Hagsater, E. AMO
Hagström, J. O. LD
Hainer, UWM
Haines, H. H. DD
Halácsy, E. von ACA, WU
Hale, G. VNC
Hale, J. NO
Hale, T. J. KNOX, WIS
Hall, E. BUF, GRA, KNOX
Hall, H. M. CM, UC
Hall, J. B. GC
Hall, M. O. HBFH
Haller, A. von GOET, MW, P (herb.)
Hallier, J. G. HBG
Hallworth, B. M. UAC
Hance, H. F. GRA
Hancock, M. HAMU
Hancock, W. BRIST, K
Handel-Mazzetti, H. W, WU
Hanes, C. R. WMU
Hanes, F. N. WMU
Hankenson, E. L. EMC
Hanmer, C. C. CONN
Hansen, B. UWFP
Hansford, C. G. PREM
Hapeman, H. RM
Hara, H. TI
Harbour, J. P. BUF, KNOX
Harger, E. B. NCBS
Haring, I. M. NY
Hariot, P. A. PC
Harkness, W. F. DLF
Harley, R. M. CEPEC
Harling, G. GB
Harmand, F. J. ANGUC, DUKE
Harmand, NCY
Harmon, W. E. MO, UMO
Harms, V. L. SASK
Harnell, H. V. PAD
Harper, R. A. NY
Harrington, H. CS, PUSC
Harris, C. J. MVC
Harris, R. C. MSC
Harris, S. K. BSN
Harris, W. UCWI
Harrison, B. F. BRY
Hart, H. C. DBN
Hart, J. UCWI
Hartford, W. G. W. BUF
Harthill, M. P. CSPU
Hartman, C. V. GH
Hartweg, K. T. CGE, LD
Harvey, F. L. AK, UARK
Harvey, L. H. MONTU, WMU
Harvey, W. H. BEL, BKL, DBN, DS,
    DWC, TCD, WELT
Harvey, FH
Harvill, A. M., Jr. FARM

Hasse, H. E. FH, LAM, NY
Hasselqvist, F. SBT
Hasselt, J. C. A. van L
Hasskarl, J. K. BO, L
Hassler, E. BAF, G, MO, SI
Hasslow, O. J. LD
Hatch, E. D. AK
Hatch, S. L. TAES
Hatcher, UWM
Hatman, IBIR
Hatschbach, G. HBR, MBM
Hattori, S. NICH
Hauck, F. L
Hauck, FH
Haught, O. COL
Hauman, L. BA, BR, BRLU (herb.)
Haussknecht, C. JE
Havaas, J. BG, DUKE
Haviland, G. D. CGE
Hawkes, J. G. BAL, BIRM, BOLV
Haworth, A. H. OXF
Hawsford, C. G. DAR
Hayashi, T. TF
Hayata, B. TI
Hayden, F. V. WAB
Hayek, A. A. von GB, GJO, WU
Haynes, C. C. FH, NY
Heald, F. D. WSP
Healy, A. J. CHR
Hebden, T. CMM
Hedberg, O. UPS
Hedgcock, G. G. BPI
Hedlund, T. UPS
Hedwig-Schwaegrichen, G
Hagelmaier, F. STU
Hegetschweiler, C. Z
Heikkinen, L. OULU
Heilbronn, A. ISTF
Heilbronn, M. ISTF
Heimburger, M. WLU
Heimerl, A. IBF
Heinrichs, E. Z
Heldreich, T. ATHU, LIV, TAU
Helin, M. TMP
Hellenius, C. N. H
Heller, A. A. BKL, DS, FMC, MO,
    MTMG, NEB, NY, RENO-NESH, RM,
    SEL, WBM, WTU
Heller, F. X. (herb.) WB
Hellerman, J. HDSM
Hellwig, R. MOVC
Henderson, L. F. ORE, OSC
Hennebert, G. L. MUCL
Hennen, J. F. IBI, PUR
Henninger, E. P. URM
Hennings, P. B
Henrickson, J. CSLA, RSA, TEX
Henry, A. CAL, CGE, DBN, HK, K, MO,
    Z
Herbich, F. CERN

Herbst, W. CANI
Héribaud, J. (herb.) BM
Heringer, E. P. IBGE, UB
Hermann, F. GAT
Hermann, F. J. MICH
Herminier, F. L. l' P
Hermsen, J. BAL
Hernandez Corzo, A. UNL
Hernández X., E. CHAPA
Herre, H. STE
Herrera, HAJB
Herter, W. G. G, PAE
Herzog, T. JE
Herzog, Z
Hesler, L. R. TENN
Hespenheide, E. B. UCWI
Hespenheide, H. A. UCWI
Heudelot, OXF
Heurck, H. F. van AWH, BR
Heyne, B. LIV
Hicken, C. M. SI
Hiern, W. P. CGE, RAMM
Hieronymus, G. H. E. W. B, BAF,
    CORD
Hieronymus, PAD
Hiesey, W. DS
Higgins, E. A. MARY
Higgins, L. C. BRY, WTS
Hildebrandt, J. M. PR, WU, Z
Hilitzer, A. (herb.) PRM
Hill, E. J. ILL
Hill, S. R. FTG, MARY, VT
Hillebrand, W. BISH
Hillebrand, W. F. WELT
Hillhouse, W. BIRM
Hillson, C. J. PAC
Hinckley, F. MAINE
Hind, W. M. IPS
Hinton, G. B. DES, ENCB, IJ, K, MEXU,
    MO, NY, TEX, UTD
Hirn, K. E. H
Hitchcock, A. S. HAC, KSC, MO, US
Hitchcock, C. L. MONTU, WTU
Hjerting, J. P. BOLV
Hladnik, LJM
Hochstetter, C. F. STU, TUB
Hodgdon, A. R. NHA
Hodge, E. OS
Hodge, W. H. ECON
Hodgson, E. A. MPN
Hoe, W. J. HAW
Hoffman, G. F. (herb.) MW
Hoffmann, W. BAL
Hohenwarth, S. GJO
Höhnel, F. X. R. von FH
Hollenberg, G. J. GMS, US
Hollick, A. SIM
Holm, K. TMP
Holm, L. UPS
Holmes, A. F. MTMG

Holmes, E. M. NOT
Holmgren, A. H. UTC
Holmgren, N. H. NY, UTC
Holm-Nielsen, L. AAU, QCA, QCNE
Holuby, J. E. PRC
Holway, E. W. D. MIN, MPPD, PUR
Holway, M. M. PUR
Holzinger, J. M. GJO, IA
Homola, R. MAINE
Honey, E. E. CUP
Hoock, J. CAY
Hoogland, R. D. CANB
Hooker, J. D. CAL, K, MH, TCD
Hooker, W. J. DWC, GL, K
Hoopes, J. DWC
Hoover, R. F. CAS, OBI, UC
Hopkins, L. S. OS
Hopkins, M. OKL
Hoppe, D. H. GJO, GZU, WU
Hoppin, R. EMC
Horak, E. LPS
Horikawa, Y. HIRO
Horneman, J. W. AWH
Horsey, W. R. GESU
Horton, O. B. UC
Horwood, A. R. NMW
Horwood, E. K. LTR
Hose, C. CGE
Hosseus, C. CORD
Houghton, D. MICH
House, H. D. NYS
Houstoun, W. CGE, XAL (photos)
Howard, G. E. WELC
Howard, H. J. K, NWH
Howard, R. A. UCWI
Howe, D. F. SD
Howe, M. A. MSM, NY, UC
Howe, R. H. FH
Howell, J. T. CAS
Howell, T. J. ORE, OSC, WTU
Hoysradt, L. H. HHH
Huber, J. MG
Huber, O. VEN
Huber-Morath, A. (herb.) BASBG
Hübner, J. W. GJO
Hudson, J. H. DAO
Hue, A. M. PC
Huerta, L. ENCB
Huertas, G. COL
Hugo, L. STE
Huguet del Villar, MAF
Hultén, E. S
Humbert, H. P
Humboldt, F. W. H. A. P
Humm, H. J. FPDB
Hunt, K. CHARL
Hunziker, J. BAB
Hürlimann, H. Z
Husnot, P. T. SMU
Hutchinson, J. PRE

Hutchison, P. C. UC, USM
Hy, F. ANGUC, COLO

Idman, R. TMP
Idrobo, J. M. COL
Ijjasz, E. MY
Illin, N. BAF
Iltis, H. H. WIS
Imler, R. H. KSC
Imshaug, H. A. MSC
Infantes, J. SMF
Inokuma, T. TOFO
Inumaru, S. HIRO
Ireland, O. L. ORE
Irish, F. M. ASU
Irmisch, T. JE
Irwin, H. S. COL, NY, UB, VIC
Isaac, W. E. NAI
Isely, D. ISC
Isle, G. de l' P
Issler, E. (herb.) BASBG
Iwatsuki, K. YUO
Iwatsuki, Z. NICH

Jaap, O. MPPD
Jabornegg, M. WU
Jackson, G. MAL
Jackson, H. S. PUR, TRTC
Jacobs, M. R. FRI
Jacot Guillarmod, A. F. M. G. ROML
Jacquemin, H. CAY
Jacquemont, V. P
Jacques-Félix, H. P
Jaeger, A. NY
Jafri, S. M. H. ULT
Jahandiez, E. (herb.) MARSSJ
Jahn, A. VEN
Jahn, E. B
James, E. P. NY
James, L. E. DAO
James, T. P. FH
Jameson, G. Q
Jameson, W. DD
Janchen, E. WU
Janczewski, E. KRAM
Janisch, AWH
Jansson, K. P. CONN, MAINE
Jaramillo, J. QCA
Jaramillo, R. COL
Jäschke, Rev. WU
Jasiewicz, A. KRAM
Jeanjean, A. F. (herb.) BORD
Jeanpert, H. E. P
Jelski, K. KRA
Jenkins, A. E. BPI, IBI
Jenkins, F. HCIO
Jenkins, L. DAO
Jenman, G. S. BRG, NY
Jennings, O. E. CM

Jepson, W. L. JEPS
Jermy, C. BM
Jermy, G. MO
Jewett, A. MICH
Jiménez, J. USD
Jimenez, TAES
John, GC
Johnsen, A. MNA
Johnson, A. W. FSSR
Johnson, J. D. CAFB
Johnson, T. DBN
Johnson, W. J. P. GRA
Johnston, I. M. ANSM, GH, TEX
Johnston, M. C. TEX
Jokela, P. S. OULU
Jolis, A. F. le (herb.) CHE
Joly, A. B. SPF
Joncheere, G. J. de YUO
Jones, A. G. ILL
Jones, D. A. NMW
Jones, G. N. ILL
Jones, G. T. MU, OC
Jones, H. L. OC
Jones, M. E. ASC, CSPU, MO, NHA, NMC, POM, RM, RSDR, UTC
Jones, S. B., Jr. GAS
Jones, T. DBN
Jones, GC
Joor, J. F. MO, NO
Jordaan, P. G. STE
Jordan, A. CGE, Z
Jordán de Urries, MA
Jørgensen, E. BG
Jörgensen, P. BAF, SI
Joseph, F. C. CANI
Jourtau, Abbé LUCH
Jump Saldivar, L. A. HHUA
Junak, S. A. SBBG
Junghuhn, F. W. L
Juratzka, J. (herb.) W
Jussieu, A. de (herb.) P
Jussieu, A. L. de (herb.) P
Jussieu, B. de (herb.) P

Kaalaas, B. BG
Kabanov, N. E. VLA
Kabát, J. E. PRC
Kaiser, A. CAIM, Z
Kajewski, S. F. BISH
Kalchbrenner, K. BRA
Kalela, A. H
Kalm, P. SBT
Kanai, H. TI
Kanda, H. NIPR
Kane, O. E. DAKAR
Kanehira, R. BISH, FU
Kaneshiro, T. KYO
Kanjilal, P. C. ASSAM
Kanjilal, U. N. ASSAM, DD
Kapp, R. ALMA

334

Kappel, A. BLA
Karamysheva, Z. V. UBA
Karapetian, R. A. ERE
Karavaev, M. A. SASY
Karelin, G. S. LE
Karl, W. LIT
Karsten, P. A. H
Karwinski, W. F. M
Käser, F. Z
Kässner, T. BR, Z
Katende, A. B. MO
Kauffman, C. H. MICH
Kausel, E. H
Kaynak, G. DUF
Kearney, T. H. ARIZ, ASC, CAS, OS, RSDR
Keck, D. D. DS, NO, NY
Keck, K. WU
Keener, C. S. PAC
Keet, J. D. STE
Keller, R. Z
Kellerman, W. A. KSC, OS, PUR
Kelley, W. A. SRCG
Kellogg, A. BUF, CAS, UC
Kellogg, J. H. MO
Kelly, J. GESU
Kelsey, F. MONT
Kendrick, W. B. WAT
Kennedy, P. B. RENO-NESH
Kenoyer, L. WMU
Kerfoot, O. J, STE
Kern, F. D. PAC, PUR
Kerner, A. WU
Kerner-Marilaun, A. J. GJO
Kerr, A. F. G. BM, K, TCD
Kerr, AAU
Kerstan, K. HAL
Ketchledge, E. H. CANI
Khalifa, M. M. ULT
Kharkevich, S. S. VLA
Khattab, A. CAIM
Kibbe, A. L. CART, WARK
Kiener, W. NEB
Kihlman, A. O. H
Killermann, M
Killick, D. J. B. PRE
Killip, E. P. COL, HAC, MO, NO, US
Kimnach, M. HNT
Kimura, A. TUS
King, B. HAMU
King, C. NSW
King, G. CAL
King, K. FDG
King, L. J. GESU
Kingdon-Ward, F. GB
Kirk, T. WELT
Kirkwood, J. E. MONTU
Kirschstein, W. B
Kistler, J. SRCG
Kitagawa, M. TI

Kitaibel, P. PR
Kitamura, S. KYO
Kitching, L. BIRM
Kitton, F. BM
Klaine, T. J. P
Klatt, F. W. S
Klävsen, AWH
Klein, J. G. LIV
Klein, R. M. HBR
Klementz, LE
Klobukova-Alisova, E. N. VLA
Klotzsch, J. F. B
Kluzák, Z. CB
Kmeť, A. BRA
Knapp, A. ZT
Knapp, J. A. WU
Knapp, J. L. BRISTM
Kneiskern, P. D. NYS
Kneucker, A. KR
Knight, C. C. WELT
Knight, H. H. NMW
Knobloch, I. W. MSC
Knoche, H. DS
Knowles, M. C. DBN
Ko, S. P. IBK
Koch, K. OSN
Koch, L. F. ILL
Koch, W. ZT
Koegeler, K. GJO
Koelz, W. N. MICH
Köhler, HAJB
Kohlmeyer, E. IMS
Kohlmeyer, J. IMS
Koidzumi, G. KYO, TI
Koidzumi, H. TNS
Kojima, S. CAFB
Kokwaro, J. O. NAI
Koldeway, K. BREM
Kolesnikov, B. P. VLA
Komarov, V. L. LE
König, J. G. SBT
Konklar, WU
Koorders, S. H. BO
Koppe, K. HAL
Körber, G. W. L
Kornaś, J. KRA
Korovin, E. P. RNMUT
Korshinsky, S. I. LE
Korthals, P. W. L
Koslowsky, J. BAF
Kostina, K. F. WIR
Kotschy, T. AWH, DS, GJO, OXF, PR, STU, W
Kotte, W. ANK
Kotula, B. KRAM
Kovalev, K. I. WIR
Kovarik, A. F. LCDI
Kraenzlin, F. W. L. AMES
Krafft, A. (herb.) BREG
Kraft, G. T. MELU

Kral, R. SMU, VDB
Krapovickas, A. CTES
Krasske, G. KASSEL
Krause, E. H. L. ROST
Krause, K. ANK
Kreisel, HAJB
Krempelhuber, A. von M, WU
Kriebel, R. PUL
Krieg, D. SBU
Krieger, L. HXBH
Krieger, W. RMS
Kristof, L. GJO
Krivda, W. DAO
Krog, H. ALA, O
Krug, H. P. IACM
Kruger, F. J. STE
Krukoff, B. A. MAD, MO, NY
Kruschke, E. P. MIL
Kučera, S. CB
Kudrjaschev, V. I. TASH
Kuhl, H. L
Kuhlmann, J. G. RB, VIC
Kuhn, M. B
Kuhnholtz-Lordat, G. MPA
Kujala, V. HFR
Kükenthal, G. B
Kultiassov, M. V. MHA, RNMUT
Kunkel, G
Kunth, K. S. SGO
Kuntze, O. NY
Kunze, G. B
Kupffer, K. R. RIG
Kurata, S. TOFO
Kurentsova, G. E. VLA
Kurtz, F. BAF, CORD
Kurz, W. S. CAL
Kusaka, M. TF
Kützing, F. T. AHW, L
Kuvaev, B. V. SASY
Kylin, H. LD

Labani, R. M. ULT
Labillardière, J. J. H. FI
Lachenal, W. de BAS
Lackschewitz, K. MONTU
Ladero, M. GDA
Laestadius, L. L. JYV
Laflin, J. CGE
Lagrèze-Fossat, A. R. A. (herb.) TL
Lahm, J. G. B, MSTR
Laing (herb.) CANU
Laitsch, J. T. YUO
Lakela, O. DUL, USF
Lamarck, J. B. A. P. M. de (herb.) P
Lamas Robles, R. CREG
Lamb, I. M. CANL, FH
Lambert, A. B. (herb.) PH
Lambert, E. L. WARK
Lamotte, M. (herb.) CLF

Lamouroux, J. V. F. CN
Lampton, R. K. VSC, WGC
Lang, A. F. (herb.) WU
Lång, G. H
Lange, J. C
Langlassé, E. GH, MEXU
Langlois, A. B. BPI
Langsdorff, G. H. von LE
Lanser, IBF
Lányi, A. SZE
Lanza, PAL
Lapeyrouse, P. P. B. de TL, TLJ
Lapham, I. A. DWC, WIS
Lara, R. R. LPB
Larsen, K. AAU
Lasser, T. VEN
Lassimone, S. E. (herb.) CLF
Latham, R. A. NYS
Latowski, POZ
La Trobe (herb.) NEU
Lau, S. K. IBK
Laubengayer, R. A. WAB
Laureano Amorín, J. INFYB
Laurila, M. H, HPP
Lauterbach, K. A. G. (herb.) WRSL
Lavarenne (herb.) CLF
Lavranos, J. MO
Lawson, G. W. GC
Lawson, M. A. MH
Laydevant, ROML
Lazăr, IBIR
Lazarides, M. CANB
Lázaro é Ibiza, B. MAF
Leach, L. ORE
Leach, L. C. SRGH
Leavenworth, W. WAB
Leblanc, QFA
Lebrun, F. BR
Lécard, T. BR
Ledebour, C. F. von LE
Ledingham, G. F. DAO
LeDoux, D. UMO
Lee, R. K. S. CANA
Leefe, J. E. BRISTM
Lees, F. A. CMM
Leeuwenberg, A. YA
Legault, A. DAO, WLU
Leggett, W. H. NY
Legrand, D. MVM
Legrand (herb.) CLF
Lehmann, F. C. K
Lehmann, J. G. MEL, PR, S
Lehr, J. H. DES
Leiberg, J. B. ORE, WTU
Leighton, W. A. NY
Leistner, O. A. KMG
Leite, J. E. FCAB
Lejeune, A. L. S. BR, LG
Lellinger, D. B. HUA
Lemann, C. M. CGE

Lemmermann, E. BREM
Lemmon, J. G. CM, NO, UC
Lems, K. MICH
Lenormand, S. R. CN, FH, P
Lenz, L. RSA
León, Brother (J. S. Sauget) CHI,
    HAC, HAJB, SV
Leonard, S. W. GAS
Lepage, E. DAO, RIM
Lepper, HAJB
Le Rat, A. J. P
Lerchenfeld, F. (herb.) SIB
LeRoy, P. V. NY
Leschenault, J. B. L. T. P
Le Sourd, MPA
Lespinasse, J. M. G. (herb.) BORD
Lesquereux, L. BUF, NEU, NY, OS,
    WTU
Letacq, Abbé COLO
Le Testu, G. M. P. C. P
Letourneau, CAIM
Letouzey, R. P. YA
Lett, H. W. DBN
Lettau, G. B
Letterman, G. W. MO
Lettors, M. DAO
Léveillé, A. A. H. E, P
Levier, E. FI, PAD
Lewis, W. H. MO
Ley, A. BIRM
L'Héritier, C. L. (herb.) NEU
Lhotsky, J. PR
Li, Y. H. HITBC
Liang, H. Y. IBK
Libert, M. A. BR, LG, LGHF
Lid, J. O
Liesner, R. MO
Lightfoot, J. K
Lillo, M. BAF, LIL
Lima, D. de A. IPA, URM
Lima, H. S. CVRD
Lindauer, V. W. AK, AKU, WELT
Lindberg, H. H
Lindberg, S. O. H
Lindemann, E. LECB
Linden, J. J. BR, CGE
Lindenberg, J. B. W. (herb.) W
Linder, D. H. FH, MO
Lindheimer, F. J. BAYLU, DUR, GH,
    GJO, MO, NHA, RENO-NESH, SMU, YU
Lindley, J. AMES, CGE, K
Lindquist, J. C. LPS, PUR
Lindsay, D. R. DAO
Lingelsheiù, PAD
Link, H. F. B
Linnaeus, C. H, LINN, LIV, S, SBT
Lino, A. M. CVRD
Linton, W. R. LIV, LIVU
Liogier, A. H. JBSD, NY, UPR
Lippold, HAJB

Lipsky, V. I. LE
Liro, J. I. H, HPP
Lisa, D. TO
Lisowski, S. BRVU, POZG
Littke, W. UKMB
Little, E. L. ASC, CHAS, COL, MAD,
    QAME
Llamas, A. de BAF
Lloyd, C. G. BPI, CINC
Lobb, T. CGE, OXF
Löfling, O. SBT
Loiseleur-Deslongchamps, J. L. A.
    (herb.) AV
Løjtnant, AAU
Lombardo, A. MVFA
Long, B. MCA
Long, D. M. CSPU
Long, F. NWH
Long, F. R. (herb.) PEU
Long, R. W. USF
Long, W. H. BPI, PUR
Longhi, H. BLA
Longpre, E. K. MSC
Lönnbohm, O. A. F. KUO
Loock, E. E. M. FFS
Loomis, N. (herb.) AHFH
Looser, G. G, PAE
López, N. de UTMC
López Figueiras, M. HAJB
Lopez Guillen, J. SMF
Lopez Ramirez, A. XALU
López, HAJB
Lorentz, P. G. BAF, CORD
Losa España, T. M. BCF
Losee, S. T. LKHD
Louis, A. BR
Louis, Frère P
Louis-Marie, Père QFA
Loureiro, J. P
Lousley, J. E. RNG
Louw, W. J. PUC
Löve, A. DAO
Löve, D. DAO
Lowe, E. N. MISS
Lowe, R. T. CGE
Lowrie, A. E. DD
Lowy, B. LSUM
Lozano, G. COL
Lucand, J. L. AUT
Lucas, A. H. S. CANB, NSW
Luchnik, Z. I. VLA
Ludlow, F. BM
Ludwig, A. B
Ludwin, C. F. MO
Luer, C. SEL
Luetzelburg, P. von R
Lugard, C. E. GRA
Lugard, E. J. GRA
Lugard, F. GRA
Lugea, BAI

Luiz, I. T. PEL
Lundell, C. L. MO, TEX, UTD
Lunell, J. MIN
Luschan, F. WU
Lusina, RO
Luteyn, J. QPNRA
Lyell, K. M. RNG
Lynch, S. P. LSUS
Lynge, B. A. O
Lyonnet, E. MEXU

Macaluso, PAL
Macbride, J. F. F, RM, WTU
Macbride, T. H. BPI, URM
MacBryde, B. QCA
MacDougal, D. T. NY, RSDR
Mac Dougall, T. MEXU
MacFadden, F. CSPU, MACF, ORE
MacFarlane, C. NSPM
Mackay, A. H. NSPM
MacKee, P
Mackenzie, K. K. NY
MacLulich, D. WLU
MacMillan, C. MIN
Macoun, J. BUF, CAN, CANA, CANM, DAO, DAOM, EMC, MO, OAC, QK, UAC, WTU
Macoun, J. M. CAN, CANM, MTMG
MacOwan, P. BUF, GRA (herb.), PREM, SAM
Madison, M. QCA, SEL
Madrigal, X. INIF
Magill, R. E. PRE
Magnus, P. W. HBG
Magnusson, A. H. GB, UPS
Maguire, B. FDG, NY, UTC, VEN
Maiden, J. H. NSW
Mains, E. B. MICH, PUR
Maire, G. CAIM
Maire, R. AL
Mäkelä, T. TMP
Makino, T. MAK, TI
Mäkisalo, I. TMP
Malaisse, BRVU
Malakates, ACA
Malme, G. O. A. S
Malos, G. BAJ
Malte, M. O. CAN
Mal'tsev, A. I. WIR
Maly, J. GJO
Malyer, H. DUF
Manakian, V. A. ERE
Mancinas Zaldivar, G. CREG
Mandon, G. GH, MPA
Maneval, W. E. UMO
Mangelsdorf, P. C. ECON
Mangieri, BAI
Manickam, V. S. RHT
Manitz, HAJB
Mann, A. US

Mann, G. ASSAM, DD
Mann, H. CU
Manning, S. A. NWH
Manning, W. E. BUPL
Marcello, A. PAD
Marchesetti, C. von FI
Marchesi, E. MVFA
Marchesoni, V. CAME
Marchesoni, FI
Marie-Victorin, Brother DAO, MT, SFS
Mariz, G. UFP
Markgraf, ANK
Markland, G. H
Markötter, E. I. STE
Marktanner-Turneretscher, G. V. GJO
Marloth, R. PRE, STE
Marr, J. W. QUE
Marroquín, J. S. ANSM, UNL
Marshall, E. S. CGE
Marshall, H. DWC
Martelli, U. FI
Martin, G. W. BPI, IA, URM
Martin, W. WELT
Martin, W. C. PUSC
Martindale, I. C. AK, NA (herb.)
Martinelli, G. RB
Martínez, M. CODAGEM, MEXU
Martínez Esquivel, S. CREG
Martínez Solorzano, EBUM
Martius, C. F. P. von BH, BR, M, PI
Mason, G. ORE, OSC
Mason, H. L. UC
Mason, R. CHR
Massalongo, C. B. PAD
Massee, G. NY
Massey, J. R. GAS
Mathews, A. CGE
Mathews, W. A. GESU
Matsson, R. LD
Matsuda, T. NIPR
Matsumura, J. TI
Mattei, G. E. PAL
Matthew, K. M. RHT
Mattirolo, O. TO
Matuda, E. CODAGEM, FCME, MEXU, TEX, UTD
Maximovicz, K. I. LE, NY
Maxwell, R. H. JEF
Maxwell, AAU
Maycock, P. F. APM
Mayebara, K. KYO
May Nah, A. INIF
Mayor, E. NEU, Z
Mayr, REG
Mazzantini, M. (herb.) GDOR
Mazzer, S. J. KE
McAlpine, D. VPRI
McCabe, T. T. UC

McCalla, W. C. ALTA
McCann, C. BLAT
McCart, W. L. HPC
McClean, A. P. D. NH
McClintock, E. CAS
McClure, F. BISH, US
McCoy, T. N. MEM, MUR
McDaniel, S. AMAZ, NATC, VDB
McIntosh, A. E. S. BAR
McIntosh, T. WLU
McMahon, J. H. WELT
McMinn, H. E. UC
McNab, J. DBN
McNab, W. R. DBN
McNabb, R. F. R. PDD
McPherson, G. D. MO
McSweeney, G. D. HIP
McVaugh, R. ENCB, IBUG, MEXU, MICH, TEX
Mead, S. B. ILL, KNOX
Meades, W. J. CDFN
Medellin-Leal, F. SLPM
Medley-Wood, J. GRA
Meijer, W. MO
Meisner, C. F. NY
Meister, Fr. ZT
Mela, A. J. KUO
Meldrum, R. H. PTH
Meliss, J. C. GRA
Melvill, J. C. MANCH
Melville, N. BDI
Melville, WAT
Mendes, E. J. S. M. LISC
Mendez, E. MERL
Mendon, PI
Mendonça, F. A. LISC
Mendonça, R. C. de IBGE
Menyhárt, L. WU
Menzies, A. CGE, LIV
Mercier, P. FI
Meredith, L. A. HO
Merev, N. KATO
Merrill, E. D. BISH, CAL, FH, NSW, PNH, UC, US
Merrill, H. W. MAINE
Merxmüller, H. WIND
Metcalf, F. P. FCU
Metcalf, O. B. NMC
Mettenius, G. H. B
Mexia, Y. MO, NO, UC, VIC
Meyer, F. G. MO
Meyer, G. Z
Meyer, G. F. W. GOET (herb.), LE
Meyer, J. A. MUCL
Meyer, HAJB
Meylan, C. LAU
Michans, S. INFYB
Michaux, A. P.
Michaux, F. A. P
Micheli, P. A. CR, FI

337

Michener, E. DWC
Mickel, J. T. NY
Middleton, R. M. MTMG
Miège, DAKAR
Miers, J. CGE, DS
Migula, W. GJO, JE
Mikhalyeva, V. I. SASY
Miki, S. OSA
Mikula, B. FARM, WILLI
Mikutowicz, J. RIG
Mildbraed, G. W. J. HBG
Milde, J. B
Militzer, M. GLM
Mille, L. QCA
Miller, E. L. BKL
Miller, H. A. FTU, MU
Miller, J. H. GAM
Miller, O. K. VPI
Milligan, J. HO
Minaya Cruz, R. N. HHUA
Minshall, W. H. DAO
Miquel, F. A. W. U
Miranda, F. CHIP, MEXU
Mishler, B. D. CSPU
Misirdali, H. DUF
Mitchell, T. CGE
Mitra, S. N. HCIO
Mitten, W. NY
Miyoshi, M. TI
Mizutani, M. NICH
Moçino, J. M. FI, MA, OXF
Mocquerys, Z
Moenkemeyer, W. HBG
Moffatt, W. S. ILL
Mogg, A. O. D. J
Moggi, G. FT
Moggridge, J. T. K
Mohamed, A. L. UKMB
Mohr, C. T. ALU, BUF, US (herb.)
Moldenke, H. N. NY, OS, TEX
Molesworth, B. E. MPN
Molfino, J. F. BAF
Molina R., A. ENCB
Molkenboer, J. H. L
Moll, E. J. NH
Möller, J. D. AWH
Monguillon, E. COLO
Montagne, J. P. F. C. PC
Montaldo, P. MY
Montes, M. SRFA
Mooney, H. F. DD
Moore, D. DBN
Moore, D. M. HIP, UARK
Moore, J. LTU
Moore, J. W. MIN
Moore, L. B. CHR
Moore, P. H. GUAM
Moore, R. J. DAO
Moore, T. K
Moquin-Tandon, C. H. B. A. FI, P

Mora O., L. E. COL, PSO, UTMC
Moraes, J. C. de EAN
Morales, G. QPNRA
Moran, R. INIF, SD
Moretti, C. CAY
Moretti, G. FI
Morgan, A. P. IA
Mori, S. A. CEPEC
Morillo, G. VEN
Moris, G. G. (herb.) SASSA, TO
Morison, R. (herb.) OXF
Morong, T. NY, VT
Morren, C. J. E. LG
Morris, A. ADW
Morris, D. UCWI
Morrison, A. PERTH
Morrison, J. L. UC
Morse, E. UC
Morthier, P. (herb.) NEU
Morton, J. K. GC, WAT
Mory, HAJB
Moseley, E. L. BGSU
Mosquin, T. DAO
Moss, C. E. J
Moss, E. H. ALTA, DAO
Mosseray, R. BR
Motelay, L. (herb.) BORD
Mouterde, G
Mouton, BR
Moxley, E. A. TRTC
Muehlenbach, V. MO
Mueller, F. von BUF
Muenscher, W. C. CU
Mühlenbeck, H. G. (herb.) STR
Muhlenberg, G. H. E. FMC, LIV, PH
    (herb.)
Muir, J. STEU
Mukherjee, S. K. CAL
Mulkidjanian, J. I. ERE
Müller, C. H, LZ
Muller, C. H. TEX, UCSB
Müller, F. von BR, GRA, MEL
Müller, G. LZ
Muller, G. SMF
Muller, J., Argoviensis G
Müller, K. KR, S, STU
Muller, K. K. SBBG
Mulligan, G. A. DAO
Müllner, F. GJO
Mülner, PAD
Mundkur, B. BLAT
Muñoz Medina, J. M. (herb.) GDA
Munz, P. A. CSPU, FSC, POM, RSA
Murata, G. KYO
Muraviova, O. A. LECB
Murbeck, S. LD
Muret, J. LAU
Murillo, M. T. COL, UTMC
Murr, J. IBF, PAE
Murrahi, MW

Murray, B. M. ALA
Murray, D. F. ALA
Murrill, W. A. FLAS, NY
Mutarelli, BAI
Mutis, J. C. COL, MA
Myers, R. M. MWI
Myrick, D. W. SBBG

Nabiev, TASH
Nádvorník, BRA
Nägeli, C. W. von HBG
Nair, N. C. PBL
Nakahara, G. TI
Nakai, T. TI
Nakano, T. HIRO
Namur, P. CHAM
Nannfeldt, J. A. UPS
Nannizzi, A. SIENA
Narayanaswami, V. CAL
Nash, G. V. NY
Naustdal, J. BG
Nava, FCME
Neal, O. MAINE
Nechaev, V. A. VLA
Nees, C. G. (herb.) STR
Nees von Esenbeck, T. BHU, GZU
Neese, E. BRY
Negri, FT
Nelson, A. NEB, RENO-NESH, RM,
    WTU
Nelson, C. TEFH
Nelson, D. J. NT
Nelson, E. RM
Nelson, J. B. UWFP
Nemetz, WU
Nessel, H. (herb.) BONN
Neto, G. G. UFMT
Neuman, L. M. LD
Neumann, A. KL (herb.), WFBVA
Nicholson, N. L. GMS
Nicholson, W. E. CGE
Niederlein, G. BA, BAF, CORD
Nieuwland, J. A. ND
Nievo, I. PAD
Nikitin, V. V. WIR
Ninan, C. A. RHT
Nissl von Mayendorf, M
Nitschke, T. B
Niven, J. DBN
Noguchi, A. NICH
Nordal, O
Norden, BALT
Nordmann, A. van H
Nordstedt, O. LD, WELT
Norlindh, T. LD
Norman, E. M. DLF
Norman, J. M. BG
Norman, O
Normann-Kämpf, A. BLA
Norris, J. N. GMS

Norrlin, J. P. H
Norton, J. B. S. MARY
Notaris, G. de FI, GJO
Notaris, de PAD, RO
Notcutt, W. L. NWH
Nott, C. P. GMS
Nowak, J. KRAM
Nozzolillo, C. OTT
Nuttall, T. DWC, GH, LIV, PR (herb.)
Nyárády, A. CLA
Nyárády (herb.) SIB
Nydegger, M. (herb.) BASBG
Nylander, W. H

Oberlin, T. J. RPM
Oborny, PRC
Oescu, IBIR
Ogilvie, R. T. UAC
Ohashi, H. TI
Ohenoja, E. OULU
Ohenoja, M. OULU
Ohwi, J. KYO, TNS
Okada, K. A. BAL
Okamura, S. NICH
Okubo, S. TI
Olaru, M. BAJ
Oldeman, R. A. A. CAY, QPNRA
Oliveira Filho, E. C. de SPF
Oliveira, J. A. de BHCB
Oliver, E. G. H. STE
Oliver, W. R. B. WELT
Øllgaard, B. AAU, QCA
Olney, S. T. BRU, UNB
Onishi, E. UB
Onno, M. WFBVA
Opiz, P. M. PRC
Orbigny, d' LR
Orcutt, C. R. DS, MO, YU
Orfila, E. N. INFYB
Orphanides, T. TAU
Orphanides, ACA, ATHU, WU
Orsini, PAD
Ørsted, C
Ortega, A. Q
Ortega, HAJB
Orton, C. R. PUR
Osbeck, P. SBT
Osborn, N. L. PUSC
Osmaston, A. E. DD
Ostafichuk, M. MSC
Osten, C. MVM
Ostenfeld, C. E. H. DBN
Osterhout, G. E. RM
Ottone, J. R. BAI
Overholts, L. O. PAC
Ownbey, M. WS

Pabot, G
Pabst, F. HAL
Pabst, G. HB

Pacher, D. (herb.) KL
Packer, J. G. ALTA
Padilla, I. Q
Padilla, R. QPNRA
Padwick, HCIO
Paget, J. NWH
Painter, H. ABD, ABS
Palacios, M. L. (herb.) GDA
Palazzi (herb.) TO
Pallas, P. S. GJO, LIV, SBT
Palmer, E. BUF, CM, MEXU, MO, US, YU
Palmer, E. J. DUR, HPH, MO, MOR, RSDR, SMS, UMO
Palmgren, A. H
Palun, M. (herb.) AV
Pampanini, R. FI, PAD
Pancher, J. A. I. P
Pangalo, K. I. WIR
Pantling, R. CAL
Pantocsek, PAD
Paoli, G. FT
Papenfuss, G. F. GRA, UC
Pappe, C. W. L. SAM
Pappi, FT
Paray, L. ENCB
Parfitt, E. TOR
Parish, S. B. ASUF, CM, DS
Parke, Davis & Co. MICH
Parker, R. N. DD
Parkinson, C. E. DD
Parks, H. E. UC
Parlatore, F. FI
Parmelee, J. A. DAO
Parodi, L. R. BAA, BAF
Parry, C. C. CM, ISC, NEB, US, YU
Pase, C. P. ALBU
Passerini, G. PARMA, PI (herb.)
Páter, B. CLA
Paterson, T. V. GRA
Patouillard, N. T. FH
Patria, TSM
Patterson, I. W. CONN
Patterson, P. NY
Pau, MA
Paula, E. J. de SPF
Paulay, WU
Paulin, A. GJO
Paum, M. BAJ
Pavón, J. A. FI, MA, OXF
Pawek, J. MAL, MO
Pawłowski, B. KRAM
Pax, CR
Payne, G. W. BM
Payson, E. B. RM
Pazia, T. K. RNMUT
Pearson, W. H. MANCH
Pease, A. S. VT
Peck, C. H. BUF, NYS, PUR

Peck, M. E. WILLU, WTU
Pedicino, N. A. PAD, RO
Peebles, W. ARIZ
Pegler, A. GRA, PRE, PREM
Pei, S. J. HITBC
Peirson, F. W. NO, RSA
Peixoto, A. L. CVRD
Pekkarinen, J. KUO
Pellegrini (herb.) PI
Pelvet, F. A. CN
Pennell, F. W. NY, SPWH
Pennington, M. S. BAF
Pennington, T. D. CHAP
Penzig, A. G. O. BO, GE, PAD
Peragallo, H. AWH
Perceval, Mrs. DAO
Pereira, B. A. da S. IBGE
Pereira, E. HB
Pereira Coutinho, A. X. LISU
Pérez-Arbeláez, E. COL
Pérez-Lara, MAF
Perfilyeva, V. I. SASY
Perrault, M. (herb.) BRE
Perrier de la Bâthie, P. E. P
Perrin, F. HO
Perris, MPA
Perrottet, G. S. DS
Perry, R. A. NT
Perry, W. G. WAR
Persaud, C. A. FDG
Persoon, C. H. L, LG
Perttulo, Q. TMP
Pételot, P
Peter, A. B
Peter, Brother CANI
Peters, T. M. ALU
Peterson, A. M. UWL
Petit-Thouars, A. du P
Petrak, F. IBI, LPS, PAD, PR, RMS, URM, W (herb.)
Petrie, D. WELT
Pfaff, PAD
Philbrick, R. N. SBBG
Philibert, H. AUT
Philippi, R. A. FI, SGO
Philippi, BAF
Phillips, A. MNA
Phillips, B. MNA
Phillips, C. E. DOV
Phillips, E. MO
Picbauer, R. (herb.) BRNM
Pichi-Sermolli, R. E. G. FT
Pichler, WU
Pickel, B. EAN, IPA, URM
Picler, PAD
Pierce, L. WCW
Pierre, J. B. L. P
Pigg, T. HAMU
Pigmigsel, BOIS
Pignatti, TSB

Pike, L. H. ORE
Pilat, I. A. (herb.) PRM
Pilger, R. K. F. VT
Pillans, N. S. BOL
Pilz, G. MO
Pinheiro Sobrinho, J. M. BHCB
Pinto E., P. COL
Pinto-Lopes, J. LISU
Piper, C. V. WCW, WS
Pires, J. M. IAN, MG, UB
Pirotta, P. R. RO
Pisano V., E. HIP
Pitard, GRO
Pittier, H. F. BR, CR, MO, US, VEN, Z
Planelles, BCC
Platter, F. BERN
Playfair, G. I. NSW
Plowman, T. ECON, HUA
Plumier, C. P
Pobéquin, P
Pocock, M. A. (herb.) GRA
Podpěra, J. (herb.) BRNM
Poelt, M
Pohl, J. E. PR
Pohl, R. W. ISC
Poilane, P
Poiret, J. L. M. P
Pole Evans, I. B. PRE
Pollard, H. M. CAS, SBBG
Pollett, F. C. CDFN
Polunin, O. LTR
Pomel, A. N. AL
Pontius, L. L. OS
Poore, M. E. D. KLU
Pope, P. WCW
Popenoe, J. FTG
Popov, M. G. RNMUT, VLA, WIR
Popov, N. A. VLA
Porcher, F. CHARL
Poroca, D. J. M. URM
Porsild, A. E. ALA, CAN
Portenschlag, F. V. GJO
Porter, C. L. RM
Porter, D. M. CDS, MO
Porter, T. C. FMC, MVSC, NHA, PH (herb.)
Pospichal (herb.) TSM
Post, G. E. BEI
Post, EGE
Potanin, G. N. LE
Potier de laVárde, R. PC
Pott, A. BLA
Potts, G. BLFU
Potzger, R. F. ND
Pourret, F. A. MAF, P
Praeger, R. DBN
Prain, D. CAL
Prance, G. T. COL, INPA, MG, NY, UFMT
Pratov, TASH

Pratt, P. D. APM
Preiss, J. A. L. DBN, HBG, MEL
Preiss, L. LD
Prescott, G. W. EMC
Prescott, J. D. OXF
Presl, J. S. PR
Presl, K. B. PR
Presl, PRC
Preston, A. W. NWH
Pretz, H. W. MCA
Preuss, C. G. T. B
Prevost, M. F. CAY
Price, S. F. MO
Priester, D. S. CHAS
Prigge, B. CSLA
Prince, A. R. UAC
Pringle, C. G. ASU, CM, EMC, FCME, MEXU, MO, MTMG, MU, NMC, NY, RM, SMU, TAES, TEX, US, UTD, VT, YU, Z
Pringle, J. S. PR
Printz, H. C. O
Prior, R. C. A. K
Pritchard, E. DLF
Pritzel, Z
Probatova, N. S. VLA
Proctor, G. R. HAC, IJ, UCWI
Prodan, I. BUCA, CLA
Prohaska, K. GJO
Prokhanov, Y. I. WIR
Proscuriakova, G. M. MHA
Proskauer, J. UC
Prosser, L. N. (herb.) PEU
Provancher, L. QPH
Prshewalski, N. M. LE
Puccinelli, B. LUCCA
Puccioni, FT
Puel, T. P
Puig, H. CSAT
Puntsag, T. UBA
Purdy, G. B. KNOX
Purpus, C. A. HPH, RSDR, UC, US
Pursell, R. A. PAC
Pursh, F. PH
Puttemans, A. IBI, UFRJ
Pyrah, G. SMS

Quartin, Dillon, R. P
Quélet, L. PC
Quézel (herb.) MARSSJ
Quibell, C. FSC
Quimby, M. MAINE
Quimio, T. H. CALP

Rabenhorst, L. B, GJO, ODU
Rabenhorst, FH, PAD
Rachkovskaya, E. I. UBA
Raciborski, M. KRA
Raddi, G. FI, PI
Radford, A. E. GAS

Rădulescu, IBIR
Rafinesque, C. S. DWC, WIS
Ragonese, A. BAI, SF
Railonsala, A. OULU
Raimondi, A. USM
Rainer-Haarbach, M. V. GJO
Raizada, M. B. DD
Ramakrishnan, T. S. HCIO
Ramamurthy, K. PBL
Rama Rao, FRC
Rambo, B. HBR
Ramia, M. MY
Ramírez-Cantú, FCME
Ramis, A. I. CAIM
Ramos, PNH
Rändel, HAJB
Range, P. SAM
Rapp, F. W. WMU
Rapp, S. FLAS
Räsänen, V. H
Rateeb, F. B. ULT
Rattan, V. DS
Ratter, J. A. UB
Ratzenberger, C. KASSEL
Rauh, W. ZSS
Rausch, W. ZSS
Rautanen, M. GRA, H, Z
Răvărut, M. IASI
Raven, P. H. DS, MO, RSA
Ravenel, H. W. CHARL
Ray, J. D., Jr. USF
Raymond, M. MTJB
Raynal, P
Raynal-Roques, A. CAY
Re, F. SPAL
Reader, Father BRIST
Rechinger, K. H. LD, W
Rechinger, AAU, G
Record, S. J. MAD
Redfearn, P. L., Jr. MO
Redfield, J. H. MO
Reekman, M. MO
Reese, H. (herb.) BASBG
Reese, W. D. LAF
Regel, C. KA, LE
Regnell, R, S
Rehm, E..PAD, S
Rehmann, A. BR, GRA, Z
Rehmann, PRE
Reichelet, PAD
Reichenbach, H. G. AMES, AWH, W (herb.)
Reinbold, M
Reinking, O. A. BPI
Reinwardt, C. G. C. L
Reitz, R. HBR
Rémy, E. J. P
Renaud, P. MPA
Renecker, L. WLU
Renteria A., E. HUA

Requien, E. (herb.) AV
Retzius, A. J. LD
Reuss, WU
Reuter, G. F. G
Reveal, J. L. MARY, OKL, UTC
Reverchon, J. SMU
Revilla, J. AMAZ, USM
Rexroat, R. T. MWI
Reyna, J. V. ANSM
Reynolds, D. CALP
Reynolds, E. M. BIRA
Reynolds, G. W. PRE
Reznicek, A. A. APM
Rhodes, D. LTU
Rhodes, H. L. DAO
Rhodes, P. G. M. BIRA
Rial Alberti, BAI
Riba, FCME
Ricardo da Cunha, LISU
Richard, A. P
Richards, C. D. MAINE
Richards, E. L. STAR
Richards, P. W. NMW
Richter, K. (herb.) WU
Richter, HBG
Rick, J. FH, IACM, PACA
Ricker, P. L. WIS
Riddell, J. NO
Riddle, L. W. FH
Riedel, L. LE, OXF
Rieter, MAAS
Riley, H. P. MEM
Rimachi, M. AMAZ, NATC
Ripart, E. COLO
Ripper, E. E. FSSR
Risso, A. P
Ritter, F. ZSS
Riva, D. FT
Rivas Goday, MAF
Rivera Lopez, D. E. HHUA
Rivola, M. CB
Rizzini, EAN
Robb, J. UNB
Robbins, FH
Robecchi-Bricchetti, FT
Robert, M. F. ANSM
Roberts, E. P. MSC
Roberts, P. DAO
Robertson, A. CDFN
Robertson, C. ILLS
Robertson, K. R. ILLS, MO
Robertson, S. A. MO
Robertson, W. HAMU
Robinson, B. L. GH
Robinson, F. NWH
Rocha, G. I. da IBGE
Rochel, A. GJO
Rochel, WU
Rock, J. F. A, BISH, HPH, NY, US,
    WELT

Rockwell, J. FSC
Rodin, R. MO, OBI
Rodrigues, M. R. BHCB
Rodrigues, W. IBGE
Rodriguez, E. M. BAI
Rodriguez, H. MY
Rodríguez, M. BAF
Rodriguez, SI
Rodway, A. NSW
Rodway, L. HO
Röell, PI
Rogers, F. A. GRA
Rogers, J. D. WSP
Rogers, R. S. AD
Rogers, R. W. BRIU
Rogerson, C. T. NY
Rogowicz, A. S. KW
Rohlena, PRC
Rohrdorf, Z
Roig, F. A. MERL
Roig, J. T. HAC, HAJB
Rojas, C. E. B. de MY
Rojas, T. SI
Rojas M., P. UNL
Roland, A. E. DAO
Röll (herb.) WB
Rolland-Germain, DAO, SFS
Rolli, RO
Rollins, R. C. GH
Romell, L. S
Romero-Castañeda, R. COL, UTMC
Rominger, J. M. ASC
Rommel, PAD
Rood, A. N. KE, YUO
Rooy, J. van PRE
Rosas, S. CHAM
Roscoe, W. LIV
Rose, F. MONTU
Rose, J. N. US
Rose, L. S. CAS, NYS
Rosengurtt, B. MVFA
Rosenstock, E. CR, M, UC
Ross, E. BDI
Ross, H. BAL
Ross, J. H. NH
Rossbach, G. B. MAINE, WVW
Rosthorn, von O
Rostrup, E. CP
Rostrup, O. C, CP
Roth, S
Rothmaler, W. JE
Rothmaler, BCF
Rottler, J. P. K, LIV
Rouleau, E. DAO, NFLD
Roumequère, C. IASI
Rousseau, J. DAO, QUE
Rousseau, J. J. P
Rousseau, M. BR
Rouy, G. C. C. (herb.) LY
Rowell, C. M. HPC, SAT

Roxburgh, W. BR, CAL
Roy, J. E. QK
Royce, R. D. PERTH
Royen, P. van BISH
Royle, J. F. LIV
Royle, J. R. DD
Rubtzoff, P. CAS
Rudatis, H. GRO, STE
Rudatis, Z
Rueppell, W. P. E. S. FR
Rugenstein, S. R. GESU
Ruiz, A. SRFA
Ruiz, H. FI, MA, OXF
Ruiz Leal, A. MERL
Ruiz-Terán, L. VEN
Rumbelow, P. E. NWH
Rump, W. G. PREM
Runemark, H. LD
Runyon, R. TEX
Ruprecht, F. J. LE
Rusby, H. H. BOLV, CM, MO, NY
Rusby, Z
Rushing, A. E. CINC
Ruspoli, FT
Russell, R. C. DAO
Rust, H. J. ID
Ruth, A. FWM, SMU
Rydberg, P. A. KSC, MONT, MONTU,
    NEB, NY, RM
Rydmon, G. TMP
Ryvarden, O
Rzedowski, J. DS, ENCB, IBUG, UNL,
    SLPM

Sa'ad, F. CAIM
Saarnijoki, S. HFR
Saarsoo, B. H
Sabidussi (herb.) KL
Saccardo, P. A. PAD, TO
Sacleux, C. P
Sadebeck, R. E. B. HBG
Sadler, M. GJO
Sagorski, E. JE
Sagot, P. A. P
Sahashi, N. YUO
Sahlberg, C. R. H
Sahni, K. C. DD
Sainsbury, G. O. K. WELT
St. Hilaire, A. de ORM, P
St. John, E. P. DLF
St. John, H. BISH, WELT, WS, WTU
Sakurai, K. MAK
Salas de Leon, S. SLPM
Saldanka, C. JCB
Salinas, F. CHAM
Salles, A. E. H. IBGE
Salt, J. SCM, SFD
Salter, J. H. NMW
Salter, T. M. BOL, NBG
Salzmann, P. AWH

Samoilov, T. P. VLA
Samoilova, T. V. VLA
Sampaio, A. J. R
Samson, R. A. CBS
Sanborn, E. I. OSC
Sanchez, H. UNL
Sanchez Mejorada, H. CODAGEM
Sanchez Vega, I. M. CPUN
Sanchir, C. UBA
Sandberg, J. H. WTU
Sande Lacoste, van der L
Sandeman, C. OXF
Sandstede, H. BREM
Sandu-Ville, C. BUCM, IBIR
Sandwith, C. I. BRIST
Sandwith, N. Y. BRIST, FDG
Sandwith, BRISTM
Sanguinetti, RO
Sanson, UAC
Santa, J. I. HUA
Santapau, Father BLAT
Santesson, R. UPS
Santisarup, JAC
Santos, E. PEL
Santos, R. LUAI
Santos, T. S. dos CEPEC
Sarasin, F. BAS, Z
Saravia, C. COL
Sardagna, WU
Sargent, F. BUPL
Sargent, F. H. BRY
Sargent, S. P. NYS
Sarnthein, IBF
Sartwell, H. P. NYS
Sarukhán, J. CHAP
Sarvas, R. HSI
Sasaoka, H. TNS
Sastre, C. TOLI
Sauleda, R. P. FTG
Saunders, A. DAO
Sauvageau, C. F. PC
Savatier-Fouillade, LR
Savery, G. B. RAMM
Savi, P. PI
Săvulescu, T. BUC, BUCA, BUCM
Saya, Ö. DUF
Sbarbaro, C. (herb.) GDOR
Schade, A. GLM
Schaeffer, R. L., Jr. MCA
Schaerer, L. E. GJO
Schaffner, J. G. MEXU, SLPM
Schaffner, J. H. OS
Schallert, P. O. SMU
Schefczik, J. GJO
Scheffler, G. GRO
Schelkownicow, A. B. ERE
Schenck, A. GRA
Schery, R. W. MO
Scheuchzer, J. J. ZT
Schickendantz, F. CORD

Schiede, C. J. W. HAL, XAL (photos)
Schiffner, V. F. FH, GJO, WU
Schildbach, C. KASSEL
Schimper, A. F. W. GRA
Schimper, G. H. W. AWH, BUF, FI, FT, GRO, TUB
Schimper, W. STU
Schinz, H. GRA, Z
Schkuhr, C. (herb.) HAL
Schlagintweit, WU
Schlechtendal, D. F. L. von HAL
Schlechter, F. R. R. AMES, GRO, Z
Schlechter, R. BAJ, BR, GRA, NSW, PR, PRE
Schlechter, CR
Schleicher, J. C. GJO, LAU (herb.)
Schleiden, M. J. JE
Schlieben, H. J. E. BR, LISC, PRE, Z
Schlieben, MAD
Schliephacke, K. JE
Schmalhausen, I. T. KW
Schmarda, C. GZU
Schmidt, J. A. HBG
Schmitz, M. ROML
Schnee, L. MY
Schneider, A. NY
Schneider, C. BKL
Schnell, R. ABT, P
Schnitzlein, A. GJO
Schoch, O. WU
Schodde, R. CANB
Schomburgk, R. AD, DS
Schonland, S. GRA
Schrader, H. A. GOET
Schreber, J. C. D. M
Schreiter, R. LIL
Schrenk, A. G. von LE
Schuabe, H. SRFA
Schultes, J. A. M
Schultes, J. H. M
Schultes, R. E. COL, ECON
Schulz, A. G. CTES
Schulz, H. KASSEL
Schulze, A. F. CONN
Schumacher, E. F. BING
Schunke, J. AMAZ, COL
Schutz, PAD
Schwacke, C. A. W. R, RB
Schwarz, O. JE
Schwarz, EGE
Schweickerdt, H. G. PUC
Schweiger, H. G. FPDB
Schweinfurth, G. B, CAIM
Schweinfurth, G. A. AMES
Schweinfurth, FT, WU
Schweinitz, L. D. von BPI, DWC, PH (herb.)
Schwenkmeyer, R. SDM
Schwinmer, BREG
Scortechini, B. CAL

Scotter, G. W. CAFB, DAO
Scoullar, H. P. MAINE
Seaver, F. J. NY
Sedgwick, L. J. BLAT
Seeley, H. M. MID
Sehnem, A. FCAB
Seki, T. HIRO
Selby, A. D. OS
Sellow, F. SGO, VT
Semper, J. MERL
Semple, J. C. WAT
Senn, H. A. DAO
Sennen, Fr. BC, BCF
Sequenza, G. (herb.) MS
Servít, M. (herb.) PRM
Sessé, M. FI, MA, OXF
Setälä, T. TMP
Setchell, W. A. UC
Setzer, R. B. AHFH
Seymour, F. C. MAINE, MCJ, MO, VT, WIS
Sezik, E. HUEF
Shabotai, J. R. CAIM
Shafer, J. A. CM, HAC, NY
Shaffer, R. L. MICH
Shantz, BOIS
Sharp, A. J. MEXU, TENN
Sharp, W. WVA
Sharsmith, C. W. UC
Sharsmith, H. K. UC
Shaver, J. VDB
Shaw, C. G. WSP
Shear, C. EMC
Shear, C. L. BPI, NY
Sheldon, C. S. NYS
Sheludyakova, V. A. SASY
Sherard, W. (herb.) OXF
Sherk, L. C. DAO
Sherriff, G. BM
Shildneck, P. ILL
Shimek, B. WET
Shinners, L. SMU
Shishkin, I. K. VLA
Shoolbred, W. A. NMW
Short, C. W. CM, DWC, KNOX, KY, PH (herb.), WIS
Shreve, F. ARIZ, ASUF
Shultz, J. BTJW
Shultz, L. BTJW
Sibthorp, J. OXF
Sickenberger, E. CAIM
Sickenberger, Z
Siddiqi, M. A. ULT
Sieber, F. W. AWH, GJO, MEL, PR
Siebold, P. F. von L
Silva, C. A. da BHCB
Silva, F. das C. e IBGE
Silva, I. A. CVRD
Silva, P. C. UC
Silveira, A. R

Silvestri, FI

Silveus, W. A. LLC, TEX

Sim, T. R. GRA, PRE

Simon, C. (herb.) BASBG

Simonian, S. A. EREM

Simony, O. WU

Simpson, G. CHR

Simpson, N. D. CAIM

Singer, R. BAFC, LPS, SGO, URM

Sinskaya, E. N. WIR

Sintenis, P. ANK, HAC, LD, PR, UCWI, WU, Z

Sipe, F. P. ORE

Siqueira, J. C. de FCAB

Skorepa, BALT

Skottsberg, C. BA, GB

Skvortsov, A. K. MHA

Slavin, B. H. HPH

Small, J. K. CU, FMC, NY

Smarods, J. RIG

Smith, A. C. BISH, MAD, MASS, NY, US

Smith, A. H. MICH

Smith, C. P. DS, UTC

Smith, D. R. GUAM

Smith, E. C. DAO

Smith, E. L. VT

Smith, G. BRISTM

Smith, G. L. NY

Smith, G. M. GMS

Smith, H. GB, UPS

Smith, H. H. CM, MIL, US

Smith, H. L. OS

Smith, J. SCM

Smith, J. D. MO, US (herb.)

Smith, J. E. LINN, LIV

Smith, J. G. NEB

Smith, J. J. AMES

Smith, L. EAN, GH, HBR

Smith, L. S. BRI

Smith, S. J. NYS

Smith, W. AWH

Smith, W. P. OC

Smuts, J. C. PRE, STE

Smythies, B. L. LTR

Snell, W. BPI, KIRI

Snider, J. A. CINC

Snyder, M. S. SCR

Soares, O. URM

Sodiro, P. L. QPLS

Sodiro S. J., L. Q

Soehner, A. G. M

Soejarto, D. D. HUA

Soepadmo, E. KLU

Solander, D. WELT

Solander, D. C. AK, MO

Solheim, W. G. LPS, WSP

Solheim, HCIO

Solis, F. F

Solla, R. PAD

Sommerfelt, S. C. O

Sommier, C. P. S. FI

Sonder, O. W. MEL, S

Sonnerat, P. P, SBT

Soper, J. H. DAO

Sorbello, R. INFYB

Soriano, A. BAB

Sormus, L. SPF

Sosnowskyi, D. TBI

Sota, E. R. de la HUA, LP

Souckup, J. SMF

Soulier, P

Sousa S., M. ENCB, MEXU

South, G. R. FPDB, NFLD

Souza, M. M. P. de BHCB

Soyaux, H. P, Z

Spach, E. P

Spada, J. CVRD

Spallanzani, L. (herb.) SPAL

Sparling, S. OBI

Sparrman, A. S

Speese, B. WILLI

Spegazzini, C. BAB, BAF, LP, LPS

Spegazzini, G. PAD

Spellenberg, R. W. NMC

Spencer, M. F. MU

Sporleder, JE

Sprague, C. J. FH

Sprague, R. WSP

Spreitzenhofer, G. C. WU

Sprengel, K. B, PR

Spring, A. F. LG

Springer, J. FSC

Springfield, H. W. ALBU

Spruce, R. AWH, BEL, BH, BR, CGE, DS, F, K, LD, MANCH, MG, NY, OXF, RB

Srinivasan, K. S. BSIS

Stahl, MAD

Stainton, BM

Stakman, E. C. MPPD

Stakman, E. L. MPPD

Standley, P. C. BPI, CR, F, MAD, MO, NMC, US

Stanford, E. E. (herb.) CPH

Stanford, J. W. HPC

Stankevich, A. K. WIR

Stanton, W. D. BRY

Stapf, WU

Stebbins, G. L. UC

Stebbins, J. FSC

Steere, W. C. ALA, MICH, NY

Stefanini, FT

Steibel, P. SRFA

Steinbach, J. BAF, SI

Steinbach, R. LPB, MO

Steindórsson, S. (herb.) AMNH

Steiner, J. KL (herb.), WU

Stelfox, A. W. BEL

Stepanova, K. D. VLA

Stephani, F. G

Stephens, F. C. HBFH

Stephenson, T. TOR

Stergios, B. G. KBSMS

Stern, MAD

Sternberg, D. UCWI

Sterneck, PRC

Sterner, R. PAD

Steudel, E. G. von OXF

Steven, C. H

Stevens, C. E. FARM

Stevens, F. L. ILL

Stevens, G. W. DUR, NWOSU, OKL

Stevens, O. A. NDA

Stevens, W. D. MO, MSC

Stevens, PUR

Stevenson, J. A. BPI

Steward, A. N. OSC

Stewart, A. CAS

Stewart, R. R. DD

Stewart, S. A. BEL

Stewart, W. N. ALTA

Stewart, ANSM

Steyermark, J. A. F, MO, SMS, UMO, VEN

Stillinger, C. R. ID

Stilwell, A. ALMA

Stirton, J. GLAM

Stizenberger, E. ZT

Stocks, J. E. LIV

Stohr, HAJB

Stojanov, N. SOM

Stokes, S. DS

Stokoe, T. P. SAM

Stolz, A. F. GRO

Stolz, Z

Stone, B. C. GUAM, KLU

Stone, D. NO

Stone, I. G. MELU

Storey, J. HAMU

Stork, H. UC

Story, R. GRA

Strauss, T. JE

Strauss, WU

Straw, R. CSLA

Strey, R. G. NH

Strobl, G. GJO

Stuckenberg, J. H. W. JHWU

Stuckert, T. CORD

Stuhlmann, F. L. GRA

Sturgeon, W. YUO

Sturgis, W. C. NY

Sturm, H. E. W. N. YUO

Sturrock, A. PTH

Stzbznü, V. SOM

Sucre, D. CVRD, RB

Sukachev, V. N. MHA

Suksdorf, W. N. GH, ORE, WS, WSP, WTU

Sulger-Büel, E. ZT

Sullivant, W. S. FH, IA, OS, WTU

Summers, R. W. SBBG
Sumnevitcz, G. P. TASH
Sun, S. C. WH
Sunding, O
Sünter, G. ISTF
Surian, J. D. P
Suringar, W. F. R. L
Sutton, B. C. CFB
Suza, J. (herb.) PRM
Suzuki, H. HIRO
Svenson, H. K. BKL, FARM
Sventenius, E. R. ORT
Svrček, M. (herb.) PRM
Swainson, W. (herb.) WELT
Swales, D. E. MTMG
Swallen, J. R. PEL
Swart, H. J. MELU
Swartz, O. LD, S, SBT
Sydon, IASI
Sydow, H. DAR, RMS
Sydow, P. PAD, S
Symoens, BRVU
Symon, D. E. ADW

Tabley, Baron de DBN
Táccari, BAI
Tagawa, M. KYO
Tai, L. Y. WH
Takaki, F. SLPM
Takhtajan, A. L. ERE
Talbot, W. A. BSI
Tamamschian, S. G. ERE
Tamayo, F. VEN
Tamin, N. UKMB
Tanger, C. Y. FMC
Tao, G. D. HITBC
Tappeiner, IBF
Tashiro, Z. KYO
Tate, R. AD
Tatnall, E. DOV
Tatnall, R. DOV
Tausch, I. F. PR
Tausch, PRC
Tavares, C. N. LISU
Tavel, F. von BERN
Taylor, C. DUR
Taylor, G. BM
Taylor, H. C. STE
Taylor, J. DUR
Taylor, M. S. ABSH
Taylor, R. DS
Taylor, R. M. MSC
Taylor, T. FH
Taylor, T. M. C. DAO
Taylor, W. R. AHFH, MICH, NFLD, US
Teague, A. J. GRA
Tehon, L. ILLS
Teijsmann, J. E. BO
Teixeira, J. B. LISJC
Tempère, J. A. AWH

Temple, A. QPNRA
Templeton, J. BEL
Teng, S. C. CUP
Tenório, E. C. HXBH
Terracciano, A. FT
Terraneo, L. (herb.) TO
Tessman, G. NY
Testu, G. le BM (herb.), LISC
Thaker, I. BSI
Tharp, B. C. UNL
Thaxter, R. FH
Theissen, L. RMS
Thellung, A. BAS
Thériot, M. H. I. PC
Theroux, M. MNA
Thieret, J. W. LAF
Thiessen, FH
Thode, J. STE
Thomas, H. (herb.) BRISTM
Thomas, J. H. DS
Thomasson, J. R. BHSC
Thompson, E. J. CONN
Thompson, G. E. GAM
Thompson, H. S. BIRM
Thompson, J. W. WTU
Thompson, M. F. STE
Thompson, S. (herb.) WELT
Thomson, J. W. WIS
Thomson, T. CAL
Thomson, MH
Thornber, J. J. ASC
Thorne, R. F. GEO, RSA
Thornhill, J. HAMU
Thothathri, K. PBL
Thouin, A. SBT
Thulin, M. UPS
Thümen, F. von GJO
Thümen, PAD
Thunberg, C. P. LD, MW, S, SBT, UPS (herb.)
Thuret, G. A. PC
Thurston, H. W. PUR
Thwaites, G. H. K. BRISTM, CAL, CGE
Thwaites, BR, MH, PDA
Tibell, L. UPS
Tidestrom, I. OGDF
Tilden, J. WELT
Tilden, J. E. FPDB, MIN, NFLD
Timbal-Lagrave (herb.) TL
Tineo, PAL
Tisserant, L. E. P
Tobisch (herb.) KL
Todaro, PAL
Tolmachev, A. I. VLA
Tommasini, M. KNOX
Tommasini (herb.) TSM
Tonduz, A. CR
Tonzig, PAD
Torges, E. JE
Torre, A. R. LISC

Torrend, C. URM
Torres, J. H. COL
Torres, UWM
Torrey, J. DWC, NY, NYS
Torrey, R. NY
Tortorelli, BAI
Tountas, ACA, TAU (herb.)
Tournefort, J. P. de P
Tovar, O. USM
Toyama, R. KYO
Trabut, L. C. AL
Tracey, J. G. BRI
Tracy, J. P. UC
Tracy, S. M. MO, PUR, TAES
Trail, J. W. H. BH
Train, P. MU, RENO-NESH
Transeau, E. ALMA
Trappe, J. MEXU
Trappe, J. M. OSC
Traunfellner, A. (herb.) KL
Traunsteiner, J. GJO
Traverse, A. HPM
Traverso, G. B. MIPV, PAD
Trelease, W. ILL, MO
Trevelyan, W. C. HAMU
Treviranus, L. C. BHU
Triana, J. J. COL
Trimen, PDA
Trinius, C. B. von LE, MW
Trinta, E. F. PEL
Tripp, N. OAC
Tristan, J. M. C. de P
Trivivño V., F. GUAY
Trochain, J.-L. P
Troiani, H. SRFA
Trow, A. H. UCSW
Trufanova, E. R. SASY
Trujillo, B. MY
Tsegmed, T. UBA
Tsetsegma, D. UBA
Tsiang, T. NAS
Tsogt, U. UBA
Tsuda, R. T. GUAM
Tuckerman, E. FH, NYS
Tuckerman, W. UCS
Tulasne, C. PC
Tulasne, E. L. R. PC
Tuntas, ATHU
Türckheim, von Z
Turczaninov, N. von CW (herb.), KW, LE
Turnan, E. A. YUO
Turner, D. NWH
Turner, G. H. ALTA, DAO
Tutcher, W. J. HK
Tutel, B. ISTF
Tutin, T. G. LTR
Tuyama, T. TI
Tweedy, F. NY
Twining, A. EVMU

Twisselman, E. CAS
Tyson, E. F. MO
Tyson, RUH

Ugadim, Y. SPF
Ugent, D. WIS
Uggla, W. NY
Ule, E. H. G. HBG, MG, PR, R
Ullepitsch, WU
Ulvinen, T. OULU
Ul'yanova, T. N. WIR
Ulziykhutag, W. UBA
Umbach, L. M. ILLS, WIS
Unamuno, P. MA
Underwood, L. M. MAINE, NY, OS
Ungar, K. (herb.) SIB
Unger, F. GJO
Urban, W. S. M. d' RAMM
Urban, HAC
Uribe U., L. COL, UTMC
Urumov, I. SOM
Uttal, L. J. VPI

Vaccari, FI
Vachell, C. T. NMW
Vachell, E. NMW
Vahl, M. C
Vail, A. M. NY
Vaillant, S. P
Vainio (herb.) TUR
Valde Lievre, IBF
Valente, BAI
Valls, J. BLA
Valverde Badillo, F. M. GUAY
Van Cleve, J. W. DMNH
Vandas, K. PR
Vanderyst, H. BR
Vaněček, J. CB
Van Ess, J. SACT
Van Faasen, P. MSC
Van Heurck, H. OS
Vanky, K. UPS
Van Rensselaer, M. SBBG
Van Schaack, G. B. WIS
Vareschi, V. VEN
Vargas, E. TEFH
Vasey, G. NEB, NHA
Vasiliev, Y. Y. VLA
Vatke, W. JE
Vaudois, LAU
Vavilov, N. I. WIR
Vazquez, M. XALU
Vázquez Sánchez, J. MEXU
Veilex (herb.) AV
Vela, L. INIF
Velarde Nuñez, O. SMF
Velenovský, J. PRC, PRM (herb.)
Velley, T. LIV
Venn, J. M. WAT
Ventura, A. ENCB

Ventura, F. ENCB
Venturi, G. TR
Venturi, S. BAF, LIL, SI
Verbniak, F. GJO
Verdoorn, F. FH
Verreaux, DS
Veselý, A. CB
Vest, L. C. von GJO
Veyret, Y. CAY
Vezda, A. STU
Vichet, J. de (herb.) MPU
Vickers, E. W. YUO
Vidal, J. R
Vidal, W. N. HXBH
Viégas, A. P. CUP, IACM, PUR
Vieillard, E. P
Viereck, L. A. ALA
Vierhapper, F. K. M. WU
Vigener, A. NY
Vihodcevsky, N. BAJ
Vilhelm, PRC
Villarreal de Puga, L. M. CREG, IBUG
Villa-Vega, J. SLPM
Vincent, C. F. TOR
Viorica, IBIR
Vital, A. URM
Vitt, D. H. ALTA, CINC, MSC
Volkart, A. ZT
Vorobiev, D. P. VLA
Voroshilov, V. N. MHA, VLA
Vos, M. P. de STE
Voss, E. G. MICH
Vöth, WU
Vriese, W. H. de L

Waddell, C. H. BEL
Wade, A. E. NMW
Wager, H. A. PRE
Wahl, H. A. PAC
Wahlstedt, L. J. LD
Wakefield, N. A. MEL
Waldron, C. B. NDA
Waldstein, F. PR
Walker, HCIO
Wallace, C. CHARL
Wallays, BR
Wallich, N. BR, CAL, CGE, DS, K,
   LIV, PR
Wallroth, K. F. PR
Walshe, S. APM
Ward, C. J. NPB
Ward, D. B. WAB
Warming, E. C, Z
Warnock, B. H. SRSC, TEX, UNL
Warnstorf, C. B
Warnstorff, PI
Watanabe, WU
Waterfall, U. T. HPC, OKL
Watson, E. E. MSC
Watson, H. C. K

Watson, S. GH, YU
Watson, S. H. WIS
Watt, D. A. MO
Watt, G. BSIS
Watts, W. W. NSW
Watzl, B. WU
Wear, S. BEL
Weatherby, C. A. NCBS
Webb, L. J. BRI
Webb, P. B. FI
Weber, C. A. BREM
Weber, D. WLU
Weber, H. MJG
Weber, W. A. COLO
Weber, W. R. SMS
Weber, CR
Weberbauer, A. MOL, USM
Weber-Van Bosse, A. A. L
Weddell, H. A. P
Wehmeyer, L. E. DAOM
Weigel, C. E. JE
Weigel, T. O. MO
Weihe, C. E. A. MSTR
Weiler, J. FSC
Weimarck, H. LD
Weinzierl, M
Weir, J. R. BPI
Weissflog, E. AHW
Welch, I. A. FDG
Welch, W. H. DPU
Welden, A. L. NO
Welden, v. REG
Wells, E. D. CDFN
Wellsted, J. R. LIV
Wellwood, A. WLU
Welsh, S. L. BRY, WTS
Welwitsch, F. LISU
Wendelbo, P. BG, O
Wendland, H. GOET
Wendland, H. L. GOET
Wendland, J. C. GOET
Wendt, T. ANSM
Wercklé, CR
Werther, W. B. DMNH
West, G. S. BIRM, BM
West, G. T. STA
West, J. UC
West, W. BIRM, BM
Westendorp, G. BR
Westerfeld, W. F. PAC
Wetmore, C. M. MSC
Wetmore, R. H. ACAD
Wettstein, R. WU
Wever, de MAAS
Weymouth, W. A. HO
Wharton, M. KY
Wheeler, C. F. EMC
Wheeler, L. C. LAM
Wheldon, J. H. NMW
Wherry, E. T. (herb.) PH

345

Whetzel, H. H. CUP, PUR
White, C. D. ORE
White, C. T. BRI
White, F. B. PTH
White, F. I. PTH
White, J. W. BRIST
White, W. L. CUP
White, FH
Whitehouse, E. SMU
Whittier, H. O. FTU
Whitwell, W. BIRA
Whyte, A. GRA
Wibbe, J. H. CANI, LV
Wieboldt, T. F. WILLI
Wiegand, K. M. CU
Wiegmann, W. H. SIM
Wiens, D. COLO
Wierzbicki, P. GJO
Wiggins, I. L. CDS, DS, RSDR
Wight, R. CAL, GL
Wight, MH
Wijk, R. van der GRO
Wilczek, E. LAU
Wild, H. GRA, SRGH
Wilde, W. de YA
Wilkinson, E. OC
Willdenow, C. L. B, HAL
Williams, H. HUBE
Williams, L. H. J. BM
Williams, Ll. F, VEN
Williams, L. O. AMES, F, RM, SEL
Williams, M. M. BRY
Williams, R. S. MONT, NY
Williams, TOR
Willing, T. N. SASK
Willis, J. H. MEL
Willis, PDA
Willkomm, H. M. (herb.) COI
Willmott, E. A. K
Wilman, M. GRA
Wilman, W. KMG
Wilson, E. H. A, HK, K
Wilson, P. NY
Wilson, S. H. MCW
Winch, N. J. HAMU

Windler, D. R. GAS
Wing-Field Dudgeon LWG
Winkler, H. HBG
Winkworth, R. E. NT
Winter, B. de PRE, WIND
Winter, G. B
Winter, H. JE
Wirtgen, NCY, REG
Wirth, V. STU
Wissmann, HBG
Wolf, C. B. DS, RSA
Wolf, H. PAE
Wolf, T. DR
Wolff, S. TEXA
Wolle, F. (herb.) PH
Wolle, J. CM (herb.), DWC
Wolle, BUF
Wołoszczak, E. KRAM
Wood, A. NY
Wood, J. M. NH, PREM, UMO
Wood, R. D. NY
Woodbury, R. O. UPR
Woodland, D. W. MTMG
Woodrow, G. M. BSI
Woodruff, J. DAO
Woods, J. G. APM
Woodson, R. MO
Wooton, E. O. MO, NMC, RM
Worley, C. L. YUO
Worley, I. A. YUO
Woytkowski, F. MO, UC, USM
Wright, B. H. DLF
Wright, C. BUF, CGE, CM, HAC, MO,
    SV, US, YU
Wright, C. H. RAMM
Wright, J. LPS
Wright, R. GRA
Wulf, E. V. WIR
Wulfen, WU
Wulffen, F. X. von GJO
Wullschlägel, H. R. BR
Wurzlow, E. C. LSU

Xavier, L. P. JPB, UFP
Xiffreda, C. INFYB

Yabe, Y. TI
Yacobi, BAI
Yacubson, D. BAI
Yamada, Y. SAP
Yasuda, A. TNS
Yatabe, R. TI
Yoder-Williams, M. P. WDNE
Young, W. STA
Yunatov, A. A. UBA
Yuncker, T. G. DPU, MO, WELT
Yuzepchuk, S. V. WIR

Zaganiaris, D. (herb.) TAU
Zahariadi, C. BUCA
Zahlbruckner, A. PAD, W (herb.),
    WU
Zanoni, T. A. SRCG
Zanten, van GRO
Zapałowicz, H. KRAM
Zederbauer, WU
Zeller, S. M. NY
Zenari, PAD
Zenker, G. GRO, HBG, MO, P, PR
Zenker, WU, Z
Zeyher, C. B. S. CM
Zeyher, C. L. P. AWH, DS, GRA, GZU,
    PR, S, STE, WU
Zeyher, K. L. SAM
Zhukovsky, P. M. WIR
Ziller, W. G. DAVFP
Zimmeter, IBF
Zippel, A. L
Zirnich (herb.) TSM
Zmuda, A. KRAM
Zodda, TENN
Zohary, M. CAIM, HUJ
Zois, LJM
Zoller, H. BAS
Zollinger, H. P
Zöllner, O. MO
Zoltai, S. C. CAFB
Zopf, W. B
Zuccarini, J. G. M
Zukowski, POZ
Zundel, G. L. PBI

II. Geographical Arrangement of the Herbaria

Herbaria marked with an (*) refer to British Institutional Herbaria mentioned in D. H. Kent, British Herbaria, London (1957) (q.v.). Herbaria marked with two asterisks (**) appear in F. N. Hepper and F. Neate, Plant collectors in West Africa, Regnum Vegetabile 74, Utrecht 1971.

AFGHANISTAN, Kabul (KABA).

ALGERIA, Alger (AL).

ANGOLA, Dundo (DIA), Luanda (LUAI), Nova Lisboa (LUA).

ARGENTINA, Anguil (ANGU), Bahía Blanca (BB), Balcarce (BAL), Buenos Aires (BA, BAA, BACP, BAF, BAFC, BAJ, BUEN, IAA, INFYB), Castelar (BAB, BAI, LCF), Chacras de Coria (MEN), Chamical (CHAM, IZAC), Cinco Saltos (ARC), Córdoba (CORD), Corrientes (CTES, CTESN), La Plata (LP, LPAG, LPD, LPS), Mendoza (MERL), Paraná (PAR), Salta (MCNS), San Carlos de Bariloche (CRP), San Isidro (SI), San Martín de los Andes (IPCN), San Miguel de Tucumán (LIL), Santa Fe (MFA, SF), Santa Rosa (SRFA), Santo Tomé (STL), Villa Mercedes (VMSL).

AUSTRALIA, *Australian Capital Territory*, Canberra (CANB, CBG, FRI, GAUBA).

— *New South Wales*, Armidale (NE), Rydalmere (DAR), Sydney (NSW, SYD, UNSW).

— *Northern Territory*, Alice Springs (NT), Darwin (DNA).

— *Queensland*, Atherton (QRS), Brisbane (BRI, BRIP, BRIU), Cairns (CAIRNS), Townsville (AIMS, JCT).

— *South Australia*, Adelaide (AD, ADU, ADW).

— *Tasmania*, Hobart (HO).

— *Victoria*, Burnley (VPRI), Melbourne (LTB, MEL, MELU, MUCV, MUH).

— *Western Australia*, Nedlands (UWA), Perth (PERTH).

AUSTRIA, Admont (ADMONT), Dornbirn (BREG), Graz (GJO, GZU), Hallstatt (HALLST), Illmitz (NBSI), Innsbruck (IB, IBF), Klagenfurt (KL), Linz (LI), Salzburg (SZB, SZL, SZU), Wien (W, WF-BVA, WHB, WNLM, WU).

AZORES, Ponta Delgada (AZ).

BARBADOS, Bridgetown (BAR).

BELGIUM, Antwerpen (AWH), Bruxelles (BRGE, BRLU, BRVU), Gembloux (LFG), Gent (GENT), Heverlee (LV), Liège (LG, LGHF), Louvain-la Neuve (MUCL), Meise (BR), Namur (NAM).

BELIZE, Belmopan (BRH).

BÉNIN, Cotonou (BENIN).

BOLIVIA, Cochabamba (BOLV, COCH), La Paz (LPB).

BOTSWANA, Gaborone (GAB, UCBG), Mahalapye (MAH).

BRAZIL, *Amapá*, Macapá (HAMAB).

— *Amazonas*, Manaus (INPA).

— *Bahía*, Cruz das Almas (IAL), Itabuna (CEPEC), Salvador (ALCB, BAH, HRB).

— *Ceará*, Fortaleza (EAC).

— *Distrito Federal*, Brasília (CEN, IBGE, UB).

— *Espírito Santo*, Linhares (CVRD).

— *Goiás*, Goiânia (UFG).

— *Maranhão*, São Luís (UFMA).

— *Mato Grosso*, Cuiabá (UFMT).

— *Minas Gerais*, Belo Horizonte (BHCB, BHMG, BHMH, HXBH, PAMG), Juiz de Fora (CESJ), Lavras (ESAL), Ouro Prêto (EM, OUPR), Paraopeba (PMG), Viçosa (VIC).

— *Pará*, Belém (HF, IAN, MG).

— *Paraíba*, Areia (EAN), João Pessoa (JPB).

— *Paraná*, Curitiba (EFC, IBP, IPB, MBM, PKDC, UPCB).

— *Pernambuco*, Recife (IPA, UFP, URM).

— *Piauí*, Teresina (TEPB).

— *Rio de Janeiro*, Niterói (NIT), Nova Friburgo (FCAB), Rio de Janeiro (GUA, HB, R, RB, RBE, RBR, RFA, RIZ, UFRJ).

— *Rio Grande do Sul*, Canoas (SALLE), Pelotas (PEL), Porto Alegre (BLA, HAS, ICN, MPUC, SFPA), Santa Maria (SMDB), São Leopoldo (PACA).

— *Santa Catarina*, Florianópolis (FLOR), Itajaí (HBR).

— *São Paulo*, Botucatu (BOTU), Campinas (IAC, IACM, UEC), Piracicaba (ESA), Rio Clara, (HRCB), São Paulo (IBI, SP, SPB, SPF, SPSF).

— *Sergipe*, Aracaju (ASE).

BRITISH HONDURAS: see Belize.

BRITISH SOLOMON ISLANDS PROTECTORATE: see Solomon Islands.

BRUNEI, Brunei (BRUN).

BULGARIA, Sofia (SO, SOA, SOM).

BURMA, Mandalay (ASM, MAND), Rangoon (RAF, RANG, RAS).

CAMEROUN (Cameroon), Victoria (SCA, VICA**, VICF**), Yaoundé (YA).

CANADA, *Alberta*, Calgary (UAC), Edmonton (ALTA, CAFB, CFB, PMAE), Grande Prairie (GPA), Lethbridge (LEA, LRS), Olds (OLDS), Vermilion (LCVA).

— *British Columbia*, Burnaby (SFUV), Castlegar (SCCBC), Kamloops (ACK), Nelson (NLSN), Vancouver (UBC), Victoria (DAVFP, DECV, UVIC, V).

— *Manitoba*, Pinawa (WNRE), Portage la Prairie (DELTA, WINDM), Winnipeg, (MDNR, MMMN, UWPG, WIN, WINF, WINFM).

— *New Brunswick*, Fredericton (AFES, FFB, UNB), Saint John (NBM).

— *Newfoundland*, Rocky Harbour (GMNP), St.

John's (CDFN, NFLD).
— *Nova Scotia*, Halifax, (DAL, NRCC, NSPM, NSRF), Truro (NSAC), Wolfville (ACAD).
— *Ontario*, Chalk River (PFES), Guelph (OAC), Hamilton (HAM, MCM), Kingston (QK), London (UWO), Mississauga (TRTE), Niagara Falls (NFO), Ottawa (CAN, CANA, CANL, CANM, CCO, DAO, DAOM, OTF, OTT), Peterborough (TUP), Sault Ste. Marie (AWL, SSMF [MFB]), Sudbury (SLU), Thunder Bay (LKHD), Toronto (TRT, TRTC, TRTS, YUTO), Waterloo (WAT, WLU), Wawa (LSP), Whitney (APM), Windsor (WOCB).
— *Prince Edward Island*, Charlottetown (PEI, UPEI).
— *Québec*, La Pocatière (QSA), La Trappe (LT), Lennoxville (BULQ), Montréal (MT, MTJB, MTMG, QPAR, UQAM), Québec (QEF, QFA, QFB, QFBE, QFS, QMP, QPH, QUC, QUE, SCFQ, ULF), Rimouski (RIM, UQAR), Sherbrooke (SFS), Trois-Rivières (UQTR).
— *Saskatchewan*, Fort Qu'Appelle (FQH), Regina (DAS, USAS), Saskatoon (SAFB, SASK), Swift Current (SCS).
CANAL ZONE: see Panama.
CANARY ISLANDS: see Spain.
CENTRAL AFRICAN REPUBLIC, Boukoko (SCB).
CEYLON: see Sri Lanka.
CHILE, Concepción (CONC), Punta Arenas (HIP), Santiago (EIF, SGO, SSUC), Valdivia (HFV, VALD), Valparaíso (VALPL).
CHINA: see People's Republic of China.
COLOMBIA, Bogotá (BOG, COL, ICA, UDBC), Bucaramanga (UIS), Cali (CUVC), Cartagena (JBGP), Ibagué (TOLI), Manizales (FAUC), Medellín (HUA, JAUM, MEDEL), Montería (HUC), Palmira (VALLE), Pasto (PSO), Popayán (CAUP), Santa Marta (UTMC), Tulua (TULV), Tunja (UPTC).
CONGO: see People's Republic of the Congo.
COSTA RICA, San José (CR, USJ), Turrialba (CATIE).
CÔTE D'IVOIRE: see Ivory Coast.
CUBA, Guantánamo (CSC), Habana (HABA, HABE, HAC, HAJB, IH, LS, SV), Matanzas (IM), Santa Clara (ULV).
CYPRUS, Nicosia (CYP).
CZECHOSLOVAKIA, Bratislava (BAV, BRA, SAV, SLO), Brno (BRNM, BRNU), Čáslav (CVM), České Budějovice (CB), Cheb (CHEB), Chomutov (CHOM), Gottwaldov (GM), Hlohovec (HLO), Hluboká (OH), Hradec Králové (HR), Humpolec (HUMP), Jihlava (MJ), Kašperské Hory (KHMS), Košice (KO), Kutná Hora (OMKH), Liberec (LIM), Litoměřice (LIT), Martin (TM), Nitra (NI), Olomouc (OL, OLM, OLP), Opava (OP), Pardubice (MP), Plzeň (PL), Poděbrady (OMP), Poprad (POP), Praha (PR, PRC, PRM), Šumperk (SUM), Tatranská Lomnica (TNP), Třebíč (ZMT), Trenčín (TRE), Trutnov (TRM), Vrchlabi (KM), Znojmo (MZ), Zvolen (ZV).

DENMARK, Aarhus (AAU), Copenhagen (C, CP).
DOMINICAN REPUBLIC, Santiago de los Caballeros (UCMM), Santo Domingo (JBSD, USD).

EAST GERMANY: see German Democratic Republic.
ECUADOR, Guayaquil (GUAY), Loja (LOJA), Puerto Ayora (CDS), Quito (Q, QAME, QCA, QCNE, QPLS, QPNRA), Santo Domingo de los Colorados (RPSC).
EGYPT, Alexandria (ALEX), Cairo (CAI, CAIA, CAIH, CAIM).
EL SALVADOR, Nueva San Salvador (TECLA), San Salvador (ITIC).
ETHIOPIA, Addis Ababa (ETH, ILCA), Dire Dawa (ACD).

FEDERAL REPUBLIC OF GERMANY, Bad Godesberg (ZVS), Berlin (B, BSB), Bonn (BNL, BONN), Bremen (BREM), Dortmund (DORT), Duisburg (DUIS), Düsseldorf (DUSS), Erlangen (ER), Frankfurt (FR), Freiburg (FB), Göttingen (GOET), Hamburg (HBG), Hannover (HAN), Heidelberg (HEID), Karlsruhe (KR), Kassel (KASSEL), Kiel (KIEL), Lindich (ERZ), Lübeck (LUB), Ludwigsburg (STU), Mainz (MJG), Marburg (MB), München (M), Münster (MSTR), Osnabrück (OSN), Regensburg (REG), Stuttgart-Hohenheim (HOH), Tübingen (TUB), Würzburg (WB, WBM).
FIJI, Suva (SUVA).
FINLAND, Forssa (FOR), Helsinki (H, HEL, HFR, HHC, HPP, HSI, KYM), Jyväskylä (JYV), Kuopio (KUO), Lahti (LHT), Oulu (OULU), Porvoo (PRV), Tampere (TMP), Tikkurila (TIK), Turku (TUR, TURA), Utsjoki (KEVO), Vaasa (VOA).
FRANCE, Angers (ANG, ANGUC), Autun (AUT), Avignon (AV), Avon (ABT), Bagnères-de-Luchon (LUCH), Banyuls-sur-Mer (ARAGO), Bayonne (BAY), Bordeaux (BORD), Brest (BRE), Brignoles (SFB), Caen (CN), Cherbourg (CHE), Clermont-Ferrand (CLF), Concarneau (CO), Dijon (DI), Dinard (DIN), Douai (DO), Grenoble (GR, GRM), La Rochelle (LR), Le Mans (LEMA), Lille (LILLE), Maisons Alfort (ALF [MAIS]), Marseille (MARS, MARSSJ), Montpellier (MPA, MPU, SIGMA), Nancy (NCY), Nantes (NTM), Nice (NICE), Orléans (ORM), Orsay (VIL), Paris (P, PAT, PC, PCU), Rennes (REN), Samoëns (JAY), Strasbourg (STR), Talence (TALE), Toulon (TLON), Toulouse (TL, TLA, TLF, TLJ, TLM, TLP), Vannes (VAN), Villeurbanne (LY).
FRENCH GUIANA, Cayenne (CAY).

GALÁPAGOS ISLANDS: see Ecuador.
GAMBIA, Yundum (YUN**).
GERMAN DEMOCRATIC REPUBLIC, Bautzen (ISIS), Berlin (BHU), Dresden (DR), Gatersleben (GAT), Görlitz (GLM), Greifswald (GFW), Halle (HAL), Jena (JE, SUJ), Leipzig (LZ), Rostock (ROST).
GERMANY: see Federal Republic of Germany and

German Democratic Republic.

GHANA, Bunso-Bosuso (BUNS**), Cape Coast (CCG, MFANT**), Kumasi (KUM [FH], KUU, SLUS**), Legon (GC, GCM), Tafo (WACRI**).

GREAT BRITAIN, *Channel Islands*, Alderney (ALD), Jersey (JEY*, JRY*, JSY*), Saint Peter Port (STP*).

—— *England*, Abingdon (ABN*), Accrington (ACC*), Alton (ALT*), Altrincham (ALM*), Aylesbury (FPRL), Bacup (BAC*), Barnsley (BLY*), Barnstaple (BPL*), Basingstoke (BAE*), Bath (BATH*, BTH*), Batley (BAT*), Bayfordbury (BFY*), Bedford (BED*), Bexhill (BEX*), Birkenhead (BHD*), Birmingham (BHM*, BIM*, BIRA, BIRM), Bognor Regis (BOR*), Bolton (BON*), Bournemouth (BMH*), Bradfield (BRD*), Bradford (BDD*, CMM, PSGB), Brighton (BTN*), Bristol (BRIST, BRISTM, BRL*), Bruton (BRN*), Buckingham (SWE*), Bury St. Edmunds (BSE*), Cambridge (AAS, CAM*, CGE, CGG), Carlisle (CLE*), Cawthorne (CNE*), Chatham (CLI*), Cheltenham (CHL*, CHM*, CHT*, CNM*), Chester (CHRG*), Chichester (CCR*), Cirencester (CIR*), Cleveland (CLD*), Clifton (CFN*, CON*), Colchester (CLR*), Coventry (COV), Crowthorne (CRO*), Croydon (CDN*), Derby (DBY*), Devizes (DZS*), Dewsbury (DSY*), Doncaster (DCR*), Dorchester (DOR*), Dorking (DKG*), Dover (DVR*), Dudley (DLY*), Durham (DHM, DURH*), Eastbourne (EBE*), Englefield Green (ENG*), Epsom (EPM*), Erith (ERH*), Eton (ETN*), Exeter (EXR, RAMM), Folkestone (FKE*), Gloucester (GLR*), Godalming (GOD*, PHG*), Goole (GOE*), Grimsby (GBY*), Halifax (HFX*, HLX*), Hampstead (HPD*), Harpenden (PPL), Harrogate (HTE*), Harrow (HWB*), Haslemere (HME*), Hastings (HGS*), Hereford (HFD*), Hertford (HTD*), Hitchin (HIN*, HTN*), Hollinwood (HWD*), Horsham (HHM*, HSM*), Huddersfield (HDD*), Hull (HLL*, HLM*, HLU*, HUL*), Ilfracome (ILF*), Ipswich (IPS), Keele (KLE), Keighely (KGY), Keswick (KSK*), Kettering (KRG*), Kew (IMI, K), Kidderminster (KDR*), King's Lynn (KLN), Lancaster (LANC), Leeds (LDS, LES*), Leicester (LEI*, LSR*, LTR*), Letchworth (LCH*, LET*), Lincoln (LCN*, LLN*), Littlehampton (LPN*), Liverpool (LIV, LIVU, LPL*, LRL*), London (BCW*, BM, BRC*, BSL*, ICST, LINN, LNHS*, MSL*, PHA*, POLY*, QMC*, SAB*, SJC*, SLBI, SMW*, STB*, STT*, WCE*, WPL*), Long Sutton (LSN*), Louth (LTH*), Ludlow (LUD*), Luton (LTN*), Maidstone (MNE*), Malham (MHM*), Malvern (MVN*), Manchester (MANCH), Marlborough (MACO, MBH*), Middlesborough (MDH*), Newark upon Trent (NWK*), Newcastle upon Tyne (HAMU, NCE*), Newton Abbot (NAT*), Northampton (NMN*, NTN*), Norwich (NCH*, NWH), Nottingham (NHM, NOT), Oldham (OHM*,

WERN), Oundle (OLE*), Oxford (BOD*, FHO [IFI], OXD*, OXF), Penrith (PEN*), Penzance (PNZ*), Peterborough (PBH*), Plymouth (PLY*), Preston (PTN*), Prestwich (PCH*), Puslinch (PUS*), Radcliffe (RFE*), Reading (RDG*, RNG, RU), Reigate (RTE*), Ripon (RPN*), Rochester (RCR*), Rugby (RGY*), Ryde (RYD*), Saffron Walden (SWN*), Saint Albans (STAL*), Salisbury (SBY*), Sheffield (SCM, SFD, SHD*), Shrewsbury (SHY*), Sidcot (SCT*), Skipton (SKN*), Southampton (SOTON, SPN), Southend-on-Sea (STD*), Southport (SPT*), Stalybridge (SGE*), Stockport (SKT*), Stoke-on-Trent (STO*), Stoneyhurst (SYT*), Stowlangtoft (SFT*), Stratford (SRD*), Streatham (STM*), Stroud (SUD*), Sunderland (SUN*), Swindon (SDN*), Taunton (TTN*), Tetbury (TTY*), Thetford (TRD), Todmorden (TDN*, TOD*), Tonbridge (TON*), Torquay (TOR), Truro (TRO*, TRU*), Tunbridge Wells (TLS*), Tyldesley (TDY*), Uppingham (UPP*), Wakefield (WKD), Walthamstow (WMW*), Warrington (WRN*), Warwick (WAR), Weston-super-Mare (WSM*), Whitby (WHY*), Whitehaven (WHN*, WVN*), Winchester (WCR*, WTR), Wisley (WSY*), Woolwich (WCH*), Worcester (WOS*), Wye (WYE*), Yeovil (YEO*), York (YK*, YRK).

—— *Isle of Man*, Castletown (CWN*), Douglas (DGS*), Ramsey (RAM*).

—— *Northern Ireland*, Armagh (ARM*), Belfast (BEL, BFT, BST*).

—— *Scotland*, Aberdeen (ABD), Aboyne (ABO*), Campbeltown (CTN*), Dumfries (DFS*), Dundee (DEE*, DUE*), Edinburgh (ACHE, E, EBH*, EDH*, EGH*), Elgin (ELN*), Forfar (FFR*), Forres (FRS*), Glasgow (GAW*, GGO*, GGW*, GL, GLAM, GLG*, GLO*, GLW*, GO*, GOW*, GSO*, GW*), Greenock (GRK*), Kelso (KSO*), Kilmarnock (KCK*), Kinross (KRS*), Kirkcudbright (KBT*), Montrose (MSE*), Paisley (PAY*, PSY*), Perth (PER, PRH*, PTH), Saint Andrews (STA), Stirling (STI), Stromness (STS*), Thornhill (THL*), Thurso (THO*).

—— *Wales*, Aberystwyth (ABS, WPBS*), Bangor (UCNW), Cardiff (BBSUK, NMW, UCSW), Newport (NPT*, NWT*), Swansea (SWA), Tenby (TBY*).

GREECE, Athens (ACA, ATH, ATHU), Patras (UPA), Thessaloniki (TAU).

GREENLAND, Disko (DISKO).

GUAM, Mangilao (GUAM).

GUATEMALA, Guatemala (GUAT, USCG, UVAL).

GUINEA (Guinée), Mamou (MAMOU**).

GUYANA, Georgetown (BRG, FDG).

HAITI, Damien (EHH).

HONDURAS, Tegucigalpa (EAP, TEFH).

HONG KONG, Hong Kong (HK).

HUNGARY, Budapest (BP, BPU), Debrecen (DE), Eger (EGR), Pécs (PECS), Szeged (SZE), Vácrátót (VBI).

ICELAND, Akureyri (AMNH), Reykjavik (ICEL).
INDIA, Allahabad (BSA), Banaras (BAN), Bangalore (JCB, RRCBI), Baroda (BARO), Bhavnagar (BHAV), Bombay (BLAT), Calcutta (BSIS, CAL, CMY, CUH), Chandigarh (PAN), Coimbatore (FRC, MH), Darbhanga (DMU), Dehra Dun (BSD, DD), Hyderabad (HY), Jaipur (RUBL), Jodhpur (BSJO, JAC), Lucknow (CIMAP, LWG, LWU), Madras (PCM), New Delhi (DUH, HCIO, IARI), Patiala (PUN), Pondicherry (HIFP), Port Blair (PBL), Pune (AMH, BSI), Shillong (ASSAM), Srinagar (KASH), Tiruchirapalli (RHT), Varanasi (BHUPP).
INDONESIA, Bandung (FIPIA), Bogor (BO [BZ], BZF), Manokwari (MAN), Pasuruan (PAS).
IRAN, Tehran (IRAN, KAR, TARI, TEH).
IRAQ, Baghdad (BAG, BUA, BUE, BUH, BUNH), Mosul (MOS).
IRELAND, Cork (CRK*), Dublin (DBN [DUB], IRDA*, TCD), Galway (GALW).
ISRAEL, Deganya Aleph (BEGO), Jerusalem (HUJ), Kefar Malal (IBL), Tel Aviv (TELA), Zichron-Yaakov (AAR).
ITALY, L'Aquila (AQUI), Bari (BI), Bassano del Grappa (BASSA), Bologna (BOLO), Cagliari (CAG), Camerino (CAME), Catania (CAT), Domodossola (DOMO), Ferrara (FER), Firenze (FI, FIAF, FIPF, FT), Genova (GDOR, GE), Lucca (LUCCA), Messina (MS), Milano (MI, MIPV), Modena (MOD), Napoli (NAP), Padova (PAD), Palermo (PAL), Parma (PARMA), Pavia (PAV), Perugia (PERU), Pisa (PI), Portici (POR), Reggio Emilia (SPAL), Roma (RO, ROPV), Sassari (SASSA, SS), Siena (SIAC, SIENA), Taranto (TAR), Torino (TO, TOM), Trento (TR), Trieste (TSB, TSM), Udine (MFU, UDM), Verona (VER).
IVORY COAST, Abidjan (ABI, UCJ), Ouagadougou (CVRS**).

JAMAICA, Kingston (IJ, UCWI).
JAPAN, Fukuoka (FU), Hachioji (TFA), Hiroshima (HIRO), Kagoshima (KAG), Kamakura (KAMA), Kanazawa (KANA), Kariya (AICH), Kukizaki (TF), Kyoto (KYO), Matsumoto (SHIN), Matsuyama (MATSU), Morioka (IUM), Nichinan (NICH), Osaka (OSA), Sapporo (SAP, SAPA, SAPS), Sendai (TUS, TUSG), Tokyo (MAK, NIPR, OCHA, TFM, TH, TI, TKU, TNS, TOFO, TOKE), Tsudanuma (TOHO), Tsukuba (TKB), Tsu Shi (TSU), Yamaguchi (YAM), Yokohama (YNU).
JAVA: see Indonesia.

KENYA, Nairobi (EA, NAI).
KOREA, Seoul (KFI, SKK, SNU).

LEBANON, Beirut (BEI).
LESOTHO, Maseru (MASE), Roma (ROML).
LIBERIA, Monrovia (LIB), Nimba (LAMCO**).
LIBYA (Libyan Arab Republic), Tripoli (ULT).

LUXEMBOURG, Luxembourg (LUX).

MADAGASCAR, Tananarive (TAN).
MADEIRA: see Portugal.
MALAWI, Dedza (NYAS), Zomba (MAL, ZOM).
MALAYSIA, Bangi (UKMB), Kepong (KEP), Kuala Lumpur (KLA, KLU), Kuching (SAR), Sandakan (SAN).
MALTA, Floriana (ARG).
MASCARENE ISLANDS: see Mauritius and Réunion.
MAURITIUS, Réduit (MAU).
MEXICO, Chiapas, Tuxtla Gutiérrez (CHIP).
–– Chihuahua, Chihuahua (RELC).
–– Coahuila, Saltillo (ANSM).
–– Distrito Federal, Coyoacán (ICF), México (AMO, ENCB, FCME, INIF, MEX, MEXU).
–– Jalisco, Guadalajara (CREG, GUADA), Zapopan (IBUG).
–– México, Chapingo (CHAP, CHAPA), Metepec (CODAGEM).
–– Michoacán, Morelia (EBUM).
–– Nuevo León, Monterrey (MEMO, UNL).
–– San Luis Potosí, San Luis Potosí (SLPM).
–– Tabasco, Cárdenas (CSAT).
–– Veracruz, Xalapa (XAL, XALU).
MONGOLIAN PEOPLE'S REPUBLIC, Ulan-Bator (UBA, UBU).
MOROCCO, Rabat (RAB, RAU).
MOZAMBIQUE (Moçambique), Maputo (LM, LMA, LMC, LMJ, LMU).

NEPAL, Lalitpur (KATH).
NETHERLANDS, Amsterdam (AMD, AVU), Baarn (CBS), Haren (GRO), Leersum (RIN), Leeuwarden (FNM), Leiden (L, NBV), Maastricht (MAAS), Rijswijk (SRR), Utrecht (U), Wageningen (WAG, WAHO, WBS).
NEW CALEDONIA, Nouméa (NOU).
NEW GUINEA: see Papua New Guinea.
NEW HEBRIDES, Port Vila (PVNH).
NEW ZEALAND, Auckland (AK, AKU, PDD), Christchurch (CANTY, CANU, CHBG, CHR), Dunedin (OTA, OTM), Levin (LEV), Palmerston North (MPN), Rotorua (NZFRI), Wellington (WELT, WELTU).
NICARAGUA, Managua (ENAG, HNMN, MGA).
NIGER, Niamey (ESN), Toukounous (TOUK**).
NIGERIA, Enugu (EFH), Ibadan (FAIB**, FHI, UCI), Ikare (VICC**), Ile-Ife (IFE), Lagos (LUH), Nsukka (UNN), Umudike (ARS**), Yaba (ULN), Zaria (SAMARU**, ZARIA**).
NORWAY, Bergen (BG), Oslo (O), Stavanger (SVG), Tromsoe (TROM), Trondheim (TRH).

PAKISTAN, Islamabad (ISL), Karachi (KUH), Lahore (LAH), Peshawar (ICP, PES, PPFI, PUP), Rawalpindi (RAW).
PANAMA, Balboa (SCZ, STRI), Panamá (PMA).
PAPUA NEW GUINEA, Lae (LAE), Port Moresby (PNG [TPNG], UPNG), Wau (WAU).

350

PARAGUAY, Asunción (AS).

PEOPLE'S REPUBLIC OF CHINA, Chengdu (SZ, WCU), Foochow (FCU), Guangzhou (CANT, IBSC, LU, SYS), Guilin (IBK), Hangzhou (HC, HHBG, HU), Huhetot (HIMC), Jinan (JSPC, SCU), Kunming (KUN, YUKU), Lusan (LUS), Lushan (LBG), Mengla (HITBC), Nanjing (N, NAS, NF, NPA, NSM), Peking (FM, PE, PEM, PET, PEY), Qingdao (TS), Shanghai (FUS, HSNU, SH, SHB, SHJ, SHMH), Shenyang (IFP), Suzhou (SU), Tianjin (TIE), Wuchang (WH), Wugong (WUK), Wuhan (HIB), Wuzhou (KU), Xiamen (AU), Xining (HNWP), Yenshan (IBY), Yiyang (YH).

PEOPLE'S REPUBLIC OF THE CONGO, Brazzaville (IEC [IRSC]).

PERU, Cajamarca (CPUN), Cuzco (CUZ), Huancayo (HCEN), Huánuco (HHUA), Iquitos (AMAZ), Lambayeque (PRG), Lima (MOL, SMF, USM), Tingo María (HTIN), Trujillo (HUT).

PHILIPPINES, Los Baños (CAHUP, CALP, CLP, LBC), Manila (PNH), Quezon City (PUH), Siniloan (PNBG).

POLAND, Katowice (KTU), Kórnik (KOR), Kraków (KRA, KRAM), Łódź (LOD), Lublin (LBL, LBLC), Poznań (POZ, POZG), Siedlce (WSRP), Toruń (TRN), Warszawa (WA), Wrocław (WRSL [BRSL]).

PORTUGAL, Caldas da Saúde (INA), Coimbra (COI), Elvas (ELVE), Funchal (MADJ, MADM, MADS), Lisboa (CRCA, LIG, LISC, LISFA, LISI, LISJC, LISM, LISU, LISVA), Oeiras (LISE), Porto (PO), Vila Real (HVR).

PORTUGUESE EAST AFRICA: see Mozambique.

PORTUGUESE WEST AFRICA: see Angola.

PUERTO RICO, Mayaguez (FPDB, MAPR, MSM), Río Piedras (RPPR, UPR).

REPUBLIC OF SINGAPORE: see Singapore.

REPUBLIC OF VENDA, Sibasa (VENDA).

REPUBLIC OF ZAMBIA: see Zambia.

REPÚBLICA DOMINICANA: see Dominican Republic.

RÉPUBLIQUE CENTRAFRICAINE: see Central African Republic.

RÉUNION, Saint Clothilde (STCR).

RHODESIA: see Zimbabwe.

ROMANIA, Bucureşti (BUC, BUCA, BUCF, BUCM), Cluj-Napoca (CL, CLA, CLCB), Craiova (CRAF, CRAI), Iasi (I, IAGB, IASI, IBIR), Sibiu (SIB).

RYUKYU ISLANDS, Shuri (URO).

SENEGAL, Bambey (BAMB**), Dakar (DAKAR, IFAN).

SEYCHELLES, Port Victoria (SEY).

SIERRA LEONE, Bo (BOSL**), Freetown (FBC, SL), Kenema (FHK), Njala (NJ).

SINGAPORE, Singapore (SING).

SOLOMON ISLANDS, Honiara (BSIP).

SOMALIA, Mogadishu (MOG).

SOUTH AFRICA, Bellville (UWC), Bloemfontein (BLFU), Cape Town (BOL, CT, NBG, SAM), Durban (NH), Empangeni (ZULU), George (SAAS), Grahamstown (GRA, RUH), Johannesburg (J), Kimberley (KMG), Mtubatuba (NPB), Pietermaritzburg (NU), Port Elizabeth (MPE, PEU), Potchefstroom (PUC), Pretoria (PRE, PREM, PRF, PRU, TRV), Skukuza (KNP), Stellenbosch (FFS, JF, STE, STEU), Winterton (CPF).

SOUTH-WEST AFRICA, Windhoek (WIND).

SPAIN, Barcelona (BC, BCC, BCF), Granada (GDA), Madrid (MA, MAF, MAFST), Malaga (MGC), Oviedo (FCO), Pamplona (PAMP**), Santiago de Compostela (SANT), Sevilla (SEV), Valencia (VAL).

–– Canary Islands, La Laguna (TFC), Las Palmas (LPA), Puerto de la Cruz (ORT), Santa Cruz de Tenerife (TFMC).

SRI LANKA, Hakgala (HAKS), Peradeniya (PDA).

SUDAN, Gezira (WM), Khartoum (KHF, KHU), Wad Medani (GRS).

SURINAME, Paramaribo (BBS).

SWEDEN, Göteborg (GB), Lund (LD), Örebro (OREB), Skara (SK), Stockholm (S, SBT, S-PA, SPL, SUNIV), Umeå (UME), Uppsala (UPS, UPSV), Visby (VI).

SWITZERLAND, Basel (BAS, BASBG), Bern (BERN), Chur (CHUR), Genève (G, G-PAE), Lausanne (LAU), Neuchâtel (NEU), Schaffhausen (SCH), Zürich (RUEB, Z, ZSS, ZT).

TAIWAN, Taipei (TAI, TAIF, TAIM).

TANGANYIKA: see Tanzania.

TANZANIA, Dar es Salaam (DSM), Lushoto (TFD).

THAILAND, Bangkok (BK, BKF).

TOGO, Lomé (TOGO), Palimé (PALIME**).

TRINIDAD, Saint Augustine (TRIN).

TUNISIA (Tunisie), Tunis (TUN).

TURKEY, Ankara (AEF, ANK, ANKO, BIA, HUB, HUEF), Diyarbakir (DUF), Erzurum (ATA), Etimesgut (ESK), Istanbul (ISTE, ISTF, ISTO), Izmir (EGE, IZ, IZEF), Trabzon (KATO).

UGANDA, Entebbe (ENT), Kampala (KAW, MHU), Nyabyeya (UFS).

UNION OF SOVIET SOCIALIST REPUBLICS (U.S.S.R.), Alma Ata (AA), Ashkhabad (ASH), Baku (BAK), Batumi (BATU), Cernǎuti (CERN), Chardjow (RSDR), Charkow (CW, CWB, CWU), Chernovzy (CHER), Dnepropetrovsk (DSU), Donskoye (VU), Dushambe (TAD), Frunze (FRU), Irkutsk (IRK), Kaunas (KA), Kazan (KAZ), Kiev (KW, KWHA), Kirovsk (KPABG), Kishinev (CHIS, CHISA), Krasnodar (KBAI), Krasnojarsk (KRAS), Leningrad (KFTA, LE, LECB, WIR [LEP]), Lwow (LW, LWA, LWD, LWS), Maikop (CSR), Makhachkala (LENUD), Minsk (MSK), Moscow (MHA, MOSM, MOSP, MW), Nalchik (AUBSN), Novo-Aleksandrovsk (NABG), Novosibirsk (NS), Odessa (MSUD), Penza (PKM), Perm (PERM), Petrozavodsk (PZV), Repetek (REP), Riga (RIG), Rostov on Don (RV), Salaspils

(LATV), Saratov (SARAT), Simferopol (SIMF), Stavropol (SBG, SMRS, SPI), Sukhumi (SUCH), Sverdlovsk (SVER), Syktyvkar (SYKO), Tartu (EAA, TAA, TAM, TU), Tashkent (RNMUT, TAK, TASH), Tbilisi (TB, TBI, TGM), Tomsk (TK), Uralsk (PPIU), Ust-Kamenogorsk (UKSPI), Uzhgorod (UU), Vedi (KSRV), Vilnius (BILAS, WI), Vladivostok (VLA), Voronezh (VOR), Yakutsk (SASY), Yalta (YALT), Yaroslavl (USPIY), Yerevan (AISIY, APIY, BGAAS, ERCB, ERE, EREM, ERHM, VIAY, YAI).

UNITED ARAB EMIRATES, Abu Dhabi (ABDH).

UNITED KINGDOM OF GREAT BRITAIN AND NORTHERN IRELAND: see Great Britain.

UNITED STATES OF AMERICA (U.S.A.), *Alabama*, Auburn (AUA), Huntsville (HALA), Saint Bernard (SB), Troy (TROY), University (ALU, UNA).
–– *Alaska*, Fairbanks (ALA), Palmer (AES), Sitka (TNFS).
–– *Arizona*, Flagstaff (ASC, FSLF, MNA), Grand Canyon (GCNP), Phoenix (DES), Tempe (ASU, ASUF), Tucson (ARIZ, TUC).
–– *Arkansas*, Fayetteville (UARK), Jonesboro (STAR), Little Rock (LRU), Russellville (APCR).
–– *California*, Alta Loma (CHAF), Anaheim (ANA), Angwin (PUA), Arcadia (LASCA), Arcata (HSC), Azusa (AZUS), Berkeley (JEPS, PFRS, UC), Borrego Springs (BSCA), Carmel Valley (CAVA), Chico (CHSC), Claremont (POM, RSA), Davis (AHUC, DAV, DAVH), Dillon Beach (PMS), Fresno (FSC), Fullerton (MACF), Hayward (HAY), Huntington Beach (HUBE), Irvine (IRVC), La Jolla (SCR, TRA), Loma Linda (LOMA), Long Beach (LOB), Los Angeles (AHFH, CSLA, LA, LAM, LOC, USC), Mineral (LVNP), Northridge (SFV), Oakland (OAKL, OMC), Pacific Grove (GMS, PGM), Pasadena (PASA), Placerville (IFGP), Pleasant Hill (DVM), Point Reyes (PORE), Pomona (CSPU), Redding (RESC), Redlands (RED), Riverside (UCR), Rohnert Park (ROPA), Sacramento (CDA [BPS], SACT), San Diego (SD, SDM, SDSU), San Francisco (CAS, DS, SAFU, SFRF, SFSU), San Jose (SJSU), San Luis Obispo (OBI), San Marcos (PASM), San Marino (HNT), Santa Barbara (SBBG, SBCC, SBM, UCSB), Santa Clara (SACL), Santa Cruz (UCSC), Santa Rosa (NCC), Stanford (CI), Stockton (CPH, SSJC), Terminal Island (TIC), Three Rivers (THRI), Turlock (SHTC), Van Nuys (VNC), Woodland Hills (LAPC), Yosemite National Park (YM), Yreka (KNFY).
–– *Colorado*, Alamosa (ALAM), Boulder (COLO, GGB), Colorado Springs (COCO), Denver (COLOM, DBG, KHD), Fort Collins (CS, FPF, USFS), Greeley (GREE), La Junta (LAJC), Lakewood (DENF), Pueblo (PUSC).
–– *Connecticut*, Middletown (WECO), New Haven (NCBS, NHES, Y, YU), Storrs (CONN).
–– *Delaware*, Dover (DOV), Newark (DELS).
–– *District of Columbia*, Washington (LCU, NA, US, USNC).

–– *Florida*, Boca Raton (FAU), Coral Gables (BUS), DeLand (DLF), Fort Pierce (HBFH), Gainesville (FLAS, PIHG), Lakeland (FSCL), Miami (FTG), Orlando (FTU), Pensacola (UWFP), Saint Petersburg (SPMS, STPE), Sarasota (MOT, SEL), Tallahassee (FSU), Tampa (USF).
–– *Georgia*, Athens (GA, GAM), Atlanta (FSSR, GEO), Carrollton (WGC), Columbus (COLG), Decatur (DECA), Experiment (GAES), Statesboro (GAS), Valdosta (VSC).
–– *Hawaii*, Honolulu (BISH, HAW, HLA), Lawai (PTBG).
–– *Idaho*, Boise (BOIS, IFGH), Caldwell (CIC), Moscow (ID, IDF), Pocatello (IDS), Rexburg (RICK).
–– *Illinois*, Carbondale (ABSH, SIU), Charleston (EIU), Chicago (CHI, F), DeKalb (DEK), Evanston (NWU), Galesburg (KNOX), Lisle (MOR), Macomb (MWI), Normal (ISU), Springfield (ISM), Urbana (CEL, ILL, ILLS), Warsaw (WARK).
–– *Indiana*, Bloomington (IND), Crawfordsville (WAB), Greencastle (DPU), Indianapolis (BUT, CAHS), Muncie (BSUH), New Albany (JEF), Notre Dame (ND, NDG), Richmond (EAR), Saint Meinrad (SMH), Terre Haute (TER), West Lafayette (PUL, PUR).
–– *Iowa*, Ames (ISC), Cedar Falls (ISTC), Davenport (BDI), Decorah (LCDI), Grinnell (GRI), Indianola (SICH), Iowa City (IA), Milford (ILH), Mount Vernon (MOVC), Waverly (WET).
–– *Kansas*, Atchison (HWBA), Emporia (KSTC), Hays (FHKSC), Lawrence (KANU), Manhattan (KSC), Pittsburg (KSP), Salina (SAL).
–– *Kentucky*, Danville (KBRYO), Highland Heights (KNK), Lexington (KY), Louisville (DHL), Murray (MUR), Richmond (EKY).
–– *Louisiana*, Baton Rouge (LSU, LSUM), Lafayette (LAF, USLH), Monroe (NLU), Natchitoches (NATC), New Orleans (NO, NOLS), Pineville (SFRP), Ruston (LTU), Shreveport (LSUS).
–– *Maine*, Lewiston (BCL), Orono (MAINE), Waterville (WAVI).
–– *Maryland*, Baltimore (BALT), Beltsville (BARC, BPI), College Park (MARY), Rockville (ATCC),
–– *Massachusetts*, Amherst (AC, MASS), Bedford (BEDF), Boston (BOSC, BSN, HNUB, MCP), Cambridge (A, AMES, ECON, FH, GH, NEBC), Jamaica Plain (AAH), Medford (TUFT), Natick (QM), Northampton (SCHN), North Dartmouth (HDSM), Salem (PM), Springfield (SPR), Wellesley (WELC), Wenham (WMGC), Woods Hole (SPWH), Worcester (CUW).
–– *Michigan*, Adrian (ADR), Albion (ALBC), Allendale (GVSC), Alma (ALMA), Ann Arbor (AFS, MICH), Berrien Springs (AUB), Bloomfield Hills (BLH), Detroit (WUD), East Lansing (MSC), Grand Rapids (AQC, GRJC), Hickory Corners (KBSMS), Holland (HCHM), Houghton (IRP, MCT, MCTC), Houghton Lake Heights (HL), Kalamazoo (WMU), L'Anse (MCTF), Marquette

(NM), Mount Pleasant (CMC), Muskegon (MUSK), Olivet (OLV), Pellston (UMBS), Pinckney (MGR), Shingleton (CUS), Ypsilanti (EMC).
— *Minnesota*, Duluth (DUL), Mankato (MANK), Moorhead (MRD), Northfield (CARL), Saint Cloud (SCL), Saint Paul (ABSL, MIN, MPPD), Winona (WINO).
— *Mississippi*, Cleveland (DSC), Columbus (MSCW), Mississippi State (IBE, MISSA), University (MISS).
— *Missouri*, Columbia (UMO), Joplin (MCJ), Liberty (WJC), Maryville (NMSU), Point Lookout (SOTO), Saint Joseph (MWSJ), Saint Louis (MO), Springfield (SMS), Warrensburg (WARM).
— *Montana*, Bozeman (MONT), Great Falls (GFC), Missoula (MONTU, MRC).
— *Nebraska*, Chadron (CSCN), Lincoln (NEB), Omaha (OMA).
— *Nevada*, Carson City (NSMC), Las Vegas (UNLV), Mercury (NTS), Reno (NESH, NSDA, RENO), Winnemucca (WDNE).
— *New Hampshire*, Durham (NHA), Hanover (HNH), Hillsboro (SPH), Keene (KESC).
— *New Jersey*, East Orange (EONJ), Newark (NCAS, NEMU), New Brunswick (CHRB, RUT, RUTPP).
— *New Mexico*, Albuquerque (ALBU, UNM), Las Cruces (NMC, NMCR), Silver City (SNM).
— *New York*, Albany (NYS), Binghamton (BING), Brockport (BROC), Brooklyn (BKL), Buffalo (BUF, CANI), Geneseo (GESU), Geneva (DH), Hamilton (GRCH), Ithaca (BH, CU, CUP), New York (NY), Oneonta (HHH), Oyster Bay (OBPF), Palisades (LGO), Poughkeepsie (VAS), Rochester (HPH, ROCH), Saint Bonaventure (SBU), Schenectady (UCS), Southampton (SOUT), Staten Island (SIM), Syracuse (SYR, SYRF).
— *North Carolina*, Boone (BOON), Chapel Hill (NCU), Charlotte (UNCC), Cullowhee (WCUH), Durham (ABSM, DUKE), Greensboro (NCATG), Laurinburg (SAPCL), Misenheimer (PFC), Morehead City (IMS), Raleigh (NCSC), Wilmington (WNC), Winston-Salem (SC, WFU).
— *North Dakota*, Fargo (NDA), Grand Forks (GFND), Jamestown (NPWRC).
— *Ohio*, Athens (BHO), Bowling Green (BGSU), Cincinnati (CINC, LLO), Cleveland (CLM), Columbus (OS), Dayton (DMNH), Delaware (OWU), Granville (DEN), Kent (KE), New Concord (MUS), Oberlin (OC), Oxford (MU), Springfield (JHWU), Waterville (PSP), Wilmington (WSFA), Youngstown (YUO).
— *Oklahoma*, Ada (ECSC), Alva (NWOSU), Chickasha (OCLA), Durant (DUR), Edmond (CSU), Norman (OKL), Stillwater (OKLA), Tahlequah (NOSU), Tulsa (TULS), Weatherford (WOH).
— *Oregon*, Ashland (SOC), Corvallis (OSC, OSUF, WILLU), Eugene (LCEU, ORE), LaGrande (LAGO), Lakeview (BLMLK, FNLO), Maryl-hurst (MARO), Monmouth (MOC), Portland (POFS), Prineville (OCNF).
— *Pennsylvania*, Allentown (MCA), Harrisburg (PAM), Indiana (IUP), Kennett Square (KEN), Lancaster (FMC), Latrobe (LAT), Lewisburg (BUPL), Merion (ABFM), Millersville (MVSC), Philadelphia (MOAR, PENN, PH, PHIL), Pittsburgh (CM), Reading (RPM), Scranton (EVMU), Slippery Rock (SLRO), Swarthmore (SWC), University Park (PAC), West Chester (DWC).
— *Rhode Island*, Kingston (KIRI), Providence (BRU).
— *South Carolina*, Charleston (CHARL, CHAS, CITA), Clemson (CLEMS), Columbia (USCH), Greenville (FUGR).
— *South Dakota*, Brookings (SDC), Sioux Falls (AUG), Spearfish (BHSC), Vermillion (SDU).
— *Tennessee*, Chattanooga (UCHT), Clarksville (APSC), Gatlinburg (GSMNP), Johnson City (ETSU), Knoxville (TENN), Memphis (MEM, SWMT), Nashville (VDB).
— *Texas*, Abilene (HSU), Alpine (SRSC), Amarillo (USSC), Austin (AHS, LL, TEX), Belton (HABAYC), Brownsville (RUNYON), Brownwood (HPC), Canyon (WTS), College Station (TAES, TAMU), Commerce (ETST), Dallas (SMU), Denton (NTSC, TCSW), Edinburg (PAUH), Fort Worth (FW, FWM), Gruver (SRCG), Houston (HOU, HPM), Huntsville (SHST), Kingsville (TAIC), Levelland (SPLT), Lubbock (TTC), Nacogdoches (ASTC), Prairie View (TPV), Richardson (UTD), San Angelo (SAT), San Antonio (LLC), Sinton (WWF), Stephenville (TAC), Temple (TEXA), Uvalde (UVST), Waco (BAYLU).
— *Utah*, Ephraim (EPHR), Logan (UTC), Milford (DERM), Ogden (OGDF, WSCO), Price (MALS, PRI), Provo (BRY, SSLP), Richfield (FNFR), Salt Lake City (SLC, UT, WANF).
— *Vermont*, Burlington (VT), Middlebury (MID), Northfield (NUV), Plainfield (FMH), Saint Johnsbury (SJFM), Winooski (SMCW).
— *Virginia*, Blacksburg (VPI), Bridgewater (BDWR), Charlottesville (VA), Emory (EHCV), Fairfax (GMUF), Farmville (FARM), Fredericksburg (MWCF), Glenns (GLEN), Harrisonburg (HAVI, JMUH), Lexington (VMIL), Lynchburg (LYN, RMWC), Middletown (LFCC), Norfolk (ODU), Petersburg (VSUH), Radford (RUHV), Richmond (VCU, VDAC), Roanoke (ROAN), Salem (SARC), Sweet Briar (SWBR), Williamsburg (WILLI), Wise (CVCW), Wytheville (WYCO).
— *Washington*, Bellingham (WWB), College Place (WCP), Ellensburg (ELRG), Friday Harbor (FHL), Lacey (OSMC), Pullman (WS, WSP), Seattle (SPC, WTU), Walla Walla (WCW).
— *West Virginia*, Buckhannon (WVW), Charleston (MVC), Fairmont (FWVA), Huntington (MUHW), Montgomery (WVIT), Morgantown (WVA), Salem (SAWV).
— *Wisconsin*, Beloit (BELC), De Pere (SNC), Fond du Lac (FDLW), Janesville (UWJ), Kenosha

(CART), La Crosse (UWL), Madison (CFMR [BFDL], MAD, WIS), Milton (MCW), Milwaukee (MIL, UWM), Oshkosh (OSH), River Falls (RIVE), Stevens Point (UWSP), Superior (SUWS).
–– *Wyoming*, Jackson (BTJW), Laramie (RM, RMS, WYAC), Yellowstone (YELLO).
URUGUAY, Montevideo (MVDA, MVFA, MVHC, MVM).

VENEZUELA, Barquisimeto (UCOB), Caracas (MYF, VEN), Guanare (PORT), Maracaibo (HERZU), Maracay (IPMY, MY), Mérida (MER, MERF).
VIRGIN ISLANDS OF THE UNITED STATES, St. Thomas (VIST).

WEST AFRICA: see Ghana, Sierra Leone.
WEST GERMANY: see Federal Republic of Germany.
WEST MALAYSIA: see Malaysia.

YUGOSLAVIA, Beograd (BEO), Ljubljana (LJM, LJU), Makarska (MAKAR), Rovinj (RI), Sarajevo (SARA), Zagreb (ADRZ, ZA, ZAHO).

ZAÏRE, Lubumbashi (EBV, LSHI), Yangambi (YBI).
ZAMBIA, Abercorn (LCS), Chilanga (MRSC, ZAD), Kitwe (NDO), Lusaka (MPR, UZL), Mbala (LCO).
ZIMBABWE, Bulawayo (BUL), Salisbury (CAH, SRGH), Umtali (UMT).

III. Herbarium Abbreviations

Extensive information may be found in the main list, under the name of the town in which the respective herbarium is located.

The Herbaria marked with an (*) are *not* to be found in the main list. They refer to British Institutional Herbaria mentioned in D. H. Kent, *British Herbaria*, London (1957) (q.v.). Herbaria marked with two asterisks (**) are also not listed in this *Index Herbariorum*, but appear in F. N. Hepper and Fioria Neate, *Plant collectors in West Africa*, Regnum Vegetabile 74, Utrecht 1971.

A	CAMBRIDGE: Herbarium, Arnold Arboretum of Harvard University, 22 Divinity Avenue, Cambridge, Massachusetts 02138, U.S.A.
AA	ALMA-ATA: Herbarium, Botanical Institute of the Academy of Sciences of the Kazakh S.S.R., Kirova St. 103, Alma-Ata 2, 480100, U.S.S.R.
AAH	JAMAICA PLAIN: Herbarium, Arnold Arboretum, Harvard University, The Arborway, Jamaica Plain, Massachusetts 02130, U.S.A.
AAR	ZICHRON-YAAKOV: Reliquae Aaronsohnianae, 40 Hameyasdina Street, Zichron-Yaakov 30-900, Israel.
AAS	CAMBRIDGE: British Antarctic Survey Herbarium, British Antarctic Survey Life Sciences Division, Plant Biology Section, Madlingley Road, Cambridge CB3 OET, England, Great Britain.
AAU	AARHUS: Herbarium Jutlandicum, Botanical Institute, University of Aarhus, 68 Nordlandsvej, DK-8240 Risskov, Denmark.
ABD	ABERDEEN: Herbarium, Department of Botany, The University, Aberdeen AB9 24D Scotland, Great Britain.
ABDH	ABU DHABI: Herbarium, Department of Biology, United Arab Emirates University, P.O. Box 15551, Al Ayn, Abu Dhabi, United Arab Emirates.
ABFM	MERION: Herbarium, Arboretum of the Barnes Foundation, Box 128, Merion, Pennsylvania 19066, U.S.A.
ABI	ABIDJAN: Herbarium, Centre ORSTOM d'Adiopodoumé, B.P. 20, Abidjan, Ivory Coast.
ABN	ABINGDON: Radley College, Abingdon, England, Great Britain.*
ABO	ABOYNE: Aboyne Castle, Aboyne (Aberdeen), Scotland, Great Britain.*
ABS	ABERYSTWYTH: The Painter Herbarium, Department of Botany, University College of Wales, Aberystwyth, Wales, Great Britain.
ABSH	CARBONDALE: The Hepatic Herbarium, The American Bryological and Lichenological Society, Department of Botany, Southern Illinois University, Carbondale, Illinois 62901, U.S.A.
ABSL	SAINT PAUL: American Bryological and Lichenological Society Herbarium, Department of Botany, University of Minnesota, 1445 Gortner Avenue, St. Paul, Minnesota 55108, U.S.A.
ABSM	DURHAM: Moss Herbarium, American Bryological Society — incorporated in DUKE.
ABT	AVON: Herbarium, Laboratoire de Botanique Tropicale, Avon, Seine et Marne, France.
AC	AMHERST: Herbarium, Amherst College, Amherst, Massachusetts 01002, U.S.A. — on permanent loan to MASS.
ACA	ATHENS: Agricultural College of Athens, Institute of Systematic Botany, Botanikos Kipos, Iera Odos 75, Athens 301, Greece.
ACAD	WOLFVILLE: E. C. Smith Herbarium, Department of Biology, Acadia University, Wolfville, Nova Scotia, Canada.
ACC	ACCRINGTON: Municipal Museum, Accrington, England, Great Britain.*
ACD	DIRE DAWA: Herbarium, Agricultural College of the Haile Selassi 1st University, c/o Agricultural College, Box 138, Dire Dawa, Ethiopia.
ACHE	EDINBURGH: Austral Cryptogamic Herbarium, Institute of Terrestrial Ecology, Bush Estate, Penicuik, Midlothian EH26 OQB, Scotland, Great Britain.
ACK	KAMLOOPS: Herbarium, Agriculture Canada Research Station, 3015 Ord Road, Kamloops, British Columbia, Canada V2B 8A9.
AD	ADELAIDE: State Herbarium of South Australia, Botanic Garden, North Terrace, Adelaide, South Australia 5000, Australia.
ADMONT	ADMONT: Benediktiner Abtei Admont "Obersteirisches Herbar," Benediktiner Abtei Admont/Naturhistorisches Museum, A-8911 Admont, Austria.
ADR	ADRIAN: Herbarium, Biology Department, Adrian College, Adrian, Michigan 49221, U.S.A.
ADRZ	ZAGREB: Herbarium Adriaticum, Instituti "R. Boškovic" Dautoniae, CIM Coastal Botany, POB 1016, Bijenicka 54, Zagreb, 41001 – Yugoslavia.
ADU	ADELAIDE: Herbarium, Botany Department, University of Adelaide, Adelaide, South Australia 5001, Australia.

ADW	ADELAIDE: Herbarium, Waite Agricultural Research Institute, The University of Adelaide, Private Bag No. 1, Glen Osmond, South Australia 5064, Australia.
AEF	ANKARA: Ankara Üniversitesi Eczacilik Fakültesi Herbaryum, Farmakognozi ve Farmasötik Botanik Kürsüsü, Tandogan, Ankara, Turkey.
AES	PALMER: Herbarium, University of Alaska Agricultural Experiment Station, Box AE, Palmer, Alaska 99645, U.S.A.
AFES	FREDERICTON: Environmental Management, Maritimes Forest Research Centre, P.O. Box 4000, Fredericton, New Brunswick, Canada E3B 5P7 -- incorporated in UNB.
AFS	ANN ARBOR: Herbarium of the American Fern Society, University of Michigan, North University Building, Ann Arbor, Michigan 48109, U.S.A. -- incorporated in MICH.
AHFH	LOS ANGELES: Herbarium, Allan Hancock Foundation, University of Southern California, Los Angeles, California 90007, U.S.A.
AHS	AUSTIN: Austin High School Herbarium, Austin, Texas 78712, U.S.A. -- discontinued.
AHUC	DAVIS: Herbarium, Department of Agronomy and Range Science, University of California, Davis, California 95616, U.S.A.
AICH	KARIYA: Herbarium, Department of Biology, Aichi Kyoiku University, Igaya-cho, Kariya-shi, Aichi-ken 448, Japan.
AIMS	TOWNSVILLE: Herbarium, Australian Institute of Marine Science, Cape Ferguson, PMB 3, Townsville, M.S.O., Queensland, Australia.
AISIY	YEREVAN: Herbarium, Department of Meadows and Pastures, Armenian Institute for the Scientific Investigation of Cattle Breeding and Veterinary, Nalbandyan St. 57, 375025 Yerevan, U.S.S.R.
AK	AUCKLAND: Auckland Institute and Museum (Cheeseman Herbarium), Private Bag, Auckland, New Zealand.
AKU	AUCKLAND: Herbarium, Botany Department, University of Auckland, Private Bag, Auckland, New Zealand.
AL	ALGER: Herbarium, Laboratoire de Botanique de la Faculté des Sciences, Université d'Alger, Alger, Algeria.
ALA	FAIRBANKS: Herbarium, University of Alaska Museum, Fairbanks, Alaska 99701, U.S.A.
ALAM	ALAMOSA: Herbarium, Adams State College, Alamosa, Colorado 81102, U.S.A.
ALBC	ALBION: Herbarium, Department of Biology, Albion College, Albion, Michigan 49224, U.S.A.
ALBU	ALBUQUERQUE: Herbarium, Rocky Mountain Forest and Range Experiment Station, Albuquerque Unit, 2205 Columbia SE, Albuquerque, New Mexico 87106, U.S.A.
ALCB	SALVADOR: Herbário Alexandre Leal Costa, Instituto de Biologia, Universidade Federal da Bahia, Campus Universitário da Federação, Ondina, 40.000 Salvador, Bahia, Brazil.
ALD	ALDERNEY: Herbarium, Alderney Society and Museum, Alderney, Channel Islands, Great Britain.
ALEX	ALEXANDRIA: Department of Botany, Faculty of Science, The University, Moharram Bey, Alexandria, Egypt.
ALF	MAISONS ALFORT: Herbarium, Institut d'Elevage et de Médecine Vétérinaire des Pays Tropicaux, 10 Rue Curie, 94700 Maisons Alfort, France.
ALM	ALTRINCHAM: Central Library, Altrincham, England, Great Britain.*
ALMA	ALMA: Herbarium, Biology Department, Alma College, Alma, Michigan 48801, U.S.A.
ALT	ALTON: Curtis Museum, Alton, England, Great Britain.*
ALTA	EDMONTON: Herbarium, Department of Botany, University of Alberta, Edmonton, Alberta, Canada T6G 2E9.
ALU	UNIVERSITY: Mohr Herbarium, Alabama Museum of Natural History, University, Alabama 35486, U.S.A. -- on permanent loan to UNA.
AMAZ	IQUITOS: Herbarium Amazonense, Universidad Nacional de la Amazonía Peruana, Jirón Próspero No. 584, Apartado 421, Iquitos, Peru.
AMD	AMSTERDAM: Herbarium, Hugo de Vries-laboratorium, Plantage Middenlaan 2A, 1018 DD Amsterdam, Netherlands.
AMES	CAMBRIDGE: Orchid Herbarium of Oakes Ames, Botanical Museum of Harvard University, 22 Divinity Avenue, Cambridge, Massachusetts 02138, U.S.A.
AMH	PUNE: Ajrekar Mycological Herbarium, Maharashtra Association for the Cultivation of Science - Research Institute, Law College Road, Pune 411003, India.
AMNH	AKUREYRI: Herbarium, Náttúrugripasafnić á Akureyri (Akureyri Museum of Natural History), Hafnarstraeti 81, P.O. Box 580, 600 Akureyri, Iceland.
AMO	MÉXICO: Herbario, Asociacion Méxicana de Orquideologia, Apartado postal 53-123, México 17, Distrito Federal, Mexico.

ANA ANAHEIM: Herbarium, Orange County Department of Agriculture, 1010 South Harbor Boulevard, Anaheim, California 92805, U.S.A.
ANG ANGERS: Herbier Lloyd, Place des Halles, Angers, France.
ANGU ANGUIL: Herbario, Estación Experimental Regional Agropecuaria, Instituto Nacional de Tecnología Agropecuaria, Casilla de Correo 11, 6326 Anguil, La Pampa, Argentina.
ANGUC ANGERS: Herbier de la Faculté Libre des Sciences, 3 Place André Leroy, B.P. 808, 49005 Angers Cedex, France.
ANK ANKARA: Ankara Üniversitesi, Fen Fakúltesi Herbariumu, Sistematik Botanik Kürsüsü, Beşevker – Ankara, Turkey.
ANKO ANKARA: Forest Research Institute Herbarium, P.K. 24, Bahçelievler, Ankara, Turkey.
ANSM SALTILLO: Herbario, Departamento de Botánica, Universidad Autónoma Agraria "Antonio Narro," Buenavista, Saltillo, Coahuila, Mexico.
APCR RUSSELLVILLE: Herbarium, School of Physical and Life Sciences, Arkansas Tech University, Russellville, Arkansas 72801, U.S.A.
APIY YEREVAN: Herbarium, Department of Botany, Abovjan Pedagogical Institute, Khandzhyana St. 5, 375000 Yerevan, U.S.S.R.
APM WHITNEY: Herbarium, Algonquin Park Museum, Algonquin Provincial Park, Ministry of Natural Resources, Box 219, Whitney, Ontario, Canada K0J 2M0.
APSC CLARKSVILLE: Herbarium, Department of Biology, Austin Peay State University, Clarksville, Tennessee 37040, U.S.A.
AQC GRAND RAPIDS: Herbarium, Aquinas College, 1607 Robinson Road, Grand Rapids, Michigan 49506, U.S.A.
AQUI L'AQUILA: Herbarium Aquilanum, Istituto Botanico dell'Università, Piazza Annunziata 1, 67100 L'Aquila, Italy.
ARAGO BANYULS-SUR-MER: Laboratoire Arago de la Faculté des Sciences de Paris, Banyuls-sur-Mer, France.
ARC CINCO SALTOS: Herbario, Facultad de Ciencias Agrarias, Universidad Nacional del Comahue, Cátedra de Botánica, Casilla de Correo 60, 8303 Cinco Saltos, Río Negro, Argentina.
ARG FLORIANA: Herbarium, Argotti Botanic Garden, Floriana, Malta.
ARIZ TUCSON: Herbarium, University of Arizona, 113 Agricultural Sciences Building, Tucson, Arizona 85721, U.S.A.
ARM ARMAGH: County Museum, Armagh, Northern Ireland, Great Britain.*
ARS UMUDIKE: Agriculture Research Station, Umudike, Nigeria.**
AS ASUNCIÓN: Jardin Botánico, Asunción, Paraguay.
ASC FLAGSTAFF: Deaver Herbarium, Department of Biology, Box 5640, Northern Arizona University, Flagstaff, Arizona 86001, U.S.A.
ASE ARACAJU: Herbário, Departamento de Biologia, Universidade Federal de Sergipe, Rua Vila Cristina, 1051, 49.000 Aracaju, Sergipe, Brazil.
ASH ASHKHABAD: Herbarium, Botanical Institute of the Turkmenia Academy of Sciences, Laboratory of Flora and Systematics of Vascular Plants, Svobody Prospect 81, 744000 Ashkhabad, U.S.S.R.
ASM MANDALAY: Herbarium, Arts and Science University, Mandalay, Burma.
ASSAM SHILLONG: Botanical Survey of India, Eastern Circle, Shillong, India.
ASTC NACOGDOCHES: Herbarium, Department of Biology, Stephen F. Austin State University, P.O. Box 13003, Nacogdoches, Texas 75962, U.S.A.
ASU TEMPE: Herbarium, Department of Botany and Microbiology, Arizona State University, Tempe, Arizona 85281, U.S.A.
ASUF TEMPE: Herbarium, Rocky Mountain Forest and Range Experiment Station, Forest Sciences Laboratory, Arizona State University, Tempe, Arizona 85281, U.S.A.
ATA ERZURUM: Atatürk Üniversitesi Herbaryumu, Fen Fakültesi, Atatürk Üniversitesi, Erzurum, Turkey.
ATCC ROCKVILLE: Herbarium, American Type Culture Collection, 12301 Parklawn Drive, Rockville, Maryland 20852, U.S.A.
ATH ATHENS: Herbarium, The Goulandris Natural History Museum, 13 Levidou Str., Kifissia, Athens, Greece.
ATHU ATHENS: Botanical Museum and Herbarium, University of Athens, Panepistimiopolis, Athens 621, Greece.
AU XIAMEN: Herbarium, Xiamen University, Xiamen, Fujian, People's Republic of China.
AUA AUBURN: Herbarium, Department of Botany, Plant Pathology, and Microbiology, Auburn University, Auburn, Alabama 36849, U.S.A.

AUB	BERRIEN SPRINGS: Herbarium, Museum of Natural History, Biology Department, Andrews University, Berrien Springs, Michigan 49104, U.S.A.
AUBSN	NALCHIK: Herbarium, Kabargin-Balkarsk Section of the All-Union Botanical Society, Chernyshevskoya St. 173, 360017 Nalchik, U.S.S.R.
AUG	SIOUX FALLS: Herbarium, Biology Department, Augustana College, Sioux Falls, South Dakota 57197, U.S.A.
AUT	AUTUN: Herbarium, Société d'Histoire Naturelle et des Amis du Muséum d'Autun, 19 Rue Saint Antoine, 71400 Autun, France.
AV	AVIGNON: Herbarium, Museum Requien, 67 Rue Joseph-Vernet, 84000 Avignon, France.
AVU	AMSTERDAM: Department of Systematic Botany, Vrije Universiteit, De Boelelaan 1087, 1081 AV Amsterdam, Netherlands.
AWH	ANTWERPEN: Dr. Henri Van Heurck Museum, Royal Zoological Society of Antwerp, Koningin Astridplein 26, B-2000 Antwerpen, Belgium.
AWL	SAULT STE. MARIE: Herbarium, Abitibi Woodlands Laboratory, Abitibi Paper Company, Sault Ste. Marie, Ontario, Canada — transferred to Lakehead University, Thunder Bay, Ontario, Canada P7S 5E1.
AZ	PONTA DELGADA: Herbarium, Museu Distrital de Ponta Delgada, Ponta Delgada, Azores.
AZUS	AZUSA: Herbarium, Department of Biological Sciences, Citrus College, 18824 E. Foothill Blvd., Azusa, California 91702, U.S.A.
B	BERLIN: Botanischer Garten und Botanisches Museum Berlin-Dahlem, Königin-Luise-Strasse 6-8, D-1000 Berlin 33, Federal Republic of Germany, BRD.
BA	BUENOS AIRES: Herbario, Museo Argentino de Ciencias Naturales "Bernardino Rivadavia" e Instituto Nacional de Investigación de las Ciencias Naturales, Avenida Angel Gallardo 470, Casilla de Correo 10, Sucursal 5, 1405 Buenos Aires, Argentina.
BAA	BUENOS AIRES: Herbario "Gaspar Xuárez," Facultad de Agronomía, Universidad de Buenos Aires, Avenida San Martín 4453, 1417 Buenos Aires, Argentina.
BAB	CASTELAR: Herbario, Departamento de Botánico Agrícola, Instituto Nacional de Tecnología Agropecuaria, 1712 Castelar, Buenos Aires, Argentina.
BAC	BACUP: Museum of the Bacup Natural History Society, Bacup, England, Great Britain.*
BACP	BUENOS AIRES: Herbario, Centro de Estudios Farmacologicos y de Principios Naturales, Serrano 661, 1414 Buenos Aires, Argentina.
BAE	BASINGSTOKE: The Museum, Basingstoke, England, Great Britain.*
BAF	BUENOS AIRES: Herbario, Museo de Botánica y Farmacología Juan A. Domínguez, Junín 954, ler. Piso, 1113 Buenos Aires, Argentina.
BAFC	BUENOS AIRES: Herbario, Departamento de Ciencias Biológicas, Facultad de Ciencias Exactas y Naturales, Universidad de Buenos Aires, II Pabellón, 4th piso, Ciudad Universitaria (Núñez), 1428 Buenos Aires, Argentina.
BAG	BAGHDAD: National Herbarium of Iraq, Ministry of Agriculture and Agrarian Reform, Abu-Ghraib, Baghdad, Iraq.
BAH	SALVADOR: Herbário Antonio Nonata Marques, Empresa de Pesquisa Agropecuária da Bahia, Avenida Ademar de Barros 967, Ondina, 40.000 Salvador, Bahia, Brazil.
BAI	CASTELAR: Herbario, Bosques Argentina Investigación, Instituto Forestal Nacional, Correo Central 42, 1708 Moron, Castelar, Buenos Aires, Argentina.
BAJ	BUENOS AIRES: Herbario, Dirección de Mantenimiento y Preservación de la Flora, Instituto Municipal de Botánica, Parque Pte. Dr. Nicolás Avellaneda, Lacarra y Directorio, 1407 Buenos Aires, Argentina.
BAK	BAKU: Herbarium, Botanical Institute of the Academy of Sciences of Azerbaijan S.S.R., Potamdarskoye Avenue 40, 370073 Baku, U.S.S.R.
BAL	BALCARCE: Herbario, Estación Experimental Regional Agropecuaria, Instituto Nacional de Tecnologia Agropecuaria, Correo Central 276, 7620 Balcarce, Buenos Aires, Argentina.
BALT	BALTIMORE: Herbarium, Department of Biological Sciences, Towson State University, 8000 York Road, Baltimore, Maryland 21204, U.S.A.
BAMB	BAMBEY: Centre de Recherches Agronomiques, Bambey, Senegal.**
BAN	BANARAS: Herbarium, Department of Botany, Banaras Hindu University, Banaras 5, India.
BAR	BRIDGETOWN: The Barbados Herbarium, Department of Biology, University of the West Indies, Cave Hill Campus, P.O. Box 64, Bridgetown, Barbados.
BARC	BELTSVILLE: U.S. National Seed Herbarium, Plant Taxonomy Laboratory, Room 238, Building 001, BARC-West, Beltsville, Maryland 20705, U.S.A.
BARO	BARODA: Herbarium, University of Baroda, Baroda, India.

BAS	BASEL: Botanisches Institut der Universität, Schönbeinstrasse 6, CH-4056 Basel, Switzerland.
BASBG	BASEL: Basler Botanische Gesellschaft, Postfach 63, CH-4020 Basel, Switzerland.
BASSA	BASSANO DEL GRAPPA: Museo-Biblioteca-Archivio (Sezione Erbario), Via Museo, 12-36061 Bassano del Grappa (Vicenza), Italy.
BAT	BATLEY: Bagshaw Museum and Art Gallery, Batley, England, Great Britain.*
BATH	BATH: Bath Natural History Society, Bath, England, Great Britain.*
BATU	BATUMI: Herbarium, Botanical Garden of Batumi, Academy of Sciences of the Georgian S.S.R., Post Office Machindzauri, 384533 Batumi, U.S.S.R.
BAV	BRATISLAVA: Slovenska Akademie Vied, Biologicky Ustav –– see SAV.
BAY	BAYONNE: Muséum d'Histoire Naturelle de Bayonne, Rue Jacques Lafitte 7, Bayonne (Bas-Pyr.), France.
BAYLU	WACO: Herbarium, Department of Biology, Baylor University, Waco, Texas 76703, U.S.A.
BB	BAHÍA BLANCA: Herbario, Departamento Ciencias Agrarias, Universidad Nacional de Sur, Rondeau 29, 8000 Bahía Blanca, Buenos Aires, Argentina.
BBS	PARAMARIBO: National Herbarium of Suriname, Faculty of Natural Resources, University of Suriname, P.O. Box 9212, Paramaribo, Suriname.
BBSUK	CARDIFF: British Bryological Society, Department of Botany, National Museum of Wales, Cardiff CF1 3NP, Wales, Great Britain.
BC	BARCELONA: Institut Botánic de Barcelona, Av. dels Muntanyans, Parc de Montjuïc, Barcelona – 4, Catalonia, Spain.
BCC	BARCELONA: Departamento de Botánica, Facultad de Biologia, Universidad de Barcelona, Gran Via, 585 Barcelona 7, Spain.
BCF	BARCELONA: Departamento de Botánica, Facultad de Farmacia, Núcleo Universitario de Pedralbes Diagonal, s/n – Barcelona, Spain.
BCL	LEWISTON: Herbarium, Department of Biology, Bates College, Lewiston, Maine 04240, U.S.A.
BCW	LONDON: Department of Biology, Bedford College for Women, London, England, Great Britain.*
BDD	BRADFORD: Bradford Natural History & Microscopical Society, Bradford, England, Great Britain.*
BDI	DAVENPORT: Herbarium, Putnam Museum, 1717 West 12th Street, Davenport, Iowa 52804, U.S.A.
BDWR	BRIDGEWATER: Herbarium, Department of Biology, Bridgewater College, Bridgewater, Virginia 22812, U.S.A.
BED	BEDFORD: Bedford Natural History and Archaeological Society, Bedford, England, Great Britain.*
BEDF	BEDFORD: Concord Field Station Herbarium of the Museum of Comparative Zoology of Harvard University, Old Causeway Road, Bedford, Massachusetts 01730, U.S.A.
BEGO	DEGANYA ALEPH: Herbarium of "Beth Gordon," The A. D. Gordon Agriculture, Nature and Kinnereth Valley Study Institute, Deganya Aleph 15 120, D. N. Emeq Ha Yarden, Israel.
BEI	BEIRUT: Post Herbarium, Faculty of Agricultural Sciences, American University of Beirut, Beirut, Lebanon.
BEL	BELFAST: Herbarium, Ulster Museum, Botanic Gardens, Belfast BT9 5AB, Northern Ireland, Great Britain.
BELC	BELOIT: Herbarium, Biology Department, Beloit College, Beloit, Wisconsin 53511, U.S.A.
BENIN	COTONOU: Herbier National du Bénin, Université Nationale du Bénin, Campus Universitaire d'Abomey-Calavi, BP 526-Cotonou (R.P.B.), Bénin.
BEO	BEOGRAD: Botaničko odeljenje, Prirodnjački muzej (Botanical Department, Natural History Museum), Njegoševa 51, Yu-11000 Beograd, Yugoslavia.
BERN	BERN: Systematisch-Geobotanisches Institut der Universität Bern, Altenbergrain 21, CH-3013 Bern, Switzerland.
BEX	BEXHILL: The Museum, Bexhill, England, Great Britain.*
BFDL	LAUREL: Beltsville Forest Disease Laboratory, Forest Service, U.S. Department of Agriculture –– relocated at Madison (CFMR).
BFT	BELFAST: The Herbarium, Department of Botany, The Queen's University –– transferred to BEL.
BFY	BAYFORDBURY: John Innes Horticultural Institution, Bayfordbury, England, Great Britain.*
BG	BERGEN: Herbariet, Botanisk Institutt, Universitetet i Bergen, Postbox 12, N-5014 Bergen – Universitetet, Norway.
BGAAS	YEREVAN: Herbarium, Department of Flora and Vegetation, Botanical Garden of the Armenian Academy of Sciences, 375063 Yerevan, U.S.S.R.

BGSU	Bowling Green: Herbarium, Department of Biological Sciences, Bowling Green State University, Bowling Green, Ohio 43403, U.S.A.
BH	Ithaca: Liberty Hyde Bailey Hortorium, Cornell University, 467 Mann Library Building, Ithaca, New York 14853, U.S.A.
BHAV	Bhavnagar: Herbarium, Central Salt and Marine Chemicals Research Institute, Bhavnagar, 364 002, India.
BHCB	Belo Horizonte: Herbário, Departamento de Botânica, Instituto de Ciências Biológicas, Universidade Federal de Minas Gerais, Avenida Antônio Carlos 6627, 30.000 Belo Horizonte, Minas Gerais, Brazil.
BHD	Birkenhead: Williamson Art Gallery and Museum, Birkenhead, England, Great Britain.*
BHM	Birmingham: Birmingham Natural History and Philosophical Society, Birmingham, England, Great Britain.*
BHMG	Belo Horizonte: Instituto Agronômico, Belo Horizonte, Minas Gerais, Brazil ‒‒ incorporated in BHMH.
BHMH	Belo Horizonte: Herbário, Museu de História Natural, Universidade Federal de Minas Gerais, Rua Gustavo da Silveira, 1035 Horto, Caixa Postal 2475, 30.000 Belo Horizonte, Minas Gerais, Brazil.
BHO	Athens: Bartley Herbarium, Department of Botany, Ohio University, Athens, Ohio 45701, U.S.A.
BHSC	Spearfish: F. L. Bennett Herbarium, Division of Science and Mathematics, Black Hills State College, Spearfish, South Dakota 57783, U.S.A.
BHU	Berlin: Bereich Botanik und Arboretum des Museums für Naturkunde der Humboldt-Universität zu Berlin, Späthstrasse 80/81, DDR-1195 Berlin ‒ Baumschulenweg, German Democratic Republic, DDR.
BHUPP	Varanasi: Herbarium, Department of Mycology and Plant Pathology, Faculty of Agriculture, Banaras Hindu University, Varanasi ‒ 221005, India.
BI	Bari: Herbarium, Istituto di Botanica dell'Università, Via Amendola 175, 70126 Bari, Italy.
BIA	Ankara: Herbarium, British Institute of Archaeology, Tahran Caddesi 21, Kavaklidere, Ankara, Turkey.
BILAS	Vilnius: Flora and Geobotanical Sector, Botanical Institute of the Lithuanian Academy of Sciences, Turistu St. 47, 232021 Vilnius, U.S.S.R.
BIM	Birmingham: Birmingham Natural History and Microscopical Society, Birmingham, England, Great Britain.*
BING	Binghamton: Herbarium, Department of Biological Sciences, State University of New York, Binghamton, New York 13901, U.S.A.
BIRA	Birmingham: Herbarium, City of Birmingham Museum and Art Gallery, Chamberlain Square, Birmingham B3 3DH, England, Great Britain.
BIRM	Birmingham: Herbarium, Department of Botany, The University, Edgbaston, Birmingham B15 2TT, England, Great Britain.
BISH	Honolulu: Herbarium Pacificum, Department of Botany, Bernice P. Bishop Museum, P.O. Box 19000-A, Honolulu, Hawaii 96819, U.S.A.
BK	Bangkok: Botanical Section, Technical Division, Department of Agriculture, Bangkok, Thailand.
BKF	Bangkok: The Forest Herbarium, Royal Forest Department, Bangkok 9, Thailand.
BKL	Brooklyn: Herbarium, Brooklyn Botanic Garden, 1000 Washington Avenue, Brooklyn, New York 11225, U.S.A.
BLA	Porto Alegre: Herbário, Departamento de Pesquisa, Instituto de Pesquisas Zootécnicas "Francisco Osório," Rua Gonçalves Dias 570, 90.000 Porto Alegre, Rio Grande do Sul, Brazil.
BLAT	Bombay: Blatter Herbarium, St. Xavier's College, Bombay 400 001, India.
BLFU	Bloemfontein: Geo Potts Herbarium, Department of Botany, University of the Orange Free State, P.O. Box 339, Bloemfontein 9300, South Africa.
BLH	Bloomfield Hills: Billington Herbarium, Cranbrook Institute of Science, Box 801, Bloomfield Hills, Michigan 48013, U.S.A.
BLMLK	Lakeview: Herbarium, Bureau of Land Management, Box 151, 1000 South Ninth Street, Lakeview, Oregon 97630, U.S.A.
BLY	Barnsley: Museum of the Barnsley Naturalist and Scientific Society, Barnsley, England, Great Britain.*
BM	London: Herbarium, British Museum (Natural History), Cromwell Road, London SW7 5BD, England, Great Britain.
BMH	Bournemouth: Museum of the Bournemouth Natural Science Society, Bournemouth, England, Great Britain.*

BM-SL	LONDON: Sloane Herbarium -- *see* BM.
BNL	BONN: Bundesforschungsanstalt für Naturschutz und Landschaftsökologie, Konstantinstrasse 110, 5300 Bonn 2, Federal Republic of Germany, BRD.
BO	BOGOR: Herbarium Bogoriense, Jalan Raya Juanda 22-24, Bogor, Indonesia.
BOD	OXFORD: Bodleian Library, Oxford, England, Great Britain.*
BOG	BOGOTÁ: Herbario, Museo del Instituto de La Salle, Calle 11 No. 1-47, Apartado Aéreo 27389, Bogotá, Colombia.
BOIS	BOISE: Herbarium, Intermountain Forest and Range Experiment Station, 316 East Myrtle Street, Boise, Idaho 83706, U.S.A.
BOL	CAPE TOWN: Bolus Herbarium, University of Cape Town, Rondebosch, 7700 South Africa.
BOLO	BOLOGNA: Herbarium, Istituto Botanico dell'Università, Via Irnerio 42, Bologna, Italy.
BOLV	COCHABAMBA: Herbario Forestal Nacional "M. Cárdenas," Centro Desarrollo Forestal, Ministerio de A.A.C.C. Agropecuarias, Casilla Correo 895, Cochabamba, Bolivia.
BON	BOLTON: Museum and Art Gallery, Bolton, England, Great Britain.*
BONN	BONN: Botanisches Institut der Universität Bonn, Abt. für Morphologie und Systematik, Meckenheimer Allee 170, D-53 Bonn 1, Federal Republic of Germany, BRD.
BOON	BOONE: Herbarium, Department of Biology, Appalachian State University, Rankin Science Building, Boone, North Carolina 28608, U.S.A.
BOR	BOGNOR REGIS: The Museum, Bognor Regis, England, Great Britain.*
BORD	BORDEAUX: Herbier du Jardin Botanique, Terrasse du Jardin Public, Place Bardineau, 33000 - Bordeaux, France.
BOSC	BOSTON: Herbarium, Department of Biology, Boston State College, 625 Huntington Avenue, Boston, Massachusetts 02115, U.S.A.
BOSL	BO: Government School Herbarium, Bo, Sierra Leone, West Africa.**
BOTU	BOTUCATU: Herbário, Departamento de Botânica, Instituto Básico de Biologia Médica e Agrícola de Botucatu, Caixa Postal 526, 18.610 Botucatu, São Paulo, Brazil.
BP	BUDAPEST: Botanical Department of The Hungarian History Museum, Könyveskálmán Krt. 40, Pf. 22, H-1476 Budapest VIII, Hungary.
BPI	BELTSVILLE: U.S. National Fungus Collections, Building 011A, BARC-West, Beltsville, Maryland 20705, U.S.A.
BPL	BARNSTAPLE: North Devon Athenaeum, Barnstaple, England, Great Britain.*
BPS	SACRAMENTO: The Gilbert L. Stout Plant Disease Herbarium, Bureau of Plant Pathology, California Department of Agriculture --*see* CDA.
BPU	BUDAPEST: Herbarium, Institute of Plant Taxonomy and Ecology of the Eötvös L. University, 1088, Muzeum Körut 4A, Budapest, Hungary.
BR	MEISE: Herbarium, Jardin Botanique National de Belgique – Nationale Plantentuin van België, Domein van Bouchout, B-1860 Meise, Belgium.
BRA	BRATISLAVA: Slovenské nàrodné múzeum, 885 36 Vajanského nábr. 2, Bratislava, Czechoslovakia.
BRC	LONDON: Botanical Record Club, London, England, Great Britain.*
BRD	BRADFIELD: Bradfield College Scientific Society, Bradfield, England, Great Britain.*
BRE	BREST: Herbarium, Faculté des Sciences, Brest, France.
BREG	DORNBIRN: Herbarium, Vorarlberger Naturschau, Marktstrasse 33, A-6850 Dornbirn, Austria.
BREM	BREMEN: Herbarium, Übersee-Museum, Bahnhofsplatz 13, D-2800 Bremen 1, Federal Republic of Germany, BRD.
BRG	GEORGETOWN: Herbarium, Department of Biology, University of Guyana, Turkeyen, Greater Georgetown, Guyana.
BRGE	BRUXELLES: Laboratoire de Génétique des Plantes Supérieures, 1850 Chaussée de Wavre, Bruxelles 16, Belgium.
BRH	BELMOPAN: Herbarium, Forestry Department, Ministry of Natural Resources, Belmopan, Belize.
BRI	BRISBANE: Queensland Herbarium, Meiers Road, Indooroopilly, Queensland 4068, Australia.
BRIP	BRISBANE: Herbarium, Plant Pathology Branch, Department of Primary Industries, Meiers Road, Indooroopilly, Queensland 4068, Australia.
BRIST	BRISTOL: Herbarium, Department of Botany, University of Bristol, Woodland Road, Bristol BS8 1RL, England, Great Britain.
BRISTM	BRISTOL: Herbarium, City of Bristol Museum and Art Gallery, Queen's Road, Bristol BS8 1RL, England, Great Britain.
BRIU	BRISBANE: Herbarium of the University of Queensland, St. Lucia, Queensland 4067, Australia.
BRL	BRISTOL: City Library, Bristol, England, Great Britain.*

BRLU	Bruxelles: Laboratoire de Botanique Systématique et d'Ecologie, 28 Avenue Paul Heger, 1050 Bruxelles, Belgium.
BRN	Bruton: Sexey's Boy's School, Bruton, England, Great Britain.*
BRNM	Brno: Herbarium, Botanical Department of the Moravian Museum, Preslova 1, 60 200 Brno, Czechoslovakia.
BRNU	Brno: Herbarium, Institute of Plant Biology, University of J. E. Purkyně, Kotlářská 2, 611 37 Brno, Czechoslovakia.
BROC	Brockport: Herbarium, Department of Biological Sciences, State University of New York, College at Brockport, Brockport, New York 14420, U.S.A.
BRSL	See WRSL.
BRU	Providence: Herbarium, Division of Biological and Medical Sciences, Brown University, Waterman Street, Providence, Rhode Island 02912, U.S.A.
BRUN	Brunei: Herbarium, Office of the Conservator of Forests, Brunei, Brunei.
BRVU	Bruxelles: Laboratorium voor Algemene Plantkunde en Natuurbeheer, Pleinlaan 2, B-1050 Bruxelles, Belgium.
BRY	Provo: Herbarium, Room 375, Monte L. Bean Life Science Museum, Brigham Young University, Provo, Utah 84602, U.S.A.
BSA	Allahabad: Botanical Survey of India, Central Circle, 10 Chatham Lines, Allahabad – 211002, India.
BSB	Berlin: Institut für Systematische Botanik und Pflanzengeographie der Freien Universität Berlin, Altensteinstr. 6, 1000 Berlin 33 (Dahlem), Federal Republic of Germany, BRD.
BSCA	Borrego Springs: Herbarium, Anza-Borrego Desert State Park, Box 428, Borrego Springs, California 92004, U.S.A.
BSD	Dehra Dun: Botanical Survey of India, Northern Circle, Dehra Dun, India.
BSE	Bury St. Edmunds: Moyse's Hall Museum, Bury St. Edmunds, England, Great Britain.*
BSI	Pune: Botanical Survey of India, Western Circle, 7-Koregaon Road, Pune 411001, Maharashtra, India.
BSIP	Honiara: Forestry Division Herbarium, Ministry of Natural Resources, Honiara, Solomon Islands.
BSIS	Calcutta: Economic Herbarium, Industrial Section, Indian Museum, Botanical Survey of India, 1 Sudder Street, Calcutta –– 700016, India.
BSJO	Jodhpur: Herbarium, Botanical Survey of India, Arid Zone Circle, D-7 Shastri Nagar, Jodhpur – 342003, Rajasthan, India.
BSL	London: Botanical Society of London, London, England, Great Britain.*
BSN	Boston: Stuart K. Harris Herbarium, Biological Science Center, Boston University, 2 Cummington Street, Boston, Massachusetts 02215, U.S.A.
BST	Belfast: Belfast Naturalists' Field Club, Belfast, Northern Ireland, Great Britain.*
BSUH	Muncie: Herbarium, Department of Biology, Ball State University, Muncie, Indiana 47306, U.S.A.
BTH	Bath: Museum of the Bath Royal Literary and Scientific Institution, Bath, England, Great Britain.*
BTJW	Jackson: Herbarium, Bridger-Teton National Forest, P.O. Box 1888, Jackson, Wyoming 83001, U.S.A.
BTN	Brighton: County Borough Art Gallery and Museum, Brighton, England, Great Britain.*
BUA	Baghdad: Herbarium, College of Agriculture, University of Baghdad, Abu Ghraib, Baghdad, Iraq.
BUC	București: Herbarium, University of București, Soseaua Cotroceni 32, 76258 București, Romania.
BUCA	București: Herbarium, Institutul de Biologie "Tr. Săvulescu" al Academici R.P.R., Spl. Independentei 296, București 17, Romania.
BUCF	București: Herbarium, Institutul de Cercetari Forestière, Sos. Pipera 46, București, Romania.
BUCM	București: Institutul de Stiinte Biologice Herbarul Micologic, Spl. Independenţei 296, R-77748 București 17, Romania.
BUE	Baghdad: Herbarium, College of Education, University of Baghdad, Baghdad, Iraq.
BUEN	Buenos Aires: Herbario, Proteccion de la Naturaleza, Santa Fe 690, Buenos Aires, Argentina –– incorporated in BA.
BUF	Buffalo: Clinton Herbarium, Buffalo Museum of Science, Humboldt Parkway, Buffalo, New York 14211, U.S.A.
BUH	Baghdad: The University Herbarium, College of Science, Baghdad, Iraq.
BUL	Bulawayo: Herbarium, National Museum of Rhodesia, 8th Avenue, Bulawayo, Zimbabwe.

BULQ	LENNOXVILLE: Herbarium, Bishop's University, Johnson Science Building, Lennoxville, Québec, Canada J1M 1Z7.
BUNH	BAGHDAD: Iraq Natural History Research Centre and Museum, University of Baghdad, Bab Al-Muadham, Baghdad, Iraq.
BUNS	BUNSO-BOSUSO: Crops Research Institute, Bunso-Bosuso, Ghana.**
BUPL	LEWISBURG: Wayne E. Manning Herbarium, Department of Biology, Bucknell University, Lewisburg, Pennsylvania 17837, U.S.A.
BUS	CORAL GABLES: Buswell Herbarium, Department of Biology, University of Miami, P.O. Box 249118, Coral Gables, Florida 33124, U.S.A.
BUT	INDIANAPOLIS: Friesner Herbarium, Department of Botany, Butler University, Indianapolis, Indiana 46208, U.S.A.
B-W	BERLIN: Herbarium Willdenow — see B.
BZ	See BO.
BZF	BOGOR: Lembaga Pusat Penjelidikan Kehutanan (Forest Research Institute), Bogor, Indonesia.
C	COPENHAGEN: Botanical Museum and Herbarium, Gothersgade 130, DK-1123 Copenhagen K, Denmark.
CAFB	EDMONTON: Herbarium, Northern Forest Research Centre, Canadian Forestry Service, Environment Canada, 5320 122 Street, Edmonton, Alberta, Canada T6H 3S5.
CAG	CAGLIARI: Istituto Botanico della Università, Viale Fra Ignazio da Laconi 13, Cagliari, Sardinia, Italy.
CAH	SALISBURY: Herbarium, University of Zimbabwe, P.O. Box MP167, Salisbury, Zimbabwe.
CAHS	INDIANAPOLIS: Crispus Attucks High School, Indianapolis, Indiana 46200, U.S.A. — discontinued.
CAHUP	LOS BAÑOS: Herbarium, College of Agriculture, University of the Philippines, Los Baños, College, Laguna, Philippines.
CAI	CAIRO: Herbarium, Department of Botany, Faculty of Science, Cairo University, Giza, Cairo, Egypt.
CAIA	CAIRO: Herbarium, Department of Botany, Faculty of Science, A'in Shams University, Abbassia, Cairo, Egypt.
CAIH	CAIRO: Herbarium, The Desert Institute, Mataria, Cairo, Egypt.
CAIM	CAIRO: The Herbarium, Flora and Phytotaxonomy Researches, P.O. Box, Ministry of Agriculture, Dokki, Cairo, A.R., Egypt.
CAIRNS	CAIRNS: Flecker Herbarium, c/o North Queensland Naturalists' Club, P.O. Box 991, Cairns, Queensland, Australia 4870 — incorporated in QRS.
CAL	CALCUTTA: Central National Herbarium, Botanical Survey of India, P.O. Botanic Garden, Howrah – 711103, India.
CALP	LOS BAÑOS: Mycological Herbarium, University of the Philippines Museum of Natural History, Los Baños, College, Laguna, Philippines.
CAM	CAMBRIDGE: St. John's College, Cambridge, England, Great Britain.*
CAME	CAMERINO: Erbario dell'Istituto di Botanica dell'Università di Camerino, Via Pontoni 5, 62032 Camerino (Macerata), Italy.
CAN	OTTAWA: Vascular Plant Section, National Herbarium of Canada, Botany Division, National Museum of Natural Sciences, National Museums of Canada, Ottawa, Ontario, Canada K1A 0M8.
CANA	OTTAWA: Phycology Section, National Herbarium of Canada, Botany Division, National Museum of Natural Sciences, National Museums of Canada, Ottawa, Ontario, Canada K1A 0M8.
CANB	CANBERRA: Herbarium Australiense, P.O. Box 1600, Canberra City, A.C.T. 2601, Australia.
CANI	BUFFALO: Herbarium, Department of Biology, Canisius College, 2001 Main Street, Buffalo, New York 14208, U.S.A.
CANL	OTTAWA: Lichenology Section, National Herbarium of Canada, Botany Division, National Museum of Natural Sciences, National Museums of Canada, Ottawa, Ontario, Canada K1A 0M8.
CANM	OTTAWA: Bryophyte Section, National Herbarium of Canada, Botany Division, National Museum of Natural Sciences, National Museums of Canada, Ottawa, Ontario, Canada K1A 0M8.
CANT	GUANGZHOU: Herbarium, Department of Forestry, College of Agriculture of South China, Shek-p'ai, Guangzhou, Guangdong, People's Republic of China.
CANTY	CHRISTCHURCH: Canterbury Museum — incorporated in CHR.
CANU	CHRISTCHURCH: Herbarium, Botany Department, University of Christchurch, Private Bag, Christchurch, New Zealand.

CARL	NORTHFIELD: Herbarium, Biology Department, Carleton College, Olin Hall, Northfield, Minnesota 55057, U.S.A.
CART	KENOSHA: Herbarium, Department of Biology, Carthage College, 2001 Alford Drive, Kenosha, Wisconsin 53141, U.S.A.
CAS	SAN FRANCISCO: Herbarium, Department of Botany, California Academy of Sciences, Golden Gate Park, San Francisco, California 94118, U.S.A.
CAT	CATANIA: Istituto di Botanica, Orto Botanico, Università di Catania, Via Antonino Longo 19, Catania, Sicilia, Italy.
CATIE	TURRIALBA: Herbario, Centro Agronómico Tropical de Investigación y Enseñanza, Turrialba, Costa Rica -- on extended loan to CR and USJ.
CAUP	POPAYÁN: Herbario, Museo de Historia Natural, Universidad del Cauca, Apartado Aéreo 1113, Popayán, Cauca, Colombia.
CAVA	CARMEL VALLEY: Herbarium, Hastings Natural History Reservation, University of California, Star Route Box 80, Carmel Valley, California 93924, U.S.A.
CAY	CAYENNE: Herbier, Centre O.R.S.T.O.M., Route de Montabo, B.P. 165, 97301 Cayenne Cedex, French Guiana.
CB	ČESKÉ BUDĚJOVICE: Herbarium, Jihočeské Muzeum, Dukelská 1, 37000 České Budějovice, Czechoslovakia.
CBG	CANBERRA: Herbarium, National Botanic Gardens, Department of the Capital Territory, P.O. Box 158, Canberra City, A.C.T. 2601, Australia.
CBS	BAARN: Herbarium, Centraalbureau voor Schimmelcultures, Oosterstraat 1, P.O. Box 273, 3740 AG Baarn, Netherlands.
CCG	CAPE COAST: Department of Botany, University of Cape Coast, Cape Coast, Ghana.
CCO	OTTAWA: Herbarium, Department of Biology, Carleton University, Ottawa, Ontario, Canada K1S 5B6.
CCR	CHICHESTER: The Museum, Chichester, England, Great Britain.*
CDA	SACRAMENTO: Herbarium, California Department of Food and Agriculture, 1220 N Street, Sacramento, California 95814, U.S.A.
CDFN	SAINT JOHN'S: Herbarium, Newfoundland Forest Research Centre, Canadian Forestry Service, Box 6028, St. John's, Newfoundland, Canada A1C 5X8.
CDN	CROYDON: Whitgift School, Croydon, England, Great Britain.*
CDS	PUERTO AYORA: Herbario, Estación Cientifica Charles Darwin, Puerto Ayora, Isla Santa Cruz, Galápagos Islands, Ecuador. (Mailing address: Casilla 58-39, Guayaquil, Ecuador).
CEL	URBANA: Herbarium, Crop Evolution Laboratory, Department of Agronomy, University of Illinois, Urbana, Illinois 61801, U.S.A.
CEN	BRASÍLIA: Herbário, Centro Nacional de Recursos Genéticos, Empresa Brasileira de Pesquisa Agropecuária, CENARGEN/EMBRAPA, Avenida W-5 Norte Parque Rural, Caixa Postal 10.2372, 70.000 Brasília, Distrito Federal, Brazil.
CEPEC	ITABUNA: Herbário de Centro de Pesquisas do Cacau, CEPEC, Caixa Postal 7, 45.600 Itabuna, Bahia, Brazil.
CERN	CERNĂUTI: Botanical Institute of the University, Cernăuti (Czernowitz), Bessarabia, U.S.S.R.
CESJ	JUIZ DE FORA: Herbário, Centro de Ensino Superior de Juiz de Fora, Caixa Postal 668, 36.100 Juiz de Fora, Minas Gerais, Brazil.
CFB	EDMONTON: Mycological Herbarium, Northern Forest Research Centre, Canadian Forestry Service, 5320 122 Street, Edmonton, Alberta, Canada T6H 3S5.
CFMR	MADISON: Herbarium, Forest Products Laboratory, Center for Forest Mycology Research, P.O. Box 5130, Madison, Wisconsin 53705, U.S.A. (formerly at Laurel, Forest Disease Laboratory, BFDL).
CFN	CLIFTON: Clifton College Natural History Society, Clifton, England, Great Britain.*
CGE	CAMBRIDGE: Herbarium, Botany School, University of Cambridge, Downing Street, Cambridge CB2 3EA, England, Great Britain.
CGE-B	CAMBRIDGE: Herbarium Babington -- see CGE.
CGG	CAMBRIDGE: Herbarium, University Botanic Garden, 1 Brookside, Cambridge CB2 1JF, England, Great Britain.
CHAF	ALTA LOMA: Herbarium, Life Science Division, Chaffey College, 5885 Haven Avenue, Alta Loma, California 91701, U.S.A.
CHAM	CHAMICAL: Herbario de la Sub-estación Experimental Agropecuaria La Rioja, Instituto Nacional de Tecnologia Agropecuaria, Casilla de Correo 6, 5380 Chamical, La Rioja, Argentina.
CHAP	CHAPINGO: Herbario, Departamento de Bosques, Universidad Autónoma Chapingo, Apartado postal 37, Chapingo, México, Mexico.

CHAPA	CHAPINGO: Herbario-Hortorio, Rama de Botánica, Colegio de Postgraduados, Chapingo, México, Mexico.
CHARL	CHARLESTON: Herbarium, The Charleston Museum, 360 Meeting Street, Charleston, South Carolina 29403, U.S.A.
CHAS	CHARLESTON: Forest Service Herbarium, Southeastern Forest Experiment Station, Forestry Sciences Laboratory, 2730 Savannah Highway, Charleston, South Carolina 29407, U.S.A.
CHBG	CHRISTCHURCH: J. B. Armstrong Herbarium, Christchurch Botanic Gardens, Parks and Recreation Department, Christchurch City Council, P.O. Box 237, Christchurch, New Zealand.
CHE	CHERBOURG: Herbarium, Société Nationale des Sciences Naturelles et Mathématiques, 21 Rue Bonhomme, 50100 Cherbourg, France.
CHEB	CHEB: Herbarium, Oblastní vlastivědné muzeum Cheb, Náměstikrále Jiřího z Poděbrad č. 3, Cheb, Czechoslovakia.
CHER	CHERNOVZY: Herbarium, Department of Botany, Chernovzy University, Fedkovicka St. 11, 274022 Chernovzy, U.S.S.R.
CHI	CHICAGO: Herbarium, Department of Biological Sciences, University of Illinois at Chicago Circle, Box 4348, Chicago, Illinois 60680, U.S.A.
CHIP	TUXTLA GUTIÉRREZ: Herbario, Instituto de Historia Natural del Estado de Chiapas, Parque Francisco I. Madero, Apartado postal 6, Tuxtla Gutiérrez, Chiapas, Mexico.
CHIS	KISHINEV: Herbarium, Botanical Garden of the Academy of Sciences of the Moldavian S.S.R., 18 Lesnaja Street, 277018 Kishinev, U.S.S.R.
CHISA	KISHINEV: Herbarium, Faculty of Agriculture, Kishinev, U.S.S.R.
CHL	CHELTENHAM: Cheltenham Grammar School, Cheltenham, England, Great Britain.*
CHM	CHELTENHAM: Art Gallery and Museum, Cheltenham, England, Great Britain.*
CHOM	CHOMUTOV: Vlastivědné muzeum Chomutov, Náměsti 1. máje 1, Chomutov, Czechoslovakia.
CHR	CHRISTCHURCH: Botany Division, Department of Scientific and Industrial Research, Private Bag, Christchurch, New Zealand.
CHRB	NEW BRUNSWICK: Chrysler Herbarium, Department of Botany, Rutgers University, Nelson Biological Labs, Busch Campus, New Brunswick, New Jersey 08903, U.S.A.
CHRG	CHESTER: Grosvenor Museum, Chester, England, Great Britain.*
CHSC	CHICO: Herbarium, Department of Biological Sciences, California State University, Chico, California 95929, U.S.A.
CHT	CHELTENHAM: Cheltenham College, Cheltenham, England, Great Britain.*
CHUR	CHUR: Herbarium, Bündner Natur-Museum, Masanserstrasse 31, 7000 Chur, Switzerland.
CI	STANFORD: Herbarium, Department of Plant Biology, Carnegie Institution of Washington, 290 Panama Street, Stanford, California 94305, U.S.A. -- incorporated in DS.
CIC	CALDWELL: Harold M. Tucker Herbarium, College of Idaho, Caldwell, Idaho 83605, U.S.A.
CIMAP	LUCKNOW: Herbarium, Central Institute of Medicinal and Aromatic Plants, Faridinagar (near Kukrail Picnic Spot), Lucknow 226010, India.
CINC	CINCINNATI: Herbarium, Department of Biological Sciences, University of Cincinnati, Cincinnati, Ohio 45221, U.S.A.
CIR	CIRENCESTER: Royal Agricultural College, Cirencester, England, Great Britain.*
CITA	CHARLESTON: Herbarium, Biology Department, The Citadel, Charleston, South Carolina 29409, U.S.A.
CL	CLUJ-NAPOCA: Herbarium Universitatis Napocensis (Herbarul Universității), Str. Republicii nr. 42, 3400 Cluj-Napoca, Romania.
CLA	CLUJ-NAPOCA: Herbarium, Institutul Agronomic "Dr. Petru Groza," Str. Mănăștur 3, 3400 Cluj-Napoca, Romania.
CLCB	CLUJ-NAPOCA: Centrul de Cercetări Biologice, Laboratorul de ecologie, Str. Republicii 48, Cluj-Napoca, Romania.
CLD	CLEVELAND: Cleveland Literary and Philosophical Society, Cleveland, England, Great Britain.*
CLE	CARLISLE: Corporated Museum and Art Gallery, Carlisle, England, Great Britain.*
CLEMS	CLEMSON: Herbarium, Department of Botany, Clemson University, Clemson, South Carolina 29631, U.S.A.
CLF	CLERMONT-FERRAND: Herbier de l'Université de Clermont II, Laboratoire de Botanique, 4 Rue Ledru, 63038 Clermont-Ferrand Cedex, France.
CLI	CHATHAM: Literary Institute, Chatham, England, Great Britain.*
CLM	CLEVELAND: Herbarium, Cleveland Museum of Natural History, Wade Oval, University Circle, Cleveland, Ohio 44106, U.S.A.
CLP	LOS BAÑOS: Herbarium, Forest Products Research and Industries Development Commission, National Science Development Board, Los Baños, College, Laguna, Philippines.

CLR	COLCHESTER: The Museum, Colchester, England, Great Britain.*
CM	PITTSBURGH: Herbarium, Carnegie Museum of Natural History, 4400 Forbes Avenue, Pittsburgh, Pennsylvania 15213, U.S.A.
CMC	MOUNT PLEASANT: Herbarium, Department of Biology, Central Michigan University, Mount Pleasant, Michigan 48859, U.S.A.
CMM	BRADFORD: Herbarium, Bradford Art Galleries and Museums, Cartwright Hall, Lister Park, Bradford, West Yorkshire BD9 4N5, England, Great Britain.
CMY	CALCUTTA: Botany Department of R. G. Kar Medical College, Calcutta, India –– discontinued.
CN	CAEN: Laboratoire d'Algologie fondamentale et appliquée, 39 Rue Desmoueux, 14000 – Caen, France.
CNE	CAWTHORNE: The Museum, Cawthorne, England, Great Britain.*
CNM	CHELTENHAM: Cheltenham Naturalists' Association, Cheltenham, England, Great Britain.*
CO	CONCARNEAU: Herbier Crouan, College de France, Laboratoire de Biologie Marine, B.P. 11, F. 29181 Concarneau, France.
COCH	COCHABAMBA: Herbario, Departamento de Botánica, Universidad Mayor de San Simón, Cochabamba, Bolivia –– discontinued.
COCO	COLORADO SPRINGS: Herbarium, Department of Biology, Colorado College, Colorado Springs, Colorado 80903, U.S.A.
CODAGEM	METEPEC: Herbario, Comision Coordinadora para el Desarrollo Agricola y Ganadero del Estado de México, Conjunto CODAGEM, Metepec, México, Mexico.
COI	COIMBRA: Botanical Institute of the University of Coimbra, 3049 Coimbra, Portugal.
COL	BOGOTÁ: Herbario Nacional Colombiano, Instituto de Ciencias Naturales, Museo de Historia Natural, Universidad Nacional, Apartado 7495, Bogotá, Colombia.
COLG	COLUMBUS: Herbarium, Department of Science/Mathematics, Columbus College, Columbus, Georgia 31906, U.S.A.
COLO	BOULDER: Herbarium, University of Colorado Museum, Campus Box 218, Boulder, Colorado 80302, U.S.A.
COLOM	DENVER: Harbarium of Colorado State Museum, Denver, Colorado 80201, U.S.A. –– incorporated in COLO, CS, and KHD.
CON	CLIFTON: Bristol, Clifton and West of England Zoological Society's Gardens, Clifton, England, Great Britain.*
CONC	CONCEPCIÓN: Herbario, Departamento de Botánica, Instituto de Biología, Universidad de Concepción, Casilla 1367, Barrio Universitario, Concepción, Chile.
CONN	STORRS: George Safford Torrey Herbarium, Biological Sciences Group, University of Connecticut, Life Sciences U-43, Storrs, Connecticut 06268, U.S.A.
CORD	CÓRDOBA: Herbario, Museo Botánico, Facultad de Ciencias Exactas, Físicas y Naturales, Casilla de Correo 495, Avda. Vélez Sarsfield 299, 5000 Córdoba, Córdoba, Argentina.
COV	COVENTRY: Herbarium, Herbert Art Gallery and Museum, Jordan Well, Coventry CV1 5QP, Warwickshire, England, Great Britain.
CP	COPENHAGEN: Herbarium, Department of Plant Pathology, Thorvaldsensvej 40, Entrance no. 8, DK-1871 Copenhagen V, Denmark.
CPF	WINTERTON: The David Killick Herbarium, Cathedral Peak Forest Research Station, Private Bag Gewaagd, P.O. Winterton, Natal, South Africa.
CPH	STOCKTON: Herbarium, Department of Biological Sciences, University of the Pacific, Stockton, California 95211, U.S.A.
CPUN	CAJAMARCA: Herbario, Departamento de Biología, Sección de Botánica, Universidad Nacional Técnica de Cajamarca, Ciudad Universitaria, Apartado 16, Cajamarca, Peru.
CR	SAN JOSÉ: Herbario Nacional de Costa Rica, Museo Nacional, P.O. Box 749, San José, Costa Rica.
CRAF	CRAIOVA: Herbarium, Catedra de fitopatologie a Universităţii, Str. Libertăţii 15, Craiova, Romania.
CRAI	CRAIOVA: Herbarium, Botany Department, University of Craiova, Libertăţii 15, 1100 Craiova, Romania.
CRCA	LISBOA: Herbarium, Instituto Dos Cereais –– transferred to LISI.
CREG	GUADALAJARA: Herbario, Departamento de Pulpa y Papel, Centro Regional de Enseñanza Técnica Industrial de Guadalajara, Calle El Chaco 3223, Fraccionamiento Providencia, Apartado Postal 6-725, Guadalajara, Jalisco, Mexico.
CRK	CORK: Department of Botany of the University College, Cork, Ireland.*
CRO	CROWTHORNE: Wellington College Natural History Society Museum, Crowthorne, England, Great Britain.*

CRP	SAN CARLOS DE BARILOCHE: Herbario Centro Regional Patagonico EERA Bariloche, Instituto Nacional de Tecnología Agropecuaria, Casilla de Correo 277, 8400 San Carlos de Bariloche, Río Negro, Argentina.
CS	FORT COLLINS: Herbarium, Department of Botany, Colorado State University, Fort Collins, Colorado 80523, U.S.A.
CSAT	CÁRDENAS: Herbario, Departamento de Ecología, Colegio Superior de Agricultura Tropical, Apartado postal 24, Cárdenas, Tabasco, Mexico.
CSC	GUANTÁNAMO: Colegio del Sagrado Corazón, Guantánamo, Cuba –– incorporated in HAC.
CSCN	CHADRON: Herbarium, Department of Biology, Chadron State College, Science Building, Chadron, Nebraska 69337, U.S.A.
CSLA	LOS ANGELES: Herbarium, Department of Biology, California State University, Los Angeles, California 90032, U.S.A.
CSPU	POMONA: Herbarium, Botany Department, California State Polytechnic University, 3801 West Temple Avenue, Pomona, California 91711, U.S.A.
CSR	MAIKOP: Herbarium, Caucasus State Reserve, Sovetskaya St. 187, Krasnodarsk Region, 352700 Maikop, U.S.S.R.
CSU	EDMOND: Herbarium, Biology Department, Central State University, 100 North University Drive, Edmond, Oklahoma 73034, U.S.A.
CT	CAPE TOWN: Guthrie Herbarium, Department of Botany, University of Cape Town, Rondesbosch, 7700 South Africa.
CTES	CORRIENTES: Herbario, Instituto de Botánica del Nordeste, Sargento Cabral 2139, Casilla de Correo 209, 3400 Corrientes, Corrientes, Argentina.
CTESN	CORRIENTES: Herbarium Humboldtianum, Facultad de Ciencias Exactas y Naturales y Agrimensura, Universidad Nacional del Nordeste, Casilla 326, San Lorenzo 690, 3400 Corrientes, Corrientes, Argentina.
CTN	CAMPBELTOWN: Free Library and Museum, Campbeltown, Scotland, Great Britain.*
CU	ITHACA: Wiegand Herbarium, Cornell University, 467 Mann Library Building, Ithaca, New York 14853, U.S.A. –– incorporated in BH.
CUH	CALCUTTA: Herbarium, Department of Botany, Calcutta University, 35 Ballygunge Circular Road, Calcutta – 700019, India.
CUP	ITHACA: Plant Pathology Herbarium, Cornell University, Ithaca, New York 14853, U.S.A.
CUS	SHINGLETON: Herbarium, Department of Natural Resources, Cusino Wildlife Research Station, Shingleton, Michigan 49884, U.S.A.
CUVC	CALI: Herbario, Departamento de Biología, Universidad del Valle, Apartado Aéreo 2188, Cali, Valle, Colombia.
CUW	WORCESTER: Herbarium, Department of Biology, Clark University, Worcester, Massachusetts 01610, U.S.A.
CUZ	CUZCO: Herbario Vargas, Facultad de Ciencias, Universidad Nacional de San Antonio Abad del Cuzco, Avenida de la Cultura, Apartado 367, Cuzco, Peru.
CVCW	WISE: Herbarium, Biology Department, Clinch Valley College of the University of Virginia, Wise, Virginia 24293, U.S.A.
CVM	ČÁSLAV: Herbarium, Městské muzeum Čáslav, Čáslav, Czechoslovakia.
CVRD	LINHARES: Herbário, Companhia Vale do Rio Doce, Reserva Florestal da Cia. Vale do Rio Doce, Km 118 da BR 101 Norte, P.O. Box 91, 22.900 Linhares, Espírito Santo, Brazil.
CVRS	OUAGADOUGOU: Centre Vétérinaire, Ouagadougou, Ivory Coast.**
CW	CHARKOW: Herbarium of the Ukrainian Institute for Scientific Research of Socialist Agriculture, Chajkovskaja 4, Charkow, Ukraine, U.S.S.R.
CWB	CHARKOW: Charkowskij Botanitscheskij Sad, Klotschkowskaja 52, Charkow, U.S.S.R.
CWN	CASTLETOWN: Ramsey Library –– changed to RAM.*
CWU	CHARKOW: University Herbarium, Charkow, U.S.S.R.
CYP	NICOSIA: Cyprus Herbarium, Department of Agriculture, Nicosia, Cyprus.
DAKAR	DAKAR: Herbarium, Département de Biologie Végétale, Faculté des Sciences, Dakar, Senegal.
DAL	HALIFAX: Herbarium, Department of Biology, Dalhousie University, Halifax, Nova Scotia, Canada B3H 4J1.
DAO	OTTAWA: Vascular Plant Herbarium, Biosystematics Research Institute, Agriculture Canada, Central Experimental Farm, Ottawa, Ontario, Canada K1A 0C6.
DAOM	OTTAWA: National Mycological Herbarium, Biosystematics Research Institute, Agriculture Canada, Central Experimental Farm, Ottawa, Ontario, Canada K1A 0C6.
DAR	RYDALMERE: Biology Branch Herbarium, Biological and Chemical Research Institute, N.S.W.

	Department of Agriculture, Private Mailbag no. 10, Rydalmere, N.S.W. 2116, Australia.
DAS	REGINA: Herbarium, Agriculture Canada, Regina Research Station, Box 440, Regina, Saskatchewan, Canada S4P 3A2.
DAV	DAVIS: Herbarium, Department of Botany, University of California, Davis, California 95616, U.S.A.
DAVFP	VICTORIA: Herbarium, Pacific Forest Research Centre, Canadian Forestry Service, 506 W. Burnside Road, Victoria, British Columbia, Canada V8Z 1M5.
DAVH	DAVIS: Herbarium, Department of Environmental Horticulture, University of California, Davis, California 95616, U.S.A.
DBG	DENVER: Herbarium of Fungi, Denver Botanic Gardens, 909 York Street, Denver, Colorado 80206, U.S.A.
DBN	DUBLIN: Herbarium, National Botanic Gardens, Glasnevin, Dublin 9, Ireland.
DBY	DERBY: County Borough Museum and Art Gallery, Derby, England, Great Britain.*
DCR	DONCASTER: County Borough Art Gallery and Museum, Doncaster, England, Great Britain.*
DD	DEHRA DUN: Herbarium, Forest Research Institute and College, P.O. New Forest, Dehra Dun 248006, U.P. India.
DE	DEBRECEN: Herbarium, Botanical Institute of L. Kossuth University, Debrecen 4010, Hungary.
DECA	DECATUR: Herbarium, Department of Biology, Agnes Scott College, Room 100-A, Campbell Hall, Decatur, Georgia 30030, U.S.A.
DECV	VICTORIA: Herbarium, Douglas Ecological Consultants Ltd., 2049 Crescent Road, Victoria, British Columbia, Canada V8S 2G9.
DEE	DUNDEE: Central Museum and Fine Art Gallery, Dundee, Scotland, Great Britain.*
DEK	DEKALB: Herbarium, Department of Biological Sciences, Northern Illinois University, DeKalb, Illinois 60115, U.S.A.
DELS	NEWARK: Herbarium, Society of Natural History of Delaware, Department of Plant Science, University of Delaware, Newark, Delaware 19711, U.S.A. -- incorporated in DOV.
DELTA	PORTAGE LA PRAIRIE: Herbarium, Delta Waterfowl Research Station, R.R. 1, Portage la Prairie, Manitoba, Canada R1N 3A1 -- incorporated in WINDM.
DEN	GRANVILLE: Herbarium, Biology Department, Denison University, Granville, Ohio 43023, U.S.A.
DENF	LAKEWOOD: Herbarium, Range and Wildlife Management, Rocky Mountain Region, U.S. Forest Service, P.O. Box 25127, 11177 West 8th Avenue, Lakewood, Colorado 80225, U.S.A.
DERM	MILFORD: Herbarium, Desert Experimental Range, Intermountain Experiment Station, Milford, Utah 84751, U.S.A.
DES	PHOENIX: Herbarium, Desert Botanical Garden, Papago Park, P.O. Box 5415, Phoenix, Arizona 85010, U.S.A.
DFS	DUMFRIES: Dumfries and Galloway Natural History and Antiquarian Society, Scotland, Great Britain.*
DGS	DOUGLAS: Manx Museum, Douglas, Isle of Man, Great Britain.*
DH	GENEVA: Herbarium, Department of Biology, Hobart & William Smith Colleges, Geneva, New York 14456, U.S.A.
DHL	LOUISVILLE: Davies Herbarium, Department of Biology, University of Louisville, Louisville, Kentucky 40208, U.S.A.
DHM	DURHAM: Herbarium, Department of Botany, University of Durham, South Road, Durham, England, Great Britain.
DI	DIJON: Laboratoire de Botanique, Faculté des Sciences de la Vie et de l'Environnement, Bâtiment Mirande, 6 Bd Gabriel, F 21.000 Dijon, France.
DIA	DUNDO: Herbarium, Museu do Dundo, Dundo, Lunda District, Angola.
DIN	DINARD: Laboratoire Maritime du Muséum National d'Histoire Naturelle, 17 Avenue George V, Dinard (Ille-et-Vilaine), France.
DISKO	DISKO: Danish Arctic Station, Disko, 3953 Godhavn, Greenland.
DKG	DORKING: Field Studies Council, Juniper Hall Field Center, Dorking, England, Great Britain.*
DLF	DELAND: Herbarium, Department of Biology, Stetson University, DeLand, Florida 32720, U.S.A.
DLY	DUDLEY: Dudley and Midland Geological and Scientific Society and Field Club, Dudley, England, Great Britain.*
DMNH	DAYTON: Herbarium, Dayton Museum of Natural History, 2629 Ridge Avenue, Dayton, Ohio 45415, U.S.A.
DMU	DARBHANGA: Herbarium, Department of Botany, Mithila University, Darbhanga 846004, India.

DNA	DARWIN: Herbarium of the Northern Territory, Division of Agriculture and Stock, Department of Primary Production, P.O. Box 5160, Darwin, N.T. 5794, Australia.
DO	DOUAI: Société Nationale d'Agriculture, Sciences et Arts, Douai, France.
DOMO	DOMODOSSOLA: Herbarium, Collegio Romini, Domodossola, Italy.
DOR	DORCHESTER: Dorset Natural History and Archeological Society, Dorchester, England, Great Britain.*
DORT	DORTMUND: Herbarium dendrologicum tremoniense, Botanischer Garten Rombergpark der Stadt Dortmund, Am Rombergpark 49, D-46 Dortmund 50, Federal Republic of Germany, BRD.
DOV	DOVER: Claude E. Phillips Herbarium, Department of Agriculture and Natural Resources, Delaware State College, Dover, Delaware 19901, U.S.A.
DPU	GREENCASTLE: Truman G. Yuncker Herbarium, Department of Botany and Bacteriology, De-Pauw University, 7 Harrison Hall, Greencastle, Indiana 46135, U.S.A.
DR	DRESDEN: Herbarium des Botanischen Gartens der Technischen Universität Dresden, Stübel-allee 2, DDR-8019 Dresden, German Democratic Republic, DDR.
DS	SAN FRANCISCO: Dudley Herbarium of Stanford University, Department of Botany, California Academy of Sciences, Golden Gate Park, San Francisco, California 94118, U.S.A.
DSC	CLEVELAND: Herbarium, Department of Biological Sciences, Delta State University, P.O. Box 3262, Cleveland, Mississippi 38733, U.S.A.
DSM	DAR ES SALAAM: Herbarium, Botany Department, University of Dar es Salaam, Dar es Salaam, Tanzania.
DSU	DNEPROPETROVSK: Herbarium, Department of Botany, Dnepropetrovsk State University, Ga-garina Prospect 72, 320625 Dnepropetrovsk, U.S.S.R.
DSY	DEWSBURY: County Borough Museum, Dewsbury, England, Great Britain.*
DUB	DUBLIN: National Botanic Gardens — see DBN.
DUE	DUNDEE: Department of Botany, Quen's College, Dundee, Scotland, Great Britain.*
DUF	DIYARBAKIR: Diyarbakir Üniversitesi Herbaryumu, Diyarbakir Üniversitesi, Fen Fakültesi, Botanik Bölümü, Diyarbakir, Turkey.
DUH	NEW DELHI: Herbarium, Department of Botany, University of Delhi, New Delhi 7, India.
DUIS	DUISBURG: Fach Botanik, Gesamthochschule Duisburg, Fachbereich 6, Lotharstrasse 65, Post-fach 101629, D 4100 Duisburg 1, Federal Republic of Germany, BRD.
DUKE	DURHAM: Herbarium, Department of Botany, Duke University, Durham, North Carolina 27706, U.S.A.
DUL	DULUTH: Olga Lakela Herbarium, Department of Biology, University of Minnesota, Duluth, Minnesota 55812, U.S.A.
DUR	DURANT: Herbarium, Department of Biology, Southeastern Oklahoma State University, Du-rant, Oklahoma 74701, U.S.A.
DURH	DURHAM: Department of Botany, University, Durham, England, Great Britain.*
DUSS	DÜSSELDORF: Botanisches Institut der Universität, Universitätstrasse 1, 4000 Düsseldorf 1, Federal Republic of Germany, BRD.
DVM	PLEASANT HILL: Herbarium, Diablo Valley College Museum, 321 Golf Club Road, Pleasant Hill, California 94523, U.S.A.
DVR	DOVER: Corporation Museum, Dover, England, Great Britain.*
DWC	WEST CHESTER: Darlington Herbarium, Department of Biology, West Chester State College, West Chester, Pennsylvania 19380, U.S.A.
DZS	DEVIZES: Museum of the Wiltshire Archaeological and Natural History Society, Devizes, En-gland, Great Britain.*
E	EDINBURGH: Herbarium, Royal Botanic Garden, Inverleith Row, Edinburgh EH3 5LR, Scot-land, Great Britain.
EA	NAIROBI: East African Herbarium, Museum Hill, P.O. Box 45166, Nairobi, Kenya, East Africa.
EAA	TARTU: Herbarium of the Chair of Botany, Plant Physiology and Phytopathology, Estonian Agricultural Academy, 366 Mitskurini Street, Tartu, Estonian S.S.R., U.S.S.R.
EAC	FORTALEZA: Herbário Prisco Bezerra, Departamento de Biologia, Centro de Ciências, Uni-versidade Federal do Ceará, C.P.D-141, 60.000 Fortaleza, Ceará, Brazil.
EAN	AREIA: Herbário Jayme Coelho de Moraes, Centro de Ciências Agrárias, Universidade Federal da Paraíba, Campus III, 58.397 Areia, Paraíba, Brazil.
EAP	TEGUCIGALPA: Herbario Paul C. Standley, Escuela Agricola Panamericana, Apartado 93, Tegu-cigalpa, Honduras.
EAR	RICHMOND: Herbarium, Department of Biology, Earlham College, Richmond, Indiana 47374, U.S.A.

369

EBE	EASTBOURNE: The Museum, Eastbourne, England, Great Britain.*
EBH	EDINBURGH: Botanical Society of Edinburgh, Edinburgh, Scotland, Great Britain.*
EBUM	MORELIA: Herbario, Escuela de Biología, Universidad Michoacana de San Nicolás de Hidalgo, Edificio "L", Ciudad Universitaria, Santiago Tapia 403, Morelia, Michoacán, Mexico.
EBV	LUBUMBASHI: Laboratoire de Biologie générale et de Botanique –– incorporated in LSHI.
ECON	CAMBRIDGE: Economic Herbarium of Oakes Ames, Botanical Museum of Harvard University, Cambridge, Massachusetts 02138, U.S.A.
ECSC	ADA: Herbarium, Biology Department, East Central Oklahoma State University, Ada, Oklahoma 74820, U.S.A.
EDH	EDINBURGH: Plinian Society, Edinburgh, Scotland, Great Britain.*
EFC	CURITIBA: Herbário, Escola de Florestas, Caixa Postal 2959, 80.000 Curitiba, Paraná, Brazil.
EFH	ENUGU: Enugu Forest Herbarium, Forestry Commission, P.M.B. 1028, Enugu, Nigeria.
EGE	IZMIR: Botanik Bahçesi ve Herbaryum Merkezi, Ege University, Faculty of Science, Bornova-Izmir, Turkey.
EGH	EDINBURGH: University of Edinburgh, Edinburgh, Scotland, Great Britain.*
E-GL	EDINBURGH: Herbarium of Glasgow ––see E.
EGR	EGER: Herbarium, Department of Botany, Ho Si Minh Teacher's College, H-3301, Eger, pf. 43, Hungary.
EHCV	EMORY: Herbarium, Biology Department, Emory and Henry College, P.O. Drawer DDD, Emory, Virginia 24327, U.S.A.
EHH	DAMIEN: Ekman Herbarium, Département de l'Agriculture, des Ressources Naturelles et du Développement Rural, Service Recherche Agronomique, Damien, Port-au-Prince, Haiti (see Addenda).
EIF	SANTIAGO: Herbario, Departamento de Silvicultura, Facultad de Ciencias Forestales, Universidad de Chile, Casilla 9206, Santiago, Chile.
EIU	CHARLESTON: Stover Herbarium, Department of Botany, Eastern Illinois University, Charleston, Illinois 61920, U.S.A.
EKY	RICHMOND: Herbarium, Department of Biological Sciences, Eastern Kentucky University, Richmond, Kentucky 40475, U.S.A.
ELN	ELGIN: Elgin and Morayshire Literary and Scientific Association Museum, Elgin, Scotland, Great Britain.*
ELRG	ELLENSBURG: Herbarium, Biology Department, Central Washington University, Ellensburg, Washington 98926, U.S.A.
ELVE	ELVAS: Herbarium, Estação de Melhoramento de Plantas, Elvas, Portugal.
EM	OURO PRÊTO: Herbário, Escola de Minas, Universidade Federal de Ouro Prêto, Praça Tiradentes 20, 35.400 Ouro Prêto, Minas Gerais, Brazil.
EMC	YPSILANTI: Herbarium, Department of Biology, Eastern Michigan University, West Cross Street, Ypsilanti, Michigan 48197, U.S.A.
ENAG	MANAGUA: Herbario, Facultad de Ciencias Agropecuarias, Universidad Nacional Autonoma de Nicaragua, Km 12$^{1}/_{2}$ Carretera Norte, Managua, Nicaragua.
ENCB	MÉXICO: Herbario, Escuela Nacional de Ciencias Biológicas, Instituto Politécnico Nacional, Carpio y Plan de Ayala, Apartado postal 17-564, México 17, Distrito Federal, Mexico.
ENG	ENGLEFIELD GREEN: Department of Botany of Royal Holloway College, Englefield Green, England, Great Britain.*
ENT	ENTEBBE: Herbarium, Ministry of Agriculture, Forestry and Cooperatives, Forest Department, P.O. Box 31, Entebbe, Uganda.
EONJ	EAST ORANGE: Herbarium, Department of Biology, Upsala College, East Orange, New Jersey 07019, U.S.A.
EPHR	EPHRAIM: Herbarium, Snow College, Ephraim, Utah 84627, U.S.A.
EPM	EPSOM: Epsom College Museum, Epsom, England, Great Britain.*
ER	ERLANGEN: Botanisches Institut der Universität Erlangen, Schlossgarten 4, Erlangen, Federal Republic of Germany, BRD.
ERCB	YEREVAN: Phanerogamic Herbarium, Department of Botany, Yerevan State University, Tsharenz Street 8, Yerevan, 375025 U.S.S.R.
ERE	YEREVAN: Herbarium, Department of Plant Taxonomy and Geography, Botanical Institute of the Academy of Sciences of the Armenian S.S.R., Yerevan 63, 375063 U.S.S.R.
EREM	YEREVAN: Herbarium Mycologicum, Department of Dendrology, Botanical Institute of the Academy of the Armenian S.S.R., Yerevan 63, 375063 U.S.S.R.
ERH	ERITH: Borough Museum, Erith, England, Great Britain.*
ERHM	YEREVAN: Cryptogamic Herbarium, Department of Botany, Yerevan State University, Tsharenz

370

Street 8, Yerevan, 375024 U.S.S.R.

ERZ   LINDICH: Fürstin-Eugenie-Institut für Arzneipflanzenforschung, 745 Hechingen, Schloss Lindich, Federal Republic of Germany, BRD.

ESA   PIRACICABA: Herbário, Escola Superior de Agricultura "Luis de Queiroz," Departamento de Botânica, Universidade de São Paulo, Caixa Postal 9, 13.400 Piracicaba, São Paulo, Brazil.

ESAL   LAVRAS: Herbário, Departamento de Biologia, Escola Superior de Agricultura de Lavras, Caixa Postal 37, 37.200 Lavras, Minas Gerais, Brazil.

ESK   ETIMESGUT: Türkiye Seker Fabrikalari A. S. Seker Enstitüsü, (Institute for Agricultural and Technological Sugar Beet Research), Etimesgut, Ankara, Turkey.

ESN   NIAMEY: Herbier, Ecole des Sciences de Niamey, Laboratoire de Biologie Végétale, BP 91, Niamey, Niger.

ETH   ADDIS ABABA: Herbarium, Biology Department, Haile Selassie I University, P.O. Box 1176, Addis Ababa, Ethiopia.

ETN   ETON: Eton College Natural History Society Museum, Eton, England, Great Britain.*

ETST   COMMERCE: Herbarium, Biology Department, East Texas State University, Commerce, Texas 75428, U.S.A.

ETSU   JOHNSON CITY: Herbarium, Department of Biological Science, East Tennessee State University, Johnson City, Tennessee 37614, U.S.A.

EVMU   SCRANTON: Alfred Twining Herbarium, Everhart Museum, Nay Aug Park, Scranton, Pennsylvania 18510, U.S.A.

EXR   EXETER: Herbarium, Department of Biological Sciences, University of Exeter, Hatherly Biological Laboratories, Prince of Wales Road, Exeter EX4 4PS, England, Great Britain.

F   CHICAGO: John G. Searle Herbarium, Field Museum of Natural History, Roosevelt Road at Lake Shore Drive, Chicago, Illinois 60605, U.S.A.

FAIB   IBADAN: Federal Agricultural Department, Ibadan, Nigeria.**

FARM   FARMVILLE: Herbarium, Longwood College, Farmville, Virginia 23901, U.S.A.

FAU   BOCA RATON: Herbarium, Department of Biological Sciences, Florida Atlantic University, Boca Raton, Florida 33431, U.S.A.

FAUC   MANIZALES: Herbario, Facultad de Agronomía, Universidad de Caldas, Apartado Aéreo 275, Manizales, Caldas, Colombia.

FB   FREIBURG: Herbarium, Institut für Biologie II, Lehrstul für Botanik — incorporated in KR.

FBC   FREETOWN: Herbarium, Department of Botany, Fourah Bay College, University of Sierra Leone, Freetown, Sierra Leone, West Africa.

FCAB   NOVA FRIBURGO: Herbarium Friburgense Colégio Anchieta, Rua General Osório 180, 28.600 Nova Friburgo, Rio de Janeiro, Brazil.

FCME   MÉXICO: Herbario, Departamento de Biología, Facultad de México, Apartado postal 70-399, México 20, Distrito Federal, Mexico.

FCO   OVIEDO: Departamento de Botánica, Universidad de Oviedo, Facultad de Ciencias (Sección Biológicas), Jesus Arias de Velasco s/n, Oviedo, Spain.

FCU   FOOCHOW: Herbarium, Fukien Christian University, Foochow, Fukien, People's Republic of China.

FDG   GEORGETOWN: Herbarium, Guyana Forestry Commission, Water Street, Georgetown, Guyana.

FDLW   FOND DU LAC: Herbarium, Department of Biology, University of Wisconsin Center, Prairie Road, Fond du Lac, Wisconsin 54935, U.S.A.

FER   FERRARA: Istituto di Botanica Università, Corso Porta Mare 2, 44100 Ferrara, Italy.

FFB   FREDERICTON: Mycological Herbarium, Forest Insect and Disease Survey, Maritimes Forest Research Centre, College Hill, P.O. Box 4000, Fredericton, New Brunswick, Canada E3B 5P7.

FFR   FORFAR: Meffan Institute, Forfar, Scotland, Great Britain.*

FFS   STELLENBOSCH: Williams Herbarium, Faculty of Forestry, University of Stellenbosch, Stellenbosch 7600, South Africa.

FH   CAMBRIDGE: Farlow Reference Library and Herbarium of Cryptogamic Botany, Harvard University, 20 Divinity Avenue, Cambridge, Massachusetts 02138, U.S.A.

(FH)   (Formerly used for KUM)**

FHI   IBADAN: Forest Herbarium, Forestry Research Institute of Nigeria, P.M.B. 5054, Ibadan, Nigeria.

FHK   KENEMA: Kenema Forestry Herbarium, Forestry Research Office, c/o Divisional Forest Office, Bambawo via Kenema, Sierra Leone, West Africa.

FHKSC   HAYS: Elam Bartholomew Herbarium, Fort Hays State University, Hays, Kansas 67601, U.S.A.

FHL   FRIDAY HARBOR: Herbarium, Friday Harbor Laboratories, University of Washington, Friday

	Harbor, Washington 98250, U.S.A.
FHO	OXFORD: Forest Herbarium, Department of Forestry, University of Oxford, South Parks Road, Oxford OX1 3RA, England, Great Britain.
FI	FIRENZE: Herbarium Universitatis Florentinae, Museo Botanico, Via Giorgio La Pira 4, I-50121 Firenze, Italy.
FIAF	FIRENZE: Erbario dell'Istituto di Botanica della Facoltà di Agraria, Piazzale delle Cascine 18-50144, Firenze, Italy.
FI-B	FIRENZE: Herbarium Beccarianum —— see FI.
FI-M	FIRENZE: Herbarium Michelianum —— see FI.
FIPF	FIRENZE: Istituto di Patologia Forestale dell'Università, Piazzale delle Cascine 28, 50144 Firenze, Italy.
FIPIA	BANDUNG: Herbarium Bandungense, Department Biologi, Fakultas Matematika + Ilmu Pasti Alam, Institut Teknologi Bandung, Jl. Ganeca 10, Bandung, Indonesia.
FI-W	FIRENZE: Herbarium Webbianum —— see FI.
FKE	FOLKESTONE: Public Museum and Art Gallery, Folkestone, England, Great Britain.*
FLAS	GAINESVILLE: Herbarium, Department of Botany, University of Florida, Gainesville, Florida 32611, U.S.A.
FLOR	FLORIANÓPOLIS: Herbário do Hôrto Botânico, Departamento de Biologia, Universidade Federal de Santa Catarina, Campus Universitário, Trindade, Caixa Postal 476, 88.000 Florianópolis, Santa Catarina, Brazil.
FM	PEKING (Beijing): Fan Memorial Institute, Beijing, People's Republic of China.
FMC	LANCASTER: Herbarium, North Museum, Franklin and Marshall College, P.O. Box 3003, Lancaster, Pennsylvania 17604, U.S.A.
FMH	PLAINFIELD: Herbarium, Goddard College, Plainfield, Vermont 05667, U.S.A.
FNFR	RICHFIELD: Herbarium, Fishlake National Forest, P.O. Box 628, 170 North Main Street, Richfield, Utah 84701, U.S.A.
FNLO	LAKEVIEW: Herbarium, Fremont National Forest, 34 North D Street, P.O. Box 551, Lakeview, Oregon 97630, U.S.A.
FNM	LEEUWARDEN: Herbarium, Fries Natuurhistorisch Museum, Heerestraat 13, 8911 LC Leeuwarden, Netherlands.
FOR	FORSSA: Herbarium, Forssa Museum of Natural History, Vapaudenkatu 5 B 17, Forssa, Finland.
FPDB	MAYAGUEZ: Herbario, Ficoteca Puertorriqueña, Departamento de Ciencias Marinas, Universidad de Puerto Rico, Recinto Universitario de Mayaguez, Mayaguez, Puerto Rico 00708.
FPF	FORT COLLINS: Forest Pathology Herbarium, U.S. Forest Service, Rocky Mountain Forest and Range Experiment Station, 240 West Prospect Street, Fort Collins, Colorado 80526, U.S.A.
FPRL	AYLESBURY: Herbarium, Building Research Establishment, Princes Risborough Laboratory, Princes Risborough, Aylesbury, Buckinghamshire HP17 9PX, England, Great Britain.
FQH	FORT QU'APPELLE: Fort Qu'Appelle Herbarium, Central Avenue, P.O. Box 1043, Fort Qu'Appelle, Saskatchewan, Canada S0G 1S0.
FR	FRANKFURT: Forschungsinstitut und Naturmuseum Senckenberg, Senckenberg – Anlage 25, Frankfurt a. M., Federal Republic of Germany, BRD.
FRC	COIMBATORE: Herbarium, Forest Research Centre, R. S. Puram P. O., Coimbatore 641002, Tamil Nadu, India.
FRI	CANBERRA: Herbarium of the Division of Forest Research, CSIRO, Banks St., Yarralumla, Canberra, A.C.T. 2600, Australia.
FRS	FORRES: Falconers' Museum, Forres, Scotland, Great Britain.*
FRU	FRUNZE: Herbarium, Laboratory of Flora, Biological Institute of Academy of Sciences of Kirghiz S.S.R., XXII Partsezda St. 265, 720071 Frunze, U.S.S.R.
FSC	FRESNO: Fresno Herbarium, Department of Biology, California State University, Fresno, California 93740, U.S.A.
FSCL	LAKELAND: Herbarium, Biology Department, Florida Southern College, MacDonald and Johnson streets, Lakeland, Florida 33802, U.S.A.
FSLF	FLAGSTAFF: Herbarium, Forestry Sciences Laboratory, Rocky Mountain Forest and Range Experiment Station, Northern Arizona University, Flagstaff, Arizona 86001, U.S.A.
FSSR	ATLANTA: Range, Timber & Wildlife, Southern Region, U.S. Forest Service, 1720 Peachtree Road, N.W., Atlanta, Georgia 30309, U.S.A.
FSU	TALLAHASSEE: Herbarium, Department of Biological Science, Unit 1, Florida State University, Tallahassee, Florida 32306, U.S.A.
FT	FIRENZE: Erbario Tropicale di Firenze, Via Giorgio La Pira 4, I-50121 Firenze, Italy.

FTG	MIAMI: Herbarium, Fairchild Tropical Garden, 10901 Old Cutler Road, Miami, Florida 33156, U.S.A. (Herbarium location: 11035 Old Cutler Road).
FTU	ORLANDO: Herbarium, Department of Biological Sciences, University of Central Florida, Orlando, Florida 32816, U.S.A.
FU	FUKUOKA: Herbarium, Laboratory of Wood Science, Faculty of Agriculture, Kyushu University, 6-10-1 Hakozaki, Higashi-ku, Fukuoka 812, Japan.
FUGR	GREENVILLE: Ives Herbarium, Department of Biology, Furman University, Poinsett Highway, Greenville, South Carolina 29613, U.S.A.
FUS	SHANGHAI: Herbarium, Department of Biology, Fudan University, Shanghai, Kiangsu, People's Republic of China.
FW	FORT WORTH: Department of Biology, Texas Christian University, Fort Worth, Texas 76129, U.S.A. -- incorporated in FWM.
FWM	FORT WORTH: Herbarium, Fort Worth Museum of Science and History, 1501 Montgomery Street, Fort Worth, Texas 76107, U.S.A.
FWVA	FAIRMONT: Herbarium, Department of Biology, Fairmont State College, Locust Avenue, Fairmont, West Virginia 26554, U.S.A.
G	GENÈVE: Herbarium, Conservatoire et Jardin botaniques de la Ville de Genève, Case postale 60, CH-1292 Chambésy/GE, Switzerland.
GA	ATHENS: Herbarium, Botany Department, University of Georgia, Plant Sciences Building, Athens, Georgia 30602, U.S.A.
GAB	GABORONE: The National Herbarium, P.O. Box 114, Gaborone, Botswana.
GAES	EXPERIMENT: Georgia Agricultural Experiment Station -- incorporated in GA.
GALW	GALWAY: Herbarium, University College, Galway, Ireland.
GAM	ATHENS: Julian H. Miller Mycological Herbarium, Department of Plant Pathology, University of Georgia, Athens, Georgia 30602, U.S.A.
GAS	STATESBORO: Herbarium, Department of Biology, Box 8042, Georgia Southern College, Statesboro, Georgia 30460, U.S.A.
GAT	GATERSLEBEN: Herbarium, Zentralinstitut für Genetik und Kulturpflanzenforschung, Corrensstr. 3, DDR 4325 Gatersleben, Kreis Aschersleben, German Democratic Republic, DDR.
GAUBA	CANBERRA: Gauba Herbarium, Department of Botany, Faculty of Science, Australian National University, Canberra, A.C.T. 2600, Australia.
GAW	GLASGOW: Eastern Botanical Society of Glasgow, Scotland, Great Britain.*
GB	GÖTEBORG: Herbarium, Botanical Museum, Carl Skottsberg Gata 22, S-413 19 Göteborg, Sweden.
G-BOIS	GENÈVE: Herbier Boissier -- see G.
G-BU	GENÈVE: Herbier Burnat -- see G.
GBY	GRIMSBY: Art and Natural History Museum, Grimsby, England, Great Britain.*
GC	LEGON: Ghana Herbarium, Department of Botany, University of Ghana, Box 55, Legon, Ghana, West Africa.
GCM	LEGON: Ghana Mycological Herbarium, University College of Ghana, Legon, Ghana -- incorporated in GC.
GCNP	GRAND CANYON: Herbarium, Grand Canyon National Park, Box 129, Grand Canyon, Arizona 86023, U.S.A.
GDA	GRANADA: Facultad de Farmacia, Catedra de Botánica, c/ Rector Lopez Argüeta s/n, Granada, Spain.
G-DC	GENÈVE: Herbier De Candolle -- see G.
G-DEL	GENÈVE: Herbier Delessert --see G.
GDOR	GENOVA: Herbarium, Museo Civico di Storia Naturale "Giacomo Doria," Via Brigata Liguria 9, I-16121 Genova, Italy.
GE	GENOVA: Erbario dell'Istituto Botanico "Hanbury" e Orto Botanico dell'Università di Genova, Corso Dagali 1/C, 16136 Genova, Italy.
GENT	GENT: Herbarium van de Rijksuniversiteit, K.L. Ledeganckstraat 35, B 9000 Gent, Belgium.
GEO	ATLANTA: Herbarium, Biology Department, Emory University, Atlanta, Georgia 30322, U.S.A.
GESU	GENESEO: Herbarium, Biology Department, State University College, Geneseo, New York 14454, U.S.A.
GFC	GREAT FALLS: Herbarium, Department of Biology, College of Great Falls, 1301 20th Street South, Great Falls, Montana 59405, U.S.A.
GFND	GRAND FORKS: Herbarium, Biology Department, University of North Dakota, Starcher Hall, Grand Forks, North Dakota 58202, U.S.A.

GFW   GREIFSWALD: Herbarium, Sektion Biologie der Ernst-Moritz-Arndt-Universität Greifswald, Grimmer Strasse 88, DDR – 22 Greifswald, German Democratic Republic, DDR.

GGB   BOULDER: Herbarium, Gesneriad Gardens, 2945 Third Street, Boulder, Colorado 80302, U.S.A.

GGO   GLASGOW: Royal Technical College, Glasgow, Scotland, Great Britain.*

GGW   GLASGOW: Botanical Society of Glasgow, Scotland, Great Britain.*

GH   CAMBRIDGE: Gray Herbarium of Harvard University, 22 Divinity Avenue, Cambridge, Massachusetts 02138, U.S.A.

GJO   GRAZ: Abteilung für Botanik, Steiermärkisches Landesmuseum Joanneum, Raubergasse 10, A-8010 Graz, Styria, Austria.

GL   GLASGOW: Herbarium, Department of Botany, University of Glasgow, Glasgow G12 8QQ, Scotland, Great Britain.

GLAM   GLASGOW: Department of Natural History, Museum and Art Gallery, Kelvin Grove, Glasgow G3 8AG, Scotland, Great Britain.

GLEN   GLENNS: Herbarium, Middle Peninsula and Northern Neck Plant Classification Depository, Rappahannock Community College, South Campus, Glenns, Virginia 23149, U.S.A.

GLG   GLASGOW: Trinity College, Glasgow, Scotland, Great Britain.*

GLM   GÖRLITZ: Herbarium, Staatliches Museum für Naturkunde Görlitz, Forschungsstelle, Am Museum 1, DDR-8900 Görlitz, German Democratic Republic, DDR.

GLO   GLASGOW: Natural History Society of Glasgow, Glasgow, Scotland, Great Britain.*

GLR   GLOUCESTER: City Museum, Gloucester, England, Great Britain.*

GLW   GLASGOW: Andersonian Naturalists' Society, Glasgow, Scotland, Great Britain.*

GM   GOTTWALDOV: Herbarium, Oblastní Muzeum Jihovychodní Moravy, Lešná u Gottwaldova, 763 14 Gottwaldov, Czechoslovakia.

GMNP   ROCKY HARBOUR: Herbarium, Gros Morne National Park, Box 130, Rocky Harbour, Newfoundland, Canada A0K 4No.

GMS   PACIFIC GROVE: Gilbert M. Smith Herbarium, Hopkins Marine Station, Stanford University, Pacific Grove, California 93950, U.S.A.

GMUF   FAIRFAX: Herbarium, Biology Department, George Mason University, 4400 University Drive, Fairfax, Virginia 22030, U.S.A.

GO   GLASGOW: Glasgow Philosophical Society, Glasgow, Scotland, Great Britain.*

GOD   GODALMING: Charterhouse School Museum, Godalming, England, Great Britain.*

GOE   GOOLE: Goole Scientific Society, Goole, England, Great Britain.*

GOET   GÖTTINGEN: Systematisch-Geobotanisches Institut der Universität Göttingen, Untere Karspüle 2, D-3400 Göttingen, Federal Republic of Germany, BRD.

GOW   GLASGOW: Clydebank High School, Glasgow, Scotland, Great Britain.*

GPA   GRANDE PRAIRIE: Herbarium, Grande Prairie Regional College, Grande Prairie, Alberta, Canada.

G-PAE   GENÈVE: Herbier Aellen --see G.

GR   GRENOBLE: Laboratoire de Botanique et Biologie Végétale de l'Université Scientifique et Médicale, Domaine Universitaire, B.P. 53X, 38041 Grenoble Cedex, France.

GRA   GRAHAMSTOWN: Herbarium, Albany Museum, Botanical Research Unit, P.O. Box 101, Grahamstown, South Africa.

GRCH   HAMILTON: George R. Cooley Herbarium, Department of Biology, Colgate University, Hamilton, New York 13346, U.S.A.

GREE   GREELEY: Herbarium, Department of Biological Sciences, University of Northern Colorado, Ross Hall, Greeley, Colorado 80639, U.S.A.

GRI   GRINNELL: Herbarium, Biology Department, Grinnell College, Grinnell, Iowa 50112, U.S.A.

GRJC   GRAND RAPIDS: Herbarium, Department of Botany, Life Science Division, Grand Rapids Junior College, 143 Bostwick Avenue N.E., Grand Rapids, Michigan 49503, U.S.A.

GRK   GREENOCK: McLean Museum and Watt Institution, Greenock, Scotland, Great Britain.*

GRM   GRENOBLE: Herbarium, Muséum d'Histoire Naturelle, 1 Rue Dolomieu, 38000 Grenoble, France.

GRO   HAREN: Herbarium, Biological Centre, Department of Systematic Botany, Kerklaan 30, P.O. Box 14, Haren (Groningen), Netherlands.

GRS   WAD MEDANI: Herbarium, Agricultural Research Division, Gezira Research Station, Wad Medani, Sudan.

GSMNP   GATLINBURG: Herbarium, Uplands Field Research Lab, Great Smoky Mountains National Park, Gatlinburg, Tennessee 37738, U.S.A.

GSO   GLASGOW: Glasgow Society of Field Naturalists, Glasgow, Scotland, Great Britain.*

GUA   RIO DE JANEIRO: Herbário Alberto Castellanos, FEEMA, DECAM, Estrada da Vista Chinesa

741, Alto da Boa Vista, 20.531 Rio de Janeiro, Rio de Janeiro, Brazil.

GUADA	GUADALAJARA: Herbario, Escuela de Biología, Universidad Autonoma de Guadalajara, Lomas del Valle, Guadalajara, Jalisco, Mexico.
GUAM	MANGILAO: Herbarium, Department of Biology, University of Guam, UOG Station, Mangilao, Guam.
GUAT	GUATEMALA: Herbario "Ulises Rojas," Museo Nacional de Historia Natural, Apartado postal 987, Guatemala, Guatemala.
GUAY	GUAYAQUIL: Herbario, Facultad de Ciencias Naturales, Universidad Estatal de Guayaquil, Avenida 25 de Julio – El Guaamo, Apartado Aereo 471, Guayaquil, Ecuador.
GVSC	ALLENDALE: Herbarium, Department of Biology, Grand Valley State Colleges, Allendale, Michigan 49401, U.S.A.
GW	GLASGOW: West of Scotland Agricultural College, Glasgow, Scotland, Great Britain.*
GZU	GRAZ: Herbarium, Institut für Botanik, Halteigasse 6, A-8010 Graz, Austria.
H	HELSINKI: Herbarium, Botanical Museum, University of Helsinki, Unioninkatu 44, SF-00170 Helsinki 17, Finland.
HABA	HABANA: Herbario, Academia de Ciencias Médicas, Fisicas y Naturales de La Habana, Calle Cuba 460, Habana, Cuba –– incorporated in HAC.
HABAYC	BELTON: Herbarium, Department of Biology, University of Mary Hardin-Baylor, Belton, Texas 76513, U.S.A.
HABE	HABANA: Herbario, Instituto de Biología, Departamento de Ecologia Forestal, Academia de Ciencias de Cuba, Capitolio Nacional, Habana, Cuba.
HAC	HABANA: Herbario, Academia de Ciencias de Cuba, Instituto de Botánica, Calzada del Cerro 1257, Habana 6, Cuba.
H-ACH	HELSINKI: Acharius Herbarium –– see H.
HAJB	HABANA: Herbario, Jardín Botánico Nacional, Universidad de La Habana, Carretera del Rocío Km 3$^1/_2$, Calabazar, Habana, Cuba.
HAKS	HAKGALA: Herbarium, Hakgala Botanic Garden, Hakgala, Sri Lanka.
HAL	HALLE: Martin-Luther-Universität, Sektion Biowissenschaften, Wissenschaftsbereich Geobotanik und Botanischer Garten, Neuwerk 21, DDR-402 Halle (Saale), German Democratic Republic, DDR.
HALA	HUNTSVILLE: Herbarium, Department of Biology, University of Alabama, P.O. Box 1247, Huntsville, Alabama 35807, U.S.A.
HALLST	HALLSTATT: Botanische Station, Hallstatt, Austria –– discontinued.
HAM	HAMILTON: Herbarium, Royal Botanical Gardens, Box 399, Hamilton, Ontario, Canada L8N 3H8.
HAMAB	MACAPÁ: Herbário Amapaense, Museu Ângelo Moreira da Costa Lima, Avenida Feliciano Coelho 1509, Macapá, Amapá, Brazil.
HAMU	NEWCASTLE UPON TYNE: Natural History Society of Northumbria, Hancock Museum, Barras Bridge, Newcastle upon Tyne NE2 4PT, England, Great Britain.
HAN	HANNOVER: Herbarium, Institut für Vegetationskunde, Nienburgerstrasse 17, 3 Hannover, Federal Republic of Germany, BRD.
HAS	PORTO ALEGRE: Herbário "Prof. Dr. Alarich R. H. Schultz," Museu de Ciências Naturais da Fundação Zoobotânica do Rio Grande do Sul, Avenida Salvador França 1427, Caixa Postal Box 1188, 90.000 Porto Alegre, Rio Grande do Sul, Brazil.
HAVI	HARRISONBURG: Herbarium, Department of Biology, Eastern Mennonite College, Harrisonburg, Virginia 22801, U.S.A.
HAW	HONOLULU: Herbarium, Department of Botany, University of Hawaii, 3190 Maile Way, Honolulu, Hawaii 96822, U.S.A.
HAY	HAYWARD: Herbarium, Department of Biological Sciences, California State University, Hayward, California 94542, U.S.A.
HB	RIO DE JANEIRO: Herbarium Bradeanum, Caixa Postal 15.005, ZC-06 20.000 Rio de Janeiro, Rio de Janeiro, Brazil.
HBFH	FORT PIERCE: Herbarium, Harbor Branch Foundation, R.R. 1, Box 196, Fort Pierce, Florida 33450, U.S.A.
HBG	HAMBURG: Herbarium, Institut für Allgemeine Botanik und Botanischer Garten, Jungiusstrasse 6-8, D-2000 Hamburg 13, Federal Republic of Germany, BRD.
HBR	ITAJAÍ: Herbário "Barbosa Rodrigues," Avenida Marcos Konder 800, 88.300 Itajaí, Santa Catarina, Brazil.
H-BR	HELSINKI: Brotherus Herbarium –– see H.

HC	HANGZHOU: Herbarium, Hangchow Christian College, Hangzhou, Zhejiang, People's Republic of China.
HCEN	HUANCAYO: Herbario Huancayo, Universidad Nacional del Centro del Perú, Calle Real 160, Apartado 138, Huancayo, Peru.
HCHM	HOLLAND: Herbarium, Biology Department, Hope College, Holland, Michigan 49423, U.S.A.
HCIO	NEW DELHI: Herbarium Cryptogamiae Indiae Orientalis, Division of Mycology and Plant Pathology, Indian Agricultural Research Institute, New Delhi 110012, India.
HDD	HUDDERSFIELD: Tolson Memorial Museum, Huddersfield, England, Great Britain.*
HDSM	NORTH DARTMOUTH: Hellerman Diatom Herbarium, Department of Biology, Southeastern Massachusetts University, North Dartmouth, Massachusetts 02747, U.S.A.
HEID	HEIDELBERG: Institut für Systematische Botanik der Universität Heidelberg, Im Neuenheimer Feld 280, D-6900 Heidelberg, Federal Republic of Germany, BRD.
HEL	HELSINKI: Herbarium, Institute of General Botany, University of Helsinki, Viikki, 00710 Helsinki 71, Finland.
HERZU	MARACAIBO: Herbario Zulia, Facultad de Agronomía, Universidad del Zulia, Apartado 526, Maracaibo, Zulia, Venezuela.
HF	BELÉM: Faculdade de Farmacia, Universidade Federal de Pará, Avenida Generalissimo Deodoro 1562, 66.000 Belém, Pará, Brazil -- discontinued.
HFD	HEREFORD: City Library, Museum, Art Gallery and Old House, Hereford, England, Great Britain.*
HFR	HELSINKI: Herbarium, Finnish Forest Research Institute (Herbarium Instituti Forestalis Fenniae), Unioninkatu 40A, SF-00170 Helsinki 17, Finland.
HFV	VALDIVIA: Herbario, Instituto de Defensa de las Plantas, Facultad de Ciencias Agrarias, Universidad Austral de Chile, Casilla 567, Valdivia, Chile.
HFX	HALIFAX: Bankfield Museum, Halifax HX3 6HG, England, Great Britain.*
HGS	HASTINGS: County Borough Museum and Art Gallery, Hastings, England, Great Britain.*
HHBG	HANGZHOU: Herbarium, Hangzhou Botanic Garden, Hangzhou, Zhejiang, People's Republic of China.
HHC	HELSINKI: Institute of Horticulture, Viikki, 00710 Helsinki 71, Finland.
HHH	ONEONTA: Hoysradt Herbarium, Hartwick College, Oneonta, New York 13820, U.S.A.
HHM	HORSHAM: Collyer's School, Horsham, England, Great Britain.*
HHUA	HUÁNUCO: Herbario, Universidad Nacional de Huánuco "Hermilio Valdizán," Jirón Dos de Mayo 680, Huánuco, Peru.
HIB	WUHAN: Herbarium, Wuhan Institute of Botany, Academia Sinica, Wuhan, Hubei, People's Republic of China.
HIFP	PONDICHERRY: Herbarium, Institut Français, 10 Saint Louis Street, Pondicherry 605001, India.
HIMC	HUHEHOT: Herbarium, Department of Biology, University of Inner Mongolia, Huhehot, Inner Mongolia, People's Republic of China.
HIN	HITCHIN: Hitchin Priory, Hitchin, (Isle of Wight), England, Great Britain.*
HIP	PUNTA ARENAS: Herbario, Instituto de la Patagonia, Casilla 102-D, Punta Arenas, Magallanes, Chile.
HIRO	HIROSHIMA: Herbarium, Botanical Institute, Hiroshima University, Higashisenda-machi 1-1-89, Naka-ku, Hiroshima 730, Japan.
HITBC	MENGLA: Herbarium of Yunnan Institute of Tropical Botany, Academia Sinica, Mengla County, Yunnan, People's Republic of China.
HK	HONG KONG: Herbarium, Agriculture and Fisheries Department, 393 Canton Road, 14/F Kowloon, Hong Kong.
HL	HOUGHTON LAKE HEIGHTS: Herbarium, Department of Natural Resources, Houghton Lake Wildlife Research Station, Box 158, Houghton Lake Heights, Michigan 48630, U.S.A.
HLA	HONOLULU: Herbarium, Harold L. Lyon Arboretum, 3860 Manoa Road, Honolulu, Hawaii 96822, U.S.A.
HLL	HULL: Department of Natural Science and Municipal Technical College, Hull, England, Great Britain.*
HLM	HULL: Mechanics' Institute, Hull, England, Great Britain.*
HLO	HLOHOVEC: Herbarium, Okresné muzeum, Hlohovec, Czechoslovakia.
HLU	HULL: Department of Botany of University College, Hull, England, Great Britain.*
HLX	HALIFAX: Ovenden Naturalists' Society, Halifax, England, Great Britain.*
HME	HASLEMERE: Educational Museum, Haslemere, England, Great Britain.*
HNH	HANOVER: Jesup Herbarium, Department of Biological Sciences, Dartmouth College, Hanover, New Hampshire 03755, U.S.A.

HNMN	MANAGUA: Herbario Nacional de Nicaragua, Apartado 4271, Managua, D.N. Nicaragua.
HNT	SAN MARINO: Herbarium, Huntington Botanical Gardens, 1151 Oxford Road, San Marino, California 91108, U.S.A.
HNUB	BOSTON: Husky Herbarium, Department of Biology, Northeastern University, 360 Huntington Avenue, Boston, Massachusetts 02115, U.S.A.
HNWP	XINING: Herbarium, Northwest Plateau Institute of Biology, Academia Sinica, 57 Xiquan Street, Xining, Qinghai, People's Republic of China.
H-NYL	HELSINKI: Nylander Herbarium — see H.
HO	HOBART: Tasmanian Herbarium, University of Tasmania, G.P.O. Box 252 C, Hobart, Tasmania 7001, Australia.
HOH	STUTTGART-HOHENHEIM: Institut für Botanik, Garbenstrasse 30, 7000 Stuttgart 70 (Hohenheim), Federal Republic of Germany, BRD.
HOU	HOUSTON: Herbarium, University of Houston, Houston, Texas, U.S.A. — discontinued.
HPC	BROWNWOOD: Herbarium, Biology Department, Howard Payne University, Brownwood, Texas 76801, U.S.A.
HPD	HAMPSTEAD: Hampstead Scientific Society, Hampstead, England, Great Britain.*
HPH	ROCHESTER: Monroe County Parks Department Herbarium, 375 Westfall Road, Rochester, New York 14620, U.S.A.
HPM	HOUSTON: Herbarium, Museum of Natural History of Houston, P.O. Box 8175, 5555 Montrose Boulevard, Houston, Texas 77030, U.S.A.
HPP	HELSINKI: Herbarium, Department of Plant Pathology, University of Helsinki, Helsinki 71, Finland.
HR	HRADEC KRÁLOVÉ: Herbarium, Krajské muzeum Hradec Králové, Přírodovědné odděleni, Husovo nám. 124, Hradec Králové, Czechoslovakia.
HRB	SALVADOR: Herbário, Projeto RADAMBRASIL, Rua Pernambuco 4, Pituba, Salvador, Bahia, Brazil.
HRCB	RIO CLARO: Herbarium Rioclarense, Instituto de Biociências, Universidade Estadual Paulista "Julio de Mesquita Filho," Avenida 24-A, Caixa Postal 178, 13.500 Rio Claro, São Paulo, Brazil.
HSC	ARCATA: Herbarium, Department of Biology, Humboldt State University, Arcata, California 95521, U.S.A.
HSI	HELSINKI: Department of Silviculture Herbarium, Helsinki University, Unioninkatu 40B, SF-00170 Helsinki 17, Finland.
HSM	HORSHAM: Christ's Hospital Natural History Society, Horsham, England, Great Britain.*
HSNU	SHANGHAI: Herbarium, Department of Biology, East China Normal University, 3663 North Zhong Shang Road, 200062 Shanghai, People's Republic of China.
H-SOL	HELSINKI: Lindberg Herbarium —see H.
HSU	ABILENE: Herbarium, Department of Biology, Hardin-Simmons University, 2200 Hickory Street, Box N, HSU Station, Abilene, Texas 79698, U.S.A.
HTD	HERTFORD: Haileybury and Imperial Services, College Natural History Society, Hertford, England, Great Britain.*
HTE	HARROGATE: Queen Ethelburga's School, Harrogate, England, Great Britain.*
HTIN	TINGO MARÍA: Herbario Tingo María, Universidad Nacional de la Selva, Tingo María, Huánuco, Peru.
HTN	HITCHIN: Urban District Council Museum, Hitchin (Isle of Wight), England, Great Britain.*
HU	HANGZHOU: Herbarium, University of Zhejiang, Hangzhou, Zhejiang, People's Republic of China.
HUA	MEDELLÍN: Herbario, Departamento de Biología, Universidad de Antioquia, Apartado Aéreo 1226, Medellín, Antioquia, Colombia.
HUB	ANKARA: Herbarium, Department of Botany, Hacettepe University, Beytepe Campus, Ankara, Turkey.
HUBE	HUNTINGTON BEACH: Herbarium, Biology Department, Golden West College, 15744 Golden West Street, Huntington Beach, California 92647, U.S.A.
HUC	MONTERÍA: Herbario, Departamento de Biología, Universidad Nacional de Córdoba, Apartado Aéreo 354, Montería, Córdoba, Colombia.
HUEF	ANKARA: Hacettepe Üniversitesi Eczacilik Fakültesi Herbaryumu, Farmakognozi ve Farmasötik Botanik Bölümü, Hacettepe 1–M Ankara, Turkey.
HUJ	JERUSALEM: Herbarium, Department of Botany, The Hebrew University, Givath Ram, Jerusalem, Israel.
HUL	HULL: Hull Literary and Philosophical Society, Hull, England, Great Britain.*
HUMP	HUMPOLEC: Herbarium, Muzeum v Humpolci, okr. Havlíčkův, Brod, Humpolec, Czechoslovakia.

HUT   Trujillo: Herbarium Truxillense, Universidad Nacional de Trujillo, Calle San Martin 392, Trujillo, Peru.

HVR   Vila Real: Herbarium, Instituto Universitário de Tras-os-Montes e Alto Douro, Apart. 202, 5001 Vila Real Codex, Portugal.

HWB   Harrow: Butler Museum, Harrow, England, Great Britain.*

HWBA   Atchison: Herbarium, Biology Department, Benedictine College, North Campus, Atchison, Kansas 66002, U.S.A.

HWD   Hollinwood: Hollinwood Botanists' and Field Naturalists' Society, Hollinwood, England, Great Britain.*

HXBH   Belo Horizonte: Herbário e Xiloteca, Fundação Centro Tecnológico de Minas Gerais, Avenida José Cândido da Silveira, 2000 Horto, Caixa Postal 2306, Belo Horizonte, Minas Gerais, Brazil.

HY   Hyderabad: Herbarium and Botanical Museum, Osmania University, Hyderabad 7, India.

I   Iaşi: Herbarium, Facultatea de Biologie-Geografie-Geologie, Universitatea "Al I. Cuza," Strada 23 August nr. 11, Iaşi, 6600 Romania.

IA   Iowa City: Herbarium, Department of Botany, University of Iowa, Iowa City, Iowa 52242, U.S.A.

(IA)   (Formerly used for ABI)**

IAA   Buenos Aires: Dirección Nacional del Antártico, Cerrito 1248, Buenos Aires, Argentina -- discontinued.

IAC   Campinas: Phanerogamic Herbarium, Instituto Agronômico de Campinas, Avenida Barão de Itapura 1481, Caixa Postal 28, 13.100 Campinas, São Paulo, Brazil.

IACM   Campinas: Mycological Herbarium, Instituto Agronômico de Campinas, Avenida Barão de Itapura 1481, Caixa Postal 28, 13.100 Campinas, São Paulo, Brazil.

IAGB   Iaşi: Herbarium, Grădina botanică, Str. Dumbrava Roşie 9, Iaşi, Romania.

IAL   Cruz das Almas: Herbário, Centro Nacional de Pesquisa de Mandioca e Fruticultura, Empresa Brasileira de Pesquisa Agropecuária, Caixa Postal 007, 44.380 Cruz das Almas, Bahia, Brazil.

IAN   Belém: Herbário, Centro de Pesquisa Agropecuária do Trópico Úmido, EMBRAPA, Trav. Enéas Pinheiro, Caixa Postal 48, 66.000 Belém, Pará, Brazil.

IARI   New Delhi: Herbarium, Division of Plant Introduction, Indian Agricultural Research Institute, New Delhi 12, India.

IASI   Iaşi: Institutul Agronomic, Aleea Sadoveanu 3, 6600 – Iaşi, Romania.

IB   Innsbruck: Herbarium, Institut für Botanik der Universität Innsbruck, Sternwartestrasse 15, A-6020 Innsbruck, Austria.

IBE   Mississippi State: Herbarium, Institute for Botanical Exploration, Box EN, Mississippi State, Mississippi 39762, U.S.A.

IBF   Innsbruck: Herbarium, Tiroler Landesmuseum Ferdinandeum, Zeughaus, Zeughausgasse 1, A-6020 Innsbruck, Austria.

IBGE   Brasília: Herbário da Reserva Ecológa do Instituto Brasileiro de Geografia e Estatística, Edifício Venâncio II, 2° andar Reserva Ecológica do IBGE, 70.302 Brasília, Distrito Federal, Brazil.

IBI   São Paulo: Herbário, Seção de Micologia Fitopatológica, Instituto Biológico, Avenida Conselheiro Rodrigues Alves 1252, Caixa Postal 7119, 04014 São Paulo, São Paulo, Brazil.

IBIR   Iaşi: Herbarium "C. Sandu-Ville," Institutul Agronomic "Ion Ionescu de la Brad," M. Madoveaunu 3, 6600 Iaşi, Romania.

IBK   Guilin: Herbarium, Guangxi Institute of Botany, Yenshan, Guilin, Guangxi, People's Republic of China.

IBL   Kefar Malal: Herbarium, Independent Biological Laboratories, P.O.B. Ramatayin, Kefar Malal, Israel.

IBP   Curitiba: Instituto de Biologia do Paraná, Curitiba, Paraná, Brazil -- incorporated in herb. Hatschbach (private).

IBSC   Guangzhou: Herbarium, Botanical Institute, Academia Sinica, Guangzhou, Guangdong, People's Republic of China.

IBUG   Zapopan: Herbario, Instituto de Botánica, Universidad de Guadalajara, Apartado postal 139, Zapopan, Jalisco, Mexico.

IBY   Yenshan: Herbarium, Botanical Institute of Guangxi, Yenshan, Guangxi, People's Republic of China.

ICA   Bogotá: Herbario Fitopatológico Colombiano, Instituto Colombiano Agropecuario, Tibaitatá, Apartado Aéreo 151123, El Dorado, 6420 Bogotá, Colombia -- incorporated in COL.

ICEL	REYKJAVIK: Herbarium, Department of Botany, Museum of Natural History, P.O. Box 5320, 125 Reykjavik, Iceland.
ICF	COYOACAN: Instituto Nacional de Investigaciones Forestales, Coyoacan, México 21, D.F., Mexico — *see* INIF.
ICN	PORTO ALEGRE: Herbário, Departamento de Botânica, Universidade Federal do Rio Grande do Sul, Avenida Paulo Gama, 90.000 Porto Alegre, Rio Grande do Sul, Brazil.
ICP	PESHAWAR: Herbarium, Islamia College, Peshawar, Pakistan.
ICST	LONDON: Herbarium, Department of Botany and Plant Technology, Imperial College of Science and Technology, Prince Consort Road, London S.W. 7, England, Great Britain.
ID	MOSCOW: Herbarium, Department of Biological Sciences, University of Idaho, Moscow, Idaho 83843, U.S.A.
IDF	MOSCOW: Research Herbarium, Forest, Wildlife, and Range Experiment Station, College of Forestry, University of Idaho, Moscow, Idaho 83843, U.S.A.
IDS	POCATELLO: Ray J. Davis Herbarium, Idaho State University, P.O. Box 8096, Pocatello, Idaho 83209, U.S.A.
IEC	BRAZZAVILLE: Herbarium, Centre ORSTOM, B.P. 181, Brazzaville, People's Republic of Congo.
IFAN	DAKAR: Herbarium, Institut Fondamental d'Afrique Noire, B.P. 206, Dakar, Senegal.
IFE	ILE-IFE: Herbarium, Department of Botany, University of Ife, Ile-Ife, Nigeria.
IFGH	BOISE: Herbarium, Idaho Department of Fish and Game, 109 W. 44th Street, Boise, Idaho 83704, U.S.A.
IFGP	PLACERVILLE: Herbarium, Institute of Forest Genetics, Pacific Southwest Forest and Range Experiment Station, 2480 Carson Road, Placerville, California 95667, U.S.A.
(IFI)	(Formerly used for FHO)**
IFP	SHENYANG: Cryptogamic Herbarium, Institute of Forestry and Pedology, Academia Sinica, Culture Road, Shenke District, Shenyang, Liaoning, People's Republic of China.
IH	HABANA: Herbario, Instituto de Segunda Enseñanza de La Habana, Agramonte y San Martín, Habana, Cuba.
IJ	KINGSTON: Herbarium, The Institute of Jamaica, 12-14 East Street, Kingston, Jamaica.
ILCA	ADDIS ABABA: Herbarium, International Livestock Centre for Africa, P.O. Box 5689, Addis Ababa, Ethiopia.
ILF	ILFRACOME: The Museum, Ilfracome, England, Great Britain.*
ILH	MILFORD: Herbarium, Iowa Lakeside Laboratory, Milford, Iowa 51351, U.S.A.
ILL	URBANA: Herbarium, Department of Botany, University of Illinois at Urbana-Champaign, Urbana, Illinois 61801, U.S.A.
ILLS	URBANA: Herbarium, Illinois State Natural History Survey, 172 Natural Resources Building, Urbana, Illinois 61801, U.S.A.
IM	MATANZAS: Herbario, Instituto de Segunda, Enseñanza de Matanzas, Matanzas, Cuba — incorporated in HAC.
IMI	KEW: Herbarium, Commonwealth Mycological Institute, Ferry Lane, Kew, Richmond, Surrey TW9 3AF, England, Great Britain.
IMS	MOREHEAD CITY: Mycological Herbarium, Institute of Marine Sciences, University of North Carolina, Morehead City, North Carolina 28557, U.S.A.
INA	CALDAS DA SAÚDE: Instituto Nun'Alvres, 4780 Caldas da Saúde, Portugal.
IND	BLOOMINGTON: Herbarium, Department of Biology, Indiana University, Bloomington, Indiana 47401, U.S.A.
INFYB	BUENOS AIRES: Herbario, Instituto Nacional de Farmacología y Bromatología, Caseros 2161, 1264 Capital Federal, Buenos Aires, Argentina.
INIF	MÉXICO: Herbario, Instituto Nacional de Investigaciones Forestales, Secretaría de Agricultura y Ganadería, Progreso 5, Coyoacán, México 21, Distrito Federal, Mexico.
INPA	MANAUS: Herbário, Instituto Nacional de Pesquisas de Amazônia, Estrada do Aleixo 1756, Coroado, Caixa Postal 478, 69.000 Manaus, Amazonas, Brazil.
IPA	RECIFE: Herbário, Empresa Pernambucana de Pesquisa Agropecuária, Avenida General San Martin 1371, Caixa Postal 1022, Bonji, 50.000 Recife, Pernambuco, Brazil.
IPB	CURITIBA: Herbário, Instituto Paranaense de Botânica, Caixa Postal 1362, 80.000 Curitiba, Paraná, Brazil.
IPCN	SAN MARTÍN DE LOS ANDES: Herbario, Instituto Patagonico de Ciencias Naturales, Coronel Rohde 1351, Casilla Correo 7, San Martín de los Andes, Neuquén, Argentina.
IPMY	MARACAY: Herbarium, Instituto Universitario Pedagógico Experimental "Rafael Alberto Escobar Lara," Apartado 288, Maracay, Aragua, Venezuela.

IPS	IPSWICH: Ipswich Museum Herbarium, The Museum, High Street, Ipswich, Suffolk IP1 3QH, England, Great Britain.
IRAN	TEHRAN: Herbarium, Plant Pests and Diseases Research Institute, P.O. Box 3178, Tehran, Iran.
IRDA	DUBLIN: Department of Agriculture, Dublin, Ireland.**
IRK	IRKUTSK: Popov Herbarium, Physiological and Biochemical Institute of the Siberian Section of Academy of Sciences of U.S.S.R., Ab. Yashch. 1243, 664039 Irkutsk, U.S.S.R.
IRP	HOUGHTON: Isle Royale National Park, 87 North Ripley Street, Houghton, Michigan 49931, U.S.A.
IRSC	BRAZZAVILLE: Institut de Recherches Scientifiques au Congo — see IEC.
IRVC	IRVINE: Herbarium, Museum of Systematic Biology, School of Biological Sciences, University of California, Irvine, California 92664, U.S.A.
ISC	AMES: Herbarium, Department of Botany, Iowa State University, Ames, Iowa 50011, U.S.A.
ISIS	BAUTZEN: Herbarium, Arbeitsgemeinschaft Isis, Bautzen, Sachsen, German Democratic Republic, DDR — transferred to GLM.
ISL	ISLAMABAD: Herbarium, Quaid-l-Azam University, Islamabad, Pakistan.
ISM	SPRINGFIELD: Herbarium, Illinois State Museum, Spring and Edwards Streets, Springfield, Illinois 62706, U.S.A.
ISTC	CEDAR FALLS: Herbarium, Department of Biology, University of Northern Iowa, Cedar Falls, Iowa 50613, U.S.A.
ISTE	ISTANBUL: Istanbul Üniversitesi Eczacilik Fakültesi Herbaryum (Herbarium of the Faculty of Pharmacy of Istanbul University), Eczacilik Fakültesi Farmasötik Botanik Kürsüsü Üniversite, Istanbul, Turkey.
ISTF	ISTANBUL: Istanbul Üniversitesi Fen Fakültesi Herbaryum, Istanbul Üniversitesi, Botanik ve Genetik Kürsüsü, Süleymaniye – Istanbul, Turkey.
ISTO	ISTANBUL: Herbarium, Istanbul Üniversitesi Orman Fakültesi, Orman botanigi Kürsüsü, Büyükdere – Istanbul, Turkey.
ISU	NORMAL: Herbarium, Department of Biological Sciences, Illinois State University, Normal, Illinois 61761, U.S.A.
ITIC	SAN SALVADOR: Herbario, Departamento de Biología, Facultad de Ciencias y Humanidades, Universidad de El Salvador, San Salvador, El Salvador.
IUM	MORIOKA: Herbarium, Department of Biology, Faculty of Education, Iwate University, 18-33 Ueda 3-chome, Morioka 020, Japan.
IUP	INDIANA: Arthur G. Shields Herbarium, Biology Department, Indiana University of Pennsylvania, Indiana, Pennsylvania 15705, U.S.A.
IZ	IZMIR: Zirai Araştirma ve Introdüksiyon Merkezi (Agricultural Research and Introduction Center), Posta kutusu 25, Karşiyaka, Izmir, Turkey.
IZAC	CHAMICAL: Herbario, Instituto de Zonas Aridas, Universidad Provincial de La Rioja, San Martin 250, 5380 Chamical, La Rioja, Argentina.
IZEF	IZMIR: Herbaryumu, Eczacilik Fakültesi, Ege Üniversitesi, Farmasötik Botanik Kürsüsü, Inciralti-Izmir, Turkey.
J	JOHANNESBURG: Moss Herbarium, Department of Botany, University of the Witwatersrand, 1 Jan Smuts Avenue, Johannesburg 2001, Republic of South Africa.
JAC	JODHPUR: Herbarium, Department of Botany, University of Jodhpur, Jodhpur, India.
JAUM	MEDELLÍN: Herbario, Fundacion Jardin Botanico "Joaquin Antonio Uribe," Carrera 52 No. 73-298, Apartado Aéreo 51-407, Medellín, Antioquia, Colombia.
JAY	SAMOËNS: Herbarium, Laboratoire de la Jäysinia, 74340 Samoëns, France.
JBGP	CARTAGENA: Herbarium, Fundación Jardín Botánico "Guillermo Piñeres," Banco de la República, Cartagena, Colombia (see Addenda).
JBSD	SANTO DOMINGO: Herbarium, Jardín Botánico Nacional "Dr. Rafael M. Moscoso," Apartado 174-2, Avenida Botánica, Los Jardines, Santo Domingo, Dominican Republic.
JCB	BANGALORE: Herbarium, Centre for Taxonomic Studies, St. Joseph's College, P.B. 5031, Bangalore 560001, India.
JCT	TOWNSVILLE: Botany Department, James Cook University of North Queensland, Post Office 4811, Townsville, Queensland, Australia.
JE	JENA: Herbarium Haussknecht, Sektion Biologie der Friedrich-Schiller-Universität, Schlossgasse, DDR-69, Jena, German Democratic Republic, DDR.
JEF	NEW ALBANY: Herbarium, Indiana University Southeast, 4201 Grant Line Road, New Albany, Indiana 47150, U.S.A.
JEPS	BERKELEY: Jepson Herbarium and Library, Department of Botany, University of California,

	Berkeley, California 94720, U.S.A.
JEY	JERSEY: Victoria College (Boys' Grammar School), Jersey, Channel Islands, Great Britain.*
JF	STELLENBOSCH: Wicht Herbarium, Jonkershoek Forestry Research Station, Private Bag 5011, Stellenbosch 7600, South Africa.
JHWU	SPRINGFIELD: Jacobs Herbarium, Wittenberg University, Springfield, Ohio 45501, U.S.A.
JMUH	HARRISONBURG: Herbarium, Department of Biology, James Madison University, Burruss Hall Rm. 303, Harrisonburg, Virginia 22807, U.S.A.
JPB	JOÃO PESSOA: Herbário Lauro Pires Xavier, Departamento de Biologia, Centro de Ciências Exatas e da Natureza, Universidade Federal da Paraíba, Campus Universitário, 58.000 João Pessoa, Paraíba, Brazil.
JRY	JERSEY: Jersey Ladies' College, Jersey, Channel Islands, Great Britain.*
JSPC	JINAN: Herbarium, Department of Biology, University of Shandong, Jinan, Shandong, People's Republic of China.
JSY	JERSEY: Société Jersiaise Museum, Jersey, Channel Islands, Great Britain.*
JYV	JYVÄSKYLÄ: Natural Science Collections, University of Jyväskylä, SF-40100 Jyväskylä 10, Finland.

K	KEW: The Herbarium, Royal Botanic Gardens, Kew, Richmond, Surrey TW9 3AB, England, Great Britain.
KA	KAUNAS: Vytauto Didžiojo Universiteto Augalu Sistematikos Kabineta, Kaunas, Freda, Lithuania, U.S.S.R.
KABA	KABUL: Herbarium, University of Kabul, Kabul, Afghanistan.
KAG	KAGOSHIMA: Herbarium, Kagoshima University, Kagoshima, Japan.
KAMA	KAMAKURA: Herbarium, Biological Institute, Yokohama University, Kamakura, Kanagawa, Japan.
KANA	KANAZAWA: Herbarium, Faculty of Science, University of Kanazawa, 1-1 Marunouchi, Kanazawa 920, Ishikawa, Japan.
KANU	LAWRENCE: Herbarium, University of Kansas, 2045 Avenue A, Campus West, Lawrence, Kansas 66044, U.S.A.
KAR	TEHRAN: Herbarium, Faculty of Agriculture, University of Tehran, Kardj, Tehran, Iran.
KASH	SRINAGAR: Herbarium, Department of Botany, University of Kashmir, Srinagar – 190006, India.
KASSEL	KASSEL: Herbarium, Phytowissenschaftliche Abteilung, Naturkundemuseum im Ottoneum, Steinweg 2, BRD-3500 Kassel 1, Federal Republic of Germany, BRD.
KATH	LALITPUR: Botanical Survey and Herbarium Section, Godawary, Lalitpur, Nepal.
KATO	TRABZON: Karadeniz Teknik Üniversitesi Orman Fakültesi Herbaryumu, Karadeniz Teknik Üniversitesi, Orman Fakültesi, Orman Botaniği Kürsüsü, Trabzon, Turkey.
KAW	KAMPALA: Kawanda Herbarium, Kawanda Research Station, P.O. Box 7065, Kampala, Uganda.
KAZ	KAZAN: Herbarium, Department of Botany, Lenin University of Kazan, Lenin St. 18, 420008 Kazan, U.S.S.R.
KBAI	KRASNODAR: Herbarium, Department of Botany, Kubansk Agricultural Institute, Kalinina St. 13, 350044, Krasnodar, U.S.S.R.
KBRYO	DANVILLE: Bryophyte Herbarium, Centre College of Kentucky, Walnut Street, Danville, Kentucky 40422, U.S.A.
KBSMS	HICKORY CORNERS: Herbarium, Kellogg Biological Station, Michigan State University, 3700 East Gull Lake Drive, Hickory Corners, Michigan 49060, U.S.A.
KBT	KIRKCUDBRIGHT: Stewartry Museum, Kirkcudbright, Scotland, Great Britain.*
KCK	KILMARNOCK: Public Library and Museum, Kilmarnock, Scotland, Great Britain.*
KDR	KIDDERMINSTER: Borough Public Library, Museum and Art Gallery, Kidderminster, England, Great Britain.*
KE	KENT: Herbarium, Department of Biological Sciences, Kent State University, Kent, Ohio 44242, U.S.A.
KEN	KENNETT SQUARE: Longwood Gardens, Kennett Square, Pennsylvania 19348, U.S.A.
KEP	KEPONG: Forest Research Institute, Kepong, Selangor, Malaysia.
KESC	KEENE: Herbarium, Biology Department, Keene State College, 229 Main Street, Keene, New Hampshire 03431, U.S.A.
KEVO	UTSJOKI: The Kevo Subarctic Research Institute, University of Turku, SF-20500 Turku 50 (winter), SF-99980 Utsjoki (summer), Finland.
KFI	SEOUL: Hongnung Arboretum, Forest Research Institute, Chongyangni, Tongdaemun-ku, Seoul, Korea.

KFTA	LENINGRAD: Herbarium, Department of Botany and Dendrology, S. M. Kirov Forest Technology Academy, Institutskii Per. 5, 194018 Leningrad, U.S.S.R.
KGY	KEIGHELY: Borough Museum — *see* CMM.
KHD	DENVER: Kathryn Kalmbach Herbarium, Denver Botanic Gardens, 909 York Street, Denver, Colorado 80206, U.S.A.
KHF	KHARTOUM: Herbarium, Forest Research and Education Institute, Soba, Khartoum, Sudan.
KHMS	KAŠPERSKÉ HORY: Herbarium, Muzeum Šumavy, přírodovedĕcké pracov., Kašperské Hory, Czechoslovakia.
KHU	KHARTOUM: Herbarium, University of Khartoum, Khartoum, Sudan.
KIEL	KIEL: Botanisches Institut der Universität Kiel, Biologiezentrum Olshausenstrasse 40-60, D-2300 Kiel, Federal Republic of Germany, BRD.
KIRI	KINGSTON: Herbarium, Department of Botany, University of Rhode Island, Kingston, Rhode Island 02881, U.S.A.
KL	KLAGENFURT: Landesherbar, Landesmuseum für Kärten, Museumgasse 2, A-9010 Klagenfurt, Austria.
K-L	KEW: Lindley Herbarium — *see* K.
KLA	KUALA LUMPUR: Herbarium, Department of Agriculture, Swettenham Road, Kuala Lumpur, Malaysia.
KLE	KEELE: E. S. Edees Herbarium, Department of Biological Sciences, Unıversity of Keele, Keele, Staffordshire ST5 5BG, England, Great Britain.
KLN	KING'S LYNN: Herbarium, Museum and Art Gallery, King's Lynn, England, Great Britain — incorporated in NWH.
KLU	KUALA LUMPUR: Herbarium, Department of Botany, University of Malaya, Pantai Valley, Kuala Lumpur, Malaysia.
KM	VRCHLABI: Herbarium, Krkonošské muzeum Vrchlabi, Vrchlabi, okr. Trutnov, Czechoslovakia.
KMG	KIMBERLEY: Herbarium, Alexander McGregor Memorial Museum, P.O. Box 316, 2 Egerton Rd., Kimberley C.P. 8300, South Africa.
KNFY	YREKA: Herbarium, Klamath National Forest, 1312 Fairlane Road, Yreka, California 96097, U.S.A.
KNK	HIGHLAND HEIGHTS: Herbarium, Northern Kentucky University, Highland Heights, Kentucky 41076, U.S.A.
KNOX	GALESBURG: Herbarium, Department of Biology, Knox College, Galesburg, Illinois 61401, U.S.A.
KNP	SKUKUZA: Herbarium, Kruger National Park, Research Institute, Private Bag X402, Skukuza 1350, South Africa.
KO	KOŠICE: Katedra biológie Prírodovedeckej fakulty Univerzity P. J. Šafárika, Kuzmányho 12, Košice, Czechoslovakia.
KOR	KÓRNIK: Herbarium, Institute of Dendrology, ul. Parkowa 5, 62-035 Kórnik (near Poznán), Poland.
KPABG	KIROVSK: Herbarium, S. M. Kirov Polar-Alpine Botanical Garden, Kolsk Branch of U.S.S.R. Academy of Science, Laboratory of Flora and Plant Resources, Kirovsk, U.S.S.R.
KR	KARLSRUHE: Herbarium, Landessamlungen f. Naturkunde, Erbprinzenstrasse 13, D-7500 Karlsruhe 1, Federal Republic of Germany, BRD.
KRA	KRAKÓW: Herbarium Universitatis Jagellonicae Cracoviensis, ul. Lubicz, 31-512 Kraków, Poland.
KRAM	KRAKÓW: Herbarium of the Botanical Institute of the Polish Academy of Sciences, ul. Lubicz 46, 31-512, Kraków, Poland.
KRAS	KRASNOJARSK: Herbarium, Krasnojarsk Pedagogical Institute, Prospect Mira 83, 660607 Krasnojarsk, U.S.S.R.
KRG	KETTERING: Borough Public Library, Art Gallery and Museum, Kettering, England, Great Britain.*
KRS	KINROSS: Marshall Museum, Kinross, Scotland, Great Britain.*
KSC	MANHATTAN: Herbarium, Division of Biology, Kansas State University, Manhattan, Kansas 66506, U.S.A.
KSK	KESWICK: Fitzpark Museum, Keswick, England, Great Britain.*
KSO	KELSO: Tweedside Physical and Antiquarian Society Museum, Kelso, Scotland, Great Britain.*
KSP	PITTSBURG: Theodore M. Sperry Herbarium, Department of Biology, Pittsburg State University, 1701 S. Broadway, Pittsburg, Kansas 66762, U.S.A.
KSRV	VEDI: Herbarium, Khosrovsk State Reserve, State Bureau of Forestry of Armenia, 378210 Vedi, U.S.S.R.

KSTC	EMPORIA: Herbarium, Department of Biology, Emporia State University, Emporia, Kansas 66801, U.S.A.
KTU	KATOWICE: Herbarium, Department of Plant Systematics, Silesian University, Jagiellońska 28, 40-032 Katowice, Poland.
KU	WUZHOU: Herbarium, Guangxi University, Wuzhou, Guangsi, People's Republic of China.
KUH	KARACHI: Herbarium, Department of Botany, University of Karachi, Karachi – 32, Pakistan.
KUM	KUMASI: Forest Herbarium, Ministry of Forestry, Kumasi, Ghana.
KUN	KUNMING: Herbarium of Kunming Institute of Botany, Academia Sinica, Helongtan, Kunming, Yunnan, People's Republic of China.
KUO	KUOPIO: Herbarium, Department of Natural History, Kuopio Museum, Kuopio, Finland.
KUU	KUMASI: Herbarium, University of Science and Technology, Kumasi, Ghana.
KW	KIEV: N. G. Kholodny Institute of Botany of the Academy of Sciences of the Ukrainian S.S.R., Repin Street 2, Kiev 252601, U.S.S.R.
K-W	KEW: Wallich Herbarium –– see K.
K-WA	KEW: Watson Herbarium –– see K.
KWHA	KIEV: Herbarium, Central Republic Botanical Garden of the Ukrainian Academy of Sciences, Timiryazevskaya Street 1, Kiev 14, Ukraine 252014, U.S.S.R.
KY	LEXINGTON: Herbarium, Thomas Hunt Morgan School of Biological Sciences, University of Kentucky, Lexington, Kentucky 40506, U.S.A.
KYM	HELSINKI: Herbarium of Kymenlaakso, Botanical Museum, Unionink 44, SF-00170 Helsinki 17, Finland.
KYO	KYOTO: Kyoto: Herbarium, Department of Botany, faculty of Science, Kyoto University, Sakyo-ku, Kyoto 606, Japan.
L	LEIDEN: Rijksherbarium, Schelpenkade 6, 2313 ZT Leiden, Netherlands.
LA	LOS ANGELES: Herbarium, University of California, 405 Hilgard Avenue, Los Angeles, California 90024, U.S.A.
LAE	LAE: Herbarium, Division of Botany, Department of Forests, P.O. Box 314, Lae, Papua New Guinea.
LAF	LAFAYETTE: Herbarium, Department of Biology, University of Southwestern Louisiana, Lafayette, Louisiana 70504, U.S.A.
LAGO	LAGRANDE: Range and Wildlife Habitat Laboratory, Pacific Northwest Forest and Range Experiment Station, U.S. Forest Service, Route 2, Box 2315, LaGrande, Oregon 97850, U.S.A.
LAH	LAHORE: Herbarium, Panjab University, Lahore, Pakistan.
LAJC	LA JUNTA: Herbarium, Biology Department, Otero Junior College, La Junta, Colorado 81050, U.S.A.
LAM	LOS ANGELES: Natural History Museum of Los Angeles County, 900 Exposition Boulevard, Los Angeles, California 90007, U.S.A.
LAMCO	NIMBA: Liberia-American Minerals Company, Nimba Reserve Herbarium, Nimba, Liberia.**
LANC	LANCASTER: Lancaster University, Department of Biological Sciences, Lancaster LA1 4YQ, England, Great Britain.
LAPC	WOODLAND HILLS: Herbarium, Los Angeles Pierce College, 6201 Winnetka Avenue, Woodland Hills, California 91371, U.S.A.
LASCA	ARCADIA: Herbarium, Los Angeles State and County Arboretum, 301 North Baldwin Avenue, Arcadia, California 91006, U.S.A.
LAT	LATROBE: Herbarium, Department of Biology, Saint Vincent College, Latrobe, Pennsylvania 15650, U.S.A.
LATV	SALASPILS: Herbarium, Laboratory of Botany, Institute of Biology of the Academy of Sciences of the Latvian S.S.R., 3 Miera Street, Salaspils, U.S.S.R.
LAU	LAUSANNE: Herbarium, Musée botanique cantonal, Avenue de Cour 14 bis, CH-1007 Lausanne, Switzerland.
LBC	LOS BAÑOS: Herbarium, College of Forestry, University of the Philippines, Los Baños, College, Laguna, Philippines.
LBG	LUSHAN: Herbarium, Lushan Botanical Garden, P.O. Box 4, Lushan, Jiangxi, People's Republic of China.
LBL	LUBLIN: Department of Plant Systematics and Geography of the University, ul. Głowackiego 2, Lublin, Poland.
LBLC	LUBLIN: Cryptogamic Herbarium (Herbarium Muscorum), Institute of Biology, University of M. Curie-Skłodowska, ul. Akademicka 19, 20-033 Lublin, Poland.
LCDI	DECORAH: Herbarium, Department of Biology, Luther College, Decorah, Iowa 52101, U.S.A.

LCEU	EUGENE: Herbarium, Science Department, Lane Community College, 4000 East 30th Avenue, Eugene, Oregon 97405, U.S.A.
LCF	CASTELAR: Herbario, Departamento de Patología Vegetal, Instituto Nacional de Tecnología Agropecuaria, Correo Central 25, 1712 Castelar, Buenos Aires, Argentina.
LCH	LETCHWORTH: Urban District Council Museum and Art Gallery, Letchworth, England, Great Britain.*
LCN	LINCOLN: City and County Museum, Lincoln, England, Great Britain.*
LCO	MBALA: Herbarium, International Red Locust Control Organisation for Central and Southern Africa — incorporated in UZL.
LCS	ABERCORN: International Red Locust Control Service — see LCO.
LCU	WASHINGTON: Herbarium, Catholic University of America, Michigan Avenue, N.E., Washington, DC 20064, U.S.A.
LCVA	VERMILION: Herbarium, Department of Biology, Lakeland College, Vermilion Campus, Vermilion, Alberta, Canada ToB 4Mo.
LD	LUND: Botanical Museum, Ö. Vallgatan 18, S-223 61 Lund, Sweden.
LDS	LEEDS: University of Leeds, Department of Plant Sciences, Leeds, West Yorkshire LS2 9JT, England, Great Britain.
LE	LENINGRAD: Herbarium of the Department of Higher Plants, V. L. Komarov Botanical Institute of the Academy of Sciences of the U.S.S.R., Prof. Popov Street 2, 197022 Leningrad, U.S.S.R.
LEA	LETHBRIDGE: Herbarium, Department of Biological Sciences, University of Lethbridge, 4401 University Drive, Lethbridge, Alberta, Canada T1K 3M4.
LECB	LENINGRAD: Herbarium of the Cathedra Botanica, Leningrad University, V.O. Quay of University 7/9, 199164 Leningrad, U.S.S.R.
LEI	LEICESTER: Leicester Literary and Philosophical Society, Leicester, England, Great Britain.*
LEMA	LE MANS: Herbarium, Academie de Caen, Centre Universitaire du Mans, C.S.U., Route de Laval, Le Mans, France.
LENUD	MAKHACHKALA: Herbarium, Department of Botany, Lenin University of Dagestan, Dzerzhinskovo St. 12, 367025 Makhachkala, U.S.S.R.
LEP	LENINGRAD: The All-Union Institute for Plant Protection, Herzen Street 42, Leningrad, U.S.S.R. — see WIR.
LES	LEEDS: City Museum, Leeds, England, Great Britain.*
LET	LETCHWORTH: Letchworth Naturalists' Society, Letchworth, England, Great Britain.*
LEV	LEVIN: Plant Health and Diagnostic Station, Horticultural Research Centre, Kimberley Road, Levin, New Zealand.
LFCC	MIDDLETOWN: Herbarium, Department of Natural Resources, Lord Fairfax Community College, P.O. Box 47, Middletown, Virginia 22645, U.S.A.
LFG	GEMBLOUX: Herbarium, Laboratoire Forestier de l'Etat, Gembloux, Belgium.
LG	LIÈGE: Herbarium et Jardin Botanique de l'Université, Département de Botanique, Sart Tilman, B-4000 Liège, Belgium.
LGHF	LIÈGE [WAISMES-ROBERTVILLE]: Station Scientifique des Hautes Fagnes (Université de Liège), Mont Rigi, B-4898 Waismes-Robertville, Belgium.
LGO	PALISADES: Herbarium, Lamont-Doherty Geological Observatory of Columbia University, Palisades, New York 10964, U.S.A.
LHT	LAHTI: Herbarium of Lahden Luonnonystävät, Savonkatu 1 A 50, Lahti, Finland.
LI	LINZ: Botanische Abteilung am Oberösterreichischen Landesmuseum, Museumstrasse 14, A-4010 Linz, Austria.
LIB	MONROVIA: Harley Herbarium, College of Agriculture and Forestry, University of Liberia, Monrovia, Liberia.
LIG	LISBOA: Herbarium, Sociedade de Geografia de Lisboa, Portas de Santo Antão, Lisboa – 2, Portugal.
LIL	SAN MIGUEL DE TUCUMÁN: Herbario, Instituto Miguel Lillo de la Fundación Miguel Lillo, Calle Miguel Lillo 251, Casilla de Correo 91, 4000 San Miguel de Tucumán, Tucumán, Argentina.
LILLE	LILLE: Fédération Universitaire et Polytechnique (Association d'Ecoles Supérieures et de Facultés Catholiques), 60 Boulevard Vauban, 59046 Lille Cedex, France.
LIM	LIBEREC: Herbarium, Severočeské Museum, Leninova 11, 460 01 Liberec 1, Czechoslovakia.
LINN	LONDON: Herbarium, The Linnean Society of London, Burlington House, Piccadilly, London WIV OLQ, England, Great Britain.
LISC	LISBOA: Herbarium, Centro de Botânica da Junta de Investigações Científicas do Ultramar, Rua da Junqueira 86, P-1300 Lisboa, Portugal.
LISE	OEIRAS: Herbarium, Estação Agronómica Nacional, Oeiras, Portugal.

LISFA	Lisboa: Herbarium, Estação de Biologia Florestal, Avenida João Crisóstomo 26-28, Lisboa, Portugal.
LISI	Lisboa: Herbarium, Instituto Superior de Agronomia, Tapada da Ajuda, 1300 Lisboa, Portugal.
LISJC	Lisboa: Herbarium, Jardim e Museum Agrícola do Ultramar, Calçada do Galvão, 1400 Lisboa, Portugal.
LISM	Lisboa: Herbarium, Missão de Estudos Agronómicos do Ultramar, Lisboa, Portugal.
LISU	Lisboa: Museu, Laboratório e Jardim Botanico, Rua da Escola Politécnica, 1294 Lisboa, Portugal.
LISVA	Lisboa: Herbarium, Laboratório de Patologia Vegetal "Veríssimo de Almeida," Lisboa, Portugal.
LIT	Litoměřice: Herbarium, Okresní Museum Litoměřice, Míroné nam, 412 01 Litoměřice, Czechoslovakia.
LIV	Liverpool: Herbarium, Merseyside County Museum, William Brown Street, Liverpool L3 8EN, England, Great Britain.
LIVU	Liverpool: Herbarium, The Hartley Botanical Laboratories, Liverpool 3, England, Great Britain.
LJM	Ljubljana: Herbarium, Prirodoslovni Muzej Slovenije, Prešernova 20, p.p. 290, 61000 Ljubljana, Yugoslavia.
LJU	Ljubljana: Botanični Inštitut, Univerza v Ljubljana, Ljubljana, Yugoslavia.
LKHD	Thunder Bay: Claude E. Garton Herbarium, Department of Biology, Lakehead University, Thunder Bay, Ontario, Canada P7B 5E2.
LL	Renner: Lundell Herbarium, Texas Research Foundation, Renner, Texas 75079, U.S.A. -- deposited at TEX.
LLC	San Antonio: Herbarium, Our Lady of the Lake College, San Antonio, Texas 78285, U.S.A.
LLN	Lincoln: Lincolnshire Naturalists' Association, Lincoln, England, Great Britain.*
LLO	Cincinnati: Lloyd Library and Museum, 309 West Court Street, Cincinnati, Ohio 45221, U.S.A.
LM	Maputo: Direcção de Agricultura e Florestas, Secção de Botânica e Ecologia -- incorporated in LMA.
LMA	Maputo: Instituto de Investigação Agronómica de Mozambique, Divisão de Botânica Sistemática e Geobotânica, P.O. Box 3658, Maputo, Mozambique.
LMC	Maputo: Instituto de Investigação Científica de Mozambique, Maputo, Mozambique -- incorporated in LMU.
LMJ	Maputo: Botanical Department of the Cotton Research Centre (Centro de Investigação Científica Algodoeira) -- incorporated in LMA.
LMU	Maputo: Herbário, Faculdade de Biologia, Universidade da Eduardo Mondlane, C.P. 257, Maputo, Mozambique.
LNHS	London: London Natural History Society Museum, London, England, Great Britain.*
LOB	Long Beach: Herbarium, Biology Department, California State University, 1250 Bellflower Boulevard, Long Beach, California 90840, U.S.A.
LOC	Los Angeles: Herbarium, Department of Biology, Occidental College, 1600 Campus Road, Los Angeles, California 90041, U.S.A.
LOD	Łódź: Herbarium, Institute of Environmental Biology, Łódź University, Banacha 12/16, PL-90-237 Łódź, Poland.
LOJA	Loja: Herbarium Universitatis Loxensis "Reinaldo Espinoza," Facultad de Ciencias Agricolas, Universidad Nacional de Loja, casilla letra B, Loja, Ecuador.
LOMA	Loma Linda: Herbarium, Department of Biology, Loma Linda University, 24971 Stewart Street, Loma Linda, California 92354, U.S.A.
LP	La Plata: Herbario, División Plantas Vasculares del Museo de La Plata, Paseo del Bosque, 1900 La Plata, Buenos Aires, Argentina.
LPA	Las Palmas: Herbarium Las Palmas, El Museo Canario, 33 Dr Chil, Las Palmas, Canary Islands, Spain.
LPAG	La Plata: Herbario, Facultad de Agronomía, Universidad Nacional de La Plata, Calle 60 y 117, 1900 La Plata, Buenos Aires, Argentina.
LPB	La Paz: Herbario Nacional de Bolivia, Universidad Mayor de San Andres, Campus Universitario Cota Cota, Casilla 20127, La Paz, Bolivia.
LPD	La Plata: Herbario, Laboratorio de Botánica de la Dirección de Agricultura, Paseo del Bosque, 1900 La Plata, Buenos Aires, Argentina.
LPL	Liverpool: Liverpool Botanical Society, Liverpool, England, Great Britain.*
LPN	Littlehampton: Public Library and Museum, Littlehampton, England, Great Britain.*

385

LPS	LA PLATA: Herbario, Instituto de Botánica "C. Spegazzini," Calle 53 No. 477, La Plata, Buenos Aires, Argentina.
LR	LA ROCHELLE: Herbarium, Muséum d'Histoire Naturelle et d'Ethnographie de la Rochelle, 28 Rue Albert 1er, 17000 La Rochelle, France.
LRL	LIVERPOOL: Historical Society of Lancashire and Cheshire, Liverpool, England, Great Britain.*
LRS	LETHBRIDGE: Herbarium, Research Station, Agriculture Canada, Lethbridge, Alberta, Canada T1J 4B1.
LRU	LITTLE ROCK: Herbarium, Biology Department, University of Arkansas at Little Rock, 33rd & University Ave., Little Rock, Arkansas 72204, U.S.A.
LS	HABANA: Herbario de La Salle, Colegio de La Salle, Calle 13 n. 608, Vedado, Habana, Cuba — incorporated in HAC.
LSHI	LUBUMBASHI: Service de Botanique Systématique et Ecologie Tropicales, Université Nationale du Zaïre, B.P. 1825, Lubumbashi, Zaïre.
LSN	LONG SUTTON: Lord Wandsworth College Natural History Society, Long Sutton (Hants.), England, Great Britain.*.
LSP	WAWA: Herbarium, Lake Superior Provincial Park, Box 1160, Wawa, Ontario, Canada P0S 1K0.
LSR	LEICESTER: City Museum and Art Gallery, Leicester, England, Great Britain.*
LSU	BATON ROUGE: Herbarium, Department of Botany, Louisiana State University, Baton Rouge, Louisiana 70803, U.S.A.
LSUM	BATON ROUGE: Mycological Herbarium, Botany Department, Louisiana State University, Baton Rouge, Louisiana 70803, U.S.A.
LSUS	SHREVEPORT: Herbarium, Museum of Life Sciences, Department of Biological Sciences, Louisiana State University, 8515 Youree Drive, Shreveport, Louisiana 71115, U.S.A.
LT	LA TRAPPE: Laboratoire de l'Institut Agronomique d'Oka, Université de Montréal — incorporated in QFA.
LTB	MELBOURNE: Herbarium, Department of Botany, La Trobe University, Bundoora, Melbourne, Victoria 3083, Australia.
LTH	LOUTH: Museum of the Louth Naturalists' Antiquity and Literary Society, Louth, England, Great Britain.*
LTN	LUTON: Public Museum and Art Gallery, Luton, England, Great Britain.*
LTR	LEICESTER: Herbarium, University of Leicester, Leicester LE1 7RH, England, Great Britain.
LTU	RUSTON: Herbarium, Department of Botany and Bacteriology, Louisiana Tech University, Ruston, Louisiana 71272, U.S.A.
LU	GUANGZHOU: Herbarium, Lingnan University, Guangzhou, Guangdong, People's Republic of China — see IBSC.
LUA	NOVA LISBOA: Herbarium, Instituto de Investigação Agronómica de Angola, C.P. 406, Nova Lisboa, Angola.
LUAI	LUANDA: Herbarium, Instituto de Investigação Científica de Angola, Centro de Estudos de Sá da Bandeira, P.O. Box 485, Sá da Bandeira, Luanda, Angola.
LUB	LÜBECK: Herbarium, Naturhistorisches Museum zu Lübeck, Mühlendamm 1-3, 2400 Lübeck, Federal Republic of Germany, BRD.
LUCCA	LUCCA: Herbarium Horti Lucensi, Via S. Micheletto n. 5, 55 100 Lucca, Italy.
LUCH	BAGNÈRES-DE-LUCHON: Société Julien Sacaze, Société Pyrénéiste d'Etudes Historiques, Archéologiques et Scientifiques du Pays de Luchon, Musée du Pays de Luchon, Château Lafont, 18 Allées d'Etigny, Bagnères-de-Luchon, Haute Garonne, France.
LUD	LUDLOW: Ludlow Natural History Society, Ludlow, England, Great Britain.*
LUH	LAGOS: Lagos University Herbarium, Department of Biological Sciences, University of Lagos, Akoka, Lagos, Nigeria.
LUS	LUSAN: Herbarium, Botanic Garden, Academia Sinica, Lusan, Gansu, People's Republic of China.
LUX	LUXEMBOURG: Herbarium, Musée d'Histoire Naturelle, Luxembourg, Luxembourg.
LV	HEVERLEE: Carnoy Instituut Laboratorium voor beschrijvende plantkunde, Kardinaal Mercierlaan 92, B-3030 Heverlee, Belgium.
LVNP	MINERAL: Herbarium, Lassen Volcanic National Park, Mineral, California 96063, U.S.A.
LW	LWOW: Zielnik ogrodu Botanicznego Universitetu J.K., sw. Mikolaja 4, Lwow, Ukraine, U.S.S.R.
LWA	LWOW: Agricultural Experiment Station, Zyblikiewicza 40, Lwow, Ukraine, U.S.S.R.
LWD	LWOW: Museum Dzieduszykick, Rutowskiega 18, Lwow, Ukraine, U.S.S.R.
LWG	LUCKNOW: Herbarium of National Botanical Research Institute, Lucknow 226001, India.

LWS	Lwow: Musée des Sciences Naturelles de la Société Scientifique de Chevtchenko Léopol, 24/II Rue Czarniecki, Lwow, Ukraine, U.S.S.R.
LWU	Lucknow: University Herbarium, Lucknow, India.
LY	Villeurbanne: Herbiers de l'Université de Lyon, Département de Biologie Végétale, 43 Bd du 11 Novembre, F-69621 Villeurbanne, France.
LYN	Lynchburg: Herbarium, Lynchburg College, Lynchburg, Virginia 24501, U.S.A.
LZ	Leipzig: Herbarium Universitatis Lipsiensis, WB Taxonomie/Ökologie und Botanischer Garten der Sektion Biowissenschaften der KMU, Talstrasse 33, DDR-701 Leipzig, German Democratic Republic, DDR.
M	München: Herbarium, Botanische Staatssammlung, Menzinger Strasse 67, D-8000 München 19, Federal Republic of Germany, BRD.
MA	Madrid: Herbarium, Jardín Botánico, Plaza de Murillo 2, Madrid 14, Spain.
MAAS	Maastricht: Herbarium, Natuurhistorisch Museum, Bosquetplein 6-7, 6211 KJ Maastricht, Netherlands.
MACF	Fullerton: Faye A. MacFadden Herbarium, Department of Biology, California State University, Fullerton, California 92634, U.S.A.
MACO	Marlborough: Herbarium, Marlborough College, Marlborough, England, Great Britain.
MAD	Madison: Herbarium, Forest Products Laboratory, Center for Wood Anatomy Research, P.O. Box 5130, Madison, Wisconsin 53705, U.S.A.
MADJ	Funchal: Herbario do Jardim Botânico de Madeira, Quinta do Bom Sucesso – Caminho de Meio, 9000 Funchal, Madeira, Portugal.
MADM	Funchal: Herbarium, Museu Municipal do Funchal, 9000 Funchal, Madeira, Portugal.
MADS	Funchal: Herbarium, Museu de História Natural do Seminário do Funchal, Madeira, Portugal.
MAF	Madrid: Herbario de la Facultad de Farmacia de Madrid, Departamento de Botánica, Facultad de Farmacia, Universidad Complutense, Madrid – 3, Spain.
MAFST	Madrid: Instituto Forestal de la Moncloa, Burjasot, Madrid, Spain –– discontinued.
MAH	Mahalapye: Herbarium, Department of Agriculture, Box 10, Mahalapye, Botswana.
MAINE	Orono: Herbarium, Department of Botany and Plant Pathology, University of Maine, Folger Library, Orono, Maine 04473, U.S.A.
MAIS	Maisons Alfort: Institut d'Elevage et de Médecine Vétérinaire des Pays Tropicaux –– see ALF.
MAK	Tokyo: Makino Herbarium, Tokyo Metropolitan University, 2-1 Fukasawa, Setagaya, Tokyo 158, Japan.
MAKAR	Makarska: Herbar Biokovskog Područja, Žrtava Fašizma 1, YU-58300 Makarska, Yugoslavia.
MAL	Zomba: The National Herbarium of Malawi, Chancellor College, P.O. Box 280, Zomba, Malawi.
MALS	Price: Herbarium, Manti-LaSal National Forest, 350 East Main Street, Price, Utah 84501, U.S.A.
MAMOU	Mamou: Department of Agriculture, Mamou, Guinée.**
MAN	Manokwari: Section of Forest Botany, Forestry Division, Manokwari, Indonesia.
MANCH	Manchester: Herbarium, The Manchester Museum, The University, Manchester 13, England, Great Britain.
MAND	Mandalay: Herbarium, Agricultural College and Research Institute, Mandalay, Burma –– discontinued.
MANK	Mankato: Herbarium, Biology Department, Mankato State University, Mankato, Minnesota 56001, U.S.A.
MAPR	Mayaguez: Herbario, Departamento de Biología, Universidad de Puerto Rico, Recinto Universitario de Mayaguez, Mayaguez, Puerto Rico 00708.
MARO	Marylhurst: Herbarium, Marylhurst College, Marylhurst, Oregon 97036, U.S.A.
MARS	Marseille: Laboratoire de Botanique, Université de Provence (U.1), Place Victor-Hugo, Centre St. – Charles, F-13331 Marseille Cedex 3, France.
MARSSJ	Marseille: Laboratoire de Botanique, Faculté des Sciences St. Jerôme, Laboratoire de Botanique et Ecologie Mediterranéen, F-13397 Marseille Cedex 4, France.
MARY	College Park: Herbarium, Department of Botany, University of Maryland, College Park, Maryland 20742, U.S.A.
MASE	Maseru: Maseru Herbarium, Maseru Experiment Station, P.O. Box 24, Maseru, Lesotho.
MASS	Amherst: Herbarium, Department of Botany, University of Massachusetts, Amherst, Massachusetts 01003, U.S.A.

MATSU   MATSUYAMA: Forestry Department, Matsuyama Agricultural College, Matsuyama, Ehime-ken, Japan.

MAU   RÉDUIT: The Mauritius Herbarium, Mauritius Sugar Industry Research Institute, Réduit, Mauritius.

MB   MARBURG: Fachbereich Biologie der Philipps-Universität, Botanik, Lahnberge, D-355 Marburg (Lahn), Federal Republic of Germany, BRD.

MBH   MARLBOROUGH: Marlborough College Natural History Society, Marlborough, England, Great Britain.*

MBM   CURITIBA: Herbário, Museu Botânico Municipal, Caixa Postal 1142, 80.000 Curitiba, Paraná, Brazil.

MCA   ALLENTOWN: Herbarium, Department of Biology, Muhlenberg College, Allentown, Pennsylvania 18104, U.S.A.

MCJ   JOPLIN: Herbarium, Biology Department, Missouri Southern State College, Joplin, Missouri 64836, U.S.A.

MCM   HAMILTON: Herbarium, Biology Department, Hamilton College, McMaster University, Hamilton, Ontario, Canada -- incorporated in HAM.

MCNS   SALTA: Herbario, Museo de Ciencias Naturales, Universidad Nacional de Salta, Mendoza 2, 4400 Salta, Salta, Argentina.

MCP   BOSTON: Herbarium, Massachusetts College of Pharmacy and Allied Health Sciences, 179 Longwood Avenue, Boston, Massachusetts 02115, U.S.A.

MCT   HOUGHTON: Herbarium, Department of Biological Sciences, Michigan Technological University, Houghton, Michigan 49931, U.S.A.

MCTC   HOUGHTON: Cryptogamic Herbarium, Department of Biological Sciences, Michigan Technological University, Houghton, Michigan 49931, U.S.A.

MCTF   L'ANSE: Herbarium, Ford Forestry Center, Michigan Technological University, L'Anse, Michigan 49946, U.S.A.

MCW   MILTON: Harbarium, Biology Department, Milton College, College Street, Milton, Wisconsin 53563, U.S.A.

MDH   MIDDLESBOROUGH: Dorman Memorial Museum, Middlesborough, England, Great Britain.*

MDNR   WINNIPEG: Herbarium, Wildlife Biological Services, Manitoba Department of Natural Resources, Box 14, 1495 St. James Street, Winnipeg, Manitoba, Canada R3H 0W9.

MEDEL   MEDELLÍN: Herbario "Gabriel Gutierrez V.," Facultad de Ciencias, Universidad Nacional de Colombia, Seccional Medellín, Apartado 568, Medellín, Antioquia, Colombia.

MEL   MELBOURNE: National Herbarium of Victoria, Royal Botanic Gardens, Birdwood Avenue, South Yarra, Victoria 3141, Australia.

MELU   MELBOURNE: Botany School Herbarium, University of Melbourne, Parkville, Victoria 3052, Australia.

MEM   MEMPHIS: Herbarium, Department of Biology, Memphis State University, Memphis, Tennessee 38152, U.S.A.

MEMO   MONTERREY: Herbario, Departamento de Biológia, Estudios Superiores de Monterrey, Avenida Eugenio Garza Sada 2501, Sucursal de Correos "J", Monterrey, Nuevo León, Mexico.

MEN   CHACRAS DE CORIA: Herbario, Facultad de Ciencias Agrarias, Universidad Nacional de Cuyo, Almirante Brown 500, Luján de Cuyo, 5505 Chacras de Coria, Mendoza, Argentina.

MER   MÉRIDA: Herbario, Facultad de Ciencias Forestales, Universidad de Los Andes, Mérida, Venezuela.

MERF   MÉRIDA: Herbario "Luis E. Ruiz Terán,"Departamento de Botánica y Farmacognosia, Facultad de Farmacia, Universidad de Los Andes, Mérida 5101, Venezuela.

MERL   MENDOZA: Herbario Ruiz Leal, Instituto Argentino de Investigaciones de las Zonas Aridas, Consejo Nacional de Investigaciones Cientificas y Técnicas, Casilla de Correo 507, Correo Central, 5500 Mendoza, Mendoza, Argentina.

MEX   MÉXICO: Herbario, Museo de Historia Natural de la Ciudad de México, México, Distrito Federal, Mexico -- discontinued.

MEXU   MÉXICO: Herbario Nacional de México, Departamento de Botánica, Instituto de Biología, Universidad Nacional Autónoma de México, Apartado postal 70-367, México 20, Distrito Federal, Mexico.

MFA   SANTA FE: Herbario, Museo Provincial de Ciencias Naturales "Florentino Ameghina," Moreno 2557, 3000 Santa Fe, Argentina.

MFANT   CAPE COAST: Mfantsipim School, Cape Coast, Ghana.**

MFB   MAPLE: Forest Pathology Laboratory, Southern Research Station -- see SSMF.

MFU   UDINE: Herbarium, Museo Friulano di Storia Naturale, Palazzo Giacomelli, via Grazzano 1, 1-

	33100 Udine, Italy.
MG	BELÉM: Herbário, Museu Paraense Emílio Goeldi, Avenida Magalhães Barata 376, Caixa Postal 399, 66.000 Belém, Pará, Brazil.
MGA	MANAGUA: Herbario, Instituto Pedagógico de Varones, Managua, Nicaragua — discontinued.
MGC	MÁLAGA: Herbario de la Facultad de Ciencias de la Universidad de Málaga, Departamento de Botánica, Camino de la Misericordia s/n, Málaga – 4, Spain.
MGR	PINCKNEY: Herbarium, Edwin S. George Reserve, University of Michigan, 9250 Kelly Road, Pinckney, Michigan 48169, U.S.A.
MH	COIMBATORE: Herbarium, Botanical Survey of India, Southern Circle, Tamil Nadu Agricultural University, Lawley Road (P.O.), Coimbatore – 641003, India.
MHA	MOSCOW: Herbarium, Main Botanic Garden, Academy of Sciences of the U.S.S.R., Botaniches-kaya Street 4, 127276 Moscow, U.S.S.R.
MHM	MALHAM: Field Studies Council, Malham Tarn Field Centre, Malham, England, Great Britain.*
MHU	KAMPALA: Makerere Herbarium, Makerere University, P.O. Box 7062, Kampala, Uganda.
MI	MILANO: Herbarium, Istituto di Scienze Botaniche, Via Giuseppe Colombo 60, 20133 Milano, Italy.
MICH	ANN ARBOR: Herbarium of the University of Michigan, North University Building, Ann Arbor, Michigan 48109, U.S.A.
MID	MIDDLEBURY: Herbarium, Biology Department, Middlebury College, Middlebury, Vermont 05753, U.S.A.
MIL	MILWAUKEE: Herbarium, Milwaukee Public Museum, 800 West Wells Street, Milwaukee, Wisconsin 53233, U.S.A.
MIN	SAINT PAUL: Herbarium, Department of Botany, University of Minnesota, St. Paul, Minnesota 55108, U.S.A.
MIPV	MILANO: Herbarium, Istituto di Patologia Vegetale dell'Università, Via Celoria 2, 20133 Milano, Italy.
MISS	UNIVERSITY: Herbarium, Biology Department, University of Mississippi, University, Mississippi 38677, U.S.A.
MISSA	MISSISSIPPI STATE: Herbarium, Department of Biological Sciences, Mississippi State University, Drawer GY, Mississippi State, Mississippi 39762, U.S.A.
MJ	JIHLAVA: Herbarium, Muzeum Vysočiny, Nám. Míru 58, Jihlava, Czechoslovakia.
MJG	MAINZ: Institut für Spezielle Botanik und Botanischer Garten der Johannes Gutenberg-Universität, Saarstr. 21, P.O. Box 3980, D-6500 Mainz, Federal Republic of Germany, BRD.
MMMN	WINNIPEG: Herbarium, Manitoba Museum of Man and Nature, 190 Rupert Street, Winnipeg, Manitoba, Canada R3B 0N2.
MNA	FLAGSTAFF: Herbarium, Museum of Northern Arizona, Route 4, Box 720, Flagstaff, Arizona 86001, U.S.A.
MNE	MAIDSTONE: Museum and Art Gallery, Maidstone, England, Great Britain.*
MO	SAINT LOUIS: Herbarium, Missouri Botanical Garden, P.O. Box 299, St. Louis, Missouri 63166, U.S.A.
MOAR	PHILADELPHIA: Herbarium, Morris Arboretum, University of Pennsylvania, 9414 Meadowbrook Avenue, Philadelphia, Pennsylvania 19118, U.S.A.
MOC	MONMOUTH: Herbarium, Oregon College of Education, 345 N. Monmouth Avenue, Monmouth, Oregon 97361, U.S.A.
MOD	MODENA: Herbarium, Istituto Botanico dell'Università, Modena, Italy.
MOG	MOGADISHU: National Herbarium, National Range Agency, P.O. Box 1759, Mogadishu, Somalia, East Africa.
MOL	LIMA: Herbario, Departamento de Biología, Sección Botánica, Universidad Nacional Agraria, Apartado 456, La Molina, Lima, Peru.
MONT	BOZEMAN: W. E. Booth Herbarium, Biology Department, Montana State University, Bozeman, Montana 59715, U.S.A.
MONTU	MISSOULA: Herbarium, Botany Department, University of Montana, Missoula, Montana 59812, U.S.A.
MOR	LISLE: Herbarium, Morton Arboretum, Lisle, Illinois 60532, U.S.A.
MOS	MOSUL: Herbarium, College of Agriculture and Forestry, Mosul, Iraq.
MOSM	MOSCOW: Herbarium, All-Union Scientific Investigation Institute of Medicinal Plants, Ministry of Medical Industry, P/O Vilar, Lenin Region, 142790 Moscow Oblast, U.S.S.R.
MOSP	MOSCOW: Herbarium, Lenin State Pedagogical Institute, Kibaltschitsch Str. 6, Moscow 129243, U.S.S.R.
MOT	SARASOTA: Herbarium, Mote Marine Laboratory, 1600 City Island Park, Sarasota, Florida 33577, U.S.A.

MOVC	MOUNT VERNON: Herbarium, Biology Department, Cornell College, Mount Vernon, Iowa 52314, U.S.A.
MP	PARDUBICE: Herbarium, Východočeské museum, 53134 Pardubice, Czechoslovakia.
MPA	MONTPELLIER: Ecole Nationale Superieure Agronomique Botanique, Laboratoire de Botanique, 34060 Montpellier Cedex, France.
MPE	PORT ELIZABETH: Port Elizabeth Museum, F. R. Long Herbarium — see PEU.
MPN	PALMERSTON NORTH: Herbarium, Botany and Zoology Department, Massey University, Palmerston North, New Zealand.
MPPD	SAINT PAUL: Department of Plant Pathology Mycological Herbarium, College of Agriculture, University of Minnesota, 304 Stakman Hall of Plant Pathology, St. Paul, Minnesota 55108, U.S.A.
MPR	LUSAKA: Mount Makulu Pasture Research Station, Lusaka, Zambia.
MPU	MONTPELLIER: Institut de Botanique, 163 rue Auguste Broussonnet, 34000 Montpellier, France.
MPUC	PORTO ALEGRE: Herbário, Museu de Ciências da Pontifícia Universidade Católica do Rio Grande do Sul, Avenida Ipiranga 6681, Prédio 10, Caixa Postal 1429, 90.000 Porto Alegre, Rio Grande do Sul, Brazil.
MRC	MISSOULA: Herbarium, Forestry Sciences Laboratory, Intermountain Forest and Range Experiment Station, Forest Service, U.S. Department of Agriculture, Drawer G, Missoula, Montana 59806, U.S.A.
MRD	MOORHEAD: Herbarium, Department of Biology, Moorhead State University, Moorhead, Minnesota 56560, U.S.A.
MRSC	CHILANGA: Herbarium, Mount Makulu Research Station, P/Bag 7, Chilanga, Zambia.
MS	MESSINA: Istituto ed Orto Botanico, Piazza XX Settembre, Messina, Italy.
MSC	EAST LANSING: Herbarium, Department of Botany and Plant Pathology, Michigan State University, East Lansing, Michigan 48824, U.S.A.
MSCW	COLUMBUS: Herbarium, Department of Biological Sciences, Mississippi University for Women, Columbus, Mississippi 39701, U.S.A.
MSE	MONTROSE: Montrose Natural History and Antiquarian Society Museum, Montrose, Scotland, Great Britain.*
MSK	MINSK: Herbarium, Biological Institute of Academy of Sciences of the Belorussya S.S.R., Stalin Street 108, Minsk, U.S.S.R.
MSL	LONDON: Medical Society of London, London, England, Great Britain.*
MSM	MAYAGUEZ: Herbarium, Department of Marine Sciences, University of Puerto Rico, Mayaguez, Puerto Rico 00708.
MSTR	MÜNSTER: Herbarium, Westfälisches Landesmuseum für Naturkunde, Himmelreichallee 50 (from 1982 Sentrupen Strasse), D-4400 Münster, Federal Republic of Germany, BRD.
MSUD	ODESSA: Herbarium, Department of Morphology and Systematics of Plants, I. I. Mecynikov State University of Odessa, Shampanskii per. 2, 270015 Odessa, U.S.S.R.
MT	MONTRÉAL: Herbier Marie-Victorin, Institut Botanique, Université de Montréal, 4101 est, rue Sherbrooke, Montréal, Québec, Canada H1X 2B2.
MTJB	MONTRÉAL: Herbarium, Jardin Botanique de Montréal, 4101 est, rue Sherbrooke, Montréal, Québec, Canada H1X 2B2.
MTMG	MONTRÉAL: McGill University Herbarium, Department of Plant Science, Box 4000, Macdonald College P.O., Ste-Anne-de-Bellevue, Québec, Canada H9X 1Co.
MU	OXFORD: Willard Sherman Turrell Herbarium, Department of Botany, Miami University, Oxford, Ohio 45056, U.S.A.
MUCL	LOUVAIN-LA NEUVE: Mycothèque de l'Université Catholique de Louvain, Place Croix du Sud 3, B-1348 Louvain-la Neuve, Belgium.
MUCV	MELBOURNE: Herbarium, Department of Botany, Monash University, Clayton, Victoria 3168, Australia.
MUH	MELBOURNE: Herbarium, Department of Botany, Melbourne University — see MELU.
MUHW	HUNTINGTON: Herbarium, Department of Biological Sciences, Marshall University, Huntington, West Virginia 25701, U.S.A.
MUR	MURRAY: Herbarium, Department of Biology, Murray State University, Murray, Kentucky 42071, U.S.A.
MUS	NEW CONCORD: Herbarium, Biology Department, Muskingum College, Science Center, New Concord, Ohio 43762, U.S.A.
MUSK	MUSKEGON: Herbarium, Life Science Department, Muskegon Community College, 221 S. Quarterline Road, Muskegon, Michigan 49442, U.S.A.
MVC	CHARLESTON: Herbarium, Department of Natural Sciences, Morris Harvey College of Arts and

Sciences, University of Charleston, 2300 MacCorkle Avenue S.E., Charleston, West Virginia 25304, U.S.A.

MVDA	MONTEVIDEO: Dirección de Agronomía, Ministerio de Ganadería y Agricultura, Calle Uruguay, Montevideo, Uruguay -- discontinued.
MVFA	MONTEVIDEO: Herbario, Laboratorio de Botánica, Facultad de Agronomía, Casilla de Correo 1238, Avenida Garzón 780, Montevideo, Uruguay.
MVHC	MONTEVIDEO: Herbario, Laboratorio de Botánica, Facultad de Hum. y Ciencias, Cerrito 73, Montevideo, Uruguay.
MVM	MONTEVIDEO: Herbario, Museo Nacional de Historia Natural de Montevideo, Casilla de Correo 399, Montevideo, Uruguay.
MVN	MALVERN: Public Library, Malvern, England, Great Britain -- incorporated in WOS.*
MVSC	MILLERSVILLE: Herbarium, Department of Biology, Millersville State College, Millersville, Pennsylvania 17551, U.S.A.
MW	MOSCOW: Herbarium, Biology – Soils Department, M. V. Lomonosov State University of Moscow, Lenin Hills, MGU, 117234 Moscow B-234, U.S.S.R.
MWCF	FREDERICKSBURG: Herbarium, Department of Biological Sciences, Mary Washington College, Fredericksburg, Virginia 22401, U.S.A.
MWI	MACOMB: R. M. Myers Herbarium, Department of Biological Sciences, Western Illinois University, Macomb, Illinois 61455, U.S.A.
MWSJ	SAINT JOSEPH: Herbarium, Department of Biology, Missouri Western State College, St. Joseph, Missouri 64507, U.S.A.
MY	MARACAY: Herbario, Facultad de Agronomía, Instituto de Botánica Agricola, Universidad Central de Venezuela, Maracay, Aragua, Venezuela.
MYF	CARACAS: Herbario Dr. Victor Manuel Ovalles, Facultad de Farmacia, Universidad Central de Venezuela, Apartado 40.109, Caracas 1040A, Venezuela.
MZ	ZNOJMO: Herbarium, Jihomoravské muzeum, Ul. Přemyslovců 6, Znojmo, Czechoslovakia.
N	NANJING: Herbarium, Department of Biology, Nanjing University, Ling-Hai-Rou, Nanjing, Jiangsu, People's Republic of China.
NA	WASHINGTON: Herbarium, U.S. National Arboretum, Washington, DC 20002, U.S.A.
NABG	NOVO-ALEKSANDROVSK: Herbarium, Sakhalin Complex Institute for Scientific Investigation, Botanical Garden, 694050 Novo-Aleksandrovsk, Sakhalin Oblast, U.S.S.R.
NAI	NAIROBI: Nairobi University Herbarium, Department of Botany, University of Nairobi, P.O. Box 30197, Nairobi, Kenya.
NAM	NAMUR: Facultés Universitaires Notre-Dame de la Paix, Laboratoire de Botanique, 61 rue de Bruxelles, B-5000 Namur, Belgium.
NAP	NAPOLI: Istituto Botanico della Università di Napoli, Via Foria 223, Napoli, Italy.
NAS	NANJING: Herbarium, Jiangsu Botanical Institute, 210014 Nanjing, Jiangsu, People's Republic of China.
NAT	NEWTON ABBOT: Seale-Hayne Agricultural College, Newton Abbot, England, Great Britain.*
NATC	NATCHITOCHES: Herbarium, Department of Biological Sciences, Northwestern State University, Natchitoches, Louisiana 71457, U.S.A.
NBG	CAPE TOWN: Compton Herbarium, National Botanic Gardens of South Africa, Kirstenbosch, Private Bag X7, Claremont 7735, South Africa.
NBM	SAINT JOHN: Herbarium, New Brunswick Museum, 277 Douglas Avenue, Saint John, New Brunswick, Canada E2K 1E5.
NBSI	ILLMITZ: Herbarium, Biologische Station Neusiedlersee, Biologische Forschungsinstitut für Burgenland, A 7142 Illmitz, Burgenland, Austria.
NBV	LEIDEN: Koninklijke Nederlandse Botanische Vereniging (Royal Botanical Society of the Netherlands), c/o Schelpenkade 6, 2313 ZT Leiden, Netherlands.
NCAS	NEWARK: Herbarium, Botany Department, Newark College of Arts and Sciences of Rutgers University, 195 University Avenue, Newark, New Jersey 07102, U.S.A.
NCATG	GREENSBORO: Herbarium, Department of Biology, North Carolina A&T State University, Greensboro, North Carolina 27411, U.S.A.
NCBS	NEW HAVEN: Herbarium, Connecticut Botanical Society, Osborn Memorial Laboratories, Yale University, New Haven, Connecticut 06520, U.S.A.
NCC	SANTA ROSA: North Coast Herbarium of California, Santa Rosa Junior College, Santa Rosa, California 95402, U.S.A. -- incorporated in ROPA.
NCE	NEWCASTLE UPON TYNE: King's College, Newcastle upon Tyne, England, Great Britain.*
NCH	NORWICH: Norwich Botanical Society, Norwich, England, Great Britain.*

NCSC	RALEIGH: Herbarium, Department of Botany, North Carolina State University, Raleigh, North Carolina 27650, U.S.A.

NCSC   RALEIGH: Herbarium, Department of Botany, North Carolina State University, Raleigh, North Carolina 27650, U.S.A.

NCU   CHAPEL HILL: Herbarium, Department of Botany, The University of North Carolina, Coker Hall 010A, Chapel Hill, North Carolina 27514, U.S.A.

NCY   NANCY: Laboratoire de Botanique, Université de Nancy I, C.O. 140, 54037 Nancy Cedex, France.

ND   NOTRE DAME: The Julius A. Nieuwland Herbarium, Department of Biology, University of Notre Dame, Notre Dame, Indiana 46556, U.S.A.

NDA   FARGO: Herbarium, Botany Department, North Dakota State University, Fargo, North Dakota 58105, U.S.A.

NDG   NOTRE DAME: The Edward Lee Greene Herbarium, Department of Biology, University of Notre Dame, Notre Dame, Indiana 46556, U.S.A.

NDO   KITWE: Herbarium, Forest Department, Ministry of Lands and Natural Resources, P.O. Box 2099, Kitwe, Zambia.

NE   ARMIDALE: Herbarium, Department of Botany, University of New England, Armidale, New South Wales 2351, Australia.

NEB   LINCOLN: C. E. Bessey Herbarium, University of Nebraska State Museum, W-532 Nebraska Hall 5U, Lincoln, Nebraska 68588, U.S.A.

NEBC   CAMBRIDGE: Herbarium, New England Botanical Club, 22 Divinity Avenue, Cambridge, Massachusetts 02138, U.S.A.

NEMU   NEWARK: Herbarium, Newark Museum, P.O. Box 540, 43 Washington Street, Newark, New Jersey 07101, U.S.A.

NESH   RENO: Nevada Agricultural Experiment Station Herbarium, Renewable Natural Resources Division, University of Nevada, Reno, Nevada 89557, U.S.A.

NEU   NEUCHÂTEL: Institut de Botanique de l'Université, 22 rue de Chantemerle, CH-2007 Neuchâtel, Switzerland.

NF   NANJING: Dendrological Herbarium, Nanjing Technological College of Forest Products, Shaoshan Road, 210037 Nanjing, Jiangsu, People's Republic of China.

NFLD   SAINT JOHN'S: Herbarium, Department of Biology, Memorial University of Newfoundland, St. John's, Newfoundland, Canada A1B 3X9.

NFO   NIAGARA FALLS: Herbarium, Niagara Parks Commission School of Horticulture, Box 150, Niagara Falls, Ontario, Canada L2E 6T2.

NH   DURBAN: Natal Herbarium, Botanical Research Unit, Botanic Gardens Road, Durban, 4001 South Africa.

NHA   DURHAM: Albion R. Hodgdon Herbarium, Department of Botany and Plant Pathology, University of New Hampshire, Nesmith Hall, Durham, New Hampshire 03824, U.S.A.

NHES   NEW HAVEN: Herbarium, Connecticut Agricultural Experiment Station, P.O. Box 1106, New Haven, Connecticut 06504, U.S.A.

NHM   NOTTINGHAM: Herbarium, Department of Botany, University of Nottingham, Nottingham, England, Great Britain.

NI   NITRA: Herbarium, Katedra rastlinnej biológie, Agromická fakulta, Vysoká škola polnohospodárska, Nitra, Czechoslovakia.

NICE   NICE: Herbarium, Muséum d'Histoire Naturelle (= Musée Barla), 60 bis Bd. Risso, 06300 Nice, France.

NICH   NICHINAN: Herbarium, Hattori Botanical Laboratory, 3888 Hon-machi, Nichinan-shi, Miyazaki-ken 889-25, Japan.

NIPR   TOKYO: Herbarium, National Institute of Polar Research, 9-10 Kaga 1-chome, Itabashi-ku, Tokyo 173, Japan.

NIT   NITERÓI: Herbário, Jardim Botânico de Niterói, Alameda São Boaventura 770, Fonseca, 24.000 Niterói, Rio de Janeiro, Brazil.

NJ   NJALA: Njala University College -- incorporated in SL.

NLSN   NELSON: Herbarium, Department of Biological Sciences, Notre Dame University, Nelson, British Columbia, Canada V1L 3C7 -- transferred to SCCBC.

NLU   MONROE: Herbarium, Biology Department, Northeast Louisiana University, Monroe, Louisiana 71209, U.S.A.

NM   MARQUETTE: Herbarium, Biology Department, Northern Michigan University, Marquette, Michigan 49855, U.S.A.

NMC   LAS CRUCES: Herbarium, Biology Department, New Mexico State University, Las Cruces, New Mexico 88003, U.S.A.

NMCR   LAS CRUCES: Range Science Herbarium, Department of Animal and Range Sciences, New

Mexico State University, Box 3I, Las Cruces, New Mexico 88003, U.S.A.

NMN   NORTHAMPTON: Northamptonshire Natural History Society and Field Club, Northampton, England, Great Britain.*

NMSU   MARYVILLE: Herbarium, Department of Biology, Northwest Missouri State University, Garrett-Strong Science Building, Maryville, Missouri 64468, U.S.A.

NMW   CARDIFF: Herbarium, Department of Botany, National Museum of Wales, Cardiff CF1 3NP, Wales, Great Britain.

NO   NEW ORLEANS: Herbarium, Department of Biology, Tulane University, New Orleans, Louisiana 70118, U.S.A.

NOLS   NEW ORLEANS: Herbarium, Department of Biological Sciences, University of New Orleans, Lakefront, New Orleans, Louisiana 70122, U.S.A.

NOSU   TAHLEQUAH: Herbarium, Division of Natural Science and Mathematics, Northeastern Oklahoma State University, Tahlequah, Oklahoma 74464, U.S.A.

NOT   NOTTINGHAM: Herbarium, Natural History Museum, Wollaton Hall, Wollaton, Nottingham NG8 2AE, England, Great Britain.

NOU   NOUMÉA: Herbarium, Centre O.R.S.T.O.M. de Nouméa, B.P. A 5 Cedex, Nouméa, New Caledonia.

NPA   NANJING: Herbarium, Institute of Geology and Paleontology, Academia Sinica, Nanjing, Jiangsu, People's Republic of China -- discontinued.

NPB   MTUBATUBA: Herbarium, Hluhluwe Game Reserve Research Centre, P.O. Box 25, Mtubatuba, 3935 South Africa.

NPT   NEWPORT: County Borough Museum and Art Gallery, Newport (Mon.), Wales, Great Britain.*

NPWRC   JAMESTOWN: Herbarium, Northern Prairie Wildlife Research Center, P.O. Box 1747, Jamestown, North Dakota 58401, U.S.A.

NRCC   HALIFAX: Herbarium, Atlantic Regional Laboratory, National Research Council of Canada, 1411 Oxford Street, Halifax, Nova Scotia, Canada B3H 3Z1.

NS   NOVOSIBIRSK: Herbarium, Siberian Central Botanical Garden, 101 Zolotodolinskaya Ul., Novosibirsk 90, U.S.S.R.

NSAC   TRURO: Herbarium, Nova Scotia Agricultural College, Box 550, Truro, Nova Scotia, Canada B2N 2V5.

NSDA   RENO: Herbarium, Nevada State Department of Agriculture, P.O. Box 11100, 350 Capitol Hill Avenue, Reno, Nevada 89510, U.S.A.

NSM   NANJING: Herbarium, Botanical Garden of Sun Yatsen Tomb and Memorial Park Commission, Nanjing, Jiangsu, People's Republic of China.

NSMC   CARSON CITY: Herbarium, Nevada State Museum, Capitol Complex, Carson City, Nevada 89710, U.S.A.

NSPM   HALIFAX: Herbarium, Nova Scotia Museum, 1747 Summer Street, Halifax, Nova Scotia, Canada B3H 3A6.

NSRF   HALIFAX: Seaweeds Division, Nova Scotia Research Foundation -- incorporated in NSPM.

NSW   SYDNEY: National Herbarium of New South Wales, Royal Botanic Gardens, Mrs. Macquaries Road, Sydney, N.S.W. 2000, Australia.

NT   ALICE SPRINGS: Herbarium of the Northern Territory of Australia, Box 2134, Arid Zone Research Institute, Alice Springs, N.T. 5750, Australia.

NTM   NANTES: Herbarium, Muséum d'Histoire Naturelle de Nantes, Place de la Monnaie, Nantes, France.

NTN   NORTHAMPTON: County Borough Central Museum, Northampton, England, Great Britain.*

NTS   MERCURY: Herbarium, Nevada Test Site, Mercury, Nevada 89023, U.S.A. (Mailing address: Janice C. Beatley, Department of Biological Sciences, University of Cincinnati, Cincinnati, Ohio 45223).

NTSC   DENTON: Benjamin B. Harris Herbarium, Department of Biological Sciences, North Texas State University, Denton, Texas 76203, U.S.A.

NU   PIETERMARITZBURG: Herbarium, Department of Botany, University of Natal, P.O. Box 375, Pietermaritzburg 3200, Natal, South Africa.

NUV   NORTHFIELD: Herbarium, Norwich University, Cabot Science Building, Northfield, Vermont 05663, U.S.A.

NWH   NORWICH: Herbarium, Norwich Castle Museum (Norfolk Museums Service), Norwich NR1 3JU, England, Great Britain.

NWK   NEWARK UPON TRENT: Gilstrap Public Library and Museum, Newark upon Trent, England, Great Britain.*

NWOSU   ALVA: Herbarium, Northwestern Oklahoma State University, Alva, Oklahoma 73717, U.S.A.

NWT   NEWPORT: Harper Adams Agricultural College, Newport (Salop), Wales, Great Britain.*

NWU   EVANSTON: Botany Department, Northwestern University, Evanston, Illinois, U.S.A. –– incorporated in F.

NY   NEW YORK: Herbarium, New York Botanical Garden, Bronx, New York 10458, U.S.A.

NYAS   DEDZA: Herbarium, Silvicultural Research Station –– incorporated in MAL.

NYS   ALBANY: Herbarium, New York State Museum, Biological Survey, 3132 CEC, Albany, New York 12230, U.S.A.

NZFRI   ROTORUA: Herbarium, Forest Research Institute, Private Bag, Whakarewarewa, Rotorua, New Zealand.

O   OSLO: Botanical Garden and Museum, Trondheimsvn. 23B, Oslo 5, Norway.

OAC   GUELPH: Herbarium, Department of Botany and Genetics, University of Guelph, Guelph, Ontario, Canada NIG 2W1.

OAKL   OAKLAND: Herbarium, Natural Sciences Department, Oakland Museum, 1000 Oak Street, Oakland, California 94607, U.S.A.

OBI   SAN LUIS OBISPO: Robert F. Hoover Herbarium, Department of Biology, California Polytechnic State University, San Luis Obispo, California 93407, U.S.A.

OBPF   OYSTER BAY: Herbarium, Planting Fields Arboretum, Box 58, Oyster Bay, New York 11771, U.S.A.

OC   OBERLIN: Herbarium, Department of Biology, Kettering Hall of Science, Oberlin College, West Lotain Street, Oberlin, Ohio 44074, U.S.A.

OCHA   TOKYO: Herbarium, Ochanomizu University, Tokyo, Japan.

OCLA   CHICKASHA: Herbarium, Department of Mathematics and Natural Science, University of Science & Arts of Oklahoma, 17th Street and Grand Avenue, Chickasha, Oklahoma 73018, U.S.A.

OCNF   PRINEVILLE: Ochoco National Forest, Box 490, Prineville, Oregon 97754, U.S.A. –– incorporated in LAGO.

ODU   NORFOLK: Herbarium, Department of Biological Sciences, Old Dominion University, Hampton Boulevard, Norfolk, Virginia 23508, U.S.A.

OGDF   OGDEN: Herbarium, U.S. Forest Service, Intermountain Region, Federal Office Building, 324 25th Street, Ogden, Utah 84401, U.S.A.

OH   HLUBOKÁ: Herbarium, Agricultural Museum of Praha, Hunting Lodge Ohrada, 373 41 Hluboká n. Vltavou, České Budějovice, Czechoslovakia.

OHM   OLDHAM: Oldham Microscopical Society and Field Club, Oldham, England, Great Britain.*

OKL   NORMAN: Robert Bebb Herbarium, Department of Botany and Microbiology, Oklahoma Biological Survey, University of Oklahoma, 770 Van Vleet Oval, Norman, Oklahoma 73019, U.S.A.

OKLA   STILLWATER: Herbarium, School of Biological Sciences, Oklahoma State University, Stillwater, Oklahoma 74078, U.S.A.

OL   OLOMOUC: Katedra botaniky, přírod. fakulty University Palackého, Leninstr. 26, Olomouc, Czechoslovakia.

OLDS   OLDS: Herbarium, Olds College, Olds, Alberta, Canada TOM 1PO.

OLE   OUNDLE: Oundle School Natural History Society, Oundle, England, Great Britain.*

OLM   OLOMOUC: Herbarium, Vlastivědný ustav – muzeum, Nám. Republiky 5, Olomouc, Czechoslovakia.

OLP   OLOMOUC: Herbarium, Katedra příodopisu pedagogická fakulty Univerzity Palackého, Žerotínovo nám. 2, 771 40 Olomouc, Czechoslovakia.

OLV   OLIVET: Herbarium, Biology Department, Olivet College, Olivet, Michigan 49076, U.S.A.

OMA   OMAHA: Herbarium, Department of Biology, University of Nebraska at Omaha, Omaha, Nebraska 68182, U.S.A.

OMC   OAKLAND: Herbarium, Biology Department, Mills College, Oakland, California 94613, U.S.A.

OMKH   KUTNÁ HORA: Herbarium, Oblastní muzeum Kutná Hora, Kutná Hora, Czechoslovakia.

OMP   PODĚBRADY: Polabské muzeum v Poděbradech, Poděbrady, Czechoslovakia.

OP   OPAVA: Slezské Muzeum, Botanical Department, Vítězného února 35, 746 46 Opava, Czechoslovakia.

ORE   EUGENE: Herbarium, Department of Biology, University of Oregon, Eugene, Oregon 97403, U.S.A.

OREB   ÖREBRO: Karolinska Högre Allmänna Läroverket, Örebro, Sweden.

ORM   ORLÉANS: Herbarium, Musée des Sciences Naturelles, 2 rue Marcel Proust, Orléans, Loiret, France.

O.R.S.T.O.M.   Organisation Recherche Scientifique et Technique d'Outre Mer.**

ORT	Puerto de la Cruz: Jardín de Aclimatación de Plantas de la Orotava, Puerto de la Cruz, Tenerife, Canary Islands, Spain.
OS	Columbus: Herbarium, Department of Botany, The Ohio State University, 1735 Neil Avenue, Columbus, Ohio 43210, U.S.A.
OSA	Osaka: Herbarium, Osaka Museum of Natural History, Nagai Park, Higashi-Sumiyoshi-ku, Osaka 546, Japan.
OSC	Corvallis: Herbarium, Department of Botany and Plant Pathology, Oregon State University, Corvallis, Oregon 97331, U.S.A.
OSH	Oshkosh: Herbarium, Department of Biology, University of Wisconsin – Oshkosh, Oshkosh, Wisconsin 54901, U.S.A.
OSMC	Lacey: Herbarium, Department of Biology, Saint Martin's College, Lacey, Washington 98503, U.S.A.
OSN	Osnabrück: Herbarium, Naturwissenschaftliches Museum der Stadt Osnabrück, Heger-Tor-Wall 28, D-4500 Osnabrück, Federal Republic of Germany, BRD.
OSUF	Corvallis: Herbarium, Department of Forest Products, School of Forestry, Oregon State University, Corvallis, Oregon 97331, U.S.A.
OTA	Dunedin: Herbarium, Botany Department, University of Otago, P.O. Box 56, Dunedin, New Zealand.
OTF	Ottawa: Dominion Forest Service, Ottawa, Ontario, Canada — housed in Chalk River with PFES.
OTM	Dunedin: Herbarium, Otago Museum, Dunedin, New Zealand.
OTT	Ottawa: Herbarium, Département de Biologie, Université d'Ottawa, 30 Somerset Street, Ottawa, Ontario, Canada K1N 9B4.
OULU	Oulu: Botanical Museum, University of Oulu, P.O. Box 191, SF-00101 Oulu 10, Finland.
OUPR	Ouro Prêto: Escola de Farmácia, Universidade Federal de Ouro Prêto, Rua Costa Sena 171, 35.400 Ouro Prêto, Minas Gerais, Brazil.
OWU	Delaware: Herbarium, Ohio Wesleyan University, Delaware, Ohio 43015, U.S.A.
OXD	Oxford: Wadham College, Oxford, England, Great Britain.*
OXF	Oxford: Fielding-Druce Herbarium, Department of Botany, University of Oxford, Botany School, South Parks Road, Oxford 0X1 3RA, England, Great Britain.
P	Paris: Muséum National d'Histoire Naturelle, Laboratoire de Phanérogamie, 16 Rue Buffon, 75005 Paris, France.
PAC	University Park: Herbarium, The Pennsylvania State University, 202 Buckhout Laboratory, University Park, Pennsylvania 16802, U.S.A.
PACA	São Leopoldo: Herbarium Anchieta, Instituto Anchietano e Unisinos, 93.000 São Leopoldo, Rio Grande do Sul, Brazil.
PAD	Padova: Istituto di Botanica e Fisiologia Vegetale, via Orto Botanico 15, 35100 Padova, Italy.
PAE	Basel: Stiftung Herbarium Paul Aellen – see G-PAE.
PAL	Palermo: Erbario Siculo and Erbario Generale, Via Archirafi 38 (Erb. Siculo), 90125 Palermo; Via Lincoln 2 (Erb. Gen.), 90133 Palermo, Italy.
PALIME	Palimé: Animal Breeding and Husbandry Station, Palimé, Togo.**
PAM	Harrisburg: Herbarium, Bureau of Plant Industry, Pennsylvania Department of Agriculture, 2301 North Cameron Street, Harrisburg, Pennsylvania 17110, U.S.A.
PAMG	Belo Horizonte: Empresa de Pesquisa Agropecuária de Minas Gerais, Avenida Amazonas 115, Caixa Postal 515, 30.000 Belo Horizonte, Minas Gerais, Brazil.
PAMP	Pamplona: Department of Botany, University, Pamplona, Spain.**
PAN	Chandigarh: Herbarium, Department of Botany, Panjab University, Sector – 14, Chandigarh, PIN-160014, India.
PAR	Paraná: Herbario, Museo de Ciencias Naturales y Antropológicas de Entre Ríos, Rivadavia 462, Casilla de Correo 71, 3100 Paraná, Entre Ríos, Argentina.
PARMA	Parma: Herbarium, Istituto Botanico dell' Università, Parma, Italy.
PAS	Pasuruan: Java Sugar Experimental Station, Pasuruan, Java, Indonesia — deposited on permanent loan at BO.
PASA	Pasadena: Herbarium, Department of Life Sciences, Pasadena City College, 1570 East Colorado Boulevard, Pasadena, California 91106, U.S.A.
PASM	San Marcos: Herbarium, Life Science Department, Palomar College, San Marcos, California 92069, U.S.A.
PAT	Paris: Laboratoire d'Ethnobotanique, Muséum National d'Histoire Naturelle, 57 Rue Cuvier, 75005 Paris, France.

PAUH	EDINBURG: Herbarium, Department of Biology, Pan American University, Edinburg, Texas 78539, U.S.A.
PAV	PAVIA: Botanical Institute, The University, P.O. Box 99, 27100 – Pavia, Italy.
PAY	PAISLEY: Paisley Philosophical Institute, Paisley, Scotland, Great Britain.*
PBH	PETERBOROUGH: Museum of the Peterborough Natural History, Scientific and Archaeological Society, Peterborough, England, Great Britain.*
PBL	PORT BLAIR: Regional Herbarium, Andaman-Nicobar Circle, Botanical Survey of India, Horti-cultural Road, Port Blair 744102, India.
PC	PARIS: Muséum National d'Histoire Naturelle, Laboratoire de Cryptogamie, 12 Rue de Buffon, 75005 Paris, France.
PCH	PRESTWICH: Prestwich and Pilkington Botanical Society, Prestwich, England, Great Britain.*
P-CHEV	PARIS: Herbier Chevalier –– see P.
PCM	MADRAS: Herbarium, Department of Botany, Presidency College, Madras 600005, (Tamil Nadu), India.
P-CO	PARIS: Durand-Cosson coll. –– see P.
PCU	PARIS: Muséum National d'Histoire Naturelle, Laboratoire de Biologie Végétale Appliquée, 61 Rue de Buffon, 75005 Paris, France.
PDA	PERADENIYA: National Herbarium, Division of Systematic Botany, Royal Botanic Gardens, Peradeniya, Sri Lanka.
PDD	AUCKLAND: Herbarium, Plant Diseases Division, Department of Scientific and Industrial Re-search, Mt. Albert Research Centre, Private Bag, Auckland, New Zealand.
P-DU	PARIS: Herbier Durand –– see P.
PE	PEKING (Beijing): Herbarium, Institute of Botany, Academia Sinica, Beijing, People's Republic of China.
PECS	PÉCS: Department of Botany, Museum of Natural History, Rák-czi ut 34, Pécs, Hungary.
PEI	CHARLOTTETOWN: Laboratory of Plant Pathology, P.O. Box 220, Charlottetown, Prince Edward Island, Canada.
PEL	PELOTAS: Herbário, Departamento de Botânica, Instituto de Biologia, Universidade Federal de Pelotas, 96.100 Pelotas, Rio Grande do Sul, Brazil.
PEM	PEKING (Beijing): Herbarium, Department of Botany, Beijing Medical College, Beijing, People's Republic of China.
PEN	PENRITH: The Museum, Penrith, England, Great Britain.*
PENN	PHILADELPHIA: Herbarium, University of Pennsylvania –– incorporated in PH.
PER	PERTH: Herbarium, City Museum, Perth, Scotland, Great Britain.
PERM	PERM: Department of Botany, A. M. Gorky University of Perm, Bukireva 15, Building 2, 614005 Perm, U.S.S.R.
PERTH	PERTH: Western Australian Herbarium, Department of Agriculture, George Street, South Perth, Western Australia 6151, Australia.
PERU	PERUGIA: Herbarium, Istituto Interfacoltà di Botanica dell' Università, 74 Borgo XX Giugno, 06100 Perugia, Italy.
PES	PESHAWAR: Herbarium, Pakistan Council of Scientific and Industrial Research, P.O. Peshawar University, Peshawar, Pakistan.
PET	PEKING (Beijing): Herbarium, National University of Peking Teachers College, Beijing, People's Republic of China ––see PE.
PEU	PORT ELIZABETH: Herbarium of the University of Port Elizabeth, P.O. Box 1600, Port Elizabeth 6000, South Africa.
PEY	PEKING (Beijing): Herbarium, Yenching University, Beijing, People's Republic of China –– see PE.
PFC	MISENHEIMER: Herbarium, Division of Natural and Health Sciences, Pfeiffer College, Misen-heimer, North Carolina 28109, U.S.A.
PFES	CHALK RIVER: Herbarium, Petawawa National Forestry Institute, Canadian Forestry Service, Environment Canada, Chalk River, Ontario, Canada.
PFRS	BERKELEY: Forest Disease Herbarium, Pacific Southwest Forest and Range Experiment Station, P.O. Box 245, Berkeley, California 94701, U.S.A.
PGM	PACIFIC GROVE: Herbarium, Museum of Natural History, 165 Forest Avenue, Pacific Grove, California 93950, U.S.A.
PH	PHILADELPHIA: Herbarium, Academy of Natural Sciences of Philadelphia, 19th and the Park-way, Philadelphia, Pennsylvania 19103, U.S.A.
PHA	LONDON: Pharmaceutical Society of Great Britain, London, England, Great Britain.*
P-HA	PARIS: Herbier Haller –– see P.

PHG	GODALMING: Peperharrow, Godalming (Surrey), England, Great Britain.*
PHIL	PHILADELPHIA: Herbarium, Department of Biology, Philadelphia College of Pharmacy & Science, 43rd St., and Kingsessing & Woodland Aves., Philadelphia, Pennsylvania 19104, U.S.A. — incorporated in NA.
PI	PISA: Herbarium Horti Pisani, Via L. Ghini 5, I-56100 Pisa, Italy.
PI-ARC	PISA: Arcangeli Herbarium — see PI.
PI-ART	PISA: Artaria Herbarium — see PI.
PI-BOTT	PISA: Bottini Herbarium — see PI.
PI-CAR	PISA: Carvel Herbarium — see PI.
PI-CITT	PISA: Cittadella Herbarium — see PI.
PI-GUAD	PISA: Guadagno Herbarium — see PI.
PIHG	GAINESVILLE: Herbarium, Division of Plant Industry, P.O. Box 1269, Gainesville, Florida 32602, U.S.A.
PI-PASS	PISA: Passerini Herbarium — see PI.
PI-PELL	PISA: Pellegrini Herbarium — see PI.
P-JU	PARIS: Herbier Jussieu — see P.
PKDC	CURITIBA: Herbário Per Karl Dusén, Fundação Instituto Agronômico do Paraná, Rua Nivaldo Braga 1225, Capão da Imbuia, Caixa Postal 1493, 80.000 Curitiba, Paraná, Brazil.
PKM	PENZA: Herbarium, V. G. Belinsk Pedagogical Institute of Penza, Lermontova St. 37, 440602 Penza, U.S.S.R.
PL	PLZEŇ: Herbarium, Západočeské Muzeum (West Bohemian Museum), Kopeckého sady 2, 301 50 Plzeň, Czechoslovakia.
P-LA	PARIS: Lamarck collection — see P.
PLY	PLYMOUTH: Plymouth Institution, Plymouth, England, Great Britain.*
PM	SALEM: Herbarium, Peabody Museum, 161 Essex Street, Salem, Massachusetts 01970, U.S.A.
PMA	PANAMÁ: Herbario, Escuela de Biología, Universidad de Panamá, Estafeta Universitaria, Panamá, Panama.
PMAE	EDMONTON: Herbarium, Provincial Museum of Alberta, 12845 102nd Avenue, Edmonton, Alberta, Canada T5N OM6.
PMG	PARAOPEBA: Horto Florestal, 35.774 Paraopeba, Minas Gerais, Brazil.
PMS	DILLON BEACH: Herbarium, Pacific Marine Station, Dillon Beach, Marin Co., California 94929, U.S.A. — discontinued.
PNBG	SINILOAN: Philippine National Botanic Herbarium, U.P. Quezon Land Grant, Siniloan, Laguna, Philippines.
PNG	PORT MORESBY: Herbarium, Department of Primary Industry, Plant Pathology Branch, P.O. Box 2417, Konedobu, Port Moresby, Papua New Guinea.
PNH	MANILA: Philippine National Herbarium, Old Congress Building, P. Burgos Street, P.O. Box 2659, Manila, Philippines.
PNZ	PENZANCE: Museum of the Penzance Natural History and Antiquarian Society, Penzance, England, Great Britain.*
PO	PORTO: Instituto de Botânica "Dr. Gonçalo Sampaio," Faculdade de Ciências da Universidade do Porto, Rua do Campo Alegre 1191, 4100 Porto, Portugal.
POFS	PORTLAND: U.S. Forest Service, R.M. Unit, Box 3623, Portland, Oregon 97208, U.S.A. — incorporated in LAGO.
POLY	LONDON: The Polytechnic, London, England, Great Britain.*
POM	CLAREMONT: Herbarium of Pomona College, Rancho Santa Ana Botanic Garden, 1500 N. College Avenue, Claremont, California 91711, U.S.A.
POP	POPRAD: Tatranské múzeum v Poprade, Czechoslovakia — incorporated in TNP.
POR	PORTICI: Istituto di Patologia vegetale dell' Università, Portici (Napoli), Italy.
PORE	POINT REYES: Herbarium, Point Reyes National Seashore, Point Reyes, California 94956, U.S.A.
PORT	GUANARE: Herbario Universitario, School of Natural Resources, Universidad Nacional Experimental de los Llanos Occidentales "Ezequiel Zamora," Guanare, Portuguesa, Venezuela.
POZ	POZNAŃ: Herbarium of the Department of Plant Taxonomy, Adam Mickiewicz University, Stalingradzka 14, 61-713 Poznań, Poland.
POZG	POZNAŃ: Herbarium of the Department of Geobotany, Adam Mickiewicz University, Stalingradzka 14, 61-713 Poznań, Poland.
PPFI	PESHAWAR: Herbarium, Pakistan Forest Institute, Peshawar, Pakistan.
PPIU	URALSK: Herbarium, Department of Botany, A. S. Pushkin Pedagogical Institute of Uralsk, Lenina Prospect 121, 417001 Uralsk, U.S.S.R.

PPL HARPENDEN: Harpenden Laboratory, Ministry of Agriculture, Fisheries and Food, Agricultural Development and Advisory Service, Hatching Green, Harpenden, Hertfordshire AL5 2BD, England, Great Britain.

PR PRAHA: Botanické oddělení Přírodověd. muzea Národního muzea v Praze (Department of Botany, National Museum in Prague), 252 43 Průhonice near Praha, Czechoslovakia.

PRC PRAHA: Herbarium, Universitatis Carolinae Facultatis Scientiae Naturalis, Institutum Botanicum, Benátská 2, 128 01 Praha 2, Czechoslovakia.

PRE PRETORIA: National Herbarium, Botanical Research Institute, 2 Cussonia Ave., P. Bag X101, Pretoria, 0001 South Africa.

PREM PRETORIA: National Mycological Herbarium, Private Bag X 134, 590 Vermeulen St., Pretoria 0001, South Africa.

PRF PRETORIA: Forestry Herbarium, South African Forestry Research Institute, Ketjen St., P.O. Box 727, Pretoria 0001, South Africa.

PRG LAMBAYEQUE: Herbario Lambayeque, Universidad Nacional Pedro Ruiz Gallo, Plaza Principal, Apartado 48, Lambayeque, Peru.

PRH PERTH: Perthshire Society of Natural Science, Perth, Scotland, Great Britain.*

PRI PRICE: Herbarium, College of Eastern Utah, 450 East 4th North, Price, Utah 84501, U.S.A.

PRM PRAHA: Mycological Department of the National Museum, Tř. Vítězného února 74, 115 79 Praha-1, Czechoslovakia.

PRU PRETORIA: H. G. W. J. Schweickerdt Herbarium, Department of Botany, University of Pretoria, Pretoria 0002, South Africa.

PRV PORVOO: Herbarium, Porvoo Museum of Natural History, Papinkatu 18, Porvoo, Finland.

PSGB BRADFORD: Herbarium, Pharmaceutical Society of Great Britain, Department of Pharmacy, University of Bradford, Richmond Rd., Bradford, West Yorkshire BD7 1DP, England, Great Britain.

PSO PASTO: Herbario, Facultad de Ciencias Agricolas, Universidad de Nariño, Ciudad Universitaria Torobajo, Apartado Aéreo 505, Pasto, Nariño, Colombia.

PSP WATERVILLE: Herbarium of Parasitic Seed Plants, c/o Nature Center, 10045 South River Road, Waterville, Ohio 43566, U.S.A.

PSY PAISLEY: Corporation and Art Gallery, Paisley, Scotland, Great Britain.*

PTBG LAWAI: Herbarium, Pacific Tropical Botanical Garden, P.O. Box 340, Lawai, Kauai, Hawaii 96765, U.S.A.

PTH PERTH: Herbarium, Perth Museum and Art Gallery, George Street, Perth, Tayside, Scotland, Great Britain.

PTN PRESTON: Preston Science Society, Preston, England, Great Britain.*

PUA ANGWIN: Herbarium, Biology Department, Pacific Union College, Angwin, California 94508, U.S.A.

PUC POTCHEFSTROOM: Herbarium, Potchefstroom University for C.H.E., Potchefstroom 2520, South Africa.

PUH QUEZON CITY: Herbarium, Department of Botany, College of Arts and Sciences, University of Philippines, Quezon City, Philippines.

PUL WEST LAFAYETTE: Kriebel Herbarium, Department of Biological Sciences, Purdue University, West Lafayette, Indiana 47907, U.S.A.

PUN PATIALA: Herbarium, Department of Botany, Punjabi University, Patiala-147 002, India.

PUP PESHAWAR: Herbarium, Botany Department, Peshawar University, Peshawar, Pakistan.

PUR WEST LAFAYETTE: Arthur Herbarium, Department of Botany and Plant Pathology, Purdue University, West Lafayette, Indiana 47907, U.S.A.

PUS PUSLINCH: Puslinch House, near Yealmpton, Puslinch, Devon, England, Great Britain.*

PUSC PUEBLO: Herbarium, Biology Department, University of Southern Colorado, 2200 Bonforte Boulevard, Pueblo, Colorado 81001, U.S.A.

PVNH PORT VILA: Herbarium, Forestry Section, Department of Agriculture, Port Vila, New Hebrides.

PZV PETROZAVODSK: Herbarium, O. V. Kuusinev State University, Lenin Street 39, Petrozavodsk, U.S.S.R.

Q QUITO: Herbario del Instituto de Ciencias Naturales, Universidad Central, Casilla 633, Quito, Ecuador.

QAME QUITO: Herbario "Luciano Andrade Marin," Centro Forestal de Conocoto, Direccion de desarrollo Forestal, Ministerio de Agricultura y Ganadería, casilla 099-B, Quito, Ecuador.

QCA QUITO: Herbario, Instituto de Ciencias, Pontificia Universidad Catolica del Ecuador, Avenida 12 de Octubre, Apartado 2184, Quito, Ecuador.

QCNE Quito: Herbario, Museo Nacional de Ciencias Naturales, Apartado 67, Quito, Ecuador.

QEF Quebec: Herbier du Laboratoire d'ecologie forestière, Ecologie forestière, Université Laval, Québec, Québec, Canada G1K 7P4.

QFA Québec: Herbier Louis-Marie, Faculté des Sciences de l'agriculture et de l'alimentation, Université Laval, Sainte-Foy, Québec, Canada G1K 7P4.

QFB Québec: Herbier, Centre de Recherches Forestières des Laurentides, Environnement Canada, P.O. Box 3800, Sainte-Foy, Québec, Canada G1V 4C7.

QFBE Québec: Environnement Canada Land Directorate Québec Region, C.P. 10100, Sainte-Foy, Québec, Canada G1V 4H5.

QFS Québec: Faculté des Sciences, Université Laval, Québec, Québec, Canada — incorporated in QFA.

QK Kingston: Fowler Herbarium, Biology Department, Queen's University, Kingston, Ontario, Canada K7L 3N6.

QM Natick: Mycology Laboratory (Culture Collection), Pioneering Research Laboratory, U.S. Army Natick Laboratories, Natick, Massachusetts 01760, U.S.A. — transferred to Northern Regional Research Center, 1815 North University Street, Peoria, Illinois 61604.

QMC London: Queen Mary College, London, England, Great Britain.*

QMP Québec: Musée du Québec, Section des sciences naturelles — incorporated in QUE.

QPAR Montreal: Herbier, Laboratoire de Recherches, Service de la Faune, Ministère du Tourisme, de la Chasse et de la Pêche du Québec, 5075 rue Fullum, Montreal 178, Québec, Canada.

QPH Québec: Herbier Provancher, Département de biologie, Faculté des Sciences, Université Laval, Québec, Québec, Canada G1K 7P4.

QPLS Quito: Herbario "P. Luis Sodiro," Biblioteca y Museo "Aurelio Espinoza Polit," Apartado 160, Quito, Ecuador.

QPNRA Quito: Herbario, Departamento de Ecologia, Programa Nacional de Regionalización, Ministerio de Agricultura y Ganadería, Casilla 099-B, Edif. La Filantrópica, Quito, Ecuador.

QRS Atherton: Herbarium, Queensland Regional Station, C.S.I.R.O., Division of Forest Research, P.O. Box 273, Atherton, Queensland 4883, Australia.

QSA La Pocatière: Herbier, Institut de technologie agricole, La Pocatière, Québec, Canada.

QUC Québec: Herbier Cardinal, Département de biologie, Faculté des Sciences, Université Laval, Québec, Québec, Canada G1K 7P4 — incorporated in QFA.

QUE Québec: Herbier du Québec, Complexe Scientifique, 2700 rue Einstein, Sainte-Foy, Québec, Canada G1P 3W8.

R Rio de Janeiro: Herbário, Departamento de Botânica, Museu Nacional, Quinta da Boa Vista, São Cristovão, 20.942 Rio de Janeiro, Rio de Janeiro, Brazil.

RAB Rabat: Institut Scientifique Chérifien, Laboratoire de Taxonomie et Ecologie des Végétaux Supérieurs, Avenue Moulay Chérif, Rabat, Morocco.

RAF Rangoon: Forest Department Herbarium, 526 Merchant Street, Rangoon, Burma.

RAM Ramsey: Ramsey Public Library, Ramsey, Isle of Man, Great Britain.*

RAMM Exeter: Herbarium, Royal Albert Memorial Museum, Queen Street, Exeter, Devon EX4 3RX, England, Great Britain.

RANG Rangoon: Herbarium, Rangoon University, Rangoon, Burma.

RAS Rangoon: Herbarium, Union of Burma Applied Research Institute, Pharmaceutical Department, Rangoon, Burma.

RAU Rabat: Herbarium, Laboratoire de Biologie Végétale, Faculté des Sciences, Avenue Moulay Chérif, Rabat, Morocco.

RAW Rawalpindi: Stewart Herbarium, Gordon College, Rawalpindi, Pakistan.

RB Rio de Janeiro: Herbário, Jardim Botânico do Rio de Janeiro, Rua Pacheco Leão 915, 20.000 Rio de Janeiro, Rio de Janeiro, Brazil.

RBE Rio de Janeiro: Herbário, Instituto de Ecologia e Exp. Agricolas, Caixa Postal 1620, Rio de Janeiro, Rio de Janeiro, Brazil.

RBR Rio de Janeiro: Herbário, Laboratório de Botânica, Escola Nacional de Agronômia, Universidade Rural, Caixa Postal 25, Rio de Janeiro, Rio de Janeiro, Brazil.

RCR Rochester: The Museum, Rochester, England, Great Britain.*

RDG Reading: County Borough Museum and Art Gallery, Reading, England, Great Britain.*

RED Redlands: Herbarium, University of Redlands, Redlands, California 92373, U.S.A.

REG Regensburg: Regensburgische Botanische Gesellschaft, Postfach Universität, 8400 Regensburg, Federal Republic of Germany, BRD.

RELC Chihuahua: Herbario, Rancho Experimental La Campana, Instituto Nacional de Investigaciones Pecuarias, Apartado postal 682, Chihuahua, Chihuahua, Mexico.

REN RENNES: Laboratoire de Botanique de la Faculté des Sciences, Avenue du Général Leclerc, 35 Rennes, France.

RENO RENO: University of Nevada Herbarium, Renewable Natural Resources Division, University of Nevada, Reno, Nevada 89557, U.S.A.

REP REPETEK: Herbarium of the Desert Experiment Station of the W.I.R., Repetek, U.S.S.R.

RESC REDDING: Herbarium, Agriculture and Natural Resources Division, Shasta College, 1065 North Old Oregon Trail, Redding, California 96001, U.S.A.

RFA RIO DE JANEIRO: Herbário, Departamento de Botânica, Instituto de Biologia, Universidade Federal do Rio de Janeiro, Cidade Universitária, Ilha do Fundão, ZC-32 Rio de Janeiro, Rio de Janeiro, Brazil.

RFE RADCLIFFE: Borough Public Library and Local History Museum, Radcliffe, England, Great Britain.*

RGY RUGBY: Rugby School Natural History Society Museum, Rugby, England, Great Britain — incorporated in WAR.*

RHT TIRUCHIRAPALLI: The Rapinat Herbarium, St. Joseph's College, Tiruchirapalli 620002, Tamilnadu, India.

RI ROVINJ: Centar za istraživanje mora, Institut "Rudjer Bošković," 52210 Rovinj, Yugoslavia.

RICK REXBURG: Herbarium, Ricks College, Rexburg, Idaho 83440, U.S.A.

RIG RIGA: Herbarium, Department of Botany, Latvian State University, Fr. Gaila Street 10, 226200 Riga, U.S.S.R.

RIM RIMOUSKI: Herbier, L'Ecole d'Agriculture, Rimouski, Québec, Canada.

RIN LEERSUM: Herbarium, Rijkinstituut voor Natuurbeheer (Research Institute for Nature Management), Kasteel Broekhuizen, Broekhuizerlaan 2, 3956 ZR Leersum, Netherlands.

RIVE RIVER FALLS: Herbarium, Department of Biology, University of Wisconsin, River Falls, Wisconsin 54022, U.S.A.

RIZ RIO DE JANEIRO: Herbário, Seção Experimental de Agrostologia, Instituto de Zootecnia, Km 47, Rio de Janeiro, Rio de Janeiro, Brazil.

RM LARAMIE: Rocky Mountain Herbarium, University of Wyoming, Laramie, Wyoming 82071, U.S.A.

RMS LARAMIE: Wilhelm G. Solheim Mycological Herbarium, University of Wyoming, Laramie, Wyoming 82071, U.S.A.

RMWC LYNCHBURG: Herbarium, Biology Department, Randolph-Macon Woman's College, Lynchburg, Virginia 24503, U.S.A.

RNG READING: Herbarium, Plant Science Laboratories, University of Reading, Whiteknights, Reading RG6 2AS, England, Great Britain.

RNMUT TASHKENT: Herbarium, Republic Nature Museum of Uzbekistan, Sagban Street 16, 700002 Tashkent, U.S.S.R.

RO ROMA: Erbario dell' Istituto Botanico dell' Università di Roma, Città Universitaria, 00100 Roma, Italy.

ROAN ROANOKE: Herbarium, Department of Biology, Virginia Western Community College, P.O. Box 4195, Roanoke, Virginia 24015, U.S.A.

ROCH ROCHESTER: Herbarium of the University of Rochester and the Rochester Academy of Science, Department of Biology, University of Rochester, Rochester, New York 14627, U.S.A — discontinued.

ROML ROMA: Roma Herbarium, National University of Lesotho, Roma, Lesotho.

ROPA ROHNERT PARK: Herbarium, Department of Biology, Sonoma State University, Rohnert Park, California 94928, U.S.A.

ROPV ROMA: Herbarium, Stazione di Patologia Vegetale, Via Casal de' Pazzi 250, 00156 Roma, Italy.

ROST ROSTOCK: Herbarium der Sektion Biologie, Botanischer Garten der Wilhelm-Pieck-Universität, Doberaner-Strasse 143, DDR 25 Rostock, German Democratic Republic, DDR.

RPM READING: Herbarium, Reading Public Museum and Art Gallery, 500 Museum Road, Reading, Pennsylvania 19611, U.S.A.

RPN RIPON: Mechanics' Institute, Ripon, England, Great Britain.*

RPPR RÍO PIEDRAS: Herbarium, Institute of Tropical Forestry, P.O. Box AQ, Río Piedras, Puerto Rico 00928.

RPSC SANTO DOMINGO DE LOS COLORADOS: Herbarium, Rio Palenque Science Center, Casilla 95, Santo Domingo de los Colorados, Pichincha, Ecuador.

RRCBI BANGALORE: Herbarium, Regional Research Center (Ay.), Government Central Pharmacy Annexe, Jayanagar, Bangalore 560011, India.

RSA	CLAREMONT: Herbarium, Rancho Santa Ana Botanic Garden, 1500 N. College Avenue, Claremont, California 91711, U.S.A.
RSDR	CHARDJOW: Herbarium of the Repetek Sandy Desert Reserve, Desert Institute of the Turkmen Academy of Sciences, Chardjow Region, Turkmen S.S.R., 746060 U.S.S.R.
RTE	REIGATE: Holmesdale Natural History Club Museum, Reigate, England, Great Britain.*
RU	READING: Department of Agricultural Botany, The University — incorporated in RNG.
RUBL	JAIPUR: Herbarium, Department of Botany, University of Rajasthan, Jaipur 302004, India.
RUEB	ZÜRICH: Geobotanisches Institut der E.T.H., Stiftung Rübel, Zürichbergstrasse 38, CH-8044 Zürich, Switzerland — incorporated in ZT.
RUH	GRAHAMSTOWN: Rhodes University Herbarium, Department of Plant Sciences, Rhodes University, P.O. Box 94, Grahamstown 6140, South Africa.
RUHV	RADFORD: Herbarium, Biology Department, Box 5792, Radford University, Radford, Virginia 24142, U.S.A.
RUNYON	BROWNSVILLE: Robert Runyon Herbarium, P.O. Box 3311, Brownsville, Texas 78520, U.S.A. — incorporated in TEX.
RUT	NEW BRUNSWICK: Department of Biological Sciences, Douglass College, Rutgers University, New Brunswick, New Jersey 08903, U.S.A. — incorporated in CHRB.
RUTPP	NEW BRUNSWICK: Herbarium, Department of Plant Pathology, Rutgers University, New Brunswick, New Jersey 08903, U.S.A.
RV	ROSTOV ON DON: Herbarium, Department of Botany, Molotov State University of Rostov, Engels Street 105, 344006 Rostov on Don, U.S.S.R.
RYD	RYDE: Isle of Wight Philosophical and Scientific Society, Ryde, England, Great Britain.*

S	STOCKHOLM: Herbarium, Swedish Museum of Natural History (Natuurhistoriska riksmuseet), Rolagsvägen 106, P.O. Box 50007, S-10405 Stockholm, Sweden.
SAAS	GEORGE: Herbarium, Saasveld Forest Research Station, Private Bag X6531, George 6530, South Africa.
SAB	LONDON: Society of Amateur Botanists, London, England, Great Britain.*
SACL	SANTA CLARA: Herbarium, Department of Biology, University of Santa Clara, Santa Clara, California 95053, U.S.A.
SACT	SACRAMENTO: Herbarium, Department of Biological Sciences, California State University, 6000 J Street, Sacramento, California 95819, U.S.A.
SAFB	SASKATOON: Forest Pathology Laboratory, Department of Forestry — incorporated in CFB.
SAFU	SAN FRANCISCO: Herbarium, University of San Francisco, San Francisco, California 94117, U.S.A. — discontinued.
SAL	SALINA: Herbarium, Department of Biology, Kansas Wesleyan, Salina, Kansas 67401, U.S.A.
SALLE	CANOAS: Instituto Geobiológico La Salle, Canoas, Rio Grande do Sul, Brazil — incorporated in ICN.
SAM	CAPE TOWN: South African Museum Herbarium, National Botanic Gardens of South Africa, Kirstenbosch, Private Bag X7, Claremont 7735, South Africa.
SAMARU	ZARIA: Agricultural Institute, Samaru, Zaria, Nigeria.**
SAN	SANDAKAN: Forest Department Herbarium, P.O. Box 1407, Sandakan, Sabah, Malaysia.
SANT	SANTIAGO DE COMPOSTELA: Herbarium, Jardin Botánico, Universidad de Santiago, Facultad de Farmacia, Avenida Las Ciencias s/n, Santiago de Compostela, La Coruña, Spain.
SAP	SAPPORO: Laboratory of Plant Taxonomy and Ecology, Botanical Institute, Faculty of Agriculture, Hokkaido, Sapporo, Japan.
SAPA	SAPPORO: Laboratory of Plant Virology and Mycology, Department of Botany, Faculty of Agriculture, Hokkaido University, Kita-9, Nishi-9, Kitaku, Sapporo 060, Japan.
SAPCL	LAURINBURG: Herbarium, Department of Biology, St. Andrews Presbyterian College, Laurinburg, North Carolina 28352, U.S.A.
SAPS	SAPPORO: Herbarium, Botanical Institute, Faculty of Science, Hokkaido University, Kita 10, Nisha 8, Kitaku, Sapporo 060, Japan.
SAR	KUCHING: Sarawak Herbarium, Forest Department Headquarters, Jalan Badruddin, Kuching, Sarawak, E. Malaysia.
SARA	SARAJEVO: Biološki Institut, Postfach 281, Sarajevo, Yugoslavia.
SARAT	SARATOV: University Herbarium, Saratov, U.S.S.R.
SARC	SALEM: Herbarium, Department of Biology, Roanoke College, Salem, Virginia 24153, U.S.A.
SASK	SASKATOON: W. P. Fraser Herbarium, Department of Plant Ecology, University of Saskatchewan, Saskatoon, Saskatchewan S7N 0W0, Canada.
SASSA	SASSARI: Herbarium, Istituto Botanica Farmaceutica, Via Muroni 23/A, 07100 Sassari, Sardinia, Italy.

SASY   Yakutsk: Herbarium, Institute of Biology of the Yakutian Branch of the Siberian Academy of Sciences, Petrovskogo Street 2, Yakutsk 677891, U.S.S.R.

SAT   San Angelo: Herbarium, Department of Biology, Angelo State University, Box 10890, A.S.U. Station, San Angelo, Texas 76901, U.S.A.

SAV   Bratislava: Botanický ústav Slovenskej akadémie vied, Dúbravská cesta 26, 80900 Bratislava, Czechoslovakia.

SAWV   Salem: Herbarium, Department of Natural Science, Salem College, Salem, West Virginia 26426, U.S.A.

SB   Saint Bernard: Herbarium, Saint Bernard College, Saint Bernard, Alabama 35138, U.S.A.

SBBG   Santa Barbara: Herbarium, Santa Barbara Botanic Garden, 1212 Mission Canyon Road, Santa Barbara, California 93105, U.S.A.

SBC   Changed to UCSB.

SBCC   Santa Barbara: Herbarium, Santa Barbara City College, 721 Cliff Drive, Santa Barbara, California 93109, U.S.A.

SBG   Stavropol: Herbarium of the Stavropol Botanical Garden, ab. Yashch 22, 355000 Stavropol, U.S.S.R.

SBM   Santa Barbara: Herbarium, Santa Barbara Museum of Natural History, 2559 Puesta Del Sol Road, Santa Barbara, California 93105, U.S.A.

SBT   Stockholm: Herbarium, Bergius Foundation, P.O. Box 50017, S-104 05 Stockholm, Sweden.

SBU   Saint Bonaventure: Herbarium, Department of Biology, Saint Bonaventure University, Saint Bonaventure, New York 14778, U.S.A.

SBY   Salisbury: Salisbury, S. Wilts and Blackmore Museum, Salisbury, England, Great Britain.*

SC   Winston-Salem: Herbarium, Salem College, Winston-Salem, North Carolina 27108, U.S.A.

SCA   Victoria: Herbarium, Victoria Botanic Garden, Victoria, Cameroun -- incorporated in YA.

SCB   Boukoko: Herbarium, Station Centrale de Boukoko, via M'Baiki, Boukoko, Oubangui-Chari, Central African Republic.

SCCBC   Castlegar: Herbarium, Department of Environmental Sciences, Selkirk College, P.O. Box 1200, Castlegar, British Columbia, Canada V1N 3J1.

SCFQ   Québec: Herbier, Service Canadien de la Faune, Région du Québec, 2700 Blvd. Laurier, C.P. 10.100, Sainte-Foy, Québec, Canada G1V 4H5.

SCH   Schaffhausen: Naturhistorisches Museum, Frauengasse, Schaffhausen, Switzerland.

SCHN   Northampton: Herbarium, Department of Biological Sciences, Smith College, Clark Science Center, Northampton, Massachusetts 01063, U.S.A.

SCL   Saint Cloud: Herbarium, Department of Biological Sciences, St. Cloud State University, St. Cloud, Minnesota 56301, U.S.A.

SCM   Sheffield: Herbarium, Sheffield City Museum, Weston Park, Sheffield 10, England, Great Britain.

SCR   La Jolla: Scripps Institution of Oceanography, University of California, La Jolla, California 92093, U.S.A.

SCS   Swift Current: Herbarium, Research Station, Agriculture Canada, Swift Current, Saskatchewan, Canada S9H 3X2.

SCT   Sidcot: Friends' School, Sidcot, England, Great Britain.*

SCU   Jinan: Herbarium, Shantung Christian University, Jinan, Shandong, People's Republic of China.

SCZ   Balboa: Canal Zone Herbarium, Apartado 2072, Balboa, Panama (formerly listed under Canal Zone).

SD   San Diego: Herbarium, San Diego Museum of Natural History, Box 1390, Balboa Park, San Diego, California 92112, U.S.A.

SDC   Brookings: Herbarium, Department of Biology, South Dakota State University, Brookings, South Dakota 57007, U.S.A.

SDM   San Diego: Herbarium, San Diego Mesa College, 7250 Mesa College Drive, San Diego, California 92111, U.S.A.

SDN   Swindon: Borough Museum, Swindon, England, Great Britain.*

SDSU   San Diego: Herbarium, Botany Department, San Diego State University, College Avenue, San Diego, California 92182, U.S.A.

SDU   Vermillion: Herbarium, Biology Department, University of South Dakota, Vermillion, South Dakota 57069, U.S.A.

SEL   Sarasota: Herbarium, The Marie Selby Botanical Gardens, 800 S. Palm Avenue, P.O. Box 4155, Sarasota, Florida 33577, U.S.A.

SEV   Sevilla: Departamento de Botanica, Avda. Reina Mercedes s/n, Sevilla, Spain.

SEY   PORT VICTORIA: Herbarium, Department of Agriculture, Mont Fleuri, Mahe, Seychelles.

SF   SANTA FE: Herbario, Dirección Ecología y Protección de la Fauna, Boulevard Pellegrini 3100, Casilla de Correo 2000, Santa Fe, Argentina.

SFB   BRIGNOLES: Salques Foundation of Brignoles for the Development of Biological Sciences, Brignoles, France.

SFD   SHEFFIELD: Herbarium, Sheffield City Museum, Weston Park, Sheffield SI0 2TP, England, Great Britain.

SFPA   PORTO ALEGRE: Herbário, Seção de Fitopatologia, Divisão de Pesquisas Agronômicas, Rua Gonçalves Dias 570, 90.000 Porto Alegre, Rio Grande do Sul, Brazil.

SFRF   SAN FRANCISCO: U.S. Forest Service Herbarium, Region Five (California), Division of Range and Wildlife Management, 630 Sansome Street, San Francisco, California 94111, U.S.A. -- incorporated in CAS.

SFRP   PINEVILLE: Herbarium, Range Management Research, Southern Forest Experiment Station, U.S. Forest Service, 2500 Shreveport Highway, Pineville, Louisiana 71360, U.S.A.

SFS   SHERBROOKE: Herbier Rolland-Germain, Département de Biologie, Université de Sherbrooke, Sherbrooke, Québec, Canada J1K 2R1.

SFSU   SAN FRANCISCO: Herbarium, Department of Biological Sciences, San Francisco State University, 1600 Holloway Avenue, San Francisco, California 94132, U.S.A.

SFT   STOWLANGTOFT: Stowlangtoft Hall, Stowlangtoft, England, Great Britain.*

SFUV   BURNABY: Herbarium, Department of Biological Sciences, Simon Fraser University, Burnaby, British Columbia, Canada V5A 1S6.

SFV   NORTHRIDGE: Herbarium, Department of Biology, California State University, 18111 Nordhoff Street, Northridge, California 91330, U.S.A.

SGE   STALYBRIDGE: The Museum, Stalybridge, England, Great Britain.*

SGO   SANTIAGO: Herbario, Seccion Botánica, Museo Nacional de Historia Natural, Casilla 787, Santiago, Chile.

SH   SHANGHAI: Herbarium, Institute of Botany, Academia Sinica, Shanghai, People's Republic of China -- incorporated in PE.

SHB   SHANGHAI: Herbarium, Shanghai Baptist College, Shanghai, People's Republic of China -- incorporated in NAS.

SHD   SHEFFIELD: Department of Botany of the University, Sheffield, England, Great Britain.*

SHIN   MATSUMOTO: Herbarium and Biological Institute, Faculty of Liberal Arts, Shinshu University, 3-1-1 Asahi, Matsumoto, Japan.

SHJ   SHANGHAI: Herbarium, St. John's University, Shanghai, People's Republic of China -- incorporated in HSNU.

SHMH   SHANGHAI: Musée Heude (Ancien Musée de Zikawei), Université l'Aurore, 223 Avenue Dubail, Shanghai, People's Republic of China -- incorporated in NAS.

SHST   HUNTSVILLE: Herbarium, Department of Life Sciences, Sam Houston State University, Huntsville, Texas 77341, U.S.A.

SHTC   TURLOCK: Stanislaus Herbarium, California State College, Stanislaus, 800 Monte Vista Avenue, Turlock, California 95380, U.S.A.

SHY   SHREWSBURY: Borough Public Library, Museum and Art Gallery, Shrewsbury, England, Great Britain.*

SI   SAN ISIDRO: Herbario, Instituto de Botanica Darwinion, Labarden 200, 1640 Martínez, San Isidro, Buenos Aires, Argentina.

SIAC   SIENA: Herbarium, Accademia del Fisiocritici, Prato S. Agostino 4, Siena, Italy.

SIB   SIBIU: Muzeul Brukenthal Sibiu, Secţia de Istorie Naturală, str. Cetăţii 1, 2400 Sibiu, Romania.

SICH   INDIANOLA: Herbarium, Department of Biology, Simpson College, Indianola, Iowa 50125, U.S.A.

SIENA   SIENA: Istituto di Botanica, Università di Siena, Via Mattioli 4, 53100 Siena, Italy.

SIGMA   MONTPELLIER: Herbarium, Station Internationale de Géobotanique Méditerranéenne et Alpine, Rue du Pioch de Boutonnet, Montpellier (Hérault), France.

SIM   STATEN ISLAND: Herbarium, Staten Island Museum, 75 Stuyvesant Place, Staten Island, New York 10301, U.S.A.

SIMF   SIMFEROPOL: Herbarium, Department of Botany of the Crimean Pedagogic Institute, ul. Lenina 17, Simferopol, Crimea, U.S.S.R.

SING   SINGAPORE: Herbarium and Library, Botanic Gardens, Cluny Road, Singapore 10, Singapore.

SIU   CARBONDALE: Herbarium, Department of Botany, Southern Illinois University, Carbondale, Illinois 62901, U.S.A.

SJC   LONDON: Department of Biology, Sir John Cass College, London, England, Great Britain.*

SJFM	SAINT JOHNSBURY: Herbarium, Fairbanks Museum and Planetarium, Main and Prospect streets, St. Johnsbury, Vermont 05819, U.S.A.
SJSU	SAN JOSE: Herbarium, California State University, San Jose, California 95192, U.S.A.
SK	SKARA: Katedralskolan, Brunsbogatan 1, S-532 00 Skara, Sweden.
SKK	SEOUL: Herbarium, Department of Biology, Sung Kyun Kwan University, 3 ga 53, Meong Lyun Dong Jong Loo Gu, Seoul 110, Korea.
SKN	SKIPTON: Craven Museum, Skipton, England, Great Britain.*
SKT	STOCKPORT: Municipal Museum, Stockport, England, Great Britain.*
SL	FREETOWN: Sierra Leone National Herbarium, Department of Biological Sciences, Njala University College, Sierra Leone, PMB Freetown, Sierra Leone, West Africa.
SLBI	LONDON: Herbarium, South London Botanical Institute, 323 Norwood Road, London S.E. 24, England, Great Britain.
SLC	SALT LAKE CITY: Department of Botany, East High School, Salt Lake City, Utah 84102, U.S.A. — incorporated in UT.
SLO	BRATISLAVA: Department of Systematic Botany of Faculty of Natural Sciences, Comenius University, Révová 39, 80100 Bratislava, Czechoslovakia.
SLPM	SAN LUIS POTOSÍ: Herbario del Instituto de Investigacion de Zonas Deserticas, Universidad Autónoma de San Luis Potosí, Alvaro Obregon 64, San Luis Potosí, San Luis Potosí, Mexico.
SLRO	SLIPPERY ROCK: Herbarium, Department of Biology, Slippery Rock State College, Slippery Rock, Pennsylvania 16057, U.S.A.
SLU	SUDBURY: Herbarium, Department of Biology, Laurentian University, Sudbury, Ontario, Canada P3E 2C6.
SLUS	KUMASI: Council for Scientific and Industrial Research, Soils and Land-use Survey, Kwadaso, Ghana.**
SMCW	WINOOSKI: Herbarium, Biology Department, Saint Michael's College, Winooski, Vermont 05404, U.S.A.
SMDB	SANTA MARIA: Herbário, Departamento de Biologia, Centro de Ciências Naturais e Exatas, Universidade Federal de Santa Maria, 97.100 Santa Maria, Rio Grande do Sul, Brazil.
SMF	LIMA: Herbario, Instituto de Botanica y Recursos Vegetales Terapeuticos, Universidad Nacional Mayor de San Marcos, Casilla 3551, Lima 1, Peru.
SMH	SAINT MEINRAD: Henrietta Herbarium, College of Liberal Arts, Saint Meinrad College, St. Meinrad, Indiana 47577, U.S.A.
SMRS	STAVROPOL: Herbarium of Stavropol Museum of Regional Studies, Dzerzhinskovo St. 135, 355000 Stavropol, U.S.S.R.
SMS	SPRINGFIELD: Ozarks Regional Herbarium, Department of Life Sciences, Southwest Missouri State University, Springfield, Missouri 65802, U.S.A.
SMU	DALLAS: Herbarium, Southern Methodist University, Dallas, Texas 75275, U.S.A.
SMW	LONDON: School of Medicine for Women, London, England, Great Britain.*
SNC	DE PERE: The Heraly MacDonald Herbarium, Division of Natural Sciences, Saint Norbert College, De Pere, Wisconsin 54115, U.S.A.
SNM	SILVER CITY: Herbarium, Department of Biological Science, Western New Mexico University, Silver City, New Mexico 88061, U.S.A.
SNU	SEOUL: The Herbarium, Seoul National University, Seoul, Korea.
SO	SOFIA: Herbarium, Department of Botany, University of Sofia, ul. Dragan Zankov N8, Sofia 1421, Bulgaria.
SOA	SOFIA: Herbarium, College of Agriculture "Georgi Dimitroff," Sofia, Bulgaria.
SOC	ASHLAND: Herbarium, Department of Biology, Southern Oregon State College, Ashland, Oregon 97520, U.S.A.
SOM	SOFIA: Botanical Institute of the Bulgarian Academy of Sciences, Str. "Akad. G. Bontshev," Clou I, 1113 Sofia, Bulgaria.
SOTO	POINT LOOKOUT: Herbarium, Biology Department, School of the Ozarks, Point Lookout, Missouri 65726, U.S.A.
SOTON	SOUTHAMPTON: Southampton University — see SPN.
SOUT	SOUTHAMPTON: Herbarium, Division of Natural Sciences, Southampton College, Long Island University, Southampton, New York 11968, U.S.A.
SP	SÃO PAULO: Herbario do Estado "Maria Eneyda P. K. Fidalgo," Instituto de Botânica, Caixa Postal 4005, 01000 São Paulo, São Paulo, Brazil.
S-PA	STOCKHOLM: Section for Palaeobotany, Naturhistoriska riksmuseet — incorporated in S.
SPAL	REGGIO EMILIA: Herbarium, Civici Musei e Gallerie, Via Spallanzani I, 42100 Reggio Emilia, Italy.

SPB	São Paulo: Herbário, Faculty of Pharmacy and Biochemistry, Universidade de São Paulo — *see* SPF.
SPC	Seattle: Herbarium, Department of Biology, Seattle Pacific College, Seattle, Washington 98119, U.S.A.
SPF	São Paulo: Herbário, Departamento de Botânica, Instituto de Biociências, Universidade de São Paulo, Caixa Postal 11.461, 01000 São Paulo, São Paulo, Brazil.
SPH	Hillsboro: Herbarium, Fox Research Forest, Center Road, Hillsboro, New Hampshire 03244, U.S.A.
SPI	Stavropol: Herbarium, Department of Botany, Stavropol Pedagogical Institute, Lenina Square 1, 355009 Stavropol, U.S.S.R.
SPL	Stockholm: Palynological Laboratory — incorporated in S.
SPLT	Levelland: Herbarium, Science Department, South Plains College, Levelland, Texas 79336, U.S.A.
SPMS	Saint Petersburg: Herbarium, Department of Marine Science, University of South Florida, 830 First Street South, St. Petersburg, Florida 33701, U.S.A.
SPN	Southampton: Herbarium, Biology Department, Southampton University, Building 44, Southampton SO9 5NH, England, Great Britain.
SPR	Springfield: Luman Andrews Herbarium, Springfield Science Museum, 236 State Street, Springfield, Massachusetts 01103, U.S.A.
SPSF	São Paulo: Herbário Bento Pickel, Instituto Florestal de São Paulo, Rua do Horto, Caixa Postal 1322, 02377 São Paulo, São Paulo, Brazil.
SPT	Southport: Botanic Gardens Museum, Southport, England, Great Britain.*
SPWH	Woods Hole: Herbarium, Marine Biological Laboratory, George M. Gray Museum, Woods Hole, Massachusetts 02543, U.S.A.
SRCG	Gruver: Herbarium, Science Research Center, 112 Main, Box 1095, Gruver, Texas 79040, U.S.A.
SRD	Stratford: Essex Field Club Museum, Stratford, England, Great Britain.*
SRFA	Santa Rosa: Herbario, Facultad de Agronomía, Universidad Nacional de La Pampa, Casilla de Correo 159, 6.300 Santa Rosa, La Pampa, Argentina.
SRGH	Salisbury: National Herbarium and Botanic Garden, P.O. Box 8100, Causeway, Salisbury, Zimbabwe.
SRR	Rijswijk: Koninklijke Shell, Exploratie en Produktie Laboratorium — discontinued.
SRSC	Alpine: Herbarium, Department of Biology, Sul Ross State University, Alpine, Texas 79830, U.S.A.
SS	Sassari: Istituto di Botanica, Facoltá di Scienze Mat. Fis. e Nat., Università di Sassari, Via Muroni 25, 07100 Sassari, Italy.
SSJC	Stockton: Herbarium, San Joaquin County Department of Agriculture, P.O. Box 1809, 1868 E. Hazelton, Stockton, California 95201, U.S.A.
SSLP	Provo: Herbarium, Shrub Sciences Laboratory, U.S. Forest Service, Intermountain Forest and Range Experiment Station, 735 N. 500 E., Provo, Utah 84601, U.S.A.
SSMF	Sault Ste. Marie: Herbarium, Great Lakes Forest Research Centre, Canadian Forestry Service, Box 490, Sault Ste. Marie, Ontario, Canada P6A 5M7 (formerly Maple Forest Pathology Laboratory — MFB).
SSUC	Santiago: Herbario, Sala de Sistematica, Departamento de Biología Ambiental y de Poblaciones, Instituto de Ciencias Biológicas, Pontificia Universidad Católica de Chile, Casilla 114-D, Santiago, Chile.
STA	Saint Andrews: Herbarium of the Department of Botany, The University, St. Andrews, Fife KY16 9AL, Scotland, Great Britain.
STAL	Saint Albans: Hertfordshire County Museum, St. Albans, England, Great Britain.*
STAR	Jonesboro: Herbarium, Department of Biological Science, Arkansas State University, State University, Arkansas 72467, U.S.A.
STB	London: St. Bartholomew's Hospital, London, England, Great Britain.*
STCR	Saint Clothilde: Herbier de la Réunion, St. Clothilde, Réunion.
STD	Southend-on-Sea: Prittlewell Priory Museum, Southend-on-Sea, England, Great Britain.*
STE	Stellenbosch: Government Herbarium, Botanical Research Unit, Natuurwetenskappe Gebou, Merriman Ave., P.O. Box 471, Stellenbosch 7600, South Africa.
STEU	Stellenbosch: Herbarium of the Department of Botany, University of Stellenbosch, Stellenbosch 7600, South Africa.
STEU-VB	Stellenbosch: Herbarium P. A. van der Byl — *see* STEU.
STI	Stirling: Herbarium, Stirling Smith Art Gallery and Museum, Albert Place, Stirling, Scotland, Great Britain.

STL SANTO TOMÉ: Herbario, Instituto Nacional de Limnología, José Macía 1933, 3016 Santo Tomé, Santa Fe, Argentina.

STM STREATHAM: Streatham Antiquarian and Natural History Society, Streatham, England, Great Britain.*

STO STOKE-ON-TRENT: City Museum and Art Gallery, Stoke-on-Trent, England, Great Britain.*

STP SAINT PETER PORT: La Société Guernesiaise Museum, St. Peter Port, Guernsey, Channel Islands, Great Britain.*

STPE SAINT PETERSBURG: Herbarium, Marine Research Laboratory, Florida Department of Natural Resources, 100 Eighth Avenue, S.E., St. Petersburg, Florida 33731, U.S.A.

STR STRASBOURG: Institut de Botanique de l'Université Louis Pasteur, 28 Rue Goethe, 67083 Strasbourg Cedex, France.

STRI BALBOA: Barro Colorado Island Herbarium, Smithsonian Tropical Research Institute, Apartado 2072, Balboa, Panama.

STS STROMNESS: Orkney Natural History Society Museum, Stromness, Scotland, Great Britain.*

STT LONDON: St. Thomas's Hospital Medical School Library, London, England, Great Britain.*

STU LUDWIGSBURG: Staatliches Museum für Naturkunde Stuttgart, Abteilung für Botanik, Arsenalplatz 3, D-7140 Ludwigsburg, Federal Republic of Germany, BRD.

SU SUZHOU: Herbarium, Suzhou University, Suzhou, Jiangsu, People's Republic of China.

SUCH SUKHUMI: Colchic Herbarium, Sukhumi Botanical Garden of the Georgian Academy of Sciences, Chavchavadze Street 20, 384933 Sukhumi, Abkhaizian A.S.S.R., U.S.S.R.

SUD STROUD: Cowie Museum, Stroud, England, Great Britain.*

SUJ JENA: Schiller University, Jena, German Democratic Republic, DDR -- discontinued.

SUM ŠUMPERK: Vlastivědný ústav v. Šumperku, Sady 1, máje 1, Šumperk, Czechoslovakia.

SUN SUNDERLAND: County Borough Public Library, Museum and Art Gallery, Sunderland, England, Great Britain.*

SUNIV STOCKHOLM: Herbarium, Institute of Botany, University of Stockholm, S-106 91 Stockholm, Sweden.

SUVA SUVA: Fiji Herbarium, Ministry of Agriculture and Fisheries, P.O. Box 358, Suva, Fiji.

SUWS SUPERIOR: Herbarium, Biology Department, University of Wisconsin – Superior, 1800 Grand Avenue, Superior, Wisconsin 54880, U.S.A.

SV HABANA: Herbario, Instituto de Agronomía, Santiago de las Vegas, Habana, Cuba -- housed at HAC.

SVER SVERDLOVSK: Herbarium of the Laboratory of Plant Ecology and Geobotany, Institute of Plant and Animal Ecology, Urals Centre Academy of Sciences, 8 Marta 202, 620008 Sverdlovsk, U.S.S.R.

SVG STAVANGER: Herbarium, Arkeologisk Museum, Stavanger, Norway.

SWA SWANSEA: Herbarium, Swansea Museum, Victoria Road, Swansea 5A1 1SN, Wales, Great Britain.

SWBR SWEET BRIAR: Herbarium, Biology Department, Sweet Briar College, Sweet Briar, Virginia 24595, U.S.A. -- incorporated in LYN.

SWC SWARTHMORE: Herbarium, Biology Department, Swarthmore College, Swarthmore, Pennsylvania 19081, U.S.A.

SWE BUCKINGHAM: Stowe School, Buckingham, England, Great Britain.*

SWMT MEMPHIS: Herbarium, Department of Biology, Southwestern at Memphis, 2000 N. Parkway, Memphis, Tennessee 38112, U.S.A.

SWN SAFFRON WALDEN: The Museum, Saffron Walden, England, Great Britain.*

SYD SYDNEY: John Ray Herbarium, University of Sydney, Botany Building A12, Sydney, N.S.W. 2006, Australia.

SYKO SYKTYVKAR: Herbarium, Laboratory of Geobotany and Plant Systematics, Biological Institute of the Komi Section of Academy of Sciences of U.S.S.R., Kommunisticheskaya St. 24, 167610 Syktyvkar, Komi, U.S.S.R.

SYR SYRACUSE: Herbarium, Department of Plant Sciences, Syracuse University, Syracuse, New York 13210, U.S.A.

SYRF SYRACUSE: Herbarium, Department of Environmental and Forest Biology, College of Environmental Science and Forestry, State University of New York, Syracuse, New York 13210, U.S.A.

SYS GUANGZHOU: Herbarium, Department of Biology, Sun Yatsen University, Guangzhou, Guangdong, People's Republic of China.

SYT STONEYHURST: Stoneyhurst College, Stoneyhurst, England, Great Britain.*

SZ CHENGDU: Herbarium, Department of Biology, National Sichuan University, Chengdu, Sichuan, People's Republic of China.

SZB SALZBURG: Herbarium, Haus der Natur, Hofstallgasse 7, Salzburg, Austria.

SZE SZEGED: Herbarium, Mora Ferenc Muzeum, Szeged, Hungary.

SZL SALZBURG: Landesherbar von Salzburg, Salzburg, Austria.

SZU SALZBURG: Institut für Botanik der Universität, Abteilung f. Systematik u. Geobotanik, Frei-saalweg 16, A5020 Salzburg, Austria.

TAA TARTU: Herbarium of the Institute of Zoology and Botany of the Academy of Sciences of the E.S.S.R., 21 Vanemuise Street, Tartu, Estonian S.S.R., U.S.S.R.

TAC STEPHENVILLE: Herbarium, Department of Biological Sciences, Tarleton State University, Box T-219, Stephenville, Texas 76402, U.S.A.

TAD DUSHAMBE: Department of Flora and Systematics of Higher Plants, Botanical Institute of the Tadzhikistan Academy of Sciences, Karamova St. 27, 734017 Dushambe, U.S.S.R.

TAES COLLEGE STATION: S. M. Tracy Herbarium, Department of Range Science, Texas A&M University, College Station, Texas 77843, U.S.A.

TAI TAIPEI: The Herbarium, Department of Botany, National Taiwan University, Taipei, Taiwan.

TAIC KINGSVILLE: Herbarium, Biology Department, Texas Arts and Industries University, P.O. Box 158, Kingsville, Texas 78363, U.S.A.

TAIF TAIPEI: Herbarium, Taiwan Forestry Research Institute, Po-A Road Botanical Garden, Taipei, Taiwan.

TAIM TAIPEI: Herbarium, Taiwan Museum, No. 2 Siangyang Road, Taipei, Taiwan.

TAK TASHKENT: Herbarium, Biology-Soils Faculty, Lenin State University, Karl Marx Street 35, 700047 Tashkent, U.S.S.R.

TALE TALENCE: Herbarium, Faculté des Sciences, Laboratoire Géologique, Talence, France.

TAM TARTU: Herbarium, State Museum of Natural Sciences, Tartu, Estonian S.S.R., U.S.S.R.

TAMU COLLEGE STATION: Herbarium, Department of Biology, Texas A&M University, College Station, Texas 77843, U.S.A.

TAN TANANARIVE: Institut de Recherche Scientifique de Madagascar, BP 434, Tananarive, Madagascar.

TAR TARANTO: Herbarium, Istituto di Biologia Marino, Via Roma 3, Taranto, Italy.

TARI TEHRAN: Botanical Institute of Iran, Karaj Road, P.O. Box 8-6096, Tehran, Iran.

TASH TASHKENT: Herbarium, Institute of Botany of the Uzbek Academy of Sciences, F. Khodzhaeva str. 32, 700125 Tashkent, U.S.S.R.

TAU THESSALONIKI: Herbarium Universitatis Thessalonicensis, Aristotle University of Thessaloniki, Department of Systematic Botany and Phytogeography, Thessaloniki, Greece.

TB TBILISI: Herbarium, Stalin State University of Tbilisi, University Street, Tbilisi, Georgia, U.S.S.R.

TBI TBILISI: Herbarium, Botanical Institute of the Academy of Sciences of the Georgian S.S.R., Kodjorskaje Highway, Tbilisi 380007, U.S.S.R.

TBY TENBY: The Museum, Tenby, Wales, Great Britain.*

TCD DUBLIN: Herbarium, School of Botany, Trinity College, Dublin 2, Ireland.

TCSW DENTON: Herbarium, Texas State University for Women, Denton, Texas 76201, U.S.A.

TDN TODMORDEN: Todmorden Botanical Society, Todmorden, England, Great Britain.*

TDY TYLDESLEY: Tyldesley Natural History Society, Tyldesley, England, Great Britain.*

TECLA NUEVA SAN SALVADOR: Herbario, Centro Nacional de Tecnologia Agropecuaria, Apartado postal 885, Nueva San Salvador, El Salvador (formerly listed as Santa Tecla).

TEFH TEGUCIGALPA: Herbario, Departamento de Biología, Universidad Nacional Autónoma de Honduras, Tegucigalpa, Honduras.

TEH TEHRAN: Herbarium, Museyeh Guiah shenacy, Faculty of Pharmacy, University of Tehran, Tehran, Iran.

TELA TEL AVIV: Herbarium, Department of Botany, Tel Aviv University, 155 Herzl St., Tel Aviv, Israel.

TENN KNOXVILLE: Herbarium, Department of Botany, University of Tennessee, Knoxville, Tennessee 37916, U.S.A.

TEPB TERESINA: Herbário Graziela Barroso, Departamento de Biologia, Fundação Universidade Federal do Piauí, 64.000 Teresina, Piauí, Brazil.

TER TERRE HAUTE: Herbarium, Life Science Department, Indiana State University, 279 Science Building, Terre Haute, Indiana 47808, U.S.A.

TEX AUSTIN: Herbarium, Department of Botany, Plant Resources Center, University of Texas, Austin, Texas 78712, U.S.A.

TEXA	TEMPLE: Herbarium, Blackland Experiment Station, P.O. Box 414, Temple, Texas 76501, U.S.A. — incorporated in TAES.
TF	KUKIZAKI: Herbarium, Silviculture Division, Forestry and Forest Products Research Institute, P.O. Box 2, Ushiku, Ibaraki 300-12, Japan.
TFA	HACHIOJI: Asakawa Herbarium of Forestry and Forest Products Institute, 1833 Nagafusa-cho, Hachioji, Tokyo 193, Japan.
TFC	LA LAGUNA: Departamento de Botanica, Facultad de Biologia, Universidad de La Laguna, La Laguna, Tenerife, Canary Islands, Spain.
TFD	LUSHOTO: Forest Division Herbarium, Silviculture Research Station, P.O. Box 95, Lushoto, Tanzania.
TFM	TOKYO: Laboratory of Forest Mycology, Government Forest Experiment Station, Shinomeguro-5, Meguro, Tokyo, Japan.
TFMC	SANTA CRUZ DE TENERIFE: Herbarium, Museo Insular de Ciencias Naturales de Tenerife, Santa Cruz de Tenerife, Tenerife, Canary Islands, Spain.
TGM	TBILISI: Herbarium, Department of Botany, S. N. Dzhanashiya State Museum of the Georgian Academy of Sciences, Ketskhoveli St. 10, 380007 Tbilisi, Georgia, U.S.S.R.
TH	TOKYO: The Laboratory of Plant Biology, University of Tokyo — incorporated in TI.
THL	THORNHILL: Grierson Museum, Thornhill (Dumfries), Scotland, Great Britain.*
THO	THURSO: Free Public Library and Museum, Thurso, Scotland, Great Britain.*
THRI	THREE RIVERS: Herbarium, Ash Mountain, Sequoia and Kings Canyon National Parks, Three Rivers, California 93271, U.S.A.
TI	TOKYO: Herbarium, Botanic Gardens Koishikawa, Hakusan 3-7-1, Bunkyo-ku, Tokyo 112, Japan.
TIC	TERMINAL ISLAND: California Department of Fish and Game, Marine Resources Operations, 511 Tuna Street, Terminal Island, California 90731, U.S.A. — discontinued.
TIE	TIANJIN: Herbarium, Musée Hoark-Ho Pai-Ho, Race Course Road, Tianjin, People's Republic of China.
TIK	TIKKURILA: Herbarium, Department of Plant Pathology, Agricultural Research Centre, Tikkurila, Finland — incorporated in H and HPP.
TK	TOMSK: P. N. Krilov Herbarium, Kuibyshev State University of Tomsk, Leninskii Prospect 36, 634010 Tomsk, U.S.S.R.
TKB	TSUKUBA: Herbarium, Institute of Biological Sciences, University of Tsukuba, Sakura-mura, Niihari-gun, Ibaraki 305, Japan.
TKU	TOKYO: Tokyo Kyoiku University, Tokyo, Japan — incorporated in TKB.
TL	TOULOUSE: Laboratoire de Botanique, Université Paul Sabatier, 39 Allées Jules Guesde, 31077 Toulouse Cedex, France.
TLA	TOULOUSE: Laboratoire de Cryptogamie, Université Paul Sabatier (Sciences), 118 route de Narbonne, 31077 Toulouse Cedex (Haute Garonne), France.
TLF	TOULOUSE: Laboratoire Forestier de Toulouse, Faculté des Sciences, Toulouse (Haute Garonne), France.
TLJ	TOULOUSE: Herbarium, Jardin Botanique, Toulouse (Haute Garonne), France.
TLM	TOULOUSE: Muséum d'Histoire Naturelle de Toulouse, Toulouse (Haute Garonne), France.
TLON	TOULON: Herbarium, Musée d'Histoire Naturelle de la Ville de Toulon, Toulon (Var), France.
TLP	TOULOUSE: Chaire de Botanique, Faculté de Medecine, Toulouse (Haute Garonne), France.
TLS	TUNBRIDGE WELLS: Municipal Museum, Tunbridge Wells, England, Great Britain.*
TM	MARTIN: Slovak National Museum — incorporated in BRA.
TMP	TAMPERE: Herbarium, Tampere Museum of Natural History, Pirkankatu 2, SF-33210 Tampere 21, Finland.
TNFS	SITKA: Herbarium, Tongass National Forest, R-10, U.S. Department of Agriculture, Box 1980, Sitka, Alaska 99835, U.S.A.
TNP	TATRANSKÁ LOMNICA: Herbarium, Museum of the Tatra National Park, 05960 Tatranská Lomnica, Czechoslovakia.
TNS	TOKYO: Herbarium, National Science Museum, Department of Botany, 3-23-1 Hyakunin-cho, Shinjuku-ku, Tokyo 160, Japan.
TO	TORINO: Museum Botanicum Horti Taurinensis, c/o Istituto ed Orto Botanico dell' Università, Viale Mattioli 25, 10125 Torino, Italy.
TOD	TODMORDEN: Free Library, Todmorden, England, Great Britain.*
TOFO	TOKYO: Herbarium, Section of Forest Botany, University Museum, University of Tokyo, Yayoi 1-1, Bunkyo-ku, Tokyo 113, Japan.
TOGO	LOMÉ: Herbier de l'Université du Bénin, Laboratoire de Biologie Végétale, Université du Bénin,

	B.P. 1515, Lomé, Togo.
TOHO	Tsudanuma: Herbarium, Toho University, Tsudanuma, Chiba, Japan.
TOKE	Tokyo: Tokyo University of Education, Tokyo, Japan -- incorporated in TKB.
TOLI	Ibagué: Herbario, Departamento de Biología, Universidad del Tolima, Ibagué, Tolima, Colombia.
TOM	Torino: Herbarium, Istituto Missioni Consolata, Corso Ferrucci 14, 10138 Torino, Italy.
TON	Tonbridge: Tonbridge School Natural History Society, Tonbridge, England, Great Britain.*
TOR	Torquay: Herbarium, Torquay Natural History Society, The Museum, Babbacombe Road, Torquay, Devon, England, Great Britain.
TOUK	Toukounous: Livestock Research Station, Toukounous, Niger.**
TPNG	Changed to PNG.
TPV	Prairie View: Herbarium, Department of Biology, Prairie View A & M University, Prairie View, Texas 77445, U.S.A. -- discontinued.
TR	Trento: Herbarium, Museo Tridentino di Scienze Naturale, Trento, Italy.
TRA	La Jolla: The Traub Herbarium of the American Plant Life Society, 2678 Prestwick Court, La Jolla, California 92037, U.S.A.
TRD	Thetford: Herbarium, Ancient House Museum, Thetford, England, Great Britain -- incorporated in NWH.
TRE	Trenčin: Herbarium, Trenčianske múzeum, Mieroné nám. 46, Trenčin, Czechoslovakia.
TRH	Trondheim: Botanical Department, Museum of the Royal Norwegian Society for Science and Letters, Erling Skakkes gt. 47, N-7000 Trondheim, Norway.
TRIN	Saint Augustine: National Herbarium of Trinidad and Tobago, Department of Biological Sciences, University of the West Indies, Saint Augustine, Trinidad.
TRM	Trutnov: Herbarium, Vlastivědné muzeum Trutnov, Trutnov, Czechoslovakia.
TRN	Torún: Department of Plant Systematics and Geography, Copernicus University, Gagarina 9, 87-100 Torún, Poland.
TRO	Truro: Royal Horticultural Society of Cornwall, Truro, England, Great Britain.*
TROM	Tromsoe: Botanical Department of Tromsoe Museum, Institute of Museum Science, University of Tromsoe, 9000 Tromsoe, Norway.
TROY	Troy: Herbarium, Department of Biological Sciences, Troy State University, Troy, Alabama 36081, U.S.A.
TRT	Toronto: Vascular Plant Herbarium, Department of Botany, University of Toronto, Toronto, Ontario, Canada M5S 1A1.
TRTC	Toronto: Cryptogamic Herbarium, Department of Botany, University of Toronto, Toronto, Ontario, Canada M5S 1A1.
TRTE	Mississauga: Herbarium, Erindale College, University of Toronto, 3359 Mississauga Road, Mississauga, Ontario, Canada L5L 1C6 (formerly listed under Toronto).
TRTS	Toronto: Herbarium, Botany Department, Scarborough College, University of Toronto, West Hill, Ontario, Canada M1C 1A4 -- discontinued.
TRU	Truro: Royal Institution of Cornwall, County Museum, Truro, England, Great Britain.*
TRV	Pretoria: Transvaal Museum -- incorporated in PRE.
TS	Qingdao: Herbarium, Department of Biology, National University of Shandong, Qingdao, Shandong, People's Republic of China.
TSB	Trieste: Istituto ed Orto Botanico dell' Università, Via A. Valerio 30, Casella Università I-34100 Trieste, Italy.
TSM	Trieste: Herbarium, Civico Museo di Storia Naturale, Direz. Piazza Hortis 4, 34100 Trieste, Italy.
TSU	Tsu Shi: Botanical Institute, Miye University, Kamihama Cho, Tsu Shi, Miye Ken, Japan.
TTC	Lubbock: E. L. Reed Herbarium, Department of Biological Sciences, Texas Tech University, Box 4149, Lubbock, Texas 79409, U.S.A.
TTN	Taunton: Somerset Archaeological and Natural History Society, Taunton, England, Great Britain.*
TTY	Tetbury: Westonbirt, Tetbury (Glos.), England, Great Britain.*
TU	Tartu: Herbarium, Department of Geobotany and Plant Systematics, Tartu State University, Michurina St. 40, 202400 Tartu, Estonian S.S.R., U.S.S.R.
TUB	Tübingen: Herbarium, Institut für Biologie I, Lehrstuhl spezielle Botanik, Auf der Morganstelle I, D-7400 Tübingen, BRD.
TUC	Tucson: Herbarium, Department of Ecology and Evolutionary Biology, University of Arizona, Tucson, Arizona 85721, U.S.A.
TUFT	Medford: Phippen-LaCroix Herbarium, Department of Biology, Tufts University, Medford,

Massachusetts 02155, U.S.A.
TULS   TULSA: Herbarium, Department of Natural Sciences, University of Tulsa, 600 South College, Tulsa, Oklahoma 74101, U.S.A.
TULV   TULUA: Herbario Jardín Botánico "Juan María Céspedes," Apartado Aéreo 5660, Cali, Valle, Colombia.
TUN   TUNIS: Laboratoire de Biologie Végétale, Faculté des Sciences, Université de Tunis, 8 Rue de Rome, Tunis, Tunisia.
TUP   PETERBOROUGH: Herbarium, Biology Department, Trent University, Peterborough, Ontario, Canada K9J 7B8.
TUR   TURKU: Herbarium, Institute of Biology, University of Turku, SF-20500 Turku 50, Finland.
TURA   TURKU (ÅBO): Herbarium, Institute of Biology, Åbo Akademi, Porthansg. 3, SF-20500 Turku 50, Finland.
TUR-V   TURKU: Herbarium Vainio — see TUR.
TUS   SENDAI: Herbarium, Biological Institute, Faculty of Science, Tohoku University, Aoba, Sendai 980, Japan.
TUSG   SENDAI: Herbarium, Botanical Garden, Tohoku University, Kawauchi, Sendai 980, Japan.

U   UTRECHT: Institute of Systematic Botany, Heidelberglaan 2, P.O. Box 80.102, 3508 TC Utrecht, Netherlands.
UAC   CALGARY: Herbarium, Department of Biology, University of Calgary, Calgary, Alberta, Canada T2N 1N4.
UARK   FAYETTEVILLE: Herbarium, Department of Botany and Bacteriology, University of Arkansas, Fayetteville, Arkansas 72701, U.S.A.
UB   BRASÍLIA: Herbário, Departamento de Biologia Vegetal, Funcação Universidade de Brasília, Caixa Postal 153081, 70.910 Brasília, Distrito Federal, Brazil.
UBA   ULAN-BATOR: Herbarium, Botanical Institute of the Academy of Sciences of the M.P.R., Marshall Zhukov Street, Ulan-Bator, Mongolian People's Republic.
UBC   VANCOUVER: Herbarium, Department of Botany, University of British Columbia, 3529-6270 University Boulevard, University Campus, Vancouver, British Columbia, Canada V6T 2B1.
UBU   ULAN-BATOR: Department of Botany, Mongolian State University, Ulan-Bator, Mongolian People's Republic.
UC   BERKELEY: Herbarium, Department of Botany, University of California, Berkeley, California 94720, U.S.A.
UCBG   GABORONE: Herbarium, Department of Biology, University College of Botswana, Private Bag 0022, Gaborone, Botswana.
UCHT   CHATTANOOGA: Herbarium, Department of Biology, University of Tennessee, Chattanooga, Tennessee 37402, U.S.A.
UCI   IBADAN: Herbarium, Department of Botany, University of Ibadan, Ibadan, Oyo State, Nigeria.
UCJ   ABIDJAN: Herbier National de Côte d'Ivoire (Université d'Abidjan), B.P. 4322, Abidjan, Ivory Coast.
UCMM   SANTIAGO DE LOS CABALLEROS: El Herbario "Rafael M. Moscoso," Universidad Católica Madre y Maestra, Santiago de los Caballeros, Dominican Republic.
UCNW   BANGOR: Herbarium, School of Biology, University College of North Wales, Bangor LL57 2UW, Wales, Great Britain.
UCOB   BARQUISIMETO: Herbario, Escuela Agronomia, Universidad Centro Occidental "Lisandro Alvarado," Barquisimeto, Lara, Venezuela.
UCR   RIVERSIDE: Herbarium, Department of Botany and Plant Sciences, University of California, Riverside, California 92521, U.S.A.
UCS   SCHENECTADY: Herbarium, Department of Biological Sciences, Union College, Schenectady, New York 12308, U.S.A.
UCSB   SANTA BARBARA: Herbarium, Department of Biological Sciences, University of California, Santa Barbara, California 93106, U.S.A.
UCSC   SANTA CRUZ: Herbarium, Division of Natural Sciences, University of California, Santa Cruz, California 95064, U.S.A.
UCSW   CARDIFF: Herbarium, Department of Botany, University College, P.O. Box 78, Cardiff CF1 1XL, Wales, Great Britain.
UCWI   KINGSTON: Herbarium, Department of Botany, University of the West Indies, Mona, Kingston 7, Jamaica.
UDBC   BOGOTÁ: Herbario Forestal, Facultad de Ingeniería Forestal, Universidad Distrital, Carrera 8a, No. 40-78, Bogotá, Colombia.

410

UDM	UDINE: Herbarium, Museo Friulano di Storia Naturale — *see* MFU.
UEC	CAMPINAS: Herbário, Departamento de Morfologia e Sistemática Vegetais, Instituto de Biologia, Universidade Estadual de Campinas (UNICAMP), Caixa Postal 1170, 13.100 Campinas, São Paulo, Brazil.
UFG	GOIÂNIA: Herbário, Departamento de Botânica, Universidade Federal de Goiás, 74.000 Goiânia, Goiás, Brazil.
UFMA	SÃO LUÍS: Herbário Atico Seabra, Laboratório de Hidrobiologia, Universidade Federal do Maranhão, Rua Treze de Maio 506, Caixa Postal 571, 65.000 São Luís, Maranhão, Brazil.
UFMT	CUIABÁ: Herbário, Universidade Federal de Mato Grosso, Avenida Fernando Corrêa da Costa, 78.000 Cuiabá, Mato Grosso, Brazil.
UFP	RECIFE: Herbário, Departamento de Botânica, Centro de Ciências Biológicas, Universidade Federal de Pernambuco, Cidade Universitária, Avenida Artur de Sá, 50.000 Recife, Pernambuco, Brazil.
UFRJ	RIO DE JANEIRO: Herbário, Departamento de Fitopatologica, Universidade Federal Rural do Rio de Janeiro, Antiga Rodovia Rio — São Paulo, Km 47, Via Campo Grande, 20.000 Rio de Janeiro, Rio de Janeiro, Brazil.
UFS	NYABYEYA: Herbarium, Uganda Forest School, P.O. Masindi, Nyabyeya, Uganda.
UIS	BUCARAMANGA: Herbario, Departamento de Biología, Universidad Industrial de Santander, Apartado Aéreo 678, Bucaramanga, Santander, Colombia.
UKMB	BANGI: Herbarium, Botany Department, Universiti Kebangsaan Malaysia, Bangi, Selangor, Malaysia.
UKSPI	UST-KAMENOGORSK: Herbarium, Department of Botany, Ust-Kamenogorsk State Pedagogical Institute, 492036 Ust-Kamenogorsk, U.S.S.R.
ULF	QUÉBEC: Herbier, Département d'ecologie et de pédologie, Faculté de foresterie et géodésie, Université Laval, Québec, Wuébec, Canada G1K 7P4 — incorporated in part in QFA.
ULN	YABA: Herbarium, School of Biological Sciences, University of Lagos, Yaba, Lagos, Nigeria.
ULT	TRIPOLI: Herbarium, Faculty of Science, Al-Faateh University, Tripoli, Libya.
ULV	SANTA CLARA: Centro Agricola Herbario, Universidad Central de Las Villas, Seccion de Canje Internacional, Santa Clara, Las Villas, Cuba.
UMBS	PELLSTON: Herbarium, University of Michigan Biological Station, Pellston, Michigan 49769, U.S.A.
UME	UMEÅ: Avdelningen för ekologisk botanik, Biologiska institutionen, Umeå universitet, 901 87 Umeå, Sweden.
UMO	COLUMBIA: Herbarium, Division of Biological Sciences, University of Missouri, 201 Tucker Hall, Columbia, Missouri 65211, U.S.A.
UMT	UMTALI: Chase Herbarium, Umtali Museum, Victory Avenue, Umtali, Zimbabwe.
UNA	UNIVERSITY: Herbarium, University of Alabama, P.O. Box 1927, University, Alabama 35486, U.S.A.
UNB	FREDERICTON: Connell Memorial Herbarium, Biology Department, University of New Brunswick, College Hill, P.O. Box 4400, Fredericton, New Brunswick, Canada E3B 5A3.
UNCC	CHARLOTTE: Herbarium, Department of Biology, University of North Carolina, Charlotte, North Carolina 28223, U.S.A.
UNL	MONTERREY: Herbario, Facultad de Ciencias Biológicas, Universidad Autónoma de Nuevo León, Ciudad Universitaria, Apartado postal 2790, Monterrey, Nuevo León, Mexico.
UNLV	LAS VEGAS: Herbarium, Department of Biological Sciences, University of Nevada, Las Vegas, Nevada 89154, U.S.A.
UNM	ALBUQUERQUE: Herbarium and Museum of Botany, Department of Biology, University of New Mexico, Albuquerque, New Mexico 87131, U.S.A.
UNN	NSUKKA: Herbarium, University of Nigeria, Nsukka, Nigeria.
UNSW	SYDNEY: The Herbarium of the University of New South Wales, Box 1, P.O., Kensington, N.S.W. 2033, Australia.
UPA	PATRAS: Botanical Institute and Botanical Museum of the University of Patras, Patras, Greece.
UPCB	CURITIBA: Herbário, Departamento de Botânica, Universidade Federal do Paraná, Centro Politécnico, 80.000 Curitiba, Paraná, Brazil.
UPEI	CHARLOTTETOWN: Herbarium, Biology Department, University of Prince Edward Island, Charlottetown, Prince Edward Island, Canada C1A 4P3.
UPNG	PORT MORESBY: University Herbarium, Department of Biology, University of Papua New Guinea, P.O. Box 4820, University, N.C.D., Papua New Guinea.
UPP	UPPINGHAM: Uppingham School Museum, Uppingham, England, Great Britain.*
UPR	RÍO PIEDRAS: Herbario, Jardin Botánico, Administracion Central, Universidad de Puerto Rico, G.P.O. Box 4984-G, San Juan, Puerto Rico 00936.

411

UPS	UPPSALA: The Herbarium, University of Uppsala, P.O. Box 541, S-751 21 Uppsala, Sweden.
UPSV	UPPSALA: Herbarium, Växtbiologiska Institutionen, Box 559, S-751 22 Uppsala, Sweden.
UPTC	TUNJA: Herbario, Departamento de Biología, Universidad Pedagógica y Técnológica de Colombia, Apartado Aéreo 1069, Tunja, Boyacá, Colombia.
UQAM	MONTRÉAL: Herbier, Département des Sciences Biologiques, Université du Québec à Montréal, Case postale 8888, Montréal, Québec, Canada H3C 3P8.
UQAR	RIMOUSKI: Herbier, Département de Biologie, Université du Québec à Rimouski, 300 avenue des Ursulines, Rimouski, Québec, Canada G5L 3A1.
UQTR	TROIS-RIVIÈRES: Herbarium, Département Chimie-Biologie, Université du Québec à Trois-Rivières, Case postale 500, Trois-Rivières, Québec, Canada G9A 5H7.
URM	RECIFE: Herbário, Departamento de Micologia, Centro de Ciências Biológicas, Universidade Federal de Pernambuco, Cidade Universitária, Avenida Prof. Artur de Sá, 50.000 Recife, Pernambuco, Brazil.
URO	SHURI: Herbarium of University of the Ryukyus, Shuri, Okinawa, Ryukyu Islands.
US	WASHINGTON: United States National Herbarium, Department of Botany, Smithsonian Institution, Washington, DC 20560, U.S.A.
USAS	REGINA: Herbarium, Biology Department, University of Regina, Regina, Saskatchewan, Canada S4S 0A2.
USC	LOS ANGELES: Herbarium, Department of Biological Sciences, University of Southern California, University Park, Los Angeles, California 90007, U.S.A. — incorporated in LAM.
USCG	GUATEMALA: Herbario, Escuela de Biología, Museo de Historia Natural y Jardín Botánico, Universidad de San Carlos de Guatemala, Avenida de la Reforma 0-43, Zona 10, Guatemala, Guatemala.
USCH	COLUMBIA: Herbarium, Department of Biology, University of South Carolina, Columbia, South Carolina 29208, U.S.A.
USD	SANTO DOMINGO: Rafael M. Moscoso Herbarium, Universidad Autónoma de Santo Domingo, Santo Domingo, Dominican Republic.
USF	TAMPA: Herbarium, Department of Biology, University of South Florida, Tampa, Florida 33620, U.S.A.
USFS	FORT COLLINS: Forest Service Herbarium, Rocky Mountain Forest and Range Experiment Station, 3825 East Mulberry, Fort Collins, Colorado 80524, U.S.A.
USJ	SAN JOSÉ: Herbario, Escuela de Biología, Universidad de Costa Rica, Ciudad Universitaria "Rodrigo Facio," San José, Costa Rica.
USLH	LAFAYETTE: Ornamental Horticulture Herbarium, Department of Plant Industry and General Agriculture, University of Southwestern Louisiana, P.O. Box 44433, Lafayette, Louisiana 70504, U.S.A.
USM	LIMA: Herbario San Marcos, Museo de Historia Natural, Universidad Nacional Mayor de San Marcos de Lima, Avenida Arenales 1256, Apartado 1109, Lima, Peru.
USNC	WASHINGTON: Non-articulated Coralline Herbarium, Department of Paleobiology, U.S. National Museum of Natural History, Smithsonian Institution, Washington, DC 20560, U.S.A.
USPIY	YAROSLAVL: Herbarium, Department of Botany, K. D. Ushinsky State Pedagogical Institute of Yaroslavl, Kotoroslnaya Embankment 46, 150000 Yaroslavl, U.S.S.R.
USSC	AMARILLO: Herbarium, U.S. Soil Conservation Service, Herring Plaza, Box H-4358, Amarillo, Texas 79101, U.S.A. — dispersed several years ago.
UT	SALT LAKE CITY: Garrett Herbarium, University of Utah, Salt Lake City, Utah 84112, U.S.A.
UTC	LOGAN: Intermountain Herbarium, Department of Biology, UMC 45, Utah State University, Logan, Utah 84322, U.S.A.
UTD	RICHARDSON: Lundell Herbarium, Plant Science Laboratory, University of Texas at Dallas, Box 688, Richardson, Texas 75080, U.S.A.
UTMC	SANTA MARTA: Herbario, Universidad Tecnológica del Magdalena, Apartado Aéreo 732, Santa Marta, Magdalena, Colombia.
UU	UZHGOROD: Herbarium, Department of Botany, Biology Faculty, Uzhgorod University, Oktyabrskaya St. 54, Uzhgorod, U.S.S.R.
UVAL	GUATEMALA: Herbario, Universidad del Valle de Guatemala, Apartado Postal 82, Guatemala, Guatemala.
UVIC	VICTORIA: Herbarium, Department of Biology, University of Victoria, P.O. Box 1700, Victoria, British Columbia, Canada V8W 2Y2.
UVST	UVALDE: Herbarium, Biology Department, Southwest Texas Junior College, Uvalde, Texas 78801, U.S.A.
UWA	NEDLANDS: Botany Department Herbarium, University of Australia, Nedlands, Western Australia 6009, Australia.

UWC   BELLVILLE: Herbarium, University of the Western Cape, Modderdam Road, Private Bag X17, Bellville 7530, South Africa.

UWFP   PENSACOLA: Herbarium, Building 58, Department of Biology, University of West Florida, Pensacola, Florida 32504, U.S.A.

UWJ   JANESVILLE: Herbarium, University of Wisconsin, Rock County Campus, Kellogg Avenue, Janesville, Wisconsin 53545, U.S.A.

UWL   LA CROSSE: Herbarium, Department of Biology, University of Wisconsin – La Crosse, La Crosse, Wisconsin 54601, U.S.A.

UWM   MILWAUKEE: Herbarium, Department of Botany, University of Wisconsin, P.O.Box 413, Milwaukee, Wisconsin 53201, U.S.A.

UWO   LONDON: Herbarium, Department of Plant Sciences, University of Western Ontario, London, Ontario, Canadá N6A 5B5.

UWPG   WINNIPEG: Herbarium, Department of Biology, University of Winnipeg, 515 Portage Avenue, Winnipeg, Manitoba, Canada R3B 2E9.

UWSP   STEVENS POINT: Herbarium, Museum of Natural History, University of Wisconsin, Stevens Point, Wisconsin 54481, U.S.A.

UZL   LUSAKA: Herbarium, Biology Department, University of Zambia, P.O. Box 32379, Lusaka, Zambia.

V   VICTORIA: Herbarium, Botany Division, British Columbia Provincial Museum, Victoria, British Columbia, Canada V8V 1X4.

VA   CHARLOTTESVILLE: University of Virginia Herbarium, Charlottesville, Virginia 22904, U.S.A.—transferred to Mountain Lake Biological Station at Pembroke, Virginia 24136 several years ago.

VAL   VALENCIA: Jardin Botánico de la Universidad, Valencia, Spain.

VALD   VALDIVIA: Herbario, Instituto de Botánica, Facultad de Ciencias, Universidad Austral de Chile, Casilla 567, Valdivia, Chile.

VALLE   PALMIRA: Herbario, Facultad de Ciencias Agropecuarias, Universidad Nacional, Seccional Palmira, Apartado Aéreo 237, Palmira, Valle, Colombia.

VALPL   VALPARAÍSO: Herbario Liquenológico, Departamento de Biología, Facultad de Matemáticas y Ciencias Naturales, Universidad de Chile, Valparaíso, Casilla 130-V, Valparaíso, Chile.

VAN   VANNES: Herbarium, Société Polymathique du Morbihan, 2 rue Noé, Vannes, Morbihan, France.

VAS   POUGHKEEPSIE: Herbarium, Department of Biology, Vassar College, Poughkeepsie, New York 12601, U.S.A.

VBI   VÁCRÁTÓT: Magyar Tudományos Akadémia Botanikai Kutatóintézete, 2163 Vácrátót, Hungary.

VCU   RICHMOND: Herbarium, Department of Biology, Virginia Commonwealth University, 816 Park Avenue, Richmond, Virginia 23284, U.S.A.

VDAC   RICHMOND: Herbarium, Virginia Department of Agriculture and Consumer Services, Room 238, Consolidated Laboratories Building, 1 North 14th Street, Richmond, Virginia 23219, U.S.A.

VDB   NASHVILLE: Herbarium, Department of Botany and Zoology, Vanderbilt University, Box 1705, Station B, Nashville, Tennessee 37235, U.S.A.

VEN   CARACAS: Instituto Botánico, Apartado 2156, Caracas, Venezuela.

VENDA   SIBASA: Venda Herbarium, Private Bag X2247, Sibasa 0970, Republic of Venda.

VER   VERONA: Erbario Generale del Museo Civico di Storia Naturale di Verona, Sezione di Botanica, Corso Cavour 11, 37121 Verona, Italy.

VI   VISBY: Högre Allmänna Läroverket, Visby, Sweden.

VIAY   YEREVAN: Herbarium, Department of Botany, Veterinarian Institute of Armenia, Teryana St. 66, 375009 Yerevan, U.S.S.R.

VIC   VIÇOSA: Herbário, Departamento de Biologia Vegetal, Universidade Federal de Viçosa, 36.570, Viçosa, Minas Gerais, Brazil.

VICA   VICTORIA: Agriculture Department Herbarium, Victoria, Cameroun.**

VICC   IKARE: Victory College, Ikare, Nigeria.**

VICF   VICTORIA: Department of Forestry, Victoria, Cameroun.**

VIL   ORSAY: Laboratoire de Biologie Végétale, Faculté des Sciences, 91405 Orsay, France.

VIST   SAINT THOMAS: Diagnostic Herbarium, Cooperative Extension Service, College of the Virgin Islands, St. Thomas, U.S. Virgin Islands 00801.

VLA   VLADIVOSTOK: Herbarium, Institute of Biology-Soils, Far Eastern Scientific Center of the Academy of Sciences of the U.S.S.R., 159 G. Stoletiya Prospect, 690022 Vladivostok, U.S.S.R.

VMIL   LEXINGTON: Herbarium, Virginia Military Institute, Lexington, Virginia 24450, U.S.A.

VMSL   VILLA MERCEDES: Herbario, Instituto Nacional de Tecnología Agropecuaria, Estación Experimental Agropecuaria San Luis, Casilla de Correo 17, 5730 Villa Mercedes, San Luis, Argentina.

VNC   VAN NUYS: Herbarium, Department of Life Sciences, Los Angeles Valley College, 5800 Fulton Avenue, Van Nuys, California 91401, U.S.A.

VOA   VAASA: Herbarium of Ostrobothnia Australis, c/o M. Malmberg, Sandögatan 12, Vaasa, Finland.

VOR   VORONEZH: Department of Morphology, Systematics and Geography of Plants, Lenin Komsomul University of Voronezh, Universitetskaya Square, 394000 Voronezh, U.S.S.R.

VPI   BLACKSBURG: Massey Herbarium, Department of Biology, Virginia Polytechnic Institute and State University, Blacksburg, Virginia 24061, U.S.A.

VPRI   BURNLEY: Plant Research Institute, Swan St., Burnley, Victoria 3121, Australia.

VSC   VALDOSTA: Herbarium, Department of Biology, Valdosta State College, Nevins Hall, Valdosta, Georgia 31601, U.S.A.

VSUH   PETERSBURG: Herbarium, Department of Life Sciences, Virginia State University, Petersburg, Virginia 23803, U.S.A.

VT   BURLINGTON: Pringle Herbarium, Department of Botany, University of Vermont, Burlington, Vermont 05405, U.S.A.

VU   DONSKOYE: Herbarium, Galichya Gora Reserve of Voronezh University, Zadonsk Region, Lipetsk Oblast, 399020 S. Donskoye, U.S.S.R.

W   WIEN: Naturhistorisches Museum, Botanische Abteilung, Burgring 7, Postfach 417, A-1014 Wien, Austria.

WA   WARSZAWA: Zakład Systematyki i Geografii Róslin, Uniwersytetu Warczawskiego, Aleje Ujazdowskie 4, 00-478 Warszawa, Poland.

WAB   CRAWFORDSVILLE: Herbarium, Biology Department, Wabash College, Crawfordsville, Indiana 47933, U.S.A.

WACRI   TAFO: West African (later Ghana) Cocoa Research Institute, Tafo, Ghana.**

WAG   WAGENINGEN: Herbarium Vadense, Laboratory for Plant Taxonomy and Plant Geography, 37 Gen. Foulkesweg, P.O. Box 8010, 6700 ED Wageningen, Netherlands.

WAHO   WAGENINGEN: Herbarium, Institute for Horticultural Plant Breeding, Mansholtlaan 15, P.O. Box 16, 6700 AA Wageningen, Netherlands.

WANF   SALT LAKE CITY: Herbarium, Wasatch National Forest, 8226 Federal Building, 125 South State Street, Salt Lake City, Utah 84138, U.S.A.

WAR   WARWICK: Herbarium, Warwickshire Museum, Market Place, Warwick CV34 4SA, England, Great Britain.

WARK   WARSAW: Herbarium, A. L. Kibbe Life Science Station, Western Illinois University, Warsaw, Illinois 62379, U.S.A.

WARM   WARRENSBURG: Herbarium, Biology Department, Central Missouri State University, Warrensburg, Missouri 64093, U.S.A.

WAT   WATERLOO: Herbarium, Department of Biology, University of Waterloo, Waterloo, Ontario N2L 3G1, Canada.

WAU   WAU: Herbarium, Wau Ecology Institute, P.O. Box 77, Wau, Morobe Province, Papua New Guinea.

WAVI   WATERVILLE: Herbarium, Biology Department, Colby College, Waterville, Maine 04901, U.S.A.

WB   WÜRZBURG: Herbarium der Universität Würzburg, Institut f. Botanik u. Pharmaz. Biologie mit Botanischem Garten, Mittlerer Dallenbergweg 64, D-8700 Würzburg, Federal Republic of Germany, BRD.

WBM   WÜRZBURG: Botanisches Institut II der Universität, Mittlerer Dallenbergweg 64, 87 Würzburg, Federal Republic of Germany, BRD.

WBS   WAGENINGEN: Herbarium, Biological Station Wijster, Biologisch Station, Kampsweg 27, Wijster (Dr.), Netherlands.

WCE   LONDON: Westfield College, London, England, Great Britain.*

WCH   WOOLWICH: Borough Museum, Woolwich, England, Great Britain.*

WCP   COLLEGE PLACE: Walla Walla College Natural History Herbarium, Department of Biological Sciences, Walla Walla College, Life Science Building 226, West Whitman Drive, College Place, Washington 99324, U.S.A.

WCR   WINCHESTER: City Museum, Winchester, England, Great Britain.*

WCU   CHENGDU: Herbarium, West China University, Chengdu, Sichuan, People's Republic of China.

WCUH   CULLOWHEE: Herbarium, Department of Biology, Western Carolina University, Cullowhee, North Carolina 28723, U.S.A.

WCW   WALLA WALLA: Herbarium, Department of Biology, Whitman College, Walla Walla, Washington 99362, U.S.A.

WDNE   WINNEMUCCA: Herbarium of the Winnemucca District, U.S. Department of the Interior, Bureau of Land Management, 705 East 4th Street, Winnemucca, Nevada 89445, U.S.A.

WECO   MIDDLETOWN: Herbarium, Department of Biology, Wesleyan University, Middletown, Connecticut 06457, U.S.A. -- incorporated in NY.

WELC   WELLESLEY: Herbarium, Department of Biological Sciences, Wellesley College, Wellesley, Massachusetts 02181, U.S.A.

WELT   WELLINGTON: Herbarium, National Museum of New Zealand, Private Bag, Wellington, New Zealand.

WELTU   WELLINGTON: The H. D. Gordon Herbarium, Botany Department, Victoria University of Wellington, Private Bag, Wellington, New Zealand.

WERN   OLDHAM: Herbarium, Werneth Park Study Centre and Natural History Museum, Frederick Street, Oldham, Lancashire, England, Great Britain.

WET   WAVERLY: Herbarium, Biology Department, Wartburg College, Waverly, Iowa 50677, U.S.A.

WFBVA WIEN: Herbarium, Forstliche Bundesversuchsanstalt, Institut f. Standort der Forstlichen Bundesversuchsanstalt, A-1131 Wien, Schöbrunn, Austria.

WFU   WINSTON-SALEM: Herbarium, Department of Biology, Wake Forest University, Winston-Salem, North Carolina 27109, U.S.A.

WGC   CARROLLTON: Herbarium, Department of Biology, West Georgia College, Carrollton, Georgia 30118, U.S.A.

WH   WUCHANG: Herbarium of Wuhan University, Department of Biology, Wuchang, Hubei, People's Republic of China.

WHB   WIEN: Herbarium, Botanisches Institut der Universität für Bodenkultur, Gregor Mendelstrasse 33, A-1180 Wien, Austria.

WHN   WHITEHAVEN: Borough Public Library and Museum, Whitehaven, England, Great Britain.*

WHY   WHITBY: Whitby Literary and Philosophical Society, Whitby, England, Great Britain.*

WI   VILNIUS: Department of Botany and Genetics, Kapsukas State University, Churlionio Street 23, 232031 Vilnius, U.S.S.R.

WILLI   WILLIAMSBURG: Herbarium, Department of Biology, The College of William and Mary, Williamsburg, Virginia 23185, U.S.A.

WILLU   SALEM: Peck Herbarium, Willamette University, Salem, Oregon 97301, U.S.A. -- housed at OSC.

WIN   WINNIPEG: Herbarium, Department of Botany, University of Manitoba, Winnipeg, Manitoba, Canada R3T 2N2.

WIND   WINDHOEK: S.W.A. Herbarium, Agricultural Buildings, 83 Leutwein Street, Private Bag X13184, 9000 Windhoek, South-West Africa.

WINDM PORTAGE LA PRAIRIE: Herbarium, Delta Marsh, University of Manitoba Field Station, Box 8, Site 2, R.R. 1, Portage la Prairie, Manitoba, Canada R1N 3A1.

WINF   WINNIPEG: Forest Research Laboratory, Department of Forestry and Rural Development -- incorporated in CAFB and CFB.

WINFM WINNIPEG: Mycological Herbarium, Forest Research Laboratory, Department of Forestry and Rural Development -- incorporated in CFB.

WINO   WINONA: Herbarium, Biology Department, Saint Mary's College, Winona, Minnesota 55987, U.S.A.

WIR   LENINGRAD: Herbarium, The All-Union Institute of Plant Industry, Herzen Street 44, 190000 Leningrad, U.S.S.R.

WIS   MADISON: Herbarium, Department of Botany, University of Wisconsin, Birge Hall, 430 Lincoln Drive, Madison, Wisconsin 53706, U.S.A.

WJC   LIBERTY: Herbarium, Department of Biology, William Jewell College, College Hill, Liberty, Missouri 64068, U.S.A.

WKD   WAKEFIELD: City Art Gallery and Museum -- see CMM.

WLU   WATERLOO: Herbarium, Department of Biology, Wilfrid Laurier University, Waterloo, Ontario, Canada N2L 3C5.

WM   GEZIRA: Wad Medani Herbarium, Ministry of Agriculture, Gezira, Sudan.

WMGC   WENHAM: Herbarium, Biology Department, Gordon College, 255 Grapevine Road, Wenham, Massachusetts 01984, U.S.A.

WMU   KALAMAZOO: Clarence R. Hanes Herbarium, Department of Biology, Western Michigan University, Kalamazoo, Michigan 49008, U.S.A.

WMW   WALTHAMSTOW: Borough Museum of Local History and Antiquities, Walthamstow, England, Great Britain.*

WNC	WILMINGTON: Herbarium, Department of Biology, University of North Carolina, Wilmington, North Carolina 28406, U.S:A.

WNLM	WIEN: Herbarium, Niederösterreichisches Landesmuseum, Herrengasse 9, A-1014 Wien, Austria.

WNRE	PINAWA: Herbarium, Whiteshell Nuclear Research Establishment, Pinawa, Manitoba, Canada ROE 1Lo.

WOCB	WINDSOR: Herbarium, Department of Biology, University of Windsor, 400 Sunset Avenue, Windsor, Ontario, Canada N9B 3P4.

WOH	WEATHERFORD: Western Oklahoma Herbarium, Biology Department, Southwestern Oklahoma State University, Weatherford, Oklahoma 73096, U.S.A.

WOS	WORCESTER: Hastings Museum and Art Gallery, Worcester, England, Great Britain.*

WPBS	ABERYSTWYTH: Welsh Plant Breeding Station, Aberystwyth, Wales, Great Britain.*

WPL	LONDON: Whitechapel Museum, London, England, Great Britain.*

WRN	WARRINGTON: Municipal Museum and Art Gallery, Warrington, England, Great Britain.*

WRSL	WROCŁAW: Herbarium, Department of Botany, Museum of Natural History, Wrocław University, ul. Sienkiewicza 21, 50-335 Wrocław, Poland.

WS	PULLMAN: Marion Ownbey Herbarium, Washington State University, Pullman, Washington 99164, U.S.A.

WSCO	OGDEN: Herbarium, Weber State College, Ogden, Utah 84408, U.S.A.

WSFA	WILMINGTON: Herbarium, Department of Biology, Wilmington College, Kettering Hall, Room 203, Box 1301, Wilmington, Ohio 45177, U.S.A.

WSM	WESTON-SUPER-MARE: Borough Public Library and Museum, Weston-super-Mare, England, Great Britain.*

WSP	PULLMAN: Mycological Herbarium, Department of Plant Pathology, Washington State University, Pullman, Washington 99164, U.S.A.

WSRP	SIEDLCE: Herbarium, Department of Botany, Wyzsza Szkoła, Rolnicze-Pedagogiczna, ul. Prusa 12, 08-110 Siedlce, Poland.

WSY	WISLEY: Royal Horticultural Society's Gardens, Wisley, England, Great Britain.*

WTR	WINCHESTER: Herbarium, Winchester College Museum, Winchester, Hampshire, England, Great Britain.

WTS	CANYON: Herbarium, Biology Department, West Texas State University, Canyon, Texas 79016, U.S.A.

WTU	SEATTLE: Herbarium, Department of Botany, University of Washington, Seattle, Washington 98195, U.S.A.

WU	WIEN: Institut für Botanik und Botanischer Garten der Universität, Rennweg 14, A-1030 Wien, Austria.

WUD	DETROIT: Herbarium, Department of Biology, Wayne State University, Detroit, Michigan 48202, U.S.A.

WUK	WUGONG: Herbarium, Northwest Botanical Institute, Academia Sinica, Wugong, Shaanxi, People's Republic of China.

WVA	MORGANTOWN: Herbarium, West Virginia University, Morgantown, West Virginia 26505, U.S.A.

WVIT	MONTGOMERY: Herbarium, West Virginia Institute of Technology, Montgomery, West Virginia 25136, U.S.A.

WVN	WHITEHAVEN: Whitehaven Scientific Association, Whitehaven, England, Great Britain.*

WVW	BUCKHANNON: George B. Rossbach Herbarium, West Virginia Wesleyan College, Buckhannon, West Virginia 26201, U.S.A.

WWB	BELLINGHAM: Herbarium, Biology Department, Western Washington University, Bellingham, Washington 98225, U.S.A.

WWF	SINTON: Herbarium, Welder Wildlife Foundation, P.O. Drawer 1400, Sinton, Texas 78387, U.S.A.

WYAC	LARAMIE: Range Management Herbarium, College of Agriculture, University of Wyoming, Laramie, Wyoming 82071, U.S.A.

WYCO	WYTHEVILLE: Herbarium, Wytheville Community College, Wytheville, Virginia 24382, U.S.A.

WYE	WYE: Wye College, Wye, England, Great Britain.*

XAL	XALAPA: Herbario, Instituto Nacional de Investigaciones sobre Recursos Bióticos, Apartado postal 63, Xalapa, Veracruz, Mexico.

XALU	XALAPA: Herbario, Facultad de Ciencias Biológicas, Universidad Veracruzana, Apartado postal 222, Xalapa, Veracruz, Mexico.

Y	New Haven: Samuel James Record Memorial Collection, School of Forestry, Yale University, New Haven, Connecticut 06511, U.S.A. — incorporated in MAD.
YA	Yaoundé: Herbier National du Cameroun, Boîte Postale 1601, Yaoundé, Cameroun.
YAI	Yerevan: Herbarium, Department of Botany, Yerevan Agricultural Institute, Teryana St. 74, 375200 Yerevan, U.S.S.R.
YALT	Yalta: Herbarium of the Nikita Botanical Gardens, 334267, Yalta, Crimea, U.S.S.R.
YAM	Yamaguchi: Herbarium, Faculty of Agriculture, Yamaguchi University, Yoshida, Yamaguchi 753, Yamaguchi Prefecture, Japan.
YBI	Yangambi: Herbarium, Institut National pour l'Etude Agronomique du Congo, Yangambi, Zaire.
YELLO	Yellowstone: Yellowstone National Park Herbarium, Mammoth Hot Springs, P.O. Box 168, Yellowstone National Park, Wyoming 82190, U.S.A.
YEO	Yeovil: Borough Public Library and Museum, Yeovil, England, Great Britain.*
YH	Yiyang: Herbarium, Lutheran College, Yiyang, Hunan, People's Republic of China.
YK	York: Bootham School Natural History Society, York, England, Great Britain.*
YM	Yosemite National Park: Herbarium, Yosemite Museum, P.O. Box 577, Yosemite National Park, California 95389, U.S.A.
YNU	Yokohama: Herbarium, Agricultural Institute, Yokohama National University, 100 Gontazaka, Hodogayaku, Yokohama, Japan.
YRK	York: Herbarium, The Yorkshire Museum, York, Yorkshire, England, Great Britain.
YU	New Haven: Herbarium, Osborn Memorial Laboratories, Yale University, 167 Prospect Street, New Haven, Connecticut 06520, U.S.A.
YUKU	Kunming: Herbarium, Yunnan University, Kunming, Yunnan, People's Republic of China.
YUN	Yundum: Department of Agriculture, Yundum, Gambia.**
YUO	Youngstown: Herbarium, Department of Biological Sciences, Youngstown State University, 410 Wick Avenue, Youngstown, Ohio 44555, U.S.A.
YUTO	Toronto: Herbarium, Department of Biology, York University, Toronto, Ontario, Canada.
Z	Zürich: Institut für systematische Botanik der Universität Zürich, Zollikerstrasse 107, CH-8008 Zürich, Switzerland.
ZA	Zagreb: Herbarium Croaticum, Department of Biology, Faculty of Science, University, Zagreb, Yugoslavia.
ZAD	Chilanga: Mt. Makulu Research Station — see MRSC.
ZAHO	Zagreb: Herbarium "Dr. Ivo Horvat," Veterinarian Faculty, University of Zagreb, Heinzelova 55, YU-41000 Zagreb, Yugoslavia.
ZARIA	Zaria: Department of Botany, University, Zaria, Nigeria.**
ZMT	Třebíč: Západomoravské muzeum v Třebíči, Zámek 1, 674 01 Třebíč, Czechoslovakia.
ZOM	Zomba: Department of Agriculture — incorporated in MAL.
ZSS	Zürich: Städtische Sukkulentensammlung, I.O.S. affiliated Reserve Collection and Herbarium, Mythenquai 88, CH-8002 Zürich, Switzerland.
ZT	Zürich: The Herbarium, Institut für Spezielle Botanik, Eidg. Technische Hochschule, Zurichbergstrasse 38, CH-8006 Zürich, Switzerland.
ZULU	Empangeni: Herbarium, University of Zululand, Private Bag Kwa-Dlangezwa, via Empangeni, Zululand, South Africa.
ZV	Zvolen: Katedra botaniky a fytocenológie Vysokej školy lesníckej a drevárskej vo Zvolene, Zvolen, Czechoslovakia.
ZVS	Bad Godesberg: Bundesanstalt für Vegetationskunde, Naturschutz und Landschaftspflege, Heerstrasse 110, 532 Bad Godesberg, Federal Republic of Germany, BRD.

IV. General Index to Personal Names

425

Hommersand, M. 58
Homola, R. 205
Homrich, M. H. 224
Honer, T. G. 301
Hong, D.-Y. 215
Hong, W. S. 103
Honsell, E. 289
Hoog, G. S. de 16
Hooper, A. D. L. 4
Hooper, R. G. 248
Hooper, S. S. 134
Hopkins, J. C. 301
Horton, J. H. 73
Horvat, M. 322
Hosford, D. 86
Hoshaw, R. W. 292
Hoshiai, T. 285
Hoshizaki, B. J. 160
Hosoi, M. 109
Hotta, M. 140
Hou, D. 148
Houedjissi, N. 72
Houngnon, P. 72
Howard, L. D. 200
Howard, R. A. 47
Howell, G. L. 176
Howell, J. T. 255
Hrapko, J. O. 86
Hrynkiewicz, J. 315
Hsu, H.-T. 244
Hsü, P.-S. 267
Hsu, W.-H. 140
Hsu, Y.-B. 316
Hu, C.-M. 105
Hu, R.-L. 267
Hu, Z.-X. 316
Huang, C.-C. 105
Huang, P.-C. 192
Huang, Y.-F. 106
Huapalla Yábar, J. P. 118
Hubbard, M. M. 276
Huber, J. 10
Hübl, E. 311
Huck, R. B. 205
Huckins, C. A. 219
Huddlestone, D. 244
Hudson, J. H. 265
Huerta, L. 178
Huertos, F. A. 120
Huggins, R. A. 117
Hughes, S. J. 208
Hugo, L. 274
Hulbary, R. L. 121
Hull, J. C. 18
Hulst, R. van 150
Hultgård, U.-M. 296
Humm, H. J. 250, 264
Humphries, C. J. 158
Hunde, A. 296
Hunt, D. R. 134

Hunt, R. S. 301
Hunter, B. 230
Hunziker, A. T. 70
Hunziker, J. H. 42
Hürlimann, H. 323
Hurtado Morales, J. 101
Husain, A. 162
Hussin, K. 19
Huszar, V. L. de M. 241
Huttleston, D. G. 132
Huynh, K.-L. 194
Hwang, S.-M- 105
Hyland, B. P. M. 12
Hyypio, P. A. 124

Ichaso, C. L. F. 242
Idrobo M., J. M. 30
Ietswaart, J. H. 7
Ifteni, L. 119
Ihlenfeldt, H.-D. 110
Iizumi, S. 267
Ikonnikov, S. S. 150
Ilan, D. 77
Ilarslan, R. 8
Illman, W. I. 207
Iltis, H. H. 167
Imaguire, N. 73
Imbamba, S. K. 191
Imkhanitskaya, N. N. 149
Immelman, K. 228
Imshaug, H. A. 83
Inca, J. 233
Ingen, T. van 298
Ingram, J. W. 124
Ingram, R. 246
Inimua, E. 116
Inoue, H. 198, 286
Ioan, G. 65
Ireland, R. R. 207
Irgang, B. E. 224
Irvine, L. M. 158
Irving, R. S. 204
Isaac, M. J. 278
Isely, D. 6
Ishihashi, N. 115
Ishin, Y. D. 201
Ismawi, O. 139
Isoviita, P. 112
Ito, M. F. 51
Ito, S. 286
Ivanova, L. I. 150
Ivanov, V. V. 296
Ives, G. P. 272
Ivimey-Cook, R. B. 88
Ivo, M. I. 237
Iwarsson, M. 296
Iwatsuki, K. 140
Iwatsuki, Z. 198
Izaguirre de Artucio, P. 184
Izco, J. 261

Jackes, B. R. 288
Jackowiak, B. 226
Jackson, D. G. 321
Jackson, J. R. 128
Jackson, M. T. 284
Jackson, R. C. 162
Jacobi, J. D. 116
Jacobs, M. 148
Jacobs, R. P. W. M. 16
Jacobs, S. W. L. 278
Jacobsen, T. D. 220
Jacobsson, S. 100
Jacquemin, H. 57
Jacquemoud, F. 98
Jacques-Felix, H. 213
Jafri, S. M. H. 290
Jäger, E. 109
Jain, H. K. 195
Jain, S. K. 46
Jain, S. S. 77
Jalani, B. S. 18
Jalas, J. 112
James, P. W. 158
James, S. H. 193
Jamnback, H. 3
Jamzad, Z. 282
Janardhanan, K. P. 46
Jancey, R. C. 159
Jangoux, J. I. G. 22
Janos, D. P. 70
Jansen, P. C. M. 171
Jansen-Jacobs, M. J. 297
Janssen, C. R. 298
Janzen, D. H. 256
Jaramillo, J. 233
Jaramillo-M., R. 30, 120
Jarrett, F. M. 134
Jarry, D. M. 185
Jarry, D. T. 185
Järvinen, I. 113
Jasiewicz, A. 139
Jayachandran, C. K. 66
Jayasuriya, A. H. M. 217
Jeanmonod, D. 98
Jefferson, R. M. 306
Jeffrey, C. 134
Jeglum, J. 266
Jelem, H. 311
Jérémie, J. 213
Jermy, A. C. 158
Jervis, R. A. 221
Jessop, J. P. 2
Jessup, L. 36
Jessup, L. G. 36
Jesus, R. M. de 154
Jeudi, R. addenda
Jimenez, A., R. 317
Jiménez Ramírez, J. 178
Johannsson, B. 239

433

Robbins, R. 181
Robbrecht, E. 174
Roberts, E. P. 69
Robertson, A. 247
Robertson, K. R. 297
Robinson, H. E. 306
Robinson, P. 33
Robles G., L. 183
Robson, N. K. B. 158
Robyns, A. 174
Rocca de Sarasola, M. A. 56
Rocha, G. I. 34
Rochelle, L. A. 220
Rodd, A. N. 278
Rodgers, C. L. 103
Rodman, J. E. 196
Rodrigues, A. F. 224
Rodrigues, I. A. 21
Rodrigues, J. D. 32
Rodrigues, S. D. 32
Rodrigues, W. A. 169
Rodrigues, de Miranda, L. 16
Rodríguez, C. 178
Rodriguez, E. M. 5
Rodriguez, H. 172
Rodríguez, M. 108
Rodríguez, R. 69
Rodriguez de Sarmiento, M. 258
Rodríguez J., L. del S. 187
Roessler, H. 189
Rogers, C. M. 78
Rogers, D. J. 270
Rogers, J. S. 230
Rogers, R. W. 36
Rogerson, C. T. 197
Rohweder, O. 323
Roivainen, H. 113
Rollins, R. C. 50
Romanczuk, C. 41
Romero, E. 42
Rominger, J. M. 91
Romo, A. 19
Rooden, J. van 297
Roon, A. C. de 297
Rooy, J. van 227
Ropke, D. 266
Roquebert, M.-F. 214
Rosa, M. T. 154
Rosa, Z. M. 224
Rosario, R. M. del 170
Rosengurtt, B. 184
Rosero, J. 214
Ross, D. 247
Ross, E. M. 36
Ross, J. H. 175
Ross, R. 158
Rossi, L. A. 56
Rossi de Ceballos, E. 258
Rostański, K. 131
Rotman, A. 256

Rotschild, D. I. de 41
Rott, E. 120
Rouane, M. L. 288
Roubal, A. 227
Rouleau, E. 185
Rourke, J. P. 53
Rousi, A. 292
Roussel, J. L. 185
Rousselle, J. 152
Roussomoustakaki-Theodoraki,
M. N. 12
Roux, C. 228
Rowe, F. 87
Rowell, C. M. 253
Rowland, R. E. 191
Rowley, G. D. 236
Roy, G. P. 5
Royen, P. van 116
Rubers, W. V. 148
Rubinoff, I. 17
Rubió de Pol, M. 56
Rudall, P. 135
Rudd, V. E. 200
Rudloff, E. von 301
Rudolph, E. D. 69
Ruffo, A. 301
Ruffo, C. K. 165
Rúgolo, Z. 256
Ruiz, Vigo, W. 46
Rumely, J. H. 33
Runemark, H. 163
Ruschi, A. 241
Rushworth, J. E. 251
Rusińska, A. 226
Russell, G. F. 306
Russell, N. 85
Ryberg, M. 275
Rycroft, H. B. 53
Ryding, O. 296
Rydzewski, W. 315
Ryman, S. 295
Rzedowski, J. 178

Sa'ad, F. M. 45
Saari, V. 129
Sabapathy, M. R. 139
Sacco, J. da C. 216, 241
Sachet, M.-H. 306
Saddi, N. 72
Saenz, A. A. 256
Sáenz-Renauld, J. A. 257
Saether, B. 290
Sagástegui Alva, A. 291
Sagawa, Y. 116
Sahid, I. 19
Şahinkaya, H. 79
Saint Antoine, J. D. de R. de 237
Saint John, H. 116
Saint-Martin, M. 288
Sakane, M. 263

Sakr, A. 46
Salamun, P. J. 181
Salas de Leon, S. 257
Salatino, A. 263
Salatino, M. L. F. 263
Salazar, N. 212
Salazar de Benavides, O. 214
Saldanha, C. J. 18
Salih, S. T. 16
Salles, A. E. H. 34
Salles, H. G. 241
Salmina, N. P. 277
Salubeni, A. J. 323
Salvo Tierra, E. 169
Samai, S. K. 132
Sameva, E. 271
Samson, R. A. 16
Samuels, G. J. 14
San Juan, C. V. 170
Sánchéz, C. 108
Sánchez, M. E. 178
Sanchez, P. 261
Sanchez Colin, S. 177
Sanchez de Garcia, E. 41
Sánchez Mejorada, H. 179
Sanchez-S., D. 174
Sánchez Salamanca, C. 322
Sanchez Vega, H. 183
Sanchez Vega, I. M. 46
Sanchez Vega, J. 46
Sanchir, C. 294
Sancho, M. 256
Sanders, A. 243
Sanders, A. E. 59
Săndová, M. 221
Sandoval Pérez, M. 317
Sandoz, H. 172
Sands, M. J. S. 134
Sanford, W. W. 120
Sangat, H. M. 29
Sanokho, A. 75
Sansing, J. L. 222
Sant'Anna, C. L. 263
Sant'Anna, W. dos R. 252
Santa S., J. I. 173
Santelices, B. 261
Santesson, R. 275
Santos, A. K. de O. 209
Santos, E. A. A. dos 241
Santos, E. C. dos 216
Santos, R. 95
Santos Guerra, A. 230
Saraçoğlu, I. 8
Saraçoğlu, M. 122
Saralegui, H. 108
Sarbhoy, A. K. 195
Sârbu, I. 119
Sareen, T. S. 58
Sarfatti, G. 269
Sarlis, G. 11

V. Addenda

Most of the information in the Addenda was received too late to be included in the Indices.

ASHEVILLE: *Herbarium, Southeastern Forest Experiment Station, U.S. Forest Service, U.S.D.A.*, **(SEFES)**, 13 Veterans Drive, Asheville, North Carolina 28805, **U.S.A.**
Telephone: 704/298-7049.
Status: U.S. Department of Agriculture, Forest Service.
Foundation: 1966. *Number of specimens:* 3.750.
Herbarium: Useful understory plants of southeastern forests; flowering plants of Kentucky, North Carolina, Virginia, and Georgia.
Director: ARNOLD KROCHMAL, 1919 (Economic botany, tropical and temperate areas).
Staff member: CONNIE KROCHMAL, 1949.
Specialization in research: Forest understory plants in National Forests along the Appalachian Trail and in parts of the Blue Ridge National Park.
Loans: To recognized herbaria.
Periodical and serial works: Structure of Tropical Rain Forests Newsletter, IUFRO Working Party.

CARTAGENA: *Herbarium, Fundación Jardín Botánico "Guillermo Piñeres,"* **(JBGP)**, Banco de la República, Cartagena, **Colombia**.
Status: Directed by Banco de la República, a private institution.
Foundation: 1977. *Number of specimens:* 2.000.
Administrator: ROBERTO BARRIGA.
Staff member: JOSEFINA ESPINA.

DAMIEN: *Ekman Herbarium, Département de l'Agriculture, des Ressources Naturelles et du Développement Rural, Service Recherche Agronomique,* **(EHH)**, Damien, Port-au-Prince, **Haiti.**
Telephone: 2-3596, ext. 42; 2-3457, ext. 42.
Status: Faculté d'Agronomie et de Médecine Vétérinaire.
Foundation: 1925. *Number of specimens:* 10.000.
Herbarium: West Indies.
Important collections: E. L. Ekman.
Curator: ROSEMOND JEUDI, 1922.
Staff member: FRÉDÉRIC KÉBREAU, Head, Department of Biology.
Exchange: Limited to southeastern U.S. forests.

MÉRIDA: *Herbario "Luis E. Ruiz Terán," Departamento de Botánica y Farmacognosia, Facultad de Farmacia, Universidad de Los Andes,* **(MERF)**, Mérida 5101, **Venezuela.**
Foundation: 1970. *Number of specimens:* 30.000.
Herbarium: Venezuelan plants, especially flora de los páramos.
Director and Curator: DAVID DÍAZ-MIRANDA, 1946 (Aquatic vascular plants; *Limnobium, Lindernia*).
Staff members: ROSA MARÍA ACOSTA DE OBANDO,

1935 (Anatomy of *Espeletia*).
ALFREDO CARABOT CUERVO, 1939 (Phytochemistry; Agavaceae; *Costus, Solanum*).
MANUEL LÓPEZ FIGUEIRAS, 1915 (Lichens; *Espeletia,* Compositae).
SANTIAGO LÓPEZ PALACIOS, 1918 (Verbenaceae of Venezuela, Colombia, and Ecuador).

ANA TILISA PEÑA DE CÁRDENAS, 1935 (Anatomy of *Libanothamnus,* Compositae).
Specialization in research: Flora de los páramos (high altitude tropical vegetation); lichens of Venezuela; phytochemistry; flora de los Andes.
Loans: To recognized botanical institutions; standard regulations.
Periodical and serial works: Revista de la Facultad de Farmacia.
Exchange: Available: Venezuela, especially the Andes. Desired: Tropical regions, especially the Andes.

OXFORD: *Herbarium, ARC Weed Research Organization,* **(WRO)**, Begbroke Hill, Sandy Lane, Yarnton, Oxford OX5 1PF, England, **Great Britain.**
Telephone: Kidlington 3761.
Status: Agricultural Research Council.
Foundation: 1967. *Number of specimens:* 3.000.
Herbarium: Mainly tropical and subtropical weed species.
Director: J. D. FRYER.
Curator: C. PARKER, 1931 (Tropical weed control, especially parasitic and perennial species).
Specialization in research: Weed biology and control.
Loans: Yes.
Exchange: Yes.

PORTICI: *Erbario dell' Istituto di Botanica della Facoltà di Agraria, Università di Napoli,* **(PORUN)**, Via Università 100, I 80055 Portici, Napoli, **Italy.**
Telephone: 0817390624; 0817395024.
Status: University of Naples.
Foundation: 1979. *Number of specimens:* 50.000.
Herbarium: Many collections of the 19th century.
Director: PAOLO PIZZOLONGO, 1928 (Taxonomy, phytogeography, embryology).
Staff members: GRAZIA G. APRILE, 1953 (Floristics; lichens).
MAURIZIO GARGIULO, 1955 (Phycology).
MATTEO GIANNATTASIO, 1940 (Medicinal plants).
FLORA DE MASI, 1936 (Phycology).
MASSIMO RICCIARDI, 1935 (Taxonomy, phytogeography; lichens).
GIACOMO TRIPODI, 1938 (Phycology).

451

GIAN FRANCO TUCCI, 1943 (Plant physiology, cytilogy).

Specialization in research: Mainly Italian flora; marine algae.

Associated botanic garden: Orto Botanico della Facoltà di Agraria.

Loans: For six months unless otherwise stated.

Exchange: Yes.